Street by Street

BIRMINGHAM
WOLVERHAMPTON
DUDLEY, SOLIHULL, STOURBRIDGE, WALSALL, WEST BROMWICH

Aldridge, Brownhills, Codsall, Coleshill, Dorridge, Halesowen, Knowle, Pelsall, Sutton Coldfield, Wombourne

GAZETTEER SYMBOL KEY

☎ - telephone number

✆ - telephone booking service

@ - email address

🖱 - web address

📄 - fax number

🅟 - map page number & grid reference

1st edition published July 2008
© Automobile Association Developments Limited 2008

 This product includes map data licensed from
Ordnance Survey® with the permission of the
Controller of Her Majesty's Stationery Office.
© Crown copyright 2008.
All rights reserved. Licence number 100021153.

The copyright in all PAF is owned by Royal Mail Group plc.

Published by AA Publishing (a trading name of Automobile Association
Developments Limited, whose registered office is Fanum House, Basing View,
Basingstoke, Hampshire RG21 4EA. Registered number 1878835).

Cartography produced by the Mapping Services Department
of The Automobile Association. (A03534)

A CIP Catalogue record for this book is available from the British Library.

Design and management for listings section by ey communications Ltd.
(www.eysite.com). Editorial services by Pam Stagg

Listings data provided by Global DataPoint Limited, London

Printed by Oriental Press in Dubai

The Automobile Association would like to thank the
following photographers, companies and picture libraries
for their assistance in the preparation of this book.

Abbreviations for the picture credits are as follows: (t) top; (b)
bottom; (l) left; (r) right; (AA) AA World Travel Library.
Front Cover AA/P Baker;
3 (t) AA/J Welsh; 3 (ct) AA/J Welsh; 3 (cb) AA/J Welsh; 3 (b) AA/
P Baker; 4 AA/J Welsh; 5 AA/R Newton; 6 AA/J Welsh; 8 AA/J
Welsh; 9 (t) AA/I Burgum; 9 (b) AA/V Greaves; 12 AA/J Welsh; 13
AA/J Welsh; 16 AA/J Welsh; 19 AA/J Welsh; 25 AA/J Welsh

Every effort has been made to trace the copyright holders, and we
apologise in advance for any accidental errors. We would be happy
to apply the corrections in the following edition of this publication.

Opposite page
Top and bottom: Birmingham Museum and Art Gallery
Centre top: A gleaming skyscraper rises above Gas Street Basin
Centre bottom: King Street, Wolverhampton

Birmingham &Wolverhampton

Birmingham, Britain's second largest city, has become one of the most vibrant centres of British culture, with an exceptionally good nightlife. The largely pedestrianised heart of the city has been completely revitalised and is now a major shopping and leisure destination. The city centres on the landmark Centenary Square and Victoria Square, an area fringed by impressive civic buildings. Around the intricate canal network, new walkways, shops and public areas have been created. Gas Street Basin, where narrowboats are often moored, makes a good starting point for waterside walks along the canal's towpaths.

In the city centre shoppers will find designer stores, stylish malls and arcades, friendly markets, the famous Jewellery Quarter and the celebrated Bullring shopping complex.

To help you make the most of your leisure time in Birmingham we have provided a useful gazetteer covering a range of attractions from outstanding museums and art galleries, to cinemas and grand theatres featuring everything from opera to live music and classical ballet – Birmingham has its own world-class symphony orchestra and ballet company. With its large student population, you'll also find one of the liveliest club scenes in the country – Gas Street Basin and Broad Street are abuzz with a wide range of bars and clubs. Wolverhampton, to the northwest, also offers a mix of shopping, art, theatre and nightlife.

Entries are listed alphabetically (ignoring The) under each category heading. The map reference denotes the map page number in the mapping section and the grid square in which the street/road is to be found, not the individual establishments. We have given the street name, town/city name, post code, telephone and fax numbers and, where possible, email and website details.

Please note: the entries listed in this gazetteer section were provided by a third party and are not in any way recommended or endorsed by the AA.

TOURIST ATTRACTIONS

Aston Hall

Throughout its 400-year history Aston Hall has survived cannon attacks; accommodated King Charles I on his way to the Battle of Edge Hill; and for 30 years it was the rented home of James Watt junior, son of the great engineer and a successful businessman in his own right. The Hall's elaborate ceilings, ornate staircases and the vast long gallery make Aston a very special place to visit.

Trinity Road, Aston, Birmingham, West Midlands B6 6JD
☎ 0121 327 0062
@ bmag.enquiries@ birmingham.gov.uk
🖰 www.bmag.org.uk/
🌐 Page 109-F1

Bantock House and Park

Bantock House is home to the Bantock family and provides an insight into the history of Wolverhampton. Exhibits include the enamels, steel jewellery and japanned ware collections. The ground floor is set in the Edwardian period with Arts and Crafts inspired decor and the first floor features a number of interactive exhibitions exploring local history. Covering over 43 acres, the park is home to all sorts of birds, animals, insects and plants. Visitors can spot mistle thrushes, blackbirds, blue tits, pied wagtails and robins among others.

Finchfield Road, Wolverhampton, West Midlands WV3 9LQ
☎ 01902 552195

@ bantockhouse@ wolverhampton.gov.uk
🖰 www.wolverhamptonart. org.uk/bantock/visit
🌐 Page 36-B4

Birmingham Botanical Gardens and Glasshouses

The Birmingham Botanical Gardens and Glasshouses were designed by J C Loudon, a leading garden planner, horticultural journalist and publisher. Opened in 1832, the gardens feature the Loudon Terrace, main lawn and bandstand as well as the cottage garden. The glasshouses have separate tropical, subtropical and Mediterranean zones for specific plants. Weekend courses and various workshops for children are organised here.

Westbourne Road, Edgbaston, Birmingham, West Midlands B15 3TR

☎ 0121 454 1860
@ admin@birmingham botanicalgardens.org.uk
🖰 www.birmingham botanicalgardens.org.uk
🌐 Page 125-H5

Birmingham Nature Centre

The Nature Centre covers an area of over 6 acres and is a habitat for 130 different species of animal including deer, otters, owls, snakes, spiders and fish. The centre's natural habitats also provide a source of food and shelter for native wildlife like newts, kingfishers and grey squirrels. Besides the wildlife, a museum with city's natural history collection is open to visitors.

Pershore Road, Edgbaston, Birmingham, West Midlands B5 7RL
☎ 0121 472 7775
@ nature.centre@ birmingham.gov.uk

🖰 www.birmingham.gov. uk/naturecentre.bcc
📄 0121 471 4997
🌐 Page 143-G3

Blakesley Hall

Blakesley Hall was built in 1590 by Richard Smalbroke, a member of one of Birmingham's leading merchant families. Exhibits include 400-year-old wall decorations in the Painted Chamber and the Long Table in the Great Hall. Beyond the Hall, the herb garden and orchard houses butterflies and birds.

Blakesley Road, Yardley, Birmingham, West Midlands B25 8RN
☎ 0121 464 2193
🖰 www.bmag.org.uk
🌐 Page 130-A3

Brindleyplace

Brindleyplace is a business environment with 8,500 people based here. Tree-lined streets, three public squares and a network

The Birmingham Botanical Gardens and Glasshouses in Edgbaston

of restored canals define Brindleyplace, while bars and restaurants, individual shops, galleries and attractions add character and life.

Brindley Place, 2 Brunswick Street, Birmingham, West Midlands B1 2JF
☎ 0121 643 6866
@ admin@
  brindleyplace.com
🖰 www.brindleyplace.com
🗎 0121 643 1771
✐ Page 2-C6

Cadbury World
Located in Birmingham, Cadbury World is an educational multimedia attraction dedicated to the story of Cadbury and chocolate. It features a demonstration area, a jungle with waterfalls and boardwalks as well as a 3D cinema screen where 'Flex6' the robot brings to life the Cadbury pack and wrap process.

Linden Road, Bourneville, Birmingham, West Midlands B30 2LD
☎ 0121 451 4767,
  0121 451 4180
🕿 0845 450 3599
🖰 www.cadburyworld.co.uk
✐ Page 159-H3

Cannon Hill Park
The park features flowerbeds, lakes, pools and a collection of trees. The conservation area within the park includes a 5-acre woodland, known as the RSPB Centenary Plantation, besides a wildflower meadow, which is sown each year with cornfield annuals such as field poppy, cornflower and corn marigold.

2 Russell Road, Moseley, Birmingham, West Midlands B13 8RD

Dudley Zoological Gardens and Castle

☎ 0121 442 4226
@ Cannon.Hill.Park@
  birmingham.gov.uk
🖰 www.birmingham.gov.
  uk/cannonhillpark.bcc
🗎 0121 449 0238
✐ Page 143-H3

Chasewater Railway, Chasewater Country Park
The Chasewater Railway is located in Chasewater Country Park and operates heritage steam and diesel trains throughout the year from its headquarters at Brownhills West to Chasetown (Church Street), with intermediate stations at Norton Lakeside and Chasewater Heaths.

Pool Road, Brownhills, West Midlands WS8 7NL

☎ 01543 452623
@ info@chasewaterrailway.
  co.uk
🖰 www.chasewaterrailway.
  co.uk
🗎 01543 452623
✐ Page 8-C1

Dudley Water Ski Centre

Highbridge Road, Dudley, West Midlands DY2 0BH
☎ 0773 170 7947,
  0774 777 0110
@ info@dudleywaterski.
  co.uk
🖰 www.dudleywaterski.
  co.uk
✐ Page 120-B1

Dudley Zoological Gardens and Castle
Dudley Zoological Gardens houses an array of endangered animals including Asiatic lions,

Sumatran tigers, lemurs, penguins, chimps and orangutans. The other attraction, Dudley Castle was used by the Earls of Dudley, responsible for founding Dudley Zoo in 1937. The zoo hosts workshops, ghost tours, Halloween specials and other children's activities.

2 The Broadway, Dudley, West Midlands DY1 4QB
☎ 01384 215313
@ admin@dudleyzoo.org.uk
🖰 www.dudleyzoo.org.uk
🗎 01384 456048
✐ Page 84-D4

Edgbaston Reservoir
Built in 1827 by Thomas Telford, the 70-acre site is mainly open water and supports a variety of birdlife. A belt of woodland and grassland encircles the

reservoir providing a unique oasis of natural beauty in an urban setting.

The Ranger's Lodge,
115 Reservoir Road,
Ladywood, Birmingham,
West Midlands B16 9EE
☎ 0121 454 1908
@ edgbaston.reservoir@
birmingham.gov.uk
🖰 www.birmingham.gov.
uk/resa.bcc
🕮 Page 125-G2

English Heritage: Halesowen Abbey
The site features the remains of Halesowen Abbey, which was founded by King John in the 13th century.

Halesowen Abbey,
Birmingham, West Midlands
B62 8RJ
☎ 0121 625 6820
🖰 www.english-heritage.
org.uk
🕮 Page 139-F5

The Falconry Centre
The centre is home to hawks, owls, falcons, vultures, kestrels, lanners and golden eagles, and also offers treatment and rehabilitation for injured birds.

Kidderminster Road South,
Hagley, Worcestershire
DY9 0JB
☎ 01562 700014
@ info@thefalconrycentre.
co.uk
🖰 www.thefalconrycentre.
co.uk
🖹 01562 700014
🕮 Page 169-E2

Hall of Memory
The Hall of Memory was opened by Prince Arthur of Connaught in 1925 to commemorate the 12,320 Birmingham citizens who died in World War I. Around the exterior are four allegorical bronze figures, by local artist Albert Toft, representing the Army, Navy, Air Force and Women's Services. Inside the Hall are three art deco panels, *Call*, *Front Line* and *Return*, by William Bloye.

Centenary Square, Broad Street, Birmingham,
West Midlands B1 2EP
☎ 0121 303 2822
🖰 www.birmingham.gov.
uk/hom.bcc
🕮 Page 2-D5

Handsworth Park
Handsworth Park occupies over 63 acres and features a varied landscape, a children's play area and a leisure centre.

Handsworth Leisure Centre,
Holly Road, Handsworth,
Birmingham, West Midlands
B20 2BY
☎ 0121 464 0305
@ Handsworth.Park@
birmingham.gov.uk
🖰 www.birmingham.gov.
uk/handsworthpark.bcc
🕮 Page 107-H1

Hawbush Urban Farm
Hawbush Urban Farm was originally set up in 1980–1 after a group of residents visited a city farm in Bristol. Although from time to time the farm does take in rescued animals it is essentially a working farm breeding livestock, some for market.

Bull Street, Hawbush,
Brierley Hill, West Midlands
DY5 3RA
☎ 01384 79813
@ hawbushfarm@aol.com
🖰 www.hawbushfarm.
freewebspace.com
🕮 Page 118-C2

Himley Hall and Park
Himley Hall stands amid 180 acres of parkland designed by 'Capability' Brown and has been home to the Ward family.

Himley Park, Dudley
Staffordshire DY3 4DF
☎ 01384 817817, 01384
817825
@ himley.hall@
dudley.gov.uk
🖰 www.himleyhall.org
🖹 01384 817818
🕮 Page 81-H2

Holland Park
Chester Road North,
Brownhills, West Midlands
WS8 7JW
☎ 01922 654 370
🖰 www.walsall.gov.uk
🕮 Page 9-F3

Kingfisher Country Park
The Kingfisher Country Park stretches along the River Cole and features many different types of landscape and wildlife habitats. Alongside the river there are areas of formal public open space, tall herbs and scrub, course grassland, wetland with several small ponds and ancient woodland.

Shard End Community Centre, Packington Avenue,

Cannon Hill Park (see entry on page 5)

Shard End, Birmingham, West Midlands B34 7RD
☎ 0121 748 3798
@ kingfisher.countrypark@ birmingham.gov.uk
🖮 www.birmingham.gov. uk/kingfisher
🏛 Page 113-F4

Kings Heath Park

Kings Heath Park covers 35 acres and has a Green Flag status. The area around the main house and conservatory features seasonal bedding schemes, herbaceous borders, alpine outcrops, heather beds, trees, shrubs and a newly refurbished pool area. From the more formal areas of the park there is a transition to more informal areas where visitors can get involved with passive and active recreational activities.

Vicarage Road, Kings Heath, Birmingham, West Midlands B14 7TQ
☎ 0121 444 2848
@ mike.hinton@ birmingham.gov.uk
🖮 www.birmingham.gov.uk/
🏛 Page 160-D2

Lickey Hills Country Park

Lickey Hills Country covers 524 acres and features mixed deciduous woodland, conifer plantations and heathland inhabited by a variety of wildlife. A tour of the visitor centre offers an insight into the flora and fauna of the region through exhibitions, displays and guided services.

The Visitor Centre, Warren Lane, Rednal, Birmingham, Worcestershire B45 8ER
☎ 0121 447 7106, 0121 445 6036
@ lickey.hills@ birmingham.gov.uk

🖮 www.birmingham.gov. uk/lickeyhills.bcc
📄 0121 447 7106
🏛 Page 188-A4

The Locksmith's House

Once the home of the Hodson family, this preserved locksmith's house and workshop is displayed as the family would have lived during the early 1900s. The house still has many of the Hodson's original furniture and belongings.

54–56, New Road, Willenhall, West Midlands WV13 2DA
☎ 0121 557 9643, 01902 634542
🖮 www.bclm.co.uk
🏛 Page 39-F4

Martineau Gardens

The site features broadleaved woodland, dominated by penduculate oak, some over 150 years old, as well as sweet chestnut, elder, beech, holly, sycamore, field maple and hazel. The pond supports lesser pond sedge, yellow flag, water crowfoot, white water lily, common duckweed and water mint.

27 Priory Road, Birmingham, West Midlands B5 7UG
☎ 0121 440 7430
@ info@martineau- gardens.org.uk
🖮 www.martineau-gardens. org.uk
🏛 Page 143-G2

National Sea Life Centre

The National Sea Life Centre takes visitors on an undersea voyage with displays of freshwater and marine life, an otter sanctuary and adventure trail.

The Waters Edge, Brindley Place, Birmingham, West Midlands B1 2HL

☎ 0121 633 4700, 0121 643 6777
@ slcbirmingham@ merlinentertainments.biz
🖮 www.sealifeeurope.com
📄 0121 633 4787
🏛 Page 2-B5

National Trust: Birmingham Back to Backs

Birmingham Back to Backs are a courtyard of working people's homes reflecting the story of the houses through the experiences of the people who lived and worked here. Visitors move through four different periods, from 1840 to the 1970s. The design of each interior reflects the varied cultures, religions and professions of the families who made their homes here.

50–54 Inge Street, 55–63 Hurst Street, Birmingham, West Midlands B5 4TE
☎ 0121 622 2442
☏ 0121 666 7671
@ backtobacks@ nationaltrust.org.uk
🖮 www.nationaltrust.org.uk
🏛 Page 3-F7

National Trust: Moseley Old Hall

Moseley Old Hall is an Elizabethan house and features panelled walls, which were often used for hiding Catholic priests. One of these cramped priest holes saved Charles II when he hid here after the Battle of Worcester in 1651, and the bed where he slept is on view. An exhibition in the barn tells the story of the King's dramatic escape from Cromwell's troops. The garden has been recreated in 17th-century style with a formal knot garden, arbour and nut walk, and

has appropriate varieties of herbs and plants.

Moseley Old Hall Lane, Fordhouses, Wolverhampton, West Midlands WV10 7HY
☎ 01902 782808
@ moseleyoldhall@ nationaltrust.org.uk
🖮 www.nationaltrust.org. uk/
🏛 Page 13-G2

National Trust: Wightwick Manor

Wightwick Manor is an example of a house built and furnished under the influence of the Arts and Crafts Movement. The many original William Morris wallpapers and fabrics, pre-Raphaelite paintings, Kempe glass and de Morgan ware help conjure up the spirit of the time.

Wightwick Bank, Wolverhampton, West Midlands WV6 8EE
☎ 01902 761400
@ wightwickmanor@ nationaltrust.org.uk
🖮 www.nationaltrust.org. uk/
📄 01902 764663
🏛 Page 34-D4

RSPB Sandwell Valley

The valley is an oasis for wildlife on the outskirts of Birmingham and supports an array of garden birds on the feeders.

20 Tan House Avenue, Great Barr, Birmingham, West Midlands B43 5AG
☎ 0121 357 7395
@ sandwellvalley@ rspb.org.uk
🖮 www.rspb.org/reserves/ guide/s/sandwellvalley
🏛 Page 73-E5

Selly Manor

Selly Manor was rebuilt by the Cadbury family and

Timber-framed Selly Manor Museum

houses oak furniture and domestic objects offering an insight into life centuries ago.

Corner Of Maple and Sycamore Road, Bourneville, Birmingham, West Midlands B30 1UB
☎ 0121 472 0199
@ sellymanor@bvt.org.uk
🖱 www.bvt.org.uk/ sellymanor
📄 0121 415 6410
📍 Page 159-H3

Sheldon Country Park
The park covers 300 acres and includes open grassland, wetlands, old hedgerows, mature woodland and a 17th-century dairy farm.

Sheldon Country Park Ranger Service, Old Rectory Farm, Ragley Drive, Church Road, Sheldon, Birmingham, West Midlands B26 3TU
☎ 0121 742 0226
@ sheldon.country.park@ birmingham.gov.uk
🖱 www.birmingham.gov. uk/sheldonpark.bcc
📍 Page 148-C1

The Shire Country Park
The Shire Country Park

features an array of wildlife including butterflies, foxes, watervoles and bats. Bird lovers can spot kingfishers, sparrowhawks, all three British species of woodpecker, a variety of warblers in the summer and redwings and fieldfares in the winter months. The Park also has willows, alders and mature oaks besides a wide range of wild flowers in spring.

Sarehole Mill Museum, Cole Bank Road, Moseley, Birmingham, West Midlands B14 0BD
☎ 0121 702 2739 / 303 4266
@ shire.countrypark@ birmingham.gov.uk
🖱 www.birmingham.gov. uk/shirecountrypark.bcc
📍 Page 162-B2

Soho House
The Soho House was the seat of the Lunar Society, who met to discuss their world-changing ideas at the dining hall. Exhibits at the house include underfloor central heating system, the ormolu Sidereal clock and exhibitions.

Soho Avenue, Handsworth, Birmingham, West Midlands B18 5LB
☎ 0121 554 9122
🖱 www.bmag.org.uk
📍 Page 108-A2

Sutton Park
Sutton Park covers an area of 2,400 acres consisting of woodlands, heathlands and wetlands. The park is a remnant of an extensive forest that used to cover much of the Midlands and includes many ancient features like prehistoric mounds and ruins, as well as a Roman road. Besides being home to wildlife, it offers walking, cycling, horse riding, fishing, jogging, kite flying, canoeing and sailing facilities to visitors.

Sutton Park Visitor Centre, Park Road, Sutton Coldfield, West Midlands B74 2YT
☎ 0121 355 6370
🖱 www.birmingham.gov.uk/
📍 Page 62-A3

Victoria Square
Victoria Square stands at the junction of three streets: New Street, Paradise Street and Colmore Row. After the Council House was built in the 1870s it was known as Council House Square. It became Victoria Square after the arrival of the statue of Queen Victoria in 1901.

New Street, Birmingham, West Midlands B1 1BD
☎ 0121 693 6300
🖱 www.birmingham.gov. uk/victoriasquare.bcc
📍 Page 2-E5

Walsall Arboretum
Walsall Arboretum is a Victorian park close to Walsall town centre and contains parkland, lakes, gardens and woodland walks.

Lichfield Street, Walsall, West Midlands WS1 2AB
☎ 01922 654370, 01922 650309
@ guest@walsall.gov.uk
🖱 www.walsall.gov. uk/index/leisure_ and_culture/tourism/ attractions/walsall_ arboretum.htm
📍 Page 5-J2

Weoley Castle
The ruins at Weoley Castle are over 700 years old and are the remains of the moated medieval manor house that once stood here. Although the ruins are not accessible to visitors there is a viewing area, with information panels, which is open to the public. There is a regular programme of activities and exhibitions.

Alwold Road, Birmingham, West Midlands B29 5RX
☎ 0121 464 2193
🖱 www.bmag.org.uk
📍 Page 141-G5

Woodgate Valley Urban Farm
The farm was established in 1988 and is home to rare breeds of cattle, sheep, pigs, goats, geese, ducks and rabbits.

12 Doulton Close, Harborne, Birmingham, West Midlands B32 2XF
☎ 0121 423 2593, 0121 426 1871
@ wvuf.development@ thephone.coop
🖱 wvurbanfarm.org.uk
📍 Page 141-F4

MUSEUMS

Birchills Canal Museum
Birchills Canal Museum houses displays on the history of Walsall's waterways, boat building tools and information, and

also includes items belonging to local boat builders.

Old Birchills, Walsall, West Midlands WS3 8QD
☎ 01922 645778
@ museum@walsall.gov.uk
🖰 www.canaljunction.com/museum/birchills.htm
🖭 Page 41-G2

Birmingham Museum and Art Gallery

The musuem and art gallery house a vast collection telling the story of the last 400,000 years of history. The art galleries include the pre-Raphaelite paintings and drawings collection, fine art from the 14th century onwards, applied arts like ceramics and metalwork, and historic collections, including everything from local archaeology to cultures of the world.

Chamberlain Square, Birmingham, West Midlands B3 3DH

☎ 01213 032834
@ bmag_enquiries@birmingham.gov.uk
🖰 www.bmag.org.uk
🖭 Page 2-E5

Birmingham Railway Museum

670 Warwick Road, Tyseley, Birmingham, West Midlands B11 2HL
☎ 0121 708 4962
🕓 0121 708 4960
@ office@binthetrains.co.uk
🖰 www.vintagetrains.co.uk/brm.htm
🖹 0121 708 4963
🖭 Page 145-H2

Bishop Asbury Cottage

This 18th-century cottage was the boyhood home of Francis Asbury, the first American Methodist Bishop. It is furnished in period style, and with memorabilia and information relating to Asbury's life both in West

The Black Country Living Museum

Bromwich and in America. There is information relating to the rise of Methodism in the Black Country, links to John Wesley's life and times and his visits to the local area.

Newton Road, Great Barr, West Midlands B43 6HN

☎ 0121 553 0759
@ pamela_haines@sandwell.gov.uk
🖰 www.laws.sandwell.gov.uk/
🖭 Page 73-E2

The Black Country Living Museum

The Museum occupies a 26-acre urban heritage park in the shadow of Dudley Castle in the centre of the Black Country conurbation of two million people. Historic buildings from all around the Black Country have been moved and authentically rebuilt at the museum to create a tribute to the traditional skills and enterprise of the people that once lived in the heart of industrial Britain.

Tipton Road, Dudley, West Midlands DY1 4SQ
☎ 012 1557 9643
@ info@bclm.co.uk
🖰 www.bclm.co.uk
🖹 0121 557 4242
🖭 Page 84-D3

Blakesley Hall

Blakesley Hall was built in 1590 by Richard Smalbroke, a member of one of Birmingham's leading

Birmingham Museum and Art Gallery

merchant families. Exhibits include 400-year-old wall decorations in the Painted Chamber and the Long Table in the Great Hall. Beyond the Hall, the herb garden and orchard are a haven for butterflies and birds.

Blakesley Road, Yardley, Birmingham, West Midlands B25 8RN
☎ 0121 464 2193
🖰 www.bmag.org.uk
🖉 Page 130-A3

Broadfield House Glass Museum

The Museum has a collection of British glass, much of it made locally, dating from the 17th century up to the present day. The programme of events and temporary exhibitions complement the glass displays and celebrate the magical art of glassmaking. There is also a glassmaking studio at the museum.

Compton Drive, Kingswinford, West Midlands DY6 9NS
☎ 01384 812745
@ glass.museum@ dudley.gov.uk
🖰 www.glassmuseum. org.uk
🖉 Page 99-H4

Dudley Museum and Art Gallery

Dudley Museum and Art Gallery possesses a collection of 19th-and 20th-century oil paintings, drawings and watercolours. The museum is also home to the Brooke Robinson Collection – a Victorian gentleman's collection of paintings, furniture and Greek and Roman pottery.

St James Road, Dudley, West Midlands DY1 1HU

☎ 01384 815575
@ dudley.museum@ dudley.gov.uk
🖰 www.dudley.gov.uk/ dudleymuseum
📄 01384 815576
🖉 Page 84-C5

Haden Hill House

A Victorian Gentleman's residence, furnished in period style, and surrounded by 55 acres of beautiful parkland. The magnificent Oak Room is licensed for civil weddings, and conference facilities are also available. Talks, tours and Victorian handling collections are available for a small charge.

Halesowen Road, Cradley Heath, West Midlands B64 7JU
☎ 01384 569444
🖰 www.lea.sandwell.gov.uk/ museums/hadenhill.htm
🖉 Page 121-F4

Jerome K Jerome Birthplace Museum

The celebrated author of *Three Men in a Boat* was born in Walsall in 1859. His birthplace home is now a Grade II listed building and houses a small museum dedicated to his life and work. It has a considerable collection of photographs, books, letters and personal items connected with Jerome.

Belsize House, Bradford Street, Walsall, West Midlands WS1 1PN
☎ 01922 653135
🖰 www.jeromekjerome. com/museum.htm
📄 01922 720885
🖉 Page 4-D5

The Lace Guild

The Lace Guild is one of the largest organisations for lacemakers in British,

with an international membership. The aim is to provide information about the craft, to promote a high standard of lacemaking, and to encourage the design, development and professional presentation of laces.

The Hollies, 53 Audnam, Stourbridge, West Midlands DY8 4AE
☎ 01384 390739
@ hollies@laceguild.org
🖰 www.laceguild.demon. co.uk
📄 01384 444415
🖉 Page 118-A3

The Lapworth Museum

The museum has some of the finest collections from the Wenlock Limestone of Dudley, famous for its fossils dating from 420 million years ago when the area was covered by a shallow, warm, tropical sea that enabled a highly diverse ecosystem to develop. From the rocks of the old Midlands coalfields are important collections of fossil plants, fish, insects, arachnids, fossil footprints and animal tracks.

University of Birmingham, Edgbaston, Birmingham, West Midlands B15 2TT
☎ 0121 414 6751, 0121 414 7294
@ lapworth@contacts. bham.ac.uk
🖰 www.lapworth.bham. ac.uk
📄 0121 414 4942
🖉 Page 142-D4

Museum of The Jewellery Quarter

The museum narrates the story of the Jewellery Quarter through live demonstrations of traditional jewellery-making skills and visitors can get

first-hand experience of what it was like to work in this noisy and busy workshop.

75–79 Vyse Street, Hockley, Birmingham, West Midlands B18 6HA
☎ 0121 554 3598
🖰 bmag.org.uk/
🖉 Page 2-C1

National Motorcycle Museum

The National Motorcycle Museum opened its doors in October 1984. The museum is home to more than 650 machines, with new acquisitions arriving daily. The museum also has conference and banqueting facilities with state-of-the-art audio-visual equipment.

Coventry Road, Bickenhill, Solihull West Midlands B92 0EJ
☎ 01675 443311
@ admin@nationalmotor cyclemuseum.co.uk
🖰 www.nationalmotor cyclemuseum.co.uk
🖉 Page 150-C4

The Red House Glass Cone

The Red House Glass Cone lies in the heart of the Stourbridge glassmaking industry. Built at the end of the 18th century the Cone was used for the manufacture of glass until 1936 and is now one of only four cones left in the United Kingdom. Reaching 100 feet into the sky, the Cone enclosed a furnace around which men made glass for 140 years.

High Street, Wordsley, Stourbridge, West Midlands DY8 4AZ
☎ 01384 812750
@ redhouse.cone@ dudley.gov.uk
🖰 www.redhousecone.co.uk

📄 01384 812751
✎ Page 118-A2

Sarehole Mill Museum

The 200-year-old mill at Sarehole is one of only two surviving watermills in Birmingham. The musuem consists of a courtyard and a mill pool, while the buildings and their machinery give an insight into the lives of the millers who once lived here.

Cole Bank Road, Hall Green, Birmingham, West Midlands B13 0BD
☎ 0121 777 6612
🖰 www.bmag.org.uk
📄 0121 236 1766
✎ Page 162-B2

Smethwick Heritage Centre

Victoria Park Lodge, High Street, Smethwick, West Midlands B66 3NJ
☎ 0121 555 7278
@ info@smethwick-heritage.co.uk
🖰 www.smethwick-heritage.co.uk
✎ Page 106-C4

Thinktank at Millennium Point

Thinktank is exactly how a modern science museum should be – interactive, informative and fun. Attractions include historic transport and stream engine collections, over 200 hands-on games and activities, characters from the past and real examples of cutting edge innovations.

Curzon Street, Digbeth, Birmingham, West Midlands B4 7XG
☎ 01564 742251, 0121 202 2222
@ findout@thinktank.ac
🖰 www.thinktank.ac/visit/
✎ Page 3-K4

Tipton Community Heritage Centre

Included in the centre are temporary displays covering various aspects of Tipton's industrial and social history, along with information about the canals. There is also a local history section within the library.

Tipton Library, Unit 19, Tipton Shopping Centre, Owen Street, Tipton, West Midlands DY4 8QE
☎ 0121 556 0683, 0121 557 1796
🖰 www.lea.sandwell.gov.uk/museums/tiptonhc.htm
✎ Page 85-E1

Walsall Leather Museum

The Leather Museum features displays on the fascinating trade which features Walsall-made leather goods, both past and present. A shop sells a wide range of Walsall-made bags, wallets and purses.

Littleton Street West, Walsall, West Midlands WS2 8EQ
☎ 01922 721153
@ leathermuseum@walsall.gov.uk
🖰 www.walsall.gov.uk/leathermuseum
📄 01922 725827
✎ Page 4-D1

Walsall Museum

Dedicated to the history of Walsall, the museum is home to a wide-ranging collection of artefacts reflecting Walsall's heritage, its many industries, and the lives of the people who lived here. In particular the museum houses the nationally important Hodson Shop collection of 20th-century working clothes.

Lichfield Street, Walsall, West Midlands WS1 1TR
☎ 01922 653116
@ museum@walsall.gov.uk
🖰 www.walsall.gov.uk
✎ Page 4-D1

Warwickshire County Cricket Club Museum

A visit to the Warwickshire County Cricket Club Museum at Edgbaston is to take a unique journey through the last 112 years of first- class cricket played at this famous ground. Photographs, memorabilia, artefacts and articles are displayed in a way that captures the interest of the visitor and provides scope for many repeat visits during a season. The ethos of the museum is the emphasis on retaining its unique items and nostalgic look, while at the same time providing regular displays and features to captivate the many thousands of visitors each year.

County Ground, Edgbaston, Birmingham, West Midlands B5 7QU
☎ 0121 446 4422
@ info@edgbaston.com
🖰 www.thebears.co.uk/history/museum/international.shtml
✎ Page 143-H2

Wednesbury Museum and Art Gallery

This Victorian art gallery, houses collections which include fine art paintings, applied art, and collections of Ruskin pottery and geology. The family room is dedicated to school and community use, and the education programme features activities such as toy handling, gallery visits, and storytelling linked to the collections.

Holyhead Road, Wednesbury, West Midlands WS10 7DF
☎ 0121 556 0683
🖰 www.lea.sandwell.gov.uk
✎ Page 70-C1

West Midlands Police Museum

The West Midlands Police Museum houses a wide range of pictures, information and items to show the development of policing in and around Birmingham. From an early watchman's lamp and staff to modern drug testing equipment, there is a complete record of the work of the police.

Sparkhill Police Station, 639 Stratford Road, Sparkhill, Birmingham, West Midlands B11 4EA
☎ 0845 113 5000, 0121 626 7181
🖰 www.westmidlands policemuseum.co.uk
📄 0121 626 7066
✎ Page 145-E3

ART GALLERIES AND VISUAL ARTS

The Barber Institute of Fine Arts

The Barber Institute of Fine Arts is housed in one of Birmingham's finest art deco buildings, purpose built and opened by Queen Mary in 1939. The Institute was designed by Robert Atkinson (1883–1952), one of Britain's leading architects of the 1920s and 30s. When it opened *The Times* described the building as 'the purest example of his work' and it continues to be regarded as one of his greatest achievements.

University of Birmingham, Edgbaston, Birmingham, West Midlands B15 2TS

The Barber Institute of Fine Arts (see entry on page 11)

☎ 0121 414 7333
@ info@barber.org.uk
🖰 www.barber.org.uk
📄 0121 414 3370
📖 Page 142-D4

Bilston Craft Gallery
Bilston Craft Gallery is a craft venue with exhibitions featuring the contemporary crafts.

Mount Pleasant, Bilston, Wolverhampton, West Midlands WV14 7LU
☎ 01902 552507
@ bilstoncraftgallery@ dial.pipex.com
🖰 www.wolverhampton art. org.uk/bilston
📖 Page 54-A2

Birmingham Botanical Gardens and Glasshouses
The Birmingham Botanical Gardens and Glasshouses were designed by J C Loudon, a leading garden planner, horticultural journalist and publisher. Opened in 1832, the gardens feature the Loudon Terrace, main lawn and bandstand as well as the cottage garden. The glasshouses have separate tropical, subtropical and Mediterranean zones for specific plants. Weekend courses and various workshops for children are organised here.

Westbourne Road, Edgbaston, Birmingham, West Midlands B15 3TR
☎ 0121 454 1860
@ admin@birmingham botanicalgardens.org.uk
🖰 www.birmingham botanicalgardens.org.uk
📖 Page 125-H5

Birmingham Institute of Art & Design
Birmingham Museum and Art Gallery boasts an unrivalled collection of pre-Raphaelite arts and crafts, and the new Waterhall Gallery has works by some of the key British Artists of the 20th and 21st centuries. Birmingham's commitment to the arts is reflected in ArtsFest an annual free festival featuring artists from all disciplines covering the wealth of arts available throughout the West Midlands.

Gosta Green, Corporation Street, Birmingham, West Midlands B4 7DX
☎ 0121 331 5800, 0121 331 5801
@ enquiries@students. uce.ac.uk
🖰 www.biad.uce.ac.uk
📄 0121 331 7814
📖 Page 3-J1

Birmingham Museum and Art Gallery
The musuem and art gallery house a vast collection telling the story of the last 400,000 years of history. The art galleries include the pre-Raphaelite paintings and drawings collection, fine art from the 14th century onwards, applied arts like ceramics and metalwork, and historic collections, including everything from local archaeology to cultures of the world.

Chamberlain Square, Birmingham, West Midlands B3 3DH
☎ 01213 032834
@ bmag_enquiries@ birmingham.gov.uk
🖰 www.bmag.org.uk
📖 Page 2-E5

Halcyon Gallery, ICC
The Halcyon Gallery, established over 20 years ago, specialises in the sale of original paintings, drawings and sculpture as well as fine art, master graphics and limited editions. A changing programme of exhibitions and a wide range of work is offered across a broad range of styles and subject matter.

International Convention Centre, Broad Street, Birmingham, B1 2EA
☎ 0121 248 8484
@ info@halcyongallery.com
🖰 www.theicc.co.uk
📄 0121 248 8585
📖 Page 2-C5

Ikon Gallery
The gallery features temporary exhibitions over two floors totalling 450 square metres. A variety of mediums are represented, including sound, film, mixed media, photography, painting, sculpture and installation.

1 Oozells Square, Birndleyplace, Birmingham, West Midlands B1 2HS
☎ 0121 248 0708
⌂ www.ikon-gallery.co.uk
🖹 0121 248 0709
✐ Page 2-B6

International Project Space

International Project Space was opened in the year 2002 and this gallery is a centre for production, exhibition and dissemination of contemporary art. The gallery hosts international, national and regional projects, exhibitions and conferences. The gallery is a resource centre for students, staff, the local community people and for the art audiences.

University of Central England, Maple Road, Birmingham, West Midlands B30 2AA
☎ 0121 331 5785
@ info@international projectspace.org
⌂ www.international projectspace.org
🖹 0121 331 5779
✐ Page 159-G3

The New Art Gallery Walsall

The New Art Gallery Walsall houses the Garman Ryan collection, featuring European art including works by Monet, Degas and Van Gogh.

Gallery Square, Walsall, West Midlands WS2 8LG
☎ 01922 654400
@ info@artatwalsall.org.uk
⌂ www.artatwalsall.org.uk
🖹 01922 654401
✐ Page 4-D3

The New Gallery

The New Gallery is an independent gallery dedicated to modern and contemporary fine art. Original paintings, monoprints, limited edition prints, photography, and other media pieces are shown in exhibitions featuring nationally and internationally known artists.

Blackthorn House, 1–2 Mary Ann Street, St Paul's Square, Birmingham, West Midlands B3 1RL
☎ 0845 226 1964
@ enquiries@ thenewgallery.co.uk
⌂ www.thenewgallery.co.uk
🖹 0845 226 1964
✐ Page 2-E2

Number Nine The Gallery

Number Nine The Gallery was established in 1999 by Lee Benson. The gallery exhibits a broad range of artwork, ranging from glass, ceramics and sculpture in a reviving commercial environment.

9 Brindleyplace, Birmingham, West Midlands B1 2JA
☎ 0121 643 9099
@ noninethegallery@ btclick.com
⌂ www.numberninethe gallery.com
🖹 0121 643 9199
✐ Page 2-B6

Purple Gallery

The gallery houses a wide range of collections including painting, sculpture, ceramics, textiles and jewellery.

229 Mary Vale Road, Bournville, Birmingham, West Midlands B30 2DL
☎ 0121 459 0941
@ jane@purplegallery.com
⌂ www.purplegallery.com
✐ Page 159-H4

Royal Birmingham Society of Artists (RBSA)

The Royal Birmingham Society of Artists is one of the oldest art societies in the UK. As early as 1807, Samuel Lines opened an academy teaching students, several of whom became famous in the art world. There are two galleries displaying a changing programme of work by members, associates, friends and visiting exhibitions. These will be available for rent by artists, craftsmen or societies, subject to availability and approval.

4 Brook Street, St Paul's, Birmingham, West Midlands B3 1SA
☎ 0121 236 4353
@ secretary@rbsa.org.uk
⌂ www.rbsa.org.uk
🖹 0121 236 4555
✐ Page 2-D3

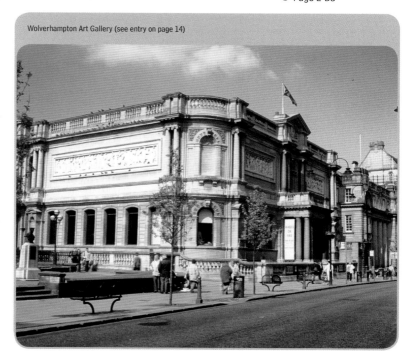
Wolverhampton Art Gallery (see entry on page 14)

Snap Galleries

Snap Galleries specialise in rare, iconic rock 'n' roll photographs which are produced in small limited editions by the master photographers.

12–13, Gibb Square,
The Custard Factory,
Birmingham, West Midlands
B9 4AA
☎ 0121 224 7345,
   0121 748 3408
@ info@snapgalleries.com
🖰 www.snapgalleries.com
🕮 Page 3-K7

St Paul's Gallery

The gallery sells original and editioned artwork. It collaborates with major worldwide galleries to bring specialist shows to Birmingham.

94–108 Northwood Street,
Birmingham, West Midlands
B3 1TH
☎ 0121 236 5800
@ info@stpaulsgallery.com
🖰 www.stpaulsgallery.com
🕮 Page 2-D2

Wolverhampton Art Gallery

Situated in the heart of Wolverhampton city centre, Wolverhampton Art Gallery was established in 1884. The gallery has an impressive collection of contemporary Pop Art, sumptuous displays of Victorian and Georgian paintings and three national awards for the way it presents art to its visitors.

Lichfield Street,
Wolverhampton, West
Midlands WV1 1DU
☎ 01902 552055
@ info@wolverhamptonart.
   org.uk
🖰 www.wolverhamptonart.
   org.uk/wolves
🕮 Page 7-F4

ART CENTRES

The Custard Factory

The award-winning first phase is home to a bohemian community of 500 artists and small creative enterprises. The studio workshops are complemented by a theatre cafe, antiques shops, meeting rooms, dance studios, holistic therapy rooms, art galleries, the Medicine Bar and the Code nightclub. The second phase, completed in 2002 comprises shops, galleries and restaurants plus the Green Man, a towering 40-foot sculpture made of earth, fire and water.

Gibb Square, Birmingham,
West Midlands B9 4AA
☎ 0121 224 7777,
   0121 224 8401
@ info@custardfactory.com
🖰 www.custardfactory.co.uk
🕮 0121 604 8888
🕮 Page 3-K7

The Dormston Centre

The Dormston Centre was built in 1997 with funding from The National Lottery and Sport England. The Centre has a sports hall with two smaller studios, a well-equipped gym, an art gallery, a bar and a 350-seat, purpose-built theatre.

Mill Bank, Sedgley, Dudley,
West Midlands DY3 1SN
☎ 01384 816389
🕘 01384 816388
🖰 www.dormstoncentre.
   dudley.gov.uk
🕮 Page 67-F3

The Drum

The Drum develops and promotes contemporary art and culture of British African, Asian and Caribbean communities. Through its various initiatives, The Drum intends to become a centre of national and international renown, firmly rooted within its local community.

144 Potters Lane, Aston,
Birmingham, West Midlands
B6 4UU
☎ 0121 333 2400
🕘 0121 333 2444
@ info@the-drum.org.uk
🖰 www.the-drum.org.uk
🕮 0121 333 2440
🕮 Page 109-E2

The Glasshouse

The Glasshouse is part of the Ruskin Mill Educational Trust. The Ruskin Glass Centre is also based on the Glasshouse site hosting workshops in glass blowing, glass cutting, glass repairs, photography and stone carving.

Wollaston Road,
Stourbridge, West Midlands
DY8 4HF
☎ 01384 399400
🖰 www.rmet.co.uk/
   glasshouse_events/
🕮 Page 118-A5

Light House

Today Light House provides production courses, new exhibitions, films, educational activities, conferences and events. In addition, there are two major annual festivals and a myriad of activities that develop and support the growing creative industries in the city and region. The emphasis is still on giving opportunities for active involvement for everyone. Light House has held to its original mission, increasing the enjoyment and understanding of different media forms and using them for the benefit of the people of Wolverhampton and beyond.

The Chubb Buildings, Fryer
Street, Wolverhampton,
West Midlands WV1 1HT
☎ 01902 716055
@ info@light-house.co.uk
🖰 www.light-house.co.uk
🕮 01902 717143
🕮 Page 7-G3

MAC: Midlands Arts Centre

MAC is the most visited arts centre in the Midlands, with over 650,000 visitors a year who come to enjoy theatre performances, music, comedy, plays for children, literature and poetry events, courses, magical family shows, films, dance performances and free exhibitions.

Cannon Hill Park,
Birmingham, West Midlands
B12 9QH
☎ 0121 440 3838
@ info@macarts.co.uk
🖰 www.macarts.co.uk
🕮 Page 143-H3

Netherton Arts Centre

Halesowen Road, Netherton,
Dudley, West Midlands
DY2 9EP
☎ 01384 815577
🖰 www.dudley.gov.
   uk/education-and-learning/
   extra-curricular-activities/
   dudley-performing-arts/
   whats-on-offer/tailor-made-
   options/netherton-arts-
   centre
🕮 Page 102-C4

Newhampton Arts Centre

Creative arts space that hosts public performances.

Dunkley Street,
Wolverhampton, West
Midlands WV1 4AN
☎ 01902 572090
🖰 www.newhamptonarts.
   co.uk
🕮 01902 572090
🕮 Page 6-E2

Northern Star Community Arts Project

Northern Star Community Arts Project organise and run events for the community from shows to playschemes to workshops as well as African drumming workshops to performance of Indian dance.

The Baptist Church Centre, Hedingham Grove, Chelmsley Wood, Solihull, West Midlands B37 7TP
☎ 0121 788 3402
@ northernstar@
  northernstararts.co.uk
www.northernstararts.co.uk
0121 788 3402
Page 132-D2

The Public

The Public works with art projects, in the arenas of print, photography, internet, video and sound.

1 Overend Street, West Bromwich, West Midlands B70 6EY
☎ 0121 524 2107
@ info@thepublic.com
www.thepublic.com
0121 525 6475
Page 87-H3

Solihull Arts Complex

Solihull Arts Complex comprises a 339-seat theatre, a multipurpose studio space and the first floor gallery, exhibiting contemporary work, community groups and heritage exhibitions.

Solihull Arts Complex, Homer Road, Solihull, West Midlands B91 3RG
☎ 0121 704 6962
@ artscomplex@
  solihull.gov.uk
www.solihull.gov.uk/artscomplex
Page 181-H2

DANCE AND PERFORMING ARTS

Arena Theatre

The Arena Theatre seats 150 and hosts dance, ballet performances and plays. The Arena also showcases work by local schools, colleges, amateur companies and community events.

Wulfruna Street, Wolverhampton, West Midlands WV1 1SE
☎ 01902 321327
01902 321321
@ arena@wlv.ac.uk
www.arenatheatre.info
01902 322599
Page 7-F3

Birmingham Hippodrome

Welcoming audiences averaging almost 500,000 per year, Birmingham Hippodrome can lay claim to the highest regular annual attendance of any single theatre in the country. It hosts a vast variety of entertainment events throughout the year.

Hurst Street, Birmingham, West Midlands B5 4TB
☎ 0870 730 5555
0870 730 1234,
  0870 730 4321
@ tickets@birmingham
  hippodrome.com
www.birmingham
  hippodrome.com
0121 689 3031
Page 3-F7

Crescent Theatre

20 Sheepcote Street, Brindleyplace, Birmingham West Midlands B16 8AE
☎ 0121 643 5859
0121 643 5858
@ admin@crescent-theatre.co.uk
www.crescent-theatre.co.uk
0121 643 5860
Page 2-B6

LIVE MUSIC VENUES

The Actress and Bishop

Hosting live music, most nights of the week.

36 Ludgate Hill, Birmingham, West Midlands B3 1EH
☎ 0121 236 7426
Page 2-E3

Adam and Eve

Bradford Street, Birmingham, West Midlands B12 0JD
☎ 0121 693 1500
@ katie@theadam.co.uk
www.theadam.co.uk
Page 127-F3

Alcatraz Rock Club

Cemetery Road, Willenhall, Wolverhampton, West Midlands WV13 1DD
☎ 01902 834777
www.Alcatrazrock.com
Page 39-G2

Arena Theatre

The Arena Theatre seats 150 and hosts dance, ballet performances and plays. The Arena also showcases work by local schools, colleges, amateur companies and community events.

Wulfruna Street, Wolverhampton, West Midlands WV1 1SE
☎ 01902 321327
01902 321321
@ arena@wlv.ac.uk
www.arenatheatre.info
01902 322599
Page 7-F3

Bar Academy Birmingham

51 Dale End, Birmingham, West Midlands B4 7LS
☎ 0121 262 3000
0870 771 2000
@ mail@birmingham-academy.co.uk
www.birmingham-academy.co.uk
0121 236 2241
Page 3-H5

Barfly, Birmingham

A live music and club night venue in Birmingham.

78 Digbeth High Street, Birmingham, West Midlands B5 6DY
☎ 0121 246 1010,
  0121 633 8311
@ carlo@barflyclub.com
www.barflyclub.com
0121 633 8344
Page 3-J7

The Barn

The Barn, which hosts a wonderful programme of entertainment and social activities, is one of the most famous and prestigious venues in clubland and throughout Britain.

Brookvale Road, Witton, Birmingham, West Midlands B6 7AJ
☎ 0121 356 5706
@ info@thebarn
  birmingham.co.uk
www.thebarn
  birmingham.co.uk
Page 91-G3

Bash Bar Lounge

The bar holds regular and popular jazz jam nights.

84b New Street, Birmingham, West Midlands B2 4BA
☎ 0121 633 3852
www.myspace.com/bashbarjam
Page 3-G5

Bear Tavern

A popular and long-standing pub with music and comedy nights at the weekend.

500 Bearwood Road, Smethwick, Birmingham, West Midlands B66 4BX
☎ 0121 429 1184
Page 124-C2

Bearwood Corks Club

558 Bearwood Road, Bearwood, Smethwick, West Midlands B66 4BT

☎ 0121 429 2091
@ bearwoodjazz@
gmail.com
🖱 www.bearwoodjazz.co.uk
🖉 Page 124-C3

Birmingham Hippodrome

Welcoming audiences averaging almost 500,000 per year, Birmingham Hippodrome can lay claim to the highest regular annual attendance of any single theatre in the country. It hosts a vast variety of entertainment events throughout the year.

Hurst Street, Birmingham, West Midlands B5 4TB
☎ 0870 730 5555
📞 0870 730 1234,
0870 730 4321
@ tickets@birmingham
hippodrome.com
🖱 www.birmingham
hippodrome.com
📄 0121 689 3031
🖉 Page 3-F7

Birmingham Town Hall

Acclaimed at its opening in 1834 as the finest music hall in the country, the Grade I listed landmark has been lovingly and painstakingly renovated by a dedicated team of conservation and construction professionals. It was designed by Joseph Aloysius Hansom for the performance of music, and today hosts a varied programme including recitals, international chamber music, world music, folk, jazz and pop.

Victoria Square, Birmingham, West Midlands B3 3DQ
☎ 0121 303 2880
🖱 www.birmingham.gov.
uk/townhall.bcc
🖉 Page 2-E5

Black Diamond Folk Club

The Globe, Blews Street, Aston, Birmingham, West

Midlands B6 4HN
☎ 0121 358 2665
🖱 www.btinternet.
com/~radical/diamond
🖉 Page 109-E4

The Bonded Warehouse

Canal Street, Stourbridge, West Midlands DY8 4LU
☎ 01384 395216
🖱 www.quests.freeuk.
com/warehouse.htm
📄 01384 395216 (daytime only)
🖉 Page 135-F1

The Bristol Pear

Hosts regular open mic nights.

676 Bristol Road, Selly Oak, Birmingham, West Midlands B29 6BJ
🖉 Page 142-C5

Broadway Casino

1–4 Broadway Plaza, 220 Ladywood Middleway, Birmingham, West Midlands B16 8LP

☎ 0121 456 5557
@ info@broadwaycasino.
co.uk
🖱 www.broadwaycasino.
co.uk
🖉 Page 126-A2

The Bull's Head

With a packed programme of entertainment, the Bull's Head has music playing on most nights of the week and a regular reggae night on Mondays.

23 St Mary's Row, Moseley, Birmingham, West Midlands B13 8HW
☎ 0121 256 7777
@ adam@diffdrum.co.uk
🖱 www.plimsoul.co.uk/
bullshead
🖉 Page 144-B4

Bull's Head

101 Birchfield Road, Birmingham, West Midlands B19 1LH
☎ 0121 523 8155
🖉 Page 108-D1

Birmingham Town Hall

Cafe One

1 Auchinleck Square,
Fiveways, Birmingham,
West Midlands B15 1DU
☎ 0121 245 0000
🖉 Page 126-B3

Carling Academy Birmingham

Carling Academy
Birmingham has fast
become Birmingham's
premier venue, offering the
best live events and club
nights in the region. It is a
focal point for nightlife in
the Midlands.

52–54 Dale End,
Birmingham, West Midlands
B4 7LS
☎ 01212 623000
@ mail@birmingham-
   academy.co.uk
🖱 www.birmingham-
   academy.co.uk
📄 01212 362241
🖉 Page 3-H5

The Ceol Castle

402 Moseley Road,
Birmingham, West Midlands
B12 9AT
☎ 0121 440 4278
@ mail@ceolcastle.com
🖉 Page 144-B2

The Chestnut Tree

The Chestnut Tree presents
a packed menu of rocking
tribute bands.

208 Sheldon Heath Road,
Birmingham, West Midlands
B26 2RY
☎ 0121 741 1931
@ keith@thenuts.info
🖱 www.thenuts.info
🖉 Page 130-C2

Coleshill Town Hall

144 High Street, Coleshill,
Birmingham, West Midlands
B46 3BG
🕾 01675 463239
🖉 Page 115-G3

Concrete

A 3,000-square foot
multipurpose venue spread
over two levels based in the
Jewellery Quarter, Hockley,
Birmingham. The venue
morphs through the week
from restaurant lounge bar
to full on live music at the
weekends, with strong club
promoters, eclectic bands
and internationally known
artists appearing regularly.

120 Vyse Street, Jewellery
Quarter, Birmingham, West
Midlands B18 6NF
☎ 0121 212 9280, 07968
366878, 07968 260276
🕾 0121 236 6446
@ info@concretebar.co.uk
🖱 www.concretebar.co.uk
🖉 Page 2-C1

Crescent Theatre

20 Sheepcote Street,
Brindleyplace, Birmingham,
West Midlands B16 8AE
☎ 0121 643 5859
🕾 0121 643 5858
@ admin@crescent-
   theatre.co.uk
🖱 www.crescent-theatre.
   co.uk
📄 0121 643 5860
🖉 Page 2-A5

Dudley Concert Hall

The largest venue in the
borough, hosting a variety
of national and local events
including concerts, shows,
dances, fashion shows,
product launches and
exhibitions.

St James's Road, Dudley,
West Midlands DY1 1HP
☎ 01384 815577
@ dudley.townhall@
   dudley.gov.uk
🖱 online.dudley.gov.
   uk/whatson/townhalls/
   index.asp
🖉 Page 84-B5

Edward's No8

A rock club in Birmingham.

Lower Severn Street,
Birmingham, West Midlands
B1 1BL
☎ 0121 643 5835
@ info@edwardsno8.
   wanadoo.co.uk
🖱 www.edwardsno8.com
🖉 Page 2-E6

Flapper & Firkin

Kingston Row, Cambrian
Wharf, Birmingham, West
Midlands B1 2NU
☎ 0121 236 2421
🕾 0121 236 2421
🖱 www.zootmusic.net
🖉 Page 2-C5

Giffard Arms

64 Victoria Street,
Wolverhampton, West
Midlands WV1 3NX
☎ 01902 426664
🖱 www.thegiffardarms.
   co.uk
🖉 Page 7-F5

The Glee Club Birmingham

Situated on the 1st floor
of The Arcadian Centre,
the club hosts live comedy
shows and music nights.

The Arcadian Centre, Hurst
Street, Birmingham, West
Midlands B5 4DP
☎ 0870 241 5093
🕾 0870 241 5093
@ duncan@glee.co.uk
🖱 www.glee.co.uk
🖉 Page 3-G7

HMV Birmingham

38 High Street, Birmingham,
West Midlands B4 7SL
☎ 0121 643 2177
🖱 www.hmv.co.uk/
🖉 Page 3-G5

Halesowen Cornbow Hall

Situated in the busy town
centre of Halesowen, this
attractive and modern

community venue comprises
a large hall, function room
and bar area.

10 Hagley Street,
Halesowen, West Midlands
B63 3AT
☎ 01384 812814
@ borough.halls@
   dudley.gov.uk
🖱 www.dudley.gov.uk/
   leisure-and-culture/arts-
   and-entertainment/
🖉 Page 138-D4

Hard Rock Cafe, Birmingham

Unit 6, Five Ways Leisure
Complex, 263 Broad Street,
Birmingham, West Midlands
B15 2HF
☎ 0121 665 6562
🖉 Page 2-C6

Harvester

Tanhouse Farm Lane,
Solihull, West Midlands
B92 9EY
☎ 0121 742 0770
🖱 www.harvesterlife.com
🖉 Page 148-A5

The Irish Club

16–20 High Street, Deritend,
Irish Quarter, Birmingham,
West Midlands B12 0LN
☎ 0121 622 2314
@ info@birmingham
   irishclub.co.uk
🖱 www.birmingham
   irishclub.co.uk
📄 0121 624 4444
🖉 Page 3-K7

island bar

At Birmingham's rock and
roll cocktail bar in Suffolk
Street, Queensway, you'll
find some of the city's
finest bartenders showing
off their skills while you
enjoy great guitar music.
DJs play a mix of old and
newer guitar classics,
live acoustic guitar music
features on many nights
of the week, there is an

open mic night for budding songwriters and the bar is also a showcase for local and national up-and-coming bands.

14–16 Suffolk Street, Queensway, Birmingham, West Midlands B1 1LT
☎ 0121 632 5296
© 0121 632 5296
@ info@bar-island.co.uk
🖰 www.bar-island.co.uk
🕮 Page 2-E6

JB's

15 Castle Hill, Dudley, West Midlands DY1 4QF
☎ 01384 253597
@ concerts@ jbsdudley.co.uk
🖰 www.jbsdudley.co.uk
🕮 Page 84-D4

The Jam House

Opened in 1999 by Jools Holland, the Jam House offers a nightly dose of duelling pianos, live rhythm 'n' blues and international cuisine. Located in the heart of the Jewellery Quarter of Birmingham the Jam House occupies a Georgian building with seating spread over three floors, boasting a capacity for up to 600 people.

1 St Paul's Square, Jewellery Quarter, Birmingham, West Midlands B3 1QU
☎ 0121 200 3030
@ info@thejamhouse.com
🖰 www.thejamhouse.com
🕮 0121 200 3044
🕮 Page 2-D3

The Jug Of Ale

The Jug of Ale is located in the area of Moseley and offers a small upstairs bar that provides a platform for local, national and international bands. The downstairs facility runs a rotating schedule of DJs to

suit the varying demands for pop, punk and other forms of music from its visitors.

43 Alcester Road, Moseley, Birmingham, West Midlands B13 8AA
☎ 0121 449 1082
@ arthur@catapultclub. freeserve.co.uk
🖰 www.jugofale.com
🕮 Page 144-B4

Katie Fitzgerald's

Originally known as the Golden Lion, Katie Fitzgerald's was a small one-roomed beerhouse, the property of Mary Faulkner. It was well positioned to attract travellers along the Stourbridge-Kinver turnpike road.

187 Enville Street, Stourbridge, West Midlands DY8 3TB
☎ 01384 374410
@ enquiries@ katiefitzgeralds.co.uk
🖰 www.katiefitzgeralds. co.uk/
🕮 Page 135-F2

Kitchen Garden Cafe

17 York Rd, Kings Heath, Birmingham, West Midlands B14 7SA
🖰 www.kitchengardencafe. co.uk/
🕮 Page 161-E2

Little Civic

Music and entertainment venue hosting comedy and special events.

North Street, Wolverhampton, West Midlands WV1 1RQ
© 0870 320 7000
🖰 www.wolvescivic.co.uk
🕮 Page 7-F4

MH Bar (Madhouse Rehearsals)

41 Hampton Street, Hockley, Birmingham, West Midlands B19 3LS

☎ 0121 233 1109
🖰 www.madhouse rehearsals.com
🕮 0121 233 1286
🕮 Page 2-E1

The Malt House

75 King Edwards Road, Birmingham, West Midlands B1 2NX
☎ 0121 633 4171
🕮 Page 2-B5

The NEC Arena

The NEC Arena is renowned for its blockbusting concerts and sporting events. Located within The NEC complex, the 12,300-seat NEC Arena receives over 1 million visitors every year. The list of concerts and entertainment events over the years is punctuated by legendary names. Since opening in 1980 with an epic performance by Queen, The NEC Arena has given the finest stage to the finest performers.

The NEC Arena, Birmingham, West Midlands B40 1NT
☎ 01217 804141
@ nec-arena@ necgroup.co.uk
🖰 www.necgroup.co.uk/ visitor/thenecarena
🕮 Page 150-A2

NIA: National Indoor Arena

King Edwards Road, Birmingham, West Midlands B1 2AA
☎ 0121 780 4444
@ nia-sales@ necgroup.co.uk
🖰 www.necgroup.co.uk
🕮 Page 2-B5

Newhampton Inn

17 Riches Street, Wolverhampton, West Midlands WV6 0DW
☎ 01902 745773
🕮 Page 36-B2

The Newt

58 Stephenson Street, Birmingham, West Midlands B2 4DH
☎ 0121 643 2969
🕮 Page 3-F6

The Old Crown

The oldest inn in Birmingham is an independently run establishment offering a delightful traditional bar, an intimate restaurant, truly unique accomodation and impressive facilities for both business conferences and special occasions.

188 High Street, Deritend, Birmingham, West Midlands B12 0LD
☎ 0121 248 1368
🖰 www.theoldcrown.com
🕮 0121 248 1369
🕮 Page 3-K7

The Old Mill

Long established as one of south Birmingham's most enduring and respected live music venues, The Old Mill has earned a reputation for showcasing some of the best live acts in the country – and for free. You can be sure of hearing your kind of music at The Old Mill with bands delivering rock, metal, reggae, pop, blues, R&B, jazz, celtic and tributes to all your favourites too. The atmosphere is relaxed and the company friendly.

30 West Heath Road, Northfield, Birmingham, West Midlands B31 3TG
☎ 0121 475 1337, 07779 582034
@ jackieheaton@ btconnect.com
🖰 www.music-at-the-mill. co.uk
🕮 Page 175-H4

The Old Moseley Arms

The club was established as the Prince of Wales Fit Men

Birmingham's NEC Arena (see entry opposite)

Cricket Club in 1981, out of the pub in Moseley of the same name. The club moved round the corner to the Old Moseley Arms at Tindal Street in about 1997.

53 Tindal Street, Balsall Heath, Birmingham, West Midlands B12 9QU
☎ 0121 440 1954
@ webmaster@ fitmen.org.uk
🖰 www.fitmen.org.uk
🥏 Page 144-B2

The Old Rep Theatre
This 383-seat theatre in the centre of Birmingham plays host to the Birmingham Stage Company and numerous amateur companies offering a wide variety of productions from plays to musicals, regular sell-out Christmas productions and specially written issued-based drama for young people.

Station Street, Birmingham, West Midlands B5 4DY
☎ 0121 605 5116
🖰 0121 303 2323
@ oldrephelpdesk@ birmingham.gov.uk
🖰 oldreptheatre.org.uk
🥏 Page 3-F7

The Place 2B
Chester Road, Sutton Coldfield, West Midlands B73 5BD
☎ 08712 071260, 0121 354 8228
🖰 www.theplace2buk.com
🥏 Page 76-C3

The Place I Love
30–31 Allison Street, Birmingham, West Midlands B5 5TY
🥏 Page 3-J6

Prince of Wales
84 Cambridge Street, Birmingham, West Midlands B1 2NP
☎ 0121 643 9460
🥏 Page 2-D5

The Rainbow
160 High Street, Digbeth, Birmingham, West Midlands B12 0LD
☎ 0121 772 8174
🖰 www.therainbowpub.com
🥏 Page 3-K7

Red Lion
95 Warstone Lane, Hockley, Birmingham, West Midlands B18 6NG
☎ 0121 236 8371
🖰 www.redlionfolkclub.com
🥏 Page 2-C2

The Roadhouse
Wharfside Leisure Complex, Lifford Lane, Stirchley, Birmingham, West Midlands B30 3DZ
☎ 0121 624 2920
@ vipervp@blueyonder.co.uk
🖰 www.roadhousevenue. co.uk
🥏 Page 160-A5

Roadhouse
Waterfront, Merry Hill, Dudley, West Midlands DY5 1XE
☎ 01384 572205l
🥏 Page 101-G5

The Robin 2
20–22 Mount Pleasant, Bilston, Wolverhampton, West Midlands WV14 7LJ
☎ 01902 401211
@ music@therobin.co.uk
🖰 www.therobin.co.uk
📄 01902 401418
🥏 Page 54-A2

Rock Cafe 2000
Rock Cafe 2000 provides a wide and varied selection of entertainment for all tastes.

Mill Race Lane, Unit 1, Stourbridge Industrial Estate, Block L, Stourbridge, West Midlands DY8 1JN
☎ 01384 390918 , 01384 833556
@ info@rockcafe2000.co.uk
🖰 www.rockcafe2000.co.uk
📄 01384 836387
🥏 Page 135-G1

Rojac Warehouse
Gibb Street, Heath Mill Lane, Birmingham, West Midlands B9 4AR
🥏 Page 3-K7

Rooty's
Unit 17, The Custard Factory, Gibb Street, Birmingham, West Midlands B9 4AA
☎ 0121 224 8458
🖉 Page 3-K7

The Rope Walk
15–20 St Paul's Square, Birmingham, West Midlands B3 1RB
☎ 0121 233 2129
🖉 Page 2-E2

Route 44
2 Westley Road, Acocks Green, Birmingham, West Midlands B27 7UH
🕐 0121 708 0108
@ info@route44.co.uk
🕂 www.route44.co.uk
🖉 Page 146-B4

The Royal Hotel
The Royal Hotel is a handsome building dating back to the mid-18th century. Retaining many of its original features, it now manages to combine the traditional elegance of the Georgian House with the hospitality and comfort of a modern hotel. Regular live acts and tribute bands.

High Street, Sutton Coldfield, West Midlands B72 1UD
☎ 0121 355 8222
@ info@the-royal-hotel.co.uk
🕂 www.the-royal-hotel.co.uk
🖺 0121 355 1837
🖉 Page 62-C3

The Sanctuary
Institute Buildings, 78 Digbeth High Street, Birmingham, West Midlands B5 6DY
☎ 0121 246 1010
🖺 0121 240 1020
🖉 Page 3-J7

Schofields
Queslett Road, Great Barr, Birmingham, West Midlands B43 7TN
☎ 0121 366 6004
🖉 Page 59-H5

Scruffy Duffy's
Broad Street, Birmingham, West Midlands B1 2JU
🖉 Page 2-C6

Scruffy Murphy's
A live rock music venue in Birmingham.

42 Newton Street, Dale End, Birmingham, West Midlands B4 7LN
☎ 0121 236 2035
@ Paulk@Scruffy Murphys.co.uk
🕂 www.scruffymurphys. co.uk
🖉 Page 3-H3

The Shed
Wedgbury Way, Brierley Hill, Dudley, West Midlands DY5 3JT
☎ 01384 482443
🖉 Page 118-D3

Smokey Mountain Country Music & Western Dance Club
Park Hall, Silver Street, Wythall, Birmingham, Worcestershire B47 6LZ
☎ 0121 459 2401
@ smokeyclub@ hotmail.com
🕂 www.smokey-mountain. ic24.net/index.htm
🖉 Page 192-A3

The Station Pub
The Station Pub hosts comedy shows in the rear function room. All comedy shows are held by Cheeky Monkey Comedy Club every two weeks.

7 High Street, Kings Heath, Birmingham, West Midlands B14 7BB

☎ 0121 444 1257
🖉 Page 161-E1

Stourbridge Town Hall
Stourbridge Town Hall is both accessible and attractive to many people. Ideal for shows, concerts, sales, exhibitions, meetings, discos, dances, and wedding receptions.

Crown Centre, Stourbridge, West Midlands DY8 1YE
☎ 01384 812960
@ stourbridge.townhall@ dudley.gov.uk
🕂 online.dudley.gov. uk/whatson/townhalls/ index.asp
🖉 Page 135-F2

Strathallan Thistle Hotel
Hagley Road, Edgbaston, Birmingham, West Midlands B16 9RY
☎ 0121 455 9777
🖉 Page 125-G3

Sutton Coldfield Library
Lower Parade, Sutton Coldfield, Birmingham West Midlands B72 1XX
☎ 0121464 0164
@ sutton.coldfield. reference.lib@ birmingham.gov.uk
🕂 www.birmingham.gov. uk/suttoncoldfieldlibrary
🖺 0121 464 0173
🖉 Page 62-C3

Sutton Coldfield Town Hall
Upper Clifton Road, Sutton Coldfield, West Midlands B73 6AB
☎ 0121 464 8990
@ Sutton_Town_Hall@ Birmingham.gov.uk
🕂 www.leisure.birmingham. gov.uk/sites/town_hall/ intro.htm
🖺 0121 464 8255
🖉 Page 62-B2

Sutton Coldfield Trad Jazz Club
Sutton Town FC, Coles Lane, Sutton Coldfield, West Midlands B72 1NL
☎ 0121 313 0385
🖉 Page 62-C5

Symphony Hall
Symphony Hall opened in 1991. In 2001 the Hall was completed with the installation of the 6000-pipe Symphony Organ. Symphony Hall's programme of events ranges from classical to jazz, world music, folk, rock and pop and stand-up comedy.

Broad Street, Birmingham, West Midlands B1 2EA
☎ 0121 200 2000
🕐 0121 780 3333
@ symphonyhall@ necgroup.co.uk
🕂 www.necgroup.co.uk/ visitor/symphonyhall/
🖺 0121 212 1982
🖉 Page 2-C5

The Tanoshi Bar
32–33 Edgbaston Shopping Centre, Hagley Road, Birmingham, West Midlands B16 8SH
🖉 Page 126-A3

Tower of Song
Acoustic and roots music in The Midlands.

107 Pershore Road South, Cotteridge, Birmingham, West Midlands B30 3JX
☎ 0121 486 1300
@ tommartin@ blueyonder.co.uk
🕂 www.towerofsong.co.uk
🖉 Page 176-D2

The Varsity Venue
Stafford Street, Wolverhampton, West Midlands WV1 1LZ
☎ 01902 711166
🖉 Page 7-F2

Vaughn's

Stratford Rd, Hall Green,
Birmingham, West Midlands
B28 9
☎ 0121 778 4006
✆ Page 162-D3

The Village Inn

152 Hurst Street,
Birmingham, West Midlands
B5 6RY
☎ 0121 622 4742
✆ www.villageinnandhotel.
com/
✆ Page 3-F7

Wagon & Horses

28 Adderley St, Bordesley
Green, Birmingham, West
Midlands B9 4ED
☎ 0121 772 1403
✆ Page 127-G3

The Waterworks Jazz Club

Birmingham United Service
Club, Gough Street,
Birmingham, West Midlands
B1 1HN
☎ 0121 445 5668
@ mason@
waterworksjazz.com
✆ www.waterworksjazz.com
✆ Page 2-E7

Wolverhampton Civic Hall

North Street,
Wolverhampton, West
Midlands WV1 1RQ
☎ 01902 552112
✆ 0870 3207000
@ info@wolvescivic.co.uk
✆ www.wolvescivic.co.uk
📄 01902 552123
✆ Page 6-E3

Wulfrun Hall

Major music and
entertainment venue.

North Street,
Wolverhampton, West
Midlands WV1 1RQ
✆ 0870 320 7000
✆ www.wolvescivic.co.uk
✆ Page 7-F3

The Yardbird Jazz Club

A bar and live music venue
pivoting on the jazz and funk
staple.

Paradise Place, Birmingham,
West Midlands B3 3HJ
☎ 0121 254 2524
✆ Page 2-E5

COMEDY CLUBS AND VENUES

The Barn

The Barn is where you
can enjoy a wonderful
programme of
entertainment and social
activities that have made
it one of the most famous
and prestigious venues in
clubland and throughout
Britain.

Brookvale Road, Witton,
Birmingham, West Midlands
B6 7AJ
☎ 0121 356 5706
@ info@thebarn
birmingham.co.uk
✆ www.thebarnbirmingham.
co.uk
✆ Page 91-G3

The Bartons Arms

144 High St, Aston,
Birmingham West Midlands
B6 4UP
☎ 0121 333 5988
✆ Page 109-E2

Birmingham Hippodrome

Welcoming audiences
averaging almost 500,000
each year, Birmingham
Hippodrome can lay claim to
the highest regular annual
attendance of any single
theatre in the country.
It hosts a vast variety
of entertainment events
throughout the year.

Hurst Street, Birmingham,
West Midlands B5 4TB
☎ 0870 730 5555
✆ 0870 730 1234,
0870 730 4321
@ tickets@birmingham
hippodrome.com
✆ www.birmingham
hippodrome.com
📄 0121 689 3031
✆ Page 3-F7

Birmingham Town Hall

Acclaimed at its opening
in 1834 as the finest music
hall in the country, the
Grade I listed landmark
has been lovingly and
painstakingly renovated
by a dedicated team
of conservation and
construction professionals.
It was designed by Joseph
Aloysius Hansom for the
performance of music,
and today hosts a varied
programme including
recitals, international
chamber music, world
music, folk and comedy.

Victoria Square,
Birmingham, West Midlands
B3 3DQ
✆ 0121 303 2880
✆ www.birmingham.gov.
uk/townhall.bcc
✆ Page 2-E5

The British Oak

1364 Pershore Road,
Stirchley, Birmingham,
West Midlands B30 2XS
☎ 0121 458 1758
✆ Page 160-A3

The Glee Club Birmingham

Situated on the 1st floor
of The Arcadian Centre,
the club hosts live comedy
shows and music nights.

The Arcadian Centre, Hurst
Street, Birmingham, West
Midlands B5 4DP
☎ 0870 241 5093
✆ 0870 241 5093
@ duncan@glee.co.uk
✆ www.glee.co.uk
✆ Page 3-G7

Jongleurs Birmingham

Jongleurs Birmingham has
a capacity of 2,400, spread
across two floors.

Quayside Tower, Broad
Street, Birmingham, West
Midlands B1 2HF
☎ 0870 011 1965
@ enquiries@jongleurs.com
✆ www.jongleurs.com
✆ Page 2-C6

Kitchen Garden Cafe

17 York Rd, Kings Heath,
Birmingham West Midlands
B14 7SA
✆ www.kitchengardencafe.
co.uk/
✆ Page 161-E2

Little Civic

Music and entertainment
venue that hosts comedy
and special events.

North Street,
Wolverhampton, West
Midlands WV1 1RQ
✆ 0870 320 7000
✆ www.wolvescivic.co.uk
✆ Page 7-F4

The Station Pub

The Station Pub hosts
comedy shows in the rear
function room. All comedy
shows are held by Cheeky
Monkey Comedy Club every
two weeks.

7 High Street, Kings Heath,
Birmingham, West Midlands
B14 7BB
☎ 0121 444 1257
✆ Page 161-E1

The Station Pub

Station Street, Sutton
Coldfield, Birmingham, West
Midlands B73 6AT
✆ 0121 350 4945
@ standupnight@
yahoo.co.uk
✆ www.comedyjunction.
co.uk
✆ Page 62-B3

Symphony Hall

Symphony Hall opened in 1991. In 2001 the Hall was completed with the installation of the 6000-pipe Symphony Organ. Symphony Hall's programme of events ranges from classical to jazz, world music, folk, rock and pop and stand-up comedy.

Broad Street, Birmingham, West Midlands B1 2EA
☎ 0121 200 2000
✆ 0121 780 3333
@ symphonyhall@ necgroup.co.uk
🖰 www.necgroup.co.uk/ visitor/symphonyhall/
🗎 0121 212 1982
🕮 Page 2-C5

Wolverhampton Civic Hall

North Street, Wolverhampton, West Midlands WV1 1RQ
☎ 01902 552112
✆ 0870 3207000
@ info@wolvescivic.co.uk
🖰 www.wolvescivic.co.uk
🗎 01902 552123
🕮 Page 6-E3

Wulfrun Hall

Major music and entertainment venue.

North Street, Wolverhampton, West Midlands WV1 1RQ
✆ 0870 320 7000
🖰 www.wolvescivic.co.uk
🕮 Page 7-F3

CLASSICAL MUSIC VENUES

Adrian Boult Hall at Birmingham Conservatoire

The ABH is a 520-seat auditorium with fine acoustics, which can accommodate a symphony orchestra and be adapted for use as an opera theatre or a conference venue. There is also a licensed bar and coffee area plus an exhibition space. The Conservatoire hosts its own varied concert programme.

Paradise Place, Birmingham, West Midlands B3 3HG
☎ 0121 331 5901, 0121 331 5902
@ conservatoire@uce.ac.uk
🖰 www.conservatoire.uce. ac.uk
🗎 0121 331 5906
🕮 Page 2-D5

The Barber Institute of Fine Arts

The Barber Institute of Fine Arts is housed in one of Birmingham's finest art deco buildings, purpose built and opened by Queen Mary in 1939. The Institute was designed by Robert Atkinson (1883–1952), one of Britain's leading architects of the 1920s and 30s. When it opened *The Times* described the building as 'the purest example of his work' and it continues to be regarded as one of his greatest achievements.

University of Birmingham, Edgbaston, Birmingham, West Midlands B15 2TS
☎ 0121 414 7333
@ info@barber.org.uk
🖰 www.barber.org.uk
🗎 0121 414 3370
🕮 Page 142-D4

Birmingham Cathedral

The church building was designed by Thomas Archer in the English baroque style, and was built between 1709 and 1715. It became a cathedral in 1905 when the Diocese of Birmingham was formed. The word 'cathedral' simply means the church that houses the chair of the bishop, and so is the central church of the diocese. There are regular concerts throughout the year with organ recitals at luchtime on one day a week.
Colmore Row, Birmingham, West Midlands B3 2QB
☎ 0121 262 1840
@ enquiries@birmingham cathedral.com
🖰 www.birmingham cathedral.com
🗎 0121 262 1860
🕮 Page 3-F4

Birmingham Hippodrome

Welcoming audiences averaging almost 500,000 each year, Birmingham Hippodrome can lay claim to the highest regular annual attendance of any single theatre in the country. It hosts a vast variety of entertainment events throughout the year.

Hurst Street, Birmingham, West Midlands B5 4TB
☎ 0870 730 5555
✆ 0870 730 1234, 0870 730 4321
@ tickets@birmingham hippodrome.com
🖰 www.birmingham hippodrome.com
🗎 0121 689 3031
🕮 Page 3-F7

Birmingham Town Hall

Acclaimed at its opening in 1834 as the finest music hall in the country, the Grade I listed landmark has been lovingly and painstakingly renovated by a dedicated team of conservation and construction professionals. It was designed by Joseph Aloysius Hansom for the performance of music, and today hosts a varied programme including recitals, international chamber music, an international concert season, world music and folk.

Victoria Square, Birmingham, West Midlands B3 3DQ
✆ 0121 303 2880
🖰 www.birmingham.gov. uk/townhall.bcc
🕮 Page 2-E5

CBSO Centre

The City of Birmingham Symphony Orchestra was founded in 1920 with its first concert conducted by Sir Edward Elgar. The Orchestra came to international prominence in the 1980s and 1990s under the leadership of Sir Simon Rattle, and continues to prosper under the baton of its current Music Director, Sakari Oramo.

Berkley Street, Birmingham, West Midlands B1 2LF
☎ 0121 616 6500
@ information@cbso.co.uk
🖰 www.cbso.co.uk
🗎 0121 616 6518
🕮 Page 2-C6

Ladywood ARC: St John's And St Peter's Church

Darnley Road, Ladywood, Birmingham, West Midlands B16 8TF
☎ 0121 454 0973
@ info@ladywoodarc. org.uk
🖰 www.stjohnpeter.org.uk
🕮 Page 125-H2

The Oratory

Hagley Road, Birmingham, West Midlands B16 8UE
☎ 0121 454 0496
🖰 www.theoratory.org.uk/
🕮 Page 125-H3

Recital Hall, Birmingham Conservatoire

UCE Birmingham Conservatoire is an international conservatoire, a full faculty of UCE Birmingham and a major concert venue for many of Birmingham's principal concert promoters and

organisations, hosting over 300 events annually. The state-of-the-art Recital Hall was recently customised for performance with live electronics.

Fletchers Walk, Birmingham, West Midlands B3 3HG
☎ 01213032323
⌂ www.conservatoire.uce.ac.uk/
❀ Page 2-D5

Symphony Hall

Symphony Hall opened in 1991. In 2001 the Hall was completed with the installation of the 6000-pipe Symphony Organ. Symphony Hall's programme of events ranges from classical to jazz, world music, folk, rock and pop and stand-up comedy.

Broad Street, Birmingham, West Midlands B1 2EA
☎ 0121 200 2000
✆ 0121 780 3333
@ symphonyhall@necgroup.co.uk
⌂ www.necgroup.co.uk/visitor/symphonyhall/
▤ 0121 212 1982
❀ Page 2-C5

Wolverhampton Civic Hall

North Street, Wolverhampton, West Midlands WV1 1RQ
☎ 01902 552112
✆ 0870 3207000
@ info@wolvescivic.co.uk
⌂ www.wolvescivic.co.uk
▤ 01902 552123
❀ Page 6-E3

CINEMAS

AMC Broadway Plaza 12

220 Ladywood Middleway, Broadway Plaza, Birmingham, West Midlands B16 8LP
☎ 0870 755 5657
@ info@broadway-plaza.com
⌂ www.amccinemas.co.uk
▤ 0121 450 6850
❀ Page 126-A3

Cineworld Wolverhampton

Bentley Bridge Park, Wednesfield Way, Wolverhampton, West Midlands WV11 1TZ
☎ 08712 208000
⌂ www.cineworld.co.uk
❀ Page 38-B1

Cineworld Birmingham Broad Street

181 Broad Street, Birmingham, West Midlands B15 1DA
☎ 0870 777 2775
✆ 08712 002000
@ customer.services@cineworld.co.uk
⌂ www.ugccinemas.co.uk
❀ Page 2-B7

Cineworld Solihull

47 Mill Lane Arcade (Upper), Touchwood, Solihull, West Midlands B91 3GS
☎ 08712 208000
⌂ www.cineworld.co.uk
❀ Page 182-A2

The Electric Cinema Birmingham

The cinema is the oldest working cinema in the UK. It first opened on 30th December 1909, and is now home to luxury sofa seating, waiter service and a full bar.

47–49 Station Street, Birmingham, West Midlands B5 4DY
☎ 0121 643 7277, 0121 643 7879
@ info@theelectric.co.uk
⌂ www.theelectric.co.uk
❀ Page 3-F6

Empire Birmingham Great Park

Bristol Road South, Rubery Great Park, Birmingham, West Midlands B45 9JL
✆ 0871 4714714
⌂ www.empirecinemas.co.uk
❀ Page 188-A1

Empire Sutton Coldfield

Maney Corner, Sutton Coldfield, West Midlands B72 1QL
☎ 08714 714714
⌂ www.empirecinemas.co.uk
❀ Page 62-B4

IMAX Birmingham

The IMAX is part of one the country's most exciting visitor attractions in the heart of Birmingham. With a screen as high as a five-storey building and as wide as four buses nose to tail, 2D presentations are spectacular enough, but the special 3D films will have people reaching out to touch the images on the screen.

Thinktank at Millennium Point, Curzon Street, Birmingham, West Midlands B4 7XG
☎ 0121 202 2222
@ findout@thinktank.ac
⌂ www.imax.ac/index.htm
❀ Page 3-K4

Odeon Birmingham

139 New Street, Birmingham, West Midlands B2 4NU
☎ 08712 244007
⌂ www.odeon.co.uk
❀ Page 3-G6

Odeon Dudley

The Merry Hill Centre, Brierley Hill, Dudley, West Midlands DY5 1SY
✆ 08712 244007
⌂ www.odeon.co.uk
❀ Page 119-H2

Piccadilly Cinema, Birmingham

372 Stratford Road, Sparkhill, Birmingham, West Midlands B11 4AB
☎ 0121 773 1658
@ info@piccadillycinemas.co.uk
⌂ www.piccadillycinema.co.uk
▤ 0121 753 3886
❀ Page 144-D2

Reel Quinton

Hagley Road West, Halesowen West Midlands B62 9AS
☎ 0121 421 5316
⌂ www.reelcinemas.co.uk/quinton/index.phtml
❀ Page 140-B1

Showcase Cinema, Birmingham

Kingsbury Road, Erdington, Birmingham, West Midlands B24 9QE
☎ 08712 201000
✆ 08712 201000
⌂ www.showcasecinemas.co.uk
❀ Page 93-H4

Showcase Cinema, Dudley

Castlegate Way, Birmingham Road, Dudley, West Midlands DY1 4TA
☎ 08712 201000
⌂ www.showcasecinemas.co.uk
❀ Page 85-E3

Showcase Cinema, Walsall

Bentley Mill Way, Walsall, West Midlands WS2 0LE
☎ 08712 201000
⌂ www.showcasecinemas.co.uk
❀ Page 40-D4

Vue Birmingham

Star City, Watson Road,
Birmingham, West Midlands
B7 5SB
☎ 08712 240240
@ guestservices@
myvue.com
🖰 www.myvue.com
🖹 0121 328 5788
🖉 Page 110-B1

OPERA VENUES

Birmingham Hippodrome

Welcoming audiences
averaging almost 500,000
each year, Birmingham
Hippodrome can lay claim to
the highest regular annual
attendance of any single
theatre in the country.
It hosts a vast variety
of entertainment events
throughout the year.

Hurst Street, Birmingham,
West Midlands B5 4TB
☎ 0870 730 5555
🖰 0870 730 1234,
0870 730 4321
@ tickets@birmingham
hippodrome.com
🖰 www.birmingham
hippodrome.com
🖹 0121 689 3031
🖉 Page 3-F7

The Old Rep Theatre

This 383-seat theatre in the
centre of Birmingham plays
host to the Birmingham
Stage Company and
numerous amateur
companies offering a wide
variety of productions
from plays to musicals,
regular sell-out Christmas
productions and specially
written issued-based drama
for young people.

Station Street, Birmingham,
West Midlands B5 4DY
☎ 0121 605 5116
🖰 0121 303 2323
@ oldrephelpdesk@
birmingham.gov.uk

🖰 oldreptheatre.org.uk
🖉 Page 3-F7

THEATRES

Alexandra Theatre

One of Birmingham's
largest theatre venues, the
Alexandra Theatre puts on
many productions all year
round.

Station Street, Birmingham,
West Midlands B5 4DS
☎ 0121 632 5554
🖰 0870 607 7533
🖰 www.birmingham
theatreguide.com
🖉 Page 3-F6

Arena Theatre

The Arena Theatre seats
150 and is spacious enough
to host dance, ballet
performances and plays. The
Arena also showcases work
by local schools, colleges,
amateur companies and
community events.

Wulfruna Street,
Wolverhampton, West
Midlands WV1 1SE
☎ 01902 321327
🖰 01902 321321
@ arena@wlv.ac.uk
🖰 www.arenatheatre.info
🖹 01902 322599
🖉 Page 7-F3

Birmingham Hippodrome

Welcoming audiences
averaging almost 500,000
each year, Birmingham
Hippodrome can lay claim to
the highest regular annual
attendance of any single
theatre in the country.
It hosts a vast variety
of entertainment events
throughout the year.

Hurst Street, Birmingham,
West Midlands B5 4TB
☎ 0870 730 5555
🖰 0870 730 1234,
0870 730 4321
@ tickets@birmingham
hippodrome.com

🖰 www.birmingham
hippodrome.com
🖹 0121 689 3031
🖉 Page 3-F7

Birmingham Repertory Theatre

Since being founded in
1913, Birmingham Repertory
Theatre has been a leading
national company. It has
introduced a range of new
and foreign plays to the
British theatre repertoire,
and has been a springboard
for many internationally
acclaimed actors, designers
and directors. The REP
produces over 20 new
productions each year.
Under the artistic direction
of Jonathan Church, The REP
has enjoyed great success
with one of its busiest and
most exciting programmes
ever.

Centenary Square, Broad
Street, Birmingham, West
Midlands B1 2EP
☎ 0121 245 2000
🖰 0121 236 4455
@ hm@birmingham-
rep.co.uk
🖰 www.birmingham-rep.
co.uk
🖉 Page 2-D5

Birmingham Town Hall

Acclaimed at its opening in
1834 as the finest music hall
in the country, the Grade I
listed landmark is now being
lovingly and painstakingly
renovated by a dedicated
team of conservation and
construction professionals.
Designed by Joseph Aloysius
Hansom for the performance
of music, political
speechmaking, public
gatherings and the use of
the urban community, the
Town Hall opened in 1834.

Victoria Square,
Birmingham, West Midlands
B3 3DQ

🖰 0121 303 2880
🖰 www.birmingham.gov.
uk/townhall.bcc
🖉 Page 2-E5

Bloxwich Library Theatre

Elmore Row, Bloxwich,
Walsall, West Midlands
WS3 2HR
☎ 01922 653183
@ pompaa@walsall.gov.uk
🖉 Page 27-F1

Crescent Theatre

20 Sheepcote Street,
Brindleyplace, Birmingham,
West Midlands B16 8AE
☎ 0121 643 5859
🖰 0121 643 5858
@ admin@crescent-
theatre.co.uk
🖰 www.crescent-theatre.
co.uk
🖹 0121 643 5860
🖉 Page 2-B6

Highbury Little Theatre

Sheffield Road, Sutton
Coldfield, West Midlands
B73 5HD
☎ 0121 373 2761
@ administration@
highburytheatre.co.uk
🖰 www.highburytheatre.
co.uk
🖉 Page 77-E4

Kitchen Garden Cafe

17 York Rd, Kings Heath,
Birmingham, West Midlands
B14 7SA
🖰 www.kitchengardencafe.
co.uk/
🖉 Page 161-E2

Library Theatre

Paradise Place, Birmingham,
West Midlands B3 3HQ
☎ 0121 303 2868
🖰 www.birmingham.gov.
uk/librarytheatre.bcc
🖉 Page 2-E5

NIA: National Indoor Arena

King Edwards Road,
Birmingham, West Midlands
B1 2AA
☎ 0121 780 4444
@ nia-sales@
  necgroup.co.uk
🖰 www.necgroup.co.uk
🖉 Page 2-B5

Old Chapel

Hollymoor Centre, 8 Manor
Park Grove, Birmingham,
West Midlands B31 5EU
☎ 0121 683 1834
🖉 Page 174-C3

Old Joint Stock Theatre

4 Temple Row West,
Birmingham, West Midlands
B2 5NY
☎ 0121 200 0946
🖰 www.oldjointstocktheatre.
  co.uk
🖉 Page 3-F4

The Old Rep Theatre

This 383-seat theatre in the
centre of Birmingham plays
host to the Birmingham
Stage Company and
numerous amateur
companies offering a wide
variety of productions
from plays to musicals,
regular sell-out Christmas
productions and specially
written issued-based drama
for young people.

Station Street, Birmingham,
West Midlands B5 4DY
☎ 0121 605 5116
🕾 0121 303 2323
@ oldrephelpdesk@
  birmingham.gov.uk
🖰 oldreptheatre.org.uk
🖉 Page 3-F7

Wolverhampton Civic Hall

North Street,
Wolverhampton West
Midlands WV1 1RQ

☎ 01902 552112
🕾 0870 3207000
@ info@wolvescivic.co.uk
🖰 www.wolvescivic.co.uk
📄 01902 552123
🖉 Page 6-F3

Wolverhampton Grand Theatre

Lichfield Street,
Wolverhampton, West
Midlands WV1 1DE
☎ 01902 573300
🕾 01902 429212
🖰 www.grandtheatre.co.uk
🖉 Page 7-G3

BARS AND PUBS

All Bar One

The Water's Edge,
Brindleyplace, Birmingham,
West Midlands B1 2HL
☎ 0121 644 5861
🖰 www.all-bar-one.co.uk/
🖉 Page 2-B6

Atticus Bar

Continental style cafe bar
that welcomes families
and features cutting edge
underground DJs.

113–114 Three Shires Oak,
Bearwood, Birmingham,
West Midlands B67 5BT
☎ 0121 429 9423
🖉 Page 124-B2

Bambu Bar

1st Floor Kotwall House,
Wrottesley Street,
Birmingham, West Midlands
B5 4BN
☎ 01216 22 4124
@ manager@
  bambubar.co.uk
🖰 www.bambubar.co.uk
🖉 Page 3-G7

Bar Academy Birmingham

51 Dale End, Birmingham,
West Midlands B4 7LS

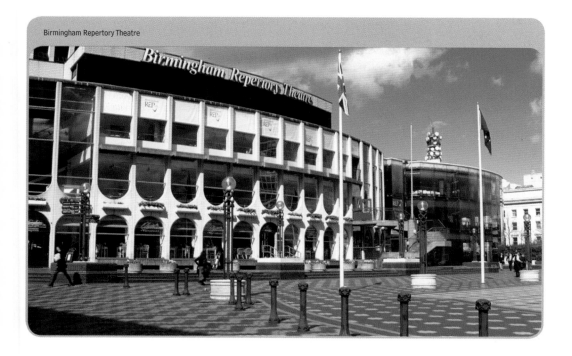
Birmingham Repertory Theatre

☎ 0121 262 3000
🕓 0870 771 2000
@ mail@birmingham-academy.co.uk
🖰 www.birmingham-academy.co.uk
🖹 0121 236 2241
🖉 Page 3-H5

Barracuda

16 Hurst St, Birmingham, West Midlands B5 4NB
☎ 0121 622 6878
@ josh@barracuda birmingham.co.uk
🖰 www.barracuda birmingham.co.uk
🖉 Page 3-F7

Bartley Green Social Club

Field Lane, Birmingham, West Midlands B32 4ES
☎ 0121 475 6825
🖉 Page 157-E2

The Bartons Arms

144 High Street, Aston, Birmingham, West Midlands B6 4UP
☎ 0121 333 5988
🖉 Page 109-E2

The Bear Tavern

500 Bearwood Road, Bearwood, Smethwick, West Midlands B66 4BX
☎ 0121 429 1184
🖉 Page 124-C2

The Beeches

116 Thornbridge Avenue, Birmingham, West Midlands B42 2AE
☎ 0121 3571380
🖉 Page 74-D4

Bull's Head

101 Birchfield Rd, Birmingham, West Midlands B19 1LH
☎ 0121 523 8155
🖉 Page 108-D1

Carling Academy Birmingham

Carling Academy Birmingham has fast become Birmingham's premier venue, offering the best live events and club nights in the region and becoming a focal point for nightlife in the Midlands.

52–54 Dale End, Birmingham, West Midlands B4 7LS
☎ 01212 623000
@ mail@birmingham-academy.co.uk
🖰 www.birmingham-academy.co.uk
🖹 01212 362241
🖉 Page 3-H5

The Case is Altered

34 Mill Street, Sutton Coldfield, Birmingham, West Midlands B72 1TJ
🖉 Page 62-C3

Chi Bar

61 Newhall Street, Birmingham, West Midlands B3 3RB
☎ 0121 233 3150
@ enquiries@ chibarrestaurant.com
🖰 www.chibar.co.uk
🖹 0121 233 3168
🖉 Page 2-E4

Chicago Rock Cafe, Manhattan

Chicago Rock Cafe offers a blend of eating, drinking and entertainment. The music played is the 'greatest classic hits of all time', catering for a wide variety of tastes and age groups, ranging from 1957–1995.

36 Pipers Row, Wolverhampton, West Midlands WV1 3JY
☎ 01902 772977
@ chicago-rock-cafe-wolverhampton@3d-entertainmentgroup.com

🖰 www.chicago-rock-cafe. co.uk/venues.asp
🖹 01902 772829
🖉 Page 7-H4

Chicago Rock Cafe, Walsall

Chicago Rock Cafe offers a blend of eating, drinking and entertainment. The music played is the 'greatest classic hits of all time', catering for a wide variety of tastes and age groups, ranging from 1957–1995.

132 Lichfield Street, Walsall, West Midlands WS1 1SL
☎ 01922 620655
@ chicago-rock-cafe-walsall@3d-entertainmentgroup.com
🖰 www.chicago-rock-cafe. co.uk/venues.asp
🖹 01922 722071
🖉 Page 5-F3

The City Bar

2–3 Kings Street, Wolverhampton, West Midlands WV1 1ST
☎ 01902 423376
🖰 www.city-bar.co.uk
🖉 Page 7-F4

The City Tavern

Bishopsgate Street, Birmingham, West Midlands B15 1ET
☎ 0121 643 8467
🖉 Page 2-B7

Concrete

A 3,000-square foot multipurpose venue spread over two levels based in the Jewellery Quarter, Hockley, Birmingham. The venue morphs through the week from restaurant lounge bar to full on live music at the weekends, with strong club promoters, eclectic bands and internationally known artists appearing regularly.

120 Vyse Street, Jewellery Quarter, Birmingham, West Midlands B18 6NF
☎ 0121 212 9280, 07968 366878, 07968 260276
🕓 0121 236 6446
@ info@concretebar.co.uk
🖰 www.concretebar.co.uk
🖉 Page 2-C1

Craven Arms Pub & Gastro Restaurant

Upper Gough Street, Birmingham, West Midlands B1 1JG
🖉 Page 126-D3

The Cross Cafe Bar

The Cross is surprisingly unpretentious. The snappy service is friendly and unobtrusive.

147 Alcester Road South, Moseley, Birmingham, West Midlands B13 8JP
☎ 0121 449 4445
@ mikethorley@ btconnect.co.uk
🖰 www.thecrossmoseley. co.uk
🖹 0121 449 6300
🖉 Page 144-B4

The Dragon Bar

Sanctuary Building, 78 Digbeth High Street, Birmingham, West Midlands B5 6DY
🖉 Page 3-J7

Dragon Eye

Bar, restaurant and nightclub in one.

193–194 Broad Street, Birmingham, West Midlands B15 1AY
☎ 0121 632 5225
@ info@dragon-eye.co.uk
🖰 www.dragon-eye.co.uk
🖉 Page 2-B7

Halfway House

151 Tettenhall Road, Wolverhampton, West Midlands WV3 9NJ
☎ 01902 429400
🖉 Page 6-A2

Hard Rock Cafe, Birmingham

Unit 6, Five Ways Leisure Complex, 263 Broad Street, Birmingham, West Midlands B15 2HF
☎ 0121 665 6562
✪ Page 2-C6

The Hare and Hounds

The Hare and Hounds offers a spectacular setting with its stunning Victorian archtecture and interior fixtures. It is also a live music and performance venue.

High Street, Kings Heath, Birmingham, West Midlands B14 7JZ
☎ 0121 444 2081
@ info@hareandhounds kingsheath.co.uk
✆ www.hareandhounds kingsheath.co.uk
✪ Page 161-E2

Harvester

Tanhouse Farm Lane, Solihull, West Midlands B92 9EY
☎ 0121 742 0770
✆ www.harvesterlife.com
✪ Page 148-A5

The Hibernian

1063 Pershore Road, Stirchley, Birmingham, West Midlands B30 2YJ
☎ 0121 471 1910
✪ Page 176-D1

Horse & Jockey

146 Walsall Road, Shelfield, Walsall, West Midlands WS9 9AJ
☎ 01543 360703
✪ Page 19-E5

The Hunters Moon

220 Coleshill Road, Castle Bromwich, Birmingham, West Midlands B36 8BE
☎ 0121 748 8951
✪ Page 112-B2

island bar

At Birmingham's rock and roll cocktail bar in Suffolk Street, Queensway, you'll find some of the city's finest bartenders showing off their skills while you enjoy great guitar music. DJs play a mix of old and newer guitar classics, live acoustic guitar music features on many nights of the week, there is an open mic night for budding songwriters and the bar is also a showcase for local and national up-and coming bands.

14–16 Suffolk Street, Queensway, Birmingham, West Midlands B1 1LT
☎ 0121 632 5296
✆ 0121 632 5296
@ info@bar-island.co.uk
✆ www.bar-island.co.uk
✪ Page 2-E6

Katie Fitzgerald's

Originally known as the Golden Lion, Katie Fitzgerald's was a small one-roomed beerhouse, the property of Mary Faulkner. It was well positioned to attract travellers along the Stourbridge-Kinver turnpike road.

187 Enville Street, Stourbridge, Wollaston, West Midlands DY8 3TB
☎ 01384 374410
@ enquiries@ katiefitzgeralds.co.uk
✆ www.katiefitzgeralds. co.uk/
✪ Page 135-F2

The Kerryman

81 Digbeth, Birmingham, West Midlands B5 6DY
☎ 0121 643 3578
✆ www.thekerryman.co.uk
✪ Page 3-J7

Lamp Tavern

116 High Street, Dudley, West Midlands DY1 1QT
☎ 01384 254129, 01384 353955
✆ www.bathams.com/ pubs_lamp_tavern.php
✪ Page 102-C1

The Light Bar

Suite 4 Chubb Building, Fryer Street, Wolverhampton, West Midlands WV1 1HT
☎ 01902 717108
✪ Page 7-G3

The Living Room, Birmingham

The Living Room in Birmingham opened on 3rd December 2001, utilising the entire top floor of Regency Wharf 2 on Broad Street. The Birmingham Living Room boasts spectacular views over the impressive skyline.

Unit 4 Regency Wharf 2, Broad Street, Birmingham, West Midlands B1 2JZ
☎ 0121 616 6820
@ birmingham@ thelivingroom.co.uk
✆ www.thelivingroom.co.uk
🖷 0870 442 2540
✪ Page 2-C6

Lost Lounge

The Lost Lounge is the perfect venue for your special occasion any night of the week.

Lower Hall Lane, The Arcade, Walsall, West Midlands WS1 1RH
☎ 01922 614382
✪ Page 4-D4

The Malt House

75 King Edwards Road, Birmingham, West Midlands B1 2NX
☎ 0121 633 4171
✪ Page 2-B5

Mechu

This hybrid venue offers an up-tempo soundtrack and fashionable lounge ambience while providing an intimate dancefloor for those who can't resist the urge to get down and party.

45 Summer Row, Birmingham, West Midlands B3 1JJ
☎ 0121 212 1661
@ info@summerrow.com
✆ www.summerrow.com
✪ Page 2-D4

Medicine Bar Birmingham

The Custard Factory, 1 Gibb Street, Birmingham, West Midlands B9 4AA
☎ 0121 693 6333
✪ Page 3-K7

Mono

Unit 202, The Arcadian Centre, Hurst Street, Birmingham, West Midlands B5 4TD
☎ 0121 622 7407
@ info@mono-bar.co.uk
✆ www.mono-bar.co.uk
✪ Page 3-F7

The Newt

58 Stephenson St, Birmingham, West Midlands B2 4DH
☎ 0121 643 2969
✪ Page 3-F6

OC's Bar

79 Digbeth Street, Digbeth, Birmingham, West Midlands B5 6DY
✪ Page 3-J7

The Old Moseley Arms

The club was established as the Prince of Wales Fit Men Cricket Club in 1981, out of the pub in Moseley of the same name. The club moved round the corner to the Old Moseley Arms at Tindal Street in about 1997.

53 Tindal Street, Balsall Heath, Birmingham, West Midlands B12 9QU

☎ 0121 440 1954
@ webmaster@
fitmen.org.uk
🖰www.fitmen.org.uk
✐ Page 144-B2

The Planet

Thornley Street,
Wolverhampton, West
Midlands WV1 1JP
☎ 01902 711301
✐ Page 7-G2

Prince of Wales

84 Cambridge Street,
Birmingham, West Midlands
B1 2NP
☎ 0121 643 9460
✐ Page 2-B5

Prince of Wales Moseley

118 Alcester Road, Moseley,
Birmingham, West Midlands
B13 8EE
☎ 01214 498284
✐ Page 144-B4

Quest Leisure

Amar House, Broad Street,
Wolverhampton, West
Midlands WV1 1HP
☎ 01902 773393
✐ Page 7-H3

R Bs

140 High Street, Solihull,
West Midlands B91 3SX
☎ 0121 705 7422
✐ Page 182-A1

RB's Bar and Nightclub

Lower Parade, Sutton
Coldfield, West Midlands
B72 1XX
☎ 0121 354 5507
🖰rbs-sutton.com
✐ Page 62-B3

The Rainbow

160 High Street, Digbeth,
Birmingham, West Midlands
B12 0LD
☎ 0121 772 8174
🖰www.therainbowpub.com
✐ Page 3-K7

Red Lion

95 Warstone Lane, Hockley,
Birmingham, West Midlands
B18 6NG
☎ 0121 236 8371
🖰www.redlionfolkclub.
com/
✐ Page 2-C2

Red Lion Folk Club

There are three hours of
folk music every Saturday
night throughout the season.

Vicarage Road, Kings Heath,
Birmingham, West Midlands
B14 7IY
☎ 0121 441 6941
@ acef@RedLionFolk
Club.com
🖰www.redlionfolkclub.co.uk
✐ Page 160-D3

Revolution Bar, Birmingham

Located in the centre of
Birmingham's thriving Broad
Street district, Revolution is
famous for the vast array of
imported vodkas and home-
made flavoured vodkas and
our sumptious cocktails and
pitchers. By night we liven up
the proceedings with live DJs
every night from 9pm. There
are loads of special events
and big parties to look out for.

Five Ways, Broad Street,
Birmingham, West Midlands
B1 2NF
☎ 0121 665 6508
@ birmingham@
revolution-bars.co.uk
🖰www.revolution-bars.
co.uk/bars
🖹 0121 665 6507
✐ Page 2-A7

Revolution Bar, Walsall

Revolution Walsall, Bridge
Street, Walsall, West
Midlands WS1 1JQ
☎ 01922 627640
🖰www.revolution-bars.
co.uk/bars
🖹 01922 627631
✐ Page 4-E3

Revolution Bar, Wolverhampton

10–12 Princess Street,
Wolverhampton, West
Midlands WV1 1HW
☎ 01902 420223
🖰www.revolution-bars.
co.uk/bars
🖹 01902 420229
✐ Page 7-G4

The Rope Walk

15–20 St Paul's Square,
Birmingham, West Midlands
B3 1RB
☎ 0121 233 2129
✐ Page 2-E2

The Royal George, Birmingham

1 Park Street, Aston,
Birmingham, West Midlands
B6 5SH
☎ 0121 6881964
✐ Page 109-G2

Scruffy Duffy's

Broad Street, Birmingham,
West Midlands B1 2JU
✐ Page 2-C6

Strathallan Thistle Hotel

Hagley Road, Edgbaston,
Birmingham, West Midlands
B16 9RY
☎ 0121 455 9777
✐ Page 125-G3

The Students' Union at UCE

The Union Building,
Franchise Street,
Birmingham, West Midlands
B42 2EN
☎ 0121 331 6801
🖰www.uceunion.com
✐ Page 90-D3

The Sunflower Lounge

76, Smallbrook Queensway,
Bimingham, West Midlands
B5 4EG
☎ 0121 6326756
✐ Page 3-G7

The Swan

65 High Street, Erdington,
Birmingham, West Midlands
B23 6SA
☎ 0121 377 2931
✐ Page 92-D2

The Thorns Inn

174 Thorns Road, Quarry
Bank, West Midlands
DY5 2JY
☎ 01384 423696
🖰 07781 474421
@ ikon@thornsinn.co.uk
🖰www.thornsinn.co.uk
✐ Page 119-G5

The Village Inn

152 Hurst Street,
Birmingham, West Midlands
B5 6RY
☎ 0121 622 4742
🖰www.villageinnandhotel.
com/
✐ Page 3-F7

Wagon & Horses

28 Adderley St, Bordesley
Green, Birmingham, West
Midlands B9 4ED
☎ 0121 772 1403
✐ Page 127-G3

West One Bar & Restaurant

159 Worcester Road, Hagley,
Worcestershire DY9 0NW
☎ 01562 885328
✐ Page 169-G1

The Yenton

Sutton Road, Erdington,
Birmingham, West Midlands
B23 5TW
☎ 0121 306 5151
✐ Page 93-E1

NIGHTCLUBS

Air

Air is a purpose-built
venue, home to two of the
biggest club nights in the
Midlands – Godskitchen and
Polysexual.

Heath Mill Lane, Digbeth,
Birmingham, West Midlands
B9 4AL
☎ 0121 7666646
@ info@airbirmingham.
co.uk
🖱 www.airbirmingham.com
▤ 0121 766 5100
✆ Page 127-G3

Arca Bar
Arcadian Centre,
Birmingham, West Midlands
B5 4TB
☎ 01216667777
✆ Page 3-G7

Bambu Bar
1st Floor Kotwall House,
Wrottesley Street,
Birmingham, West Midlands
B5 4BN
☎ 01216 22 4124
@ manager@
bambubar.co.uk
🖱 www.bambubar.co.uk
✆ Page 3-G7

Bar Academy Birmingham
51 Dale End, Birmingham,
West Midlands B4 7LS
☎ 0121 262 3000
✆ 0870 771 2000
@ mail@birmingham-
academy.co.uk
🖱 www.birmingham-
academy.co.uk
▤ 0121 236 2241
✆ Page 3-H5

Bar Risa
Centrally located on one of
Birmingham's busiest 'going
out' streets, Broad Street.
With six rooms and seven
bars, the club has been
designed to ensure there
is an area to suit every
mood or occasion. Also
incorporates Jongleurs, the
UKs largest comedy club.

Quayside Tower, 252–259
Broad Street, Birmingham,
West Midlands BH1 2HF

☎ 01216 324936
@ info@risa-
birmingham.co.uk
🖱 www.risa-birmingham.
co.uk
✆ Page 2-C6

Bar Room Bar
166–168 Wharfside Street,
The Mailbox, Birmingham,
West Midlands B1 1RL
☎ 0121 632 1199
@ birmingham@
barroombar.com
🖱 mailbox.barroombar.com
✆ Page 2-D7

Barfly, Birmingham
A live music and club night
venue in Birmingham.

78 Digbeth High Street,
Birmingham, West Midlands
B5 6DY
☎ 0121 246 1010, 0121 633
8311
@ carlo@barflyclub.com
🖱 www.barflyclub.com
▤ 0121 633 8344
✆ Page 3-J7

Barley Mow
2 Poplar Road, Solihull, West
Midlands B91 3AB
☎ 0121 705 1379
✆ Page 182-A1

Barracuda
16 Hurst Street,
Birmingham, West Midlands
B5 4NB
☎ 0121 622 6878
@ josh@barracuda
birmingham.co.uk
🖱 www.barracuda
birmingham.co.uk
✆ Page 3-F7

Basement
Purpose built underground
club which lies beneath
the city.

Holloway Circus,
Birmingham, West Midlands
B1 1EG

@ basementclub@
hotmail.co.uk
🖱 www.myspace.com/
basementbirmingham
✆ Page 3-F7

The Billesley Pub
Brook Lane, Kings Heath,
Birmingham, West Midlands
B13 0AB
☎ 0121 4443563
▤ 0121 4432642
✆ Page 161-F2

The Boiler Room
The Big Peg, 120 Vyse
Street, The Jewellery
Quarter, Birmingham, West
Midlands B18 6NF
☎ 01212484999
🖱 www.theboilerroom.
me.uk
✆ Page 2-C1

Brannigans
Cumberland House, 196–209
Broad Street, Birmingham,
West Midlands B15 1AY
☎ 0121 616 1888
🖱 www.brannigansbars.com
▤ 0121 616 1999
✆ Page 2-C6

Cafe One
1 Auchinleck Square,
Fiveways, Birmingham,
West Midlands B15 1DU
✆ 0121 245 0000
✆ Page 126-B3

Canal Club
The nightclub has two rooms
offering high-tech sound,
visuals and light shows.

British Waterways
Depot, Broad Street,
Wolverhampton, West
Midlands WV1 1JA
@ info@thecanalclub.co.uk
🖱 www.thecanalclub.co.uk
✆ Page 7-G3

Carling Academy Birmingham
Carling Academy
Birmingham has fast

become Birmingham's
premier venue, offering the
best live events and club
nights in the region and
becoming a focal point for
nightlife in the Midlands.

52–54 Dale End,
Birmingham, West Midlands
B4 7LS
☎ 01212 623000
@ mail@birmingham-
academy.co.uk
🖱 www.birmingham-
academy.co.uk
▤ 01212 362241
✆ Page 3-H5

Club DV8
Gay-friendly venue that
plays host to some of the
busiest club nights in town.

16 Lower Essex Street,
Birmingham, West Midlands
B5 6RD
☎ 0121 666 6366
@ info@clubdv8.co.uk
🖱 www.clubdv8.co.uk
▤ 0121 666 6366
✆ Page 127-E3

Concrete
A 3,000-square foot
multipurpose venue spread
over two levels based in the
Jewellery Quarter, Hockley,
Birmingham. The venue
morphs through the week
from restaurant lounge bar
to full on live music at the
weekends, with strong club
promoters, eclectic bands
and internationally known
artists appearing regularly.

120 Vyse Street, Jewellery
Quarter, Birmingham, West
Midlands B18 6NF
☎ 0121 212 9280, 07968
366878, 07968 260276
✆ 0121 236 6446
@ info@concretebar.co.uk
🖱 www.concretebar.co.uk
✆ Page 2-C1

The Cotton Club
Weekly club nights in a
300-capacity venue with

VIP areas. Plus monthly jazz nights.

Arcadian Centre, 70 Hurst Street, Birmingham, West Midlands B5 4TD
☎ 0121 622 5250
@ info@cottonclub.tv
🖰 www.cottonclub.tv
📄 0121 666 6563
📍 Page 3-G7

The Custard Factory

The award-winning first phase is home to a bohemian community of 500 artists and small creative enterprises. The studio workshops are complemented by a theatre cafe, antiques shops, meeting rooms, dance studios, holistic therapy rooms, art galleries, the Medicine Bar and the Code nightclub. The second phase, completed in 2002 comprises shops, galleries and restaurants plus the Green Man, a towering 40-foot sculpture made of earth, fire and water.

Gibb Square, Birmingham, West Midlands B9 4AA
☎ 0121 224 7777,
   0121 224 8401
@ info@custardfactory.com
🖰 www.custardfactory.co.uk
📄 0121 604 8888
📍 Page 3-K7

The Dragon Bar

Sanctuary Building, 78 Digbeth High Street, Birmingham, West Midlands B5 6DY
📍 Page 3-J7

Dragon Eye

193–194 Broad Street, Birmingham, West Midlands B15 1AY
☎ 0121 632 5225
🖰 dragon-eye.co.uk
📍 Page 2-B7

Edward's No 8

A rock club in Birmingham.

Lower Severn Street, Birmingham West Midlands B1 1BL
☎ 0121 643 5835
@ info@edwardsno8.
   wanadoo.co.uk
🖰 www.edwardsno8.com
📍 Page 2-C6

Factory Club

The Factory Club has a reputation for underground music, an atmosphere similar to that of warehouse rave parties. The venue hosts a wide variety of events, including live bands, and high profile international DJs of all genres.

The Custard Factory, Digbeth, Birmingham, West Midlands B9 4AA
☎ 0121 693 6333
🕿 0870 754 4445
@ estondj@hotmail.com
🖰 www.factoryclub.co.uk
📍 Page 3-K7

G2 Bar Club

G2 Bar Club hosts regular nights featuring DJs playing funky house and it has salsa classes for beginners and improvers.

Holloway Circus, Birmingham, West Midlands B1 1EQ
☎ 0121 643 8949, 07949 150205
@ inquiries@
   gemstwo.co.uk
🖰 www.gemstwo.co.uk
📍 Page 3-F7

Heroes, Wolverhampton

Garrick Street, Wolverhampton, West Midlands WV1 3AB
☎ 01902 426888
@ heroes.wolverhampton@
   nightclub.co.uk
📍 Page 7-G5

Holly Bush Ale House

53 Newtown Lane, Cradley Heath, West Midlands B64 5EA
☎ 07949 594484
🖰 www.hollybushpub.net
📍 Page 120-D3

Indi

Arcadian Centre, Birmingham, West Midlands B5 4TD
☎ 01216224858
📍 Page 3-G7

Ipanema Restaurant and Bar

9 Brindley Place, 60 Broad Street, Birmingham, West Midlands B1 2HJ
☎ 0121 643 5577
@ info@ipanema.co.uk
📄 0121 643 5588
📍 Page 2-C6

island bar

At Birmingham's rock and roll cocktail bar in Suffolk Street, Queensway, you'll find some of the city's finest bartenders showing off their skills while you enjoy great guitar music. DJs play a mix of old and newer guitar classics, live acoustic guitar music features on many nights of the week, there is an open mic night for budding songwriters and the bar is also a showcase for local and national up-and coming bands.

14–16 Suffolk Street, Queensway, Birmingham, West Midlands B1 1LT
☎ 0121 632 5296
🕿 0121 632 5296
@ info@bar-island.co.uk
🖰 www.bar-island.co.uk
📍 Page 2-E6

Liberty's Nightclub

184 Hagley Road, Edgbaston, Birmingham, West Midlands B16 9NY

☎ 0121 454 4444
@ info@libertysnightclub.
   co.uk
🖰 www.libertysnightclub.
   co.uk
📄 0121 455 7179
📍 Page 125-F4

The Moon Lounge

Hurst Street, Birmingham, West Midlands B5 4ST
☎ 0121 622 5700
📍 Page 3-F7

Nightingale Club

Kent Street, Birmingham, West Midlands B5 6RD
🖰 www.nightingaleclub.
   co.uk
📍 Page 127-E4

OC's Bar

79 Digbeth Street, Digbeth, Birmingham, West Midlands B5 6DY
📍 Page 3-J7

Oceana Birmingham

Hurst Street, Birmingham, West Midlands B5 4AS
☎ 0121 632 6273
@ birmingham@
   oceanaclubs.com
🖰 www.oceanaclubs.com
📄 0121 632 6274
📍 Page 3-F7

Opal Lounge

The Opal Lounge hosts regular nights featuring DJs playing indie, funk, soul, northern hip hop, retro classic dance music, house music with the fundamental 80s funk and soul.

76b High Street, Solihull, West Midlands B91 3TA
☎ 0121 705 9944
@ info@opal-lounge.com
🖰 www.opal-lounge.com
📄 0121 711 8507
📍 Page 182-A1

The Patrick Kavanagh

142 Trafalgar Road, Moseley,
Birmingham, West Midlands
B13 8BX
☎ 0121 449 2598
✆ Page 144-B4

Poppy Red

The Arcadian, Hurst Street,
Birmingham, West Midlands
B5 4TD
☎ 0121 687 1200
🖱www.poppy-red.com/
✆ Page 3-G7

Q Club

Recently refurbished venue
which plays host to some of
Birmingham's top clubbing
events.

212 Corporation Street,
Birmingham, West Midlands
B4 6QB
☎ 0121 212 1212
@ info@qclub.co.uk
🖱www.qclub.co.uk
✆ Page 3-H3

Quadrant Lounge

25–27 Lichfield Street,
Wolverhampton, West
Midlands WV1 1EQ
☎ 01902 653411
@ quadlounge@aol.com
🖱www.quadrantlounge.
   co.uk/index.htm
✆ Page 7-F4

R B's Bar & Nightclub

The Lower Parade, Sutton
Coldfield, West Midlands
B72 1XX
☎ 0121 3545507
🖱www.rbs-sutton.com
✆ Page 62-B3

Rojac Warehouse

Gibb Street, Heath Mill Lane,
Birmingham, West Midlands
B9 4AR
✆ Page 3-K7

Route 2

A gay bar and club hosting
an array of club nights
ranging from 80s nights to

funky house, seven days a
week.

139 Hurst Street,
Birmingham, West Midlands
B5 6SD
☎ 0121 622 3366
📞 07716 666 313
🖱www.routetwo.co.uk
✆ Page 3-F7

Snobs Nightclub

Birmingham's longest
running alternative/student
nightclub.

29 Paradise Circus,
Queensway, Birmingham,
West Midlands B1 2BJ
☎ 0121 643 5551
@ enquiries@
   snobsnightclub.co.uk
🖱www.snobsnightclub.
   co.uk
✆ Page 2-D4

The Sports Cafe, Birmingham

240 Broad Street,
Birmingham, West Midlands
B1 2HG
☎ 0121 633 4000
🖱www.thesportscafe.net/
✆ Page 2-C6

St Anne's Club

Alcester Street, Digbeth,
Birmingham, West Midlands
B12 0PH
☎ 0121 772 7375
🖱www.latinmotion.co.uk/
   St_Annes/SA_FRI.htm
✆ Page 127-F4

Subway City

Subway city is a large
underground nightclub
venue comprising of four
large, high roofed brick
arches underneath the train
lines. Within this space
there is room for 1,000
people covering seven
rooms, including five bars
and a restaurant, featuring
DJs playing chart classics,
80s hits, and indie anthems.

27 Water Street,
Birmingham, West Midlands
B3 1HL
☎ 0121 233 0310
@ info@subwaycity.net
🖱www.subwaycity.net
📠 0121 236 1522
✆ Page 2-E3

Type 3

Lower Parade, Sutton
Coldfield, Birmingham,
West Midlands B72 1XX
✆ Page 62-B3

Vaughn's

Stratford Road, Hall Green,
Birmingham, West Midlands
B28 9
☎ 0121 778 4006
✆ Page 162-D3

Walkabout, Birmingham

Langley Building, Regency
Wharf, 266A–271 Broad
Street, Birmingham, West
Midlands B1 2DS
☎ 0121 632 5712
@ wbi.birmingham@
   walkabout.eu.com
🖱www.walkabout.
   eu.com/010/WAI/intro.
   html
📠 0121 616 0001
✆ Page 2-C6

The Works, Birmingham

182 Broad Street,
Birmingham, West Midlands
B15 1DA
☎ 0121 633 1520
🖱www.theworks
   birmingham.com
✆ Page 2-C6

SPECIAL EVENTS' VENUES

BBC Screen, Birmingham

Chamberlain Square,
Birmingham, West Midlands
B3 3HQ
✆ Page 2-E5

Birmingham Town Hall

Acclaimed at its opening in
1834 as the finest music hall
in the country, the Grade I
listed landmark has been
lovingly and painstakingly
renovated by a dedicated
team of conservation and
construction professionals.
It was designed by Joseph
Aloysius Hansom for the
performance of music,
and today hosts a varied
programme including
recitals, international
chamber music, an
international concert
season, world music and
folk.

Victoria Square,
Birmingham, West Midlands
B3 3DQ
📞 0121 303 2880
🖱www.birmingham.gov.
   uk/townhall.bcc
✆ Page 2-E5

Centenary Square

Centenary Square,
Birmingham, B1 2DR
🖱www.birminghamuk.
   com/centenary.htm
✆ Page 2-D5

Little Civic

Music and entertainment
venue that hosts comedy
and special events.

North Street,
Wolverhampton West
Midlands WV1 1RQ
📞 0870 320 7000
🖱www.wolvescivic.co.uk
✆ Page 7-F4

Millennium Point

Millennium Point is
Birmingham's flagship
Millennium project, built to
celebrate and encourage
science, technology and
education in Birmingham
and the wider region.
Millennium Point is also
home to two pioneering
education initiatives for

school aged children
– the University of the
First Age and the Young
People's Parliament - as
well as many other firms
and organisations from
the public and private
sectors. The public areas of
Millennium Point, including
the stunning central 'Hub'
with its soaring atrium, are
open free of charge every
day except 25 December.
Events and exhibitions.

Curzon Street, Birmingham,
West Midlands B4 7XG
☎ 121 202 2200
@ info@millenniumpoint.
  org.uk
🖰 www.millenniumpoint.
  org.uk
✆ Page 3-K4

Molineux Stadium

Molineux Stadium is
the homeground of
Wolverhampton Wanderers
Football Club but also hosts
several other events, such
as live music concerts,
conferences and banquets.

Waterloo Road,
Wolverhampton, West
Midlands WV1 4QR
☎ 0870 442 0123
@ info@wolves.co.uk
🖰 www.molineuxstadium.
  co.uk
📄 01902 687055
✆ Page 6-E1

NEC: National Exhibition Centre

The National Exhibition
Centre is the busiest
exhibition centre in Europe,
staging more than 180

exhibitions each year,
ranging from world-famous
public shows such as Crufts
Dog Show and Clotheshow
Live to international trade
exhibitions like IPEX and
Spring Fair, Birmingham. Up
to four million people visit
the centre each year.

National Exhibition Centre,
Birmingham, West Midlands
B40 1NT
☎ 0121 780 4141
🕓 0870 730 0196
@ info@necgroup.co.uk
🖰 www.necgroup.co.uk
✆ Page 150-A2

NIA: National Indoor Arena

King Edwards Road,
Birmingham, West Midlands
B1 2AA
☎ 0121 780 4444
@ nia-sales@
  necgroup.co.uk
🖰 www.necgroup.co.uk
✆ Page 2-B5

Villa Park

Villa Park is the homeground
of Aston Villa Football Club
but also hosts other events,
such as live music concerts.

Villa Park, Birmingham
West Midlands B6 6HE
☎ 0121 327 2299
🖰 www.avfc.premiumtv.
  co.uk/
✆ Page 91-F5

West Bromwich Albion Football Club

West Bromwich Albion
Football Club hosts events
such as live music concerts.

The Hawthorns, Halfords
Lane, West Bromwich,
West Midlands B71 4LF
☎ 08700 66 8888
  08700 66 2840
@ enqiries@wbafc.co.uk
🖰 www.wba.premiumtv.
  co.uk/
✆ Page 88-C5

Street by Street

BIRMINGHAM
WOLVERHAMPTON
DUDLEY, SOLIHULL, STOURBRIDGE, WALSALL, WEST BROMWICH

Aldridge, Brownhills, Codsall, Coleshill, Dorridge, Halesowen, Knowle, Pelsall, Sutton Coldfield, Wombourne

Key to map pages	ii-iii
Key to map symbols	iv-1
Enlarged map pages	2-7
Main map pages	8-199
Index – towns & villages	200
Index – streets	201-243
Index – featured places	243-252
Acknowledgements	252

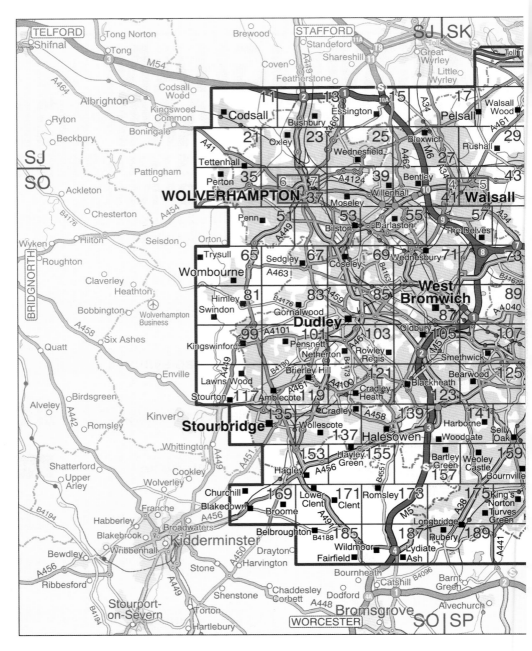

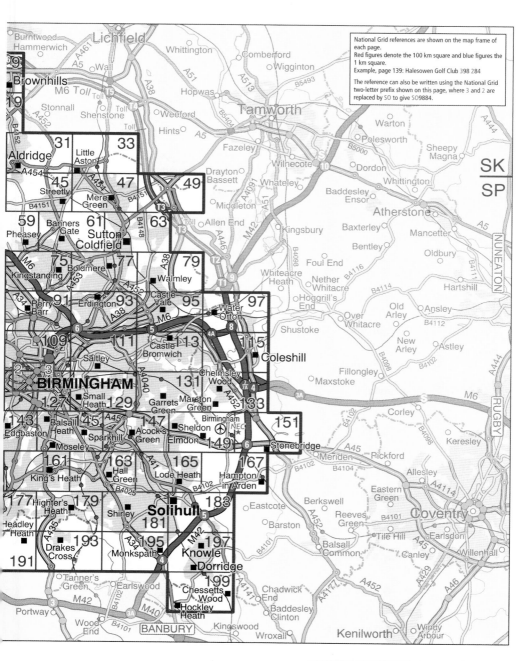

National Grid references are shown on the map frame of each page.
Red figures denote the 100 km square and blue figures the 1 km square.
Example, page 139: Halesowen Golf Club 398 284

The reference can also be written using the National Grid two-letter prefix shown on this page, where 3 and 2 are replaced by SO to give SO9884.

4.2 inches to 1 mile   Scale of main map pages   1:15,000

iv

Junction 9	Motorway & junction	*LC*	Level crossing
Services	Motorway service area		Tramway
	Primary road single/dual carriageway		Ferry route
Services	Primary road service area		Airport runway
	A road single/dual carriageway		County, administrative boundary
	B road single/dual carriageway		Mounds
	Other road single/dual carriageway	**17**	Page continuation 1:15,000
	Minor/private road, access may be restricted	**3**	Page continuation to enlarged scale 1:10,000
	One-way street		River/canal, lake, pier
	Pedestrian area		Aqueduct, lock, weir
	Track or footpath	465 ▲ Winter Hill	Peak (with height in metres)
	Road under construction		Beach
	Road tunnel		Woodland
P	Parking		Park
P+	Park & Ride		Cemetery
	Bus/coach station		Built-up area
	Railway & main railway station		Industrial/business building
	Railway & minor railway station		Leisure building
⊖	Underground station		Retail building
⊖	Light railway & station		Other building
+++++++++	Preserved private railway	**IKEA**	IKEA store

⊓⊔⊓⊔⊓⊔	City wall		♟	Castle
A&E	Hospital with 24-hour A&E department		⌷	Historic house or building
PO	Post Office		Wakehurst Place (NT)	National Trust property
📖	Public library		Ⓜ	Museum or art gallery
i	Tourist Information Centre		♟	Roman antiquity
i	Seasonal Tourist Information Centre		⚊	Ancient site, battlefield or monument
▮ ▮	Petrol station, 24 hour Major suppliers only		⊞	Industrial interest
†	Church/chapel		✿	Garden
🚻	Public toilets		◉	Garden Centre Garden Centre Association Member
♿	Toilet with disabled facilities		♣	Garden Centre Wyevale Garden Centre
PH	Public house AA recommended		♠♠	Arboretum
❶	Restaurant AA inspected		⛟	Farm or animal centre
Madeira Hotel ▬	Hotel AA inspected		⚏	Zoological or wildlife collection
🎭	Theatre or performing arts centre		⚘	Bird collection
🎥	Cinema		⚬	Nature reserve
⚑	Golf course		⇔	Aquarium
▲	Camping AA inspected		V	Visitor or heritage centre
🚐	Caravan site AA inspected		♆	Country park
▲🚐	Camping & caravan site AA inspected		⌒	Cave
⚶	Theme park		✹	Windmill
⛪	Abbey, cathedral or priory		⛃	Distillery, brewery or vineyard

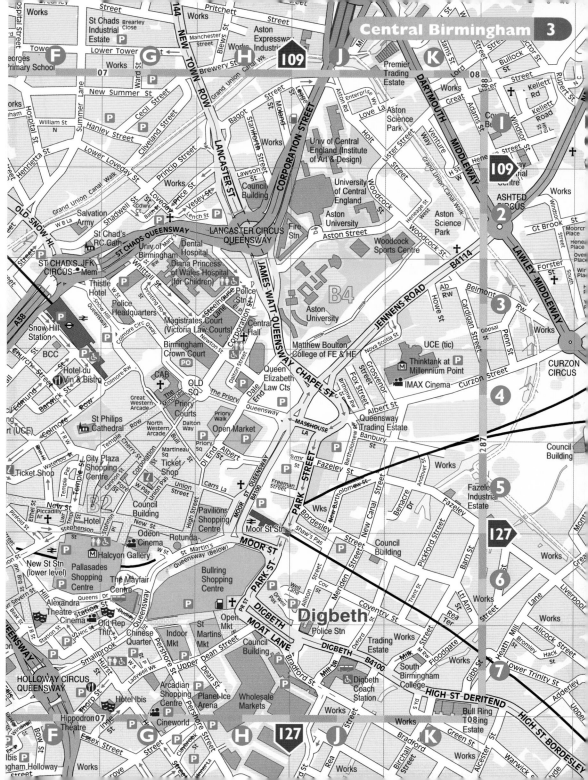

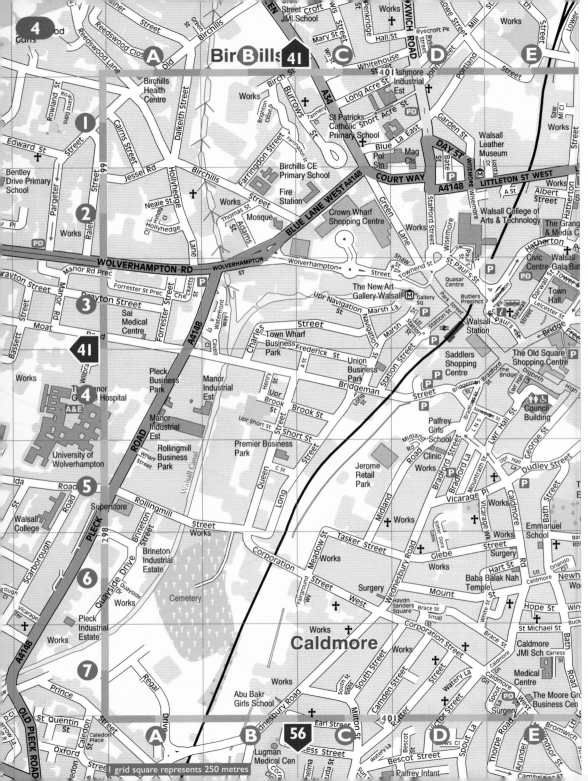

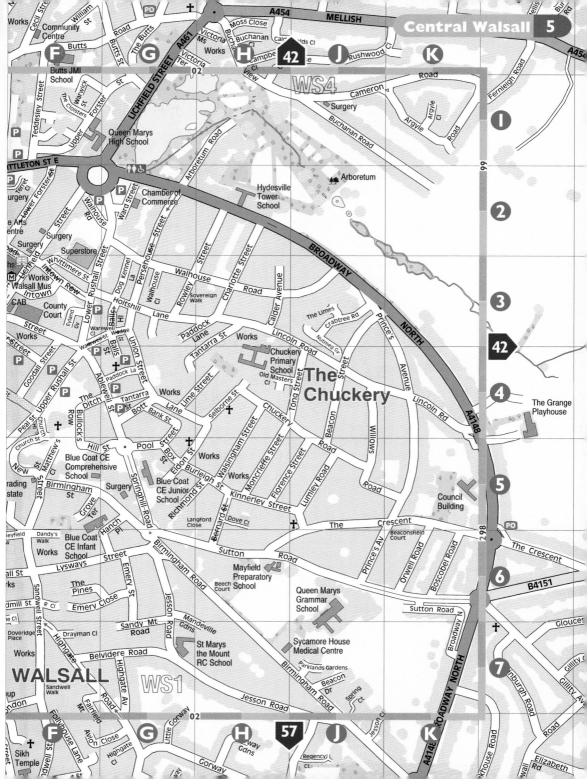

Central Walsall 5

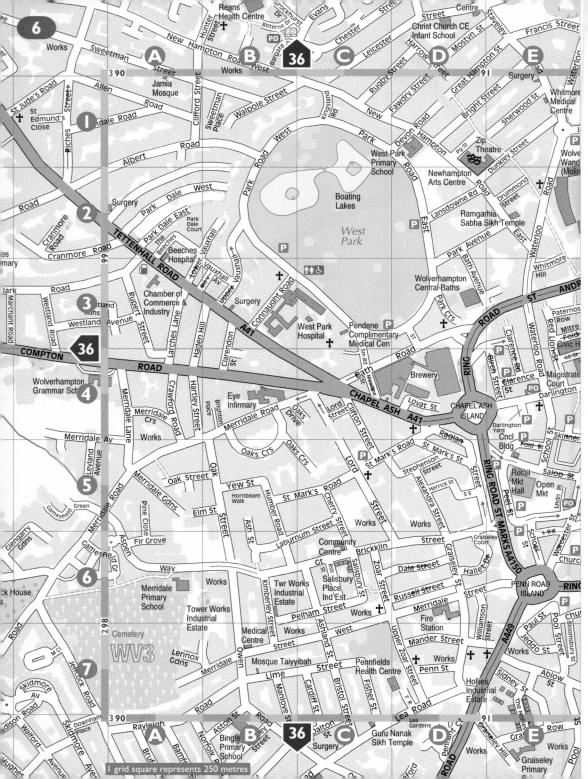

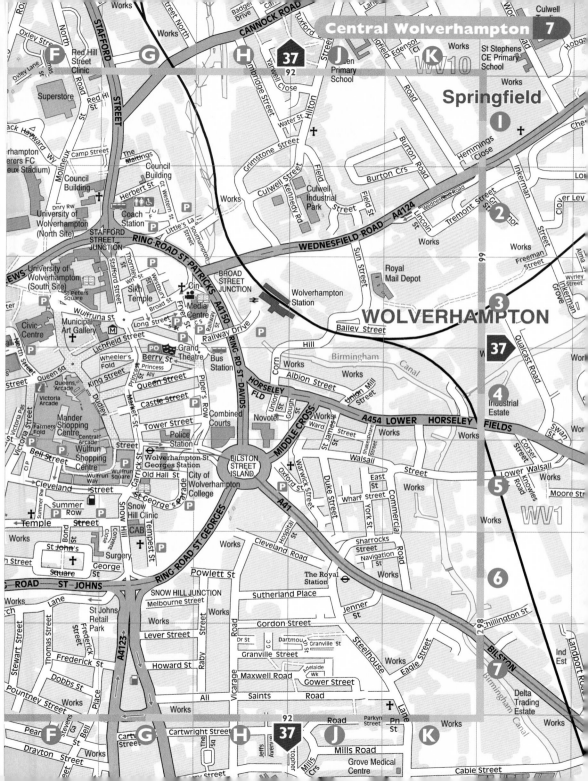

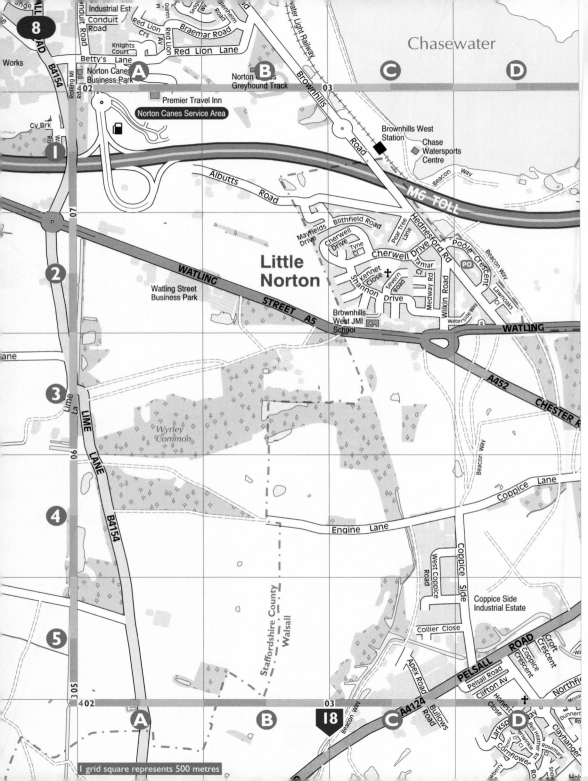

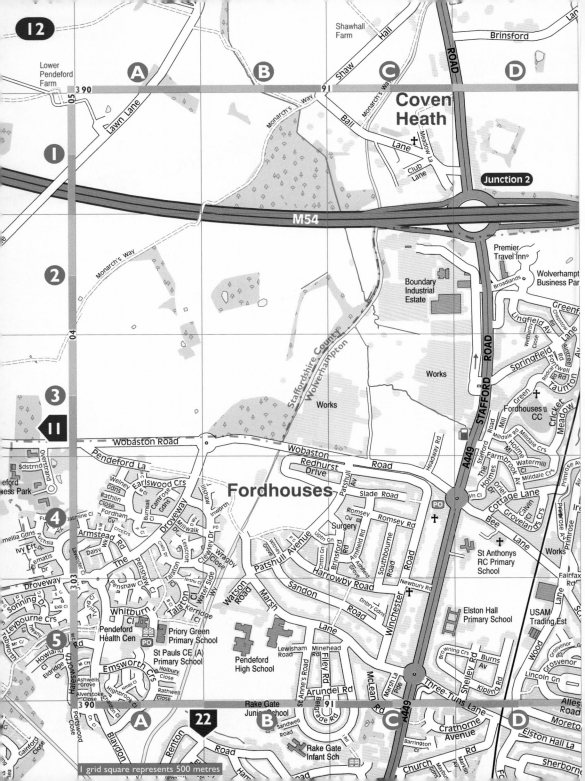

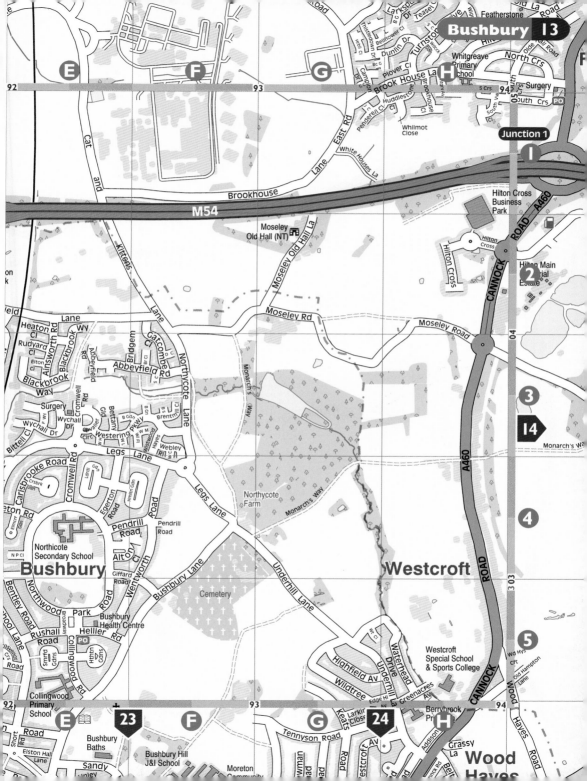

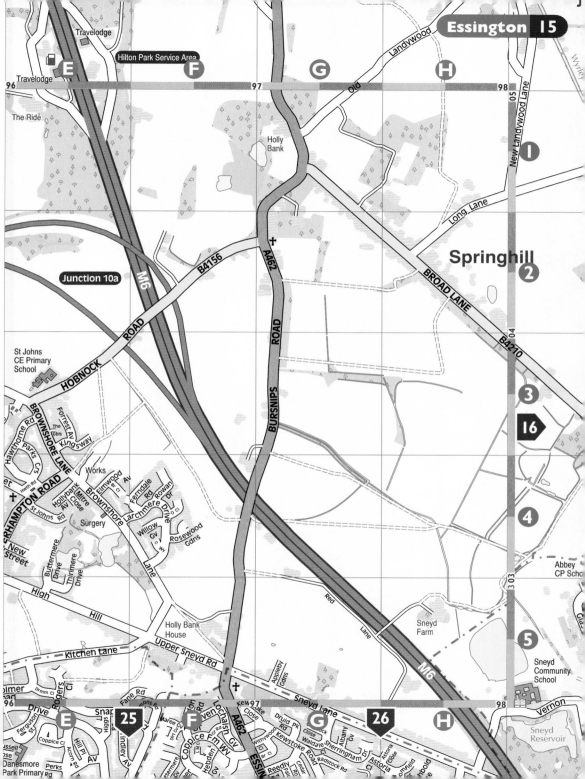

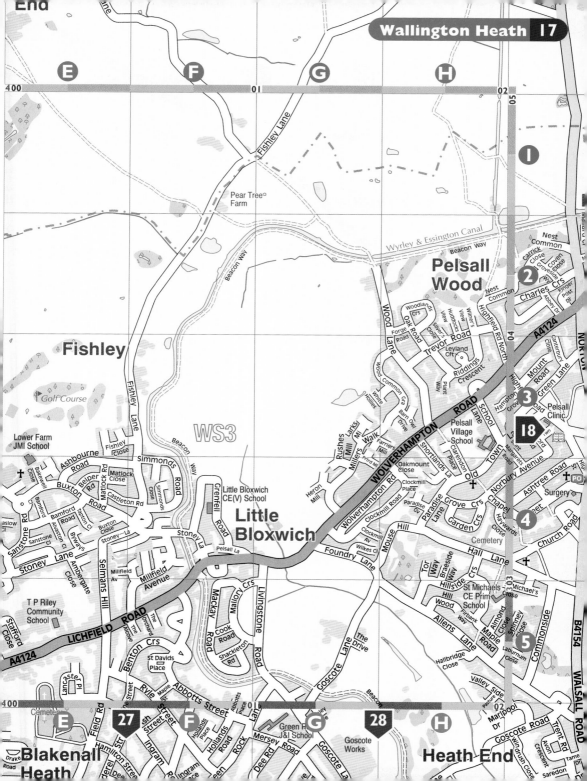

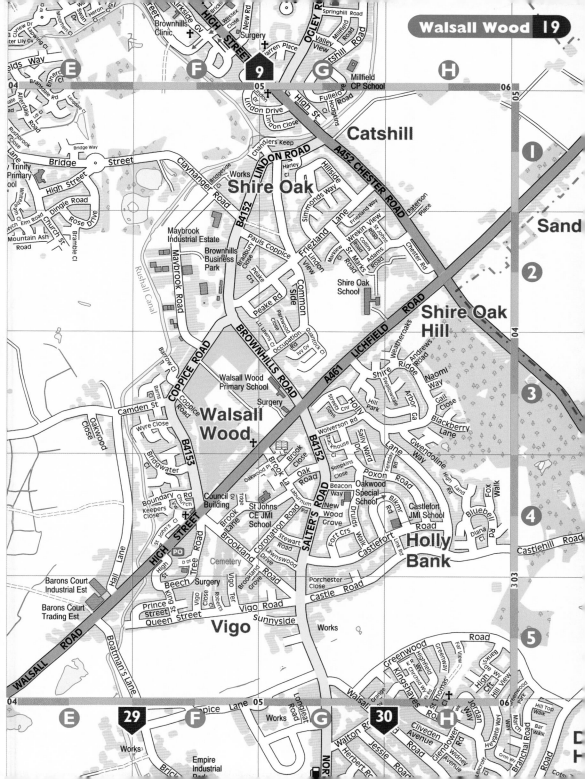

Brownhills
Clinic

Surgery

Springhill Road

Valley
View

Millfield
CP School

Catshill

Shire Oak

Warren Place

Chandlers Keep

Harley
Cl

Maybrook
Industrial Estate

Brownhills
Business
Park

Pauls Coppice

Peake Rd

Bradbury
Cl

Peake
Crs

Simmonds Way

Hillside
Lane

Wrekin View

Friezland Way

St Johns

Collins

Markew

St Marks

Adams
Road

Common
Side

Parkwood

Occupation
Rd

Ivy Gv

Shire Oak
School

Paterson
Place

Sand

**Shire Oak
Hill**

Andrews
Road

Shire
Ridge

Naomi
Way

Gail
Close

Blackberry
Lane

Weathercoaks

Arbor
Ca

Rushall Canal

Maybrook
Road

**Walsall
Wood**

Walsall Wood
Primary School

Surgery

Camden St

Barns

Wyre Close

Bridgwater
Cl

Coppice
Road

Oakwood
Close

Boundary
Keepers Close

Council
Building

St Johns
CE JMI
School

Brook
Lane

Cemetery

Brook Pl

Oak
Road

Brook
Close

Laburnum

Wolverson Rd

Sally
Ward
Dr

Streets
Cnr

Holly

Stack
House

Simpkins
Close

Hill
Park

Swallowdale

Lane
Rd

Gwendoline
Way

High
Land

Fox
Walk

Bluebell
Rd

Diana
Cl

New
Wood
Grove

Druids
Walk

Poxon
Road

Oakwood
Special
School

Stewart
Road

Fort Crs

Castlefort

Blkmr
Rd

Castlefort
JMI School
Road

**Holly
Bank**

Castlehill Road

Barons Court
Industrial Est

Barons Court
Trading Est

High
St

Beech

Tree
Road

PO

Prince
Street

King St

Queen street

Vigo
Close

Roberts

Vigo Ter

Brookland
Road

Lawnswood
Drive

Coronation
Road

Porchester
Close

Castle
Road

Vigo

sunnyside

Works

Greenwood
Road

Fat View

Greenway

Highfield

Banks

High
Cft

Hill View

Jordan
Cl

Cliveden
Avenue

Glendower
Avenue

Widney

St Thomas'
Cl

Kingshaves

Walsall Road

Boatman's Lane

Works

Empire
Industrial
Park

Works

Longleat
Road

Walton
Road

Herbert Rd

Jessie
Road

Glendower
Rd

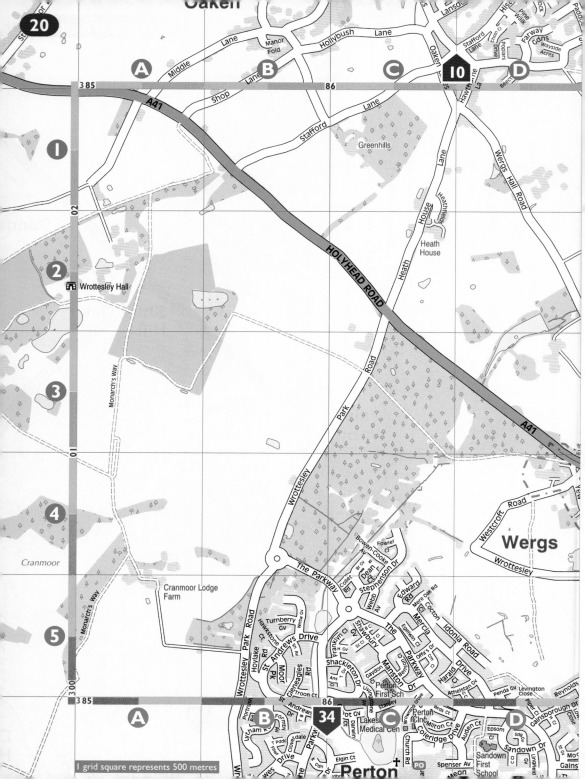

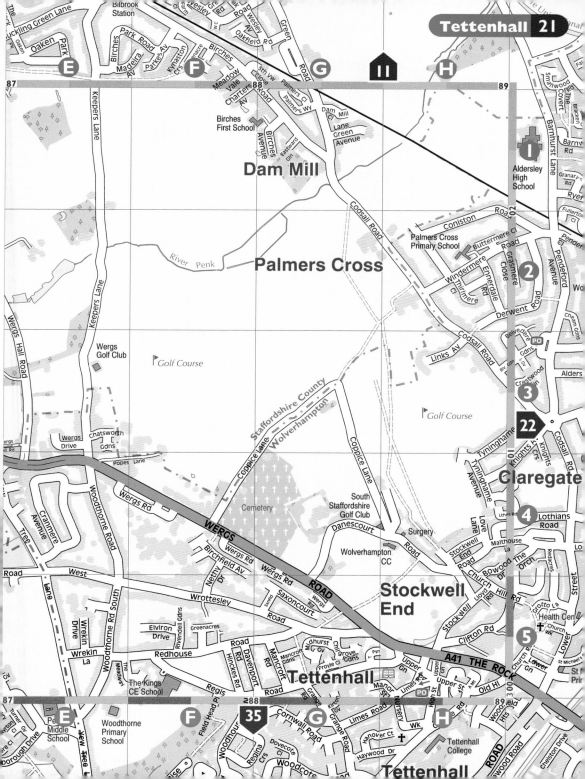

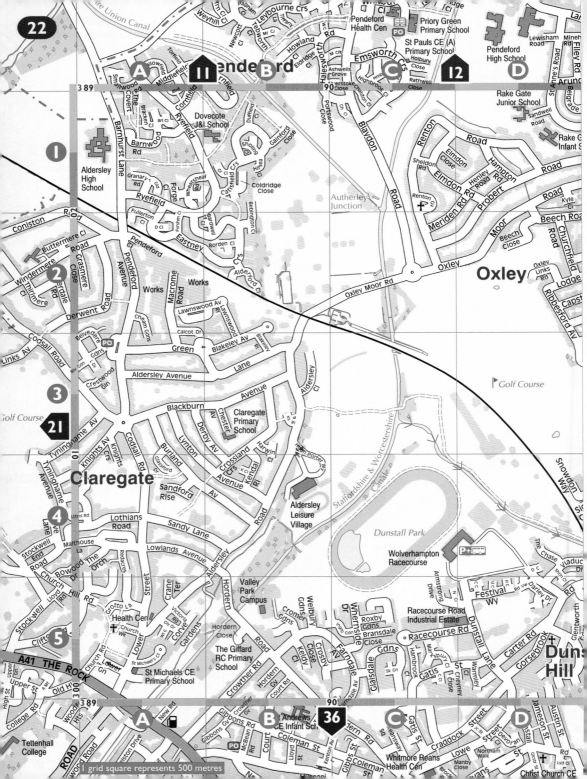

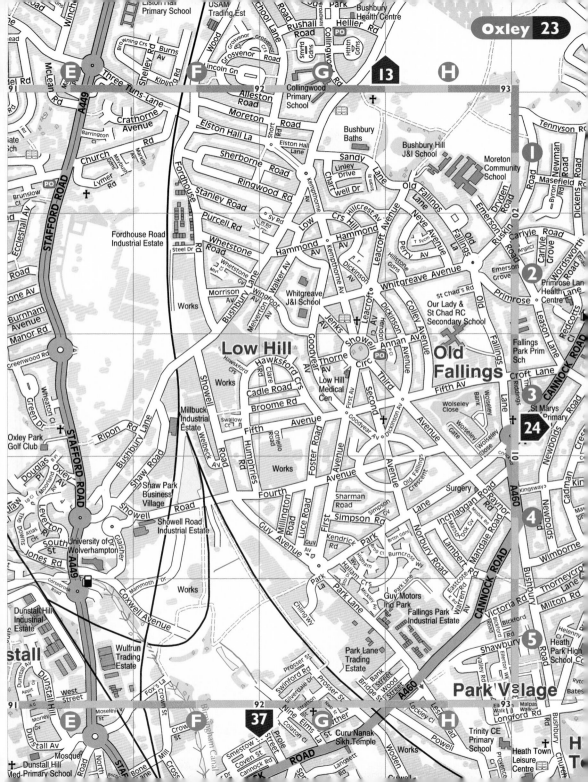

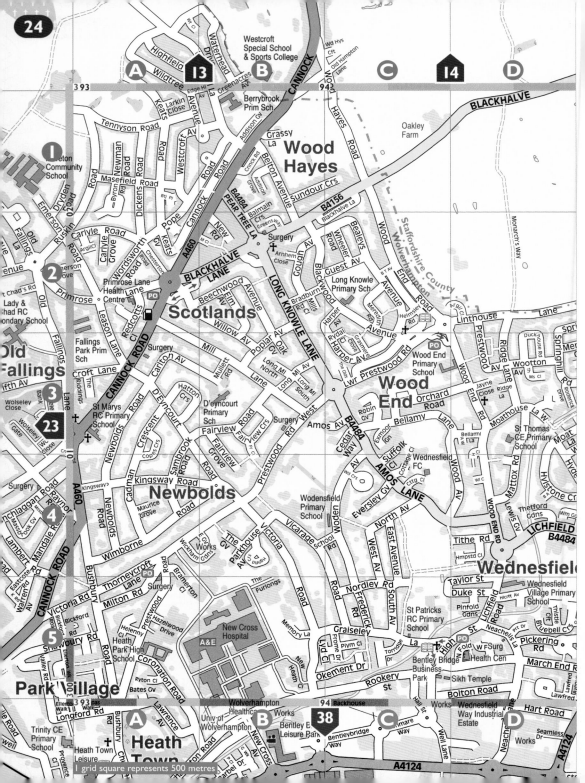

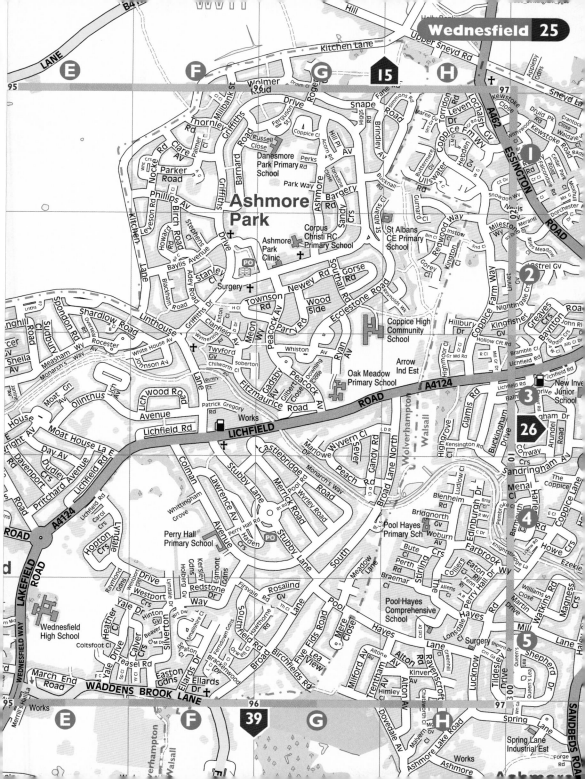

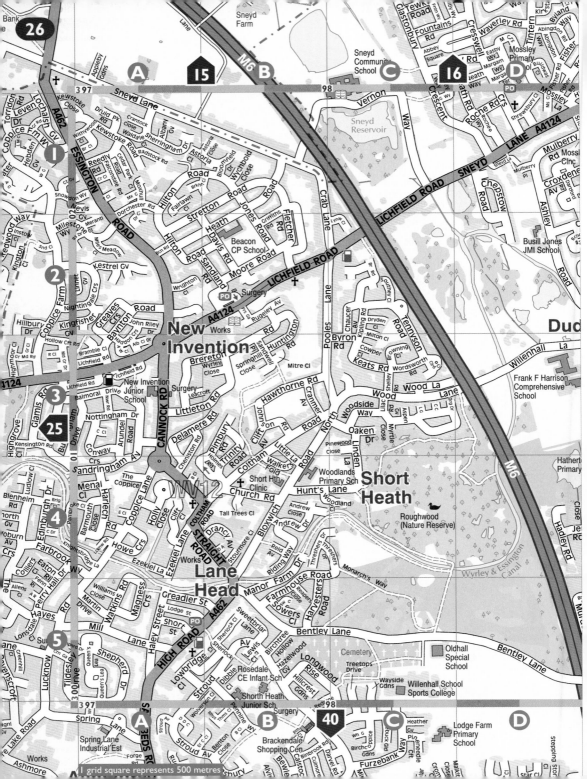

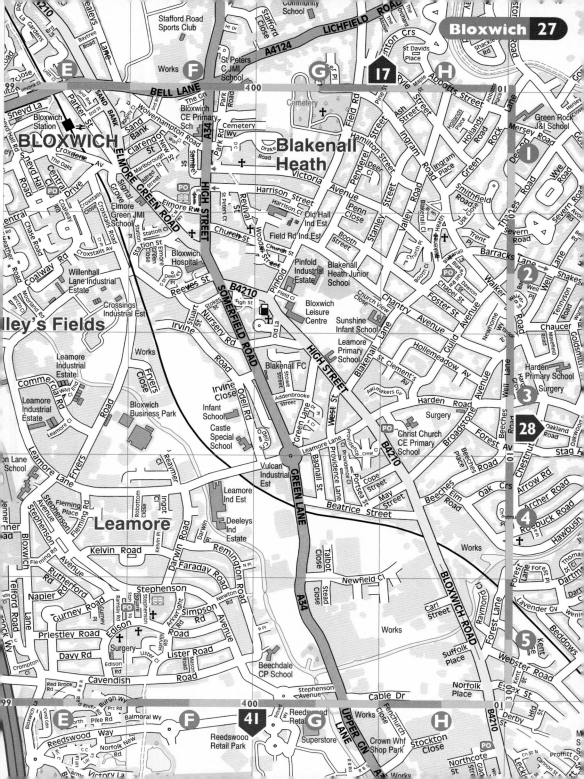

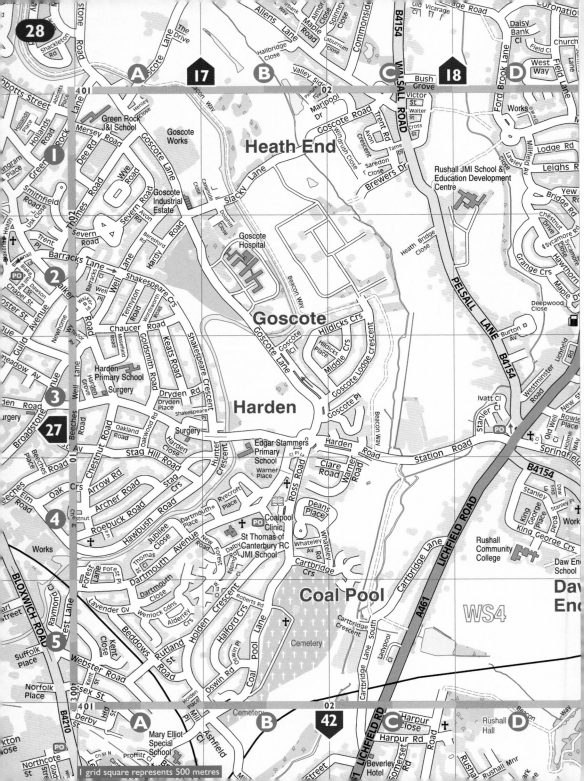

High Heath

Stubber's Green

Shelfield

Rushall

ALDRID

Walsall Road

A46104 WALSALL ROAD

E F G 19 H

I

2 Lei

3

30

4

5

E F 43 G H

BOSTY LANE

Rushall Canal
Brickyard Road

Empire Industrial Park
Empire Industrial Park
Lion Industrial Park
Northgate Way
Hayward Industrial Park
Merchants Way
Vigo Place
Lockside
Wharf Approach

Baron's Court Trading Est
Queen Street
Sunnyside
Coppice Lane
Longleat Road
Works
Works
NORTHGATE
Northgate Way
Leighswood

Works
Works
Works
Works

Boatman

Greenfield Road
New Street
Woodbridge Close
School Street
Schoolgate Close
Spring Road
Springhill Close
Stream Meadow Drive
Watermeadow Drive
Woodham Road
Meadow Road
Broadheath Drive
Streamside Way
Watermere Way
The Parkway
The Parkway
Bickfield Close
Rischale Way
Barns Lane
Pool View
Barns Lane
WD Dr
Sherwo
Stubbers Green Road
Dumbledeerry Lane
Dumbledeerry Lane

The Swag

St Francis RC Primary School
Four Crosses Rd
Spring Close
The Drive
Highfield Avenue
Gladeside
Meadowlands Drive
Wilsford Close
Parkstone Close
Brook Close
Sedgemere Gv
Highfield Avenue
Shelfield Clinic
Greenfield Primary Sch
The Longcroft
Briarbeck
Fernbourn Close

Bickley Rd
Queens Road
Linley Rd
Earls Road
York Rd
Kings Dr
Dean Rd
Bickley Road
Countess Dr
Radleys Primary School
Winterley Lane
Radley Road
Edinburgh Drive
Windsor Way
Balmoral
Chatsworth Crescent
Tintagel Wy
Tintagel Way
Westgate
Rufford Way
Red Rooster Industrial Estate
Lindley Lodge Industrial Estate
Westgate Trading Estate
Anglian Rd
Redhouse Industrial Estate
Middlemore Lane
WEST
Middlemore Business Park
Redhouse JMI School
Linley Wood Road
The Leasow
Berryfields
Gretton Crs
High Ridge
Gretton Rd
Bonner
Honiton Way
Westbrook
Red House Lane
Dilke Rd
Stapleton
Avenue
Dartmouth Drive
Lynmouth Close
Speedwell Close
Moss Close
Station Rd
Hilary Drive
Oakley Av
Walsall Road
Tynings
Aldridge School
Hepburn Close
Whitehouse Way
Quicksand Lane
Walsall Rd
Berryfields Farm

Beacon Trading Estate
Redhouse Industrial Estate
Westfie Dr

WALSALL ROAD

BOSTY LANE

Daw End Lane
DAW END
Floyds La
Park Rd
Friary Crs
Abbots Close
Lime Cv
Beacon Way
Limehurst Road

Middlemore

The Longcroft

PO
PO
PO

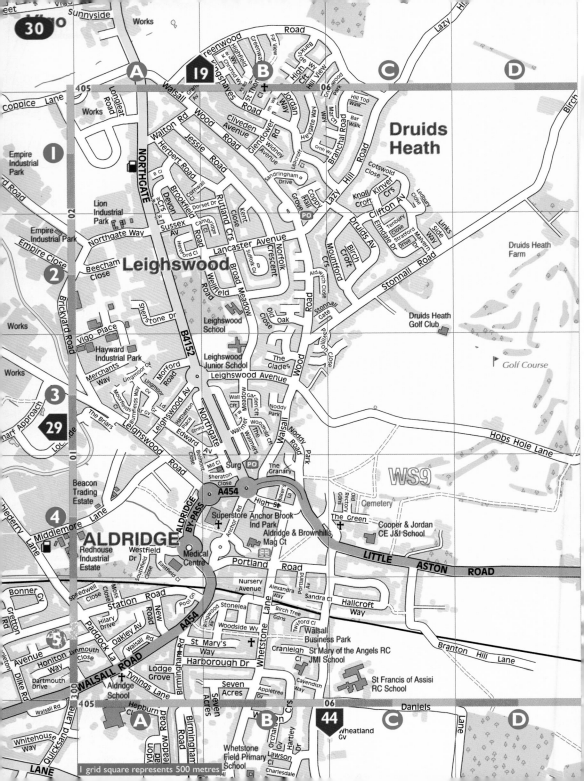

E   F   Gainsborough Hill Farm   G   H

08   09

I

Bosses

CHESTER ROAD

A452

Wood Lane

Forge Lane

Forge Farm

02

2

PH

Holly Lane

Mill Green

3

Back Lane

32

Forge   Lane

Mill Lane

10

Gould   Firm   Lane

Walsall

Staffordshire County

4

Best Western The Fairlawns at Aldridge

ALDRIDGE   ROAD

A454

WALSAL

Green Lane

A452

Fotherley Brook Road

Lakeside

The Spinney

Little Aston Hall Drive

Roman

Roman Road

5

Squirrel Walk

Bourne Farm

Beech Gate

Little A

07

E   F   G   H   Little

08   09

45

Golf Cour

Cottage Ms

A

Staffordshire Count

Walsall

Little Aston Golf Club

3000

32

A   B   C   D

409

10 Moor Lane

Footherley Lane

Back Lane

Bosses

1

Forge Lane

Forge Farm

02

2

Golf Course

3

Watford Gap

31

01

Aston Wood Golf Club

Blake Street Station

A4026

Kts Cl

B Cft

Wynn

Rykrofa

Station Ap

Shelley Drive

Belghton Close

Tennyson Av

Saxton Drive

Yates

Vaughan Close

4

Little Aston CP School

Council Building

Little Aston Lane

STREET

Hill Hook

Lydia Cft

Lowercroft

Mr C Rd

Shys Cl

Hill

Bradgate Drive

Netherstone Gv

Bishops Way

Cranmer Cl

CPt

Mr C Cl

Becket Cl

LITTLE ASTON LANE

BLAKE

WALSALL ROAD

The Grove

Poplar Rise

Rosemary Nook

Regency Wk

Vernon Close

Bickley Av

Clarence Road

HOOK ROAD

Bishops Ct

LChfrd Rd

Lakeside

The Spinney

Roman Cr

Woodside Drive

Birch Drive

Loxton Close

Knighton Road

Silver Birch Coppice

St Georges Ct

Kesterton Road

Blackberry Lane

Netherstone

Bishops

Agstn

Prt Dr

5

Roman Road

Squirrel Walk

A454

Keepers Road

Beechwood Croft

Hornton Close

Four Oaks Saints CC

Harrison Road

Ensford Close

Aylesford Drive

Kensington Dr

Sandhurst Rd

Balmoral Road

Beech Gate

Little Aston

Longfield Dr

Selwyn Wk

409

WALSALL ROAD

300

A   B   **46**   C   D

Little Aston Golf Club

Park

Drive

Chartwell Dr

Woodstock Dr

Rarkswell Rd

Edge Hill Road

White Farm Road

Blackberry

Weymouth Dr

Kny Bridge

Clarence

Chelsea

Wall Dr

Four Oaks J&I School

I grid square represents 500 metres

E F G H

I

2

3

4

5

A5127

Shenstone Woodend

Little Hay Lane

✝

Little Hay

Green Barn

Green Barns Lane

Green Barns Lane

Alder Farm

Camp Farm

Little Hay Lane

BIRMINGHAM RD

Woodland Ct

Smarts Avenue

A5127

Watford Gap Road

Common Road

Hillwood

LICHFIELD ROAD

✝

Staffordshire County

Birmingham

Camp Road

Hill Wood Road

Hill

Hill Wood

02

01

00

E F G H

47

Haycroft Drive

Keating Gdns

St Cl

Dunton Close

Dunton Close

WC

WC

Hill

Beech

Hathaway Road

Ws

Mc

A5127

Woodside

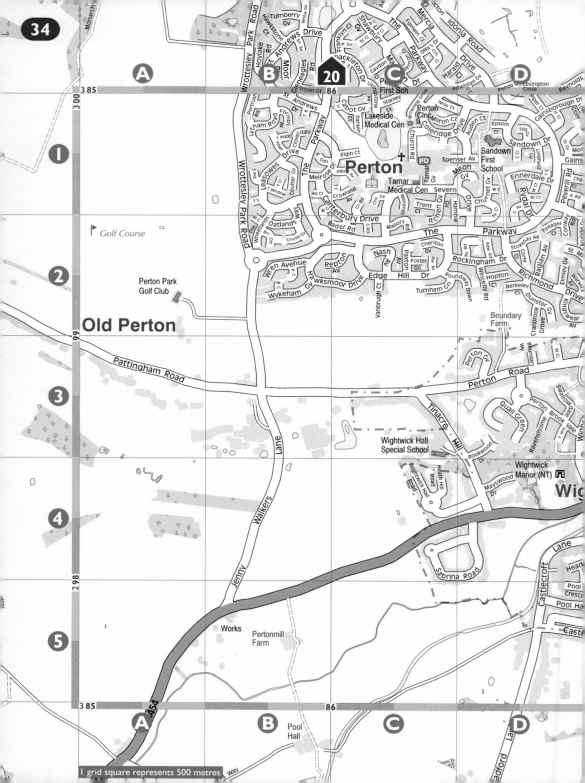

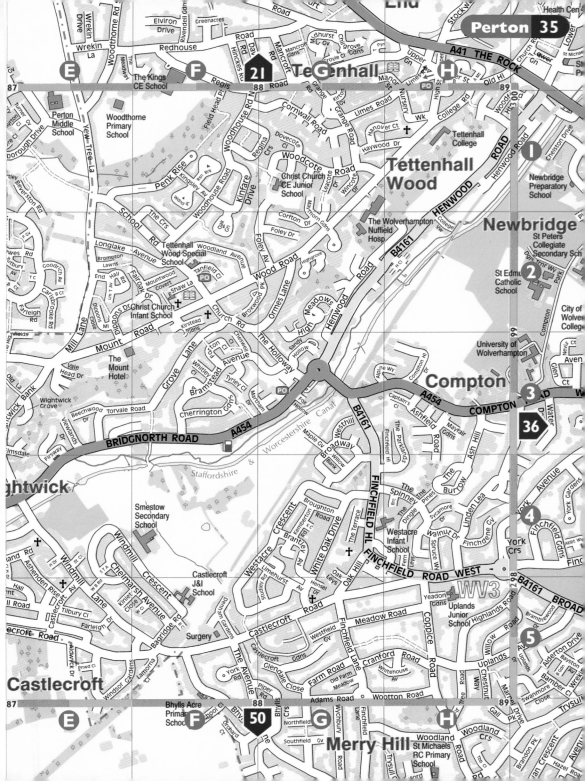

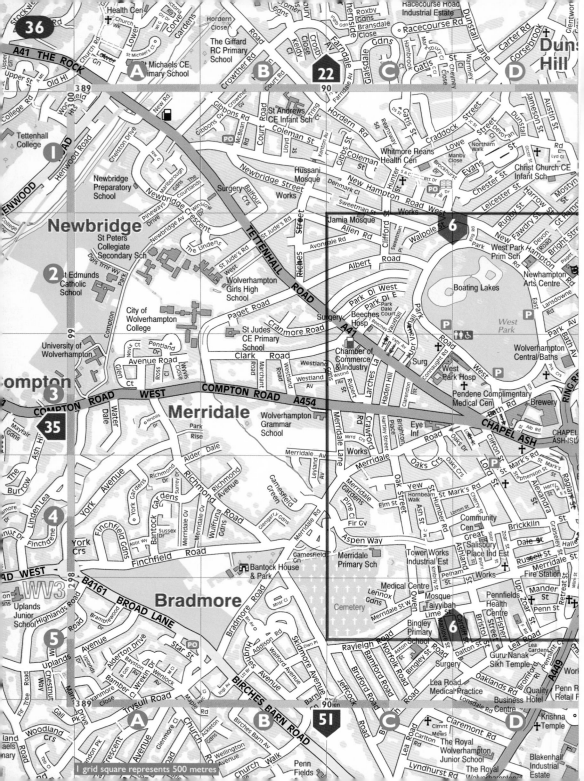

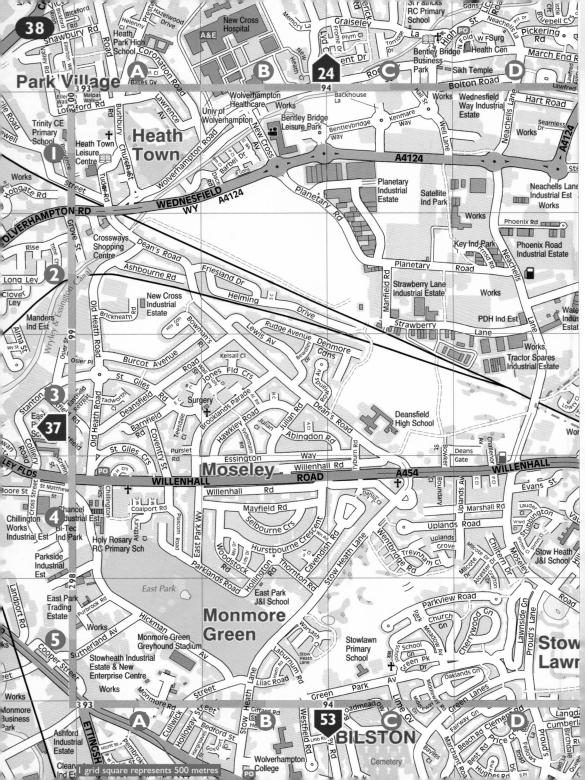

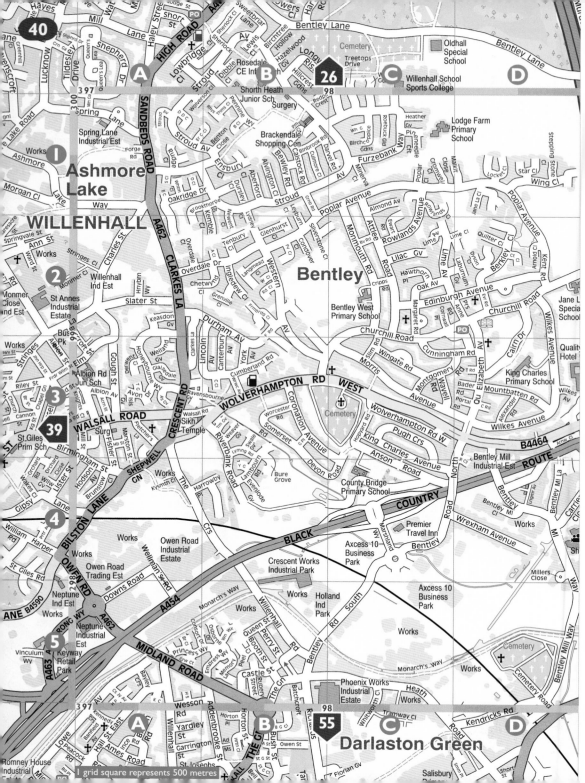

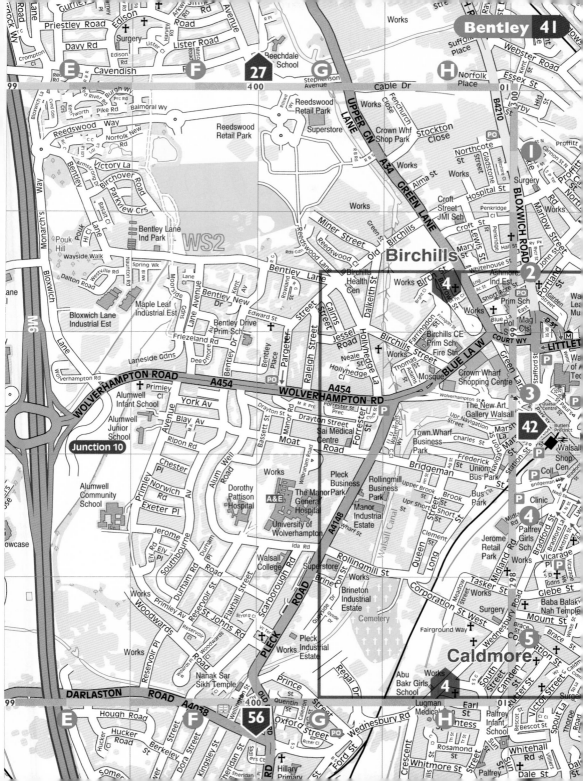

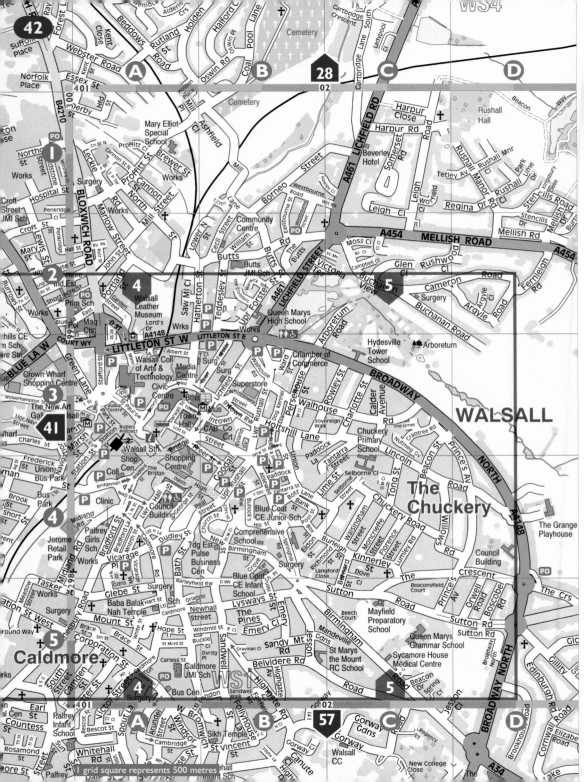

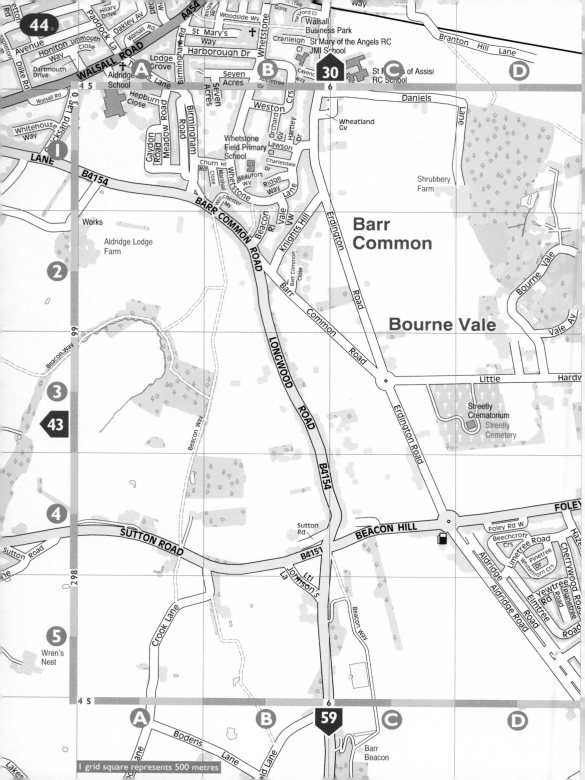

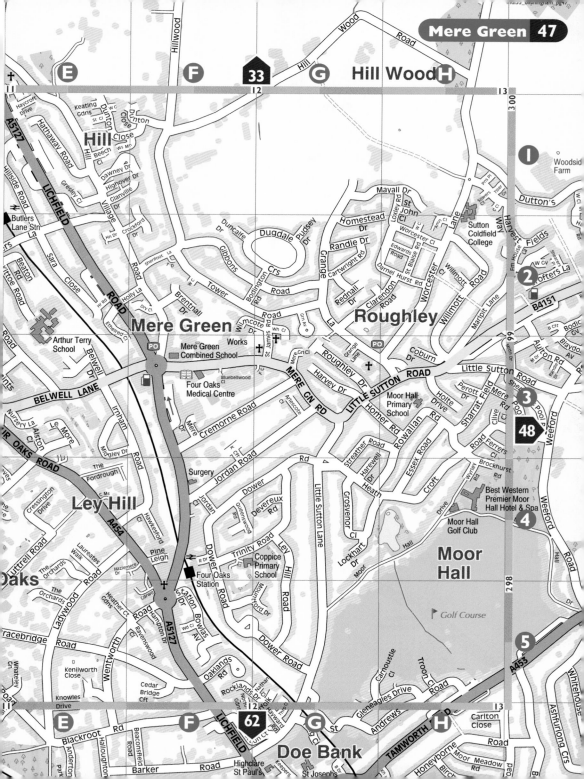

CRANEBROOK HILL

E F G H

15 16 17

300

CARROWAY HEAD HILL

Head

Shirral Drive

Shirral Drive

A453

Shirrall Hall
Farm

I

Staffordshire County

Warwickshire County

Trickley
Coppice

2

per House
Farm

99

Coppice Lane

3

Wood
Farm

4

298

LONDON ROAD

New Park
Wood

Langley Brook

5

**Littleworth
End**

thy Hill Road

A38

15 16 17

E F G H

M6 Toll

Langley Mill
Farm

Hill
Farm

LONDO

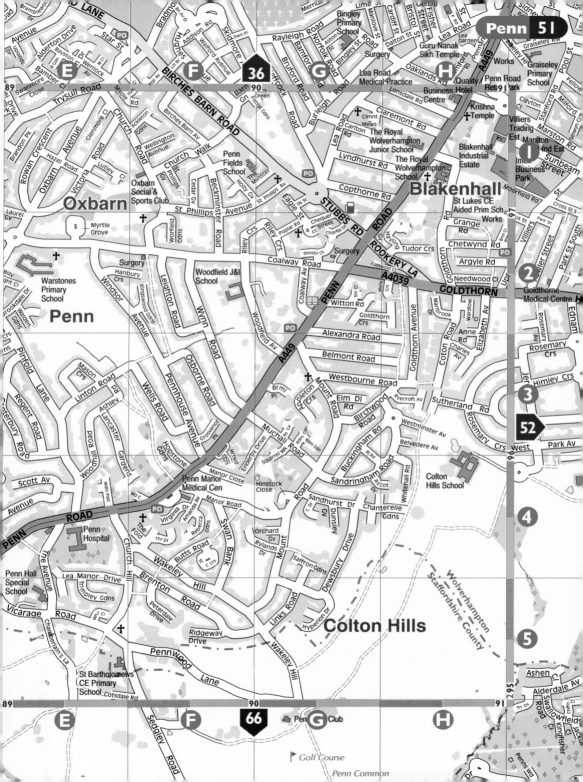

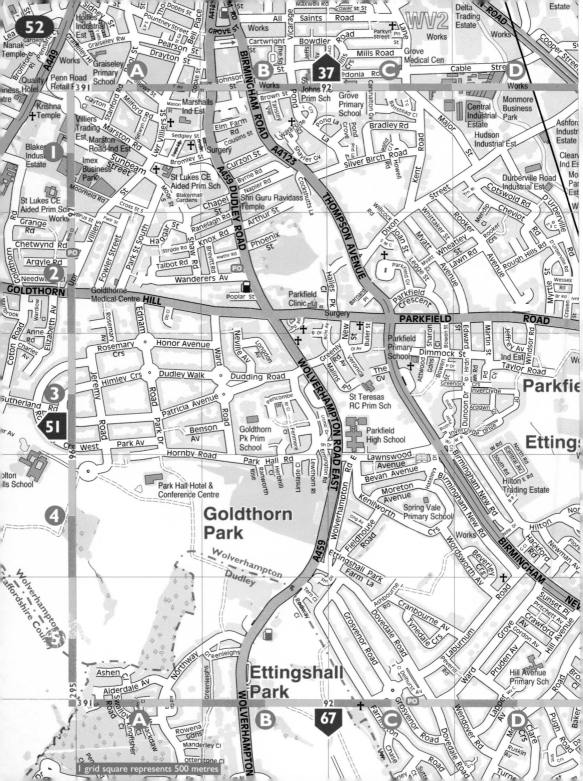

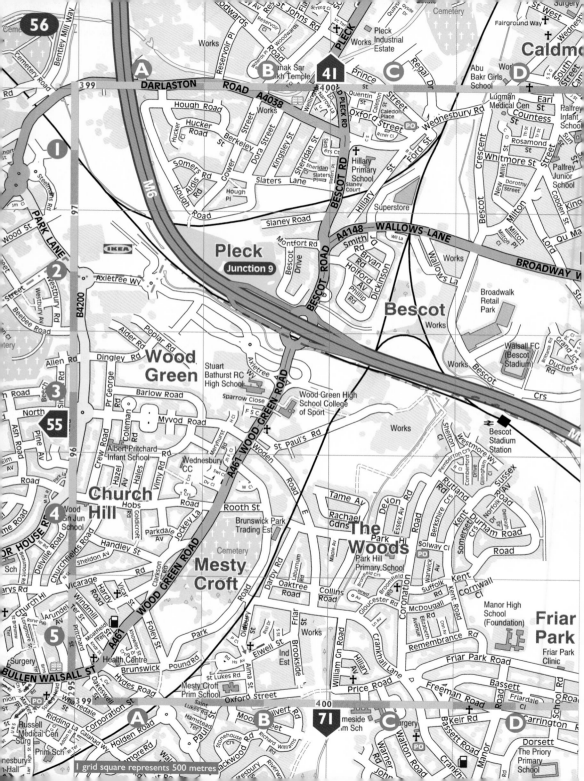

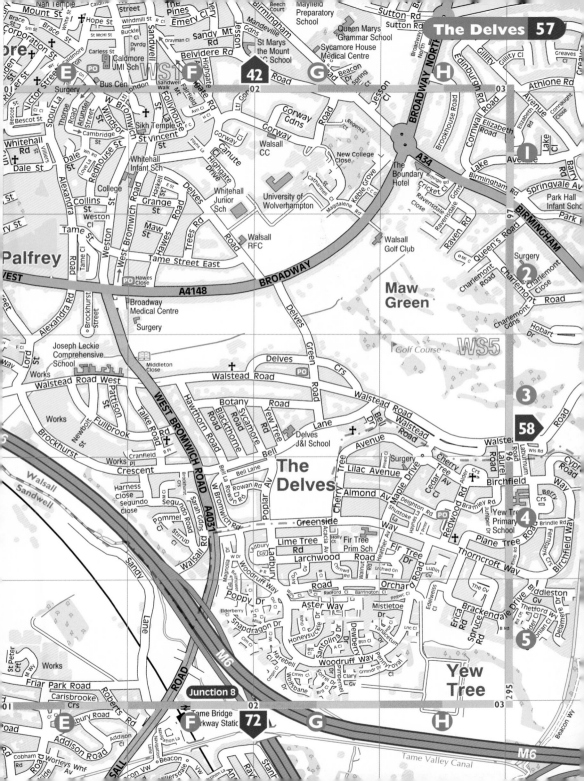

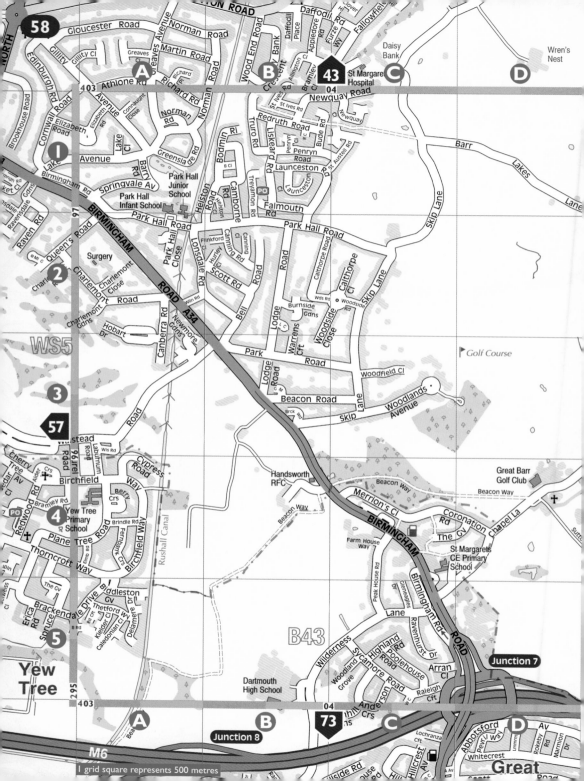

58

Gloucester Road
Norman Road
ON ROAD
Daffodil
Fallowfiel
Wren's
Nest

Edinburgh Rd
Cornwall Road
Gillity
Gillity Cl
Greaves
Greaves Avenue
Martin Road
Richard Rd
Norman Road
Wood End Road
Daffodil Place
Appledore Rd
Furze Wy
Daisy Bank

A **B** **43** St Margare Hospital **C** **D**

403
Athlone Rd
04
Newquay Road

Brookhouse Road
Avenue
Elizabeth Road
Elizabeth Rd
Connaught Close
Norman Rd
Bodmin Rl
St Ives Rd
Newquay
Redruth Road
Bude Rd
Barr

Raven Rd
Ravensdale Gns
1
Lake
Birmingham Road
Springvale Av
Park Hall Infant School
Park Hall Junior School
Helston Road
Truro Road
Liskeard Rd
Penryn
St Austell Rd
Launceston
Lakes Lane

Queen's Road
2
Surgery
Camborne Road
Trevarnon Rd
PO
Launcestion
Falmouth
Skip Lane

Charlemont
Charlemont Road
Charlemont Close
Park Hall Road
Park Hall Close
Lonsdale Rd
Flinkford
Falmouth Rd
Park Hall Road
Calthorpe Road
Calthorpe Cl

WS5
Charlemont Gdns
Hobart Dr
Canberra Rd
Newmore Gdns
Scott Rd
Canning Rd
Hurley
Bell
Lodge Road
Burnside Gdns
Woodside Close
Wds Rd
Woodside
Skip Lane
Golf Course

3
Park Road
Warrens Cft
Woodfield Cl
Woodlands Avenue

57
Walstead Road
96 rel
Laburnum
Wis Rd
Cypress Road
Lodge Road
Beacon Road
Skip Lane

Cherry Tree Av
Alder Crs
Redwood Rd
Birchfield
Berry Crs
Bramley Rd
Brindle Cl
Handsworth RFC
Beacon Way
Merrion's Cl
Coronation Rd
The Gv
Great Barr Golf Club
Beacon Way

PO
4
Yew Tree Primary School
Ferndale Crs
Fernbank Crs
Birchfield Way
Rushall Canal
Beacon Way
BIRMINGHAM
St Margarets CE Primary School
Chapel La

Plane Tree Road
Thorncroft Way
Elmo Rd
Farm House Way
Peak House Road
The Gv
Glendene Rd
Gleneagles
ROAD

Erica Rd
Spruce Rd
Biddleston Gv
Thetford Wy
Delamere
Caledonian Cl
Kielder Cl
B43
Wilderness Lane
Highland Rd
Poolehouse Road
Ravenhurst Dr
Junction 7

5
Brackendale Drive
Woodland Grove
Sycamore Road
Anderson
Arran Cl
Raleigh Cft

Yew Tree
403
Dartmouth High School
04
73
Lochranza Cft
Abbotsford Av
Peri Way
Rokeby Rd
Marmion
Whitecrest

A **B** Junction 8 **C** **D**
Junction 7

Hillcrest Av
Great

M6

I grid square represents 500 metres

E   F   44   G   H

05   06   07

1

Crook Lane

Bodens Lane

Pinfold Lane

Barr Beacon

Beacon Farm

Crook Lane

Aldridge Road

Oakwood

Alder Av

Ashwood

Laurel Dr

Maxholm Road

Lilac Av

97

Bridle Lane

2

Crook House

Pinfold Lane

BEACON ROAD

Doe Bank Lane

Doe Bank Wood

Chapel Lane

Old Hall

Old Hall La

B4154

The Barr Beacon School

Meadow View JMI School

Doe Ba

3

60

96

Yeames Close

Wimperis

Beechfield Close

Lorimer

Stanfield Rd

Frampton Way

Brooking Close

Stanhope Way

Godwin

Clausen Gv

A4041 Road

Hallswelle

Pomeroy

Horsley Rd

Way

Romney

Cooksley

Stanhope

Sundridge

Sheen

Sundridge Primary S

Brock

Brom

Aviemore Crs

Kinross Crs

Berwick Gv

Dunbar Gv

Nevison Gv

Raymout Gv

Roxburgh Gv

Beacon Rd

Morland Road

Rippingille Rd

Pheasey Park Farm Primary School

Way

sthr Cl

P Cl

Bnn Wy

Sargent Close

WK

Crs

Pheasey

Gainsborough Crescent

Chantrey

QUESLETT ROAD

Lambeth

Copthorne

Penge

Drive

Waverley Av

Crail Gv

Garnet Av

Comsey Rd

Selvey Av

Pinley Gv

Stonehurst Road

BEACON RD B4154

Collingwood Dr

Linton Rd

Raeburn Road

Leighton Cl

Tyndale Av

Hillingford Av

Surgery

BC

Crome Road

Eastlake Close

Cattermole Close

Collingwood Dr

Farrier Cl

Surgery

Kings Business Park

Trivet Cl

5

Century Industrial Estate

David Lloyd Birmingham

Handsworth

Park Farm Road

Kelway

Ivanhoe Rd

Foxwood Av

Moreton Av

PO

B4154

Pheasey Clinic

Hillingford Av

Gorsman Close

Crescent

QUESLETT ROAD A4041 Queslett Road

Queslett Road

Brackenfield

Works

Road

Calver Gv

Churchdale Road

Works

Winster Grove Industrial Estate

Shady

Fairbur

05   06   07

E   F   74   G   H

Whitecrest Primary

Que:

Sub Store

Horns Crs

Ringinglow Road

Ashgrove Road

Select Avenue

Winster Grove Industrial Cen

Shady Lane

Winster Grove

Ar

Sutton Park

Upper Nut Hurst

Blackroot Pool

Keeper's Pool

Holly Hurst

Rowton's Well

Golf Course

Powell's Pool

Boldmere Golf Club

Monmouth Drive

Rushbrooke Dr

Durley Dr

Lowe Dr

Alcester Dr

Alcester Dr

Grendon Drive

Markham Road

Jevons

Avery Road

Milcote Dr

Dunchurch Cres

Kaneta

Road

Avery Road

Warwick Rd

C Rd

Churchill

Tudor Ct

Halton Road

Denholm R

Falstone Rd

Dalkeith Rd

CHESTER ROAD NORTH

Greenway Dr

Weishmans

Weishmans Hl

Honiley Dr

Parkwood Dr

B73

Carnwath Rd

Melrose Avenue

Stonehouse Rd

Corbridge Road

Stonehouse Road

Monmouth Drive

Braemar

Mountford Road

Elwin Rd

Roxburgh Rd

Wyndley Leisure Centre

Wyndley Pool

Wyndley

Superstore

St Nicholas RC JMI School

JOCKEY

A453

Hartopp Road

Parkland Gn

High Ct

Coombe

Whateley Gn

Ken Clos

Knowle Drive

Anderton Park Rd

Blac

Park Rdg

46

62

76

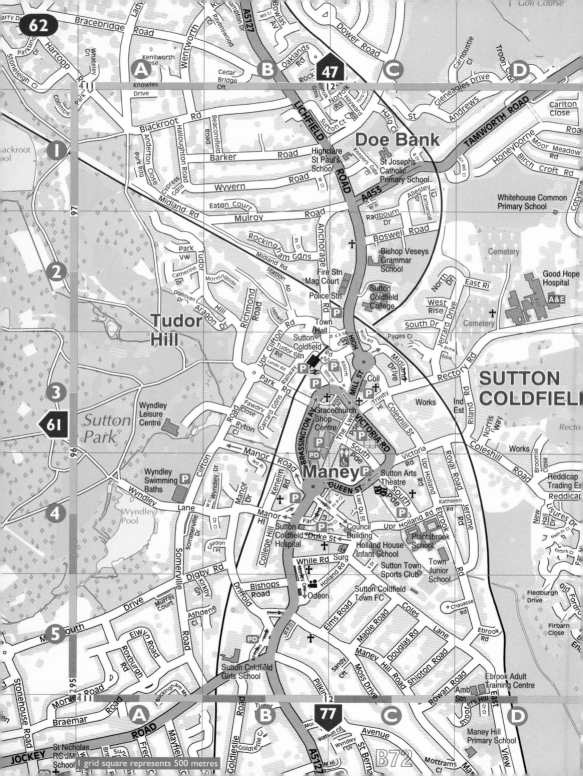

64

A · B · C · **D**Orton

Holloway

Orton Lane

Blackpit

385
95

86

Flash Lane

Awbridge Bridge

1

Union Lane

Staffordshire & Worcestershire Canal

Monarch's Way

Lane

Bell Road

Bell Road

Trysull Road

2

Manor House

White RW

School Road

School Cl

† **Trysull**

94

All Saints CE Primary School

3

Fl Rd

Woodford Lane

Common Road

Bratch Park

Tree Tops

Hillside Wy

The Bratch

Felashill Road

Hellier Dr

Dalton Ct

Monarch's Way

Bumblehole Meadows

Penleigh Gdns

Wdgwd Cl

Close

Bt Dr

4

Tollhouse

Lockside

Apse Cl

Woden Cl

Mount Pleasant Avenue

Grn

Bratch

Ounsdale Road

West...

Felashill Cl

293

Waterbridge La

Clap Gate Rd

Holendene

Wombrook Business Cen

Works

Ounsdale High School

Ounsdale Sports Centre

5

385
Smestow Gate

Smestow Bridge Industrial Estate

Works

WOMBOURNE

Wombrook Ind Est

The Meadlands

quendale

Cm Cl

Cln

Ounsdale

St Bernadettes RC Primary School

Lindale Drive

Spines Clnc

Windsor

Kirksto

Bride's

Sandringham Rd

Pool House Road

Forge Va Wy

Clp Gt Gv

Brn Cl

Green Meadow

Marlburn Way

Giggetty

Works

Cherry Trees Special School

Brook Road

W Cl

Elder

Lilac Dr

Wood Hill Drive

Birch

Crs

Lamb

176

BRIDGNORTH ROAD

A

B

Heathfields

Heath House

Mill

Miller's Vale

80

Swinford Way

Waterco

Holloway Drive

Furnace Cl

C

Lane

Jenks Road

Van

D

Birch Cl

Westleigh

Ch Dr

Calvin

† PO

Giggetty

86

1 grid square represents 500 metres

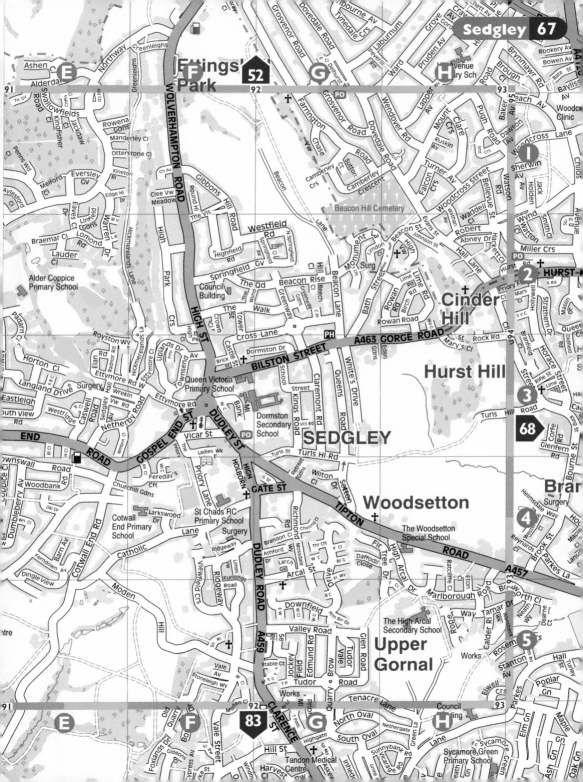

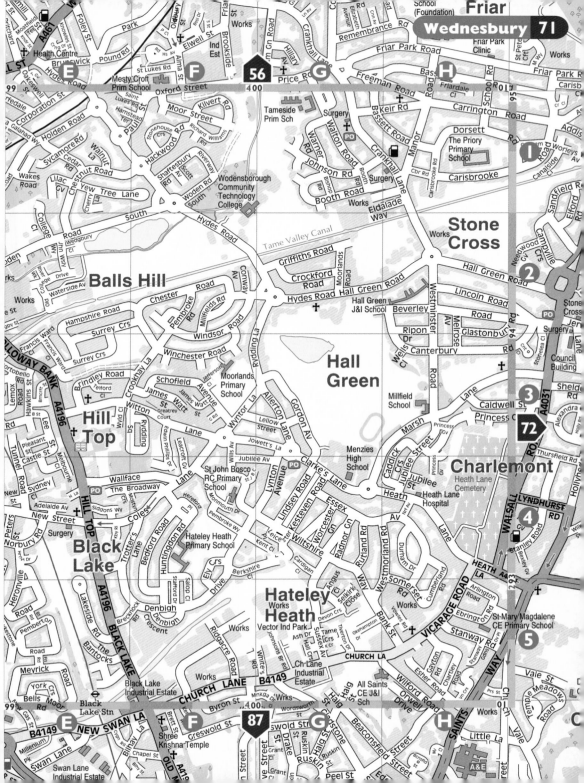

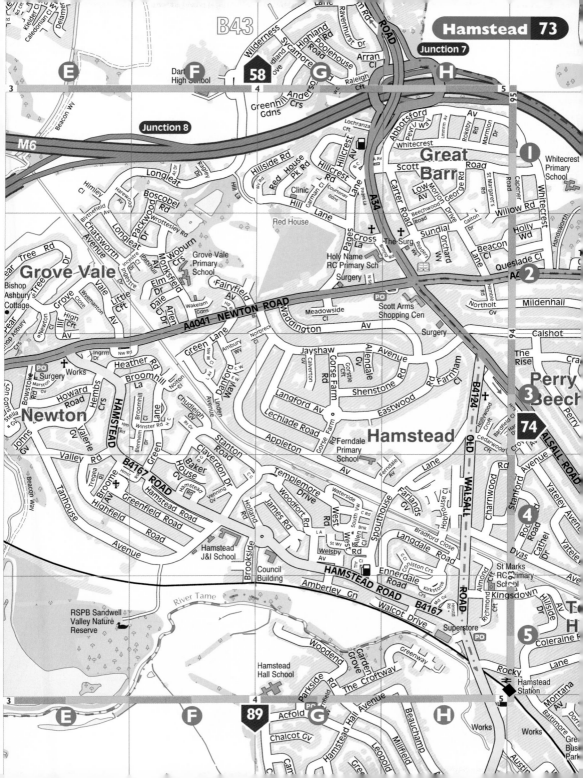

B43

E   F   G   H

58   Dart High School

Junction 8

M6

Wilderness La
Woodland Gve
Sycamore Road
Highland Road
Poolehouse Rd
Ravenhurst Dr
Arran Cl
Raleigh Cft
Greenhill Crs
Anderson
Greenhill Gdns

Lochranza Cft

Great Barr

Abbotsford Rd
Whitecrest
Scott
Low Av
Carter Road
George Rd
St Margaret's Rd
Rokeby
Marmion Dr
Willow Rd

Whitecrest Primary School

I

2

Longleat Cl
Himley Cl
Harewood Av
Blythfield Av
Chatsworth Av
Boscobel Rd
Packwood Dr
Wrottesley Rd
Woburn Crs
Monksfield Av
Elm Cft
Dale
Arlen Dr
Wakelam Gdns
Longleat Avenue
Incestre
Barshall
Wyemanton
Vale Close
Little Cft
High Cft
Av
Newton

Hillside Rd
Red House Pk Rd
Radley
Hill La
Hillcrest Rd
Hillcrest Lane
Clinic
Carman
Courtenay Gdns
Hill Lane
Red House

A34
Cross La
Pages La
The Surg
Holy Name RC Primary Sch
Surgery
Beechwood Road
Calton Dr
Sundial Lane
Orchard Wy
Beacon Cl
Holly Wd
Queslade Cl
Handsworth

Mildenhall
Northolt Gv
Hamle Rd
Calshot
The Rise
Cra

Grove Vale
Bishop Ashbury's Cottage
Pear Tree Rd
Grove Close
Bishop Ashbury

Grove Vale Primary School
Fairyfield Av

A4041 **NEWTON ROAD**
Meadowside Cl
Waddington Av
PO
Scott Arms Shopping Cen
Surgery

PO
Perry Beech
3

Surgery
Works
Heather Rd
Broomhill La
Howard Road
Hembs Crs
Valley Rd
Valerie Gv
Johns Gv

Green Lane
Norton Cl
Chudleigh Gv
Linden Avenue
Danford Way
Ambury Wy
Jayshaw Av
Calverton
Corse Cft
Corse Farm Rd
Langford Av
Lechlade Road
Appleton Av
Corstie Cft
Shenstone Rd
Eastwood Rd
Allendale Av
Avenue
Farnham Rd
Ferndale Primary School
Lane

Hamstead

B4124
OLD
WALSALL
74
ALSALL ROAD
Stanford Avenue
Rocky Road
Cathel
Dyas Av
Perry

4

Newton
HAMSTEAD
B4167 ROAD
Tregea Rd
Brooke Rd
Greenfield Road
Highfield Road
Avenue
Tanhouse
Beacon Way
Blenheim Cl
Winster Rd
Green Lane
Baker House Gv
Claverdon Dr
Stanton Road
Hamstead Rd
Venning Gv
Templemore Drive
Holland
Woodfort Rd
James Rd
Waterside
West Vw
South Vw
Welsby Av
Spouthouse La
Farlands Gv
House Cl
Bradford Close
Langdale Road
Charnwood Rd
Cedarwood
Holtwood Rd
Croft
Bardfield Cl
St Marks RC Primary School
Kingsdown
Richmond Cft
Almond
Hillside Dr

5

Hamstead J&I School
Brookside
Council Building
Amberley Gn
HAMSTEAD ROAD
Ennerdale Road
Kirkstone
B4167
Walcot Drive
Superstore
PO
Coleraine Lane
River Tame

RSPB Sandwell Valley Nature Reserve

Hamstead Hall School
Woodend
Garden Grove
Greenway
Parkside Rd
The Croftway
Rocky
Hamstead Station
Montana Av
Baltimore

Acfold Rd
Chalcot Gv
Hamstead Hall Avenue
Beauchamp
Millfield
Leopold
Austin
Works
Works

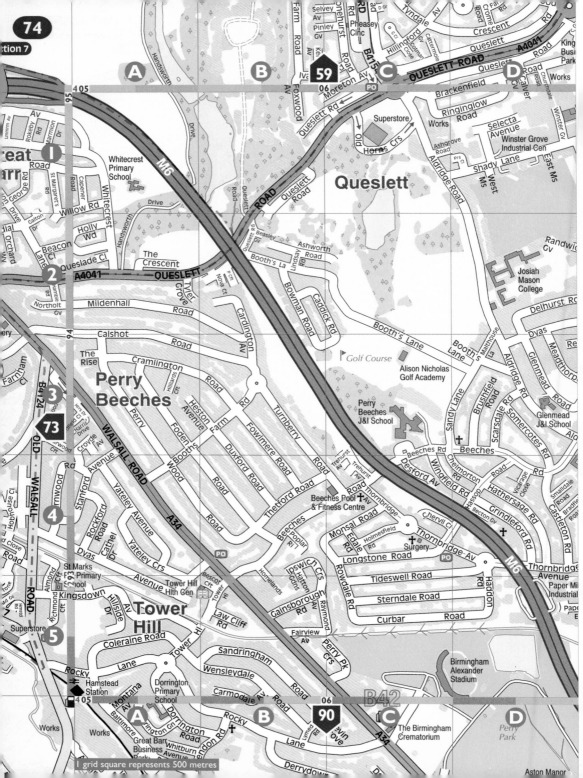

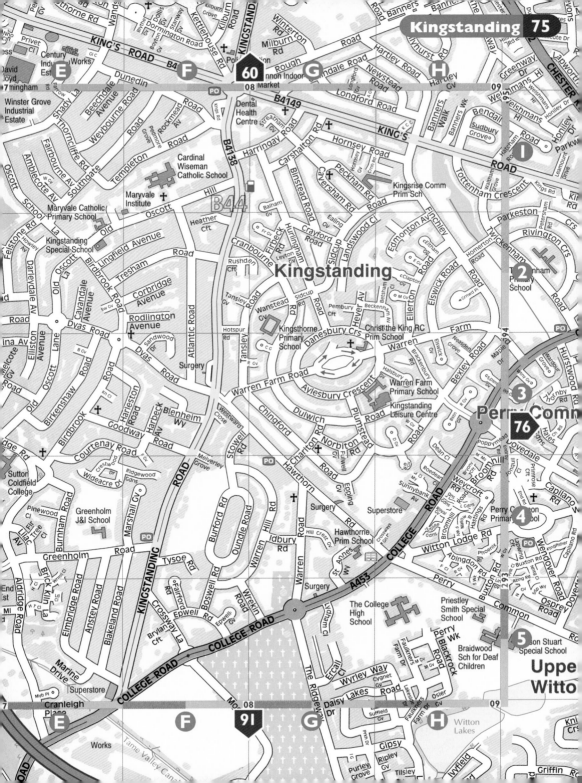

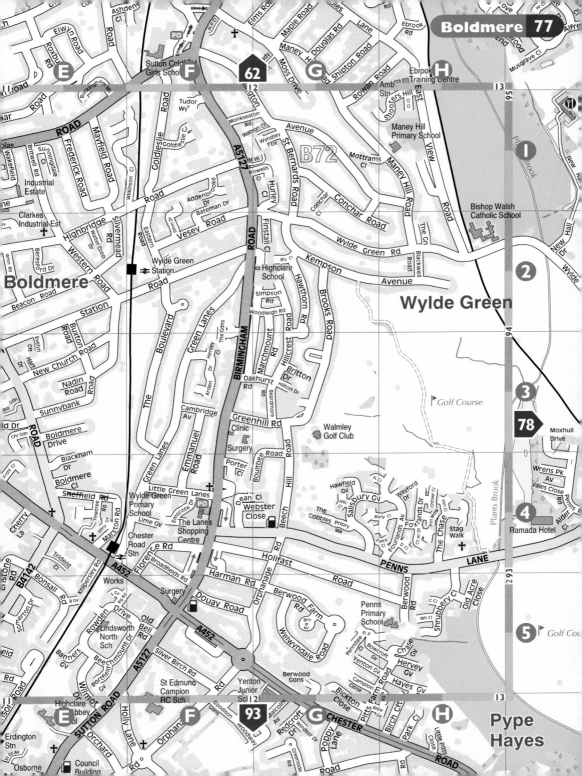

Woody

The Foxhills

E The Broadway F 65 G H Park Farm 89 Bagg Cour

87 88 92 I

Blakeley

Redhill Av Glendale Dr Pinewood Lennon Road High Mdw Copper Beech Rise Poplar Greenhill Gdns Beggars Bush La

Redcliffe Drive Rookery Rise Surg

The Longlands

Bl H Dr Whites Wood Woodlands Richmond Oaks Dr Cedars Chant Dr

Greenfields Road Griffiths Dr Sytch Lane

Blakeley Heath Primary Sch

Dickinson Rd Neachless Av Bossgate

Greenhill Farm

Greenhill Cotts

Rock Pool

2 Golf Cou

Himley Hall Golf Centre

Nature Reserve

Plantation Lane

Himley Plantation

Bridgnorth Road

School Road

Churns Hill Lane

Cherry Lane

Himley Country Hotel

Himley La

Great Pool

Himley Hall & Park

3

82

Himley A449 Himley House Hotel DUDLEY ROAD

B4176

Works

Home Farm

91

4

Staffordshire County
Dudley

Maidensbridge Primary School

Beachcroft Road

Claydon Road

Holcroft Road

Beachwood Av

Maidensbridge Rd

Victoria St

Brook Street Victoria St

Cross Street Albert St Albion St

Forge Lane Blaze Park Blaze Hill Road

E F 99 G H

7 Vctr St 88 WOLVERHAMPTON

Holbeache Lane

Collindale Dr Ct Camden Way

Copper Beech Dr Rowewood Keyes Drive Monteagle Drive

Oakdale Trading Estate

5 Oakdale Lane Oakdale Trading Est

Charterfield Drive Charterfield

Cincel Industrial Est

Charterfield Shopping Cen

Midland House

Wall Enville Rd DUDLE B4175

82

Woody Park

Park Farm

A 389

B

66 90

C Sandyfields Road

Sedgley Golf C

Golf Course

D

Baggeridge Country Park

I

Spring Pool

Island Pool

DY3

Shelley Cl

Ruskin Av

Milton Crs

Addison Cft

Kipling Road

Sandyfields Rd

Keats Close

The Straits

Meredith Rd

Straits Primary School

St Michaels Road

Byron Cft

Chaucer Av

Tennyson Rd

Kingsley Gv

Longfellow

Wordsworth Rd

Himley Gdns

PO

Irving Ct

The Straits

Browning Rd

Masefield Rd

Shakespeare Rd

Road

Cotwall End Road

2

Rock

Himley Hall Golf Centre

Golf Course

Higharcal Wood

High Arcal Road

Surgery

Rhodes

Burns Cl

Spencer Rd

E Cl

Coleridge Rd

Straits

Crofton Gdns

Musk La

The Alv

imley Hall ark

Wallows Wd

The Straits

St Andrew's Cl

Straits Gn

Acton Gdns

Orchard

Straits

St Chads

3 HIMLEY ROAD B4176

Himley Wood

Staffordshire County Dudley

Ladbrook Gv

Straits

Brick Kiln Lane

Eaton Crs

Manor

Hopyard

Musk Road

Louis

Summit Pl

81 91

Home Farm

HIMLEY

Oakland Dr

Elm Cl

Guys Lane

Maple Dr

Brookbank Rd

Flave

hire County Dudley

4

Windsor

Brookbank Gdns

Sandfield Gv

SANDFIELD BR

CINDI

Lane

Works

Works

Works

Oak Lane

Works

5 Monteague

Collingdale Ct

Camden Way

Ham Lane

The Oak Industrial Park

Central Trading Estate

The Pensnett Trading Estate

STALLING'S LA B4175

Tansey

Ta een Trading Estate

Beach Dr

Rokewood

Keyes Drive

Oakdale Trading Estate

Works

Chancel Industrial Est

Chancel Industrial Est

A

Hinsford Close

B

STALLINGS LANE

Works

90

100

First Av

First Av

C

Works

D

Charterfield Dr

Catesby Dr

Jay Road

Redruth Cl

Digby Rd

382 akdale Trading Est

Charterfield Shopping Cen

Avondale Road

Crmw Cl

Pensnett Trading Estate

The Pensnett Trading Estate

Works

B4175

Midl 1 grid square represents 500 metres

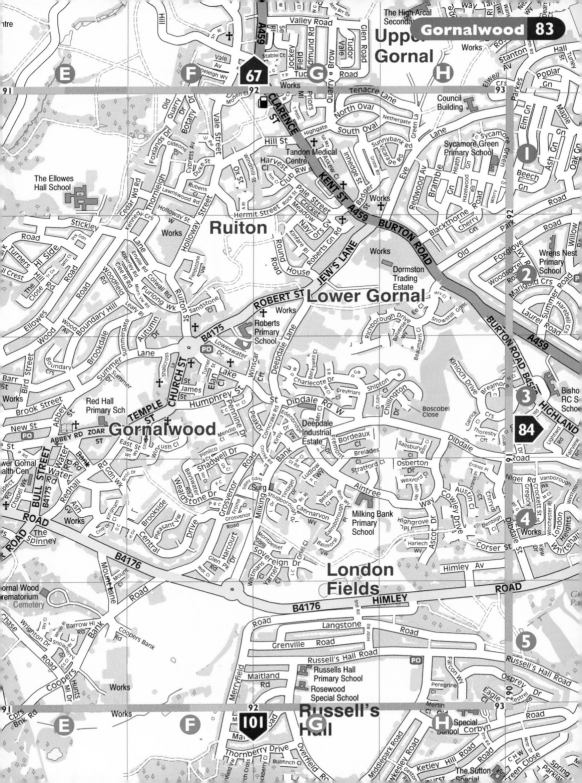

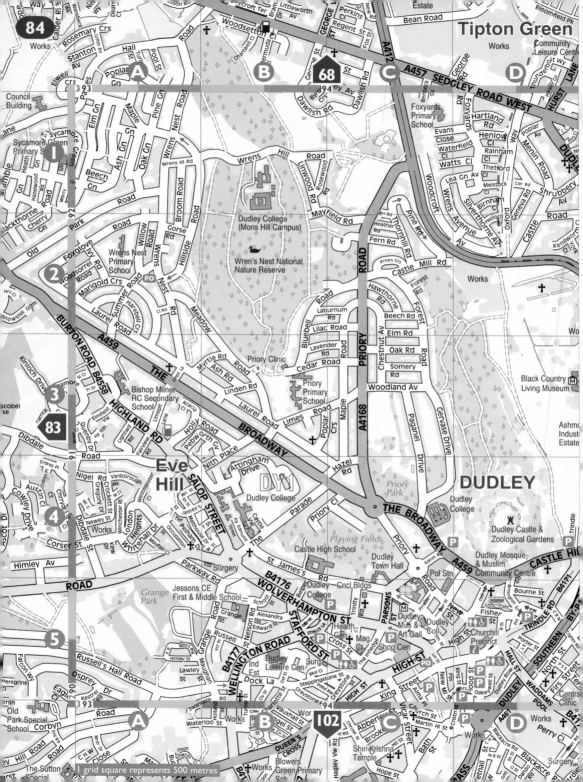

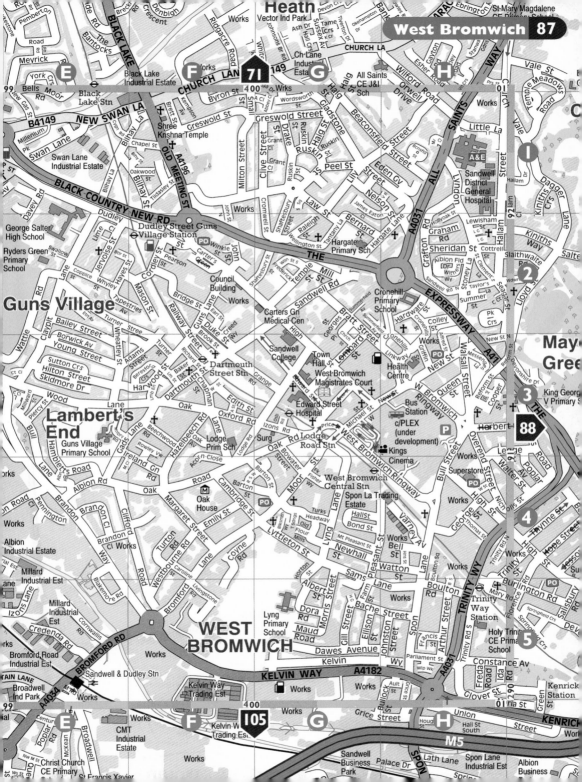

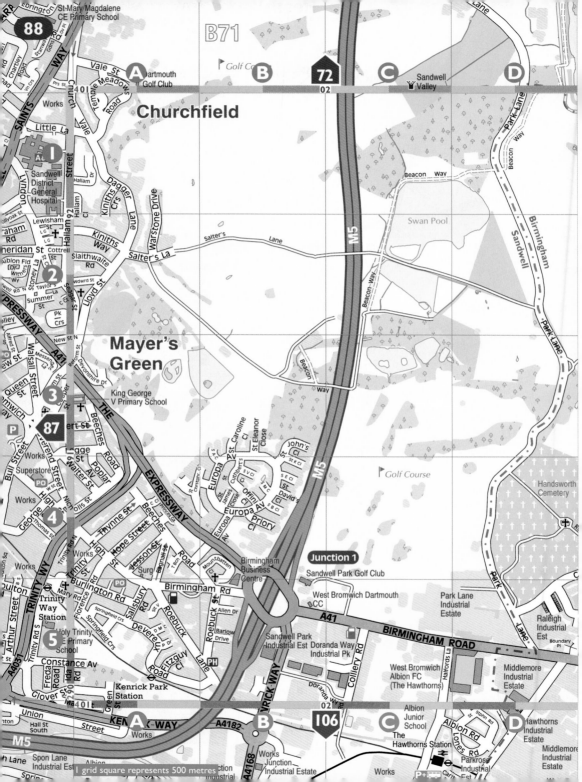

RSPB Sandwell Valley Nature Reserve

E **F** **73** Hamstead School **G** The Croftway **H**

Woodend Garden Grove Greenway Rocky Lane

Parks Rd Barnfield Hamstead Station

03 04 05 **I**

Hamstead Hall Avenue Beauchamp Works Works Montana Baltimore Road Great Business Park

Acfold Rd Leopold Millfield Austin Way B4124 Works

Chalcot Gv Greenridge Rd Underwood Road Deerhurst Avenue Manway Cl Check Rd Hudson Rd Breton Rd Epley Rd Lloyd Road Orchard

Camplin Crs Elmbank Gv Sedgley Gv St Davids Hamstead Hill West Coo

Golf Course Craythorne Bewlys Av Vernon Avenue HAMSTEAD HILL St Christophers Cl St Annes Avenue **2**

Handsworth Golf Club Westover Road Medcroft Av Wesfd Park Hl Dr St Davids Coopers Everest Rd PO

Avenue Sunningdale Cl Grestone Primary School The Spinney High Trees Englestede Cl The Silver **3**

Park Farm Brosil Av Birmingham City Council Hawthorn May Tree Gv **Brown's Green** B20 B4124 HAM Butler's

Golf Course Grestone Avenue Wheaton Vale Browns Green Taverner's Gn Richmond **90**

Hilltop Public Golf Course Ashcmb Av Woodcroft Shireland Cl Bett Rd Devonshire Road Butler's Close St R

Silvercroft Av Silvercroft Av Friary Lofthouse Road Mitton Rd Earlswood WORTHWOOD ROA

Cradley Cft Posey Cl College Road Cornwall Road Somerset Oaklands Handsworth Wood Girls School Sixth Form Centre Selborne Rd Endwood Cl **4**

The Leverets St John Wall RC School **Handsworth** Friary Gdns Windermere Rd Rosedene Drive Calder Gv Winfield Rd

Oxhill Rd St Augustines Catholic Primary School Larch Av Avenue Rd Stockwell Road Singh Sabha Gurudwara Temple Copper Beech Gdns Surgery

Oxhill Rd Road PO **A4040** **OXHILL ROAD** PO **A4040** **CHURCH LANE**

Linchmere Road Cranbrook Road Greenhill Road Grove Gdns Grove Hl Kilbys Gv **5**

Copthall Rd Landgate Rd Fell Gv Uplands Road Farnham Road Works Laurel Road Philip Victor Rd Hinstock Road

Bush Gv SANDWELL ROAD Newcombe Road Elmhurst Rd Andrew Mount Pleasant Av Orchard Grove Hl Rd Pike Cl

Farcroft Rd Mervyn Road L Cdn Rookery Primary School Laurel Road Brunswick Rd Herbert Rd

ISLAND RD A4040 Astley Road Clent Rd Aylesford Rd Antrobus Wilkes Green J&I School Centenary Road

Willow Dr Works Holly Grafton Rd Albion Road PO Maple Cl Maple Cl

Austin Rd B21 Onibury Road Carlton Rd Albert Road

Belmont Rd Nijon St James CE Primary School Farcroft AV Westbourne Road A4040

E A41 HOLYHEAD ROAD **F** **107** **G** **H** Handsworth Leisure Centre

PO Green Lane New Inns Lane Hamilton Special School Oakland Rd Douglas Road Holly

Kentish Road Raglan Road Clarence Road St James Rd Holyhead Trafalgar Rd Surgery Wilfred Road Murdock Rd Chantry Road Woodstock Rd Grove School Leyton Rd Osborne Rd Mostyn Rd Thornhill Honey Close

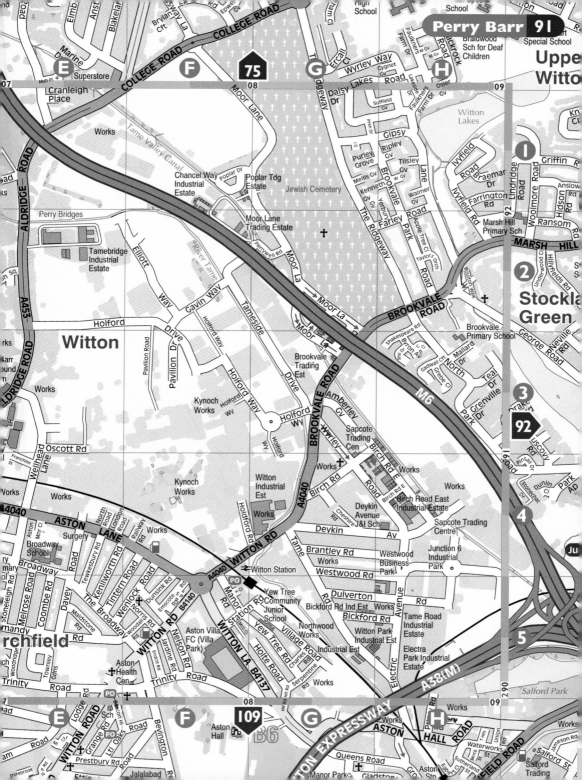

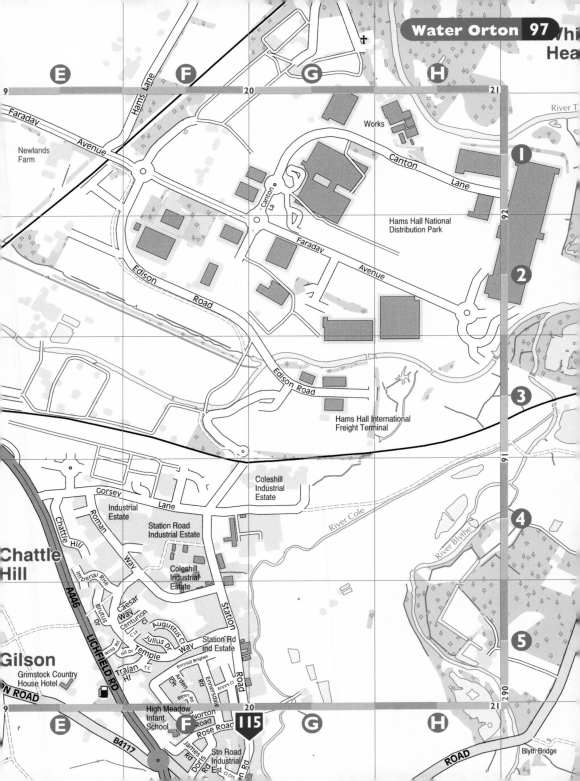

98

A **B** **80** **C** **D**

3 85 86

90

Chasepool
Farm

1

Camp
Farm

2

89

3

Greensforge

Chasepool Road

Staffordshire & Worcestershire Canal

Monarch's Way

Swindon Road

Mile Flat

Hinks

Hinksford Lane

The Br

Way

4

Ashwood

Smestow Brook

Ashwood Lower Lane

Doctors Lane

2 88

Great Checkhill Road

5

Checkhill
Farm

Little Checkhill Lane

Greensforge Lane

3 85 86

A **B** **116** **C** **D**

Ashwood Lo

I grid square represents 500 metres

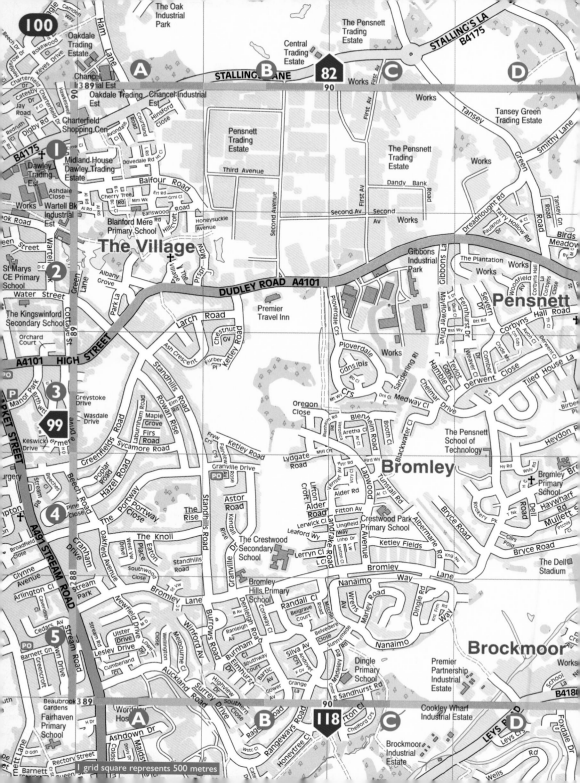

1 grid square represents 500 metres

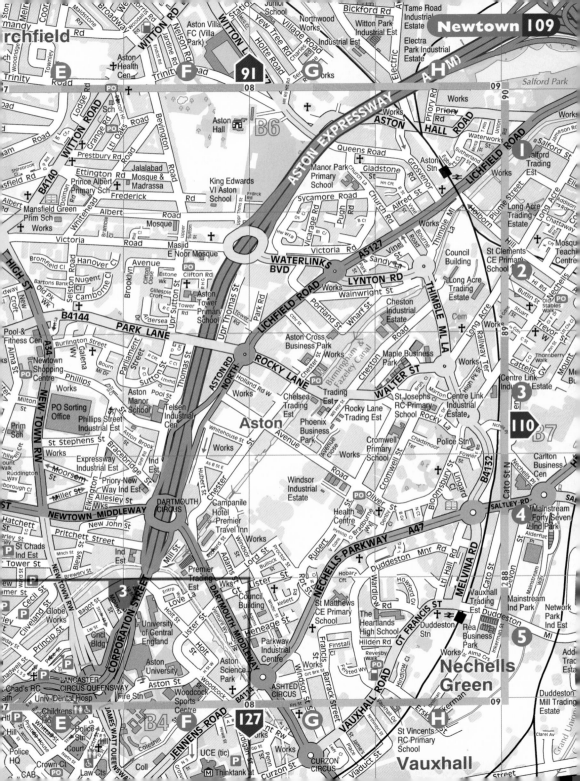

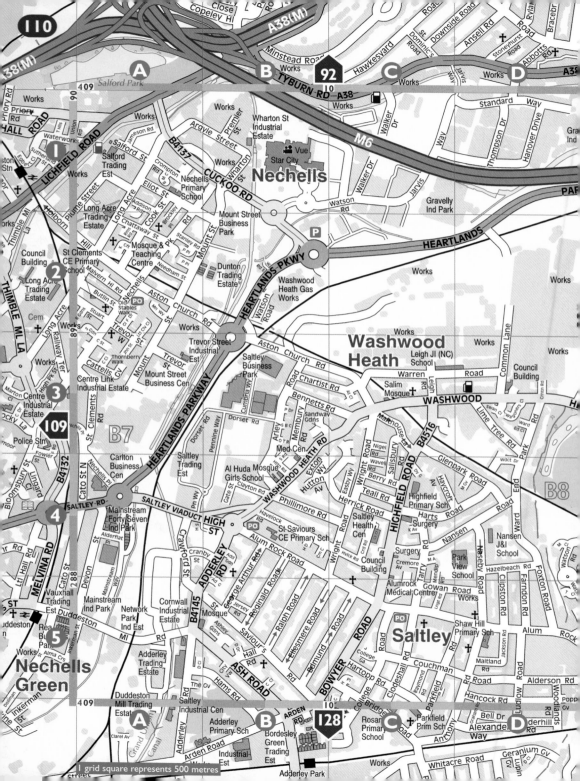

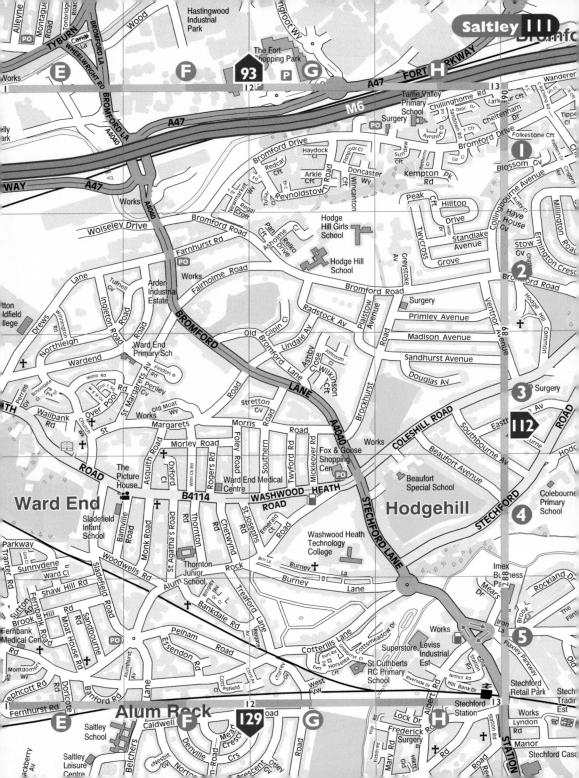

112

Bromford

River Tame

t PARKWAY
A452

| A | B | 94 | Junct C | D |

Kingsleigh Dr
Solihull Way
Danzey

413
Hyperion
Berrandale Rd
The Moors
B4147
14

Chillinghome Rd
Larkspur Cft
Catching Rd
Papyrus Wy
Chester Rd
Rectory Lane
Kyter Lane
Wasperton Cl
Impsley Cl
Bee

Sandown Rd
Cheltenham Dr
Trigo Cft
Tippet Cl
Riddfield Road
Kempson Road
Edstone Ms
Solihull Way
St.Mary & St Margarets CE Primary School

Oxpe Cl
Folkestone Cft
Palmers Gv
Pines Special School
St Wilfrids RC Primary School
Castle Bromwich Hall Gardens
Larkfield Av
Woodford Av
Chestnut
B36
CHESTER RD

I Bromford Drive
Blossom Gv
Chipperfield Road
Dregborn Road
Firs Primary School
Dr Hea Gv
PI Cl
Birmingham Road
Castle Hills Drive
HALL ROAD
Southfield Av
The Green

Hilltop Drive
Collingbourne Avenue
Haye House Gv
Millington Road
Oakdale Rd
Newport Rd
Hill Well
Broomdene Av
BRADFORD
Southwood AV
B4114
R

2 Standlake Avenue
Grove
Stow Gv
Ermington Crescent
Shawsdale Road
COLESHILL ROAD
Ashville
Heathland Av
Shopton
Hernefield Road
Priestland Rd
The Oaks
School Cl
Cat La
Fennel Cft
Pencroft

Bromford Road
PO
Heathlands Primary (NC) School
Flamborough Cl
Wellcroft Rd
Council Building
Brownmere Primary School

ley Avenue
son Avenue
hurst Avenue
las Av
Ventnor Avenue
Hodge Hill Common
Surgery
Heath Way
Way
Surgery
Heath
Pencroft

3 Eastbourne Av
Westbourne
 bourne Av
Surgery
Orkney Av
Chorley Av
Bucklands
Arran Road
Fowey Rd
End
Teesdale Avenue
Galloway Avenue
Darley Av
Lane
Haxby Av
PO
Buckland End
Hartshill Rd
Moorfield Rd
Bridgeford Rd
Buckland End
Brook Meadow Road
B34
Old Forest Wy
Woodstile
Cherry
Heath

L ROAD
III
B4147
Rymond Road
Hill
Hodge
Falmouth Road
Avenue
Maryland
Surgery
Settle
Gilling Gv
Embleton Gv
Wabry
Cole
Mt
Rivermead Pk
Hall

STECHFORD
4
Colebourne Primary School
River Cole
Kingfisher Velw
Middle
Broomy
Greetvine Cl
Leaford
Watland Gn
Slade
Lanker
Colehall

5
Imex Business Park
Mears Dr
Rockland Dr
Wyndhurst Road
Harrowfield Rd
The Flintway
The Riddings
Webbcroft Rd
Swancote Rd
Neachley Gv
Plowden Rd
Lyme Gn Road
Bushpury
Betley Gv
Crofton Gv
Surg
Howden PI
Hedgley Gv
Easthope Road
Cole Hall La
Crossfield Road
Works
Works

Works
wiss Industrial
Iron La
Brook
Old Farm Road
Audley Road
Ipstones Av
Fellbrook Close
Glebe Farm
Surgery
PO
Peplow Road
Lydbury Gv
Ridge Gv
Kempe Rd

413
14

| A | B | 130 | C | D |

Stechford Retail Park
Stechford Trading
Lyndon Rd
Manor Road
Stechford Cascades
Inglefield Road
Rudyington
Stud
Church Lane Cen
Flaxley Road
South Roundhay
N Roundhay
Elmore Rd
Crossfield Road
Hurstcroft Road
Haydon Cft
Ridpool Primary
Hallmoor Special

Stechford Station
STATION

1 grid square represents 500 metres

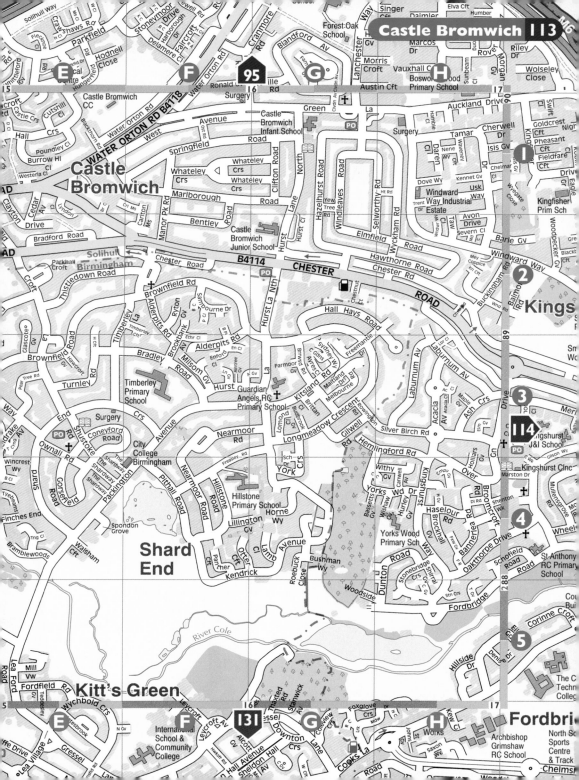

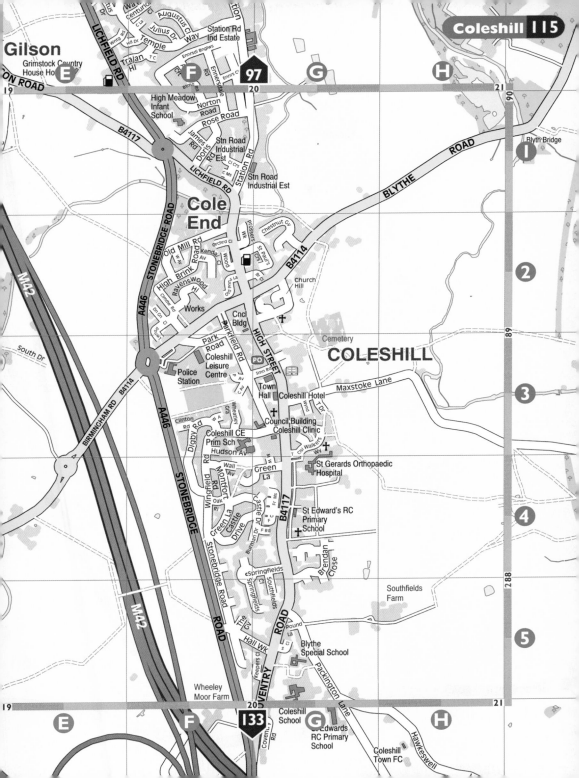

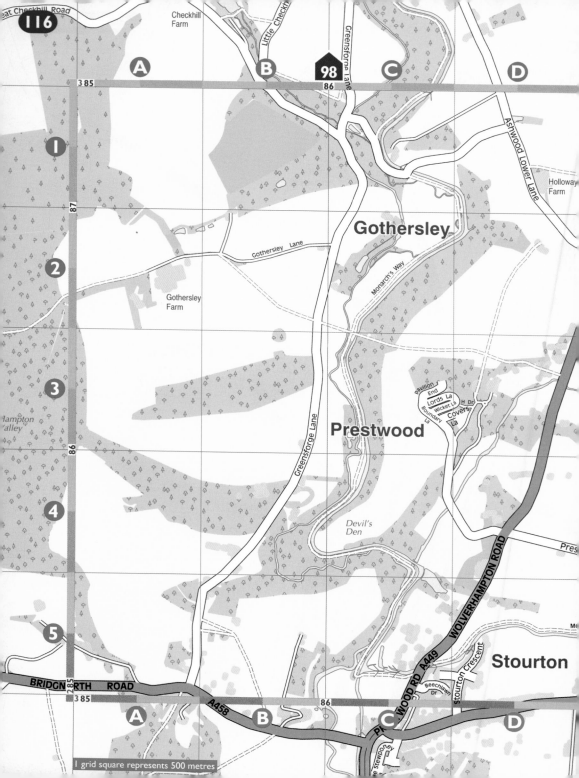

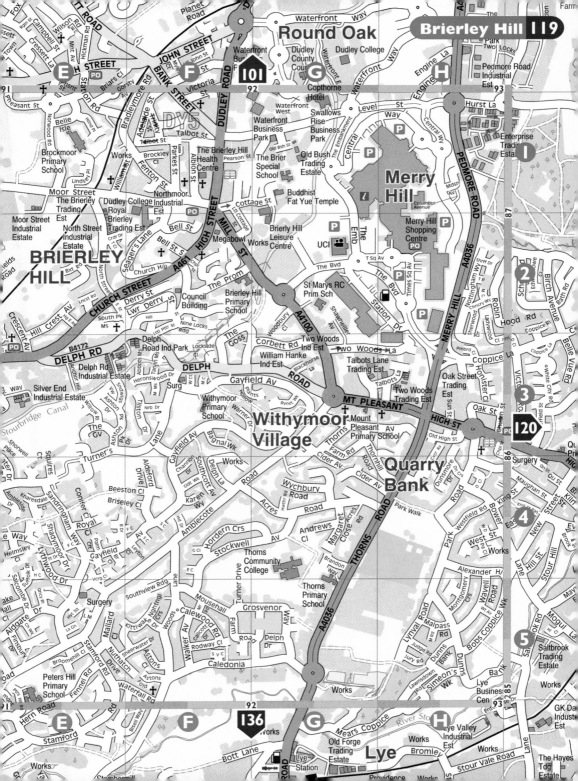

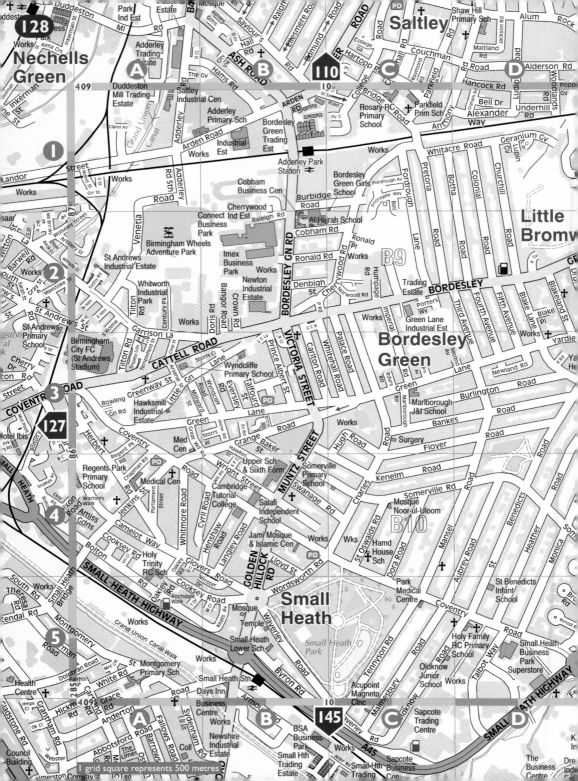

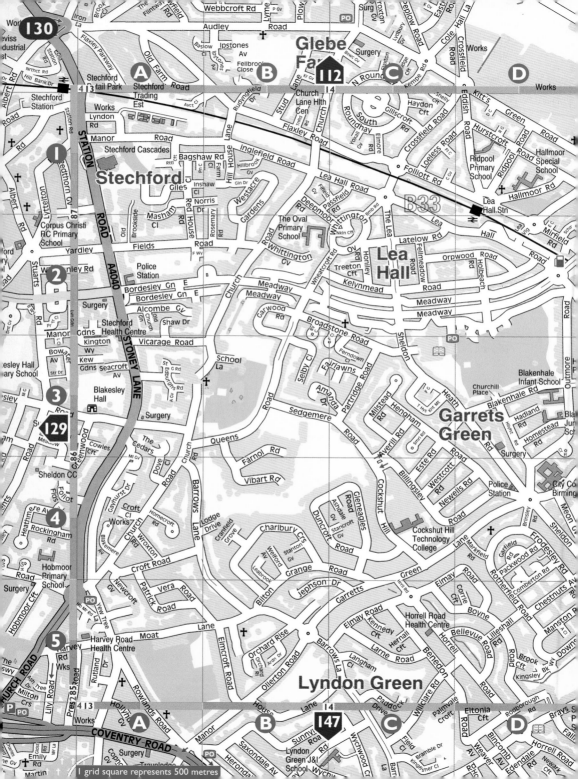

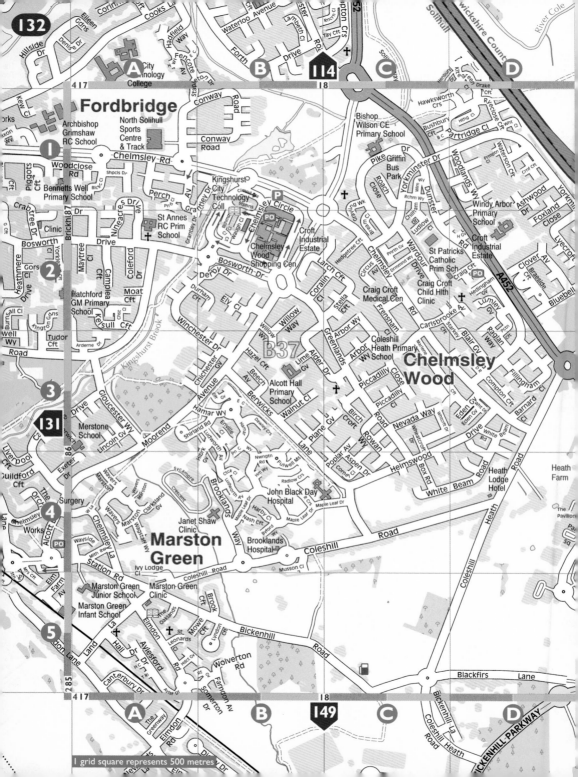

E   F   **115**   G   H

I

The Gr
ROAD
Hall Wk
Pound La
s
ers Cl

Blythe
Special School

Wheeley
Moor Farm

Coleshill
School

COVE...
Coventry Rd

St Edwards
RC Primary
School

Packington Lane

Coleshill
Town FC

Hawkeswell Lane

Packington Lane
Farm

Hawkeswell
Farm

Hawke
La..

21

2

Pool Farm

A446

M42

Road

M6

Heath

Coleshill

M6

M6

Junction 4

Junction 7/7a

Coleshill
Pool

Packington Lane

86

3

Bannerley
Pool

Drive

ive

King's
Court

he

Crescent

Solihull

CHESTER ROAD

Trident
Court

PARKWAY

Bishop's
Court

STONEBRIDGE

A452

M42

4

Birmingham
Business
Park

Knights
Court

eside

Solihull Pkwy

5

Solihull Parkway

Lane

285

Blackfirs

A438

Premier
Travel
Inn

M42

ROAD

A452

Garden
Centre

A4

20

150

21

E   F   **150**   G   H

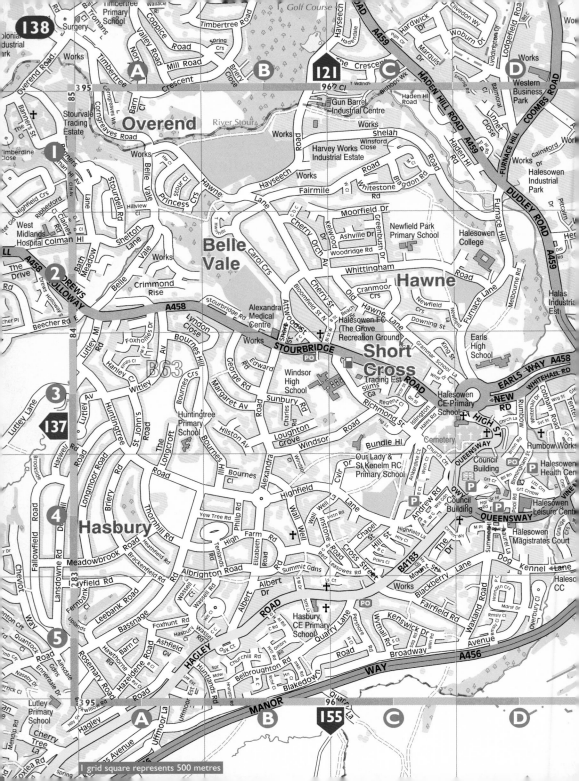

I grid square represents 500 metres

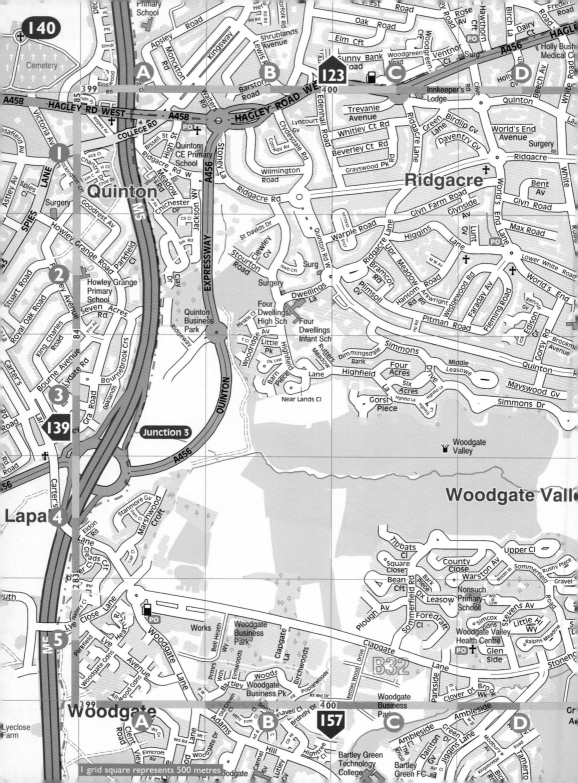

1 grid square represents 500 metres

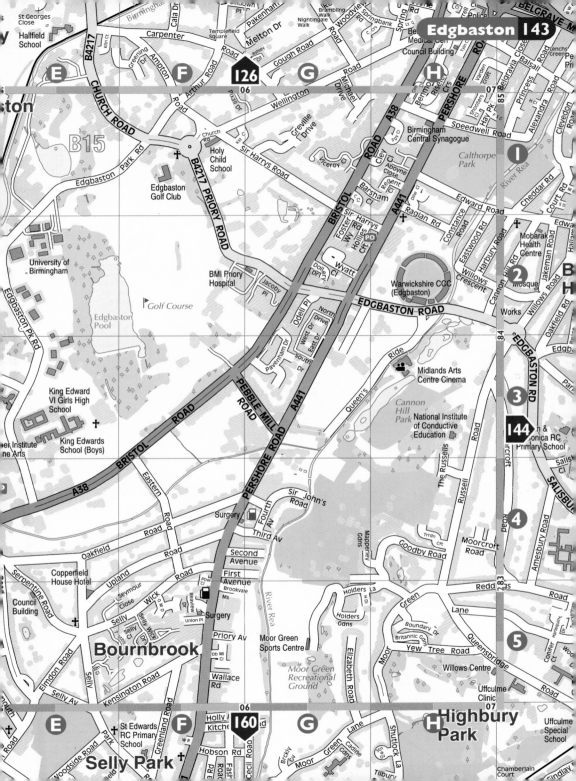

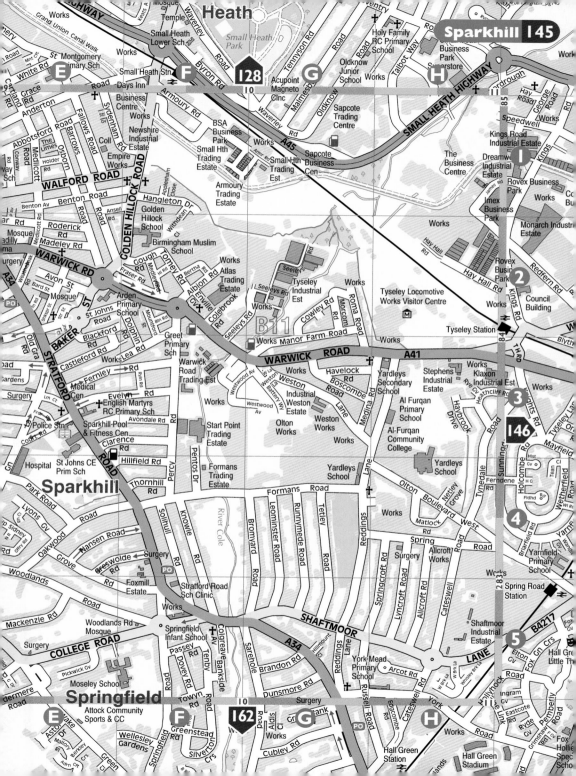

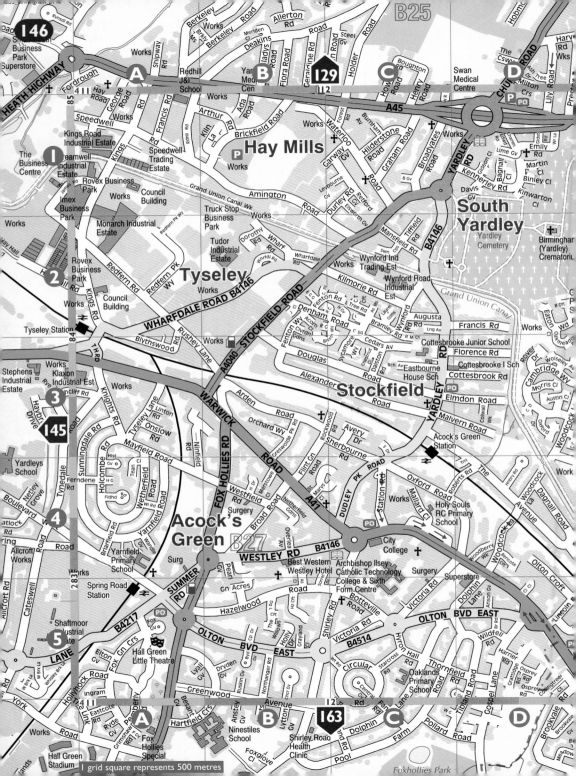

Infant School

Marston Green

The Oaklands

St Leonards

Bickenhill Road

Wolverton Rd

Aylesford Dr

Canterbury Dr

Elmdon Rd

The Greenway

Newlands La

Elmdon La

Digby Dr

The Fordrift

Somerton Dr

Farndon Av

E

F

132

G

Blackfirs

H

Blackfirs

B4438

I

BICKENHILL PARKWAY

Bickenhill La

Coleshill Heath Road

Starley Way

Starley Wy

Elmdon Trading Estate

Bickenhill Trading Estate

Bickenhill Plantations

B40

2

National Exhibition Centre

P

Ramp Rd

Exhibition Way

Perimeter

The Underpass

Road

Birmingham International Airport

Novotel

Somer Rd

Trident Rd

Ambassador Rd

Concorde Rd

Trident Rd

Elmdon Rd

Vanguard Rd

Stn Link Rd

P

P

P

P

B4438

Birmingham International Stn

i

3

150

Perimeter Rd

Perimeter Rd

Perimeter Road

PK Rd

S Car

Birmingham International Airport

Hermes Rd

P

BICKENHILL LANE

P

P

4

Pe

Hangar Rd

Commissary Rd

P

Forward Rd

Works Rd

Elmdon

Elmdon Lane

Airport Way

Airport Wy

Airport Way

Catherine Barnes La

cle

Trinity Business Park

P

5

A45

Damson

Lane

COVENTRY ROAD

A45

B4438

Clock Lane

LANE

Pitt La

Lane

Birmingham Area Civil Service Sports Club

Dunstan Farm

Arden Hotel & Leisure Club

Welsh RFC

Church La

Works

E

F

166

G

H

Bickenhi

150

Solihull Parkway

Lane

Lane

Black

A

Premier Travel Inn

B

ROAD

133

20

Garden Centre

C

A452

A446

D

PARKWAY

Lane

85 4 19 38

I

Bickenhill Plantations

2

B40

National Exhibition Centre

North Av

North Av

Northway

P

P

P

P

Little Packi

Fishpool Lane

Packington Lane

Park Farm

Little

Perimeter

The Underpass

Road

Pendigo Wy

Harbet Dr

Pendigo Way

E Car Pk Rd

P

P

Middle Bickenhill Lane

Warwickshire County

Solihull

CHE

Birmingham International

3

149

Perimeter Rd

Perimeter Road

Pendigo Wy

Pendigo Lake

Pendigo Wy

East Way

Middle Bickenhill

P

Pendigo Wy

Pendigo Way

S Car Pk Rd

S Car Pk Rd

South Way

P

P

S Car Pk Rd

4

Perimeter Rd

Trinity Business Park

P

East Way

Coventry Road

National Motorcycle Museum

Stonebridge

Pasture Farm

5

283

Lane

Pitt La

Works

Chur 419

†

A

Bickenhill

B

167

20

M42

Old Station Road

Junction 6

C

D

1 grid square represents 500 metres

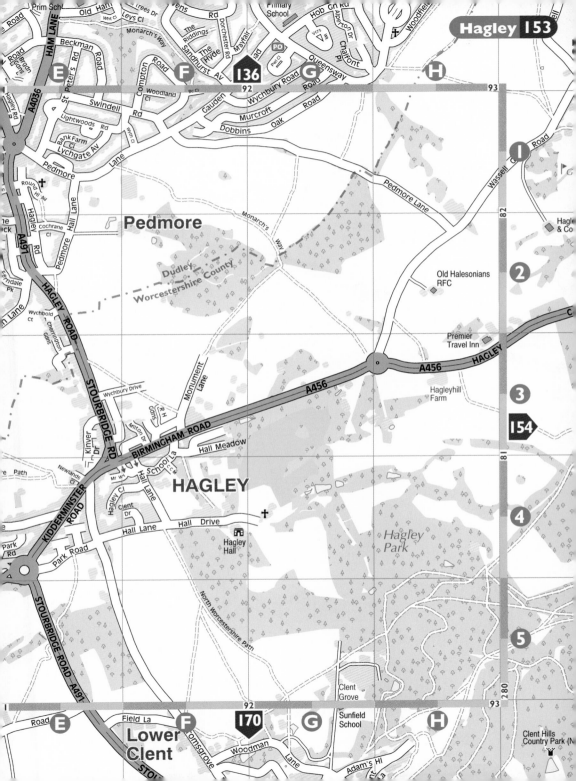

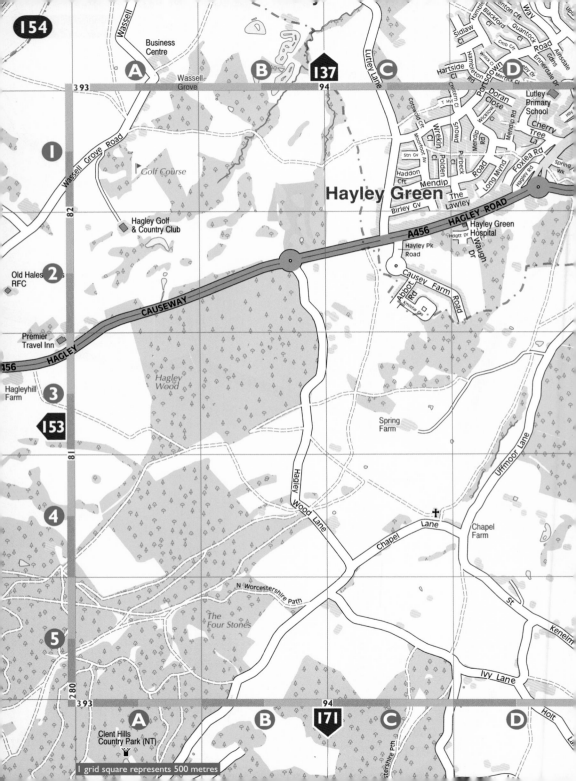

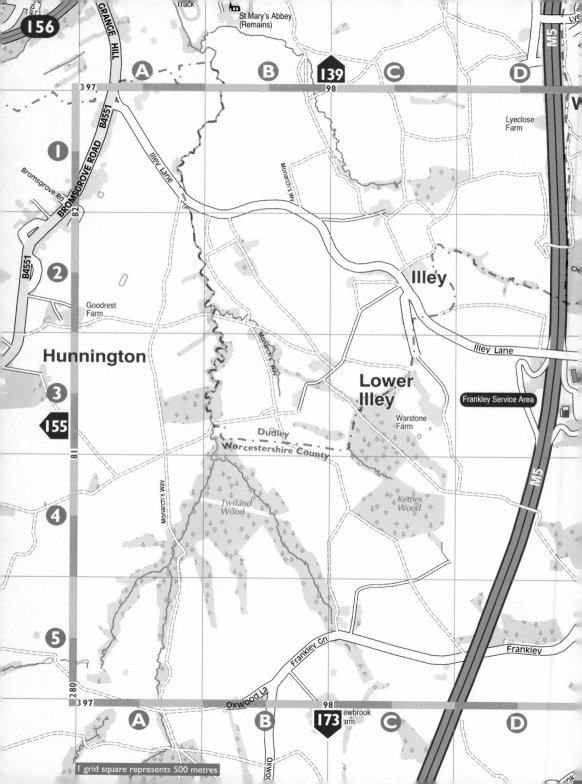

156

139

173

155

St Mary's Abbey
(Remains)

Track

Lyeclose
Farm

Illey

Lower
Illey

Frankley Service Area

Warstone
Farm

Dudley
Worcestershire County

Kettles
Wood

Twiland
Wood

Frankley Gn

Frankley

Oxwood La

ewbrook
arm

Goodrest
Farm

Hunnington

Bromsgrove Rd

BROMSGROVE ROAD B4551

GRANGE HILL

B4551

Illey Lane

Illey Lane

Monarch's Wy

Monarch's Way

Monarch's Way

M5

A B 139 C D

I

2

3

4

5

A B 173 C D

3 97

98

2 80

3 97

98

82

81

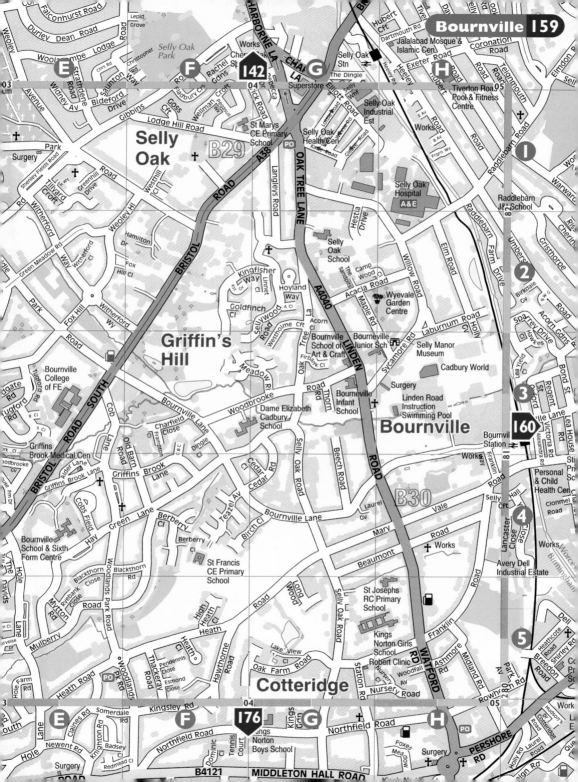

Moseley

Wake Green

King's
Heath

Billesley
Common

B13

B14

Golf Course

Moseley Golf Club

Swanshurst
Girls School

Wheelers Lane
Technology
College

Kings Heath
Boys School

Uffculme
Special
School

Josiah
Mason
College

The Bishop
Challoner
RC School

St Dunstans
RC Primary
School

Billesley
Primary
School

Woodthorpe
Primary
School

Kings Heath
CC

Cocks Moors W
Leisure Centre

Primary
School

CE Primary
School

Golf

E   F   144   G   H   I

2

3   162

4

5

E   F   178   G   H

Hall Green 163

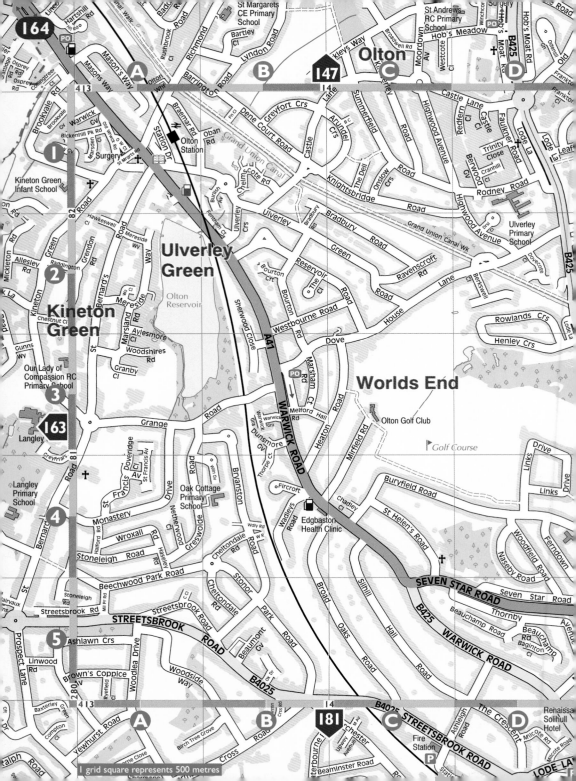

Elmdon
Heath

Lode Heath

Cath
de-B

Pasture Farm

E F **150** G H

9

20

21

Bickenhill

I

Diddington Lane

82

The Grove

2

O S R

Fiddlers Green

Meriden Rd

MERIDEN RO

Meriden Rd

Corberts Close

Lap Wing

Drive

Nesfield Grove

3

Lane

Hampton in Arden Station

Hampton in Arden

The Crescent

Station Road

81

HIGH STREET

Fentham Road

Meadow Drive

Fentham

George Fentham Endowed Primary School

Peel Close

4

Hampton Manor Homes

PH PO

Elm Tree

Bellemere Road

Belle Vue Ter

Surgery

M42

ROAD B4102

Eastcote Lane

Marsh Lane

Hook End

5

280

21

9

20

21

E F G H

Eastcote Lane

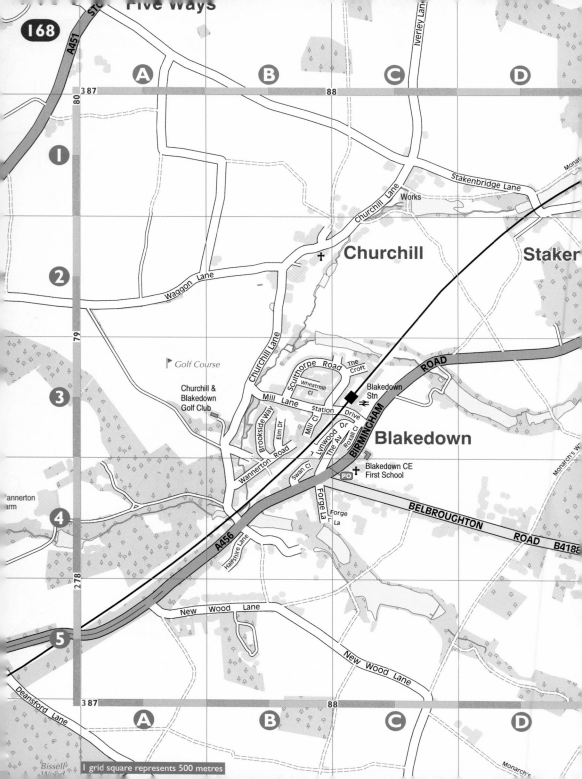

E
F
G
H

152

90

91
80

I

Field House

2

3

170

4

278

5

E
F
G
H

Haybridge
Avenue

Sweetpool

The Crescent

Sycan Works

Church St

Chapel
Street

PO

Worceste...

Kidderminster Rd

A456

KID...

Brook
Crs

Brookland
Rd

Road

Brake Mill
Farm

The Greenway

Willow Close

The Oaks

Chestnut Dr

Cavendish Dr

Milestone Dr

Milestone Dr

Meadow Croft

Spring
Cl

Long
Cl

Milestone Dr

Summervale Rd

WORCESTER ROAD

Newfield
Pl

South Rd

Newfield
Gdns

South
Gdns

Western
Road

Thicknall
Ryefield
Cl

Orchard

Western
Road

Beeches Mews

Pinewoods Av

Pinewoods
Cl

Ml Pool Cl

Newfield
Road

Thicknall
Road

Stakenbridge Lane

Stoney Lane

KIDDERMINSTER ROAD SOUTH A456

A456

A450

WORCESTER ROAD

...ridge

Garden
Centre

Thicknall
Farm

Thicknall Lane

79

Broome Lane

Broome Lane

A450

Broome

3

Red
Hall

STOURBRIDGE ROAD

Stourbridge
Rd

**Hackman's
Gate**

Knoll
Hill

HACKMAN'S

GATE

Hossll Lane

Manor
House

Egg Lane

Watery Lane

90

HACKMAN'S GATE

91

WORCE... RD

WORCE... RD

Garden
Centre

Yieldingtree

LANE

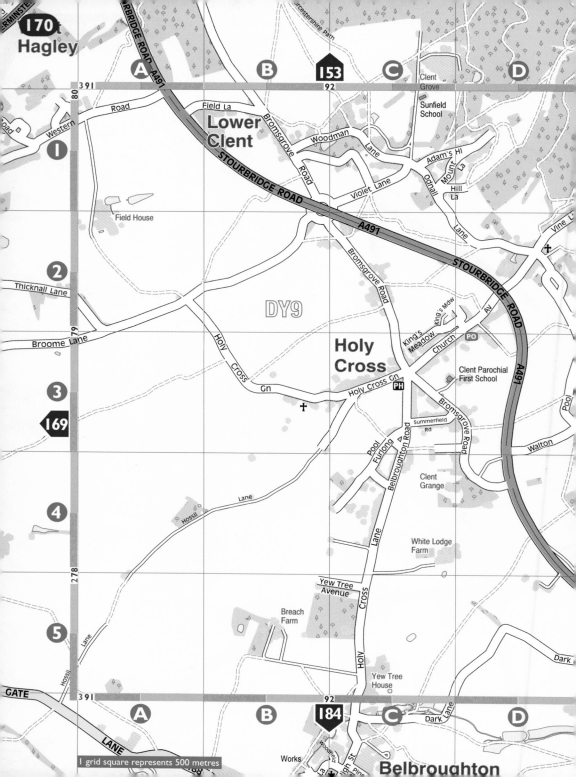

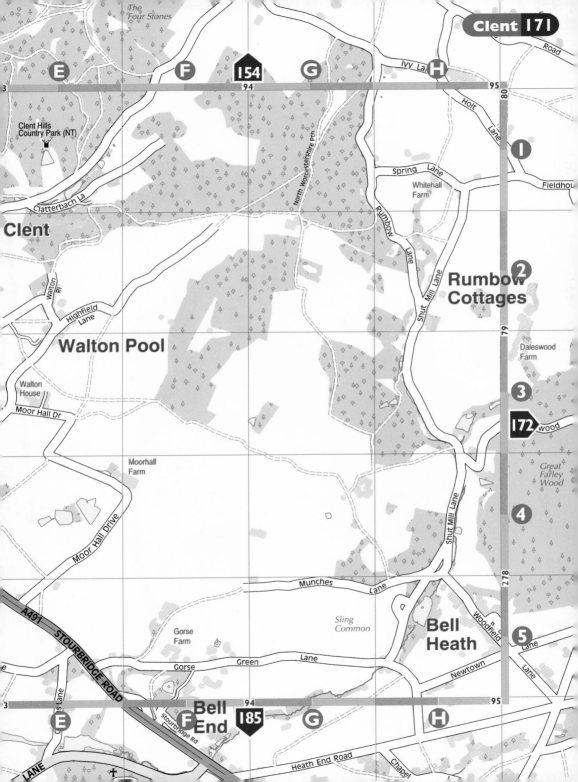

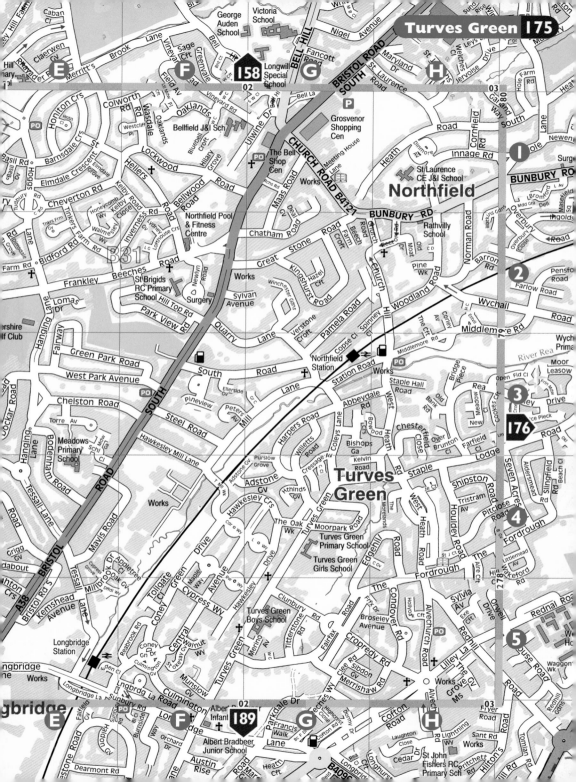

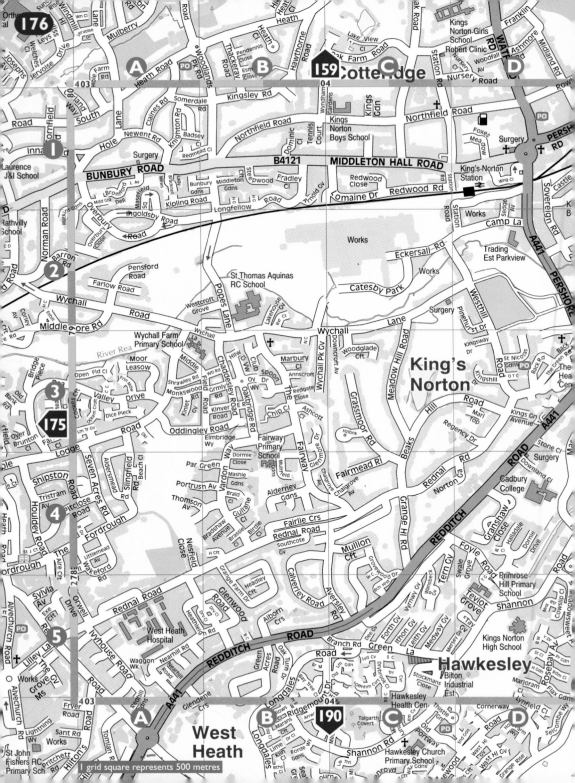

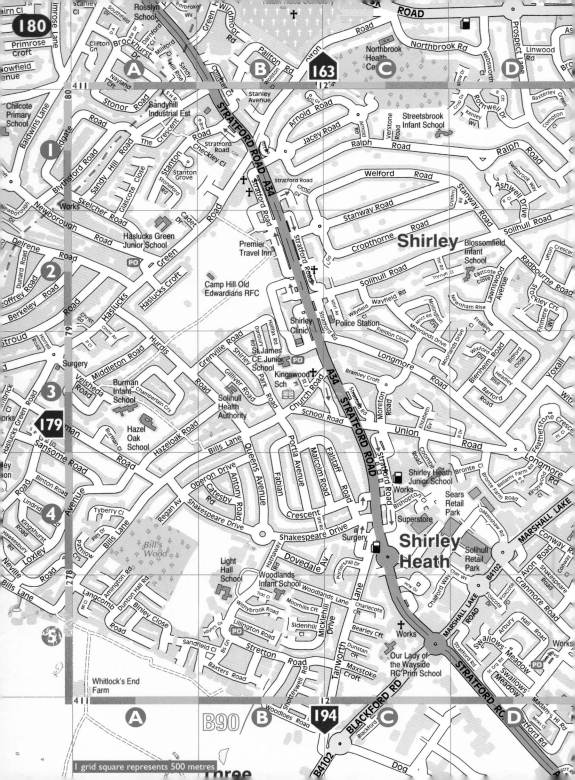

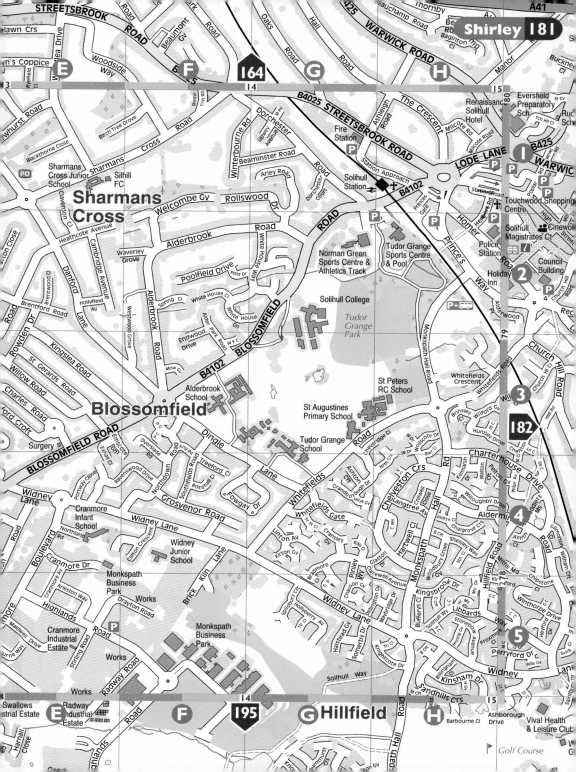

de-Barnes

HAMPTON

Hall Farm

E 2

F

166

G

H

7   18   19

80

Berry

Hall   Lane

Ravenshaw   Lane

Friday   Lane

I

Catherines Cl

Henwood

River Blythe

Lane

Barston Lane

Barston La

2

M42

79

Eastc

Cow Hayes

Grand Union Canal Walk

Barston Lane

Barston Lane

Works

Henwood Hall Farm

3

Knowle

Ravenshaw   Way

Junction 5

Grove Farm

4

River Blythe

Copt Heath

Jacobean Lane

Jc La

278

Road

A4141

WARWICK   ROAD

Grand Union Canal Walk

Copt Heath Golf Club

Jacobean Lane

Queen Minster Cl

Eleanors Dr

Warwick Rd

Golf Course

Broadfern Road

Holland Av

Hampton Road

5

Lghtwd Cl

Longdon   Croft

WARWICK RD

Wychwood Avenue

Alveston Grove

Longdon Hall

7   183   19

E

Barnbrook Rd

F

197

Ragley Close

G

H

High Trees Rd

Langfield Road

Abbots Cl

Road

WARW

Arden Vale Road

Wh Rd

Hall

Hampton Rd

Knowle FC

Knowle Village

Kixley

Sling Common

Bell Heath

Gorse Farm

STOURBRIDGE ROAD

A491

Gorse Green Lane

E 94 **F** **171** **G** **H** Newtown 95

Caltons Lane

Stourbridge Rd

Bell End

LANE

Heath End Road

Chapel Lane

Madeley Road

I

Made Heath

Bonfire Hill

Bell Hall

Castle Bourne

A491

STOURBRIDGE ROAD

Lower Madeley Farm

2

Lane

Mearse Lane

Hagley Hill Farm

Mearse Farm

3

Stourbridge Rd

186 A491

Fairfield Court

76

4

Fairfield

Swan Lane

Pepperwood Cl

Fairfield Villa FC

Fairfield First School

B4091

PO

5

275

Wood Lane

Monarch's Way

E 94 **F** Pepper **G** **H** Orchard Vis

Bournheath Road

Yew Tree Lane

STOURBRIDGE RO
95

Bell Heath **186**

Woodfield Lane

Hayes Farm

Farley Lane

Newtown Lane

A   **B**   **172**   **C**   B4551   **D**

3 95   Quantry Lane   96   M5

The Gutter

The Gutter

1

Lane

Madeley Road

Madeley Heath

77

Bonfire Hill

Chadwich Lane

LANE

2

Lower Madeley Farm

Harbours

MONEY

Hill

3

185   A491   Sandy La   **SANDY**   **LANE**

76

Works

Mo

M5

4

Middle Road

Road

Top Road

Third Road

Wildmoor Lane

Junction 4

Wildmoor

Swan

Monarch's Way

Rd

Lane

Fairfield Villa FC

5

First School

Mill Lane

B4091

275

Orchard Vls

3 95   **A**   **B**   96   **C**   **D**

STOURBRIDGE

Yew Tree Lane

Bournheath

Wildmoor Lane

Woodrow Lane

1 grid square represents 500 metres

Great Park

Romsley Cl
Waseley
Crs
Road
Leasowe Rd

E Waseley Hills Country

F

173

Cleves Road
Rea Av
G
Windmill Avenue
H
Segbourne Rd
Deelands Rd
Rubery Farm
Spencer
WK
Rubery
Cock Hill
Sandstone Av
Bristol Rd

North Worcestershire Path

North Worcestershire Path

Beeche Cl
98
I'view
Cleves Dr
Richmond Road
Rubery Clinic
A38
brookend Dr
Callowbridge Rd
Fromehead
99
A38
I

Woodlands Rd

Bowes Rd
The Av
Brook Rd
Callowbrook
Malcolm Gv
Graham Road

Holywell Primary School

Barrington Road

Works
Kineton Rd
Rochford Cl
Heron Wy
St Chad's Rd
Police Station
Heath La
Rushmead

I

Cumner Lane

Lyndon Rd
PO
New
Graham Road
Sharps

Waseley Hills High School

School Lane

Gannow Rd
Gannow Walk
A38
Birch Rd
Whetty
Chad's La
Leach
Beacon Cl
Belmont Road
Hagley Pk Dr

Whettybridge Road

Maple Rd
Chapfield MS
Chapfield
Holmes Drive
Eachway
Beacon Rd
Rednal
2
Lander

Holywell Lane

Beaconside Primary School

Hazel Road
Shearwater Cl
Heather Dr
Stockhill Dr
Eachway
Farm Road
Way

Eachway

Fairway Dr
Cottage Gdns
Valley
Links
Bilberry Road

Redhill
Redhill Farm

A38 ROAD

Golf Co

3

Beacon Hill

188

Manor Lane

BIRMINGHAM ROAD

A38

North Worcestershir

Lickey Hills Country Park
4

Beacon Lane

Monument Lane

Lick

Lydiate Ash

Lydiate Ash Rd
LAR

5

Beacon Lane

Alvechurch Highway

Lynwood Wy

E
F
Lane
98
Alvec G Highway
Lickey Hills mary School
99
H

BIRMINGHAM ROAD

High House Dr
275

Clayton Gdns
Malvern Rd
Lickey Square
The Badgers

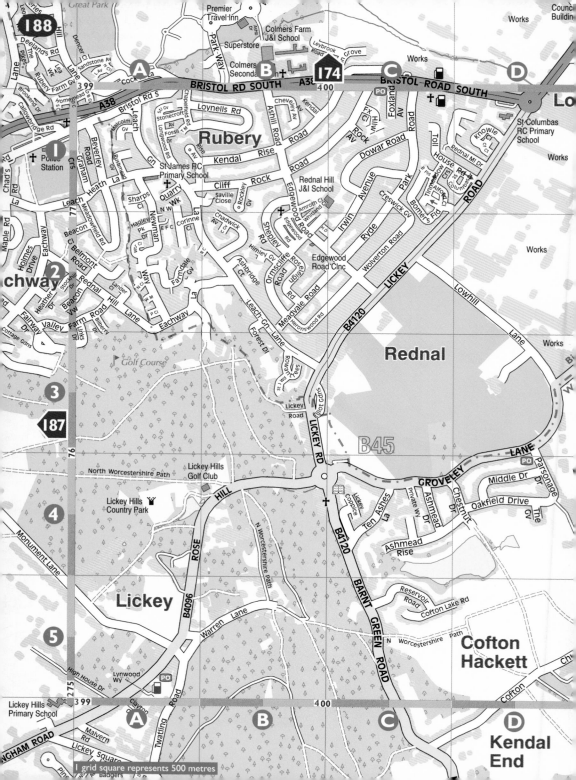

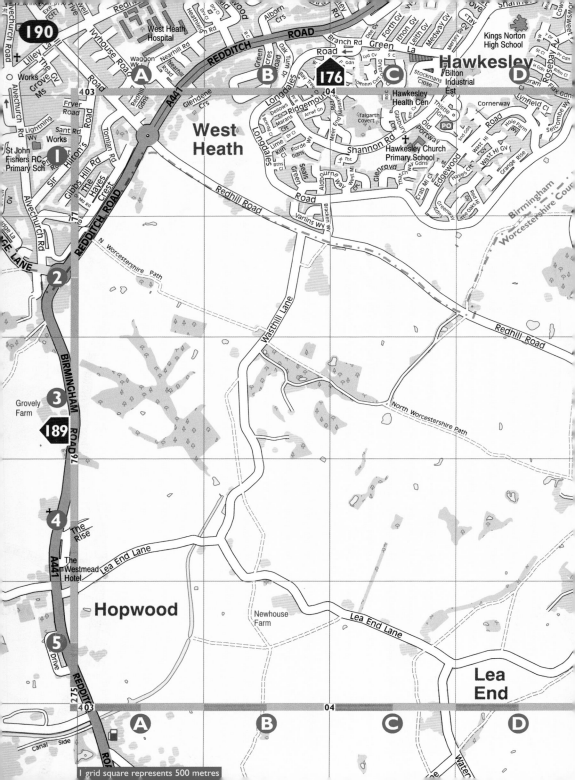

190

West Heath Hospital

REDDITCH ROAD

Branch Rd

Green La

Kings Norton High School

Hawkesley

Bilton Industrial Est

176

Hawkesley Health Cen

Cornerway

A
B
C
D

West Heath

St John Fishers RC Primary Sch

Works

1

Hawkesley Church Primary School

Shannon Rd

Redhill Road

Varlins Wy

Bracken Wy

2

N Worcestershire Path

Wasthill Lane

Redhill Road

BIRMINGHAM

3

Grovely Farm

189

North Worcestershire Path

Birmingham Worcestershire Coun

4

The Rise

Lea End Lane

The Westmead Hotel

A441

Hopwood

Newhouse Farm

Lea End Lane

5

REDDITCH

Lea End

Canal Side

A
B
C
D

177

E **F** **G** **H**

05 06 07

Longdales Road

Ontario Close

Winnipeg

Ivy

Primrose Hill

Hill Lane

Crabmill Lane

HOLLYWO

B38

Lilycroft Lane

Icknield Street

Dark Lane

I

BaCa

77

Works

Grimpits Lane

Headley Heath Lane

Middle Lane

**Headley
Heath**

† Glenfield
House

Packhorse Lane

2

HOLLYWOOD

Icknield Street

Bell Green Lane

Middle Lane

3

192

76 Silver

Woodrush
RFC

Clewshaw Lane

4

Forhill

Wor

Clewshaw Lane

PH

Lea End Lane

North Worcestershire Path

Blackgreves
Farm

275

5

Forhill
Ash

Brockhill Lane

Severn Way

Avon Dr

T Ct

† Church
View

E **F** **G** **H**

05 06 07

Icknield Street

▶ *Golf Course*

E

Major's
Freer **179**

G

H

I

The Fordrough

Romma Cl

mans

Road

Manhurst Cl

Wy Gv

Three Corner
Close

Rolan
Drive

Littlemead Road

Haslucks Green Road

Whitlock's End
Farm

Nursery
Gdns

Rushleigh Rd

Rwor Cl

Fords
Rd

Haslucks Cl

Cambria Cl

Heath   Lane

Lane

Trueman's
Heath

Haslucks Green Road

Whitlock's
End Station

Whi Church
La

Tythe   Barn

Highgate
United
FC

Horse Shoe
Associated
FC

Lane

Tythe Barn

Three Acres La

Tythebarn La

2

Houndsfield   Lane

Dickens Heath
Primary School

Works

†

Meadow Pleck

Dckn

Lea

Green

Whitlock's
End

Mdw pleck
Lane

Boundary
La

Dckmrs Heath R

Cmpn
Wy

Wl Wy

Lane

Fulford
Cl

Birchy Leasowes Lane

Birchy Close

Fishers
Dr

Dckmrs
La

Main St

3

Selsdon
Cl

Tilehouse Lane

Heath   Road

E Wy

Lane

bush Lane

194

Clay
Pit La

Kiln Lane

176

Rd

Lea Gn
Dr

Wythall
Station

Dickens

Tidbury
Green Primary
School

Rumbush

Hird

4

Littleshaw
Croft

Littleshaw

Lowbrook   La

Tidbury Green

Lane

Surgery

Worcestershire County

Solihull

Norton

Lane

Rumbush

Cleobury Far

5

Cleobury Lane

River Cole

Fulford
Hall

Fulford Hall Road

Rumbush

E

F

G

H

Fulford
Heath

River Cole

North Worcestershire Path

Golf Course

Longdon
Hall

E

F

183

G

H

Broadfern

Wychwood Avenue

Holland Av

Warwick

Lghtwa Cl

Hampton

Lndon Croft

I

Kixley
Farm

Knowle
FC

Knowle Village
CC

Alwe...

...rry Heath Crs

Whateley Hall
Rd

Ragley
Close

Arden Vale
Road

Pk Key

Mock
Rd

Hampton Road

Barnbrook Rd

High Trees
Rd

Langfield

Abbots Cl

Newton Road

Warwick Road

Whitacre

Copt Heath Drive

Holbeche Rd

Shortland

Blackdown
Road

Beausale Dr

Crabmill Close

Knowle CE
Primary
School

Kixley Lane

WARWICK RD A4141

2

Longdon

Road

Spiers Cl

St Annes
Grove

Annes
Rd

Landor Road

Austrey
Close

Arrow
Cl

Landor Rd

Uilenhall Rd

croft
Way

ansborough Rd

Trehern Close

Lodge Road

St Johns

DFC

PO

St
Lawrence Close

Lodge
Crt

HIGH ST

Knowle

Knlwrth Rd

WILSONS

RD Cook Cl

Golden Erd
Dr

KENILWORTH

Starbold
Crescent

Hilmt Rd

HC

Starbold
Crescent

Starbold
Crescent

LODGE ROAD

B4101

Milverton Rd

WARWICK RD

Batts
Hall

**Tilehouse
Green**

Pettyfields Cl

Woodrow Cl

Woodrow Crs

Purnells Way

Barcheston Rd

Hollywell Rd

Arden School

3

Knowle
Hall

Grand Union Canal Wlk

Gilberry Cl

Hollywell Road

Easenhall Cl

Barcheston
Rd

STATION

ney Road

Downing Cl

wdsd Crs

4

Dowling
Close Health
Clinic

Hertford Rd

Mdl Av Wy

Grove Road

Barton Dr

Lansdowne

A4141

St George &
St Teresa RC
Primary School

Knowle & Dorridge
CC

Warren Drive

Longford

Grove Road

Stockton Cl

**Rotten
Row**

rridge
School

Bs Dr

Foxbury
Dr

Knowle Wood Road

Grove Road

Inkeeper's
Lodge

Warwick Road

5

Avenue

Templeton

Temple Road

DORRIDGE

urgery

Brksby Gv

Gladstone Rd

**Knowle
Grove**

Granville Rd

Weston Cl

Woodcote
Dr

B93

Lane

WARWICK ROAD

STATION ROAD

101

E

F

199

G

H

Brooksby Gv

Dorridge

Paddock Drive

**Norton
Green**

Blue

Grand Union Canal

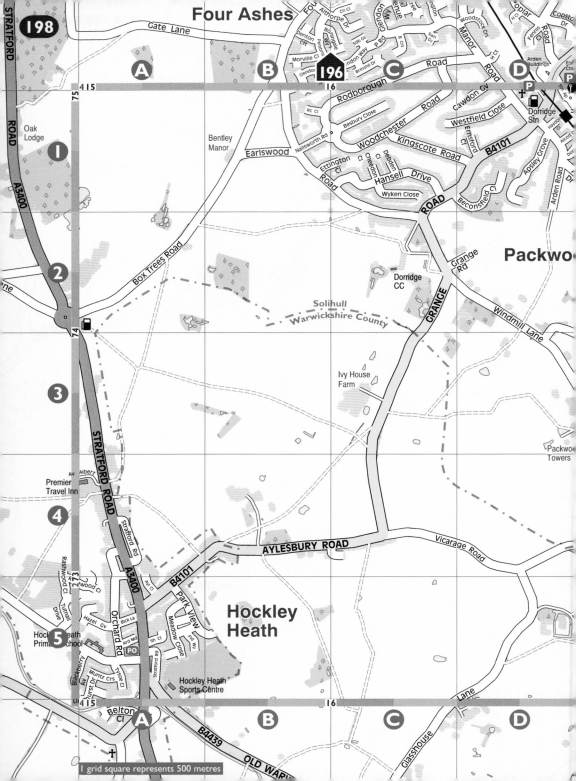

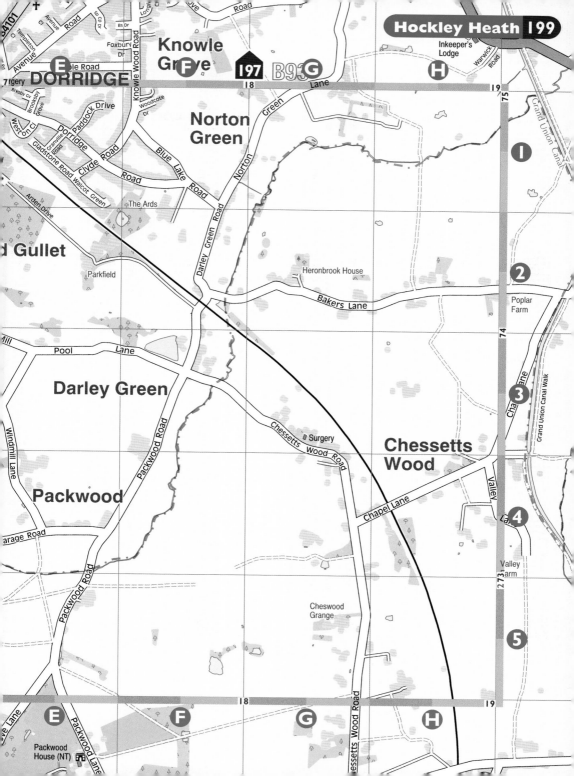

DORRIDGE

E

Knowle Grove

F

197 B93 **G**

Inkeeper's Lodge

H

I

Norton Green

Warwick Road

Grand Union Canal

Grand Union Canal Walk

Lane

Green

Norton

Knowle Wood Road

Woodcote Dr

Blue Lake Road

Clyde Road

Darley Green Road

Dorridge

Gladstone Road

Walcot Green

Granville Road

Paddock Drive

Avenue

Templecroft

Road

Foxbury Dr

Brooksby Grove

Weston Cl

Arden Drive

The Ards

Parkfield

Heronbrook House

Bakers Lane

Poplar Farm

2

74

75

Chapel Lane

Pool Lane

Darley Green

Packwood Road

Windmill Lane

Packwood

Garage Road

Chessetts Wood Road

Surgery

Chessetts Wood

Valley Lane

3

4

Valley Farm

273

Cheswood Grange

5

E

F

G

H

Cove Lane

Packwood Lane

Packwood House (NT)

Chessetts Wood Road

18

19

d Gullet

Acock's Green	146 A4
Alcester Lane's End	160 D4
Aldridge	30 A4
Alum Rock	129 E1
Amblecote	118 B5
Ashmore Lake	39 H1
Ashmore Park	25 F1
Ashwood	98 C4
Aston	109 F3
Bacon's End	114 C5
Bails Hill	71 E2
Balsall Heath	144 A2
Banners Gate	60 C4
Baptist End	102 C3
Barr Common	44 C2
Bartley Green	157 H2
Bateman's Green	192 B1
Bearwood	124 C2
Beech Lanes	124 A5
Belbroughton	184 C1
Bell End	185 F1
Belle Vale	138 B2
Bell Heath	171 H5
Bentley	40 B2
Bentley Heath	196 C3
Bescot	56 C2
Bickenhill	166 D1
Bilbrook	11 E3
Billesley	162 A4
Billesley Common	161 G3
Bilston	53 G1
Birch End	72 A4
Birches Green	93 E3
Birchfield	90 D5
Birchills	41 H2
Birmingham	2 C7
Blackheath	121 H2
Black Lake	71 E4
Blakedown	168 C3
Blakeley	81 E1
Blakenall Heath	27 G1
Blakenhall	51 H1
Bloomfield	69 F5
Blossomfield	181 E3
Bloxwich	27 E1
Boldmere	77 E2
Bordesley	127 G2
Bordesley Green	128 C3
Bournbrook	143 E5
Bourne Vale	44 C2
Bournville	159 H3
Bowling Green	120 D1
Brades Village	86 B5
Bradley	53 H5
Bradmore	36 A5
Bramford	68 A4
Brandwood End	177 H1
The Bratch	64 D3
Brierley Hill	119 E2
Bristnall Fields	123 F1
Brockmoor	100 D5
Bromford	94 A5
Bromley	100 C4
Broome	169 G3
Broom Hill	184 B5
Brownhills	9 G4
Brown's Green	89 H2
Buckland End	112 C2
Buckpool	118 B2
Burnt Tree	85 F4
Bushbury	13 E4
Caldmore	4 B7
California	141 F5
Carroway Head	48 D1
Castle Bromwich	113 E1
Castlecroft	35 E5
Castle Vale	94 C3
Catherine-de-Barnes	166 A5
Catshill	19 G1
Causeway Green	122 D1
Chad Valley	125 H5
Chapman's Hill	172 D4
Charlemont	71 H4
Chattle Hill	97 E4
Chelmsley Wood	132 C3
Chessetts Wood	199 H3
Cheswick Green	195 E4
The Chuckery	5 J4
Churchfield	88 A1
Church Hill	56 A4
Churchill	168 C2
Cinder Hill	67 H2
Claregate	24 B4
Clayhanger	18 D1
Clent	171 E2
Coal Pool	28 B5
Codsall	10 B3
Cofton Common	189 F2
Cofton Hackett	188 D5
Cole End	115 F1
Colehall	112 D4
Coleshill	115 G3
Colton Hills	51 G5
Compton	35 H3
Coombeswood	139 E1
Copt Heath	183 E4
Coseley	68 C2

Cotteridge	159 G5
Coven Heath	12 C1
Cradley	137 G1
Cradley Heath	120 C4
Dam Mill	21 F1
Darby End	102 D5
Darby's Hill	103 H2
Darlaston	54 D1
Darlaston Green	55 G1
Darley Green	199 E3
Daw End	28 D5
Dayhouse Bank	172 D3
Deepfields	68 B2
The Delves	57 G4
Dickens Heath	194 A3
Digbeth	3 J6
Doe Bank	62 C1
Dorridge	197 E5
Drakes Cross	192 C2
Druids Heath	30 C1
Dudley	84 D4
Dudley Port	86 A2
Dudley's Fields	26 D2
Dudley Wood	120 C2
Dunstall Hill	22 D5
Eachway	187 H2
Edgbaston	142 D1
Elmdon	149 E4
Elmdon Heath	165 G3
Erdington	93 E3
Essington	14 D4
Ettingshall	52 D3
Ettingshall Park	52 B5
Eve Hill	84 A4
Fairfield	185 G5
Falcon Lodge	63 H2
Fallings Heath	55 G3
Fishley	17 E5
Fordbridge	132 A1
Fordhouses	12 B4
Forhill	191 E4
Four Ashes	196 A5
Four Oaks	46 C2
Four Oaks Park	46 D5
Frankley	157 F5
Frankley	173 H3
Frankley Green	173 G2
Frankley Hill	173 H2
Friar Park	56 D5
Garrets Green	130 C3
Gib Heath	108 A2
Giggetty	30 C1
Gilbertstone	147 F1
Gilson	97 E5
Glebe Farm	112 B5
Golds Green	70 C3
Goldthorn Park	52 B4
Gornalwood	83 E3
Goscote	28 B2
Gospel End Village	66 B3
Gothersley	116 C2
Gravelly Hill	92 D4
Great Barr	73 H1
Great Bridge	69 H5
Greenforge	98 B3
Griffinis Hill	159 F3
Grimes Hill	192 D4
Grove Vale	73 E2
Gunstone	10 C1
Guns Village	87 E2
The Gutter	186 A1
Hackman's Gate	169 F4
Haden Cross	121 G4
Hagley	158 A4
Halesowen	139 E3
Hall Green	71 G3
Hall Green	163 E3
Hampton in Arden	167 F3
Hamstead	73 G5
Handsworth	89 F4
Handsworth Wood	90 B3
Harborne	141 G1
Hardware	28 B3
Hardwick	45 F3
Hartle	184 D2
Hart's Hill	101 G4
Harvills Hawthorn	70 B4
Hasbury	138 A4
Hasluck's Green	179 G5
Hateley Heath	71 G5
Hawkesley	176 C5
Hawne	138 C2
Hayley Green	154 C1
Hay Mills	146 B1
Headley Heath	191 G1
Heath End	28 B1
Heath Town	38 A1
Highbridge	18 A1
Highbury Park	160 D1
Highgate	127 F4
High Heath	18 C5
High Heath	48 D5
Highter's Heath	178 D5
Hill	47 E1
Hillfield	195 G1
Hill Hook	32 C4
Hill Top	71 E3

Hill Wood	33 G5
Himley	81 F3
Hinksford	98 D1
Hockley Heath	198 B5
Hodgehill	111 H4
Holly Bank	19 H4
Hollywood	178 D5
Holy Cross	170 C5
Hook End	167 H5
Hopwood	190 A5
Horseley Heath	86 A1
Hunnington	155 H3
Hurst Green	122 D4
Hurst Hill	67 H5
Iley	156 C2
Kates Hill	85 E5
Kineton Green	163 H2
King's Heath	161 E3
King's Hill	55 G5
Kingshurst	131 H2
King's Norton	176 C3
Kingstanding	75 G2
Kingswinford	99 F3
Kitt's Green	113 E5
Kitwell	157 E3
Knowle	197 G2
Knowle Grove	197 F5
The Knowle	103 G4
Ladywood	126 A2
Lambert's End	87 E3
Lane Green	11 E4
Lane Head	26 A4
Lanesfield	53 E4
Langley	104 D4
Langley Green	105 F5
Lapal	139 H4
Lawns Wood	117 F1
Lea End	190 D5
Lea Hall	130 C2
Leamore	27 E4
Lee Bank	126 C4
Leighswood	30 A2
Ley Hill	47 E4
Lickey	188 A5
Lifford	177 F1
Little Aston	32 A5
Little Bloxwich	27 H1
Little Bromwich	128 D2
Little Hay	33 G1
Little Norton	8 B2
Little Packington	150 D1
Littleworth End	49 E5
Lode Heath	165 E4
Lodge Hill	141 H5
Londonderry	105 G5
London Fields	83 E4
Longbridge	188 D1
Lower Bradley	54 B4
Lower Clent	170 D1
Lower Gornal	83 G2
Lower Iley	156 C3
Low Hill	23 F5
Lozells	108 C2
The Lunt	54 B5
Lutley	137 F5
Lydiate Ash	187 E5
Lye	136 C1
Lyndon Green	130 B5
Madeley Heath	186 A1
Major's Green	179 F5
Maney	62 B4
Marston Green	132 A4
Maw Green	57 H2
Mayer's Green	88 A3
Mere Green	47 F2
Merridale	36 A3
Merry Hill	50 C1
Merry Hill	119 H1
Mesty Croft	56 A4
Middle Bickenhill	150 C4
Mill Green	31 G3
Minworth	95 E1
Monksath	195 G5
Monmore Green	38 B5
Moor Hall	47 H4
Moseley	38 B4
Moseley	144 B5
Moxley	54 D4
Mushroom Green	120 B3
Nechells	110 B1
Nechells Green	109 H5
Netherton	102 B4
Newbolds	24 A4
Newbridge	35 H2
New Invention	26 A2
New Oscott	76 B1
Newton	73 E3
New Town	9 H2
New Town	86 B2
Newtown	16 C2
Newtown	108 C4
Northfield	158 B3
Norton	135 E5
Norton Green	199 F1
Oakham	103 F2
Ocker Hill	70 A2
Oldbury	105 E4

Old Fallings	23 H3
Old Hill	121 G3
Old Perton	34 A2
Old Swinford	135 G4
Olton	147 G5
Orton Hill	65 E1
Ounsdale	64 D5
Overend	138 A1
Over Green	79 H2
Oxbarn	51 E1
Oxley	22 D2
Packwood	199 E4
Packwood Gullet	198 D2
Palfrey	56 D2
Palmers Cross	21 F2
Parkfield	52 D3
Park Village	23 H5
Pedmore	153 F2
Pelsall	18 B4
Pelsall Wood	17 H2
Pendeford	11 G5
Penn	51 E2
Pensnett	100 D2
Perry Barr	90 B1
Perry Beeches	74 A3
Perry Common	75 H5
Perton	34 C1
Pheasey	59 G4
Pleck	56 B2
Portobello	39 E3
Portway	104 A3
Prestwood	116 C3
Priestfield	53 F2
Primrose Hill	102 D5
Princes End	69 E2
Pype Hayes	93 H1
Quarry Bank	119 H4
Queslett	74 C1
Quinton	140 A1
Reddicap Heath	63 G4
Rednal	188 C3
Ridgacre	140 C1
Romsley	172 C1
Romsley Hill	172 C3
Rood End	105 G3
Roseville	68 A5
Rotten Row	197 G4
Rotton Park	107 G5
Roughley	47 G2
Round Oak	101 G5
Rounds Green	104 C1
Rowley Regis	103 H4
Rubery	188 A1
Ruiton	83 F2
Rumbow Cottages	171 H2
Rumbush	195 G5
Rushall	29 E5
Russell's Hall	101 G1
Saltley	110 C5
Sandwell	106 C3
Scotlands	24 A3
Sedgley	67 G3
Selly Oak	159 F1
Selly Park	160 A1
Shard End	113 F4
Sharmans Cross	181 E1
Sheldon	147 H2
Shelfield	29 E2
Shenley Fields	158 A5
Shenstone Woodend	33 E1
Shire Oak	19 F1
Shire Oak Hill	19 H2
Shirley	180 C2
Shirley Heath	180 C4
Short Cross	138 C3
Short Heath	26 D4
Short Heath	76 D5
Silver End	118 D3
Silver Street	192 A3
Small Heath	128 B5
Smestow	80 A2
Smethwick	106 A4
Soho	107 E3
Solihull	182 A3
Solihull Lodge	179 E3
South Yardley	146 D1
Sparkbrook	127 H5
Sparkhill	145 E4
Springfield	105 F1
Springfield	103 F4
Springfield	162 A1
Springhill	15 H2
Spring Hill	50 C4
Stakenbridge	168 D2
Stambermill	136 A2
Stechford	130 A1
Stirchley	160 A3
Stockfield	146 C3
Stockland Green	92 A2
Stockwell End	21 G5
Stonebridge	150 D5
Stone Cross	71 H2
Stourbridge	134 D3
Stourton	116 D5
Stow Lawn	38 D5
The Straits	82 D1
Streetly	45 H4

Stubber's Green	29 G2
Summer Hill	69 G2
Sutton Coldfield	62 D3
Swan Village	86 D2
Swindon	80 D4
Tansley Hill	103 F2
Tat Bank	105 E2
Ten Acres	160 B2
Tettenhall	21 G5
Tettenhall Wood	35 H1
Thimble End	78 C2
Three Maypoles	194 B1
Tidbury Green	193 G4
Tile Cross	131 G2
Tilehouse Green	197 E4
Tipton	69 G4
Tipton Green	68 D5
Tividale	85 H5
Toll End	69 H5
Tower Hill	74 A4
Trueman's Heath	193 E1
Trysull	64 A2
Tudor Hill	62 A2
Turves Green	175 G4
Tyburn	94 A4
Tyseley	146 A2
Ulverley Green	164 A2
Upper Gornal	67 G5
Upper Witton	76 A5
Vauxhall	127 H1
Vigo	19 F5
The Village	100 A2
Wake Green	161 G1
Walker's Heath	177 F4
Wallbrook	68 C4
Wall Heath	99 F1
Wallington Heath	16 C4
Walmley	78 B3
Walmley Ash	78 D4
Walsall	5 F7
Walsall Wood	19 F3
Walton Pool	171 E4
Ward End	111 E1
Warley Woods	124 A3
Warstock	179 E2
Washwood Heath	110 C3
Water Orton	96 B3
Watford Gap	32 D3
Wednesbury	70 B1
Wednesbury Oak	69 F2
Wednesfield	26 D4
Weoley Castle	158 D1
Wergs	20 D4
West Bromwich	87 F5
Westcroft	13 H4
West Hagley	152 D5
West Heath	190 A1
Whitehealth Gate	104 C5
Whitehouse Common	63 G1
Whitlock's End	193 G2
Wightwick	34 D4
Wildmoor	186 B4
Willenhall	39 H2
Winson Green	107 G4
Withymoor Village	119 G3
Witton	91 G3
Wollaston	135 E1
Wollescote	136 C5
Wolverhampton	7 J3
Wombourne	64 B5
Woodcock Hill	158 A2
Wood End	24 C3
Woodgate	156 D1
Woodgate Valley	140 C4
Wood Green	56 A3
Wood Hayes	24 B1
Woods Bank	55 F3
Woodsetton	67 G4
Woodside	101 H3
The Woods	56 C4
Wordsley	118 A1
Worlds End	164 C3
Wylde Green	77 H2
Yardley	147 F4
Yardley Wood	179 G1
Yew Tree	57 H5

USING THE STREET INDEX

Street names are listed alphabetically. Each street name is followed by its postal town or area locality, the Postcode District, the page number, and the reference to the square in which the name is found.

Standard index entries are shown as follows:

Abberley Cl *HALE* B63 .... **138** B5

Street names and selected addresses not shown on the map due to scale restrictions are shown in the index with an asterisk:

Aaron Manby Ct *TPTN/OCK* DY4 * ..**69** F3

GENERAL ABBREVIATIONS

ACC....ACCESS	CTYD....COURTYARD	HLS....HILLS	MWY....MOTORWAY	SE....SOUTH EAST
ALY....ALLEY	CUTT....CUTTINGS	HO....HOUSE	N....NORTH	SER....SERVICE AREA
AP....APPROACH	CV....COVE	HOL....HOLLOW	NE....NORTH EAST	SH....SHORE
AR....ARCADE	CYN....CANYON	HOSP....HOSPITAL	NW....NORTH WEST	SHOP....SHOPPING
ASS....ASSOCIATION	DEPT....DEPARTMENT	HRB....HARBOUR	O/P....OVERPASS	SKWY....SKYWAY
AV....AVENUE	DL....DALE	HTH....HEATH	OFF....OFFICE	SMT....SUMMIT
BCH....BEACH	DM....DAM	HTS....HEIGHTS	ORCH....ORCHARD	SOC....SOCIETY
BLDS....BUILDINGS	DR....DRIVE	HVN....HAVEN	OV....OVAL	SP....SPUR
BND....BEND	DRO....DROVE	HWY....HIGHWAY	PAL....PALACE	SPR....SPRING
BNK....BANK	DRY....DRIVEWAY	IMP....IMPERIAL	PAS....PASSAGE	SQ....SQUARE
BR....BRIDGE	DWGS....DWELLINGS	IN....INLET	PAV....PAVILION	ST....STREET
BRK....BROOK	E....EAST	IND EST....INDUSTRIAL ESTATE	PDE....PARADE	STN....STATION
BTM....BOTTOM	EMB....EMBANKMENT	INF....INFIRMARY	PH....PUBLIC HOUSE	STR....STREAM
BUS....BUSINESS	EMBY....EMBASSY	INFO....INFORMATION	PK....PARK	STRD....STRAND
BVD....BOULEVARD	ESP....ESPLANADE	INT....INTERCHANGE	PKWY....PARKWAY	SW....SOUTH WEST
BY....BYPASS	EST....ESTATE	IS....ISLAND	PL....PLACE	TDG....TRADING
CATH....CATHEDRAL	EX....EXCHANGE	JCT....JUNCTION	PLN....PLAIN	TER....TERRACE
CEM....CEMETERY	EXPY....EXPRESSWAY	JTY....JETTY	PLNS....PLAINS	THWY....THROUGHWAY
CEN....CENTRE	EXT....EXTENSION	KG....KING	PLZ....PLAZA	TNL....TUNNEL
CFT....CROFT	F/O....FLYOVER	KNL....KNOLL	POL....POLICE STATION	TOLL....TOLLWAY
CH....CHURCH	FC....FOOTBALL CLUB	L....LAKE	PR....PRINCE	TPK....TURNPIKE
CHA....CHASE	FK....FORK	LA....LANE	PREC....PRECINCT	TR....TRACK
CHYD....CHURCHYARD	FLD....FIELD	LDG....LODGE	PREP....PREPARATORY	TRL....TRAIL
CIR....CIRCLE	FLDS....FIELDS	LGT....LIGHT	PRIM....PRIMARY	TWR....TOWER
CIRC....CIRCUS	FLS....FALLS	LK....LOCK	PROM....PROMENADE	U/P....UNDERPASS
CL....CLOSE	FM....FARM	LKS....LAKES	PRS....PRINCESS	UNI....UNIVERSITY
CLFS....CLIFFS	FT....FORT	LNDG....LANDING	PRT....PORT	UPR....UPPER
CMP....CAMP	FTS....FLATS	LTL....LITTLE	PT....POINT	V....VALE
CNR....CORNER	FWY....FREEWAY	LWR....LOWER	PTH....PATH	VA....VALLEY
CO....COUNTY	GA....GATE	MAG....MAGISTRATE	PZ....PIAZZA	VIAD....VIADUCT
COLL....COLLEGE	GAL....GALLERY	MAN....MANSIONS	QD....QUADRANT	VIL....VILLA
COMM....COMMON	GDN....GARDEN	MD....MEAD	QU....QUEEN	VIS....VISTA
COMM....COMMISSION	GDNS....GARDENS	MDW....MEADOWS	QY....QUAY	VLG....VILLAGE
CON....CONVENT	GLD....GLADE	MEM....MEMORIAL	R....RIVER	VLS....VILLAS
COT....COTTAGE	GLN....GLEN	MI....MILL	RBT....ROUNDABOUT	VW....VIEW
COTS....COTTAGES	GN....GREEN	MKT....MARKET	RD....ROAD	W....WEST
CP....CAPE	GND....GROUND	MKTS....MARKETS	RDG....RIDGE	WD....WOOD
CPS....COPSE	GRA....GRANGE	ML....MALL	REP....REPUBLIC	WHF....WHARF
CR....CREEK	GRG....GARAGE	MNR....MANOR	RES....RESERVOIR	WK....WALK
CREM....CREMATORIUM	GT....GREAT	MS....MEWS	RFC....RUGBY FOOTBALL CLUB	WKS....WALKS
CRS....CRESCENT	GTWY....GATEWAY	MSN....MISSION	RI....RISE	WLS....WELLS
CSWY....CAUSEWAY	GV....GROVE	MT....MOUNT	RP....RAMP	WY....WAY
CT....COURT	HGR....HIGHER	MTN....MOUNTAIN	RW....ROW	YD....YARD
CTRL....CENTRAL	HL....HILL	MTS....MOUNTAINS	S....SOUTH	YHA....YOUTH HOSTEL
CTS....COURTS		MUS....MUSEUM	SCH....SCHOOL	

POSTCODE TOWNS AND AREA ABBREVIATIONS

ACGN....Acock's Green
ALDR....Aldridge
ALE/KHTH/YWD...Alcester Lane's End/ King's Heath/Yardley Wood
ALVE....Alvechurch
AST/WIT....Aston/Witton
BDMR/CCFT....Bradmore/ Castlecroft
BFLD/HDSWWD....Birchfield/ Handsworth Wood
BHAMNEC....Birmingham N.E.C.
BHTH/HG....Balsall Heath/Highgate
BILS/COS....Bilston/Coseley
BKDE/SHDE....Buckland End/ Shard End
BKHL/PFLD....Blakenhall/Priestfield
BLKHTH/ROWR....Blackheath/ Rowley Regis
BLOX/PEL....Bloxwich/Pelsall
BNTWD....Burntwood
BORD....Bordesley
BRGRVE....Bromsgrove east
BRGRVW....Bromsgrove west
BRLYHL....Brierley Hill
BRWNH....Brownhills
BVILLE....Bournville

CBHAM....Central Birmingham
CBHAMNE....Central Birmingham northeast
CBHAMNW....Central Birmingham northwest
CBHAMW...Central Birmingham west
CBROM....Castle Bromwich
CDSL....Codsall
CDYHTH....Cradley Heath
CHWD/FDBR/MGN...Chelmsley Wood/ Fordbridge/Marston Green
CNCK/NC....Cannock/Norton Canes
COVEN....Coven
CSCFLD/WYGN.......Central Sutton Coldfield/Wylde Green
CSHL/WTROR....Coleshill/Water Orton
CVALE....Castle Vale
DARL/WED....Darlaston/Wednesbury
DIG/EDG....Digbeth/Edgbaston
DOR/KN....Dorridge/Knowle
DSYBK/YTR....Daisy Bank/Yew Tree
DUDN....Dudley north
DUDS....Dudley south
DUNHL/THL/PER.....Dunstall Hill/ Tettenhall/Perton
EDG....Edgbaston

ERDE/BCHGN.......Erdington east/ Birches Green
ERDW/GRVHL........Erdington west/ Gravelly Hill
ETTPK/GDPK/PENN ..Ettingshall Park/ Goldthorn Park/Penn
FOAKS/STRLY.....Four Oaks/Streetly
GTB/HAM....Great Barr/Hamstead
GTWY....Great Wyrley
HAG/WOL....Hagley/Wollescote
HALE....Halesowen
HDSW....Handsworth
HHTH/SAND..Hateley Heath/Sandwell
HIA/OLT....Hampton in Arden/Olton
HLGN/YWD....Hall Green/ Yardley Wood
HLYWD....Hollywood
HOCK/TIA.......Hockley Heath/ Tanworth-in-Arden
HRBN....Harborne
HWK/WKHTH.......Walker's Heath
KGSTG....Kingstanding
KGSWFD....Kingswinford
KIDD....Kidderminster
KINVER....Kinver

LDYWD/EDGR........Ladywood/ Edgbaston Reservoir
LGLGYN/QTN..Langley Green/Quinton
LGN/SDN/BHAMAIR....Lyndon Green/ Sheldon/Birmingham Airport
LICHS....Lichfield south
LOZ/NWT....Lozells/Newtown
MCN/WHC..........Mere Green/ Whitehouse Common
MOS/BIL....Moseley/Billesley
NFLD/LBR........Northfield/Longbridge
OLDBY....Oldbury
PBAR/PBCH.............Perry Bar/ Perry Beeches
POL/KGSB/FAZ........Polesworth/ Kingsbury/Fazeley
RBRY....Rubery
RCOVN/BALC/EX.....Rural Coventry north/Balsall Common/Exhall
RIDG/WDGT....Ridgacre/Woodgate
RMSLY....Romsley
RUSH/SHEL........Rushall/Sheffield
SCFLD/BOLD.......Sutton Coldfield/ Boldmere
SEDG....Sedgley
SHHTH....Short Heath

SHLY....Shirley
SLYOAK....Selly Oak
SMHTH....Small Heath
SMTHWK....Smethwick
SMTHWKW....Smethwick west
SOLH....Solihull
SPARK....Sparkhill/Sparkbrook
STETCH....Stetchford
STRBR....Stourbridge
TPTN/OCK....Tipton/Ocker Hill
VAUX/NECH....Vauxhall/Nechells
WALM/CURD....Walmley/Curdworth
WASH/WDE....Washwood Heath/ Ward End
WBROM....West Bromwich
WLNHL....Willenhall
WMBN....Wombourne
WNSFLD....Wednesfield
WOLV....Wolverhampton
WOLVN....Wolverhampton north
WSL....Walsall
WSLW....Walsall west
WSNGN....Winson Green
YDLY....Yardley

Index - streets

Aar - Alb

A

Aaron Manby Ct
TPTN/OCK DY4 *..........69 F3
Abberley Cl HALE B63.....138 B5
Abberley Rd
LGLGYN/QTN B68.........123 F4
SEDG DY3......83 E2
Abberley St DUDS DY2....102 C1
SMTHWK B66......107 G5
Abberton Cl HALE B63.........139 H4
Abberton Gv SHLY B90.....195 H1
Abbess Gv YDLY B25........130 A3
Abbey Cl HHTH/SAND B71....87 C1
Abbey Crs HALE B63........137 H3
LGLGYN/QTN B68.........123 H5
Abbeydale Rd NFLD/LBR B31 ...175 G3
Abbey Dr BLOX/PEL WS3.......18 A2
Abbeyfield Rd
ERDW/GRVHL B23.........76 C3
WOLVN WV10......13 E5
Abbey Rd DUDS DY2.....102 D3
ERDW/GRVHL B23.....92 B4
HALE B63......137 G3
HRBN B17......142 B2
SEDG DY5......83 E3
SMTHWKW B67......123 H5
Abbey Sq BLOX/PEL WS3......16 A5
Abbey St SEDG DY3......83 E3
WSNGN B18......108 A4
Abbey St North WSNGN B18...108 A4
Abbot Rd HALE B63......154 C2
Abbots Cl DOR/KN B93......197 E1
RUSH/SHEL WS4......29 E4
Abbotsford Av GTB/HAM B43...73 H1
Abbotsford Dr DUDN DY1....101 G2
Abbotsford Rd SPARK B11....145 E1
Abbots Ms BRLYHL DY5......119 F3

Abbots Rd
ALE/KHTH/YWD B14....161 E3
Abbots Wy BDMR/CCFT WV3....36 A4
WSNGN B18......108 B3
Abbotts Pl BLOX/PEL WS3...27 H1
Abbotts Rd ERDE/BCHGN B24....92 D5
Abbotts St BLOX/PEL WS3....17 F5
Abdon Av SLYOAK B29.....158 D3
Aberdeen St WSNGN B18....107 G5
Aberford Cl SHHTH WV12....40 B1
Abigails Cl
LGN/SDN/BHAMAIR B26...130 D5
Abingdon Cl WOLV WV1......38 B3
Abingdon Rd BLOX/PEL WS3....16 B5
DUDS DY2......120 D1
ERDW/GRVHL B23......75 H5
WOLV WV1......38 B3
Abingdon Wy BLOX/PEL WS3...16 B5
CVALE B35......94 C3
Ablewell St WSL WS1......5 F4
Ablow St BKHL/PFLD WV2......6 E7
Abney Dr BILS/COS WV14......67 F2
Abney Gv BCBHAMNE B4.......3 K3
Acacia Av
CHWD/FDBR/MGN B37....113 H3
DSYBK/YTR WS5......57 G4
Acacia Cl
CHWD/FDBR/MGN B37....113 H3
DUDN DY1......84 A3
OLDBY B69......69 H4
Acacia Crs CDSL WV8......10 D4
Acacia Dr BILS/COS WV14......68 A4
Acacia Rd BVILLE B30......159 G2
Accord Ms DARL/WED WS10...55 F1
Acfold Rd BFLD/HDSWWD B20...89 G1
Acheson Rd HLGN/YWD B28...179 H2
Ackleton Gdns
BDMR/CCFT WV3......51 F1
Ackleton Gv SLYOAK B29....158 B2

Acorn Cl ACGN B27......146 B2
BVILLE B30......159 G2
WBROM B70......87 F4
Acorn Gdns SLYOAK B29....160 A2
Acorn Gv CBHAMW B1......2 A4
CDSL WV8......10 A5
STRBR DY8......118 A3
Acorn Rd RMSLY B62......122 A4
WNSFLD WV11......25 G1
Acorn St WLNHL WV13......40 A3
Acre Ri SHHTH WV12......25 H5
Acres Rd BRLYHL DY5......119 G4
Acton Dr SEDG DY3......82 D3
Acton Gv BILS/COS WV14......55 G1
KGSTG B44......73 G1
Adams Brook Dr
RIDG/WDGT B32......157 F1
Adams Cl SMTHWK B66....105 H2
TPTN/OCK DY4......69 F2
Adam's Hi HAG/WOL DY9...170 C1
RIDG/WDGT B32......157 F1
Adams Rd BDMR/CCFT WV3...50 C1
BRWNH WS8......19 G2
Adams St VAUX/NECH B7......3 J1
WBROM B70......87 E3
WSLW WS2......4 B2
Ada Rd SMTHWK B66......124 D1
YDLY B25......146 D1
Ada Wrighton Cl SHHTH WV12...26 A3
Adcock Dr
SCFLD/BOLD B73......77 F1
Addenbrooke Dr
SCFLD/BOLD B73......77 F1
Addenbrooke Rd
SMTHWKW B67......124 B1
Addenbrooke St
BLOX/PEL WS3......27 G3
DARL/WED WS10......40 B5
Addenbrooke Wy
TPTN/OCK DY4......70 B3
Adderley Gdns
WASH/WDE B8......110 B5

Adderley Park Cl
WASH/WDE B8 *......110 C5
Adderley Rd WASH/WDE B8....128 A1
Adderley Rd South
WASH/WDE B8......128 A1
Adderley St BORD B9......127 G3
Addington Wy OLDBY B69....86 B3
Addison Cl DARL/WED WS10...72 A1
Addison Cft SEDG DY5......82 C1
Addison Gv WNSFLD WV11....24 B1
Addison Pl BILS/COS WV14....54 B1
CSHL/WTROR B46......96 B5
Addison Rd
ALE/KHTH/YWD B14......161 F3
BDMR/CCFT WV3......36 B5
BRLYHL DY5......118 D2
DARL/WED WS10......72 A1
Addison St DARL/WED WS10 *...70 D1
Adelaide Av WBROM B70......71 E4
Adelaide St BHTH/HG B12....127 F4
BRLYHL DY5......119 F1
Adey Rd WNSFLD WV11......25 F2
Adkins La SMTHWKW B67....124 B3
Admington Rd STECH B33....131 E4
Admiral Pl MOS/BIL B13......144 B3
Admirals Wy
BLKHTH/ROWR B65......121 F2
Adrian Cft MOS/BIL B13......162 A1
Adria Rd SPARK B11......144 C5
Adshead Rd DUDS DY2......102 C2
Adstone Gv NFLD/LBR B31....144 C1
Advent Gdns WBROM B70 *...87 F3
Adwalton Rd
DUNHL/THL/PER WV6......34 D2
Agenoria Dr STRBR DY8......135 F2
Ainsdale Cl STRBR DY8......135 F5
Ainsdale Gdns HALE B63....137 H5

Ainsworth Rd WOLVN WV10....13 E3
Aintree Gv BKDE/SHDE B34...113 F5
Aintree Rd WOLVN WV10......12 D5
Aintree Wy DUDN DY1......83 G4
Aire Cft NFLD/LBR B31......175 H4
Airfield Dr ALDR WS9......43 G2
Airport Wy HIA/OLT B92......149 G4
Akrill Cl WBROM B70 *......87 F1
The Akrill Cottage Homes
WBROM B70 *......87 F1
Alamein Rd WLNHL WV13......39 E4
Albany Crs BILS/COS WV14....53 G2
Albany Gdns SOLH B91......182 D3
Albany Gv KGSWFD DY6......100 A2
WNSFLD WV11......26 A1
Albany Rd HRBN B17......142 A1
DUNHL/THL/PER WV6......92 B3
HALE B65......138 B5
HDSW B21......89 G5
HRBN B17......141 H2
LGLGYN/QTN B68......123 G4
STETCH B33......129 H1
Albert Cl BRLYHL DY5......101 F2
DARL/WED WS10......70 C1
DIG/EDG B5......J4
HAG/WOL DY9......136 C2
KGSWFD DY6......99 F1
OLDBY B69......105 E1
STRBR DY8......135 F2
TPTN/OCK DY4......69 G3

WBROM B70 87 G5
WSLW WS2 4 E2
Albert St East OLDBY B69 105 F2
Albion Av WLNHL WV13 40 A3
Albion Field Dr
HHTH/SAND B71 87 H2
Albion Industrial Est
WBROM B70 86 D4
Albion Rd BRWNH WS8 9 E4
HDSW B21 89 F5
HHTH/SAND B71 106 C1
SPARK B11 145 F2
WBROM B70 86 D4
Albion St BILS/COS WV14 54 A2
BRLYHL DY5 119 F1
CBHAMW B1 2 B3
KGSWFD DY6 99 F1
OLDBY B69 86 C5
TPTN/OCK DY4 85 F1
WLNHL WV13 39 H3
WOLV WV1 7 H4
Alborn Crs HWK/WKHTH B38 176 B5
Albrighton Rd HALE B63 138 A4
Albright Rd LGLYGN/QTN B68 105 H5
Albury Wk SPARK B11 127 G5
Albutts Rd CNCK/NC WS11 8 B1
Alcester Dr SCFLD/BOLD B73 61 F5
WLNHL WV13 38 D5
Alcester Rd HLYWD B47 192 B4
MOS/BIL B13 144 B4
Alcester Rd South
ALE/KHTH/YWD B14 178 B4
Alcester St BHTH/HG B12 127 F4
Alcombe Gv STETCH B33 130 A2
Alcott Cl DOR/KN B93 198 D1
Alcott Gv STETCH B33 131 F1
Alcott La
CHWD/FDBR/MGN B37 131 H4
The Alcove BLOX/PEL WS3 17 F5
Aldbourne Wy
HWK/WKHTH B38 190 B1
Aldbury Rd
ALE/KHTH/YWD B14 178 C3
Aldeburgh Cl BLOX/PEL WS3 16 C4
Aldeford Dr BRLYHL DY5 119 F4
Alderbrook Cl SEDG DY3 66 D2
Alderbrook Rd SOLH B91 181 F2
Alder Cl HLYWD B47 192 D2
WALM/CURD B76 78 A4
Alder Coppice SEDG DY3 52 A5
Alder Crs DSYBK/YTR WS5 57 H4
Alder Dl BDMR/CCFT WV3 36 A4
Alderdale Av SEDG DY3 52 A5
Alderdale Crs HIA/OLT B92 165 G3
Alder Dr
CHWD/FDBR/MGN B37 132 B3
Alderflat Pl VAUX/NECH B7 110 A4
Alderford Cl CDSL WV8 22 B2
Alder Gv RMSLY B62 139 G1
Alderham Cl SOLH B91 182 C1
Alderhithe Gv
FOAKS/STRLY B74 45 H2
Alder La BVILLE B30 159 E4
Alderlea Cl STRBR DY8 135 G5
Alderley Crs BLOX/PEL WS3 28 A5
Alderminster Rd SOLH B91 181 H4
Aldermore Dr MGN/WHC B75 * 63 F2
Alderney Gdns
HWK/WKHTH B38 176 B4
Alder Park Rd SOLH B91 181 F3
Alderpits Rd BKDE/SHDE B34 113 F3
Alder Rd DARL/WED WS10 56 A2
KGSWFD DY6 100 C4
MOS/BIL B13 144 C3
Aldersea Dr AST/WIT B6 109 F2
Aldershaw Rd
LGN/SDN/BHAMAIR B26 147 E2
Aldershaws SHLY B90 194 A3
Aldersley Av
DUNHL/THL/PER WV6 22 A3
Aldersley Cl
DUNHL/THL/PER WV6 22 B3
Aldersley Rd
DUNHL/THL/PER WV6 22 B5
Aldersmead Rd NFLD/LBR B31 176 A4
Alderson Rd WASH/WDE B8 110 D5
The Alders RMSLY B62 172 B1
Alderton Cl SOLH B91 181 H4
Alderton Dr BDMR/CCFT WV3 36 A5
Alder Wy FOAKS/STRLY B74 45 E5
Alderwood Pl SOLH B91 181 H2
Alderwood Ri SEDG DY3 83 F1
Aldgate Dr BRLYHL DY5 119 E5
Aldgate Gv LOZ/NWT B19 108 D4
Aldis Cl HLGN/YWD B28 162 C1
WSLW WS2 * 56 A1
Aldis Rd WSLW WS2 56 A1
Aldridge By-Pass ALDR WS9 30 A4
Aldridge Cl LGLYGN/QTN B68 105 G5
STRBR DY8 118 A4
Aldridge Rd ALDR WS9 31 G5
FOAKS/STRLY B74 44 D5
KGSTG B44 74 C1
LGLYGN/QTN B68 123 F4
RUSH/SHEL WS4 42 D2
Aldridge St DARL/WED WS10 55 F1
Aldwych Cl ALDR WS9 30 B2
Aldwyck Dr BDMR/CCFT WV3 35 E5
Alexander Gdns
PBAR/PBCH B42 90 D3
Alexander Hl BRLYHL DY5 119 H4
Alexander Rd ACGN B27 146 B3
CDSL WV8 11 E4
SMTHWKW B67 124 A2
WSLW WS2 40 D3
Alexander Ter
SMTHWKW B67 * 106 B3
Alexander Wy WASH/WDE B8 128 D1
Alexandra Av HDSW B21 107 F2
Alexandra Crs HHTH/SAND B71 72 A3
Alexandra Pl BILS/COS WV14 53 H2
Alexandra Rd BVILLE B30 160 A3
DARL/WED WS10 55 G2
DIG/EDG B5 144 A1
ETTPK/GDPK/PENN WV4 51 G3
HALE B63 138 B4
HDSW B21 107 F2
TPTN/OCK DY4 85 G1
WSL WS1 57 E3
Alexandra St BDMR/CCFT WV3 6 D5
DUDN DY1 84 B5
Alexandra Wy ALDR WS9 30 B5
OLDBY B69 85 G4
Alford Cl RBRY B45 188 C1
Alfreda Av HLYWD B47 178 B5
Alfred Rd HDSW B21 107 G1
SPARK B11 144 D2
Alfred St ALE/KHTH/YWD B14 161 F3
AST/WIT B6 109 H1
BHTH/HG B12 144 D2
BLOX/PEL WS3 27 F1
DARL/WED WS10 55 E3
SMTHWK B66 106 D2
WBROM B70 87 H2
Algernon Rd
LDYWD/EDGR B16 107 F5
Alice St BILS/COS WV14 53 H2
Alison Cl TPTN/OCK DY4 69 G1
Alison Dr STRBR DY8 135 E5
Alison Rd RMSLY B62 139 G4
Allan Cl STRBR DY8 118 B3
Allbut St CDYHTH B64 120 D3
Allcock St BORD B9 127 G3
TPTN/OCK DY4 70 A3
Allcroft Rd SPARK B11 145 H5
Allenby Cl KGSWFD DY6 100 C4
Allen Cl GTB/HAM B43 73 G4
Allendale Gv GTB/HAM B43 73 G3
Allendale Rd WALM/CURD B76 78 A3
YDLY B25 129 F5
Allen Dr DARL/WED WS10 55 E2
WBROM B70 88 B5
Allen Rd DARL/WED WS10 55 H3
TPTN/OCK DY4 69 F2
Allens Av WSNGN B18 * 107 H3
Allens Cl SHHTH WV12 25 H5
Allens Croft Rd
ALE/KHTH/YWD B14 160 B5
Allens Farm Rd NFLD/LBR B31 174 D2
Allens La BLOX/PEL WS3 17 H5
Allens Rd WSNGN B18 107 H3
Allen St WBROM B70 87 F3
Allerdale Rd BRWNH WS8 19 E1
Allerton La HHTH/SAND B71 71 G3
Allerton Rd YDLY B25 129 F5
Allesley Cl FOAKS/STRLY B74 62 C1
Allesley Rd HIA/OLT B92 163 H2
Allesley St AST/WIT B6 109 E4
Alleston Rd WOLVN WV10 23 F1
Alleyne Gv ERDE/BCHGN B24 93 E4
Alleyne Rd ERDE/BCHGN B24 93 E5
The Alley SEDG DY3 82 D3
Allingham Gv GTB/HAM B43 59 H4
Allington Cl DSYBK/YTR WS5 43 F5
Allison St DIG/EDG B5 3 J6
Allman Rd ERDE/BCHGN B24 93 F2
Allmyn Dr FOAKS/STRLY B74 60 C2
All Saints Dr FOAKS/STRLY B74 46 D3
All Saints Rd
ALE/KHTH/YWD B14 161 E3
BKHL/PFLD WV2 7 J7
DARL/WED WS10 55 G2
WSNGN B18 108 B4
All Saints' St WSNGN B18 108 A4
All Saints Wy HHTH/SAND B71 87 H1
Allsops Cl BLKHTH/ROWR B65 103 F5
Allwell Dr ALE/KHTH/YWD B14 178 B3
Allwood Gdns
RIDG/WDGT B32 140 A5
Alma Av TPTN/OCK DY4 69 G4
Alma Crs VAUX/NECH B7 109 H5
Alma Pl DUDS DY2 84 C5
Alma St DARL/WED WS10 55 E2
HALE B63 137 G2
LOZ/NWT B19 109 E3
SMTHWK B66 107 E3
WLNHL WV13 39 H3
WOLVN WV10 37 H2
WSLW WS2 41 H1
Alma Wy LOZ/NWT B19 108 D2
Almond Av DSYBK/YTR WS5 57 G4
WSLW WS2 40 C1
Almond Cl BLOX/PEL WS3 17 H5
SLYOAK B29 158 C4
Almond Cft PBAR/PBCH B42 73 H5
Almond Gv
DUNHL/THL/PER WV6 37 E1
Almond Rd KGSWFD DY6 100 A1
Alnwick Rd BLOX/PEL WS3 16 C3
Alperton Dr HAG/WOL DY9 136 C5
Alpha Cl BHTH/HG B12 144 A1
Alpine Dr DUDS DY2 102 B5
Alpine Wy BDMR/CCFT WV3 35 G3
Alport Cft BORD B9 127 H2
Alston Cl FOAKS/STRLY B74 47 E3
SOLH B91 165 F4
Alston Gv BORD B9 129 F1
Alston Rd BORD B9 129 F1
OLDBY B69 104 C2
SOLH B91 165 F4
Alston St LDYWD/EDGR B16 125 H2
Althorpe Dr DOR/KN B93 196 B5
Alton Av SHHTH WV12 25 H5
Alton Cl WOLVN WV10 13 E4
Alton Cottages
ETTPK/GDPK/PENN WV4 * 66 B2
Alton Gv DUDS DY2 85 E5
HHTH/SAND B71 72 A4
Alton Rd SLYOAK B29 142 D4
Alum Dr BORD B9 129 E1
Alumhurst Av WASH/WDE B8 111 F5
Alum Rock Rd WASH/WDE B8 110 B4
Alumwell Cl WSLW WS2 * 41 F4
Alum Well Rd WSLW WS2 41 F4
Alvaston Cl BLOX/PEL WS3 17 E4
Alvechurch Hwy BRGRVE B60 187 E5
Alvechurch Rd HALE B63 138 B5
NFLD/LBR B31 189 H1
Alverley Cl KGSWFD DY6 99 F1
Alverstoke Cl COVEN WV9 11 H5
Alveston Gv BORD B9 129 F2
DOR/KN B93 197 F1
Alveston Rd HLYWD B47 192 C1
Alvin Cl RMSLY B62 122 D4
Alvington Cl SHHTH WV12 40 B1
Alwen St STRBR DY8 118 B3
Alwin Rd BLKHTH/ROWR B65 121 H2
Alwold Rd SLYOAK B29 141 G5
Amanda Av
ETTPK/GDPK/PENN WV4 51 F4
Amanda Dr LGN/SDN/BHAMAIR B26
130 B3
Ambassador Rd LGN/SDN/BHAMAIR
B26 149 G3
Amber Dr OLDBY B69 * 105 E4
Ambergate Cl BLOX/PEL WS3 17 E4
Ambergate Dr KGSWFD DY6 99 G1
Amberley Gn GTB/HAM B43 73 G5
Amberley Gv AST/WIT B6 91 G3
Amberley Rd HIA/OLT B92 147 F4
Amberley Wy FOAKS/STRLY B74 45 E4
Amber Wy RMSLY B62 138 D1
Amberwood Cl WSLW WS2 40 B2
Amblecote Av KGSTG B44 75 E1
Amblecote Rd BRLYHL DY5 119 F4
Ambleside RIDG/WDGT B32 157 G1
Ambleside Cl BILS/COS WV14 54 A4
Ambleside Dr BRLYHL DY5 119 E4
Ambleside Gv SHHTH WV12 25 H1
Ambleside Wy KGSWFD DY6 99 H3
Ambrose Cl WLNHL WV13 39 E3
Ambrose Crs KGSWFD DY6 99 H1
Ambury Wy GTB/HAM B43 73 F3
Amelas Cl BRLYHL DY5 118 C4
Amersham Cl RIDG/WDGT B32 141 E2
Amesbury Rd MOS/BIL B13 144 A4
Ames Rd DARL/WED WS10 55 E1
Amherst Av
BFLD/HDSWWD B20 90 A3
Amington Cl MGN/WHC B75 47 H2
Amington Rd SHLY B90 180 A5
YDLY B25 146 B1
Amiss Gdns SMHTH B10 128 A4
Amity Cl SMTHWK B66 * 106 D4
Amos Av WNSFLD WV11 24 B3
Amos La WNSFLD WV11 24 C4
Amos Rd HAG/WOL DY9 136 D5
Amphlett Cft TPTN/OCK DY4 85 H2
Amphletts Cl DUDS DY2 121 E1
Ampleforth Dr WLNHL WV13 39 H5
Ampton Rd EDG B15 126 B5
Amroth Cl RBRY B45 188 B1
Amwell Gv
ALE/KHTH/YWD B14 178 B2
Anchorage Rd
ERDW/GRVHL B23 92 B3
FOAKS/STRLY B74 62 B2
Anchor Cl LDYWD/EDGR B16 125 G3
Anchor Crs WSNGN B18 107 H4
Anchor Dr TPTN/OCK DY4 85 G3
Anchor Hl BRLYHL DY5 119 E3
Anchor La BILS/COS WV14 68 B1
SOLH B91 165 F4
Anchor Rd ALDR WS9 30 B4
BILS/COS WV14 68 C1
Andersleigh Dr BILS/COS WV14 68 A3
Anderson Crs GTB/HAM B43 73 G1
Anderson Rd ERDW/GRVHL B23 76 C5
SMTHWK B66 124 C3
TPTN/OCK DY4 85 G1
Anderton Cl FOAKS/STRLY B74 62 A1
Anderton Park Rd
MOS/BIL B13 144 C4
Anderton Rd SPARK B11 145 E1
Anderton St CBHAMW B1 2 A4
Andover Crs KGSWFD DY6 100 B5
Andover St DIG/EDG B5 3 K5
Andrew Cl SHHTH WV12 26 B4
Andrew Dr SHHTH WV12 26 B4
Andrew Gdns HDSW B21 89 G5
Andrew Rd HALE B63 138 C4
HHTH/SAND B71 72 B1
TPTN/OCK DY4 69 G2
Andrews Cl BRLYHL DY5 119 G4
Andrews Rd ALDR WS9 19 H3
Anerley Gv KGSTG B44 60 B4
Anerley Rd KGSTG B44 60 B4
Angela Av BLKHTH/ROWR B65 104 B5
Angela Pl BILS/COS WV14 53 H2
Angelica Cl DSYBK/YTR WS5 57 G5
Angelina St BHTH/HG B12 127 F5
Angel Pas STRBR DY8 135 G2
Angel St DUDN DY1 102 B1
Anglesey Av CBROM B36 114 B3
Anglesey Crs BRWNH WS8 9 F2
Anglesey Rd BRWNH WS8 9 F2
Anglesey St LOZ/NWT B19 108 C2
Anglian Rd ALDR WS9 29 F4
Angus Cl HHTH/SAND B71 71 G5
Anita Av TPTN/OCK DY4 85 G4
Anita Cft ERDW/GRVHL B23 92 C4
Ankadine Rd STRBR DY8 135 H1
Ankerdine Ct HALE B63 138 C4
Ankermoor Cl
BKDE/SHDE B34 112 D3
Annan Av WOLVN WV10 23 G3
Ann Cft
LGN/SDN/BHAMAIR B26 148 B3
Anne Cl WBROM B70 86 C3
Anne Gv TPTN/OCK DY4 69 H2
Anne Rd BRLYHL DY5 120 A3
ETTPK/GDPK/PENN WV4 51 H3
SMTHWK B66 107 E2
Ann Rd HLYWD B47 192 C5
Annscroft HWK/WKHTH B38 176 B3
Ann St WLNHL WV13 39 H2
Ansbro Cl WSNGN B18 107 H4
Ansculf Rd BRLYHL DY5 118 D3
Ansell Rd ERDE/BCHGN B24 92 D5
SPARK B11 145 E1
Anslow Gdns WNSFLD WV11 25 F1
Anslow Rd ERDW/GRVHL B23 92 A1
Anson Cl DUNHL/THL/PER WV6 20 C5
Anson Gv ACGN B27 146 D5
Anson Rd WBROM B70 70 C4
WSLW WS2 40 C3
Anstey Cft
CHWD/FDBR/MGN B37 * 114 A5
Anstey Gv ACGN B27 163 F1
Anstey Rd KGSTG B44 75 E5
Anston Wy WNSFLD WV11 24 D3
Anstruther Rd EDG B15 125 G5
Anthony Rd WASH/WDE B8 128 C1
Anton Dr WALM/CURD B76 78 C5
Antony Rd SHLY B90 180 B4
Antringham Gdns EDG B15 125 F4
Antrobus Rd HDSW B21 89 G5
SCFLD/BOLD B73 76 C2
Anvil Crs BILS/COS WV14 68 C1
Anvil Dr OLDBY B69 104 C3
Apex Rd BRWNH WS8 8 C5
Apley Rd STRBR DY8 118 A5
Apollo Cft ERDE/BCHGN B24 93 H3
Apollo Rd HAG/WOL DY9 137 E2
LGLYGN/QTN B68 105 G3
Apollo Wy BFLD/HDSWWD B20 90 C5
Apperley Wy HALE B63 120 B5
Appian Cl ALE/KHTH/YWD B14 161 E5
Appian Wy SHLY B90 194 D4
Appleby Cl ALE/KHTH/YWD B14 160 D5
Appleby Gdns WNSFLD WV11 15 G5
Appleby Gv SHLY B90 195 H2
Applecross FOAKS/STRLY B74 46 D4
Appledore Rd DSYBK/YTR WS5 43 F5
Appledorne Gdns
BKDE/SHDE B34 112 D3
Applesham Cl SPARK B11 145 F1
Appleton Av GTB/HAM B43 73 G3
STRBR DY8 135 G5
Appleton Cl BVILLE B30 159 G2
Appleton Crs
ETTPK/GDPK/PENN WV4 51 G3
Apple Tree Cl ERDW/GRVHL B23 91 H2
Appletree Cl NFLD/LBR B31 175 E4
SOLH B91 166 B5
Appletree Gv ALDR WS9 30 B5
DUNHL/THL/PER WV6 23 E5
Applewood Gv CDYHTH B64 121 F4
April Cft MOS/BIL B13 144 D5
Apse Cl WMBN WV5 64 D4
Apsley Cl LGLYGN/QTN B68 123 E5
Apsley Gv DOR/KN B93 198 D1
ERDE/BCHGN B24 93 E4
Apsley Rd LGLYGN/QTN B68 123 E5
Aqueduct Rd SHLY B90 179 G3
Aragon Dr SCFLD/BOLD B73 62 A2
Arboretum Rd WSL WS1 5 G2
Arbor Ga ALDR WS9 19 H3
Arbor Wy
CHWD/FDBR/MGN B37 132 C3
Arbury Dr STRBR DY8 117 H1
Arbury Hall Rd SHLY B90 180 D5
Arcal St SEDG DY3 67 G4
Archer Cl DARL/WED WS10 55 G5
LGLYGN/QTN B68 * 105 F5
Archer Ct HAG/WOL DY9 136 C5
Archer Gdns CDYHTH B64 120 C3
Archer Rd
ALE/KHTH/YWD B14 179 E1
BLOX/PEL WS3 28 A4
Archers Cl ERDW/GRVHL B23 76 A3
Archer Wy BLKHTH/ROWR B65 122 B3
The Arches SMHTH B10 * 127 H4
Arch Hill St DUDS DY2 102 C4
Archibald Rd LOZ/NWT B19 108 C1
Arcot Rd HLGN/YWD B28 145 H5
Ardath Rd HWK/WKHTH B38 177 E3
Ardav Rd WBROM B70 70 D3
Arden Buildings DOR/KN B93 196 D5
Arden Cl STRBR DY8 135 E1
Ardencote Rd MOS/BIL B13 161 G4
Arden Ct HIA/OLT B92 * 167 G3
Arden Cft CSHL/WTROR B46 97 F5
HIA/OLT B92 148 A3
Arden Dr DOR/KN B93 198 D1
LGN/SDN/BHAMAIR B26 130 B5
MGN/WHC B75 63 H3
SCFLD/BOLD B73 77 F3
Arden Gv LDYWD/EDGR B16 126 A3
OLDBY B69 105 E4
Ardenleigh Wy
ERDE/BCHGN B24 93 E4
Arden Meads HOCK/TIA B94 198 A5
Arden Oak Rd
LGN/SDN/BHAMAIR B26 148 B2
Arden Pl BILS/COS WV14 54 D4
Arden Rd ACGN B27 146 B3
AST/WIT B6 108 D1
DOR/KN B93 198 D1
HLYWD B47 192 C2
RBRY B45 174 A4
SMTHWKW B67 106 C5
WASH/WDE B8 128 B1
Arden Vale Rd DOR/KN B93 197 F1
Arderne Dr
CHWD/FDBR/MGN B37 132 A3
Ardgowan Gv
ETTPK/GDPK/PENN WV4 52 D3
Ardingley Wk BRLYHL DY5 118 D5
Ardley Cl DUDS DY2 102 D1
Ardley Rd ALE/KHTH/YWD B14 161 G5
Aretha Cl KGSWFD DY6 100 C3
Argil Cl WOLVN WV10 24 A2
Argus Cl WALM/CURD B76 63 F5
Argyle Cl RUSH/SHEL WS4 5 K1
STRBR DY8 118 A3
Argyle Rd BKHL/PFLD WV2 51 H2
RUSH/SHEL WS4 5 K1
Argyle St VAUX/NECH B7 110 A1
Arkle Cft BLKHTH/ROWR B65 103 F3
CBROM B36 111 G1
Arkley Gv HLGN/YWD B28 163 F3
Arkley Rd HLGN/YWD B28 163 F3
Arkwright Rd RIDG/WDGT B32 140 C2
WSLW WS2 27 F5
Arlen Dr GTB/HAM B43 73 F2
Arlescote Cl MGN/WHC B75 47 G3
Arlescote Rd HIA/OLT B92 148 A5
Arleston Wy SHLY B90 181 E5
Arley Cl OLDBY B69 104 B4
Arley Dr STRBR DY8 135 E4
Arley Gv
ETTPK/GDPK/PENN WV4 50 D3
Arley Rd SLYOAK B29 142 D4
SOLH B91 181 G1
WASH/WDE B8 110 B3
Arley Vls WSNGN B18 * 107 F5
Arlidge Cl BILS/COS WV14 53 H4
Arlington Cl KGSWFD DY6 99 H5
Arlington Ct STRBR DY8 135 H3
Arlington Gdns STRBR DY8 * 135 H3
Arlington Gv
ALE/KHTH/YWD B14 178 D3
Arlington Rd
ALE/KHTH/YWD B14 178 D2
HHTH/SAND B71 71 H5
Armada Cl ERDW/GRVHL B23 92 B5
Armoury Rd SPARK B11 145 G1
Armside Cl BLOX/PEL WS3 18 B3
Armstead Rd COVEN WV9 12 A4
Armstrong Cl STRBR DY8 135 H1
Armstrong Dr CBROM B36 95 H5
DUNHL/THL/PER WV6 22 C4
WSLW WS2 41 E1
Armstrong Wy WLNHL WV13 39 H5
Arnhem Cl WNSFLD WV11 24 B2
Arnhem Rd WLNHL WV13 39 E5
Arnhem Wy TPTN/OCK DY4 86 A1
Arnold Cl WSLW WS2 40 D2
Arnold Gv BVILLE B30 176 B1
SHLY B90 180 B1
Arnold Rd SHLY B90 180 C1
Arnwood Cl WSLW WS2 40 D3
Arosa Dr HRBN B17 141 H4
Arps Rd CDSL WV8 10 B4
Arran Cl GTB/HAM B43 58 C5
Arran Rd BKDE/SHDE B34 112 B3
Arran Wy CBROM B36 114 A2
Arras Rd DUDN DY1 85 E4
Arrow Cl DOR/KN B93 197 E2
Arrowfield Gn
HWK/WKHTH B38 190 B1
Arrow Rd BLOX/PEL WS3 28 A4
Arrow Wk HWK/WKHTH B38 177 F4
Arsenal St BORD B9 128 A3
Arter St BHTH/HG B12 144 B1
Arthur Gunby Cl
MGN/WHC B75 * 63 F1
Arthur Harris Cl SMTHWK B66 124 D1
Arthur Pl CBHAMW B1 2 B4
Arthur Rd EDG B15 143 F1
ERDE/BCHGN B24 93 F2
HDSW B21 107 H1
TPTN/OCK DY4 69 G5
YDLY B25 146 A1
Arthur St BILS/COS WV14 * 53 H2
BKHL/PFLD WV2 52 B2
SMHTH B10 127 H3
WBROM B70 87 H5
Artillery St BORD B9 127 H2
Arton Cft ERDE/BCHGN B24 92 D4
Arundel Av DARL/WED WS10 55 H5
Arundel Crs HIA/OLT B92 164 C1
Arundel Dr OLDBY B69 103 F1
Arundel Gv
DUNHL/THL/PER WV6 35 E2
Arundel Pl SPARK B11 144 C1
Arundel Rd
ALE/KHTH/YWD B14 178 C4
SHHTH WV12 26 A3
STRBR DY8 117 G2
WOLVN WV10 12 B5
Arundel St WSL WS1 57 E1
Arun Wy WALM/CURD B76 78 C2
Asbury Rd DARL/WED WS10 72 A1
Ascot Cl LDYWD/EDGR B16 125 H2
OLDBY B69 104 C3
Ascot Dr DUDN DY1 83 H4
ETTPK/GDPK/PENN WV4 51 G4
Ascote La SHLY B90 194 A3
Ascot Gdns STRBR DY8 117 H2
Ascot Rd MOS/BIL B13 144 B5
Ash Av BHTH/HG B12 144 C2
Ashborough Dr SOLH B91 195 H1
Ashbourne Gv AST/WIT B6 * 109 E1
Ashbourne Rdg HALE B63 137 H2
Ashbourne Rd BLOX/PEL WS3 17 E4
ETTPK/GDPK/PENN WV4 52 C5
LDYWD/EDGR B16 125 F1
WOLV WV1 38 A2
Ashbourne Wy SHLY B90 180 D5
Ashbridge Ct RBRY B45 188 B2
Ashbrook Crs SOLH B91 182 A5
Ashbrook Dr RBRY B45 174 B5
Ashbrook Gv BVILLE B30 160 C2
Ashbrook Rd BVILLE B30 160 C2
Ashburn Gv WLNHL WV13 40 A3
Ashburton Rd
ALE/KHTH/YWD B14 160 D5
Ashbury Covert BVILLE B30 177 G2
Ashby Cl WASH/WDE B8 111 G3
Ashby Ct SOLH B91 182 A4
Ash Cl CDSL WV8 10 C4
Ashcombe Av
BFLD/HDSWWD B20 89 G3
Ashcombe Gdns
ERDE/BCHGN B24 93 H3
Ashcott Cl HWK/WKHTH B38 176 B3
Ash Crs
CHWD/FDBR/MGN B37 113 H3
KGSWFD DY6 100 A3
Ashcroft SMTHWK B66 * 107 E4
TPTN/OCK DY4 * 85 G4
Ashcroft Gv
BFLD/HDSWWD B20 90 D4
Ashdale Cl KGSWFD DY6 99 H1
Ashdale Dr
ALE/KHTH/YWD B14 178 C4
Ashdale Gv
LGN/SDN/BHAMAIR B26 130 C4
Ashdene Cl SCFLD/BOLD B73 62 A5
Ashdene Gdns STRBR DY8 117 G2
Ashdown Cl MOS/BIL B13 161 G1
RBRY B45 174 A3
Ashdown Dr STRBR DY8 118 A1
Ash Dr HHTH/SAND B71 71 G5
NFLD/LBR B31 174 C4
Ashen Cl SEDG DY3 52 A5
Ashenden Ri BDMR/CCFT WV3 35 E4
Ashenhurst Rd DUDN DY1 101 H1
Ashes Rd OLDBY B69 104 D5
Ashfern Dr WALM/CURD B76 78 B4
Ashfield Av
ALE/KHTH/YWD B14 161 F1
Ashfield Cl BLOX/PEL WS3 42 A1
Ashfield Crs DUDS DY2 120 C1
HAG/WOL DY9 136 D4
Ashfield Gv HALE B63 138 A5
WOLVN WV10 12 C4
Ashfield Rd
ALE/KHTH/YWD B14 161 F1
BDMR/CCFT WV3 35 H3
BILS/COS WV14 54 C5
WOLVN WV10 12 C4
Ashford Cl ERDE/BCHGN B24 93 H2
Ashford Dr SEDG DY3 67 G4
WALM/CURD B76 94 A1
Ashfurlong Crs MGN/WHC B75 63 E1
Ash Gn DUDN DY1 84 A1
Ash Gv BORD B9 * 127 H2

HAG/WOL DY9 136 B4
SEDG DY3 83 E4
Ashgrove Rd KGSTG B44 74 C1
Ash Hl BDMR/CCFT WV3 35 H4
Ashill Rd RBRY B45 188 B1
Ashland St BDMR/CCFT WV3 6 C6
Ashlawn Crs SOLH B91 163 H5
Ashleigh Dr
BFLD/HDSWWD B20 90 B4
Ashleigh Gv MOS/BIL B13 161 H1
Ashleigh Rd OLDBY B69 104 A1
SOLH B91 181 H1
Ashley Cl EDG B15 126 C5
KGSWFD DY6 99 G5
STRBR DY8 134 D5
Ashley Gdns CDSL WV8 10 B3
WASH/WDE B8 110 B5
Ashley Mt
DUNHL/THL/PER WV6 21 H5
Ashley Rd BLOX/PEL WS3 26 D1
ERDW/GRVHL B23 92 C3
ETTPK/GDPK/PENN WV4 51 E3
SMTHWK B66 107 E5
Ashley St BILS/COS WV14 54 A2
BLKHTH/ROWR B65 122 A3
Ashley Ter SLYOAK B29 * 159 G1
Ashmead Dr RBRY B45 188 C4
Ashmead Gv ERDE/BCHGN B24 93 E4
Ashmead Ri RBRY B45 188 C4
Ash Ms ACGN B27 146 C2
Ashmole Rd WBROM B70 70 D4
Ashmore Av WNSFLD WV11 25 G1
Ashmore Lake Rd SHHTH WV12 39 H1
Ashmore Lake Wy
SHHTH WV12 39 H1
Ashmore Rd BVILLE B30 159 H5
Ashold Farm Rd
ERDE/BCHGN B24 93 G4
Asholme Cl CBROM B36 111 G2
Ashorne Cl HLGN/YWD B28 163 F3
Ash Rd DARL/WED WS10 55 H3
DUDN DY1 84 B3
TPTN/OCK DY4 85 E2
WASH/WDE B8 110 B5
Ashstead Cl WALM/CURD B76 78 D5
Ash St BDMR/CCFT WV3 6 B5
BILS/COS WV14 54 A5
BLOX/PEL WS3 27 H1
CDYHTH B64 121 E2
Ashted Circ CBHAMNE B4 109 G5
Ash Ter OLDBY B69 85 H5
Ashton Cft LDYWD/EDGR B16 126 A2
SOLH B91 181 G4
Ashton Dr RUSH/SHEL WS4 18 C4
Ashton Park Dr BRLYHL DY5 119 E3
Ashton Rd YDLY B25 129 F5
Ashtree Cl BRLYHL DY5 118 C4
Ash Tree Dr YDLY B25 129 H5
Ashtree Gv BILS/COS WV14 54 D5
Ashtree Rd BLOX/PEL WS3 18 A4
Ash Tree Rd BVILLE B30 160 A4
Ashtree Rd OLDBY B69 104 B1
Ashurst Rd WALM/CURD B76 78 B5
Ashville Av BKDE/SHDE B34 112 B2
Ashville Dr HALE B63 138 C2
Ashwater Dr
ALE/KHTH/YWD B14 177 H3
Ash Wy ERDW/GRVHL B23 76 A3
SPARK B11 144 D2
Ashwell Dr SHLY B90 180 D1
Ashwells Gv COVEN WV9 11 H5
Ashwin Rd HDSW B21 107 H2
Ashwood Av STRBR DY8 117 G2
Ashwood Cl FOAKS/STRLY B74 45 E5
OLDBY B69 104 D5
Ashwood Dr
CHWD/FDBR/MGN B37 132 D1
Ashwood Gv
ETTPK/GDPK/PENN WV4 51 G3
Ashwood Lower La
KGSWFD DY6 98 C4
KINVER DY7 116 D1
Ashworth Rd PBAR/PBCH B42 74 B2
Askew Bridge Rd SEDG DY3 * 82 D3
Askew Cl SEDG DY3 83 G1
Aspbury Cft CBROM B36 95 F5
Aspen Cl ACGN B27 146 B5
WALM/CURD B76 78 B1
Aspen Dr
CHWD/FDBR/MGN B37 132 C4
Aspen Gdns
BFLD/HDSWWD B20 90 B5
Aspen Gv BORD B9 129 E1
HLYWD B47 192 D3
SHHTH WV12 26 C3
Aspen Wy BDMR/CCFT WV3 6 A6
Asquith Dr OLDBY B69 86 B4
Asquith Rd WASH/WDE B8 111 F4
Asra Cl SMTHWK B66 106 C1
Astbury Av SMTHWK B67 124 B1
Astbury Cl BLOX/PEL WS3 16 C3
WOLV WV1 38 A4
Aster Wk COVEN WV9 12 A4
Aster Wy DSYBK/YTR WS5 57 G5
Astley Av RMSLY B62 139 H1
Astley Cl TPTN/OCK DY4 70 B5
Astley Rd HDSW B21 89 F5
Aston Brook Gn AST/WIT B6 * 109 F4
Aston Brook St AST/WIT B6 109 E3
Aston Brook St East
AST/WIT B6 109 F4
Aston Bury EDG B15 125 G4
Aston Church Rd
VAUX/NECH B7 110 A2
Aston Cl BILS/COS WV14 54 C4
Aston Hall Rd AST/WIT B6 109 G1
Aston La BFLD/HDSWWD B20 91 E4
Aston Manor Cl
BFLD/HDSWWD B20 91 E4
Aston Rd OLDBY B69 85 G5
VAUX/NECH B7 3 J1
WLNHL WV13 39 E3
Aston Rd North AST/WIT B6 109 F3
Astons Cl BRLYHL DY5 119 F5
Astons Fold BRLYHL DY5 119 F5
Aston St BDMR/CCFT WV3 36 C5
CBHAMNE B4 3 J2
TPTN/OCK DY4 70 A5
Astor Dr MOS/BIL B13 162 A1
Astoria Cl SHHTH WV12 26 B1
Astor Rd FOAKS/STRLY B74 45 G4
KGSWFD DY6 100 B4
Athelney Ct BLOX/PEL WS3 * 18 A4
Athelstan Gv
DUNHL/THL/PER WV6 20 C5
Atherstone Cl SHLY B90 179 G3
Atherstone Rd WOLV WV1 38 B3
Athlone Rd DSYBK/YTR WS5 43 E5
Athol Cl RIDG/WDGT B32 157 H2
Athole St BHTH/HG B12 127 G5
Atlantic Rd KGSTG B44 75 F3
Atlantic Wy DARL/WED WS10 70 C2
Atlas Cft WOLVN WV10 23 E4
Atlas Est AST/WIT B6 * 91 G4
Atlas Gv WBROM B70 86 D3
Attenborough Cl
LOZ/NWT B19 108 D4
Attingham Dr DUDN DY1 84 B4
GTB/HAM B43 73 F1
Attleborough La
CSHL/WTROR B46 96 A5
Attlee Cl OLDBY B69 86 B4
Attlee Crs BILS/COS WV14 69 E1
Attlee Rd WSLW WS2 40 C2
Attwell Pk BDMR/CCFT WV3 50 D1
Attwell Rd TPTN/OCK DY4 69 F2
Attwood Cl WASH/WDE B8 110 C3
Attwood Gdns
ETTPK/GDPK/PENN WV4 52 C3
Attwood St HAG/WOL DY9 136 D2
HALE B63 138 B2
Aubrey Rd RIDG/WDGT B32 124 A5
SMTHH B10 128 D5
Auchinleck Sq EDG B15 * 126 B3
Auckland Dr CBROM B36 113 H1
Auckland Rd KGSWFD DY6 100 A5
SMTHWKW B67 106 A4
SPARK B11 127 G5
Auden Ct DUNHL/THL/PER WV6 34 D1
Audley Rd STETCH B33 112 A5
Augusta Rd ACGN B27 146 C2
MOS/BIL B13 144 A3
Augusta Rd East MOS/BIL B13 144 B3
Augusta St WSNGN B18 2 C1
Augustine Gv FOAKS/STRLY B74 52 D5
WSNGN B18 107 H3
Augustus Cl CSHL/WTROR B46 97 F5
Augustus Ct EDG B15 125 H4
Augustus Rd EDG B15 125 G4
Augustus St WSLW WS2 4 C4
Aulton Rd MGN/WHC B75 48 A3
Ault St WBROM B70 87 H5
Austcliff Dr SOLH B91 182 A5
Austen Pl EDG B15 126 B4
Austin Cl ACGN B27 146 D3
DUDN DY1 83 H4
Austin Cft CBROM B36 95 G5
Austin Ri NFLD/LBR B31 189 F1
Austin Rd HDSW B21 89 E5
Austin St DUNHL/THL/PER WV6 36 D1
Austin Wy BFLD/HDSWWD B20 90 A1
Austrey Cl DOR/KN B93 197 E2
Austrey Gv SLYOAK B29 * 158 C2
Austrey Rd KGSWFD DY6 100 C4
Austy Cl CBROM B36 112 A1
Autherley Jct COVEN WV9 * 22 C1
Autumn Berry Gv SEDG DY3 67 G5
Autumn Cl RUSH/SHEL WS4 18 C5
Autumn Dr RUSH/SHEL WS4 18 C5
SEDG DY3 83 F3
Autumn Gv LOZ/NWT B19 108 C3
Avalon Cl ERDE/BCHGN B24 93 F2
Avebury Gv BVILLE B30 160 C3
Avebury Rd BVILLE B30 160 C2
Ave Maria Cl CDYHTH B64 121 E3
Avenbury Dr SOLH B91 182 C1
Avenue Albert HOCK/TIA B94 198 A4
Avenue Cl DOR/KN B93 197 E5
VAUX/NECH B7 109 G4
Avenue Rd
ALE/KHTH/YWD B14 160 D2
AST/WIT B6 109 G3
BDMR/CCFT WV3 36 A3
BILS/COS WV14 68 C3
BLKHTH/ROWR B65 122 B3
DARL/WED WS10 55 F2
DOR/KN B93 197 E5
DUDN DY1 101 G3
ERDW/GRVHL B23 92 D2
HDSW B21 89 F4
The Avenue ACGN B27 146 D4
BDMR/CCFT WV3 35 F5
BLKHTH/ROWR B65 121 G1
DARL/WED WS10 54 D1
ETTPK/GDPK/PENN WV4 51 E4
KIDD DY10 168 B3
RBRY B45 187 G1
WALM/CURD B76 78 A2
Averill Rd
LGN/SDN/BHAMAIR B26 130 C4
Avern Cl TPTN/OCK DY4 69 H5
Aversley Rd HWK/WKHTH B38 176 B5
Avery Cft CVALE B35 94 B4
Avery Dell BVILLE B30 * 160 B5
Avery Dr ACGN B27 146 C3
Avery Myers Cl
LGLYGN/QTN B68 105 F4
Avery Rd SCFLD/BOLD B73 76 A1
SMTHWK B66 107 F3
Aviemore Crs GTB/HAM B43 59 F4
Avington Cl SEDG DY3 67 F4
Avion Cl WSL WS1 57 F1
Avocet Cl STETCH B33 130 A1
Avon Cl BRLYHL DY5 100 D2
DUNHL/THL/PER WV6 34 D2
Avon Crs BLOX/PEL WS3 28 C1
Avondale Cl KGSWFD DY6 100 A1
Avondale Rd
DUNHL/THL/PER WV6 36 B2
SPARK B11 145 F3
Avon Dr CBROM B36 113 H2
MOS/BIL B13 144 D5
WLNHL WV13 40 A3
Avon Gv DSYBK/YTR WS5 57 G5
Avon Ms STRBR DY8 * 117 G2
Avon Rd BLOX/PEL WS3 28 A1
HALE B63 137 F2
SHLY B90 180 D5
STRBR DY8 135 F4
Avon St SPARK B11 145 E2
Avro Wy CVALE B35 94 D3
Awbridge Br WMBN WV5 64 C1
Awbridge Rd DUDS DY2 120 C1
Awefields Crs SMTHWKW B67 105 H5
Awlmakers Gv BLOX/PEL WS3 27 G3
Axletree Wy DARL/WED WS10 56 B3
Ayala Cft CBROM B36 112 A1
Aylesbury Cl HOCK/TIA B94 198 A5
Aylesbury Crs KGSTG B44 75 G3
Aylesbury Rd HOCK/TIA B94 198 B4
Aylesford Cl SEDG DY3 66 D1
Aylesford Dr
CHWD/FDBR/MGN B37 132 A5
FOAKS/STRLY B74 32 C5
Aylesford Rd HDSW B21 89 F5
Aylesmore Cl HIA/OLT B92 164 A2
RIDG/WDGT B32 157 G1
Ayre Rd ERDE/BCHGN B24 93 F2
Ayres Cl BKDE/SHDE B34 113 G3
Ayrshire Cl CBROM B36 111 H1
Ayrton Cl DUNHL/THL/PER WV6 35 E1
Azalea Cl CDSL WV8 10 D4
Azalea Gv BORD B9 128 D2
Aziz Isaac Cl
LGLYGN/QTN B68 * 105 G3

B

Babington Rd HDSW B21 107 G2
Bablake Cft HIA/OLT B92 164 C1
Babors Fld BILS/COS WV14 53 E5
Babworth Cl COVEN WV9 12 A5
Baccabox La HLYWD B47 192 A1
Bacchus Rd WSNGN B18 107 H3
Bache St WBROM B70 87 G5
Bach Mill Dr HLGN/YWD B28 179 F2
Backhouse La WNSFLD WV11 38 C1
Back La ALDR WS9 31 F3
LICHS WS14 32 B1
SHLY B90 194 A3
Back Rd HWK/WKHTH B38 176 D3
KGSWFD DY6 99 H2
Baddesley Rd HIA/OLT B92 147 E5
Bader Rd DUNHL/THL/PER WV6 34 B2
WSLW WS2 40 D3
Bader Wk CVALE B35 94 B4
Badger Cl SHLY B90 194 D4
Badger Dr WOLVN WV10 37 F1
Badgers Bank Rd
FOAKS/STRLY B74 32 D5
Badgers Cl BLOX/PEL WS3 18 A2
Badgers Cft RMSLY B62 121 H5
Badger St HAG/WOL DY9 136 C1
SEDG DY3 83 G1
Badminton Cl DUDN DY1 83 H3
Badon Covert
ALE/KHTH/YWD B14 177 H3
Badsey Cl NFLD/LBR B31 176 A1
Badsey Rd OLDBY B69 104 B4
Baggeridge Cl SEDG DY3 66 C3
Baggott St BKHL/PFLD WV2 52 A1
Baginton Cl SOLH B91 164 D5
Baginton Rd CVALE B35 94 D2
Bagley St HAG/WOL DY9 136 A1
Bagnall Cl YDLY B25 146 D1
Bagnall Rd BILS/COS WV14 53 G2
Bagnall St BLOX/PEL WS3 27 G3
TPTN/OCK DY4 70 A2
WBROM B70 88 A4
Bagnall Wk BRLYHL DY5 119 F3
Bagnell Rd MOS/BIL B13 161 F3
Bagot St CBHAMNE B4 3 H1
Bagridge Cl BDMR/CCFT WV3 35 F5
Bagridge Rd BDMR/CCFT WV3 35 F5
Bagshawe Cft
ERDW/GRVHL B23 76 B4
Bagshaw Rd STETCH B33 130 A1
Bailey Rd BILS/COS WV14 53 F1
Bailey St WBROM B70 87 E2
WOLVN WV10 7 J3
Baker Av BILS/COS WV14 67 H1
Baker House Gv GTB/HAM B43 73 F4
Baker Rd BILS/COS WV14 54 A5
Bakers Gdns CDSL WV8 10 A3
Baker's La ALDR WS9 30 B4
DOR/KN B93 199 G2
FOAKS/STRLY B74 60 B3
Baker St HDSW B21 107 H1
SMTHH B10 128 B3
SPARK B11 145 E3
TPTN/OCK DY4 85 E2
WBROM B70 87 F3
Bakers Wy CDSL WV8 10 A3
Bakewell Cl BLOX/PEL WS3 17 E4
Balaams Dr NFLD/LBR B31 174 B4
Balaams Wood Dr
NFLD/LBR B31 174 B4
Balaclava Rd
ALE/KHTH/YWD B14 161 E2
Balcaskie Cl EDG B15 125 G5
Balden Rd RIDG/WDGT B32 124 A5
Baldmoor Lake Rd
ERDW/GRVHL B23 76 D4
Bald's La HAG/WOL DY9 136 D2
Baldwin Cl OLDBY B69 86 B4
Baldwin Rd BVILLE B30 177 E2
Baldwins La HLGN/YWD B28 179 H1
Baldwin St BILS/COS WV14 54 B4
SMTHWK B66 106 D3
Baldwin Wy SEDG DY3 80 C4
Balfour Crs
DUNHL/THL/PER WV6 36 B1
Balfour Dr OLDBY B69 86 B4
Balfour Rd KGSWFD DY6 100 A1
Balfour St BHTH/HG B12 144 A1
Balham Gv KGSTG B44 75 G1
Balking Cl BILS/COS WV14 53 F5
Ballarat Wk STRBR DY8 135 F2
Ballard Crs DUDS DY2 102 D4
Ballard Rd DUDS DY2 102 D4
Ballard Wk
CHWD/FDBR/MGN B37 114 A3
Ball Flds TPTN/OCK DY4 86 A1
Ball La WOLVN WV10 12 C1
Ballot St SMTHWK B66 106 D4
Balls Hl WSL WS1 5 G3
Balls St WSL WS1 5 G3
Balmain Crs WNSFLD WV11 24 B2
Balmoral Cl RMSLY B62 121 H5
RUSH/SHEL WS4 29 F3
Balmoral Dr SHHTH WV12 25 H3
WMBN WV5 65 E2
Balmoral Rd CBROM B36 114 A2
ERDW/GRVHL B23 92 D1
ETTPK/GDPK/PENN WV4 51 G3
FOAKS/STRLY B74 32 D5
RIDG/WDGT B32 157 F3
STRBR DY8 117 G2
Balmoral Vw DUDN DY1 83 G4
Balmoral Wy
BLKHTH/ROWR B65 104 B5
WSLW WS2 41 E1
Balsall Heath Rd DIG/EDG B5 127 E5
Baltimore Rd PBAR/PBCH B42 90 A1
Balvenie Wy DUDN DY1 83 H3
Bamber Cl BDMR/CCFT WV3 36 A5
Bamford Cl BLOX/PEL WS3 17 E4
Bamford Rd BDMR/CCFT WV3 36 C5
BLOX/PEL WS3 17 E4
Bampfylde Pl PBAR/PBCH B42 * 74 C4
Bamville Rd WASH/WDE B8 111 E4
Banbery Dr WMBN WV5 80 D2
Banbrook Cl HIA/OLT B92 165 F2
Banbury Cl SEDG DY3 67 G5
Banbury Cft
CHWD/FDBR/MGN B37 131 H2
Banbury St DIG/EDG B5 3 J5
Bancroft Cl BILS/COS WV14 68 B4
Bandywood Rd KGSTG B44 60 A4
Banfield Av DARL/WED WS10 55 E1
Banfield Rd DARL/WED WS10 55 E4
Banford Rd WASH/WDE B8 111 E5
Bangham Pit Rd
NFLD/LBR B31 158 A3
Bangor Rd BORD B9 128 B2
Bangor Vls DARL/WED WS10 * 55 H2
Bankdale Rd WASH/WDE B8 111 F5
Bankes Rd SMTHH B10 128 C3
Bank Farm Cl HAG/WOL DY9 153 E1
Bankfield Rd BILS/COS WV14 53 H3
TPTN/OCK DY4 70 A3
Banklands Rd DUDS DY2 103 E3
Bank Rd DUDS DY2 102 D3
SEDG DY3 83 E3
Bankside GTB/HAM B43 73 G4
MOS/BIL B13 145 F5
WMBN WV5 64 D4
Bankside Crs FOAKS/STRLY B74 60 B1
Bankside Wy ALDR WS9 19 H5
Banks St WLNHL WV13 39 G3
Bank St ALE/KHTH/YWD B14 161 E2
BILS/COS WV14 68 C3
BRLYHL DY5 101 F5
DUDS DY2 120 C3
HAG/WOL DY9 136 D2
HHTH/SAND B71 71 G5
WOLVN WV10 23 G5
WSL WS1 5 G4
Bankwell St BRLYHL DY5 101 F5
Bannerlea Rd
CHWD/FDBR/MGN B37 113 H4
Bannerley Rd STETCH B33 131 F3
Banners Ct SCFLD/BOLD B73 * 60 D5
Banners Gate Rd
SCFLD/BOLD B73 60 D5
Banners Gv ERDW/GRVHL B23 77 E5
Banners La HALE B63 137 H1
Banners St HALE B63 137 H1
Banners Wk KGSTG B44 75 H1
Bannister Rd DARL/WED WS10 70 B1
Bannister St CDYHTH B64 120 D2
Banstead Cl BKHL/PFLD WV2 52 C1
Bantams Cl STETCH B33 131 E2
Bantock Av BDMR/CCFT WV3 36 B5
Bantock Gdns
BDMR/CCFT WV3 36 A4
The Bantocks WBROM B70 71 E5
Bantock Wy HRBN B17 142 B2
Banton Cl ERDW/GRVHL B23 76 B3
Bantry Cl
LGN/SDN/BHAMAIR B26 148 A3
Baptist End Rd DUDS DY2 102 C4
Barbara Rd HLGN/YWD B28 179 G2
Barbel Dr WOLVN WV10 38 B1
Barbers La HIA/OLT B92 166 C4
Barbourne Cl SOLH B91 195 H1
Barbrook Dr BRLYHL DY5 118 D5
Barcheston Rd DOR/KN B93 197 E4
SLYOAK B29 158 C1
Barclay Rd SMTHWKW B67 124 A3
Barcroft WLNHL WV13 39 H2
Bardenholme Gdns
HAG/WOL DY9 136 B4
Bardfield Cl PBAR/PBCH B42 73 H3
Bardon Dr SHLY B90 180 D3
Bard St SPARK B11 145 E2
Bardwell Cl CDSL WV8 22 B2
Barford Cl DARL/WED WS10 40 A5
WALM/CURD B76 63 F4
Barford Crs HWK/WKHTH B38 177 G3
Barford Rd SHLY B90 180 D3
WSNGN B18 107 G5
Barford St DIG/EDG B5 127 F3
Bargate Dr
DUNHL/THL/PER WV6 36 C1
Bargery Rd WNSFLD WV11 25 G1
Barham Cl SHLY B90 195 G3
Barker Rd FOAKS/STRLY B74 62 B1
Barker St LGLYGN/QTN B68 105 G4
LOZ/NWT B19 108 B2
Bark Piece RIDG/WDGT B32 140 C4
Barlands Cft BKDE/SHDE B34 112 D3
Barle Gv CBROM B36 113 H2
Barley Cl ALDR WS9 45 E3
CDSL WV8 22 A1
SEDG DY3 * 67 H4
Barley Cft
DUNHL/THL/PER WV6 34 B2
Barleyfield Ri KGSWFD DY6 99 E1
Barleyfield Rw WSL WS1 4 E6
Barlow Cl LGLYGN/QTN B68 123 E1
RBRY B45 173 G3
Barlow Dr WBROM B70 88 B5
Barlow Rd DARL/WED WS10 56 A3
Barlows Rd EDG B15 142 B2
Barmouth Cl SHHTH WV12 26 A4
Barnabas Rd ERDW/GRVHL B23 92 D2
Barnaby Sq WOLVN WV10 13 F3
Barnard Cl
CHWD/FDBR/MGN B37 132 D3
Barnard Pl BKHL/PFLD WV2 52 C2
Barnard Rd MGN/WHC B75 63 E1
WNSFLD WV11 25 F1
Barn Av SEDG DY3 67 E4
Barnbrook Rd DOR/KN B93 197 E1
Barn Cl BVILLE B30 160 B4
HAG/WOL DY9 136 A3
HALE B63 138 A5
Barn Cft RIDG/WDGT B32 158 A1
Barncroft Rd OLDBY B69 103 G1
Barncroft St WBROM B70 71 E3
Barnes Cl STETCH B33 131 G2
Barnes Hl SLYOAK B29 141 F5
Barnes Meadow Pl
BILS/COS WV14 68 B3
Barnesville Cl SMTHH B10 129 E4
Barnet Rd ERDW/GRVHL B23 92 B1
Barnett Cl BILS/COS WV14 53 H4
KGSWFD DY6 99 H5
Barnett Gn STRBR DY8 99 H5
Barnett La KGSWFD DY6 99 H4
STRBR DY8 117 H1
Barnett Rd WLNHL WV13 39 E4
Barnetts La BRWNH WS8 9 G3
Barnett St STRBR DY8 117 H1
TPTN/OCK DY4 85 G4
Barney Cl TPTN/OCK DY4 85 F3
Barn Farm Cl BILS/COS WV14 54 C1
Barnfield Dr HIA/OLT B92 165 H4
Barnfield Gv
BFLD/HDSWWD B20 89 G1
Barnfield Rd RMSLY B62 122 B5
TPTN/OCK DY4 69 E4
WOLV WV1 38 A3
Barnford Cl SMTHH B10 * 128 A3
Barnford Crs LGLYGN/QTN B68 123 E1
Barnfordhill Cl
LGLYGN/QTN B68 105 F5
Barn Gn BDMR/CCFT WV3 51 F1
Barnhurst La CDSL WV8 11 F4
Barn La HDSW B21 107 G2
HIA/OLT B92 147 E3
MOS/BIL B13 161 G3
Barn Meadow YDLY B25 129 H3
Barnmoor Ri SOLH B91 165 E3
Barn Owl Dr BLOX/PEL WS3 17 H3
Barnpark Covert
ALE/KHTH/YWD B14 177 G3
Barn Piece RIDG/WDGT B32 140 B3
Barnsbury Av
CSCFLD/WYGN B72 77 G5
Barns Cl ALDR WS9 19 F3
Barns Cft FOAKS/STRLY B74 45 H2
Barnsdale Crs NFLD/LBR B31 175 E1
Barns La ALDR WS9 29 F3
Barnsley Rd HRBN B17 124 C3
Barnstaple Rd SMTHWK B66 106 D4
Barn St DIG/EDG B5 3 K6
Barnswood Cl HALE B63 137 G2
Barnt Green Rd RBRY B45 188 C5
Barnwood Rd CDSL WV8 22 A1
RIDG/WDGT B32 141 F3
Barons Cl HRBN B17 141 H1
Barrack Cl MGN/WHC B75 63 G2
Barrack La HALE B63 137 F1
Barracks Cl BLOX/PEL WS3 28 A2
Barracks La BLOX/PEL WS3 27 H2
Barrack St VAUX/NECH B7 109 G5
WBROM B70 71 E3
Barra Cft CVALE B35 94 D2
Barrar Cl STRBR DY8 118 A4
Barratts Cft BRLYHL DY5 83 E5
Barratts Rd HWK/WKHTH B38 177 E4
Barr Common Cl ALDR WS9 44 B2
Barr Common Rd ALDR WS9 44 B2
Barrett St LDYWD/EDGR B16 107 E5
Barrhill Cl GTB/HAM B43 73 G1
Barrington Cl DSYBK/YTR WS5 57 G5
WOLVN WV10 23 E1
Barrington Rd HIA/OLT B92 147 E5
RBRY B45 187 G1
Barr Lakes La DSYBK/YTR WS5 58 C1
Barron Rd NFLD/LBR B31 175 H2
Barrow Cl ALDR WS9 19 F3
Barrow Hill Rd BRLYHL DY5 83 E5
Barrows La
LGN/SDN/BHAMAIR B26 147 G2
Barrows Rd SPARK B11 145 E1
Barrow Wk DIG/EDG B5 127 E5
Barrs Crs CDYHTH B64 121 F4
Barrs Rd CDYHTH B64 121 F4
Barrs St LGLYGN/QTN B68 105 E5
Barr St LOZ/NWT B19 108 C4
SEDG DY3 83 E3
Barry Rd DSYBK/YTR WS5 58 A1
Barsham Cl DIG/EDG B5 143 G1
Barsham Dr BRLYHL DY5 119 E4
Barston La SOLH B91 182 D3
Barston Rd LGLYGN/QTN B68 140 B1
Bartholomew Rw DIG/EDG B5 3 J4
Bartholomew St DIG/EDG B5 3 J5
Bartic Av KGSWFD DY6 100 B5
Bartleet Rd SMTHWK B67 105 H4
Bartlett Cl TPTN/OCK DY4 69 H2
Bartley Cl HIA/OLT B92 147 F5
Bartley Dr NFLD/LBR B31 158 A2
Bartley Ms NFLD/LBR B31 158 A2
Bartley Woods
RIDG/WDGT B32 140 B5
Barton Cft HLGN/YWD B28 179 H1
Barton Dr DOR/KN B93 197 F4
Barton La KGSWFD DY6 99 G1
Barton Lodge Rd
HLGN/YWD B28 179 G1
Barton Rd
ETTPK/GDPK/PENN WV4 52 D4
Bartons Bank AST/WIT B6 109 E2
Barton St WBROM B70 87 G4
Bar Wk ALDR WS9 30 C1
Barwell Cl DOR/KN B93 196 C4
Barwell Rd BORD B9 127 H2
Barwick St CBHAMNW B3 3 F4
Basalt Cl WSLW WS2 41 E1
Basil Gv NFLD/LBR B31 175 E1
Basil Rd NFLD/LBR B31 175 E1
Baslow Cl BLOX/PEL WS3 16 D4
STETCH B33 112 A5

Baslow Rd BLOX/PEL WS3........16 D4
Basons La LGLYGN/QTN B68...105 G4
Bassano Rd
  BLKHTH/ROWR B65........122 A3
Bassenthwaite Ct KGSWFD DY6..99 H3
Bassett Cl
  ETTPK/GDPK/PENN WV4.....50 C2
  SHHTH WV12................40 B1
  WALM/CURD B76............63 E4
Bassett Cft SMHTH B10......127 H4
Bassett Rd DARL/WED WS10...71 C1
  HALE B63.................137 E1
Bassetts Gv
  CHWD/FDBR/MGN B37....113 G4
Bassett St WSLW WS2........41 G3
Bassnage Rd HALE B63......138 A5
Batchcroft BILS/COS WV14....53 H5
  DARL/WED WS10............40 B5
Batchelor Cl STRBR DY8....118 B4
Bateman Rd SCFLD/BOLD B73..77 F2
Bateman Rd
  CSHL/WTROR B46..........97 F5
Batemans La HLYWD B47.....192 A3
Bates Cl WALM/CURD B76....78 C4
Bates Gv WNSFLD WV11......24 A5
Bate St
  ETTPK/GDPK/PENN WV4....53 E5
  WSL2......................4 D1
Bath Av WOLV WV1..........6 D2
Bathnaston Cl
  HWK/WKHTH B38...........190 B1
Bath Meadow HALE B63......138 A2
Bath Pas DIG/EDG B5........3 G7
Bath Rd BDMR/CCFT WV5.....3 C4
  BRLYHL DY5...............120 A2
  STRBR DY8................135 F1
  TPTN/OCK DY4.............85 C1
  WSL WS1...................4 E5
Bath Wk BHTH/HG B12.......144 A2
Batmans Hill Rd
  BILS/COS WV14.............68 C1
Batson Rl STRBR DY8.........118 C4
Battenhall Rd HRBN B17....141 G2
Battery Wy SPARK B11.......145 G3
Battlefield Hl WMBN WV5....65 F4
Battlefield La WMBN WV5....65 F5
Bavaro Gdns BRLYHL DY5...120 A2
Baverstock Rd
  ALE/KHTH/YWD B14.......178 B3
Baxterley Gn SOLH B91.....180 D1
  WALM/CURD B76............63 F4
Baxter Rd BRLYHL DY5......119 E2
Baxters Gn SHLY B90........180 B5
Baxters Rd SHLY B90........180 B5
Bay Av BILS/COS WV14.......54 B4
Bayer St BILS/COS WV14.....68 C3
Bayford Av
  LGN/SDN/BHAMAIR B26...148 A3
  NFLD/LBR B31............189 E2
Bayley Crs DARL/WED WS10...40 A5
Bayleys La TPTN/OCK DY4....85 H3
Baylie St STRBR DY8.........135 F3
Baylis Av WNSFLD WV11......25 F2
Bayliss Av
  ETTPK/GDPK/PENN WV4....68 A1
Bayliss Cl BILS/COS WV14....53 C1
  NFLD/LBR B31.............158 D5
Baynton Rd SHHTH WV12.....26 A3
Bayston Av BDMR/CCFT WV3...36 A5
Bayston Rd
  ALE/KHTH/YWD B14.......178 A1
Bayswater Rd
  BFLD/HDSWWD B20..........90 D5
  SEDG DY3.................83 H4
Baytree Cl BLOX/PEL WS3....16 C5
Bay Tree Cl HWK/WKHTH B38.176 B5
Baytree Rd BLOX/PEL WS3....16 C5
Baywell Cl SHLY B90.......195 G1
Beach Av BILS/COS WV14.....68 A1
Beach Brook Cl SPARK B11..144 D2
Beachburn Wy
  BFLD/HDSWWD B20..........90 A3
Beachcroft Rd KGSWFD DY6..99 E5
Beach Dr HALE B63.........138 C2
Beach Rd BILS/COS WV14.....53 H1
  SPARK B11................144 D2
Beachwood Av KGSWFD DY6...81 C5
Beacon Cl GTB/HAM B43.....73 H2
  RBRY B45.................187 H2
  SMTHWK B66..............106 C2
Beacon Dr WSL WS1..........5 J7
Beacon Hl ALDR WS9.........44 C1
  AST/WIT B6...............109 E1
  RBRY B45.................187 G3
Beacon La BRCRVE B60......187 F5
  SEDG DY3.................67 G2
Beacon Rd ALDR WS9.........59 F1
  DSYBK/YTR WS5............58 B5
  KGSTG B44...............74 B3
  SCFLD/BOLD B73...........77 E2
  SHHTH WV12...............26 A2
Beaconsfield Av
  ETTPK/GDPK/PENN WV4....52 B3
Beaconsfield Ct WSL WS1....5 K6
Beaconsfield Crs
  BHTH/HG B12*............144 A2
Beaconsfield Dr
  ETTPK/GDPK/PENN WV4....52 B3
Beaconsfield Rd
  BHTH/HG B12.............144 A3
  FOAKS/STRLY B74..........62 B1
Beacon St
  HHTH/SAND B71............87 H1
Beacon St BILS/COS WV14...67 H2
  WSL WS1...................5 J5
Beacon Vw RBRY B45........187 H2

Beacon View Dr
  FOAKS/STRLY B74..........60 B4
Beacon View Rd
  HHTH/SAND B71............72 B1
Beacon Wy Bl ALDR WS9......19 C4
  RUSH/SHEL WS4............42 D1
Beakes Rd BLKHTH/WKW B67.124 B1
Beaks Farm Gdns
  LDYWD/EDGR B16.........125 F2
Beaks Hill Rd
  HWK/WKHTH B38...........176 C4
Beak St CBHAMW B1..........3 F6
Beale Cl CVALE B35.........94 C4
Beales St AST/WIT B6......109 H1
Beale St STRBR DY8.........135 F2
Bealeys Av WNSFLD WV11....24 C2
Bealeys La BLOX/PEL WS3....16 C5
Beamans Cl HIA/OLT B92....147 G3
Beaminster Rd SOLH B91....181 F1
Bean Cft RIDG/WDCT B32....140 C5
Bean Rd DUDS DY2..........102 C4
  TPTN/OCK DY4.............68 C5
Beardmore Rd
  CSCFLD/WYGN B72.........77 C3
Bearing Dr WNSFLD WV11.....39 E1
Bearley Cft SHLY B90......180 C5
Bearmore Rd CDYHTH B64...121 E3
Bearnett Dr
  Bearnett La WMBN WV5.....65 C1
Bearnett La WMBN WV5......65 F2
Bearwood Rd SMTHWK B66...124 C2
Beasley Gv GTB/HAM B43....74 B2
Beaton Cl WLNHL WV13......39 E3
Beaton Rd FOAKS/STRLY B74..47 E2
Beatrice St BLOX/PEL WS3...27 G4
Beatrice Wk OLDBY B69.....85 C4
Beaubrook Gdns KGSWFD DY6.117 H1
Beauchamp Av
  BFLD/HDSWWD B20.........89 H1
Beauchamp Cl
  CHWD/FDBR/MGN B37.....132 B2
  WALM/CURD B76............78 D4
Beauchamp Rd MOS/BIL B13.161 H5
  SOLH B91................164 D5
Beaudesert Cl HLYWD B47...192 C2
Beaudesert Rd
  BFLD/HDSWWD B20.........108 B1
  HLYWD B47...............192 C2
Beaufort Av HLYWD B47.....192 C2
Beaufort Rd
  LDYWD/EDGR B16.........125 H3
Beaufort Wy ALDR WS9......44 B1
Beaulieu Av KGSWFD DY6....100 B5
Beaumaris Cl DUDN DY1.....83 H3
Beaumont Cl TPTN/OCK DY4..69 E5
Beaumont Dr BRLYHL DY5...118 D5
  HRBN B17................141 H3
Beaumont Gdns WSNGN B18..107 H3
Beaumont Gv SOLH B91.....164 B5
Beaumont Rd BVILLE B30...159 C4
  DARL/WED WS10............55 H4
  RMSLY B62...............122 C4
Beausale Dr DOR/KN B93....197 F1
Beauty Bank CDYHTH B64....121 F4
Beauty Bank Crs STRBR DY8.135 E1
Beaver Cl WNSFLD WV11.....25 F5
Bebington Cl CDSL WV8......22 B1
Beccles Dr WLNHL WV13.....39 F5
Beckbury Av
  ETTPK/GDPK/PENN WV4....50 C3
Beckbury Rd SLYOAK B29...158 C1
Beck Cl SMTHWK B66........106 C5
Beckenham Av KGSTG B44....75 C2
Beckensall Cl DUDN DY1.....84 B5
Becket Cl FOAKS/STRLY B74..32 D4
Beckett St BILS/COS WV14...54 A2
Beckfield Cl
  ALE/KHTH/YWD B14.......178 A3
  RUSH/SHEL WS4............29 E2
Beckford Cft DOR/KN B93*..196 D5
Beckman Rd HAG/WOL DY9...136 A5
Beckminster Rd BDMR/CCFT WV3551 F1
Beconsfield Cl DOR/KN B93..198 D1
Becton Gv PBAR/PBCH B42..74 D4
Bedcote Pl STRBR DY8......135 H2
Beddoe Cl TPTN/OCK DY4.....86 B1
Beddow Av BILS/COS WV14....68 C4
Beddows Rd BLOX/PEL WS3...28 A5
Bedford Dr MGN/WHC B75....63 E2
Bedford Rd BHTH/HG B12...127 C4
  HHTH/SAND B71............71 H4
  MGN/WHC B75.............63 E1
Bedford St TPTN/OCK DY4....85 H1
  WOLV WV1.................53 E1
Bedford Ter LOZ/NWT B19*.108 D1
Bedlam Wood Rd
  NFLD/LBR B31............174 C4
Bedworth Cft TPTN/OCK DY4..85 H2
Bedworth Gv BORD B9........129 F2
Beebee Rd DARL/WED WS10...55 H2
Beecham Cl ALDR WS9........30 A2
Beech Av BHTH/HG B12......128 B3
  CHWD/FDBR/MGN B37.....132 B3
  RIDG/WDCT B32...........140 D1
  RMSLY B62...............122 A4
Beech Cl MGN/WHC B75.......47 E1
  SEDG DY3.................67 G4
  WOLV WV10................22 D2
Beech Ct SMTHWK B66......105 C2
  WSL WS1...................5 H6
Beech Crs DARL/WED WS10...55 H3
  TPTN/OCK DY4............70 A3
Beechcroft Av
  HLGN/YWD B28............162 D4
Beechcroft Crs
  FOAKS/STRLY B74..........44 D4
Beechcroft Est HALE B63...137 C1
Beechcroft Pl WOLVN WV10...23 E4
Beechcroft Rd CBROM B36...112 D1
  CDYHTH B64..............121 E3
Beechdale Av KGSTG B44....75 E1
Beechdale Rd BLOX/PEL WS3..26 D2
Beech Dene Gv
  ERDW/GRVHL B23..........92 C1
Beecher Pl HALE B63.......137 H2
Beecher Rd East HALE B63..137 H2
Beecher St HALE B63.......137 G2
Beeches Av ACGN B27.......146 C3
Beeches Cl KGSWFD DY6.....99 H4
  RBRY B45................187 F1

Beeches Dr ERDE/BCHGN B24..93 G2
Beeches Farm Dr
  NFLD/LBR B31............189 G1
Beeches Ms HAG/WOL DY9...169 E1
Beeches Pl BLOX/PEL WS3....27 H3
Beeches Rd
  BLKHTH/ROWR B65.........121 H3
  BLOX/PEL WS3.............27 H4
  LGLYGN/QTN B68..........123 G1
  PBAR/PBCH B42............74 B4
  WBROM B70................88 A4
The Beeches EDG B15.......126 C4
  WBROM B70................88 A4
  WOLV WV1..................6 A2
Beeches View Av HALE B63.137 G3
Beeches Wk SCFLD/BOLD B73..62 B5
Beeches Wy NFLD/LBR B31..189 G1
Beechey Cl GTB/HAM B43....59 H5
Beech Farm Cft NFLD/LBR B31175 G2
Beechfield Cl RMSLY B62...122 A4
Beechfield Gv BILS/COS WV14..68 B4
Beechfield Rd SMTHWKW B67.106 B5
  SPARK B11...............144 D1
Beech Gdns CDSL WV8.......10 B5
Beech Ga FOAKS/STRLY B74...31 H5
Beechglade
  BFLD/HDSWWD B20.........89 H2
Beech Gn DUDN DY1.........84 A1
Beech Gv ALE/KHTH/YWD B14.177 H3
Beech Hill Rd
  CSCFLD/WYGN B72.........77 G4
Beech Hurst HWK/WKHTH B38.176 C5
Beechlawn Dr KINVER DY7...116 C5
Beechmere Rd
  LGN/SDN/BHAMAIR B26...147 F2
Beechmount Dr
  ERDW/GRVHL B23..........77 E5
Beechnut Cl SOLH B91.....165 G5
Beechnut La SOLH B91.....165 G5
Beech Rd BVILLE B30.......159 G3
  DARL/WED WS10............55 H1
  DUDN DY1.................84 C2
  ERDW/GRVHL B23..........76 D4
  HLYWD B47...............192 D2
  KGSWFD DY6..............99 H4
  OLDBY B69...............105 G1
  STRBR DY8...............135 E4
  WLNHL WV13...............39 E3
  WOLVN WV10..............22 D2
Beechtree Av WNSFLD WV11..24 C2
Beech Tree Cl SOLH B91.....19 F5
Beech Tree Rd ALDR WS9....30 A3
Beech Wk HWK/WKHTH B38..176 D5
Beech Wy SMTHWK B66......106 D4
Beechwood Av WNSFLD WV11..24 B2
Beechwood Cl BLOX/PEL WS3..16 C5
  SHLY B90................194 D4
Beechwood Ct
  DUNHL/THL/PER WV6*......35 G2
Beechwood Cft
  FOAKS/STRLY B74..........32 B5
Beechwood Dr
  DUNHL/THL/PER WV6.......35 E3
Beechwood Park Rd
  SOLH B91................164 A5
Beechwood Rd
  ALE/KHTH/YWD B14.......161 F5
  DUDS DY2.................85 H2
  GTB/HAM B43.............73 G2
  SMTHWKW B67............124 A4
  WBROM B70................87 F3
Bee La WOLVN WV10.........12 D4
Beecroft Cl AST/WIT B6....109 G2
  BRLYHL DY5..............119 E2
Beeton Rd WSNGN B18......107 G3
Beet St BLKHTH/ROWR B65...122 A3
Beever Rd TPTN/OCK DY4....70 B4
Beggars Bush La WMBN WV5...81 F1
Beighton Cl FOAKS/STRLY B74.32 D4
Beilby Rd BVILLE B30......160 B4
Belbroughton Rd
  HAG/WOL DY9.............170 C4
  HALE B63................138 B5
  KIDD DY10...............168 C4
  STRBR DY8...............135 E4
Belchers La BORD B9.......129 F1
Beldray Rd BILS/COS WV14...54 A2
Belfry Cl BILS/COS WV14....16 C4
Belfry Dr STRBR DY8.......135 E1
The Belfry
  DUNHL/THL/PER WV6.......34 B1
Belgrade Rd WOLVN WV10....12 B5
Belgrave Ct KGSWFD DY6....100 B5
Belgrave Int DIG/EDG B5...126 D5
Belgrave Middleway
  DIG/EDG B5..............127 E5
Belgrave Rd BHTH/HG B12..144 B1
  RMSLY B62...............122 B4
Belgrave Ter HDSW B21....108 A2
Belgrave Wk WSLW WS2......41 F2
Belgravia Cl DIG/EDG B5...127 E5
Belgrove Cl EDG B15......142 C1
Belinda Cl WLNHL WV13.....41 F2
Bellamy Cl SHLY B90......180 D4
Bellamy Farm Rd SHLY B90.180 D4
Bellamy La WNSFLD WV11....24 D3
Bell Barn Rd DIG/EDG B5..126 C5
Bell Cl BORD B9...........128 C1
  CBROM B36...............112 B4
  DARL/WED WS10............55 F1
Bellcroft LDYWD/EDGR B16...2 A6
Bell Dr DSYBK/YTR WS5......57 G3
  WASH/WDE B8.............128 C1
Bellefield Av WSNGN B18..107 G5
Bellefield Rd WSNGN B18..107 G5
Belle Isle BRLYHL DY5.....119 E1
Bellemere Rd HIA/OLT B92..167 H5
Bellencroft Gdns
  BDMR/CCFT WV3...........50 B1
Bell End BLKHTH/ROWR B65..122 A1
Belle V ALDR WS9..........138 A2
Bellevue DIG/EDG B5......126 D5
Belle Vue STRBR DY8.......117 G2
Belle Vue Dr RMSLY B62...139 G1
Belle Vue Gdns
  BLKHTH/ROWR B65*.......122 A1

Belle Vue Rd BRLYHL DY5...120 A3
Bellevue Rd BILS/COS WV14..67 H1
  LGN/SDN/BHAMAIR B26...130 C5
Bellevue St BILS/COS WV14..67 H1
Belle Vue Ter HIA/OLT B92.167 G4
Bell La ALE/KHTH/YWD B14..177 H3
  BLOX/PEL WS3............27 H4
  WALM/CURD B76...........63 E4
  WBROM B70*..............88 D1
Bell Green
  HWK/WKHTH B38...........191 F3
Bell Heather Rd BRWNH WS8..18 D1
Bell Heath Wy
  RIDG/WDCT B32...........140 B5
Bell Hl NFLD/LBR B31......175 G1
Bell Holloway NFLD/LBR B31.158 B5
Bellington Cft SHLY B90...195 G2
Bellis St LDYWD/EDGR B16..125 H3
Bell La BLOX/PEL WS3*......16 C4
Bell Meadow HAG/WOL DY9..152 D2
Bell Pl BKHL/PFLD WV2......37 E5
Bell Rd DSYBK/YTR WS5.....58 B2
  DUDS DY2................102 C4
  WMBN WV5................64 B2
Bells Farm Cl
  ALE/KHTH/YWD B14.......177 H3
Bells La ALE/KHTH/YWD B14.177 H3
  STRBR DY8...............117 H3
Bells Moor Rd WBROM B70...71 E5
  SOLH B91................164 C5
Bell St BILS/COS WV14.....68 A3
  SOLH B91................164 C5
Bell St South BRLYHL DY5..119 F2
Bell Vue Rd
  BLKHTH/ROWR B65.........122 A2
Bellwood Rd NFLD/LBR B31.175 F1
Belmont Cl ALDR WS9.......30 A3
  TPTN/OCK DY4............69 F5
Belmont Covert
  ALE/KHTH/YWD B14.......158 D5
Belmont Crs NFLD/LBR B31.158 D4
Belmont Gdns BILS/COS WV14.54 C4
Belmont Pas BORD B9......127 G2
Belmont Rd BRLYHL DY5....158 A5
  ETTPK/GDPK/PENN WV4....51 G5
  HAG/WOL DY9.............136 C5
  HDSW B21...............107 E1
  RBRY B45................187 H2
Belmont Rd East HDSW B21.107 E1
Belmont Rw CBHAMNE B4.....3 K3
Belmont St BILS/COS WV14..54 C4
Belper DUDN DY1............84 B5
Belper Rd BLOX/PEL WS3....17 E4
  WBROM B70...............86 C5
Belper Rw DUDS DY2.......103 E5
Belstone Cl
  ALE/KHTH/YWD B14.......160 D5
Belton Av WNSFLD WV11.....24 B1
Belton Gv RBRY B45........174 C5
Belvedere Av
  ETTPK/GDPK/PENN WV4....51 H3
Belvedere Cl KGSWFD DY6...100 B5
Belvedere Gdns
  DUNHL/THL/PER WV6.......21 H3
Belvedere Rd
  ERDE/BCHGN B24..........93 E4
Belvide Gdns CDSL WV8.....10 B3
Belvide Gv SLYOAK B29....159 F2
Belvidere Gdns SPARK B11.144 D3
Belvidere Rd WSL WS1.......5 F7
Belvoir Cl DUDN DY1.......83 G4
Belwell Dr FOAKS/STRLY B74.47 E3
Belwell La FOAKS/STRLY B74.47 E3
Bembridge Cl SHHTH WV12...25 H2
Bembridge Rd STETCH B33..130 C2
Benacre Dr DIG/EDG B5....127 E3
Benbeck Gv TPTN/OCK DY4...84 C1
Bencroft CDSL WV8.........10 D3
Bendall Rd KGSTG B44......75 H1
Benedon Rd
  LGN/SDN/BHAMAIR B26...130 C5
Benmore Av DIG/EDG B5....143 H1
Bennett Av DUDN DY1.......68 B5
Bennett Rd FOAKS/STRLY B74.46 B2
  DUDS DY2................103 E1
Bennetts Rd WASH/WDE B8.110 B3
Ben Nevis Wy STRBR DY8...135 C1
Benson Av
  ETTPK/GDPK/PENN WV4....52 A3
Benson Cl
  DUNHL/THL/PER WV6......21 E5
Benson Rd
  ALE/KHTH/YWD B14.......178 D4
  WSNGN B18..............107 F3
Bent Av RIDG/WDCT B32....140 D1
Bentham Ct NFLD/LBR B31..158 B5
Bentley Bridge Pk
  WNSFLD WV11*............38 B1
Bentley Dr CDSL WV8.......10 B3
  WSLW WS2.................40 C3
Bentley Farm Cl DOR/KN B93.196 C4
Bentley Gv SLYOAK B29....158 B2
Bentley Hts WLNHL WV13....26 B5
  WSLW WS2.................41 E1
Bentley Mill Cl WSLW WS2..40 C4
Bentley Mill La WSLW WS2..40 C4
Bentley Mill Wy WSLW WS2..40 C4
Bentley New Dr WSLW WS2...41 F2
Bentley Pl WSLW WS2.......40 D4
Bentley Rd CBROM B36.....113 G2
  WOLVN WV10..............13 E5
Bentley Rd North WSLW WS2.40 B5
Bentley Rd South
  DARL/WED WS10...........40 B5
Bentmead Gv
  HWK/WKHTH B38..........177 G4
Benton Av SPARK B11......145 E1
Benton Cl SHHTH WV12......40 B1

Benton Crs BLOX/PEL WS3....17 F5
Benton Rd SPARK B11......145 E1
Bentons Mill Cft
  VAUX/NECH B7............110 A1
Bent St BRLYHL DY5........101 F5
Ben Willetts Wk
  BLKHTH/ROWR B65.........122 A3
Beoley Cl CSCFLD/WYGN B72..77 G2
Beoley Gv RBRY B45........188 A1
Berberry Cl BVILLE B30....159 F4
Beresford Crs WBROM B70...87 F3
Beresford Dr SCFLD/BOLD B73..77 F2
Beresford Rd BLOX/PEL WS3..28 A2
  OLDBY B69...............105 G2
The Berets MGN/WHC B75....63 F2
Bericote Cft ACGN B27....146 D4
Berkeley Cl
  DUNHL/THL/PER WV6.......34 C2
  WSLW WS2.................40 D2
Berkeley Dr KGSWFD DY6....99 G2
Berkeley Ms SLHL B25.....129 E5
Berkeley Rd SHLY B90......179 H2
  YDLY B25................129 E5
Berkeley Rd East YDLY B25.129 F5
Berkeley St WSLW WS2......56 B1
Berkeley Cl WSLW WV2......40 D2
Berkley St CBHAMW B1......2 E5
Berkswell Cl DUDN DY1....83 G3
  FOAKS/STRLY B74..........46 C1
Berkswell Rd ERDE/BCHGN B24..93 F2
Bermuda Cl DUDN DY1.......68 B5
Bernard Pl WSNGN B18*....107 H4
Bernard Rd HRBN B17......124 D2
  LGLYGN/QTN B68.........123 C2
  TPTN/OCK DY4............69 G4
Bernard St HHTH/SAND B71..87 G2
  WSL WS1...................5 H6
Berners St LOZ/NWT B19...108 C2
Bernhard Dr HDSW B21......107 E1
Bernwall Cl STRBR DY8......88 B5
Berrandale Rd CBROM B36...94 B5
Berriage Rd BRLYHL DY5....68 B3
Berrington Gv ALE/KHTH/YWD B14..68 B3
Berrington Wk DIG/EDG B5.127 E5
Berrow Dr EDG B15........125 G5
Berrowside Rd
  BKDE/SHDE B34..........113 G3
Berry Av DARL/WED WS10...54 D2
Berrybush Gdns SEDG DY3...67 G4
Berry Cl LOZ/NWT B19.....108 D3
Berry Crs DSYBK/YTR WS5...58 B4
Berry Dr ALDR WS9.........29 G5
  SMTHWK B66..............106 C1
Berryfield Rd
  LGN/SDN/BHAMAIR B26...148 B2
Berryfields ALDR WS9......29 G5
Berry Hall La SOLH B91...182 B5
Berrymound Vw HLYWD B47..193 E1
Berry Rd DUDN DY1........84 A1
  WASH/WDE B8............110 C4
Berry St WOLV WV1........110 C1
  WSNGN B18..............107 E2
Bertha Rd SPARK B11......145 F2
Bertram Cl TPTN/OCK DY4...70 A2
Bertram Rd BORD B9.......128 B3
  SMTHWKW B67............106 A3
Berwick Gv GTB/HAM B43....59 F5
  NFLD/LBR B31...........174 D2
Berwicks La
  CHWD/FDBR/MGN B37.....132 B3
Berwood Farm Rd
  ERDE/BCHGN B24..........77 G5
Berwood Gdns
  ERDE/BCHGN B24..........77 G5
Berwood La ERDE/BCHGN B24..94 A3
Berwood Pk CVALE B35......94 D4
Berwood Rd
  CSCFLD/WYGN B72.........77 H5
Besant Gv ACGN B27.......146 A5
Besbury Cft DOR/KN B93...198 C1
Bescot Crs WSL WS1........56 D3
Bescot Cft PBAR/PBCH B42..74 B4
Bescot Dr WSLW WS2........56 C2
Bescot Rd WSLW WS2........56 C1
Bescot St WSL WS1.........57 E1
Besford Gv NFLD/LBR B31..174 C3
  SHLY B90................195 F2
Bessborough Rd YDLY B25..129 H4
Best Rd BILS/COS WV14.....53 H1
Best St CDYHTH B64.......121 F2
Beta Gv ALE/KHTH/YWD B14.179 F1
Bethesda Gdns HALE B63...120 C5
Betjeman Pl WOLVN WV10...24 A1
Betley Gv STETCH B33.....112 C5
Betony Cl DSYBK/YTR WS5...57 G5
Betsham Cl KGSTG B44.....75 H1
Bettany Gld WOLVN WV10....13 E3
Betteridge Dr WALM/CURD B76..63 E4
Bett Rd BFLD/HDSWWD B20...89 G3
Betton Av
  ETTPK/GDPK/PENN WV4....52 C4
Bevan Cl BILS/COS WV14....54 B2
  RUSH/SHEL WS4...........29 E1
Bevan Rd BRLYHL DY5......118 C2
  TPTN/OCK DY4............85 G3
Bevan Wy SMTHWK B66.....106 B1
Beverley Cl CSCFLD/WYGN B72..77 G4
Beverley Court Rd
  RIDG/WDCT B32..........140 C1
Beverley Cft
  ERDW/GRVHL B23..........92 B5
Beverley Crs WOLV WV4....52 C4
  KGSWFD DY6..............99 G2
Beverley Gv
  LGN/SDN/BHAMAIR B26...147 H2
Beverley Rd HHTH/SAND B71..71 H2
  RBRY B45................188 A1
Beverston Rd
  DUNHL/THL/PER WV6.......35 E1
  TPTN/OCK DY4............69 H1
Bevin Rd WSLW WS2........40 C2

Bewdley Av BHTH/HG B12 144 C1
Bewdley Dr WOLV WV1 38 B3
Bewdley Rd BVILLE B30 160 B2
Bewdley Vls WSNGN B18 * 107 F5
Bewlay Cl BRLYHL DY5 118 D5
Bewley Rd SHHTH WV12 40 B1
Bewlys Av BFLD/HDSWWD B20 89 G2
Bexhill Gv EDG B15 126 C3
Bexley Gv HHTH/SAND B71 72 A4
Bexley Rd KGSTG B44 75 H3
Bhylls Crs BDMR/CCFT WV3 50 C1
Bhylls La BDMR/CCFT WV3 50 B1
Bibbey's Gn WOLVN WV10 13 F3
Bibsworth Av MOS/BIL B13 162 B2
Bibury Rd HLGN/YWD B28 162 C3
Bicester Sq CVALE B35 94 D2
Bickenhill La
CHWD/FDBR/MGN B37 132 C5
HIA/OLT B92 166 C4
LGN/SDN/BHAMAIR B26 149 G3
Bickenhill Park Rd
HIA/OLT B92 163 H1
Bickenhill Pkwy
CHWD/FDBR/MGN B37 149 H1
Bickenhill Rd
CHWD/FDBR/MGN B37 132 B5
Bickford Rd AST/WIT B6 91 G5
WOLVN WV10 23 H5
Bickington Rd RIDG/WDGT B32 157 H1
Bickley Av FOAKS/STRLY B74 32 C5
SPARK B11 * 145 E1
Bickley Gv
LGN/SDN/BHAMAIR B26 147 H2
Bickley Rd BILS/COS WV14 54 C2
RUSH/SHEL WS4 29 E3
Bicknell Cft
ALE/KHTH/YWD B14 178 A3
Bickton Cl ERDE/BCHGN B24 77 G5
Biddings La BILS/COS WV14 68 B1
Biddlestone Pl
DARL/WED WS10 54 D1
Biddleston Gv DSYBK/YTR WS5 58 A5
Bideford Dr SLYOAK B29 159 E1
Bideford Rd SMTHWK B66 106 D4
Bidford Cl SHLY B90 180 D3
Bidford Rd NFLD/LBR B31 175 E2
Bierton Rd YDLY B25 129 G4
Biggin Cl CVALE B35 94 C3
DUNHL/THL/PER WV6 20 C5
The Big Peg WSNGN B18 * 2 C2
Bigwood Dr MGN/WHC B75 63 G2
RIDG/WDGT B32 157 G1
Bilberry Crs WALM/CURD B76 63 E5
Bilberry Dr RBRY B45 188 A2
Bilberry Rd
ALE/KHTH/YWD B14 160 C4
Bilboe Rd BILS/COS WV14 54 B5
Bilbrook Ct CDSL WV8 10 D4
Bilbrook Gv CDSL WV8 10 D4
SLYOAK B29 141 F5
Bilbrook Rd CDSL WV8 10 C3
Bilhay La WBROM B70 87 E1
Bilhay St WBROM B70 87 F1
Billau Rd BILS/COS WV14 68 D1
Billesley La MOS/BIL B13 161 G2
Billingham Cl SOLH B91 181 H5
Billingsley Rd
LGN/SDN/BHAMAIR B26 130 C4
Bills La SHLY B90 179 H5
Billsmore Gn HIA/OLT B92 165 E3
Bills St DARL/WED WS10 55 G2
Billy Buns La WMBN WV5 65 E3
Billy Wright Cl
ETTPK/GDPK/PENN WV4 50 D2
Bilport La DARL/WED WS10 70 D3
Bilston La WLNHL WV13 39 H5
Bilston Rd BKHL/PFLD WV2 37 H5
DARL/WED WS10 55 F5
TPTN/OCK DY4 69 H1
WLNHL WV13 54 C1
Bilston St DARL/WED WS10 55 F2
SEDG DY3 67 F3
WLNHL WV13 39 G4
Bilston Street Island WOLV WV1 7 H5
Bilton Grange Rd
LGN/SDN/BHAMAIR B26 130 B5
Binbrook Rd SHHTH WV12 40 B1
Bincomb Av
LGN/SDN/BHAMAIR B26 147 H1
Binfield St TPTN/OCK DY4 85 G2
Bingley Av WASH/WDE B8 111 F5
Bingley St BDMR/CCFT WV3 36 C5
Binley Cl SHLY B90 180 A5
YDLY B25 146 D1
Binstead Rd KGSTG B44 75 G1
Binswood Rd RMSLY B62 123 E5
Binton Cft MOS/BIL B13 161 F2
Binton Rd SHLY B90 179 H4
Birbeck Pl BRLYHL DY5 100 D3
Birchall St BHTH/HG B12 127 F3
Birch Av BRLYHL DY5 120 A2
BRWNH WS8 9 E4
NFLD/LBR B31 174 C4
Birch Cl BVILLE B30 159 F4
WALM/CURD B76 78 B4
Birch Coppice BRLYHL DY5 120 B2
WMBN WV5 64 C5
Birchcoppice Gdns
SHHTH WV12 40 C1
Birch Crs OLDBY B69 85 H5
Birch Cft ALDR WS9 30 C2
CHWD/FDBR/MGN B37 132 C3
ERDE/BCHGN B24 93 H1
Birchcroft SMTHWK B66 * 107 E4
Birch Croft Rd MGN/WHC B75 62 D1
Birchdale BILS/COS WV14 53 H1
Birchdale Av ERDW/GRVHL B23 92 C3
Birchdale Rd ERDW/GRVHL B23 92 B1
Birch Dr FOAKS/STRLY B74 32 B5
MGN/WHC B75 63 F1
RMSLY B62 122 C3
STRBR DY8 135 E1
Birches Av CDSL WV8 21 G1
Birches Barn Av
BDMR/CCFT WV3 51 F1
Birches Barn Rd
BDMR/CCFT WV3 36 B5
Birches Cl MOS/BIL B13 161 F1
Birches Green Rd
ERDE/BCHGN B24 93 F4
Birches Park Rd CDSL WV8 10 C5
Birches Ri WLNHL WV13 39 F4
Birches Rd CDSL WV8 10 D5
Birchfield Av
DUNHL/THL/PER WV6 21 F4
Birchfield Cl HALE B63 138 A5
Birchfield Crs HAG/WOL DY9 136 D4
Birchfield Gdns AST/WIT B6 * 108 D1
Birchfield La OLDBY B69 104 C5
Birchfield Rd
BFLD/HDSWWD B20 90 D5
HAG/WOL DY9 136 D4
LOZ/NWT B19 108 D1
Birchfields Rd WNSFLD WV11 25 G5
Birchfield Wy DSYBK/YTR WS5 57 H4
Birchgate HAG/WOL DY9 136 D3
Birchglade BDMR/CCFT WV3 35 H4
Birch Gv LGLYGN/QTN B68 123 H5
Birch Hill Av WMBN WV5 80 D1
Birch Hollow EDG B15 142 D1
Birchill Pl WMBN WV5 80 D1
Birchills St WSLW WS2 4 A2
Birch La ALDR WS9 30 D1
LGLYGN/QTN B68 123 H5
RUSH/SHEL WS4 29 E1
Birchley Park Av OLDBY B69 104 C3
Birchley Ri HIA/OLT B92 147 F2
Birchmoor Cl HLGN/YWD B28 163 F3
Birchover Rd WSLW WS2 41 E1
Birch Rd AST/WIT B6 91 G4
LGLYGN/QTN B68 123 H5
RBRY B45 187 G2
SEDG DY3 67 H2
WNSFLD WV11 25 F1
Birch Rd East AST/WIT B6 91 H4
Birch St LGLYGN/QTN B68 105 G3
TPTN/OCK DY4 85 F1
WOLV WV1 6 E4
WSLW WS2 4 B1
Birch Ter DUDS DY2 102 C5
Birch Tree Gdns ALDR WS9 30 B5
Birchtree Gdns BRLYHL DY5 120 A3
Birch Tree Gv SOLH B91 181 E1
Birchtree Hollow SHHTH WV12 26 B5
Birchtrees ERDE/BCHGN B24 93 H2
Birchtrees Cft
LGN/SDN/BHAMAIR B26 146 D2
Birchtrees Dr STETCH B33 131 F1
Birch Wk LGLYGN/QTN B68 123 H5
Birchwood Cl WNSFLD WV11 15 E4
Birchwood Crs BHTH/HG B12 144 C3
Birchwood Rd BHTH/HG B12 144 D3
ETTPK/GDPK/PENN WV4 51 G3
Birchwoods RIDG/WDGT B32 140 B5
Birchy Cl SHLY B90 193 H2
Birchy Leasowes La SHLY B90 193 G3
Birdbrook Rd KGSTG B44 75 E3
Bird End HHTH/SAND B71 72 B3
Birdie Cl HWK/WKHTH B38 176 B4
Birdlip Gv RIDG/WDGT B32 140 C1
Birds Meadow BRLYHL DY5 100 D2
Bird St SEDG DY3 83 E3
Birdwell Cft MOS/BIL B13 161 F4
Birkdale Av SLYOAK B29 159 H1
Birkdale Cl STRBR DY8 152 B1
WOLV WV1 38 A3
Birkdale Dr OLDBY B69 103 G2
Birkdale Gv SLYOAK B29 160 A2
Birkdale Rd BLOX/PEL WS3 16 C4
Birkenshaw Rd KGSTG B44 75 E3
Birley Gv HALE B63 154 C2
Birmingham New Rd
DUDN DY1 85 E2
ETTPK/GDPK/PENN WV4 52 D4
Birmingham Rd ALDR WS9 44 A1
BKHL/PFLD WV2 37 F5
BLKHTH/ROWR B65 122 A2
BRGRVW B61 187 E4
CBROM B36 112 C1
CHWD/FDBR/MGN B37 114 C4
CSCFLD/WYGN B72 77 F3
DSYBK/YTR WS5 57 H1
DUDN DY1 85 E4
HAG/WOL DY9 153 F4
HALE B63 138 D4
KIDD DY10 168 C3
LICHS WS14 33 E3
NFLD/LBR B31 189 H3
OLDBY B69 105 F2
RCOVN/BALC/EX CV7 151 F4
WBROM B70 88 A5
WSL WS1 5 H7
Birmingham St
DARL/WED WS10 55 F2
DUDS DY2 84 D5
HALE B63 138 D4
OLDBY B69 105 E1
STRBR DY8 135 H2
WLNHL WV13 39 H3
WSL WS1 5 F5
Birnham Cl TPTN/OCK DY4 84 D1
Bisbrook Cft SOLH B91 165 F4
Bisell Wy BRLYHL DY5 136 B1
Bishbury Cl EDG B15 125 G4
Bishop Asbury Crs
GTB/HAM B43 72 D3
Bishop Cl RBRY B45 173 G4
Bishop Rd DARL/WED WS10 71 G1
Bishops Cl DUDS DY2 103 E1
SMTHWK B66 107 E5
Bishop's Ct
CHWD/FDBR/MGN B37 133 E4
Bishops Ga NFLD/LBR B31 175 G3
Bishopsgate St EDG B15 2 B7
Bishops Meadow
MGN/WHC B75 48 A2
Bishops Rd SCFLD/BOLD B73 62 B5
Bishop St DIG/EDG B5 127 E4
Bishops Wk CDYHTH B64 138 C1
Bishops Wy FOAKS/STRLY B74 32 D5
Bishopton Cl SHLY B90 180 C4
Bishopton Rd SMTHWKW B67 124 B3
Bishton Gv DUDS DY2 102 D5
Bissel Dr DARL/WED WS10 56 B5
Bissell Cl HLGN/YWD B28 162 D4
Bissell St DIG/EDG B5 127 E4
RIDG/WDGT B32 140 A1
Bissel St BILS/COS WV14 54 B3
Biton Cl HRBN B17 141 H2
Bittell Cl NFLD/LBR B31 189 F1
WOLVN WV10 13 E3
Bitterne Dr DUNHL/THL/PER WV6 36 C1
Blackacre Rd DUDS DY2 102 D1
Blackberry Av BORD B9 129 E1
Blackberry Cl DUDN DY1 101 G1
Blackberry La ALDR WS9 19 H3
BLKHTH/ROWR B65 103 F4
FOAKS/STRLY B74 46 C1
HALE B63 138 C5
Blackbird Cft CBROM B36 114 A2
Blackbrook Cl DUDS DY2 120 A1
Blackbrook Rd DUDS DY2 102 A4
Blackbrook Wy WOLVN WV10 13 E3
Blackburn Av
DUNHL/THL/PER WV6 22 A3
Blackburne Rd
HLGN/YWD B28 162 D4
Blackbushe Cl HRBN B17 124 B5
Blackcat Cl
CHWD/FDBR/MGN B37 132 A1
Black Country New Rd
DARL/WED WS10 54 C2
Black Country Route
BILS/COS WV14 54 B2
DARL/WED WS10 40 B4
Blackdown Cl RBRY B45 174 A3
Blackdown Rd DOR/KN B93 197 F2
Blackfirs La BHAMNEC B40 133 E5
CHWD/FDBR/MGN B37 132 D5
Blackford Cl HALE B63 137 H5
Blackford Rd SHLY B90 194 C1
SPARK B11 145 E3
Blackford St WSNGN B18 107 G4
Blackhalve La WNSFLD WV11 24 B2
Blackham Dr SCFLD/BOLD B73 77 E4
Blackham Rd WNSFLD WV11 25 F2
Black Haynes Rd SLYOAK B29 158 C3
Black Horse Cl
DARL/WED WS10 55 F3
Blackhorse La BRLYHL DY5 119 G3
Black Lake WBROM B70 71 E5
Blackmoor Cft STETCH B33 131 F2
Blackrock Rd
ERDW/GRVHL B23 75 H5
Blackroot Rd FOAKS/STRLY B74 62 A1
Blacksmith Dr MGN/WHC B75 48 A2
Blacksmiths La HOCK/TIA B94 198 A5
Blacksmith Wy WBROM B70 87 G4
Blackthorn Cl BVILLE B30 159 E5
Blackthorne Cl SOLH B91 181 E1
Blackthorne Rd
DSYBK/YTR WS5 57 F3
DUDN DY1 83 H2
SMTHWKW B67 105 H5
Blackthorn Rd BVILLE B30 159 E4
CBROM B36 113 E1
STRBR DY8 118 B3
Blackwater Cl KGSWFD DY6 100 C4
Blackwell Rd
CSCFLD/WYGN B72 77 H2
Blackwood Av WNSFLD WV11 24 B2
Blackwood Dr
FOAKS/STRLY B74 45 E5
Blackwood Rd
FOAKS/STRLY B74 45 E4
Blades Rd WBROM B70 86 B2
Blaenwern Dr HALE B63 120 B5
Blagdon Rd HALE B63 138 C1
Blair Gv
CHWD/FDBR/MGN B37 132 D3
Blakedon Rd DARL/WED WS10 55 G5
Blakedown Rd HALE B63 138 B5
Blake Hall Cl BRLYHL DY5 118 D5
Blakeland Rd KGSTG B44 75 E5
Blakeland St BORD B9 128 D2
Blake La BORD B9 128 D2
Blakeley Av
DUNHL/THL/PER WV6 22 B3
Blakeley Hall Gdns OLDBY B69 105 F2
Blakeley Hall Rd OLDBY B69 105 F2
Blakeley Heath Dr WMBN WV5 81 E1
Blakeley Ri
DUNHL/THL/PER WV6 22 B3
Blakeley Wood Rd
TPTN/OCK DY4 70 A3
Blakely Hall Rd OLDBY B69 105 F1
Blakemere Av YDLY B25 130 A4
Blakemore Cl RIDG/WDGT B32 141 F4
Blakemore Dr MGN/WHC B75 63 F2
Blakemore Rd ALDR WS9 19 H4
WBROM B70 87 E4
Blakenall Cl BLOX/PEL WS3 27 H1
Blakenall Heath BLOX/PEL WS3 27 H2
Blakenall La BLOX/PEL WS3 27 H2
Blakenall Rw BLOX/PEL WS3 27 H2
Blakeney Av HRBN B17 124 C5
STRBR DY8 134 D1
Blakeney Cl SEDG DY3 67 E3
Blakenhale Rd STETCH B33 130 D3
Blakenhall Gdns
BKHL/PFLD WV2 52 B1
Blake Pl BORD B9 128 D2
Blakesley Cl WALM/CURD B76 94 B1
Blakesley Ms YDLY B25 129 H4
Blakesley Rd STETCH B33 129 G3
Blakesley Wy STETCH B33 129 H2
Blake St FOAKS/STRLY B74 32 C4
Blakewood Cl
BKDE/SHDE B34 113 E4
Blandford Av CBROM B36 95 G5
Blandford Dr STRBR DY8 118 A2
Blandford Rd RIDG/WDGT B32 141 E2
Blanefield CDSL WV8 22 A1
Blay Av WSLW WS2 41 F3
Blaydon Av MGN/WHC B75 48 A3
Blaydon Rd COVEN WV9 22 C1
Blaythorn Av HIA/OLT B92 147 G4
Blaze Hill Rd KGSWFD DY6 99 E1
Blaze Pk KGSWFD DY6 99 E1
Bleak Hill Rd ERDW/GRVHL B23 92 A1
Bleakhouse Rd
LGLYGN/QTN B68 123 G3
Bleak St SMTHWKW B67 106 B3
Blenheim Cl RUSH/SHEL WS4 29 F3
Blenheim Dr DARL/WED WS10 55 H3
Blenheim Rd
GTB/HAM B43 73 F3
Blenheim Rd KGSWFD DY6 100 C3
MOS/BIL B13 161 F1
SHHTH WV12 25 H4
SHLY B90 180 D3
Blenheim Wy CVALE B35 94 C4
DUDN DY1 83 G4
KGSTG B44 75 F3
Bletchley Rd ERDE/BCHGN B24 94 A2
Blewitt Cl CBROM B36 95 F4
Blewitt St BRLYHL DY5 101 E3
Blews St AST/WIT B6 109 E4
Blithe Cl STRBR DY8 118 C4
Blithfield Dr BRLYHL DY5 118 D5
Blithfield Gv ERDE/BCHGN B24 93 G1
Blithfield Rd BRWNH WS8 8 C2
Blockall DARL/WED WS10 55 F1
Bloomfield Cl WMBN WV5 64 B5
Bloomfield Dr SHHTH WV12 26 B1
Bloomfield Pk TPTN/OCK DY4 68 D5
Bloomfield Rd MOS/BIL B13 144 C4
TPTN/OCK DY4 69 E4
Bloomfield St North HALE B63 138 B2
Bloomfield St West HALE B63 138 B3
Bloomfield Ter TPTN/OCK DY4 68 D5
Bloomsbury Gv
ALE/KHTH/YWD B14 160 C3
Bloomsbury St BKHL/PFLD WV2 6 E6
VAUX/NECH B7 109 H4
Bloomsbury Wk
VAUX/NECH B7 * 109 H4
Bloor Mill Cl WLNHL WV13 * 39 F4
Blossom Av SLYOAK B29 * 142 D5
Blossomfield Cl
HWK/WKHTH B38 176 B5
KGSWFD DY6 100 A1
Blossomfield Rd SOLH B91 181 F3
Blossom Gv CBROM B36 111 H1
Blossom Hl ERDE/BCHGN B24 93 E2
Blossom Rd ERDE/BCHGN B24 93 G2
Blossomville Wy ACGN B27 146 B3
Blowers Green Crs DUDS DY2 102 B2
Blower's Green Rd DUDS DY2 102 B2
Bloxcidge St LGLYGN/QTN B68 105 F4
Bloxwich La WSLW WS2 41 E2
Bloxwich Rd WSLW WS2 27 H4
Bloxwich Rd North
SHHTH WV12 26 B4
Bloxwich Rd South
WLNHL WV13 39 G2
Blucher St CBHAMW B1 2 E7
Blue Ball La HALE B63 137 G1
Bluebell Cl STRBR DY8 117 G2
Bluebell Crs WNSFLD WV11 24 D5
Bluebell Cft ERDW/GRVHL B23 76 A4
NFLD/LBR B31 175 F1
Bluebell Dr
CHWD/FDBR/MGN B37 132 D2
Bluebell Rd ALDR WS9 19 H4
CDYHTH B64 121 E1
DUDN DY1 84 B3
Bluebellwood Cl
FOAKS/STRLY B74 46 D4
MGN/WHC B75 47 F3
WALM/CURD B76 63 G5
Blue Cedar Dr
FOAKS/STRLY B74 60 B1
Blue Cedars STRBR DY8 134 C1
Blue Lake Rd DOR/KN B93 199 F1
Blue La East WSLW WS2 4 D1
Blue La West WSLW WS2 4 B2
Blue Rock Pl OLDBY B69 104 A3
Blundell Rd SPARK B11 145 F2
Blythefield Av GTB/HAM B43 73 E2
Blythe Gdns CDSL WV8 10 B3
Blythe Ga SHLY B90 195 G5
Blythe Gv KGSTG B44 60 B5
Blythe Rd CSHL/WTROR B46 115 H1
Blytheway SOLH B91 182 C2
Blythewood Cl SOLH B91 182 D4
Blythsford Rd HLGN/YWD B28 179 H1
Blythswood Rd SPARK B11 146 A3
Blyton Cl LDYWD/EDGR B16 107 H5
Board School Gdns SEDG DY3 67 G5
Boar Hound Cl WSNGN B18 * 108 A5
Boatman's La ALDR WS9 19 E5
Bobbington Wy DUDS DY2 102 D4
Bobs Coppice Wk BRLYHL DY5 119 H5
Bodenham Rd
LGLYGN/QTN B68 123 F4
NFLD/LBR B31 175 E3
Boden Rd HLGN/YWD B28 163 E3
Bodens La ALDR WS9 59 E1
Bodiam Ct
DUNHL/THL/PER WV6 35 E2
Bodicote Gv MGN/WHC B75 48 A2
Bodington Rd MGN/WHC B75 47 F2
Bodmin Cl DSYBK/YTR WS5 58 B1
Bodmin Gv VAUX/NECH B7 109 H4
Bodmin Ri DSYBK/YTR WS5 58 B1
Bodmin Rd DUDS DY2 120 D2
Bognop Rd WNSFLD WV11 14 B3
Boldmere Cl SCFLD/BOLD B73 77 E4
Boldmere Dr SCFLD/BOLD B73 77 E3
Boldmere Gdns
SCFLD/BOLD B73 77 E3
Boldmere Ga
SCFLD/BOLD B73 * 61 H5
Boldmere Rd SCFLD/BOLD B73 76 D2
Boldmere Ter SLYOAK B29 * 159 G1
Boleyn Rd RBRY B45 173 G4
Bolney Rd RIDG/WDGT B32 141 E2
Bolton Rd SMTHH B10 127 H4
SMTHH B10 128 A4
WNSFLD WV11 24 C5
Bolton St BORD B9 127 H2
Bolton Wy BLOX/PEL WS3 16 B4
Bomers Fld RBRY B45 188 C1
Bond Dr CVALE B35 94 C4
Bondfield Rd MOS/BIL B13 161 H4
Bond Sq WSNGN B18 108 A5
Bond St BILS/COS WV14 68 A3
BKHL/PFLD WV2 7 F6
BLKHTH/ROWR B65 122 C1
BVILLE B30 160 A3
LOZ/NWT B19 2 E2
WBROM B70 87 G4
Bone Mill La WOLV WV1 37 E1
Bonfire Hl HAG/WOL DY9 186 A2
Bonham Gv YDLY B25 129 H3
Boningale Wy DOR/KN B93 196 B5
Bonner Dr WALM/CURD B76 94 B1
Bonner Gv ALDR WS9 29 H5
Bonnington Wy GTB/HAM B43 59 H4
Bonsall Rd ERDW/GRVHL B23 77 E5
Bonville Gdns WOLVN WV10 13 E3
Booth Cl BLOX/PEL WS3 27 H2
KGSWFD DY6 100 C3
Booth Rd DARL/WED WS10 71 G1
Booths Farm Rd
PBAR/PBCH B42 74 A4
Booth's La PBAR/PBCH B42 74 B2
Booth St BLOX/PEL WS3 27 G2
DARL/WED WS10 40 B5
HDSW B21 107 E2
Bordeaux Cl DUDN DY1 83 G3
Borden Cl CDSL WV8 22 B2
Bordesley Circ SMTHH B10 127 H3
Bordesley Cl BORD B9 129 E2
Bordesley Gn BORD B9 128 C2
Bordesley Gn East
STETCH B33 130 A2
Bordesley Green Rd BORD B9 128 B2
Bordesley Park Rd
SMTHH B10 127 H3
Bordesley St DIG/EDG B5 3 J5
Borneo St RUSH/SHEL WS4 42 B1
Borough Crs OLDBY B69 104 C4
STRBR DY8 135 E2
Borrowdale Cl BRLYHL DY5 118 D4
Borrowdale Gv NFLD/LBR B31 174 D2
Borrowdale Rd NFLD/LBR B31 174 C2
Borrow St WLNHL WV13 39 G2
Borwick Av WBROM B70 87 E3
Boscobel Av TPTN/OCK DY4 85 F2
Boscobel Cl DUDN DY1 83 H3
Boscobel Crs WOLV WV1 37 E1
Boscobel Rd GTB/HAM B43 73 F1
SHLY B90 194 D3
WSL WS1 5 K6
Boscombe Av SPARK B11 * 145 E1
Boscombe Rd SPARK B11 145 G3
Boss Dr DUDS DY2 102 C2
Bossgate Cl WMBN WV5 81 E1
Boston Gv KGSTG B44 75 H3
Bosty La ALDR WS9 29 F5
Boswell Cl TPTN/OCK DY4 70 A2
Boswell Rd BILS/COS WV14 54 B1
FOAKS/STRLY B74 62 C2
KGSTG B44 75 F5
Bosworth Cl SEDG DY3 67 H5
Bosworth Dr
CHWD/FDBR/MGN B37 131 H2
Bosworth Rd
LGN/SDN/BHAMAIR B26 147 E3
Botany Dr SEDG DY3 83 F1
Botany Rd DSYBK/YTR WS5 57 F3
Botany Wk
LDYWD/EDGR B16 * 126 A2
Botha Rd BORD B9 128 D2
Botteley Rd WBROM B70 71 E5
Botterham La SEDG DY3 80 C3
Bottetourt Rd SLYOAK B29 141 G5
Botteville Rd ACGN B27 146 C5
Bott La HAG/WOL DY9 136 B1
WSL WS1 5 G4
Boughton Rd YDLY B25 129 G5
The Boulevard BRLYHL DY5 119 G2
SCFLD/BOLD B73 77 F3
Boultbee Rd
CSCFLD/WYGN B72 77 G4
Boulton Middleway
WSNGN B18 108 B4
Boulton Retreat HDSW B21 * 107 G1
Boulton Rd HDSW B21 107 G2
SOLH B91 165 E3
WBROM B70 87 H5
Boulton Sq WBROM B70 87 H5
Boulton Wk ERDW/GRVHL B23 91 H2
Boundary Av
BLKHTH/ROWR B65 122 C2
Boundary Cl WLNHL WV13 38 C4
Boundary Crs SEDG DY3 83 E3
Boundary Dr MOS/BIL B13 143 H5
Boundary Hl SEDG DY3 83 E2
Boundary La KINVER DY7 116 C3
SHLY B90 194 A2
Boundary Pl HDSW B21 88 D5
Boundary Rd ALDR WS9 19 F4
ERDW/GRVHL B23 92 C2
FOAKS/STRLY B74 60 B1
Boundary Wy
DUNHL/THL/PER WV6 34 D3
ETTPK/GDPK/PENN WV4 50 C2
Bourlay Cl RBRY B45 173 G3
Bournbrook Rd SLYOAK B29 142 D4
Bourne Av RMSLY B62 139 H3
TPTN/OCK DY4 70 A4
Bournebrook Cl DUDS DY2 102 C4
Bournebrook Crs RMSLY B62 140 A3
Bourne Cl MOS/BIL B13 162 A4
SOLH B91 165 G4
Bourne Gn RIDG/WDGT B32 141 E1
Bourne Hill Cl DUDS DY2 103 E5
Bourne Rd AST/WIT B6 109 H2
Bournes Cl HALE B63 138 B4
Bournes Crs HALE B63 138 A3
Bournes Hl HALE B63 138 A3
Bourne St DUDS DY2 84 D5
SEDG DY3 68 A4
Bourne V ALDR WS9 44 D2
Bourne Way Gdns SLYOAK B29 160 A2
Bourn Mill Dr AST/WIT B6 109 E3
Bournville La BVILLE B30 159 G4
Bourton Cl DSYBK/YTR WS5 57 G5
Bourton Cft HIA/OLT B92 164 B2
Bourton Rd HIA/OLT B92 164 B2
Bovey Cft WALM/CURD B76 78 C4
Bovingdon Rd CVALE B35 94 C3
Bowater Av STETCH B33 129 H3
Bowater St WBROM B70 87 G3
Bowbrook Av SHLY B90 195 G3
Bowcroft Gv ERDE/BCHGN B24 77 G5
Bowden Rd SMTHWKW B67 106 A3
Bowdler Rd BKHL/PFLD WV2 37 F5
Bowen Av
ETTPK/GDPK/PENN WV4 53 E5
Bowen-Cooke Av
DUNHL/THL/PER WV6 20 C4
Bowen St
ETTPK/GDPK/PENN WV4 52 C3
Bowercourt Cl SOLH B91 181 H4
Bower La BRLYHL DY5 119 H4
Bowes Rd RBRY B45 187 G1
Bowker St WLNHL WV13 38 C3

Bowlas Av FOAKS/STRLY B74 ....47 F5
Bowling Green Cl
   DARL/WED WS10 ....55 F1
   ERDW/GRVHL B23 ....76 C4
Bowling Green Dr
   SMTHWKW B67 ....124 A2
Bowling Green La
   BFLD/HDSWWD B20 ....108 A1
Bowling Green Rd DUDS DY2 ....120 D1
   SMHTH B10 ....128 A3
   STRBR DY8 ....135 E2
Bowman Rd PBAR/PBCH B42 .....74 A2
Bowman's Rd WSL WS1 ....38 A3
Bowood Crs NFLD/LBR B31 ......175 C3
Bowood Dr
   DUNHL/THL/PER WV6................21 H5
Bowood End WALM/CURD B76 ....62 D5
Bowshot Cl CBROM B36 ....95 H5
Bowstoke Rd GTB/HAM B43 ....75 E3
Bow St BILS/COS WV14 ....54 A2
   CBHAMW B1 ....126 D5
   WLNHL WV15 ....23 E2
Bowyer Rd WASH/WDE B8.........110 C5
Bowyer St BORD B9 ....127 G3
Boxhill Cl AST/WIT B6 ....109 F5
Box Rd CHWD/FDBR/MGN B37 ..132 C4
Box St WSL WS1 ....41 G4
Box Trees Rd HOCK/TIA B94.....198 A2
Boyd Gv ACGN B27 ....146 B5
Boyleston Cl RDNG/SHDW B30 ....53 E2
Boyleston Rd HLGN/YWD B28 ...163 E4
Boyne Rd
   LGN/SDN/BHAMAIR B26 ....130 D5
Boyton Gv KGSTG B44...................60 B5
Brabazon Gv CVALE B35 ....94 B3
Brabham Crs FOAKS/STRLY B74 ..66 B2
Bracadale Av ERDE/BCHGN B24 ..33 E2
Bracebridge Rd
   ERDE/BCHGN B24 ....92 D5
   FOAKS/STRLY B74 ....47 E5
Bracebridge St AST/WIT B6 ....109 E3
Braceby Av MOS/BIL B13 ....162 A3
Brace St WSL WS1 ....4 D7
Brackenbury Rd KGSTG B44........75 H3
Bracken Cl CDSL WV8 ....22 A1
Bracken Cft
   CHWD/FDBR/MGN B37 ....132 C1
Brackendale Dr
   DSYBK/YTR WS5 ....57 H5
Brackendale Wy
   HAG/WOL DY9 ....136 B3
Bracken Dr MGN/WHC B75 ....63 G3
Brackenfield Rd HALE B63 ....138 A4
   KGSTG B44 ....74 C1
Brackenfield Vw DUDN DY1 ......101 F1
Bracken Park Gdns
   STRBR DY8 ....118 B2
Bracken Rd ERDE/BCHGN B24 ....93 G4
Bracken Wy FOAKS/STRLY B74 ....55 E3
   HWK/WKHTH B38 ....190 B1
Bracken Wd DSYBK/YTR WS5 .....58 B3
Brackenwood Dr
   WNSFLD WV11 ....25 F5
Brackley Av
   BFLD/HDSWWD B20 ....90 C5
Brackleys Wy HIA/OLT B92 ....137 F5
Bradburn Rd WNSFLD WV11 ....24 B2
Bradburne Wy VAUX/NECH B7 ...109 G4
Bradbury Rd HIA/OLT B92 ....137 F5
Bradbury Rd BRWNH WS8 ....19 F2
Bradbury Rd HIA/OLT B92 ....164 B2
Braden Rd
   ETTPK/GDPK/PENN WV4........50 D4
Brades Cl HALE B63 ....120 B5
Brades Ri OLDBY B69 ....104 B1
Brades Rd OLDBY B69 ....104 C1
Bradewell Rd CBROM B36 ....95 F5
Bradfield Rd PBAR/PBCH B42 .....74 B4
Bradford Cl GTB/HAM B43 ....73 H4
Bradford La HLGN/YWD DY9 .....184 B5
Bradford Rd BKDE/SHDE B34 ...112 C2
   BRWNH WS8 ....9 E4
   CBROM B36 ....113 E2
   DUDS DY2 ....101 H5
Bradford St DIC/EDG B5 ....3 H3
   WSL WS1 ....5 J4
Bradgate Cl WMBN WV5 ....64 C4
Bradgate Dr FOAKS/STRLY B74 ..32 C5
Bradley La BILS/COS WV14 ....54 B5
Bradleymore Rd BRLYHL DY5 ....121 E5
Bradley Rd BKDE/SHDE B34 ....113 F3
   BKHL/PFLD WV2 ....52 C1
   STRBR DY8 ....135 F1
Bradleys Cl DYHTH B64 ....121 E5
Bradley's La BILS/COS WV14 ....54 B4
Bradley's Rd BILS/COS WV14 ......54 B4
   BRLYHL DY5 ....100 D2
   TPTN/OCK DY4 ....85 F4
Bradmore Cl SOLH B91 ....181 E1
Bradmore Gv SLYOAK B29 ....158 C2
Bradmore Rd BDMR/CCFT WV3 ..36 B5
Bradshaw Av DARL/WED WS10 ....54 C1
   HWK/WKHTH B38 ....176 B4
Bradshaw Cl EDG B15 ....126 C4
   TPTN/OCK DY4 ....85 G3
Bradshawe Cl
   HLGN/YWD B28 ....179 F2
Bradshaw St WOLV WV1 * 7 H4
Bradstock Rd BVILLE B30 ....177 G1
Bradwell Cft MGN/WHC B75 ....48 A2
Braemar Av STRBR DY8 ....117 G3
Braemar Cl SEDG DY3 ....67 E2
   SHHTH WV12 ....26 C4
Braemar Dr ERDW/GRVHL B23 ....91 H1
Braemar Rd HIA/OLT B92 ....164 A1
   SCFLD/BOLD B73 ....76 D1
Braeside Cft
   CHWD/FDBR/MGN B37 ....132 D2
Braeside Wy BLOX/PEL WS3 ....17 H4
Bragg Rd BFLD/HDSWWD B20 ....90 D4
Braggs Farm La SHLY B90 ....194 A4
Braid Cl HWK/WKHTH B38 ....176 A4
Brailes Cl HIA/OLT B92 ....165 G3
Brailes Dr WALM/CURD B76 ....63 F5
Brailes Gv BORD B9 ....129 F3
Brailsford Cl WNSFLD WV11 ....24 D5
Brailsford Dr SMTHWK B66 ....106 C4
Braithwaite Dr KGSWFD DY6 ......99 H5
Braithwaite Rd SPARK B11 ....127 H5

Brake La STRBR DY8 ....152 A4
Bramah Wy TPTN/OCK DY4 ....70 A5
Bramber Dr WMBN WV5 ....64 D5
Bramber Wy STRBR DY8 ....135 F5
Bramble Cl AST/WIT B6 ....109 E2
   WMBN WV5 ....19 E2
   CDYHTH B64 ....103 F5
   CSHL/WTROR B46 ....113 H1
   NFLD/LBR B31 ....158 B5
   SHHTH WV12 ....26 A3
Bramble Dell BORD B9 ....129 E1
Bramble Dr
   LGN/SDN/BHAMAIR B26 ....147 G1
Bramble Gn DUDN DY1 ....83 H1
Brambleside STRBR DY8 ....118 B3
The Brambles HAG/WOL DY9 .....136 B4
   WALM/CURD B76 ....78 C3
Bramblewood WMBN WV5 ....65 E4
Bramblewood Dr
   BDMR/CCFT WV3 ....36 A5
Bramblewoods
   BKDE/SHDE B34 ....113 E4
Brambling Wk EDG B15 ....126 C5
Bramcote Dr SOLH B91 ....165 E3
Bramcote Ri FOAKS/STRLY B74 ..62 C1
Bramcote Rd RIDG/WDGT B32 ...140 C2
Bramerton Cl WNSFLD WV11 ....11 A5
Bramford Dr DUDN DY1 ....68 B5
Bramley Cl DSYBK/YTR WS5 ....43 F5
   CTB/HAM B43 ....59 H5
Bramley Cft SHLY B90 ....180 C3
Bramley Dr
   BFLD/HDSWWD B20 ....90 B3
   HLYWD B47 ....192 D2
Bramley Mews Ct ACGN B27 .....146 C3
Bramley Rd ACGN B27 ....146 C2
   DSYBK/YTR WS5 ....57 H4
Brampton Av HLGN/YWD B28 ....163 E4
Brampton Crs SHLY B90 ....163 F4
Bramshall Dr DOR/KN B93 ....196 C5
Bramshaw Cl
   ALE/KHTH/YWD B14 ....178 B3
Bramstead Av
   DUNHL/THL/PER WV6................35 F3
Branchal Rd ALDR WS9 ....30 C1
Branch Rd HWK/WKHTH B38 .....176 B5
Brandhall Rd
   LGLYGN/QTN B68 ....123 F3
Brandon Cl ALDR WS9 ....45 F2
   SEDG DY3 ....67 G4
   WBROM B70 ....87 F4
Brandon Gv NFLD/LBR B31 ....189 F1
Brandon Pk BDMR/CCFT WV3 .....51 E1
Brandon Pl BKDE/SHDE B34 .....113 F2
Brandon Rd HLGN/YWD B28 ......145 G5
   RMSLY B62 ....122 C5
   SOLH B91 ....165 E3
Brandon Wy BRLYHL DY5 ....119 G4
   WBROM B70 ....87 E4
Brandwood Crs BVILLE B30 ....177 H2
Brandwood Dr
   ALE/KHTH/YWD B14 ....160 D5
Brandwood Park Rd
   ALE/KHTH/YWD B14 ....177 G1
Brandwood Rd
   ALE/KHTH/YWD B14 ....160 D5
Branfield Cl BILS/COS WV14 ....68 A2
Branksome Av HDSW WS7 ....107 H1
Branscombe Cl
   ALE/KHTH/YWD B14 ....160 D5
Bransdale Cl
   DUNHL/THL/PER WV6................22 C5
Bransdale Rd BRWNH WS8 ....9 E5
Bransford Ri SOLH B91 ....166 B5
Brantford Rd YDLY B25 ....129 C4
Branthill Cft SOLH B91 ....181 H4
Brantley Av BDMR/CCFT WV3 .....35 G4
Brantley Rd AST/WIT B6 ....91 H4
Branton Hill La ALDR WS9 ....30 C5
Brasshouse La SMTHWK B66 .....106 B3
Brassie Cl HWK/WKHTH B38 .....176 B4
Brassington Av
   CSCFLD/WYGN B72 ....62 C3
Bratch Cl DUDS DY2 ....120 C1
Bratch Common Rd
   WMBN WV5 ....64 C4
Bratch Hollow WMBN WV5 ....65 E3
Bratch La WMBN WV5 ....64 C3
Bratch Pk WMBN WV5 ....64 C3
Bratt St WBROM B70 ....87 G2
Braunston Cl WALM/CURD B76 ....78 C1
Brayford Av BRLYHL DY5 ....118 D5
Braymoor Rd STETCH B33 ....131 G3
Brays Rd
   LGN/SDN/BHAMAIR B26 ....147 H1
Bray St WLNHL WV13 ....39 H3
Bream Cl
   CHWD/FDBR/MGN B37 ....132 C2
   WOLN WV10 ....38 B1
Breamore Crs DUDN DY1 ....83 H1
Brean Av
   LGN/SDN/BHAMAIR B26 ....147 F2
Brearley Cl LOZ/NWT B19 ....108 D4
Brearley St HDSW B21 ....107 F1
   LOZ/NWT B19 ....108 D4
Brecknock Rd WBROM B70 ....71 E5
Brecon Dr STRBR DY8 ....135 H1
Brecon Rd
   BFLD/HDSWWD B20 ....108 B1
Bredon Av HAG/WOL DY9 ....136 A2
Bredon Cl HALE B63 ....138 C4
Bredon Cft WSNGN B18 ....108 A4
Bredon Rd OLDBY B69 ....104 B4
   STRBR DY8 ....135 G1
Breech Cl FOAKS/STRLY B74 ....60 A1
Breedon Rd BVILLE B30 ....160 A5
Breedon Ter WSNGN B18 ....108 A4
Breedon Wy RUSH/SHEL WS4 .....29 F1
Breen Rydding Dr
   BILS/COS WV14 ....68 B2
Brelades Cl DUDN DY1 ....83 C3
Brendan Cl CSHL/WTROR B46 ...115 C4
Brennand Rd
   LGLYGN/QTN B68 ....123 F3
Brentford Rd
   ALE/KHTH/YWD B14 ....161 F5
   SHLY B90 ....181 E2
Brentmill Cl WOLN WV10 ....13 F3
Brentnall Dr MGN/WHC B75 ....47 F2

Brenton Rd
   ETTPK/GDPK/PENN WV4.........51 F4
Brent Rd BVILLE B30 ....160 C2
Brentwood Cl SOLH B91 ....181 E2
Brentwood Gv KGSTG B44............75 E3
Brenwood Cl KGSWFD DY6 ....99 F2
Brereton Cl DUDS DY2 ....85 H5
Brereton Rd SHHTH WV12 ....26 A3
Bretby Cl DOR/KN B93 ....196 D3
Bretby Gv ERDW/GRVHL B23 ....77 E5
Brethsall Cl SHLY B90 ....195 F5
Brett Cl SHLY B90 ....195 E5
Brett Dr RIDG/WDGT B32 ....157 G2
Brettell La STRBR DY8 ....118 B4
Brettell St DUDS DY2 ....102 B2
Bretton Gdns WOLN WV10 ....23 H4
Bretton Rd ACGN B27 ....146 D5
Brett St HHTH/SAND B71..............87 F1
Brevitt Rd BKHL/PFLD WV2 ....52 B2
Brewers Dr BLOX/PEL WS3 ....28 C1
Brewer St WSL WS1 ....5 K2
Brewery St AST/WIT B6 ....109 E4
   DUDS DY2 ....85 C5
   HDSW B21 ....107 F1
Brewster St DUDS DY2 ....106 B3
Brewins Wy BRLYHL DY5 ....101 H5
Breydon Gv WLNHL WV15 ....39 F5
Brian Rd SMTHWKW B67 ....106 A3
Briar Av FOAKS/STRLY B74 ....45 G4
Briarbeck RUSH/SHEL WS4 ....29 F2
Briar Cl ERDE/BCHGN B24 ....93 E2
Briarfield Rd SPARK B11 ....146 A4
Briars Cl BRLYHL DY5 ....101 E5
The Briars ALDR WS9 ....30 A3
   HAG/WOL DY9 * 169 F1
Briar Wy HWK/WKHTH B38 ....177 E5
Briar Wood Cl BKHL/PFLD WV2 ..51 E3
Briarwood Cl SHLY B90 ....194 D4
Brickbridge La WMBN WV5 ....80 C1
Brickfield Rd YDLY B25 ....146 B1
Brickheath Rd WOLV WV1 ....38 A2
Brickhill Dr
   CHWD/FDBR/MGN B37 ....132 A2
Brickhouse La South
   TPTN/OCK DY4 ....70 B5
Brickhouse Rd
   BLKHTH/ROWR B65 ....103 C5
Brickiln St SMTHWK WS8 ....9 F5
Brick Kiln La HLYWD B47 ....192 B4
   KGSTG B44 ....59 G5
   SEDG DY3 ....82 C3
   SHLY B90 ....181 F5
Brick Kiln St BRLYHL DY5 ....101 G4
   TPTN/OCK DY4 ....69 E5
Brickkiln St WLNHL WV15 ....39 F4
Brick St SEDG DY3 ....67 F4
Brickyard Rd ALDR WS9 ....29 H2
Briddsland Rd STETCH B33 ....131 G2
Bridge Av TPTN/OCK DY4 ....70 A4
Bridgeburn Rd NFLD/LBR B31 ...158 A5
Bridge Cl MOS/BIL B13 ....144 D4
Bridge Cft BHTH/HG B12 ....144 A1
Bridgeford Rd
   BKDE/SHDE B34 ....112 D3
Bridgelands Wy
   BFLD/HDSWWD B20 ....90 D5
Bridgeman Cft CBROM B36 ....113 E1
Bridgeman St WSL WS1 ....4 D4
Bridgemary Cl WOLN WV10 ....13 F3
Bridge Meadow Dr
   DOR/KN B93 ....196 D5
Bridgend Cft BRLYHL DY5 ....100 D3
Bridge Piece NFLD/LBR B31 ......175 H5
Bridge Rd RUSH/SHEL WS4 ....28 D1
   TPTN/OCK DY4 ....70 A4
   WASH/WDE B8 ....128 C1
Bridgeside Cl BRWNH WS8 ....19 F1
Bridge St BILS/COS WV14 ....68 C5
   BRWNH WS8 ....16 C5
   CBHAMW B1 ....2 D7
   DARL/WED WS10 ....70 D1
   HALE B63 ....120 C5
   OLDBY B69 ....69 F5
   STRBR DY8 ....118 A3
   WBROM B70 ....87 F2
   WLNHL WV13 ....39 H4
   WOLN WV10 ....23 C5
   WSL WS1 ....4 E5
Bridge St North SMTHWK B66 ...106 D3
Bridge St South SMTHWK B66 ...106 D3
Bridge St West LOZ/NWT B19 ....108 D3
The Bridge WSL WS1 ....4 F4
Bridge Vw CSHL/WTROR B46 * ..115 F2
Bridge Wy ACGN B27 * 146 D4
Bridgewater Av OLDBY B69 ....105 E5
Bridgewater Crs DUDS DY2 ....85 E5
Bridgewater Dr BILS/COS WV14 ..68 A4
   WMBN WV5 ....64 D4
Bridge Wy BRWNH WS8 ....19 E1
Bridgnorth Av WMBN WV5 ....80 D2
Bridgnorth Gv SHHTH WV12 ....25 H4
Bridgnorth Rd
   DUNHL/THL/PER WV6................35 E3
   SEDG DY3 ....80 A1
   STRBR DY8 ....134 C1
Bridgwater Cl ALDR WS9 ....19 H5
Bridle Gv HHTH/SAND B71 ....72 B3
Bridle La ALDR WS9 ....59 H2
   FOAKS/STRLY B74 ....45 F5
Bridle Md HWK/WKHTH B38 ......176 B5
The Bridle Pth SHLY B90 ....163 F5
Bridle Rd STRBR DY8 ....134 D1
Bridlewood
   FOAKS/STRLY B74 ....45 F5
Brierley Hill Rd STRBR DY8 ....118 A2
Brierley La BILS/COS WV14 ....69 E1
Brier Mill Rd HALE B63 ....139 E4
Briery Cl CDYHTH B64 ....121 F5
Briery Rd HALE B63 ....138 A4
Brigadoon Gdns
   HAG/WOL DY9 ....136 A5
Brigfield Crs MOS/BIL B13 ....161 H5
Brigfield Rd MOS/BIL B13 ....161 H5
Brighton Cl WSLW WS2 ....4 B1
Brighton Pl WOLV WV3 ....36 D4
Brighton Rd BHTH/HG B12 ....144 B2
Bright Rd LGLYGN/QTN B68 ......105 F4
Brightstone Cl WOLN WV10 ....11 H3
Brightstone Rd RBRY B45 ....174 B3

Bright St DARL/WED WS10 ....55 F3
   STRBR DY8 ....134 D2
   WOLV WV1 ....6 D1
Brightwell Crs DUNHL/THL/PER WV6 *36 E2
Brimfield Pl DUNHL/THL/PER WV6 *36
   E2
Brindle Cl LGN/SDN/BHAMAIR B26147
   E2
Brindlefields Wy TPTN/OCK DY4 .85 G4
Brindle Rd DSYBK/YTR WS5 ....58 A4
Brindley Cl WNSFLD WV11 ....25 C1
Brindley Ct STRBR DY8 ....118 A3
   WMBN WV5 ....64 B5
   WSLW WS2 ....48 B5
Brindley Ct LGLYGN/QTN B68 * ..123 F5
Brindley Dr CBHAMW B1 ....2 B6
Brindley Pl CBHAMW B1 ....2 B6
Brindley Rd HHTH/SAND B71 ....71 E3
Brindley Wy SMTHWK B66 * 107 E4
Brineton Gv SLYOAK B29 ....158 C1
Brineton St WSLW WS2 ....4 A6
Bringewood Gv
   RIDG/WDGT B32 ....157 F2
Brinklow Dr BKDE/SHDE B34 .....113 F2
Brinklow Rd SLYOAK B29 ....141 F5
Brinley Wy KGSWFD DY6 ....99 C3
Brinsford Rd WOLN WV10 ....12 C4
Brinsley Cl SOLH B91 ....181 H5
Brinsley Rd
   LGN/SDN/BHAMAIR B26 ....130 D4
Brisbane Rd SMTHWK B67 ....106 A3
Briseley Cl BRLYHL DY5 ....119 C4
Bristam Cl OLDBY B69 ....104 C3
Bristnall Hall La
   LGLYGN/QTN B68 ....123 C1
Bristnall Hall Rd
   LGLYGN/QTN B68 ....123 C1
Bristol Rd DUDS DY2 ....120 D2
   ERDW/GRVHL B23 ....92 C3
   SLYOAK B29 ....159 F2
Bristol Rd South RBRY B45 ....188 A1
Bristol St BDMR/CCFT WV3 ....6 C7
   BILS/COS WV14 ....53 H3
   DIG/EDG B5 ....142 D1
Briston Cl BRLYHL DY5 ....119 E4
Britannia Gdns
   BLKHTH/ROWR B65 ....122 A1
Britannia Pk DARL/WED WS10 * .70 B1
Britannia Rd BILS/COS WV14 ....54 B5
   BLKHTH/ROWR B65 ....122 A1
Britannia St TP OLDBY B69 ....86 A4
Britannic Gdns MOS/BIL B13 .....143 H5
Britford Cl
   ALE/KHTH/YWD B14 ....178 B2
Britannia Rd WSL WS1 ....56 D3
Britton Dr CSCFLD/WYGN B72 .....77 G3
Britwell Rd SCFLD/BOLD B73 ......77 E1
Brixfield Wy SHLY B90 ....194 A3
Brixham Rd LDYWD/EDGR B16 ..107 F5
Broad Acres NFLD/LBR B31 ....158 A4
Broad Cft TPTN/OCK DY4 ....70 A5
Broadfern Rd DOR/KN B93 ....183 F5
Broadfield Cl HHTH/SAND B71 ....72 B5
   KGSWFD DY6 ....99 H4
Broadfields HAG/WOL DY9 ....152 C4
Broadfields Rd
   ERDW/GRVHL B23 ....77 F4
Broadheath Wk
   LDYWD/EDGR B16 ....2 B7
Broadheath Dr
   RUSH/SHEL WS4 ....29 F2
Broadidley Dr
   RIDG/WDGT B32 ....157 F1
Broadlands WOLN WV10 ....12 D2
Broadlands Dr BRLYHL DY5 ....101 C4
Broad La ALE/KHTH/YWD B14 ...177 H2
   BDMR/CCFT WV3 ....16 C5
   BLOX/PEL WS3 ....29 E1
   RUSH/SHEL WS4 ....29 E1
   WNSFLD WV11 ....15 H2
Broad Lane Gdns
   BLOX/PEL WS3 ....16 C5
Broad La North WNSFLD WV11 ....25 H4
Broad Lanes BILS/COS WV14 ......53 C4
Broad Lanes South WNSFLD WV14 25 F5
Broad Meadow ALDR WS9 ....30 B2
Broadmeadow Cl BVILLE B30 .....177 F2
Broadmeadow Gv
   BILS/COS WV14 ....53 C1
Broad Meadow La BVILLE B30 ...177 F2
Broadmeadows Rd
   SHHTH WV12 ....26 C2
Broadmoor Av
   LGLYGN/QTN B68 ....123 H2
Broadmoor Rd BILS/COS WV14 ...53 C4
Broad Oaks WALM/CURD B76 .....78 C3
Broad Oaks Rd SOLH B91 ....164 B5
Broad Rd ACGN B27 ....146 B4
Broadstone Av
   BLOX/PEL WS3 ....27 H3
   HALE B63 ....137 F3
Broadstone Cl
   ETTPK/GDPK/PENN WV4........52 B3
Broadstone Rd
   LGN/SDN/BHAMAIR B26 ....130 D2
Broad St BILS/COS WV14 ....68 C3
   BRLYHL DY5 ....101 E3
   EDG B15 ....2 B7
   KGSWFD DY6 ....99 C3
   OLDBY B69 ....105 E4
   WOLV WV1 ....7 G3
Broad Street Jct WOLV WV1 ....7 H3
Broadwaters Av
   DARL/WED WS10 ....55 E4
Broadwaters Rd
   DARL/WED WS10 ....55 E4
Broadway Rd RUSH/SHEL WS4 ...18 C5
   CDSL WV8 ....10 C5
   HAG/WOL DY9 ....136 C1
Broadway BDMR/CCFT WV3 ....52 D2
   CDSL WV8 ....10 D5
   SHLY B90 ....179 H4
   STETCH B33 ....112 A5
   WOLV WV10 ....17 E5
   WSL WS1 ....57 E3
Broadway Cft
   LGLYGN/QTN B68 ....123 G3
   LGN/SDN/BHAMAIR B26 ....147 G1

Broadway North WSL WS1 ....5 J2
The Broadway
   BFLD/HDSWWD B20 ....90 D4
   DUDN DY1 ....84 A3
   HHTH/SAND B71 ....71 E4
   STRBR DY8 ....134 D5
   WMBN WV5 ....65 G5
Broadway West WSL WS1 ....56 D2
Broadwell Rd HIA/OLT B92 ....147 G5
   OLDBY B69 ....105 E1
Broadyates Gv YDLY B25 ....146 C1
Broadyates Rd YDLY B25 ....146 C1
Brobury Cft SOLH B91 ....180 C1
Brock Cl RBRY B45 ....174 A4
Brockeridge Cl SHHTH WV12 ......26 A1
Brockhall Gv
   CHWD/FDBR/MGN B37 ....113 H4
Brockhill La ALVE B48 ....191 H5
Brockhurst Crs
   DSYBK/YTR WS5 ....57 F4
Brockhurst Dr
   DUNHL/THL/PER WV6................35 C1
   HLGN/YWD B28 ....163 E5
Brockhurst Pl DSYBK/YTR WS5 ...57 F5
Brockhurst Rd CBROM B36 ....111 G3
   MGN/WHC B75 ....47 H4
Brockhurst St WSL WS1 ....57 F4
Brinsley Cl BRLYHL DY5 ....119 F1
Brockley Cl BRLYHL DY5 ....101 G4
Brockley Gv MOS/BIL B13 ....160 C1
Brockley Pl VAUX/NECH B7 ....110 A2
Brockmoor Cl HAG/WOL DY9 .....136 A5
Brock Rd TPTN/OCK DY4 ....85 F1
Brockwell Gv KGSTG B44 ....60 A4
Brockwell Rd KGSTG B44 ....60 A4
Brockworth Rd
   ALE/KHTH/YWD B14 ....177 C3
Brocton Cl BILS/COS WV14 ....53 E5
   BLOX/PEL WS3 ....27 E2
Brogden Cl HHTH/SAND B71 ....72 B3
Bromfield Cl AST/WIT B6 ....109 E2
Bromfield Ct
   DUNHL/THL/PER WV6................35 F2
Bromfield Crs DARL/WED WS10 ..56 C5
Bromford Cl ERDW/GRVHL B23 ...92 C1
Bromford Crs
   ERDE/BCHGN B24 ....93 E4
Bromford Di
   DUNHL/THL/PER WV6................36 D2
Bromford Dell NFLD/LBR B31 ....176 A1
Bromford Dr CBROM B36 ....111 H4
Bromford Hl
   BFLD/HDSWWD B20 ....90 C3
Bromford La ERDE/BCHGN B24 ...93 E5
   ERDE/BCHGN B24 ....111 E1
Bromford Ri BDMR/CCFT WV3 ....36 C5
Bromford Rd CBROM B36 ....111 G2
   CBROM B36 ....112 A2
   DUDS DY2 ....101 H5
   WBROM B70 ....87 E5
Bromley BRLYHL DY5 ....100 D4
Bromley Gdns CDSL WV8 ....10 C3
Bromley La KGSWFD DY6 ....100 A5
Bromley Pl
   ETTPK/GDPK/PENN WV4........51 G3
Bromley St BKHL/PFLD WV2 ....51 G3
   BORD B9 ....126 D1
   HAG/WOL DY9 ....136 D1
Brompton Lawns
   DUNHL/THL/PER WV6................35 E2
Brompton Pool Rd
   HLGN/YWD B28 ....179 G2
Brompton Rd KGSTG B44 ....60 A4
Bromsgrove Rd
   HAG/WOL DY9 ....170 B3
   HALE B63 ....139 E4
   RMSLY B62 ....172 C2
Bromsgrove St DIG/EDG B5 ....126 D3
Bromwall Rd MOS/BIL B13 ....161 H4
Bromwich Dr MGN/WHC B75 ....62 C1
Bromwich La HAG/WOL DY9 ......152 B3
Bromwynd Cl BKHL/PFLD WV2 ....51 H2
Bromyard Av WALM/CURD B76 ....78 C3
Bromyard Rd SPARK B11 ....145 G4
Bronte Cl SHLY B90 ....180 D4
Bronte Dr DUDS DY2 ....120 C2
Bronte Farm Rd SHLY B90 ....180 D4
Bronte Rd BKHL/PFLD WV2 ....52 D2
Bronwen Rd BILS/COS WV14 ......68 C4
Bronwen Vls
   DARL/WED WS10 * 55 F2
Brookbank Av
   BKDE/SHDE B34 ....113 E3
Brookbank Gdns SEDG DY3 ....82 D4
Brook Cl ALDR WS9 ....19 C4
   SHLY B90 ....179 H4
   STETCH B33 ....112 A5
Brook Crs HAG/WOL DY9 ....152 D5
   KGSWFD DY6 ....99 G2
Brook Cft
   CHWD/FDBR/MGN B37 ....132 B5
   LGN/SDN/BHAMAIR B26 ....130 D5
Brookdale Cl RBRY B45 ....174 B3
Brookdale Dr
   ETTPK/GDPK/PENN WV4........50 D2
Brook Dr RIDG/WDGT B32 ....157 H1
Brookend Dr RBRY B45 ....187 H1
Brookes Cl OLDBY B69 ....105 E1
Brook End St DUDS DY2 ....102 C1
Brookfield Cl ALDR WS9 ....30 A1
   BVILLE B30 ....177 H2
   CDSL WV8 ....10 B3
   WSNGN B18 ....107 H4
Brookfields Rd
   LGLYGN/QTN B68 ....105 G5
Brookfield Wy HIA/OLT B92 ....163 H3
   TPTN/OCK DY4 ....69 C5
Brook Gv CDSL WV8 ....10 C5
Brookhill Cl SHHTH WV12 ....26 A1
Brook Hill Rd WASH/WDE B8 .....111 F5
Brook Holloway
   HAG/WOL DY9 ....136 C4
Brookhouse La WOLN WV10 ....13 F1
Brook House La WOLN WV10 ....13 F1
Brookhouse Rd
   DSYBK/YTR WS5 ....57 H1

Brookhus Farm Rd WALM/CURD B76......78 C3
Brooking Cl GTB/HAM B43......59 H4
Brookland Gv ALDR WS9......19 F5
Brookland Rd ALDR WS9......19 F5
HAG/WOL DY9......152 C5
Brooklands STRBR DY8......118 B3
Brooklands Cl HLGN/YWD B28..162 D1
Brooklands Dr
ALE/KHTH/YWD B14......161 E5
Brooklands Gv ALDR WS9......19 F5
Brooklands Pde WOLV WV1......38 B3
Brooklands Rd
HLGN/YWD B28......162 D1
The Brooklands SEDG DY3......80 C5
Brooklands Wy
CHWD/FDBR/MGN B37......132 B4
Brook La ALDR WS9......19 G4
ALE/KHTH/YWD B14......161 F2
CDYHTH B64......121 E2
HIA/OLT B92......163 H2
RIDG/WDGT B32......141 F2
Brooklea Gv HWK/WKHTH B38...177 E4
Brooklyn Av AST/WIT B6......109 F2
Brooklyn Gv BILS/COS WV14....99 F1
KCSWFD DY6
Brookmans Av
RIDG/WDGT B32......140 D3
Brookmeadow Ct
HLGN/YWD B28......162 B4
Brookmeadow Wy
BKDE/SHDE B34......112 C5
RUSH/SHEL WS4......29 F2
Brook Mdw EDG B15......125 G5
LGLYGN/QTN B68......123 E2
RBRY B45......187 H1
STRBR DY8......135 H4
WLNHL WV5......39 E4
WMBN WV5......64 B5
Brooks Rd
CSCFLD/WYGN B72......77 G2
Brook St BILS/COS WV14......54 A3
BRLYHL DY5......120 A4
CBHAMNW B3......2 D3
HAG/WOL DY9......136 D2
KCSWFD DY6......81 F5
SEDG DY3......85 E3
SMTHWK B66......106 D5
STRBR DY8......135 H4
TPTN/OCK DY4......69 E5
WBROM B70......43 F2
WSLW WS2......4 B4
Brook Ter BILS/COS WV14....54 A5
Brookthorpe Dr SHHTH WV12...12 A4
Brookvale Gv HIA/OLT B92....163 H1
Brookvale Park Rd
ERDW/GRVHL B23......91 H2
Brookvale Rd ALDR WS6......91 G3
HIA/OLT B92......163 H1
Brookview SMTHKW B67 *....124 B1
Brook View Cl LOZ/NWT B19...108 C3
Brook Wk RIDG/WDGT B32....140 D5
Brookwillow Rd HALE B63......137 H5
Brookwood Av
HLGN/YWD B28......162 B5
Broomcroft Rd
CHWD/FDBR/MGN B37......113 H4
Broomdene Av
BKDE/SHDE B34......112 C3
Broome Dr ALE.KHTH/YWD B14..178 A1
Broome Av GTB/HAM B43......73 E4
Broome Cl HALE B63......138 C4
Broome Gdns MGN/WHC B75...62 C3
Broomehill Cl BRLYHL DY5....119 E5
Broome La KIDD DY10......169 E2
Broome Rd WOLV WV10......23 F5
Broomfield SMTHKW B67......106 B4
Broomfield Rd
DARL/WED WS10......56 C5
ERDW/GRVHL B23......92 B4
Broomfields Cl SOLH B91......165 F5
Broomhall Av WNSFLD WV11...24 D4
Brom Hall Ct ACGN B27......163 G5
Broom Hall Gv ACGN B27......163 G3
Broomhill Cl GTB/HAM B43....73 E3
Broomhill La GTB/HAM B43...73 E3
Broomhill Rd
ERDW/GRVHL B23......75 H4
Broomhurst
LDYWD/EDGR B16......125 G4
Broomie Cl MGN/WHC B75.....62 D4
Broom La SHLY B90......194 A2
Broom Rd DSYBK/YTR WS5....57 H5
DUDN DY1......84 A2
Broomy Cl BKDE/SHDE B34..112 C4
Broseley Av NFLD/LBR B31....175 H5
Broseley Brook Cl BORD B9...128 A3
Brosil Av BFLD/HDSWWD B20...89 C3
Brougham St LOZ/NWT B19...108 B2
Brough Cl
ETTPK/GDPK/PENN WV4...52 D5
VAUX/NECH B7......109 H3
Broughton Ct
DUNHL/THL/PER WV6.....35 E2
Broughton Crs NFLD/LBR B31..174 D5
Broughton Rd
BDMR/CCFT WV3......35 G4
BFLD/HDSWWD B20......108 A1
HAG/WOL DY9......136 B4
Brownfield Rd
BKDE/SHDE B34......113 F2
Brownhills Rd BRWNH WS8...19 F2
Browning Cl SHHTH WV12....26 C3
Browning Gv WOLV WV10....12 C5

Browning Gv
DUNHL/THL/PER WV6......34 C1
Browning Rd SEDG DY5......82 C2
Brownley Rd SHLY B90......195 E1
Brown Lion St TPTN/OCK DY4...69 E4
Brown Rd DARL/WED WS10....55 E1
Brown's Coppice Av SOLH B91.163 H5
Browns Dr SCFLD/BOLD B73...76 D5
Browns Dr RBRY B45......173 G4
Brownsea Dr CBHAMW B1.....2 E7
Browns Gn BFLD/HDSWWD B20..89 F1
Brownshore La WNSFLD WV11..15 H4
Browns La DOR/KN B93......196 C2
Brownsover Cl CBROM B36....94 D5
Browns St BKHL/PFLD WV2....52 B1
Brownswall Rd SEDG DY3....66 B4
Broxwood Pk
DUNHL/THL/PER WV6......35 F2
Brueton Av SOLH B91......182 B2
Brueton Dr ERDE/BCHGN B24...93 E3
Brueton Rd BILS/COS WV14....54 C1
Bruford Rd BDMR/CCFT WV3...36 C5
Brunel Cl BHTH/HG B12......144 C2
Brunel Ct BILS/COS WV14....69 E2
Brunel Dr TPTN/OCK DY4......69 E2
Brunel Gv
DUNHL/THL/PER WV6......20 C4
Brunel Rd OLDBY B69......104 B3
Brunel St CBHAMW B1......2 C6
Brunel Wk DARL/WED WS10 *...55 H2
Brunel Wy BKHL/PFLD WV2...53 E1
Brunslow Cl WLNHL WV13....40 A4
WOLV WV10......23 E1
Brunswick Ga STRBR DY8....152 C1
Brunswick Park Rd
DARL/WED WS10......56 A5
Brunswick Rd BHTH/HG B12..144 C2
BORD B9......89 H5
Brunswick Sq CBHAMW B1.....2 B6
Brunswick St CBHAMW B1.....2 B6
WSLW WS2......56 C1
Brunswick Ter
DARL/WED WS10......55 H5
Brunton Rd SMHTH B10......128 D5
Brushfield Rd PBAR/PBCH B42..74 D3
Brutus Dr CSHL/WTROR B46...97 E5
Bryan Av
ETTPK/GDPK/PENN WV4...50 D5
Bryan Rd WSLW WS2......56 C2
Bryanston Ct SOLH B91 *.....166 B3
Bryanston Rd SOLH B91......164 B4
Bryant St WSNGN B18......107 G4
Bryce Rd BRLYHL DY5......100 B4
Brylan Cft KGSTG B44......75 F5
Bryn Arden Rd
LGN/SDN/BHAMAIR B26...147 E2
Bryndale Av
ALE/KHTH/YWD B14......160 C5
Brynmawr Rd BILS/COS WV14..52 D5
Brynside Cl
ALE/KHTH/YWD B14......177 H3
Bryony Cft ERDW/GRVHL B23...75 H4
Bryony Gdns DARL/WED WS10..55 F1
Bryony Rd SLYOAK B29......158 D3
Buchanan Cl RUSH/SHEL WS4...42 C2
Buchanan Rd BILS/COS WV14...54 J1
Buckbury Cl HAG/WOL DY9....153 F1
Buckbury Cft SHLY B90......195 H2
Buckingham Cl
DARL/WED WS10......56 C4
Buckingham Dr SHHTH WV12...25 H5
Buckingham Gv KCSWFD DY6...99 G2
Buckingham Ms
SCFLD/BOLD B73......77 E1
Buckingham Rd
BLKHTH/ROWR B65......104 B5
CBROM B36......113 H2
ETTPK/GDPK/PENN WV4...2 E1
LGN/SDN/BHAMAIR B26
LOZ/NWT B19......2 E1
Buckland End La
BKDE/SHDE B34......112 C3
Bucklands End La
BKDE/SHDE B34......112 B3
Buckle Cl WSL WS1......4 E7
Buckley Rd
ETTPK/GDPK/PENN WV4...50 D3
Buckminster Dr DOR/KN B93..196 C4
Bucknall Crs RIDG/WDGT B32..157 E2
Bucknall Rd WNSFLD WV11...25 G1
Bucknell Cl SOLH B91......165 G5
Buckridge Cl
HWK/WKHTH B38......190 B1
Buckridge La SHLY B90......194 A3
Buckton Cl MGN/WHC B75....48 A3
Budbrook Gv BKDE/SHDE B34..113 G3
Budden Rd BILS/COS WV14....68 D4
Bude Rd DSYBK/YTR WS5......58 B2
Buffery Rd DUDN DY1......102 D2
Bufferys Cl SOLH B91......181 H5
Buildwas Cl BLOX/PEL WS3...16 B5
Bulford Cl
ALE/KHTH/YWD B14......178 B3
Bulger Rd BILS/COS WV14....53 G1
Bullace Cft EDG B15......142 B4
Buller St
ETTPK/GDPK/PENN WV4...52 C3
Bullfields Cl
BLKHTH/ROWR B65......103 F4
Bullfinch Cl DUDN DY1......101 G1
Bullivents Cl DOR/KN B93....196 D5
Bull La BILS/COS WV14......54 D5
WBROM B70......87 H1
WMBN WV5......65 F4
Bullmeadow La WMBN WV5...65 E4
Bullock's Rw WSL WS1......5 H4
Bullock St VAUX/NECH B7....109 G4
WBROM B70......105 H1
Bullows Rd BRWNH WS8......18 C1
Bull Ring HALE B63......138 D4
Bull St La WALM/CURD B76...78 D7
CBHAM B2......3 G5
DARL/WED WS10......56 A1
DUDN DY1......102 A1
HRBN B17......142 B1
SEDG DY3......83 E4
WBROM B70......87 H4
Bulrush Cl BRWNH WS8......9 E5
Bulwell Cl BHTH/HG B12......109 G2

Bumblehole Mdw WMBN WV5...64 D4
Bunbury Gdns BVILLE B30....176 A1
Bunbury Rd NFLD/LBR B31....175 G2
Bundle Hl HALE B63......138 C3
The Bungalows WBROM B70 *...70 D5
Bunkers Hill La BILS/COS WV14..39 E5
Bunn's La DUDS DY2......85 E5
Burbage Cl WOLV WV10......23 C4
Burbidge Rd BORD B9......128 B1
Burbury St LOZ/NWT B19....108 C3
Burbury St South
LOZ/NWT B19......108 C3
Burcot Av WOLV WV1......38 A3
Burcote Rd ERDE/BCHGN B24...93 H5
Burdock Cl DSYBK/YTR WS5...57 C5
Burdock Rd SLYOAK B29......158 C4
Burdons Cl BKDE/SHDE B34...112 C4
Bure Gv WLNHL WV13......40 A4
Burfield Rd HALE B63......137 G1
Burford Cl DSYBK/YTR WS5...57 H5
HIA/OLT B92......147 G4
Burford Rd HLYWD B47......192 B2
KGSTG B44......75 F4
Burford Park Rd
HWK/WKHTH B38......190 D1
Burgess Cft HIA/OLT B92.....165 H5
Burghley Dr HHTH/SAND B71...72 B1
Burghley Wk BRLYHL DY5....118 D4
Burgh Wy WSLW WS2......41 E1
Burhill Wy
CHWD/FDBR/MGN B37......114 B5
Burkitt Dr TPTN/OCK DY4......70 A3
Burland Av
DUNHL/THL/PER WV6......22 A3
Burleigh Cl SHHTH WV12....25 H4
Burleigh Rd BDMR/CCFT WV3...51 C1
Burleigh St WSL WS1......5 G5
Burleton Rd STETCH B33......131 C2
Burley Cl SHLY B90......194 B2
Burlington Rd SMHTH B10....128 C5
WBROM B70......87 H5
Burlington St AST/WIT B6.....109 E5
Burlish Av HIA/OLT B92......164 B1
Burman Cl SHLY B90......194 D1
Burman Dr CSHL/WTROR B46..115 F4
Burman Rd SHLY B90......179 H5
Burmese Wy
BLKHTH/ROWR B65......103 F3
Burnaston Crs SHLY B90......196 A1
Burnaston Rd HLGN/YWD B28..162 C2
Burnbank Gv
ERDE/BCHGN B24......93 F2
Burnbush Cl CROM B36......106 C5
Burncross Wy WOLV WV10....10 A1
Burnell Gdns BDMR/CCFT WV3..36 A5
Burnett Rd FOAKS/STRLY B74...44 C5
Burnett Rd FOAKS/STRLY B74...45 E5
Burnett Dr WASH/WDE B8....111 G5
Burnfields Av ALDR WS9......30 A3
Burnham Av WOLV WV10......23 A3
YDLY B25......146 C1
Burnham Meadow
HLGN/YWD B28......163 E4
Burnham Rd KGSTG B44......75 E4
Burnlea Gv SLYOAK B29......158 C2
Burnlea Gv BLOX/PEL WS3...16 D5
Burnsall Cl
CHWD/FDBR/MGN B37......131 H2
COVEN WV9......12 A4
Burns Av TPTN/OCK DY4......69 G4
Burns Cl STRBR DY8......118 C4
Burns Gv SEDG DY3......82 C2
Burnside Gdns DSYBK/YTR WS5..58 B2
Burnside Wy NFLD/LBR B31....189 F1
Burns Pl DARL/WED WS10....54 C3
Burnt Oak Dr STRBR DY8....135 G2
Burnthurst Crs SHLY B90....195 G1
Burnt Tree TPTN/OCK DY4....85 H1
Burrington Rd
RIDG/WDGT B32......157 E2
Burrowes St WSL WS1......4 C1
Burrow Hill Cl CBROM B36....113 E1
Burrows Rd KCSWFD DY6....100 B5
Burrows St WSLW WS2......56 D1
Bursnips Rd WNSFLD WV11...15 C5
Burston Av RUSH/SHEL WS4...28 D3
Burton Crs WOLV WV10......7 J2
Burton Farm Rd
RUSH/SHEL WS4......42 D2
Burton Gv CDYHTH B64......103 H2
Burton Rd DUDN DY1......83 H2
WOLV WV10......7 K1
Burton Wood Dr
BFLD/HDSWWD B20......90 D4
Buryfield Rd SOLH B91......164 C4
Bury Hill Rd OLDBY B69......104 B2
Bush Av SMTHWK B66......107 F4
Bushbury Cft
CHWD/FDBR/MGN B37......132 C1
Bushbury La WOLV WV10.....23 H3
Bushbury Rd STETCH B33....112 C4
WOLV WV10......24 A1
Bushell Dr SOLH B91......182 B1
Bushey Cl FOAKS/STRLY B74...44 C1
Bushey Fields Rd DUDN DY1..101 G2
Bush Gv BLOX/PEL WS3......16 A4
HDSW B21......89 F4
Bushley Cft SOLH B91......181 H5
Bushman Wy BKDE/SHDE B34..113 G4
Bushmore Rd HLGN/YWD B28..162 D2
Bush Rd DUDS DY2......120 C2
TPTN/OCK DY4......84 D5
Bush St DARL/WED WS10....55 F1
Bushway Cl BRLYHL DY5....118 C2
Bushwood Dr DOR/KN B93....197 E5
Bushwood Rd SLYOAK B29....158 D1
Bustleholme Av
HHTH/SAND B71......72 B2
Bustleholme Crs
HHTH/SAND B71......72 A1
Bustleholme La
HHTH/SAND B71......72 B1
Butchers La HALE B63......137 E5
Butchers Rd HIA/OLT B92....167 G4
Butcroft Gdns
DARL/WED WS10......55 G2

Bute Cl RBRY B45......173 C4
SHHTH WV12......25 H4
Butler Rd HIA/OLT B92......147 F4
Butlers Cl BFLD/HDSWWD B20..90 A3
ERDW/GRVHL B23......76 B2
Butlers La FOAKS/STRLY B74...46 D3
Butlers Prec WSL WS1......4 D5
Butler's Rd BFLD/HDSWWD B20..90 A3
Butler St WBROM B70......87 E2
Butlin St VAUX/NECH B7......110 A2
Buttercup Cl DSYBK/YTR WS5...57 G5
Butterfield Cl
DUNHL/THL/PER WV6......34 B2
Butterfield Rd BRLYHL DY5...118 D5
Butterfield Cn BRLYHL DY5....100 D2
Buttermere Ct
RIDG/WDGT B32......141 F4
WNSFLD WV11......15 E5
Buttermere Gv SHHTH WV12...12 A4
Butterworth Cl BILS/COS WV14..68 A2
Butt La SMTHWKW B67......106 A3
Buttons Farm Rd
ETTPK/GDPK/PENN WV4...50 D5
Buttress Wy SMTHWK B66....106 C3
Butts Rd
ETTPK/GDPK/PENN WV4....51 F4
RUSH/SHEL WS4......42 B2
Butts St RUSH/SHEL WS4....42 B2
The Butts RUSH/SHEL WS4...42 B2
Buxton Cl BLOX/PEL WS3....17 E4
Buxton Rd BLOX/PEL WS3....17 E4
DUDS DY2......102 A3
ERDW/GRVHL B23......75 H3
SCFLD/BOLD B73......77 E2
Byfield Cl STETCH B33......131 G3
Byfleet Cl
ETTPK/GDPK/PENN WV4....55 E5
Byford Wy
CHWD/FDBR/MGN B37......132 B4
Byland Wy BLOX/PEL WS3....16 B5
Byrchen Moor Gdns
BRLYHL DY5......100 D2
Byrne Rd BKHL/PFLD WV2....52 B1
Byron Av PBAR/PBCH B42....73 H5
Byron Cl SMHTH B10 *......128 D5
Byron Crs DUDN DY1......84 B1
SEDG DY3......66 C4
Byron Gdns HHTH/SAND B71...87 F1
Byron Rd SMHTH B10 *......128 D5
WOLV WV10......24 A1
Byron St BRLYHL DY5......101 F2
HHTH/SAND B71......87 F1
Byways BLOX/PEL WS3......17 E4

C

Caban Cl NFLD/LBR B31......158 A5
Cable Dr WSLW WS2......41 G1
Cable St BKHL/PFLD WV2.....52 B1
Cabot Gv DUNHL/THL/PER WV6..34 C1
Cadbury Dr CVALE B35......94 B5
Cadbury Rd BILS/COS WV14....13 H3
Cadbury Wy HRBN B17......141 H2
Caddick Crs HHTH/SAND B71...71 H4
Caddick Rd PBAR/PBCH B42...74 B2
Caddick St BILS/COS WV14....53 H5
Cader Dr SHLY B90......180 B1
Cadgwith Gdns BILS/COS WV14..69 G1
Cadine Gdns MOS/BIL B13....160 D1
Cadle Rd WOLV WV10......23 F3
Cadman Crs WOLV WV10....24 A4
Cadnam Cl HRBN B17......142 A4
WLNHL WV13......39 H3
Caen Cl FOAKS/STRLY B74....45 H1
Caernarvon Cl SHHTH WV12...26 A3
Caernarvon Wy DUDN DY1....83 G4
Caesar Wy CSHL/WTROR B46...97 F5
Cairn Dr WSLW WS2......40 D3
Cairns St WSLW WS2......41 G1
Caister Dr WLNHL WV13......39 F5
Cakemore Rd
BLKHTH/ROWR B65......122 C2
Cala Dr EDG B15......126 B5
Calcot Dr DUNHL/THL/PER WV6..22 A3
Calcutt Wy SHLY B90......194 A2
Caldecote Gv BORD B9......129 G3
Calder Av WSL WS1......5 K3
Calder Dr WALM/CURD B76....78 C3
Calderfields Cl RUSH/SHEL WS4..42 C2
Calder Gv KGSTG B44......74 B4
Caldmore Gn WSL WS1......4 E6
Caldmore Rd WSL WS1......4 E6
Caldwell Gv SOLH B91......165 F2
Caldwell Rd BORD B9......129 G1
WASH/WDE B8......111 H4
Caldy Wk ERDW/GRVHL B23...76 C2
Caledonia BRLYHL DY5......119 F5
Caledonia Rd DSYBK/YTR WS5..119 G4
Caledonian Cl DSYBK/YTR WS5..58 C2
Caledon Pl WSLW WS2......56 B2
Caledon St WSLW WS2......56 B2
Calewood Rd BRLYHL DY5....119 F5
California Rd OLDBY B69......104 A2
California Wy RIDG/WDGT B32..141 H4
Callaghan Dr OLDBY B69......86 A5
Callcott Dr BRLYHL DY5......119 E5
Callear Rd DARL/WED WS10...70 A1
Callers Cl HHTH/SAND B71....71 H3
Callowbridge Rd RBRY B45...187 H1
Callowbrook La RBRY B45....187 G1
Calshot Rd PBAR/PBCH B42...74 A1
Calstock Rd SHHTH WV12....26 A3
Calthorpe Man EDG B15 *....126 B3
Calthorpe Rd
BFLD/HDSWWD B20......90 C4
DSYBK/YTR WS5......58 C1
EDG B15......126 A4
Calver Crs WNSFLD WV11....25 G2
Calver Gv KGSTG B44......59 H5
Calverley Rd
HWK/WKHTH B38......176 B4

Calverton Gv GTB/HAM B43....73 G3
Calves Cft WALM/CURD WV13...39 G2
Calvin Cl WMBN WV5......80 D1
WOLV WV10......12 D4
Camberidge Ms
CSHL/WTROR B46......115 F1
Camberley Crs
ETTPK/GDPK/PENN WV4...67 G1
Camberley Dr
ETTPK/GDPK/PENN WV4...51 G4
Camberley Gv
ERDW/GRVHL B23......76 C5
Camberley Ri HHTH/SAND B71...72 B2
Camberley Rd KCSWFD DY6...100 C5
Camborne Cl AST/WIT B6.....109 G2
Camborne Rd DSYBK/YTR WS5..58 B1
Cambourne Rd
BLKHTH/ROWR B65......122 A1
Cambrai Dr HLGN/YWD B28....162 A1
Cambria Cl SHLY B90......193 G1
Cambrian Cl ALDR WS9......30 A2
Cambric Cl CBROM B36......126 D5
Cambridge Dr
CHWD/FDBR/MGN B37......131 H3
Cambridge Rd DUDS DY2....102 A2
MOS/BIL B13......161 F1
SMTHWK B66......106 C2
Cambridge St CBHAMW B1.....2 D5
WBROM B70......87 F4
WOLV WV10......37 F1
WSL WS1......5 G7
Cambridge Wy ACGN B27....146 D3
Camden Cl CBROM B36......112 C1
DSYBK/YTR WS5 *......57 G4
Camden Dr CBHAMW B1......2 D5
Camden St ALDR WS9......19 E3
WSL WS1......4 C7
WSNGN B18......2 A2
Camden Wy KCSWFD DY6....81 H5
Camellia Gdns COVEN WV9....11 H4
Camelot Wy SMHTH B10......128 A4
Cameo Dr STRBR DY8......118 B4
Cameron Rd RUSH/SHEL WS4...5 J1
Camford Gv
ALE/KHTH/YWD B14......178 B2
Cam Gdns BRLYHL DY5......100 D2
Camino Rd RIDG/WDGT B32...141 E4
Camomile Cl RUSH/SHEL WS5...57 G5
Campbell Cl RUSH/SHEL WS4..42 C2
Campbells Gn
LGN/SDN/BHAMAIR B26...147 H2
Campbell St BRLYHL DY5....101 E5
Campden Gn HIA/OLT B92....147 G4
Camp Hl BHTH/HG B12......127 G4
STRBR DY8......118 A3
Camp Hill Cl BHTH/HG B12...127 G4
Camphill La DARL/WED WS10...70 D1
Camp Hill Middleway
BHTH/HG B12......127 G5
Campion Cl DSYBK/YTR WS5...57 G5
ERDE/BCHGN B24......77 G5
WMBN WV5......64 B5
Campion Gv HALE B63......137 H4
Campion Wv SHLY B90......194 A3
Camp La HDSW B21......88 D4
WMBN WV5......78 B4
Camplea Cft
CHWD/FDBR/MGN B37......132 A2
Camplin Crs
BFLD/HDSWWD B20......89 G1
Camp Rd MGN/WHC B75......33 H4
Camp St BORD B9......128 A3
DARL/WED WS10......56 D1
WOLV WV1......37 F1
Campville Crs HHTH/SAND B71..72 A2
Campville Gv
CHWD/FDBR/MGN B37......113 H4
Camp Wood Cl BVILLE B30....159 G2
Camrose Cft BHTH/HG B12...144 A1
BKDE/SHDE B34......112 D3
Camrose Gdns COVEN WV9....12 A4
Canal La ERDE/BCHGN B24....93 E5
Canalside Cl BLOX/PEL WS3...28 A1
WOLV WV10......72 A1
Canal Side Dr
HWK/WKHTH B38......176 D4
Canal St BRLYHL DY5......101 G4
OLDBY B69......104 D2
STRBR DY8......135 F1
TPTN/OCK DY4......85 G3
Canary Gv LOZ/NWT B19.....108 C1
Canberra Gdns
BKDE/SHDE B34......113 G3
Canberra Rd DSYBK/YTR WS5..58 A3
Canberra Wy BHTH/HG B12 *..127 F4
Canford Cl BHTH/HG B12....127 F4
Canford Crs CDSL WV8......10 A4
Canning Cl DSYBK/YTR WS5...58 B2
Canning Gdns WSNGN B18....107 C5
Canning Rd DSYBK/YTR WS5...58 B2
Cannock Rd SHHTH WV12.....25 H5
WOLV WV10......23 H5
Cannon Dr BILS/COS WV14....68 C1
Cannon Hill Gv
BHTH/HG B12 *......144 A2
Cannon Hill Pl BHTH/HG B12 *.144 A2
Cannon Hill Rd BHTH/HG B12..143 H2
Cannon Rd WMBN WV5......65 E3
Cannon St CBHAM B2......3 G5
WLNHL WV13......39 H3
WSL WS1......5 G5
Cannon St North WSLW WS2...42 A1
Canterbury Av WLNHL WV13...40 B2
Canterbury Cl
BLKHTH/ROWR B65......104 C5
BLOX/PEL WS3 *......18 A2
ERDW/GRVHL B23......92 B4
KDMR/MOOR DY11 *......72 A1
Canterbury Dr
CHWD/FDBR/MGN B37......132 A5
DUNHL/THL/PER WV6......34 B1
Canterbury Rd
BFLD/HDSWWD B20......90 D5
ETTPK/GDPK/PENN WV4...66 D1
HHTH/SAND B71......71 H3
Canton La WALM/CURD B76...79 H4

Canute Cl WSL WS1................57 F1
Canvey Cl RBRY B45................173 G4
Canwell Av
  CHWD/FDBR/MGN B37....113 H4
Canwell Gdns BILS/COS WV14....53 F4
Canwell Ga MGN/WHC B75.......48 A1
Capcroft Rd MOS/BIL B13........161 H4
Cape Hl SMTHWK B66................106 D5
Capener Rd GTB/HAM B43........74 A1
Capern Gv RIDG/WDGT B32......141 F2
Cape St WBROM B70................86 C2
  CDYHTH B64.....................107 F5
Capethorn Rd SMTHWK B66....124 C1
Capilano Rd ERDW/GRVHL B23...76 A4
Capponfield Cl BILS/COS WV14...53 F5
Capstone Av WLNHL WV13.......22 D2
  WSNGN B18........................108 A5
Captain's Cl BDMR/CCFT WV3...35 H3
Carcroft Rd YDLY B25.............159 E4
Cardale St BLKHTH/ROWR B65..122 B2
Carden Cl WBROM B70.............85 E4
Carder Crs BILS/COS WV14.......53 H4
Carder Dr BRLYHL DY5.............119 E2
Cardiff St BDMR/CCFT WV3......6 C7
Cardigan Cl HHTH/SAND B71.....71 G4
Cardigan Dr SHHTH WV12........159 H4
Cardigan St CBHAMNE B4.......3 K3
Cardinal Cl HRBN B17.............124 C2
Cardington Av PBAR/PBCH B42...74 B2
Cardoness Pl DUDN DY1...........83 H4
Careless Gn HAG/WOL DY9.......136 D3
Carhampton Rd
  MGN/WHC B75....................63 G2
Carillon Gdns
  BLKHTH/ROWR B65.............122 A1
Carisbrooke Av
  CHWD/FDBR/MGN B37.........132 C2
Carisbrooke Cl
  DARL/WED WS10................72 A1
Carisbrooke Crs
  DARL/WED WS10................72 A1
Carisbrooke Dr RMSLY B62......139 F4
Carisbrooke Gdns
  WOLVN WV10....................13 E4
Carisbrooke Rd
  DARL/WED WS10................71 H1
  DUNHL/THL/PER WV6..........35 E2
  HRBN B17........................124 C2
  WOLVN WV10...................13 E4
Carless Av HRBN B17.............124 D5
Carless St WSL WS1................4 E7
Carless La WSNGN B18.............107 G4
Carl St WSLW WS2..................27 H5
Carlton Av BILS/COS WV14.......54 B1
  FOAKS/STRLY B74...............45 F3
  HAG/WOL DY9...................136 C4
  HDSW B21........................89 G5
  WNSFLD WV11..................24 A3
Carlton Cl DUDN DY1..............68 C5
  MGN/WHC B75...................62 D1
Carlton Crs FOAKS/STRLY B74...45 G3
Carlton Ms CBROM B36...........113 F2
Carlton Rd BDMR/CCFT WV3....51 G1
  BORD B9..........................128 B3
  HDSW B21........................106 C1
Carlyle Gv WOLVN WV10..........14 C3
Carlyle Rd BLKHTH/ROWR B65...122 A2
  LDYWD/EDGR B16...............125 G3
  LOZ/NWT B19....................108 C1
  WOLVN WV10....................14 C3
Carmel Gv RIDG/WDGT B32.....157 F1
Carmodale Av PBAR/PBCH B42...74 B5
Carnegie Av TPTN/OCK DY4.....85 G2
Carnegie Dr DARL/WED WS10...56 A5
Carnegie Rd
  BLKHTH/ROWR B65.............121 H2
Carnford Rd
  LGN/SDN/BHAMAIR B26.......147 H1
Carnforth Cl KGSWFD DY6.......99 F2
Carnoustie Cl BDMR/CCFT WV3...16 C4
  MGN/WHC B75...................47 H5
Carnwath Rd SCFLD/BOLD B73...76 C1
Carol Crs HALE B63................138 B2
  WNSFLD WV11...................25 E5
Carol Gdns STRBR DY8............118 B4
Caroline Rd MOS/BIL B13........144 B3
Caroline St CBHAMNW B3.......2 D2
  DUDS DY2.........................85 E5
  WBROM B70......................86 C3
Carpenter Old HALE B63.........137 H2
Carpenter Rd EDG B15...........126 B5
Carpenters Cl BHTH/HG B12 *...127 F4
Carpenter's Rd LOZ/NWT B19...108 C2
Carrick Cl BLOX/PEL WS3.........18 A2
Carriers Cl WSLW WS2............40 C4
Carriers Fold WMBN WV5.........65 F4
Carrington Rd
  DARL/WED WS10.................71 H1
Carisbrooke Rd
  DARL/WED WS10.................71 H1
Carroway Head Hl
  MGN/WHC B75...................49 E1
Carrs La CBHAMNE B4............3 H5
Carshalton Dr BKHL/PFLD WV2...37 G5
Carshalton Rd KGSTG B44.......75 C1
Cartbridge Crs BLOX/PEL WS3...28 C5
Cartbridge La RUSH/SHEL WS4...28 C5
Cartbridge La South
  RUSH/SHEL WS4.................28 C5
Carter Av CDSL WV8...............10 D4
Carter Rd
  DUNHL/THL/PER WV6..........22 D5
  GTB/HAM B43....................73 H1
Carter's Cl WALM/CURD B76....63 F5
Carters Gn WBROM B70..........87 F2
Carters Hurst STETCH B33.......130 D3
Carter's La RMSLY B62...........139 H4
Cartland Rd BVILLE B30...........160 C1
  SPARK B11.......................128 A5
The Cartway
  DUNHL/THL/PER WV6..........34 B1
Cartwright Gdns OLDBY B69....86 A4
Cartwright Rd MGN/WHC B75...47 G2
Cartwright St BKHL/PFLD WV2...37 F5
Carver Ct TPTN/OCK DY4 *......69 G2
Carver Gdns STRBR DY8.........135 E5
Carver St CBHAMNW B3.........2 C2
Casern Vw MGN/WHC B75......63 G2
Casewell Rd KGSWFD DY6.......99 G1
Casey Av ERDW/GRVHL B23.....76 B3

Cash Joynson Av
  DARL/WED WS10................40 A5
Caslon Crs STRBR DY8............134 D3
Caslon Rd HALE B63...............137 G1
Cassandra Cl BRLYHL DY5.......83 E5
Cassowary Rd
  BFLD/HDSWWD B20............89 H3
Castello Dr CBROM B36..........95 F5
The Castings BILS/COS WV14...68 D1
Castlebridge Rd WNSFLD WV11..25 G3
Castle Cl BRWN WS8...............9 F2
  CDYHTH B64.....................121 H3
  HIA/OLT B92.....................164 D1
Castle Crs CBROM B36...........113 E1
Castlecroft Av
  BDMR/CCFT WV3................35 E5
Castlecroft Gdns
  BDMR/CCFT WV3................35 F5
Castlecroft La
  BDMR/CCFT WV3................34 D5
Castlecroft Rd
  BDMR/CCFT WV3................34 D5
  BILS/COS WV14.................54 A1
Castle Dr CSHL/WTROR B46....115 F4
  SHHTH WV12....................25 H5
Castleford Gv SPARK B11........145 E3
Castleford Rd SPARK B11........145 E3
Castlefort Rd ALDR WS9.........19 G4
Castlegate Dr DUDN DY1........85 E4
Castlegate Wy DUDN DY1.......85 E4
Castle Grounds DUDN DY1 *...84 D4
Castle Hts CDYHTH B64 *.......121 H4
Castle Hl DUDN DY1..............84 D4
Castlehills Dr CBROM B36......112 C1
Castle La HIA/OLT B92...........164 C1
Castle Mill Rd DUDN DY1.......68 C3
Castle Rd ALDR WS9.............19 C5
  BVILLE B30......................176 D1
  SLYOAK B29.....................158 D1
  TPTN/OCK DY4..................84 D2
Castle Rd East
  LGLYGN/QTN B68..............123 H4
Castle Rd West
  LGLYGN/QTN B68..............123 G4
Castle St BILS/COS WV14.......68 C5
  BRWNH WS8......................9 F2
  DARL/WED WS10................84 D5
  DUDN DY1.......................84 D4
  SEDG DY3........................67 F5
  TPTN/OCK DY4..................85 E1
  WBROM B70......................71 E4
  WOLV WV1.......................7 C4
Castleton Rd BLOX/PEL WS3....17 E4
  PBAR/PBCH B42.................74 D4
Castle St DUDS DY2..............102 C4
Castle Vw DUDN DY1............84 B4
Castle View Cl
  DARL/WED WS10................54 C4
Castle View Rd
  DARL/WED WS10................54 C4
Caswell Rd SEDG DY3.............67 E3
Catalpa Gv FOAKS/STRLY B74...60 A2
Cater Dr WALM/CURD B76.......63 E4
Caterham Dr KGSWFD DY6......118 B1
Catesby Dr KGSWFD DY6.........99 H1
Catesby Pk HWK/WKHTH B38...176 C2
Catesby Rd SHLY B90.............180 B4
Cateswell Rd HLGN/YWD B28...162 D1
  SPARK B11.......................145 H5
Cathcart Rd STRBR DY8.........135 E2
Cathedral Cl TPTN/OCK DY4....85 E1
Cathel Dr PBAR/PBCH B42......74 A4
Catherine De Barnes La
  HIA/OLT B92.....................166 C4
Catherine Dr SCFLD/BOLD B73...76 C4
Catherine Rd BILS/COS WV14...68 A2
Catherines Cl SOLH B91.........183 F1
Catherine St AST/WIT B6.......110 A4
Catherton Cl TPTN/OCK DY4...70 A1
Catholic La SEDG DY3............67 E4
Catisfield Crs CDSL WV8.........22 B1
Cat & Kittens La WOLVN WV10...53 G1
Cato La BRDE/SHDE B34.........112 D2
Caton Gv HLGN/YWD B28.......163 E3
Cato St VAUX/NECH B7..........109 H5
Cato St North VAUX/NECH B7...110 A4
Catshill Rd BRWNH WS8.........9 G5
Cattell Dr MGN/WHC B75.......63 H5
Cattell Rd BORD B9...............128 A3
Cattells Gv VAUX/NECH B7.....110 A3
Cattock Hurst Dr
  SCFLD/WYGN B72...............77 H4
Causeway BLKHTH/ROWR B65..122 A2
Causeway Green Rd
  LGLYGN/QTN B68...............123 E1
Causeway Rd BILS/COS WV14...68 D5
The Causeway YDLY B25.........129 H5
Causey Farm Rd HALE B63.....154 D2
Cavalier Circ WOLVN WV10.....13 E5
Cavalier Dr HALE B63............138 C4
Cavandale Av KGSTG B44.......75 E2
Cavell Closet WSLW WS2.........4 B3
Cavell Rd DUDS DY2..............85 F5
Cavendish Cl
  HWK/WKHTH B38...............177 F4
  KGSWFD DY6.....................99 H5
Cavendish Dr HAG/WOL DY9...169 F1
Cavendish Gdns WSLW WS2....41 E1
Cavendish Rd
  LDYWD/EDGR B16..............125 F1
  RMSLY B62......................139 H3
  WOLV WV1.......................38 B4
  WSLW WS2.......................27 E5
Cavendish Wy ALDR WS9.......19 C5
Caversham Rd KGSTG B44......75 G1
Cawdon Gv DOR/KN B93.........198 C1
Cawdor Crs LDYWD/EDGR B16..125 H3
Caxton Gv KGSTG B44...........76 A2
Caynham Rd RIDG/WDGT B32..157 F2
Cayton Gv ERDW/GRVHL B23...76 D5
Cecil Dr OLDBY B69...............86 B4
Cecil Rd ERDE/BCHGN B24.....92 D3
  SLYOAK B29......................159 E4
Cecil St LOZ/NWT B19............3 G1
  RUSH/SHEL WS4.................42 B2
  STRBR DY8.......................135 F2
Cedar Av BILS/COS WV14.......68 A4

BRWNH WS8...........................9 G4
  CBROM B36.......................113 E2
Cedar Bridge Cft
  FOAKS/STRLY B74..............47 F5
Cedar Cl BVILLE B30.............159 F4
  DSYBK/YTR WS5................57 H4
  LGLYGN/QTN B68..............123 G4
  STRBR DY8........................134 D5
Cedar Dr ERDE/BCHGN B24....93 C1
  FOAKS/STRLY B74...............45 E4
  NFLD/LBR B31...................189 H1
Cedar Gv BDMR/CCFT WV5.....51 F1
  CDSL WV8.........................10 D4
  HAG/WOL DY9...................152 C4
Cedarhurst RIDG/WDGT B32...141 G2
  SOLH B91.........................182 A2
Cedar Park Rd SHHTH WV12....26 A1
Cedar Rd BVILLE B30.............159 G4
  DARL/WED WS10.................71 E1
  DUDN DY1........................84 B5
  WLNHL WV13....................39 E3
Cedars Av ACCN B27.............146 C3
  KGSWFD DY6.....................99 H5
  WMBN WV5......................81 E1
The Cedars
  DUNHL/THL/PER WV6 *.......36 B2
  YDLY B25.........................130 A3
Cedar Wy NFLD/LBR B31.......175 F4
  WNSFLD WV11...................24 C3
Cedarwood FOAKS/STRLY B74...47 F5
Cedarwood Cft
  PBAR/PBCH B42.................73 H5
Cedar Wood Rd SEDG DY3.....83 E2
Celandine Cl KGSWFD DY6.....99 G5
Celandine Rd DUDN DY1........84 A2
The Celandines WMBN WV5...64 C5
Celbury Wy GTB/HAM B43......73 F3
Celts Cl BLKHTH/ROWR B65....104 A5
Cemetery La WSNGN B18........108 B4
Cemetery Rd DARL/WED WS10..40 D5
  HAG/WOL DY9...................136 B2
  LGLYGN/QTN B68..............105 C3
  WLNHL WV13....................39 G2
Cemetery St BILS/COS WV14...53 G2
  BLOX/PEL WS3...................27 F1
Central Av BILS/COS WV14.....68 D4
  BLOX/PEL WS3...................28 D2
Central City BLOX/PEL WS3 *...27 E1
Central Dr BILS/COS WV14.....68 D4
  BLOX/PEL WS3...................28 D2
  SEDG DY3........................83 F4
Central Gv ACGN B27............146 C5
Central Pk Dr DUDS DY2 *......121 E1
Central Park Dr BHAMAIR B18...107 H4
Central Sq ERDW/GRVHL B23 *...93 E2
Central Wy BRLYHL DY5.........119 H1
Centre La HALE B63...............138 C4
The Centreway
  ALE/KHTH/YWD B14...........179 F1
Centurion Cl CSHL/WTROR B46...97 E5
Century Pk BORD B9..............128 A2
Century Rd OLDBY B69...........105 E1
Ceolmund Crs
  CHWD/FDBR/MGN B37.......132 B1
Chaceley Gv
  ERDW/GRVHL B23 *.............76 B4
Chadbury Cft SOLH B91.........181 H5
Chadbury Rd HALE B63..........139 E4
Chaddersley Cl OLDBY B69....104 B4
Chaddesley Dr HAG/WOL DY9..152 D1
Chaddesley Rd HALE B63.......138 D5
  NFLD/LBR B31...................176 B3
Chadley Cl SOLH B91............164 C4
Chad Rd DUDN DY1..............68 B4
  EDG B15..........................125 H4
Chadsmoor Ter
  VAUX/NECH B7..................109 H3
Chadstone Cl SHLY B90.........195 H2
Chad Valley Cl HRBN B17......142 B1
Chadwell Gdns CDSL WV8.......10 B3
Chadwick La HAG/WOL DY9....186 A2
Chadwick Av RBRY B45..........188 B2
Chadwick Cl
  ETTPK/GDPK/PENN WV4.....50 C2
Chadwick Ct SOLH B91 *........183 F2
Chadwick Rd MGN/WHC B75...63 F3
Chaffcombe Rd DOR/KN B93...196 D4
Chaffinch Cl SEDG DY3..........67 E1
Chaffinch Dr CBROM B36......114 B2
Chaffinch Rd STRBR DY8.......134 A4
Chainmakers Cl BILS/COS WV14..53 G5
Chain Wk LOZ/NWT B19.........108 C1
Chalcot Gv BFLD/HDSWWD B20..89 G1
Chaldon Cl COVEN WV9.........12 A5
Chale Gv ALE/KHTH/YWD B14..179 G2
Chalfont Pl HAG/WOL DY9.....136 C5
Chalfont Rd LOZ/NWT B19.....108 C1
Chalford Rd ERDW/GRVHL B23..76 A3
Chalford Wy SHLY B90...........180 B2
Chalgrove Av
  HWK/WKHTH B38...............176 C4
Chalgrove Crs SOLH B91........181 H4
Challenge Wy WOLVN WV10....23 G5
Challenor Av WLNHL WV13.....38 D3
Chalybeate Cl RBRY B45........173 H4
Chamberlain Cl OLDBY B69....86 D4
Chamberlain Ct
  ALE/KHTH/YWD B14...........161 E1
  WSNGN B18......................108 A4
Chamberlain Crs SHLY B90....180 A3
Chamberlain Rd MOS/BIL B13..161 F4
Chamberlain's La
  ETTPK/GDPK/PENN WV4.....51 E5
Chamberlain Sq CBHAMNW B3..2 E5
Chamberlain Wk
  CSHL/WTROR B46 *.............115 F2
  SMTHWK B66....................106 C3
Chance Cft LGLYGN/QTN B68..123 F4

Chancellor's Cl EDG B15.........125 G4
Chancel Wy RMSLY B62..........139 G2
Chancery Wy BRLYHL DY5......119 H2
Chandler Dr
  ETTPK/GDPK/PENN WV4.....50 D5
Chandlers Cl COVEN WV9.......22 C1
  WSNGN B18......................107 H4
Chandlers Keep BRWNH WS8...19 F1
Channon Dr BRLYHL DY5........118 C5
Chanston Av
  ALE/KHTH/YWD B14...........178 A1
Chanterelle Gdns
  ETTPK/GDPK/PENN WV4.....51 G4
Chantrey Crs BILS/COS WV14...54 B1
  GTB/HAM B43....................59 H4
Chantry Av BLOX/PEL WS3.....27 G1
Chantry Cl HLYWD B47..........192 C1
Chantry Dr RMSLY B62..........139 H1
Chantry Heath Crs
  DOR/KN B93.....................183 F5
Chantry Rd HDSW B21..........107 H1
  KINVER DY7......................117 C5
  MOS/BIL B13.....................144 A3
Chapel Ash Island
  BDMR/CCFT WV3................6 D4
Chapel Av BRWNH WS8.........9 G4
Chapel Cl CDYHTH B64.........121 H4
  WMBN WV5......................80 D1
Chapel Dr BRWNH WS8.........9 G4
  HLYWD B47.......................192 B5
Chapelfield Ms RBRY B45.......187 H2
  STRBR DY8........................135 G3
Chapelfield Rd RBRY B45.......174 A5
Chapel Fields Rd HIA/OLT B92..147 F5
Chapel Gn WLNHL WV13.......39 H3
Chapel House La HALE B63.....137 G2
Chapelhouse Rd
  CHWD/FDBR/MGN B37........131 H2
Chapel House St BHTH/HG B12 *..3 K7
Chapel La CDSL WV8.............10 D4
  GTB/HAM B43....................58 D5
  HAG/WOL DY9...................185 H1
  HOCK/TIA D94...................199 G4
  KGSWFD DY6.....................99 F1
  OLDBY B69.......................104 C2
  TPTN/OCK DY4..................85 E1
  WBROM B70......................87 F1
  WMBN WV5......................80 D1
Chapel Sq BILS/COS WV14......54 B4
  BKHL/PFLD WV2.................52 B1
  BLOX/PEL WS3...................27 H2
  BRLYHL DY5......................101 E2
  CBHAMNE B4....................3 J4
  DARL/WED WS10................70 C1
  DUDS DY2........................102 D5
  HAG/WOL DY9...................152 C5
  HALE B63........................138 C4
  HDSW B21........................107 H1
  KGSWFD DY6.....................99 F1
  OLDBY B69.......................104 C2
  TPTN/OCK DY4..................85 E1
  WBROM B70......................87 F1
  WMBN WV5......................80 D1
Chapel Vw SMTHWKW B67.....106 B5
Chapel Wk BVILLE B30..........177 E4
  SEDG DY3.........................83 E4
Chapelwood Gv
  PBAR/PBCH B42 *................90 D1
Chapman Rd SMTH B10.........128 A4
Chapmans Hl RMSLY B62......172 D5
Chapmans Pas CBHAMW B1 *..2 C7
Chapman St WBROM B70.......87 F3
Chapter House Rd DOR/KN B93..198 D1
Charfield Cl BVILLE B30.........159 F3
Charingworth Rd HIA/OLT B92..148 A5
Charlbury Av
  CHWD/FDBR/MGN B37........131 H2
Charlbury Crs
  LGN/SDN/BHAMAIR B26......130 B4
Charlecote Dr DUDN DY1......83 C3
  ERDW/GRVHL B23..............76 C4
Charlecote Gdns
  SCFLD/BOLD B73................77 E3
Charlecote Ri WLNHL WV13....39 F4
Charlecott Cl MOS/BIL B13....162 B3
Charlemont Av
  HHTH/SAND B71.................72 B5
Charlemont Cl DSYBK/YTR WS5..58 A2
Charlemont Crs
  HHTH/SAND B71.................72 A3
Charlemont Rd
  DSYBK/YTR WS5.................57 H2
  HHTH/SAND B71.................72 A3
Charles Av BLKHTH/ROWR B65..104 A3
  ETTPK/GDPK/PENN WV4.....51 H3
  WNSFLD WV11...................25 G5
Charles Cl WASH/WDE B8.......110 B5
Charles Crs BLOX/PEL WS3.....18 A4
Charlesdale Dr ALDR WS9......44 B1
Charles Dr VAUX/NECH B7.....109 H3
Charles Edward Rd
  LGN/SDN/BHAMAIR B26......146 D1
Charles Foster St
  DARL/WED WS10................55 E2
Charles Henry St
  BHTH/HG B12....................127 E4
Charles Holland St
  WLNHL WV13....................39 H3
Charles Rd AST/WIT B6..........90 C5
  BFLD/HDSWWD B20............90 C1
  BRLYHL DY5......................120 A5
  HALE B63.........................138 B3
  SMTH B10........................145 E1
  SOLH B91.........................181 G3
  STRBR DY8........................135 E5
  TPTN/OCK DY4..................85 G4
Charles St SMTHWK B66........107 G2
  WBROM B70......................70 C3
  WLNHL WV13....................40 A2
  WSLW WS2.......................4 B4
Charles Wk
  BLKHTH/ROWR B65.............104 A4
Charles Wesley Ct
  BDMR/CCFT WV3................51 G1
Charlesworth Av SHLY B90.....195 H2
Charleville Rd LOZ/NWT B19...108 B2
Charlotte Cl OLDBY B69........87 F4

Charlotte Gdns SHLY B90.......180 A2
Charlotte Rd BVILLE B30.......160 A4
  DARL/WED WS10................70 B2
  EDG B15..........................126 C4
Charlotte St CBHAMNW B3.....2 D4
  DUDN DY1........................102 B1
  WSL WS1..........................5 H5
Charlton Dr CDYHTH B64.......120 D5
Charlton Rd KGSTG B44........75 C4
Charlton St BRLYHL DY5........118 C1
  DUDN DY1........................102 A2
Charminster Av YDLY B25......129 H4
Charnwood Av SEDG DY3......67 F1
Charnwood Cl BILS/COS WV14..54 D5
  BRLYHL DY5......................118 D5
  RBRY B45.........................188 A2
Charnwood Ct
  DSYBK/YTR WS5.................57 G4
Charnwood Rd
  DSYBK/YTR WS5.................57 G4
  PBAR/PBCH B42.................73 H4
Charter Crs CDYHTH B64........121 H4
Charterfield Dr KGSWFD DY6...99 H1
Charterhouse Dr SOLH B91....181 H4
Charter Rd TPTN/OCK DY4.....70 A2
Charters Av CDSL WV8...........11 E3
Charter St BRLYHL DY5..........101 G4
Chartist Rd WASH/WDE B8....110 B3
Chartley Cl DOR/KN B93........196 C5
  DUNHL/THL/PER WV6.........35 F3
Chartley Rd ERDW/GRVHL B23..92 A5
  HHTH/SAND B71.................71 H5
The Chartway BLOX/PEL WS3..18 B3
Chartwell Cl DUDN DY1........68 B5
Chartwell Dr FOAKS/STRLY B74..46 B1
  SHLY B90.........................194 D4
  WMBN WV5......................80 D1
  WOLVN WV10....................23 G1
Chase Gv ERDE/BCHGN B24....77 H4
The Chase Link BRWNH WS8 *..9 G5
Chasepool Rd SEDG DY3.......98 A2
Chase Rd BLOX/PEL WS3........27 E2
  BRWNH WS8......................9 G4
  SEDG DY3.........................82 D5
The Chase
  DUNHL/THL/PER WV6..........21 E3
  WALM/CURD B76................77 H4
Chase Vw
  ETTPK/GDPK/PENN WV4.....67 G1
Chaters Cl TPTN/OCK DY4.....78 C2
Chatham Rd NFLD/LBR B31....175 G2
Chatsworth Cl
  CSCFLD/WYGN B72.............77 H4
  SHHTH WV12....................39 H1
  SHLY B90..........................194 D3
Chatsworth Crs
  RUSH/SHEL WS4.................29 F3
Chatsworth Gdns
  DUNHL/THL/PER WV6..........21 E3
Chatsworth Ms STRBR DY8 *...117 G2
Chatsworth Rd RMSLY B62.....121 G5
Chattaway St VAUX/NECH B7...110 A2
Chattle Hl CSHL/WTROR B46...97 E4
Chatwell Gv SLYOAK B29......141 H5
Chatwin Pl BILS/COS WV14....54 A5
Chatwin St SMTHWK B66.......106 B2
Chatwins Wfmt TPTN/OCK DY4..85 F1
Chaucer Av SEDG DY3...........82 C1
  SHHTH WV12....................25 H5
  TPTN/OCK DY4..................85 G4
Chaucer Cl BILS/COS WV14....68 D3
  STRBR DY8........................91 H5
  STRBR DY8........................118 C4
Chaucer Gv ACGN B27..........163 F1
Chaucer Rd BLOX/PEL WS3....28 A2
Chauson Gv SOLH B91..........181 G5
Chavasse Rd
  CSCFLD/WYGN B72.............62 D5
Chawn Hl HAG/WOL DY9.......136 A4
Chawnhill Cl HAG/WOL DY9...136 A4
Chawn Park Dr HAG/WOL DY9..136 A4
Chaynes Gv STETCH D33.......131 F2
Cheadle Dr ERDW/GRVHL B23..76 B3
Cheam Gdns
  DUNHL/THL/PER WV6..........22 A2
Cheapside BHTH/HG B12........127 F4
  WLNHL WV13....................39 G4
Cheatham St VAUX/NECH B7...110 A3
Checketts St WSLW WS2........4 A3
Checkley Cl SHLY B90...........180 A4
Checkley Cft WALM/CURD B76..78 B3
Cheddar Rd BHTH/HG B12....144 A1
Chedworth Cl KGSWFD DY6...118 C1
Cheedon Cl DOR/KN B93.......198 C1
Chells Gv MOS/BIL B13.........161 H5
Chelmar Cl CBROM B36........113 H1
Chelmar Dr BRLYHL DY5.......100 B5
Chelmarsh Av
  BDMR/CCFT WV3................35 E4
Chelmorton Rd
  PBAR/PBCH B42.................74 C3
Chelmsley Av
  CSHL/WTROR B46...............115 F3
Chelmsley Cl
  CHWD/FDBR/MGN B37........132 B2
Chelmsley Gv STETCH B33....131 G1
Chelmsley La
  CHWD/FDBR/MGN B37........131 H4
Chelsea Cl RIDG/WDGT B32...141 F3
Chelsea Dr FOAKS/STRLY B74..46 D1
Chelsea Wy KGSWFD DY6.......99 G3
Chelston Dr
  DUNHL/THL/PER WV6..........36 A1
Chelston Rd NFLD/LBR B31....175 E5
Cheltenham Cl
  DUNHL/THL/PER WV6..........22 D5
Cheltenham Dr CBROM B36...111 H1
  KGSWFD DY6.....................99 F5
Cheltenham Ms
  FOAKS/STRLY B74...............47 E4
Chelthorn Wy SOLH B91.......182 A3
Cheltondale Rd SOLH B91......164 B5
Chelveston Crs SOLH B91......181 G5
Chelwood Gdns
  BILS/COS WV14..................53 F5

Chelworth Rd
HWK/WKHTH B38 ....177 F3
Chem Rd BILS/COS WV14....53 F3
Chenston CI
DUNHL/THL/PER WV6.......34 D1
Chepstow Gv RBRY B45 ......188 B2
Chepstow Rd BLOX/PEL WS3....26 D1
WOLVN WV10 ....12 D2
Chepstow Vls BHTH/HG B12 * ..144 D2
Chequerfield Dr
BDMR/CCFT WV3.............51 G2
Chequers Av WMBN WV5 ......65 E2
Chequer St BDMR/CCFT WV3...51 G2
Cherhill Covert
ALE/KHTH/YWD B14............177 G3
Cherington Rd SLYOAK B29 ....160 A2
Cheriton Gv
DUNHL/THL/PER WV6.......34 C2
Cherrington CI NFLD/LBR B31..158 A3
Cherrington Gdns
DUNHL/THL/PER WV6.......35 F3
Cherrington Wy SOLH B91....181 H4
Cherry Cl ERDE/BCHGN B24....92 D3
Cherrydale Ct DUDN DY1 ....83 H4
Cherry Dr BORD B9 ....127 H5
Cherry Gn DUDN DY1 ....83 H2
Cherry Gv SMTHWK B66 ......107 E4
STRBR DY8....................135 E3
Cherry Lea DARL/WED WS10 ..71 E1
SCFLD/BOLD B73 ....77 E4
SEDG DY3......................81 F3
Cherry Orch CDSL WV8 ......112 D3
CDYHTH B64 ....121 F3
Cherry Orchard Av HALE B63 ..138 B2
Cherry Orchard Crs HALE B63 ..138 B2
Cherry Orchard Rd
BFLD/HDSWWD B20...........89 H1
Cherry Rd TPTN/OCK DY4.....69 H5
Cherry St BDMR/CCFT WV3....6 C5
CBHAM B2 ....3 G5
HALE B63.....................138 B2
STRBR DY8....................135 E3
Cherry Tree Av DSYBK/YTR WS5..57 H4
Cherrytree Cl HAG/WOL DY9 ..136 C4
Cherry Tree Cft ACGN B27....146 C2
Cherry Tree Gdns CDSL WV8 ..10 D4
Cherry Tree La CDSL WV8 ....10 D4
HALE B63 ....154 D1
Cherry Tree Rd KGSWFD DY6..100 A1
Cherry Wk HLYWD B47.......192 D5
Cherrywood Cl BILS/COS WV14..68 C2
Cherrywood Crs SOLH B91 ..182 A5
Cherrywood Gn
BILS/COS WV14 ....38 D5
Cherrywood Rd BORD B9 ....128 B2
FOAKS/STRLY B74............44 D4
Cherrywood Wy
FOAKS/STRLY B74............46 B1
Chervil CI PBAR/PBCH B42....74 C4
Chervil Ri WOLVN WV10......37 H2
Cherwell Dr BRWNH WS8 ......8 C2
CBROM B36.....................113 H1
Cherwell Gdns AST/WIT B6 * ..108 D1
Cheshire CI STRBR DY8 ......135 H1
Cheshire Ct AST/WIT B6........91 G4
Cheshire Gv
DUNHL/THL/PER WV6.......44 C2
Cheshire Rd AST/WIT B6........91 G4
SMTHWK B67 ....40 D3
WSLW WS2.....................40 D5
Chesholm Rd
DUNHL/THL/PER WV6.......22 B3
Chester Av
DUNHL/THL/PER WV6.......36 D1
VAUX/NECH B7 ....109 H4
Chesterfield CI NFLD/LBR B31..175 H3
Chesterfield Ct ALDR WS9 * 19 F3
Chester Gdns SCFLD/BOLD B73..76 C2
Chestergate Cft
ERDE/BCHGN B24...........93 H2
Chester Ri LGLYGN/QTN B68..123 C4
Chester Rd ALDR WS9 ....6 D2
BRWNH WS8...................19 H2
CBROM B36.....................112 D1
CDYHTH B64..................120 C4
CHWD/FDBR/MGN B37.......148 B5
DUDS DY2....................120 D2
ERDE/BCHGN B24...........95 G1
FOAKS/STRLY B74............60 C1
HHTH/SAND B71............71 F2
HIA/OLT B92..................147 F4
SCFLD/BOLD B73 ....76 C3
Chester St
DUNHL/THL/PER WV6.......36 D1
Chesterton CI SOLH B91......164 A5
Chesterton Rd BHTH/HG B12..144 C2
WOLVN WV10 ....12 C4
Chesterwood ALDR WS9 ......45 E3
HLYWD B47...................192 C2
Chesterwood Gdns
BFLD/HDSWWD B20...........90 D4
Chesterwood Rd
MOS/BIL B13...................161 F4
Chestnut Av DUDN DY1 ......84 C3
TPTN/OCK DY4 ....69 F4
Chestnut CI ACGN B27........146 C5
FOAKS/STRLY B74.............45 C3
HIA/OLT B92..................163 H2
STRBR DY8....................134 C5
Chestnut Ct BKDE/SHDE B34..113 G2
ERDE/BCHGN B24...........92 C2
RBRY B45.......................188 C4
WMBN WV5.....................81 E1

Chestnut Gv
CSHL/WTROR B46..............115 C2
HRBN B17.......................142 E2
KGSWFD DY6..................100 B3
Chestnut Pl BLOX/PEL WS3....27 H4
Chestnut Rd BLOX/PEL WS3...28 A4
DARL/WED WS10...............71 E1
LGLYGN/QTN B68 ....123 C5
MOS/BIL B13...................144 C3
Chestnuts Av
LGN/SDN/BHAMAIR B26....130 D5
Chestnut Wy BRLYHL DY5 ...119 G5
Chestom Rd
ETTPK/GDPK/PENN WV4.....53 F3
Cheston Rd VAUX/NECH B7 ..109 G3
Cheswell CI
DUNHL/THL/PER WV6.......35 F3
Cheswick CI WLNHL WV13 ....59 F5
Cheswick Wy SHLY B90.......194 D5
Cheswood Dr WALM/CURD B76..78 D5
Chetland Cft HIA/OLT B92....165 H3
Chettle Rd BILS/COS WV14....54 B5
Chetton Gn WOLVN WV10....12 B4
Chetwood CI
DUNHL/THL/PER WV6.......22 C5
Chetwynd CI WSLW WS2......40 A2
Chetwynd Rd BHTH/HG B12...51 H2
WASH/WDE B8.................111 F4
Cheveley Av RBRY B45.......188 B1
Chevening CI SEDG DY3.......67 G4
Cheveridge CI SOLH B91.....181 G4
Cheverton Rd NFLD/LBR B31..175 E2
Cheviot Rd BKHL/PFLD WV2 ..52 D1
STRBR DY8....................135 G1
Cheviot Wy HALE B63.........137 H4
Cheylesmore CI
SCFLD/BOLD B73 ....62 B4
Cheyne Gdns HLGN/YWD B28..179 C2
Cheyne Wk BRLYHL DY5 .....119 E5
Cheyney CI
DUNHL/THL/PER WV6.......22 C5
Chichester Av DUDS DY2 ....102 D4
Chichester Ct
SCFLD/BOLD B73 * 62 B3
Chichester Dr RIDG/WDGT B32..140 A2
Chichester Gv
CHWD/FDBR/MGN B37.......132 B3
Chigwell CI CVALE B35.........94 C3
Chilcote CI HLGN/YWD B28....179 H1
Chilham Dr
CHWD/FDBR/MGN B37.......132 C2
Chillinghome Rd CBROM B36..111 H1
Chillington Dr CDSL WV8......10 B3
DUDN DY1.....................83 H3
Chillington Flds WOLV WV1....38 A4
Chillington Pl BILS/COS WV14..53 C5
Chillington Rd TPTN/OCK DY4..70 A2
Chillington St HHTH/SAND B71..37 H5
Chiltern Av HALE B63.........137 C5
SEDG DY3......................83 F3
Chiltern Dr WLNHL WV13 ....59 H1
Chiltern Rd STRBR DY8.......135 H1
Chilton Rd
ALE/KHTH/YWD B14.........179 F1
Chilwell CI SOLH B91.........148 A4
Chilwell Cft LOZ/NWT B19...109 E3
Chilworth Av WNSFLD WV11...25 F3
Chilworth CI AST/WIT B6......109 F3
Chimes CI STETCH B33.......131 C3
Chimney Rd TPTN/OCK DY4 ..70 A2
Chingford Cl STRBR DY8......99 C5
Chingford Rd KGSTG B44.....75 C3
Chinley Gv KGSTG B44........76 A2
Chinn Brook Rd MOS/BIL B13..161 H5
Chip Cl HWK/WKHTH B38....196 B5
Chipperfield Rd CBROM B36..112 A1
Chipstead Rd
ERDW/GRVHL B23............76 B4
Chirbury Gv NFLD/LBR B31..175 H4
Chirton Gv
ALE/KHTH/YWD B14.........160 D4
Chiseldon Cft
ALE/KHTH/YWD B14.........178 C2
Chisholm Gv ACGN B27.......163 C2
Chiswell Rd WSNGN B18....107 G5
Chivington Cl SHLY B90......195 H2
Chorley Av BKDE/SHDE B34..112 B2
Chorley Gdns BILS/COS WV14..53 F3
Christchurch Cl EDG B15....125 C4
Christ Church Gv WSL WS1....57 G1
Christina Ct HHTH/SAND B71..87 H2
Christina Rd TPTN/OCK DY4 ..70 A4
Christopher Rd
BKHL/PFLD WV2 ....37 C5
RMSLY B62.....................149 E5
SLYOAK B29 ....142 B5
Chubb St WOLV WV1...........7 H3
Chuckery Rd WSL WS1.........5 H4
Chudleigh Gv GTB/HAM B43 ..75 F3
Chudleigh Rd
ERDW/GRVHL B23............92 C2
Church Av
BFLD/HDSWWD B20 * 90 C5
HAG/WOL DY9..................170 C3
MOS/BIL B13 * 144 B4
STRBR DY8....................118 C5
Churchbridge OLDBY B69....104 D3
Church CI
CHWD/FDBR/MGN B37.......114 A3
HLYWD B47...................192 B5
Church Cft HALE B63.........138 C3
HRBN B17.....................141 H3
Church Cross Vw DUDN DY1..101 F1
Churchdale Rd KGSTG B44...59 H5
Church Dr BVILLE B30.........160 B3
Churchfield Av TPTN/OCK DY4..70 A3
Churchfield Cl VAUX/NECH B7..110 A3
Churchfield Rd WOLVN WV10..22 D2
Churchfields Rd
BFLD/HDSWWD B20 * 90 B5

MOS/BIL B13...................162 A5
Church HI BRLYHL DY5 ....119 F2
Church Hill
CDSL WV8 ....10 B2
CSHL/WTROR B46............163 C5
DARL/WED WS10...............55 H5
ETTPK/GDPK/PENN WV4....51 E4
HAG/WOL DY9..................184 B2
NFLD/LBR B31.................175 C2
SEDG DY3......................157 E5
WSL WS1.........................5 F4
Church Hill CI SOLH B91......182 A3
Church Hill Rd
BFLD/HDSWWD B20...........90 B5
Reverton Rd NFLD/LBR B31 ..21 H4
SOLH B91.....................182 A3
Church Hill St SMTHWK B67..106 B3
Churchill CI OLDBY B69........86 A4
Churchill Dr
BLKHTH/ROWR B65...........121 H2
STRBR DY8....................118 C5
Churchill Gdns SEDG DY3.....67 E4
Churchill La KIDD DY10......168 C2
Churchill Pl
LGN/SDN/BHAMAIR B26....130 D3
Churchill Rd BORD B9........128 D2
HALE B63.....................138 B5
MGN/WHC B75.................63 G5
SCFLD/BOLD B73 ....76 A1
WSLW WS2.....................40 D2
Church La AST/WIT B6........109 G1
BFLD/HDSWWD B20...........89 H4
BKHL/PFLD WV2 ....6 D6
CDSL WV8 ....10 B3
HALE B63.....................138 D3
HHTH/SAND B71............87 F1
HIA/OLT B92..................166 D1
STETCH B33..................130 B1
WALM/CURD B76..............79 H2
Church Moat Wy
WALM/CURD B76..............77 H5
Church PI BLOX/PEL WS3 ....27 F2
Churchover CI
WALM/CURD B76..............77 H5
Church Rd AST/WIT B6........109 G1
BILS/COS WV14 ....51 E1
BILS/COS WV14 ....68 D2
BLKHTH/ROWR B65...........122 A1
BLOX/PEL WS3................10 B3
DUDS DY2....................102 B4
EDG B15......................143 F1
ERDE/BCHGN B24...........93 E2
HAG/WOL DY9..................184 B1
HALE B63.....................137 G1
LGN/SDN/BHAMAIR B26....148 A2
MOS/BIL B13..................144 C4
NFLD/LBR B31.................175 G2
PBAR/PBCH B42...............90 D1
SEDG DY3......................80 C4
SHFTH WV12...................26 B4
SHLY B90.....................163 G5
SMTHWK B67.................130 B2
STRBR DY8....................135 H4
WMBN WV5.....................65 E1
WOLVN WV10 ....23 E1
YDLY B25.....................129 C5
Churchside Vw ALDR WS9....19 H5
Church Sq OLDBY B69 * 86 A4
Church St BILS/COS WV14....53 H5
BKHL/PFLD WV2 ....6 E6
BLOX/PEL WS3................10 B3
BRLYHL DY5...................119 E2
CBHAMNW B3 ....3 F4
CDYHTH B64 ....121 E3
DARL/WED WS10...............54 D4
DUDS DY2....................102 B2
HAG/WOL DY9..................152 C5
LGLYGN/QTN B68 ....108 C2
OLDBY B69...................105 E1
RMSLY B62....................122 B3
SEDG DY3......................83 F3
STRBR DY8....................135 C2
TPTN/OCK DY4.................87 C3
WBROM B70...................87 E5
WLNHL WV13..................39 H5
WOLVN WV10 ....38 A1
WSL WS1.........................5 F5
Church Ter MGN/WHC B75 *....47 C2
STETCH B33 *.................130 A3
Church V BFLD/HDSWWD B20..90 B5
WASH/WDE B8.................111 E3
Church Vw ALDR WS9........19 H4
Church View Cl BLOX/PEL WS3..27 G2
Church View Dr CDYHTH B64..121 F3
Church Vls
BFLD/HDSWWD B20 * 89 G4
Church Wk BDMR/CCFT WV3..34 D4
DUNHL/THL/PER WV6.......35 G4
WASH/WDE B8.................111 E3
Churnet Gv
DUNHL/THL/PER WV6.......34 D1
Churn Hill Rd ALDR WS9......44 A1
Churns Hill La SEDG DY3.....99 E3
Churston CI BLOX/PEL WS3...16 C4
Cinder Bank DUDS DY2......119 G4
Cinder Rd SEDG DY3..........82 D4
Cinderway DARL/WED WS10...55 G5
Cinquefoil Leasow
CBROM B36.....................94 A2
Circular Rd ACGN B27........146 D5
Circus Av
CHWD/FDBR/MGN B37.......132 C2
City Plaza CBHAM B2 * 3 C5
City Rd LDYWD/EDGR B16...125 E2
City Vw ERDW/GRVHL B23....92 C3
WASH/WDE B8.................110 B5
Civic CI CBHAMW B1...........2 C5

Claerwen Gv NFLD/LBR B31..158 A5
Claines Rd HALE B63...........21 H5
NFLD/LBR B31.................176 A1
Clairvaux Gdns HIA/OLT B92..163 H5
Clandon CI ALE/KHTH/YWD B14..177 F3
Clanfield Av WNSFLD WV11...25 C5
Clapgate Gdns BILS/COS WV14..53 E5
Clap Gate La RIDG/WDGT B32..140 C5
Clapton Gv KGSTG B44........75 H2
Clare Crs BILS/COS WV14......67 H1
Clare Dr EDG B15...............125 H4
Clare Rd WSLW WV11..........25 F1
Clarel Av WASH/WDE B8......128 A1
Claremont Ms
BDMR/CCFT WV3..............51 G1
Claremont Pl WSNGN B18 *..107 E4
Claremont Rd BDMR/CCFT WV3..51 G1
SEDG DY3......................67 F1
SMTHWK B66.................106 D5
SPARK B11...................145 G1
WSNGN B18...................107 E4
Claremont St BILS/COS WV14..53 C2
CDYHTH B64..................121 E3
Claremont Wy HALE B63.....138 C4
Clarence Av HDSW B21 * 107 C1
Clarence Ct LGLYGN/QTN B68..123 C2
Clarence Gdns
FOAKS/STRLY B74.............46 D3
Clarence Rd BILS/COS WV14..54 A1
DUDS DY2....................92 B3
ERDW/GRVHL B23............92 D5
FOAKS/STRLY B74.............32 C5
HDSW B21...................107 E1
HRBN B17.....................142 B1
MOS/BIL B13..................161 G2
SPARK B11....................145 E3
Clarence St SEDG DY3.........6 C1
WOLV WV1.......................6 E4
Clarenden PI HRBN B17......142 A2
Clarendon Dr TPTN/OCK DY4..70 A5
Clarendon Dr BLOX/PEL WS3..17 H1
RMSLY B62....................139 H1
Clarendon Rd
LDYWD/EDGR B16............125 C3
MGN/WHC B75.................47 C2
RUSH/SHEL WS4.............58 C5
SMTHWK B67.................106 B5
Clarendon St BDMR/CCFT WV3..6 C4
BLOX/PEL WS3................27 F1
CDYHTH B64..................121 F3
Clare Rd BLOX/PEL WS3......28 B4
WOLVN WV10 ....23 C5
Clarewell Av SOLH B91......181 G4
Clarkes Gv TPTN/OCK DY4...70 A5
Clarke's La HHTH/SAND B71...71 C4
WLNHL WV13..................40 A3
Clark Rd BDMR/CCFT WV3....36 A5
Clarksland Gv
CHWD/FDBR/MGN B37.......132 A4
Clarks La SHLY B90...........194 A2
Clarkson Rd DARL/WED WS10..54 B4
Clark St LDYWD/EDGR B16...124 D2
Claughton Rd DUDS DY2.....102 D1
Claughton Rd North DUDS DY2..84 D5
Clausen CI GTB/HAM B43.....60 A4
Claverdon CI BILS/COS WV14..68 A3
Claverdon CI BRWNH WS8 *...8 C4
SOLH B91.....................181 E1
Claverdon Dr FOAKS/STRLY B74..45 H1
GTB/HAM B43..................73 F3
Claverdon Gdns ACGN B27..146 B2
Claverley Dr
ETTPK/GDPK/PENN WV4....50 D3
Claybrook St CBHAM B5.......3 C7
Claycroft Ter DUDN DY1......68 B5
Clay Dr
ALE/KHTH/YWD B14.........178 C2
Clay La RIDG/WDGT B32......140 A2
Clayhanger La BRWNH WS8...18 D1
Clayhanger Rd BRWNH WS8..19 F1
Clay La
LGN/SDN/BHAMAIR B26....147 E3
OLDBY B69...................105 E5
Claypit CI WBROM B70.........87 E4
Clay Pit La SHLY B90.........194 A5
Claypit La WBROM B70........87 E4
Clayton Cl BKHL/PFLD WV2 ..52 A1
Clayton Dr CBROM B36......113 E1
Clayton Gdns RBRY B45.....188 C5
WASH/WDE B8.................110 B4
Clayton Rd BILS/COS WV14...68 B3
WASH/WDE B8.................110 B4
Clear Vw KGSWFD DY6........99 F3
Clearwell Gdns DUDN DY1...83 H5
Clee Hill Dr BDMR/CCFT WV3..34 D4
Clee Hill Rd SEDG DY3.........81 C4
Clee Rd DUDN DY1............102 A2
LGLYGN/QTN B68 ....105 E3
NFLD/LBR B31.................175 C5
OLDBY B69...................105 E2
Cleeve Dr FOAKS/STRLY B74..45 G2
Cleeve Rd ALE/KHTH/YWD B14..179 E1
BLOX/PEL WS3................16 B5
Cleeve Wy BLOX/PEL WS3....16 B5
Clee View Meadow SEDG DY3..67 F1
Clee View Rd WMBN WV5.....64 B5
Clematis Dr COVEN WV9.......11 H4
Clement PI BILS/COS WV14 *..53 H1
Clement Rd BILS/COS WV14...68 D1
RMSLY B62....................122 B5
Clements CI OLDBY B69......104 D1
Clements Rd YDLY B25.......129 H4
Clements St WASH/WDE B8..111 E3
Clemson St WLNHL WV13....39 C5
Clent Dr LGN/SDN/BHAMAIR B26..147 C2
Clent Hill Dr
BLKHTH/ROWR B65...........103 G4
Clent Rd HDSW B21...........107 C1
LGLYGN/QTN B68 ....123 C1
RBRY B45.......................188 C4
STRBR DY8....................135 G1
Clent View Rd HALE B63.....137 G3
RIDG/WDGT B32..............157 G1

STRBR DY8....................134 D5
Clent Vls BHTH/HG B12 *......144 D3
Clent Wy RIDG/WDGT B32...156 D2
Cleobury La HOCK/TIA B94..194 A5
Cleton St TPTN/OCK DY4.....85 C1
Clevedon Av CBROM B36.....113 C1
Clevedon Rd BHTH/HG B12..144 A1
Cleveland CI WLNHL WV13....38 D4
WNSFLD WV11..................7 F5
Cleveland Pas BKHL/PFLD WV2..7 H6
Cleveland Rd DUDN DY1......84 B5
STRBR DY8....................135 E3
WOLV WV1.......................7 F5
Cleves Dr RBRY B45...........187 C1
Cleves Rd RBRY B45..........173 C5
Clewley Dr COVEN WV9.......12 A4
Clewley Gv RIDG/WDGT B32..140 B2
Clews Cl WSL WS1.............57 E1
Clewshaw La
HWK/WKHTH B38............191 C4
Cley CI DIG/EDG B5...........143 H1
Cliffe Dr STETCH B33........130 D1
Clifford Rd DOR/KN B93.....196 D4
SMTHWK B67.................124 B3
WBROM B70...................87 E4
Clifford St DUDN DY1.........102 B1
DUNHL/THL/PER WV6.......6 A1
LOZ/NWT B19.................108 D2
Clifford Wk LOZ/NWT B19...108 D1
Cliff Rock Rd RBRY B45......188 B1
Clift Av WNSFLD WV11........26 A4
Clift CI SHHTH WV12...........26 A4
Clifton Av ALDR WS9..........30 C2
BRWNH WS8....................18 D1
Clifton Ct AST/WIT B6........109 F2
OLDBY B69...................104 D5
Clifton Crs SOLH B91.........181 F4
Clifton Gdns CDSL WV8.......11 E4
Clifton Gv ALE/KHTH/YWD B28..163 E5
Clifton La HHTH/SAND B71....71 F4
Clifton Rd AST/WIT B6........109 F2
BHTH/HG B12.................144 C2
CBROM B36...................113 C1
DUNHL/THL/PER WV6.......22 B4
RMSLY B62....................122 B3
SCFLD/BOLD B73 ....62 A4
SMTHWK B67.................106 B5
Clifton St BDMR/CCFT WV3....6 C4
BILS/COS WV14 ....54 C1
CDYHTH B64..................121 F3
STRBR DY8....................135 C2
Clifton Ter ERDW/GRVHL B23 *..92 D2
Clinic Dr HAG/WOL DY9......136 C2
Clinton Gv SHLY B90.........180 D4
Clinton Rd BILS/COS WV14...54 C1
CSHL/WTROR B46............115 F5
SHLY B90.....................180 D5
Clinton St WSNGN B18......107 G4
Clipper Vw LDYWD/EDGR B16..125 G3
Clipston Rd WASH/WDE B8..110 D4
Clissold CI BHTH/HG B12....127 E5
Clissold Pas WSNGN B18....108 A5
Clissold St WSNGN B18.....108 A5
Clive CI MGN/WHC B75........47 H3
Cliveden Av ALDR WS9........30 B1
RBRY B45.......................90 C2
Cliveden Coppice
FOAKS/STRLY B74............46 A4
Clivedon Wy RMSLY B62....121 C5
Cleveland St LOZ/NWT B19....3 G1
Clive Rd CHWD/FDBR/MGN B37..132 B3
Clive St HHTH/SAND B71......87 F2
Clockfields Dr BRLYHL DY5..118 C3
Clock La HIA/OLT B92........149 H5
Clockmill Av BLOX/PEL WS3..17 C4
Clockmill Rd BLOX/PEL WS3..17 C4
Clodeshall Rd WASH/WDE B8..110 C5
Cloister Dr RMSLY B62.......139 F4
The Cloisters RUSH/SHEL WS4..5 F1
Cloncurry End BVILLE B30...160 A4
Clonmel Rd BVILLE B30......160 A4
Clopton Crs
CHWD/FDBR/MGN B37.......114 C5
Clopton Rd STETCH B33.....131 E4
The Close DARL/WED WS10...55 C5
HALE B63.....................138 A2
HIA/OLT B92..................164 B2
HLYWD B47...................192 C3
HRBN B17.....................124 B5
RMSLY B62....................149 E5
SEDG DY3......................80 C4
SEDG DY3......................81 C1
SLYOAK B29 *.................159 F2
Clothier Gdns WLNHL WV13..39 G2
Clothier St WLNHL WV13.....39 G2
Cloudbridge Dr HIA/OLT B92..165 H3
Cloudsley Gv HIA/OLT B92..147 F4
Clover Av
DUNHL/THL/PER WV6.......34 D2
Cloverdale
DUNHL/THL/PER WV6.......34 D2
Clover Dr RIDG/WDGT B32...140 C5
Clover HI DSYBK/YTR WS5....45 G5
Clover La KGSWFD DY6........99 E4
Clover Lea Sq WASH/WDE B8..111 E3
Clover Ley WOLVN WV10......37 H2
Clover Piece TPTN/OCK DY4...70 A5
Clover Rd SLYOAK B29........159 C5
Club La WOLVN WV10..........12 C1
Club Rw SEDG DY3.............83 C1
Club Vw HWK/WKHTH B38...176 B5
Clunbury Cft BKDE/SHDE B34..112 C4
Clunbury Rd NFLD/LBR B31..175 C5
Clun CI OLDBY B69............85 E3
Clun Rd NFLD/LBR B31......158 B4
Clyde Av HALE B63...........122 C4
Clyde Ms BRLYHL DY5........100 D3
Clyde Rd DOR/KN B93........199 E1
Clydesdale
LGN/SDN/BHAMAIR B26....147 G2
Clydesdale Rd
BLKHTH/ROWR B65...........103 C4
Clyde St BHTH/HG B12.......127 C4
CDYHTH B64..................121 E3
Clyde Tower LOZ/NWT B19 *..108 D1
Coalbourn La STRBR DY8....118 B5
Coalheath La RUSH/SHEL WS4..29 E2
Coal Pool La BLOX/PEL WS3..28 B5
Coalport Rd WOLV WV1.......38 A4

Coalway Av BDMR/CCFT WV3 51 G2
LGN/SDN/BHAMAIR B26 148 A3
Coalway Gdns
BDMR/CCFT WV3 50 D2
Coalway Rd BDMR/CCFT WV3 51 G2
BLOX/PEL WS3 27 E2
ETTPK/GDPK/PENN WV4 50 D2
The Cobbles CSCFLD/WYGN B72 77 G4
Cobble Wk WSNGN B18 * 108 A4
Cobden Cl DARL/WED WS10 55 H2
TPTN/OCK DY4 69 F3
Cobden Gdns BHTH/HG B12 144 A2
Cobden St DARL/WED WS10 55 H2
STRBR DY8 134 D1
WSL WS1 56 D1
Cobham Cl CVALE B35 94 B3
Cobham Court Ms
HAG/WOL DY9 153 F4
Cobham Rd BORD B9 128 B2
DARL/WED WS10 72 A1
HALE B63 138 D3
STRBR DY8 135 G5
Cob La BVILLE B30 159 E3
Cobs Fld BVILLE B30 159 E4
Coburg Cft TPTN/OCK DY4 70 A5
Coburn Dr MGN/WHC B75 47 H3
Cochrane Cl HAG/WOL DY9 153 E2
TPTN/OCK DY4 * 70 A5
Cochrane Rd DUDS DY2 101 H4
Cock Hill La RBRY B45 173 H5
Cocksheds La RMSLY B62 122 A4
Cockshut Hl
LGN/SDN/BHAMAIR B26 130 C4
Cockshutt La BKHL/PFLD WV2 * 52 B1
Cockshutts La BKHL/PFLD WV2 52 B1
Cocksmead Cft
ALE/KHTH/YWD B14 160 D5
Cockthorpe Cl HRBN B17 124 B5
Cocton Cl
DUNHL/THL/PER WV6 20 C5
Codsall Gdns CDSL WV8 10 A3
Codsall Rd CDSL WV8 21 G1
CDYHTH B64 121 E4
Cofield Rd SCFLD/BOLD B73 76 D2
Cofton Ct RBRY B45 188 D1
Cofton Gv NFLD/LBR B31 189 E2
Cofton Lake Rd RBRY B45 188 C5
Cofton Rd NFLD/LBR B31 189 H1
Cokeland Pl CDYHTH B64 120 D4
Colaton Cl WOLVN WV10 37 G1
Colbourne Rd TPTN/OCK DY4 85 G2
Coldbath Rd MOS/BIL B13 161 H2
Coldridge Cl CDSL WV8 22 B1
Coldstream Dr STRBR DY8 118 A1
Coldstream Rd
WALM/CURD B76 78 A3
Cole Bank Rd HLGN/YWD B28 162 C2
Colebourne Rd MOS/BIL B13 162 B4
Colebridge Crs
CSHL/WTROR B46 115 F1
Colebrook Cft SHLY B90 179 H3
Colebrook Rd SHLY B90 179 G3
SPARK B11 145 F2
Cole Ct CHWD/FDBR/MGN B37 132 B2
Coleford Cl STRBR DY8 117 G2
Coleford Dr
CHWD/FDBR/MGN B37 132 A2
Cole Gn SHLY B90 179 G3
Cole Hall La BKDE/SHDE B34 112 D4
Colehurst Cft SHLY B90 195 F2
Coleman Rd DARL/WED WS10 56 A3
Coleman St
DUNHL/THL/PER WV6 36 C1
Colemeadow Rd
CSHL/WTROR B46 115 F2
MOS/BIL B13 161 H5
Colenso Rd LDYWD/EDGR B16 107 E5
Coleraine Rd PBAR/PBCH B42 74 A5
Coleridge Cl BLOX/PEL WS3 * 18 A2
SHHTH WV12 26 C3
Coleridge Dr
DUNHL/THL/PER WV6 34 C1
Coleridge Pas CBHAMNE B4 3 H3
Coleridge Ri SEDG DY3 82 C2
Coleridge Rd GTB/HAM B43 73 G4
Colesbourne Av
ALE/KHTH/YWD B14 177 G3
Colesbourne Rd HIA/OLT B92 147 H4
Coleshill Heath Rd
CHWD/FDBR/MGN B37 149 G1
Coleshill Rd CBROM B36 112 B2
CHWD/FDBR/MGN B37 132 A5
MGN/WHC B75 62 D3
WALM/CURD B76 96 B1
Coleshill St CSCFLD/WYGN B72 62 C3
Coleside Av MOS/BIL B13 162 B3
Coles La CSCFLD/WYGN B72 62 C5
HHTH/SAND B71 71 E4
The Colesleys
CSHL/WTROR B46 115 G3
Cole St DUDS DY2 103 E5
Cole Valley Rd HLGN/YWD B28 162 B4
Coleview Crs STETCH B33 131 G1
Coleville Rd WALM/CURD B76 78 D5
Coleys La NFLD/LBR B31 175 G3
Colgreave Av MOS/BIL B13 145 F5
Colindale Rd KGSTG B44 60 C5
Colleen Av BVILLE B30 177 F2
College Cl DARL/WED WS10 71 E1
College Dr BFLD/HDSWWD B20 89 H4
College Farm Dr
ERDW/GRVHL B23 76 B3
College Ga WASH/WDE B8 110 C5
College Gv
BFLD/HDSWWD B20 * 108 B2
College Hl SCFLD/BOLD B73 62 B4
College Rd
BFLD/HDSWWD B20 89 G4
DUNHL/THL/PER WV6 35 H1
KGSTG B44 91 E1
MOS/BIL B13 145 E5
RMSLY B62 128 A1
STRBR DY8 135 G3
WASH/WDE B8 111 G5
College St WSNGN B18 108 A5
College Vw
DUNHL/THL/PER WV6 35 H2
Collet Rd DUNHL/THL/PER WV6 20 C5
Collets Brook MGN/WHC B75 48 C3
Collett Cl STRBR DY8 135 G1
Colletts Gv
CHWD/FDBR/MGN B37 113 H5
Colley Av WOLVN WV10 23 H2
Colley Ga HALE B63 137 G1
Colley La HALE B63 137 G1
Colley Orch HALE B63 137 G1
Colley St WBROM B70 87 H2
Collier Cl BRWNH WS8 8 C5
Colliers Cl SHHTH WV12 25 H4
Colliers Fold BRLYHL DY5 100 D4
Colliery Dr BLOX/PEL WS3 16 B4
Colliery Rd HHTH/SAND B71 106 C1
WOLV WV1 37 H3
Collindale Ct KGSWFD DY6 81 H5
Collingbourne Av CBROM B36 111 H2
Collingdon Av
LGN/SDN/BHAMAIR B26 148 A1
Collingtree Ct ACGN B27 146 D5
Colling Wk
CHWD/FDBR/MGN B37 114 A4
Collingwood Dr GTB/HAM B43 59 H5
Collingwood Rd BVILLE B30 177 H2
WOLVN WV10 13 E5
Collins Cl RIDG/WDGT B32 140 A2
Collins Rd BRWNH WS8 19 G2
DARL/WED WS10 56 B5
Collins St WBROM B70 86 C3
WSL WS1 57 E1
Collis St STRBR DY8 118 C4
Collister Cl SHLY B90 163 F5
Colly Cft
CHWD/FDBR/MGN B37 113 H4
Collycroft Pl ACGN B27 146 B2
Colman Av WNSFLD WV11 25 F4
Colman Crs LGLYGN/QTN B68 123 G2
Colman Hl HALE B63 137 H2
Colman Hill Av HALE B63 137 H1
Colmore Av
ALE/KHTH/YWD B14 160 D3
Colmore Circ Queensway
CBHAMNW B3 3 G3
Colmore Crs MOS/BIL B13 161 H1
Colmore Dr MGN/WHC B75 63 G3
Colmore Flats LOZ/NWT B19 * 3 F1
Colmore Rd
ALE/KHTH/YWD B14 160 D3
Colmore Rw CBHAMNW B3 3 G4
Coln Cl NFLD/LBR B31 158 B4
Colonial Rd BORD B9 128 D2
Colshaw Rd STRBR DY8 135 E3
Colston Rd ERDE/BCHGN B24 93 F4
Colt Cl FOAKS/STRLY B74 60 A1
Coltham Rd SHHTH WV12 26 B4
Coltishall Cft CVALE B35 94 B4
Coltsfoot Cl WNSFLD WV11 25 E5
Columbia Cl DIG/EDG B5 143 H1
Columbine Cl DSYBK/YTR WS5 57 F5
Columbus Av BRLYHL DY5 119 H1
Colville Cl TPTN/OCK DY4 70 B3
Colville Rd BHTH/HG B12 144 D2
Colwall Rd SEDG DY3 83 F2
Colwall Wk ACGN B27 146 D3
Colworth Rd NFLD/LBR B31 175 E1
Colyns Gv STETCH B33 112 B4
Comber Cft MOS/BIL B13 162 B2
Comber Dr BRLYHL DY5 100 D3
Comberford Ct
DARL/WED WS10 * 56 A5
Comberford Dr
DARL/WED WS10 56 D4
Comberton Rd
LGN/SDN/BHAMAIR B26 130 D5
Combine Cl MGN/WHC B75 47 H1
Comet Rd
LGN/SDN/BHAMAIR B26 149 G3
Commercial Rd WOLV WV1 7 K5
WSLW WS2 27 E3
Commercial St CBHAMW B1 2 D7
Commissary Rd
LGN/SDN/BHAMAIR B26 149 E4
Commonfield Cft
WASH/WDE B8 110 B4
Common La
LGN/SDN/BHAMAIR B26 147 G2
WASH/WDE B8 110 D3
Common Rd WMBN WV5 80 D2
Commonside BLOX/PEL WS3 18 A5
BRLYHL DY5 101 E3
Common Side BRWNH WS8 19 G2
Communication Rw EDG B15 126 C3
Compton Cl SOLH B91 180 D1
Compton Cft
CHWD/FDBR/MGN B37 132 D3
Compton Dr DUDS DY2 103 F1
FOAKS/STRLY B74 60 A1
KGSWFD DY6 99 H4
Compton Gv HALE B63 137 G3
KGSWFD DY6 99 H4
Compton Hill Dr
BDMR/CCFT WV3 35 H3
Compton Pk BDMR/CCFT WV3 36 A3
Compton Rd BDMR/CCFT WV3 36 B3
CDYHTH B64 120 C3
ERDW/GRVHL B23 92 C5
HAG/WOL DY9 153 F1
RMSLY B62 139 H2
Compton Rd West
BDMR/CCFT WV3 35 H3
Comsey Rd GTB/HAM B43 59 F5
Comwall Cl BLOX/PEL WS3 27 G3
Conchar Cl CSCFLD/WYGN B72 77 G2
Conchar Rd CSCFLD/WYGN B72 77 G1
Concorde Dr CVALE B35 94 B4
Concorde Rd
LGN/SDN/BHAMAIR B26 149 G3
Condover Cl WSLW WS2 40 B2
Condover Rd NFLD/LBR B31 175 H5
Coneyford Rd
BKDE/SHDE B34 113 E3
Coney Gn STRBR DY8 135 H2
Coney Green Dr
NFLD/LBR B31 175 F5
Coneygree Rd TPTN/OCK DY4 85 G3
Conifer Cl BRLYHL DY5 119 E4
Conifer Ct MOS/BIL B13 144 A5
Conifer Dr HDSW B21 107 G2
NFLD/LBR B31 175 H2
Conifer Paddock RMSLY B62 122 C4
Conifer Rd FOAKS/STRLY B74 45 E5
Conington Gv HRBN B17 141 G2
Coniston Av HIA/OLT B92 147 F3
Coniston Cl HLGN/YWD B28 162 D3
Coniston Crs GTB/HAM B43 73 H4
Coniston Dr KGSWFD DY6 99 F2
Coniston Rd
DUNHL/THL/PER WV6 21 H2
ERDW/GRVHL B23 92 B1
FOAKS/STRLY B74 45 F2
Connaught Av
DARL/WED WS10 56 C5
Connaught Cl DSYBK/YTR WS5 58 A1
Connaught Dr WMBN WV5 65 E2
Connaught Rd BILS/COS WV14 54 B1
WOLV WV1 6 B3
Connops Wy HAG/WOL DY9 136 C2
Connor Rd HHTH/SAND B71 72 A3
Conolly Dr RBRY B45 174 B4
Conrad Cl BHTH/HG B12 127 G5
Consort Crs BRLYHL DY5 101 E3
Consort Dr DARL/WED WS10 40 A5
Consort Rd BVILLE B30 177 E2
Constable Cl GTB/HAM B43 59 G5
The Constables
LGLYGN/QTN B68 123 F2
Constance Av WBROM B70 87 H5
Constance Rd DIG/EDG B5 143 H2
Constantine La
CSHL/WTROR B46 97 F5
Constantine Wy
BILS/COS WV14 69 G1
Constitution Hl DUDS DY2 102 D1
LOZ/NWT B19 2 E1
Constitution Hl East
DUDS DY2 102 D1
Convent Cl BKHL/PFLD WV2 7 G5
Conway Av HHTH/SAND B71 71 F2
LGLYGN/QTN B68 123 F2
RIDG/WDGT B32 140 B1
Conway Cl DUDN DY1 68 C5
KGSWFD DY6 100 B5
SHLY B90 180 D4
Conway Crs SHHTH WV12 26 A3
Conway Dr
BLKHTH/ROWR B65 122 A2
Conway Gv GTB/HAM B43 73 F4
Conway Rd
CHWD/FDBR/MGN B37 132 B1
DUNHL/THL/PER WV6 34 D2
SHLY B90 180 D4
SPARK B11 145 E1
Conwy Cl WSLW WS2 41 E1
Conybere St BHTH/HG B12 127 F5
Conyworth Cl ACGN B27 146 D3
Cook Av DUDS DY2 102 D2
Cook Cl DOR/KN B93 197 G2
DUNHL/THL/PER WV6 34 C1
Cookes Cft NFLD/LBR B31 176 A3
Cookesley Cl GTB/HAM B43 59 H4
Cooke St BKHL/PFLD WV2 52 A1
Cookley Cl HALE B65 138 B5
Cooknell Dr STRBR DY8 118 A2
Cook Rd BLOX/PEL WS3 17 F5
Cooksey La KGSTG B44 60 B4
Cooksey Rd SMHTH B10 127 H4
Cooks La
CHWD/FDBR/MGN B37 114 B4
Cook St DARL/WED WS10 55 H2
VAUX/NECH B7 110 A2
Coombe Cft COVEN WV9 * 12 A4
Coombe Hl CDYHTH B64 121 H4
Coombe Pk FOAKS/STRLY B74 61 H1
Coombe Rd
BFLD/HDSWWD B20 91 E5
SHLY B90 180 C3
Coombes La NFLD/LBR B31 189 F2
Coombs Rd RMSLY B62 138 D1
Coombswood Wy RMSLY B62 121 H4
Cooper Av BRLYHL DY5 118 C2
Cooper Cl WBROM B70 88 A4
Coopers Bank Rd BRLYHL DY5 101 E1
Coopers La SMTHWK B66 106 C4
Coopers Rd
BFLD/HDSWWD B20 90 A3
Cooper St BKHL/PFLD WV2 37 H5
WBROM B70 87 H3
Copeley Hl ERDW/GRVHL B23 92 A5
Copes Crs WOLVN WV10 24 A4
Cope St BLOX/PEL WS3 27 G4
DARL/WED WS10 55 G2
WSNGN B18 126 A1
Cophall St TPTN/OCK DY4 86 B1
Cophams Cl HIA/OLT B92 148 A5
Coplow Cottages
LDYWD/EDGR B16 * 125 H1
Coplow St LDYWD/EDGR B16 125 H1
Copnor Gv
LGN/SDN/BHAMAIR B26 147 E1
Coppenhall Gv STETCH B33 130 C1
Copperbeach Dr
BHTH/HG B12 144 C2
Copperbeech Cl
RIDG/WDGT B32 141 F2
Copperbeech Dr
BHTH/HG B12 * 144 C2
Copper Beech Dr KGSWFD DY6 81 H5
WMBN WV5 65 F5
Copper Beech Gdns
BFLD/HDSWWD B20 89 H4
Coppice Av HAG/WOL DY9 136 D4
Coppice Cl ERDE/BCHGN B24 92 D3
RBRY B45 187 H1
SEDG DY3 67 E4
SHLY B90 194 C4
SOLH B91 * 164 C3
WNSFLD WV11 25 G1
Coppice Crs BRWNH WS8 8 D5
Coppice Dr ACGN B27 146 B5
Coppice Farm Wy SHHTH WV12 25 H3
Coppice Gdns HLYWD B47 192 C1
Coppice Hollow
RIDG/WDGT B32 157 F1
Coppice La ALDR WS9 29 H1
BRLYHL DY5 119 H3
BRWNH WS8 8 D4
DUNHL/THL/PER WV6 21 G3
POL/KGSB/FAZ B78 49 E3
SHHTH WV12 26 A4
Coppice Ri BRLYHL DY5 120 A2
Coppice Rd ALDR WS9 19 F3
BDMR/CCFT WV3 35 H5
BILS/COS WV14 68 A3
CDYHTH B64 121 E5
HIA/OLT B92 165 G3
MOS/BIL B13 144 C4
Coppice Side BRWNH WS8 8 D4
Coppice St TPTN/OCK DY4 69 E5
WBROM B70 87 E2
The Coppice
BFLD/HDSWWD B20 90 A4
NFLD/LBR B31 174 C3
SHHTH WV12 26 A4
STRBR DY8 152 B5
TPTN/OCK DY4 70 A2
Coppice View Rd
SCFLD/BOLD B73 60 C4
Coppice Wk SHLY B90 194 C4
Copplestone Cl
BKDE/SHDE B34 112 D3
Coppy Hall Gv ALDR WS9 30 B1
Copse Cl NFLD/LBR B31 175 G3
Copse Crs BLOX/PEL WS3 18 A3
Copse Rd DUDS DY2 120 B1
The Copse FOAKS/STRLY B74 46 D4
MOS/BIL B13 144 D5
Copson Cl WBROM B70 87 E3
Copstone Dr DOR/KN B93 196 D5
Copston Gv SLYOAK B29 158 D2
Copthall Rd HDSW B21 89 E4
Copt Heath Cft DOR/KN B93 183 F5
Copt Heath Dr DOR/KN B93 197 E1
Copthorne Rd
BDMR/CCFT WV3 51 G1
KGSTG B44 60 A5
Coralin Cl
CHWD/FDBR/MGN B37 132 B2
Corbett Crs STRBR DY8 118 C5
Corbett Rd BRLYHL DY5 119 G3
HLYWD B47 192 C1
Corbetts Cl HIA/OLT B92 167 H3
Corbett St SMTHWK B66 106 D5
Corbridge Av KGSTG B44 75 F2
Corbridge Rd SCFLD/BOLD B73 76 D1
Corbyn Rd BORD B9 129 F1
DUDN DY1 101 H1
Corbyns Cl BRLYHL DY5 100 D2
Corbyns Hall La BRLYHL DY5 100 D2
Corbyns Hall Rd BRLYHL DY5 100 D2
Cordley St WBROM B70 87 F2
Corfe Cl DUNHL/THL/PER WV6 34 D2
RIDG/WDGT B32 141 F2
Corfe Dr OLDBY B69 103 G1
Corfe Rd BILS/COS WV14 68 A3
Corfton Dr
DUNHL/THL/PER WV6 35 G2
Coriander Cl RBRY B45 174 B4
Corinne Cl RBRY B45 188 A2
Corinne Cft
CHWD/FDBR/MGN B37 114 A5
Corisande Rd SLYOAK B29 142 A5
Corley Av NFLD/LBR B31 175 H2
Corley Cl SHLY B90 179 G4
Cornbrook Rd SLYOAK B29 158 B4
Cornbury Gv SOLH B91 180 D1
Corncrake Cl
CSCFLD/WYGN B72 77 H1
Corncrake Dr CBROM B36 114 A1
Corncrake Rd DUDN DY1 83 G3
Cornel Cl
CHWD/FDBR/MGN B37 132 C4
Cornerway HWK/WKHTH B38 190 D1
Cornfield CDSL WV8 22 A1
Cornfield Cl KGSWFD DY6 99 E1
Cornfield Cft
CHWD/FDBR/MGN B37 132 D1
WALM/CURD B76 63 F5
Cornfield Rd
BLKHTH/ROWR B65 103 F5
NFLD/LBR B31 175 H1
WALM/CURD B76 78 B2
Cornflower Crs DUDS DY2 103 F1
Cornflower Rd BRWNH WS8 18 D1
Corngreaves Rd CDYHTH B64 120 D4
The Corngreaves
BKDE/SHDE B34 113 E3
Corngreaves Wk CDYHTH B64 121 E5
Corn Hl DSYBK/YTR WS5 43 G5
WOLV WV1 7 H4
Cornhill Gv BVILLE B30 160 C4
Corn Mill Cl RIDG/WDGT B32 158 A1
WALM/CURD B76 78 B2
Cornmill Cl WSL WS1 56 D1
Cornmill Gv
DUNHL/THL/PER WV6 34 B2
Cornovian Cl
DUNHL/THL/PER WV6 20 C5
Corns Gv WMBN WV5 80 D1
Cornwall Av LGLYGN/QTN B68 123 F4
Cornwall Cl ALDR WS9 30 A1
DARL/WED WS10 56 D5
KGSWFD DY6 99 H1
Cornwall Ga SHHTH WV12 25 H5
Cornwallis Rd WBROM B70 87 E5
Cornwall Pl WSLW WS2 40 C2
Cornwall Rd
BFLD/HDSWWD B20 89 H4
DSYBK/YTR WS5 57 H1
DUNHL/THL/PER WV6 35 G1
RBRY B45 173 G3
SMTHWK B66 106 D2
STRBR DY8 117 H4
Cornwall St CBHAMNW B3 2 E4
Cornwell Cl TPTN/OCK DY4 85 G1
Cornwood La SHLY B90 194 A3
Cornyx La SOLH B91 165 F4
Coronation Av WLNHL WV13 40 B3
Coronation Rd ALDR WS9 19 F4
BILS/COS WV14 53 G2
DARL/WED WS10 56 C5
GTB/HAM B43 58 C4
RUSH/SHEL WS4 18 B5
SLYOAK B29 142 D5
TPTN/OCK DY4 69 H3
WASH/WDE B8 110 D3
WNSFLD WV11 24 A5
Corporation Rd DUDS DY2 85 F5
Corporation St CBHAM B2 3 G5
DARL/WED WS10 71 E1
WOLV WV1 6 E4
WSL WS1 4 D7
Corporation St West WSLW WS2 4 B6
Corrie Cft
LGN/SDN/BHAMAIR B26 130 D5
RIDG/WDGT B32 157 F3
Corrin Gv KGSWFD DY6 99 G1
Corron Hl HALE B63 * 138 D3
Corser St DUDN DY1 83 H4
STRBR DY8 135 G4
WOLV WV1 37 H4
Corsican Cl SHHTH WV12 26 C3
Corvedale Rd SLYOAK B29 158 C4
Corve Gdns
DUNHL/THL/PER WV6 22 A5
Corve Vw SEDG DY3 * 67 E2
Corville Gdns
LGN/SDN/BHAMAIR B26 147 H3
Corville Rd RMSLY B62 139 H1
Corwen Cft NFLD/LBR B31 157 H3
Cory Cft TPTN/OCK DY4 85 G1
Coseley Rd BILS/COS WV14 53 G4
Cosford Crs CVALE B35 94 C3
Cosford Dr DUDS DY2 103 E4
Cossington Rd
ERDW/GRVHL B23 76 B4
Costock Cl
CHWD/FDBR/MGN B37 132 B4
Cosyll Gdns DUDN DY1 102 B1
Cotford Rd
ALE/KHTH/YWD B14 178 C3
Cotheridge Cl SHLY B90 196 A2
Cot La KGSWFD DY6 99 G4
Cotleigh Gv GTB/HAM B43 59 H5
Cotman Cl GTB/HAM B43 59 G5
Coton Gv SHLY B90 179 G3
Coton La ERDW/GRVHL B23 92 D2
Coton Rd
ETTPK/GDPK/PENN WV4 51 H3
Cotsdale Rd
ETTPK/GDPK/PENN WV4 51 E5
Cotsford SOLH B91 * 181 G2
Cotswold Cl ALDR WS9 30 C1
OLDBY B69 104 C4
RBRY B45 174 A4
Cotswold Ct BKHL/PFLD WV2 51 G2
Cotswold Cft HALE B63 154 C1
Cotswold Gv SHHTH WV12 25 H1
Cotswold Rd BKHL/PFLD WV2 52 D1
STRBR DY8 135 H1
Cottage Cl WNSFLD WV11 24 C4
Cottage Gdns RBRY B45 187 H2
Cottage La WALM/CURD B76 79 F5
WOLVN WV10 12 D4
Cottage Ms ALDR WS9 * 30 D4
Cottage St BRLYHL DY5 119 F1
KGSWFD DY6 99 H2
Cottage Vw CDSL WV8 10 D3
Cotteridge Rd BVILLE B30 177 E1
Cotterills Av WASH/WDE B8 111 F5
Cotterills La WASH/WDE B8 111 G5
Cotterills Rd TPTN/OCK DY4 69 G5
Cottesbrook Rd ACGN B27 146 C3
Cottesfield Cl WASH/WDE B8 111 F5
Cottesmore Cl HHTH/SAND B71 72 B3
Cottle Cl WSLW WS2 40 D2
Cotton La MOS/BIL B13 144 C5
Cottrell St HHTH/SAND B71 87 H2
Cottsmeadow Dr
WASH/WDE B8 111 G5
Cotwall End Rd SEDG DY3 82 D2
Cotysmore Rd MGN/WHC B75 62 D1
Couchman Rd WASH/WDE B8 110 C5
Coulter Gv
DUNHL/THL/PER WV6 34 B1
Counterfield Dr
BLKHTH/ROWR B65 103 F4
Countess Dr RUSH/SHEL WS4 29 F3
Countess St WSL WS1 56 D1
Country Park Vw
WALM/CURD B76 78 A2
County Cl BVILLE B30 160 C4
RIDG/WDGT B32 140 C4
County Park Av RMSLY B62 139 F4
Court Crs KGSWFD DY6 99 G4
Courtenay Gdns GTB/HAM B43 73 G1
Courtenay Rd KGSTG B44 75 E4
Court Farm Rd
ERDW/GRVHL B23 76 C5
Courtland Rd KGSWFD DY6 100 A1
Courtlands Cl DIG/EDG B5 143 G1
The Courtlands
DUNHL/THL/PER WV6 36 A1
Court La ERDW/GRVHL B23 76 C5
Court Oak Gv RIDG/WDGT B32 141 F1
Court Oak Rd RIDG/WDGT B32 141 E1
Court Pas DUDN DY1 * 84 C5
Court Rd BHTH/HG B12 144 A1
DUNHL/THL/PER WV6 36 B1
ETTPK/GDPK/PENN WV4 53 E4
SPARK B11 145 E3
Court St CDYHTH B64 121 E3
Court Wy WSLW WS2 4 C2
Courtway Av
ALE/KHTH/YWD B14 178 D4
The Courtyard
CSHL/WTROR B46 * 97 F4
Cousins St BKHL/PFLD WV2 52 B1
Coveley Gv WSNGN B18 108 A4
Coven Cl BLOX/PEL WS3 18 A2
Coven Gv SLYOAK B29 141 H5
Coven St WOLVN WV10 37 F1
Coventry Rd
CSHL/WTROR B46 133 G1
HIA/OLT B92 150 D4
LGN/SDN/BHAMAIR B26 147 E1
SMHTH B10 127 H3
Coventry St DIG/EDG B5 3 J6
STRBR DY8 135 G2
WOLV WV1 38 A3
Cover Cft WALM/CURD B76 78 C2
Coverdale Rd HIA/OLT B92 147 G3
Covers La KINVER DY7 116 C3
The Covert CDSL WV8 22 A1
Cowles Cft YDLY B25 130 A3
Cowley Cl CBROM B36 95 H5
Cowley Dr ACGN B27 146 D3
DUDN DY1 83 H4
Cowley Rd SPARK B11 145 G2
Cowper Cl SHHTH WV12 26 C3
Cowslip Cl HWK/WKHTH B38 176 D5
SLYOAK B29 158 C3
Coxcroft Av BRLYHL DY5 119 H4

Coxmoor CI BLOX/PEL WS3 * 16 B4
Cox Rd BILS/COS WV14 ......69 E2
Cox's La CDYHTH B64 ......121 F2
Cox St CBHAMNW B3 2
Coxwell Av WOLVN WV10 ......23 E5
Coxwell Gdns
  LDYWD/EDGR B16 ......125 H2
Coyne CI TPTN/OCK DY4 ......84 D1
Coyne Rd WBROM B70 ......87 F4
Crabbe St HAG/WOL DY9 ......136 D2
Crab La SHHTH WV12 ......26 B1
Crabmill CI DOR/KN B93 ......197 G1
Crab Mill CI HWK/WKHTH B38 ......190 C1
Crabmill La HWK/WKHTH B38 ......177 G5
Crabourne Rd DUDS DY2 ......120 C2
Crabtree CI HAG/WOL DY9 ......152 D4
  HHTH/SAND B71 ......72 B3
Crabtree Dr
  CHWD/FDBR/MGN B37 ......131 H1
Crabtree Rd WSL WS1 ......5 J3
Crackley Wy DUDS DY2 ......102 A3
Craddock Rd SMTHWKW B67 ......106 A3
Craddock St
  DUNHL/THL/PER WV6 ......36 C1
Cradley Fids HALE B63 ......137 H2
Cradley Forge HALE B63 ......120 A4
Cradley Park Rd DUDS DY2 ......120 C2
Cradley Rd CDYHTH B64 ......120 C4
Cradock Rd WASH/WDE B8 ......110 C4
Craig Cft
  CHWD/FDBR/MGN B37 ......132 D2
Crail Gv GTB/HAM B43 ......59 F5
Cramlington Rd
  PBAR/PBCH B42 ......74 A3
Cramnore CI TPTN/OCK DY4 ......69 C3
Cramp HI DARL/WED WS10 ......55 F2
Cramnourne Av
  ETTPK/GDPK/PENN WV4 ......52 C5
Cranbourne CI RBRY B45 ......174 B3
Cranbourne Gv KGSTG B44 ......75 G3
Cranbourne PI
  HHTH/SAND B71 * 87 H2
Cranbourne Rd KGSTG B44 ......75 F2
  STRBR DY8 ......135 G3
Cranbrook Gv
  DUNHL/THL/PER WV6 ......34 D2
Cranbrook Rd HDSW B21 ......89 E5
Cranby St WASH/WDE B8 ......110 A4
Craneberry Rd
  CHWD/FDBR/MGN B37 ......131 G1
Crane Hollow WMBN WV5 ......80 C1
Cranehouse Rd KGSTG B44 ......75 G1
Cranemoor CI
  VAUX/NECH B7 * 110 A3
Crane Rd BILS/COS WV14 ......54 B5
Cranesbill Rd SLYOAK B29 ......158 C4
Cranes Park Rd
  LGN/SDN/BHAMAIR B26 ......148 A2
Crane Ter
  DUNHL/THL/PER WV6 ......22 B5
Cranfield Gv
  LGN/SDN/BHAMAIR B26 ......130 B4
Cranford PI DSYBK/YTR WS5 ......57 F4
Cranford Gv SOLH B91 * 182 A4
Cranford Rd BDMR/CCFT WV3 ......35 G5
Cranford St SMTHWK B66 ......107 E4
Cranford Wy SMTHWK B66 ......107 E4
Cranham Dr KGSWFD DY6 ......99 H4
Cranhill CI HIA/OLT B92 ......164 D1
Cranleigh La DARL/WED WS10 ......71 G1
Cranleigh CI ALDR WS9 ......30 B5
  SHHTH WV12 ......26 A1
Cranleigh PI KGSTG B44 ......91 E1
Cranley Dr CDSL WV8 ......10 B3
Cranmer Av SHHTH WV12 ......26 B3
Cranmere Av
  DUNHL/THL/PER WV6 ......21 E4
Cranmere Ct
  DUNHL/THL/PER WV6 * 21 E4
Cranmoor Crs HALE B63 ......138 C2
Cranmore Av HDSW B21 ......107 F2
  SHLY B90 ......181 E5
Cranmore Bvd SHLY B90 ......180 D5
Cranmore Dr SHLY B90 ......181 E4
Cranmore Rd BDMR/CCFT WV3 ......36 B2
  CBROM B36 ......95 G5
  SHLY B90 ......180 D5
Cransley Gv SOLH B91 ......181 G1
Crantock CI WNSFLD WV11 ......26 A1
Crantock Rd PBAR/PBCH B42 ......90 C2
Cranwell Gn WMBN WV5 ......80 D1
Cranwell Gv ERDE/BCHGN B24 ......93 H5
Cranwell Wy CVALE B35 ......61 G1
Crathorne Av WOLVN WV10 ......23 E1
Craufurd Ct STRBR DY8 ......135 G4
Craven St
  ETTPK/GDPK/PENN WV4 ......52 D2
Crawford Av DARL/WED WS10 ......55 E1
  ETTPK/GDPK/PENN WV4 ......52 D5
  SMTHWKW B67 ......106 A4
Crawford Rd BDMR/CCFT WV3 ......6 A4
  WALM/CURD D76 ......78 C1
Crawford St WASH/WDE B8 ......110 A4
Crawshaws Rd CBROM B36 ......95 E5
Crayford Rd KGSTG B44 ......75 G2
Craythorne Av
  BFLD/HDSWWD B20 ......89 G1
Crecy CI WALM/CURD D76 ......63 E4
Credenda Rd WBROM B70 ......87 E5
Credon Gv EDG B15 ......142 D2
Creed Wy WBROM B70 ......87 F4
Cregoe St EDG B15 ......126 C5
Cremore Av WASH/WDE B8 ......110 C4
Cremore Rd MGN/WHC B75 * 47 F3
Crendon Rd
  BLKHTH/ROWR B65 ......103 G5
Crescent Av SOLH B91 ......182 A1
Crescent Av BRLYHL DY5 ......119 E2
The Crescent Grange
  HAG/WOL DY9 * 136 A3
Crescent Rd DARL/WED WS10 ......55 F2
  DUDN DY1 ......84 C2
  WLNHL WV13 ......40 A3
Crescent Studios WSNGN B18 * 108 D3
The Crescent BILS/COS WV14 ......53 H2

CDYHTH B64 ......121 C5
CHWD/FDBR/MGN B37 ......133 E4
DARL/WED WS10 ......56 A4
DUDN DY1 ......85 E2
DUNHL/THL/PER WV6 ......35 F2
GTB/HAM B43 ......74 A2
HIA/OLT B92 ......167 H3
SHLY B90 ......180 A1
SOLH B91 ......181 H1
STRBR DY8 ......152 B5
WLNHL WV13 ......40 A4
WSL WS1 ......5 J5
WSNGN B18 ......108 D5
Cressage Av NFLD/LBR B31 ......175 G4
Cressett Av BRLYHL DY5 ......100 D5
Cressett La BRLYHL DY5 ......101 E5
Cressington Dr
  FOAKS/STRLY B74 ......47 E4
Cresswell Crs BLOX/PEL WS3 ......16 B5
Cresswell Gv ERDE/BCHGN B24 ......93 H2
Cressy CI ALE/KHTH/YWD B14 ......177 G1
The Crest NFLD/LBR B31 ......189 H2
Crest Vw FOAKS/STRLY B74 ......45 F4
Crestwood Dr KGSTG B44 ......75 E4
Crestwood Gln
  DUNHL/THL/PER WV6 ......22 A3
Creswick Gv ERDW/GRVHL B23 ......168 F5
Creswick Gv RBRY B45 ......188 C1
Crewe Dr TPTN/OCK DY4 ......85 G4
Crew Rd DARL/WED WS10 ......56 A4
Creynolds CI SHLY B90 ......194 D4
Creynolds La SHLY B90 ......195 F3
Cricket Ct DSYBK/YTR WS5 ......57 H1
Cricketers Meadow
  CDYHTH B64 ......121 F5
Cricket Meadow SEDG DY3 ......85 G1
  WOLVN WV10 ......12 D3
Crick La BFLD/HDSWWD B20 ......108 A1
Cricklewood Dr RMSLY B62 ......139 F4
Crimmond RI HALE B63 ......138 A2
Crimscote CI SHLY B90 ......195 F2
Cripps Rd WSLW WS2 ......40 C2
Crocketts Av HDSW B21 * 107 F2
Crockett's La SMTHWK B66 ......106 C4
Crocketts Rd HDSW B21 ......107 F2
Crockett St DUDN DY1 ......84 A4
Crockford Dr MGN/WHC B75 ......47 E2
Crockford Rd HHTH/SAND B71 ......71 G2
Crocus Crs COVEN WV9 ......12 A5
Croft CI YDLY B25 ......130 A4
Croft Ct CBROM B36 * 112 D1
Crofts BRWNH WS8 ......8 D5
Croft Down Rd HIA/OLT B92 ......148 B3
Croftdown Rd HRBN B17 ......141 F1
Crofters CI STRBR DY8 ......135 H5
Crofters Ct EDG B15 ......142 C1
Crofters La MGN/WHC B75 ......48 A2
Crofteigh Gdns SOLH B91 * 181 F5
Croft Rd
  LGN/SDN/BHAMAIR B26 ......130 A4
Crofts CI WALM/CURD D76 ......78 C4
  WSLW WS2 ......41 H2
The Croft DSYBK/YTR WS5 ......43 F5
  DUDS DY2 ......101 H3
  KIDD DY10 ......168 A5
  NFLD/LBR B31 ......175 H2
  SEDG DY3 ......67 G2
  WLNHL WV13 ......39 G3
  WMBN WV5 ......80 B1
The Croftway
  BFLD/HDSWWD B20 ......73 C5
Croftwood Rd HAG/WOL DY9 ......136 B3
Cromdale Dr HALE B63 ......137 H4
Cromer Gdns
  DUNHL/THL/PER WV6 ......22 B5
Crome Rd GTB/HAM B43 ......59 H5
Cromer Rd BHTH/HG B12 ......144 B2
Crompton Av
  BFLD/HDSWWD B20 * 90 C5
Crompton CI WSLW WS2 ......27 E5
Crompton Ct CDSL WV8 ......10 D5
Crompton Rd
  BFLD/HDSWWD B20 ......108 C1
  RBRY B45 ......173 H4
  TPTN/OCK DY4 ......85 G2
  VAUX/NECH B7 ......110 A1
Cromwell CI
  BLKHTH/ROWR B65 ......103 F4
  WSLW WS2 ......40 C1
Cromwell Gn DUDS DY2 * 103 F1
Cromwell La NFLD/LBR B31 ......157 H2
Cromwell Rd WOLVN WV10 ......13 E4
Cromwell St DUDS DY2 ......103 E1
  HHTH/SAND B71 ......72 A5
  VAUX/NECH B7 ......109 H4
Crondal Rd EDG B15 ......126 B5
Cronehills Linkway
  WBROM B70 ......87 H3
Cronehills St WBROM B70 ......87 H2
Crookham CI HRBN B17 ......124 D5
Crookhay La HHTH/SAND B71 ......71 E3
Crook La ALDR WS9 ......59 E2
Croome CI SPARK B11 ......144 D4
Cropredy Rd NFLD/LBR B31 ......175 G5
Cropthorne Dr HWNLD B47 ......192 D1
Cropthorne Gdns SHLY B90 ......180 C2
Cropthorne Rd SHLY B90 ......180 D1
Crosbie Rd HRBN B17 ......141 H1
Crosby CI CBHAMNW B1 ......2 A4
  DUNHL/THL/PER WV6 ......22 B5
Cross CI CDYHTH B64 ......121 F2
Cross Farm Rd HRBN B17 ......142 B3
Cross Farms La RBRY B45 ......173 H4
Crossfield Rd STETCH B33 ......130 C1
Crossfield Wy BILS/COS WV14 ......54 A3
Crossgate Rd DUDS DY2 ......101 H5
Crossings Gv STETCH B33 ......131 G2
Crossland Crs
  DUNHL/THL/PER WV6 ......22 B4
Cross La GTB/HAM B43 ......73 G2
  SEDG DY3 ......67 F5
Cross St DUDS DY2 ......102 D5
Cross PI SEDG DY3 ......67 G2
Cross St BILS/COS WV14 ......69 D1
  BLKHTH/ROWR B65 ......122 A3
  BLOX/PEL WS3 ......28 C1
  DARL/WED WS10 ......55 G5
  DUDN DY1 ......84 C5

HALE B63 ......138 C4
HDSW B21 ......107 E1
KGSWFD DY6 ......99 F1
LGLYGN/QTN B68 ......106 C5
SMTHWK B66 ......106 C5
STRBR DY8 ......135 E2
WLNHL WV13 ......39 G4
WOLV WV1 ......37 H4
Cross St North WOLV WV1 ......37 F1
Cross St South BKHL/PFLD WV2 ......52 A1
Cross Walks Rd HAG/WOL DY9 ......136 C2
Crossway La KGSTG B44 ......75 F5
Crossways KGSTG B44 ......75 H4
Crosswells Rd
  LGLYGN/QTN B68 ......105 F4
Crowberry CI BRWNH WS8 ......18 D1
Crowesbridge Ms
  BILS/COS WV14 ......68 B3
Crowhurst Rd NFLD/LBR B31 ......189 E1
Crowland Av
  DUNHL/THL/PER WV6 ......34 C1
Crowle Dr HAG/WOL DY9 ......136 A2
Crown CI BLKHTH/ROWR B65 ......104 B5
  SEDG DY3 ......67 F2
Crown Ct DARL/WED WS10 ......40 A5
Crown La FOAKS/STRLY B74 ......46 C3
  STRBR DY8 ......135 F1
Crownmeadow Dr
  TPTN/OCK DY4 ......70 B4
Crownoakes Dr STRBR DY8 ......118 A2
Crown Rd BORD B9 ......128 B2
  BVILLE B30 ......145 H5
Crown St WOLV WV1 ......37 F1
Crown Wk TPTN/OCK DY4 ......85 G4
Crows Nest CI WALM/CURD D76 ......63 F5
Crowther Gdns HALE B63 ......120 C5
Crowther Gv
  DUNHL/THL/PER WV6 ......36 B1
Crowther Rd
  DUNHL/THL/PER WV6 ......36 B1
  ERDW/GRVHL B23 ......92 B1
Crowther St WOLVN WV10 ......37 G1
Croxall Wy SMTHWK B66 ......106 D4
Croxdene Av BLOX/PEL WS3 ......26 D1
Croxley Gdns WLNHL WV13 ......39 F5
Croxstalls Av BLOX/PEL WS3 ......27 E2
Croxstalls CI BLOX/PEL WS3 ......27 E1
Croxstalls PI BLOX/PEL WS3 ......27 E1
Croxstalls Rd BLOX/PEL WS3 ......27 E2
Croxton Gv STETCH B33 ......112 C5
Croyde Av PBAR/PBCH B42 ......74 A3
Croydon Rd ERDE/BCHGN B24 ......93 E5
  SLYOAK B29 ......142 D5
Croy Dr CVALE B35 ......61 H1
The Crucible BILS/COS WV14 ......68 C1
Crusader CI RMSLY B62 ......100 C4
Crychan CI RBRY B45 ......174 B3
Cryersoak CI SHLY B90 ......195 G1
Crystal Av STRBR DY8 ......118 B3
Crystal Dr SMTHWK B66 ......105 C1
Cubley Rd HLGN/YWD B28 ......162 C1
Cuckoo CI VAUX/NECH B7 * 110 B1
Cuin Rd SMTHWK B66 ......107 E4
Culey Gv STETCH B33 ......131 F2
Culford Dr RIDG/WDGT B32 ......157 G2
Culham CI ACGN B27 ......146 D5
Culmington CI SHLY B90 ......195 H2
Culmington Rd NFLD/LBR B31 ......175 F5
Culmore CI SHHTH WV12 ......40 B1
Culmore Rd RMSLY B62 ......122 C3
Culverhouse Dr BRLYHL DY5 ......118 D3
Culverley Crs DOR/KN B93 ......196 D2
Culvert Wy SMTHWK B66 ......105 H2
Culwell St WOLVN WV10 ......37 H2
Cumberford Av STETCH B33 ......131 G3
Cumberland CI KGSWFD DY6 ......100 A5
Cumberland Rd BILS/COS WV14 ......54 A5
  HHTH/SAND B71 ......71 H5
  LGLYGN/QTN B68 ......123 F4
  WLNHL WV13 ......39 G4
Cumberland St CBHAMW B1 ......2 C6
Cumbrian Cft HALE B63 ......137 H5
Cumbria Wy WASH/WDE B8 ......110 B3
Cunningham Rd
  DUNHL/THL/PER WV6 ......34 C1
  WSLW WS2 ......40 C3
Cupfields Av TPTN/OCK DY4 ......70 A3
Cupfields Crs TPTN/OCK DY4 ......70 A4
Curbar Rd PBAR/PBCH B42 ......74 C5
Curdale Rd RIDG/WDGT B32 ......157 F2
Curdworth La
  WALM/CURD D76 ......79 H2
Curlew CI BRWNH WS8 ......9 E5
Curlew Dr DUDN DY1 ......83 H2
Curral Rd BLKHTH/ROWR B65 ......121 H1
Curtin Dr DARL/WED WS10 ......54 D4
Curtis CI SMTHWK B66 ......107 G5
Curzon Circ CBHAMNE B4 ......127 G1
Curzon St BORD B9 ......127 H1
  DUDS DY2 ......102 D3
  WOLV WV1 ......37 G3
Cutlers Rough CI
  NFLD/LBR B31 ......158 B5
Cutler St SMTHWK B66 ......106 D4
Cutsdean CI NFLD/LBR B31 ......158 B5
Cutshill CI CBROM B36 ......113 E1
The Cutting RUSH/SHEL WS4 ......42 B1
Cutworth CI WALM/CURD D76 ......63 G5
Cygnet CI WMBN WV5 ......80 D1
Cygnet Dr BRWNH WS8 ......9 E5
Cygnet La BRLYHL DY5 ......101 G1
Cygnet Rd WBROM B70 ......87 E1
Cygnus Wy WBROM B70 ......86 D1
Cypress Av SEDG DY3 ......83 F1
Cypress Gdns
  FOAKS/STRLY B74 ......62 A1
  KGSWFD DY6 ......99 G5
Cypress Rd DSYBK/YTR WS5 ......58 A4
  DUDS DY2 ......103 E4
Cypress Sq ACGN B27 ......146 C2
Cypress Wy NFLD/LBR B31 ......175 F5
Cyprus CI SLYOAK B29 ......158 C3
Cyprus St BKHL/PFLD WV2 ......51 H2
  OLDBY B69 ......104 C1
Cyril Gv SMHTH B10 ......128 A4
Cyril Rd SMHTH B10 ......128 B4

Dacer Rd BVILLE B30 ......160 B5
Dace Rd WOLVN WV10 ......38 B1
Dadford Vw BRLYHL DY5 ......118 D2
Dad's La MOS/BIL B13 ......160 D1
Daffodil CI SEDG DY3 ......67 G4
Daffodil PI DSYBK/YTR WS5 ......43 F5
Daffodil Rd DSYBK/YTR WS5 ......43 F5
Daffodil Wy NFLD/LBR B31 ......188 A1
Dagnall Rd ACGN B27 ......146 D4
Dahlia CI WOLV WV1 ......38 C4
Daimler CI CBROM B36 ......95 H5
Daimler Rd
  ALE/KHTH/YWD B14 ......179 F2
Dainton Gv RIDG/WDGT B32 ......157 G3
Dairy Ct LGLYGN/QTN B68 ......123 H5
Dairy Bank CI BLOX/PEL WS3 ......18 B5
Daisy Bank Crs DSYBK/YTR WS5 ......43 F5
Daisy Dr ERDW/GRVHL B23 ......91 G1
Daisy Farm Rd
  ALE/KHTH/YWD B14 ......178 D5
Daisy Meadow TPTN/OCK DY4 ......70 A5
Daisy St BILS/COS WV14 ......69 E1
  DUNHL/THL/PER WV6 ......36 C1
Daisy Wk COVEN WV9 ......12 A4
Dalbeg CI CDSL WV8 ......22 A2
Dalbury Rd HLGN/YWD B28 ......162 C5
Dale CI GTB/HAM B43 ......74 D1
  SMTHWKW B67 ......124 C1
  TPTN/OCK DY4 ......86 B1
Dalecote Av HIA/OLT B92 ......165 G2
Dale End CBHAMNE B4 ......3 H5
  SLYOAK B29 ......142 C4
  STRBR DY8 ......135 F5
Dales CI DUNHL/THL/PER WV6 ......22 D4
Dalesman CI KGSWFD DY6 ......99 F2
Dale St BDMR/CCFT WV3 ......6 C6
  BILS/COS WV14 ......54 B3
  DARL/WED WS10 ......55 C5
  SMTHWK B66 ......124 C1
  WSL WS1 ......57 E1
Daleswood Pk RMSLY B62 * 172 B5
Dale Ter OLDBY B69 ......104 A1
Daleview Rd
  ALE/KHTH/YWD B14 ......179 E2
Dalewood Cft
  LGN/SDN/BHAMAIR B26 ......147 F1
Dalewood Rd
  CHWD/FDBR/MGN B37 ......113 H4
Daley CI CBHAMW B1 ......2 A4
Daley Rd BILS/COS WV14 ......69 F1
Dalkeith Rd SCFLD/BOLD B73 ......76 C1
Dalkeith St WSLW WS2 ......4 A1
Dallas Rd ERDW/GRVHL B23 ......92 A2
Dallimore CI HIA/OLT B92 ......164 D1
Dalloway Cl DIG/EDG B5 ......143 H1
Dalston CI DUDS DY2 ......102 D3
Dalston Rd ACGN B27 ......146 C4
Dalton Ct WMBN WV5 ......64 C4
Dalton Rd WSLW WS2 ......41 E2
Dalton St WOLV WV1 ......37 G3
  CBHAMNE B4 ......3 H4
Dalvine Rd DUDS DY2 ......120 B2
Dalwood CI BILS/COS WV14 ......68 B4
Damar Cft
  ALE/KHTH/YWD B14 ......177 H1
Damien CI SMTHWKW B67 ......106 B4
Dam Mill CI CDSL WV8 ......21 G1
Damson CI SHHTH WV12 ......25 G5
Damson Pkwy HIA/OLT B92 ......165 H5
Danbury CI WALM/CURD D76 ......78 C1
Danbury Gdns WOLVN WV10 ......12 C5
Danby Gv ERDE/BCHGN B24 ......93 G4
Danby Rd DUDS DY2 ......102 D1
Dandy Bank Rd KGSWFD DY6 ......100 C1
Dandy's Wk WSL WS1 ......5 F6
Dane Gv BVILLE B30 ......160 D2
Danescourt Crs KGSTG B44 ......75 H5
Danescourt Rd
  DUNHL/THL/PER WV6 ......21 G4
Danesmore Dr ALDR WS9 ......19 F4
Dane Ter BLKHTH/ROWR B65 ......104 A4
Daneways CI FOAKS/STRLY B74 ......45 G5
Danford CI STRBR DY8 ......135 G3
Danford Gdns SMHTH B10 ......128 A4
Danford La SOLH B91 ......181 E2
Danford Rd HWNLD B47 ......192 B1
Danford Wy GTB/HAM B43 ......73 F5
Dangerfield La
  DARL/WED WS10 ......55 E1
Daniel Av WLSN WV5 ......64 C1
Daniels La ALDR WS9 ......44 C1
Daniels Rd BORD B9 ......129 E2
Danks St TPTN/OCK DY4 ......85 G5
Danzey Green Rd CBROM B36 ......94 D5
Danzey Gv
  ALE/KHTH/YWD B14 ......177 G2
Darby CI BILS/COS WV14 ......68 B3
Darby End Rd DUDS DY2 ......103 E5
Darby Rd DARL/WED WS10 ......55 H5
Darbys Hill Rd OLDBY B69 ......103 H2
Darby St BLKHTH/ROWR B65 ......122 A3
Darbys Wy TPTN/OCK DY4 ......85 H1
Darell Cft WALM/CURD D76 ......78 C5
Darenth Rd KGSTG B44 ......74 D4
  WSL WS1 ......57 F1
Darfield Wk BHTH/HG B12 * 127 G5
Darkhouse La BILS/COS WV14 ......53 H4
Dark La HAG/WOL DY9 ......184 C1
  HWK/WKHTH B38 ......191 H1
  RMSLY B62 ......172 B1
Darlaston La BILS/COS WV14 ......54 C1
Darlaston Rd DARL/WED WS10 ......55 E3
  WSLW WS2 ......40 D4
Darley Av BKDE/SHDE B34 ......112 B3
Darleydale Av KGSTG B44 ......75 E2

Darley Dr DUNHL/THL/PER WV6 ..22 D5
Darley Green Rd DOR/KN B93 ...199 F3
Darley Wy FOAKS/STRLY B74 ......60 B1
Darlington St DARL/WED WS10 ...55 F5
Darlington St WOLV WV1 ......6 E4
Darnel Cft SMHTH B10 ......128 A2
Darnel Hurst Rd MGN/WHC B75 ..47 G2
Darnford CI ERDE/BCHGN B24 ...93 G5
  HLGN/YWD B28 ......163 E5
Darnick Rd SCFLD/BOLD B73 ......76 B1
Darnley Rd LDYWD/EDGR B16 ...125 H2
Dart CHWD/FDBR/MGN B37 ......132 A1
Dartford Rd BLOX/PEL WS3 ......26 D1
Dartmoor CI RBRY B45 ......174 A3
Dartford Rd BLOX/PEL WS3 ......28 A5
  STRBR DY8 ......117 H1
Dartmouth Av AST/WIT B6 ......109 F4
Dartmouth Circ AST/WIT B6 ......109 F4
Dartmouth CI BILS/COS WV14 ...28 A5
Dartmouth Crs BILS/COS WV14 ...54 C1
Dartmouth Dr ALDR WS9 ......29 H5
Dartmouth Middleway
  VAUX/NECH B7 ......3 K1
Dartmouth PI BLOX/PEL WS3 ......28 A4
Dartmouth Rd SLYOAK B29 ......142 D5
  SMTHWK B66 ......106 B2
Dartmouth St BKHL/PFLD WV2 ...7 H7
  WBROM B70 ......87 F3
Dart St BORD B9 ......127 H3
Darvel Rd SHHTH WV12 ......40 B1
Darwall St WSL WS1 ......4 E3
Darwin Ct
  DUNHL/THL/PER WV6 ......34 C1
Darwin Gv WSLW WS2 ......27 F4
Darwin Rd WSLW WS2 ......27 F4
Darwin St DIG/EDG B12 ......127 F4
Dassett Gv BORD B9 ......129 G2
Dassett Rd DOR/KN B93 ......196 D4
Dauntsey Covert
  ALE/KHTH/YWD B14 ......177 H3
Davena Dr RIDG/WDGT B32 ......141 E5
Davena Gv BILS/COS WV14 ......54 A5
Davenport Rd
  DUNHL/THL/PER WV6 ......21 F5
  WNSFLD WV11 ......25 H2
Daventry Gv RIDG/WDGT B32 ...140 C1
Davey Rd BFLD/HDSWWD B20 ...91 E5
  WBROM B70 ......87 G2
David Harman Dr
  HHTH/SAND B71 ......72 B4
David Peacock CI
  TPTN/OCK DY4 ......85 G1
David Rd BFLD/HDSWWD B20 ...90 B4
  TPTN/OCK DY4 ......70 A4
The Davids NFLD/LBR B31 ......159 E4
Davies Av BILS/COS WV14 ......53 H5
Davis Av TPTN/OCK DY4 ......85 G2
Davis Gv YDLY B25 ......146 D1
Davison Rd SMTHWKW B67 ......124 B1
Davis Rd SHHTH WV12 ......26 B2
Davy Rd WSLW WS2 ......27 E5
Dawberry CI
  ALE/KHTH/YWD B14 ......160 C5
Dawberry Fields Rd
  ALE/KHTH/YWD B14 ......160 C5
Dawberry Rd
  ALE/KHTH/YWD B14 ......160 C5
Daw End RUSH/SHEL WS4 ......29 E4
Daw End La RUSH/SHEL WS4 ......29 F4
Dawes Av WBROM B70 ......87 G5
Dawes La BRWNH WS8 ......9 G3
Dawley Brook Rd KGSWFD DY6 ..99 H2
Dawley CI WSLW WS2 ......56 B1
Dawley Crs
  CHWD/FDBR/MGN B37 ......132 B3
Dawley Rd KGSWFD DY6 ......99 G1
Dawlish Rd DUDN DY1 ......84 C1
  SLYOAK B29 ......142 D5
  SMTHWK B66 ......106 C5
Dawn Dr TPTN/OCK DY4 ......70 A1
Dawney Dr MGN/WHC B75 ......47 E1
Dawn Rd NFLD/LBR B31 ......158 A4
Dawson Av BILS/COS WV14 ......67 H1
Dawson Rd HDSW B21 ......107 G2
Dawson Sq BILS/COS WV14 * 53 C3
Dawson St BLOX/PEL WS3 ......27 H2
  SMTHWK B66 ......106 C2
Day Av WNSFLD WV11 ......25 E5
Daykin Rd DSYBK/YTR WS5 ......57 H4
Dayhouse Bank RMSLY B62 ......172 D5
Daylesford Rd HIA/OLT B92 ......147 G4
Day St WSLW WS2 ......4 D1
Deakin Av BRWNH WS8 ......9 F3
Deakin Rd ERDE/BCHGN B24 ......92 D5
  WALM/CURD D76 ......63 G5
Deakins Rd YDLY B25 ......129 H5
Deal Dr OLDBY B69 ......85 F5
Deal Gv NFLD/LBR B31 ......158 A4
Deanbrook CI SHLY B90 ......195 G2
Dean CI CSCFLD/WYGN B72 ......77 E4
  KGSTG B44 ......75 H3
  STRBR DY8 ......135 H1
Dean Ct CHWD/FDBR/MGN B37 ...20 C5
Deanery Rd WOLV WV1 ......7 J2
Dean Rd ERDW/GRVHL B23 ......92 D1
  RUSH/SHEL WS4 ......29 E3
  WMBN WV5 ......79 H5
Deansfield Rd WOLV WV1 ......38 B5
Deans Ga WLNHL WV13 ......38 D5
Dean St BILS/COS WV14 ......68 C3
  DIG/EDG B5 ......3 H7
Dean's Rd WOLV WV1 ......38 B3
Dearman Brd SPARK B11 ......127 H5
Dearmont Rd NFLD/LBR B31 ...189 E1
Dearne Ct SEDG DY3 ......68 A5
Debden CI DOR/KN B93 ......198 C1
Debenham Crs YDLY B25 ......129 H4
Debenham Rd YDLY B25 ......129 H4
Deblen Dr LDYWD/EDGR B16 ...125 F3
Deborah CI BKHL/PFLD WV2 ......52 A2
Dee Gv HWK/WKHTH B38 ......190 C1
Deedmore Rd RBRY B45 ......145 H5
Deeley CI CDYHTH B64 ......121 E5
  EDG B15 ......126 C5
Deeley PI BLOX/PEL WS3 ......27 F2
Deeley St BLOX/PEL WS3 ......27 F2
  BRLYHL DY5 * 119 G3

Deepdale Av
  LGN/SDN/BHAMAIR B26 ....147 H3
Deepdale La DUDN DY1 ....83 C3
Deepdales WMBN WV5 ....64 C5
Deeplow Cl
  CSCFLD/WYGN B72 * 62 C4
Deepmoor Rd STETCH B33......130 B1
Deepmore Av WSLW WS2 ....41 F3
Deepwood Cl RUSH/SHEL WS4 ...28 D2
Deer Cl BLOX/PEL WS5 ....27 G1
Deerhurst Rd
  BFLD/HDSWWD B20 ....89 H1
Dee Rd BLOX/PEL WS5 ....28 A1
Deer Park Wy SOLH B91 ....182 A4
Defford Av RUSH/SHEL WS4 ....29 E1
Defford Dr LGLYGN/QTN B68 ..105 F5
De Havilland Dr CVALE B35 .....94 C4
Deighton Rd DSYBK/YTR WS5 ...57 G1
Delamere Cl CBROM B36 ....95 F5
Delamere Dr DSYBK/YTR WS5 ...54 C4
Delamere Rd HLGN/YWD B28 ...162 D3
  SHHTH WV12 ....24 B1
Delancey Keep MGN/WHC B75 ...63 C3
Delhurst Av
  ETTPK/GDPK/PENN WV4 ....52 C5
Delhurst Rd KGSTG B44 ....74 D2
Delius St STCHFD B33 ....77 H3
Dell Farm Cl DOR/KN B93 ......197 F2
Dellows Cl HWK/WKHTH B38 ...190 B1
Dell Rd BRLYHL DY5 ....100 D4
  BVILLE B30 ....160 A5
The Dell HIA/OLT B92 ....164 C1
  LDYWD/EDGR B16 * 125 H2
  NFLD/LBR B31 ....157 H4
  STRBR DY8 ....135 E3
Delmore Wy WALM/CURD B76 ....78 C5
Delph Dr BRLYHL DY5 ....119 G5
Delphinium Cl BORD B9 ....128 D1
Delph La BRLYHL DY5 ....119 G5
Delph Rd BRLYHL DY5 ....119 F3
Delrene Rd HLGN/YWD B28 ....179 H2
Delves Crs DSYBK/YTR WS5 .....57 G3
Delves Green Rd
  DSYBK/YTR WS5 ....57 G2
Delves Rd WSL WS1 ....57 F1
Delville Rd DARL/WED WS10 ...55 H3
De Marnham Cl WBROM B70 .....88 A5
De Moram Gv HIA/OLT B92 ....165 H3
Demuth Wy OLDBY B69 ....104 D4
Denaby Gv
  ALE/KHTH/YWD B14 ....179 F1
Denbigh Cl DUDN DY1 ....83 H4
Denbigh Crs HHTH/SAND B71 ...71 F5
Denbigh Dr DARL/WED WS10 ...56 D4
  HHTH/SAND B71 ....71 F5
Denbigh Rd TPTN/OCK DY4 ......86 A2
Denbigh St BORD B9 ....128 B2
Denby Cl VAUX/NECH B7 ....109 H4
Denby Cft SHLY B90 ....195 F2
Dencer Cl RBRY B45 ....173 H5
Dencil Cl HALE B63 ....137 H2
Dene Av KGSWFD DY6 ....99 G5
Dene Court Rd HIA/OLT B92 ...164 B1
Denegate Cl WALM/CURD B76 ...78 D5
Dene Hollow MOS/BIL B13 .....162 A4
Dene Rd STRBR DY8 ....135 F4
Denewood Av
  BFLD/HDSWWD B20 ....90 B4
Denford Gv
  ALE/KHTH/YWD B14 ....160 D5
Denham Gdns
  BDMR/CCFT WV3 ....35 F5
Denham Rd ACGN B27 ....146 B2
Denholme Gv
  ALE/KHTH/YWD B14 ....178 C2
Denholm Rd SCFLD/BOLD B73 ...61 F5
Denise Dr BILS/COS WV14 ......68 D3
  CHWD/FDBR/MGN B37 ....113 H5
  HRBN B17 ....142 A3
Denleigh Rd KGSWFD DY6 .....100 B5
Denmark Cl
  DUNHL/THL/PER WV6 ....36 C1
Denmead Dr WNSFLD WV11 ......25 F2
Denmore Gdns WOLV WV1 ....38 B3
Dennis Hall Rd STRBR DY8 ....118 C4
Dennis Rd BHTH/HG B12 ....144 D3
Dennis St STRBR DY8 ....118 B4
Denshaw Rd
  ALE/KHTH/YWD B14 ....160 D4
Denton Cft DOR/KN B93 ......196 B5
Denton Dr GTB/HAM B43 ....73 F4
  STETCH B33 ....129 H2
Denton Rd HAG/WOL DY9 .....137 E3
Denver Rd
  ALE/KHTH/YWD B14 ....178 C3
Denville Ct BILS/COS WV14 ...54 A1
Denville Crs BORD B9 ....129 F1
Depwo Gv RIDG/WDGT B32 ...157 F2
Derby Av WOLV WV1 ....22 C2
Derby Dr
  CHWD/FDBR/MGN B37 ....132 B2
Derby St BORD B9 ....127 G2
  WSLW WS2 ....41 H1
Dereham Cl WASH/WDE B8 ....110 A5
Dereham Wk BILS/COS WV14 ...69 E1
De Quincy Cl DUDN DY1 ......101 C2
Derron Av
  LGN/SDN/BHAMAIR B26 ......147 E2
Derry Cl HRBN B17 ....141 C4
Derrydown Cl
  ERDW/GRVHL B23 ....92 C3
Derrydown Rd
  PBAR/PBCH B42 ....90 B1
Derry St BRLYHL DY5 ....37 F5
  BRLYHL DY5 ....119 E2
Derwent Cl BRLYHL DY5 ....100 D3
  FOAKS/STRLY B74 ....45 F3
  WLNHL WV13 ....40 A3
Derwent Gv BVILLE B30 ....160 C1
Derwent Rd BVILLE B30 ....160 C2
  DUNHL/THL/PER WV6 ....21 H2
Desford Av PBAR/PBCH B42 ....74 C4
Dettonford Rd
  RIDG/WDGT B32 ....157 F2
Devereux Cl BDMR B36 ....113 E1
Devereux Rd MGN/WHC B75 ....47 C4
  WBROM B70 ....88 A5
Devey Dr TPTN/OCK DY4 ....70 B5
Devine Cft TPTN/OCK DY4 ......85 F5
Devitts Cl SHLY B90 ....195 F1

Devon Crs ALDR WS9 ....30 A1
  DUDS DY2 ....101 H2
  HHTH/SAND B71 ....71 G5
Devon Rd DARL/WED WS10 .....56 C4
  RBRY B45 ....173 H4
  SMTHWKW B67 ....124 A5
  STRBR DY8 ....117 H5
  WLNHL WV13 ....40 B4
  WOLV WV1 ....6 D1
Devonshire Av WBROM B18 ...107 H3
Devonshire Dr WBROM B70 .....88 A3
Devonshire Rd
  BFLD/HDSWWD B20 ....89 H4
  SMTHWKW B67 ....106 A3
Devonshire St WSNGN B18 ....107 H3
Devon St VAUX/NECH B7 ....110 A5
Devoran Cl
  DUNHL/THL/PER WV6 ....9 H5
Dewberry Rd DSYBK/YTR WS5 ...57 C5
Dewberry Rd STRBR DY8 ......118 B3
Dewhurst Cft STETCH B33 ....130 D1
Dewsbury Cl STRBR DY8 ......118 A1
Dewsbury Dr
  ETTPK/GDPK/PENN WV4 ....51 C5
Dewsbury Gv PBAR/PBCH B42 ...90 C1
Deykin Av AST/WIT B6 ....91 G4
D'Eyncourt Rd WOLV WV10 ....24 A5
Dial Cl ALE/KHTH/YWD B14 ...178 A3
Dial La STRBR DY8 ....118 A4
  WBROM B70 ....70 D5
Diamond Park Dr STRBR DY8 ..118 A3
Diana Cl ALDR WS9 ....19 G4
Diane Cl TPTN/OCK DY4 ....69 H1
Dibble Cl SHHTH WV12 ....26 B5
Dibble Rd SMTHWKW B67 .....106 B3
Dibdale Rd DUDN DY1 ....83 H5
Dibdale St West DUDN DY1 ...83 H5
Dibdale St DUDN DY1 ....83 H4
Dice Pleck NFLD/LBR B31 ....176 A3
Dickens Cl SEDG DY3 ....82 D1
Dickens Heath Rd SHLY B90 ..193 C4
Dickens Rd BILS/COS WV14 ....68 D1
  WOLV WV10 ....24 A2
Dickinson Av WOLV WV10 ......23 H5
Dickinson Dr WALM/CURD B76 ..63 E4
  WSLW WS2 ....56 C2
Dickinson Rd WMBN WV5 ......81 E2
Dick Sheppard Av
  TPTN/OCK DY4 ....69 H5
Diddington Av
  HLGN/YWD B28 ....163 E5
Didgley Gv
  CHWD/FDBR/MGN B37 ....114 A4
Digbeth DIG/EDG B5 ....3 J7
Digby Cl CSHL/WTROR B46 .....96 B3
Digby Dr
  CHWD/FDBR/MGN B37 ....149 F1
Digby Rd CSHL/WTROR B46 ...115 F3
  KGSWFD DY6 ....99 H1
  SCFLD/BOLD B73 ....62 A5
Dilke Rd ALDR WS9 ....29 H5
Dilloways La WLNHL WV13 .....39 E4
Dimbles Hill SOLH B91 ....181 G4
  WLNHL WV13 ....39 C1
Dingle Av CDYHTH B64 ....83 H5
Dingle Cl BVILLE B30 ....159 F5
  DUDS DY2 ....103 E2
Dingle Hollow OLDBY B69 .....104 B1
Dingle La SOLH B91 ....181 F5
  WLNHL WV13 ....39 C1
Dingle Rd BRWNH WS8 ....19 E2
  DUDS DY2 ....103 E2
  HAG/WOL DY9 ....135 H5
  KGSWFD DY6 ....100 C5
  WMBN WV5 ....64 C5
Dingle St OLDBY B69 ....104 B1
The Dingle BDMR/CCFT WV3 ....35 H4
  OLDBY B69 ....104 B1
  SEDG DY3 ....194 D5
  SLYOAK B29 ....142 C5
Dingle Vw SEDG DY3 ....67 E4
Dingley Rd DARL/WED WS10 ....56 A3
Dinham Gdns DUDN DY1 ....83 G3
Dinmore Av NFLD/LBR B31 ...175 H1
Dippons Dr
  DUNHL/THL/PER WV6 ....35 E3
Dippons Mill Cl
  DUNHL/THL/PER WV6 ....35 E2
Dirtytoot La
  ETTPK/GDPK/PENN WV4 ....50 A3
Discovery Cl TPTN/OCK DY4 ....86 A1
The Ditch WSL WS1 ....5 F4
Ditton Gv NFLD/LBR B31 .....189 F2
Dixon Cl CVALE B35 ....94 C4
  TPTN/OCK DY4 ....70 A5
Dixon Rd SMHTH B10 ....127 H4
Dixon's Green Rd DUDS DY2 ..103 E1
Dixon St BKHL/PFLD WV2 ....52 C2
Dobbins Oak Rd
  HAG/WOL DY9 ....153 F1
Dobbs Mill Cl SLYOAK B29 ...143 F5
Dobbs St BKHL/PFLD WV2 ....7 F7
Dockar Rd NFLD/LBR B31 .....175 E5
Dock La CDSL WV8 ....84 B5
Dock Meadow Dr
  ETTPK/GDPK/PENN WV4 ....53 E4
Dock Rd STRBR DY8 ....118 B2
The Dock HAG/WOL DY9 ....136 D2
Doctors HI HAG/WOL DY9 ......136 A4
Doctors La KGSWFD DY6 ....98 D4
Doctor's Piece WLNHL WV13 ...39 H3
Doddington Gv
  RIDG/WDGT B32 ....157 F2
Dodford Cl RBRY B45 ....187 H1
Doe Bank La TPTN/OCK DY4 ....70 A2
Doe Bank Rd TPTN/OCK DY4 ....70 A2
Doe Bank La WALM/CURD B76 ...59 H2
Dog Kennel La HALE B63 .....138 C4
Dogkennel La
  LGLYGN/QTN B68 ....105 G4
Dog Kennel La SHLY B90 .....194 D1
  WSL WS1 ....5 G5
Dogpool La BVILLE B30 ....160 B1

Doidge Rd ERDW/GRVHL B23 ....92 B3
Dollery Dr DIG/EDG B5 ....143 C2
Dollis Gv KGSTG B44 ....60 B5
Dolliman St VAUX/NECH B7 ...127 H1
Dolman Rd AST/WIT B6 ....109 E1
Dolobran Rd SPARK B11 ......127 H5
Dolphin Cl BLOX/PEL WS5 ......28 B1
Dolphin La ACGN B27 ....163 G1
Dolphin Rd SPARK B11 ....145 F2
Dolton Wy TPTN/OCK DY4 ......69 E5
Dominic Cl BVILLE B30 ....176 B1
Doncaster Wy CBROM B36 .....111 G1
Don Cl EDG B15 ....125 F4
Donegal Rd FOAKS/STRLY B74 ...60 C5
Donibristle Cft CVALE B35 ....94 C2
Donovan Dr SCFLD/BOLD B73 ...62 A2
Dooley Cl WLNHL WV13 ....39 E3
Doran Cl HALE B63 ....137 H4
Doranda Wy HHTH/SAND B71 ...88 B5
Dora Rd HDSW B21 ....107 G2
  SMHTH B10 ....128 C5
  WBROM B70 ....87 G5
Dora St WSLW WS2 ....42 A3
Dorchester Ct SHHTH WV12 ....26 A2
Dorchester Ct SOLH B91 .....181 G1
Dorchester Dr HRBN B17 .....141 H5
Dorchester Rd HAG/WOL DY9 ..136 D5
  SHHTH WV12 ....26 A2
  SOLH B91 ....181 G1
Dordale Cl NFLD/LBR B31 ....174 C4
Dordale Rd HAG/WOL DY9 ....184 B5
Doreen Gv ERDE/BCHGN B24 ...93 F4
Doris Rd BORD B9 ....128 B3
  CSHL/WTROR B46 ....115 F1
  SPARK B11 ....144 D3
Doricote Rd WASH/WDE B8 ....111 F3
Dormie Cl HWK/WKHTH B38 ...176 B4
Dormington Rd KGSTG B44 ......60 B5
Dormston Cl SOLH B91 ....182 A5
Dormston Dr SEDG DY3 ....67 E5
  SLYOAK B29 ....141 F5
Dormy Dr NFLD/LBR B31 .....189 G1
Dorncliffe Av STECH B33 ....131 F5
Dornie Dr HWK/WKHTH B38 ...176 D4
Dornton Rd BVILLE B30 ......160 C2
Dorothy Adams Cl
  CDYHTH B64 ....121 E4
Dorothy Rd SMTHWKW B67 ....124 C1
  SPARK B11 ....145 H2
Dorothy St WSL WS1 ....56 D1
Dorridge Cft DOR/KN B93 ....198 D1
Dorridge Rd DOR/KN B93 .....199 E1
Dorrington Gn PBAR/PBCH B42 ...90 A1
Dorrington Rd PBAR/PBCH B42 ..90 A1
Dorset Cl RBRY B45 ....173 H5
Dorset Rd HRBN B17 ....124 D1
  STRBR DY8 ....117 H5
  WASH/WDE B8 ....110 D3
Dorset Tower WSNGN B18 * 2 A2
Dorsett Pl BLOX/PEL WS5 ......27 G3
Dorsett Rd DARL/WED WS10 ....55 H2
Dorsett Road Ter
  DARL/WED WS10 ....55 E2
Dorsheath Gdns
  ERDW/GRVHL B23 ....92 D2
Dorsington Rd ACGN B27 .....163 H1
Dorstone Covert
  ALE/KHTH/YWD B14 ....177 G3
Dorville Cl HWK/WKHTH B38 ..176 B5
Douay Rd ERDW/GRVHL B23 ....77 F5
Double Rw DUDS DY2 ....105 E5
Doughty St TPTN/OCK DY4 .....69 H1
Douglas Av CBROM B36 ....111 H3
Douglas Davies Cl SHHTH WV12 ...40 A1
Douglas Pl WOLV WV10 ....23 E4
Douglas Rd ACGN B27 ....146 B3
  BILS/COS WV14 ....68 D3
  CSCFLD/WYGN B72 ....62 C5
  HDSW B21 ....107 C1
  HLYWD B47 ....192 C1
  LGLYGN/QTN B68 ....105 H5
  RMSLY B62 ....122 C3
Douglass Rd DUDS DY2 ....102 D1
Douglas Turner Wy
  BDMR/CCFT WV3 ....36 A2
Doulton Cl RIDG/WDGT B32 ...141 F4
Doulton Dr SMTHWK B66 .....106 C3
Doulton Rd
  BLKHTH/ROWR B65 ....103 G5
Dovebridge Cl
  WALM/CURD B76 ....63 F4
Dove Cl DARL/WED WS10 ......56 B4
  WSL WS1 ....5 H5
  VDLY B25 ....130 A4
Dovecote Cl
  DUNHL/THL/PER WV6 ....35 G1
  SOLH B91 ....164 D2
  TPTN/OCK DY4 ....70 A5
The Dovecotes MGN/WHC B75 ...47 F2
Dovedale Av BLOX/PEL WS5 ....18 A2
  SHHTH WV12 ....39 G1
  SHLY B90 ....180 B4
Dovedale Ct
  ETTPK/GDPK/PENN WV4 ....67 H1
Dovedale Dr HLGN/YWD B28 ..162 D4
Dovedale Rd ERDW/GRVHL B23 ...76 A5
  ETTPK/GDPK/PENN WV4 ....67 G1
  KGSWFD DY6 ....100 A1
Dove Dr STRBR DY8 ....118 C5
Dove Gdns HWK/WKHTH B38 ..177 F3
Dove House La SOLH B91 .....164 B4
Dovehouse Pool Rd
  AST/WIT B6 ....109 E1
Dover Cl RIDG/WDGT B32 ....157 E5
Dovercourt Rd
  LGN/SDN/BHAMAIR B26 ......148 A2
Doverdale Cl HALE B63 ....137 H2
Dove Rdg STRBR DY8 ....118 C5
Doveridge Cl SOLH B91 ......164 A4
Doveridge Pl WSL WS1 ....5 F7
Doveridge Rd HLGN/YWD B28 ..162 C5
Doversley Rd
  ALE/KHTH/YWD B14 ....160 C5
Dover St BILS/COS WV14 ....54 B5
  WSNGN B18 ....107 H3
Dovey Dr WALM/CURD B76 ......78 C4

Dovey Gv BLKHTH/ROWR B65 ..121 H2
Dovey Rd MOS/BIL B13 ....145 H4
  OLDBY B69 ....104 B1
Dovey Tower VAUX/NECH B7 * ..3 K2
Dowar Rd RBRY B45 ....188 C1
Dowells Cl MOS/BIL B13 .....144 B5
Dower Rd MGN/WHC B75 ....47 G5
Dowles Cl SLYOAK B29 ....158 D4
Downcroft Av HWK/WKHTH B38 ...176 C5
Downend Cl WOLV WV10 ....13 F3
Downes Ct TPTN/OCK DY4 ......85 E1
Downey Cl SPARK B11 ....127 H3
Downfield Cl BLOX/PEL WS5 ....16 C5
Downfield Dr SEDG DY3 ....67 G5
Downham Cl DSYBK/YTR WS5 ...43 G4
Downham Pl BDMR/CCFT WV3 ...36 B5
Downie Rd CDSL WV8 ....11 E4
Downing Cl
  BLKHTH/ROWR B65 ....122 A3
  DOR/KN B93 ....197 E4
  WNSFLD WV11 ....25 C3
Downing St HALE B63 ....138 C2
  SMTHWK B66 ....107 E2
Downland Cl
  HWK/WKHTH B38 ....176 D4
Downsfield Rd
  LGN/SDN/BHAMAIR B26 ......130 D5
Downside Rd
  ERDE/BCHGN B24 ....92 C5
Downs Rd WLNHL WV13 ....40 A5
The Downs ALDR WS9 ....45 E5
  WOLV WV10 ....23 E4
Downton Crs STETCH B33 ....131 G1
Dowty Wy COVEN WV9 ....12 A4
Doyle Dr BLOX/PEL WS5 ....27 F1
Drake Cft
  CHWD/FDBR/MGN B37 ....114 D5
Drake Rd BLOX/PEL WS5 ....27 G1
  ERDW/GRVHL B23 ....92 A3
  SMTHWK B66 ....106 C2
Drakes Cl HLYWD B47 ....192 B3
Drakes Cross Pde HLYWD B47 ..192 C3
Drake's Gn BILS/COS WV14 ....54 B5
Drakes Hill Cl STRBR DY8 ...134 C3
Drake St HHTH/SAND B71 ......87 G1
Drancy Av SHHTH WV12 ....26 B4
Drawbridge Rd SHLY B90 .....179 G5
Draycote Cl HIA/OLT B92 ....165 H3
Draycott Av ERDW/GRVHL B23 ...92 B2
Draycott Cl
  ETTPK/GDPK/PENN WV4 ....50 C3
Draycott Dr NFLD/LBR B31 ...158 A3
Draycott Rd SMTHWK B66 ....106 A2
Drayman's Cl WSL WS1 ....42 D4
Drayton Cl MGN/WHC B75 ......47 F2
Drayton Rd
  ALE/KHTH/YWD B14 ....160 E2
  HAG/WOL DY9 ....184 B2
  SHLY B90 ....180 D5
  SMTHWK B66 ....124 C3
Drayton St BKHL/PFLD WV2 .....7 F5
  WSLW WS2 ....41 G5
Dreadnought Rd BRLYHL DY5 ..100 D2
The Dreel EDG B15 ....125 G5
Dreghorn Rd CBROM B36 ......112 A1
Drem Cft CVALE B35 ....94 C4
Dresden Cl
  ETTPK/GDPK/PENN WV4 ....53 E4
Drew Crs HAG/WOL DY9 ....136 B4
Drew Rd HAG/WOL DY9 ....136 B4
Drews Holloway HALE B63 ....137 H2
Drews Holloway South
  HALE B63 ....137 H2
Drews Meadow Cl
  ALE/KHTH/YWD B14 ....177 G3
Driffold SCFLD/BOLD B73 ......62 B5
Driftwood Cl
  HWK/WKHTH B38 ....190 B1
Drive Flds
  ETTPK/GDPK/PENN WV4 ....50 B2
The Drive ALVE B48 ....209 H5
  BFLD/HDSWWD B20 ....90 A4
  BLOX/PEL WS5 ....17 G5
  BRLYHL DY5 ....101 E4
  CDSL WV8 ....10 B4
  CSHL/WTROR B46 ....96 C5
  DUNHL/THL/PER WV6 ....21 C5
  ERDW/GRVHL B23 ....92 C4
  HALE B63 ....137 H2
  RUSH/SHEL WS4 ....29 E1
The Droveway COVEN WV9 .....11 H5
Druids Av ALDR WS9 ....19 G4
Druids La ALE/KHTH/YWD B14 ..177 H4
Druids Wk ALDR WS9 ....19 G4
Drummond Cl WNSFLD WV11 ....15 E5
Drummond Gv GTB/HAM B43 ....59 G5
Drummond Rd BORD B9 ....128 D2
  HAG/WOL DY9 ....136 D3
Drummond St WOLV WV1 ....6 E2
Drummond Wy
  CHWD/FDBR/MGN B37 ....132 C2
Drury La CDSL WV8 ....10 B3
  SOLH B91 ....182 A2
  STRBR DY8 ....118 C5
Drybrook Cl HWK/WKHTH B38 ..176 C5
Dryden Cl SHHTH WV12 ....26 C2
  TPTN/OCK DY4 ....85 F4
Dryden Gv ACGN B27 ....146 B5
Dryden Pl BLOX/PEL WS5 ......28 A3
Dryden Rd BLOX/PEL WS5 ......28 A3
  WOLV WV10 ....23 H1
Drylea Gv CBROM B36 ....112 B1
Dubarry Av KGSWFD DY6 ....99 G2
Duchess Pde WBROM B70 * 87 H3
Duchess Rd LDYWD/EDGR B16 ..126 A3
  WSL WS1 ....56 D3
Duckhouse Rd WNSFLD WV11 ...24 D3
Duck La CDSL WV8 ....10 D5
Duckworth Dr MGN/WHC B75 ...47 H1
Duddeston Dr WASH/WDE B8 ..110 B5
Duddeston Manor Rd
  VAUX/NECH B7 ....109 C4
Duddeston Mill Rd
  VAUX/NECH B7 ....109 H5
Dudding Rd
  ETTPK/GDPK/PENN WV4 ....52 B3

Dudhill Rd BLKHTH/ROWR B65 ..121 G1
Dudley Cl BLKHTH/ROWR B65 ..103 F3
Dudley Crs WNSFLD WV11 ......25 E4
Dudley Park Rd ACGN B27 ...146 C4
Dudley Port TPTN/OCK DY4 ....86 B3
Dudley Rd BKHL/PFLD WV2 .....52 B1
  BLKHTH/ROWR B65 ....119 F3
  BRLYHL DY5 ....119 F1
  HAG/WOL DY9 ....136 C1
  HALE B63 ....138 D2
  KGSWFD DY6 ....99 C1
  OLDBY B69 ....69 F4
  SEDG DY3 ....67 F4
  STRBR DY8 ....118 B1
  WSNGN B18 ....107 F5
Dudley Rd East OLDBY B69 ....86 A4
Dudley Rd West OLDBY B69 ....85 H4
Dudley Rw DUDS DY2 ....84 D3
Dudley Southern By-Pass
  DUDS DY2 ....102 A2
Dudley St BILS/COS WV14 .....53 H4
  DARL/WED WS10 ....70 C1
  DIG/EDG B5 ....3 G5
  SEDG DY3 ....67 F5
  WBROM B70 ....87 E1
  WOLV WV1 ....7 F4
  WSL WS1 ....5 J3
Dudley Wk
  ETTPK/GDPK/PENN WV4 ....52 A3
Dudley Wood Av DUDS DY2 ...120 C3
Dudley Wood Rd DUDS DY2 ...120 C5
Dudnill Gv RIDG/WDGT B32 ...157 E2
Duffield Cl CDSL WV8 ....22 B1
Dufton Rd RIDG/WDGT B32 ...141 G3
Dugdale Crs MGN/WHC B75 ....47 G2
Dugdale St WSNGN B18 ....107 F5
Dukes Rd BVILLE B30 ....177 E1
Duke St BDMR/CCFT WV3 ....51 C1
  BLKHTH/ROWR B65 ....122 B4
  CSCFLD/WYGN B72 ....83 F1
  STRBR DY8 ....135 G2
  WBROM B70 ....87 F2
  WNSFLD WV11 ....7 J5
  WOLV WV1 ....7 J5
Dulvern Gv
  ALE/KHTH/YWD B14 ....160 D5
Dulverton Rd AST/WIT B6 ......91 G5
Dulwich Gv KGSTG B44 ....75 C3
Dulwich Rd KGSTG B44 ....75 C5
Dumbleberry Av SEDG DY3 .....67 E4
Dumbledery La ALDR WS9 ......29 G2
Dunard Rd SHLY B90 ....179 H2
Dunbar Gv GTB/HAM B43 ....59 F4
Duncafe Dr MGN/WHC B75 .....47 F2
Duncan Edwards Cl
  DUDN DY1 ....102 A1
Duncan Gv St BKHL/PFLD WV2 ..52 A1
Dunchurch Crs
  SCFLD/BOLD B73 ....61 H5
Dunchurch Dr NFLD/LBR B31 ..158 A3
Duncombe Gn
  CSHL/WTROR B46 ....115 F2
Duncombe Gv HRBN B17 ......124 B5
Duncombe St STRBR DY8 .....134 D1
Duncroft Rd
  LGN/SDN/BHAMAIR B26 ......130 B4
Duncumb Rd MGN/WHC B75 ....63 G3
Dundas Av DUDS DY2 ....103 F1
Dunedin Rd KGSTG B44 ....60 A5
Dunham Cft DOR/KN B93 .....196 B5
Dunkirk Av WBROM B70 ....86 C2
Dunkley St WOLV WV1 ....6 E2
Dunley Cft SHLY B90 ....195 F2
Dunlin Cl ERDW/GRVHL B23 ....76 A5
  KGSWFD DY6 ....100 C5
Dunlop Wy CVALE B35 ....94 A5
Dunnerdale Rd BRWNH WS8 ....18 D1
Dunnigan Rd RIDG/WDGT B32 ..141 F4
Dunns Bank BRLYHL DY5 .....119 H5
Dunoon Dr
  ETTPK/GDPK/PENN WV4 ....52 D3
Dunsfold Cl BILS/COS WV14 ...53 E5
Dunsfold Cft AST/WIT B6 ......109 F3
Dunsford Cl BRLYHL DY5 .....118 D5
Dunsford Rd SMTHWK B66 ....124 C2
Dunsink Rd AST/WIT B6 ....91 F5
Dunslade Crs BRLYHL DY5 ...119 H4
Dunslade Rd ERDW/GRVHL B23 ...76 C4
Dunsley Dr STRBR DY8 ....118 A1
Dunsley Gv
  ETTPK/GDPK/PENN WV4 ....51 G4
Dunsmore Dr BRLYHL DY5 ....119 H4
Dunsmore Gv SOLH B91 ......164 B3
Dunsmore Rd HLGN/YWD B28 ..162 C1
Dunstall Av
  DUNHL/THL/PER WV6 ....37 E1
Dunstall Gv SLYOAK B29 .....158 B2
Dunstall HI
  DUNHL/THL/PER WV6 ....23 E5
Dunstall La
  DUNHL/THL/PER WV6 ....22 D5
Dunstall Rd
  DUNHL/THL/PER WV6 ....36 D1
  HALE B63 ....137 H4
Dunstan Cft SHLY B90 ....180 C5
Dunstan Rd DUDS DY2 ....103 H1
Dunster Cl BVILLE B30 ....177 F1
Dunster Gv
  CHWD/FDBR/MGN B37 ....34 C2
Dunster Rd
  CHWD/FDBR/MGN B37 ....132 C1
Dunston Cl KGSWFD DY6 ....99 H2
Dunton Cl MGN/WHC B75 ....47 F1
Dunton Rd SHLY B90 ....180 A5
Dunton Rd
  CHWD/FDBR/MGN B37 ....113 H5
Dunvegan Rd
  ERDE/BCHGN B24 ....93 G2
Durant Cl RBRY B45 ....173 F4
Durban Rd SMTHWK B66 ......107 E5
D'Urberville Rd
  BKHL/PFLD WV2 ....52 D2
Durham Av WLNHL WV13 ....40 A2
Durham Cft
  CHWD/FDBR/MGN B37 ....132 A2
Durham Pl WSLW WS2 ....41 F4
Durham Rd
  BLKHTH/ROWR B65 ....104 C5

DARL/WED WS10 ....56 D4
DUDS DY2 ....120 D2
SPARK B11 ....144 D3
STRBR DY8 ....117 H4
Durley Dean Rd SLYOAK B29 ..142 A5
Durley Dr WALM/CURD B76 ....61 E5
Durley La RBRY B45 ....188 A2
Durston Cv HLGN/YWD B28 ..163 E2
Durnford Cft
ALE/KHTH/YWD B14........178 A4
Dursley Cl HIA/OLT B92 ....164 D2
SHHTH WV12 ....48 A1
Dutton's La MGN/WHC B75 ....48 A1
Duxford Rd PBAR/PBCH B42 ..74 B3
Dwellings La RIDG/WDGT B32 .140 B2
Dyas Av PBAR/PBCH B42 ......74 A4
Dyas Rd HLYWD B47 ....192 C1
                    KGSTG B44 ....74 D3
Dyce Cl CVALE B35 ....94 C2
Dymoke St BHTH/HG B12 ....127 F4
Dynes Wk SMTHWKW B67 ....106 C4
Dyott Rd MOS/BIL B13 ....161 G1
Dyson Cl WSLW V1 ....40 D2
Dysons Gdns WASH/WDE B8 ..110 C4

E

Eachelhurst Rd
ERDE/BCHGN B24 ....94 A2
Eachus Rd BILS/COS WV14 ....68 C3
Eachway RBRY B45 ....187 H2
Eachway Farm Cl RBRY B45 ..188 A2
Eachway La RBRY B45 ....188 A2
Eagle Ct BDMR/CCFT WV3 ....51 G1
Eagle Cft ALE/KHTH/YWD B14 178 A3
Eagle Gdns ERDE/BCHGN B24 .93 E4
Eagle Gv CBROM B36 ....114 A1
Eagle La TPTN/OCK DY4 ....70 B5
Eagle St BDMR/CCFT WV3 ....51 G1
                    BKHL/PFLD WV2 * 70 A4
                    TPTN/OCK DY4 ....70 A5
Ealing Gv KGSTG B44 ....75 G2
Eanbrook Gdns
BFLD/HDSWWD B20 ....90 D5
Earls Court Rd HRBN B17 ....141 G1
Earls Ferry Gdns
RIDG/WDGT B32 ....157 F3
Earlsmead Rd HDSW B21 ....107 E1
Earls Rd RUSH/SHEL WS4 ......29 E5
Earlston Wy GTB/HAM B43 ....73 F3
Earl St BILS/COS WV14 ....68 D3
                    KGSWFD DY6 ....99 H5
                    WBROM B70 ....87 F2
                    WSL WS1 ....56 D1
Earls Wy HALE B63 ....138 D3
Earlswood Ct
BFLD/HDSWWD B20 ....90 A4
Earlswood Crs COVEN WV9 ...12 A4
Earlswood Dr
FOAKS/STRLY B74 ....62 C1
Earlswood Rd DOR/KN B93 ..198 B1
                    KGSWFD DY6 ....100 A2
Easby Wy BLOX/PEL WS3 ......9B
WASH/WDE B8 ....110 C4
Easenhall Cl DOR/KN B93 ....197 E4
Easmore Cl
ALE/KHTH/YWD B14 ....177 H3
East Acre WLNHL WV13 ....39 G4
East Av OLDBY B69 ....104 A2
                    WNSFLD WV11 ....24 C4
Eastbourne Av
BKDE/SHDE B34 ....111 H3
Eastbourne St
RUSH/SHEL WS4 ....42 B2
Eastbrook Cl SHLY B90 * .... (?)
Eastbury Dr HIA/OLT B92 ....147 G5
East Car Park Rd
BHMNEC B40 ....150 B3
Eastcote La SHLY B90 ....180 D2
Eastcote La HIA/OLT B92 ....167 G5
Eastcote Rd ACGN B27 ....163 E1
                    WOLV WV10 ....23 H5
East Croft Rd
ETTPK/GDPK/PENN WV4 ..50 C4
Eastdean Cl ERDW/GRVHL B23 .76 B5
East Dr DIG/EDG B5 ....143 G3
Eastern Av BRLYHL DY5 ....118 D2
Eastern Cl DARL/WED WS10 ...55 E5
Eastern Rd SCFLD/BOLD B73 ..77 F2
                    SLYOAK B29 ....143 F4
Easterton Cft
ALE/KHTH/YWD B14 ....178 A3
East Farm Cft SMHTH B10 ...128 B4
Eastfield Cl ALDR WS9 ....30 A4
Eastfield Dr HIA/OLT B92 ....165 G1
Eastfield Gv WOLV WV1 ....37 H3
Eastfield Retreat WOLV WV1 ..37 H3
Eastfield Rd BORD B9 ....129 G2
                    TPTN/OCK DY4 ....69 G3
                    WOLV WV1 ....37 H3
East Ga LDYWD/EDGR B16 ...125 G1
East Gn
ETTPK/GDPK/PENN WV4 ...50 D2
Eastham Rd MOS/BIL B13 ....162 A4
East Holme BORD B9 ....128 A2
Easthope Rd STETCH B33 ....112 C5
Eastlake Cl GTB/HAM B43 .....59 H5
Eastlands Rd MOS/BIL B13 ...162 A4
Eastleigh DUDN DY1 ....66 D5
Eastleigh Cft WALM/CURD B76 .78 C5
Eastleigh Dr RMSLY B62 .....172 C1
Eastleigh Gv YDLY B25 ....129 H4
East Meadway STETCH B33 ..131 G1
East Mr KGSTG B44 ....74 D2
Eastmoor Cl FOAKS/STRLY B74 .45 H3
Eastney Crs CDSL WV8 ....22 A2
Easton Gdns WNSFLD WV11 ..25 F5
Easton Gv ACGN B27 ....162 C1
                    HLYWD B47 ....192 D1
East Park Wy WOLV WV1 ....38 A4
East Pathway HRBN B17 .....142 A1
East Ri MGN/WHC B75 ....62 D2
East Rd
ETTPK/GDPK/PENN WV4 ...52 D4

TPTN/OCK DY4 ....69 H3
WOLV WV10 ....13 G1
East St BRLYHL DY5 ....120 A4
DUDS DY2 ....105 E1
SEDG DY3 ....85 E5
WOLV WV1 ....57 F1
East View Rd
CSCFLD/WYGN B72 ....62 D5
Eastville NFLD/LBR B31 ......175 H2
Eastward Gln CDSL WV8 ....21 G1
East Wy BHAMNEC B40 ......150 B4
Eastway HRBN B17 .... (?)
Eastwood Rd BHTH/HG B12 ..143 H2
                    DUDS DY2 ....103 E3
                    GTB/HAM B43 ....73 G3
Eatesbrook Rd STETCH B33 ..131 E1
Eathorpe Cl BKDE/SHDE B34 .113 F3
Eaton Av WBROM B70 ....87 E2
Eaton Ct FOAKS/STRLY B74 ...62 B1
Eaton Pl SEDG DY3 ....85 E5
Eaton Rl KGSWFD DY6 ....100 A4
Eaton Rl SHHTH WV12 ....25 H3
Eaton Wd ERDE/BCHGN B24 ..93 H5
Eaton Wood Dr
LGN/SDN/BHAMAIR B26 ..146 D2
Eaves Court Dr SEDG DY3 ....67 E1
Eaves Green Gdns ACGN B27 .146 B2
Ebenezer St BILS/COS WV14 ..68 B3
                    WBROM B70 ....70 D5
Ebley Rd BFLD/HDSWWD B20 .90 A2
Ebmore Dr
ALE/KHTH/YWD B14 ....177 H3
Ebrington Av HIA/OLT B92 ...147 H4
Ebrington Cl
ALE/KHTH/YWD B14 ....177 H1
Ebrington Rd HHTH/SAND B71 .71 H5
Ebrook Rd CSCFLD/WYGN B72 .62 D5
Ebury Rd BVILLE B30 ....177 F1
Eccleshall Av WOLV WV10 .....25 E2
Ecclestone Rd WNSFLD WV11 ..25 G2
Echo Wy
ETTPK/GDPK/PENN WV4 ...53 E4
Eckersall Rd HWK/WKHTH B38 .176 C2
Edale Cl
ETTPK/GDPK/PENN WV4 ...52 C5
                    KGSWFD DY6 ....99 F2
Edale Rd PBAR/PBCH B42 .....74 C4
Eddish Rd STETCH B33 ....112 D5
Eddison Rd CSHL/WTROR B46 * .97 E2
Eddiweiss Cl DSYBK/YTR WS5 ..57 H5
Edenbridge Rd
HLGN/YWD B28 ....163 F2
Edenbridge Vw DUDN DY1 .....83 G3
Eden Cl NFLD/LBR B31 ....175 E5
                    OLDBY B69 ....86 B4
Edendale Rd
LGN/SDN/BHAMAIR B26 ..147 H1
Eden Gdns
BLKHTH/ROWR B65 ....121 H2
                    SEDG DY3 ....67 G2
Eden Gv
BLKHTH/ROWR B65 ....121 H2
Edenhall Rd RIDG/WDGT B32 .140 B1
Edenhurst Rd NFLD/LBR B31 .189 F2
Eden Pl CBHAMNW B3 ....2 E5
Eden Rd HIA/OLT B92 ....148 B4
Edensor Cl WOLV WV10 ....37 G1
Edgbaston Park Rd EDG B15 ..143 E2
Edgbaston Rd BHTH/HG B12 ..143 G2
                    DIG/EDG B5 ....143 G2
                    SMTHWK B66 ....106 C4
Edgbaston Rd East
BHTH/HG B12 ....144 B3
Edgcombe Rd HLGN/YWD B28 .162 D1
Edge Hill Av
DUNHL/THL/PER WV6 ....34 C2
Edge Hill Dr
DUNHL/THL/PER WV6 ......(?)
                    SEDG DY3 ....67 E1
Edge Hill Rd FOAKS/STRLY B74 .46 C1
Edge Rd NFLD/LBR B31 ....175 G4
Edgemond Av
ERDE/BCHGN B24 ....94 B2
Edgewood Cl CDYHTH B64 ...121 F4
Edgewood Rd
HWK/WKHTH B38 ....190 C1
                    RBRY B45 ....188 B2
Edgeworth Cl SHHTH WV12 ...40 A1
Edgware Rd ERDW/GRVHL B23 .92 B1
Edgwick Rd WSLW WS2 ....40 C2
Edinburgh Ct
ERDE/BCHGN B24 ....93 H2
Edinburgh Crs STRBR DY8 ...117 H3
Edinburgh Dr RUSH/SHEL WS4 .29 H4
                    SHHTH WV12 ....25 H4
Edinburgh La BILS/COS WV14 .54 B5
                    DSYBK/YTR WS5 ....42 D5
Edinburgh Rd BILS/COS WV14 .54 B5
                    DUDS DY2 ....103 G3
                    LGLYGN/QTN B68 ....123 F4
Edison Gv RIDG/WDGT B32 ...140 D2
Edison Rd CSHL/WTROR B46 ...97 G3
Edith Rd SMTHWK B66 ....124 D1
Edith St WBROM B70 ....87 F3
Edmonds Cl STETCH B33 ....130 D2
Edmonds Rd LGLYGN/QTN B68 .123 G2
Edmonton Av KGSTG B44 ....75 H2
Edmoor Cl SHHTH WV12 ......26 A4
Edmund Rd SEDG DY3 ....67 G2
                    WASH/WDE B8 ....110 C5
Edmund St CBHAMNW B3 ......2 E4
Ednam Cl HHTH/SAND B71 ....72 B3
Ednam Gv WMBN WV5 ....65 E2
Ednam Rd DUDN DY1 ....84 C4
                    ETTPK/GDPK/PENN WV4 ...52 A2
Edsome Wy CBROM B36 ......112 C2
Edstone Cl BVILLE B30 ....177 H2
                    DOR/KN B93 ....196 D5
Edstone Ms CBROM B36 .....112 B1
Edward Av ALDR WS9 ....30 A3
Edward Cl BILS/COS WV14 .....54 A5
Edward Fisher Dr
TPTN/OCK DY4 ....85 G1
Edward Rd
ALE/KHTH/YWD B14 ....178 B4
                    BHTH/HG B12 ....144 A2
                    CSHL/WTROR B46 ....96 C5

DIG/EDG B5 ....143 H1
DUNHL/THL/PER WV6 ....35 F2
HALE B63 ....138 B3
LGLYGN/QTN B68 ....123 C4
SMTHWKW B67 ....106 B5
TPTN/OCK DY4 ....69 C4
Edwards Rd DUDS DY2 ....102 C5
                    ERDE/BCHGN B24 ....93 E1
Edward St CBHAMW B1 ....2 B5
                    DARL/WED WS10 ....55 G5
                    DUDN DY1 ....84 B5
                    ETTPK/GDPK/PENN WV4 ...53 D2
                    LGLYGN/QTN B68 ....105 E5
                    WBROM B70 ....87 G2
                    WSLW WS2 ....41 F2
Edwin Phillips Dr
HHTH/SAND B71 ....71 F3
Edwin Rd BVILLE B30 ....160 B3
Edwinstowe Cl BRLYHL DY5 ..120 B2
Eel St OLDBY B69 ....104 D2
Effingham Rd MOS/BIL B13 ..162 A3
Egbert Cl AST/WIT B6 ....109 H1
Egelwin Cl
DUNHL/THL/PER WV6 ....20 C5
Egerton Rd ERDE/BCHGN B24 .93 H3
                    FOAKS/STRLY B74 ....46 B1
                    KGSTG B44 ....74 D1
                    WOLV WV10 ....13 G4
Egghill La RBRY B45 ....174 A1
Eggington Rd STRBR DY8 ....117 H5
Egginton Rd HLGN/YWD B28 .162 C5
Egmont Gdns WNSFLD WV11 ..25 F5
Eileen Gdns
CHWD/FDBR/MGN B37 ....114 A5
Eileen Rd SPARK B11 ....144 D4
Elan Cl SEDG DY3 ....83 F3
Elan Rd NFLD/LBR B31 ....174 C5
                    SEDG DY3 ....67 E3
Elbow St CDYHTH B64 ....121 F2
Elbury Cft DOR/KN B93 ....196 D3
Elcock Dr PBAR/PBCH B42 ....90 D1
Eldalade Wy DARL/WED WS10 .71 G2
Elderberry Cl DSYBK/YTR WS5 .57 F5
                    STRBR DY8 ....134 C4
Elder Cv WMBN WV5 ....64 D5
                    WNSFLD WV11 ....24 A4
Eldersfield Gv SHLY B90 .....195 H1
Elder Cl SEDG DY3 ....83 F3
Elderfield Cl BRWNH WS8 .....9 G5
Elder Wy ERDW/GRVHL B23 ...92 B4
Eldon Dr WALM/CURD B76 ....78 A4
Eldon Rd LDYWD/EDGR B16 ..125 H3
                    RMSLY B62 ....140 A4
Eldon St DARL/WED WS10 ....55 C5
                    WSL WS1 ....5 G5
Eldridge Cl COVEN WV9 ....11 H5
Eleanor Rd BILS/COS WV14 ...54 A3
Electric Av AST/WIT B6 ....109 H3
Elford Cl ALE/KHTH/YWD B14 .161 E5
                    FOAKS/STRLY B74 ....45 G3
Elford Gv BILS/COS WV14 .....68 D1
                    CHWD/FDBR/MGN B37 ....132 B3
Elford Rd HHTH/SAND B71 ....71 H4
                    HRBN B17 ....141 H4
Elgar Crs BRLYHL DY5 ....101 F2
Elgar Ms LICH/LICHF B1 * ......(?)
Elgin Cl SEDG DY3 ....67 G2
                    STRBR DY8 ....118 C5
Elgin Gv YDLY B25 ....129 G5
Elgin Rd BLOX/PEL WS3 ....16 C3
Eliot Cft BILS/COS WV14 ......68 D1
Eliot St VAUX/NECH B7 ....110 A3
Elizabeth Av BILS/COS WV14 ..54 B5
                    DARL/WED WS10 ....56 C5
                    ETTPK/GDPK/PENN WV4 ..51 H3
Elizabeth Crs
LGLYGN/QTN B68 ....123 H2
Elizabeth Gv DUDS DY2 ......103 F2
                    SHLY B90 ....180 C5
Elizabeth Ms OLDBY B69 .....85 C4
Elizabeth Rd DSYBK/YTR WS5 .57 H1
                    HALE B63 ....138 B4
                    MOS/BIL B13 ....143 G5
                    SCFLD/BOLD B73 ....76 A2
                    STETCH B33 ....129 H1
Elizabeth Wk TPTN/OCK DY4 ..69 H3
Elkington Cft SHLY B90 ......195 F3
Elkington St AST/WIT B6 ....109 H2
Elkstone Cl HIA/OLT B92 ....147 H4
Elkstone Covert
ALE/KHTH/YWD B14 ....177 G3
Elland Gv ACGN B27 ....162 C1
Ellards Dr WNSFLD WV11 .....25 F5
Ellen St WSNCN B18 ....2 A1
Ellenvale Cl BILS/COS WV14 ..54 A5
Ellerby Gv ERDE/BCHGN B24 .94 A2
Ellerside Gv NFLD/LBR B31 ..175 F3
Ellerslie Cl BRLYHL DY5 .....119 F4
Ellerslie Rd MOS/BIL B13 ....162 A3
Ellerton Rd KGSTG B44 ....75 E1
Ellerton Wk WOLV WV10 ......24 A1
Ellesboro' Rd HRBN B17 ....124 D4
Ellesmere Rd WASH/WDE B8 .110 B2
Ellice Dr CBROM B36 ....114 B2
Ellicer Gdns RBRY B45 ....188 B3
Elliott Rd SLYOAK B29 ....143 G5
Elliotts La CDSL WV8 ....10 C4
Elliott's Rd TPTN/OCK DY4 ...85 H2
Elliott Wy AST/WIT B6 ....91 F2
Ellis Av BRLYHL DY5 ....118 C2
Ellison St WBROM B70 ....87 G5
Ellowes Rd SEDG DY3 ....82 B3
Elm Av BHTH/HG B12 ....144 C3
                    BILS/COS WV14 ....53 H2
                    DARL/WED WS10 ....55 H4
                    WNSFLD WV11 ....24 A4
Elmay Rd
LGN/SDN/BHAMAIR B26 ..130 C5
Elm Bank MOS/BIL B13 ....144 (?)
Elmbank Gv
BFLD/HDSWWD B20 ....89 G1
Elmbank Rd DSYBK/YTR WS5 ..58 A4
Elmbridge Cl HALE B63 ....137 H2
Elmbridge Dr WNSFLD WV11 ..25 H3
Elmbridge Rd KGSTG B44 .....75 E5
Elmbridge Wy
HWK/WKHTH B38 ....176 B3

SEDG DY3 ....67 C5
STRBR DY8 ....134 C5
Elm Cl LI SEDG DY3 ....82 D4
                    STRBR DY8 ....134 C5
Elm Cft LGLYGN/QTN B68 ....125 F1
Elmcroft Av RIDG/WDGT B32 .157 G5
Elmcroft Gdns WOLV WV10 ...13 E4
Elmcroft Rd
LGN/SDN/BHAMAIR B26 ..130 D5
Elmdale RMSLY B62 ....155 E5
Elmdale Crs NFLD/LBR B31 ..175 F1
Elmdale Dr ALDR WS9 ....30 C2
Elmdale Gv NFLD/LBR B31 ...175 F1
Elmdale Rd BILS/COS WV14 ...68 A4
Elm Dale Rd
ETTPK/GDPK/PENN WV4 ..51 H3
                    WOLV WV10 ....12 B1
Elmdon Cl HIA/OLT B92 ......148 B5
                    WOLV WV10 ....10 B1
Elmdon Coppice HIA/OLT B92 .165 H3
Elmdon La
LGN/SDN/BHAMAIR B26 ..149 E4
Elmdon Park Rd HIA/OLT B92 .148 B5
Elmdon Rd ACGN B27 ....146 C5
                    CHWD/FDBR/MGN B37 ....146 C5
                    SLYOAK B29 ....143 E5
Elm Farm Av
CHWD/FDBR/MGN B37 ....131 H5
Elm Farm Rd BKHL/PFLD WV2 .52 A2
Elmfield Av ERDE/BCHGN B24 .94 A2
Elmfield Crs MOS/BIL B13 ...144 B5
Elmdon Rd ACGN B27 ....146 C5
Elmfield Vw DUDN DY1 ....84 A3
Elm Gn DUDN DY1 ....84 A1
Elm Gv CDSL WV8 ....10 C4
                    CHWD/FDBR/MGN B37 ....113 H5
Elmhurst Av
BLKHTH/ROWR B65 ....122 A1
Elmhurst Dr KGSWFD DY6 ...100 B5
Elmhurst Rd HDSW B21 ....89 C5
Elmley Cl BILS/COS WV14 .....68 C3
Elmley Gv BVILLE B30 ....177 F2
                    KGSTG B44 ....75 F5
Elm Ldg HIA/OLT B92 * 167 C3
Elmore Cl
BFLD/HDSWWD B20 ....89 H3
Elmore Green Cl BLOX/PEL WS3 * .(?)
Elmore Green Rd
BLOX/PEL WS3 ....27 E1
Elmore Rd STETCH B33 ......130 C1
Elm More Rw BLOX/PEL WS3 ..27 F1
Elm Rd BLOX/PEL WS3 ....28 A4
                    BVILLE B30 ....159 H2
                    DUDN DY1 ....84 C3
                    KGSWFD DY6 ....100 A3
                    WALM/CURD B76 ....78 B1
Elms Cl SOLH B91 ....165 F5
Elmsdale DUNHL/THL/PER WV6 .34 C4
Elmstead Cl STETCH B33 ....131 F5
Elmstead Ct DUNHL/THL/PER WV6 .43 C4
Elmstead Wd DSYBK/YTR WS5 .58 B5
The Elms LDYWD/EDGR B16 * ..(?)
Elmstone Cl DUDN DY1 ....83 H2
Elm St BDMR/CCFT WV3 ....6 A5
                    WLNHL WV13 ....39 H3
Elmsworth Rd NFLD/LBR B31 .176 B5
Elm Ter OLDBY B69 ....80 D1
Elm Tree Cv HALE B63 ....138 B3
Elm Tree Cv HALE B63 * 137 H1
Elm Tree Gv HALE B63 ....137 H1
Elm Tree Ri HIA/OLT B92 ....164 C4
Elm Tree Rd HRBN B17 ....141 G1
                    BVILLE B30 ....160 A4
Elmtree Rd SCFLD/BOLD B73 ..76 C5
Elm Tree Wy CDYHTH B64 ...121 F3
Elmwood Av WNSFLD WV11 ...15 E4
Elmwood Gdns
BFLD/HDSWWD B20 ....90 B4
Elmwood Rd RIDG/WDGT B32 .192 C2
Elmwood Ri SEDG DY3 ....66 D2
Elmwood Rd ERDE/BCHGN B24 .94 C2
                    FOAKS/STRLY B74 ....60 C2
                    STRBR DY8 ....117 C1
Elmwoods RIDG/WDGT B32 ..140 B5
Elphinstone End
ERDE/BCHGN B24 ....94 C1
Elsma Rd LGLYGN/QTN B68 ..123 C4
Elston Hall La WOLV WV10 * ...23 C1
Elstree Rd ERDW/GRVHL B23 ..92 B1
Elswick Gv KGSTG B44 ....75 H2
Elswick Rd KGSTG B44 ....75 H2
Elsworth Gv YDLY B25 ....129 H3
Eltham Gv KGSTG B44 ....76 A5
Elton Cl WOLV WV10 ....13 E3
Elton Gv HLGN/YWD B28 .....162 B3
Eltonia Cft
LGN/SDN/BHAMAIR B26 ..147 H1
Elva Cft CBROM B36 ....95 H5
Elvaston Wy SHLY B90 ....180 C5
Elveetham Rd EDC B15 ....126 C5
Elviron Dr
DUNHL/THL/PER WV6 ....34 B3
Elwell Crs DUDN DY1 ....67 H5
Elwells Cl BILS/COS WV14 .....53 E5
Elwell St DARL/WED WS10 ....56 C4
                    WBROM B70 ....86 C1
Elwyn Rd SCFLD/BOLD B73 ...76 A5
Ely Cl BLKHTH/ROWR B65 ....104 C5
                    CHWD/FDBR/MGN B37 ....132 B2
Ely Crs HHTH/SAND B71 ......71 G4
Ely Pl WSLW WS2 ....41 F4
Ely Rd WSLW WS2 ....41 F4
Emay Cl WBROM B70 ....70 D5
The Embankment
BRLYHL DY5 ....119 G2
Embassy Dr EDG B15 ....126 A4
                    OLDBY B69 ....104 C1
Embassy Rd OLDBY B69 .....104 C1
Embleton Gv BKDE/SHDE B34 .112 A2
Emerald Ct WASH/WDE B8 ...111 C4
Emerson Cl SEDG DY3 ....82 D1
Emerson Gv WOLV WV10 .....23 G4
Emerson Rd HRBN B17 ....142 A1
                    WOLV WV10 ....23 H1

Emery Cl ERDW/GRVHL B23 ...92 B5
                    WSL WS1 ....5 F6
Emery St WSL WS1 ....5 G6
Emily Gdns LDYWD/EDGR B16 .125 H1
Emily Rd
LGN/SDN/BHAMAIR B26 ..146 D1
Emily St BHTH/HG B12 ....127 F4
                    WBROM B70 ....87 F4
Emmanuel Rd SCFLD/BOLD B73 .77 F4
Emmeline St BORD B9 ....127 H5
Empire Cl ALDR WS9 ....29 H2
Empress Wy DARL/WED WS10 .40 B5
Emscote Dr SCFLD/BOLD B73 .77 F4
Emscote Gn SOLH B91 ....181 E5
Emscote Rd AST/WIT B6 ....91 F5
Emsworth Crs COVEN WV9 ...12 A5
Emsworth Gv
ALE/KHTH/YWD B14 ....160 D4
Enderby Cl DOR/KN B93 .....196 D4
Enderby Dr
ETTPK/GDPK/PENN WV4 ...51 F4
Enderley Cl BLOX/PEL WS3 ...16 C4
Enderley Dr BLOX/PEL WS3 ...16 C4
End Hall Rd
DUNHL/THL/PER WV6 ......35 E2
Endhill Rd KGSTG B44 ....60 C5
Endicott Rd AST/WIT B6 ....91 F5
Endmoor Gv ERDW/GRVHL B23 .76 B5
Endsleigh Gv HLGN/YWD B28 .163 E2
Endwood Court Rd
BFLD/HDSWWD B20 ....90 A4
Endwood Dr FOAKS/STRLY B74 .46 A1
                    SOLH B91 ....181 F5
Enfield Cl ERDW/GRVHL B23 ...76 A4
Enfield Rd BLKHTH/ROWR B65 .122 B1
                    EDG B15 ....126 A4
Enford Cl BKDE/SHDE B34 ...113 H2
Engine La BRLYHL DY5 ....119 H1
                    BRWNH WS8 ....8 B4
                    DARL/WED WS10 ....56 B2
                    HAG/WOL DY9 ....136 B2
Engine St OLDBY B69 ....105 E5
                    SMTHWK B66 ....106 C3
Englestede Cl
BFLD/HDSWWD B20 ....89 H3
Englewood Dr
HLGN/YWD B28 ....163 E2
Ennerdale Cl BRWNH WS8 ....9 G3
Ennerdale Dr
DUNHL/THL/PER WV6 ....34 D1
                    HALE B63 ....137 H5
Ennerdale Rd
DUNHL/THL/PER WV6 ....21 H2
                    GTB/HAM B43 ....73 C4
Ennersdale Bungalows
CSHL/WTROR B46 ....97 F5
Ennersdale Cl
CSHL/WTROR B46 ....97 F5
Ennersdale Rd
CSHL/WTROR B46 ....97 F5
Ensall Dr STRBR DY8 ....118 A3
Ensbury Cl SHHTH WV12 ......40 B1
Ensdale Rw WLNHL WV13 .....39 G4
Ensdon Gv KGSTG B44 ....75 H2
Ensford Cl FOAKS/STRLY B74 ..46 C1
Ensign Cl BILS/COS WV14 ....101 H1
                    ERDW/GRVHL B23 ....76 C5
Enterprise Dr FOAKS/STRLY B74 .46 C5
                    HAG/WOL DY9 ....136 D1
Enterprise Gv BLOX/PEL WS3 .18 B3
Enterprise Wy VAUX/NECH B7 .3 J1
Enville Cl BLOX/PEL WS3 .....16 C4
Enville Gv SPARK B11 ....145 F2
Enville Pl STRBR DY8 * 135 F2
Enville Rd
ETTPK/GDPK/PENN WV4 ...50 C3
                    KGSWFD DY6 ....99 F1
                    SEDG DY3 ....83 F2
Epping Cl BLOX/PEL WS3 .....28 B4
                    RBRY B45 ....174 B3
Epping Gv KGSTG B44 ....75 H1
Epsom Cl DUNHL/THL/PER WV6 .34 D1
Epsom Gv KGSTG B44 ....75 H1
Epwell Gv KGSTG B44 ....75 E3
Epwell Rd KGSTG B44 ....75 E3
Equipoint YDLY B25 * 146 D1
Erasmus Rd SPARK B11 ......127 C5
Ercall Cl ERDW/GRVHL B23 ...75 H5
Erdington Hall Rd
ERDE/BCHGN B24 ....92 D4
Erdington Rd ALDR WS9 ......44 C3
Erica Cl SLYOAK B29 ....158 C2
Erica Rd DSYBK/YTR WS5 .....58 B4
Ermington Crs CBROM B36 ..112 A2
Ermington Rd
ETTPK/GDPK/PENN WV4 ...51 F5
Ernest Clarke Cl SHHTH WV12 .25 H4
Ernest Rd BHTH/HG B12 .....144 A2
                    DUDS DY2 ....85 F5
                    SMTHWKW B67 ....106 A3
Ernest St CBHAMW B1 ....126 D1
Ernsford Cl DOR/KN B93 .....198 D1
Erskine St VAUX/NECH B7 ....127 H1
Erdington Rd ALDR WS9 ......44 C3
Esher Rd HHTH/SAND B71 ....71 H5
                    KGSTG B44 ....60 C5
Eskdale Cl WOLV WV1 ....38 A3
Eskdale Wk BRLYHL DY5 ....118 D4
Esme Rd SPARK B11 ....144 C4
Esmond Cl BVILLE B30 ....159 F5
Essendon Rd WASH/WDE B8 .111 F4
Essex Av DARL/WED WS10 ....71 G4
                    KGSWFD DY6 ....99 F4
Essex Gdns STRBR DY8 ......117 H3
Essex Rd DUDN DY1 ....67 H5
Essex St DIG/EDG B5 ....127 E3
                    WSLW WS2 ....42 C1
Essington Cl STRBR DY8 ....118 A4
Essington Rd SHHTH WV12 ...25 H1
Essington St LDYWD/EDGR B16 .2 A7
Essington Wy WOLV WV1 .....38 B4
Este Rd
LGN/SDN/BHAMAIR B26 ..130 C5
Estone Wk AST/WIT B6 ......109 F2
Estria Rd EDG B15 ....126 B5

Ethelfleda Ter *DARL/WED* WS10...**55** H5
Ethelred Cl *FOAKS/STRLY* B74...**47** E2
Ethel Rd *HRBN* B17...**142** B2
Ethel St *CBHAM* B2...**3** F5
 LCLYGN/QTN B68...**105** E5
 SMTHWKW B67...**124** B2
Etheridge Rd *BILS/COS* WV14...**53** H1
Eton Cl *SEDG* DY3...**67** H4
Eton Dr *STRBR* DY8...**135** G4
Eton Rd *BHTH/HG* B12...**144** D4
Eton Wk *HAG/WOL* DY9...**152** C4
Etruria Wy *BILS/COS* WV14...**54** A1
Etta Cl *KGSTG* B44...**60** A4
Ettingshall Park Farm La
 ETTPK/GDPK/PENN WV4...**52** B4
Ettingshall Rd *BILS/COS* WV14...**68** A2
 BKHL/PFLD WV2...**53** E1
Ettington Cl *DOR/KN* B93...**198** B1
Ettington Rd *AST/WIT* B6...**109** E1
Ettymore Cl *SEDG* DY3...**67** F3
Ettymore Rd *SEDG* DY3...**67** F3
Ettymore Rd West *SEDG* DY3...**67** E3
Etwall Rd *HIA/OLT* B92...**162** C5
Euan Cl *HRBN* B17...**124** B2
Europa Av *WBROM* B70...**88** B4
Evans Cl *TPTN/OCK* DY4...**84** C1
Evans Pl *BILS/COS* WV14...**54** A1
Evans St *BILS/COS* WV14...**54** A4
 DUNHL/THL/PER WV6...**36** D1
 WLNHL WV13...**38** D4
Eva Rd *CBROM* B36...**106** B1
Evelyn Cft *SCFLD/BOLD* B73...**77** E5
Evelyn Rd *SPARK* B11...**145** E3
Evenlode Gv *WLNHL* WV13...**40** B4
Evenlode Rd *HIA/OLT* B92...**147** G4
Everest Cl *SMTHWK* B66...**106** B1
Everest Rd *BFLD/HDSWWD* B20...**90** A3
 WSLW WS2...**40** D2
Evergreen Cl *BILS/COS* WV14...**68** B5
Everitt Dr *DOR/KN* B93...**197** F2
Eversley Dr *ERDE/BCHGN* B24...**35** E4
Eversley Gv *SEDG* DY3...**67** E1
 WNSFLD WV11...**24** C4
Eversley Rd *BORD* B9...**128** B3
Evers St *BRLYHL* DY5...**120** D5
Everton Rd *WASH/WDE* B8...**111** G5
Evesham Crs * DLOX/PEL* WS3...**16** D1
Evesham Ri *DUDS* DY2...**120** D1
Eveson Ct *STRBR* DY8...**135** E4
Eveson Rd *STRBR* DY8...**134** D5
Evington Pl *YDLY* B25...**129** E5
Ewart Rd *WSLW* WS2...
Ewell Rd *ERDE/BCHGN* B24...**93** F2
Ewhurst Av *SLYOAK* B29...**159** H1
Ewhurst Cl *WLNHL* WV13...**39** F5
Exbury Cl *COVEN* WV9...**11** H1
Excelsior Gv *BLOX/PEL* WS3...**18** B2
Exchange St *BRLYHL* DY5...**105** H1
The Exchange *BLOX/PEL* WS3 *...**27** F1
Exe Cft *NFLD/LBR* B31...**175** H5
Exeter Dr
 CHWD/FDBR/MGN B37...**131** H4
Exeter Pas *CBHAMW* B1...**126** D3
Exeter Pl *WSLW* WS2...**41** F4
Exeter Rd *DUDS* DY2...**102** D1
 SLYOAK B29...**142** D5
 SMTHWK B66...**106** D4
Exeter St *CBHAMW* B1...**2** E7
Exford Cl *BRLYHL* DY5...**118** D5
Exhall Cl *SOLH* B91...**181** E3
Exhibition Wy *BHAMNEC* B40...**149** H5
Exmoor Gn *WNSFLD* WV11...**24** C3
The Expressway *WBROM* B70...**87** G2
Exton Cl *WNSFLD* WV11...**25** F2
Exton Gdns *SMTHWK* B66 *...**107** F3
Exton Wy *WASH/WDE* B8...**110** B4
Eyland Gv *WSL* WS1...**5** F5
Eymore Cl *SLYOAK* B29...**158** D4
Eyre St *WSNGN* B18...**126** A1
Eyston Av *TPTN/OCK* DY4...**70** B5
Eyton Cft *BHTH/HG* B12...**127** F5
Ezekiel La *SHHTH* WV12...**26** A4

F

Fabian Cl *RBRY* B45...**173** H3
Fabian Crs *SHLY* B90...**180** B4
Facet Rd *HWK/WKHTH* B38...**177** E3
Factory Rd *TPTN/OCK* DY4...**69** E5
 WSNGN B18...**107** H3
Factory St *DARL/WED* WS10...**55** E2
Fairbourne Av
 BLKHTH/ROWR B65...**104** C5
 KGSTG B44...**75** E1
Fairburn Crs *BLOX/PEL* WS3...**18** D2
Faircroft Av *WALM/CURD* B76...**78** B5
Faircroft Rd *CBROM* B36...**95** F5
Fairfax Dr *NFLD/LBR* B31...**175** G5
Fairfax Rd *MGN/WHC* B75...**63** F4
 WOLVN WV10...**12** D4
Fairfield Dr *BLOX/PEL* WS3...**18** B3
 CDSL WV8...**10** A4
 RMSLY B62...**122** C3
Fairfield Gv *RMSLY* B62...**122** C3
Fairfield Mt *WSL* WS1...**5** F7
Fairfield Ri *STRBR* DY8...**134** C2
Fairfield Rd
 ALE/KHTH/YWD B14...**161** E2
 DUDS DY2...**102** D2
 HALE B63...**138** C5
 RMSLY B62...**122** C3
 STRBR DY8...**118** B2
Fairford Gdns *STRBR* DY8...**118** A1
Fairford Rd *KGSTG* B44...**75** F5
Fairgreen Gdns *BRLYHL* DY5...**101** E4
Fairgreen Wy
 FOAKS/STRLY B74...**45** G4
 SLYOAK B29...**159** H1
Fairground Wy *WSL* WS1...**4** C6
Fairhaven Cft *RMSLY* B62...**122** C3
Fairhills *SEDG* DY3...**67** F5
Fairhill Wy *SPARK* B11...**127** H5
Fairholme Rd *CBROM* B36...**111** F2

Fairlawn *EDG* B15 *...**126** A3
Fairlawn Cl *WLNHL* WV12...**26** A1
Fairlawn Dr *KGSWFD* DY6...**99** H5
Fairlawns
 LGN/SDN/BHAMAIR B26...**130** B3
 WALM/CURD B76...**78** C5
Fairlawn Wy *HWK/WKHTH* B38...**176** B4
Fairmead Ri *HWK/WKHTH* B38...**176** D4
Fairmile Rd *HALE* B63...**138** B1
Fairoak Dr
 DUNHL/THL/PER WV6...**35** G2
Fairview Av *PBAR/PBCH* B42...**74** B5
Fairview Cl *WNSFLD* WV11...**24** B3
Fairview Crs *KGSWFD* DY6...**100** B5
 WNSFLD WV11...**24** B3
Fairview Gv *WNSFLD* WV11...**24** B3
Fairview Ms
 CSHL/WTROR B46 *...**115** F2
Fairview Rd *DUDN* DY1...**84** A4
 ETTPK/GDPK/PENN WV4...**50** C4
 WNSFLD WV11...**24** B3
Fairway *NFLD/LBR* B31...**175** E3
 RUSH/SHEL WS4...**29** F1
Fairway Av *OLDBY* B69...**103** G1
Fairway Dr *RBRY* B45...**187** H2
Fairway Gn *BILS/COS* WV14...**53** C1
Fairway Rd *OLDBY* B69...**103** G1
Fairways Av *STRBR* DY8...**135** G5
Fairways Ct *STRBR* DY8...**135** E5
The Fairways *WALM/CURD* B76...**78** B5
The Fairway *HWK/WKHTH* B38...**176** B3
Fairyfield Av *GTB/HAM* B43...**73** F2
Fakenham Cft *HRBN* B17...**124** B5
Falcon Crs *BILS/COS* WV14...**67** H1
Falcondale Rd *SHHTH* WV12...**26** A1
Falconhurst Rd *SLYOAK* B29...**142** A5
Falcon Lodge Crs
 MGN/WHC B75...**63** C3
Falcon Pl *OLDBY* B69...**104** A2
Falcon Rd *LCLYGN/QTN* B68...**122** D2
The Falcons *MGN/WHC* B75...**63** H3
Falcon Wy *DUDN* DY1...**85** H5
Falfield Cl *BLKHTH/ROWR* B65...**104** B3
Falfield Gv *NFLD/LBR* B31...**189** E1
Falkland Cft *BVILLE* B30...**160** D4
Falklands Cl *SEDG* DY3...**80** C1
Falkland Wy *CBROM* B36...**114** B4
Falkwood Gv *DOR/KN* B93...**196** D2
Fallindale Rd
 DARL/WED WS10...**55** H1
Fallowfield *CDSL* WV8...**11** C5
Fallow Fld *FOAKS/STRLY* B74...**45** H2
Fallowfield Av *HLGN/YWD* B28...**162** D5
Fallow Field Rd
 BLKHTH/ROWR B65...**121** C1
Fallowfield Rd *DSYBK/YTR* WS5...**43** C5
 HALE B63...**137** H4
 HIA/OLT B92...**148** A5
Fallows Rd *SPARK* B11...**145** E1
Falmouth Rd *BKDE/SHDE* B34...**96** C2
 DSYBK/YTR WS5...**58** B1
Falstaff Av *HLYWD* B47...**192** C2
Falstaff Cl *WALM/CURD* B76...**78** C4
Falstaff Rd *SHLY* B90...**180** C5
Falstone Rd *SCFLD/BOLD* B73...**76** B1
Fancott Rd *NFLD/LBR* B31...**158** C5
Fancourt Av
 ETTPK/GDPK/PENN WV4...**50** D3
Fane Rd *WNSFLD* WV11...**25** H2
Fanshawe Rd *ACGN* B27...**163** G1
Faraday Av *RIDG/WDGT* B32...**140** D2
 WALM/CURD B76...**97** E1
Faraday Rd *WSLW* WS2...**27** F4
Faraday Wharf *VAUX/NECH* B7 *...**3** K1
Farbrook Wy *SHHTH* WV12...**25** H4
Farcroft Av *HDSW* B21...**107** F1
Farcroft Gv *HDSW* B21...**89** F5
Farcroft Rd *HDSW* B21...**89** F5
Farcroft Wy *ERDW/GRVHL* B23...**76** B3
Fareham Crs
 ETTPK/GDPK/PENN WV4...**50** C2
Farfield Cl *NFLD/LBR* B31...**175** H5
Far High Dr *TPTN/OCK* DY4...**85** H1
Far Highfield *WALM/CURD* B76...**62** H4
Far Hill Cl *HHTH/SAND* B71...**72** B3
Farlands Dr *STRBR* DY8...**135** C4
Farlands Gv *GTB/HAM* B43...**73** H4
Farlands Rd *STRBR* DY8...**135** C4
Farleigh Dr *BDMR/CCFT* WV3...**35** E5
Farleigh Rd
 DUNHL/THL/PER WV6...**35** E2
Farley La *RMSLY* B62...**172** B4
Farley Rd *ERDW/GRVHL* B23...**91** H2
Farley St *TPTN/OCK* DY4...**70** C5
Farlow Cft
 CHWD/FDBR/MGN B37...**131** H5
Farlow Rd *NFLD/LBR* B31...**158** D3
Farmacre *BORD* B9...**127** H2
Farm Av *LGLYGN/QTN* B68...**123** E1
Farmbridge Cl *WSLW* WS2...**40** B2
Farmbridge Rd *WLNHL* WV13...**40** B3
Farmbrook Av *WOLVN* WV10...**12** D4
Farm Cl *CDSL* WV8...**10** D5
 HIA/OLT B92...**148** A5
 SEDG DY3...**66** B4
 STECH B33...**130** B1
Farmcote Rd *STECH* B33...**130** C5
Farm Cft *LOZ/NWT* B19...**108** C5
Farmcroft Rd *HAG/WOL* DY9...**136** D3
Farmdale Gv *RBRY* B45...**188** A2
Farm End *HHTH/SAND* B71...**72** B2
Farmer Rd *SMTH* B10...**128** B5
Farmers Cl *WALM/CURD* B76...**63** E4
Farmers Ct *HALE* B63...**138** B3
Farmers Fold *WOLV* WV1...**7** F4
Farmer Wy *TPTN/OCK* DY4...**69** H2
Farm House La *MGN/WHC* B75...**48** A2
Farm House Wy *GTB/HAM* B43...**58** D4
Farmhouse Wy *SHLY* B90...**195** G1
Farmoor Gv *BKDE/SHDE* B34...**113** C3
Farmoor Wy *WOLVN* WV10...**13** E5
Farm Rd *BDMR/CCFT* WV3...**35** G5
 BLKHTH/ROWR B65...**103** C5
 BRLYHL DY5...**119** C3

 DUDS DY2...**102** A5
 LGLYGN/QTN B68...**123** E1
 SMTHWKW B67...**124** A1
 SPARK B11...**127** H5
 TPTN/OCK DY4...**69** H4
Farmside Cl *HAG/WOL* DY9...**137** E4
Farmside Gn *COVEN* WV9...**11** H5
Farmstead Cl *WSL* WS1...**57** E5
Farmstead Rd *HIA/OLT* B92...**148** A5
Farm St *LOZ/NWT* B19...**108** C5
 WBROM B70...**87** C5
 WSLW WS2...**42** A1
Farnborough Ct
 MGN/WHC B75...**47** C3
Farnborough Dr *SHLY* B90...**195** F2
Farnborough Rd *CBROM* B36...**94** D3
Fanbury Cft
 HWK/WKHTH B38...**177** F5
Farncote Dr *FOAKS/STRLY* B74...**46** D2
Farndale Av
 CHWD/FDBR/MGN B37...**132** B5
Farndon Av *WASH/WDE* B8...**110** D4
Farndon Rd *SMTH* B10...**128** A5
Farnham Cl *GTB/HAM* B43...**73** H5
Farnham Rd *HDSW* B21...**89** F4
Farnhurst Rd *WASH/WDE* B8...**111** F2
Farnol Rd
 CHWD/FDBR/MGN B37...**132** B5
Farnworth Gv *CBROM* B36...**95** C5
Farquhar Rd *EDG* B15...**142** D1
 MOS/BIL B13...**144** B4
Farquhar Rd East *EDG* B15...**142** D1
Farren Rd *NFLD/LBR* B31...**174** D4
Farrier Cl *WALM/CURD* B76...**78** B5
Farrier Rd *GTB/HAM* B43...**59** H5
Farriers Mi *BLOX/PEL* WS3...**17** G3
The Farriers
 LGN/SDN/BHAMAIR B26...**147** H2
Farrier Wy *KGSWFD* DY6...**99** E2
Farringdon St *WSLW* WS2...**42** A1
Farrington Rd
 ERDW/GRVHL B23...**91** H1
 ETTPK/GDPK/PENN WV4...**67** C1
Farrow Rd *KGSTG* B44...**60** A5
Farthing La *CSCFLD/WYGN* B72...**62** A4
Farthing Pools Cl
 CSCFLD/WYGN B72...**62** C4
Farthings La *DUDS* DY2...**102** A2
The Farthings *HRBN* B17...**142** B2
Farvale Rd *WALM/CURD* B76...**79** E5
Far Vw *ALDR* WS9...**19** H5
Farway Gdns *CDSL* WV8...**10** B5
Far Wood Rd *NFLD/LBR* B31...**158** A2
Fashoda Rd *SLYOAK* B29...**160** B1
Fastlea Rd *RIDG/WDGT* B32...**157** H1
Fastmoor Ov *STECH* B33...**131** G3
Fast Pits Rd *YDLY* B25...**129** F4
Fatherless Barn Crs *HALE* B63...**137** F4
Faulkland Crs *WOLV* WV1...**7** C2
Faulkner Cl *STRBR* DY8...**135** F3
Faulkner Rd *HIA/OLT* B92...**164** D1
Faulkners Farm Dr
 ERDW/GRVHL B23...**91** H1
Faulkner Dr *BRLYHL* DY5...**100** D3
Faversham Cl *CDSL* WV8...**22** A2
 WSLW WS2...**40** B2
Fawdry Cl *SCFLD/BOLD* B73...**62** A5
Fawdry St *CBHAMNE* B4...**127** C2
 SMTHWK B66...**107** E4
 WOLV WV1...**6** D1
Fawley Cl *WLNHL* WV13...**39** F5
Fawley Gv *BVILLE* B30...**160** B5
Fazeley Ct *SOLH* B91...**182** B1
Fazeley St *DIG* B5...**3** K5
Fearon Pl *SMTHWK* B66 *...**106** C3
Featherstone Cl *SHLY* B90...**180** D3
Featherstone Crs *SHLY* B90...**180** D4
Featherstone Rd
 ALE/KHTH/YWD B14...**161** E4
Featherston Rd
 FOAKS/STRLY B74...**45** C3
Feilshill Rd *SEDG* DY3...**80** B3
Felbrigg Cl *BRLYHL* DY5...**119** F4
The Feldings *ERDE/BCHGN* B24...**93** G2
Feldon La *RMSLY* B62...**122** C5
Felgate Cl *SHLY* B90...**195** G2
Fellbrook Ct *STETCH* B33...**112** B5
Fell Gv *HDSW* B21...**89** E5
Fellmeadow Rd *STECH* B33...**130** C2
Fellmeadow Wy *SEDG* DY3...**67** C5
Fellows Av *KGSWFD* DY6...**99** G1
Fellows La *HRBN* B17...**141** G1
Fellows Park Gdns
 WSL WS2 *...**56** B2
Fellows Rd *BILS/COS* WV14...**53** H1
Fellows St *BKHL/PFLD* WV2...**37** E5
Felsted Wy *VAUX/NECH* B7...**109** G5
Felstone Rd *KGSTG* B44...**75** E2
Feltham Cl *STETCH* B33...**131** C3
Felton Cft *STECH* B33...**130** C5
Felton Gv *SOLH* B91...**181** H4
Fenbourne Cl *RUSH/SHEL* WS4...**29** H2
Fenchurch Cl *WSLW* WS2...**41** H1
Fencote Av
 CHWD/FDBR/MGN B37...**114** A5
Fenmere Cl
 ETTPK/GDPK/PENN WV4...**52** D3
Fennel Cft *BKDE/SHDE* B34...**112** D2
Fennel Rd *BRLYHL* DY5...**119** E5
Fennis Cl *DOR/KN* B93...**196** D5
Fenn Ri *SHHTH* WV12...**25** H4
 STRBR DY8...**117** G1
Fens Crs *BRLYHL* DY5...**101** E4
Fens Pool Av *BRLYHL* DY5...**101** F4
The Fensway *BKDE/SHDE* B34...**112** D2
Fenter Cl *MOS/BIL* B13...**144** B3
Fentham Cl *HIA/OLT* B92...**167** H4
Fentham Ct *HIA/OLT* B92...**164** C1
Fentham Gn *HIA/OLT* B92...**167** C3
Fentham Rd *AST/WIT* B6...**108** D1
 ERDW/GRVHL B23...**92** B3
 HIA/OLT B92...**167** G3
Fenton Rd *ACGN* B27...**146** B3
 HLYWD B47...**192** C1
Fenton St *BRLYHL* DY5...**119** F1
 SMTHWK B66...**106** D4
Fenton Wy *ACGN* B27...**146** B3
Fereday Rd *ALDR* WS9...**19** H4

Fereday's Cft *SEDG* DY3...**67** F4
Fereday St *TPTN/OCK* DY4...**69** F3
Ferguson Dr *TPTN/OCK* DY4...**69** H5
Ferguson Rd *LGLYGN/QTN* B68...**105** H4
Ferguson St *WNSFLD* WV11...**25** G1
Fern Av *TPTN/OCK* DY4...**69** F4
Fernbank Cl *HALE* B63...**137** H5
Fernbank Crs *DSYBK/YTR* WS5...**58** A4
Fernbank Rd *WASH/WDE* B8...**111** E5
Ferncliffe Rd *HRBN* B17...**141** H5
Fern Cl *BILS/COS* WV14...**68** B3
 RUSH/SHEL WS4...**29** E1
Ferndale Av *GTB/HAM* B43...**73** H4
Ferndale Cl *HAG/WOL* DY9...**152** C5
Ferndale Ct *CSHL/WTROR* B46...**115** G4
Ferndale Crs *BHTH/HG* B12...**127** G4
Ferndale Ms
 CSHL/WTROR B46...**115** G4
Ferndale Pk *HAG/WOL* DY9...**153** E2
Ferndale Rd *CSHL/WTROR* B46...**115** G4
 FOAKS/STRLY B74...**45** F5
 HLGN/YWD B28...**162** B5
 LGLYGN/QTN B68...**123** E2
 STRBR DY8...**134** C1
Fern Dell Cl *ERDW/GRVHL* B23...**6** A6
Ferndene Rd *SPARK* B11...**145** H4
Ferndown Cl *BLOX/PEL* WS3...**16** D3
 LGN/SDN/BHAMAIR B26...**130** C3
Ferndown Gdns *WNSFLD* WV11...**25** F5
Ferndown Rd *SOLH* B91...**164** D4
Fernhill Gv *KGSTG* B44...**60** B5
Fernhill Rd *HIA/OLT* B92...**147** E5
Fernhurst Dr *BRLYHL* DY5...**100** D2
Fernhurst Rd *WASH/WDE* B8...**129** E1
Fernleigh Gdns *STRBR* DY8...**117** G1
Fernleigh Rd *RUSH/SHEL* WS4...**42** D2
Fern Leys *SPARK* B11...**145** E5
Fernside Rd *WLNHL* WV13...**39** E3
Fern Rd *BDMR/CCFT* WV3...**6** D7
 DUDN DY1...**84** C2
 ERDE/BCHGN B24...**93** E2
Fernside Gdns *MOS/BIL* B13...**144** D4
Fernside Rd *WLNHL* WV13...**38** D2
Fern Vls *DARL/WED* WS10...**55** C2
Fernwood Cl *SCFLD/BOLD* B73...**76** C2
Fernwood Cft
 ALE/KHTH/YWD B14...**161** E4
 TPTN/OCK DY4...**85** F2
Fernwood Rd *SCFLD/BOLD* B73...**76** C3
Fernwoods *RIDG/WDGT* B32...**140** B5
Ferrers Cl *MGN/WHC* B75...**47** H5
Ferrie Gv *BRWNH* WS8...**9** H4
Ferris Gv *ACGN* B27...**163** E1
Festival Av *DARL/WED* WS10...**55** E4
Festival Wy
 DUNHL/THL/PER WV6...**22** D5
Ffernfald Ct *ERDW/GRVHL* B23...**92** C1
Fibbersley *WLNHL* WV13...**39** G1
Fibbersley Bank *WLNHL* WV13...**39** F1
Fiddlers Gn *HIA/OLT* B92...**167** G3
Field Av *NFLD/LBR* B31...**158** B5
Field Cl *BLOX/PEL* WS3...**27** G2
 LGN/SDN/BHAMAIR B26...**147** G1
 RUSH/SHEL WS4...**18** B5
 STRBR DY8...**135** G2
Field Cottage Dr *STRBR* DY8...**135** H4
Fieldfare Cl *DUDS* DY2...**103** F5
Fieldfare Cft *CBROM* B36...**114** A1
Fieldfare Rd *HAG/WOL* DY9...**136** D3
Field Head Pl
 DUNHL/THL/PER WV6...**35** F1
Fieldhead Rd *SPARK* B11...**146** A3
Fieldhouse La *RMSLY* B62...**172** A1
Fieldhouse Rd
 ETTPK/GDPK/PENN WV4...**52** C4
 YDLY B25...**129** E5
Field La *HAG/WOL* DY9...**170** A1
 RIDG/WDGT B32...**157** E2
 RUSH/SHEL WS4...**18** B5
 SOLH B91...**166** A5
 STRBR DY8...**135** G2
Field Maple Rd
 FOAKS/STRLY B74...**60** B2
Field Ms *DUDS* DY2...**121** E2
Fieldon Cl *SHLY* B90...**180** C2
Field Rd *BLOX/PEL* WS3...**27** G1
 DUDS DY2...**102** B1
 HHTH/SAND B71...**72** A1
 WLNHL WV13...**39** G3
Fields Vw *BILS/COS* WV14...**68** D1
Field View Dr
 BLKHTH/ROWR B65...**104** C4
Field Wy *ALDR* WS9...**30** B3
Field Wy *HOCK/TIA* B94...**198** A5
Fieldways Cl *HLYWD* B47...**192** C1
Fifield Cl *STETCH* B33...**130** B1
Fifth Av *BORD* B9...**128** B2
 WOLVN WV10...**12** D2
Fifth Wy *WOLVN* WV10...**12** C1
Fillingham Cl
 CHWD/FDBR/MGN B37...**132** D3
Filton Cft *CVALE* B35...**94** C2
Fimbrell Cl *BRLYHL* DY5...**118** C4
Finbury Cl *HIA/OLT* B92...**164** D1
Finchall Cft *HIA/OLT* B92...**165** G3
Fincham Cl *COVEN* WV9...**11** H5
Finch Cl *BLKHTH/ROWR* B65...**104** A2
Finchdene Gv *BDMR/CCFT* WV3...**35** H4
Finch Dr *FOAKS/STRLY* B74...**60** C5
Finches End *BKDE/SHDE* B34...**113** E4
Finchfield Cl *STRBR* DY8...**134** C3
Finchfield Gdns
 BDMR/CCFT WV3...**36** A4
Finchfield Hl *BDMR/CCFT* WV3...**35** H3
Finchfield La *BDMR/CCFT* WV3...**50** C1
Finchfield Rd *BDMR/CCFT* WV3...**36** A4
Finchfield Rd West
 BDMR/CCFT WV3...**35** G4
Finchley Av *LOZ/NWT* B19 *...**108** C3
Finchley Cl *SEDG* DY3...**83** H1
Finchley Rd *KGSTG* B44...**61** H5
Finchmead Rd *STECH* B33...**131** G2
Finchpath Rd *WBROM* B70...**71** F5
Finch Rd *LOZ/NWT* B19...**108** C3
Findlay Rd
 ALE/KHTH/YWD B14...**161** E1

Findon Rd *WASH/WDE* B8...**111** F3
Finger Post Dr *BLOX/PEL* WS3...**18** A2
Finlarigg Dr *EDG* B15...**142** D1
Finmere Rd *HAG/WOL* DY8...**162** D2
Finmere Wy *SHLY* B90...**180** D3
Finnemore Rd *BORD* B9...**129** E2
Finney Well Cl *BILS/COS* WV14...**53** F5
Finsbury Dr *BRLYHL* DY5...**119** E5
Finsbury Gv *ERDW/GRVHL* B23...**76** B5
Finstall Cl *CSCFLD/WYGN* B72...**77** C2
 VAUX/NECH B7...**109** C5
Finwood Cl *HIA/OLT* B92...**165** G2
Fir Av *BHTH/HG* B12...**144** C2
Firbank Cl *BVILLE* B30...**159** G3
Firbank Wy *BLOX/PEL* WS3...**17** H5
Firbarn Cl *WALM/CURD* B76...**62** D5
Firbeck Gv *KGSTG* B44...**75** C2
Firbeck Rd *KGSTG* B44...**75** C2
Fircroft *BILS/COS* WV14...**53** C4
Fir Cft *BRLYHL* DY5...**119** E4
Fircroft *NFLD/LBR* B31...**158** B2
 SOLH B91...**164** B4
Firecrest Cl *ERDW/GRVHL* B23...**75** H4
Fir Gv *ALE/KHTH/YWD* B14...**161** F5
 BDMR/CCFT WV3...**6** A6
 STRBR DY8...**134** C1
Firhill Cft *ALE/KHTH/YWD* B14...**177** H3
Firmstone St *STRBR* DY8...**118** A5
Firsbrook Cl
 DUNHL/THL/PER WV6...**22** C5
Firsby Rd *RIDG/WDGT* B32...**141** E2
Firs Cl *SMTHWKW* B67...**106** C4
Firs Dr *SHLY* B90...**180** A4
Firs Farm Dr *CBROM* B36...**112** D2
Firsholm Cl *SCFLD/BOLD* B73...**77** E2
Firs Rd *KGSWFD* DY6...**100** A3
Firs St *DUDS* DY2...**84** D5
First Av *BORD* B9...**128** C3
 BRWNH WS8...**9** G4
 KGSWFD DY6...**82** C5
 SLYOAK B29...**143** F4
 WOLVN WV10...**14** C4
 WOLVN WV10...**23** G4
First Exhibition Av
 BHAMNEC B40...**149** H3
First Meadow Piece
 RIDG/WDGT B32...**141** E3
Fir St *SEDG* DY3...**66** B4
Firsvale Rd *WNSFLD* WV11...**25** F5
Firsway *DUNHL/THL/PER* WV6...**35** E4
Firswood Rd *STETCH* B33...**131** E3
Firth Dr *ALE/KHTH/YWD* B14...**161** H5
 RMSLY B62...**122** C4
Firth Park Crs *RMSLY* B62...**122** C4
Fir Tree Cl *KGSTG* B44...**75** E4
Fir Tree Dr *DSYBK/YTR* WS5...**57** G4
 SEDG DY3...**67** C4
Fir Tree Gv *SCFLD/BOLD* B73...**76** D2
Fir Tree Rd *ERDE/BCHGN* B24...**93** F4
Fisher Rd *BLOX/PEL* WS3...**27** G3
 OLDBY B69...**105** G2
Fishers Dr *SHLY* B90...**193** H3
Fisher St *BDMR/CCFT* WV3...**6** C7
 BRLYHL DY5...**119** C1
 DUDN DY1...**84** D5
 TPTN/OCK DY4...**85** G5
 WLNHL WV13...**39** F3
Fishley Cl *BLOX/PEL* WS3...**17** E3
Fishley La *BLOX/PEL* WS3...**17** E1
Fishpool Cl *CBROM* B36...**111** G1
Fishpool La
 RCOVN/BALC/EX CV7...**150** D1
Fitters Mill Cl *DIG/EDG* B5 *...**144** A1
Fitton Av *KGSWFD* DY6...**100** D4
Fitzgerald Pl *BRLYHL* DY5...**135** H1
Fitzguy Cl *WBROM* B70...**88** A5
Fitzmaurice Rd *WNSFLD* WV11...**25** F5
Fitz Roy Av *HRBN* B17...**124** B5
Five Broadway *EDG* B15 *...**126** B3
Five Fields Rd *SHHTH* WV12...**25** G5
Five Oaks Rd *WLNHL* WV13...**39** E5
Five Ways *LGHYD/EDGR* B16...**126** B3
Flackwell Rd *ERDW/GRVHL* B23...**76** C4
Fladbury Cl *DUDS* DY2...**120** D1
Fladbury Crs *SLYOAK* B29...**142** B5
Fladbury Gdns
 LOZ/NWT B19 *...**108** C3
Fladbury Pl *LOZ/NWT* B19 *...**108** C2
Flamborough Wy
 BILS/COS WV14...**68** B4
Flanders Dr *KGSWFD* DY6...**99** H1
Flash La
 ETTPK/GDPK/PENN WV4...**64** C1
Flash Rd *OLDBY* B69...**105** E2
Flatlea *NFLD/LBR* B31...**175** F1
The Flatts *DARL/WED* WS10...**55** E2
Flavell Av *BILS/COS* WV14...**68** C2
Flavell Cl *RIDG/WDGT* B32...**157** F1
Flavell St *DUDN* DY1...**84** D2
Flavells La *SEDG* DY3...**82** C2
 YDLY B25...**129** G4
Flavell St *DUDN* DY1...**68** B1
Flaxhall St *WSL* WS2...**41** H1
Flax Gdns *HWK/WKHTH* B38...**176** D5
Flaxhall St *WSL* WS2...**41** H5
Flaxley Pkwy *STETCH* B33...**112** A5
Flaxley Rd *STETCH* B33...**112** A4
Flaxton Gv *STETCH* B33...**112** C5
Flecknoe Cl *CBROM* B36...**95** H5
Fledburgh Dr *WALM/CURD* B76...**62** D5
Fleet St *CBHAMW* B3...**2** C4
 LGN/SDN/BHAMAIR B26...**130** C3
Fleming Pl *WSLW* WS2...**27** E4
Fleming Rd *RIDG/WDGT* B32...**140** D2
 WSLW WS2...**27** F4
Flemming Cl *CDSL* WV8...**10** A3
Fletcher Gv *DOR/KN* B93...**197** F4
Fletcher Rd *SHHTH* WV12...**26** B2
Fletcher's La *WLNHL* WV13...**39** G2
Fletcher St *HAG/WOL* DY9...**136** D2
Fletton Gv
 ALE/KHTH/YWD B14...**162** B5
Flinkford Cl *DSYBK/YTR* WS5...**58** A2
Flint Green Rd *ACGN* B27...**146** B4
Flintham Cl *ACGN* B27...**147** E4

The Flintway *STECH* B33 ....112 A5
Floodgate St *DIG/EDG* B5 ....3 K7
Flood St *DUDS* DY2 ....84 D5
Flora Rd *YDLY* B25 ....129 F5
Florence Av
  ETTPK/GDPK/PENN WV4 ......52 D4
  SPARK B11 ....148 D2
Florence Gv *HHTH/SAND* B71 ...72 A2
Florence Rd *ACGN* B27 ....146 D3
  ALE/KHTH/YWD B14 ....161 F2
  WSNGN B18 ....107 G5
  ERDW/GRVHL B23 ....77 F4
  HDSW B21 ....107 F1
  OLDBY B69 ....104 B2
  TPTN/OCK DY4 ....106 D5
  WBROM B70 ....88 A5
Florence St *CBHAMW* B1 ....126 D3
  WSL WS1 ....5 H5
Florence Vis *SPARK* B11 * 128 A5
Florian Gv *DARL/WED* WS10 .....55 C1
Florida Wy *KGSWFD* DY6 ....100 C4
Flowerdale Cl *BILS/COS* WV14 ..68 B3
Floyds La *RUSH/SHEL* WS4 ....9 D3
Floyer Rd *SMHTH* B10 ....128 C3
Flyford Cft *SLYOAK* B29 ....141 F5
Foden Rd *PBAR/PBCH* B42 ....74 A3
Foinavon Cl
  BLKHTH/ROWR B65 ....103 F3
Fold St *WOLV* WV1 ....6 E5
The Fold *DARL/WED* WS10 ....55 F2
  ETTPK/GDPK/PENN WV4 ......51 F4
Foldyard Cl *WALM/CURD* B76 ....78 C5
Fosey Av *DUNHL/THL/PER* WV6 .35 F2
Foley Church Cl
  FOAKS/STRLY B74 ....45 G3
Foley Dr *DUNHL/THL/PER* WV6 .35 G2
Foley Gv *WMBN* WV5 ....30 A5
Foley Rd *HAG/WOL* DY9 ....135 H5
  WASH/WDE B8 ....111 F3
Foley Rd East
  FOAKS/STRLY B74 ....45 F4
Foley Rd West
  FOAKS/STRLY B74 ....44 D4
Foley St *DARL/WED* WS10 ....56 A5
Foley Wood Cl
  FOAKS/STRLY B74 ....45 E4
Folkes Rd *HAG/WOL* DY9 ....137 E1
Folliott Rd *STECH* B33 ....132 A1
Follyhouse Cl *WSL* WS1 ....57 F1
Follyhouse La *WSL* WS1 ....5 F7
  WSL WS1 ....57 F1
Fontley Cl
  LGN/SDN/BHAMAIR B26 ....130 C3
Fontwell Rd *WOLVN* WV10 ....12 D3
Footherley La *LICHS* WS14 ....32 D1
Fordbridge Rd
  CHWD/FDBR/MGN B37 ......113 H5
Ford Brook La *BLOX/PEL* WS3 ..16 B1
Forder Gv
  ALE/KHTH/YWD B14 ....178 C3
Forde Way Gdns
  HWK/WKHTH B38 ....190 B1
Fordfield Rd *STECH* B33 ....113 E5
Fordham Gv *COVEN* WV9 ....12 A4
Fordhouse La *BVILLE* B30 ....160 B4
Fordhouse Rd *WOLVN* WV10 ....23 F1
Fordraught La *RMSLY* B62 ....172 D4
The Fordrift
  CHWD/FDBR/MGN B37 ......149 E2
Fordrough *YDLY* B25 ....128 D5
Fordrough Av *BORD* B9 ....128 C1
Fordrough La *BORD* B9 ....128 C2
The Fordrough
  FOAKS/STRLY B74 ....47 E4
  NFLD/LBR B31 ....175 H5
  SHLY B90 ....193 G5
Ford St *SMTHWKW* B67 ....106 B3
  WSL WS2 ....56 C1
  WSNGN B18 ....108 B4
Fordwater Rd
  FOAKS/STRLY B74 ....60 B2
Foredraft Cl *RIDG/WDGT* B32 .140 C5
Foredraft St *HALE* B63 ....137 G2
Foredrove La *HIA/OLT* B92 .....165 G4
Forest Cl *FOAKS/STRLY* B74 .....60 A1
  SMTHWK B66 ....106 A2
Forest Ct *DOR/KN* B93 ....196 D5
Forest Dl *RBRY* B45 ....176 D5
Forest Dr *CDYHTH* B64 ....121 F2
  HRBN B17 ....142 B1
Forest Ga *SHHTH* WV12 ....26 B2
Forest Hill Rd
  LGN/SDN/BHAMAIR B26 ....148 A2
Forest La *BLOX/PEL* WS3 ....28 A5
  WSLW WS2 ....27 H5
Forest Pk *WALM/CURD* B76 .....63 E4
Forest Pl *BLOX/PEL* WS3 ....28 A4
Forest Rd *CBHAM* B2 ....5 C5
Forest Rd *DOR/KN* B93 ....197 E5
  DUDN DY1 ....84 C2
  LGLYGN/QTN B68 ....123 G5
  MOS/BIL B13 ....144 C3
  WSL WS1 ....146 C1
Forest Wy *HLYWD* B47 ....192 D2
Forge Cl *DSGL* WV8 ....22 A1
Forge Cft *WALM/CURD* B76 .....78 D5
Forge La *ALDR* WS9 ....32 A4
  CDYHTH B64 ....120 B4
  FOAKS/STRLY B74 ....32 A4
  HAG/WOL DY9 ....184 B1
  HHTH/SAND B71 ....72 C5
  KGSWFD DY6 ....81 F4
  KIDD DY10 ....168 B4
  RMSLY B62 ....139 E2
  WALM/CURD B76 ....94 D1
Forge Leys *WMBN* WV5 ....64 C5
Forge Rd *BLOX/PEL* WS3 ....18 C5
  DARL/WED WS10 ....54 D2
  SHHTH WV12 ....40 A1
  STRBR DY8 ....135 F1
The Forge *HALE* B63 ....120 A4
Forge Valley Wy *WMBN* WV5 ....64 A5
Forge Wy *OLDBY* B69 ....104 C3

Formans Rd *SPARK* B11 ....145 G4
Formby Av
  DUNHL/THL/PER WV6 ....34 B1
Formby Wy *BLOX/PEL* WS3 ......16 C4
Forrell Gv *NFLD/LBR* B31 ....189 H1
Forrest Av *WNSFLD* WV11 ....15 E3
Forrest St *WSLW* WS2 ....4 A3
Forrester Street Prec
  WSLW WS2 ....4 A3
Forster Rd *SMTHWKW* B67 ....106 A2
  VAUX/NECH B7 ....127 G1
Forsythia Cl *NFLD/LBR* B31 ...158 B2
Forsythia Gv *CDSL* WV8 ....10 C4
Fort Crs *ALDR* WS9 ....19 G4
Forth Dr
  CHWD/FDBR/MGN B37 ......114 B5
Forth Gv *HWK/WKHTH* B38 ....176 C5
Forth Wy *RMSLY* B62 ....122 C4
Fortnum Cl *STECH* B33 ....131 E2
Forton Cl *DUNHL/THL/PER* WV6 .35 F3
Fort Pkwy *ERDE/BCHGN* B24 ...93 H5
Forward Rd
  LGN/SDN/BHAMAIR B26 ....149 E4
Fosbrooke Rd *SMHTH* B10 ......129 E4
Fosseway Dr *ERDW/GRVHL* B23 .76 C3
Fossil Dr *RBRY* B45 ....188 A1
Foster Av *BILS/COS* WV14 ....68 B2
Foster Gdns *WSNGN* B18 * 107 H3
Foster Gn
  DUNHL/THL/PER WV6 ....34 C2
Foster Pl *STRBR* DY8 ....135 E1
Foster Rd *WOLVN* WV10 ....23 G4
Foster St *BLOX/PEL* WS3 ....27 H2
  DARL/WED WS10 ....55 F1
Foster St East *STRBR* DY8 .....135 G2
Foster Wy *DIG/EDG* B5 ....143 G2
Fotherley Brook Rd *ALDR* WS9 .31 F3
Foundry La *BLOX/PEL* WS3 ....17 G4
  SMTHWK B66 ....107 F2
Foundry St *BILS/COS* WV14 .....68 C2
  KGSWFD DY6 ....99 F1
  TPTN/OCK DY4 ....85 H2
Fountain Arcade Chambers
  DUDN DY1 * 84 C5
Fountain Cl *NFLD/LBR* B31 ....189 G1
Fountain Ct *CBHAMNE* B4 * 3 G3
Fountain La *BILS/COS* WV14 ....68 D3
  OLDBY B69 ....86 D5
Fountain Rd *HRBN* B17 ....124 D3
Fountains Rd *BLOX/PEL* WS3 ...16 A5
Fountains Wy *BLOX/PEL* WS3 ...16 A5
Four Acres *RIDG/WDGT* B32 ...140 C3
Four Ashes Rd *DOR/KN* B93 ...196 C4
Four Crosses Rd
  RUSH/SHEL WS4 ....29 E1
Fourlands Av
  CSCFLD/WYGN B72 ....77 H4
Fourlands Rd *NFLD/LBR* B31 ..158 A4
Four Oaks Common Rd
  FOAKS/STRLY B74 ....46 C2
Four Oaks Rd *FOAKS/STRLY* B74 .46 D3
Four Stones Cl *SOLH* B91 ......181 G4
Four Stones Gv *DIG/EDG* B5 ...143 H1
Fourth Av *BORD* B9 ....128 D2
  BRWNH WS8 ....9 G4
  SLYOAK B29 ....143 G4
  WOLVN WV10 ....23 F4
Four Winds Rd *DUDS* DY2 ....103 E2
Fowey Cl *WALM/CURD* B76 ......78 C4
Fowey Rd *BKDE/SHDE* B34 ....112 B5
Fowgay Dr *SOLH* B91 ....181 F4
Fowler Cl
  DUNHL/THL/PER WV6 ....20 C4
  SMTHWK B66 ....106 C1
Fowler Rd *MGN/WHC* B75 ....65 G3
Fowler St *BKHL/PFLD* WV2 ....52 A2
  VAUX/NECH B7 ....109 H4
Fowlmere Rd
  PBAR/PBCH B42 ....74 B3
Foxbury Dr *DOR/KN* B93 ....197 E5
Fox Cl *MGN/WHC* B75 ....63 F1
Foxcote Av *HDSW* B21 ....107 G3
Foxcote Cl *SHLY* B90 ....180 D5
Foxcote Dr *SHLY* B90 ....180 D5
Foxcote La *HAG/WOL* DY9 .....137 G4
Fox Covert *STRBR* DY8 ....135 E2
Fox Crs *SPARK* B11 * 145 F5
Foxdale Dr *BRLYHL* DY5 ....118 D1
Foxdale Gv *STECH* B33 ....131 E2
Foxfield Dr *STRBR* DY8 ....135 G4
Fox Foot Dr *BRLYHL* DY5 ....101 E5
Foxford Cl *CBROM* B36 ....95 F5
  CSCFLD/WYGN B72 ....77 G4
Foxglove Cl *ACGN* B27 ....163 F1
  BLOX/PEL WS3 ....18 A2
  WNSFLD WV11 ....25 C5
Foxglove Crs
  CHWD/FDBR/MGN B37 ......131 C1
Foxglove Rd *DUDN* DY1 ....83 H2
Foxglove Wy
  ERDW/GRVHL B23 ....75 H4
  HDSW B21 ....107 F2
Fox Green Crs *ACGN* B27 ....146 A5
Fox Gv *ACGN* B27 ....146 A5
Fox Hi *SLYOAK* B29 ....159 E2
Fox Hill Cl *SLYOAK* B29 ....159 E2
Fox Hill Rd *MGN/WHC* B75 ....48 C3
Foxhills Pk *DUDS* DY2 ....102 C5
Foxhills Rd
  ETTPK/GDPK/PENN WV4 ......50 C5
  STRBR DY8 ....117 H5
Foxhollies Dr *HALE* B63 ....138 A3
Fox Hollies Rd *ACGN* B27 .....146 B4
  WALM/CURD B76 ....78 B3
Fox Hollow
  DUNHL/THL/PER WV6 ....35 G3
Fox Hollow Cl *RBRY* B45 ....188 C1
Foxhope Cl *HWK/WKHTH* B38 .177 F4
Foxhunt Rd *HALE* B63 ....138 A5
Foxland Av *RBRY* B45 ....188 C1
Foxland Cl
  CHWD/FDBR/MGN B37 ......132 D2
  SHLY B90 ....194 D4
Foxlands Av
  ETTPK/GDPK/PENN WV4 ......50 D5

Foxlands Crs
  ETTPK/GDPK/PENN WV4 ......50 C5
Foxlands Dr *CSCFLD/WYGN* B72.77 H4
  ETTPK/GDPK/PENN WV4 ......50 C5
  SEDG DY3 ....83 F1
Foxlea Rd *HALE* B63 ....154 D1
Foxley Dr *SOLH* B91 ....166 B5
Foxmeadow Cl *SEDG* DY3 ....67 G4
Foxoak St *CDYHTH* B64 ....120 C3
Fox's La *WOLV* WV1 ....23 F5
Fox St *DIG/EDG* B5 ....3 J5
  DUDN DY1 ....68 C5
Foxton Rd *WASH/WDE* B8 .....110 D4
Fox Wk *ALDR* WS9 ....19 H4
Foxwell Gv *BORD* B9 ....129 F2
Foxwell Rd *BORD* B9 ....129 F2
Foxwood Av *GTB/HAM* B43 ....149 F5
Foxwood Gv
  CHWD/FDBR/MGN B37 ......113 H4
Foxwood Rd
  CHWD/FDBR/MGN B37 ......113 H4
Foxyards Cl *TPTN/OCK* DY4 .....84 D1
Foxyards Rd *TPTN/OCK* DY4 ....84 D1
Foyle Rd *HWK/WKHTH* B38 ....176 D4
Fozen Cr *BILS/COS* WV14 ....68 D1
Fradley Cl *BVILLE* B30 ....176 B1
Framefield Dr *SOLH* B91 ....182 A2
Framlingham Gv
  DUNHL/THL/PER WV6 ....35 E2
Frampton Cl *BVILLE* B30 ....159 F3
  CHWD/FDBR/MGN B37 ......132 D1
Frampton Wy *GTB/HAM* B43 ..159 H4
Frances Dr *BLOX/PEL* WS3 ......16 D4
Frances Rd *BVILLE* B30 ....160 A5
  ERDW/GRVHL B23 ....92 B3
  LOZ/NWT B19 ....108 C1
Franchise Gdns
  DARL/WED WS10 ....55 H2
Franchise St *DARL/WED* WS10 ..55 H3
  PBAR/PBCH B42 ....91 E4
Francis Cl *FOAKS/STRLY* B74 ...44 C5
  KGSWFD DY6 ....99 H1
Francis Rd *LDYWD/EDGR* B16 .109 G5
  SMTHWKW B67 ....105 H4
  STECH B33 ....129 H1
  STRBR DY8 ....135 G2
Francis Sharp Cl *VAUX/NECH* B7.109 C5
  WBROM B70 ....87 H5
  WOLV WV1 ....37 E1
Francis St *NFLD/LBR* B31 ......189 G1
Francis Ward Cl
  HHTH/SAND B71 ....71 E3
Frankburn Rd
  FOAKS/STRLY B74 ....45 E5
Frank Fisher Wy *WBROM* B70 ...87 H4
Frankfort St *LOZ/NWT* B19 ....108 D4
Frankholmes Dr *SHLY* B90 .....195 G2
Frankley Av *RMSLY* B62 ....139 H2
Frankley Beeches Rd
  NFLD/LBR B31 ....174 D2
Frankley Gn *RIDG/WDGT* B32 .156 B5
Frankley Green La
  RIDG/WDGT B32 ....156 D5
Frankley Hill La
  RIDG/WDGT B32 ....157 G4
Frankley Lodge Rd
  NFLD/LBR B31 ....174 D1
Frankley Rd *LGLYGN/QTN* B68 .123 G4
Frankley Ter *HRBN* B17 * 141 H2
Franklin St *LOZ/NWT* B19 ......108 B2
Franklin St *WSNGN* B18 ....107 H2
Franklin Wy *BVILLE* B30 ....159 H5
Frank Rd *SMTHWKW* B67 ......106 A4
Frank St *BHTH/HG* B12 ....127 F5
Franks Wy *STECH* B33 ....130 A2
Frank Tommey Cl
  BLKHTH/ROWR B65 * 122 A3
Frankton Cl *HIA/OLT* B92 .....147 H5
Frankton Gv *BORD* B9 ....129 E2
Fraser Rd *SPARK* B11 ....145 E2
Fraser St *BILS/COS* WV14 ....54 A2
Frayne Av *KGSWFD* DY6 ....99 G2
Freasley Cl *SHLY* B90 ....180 D2
Freasley Rd *BKDE/SHDE* B34 .113 F4
Freda Rd *WBROM* B70 ....87 H5
Fredas Gv *HRBN* B17 ....141 G3
Frederick Rd *AST/WIT* B6 ......109 F1
  EDG B15 ....125 H3
  ERDW/GRVHL B23 ....92 B4
  LGLYGN/QTN B68 ....123 H5
  SCFLD/BOLD B73 ....77 E1
  SLYOAK B29 ....142 B5
  SPARK B11 ....145 E3
  STECH B33 ....129 H1
  WNSFLD WV11 ....25 E4
Fredericks Cl *STRBR* DY8 ....135 E5
Frederick St *BKHL/PFLD* WV2 ....7 F7
  LOZ/NWT B19 ....2 D1
  WBROM B70 ....87 G2
  WSLW WS2 ....4 B4
Frederick William St
  WLNHL WV13 ....39 H3
Fred Smith Cl *DARL/WED* WS10.56 B3
Freeland Gv *KGSWFD* DY6 ....100 B5
Freeman Dr *WALM/CURD* B76 ..63 F4
Freeman Pl *BILS/COS* WV14 .....39 E5
Freeman Rd *DARL/WED* WS10 ..56 D3
  VAUX/NECH B7 ....109 H4
Freeman St *DIG/EDG* B5 ....3 H5
  WOLVN WV10 ....23 H4
Fremantle Dr
  BKDE/SHDE B34 ....113 G3
Freer Rd *AST/WIT* B6 ....108 D1
Freer St *WSL* WS1 ....4 E3
Freeth Rd *BRWNH* WS8 ....9 G3
Freeth St *LDYWD/EDGR* B16 ...125 H2
  OLDBY B69 ....104 D1
Freezeland St *BILS/COS* WV14 ..53 H2
Fremont Dr *DUDN* DY1 ....83 G3
French Rd *DUDS* DY2 ....103 E1
Frensham Cl
  CHWD/FDBR/MGN B37 ......132 C2
Frensham Wy *HRBN* B17 ....142 A1
Frenshaw Gv *KGSTG* B44 ....75 F3
Freshwater Dr *BRLYHL* DY5 ...118 D5

Friardale Cl *DARL/WED* WS10 ..56 D5
Friar Park Rd *DARL/WED* WS10.56 D5
Friars Cl *STRBR* DY8 ....117 G1
Friars Gorse *KINVER* DY7 ......117 G5
Friar St *DARL/WED* WS10 ....56 D5
Friary Av *SHLY* B90 ....195 G2
Friary Crs *RUSH/SHEL* WS4 .....29 E4
Friary Dr *FOAKS/STRLY* B74 ....46 D2
Friary Gdns *HDSW* B21 ....89 F4
Friary Rd *BFLD/HDSWWD* B20..89 F4
Friday La *HIA/OLT* B92 ....183 H1
Friesland Dr *WOLV* WV1 ....38 B2
Frieze Av *WSLW* WS2 ....41 F5
Friezeland La *BRWNH* WS8 ......19 G2
Friezland Wy *BRWNH* WS8 ......19 G2
Frinton Gv *HDSW* B21 ....107 E2
Friston Av *LDYWD/EDGR* B16 ...2 A7
Frodesley Rd
  LGN/SDN/BHAMAIR B26 ....130 D4
Froggatt Rd *BILS/COS* WV14 ....53 H1
Froggatts Ride
  WALM/CURD B76 ....63 F5
Frogmill Rd *RBRY* B45 ....174 B3
Frome Dr *WNSFLD* WV11 ....24 C5
Frome Wy
  ALE/KHTH/YWD B14 ....160 D4
Frost St *BKHL/PFLD* WV2 ....7 J7
Froxmere Cl *SOLH* B91 ....181 H5
Froyle Cl *DUNHL/THL/PER* WV6..21 G5
Froysell St *WLNHL* WV13 ....39 H3
Fryer Rd *NFLD/LBR* B31 ....189 H1
Fryers Cl *BLOX/PEL* WS3 ....27 F1
Fryers Rd *WSL* WS2 ....28 B1
Fryer St *WOLV* WV1 ....7 G3
Fuchsia Dr *COVEN* WV9 ....11 H4
Fugelmere Cl *HRBN* B17 ....124 D5
Fulbrook Gv *SLYOAK* B29 ......158 B2
Fulbrook Rd *DUDN* DY1 ....84 A5
Fulford Cl *HLYWD* B47 ....192 B4
Fulford Dr *WALM/CURD* B76 ....94 D1
Fulford Gv
  LGN/SDN/BHAMAIR B26 ....130 D4
Fulford Hall Rd *HOCK/TIA* B94.193 F5
Fulham Rd *SPARK* B11 ....144 D2
Fullbrook Cl *DSYBK/YTR* WS5 ..57 E5
Fullelove Rd *BRWNH* WS8 ....19 H2
Fullerton Cl *CDSL* WV8 ....22 A1
Fullwood Crs *DUDS* DY2 ....84 B5
Fullwoods End *BILS/COS* WV14..68 A3
Fulmer Wk *WSNGN* B18 * 126 A1
Fulwell Gv *KGSTG* B44 ....75 G3
Fulwell Ms
  CHWD/FDBR/MGN B37 ......132 B4
Fulwood Av *RMSLY* B62 ....122 B3
Furber Pl *KGSWFD* DY6 ....100 B3
Furlong La *HALE* B63 ....137 G1
Furlong Meadow
  NFLD/LBR B31 ....176 A3
Furlongs Rd *SEDG* DY3 ....67 F5
The Furlongs *STRBR* DY8 ......135 H4
  WNSFLD WV11 ....24 B5
The Furlong *DARL/WED* WS10 ..55 F2
Furnace Hl *HALE* B63 ....138 D1
Furnace La *HALE* B63 ....138 C1
Furnace La *HALE* B63 ....138 D2
Furnace Pde *TPTN/OCK* DY4 ...85 E1
Furnace Rd *DUDS* DY2 ....102 C1
Furness Cl *BLOX/PEL* WS3 ......16 B4
Furst St *BRWNH* WS8 ....19 E1
Furzebank Wy *SHHTH* WV12 ...40 D2
Furze Wy *DSYBK/YTR* WS5 ....43 F5

The Gables *ERDE/BCHGN* B24 ..93 H2
  WNSFLD WV11 ....15 E3
Gaddesby Rd
  ALE/KHTH/YWD B14 ....161 F2
Gadds Dr *BLKHTH/ROWR* B65 .104 B5
Gadsby Av *WNSFLD* WV11 ....25 D3
Gads Gn *DUDS* DY2 ....102 D4
Gads Green Crs *DUDS* DY2 ....103 E5
Gads La *DUDN* DY1 ....84 C5
  WBROM B70 ....87 E3
Gadwall Cft *ERDW/GRVHL* B23 .91 H3
Gail Av *ALDR* WS9 ....19 H3
Gailey Cft *KGSTG* B44 ....60 A5
Gailey Pk *WOLVN* WV10 ....12 C1
Gail Pk *BDMR/CCFT* WV3 ....50 C5
Gainford Cl *CDSL* WV8 ....8 A5
Gainford Rd *KGSTG* B44 ....76 A2
Gainsborough Crs
  DOR/KN B93 ....197 G2
  GTB/HAM B43 ....59 H4
Gainsborough Dr
  DUNHL/THL/PER WV6 ....34 D1
Gainsborough Hl *STRBR* DY8 ..135 G4
Gainsborough Pl *DUDN* DY1 ....83 G3
Gainsborough Rd
  PBAR/PBCH B42 ....74 B5
Gairloch Rd *SHHTH* WV12 ....25 H1
Gaitskell Ter *OLDBY* B69 ....86 B4
Gaitswell Wy *SMTHWK* B66 ...106 B2
Galahad Wy *DARL/WED* WS10 ..71 E1
Galbraith Cl *BILS/COS* WV14 ....68 C2
Galena Wy *AST/WIT* B6 ....109 E3
Gale Wk *BLKHTH/ROWR* B65 ..103 F4
Gallery Sq *WSLW* WS2 ....4 D3
Galloway Av *BKDE/SHDE* B34 .112 B5
Galton Cl *ERDE/BCHGN* B24 ....94 D2
  TPTN/OCK DY4 ....70 A5
Galton Dr *DUDS* DY2 ....102 B3
  GTB/HAM B43 ....59 H3
Galton Rd *SMTHWKW* B67 ....124 D3
Galtons La *HAG/WOL* DY9 .....185 E1
Gamesfield Gn
  BDMR/CCFT WV3 ....36 B4
Gammage St *DUDS* DY2 ....102 B1
Gandy Rd *SHHTH* WV12 ....25 G4
Gannah Farm Cl
  WALM/CURD B76 ....63 F5
Gannow Green La *RBRY* B45 ..173 E4
Gannow Manor Crs *RBRY* B45 .173 G4

Gannow Manor Gdns
  RBRY B45 ....173 H4
Gannow Rd *RBRY* B45 ....187 G1
Gannow Wk *RBRY* B45 ....187 G1
Garden Cl *DOR/KN* B93 ....196 D2
Garden Ct *BLOX/PEL* WS3 ....16 C3
  RBRY B45 ....174 A3
  WASH/WDE B8 ....111 E4
Garden Crs *BLOX/PEL* WS3 .....17 H4
Garden Cft *ALDR* WS9 ....30 C5
Gardeners Wy *WMBN* WV5 ......80 C2
Garden Gv *BFLD/HDSWWD* B20.73 G5
The Gardens
  CSCFLD/WYGN B72 ....77 F3
  RBRY B45 ....92 C3
Garden St *WSLW* WS2 ....4 D1
Garden Wk *BILS/COS* WV14 .....54 B2
  SEDG DY3 ....83 E4
Garfield Rd
  LGN/SDN/BHAMAIR B26 ....130 D4
Garland Crs *RMSLY* B62 ....122 C4
The Garlands *WNSFLD* WV11 ...24 C3
Garland St *BORD* B9 ....128 A1
Garland Wy *NFLD/LBR* B31 ...175 H1
Garman Cl *GTB/HAM* B43 ....73 C1
Garner Cl *BILS/COS* WV14 ....53 H5
Garnet Av *GTB/HAM* B43 ....73 C4
Garnett Dr *MGN/WHC* B75 ......63 E2
Garrard Gdns *SCFLD/BOLD* B73.62 A3
Garrat St *BRLYHL* DY5 ....101 G4
Garratt Cl *LGLYGN/QTN* B68 ..105 C5
Garratt's La *CDYHTH* B64 ......121 F2
Garratt Cl *KGSWFD* DY6 ....81 H5
Garretts Green La
  LGN/SDN/BHAMAIR B26 ....130 C5
Garrick Cl *DUDN* DY1 ....83 H5
Garrick St *WOLV* WV1 * 7 G5
Garrington St *DARL/WED* WS10.55 F1
Garrison Circ *CBHAMNE* B4 ...127 G2
Garrison La *BORD* B9 ....127 H2
Garrison St *BORD* B9 ....127 H2
The Garth *ALE/KHTH/YWD* B14.179 F1
Garway Gv *YDLY* B25 ....146 B1
Garwood Rd
  LGN/SDN/BHAMAIR B26 ....130 B2
Gas St *CBHAMW* B1 ....2 C6
Gatacre St *SEDG* DY3 ....83 F3
Gatcombe Cl *WOLVN* WV10 .....13 F3
Gatcombe Rd *DUDN* DY1 ....83 G4
Gatehouse Fold *DUDS* DY2 * ...84 D5
Gate La *DOR/KN* B93 ....196 A5
  SCFLD/BOLD B73 ....76 D1
Gateley Rd *LGLYGN/QTN* B68 .123 H5
Gate St *DUDS* DY2 ....85 G5
  TPTN/OCK DY4 ....70 A5
  WASH/WDE B8 ....110 B4
Gatis St *DUNHL/THL/PER* WV6 ..36 C1
Gatwick Rd *CVALE* B35 ....94 D2
Gauden Rd *HAG/WOL* DY9 .....153 F1
Gavin Wy *AST/WIT* B6 ....93 H4
Gawne La *CDYHTH* B64 ....103 E5
Gaydon Cl
  DUNHL/THL/PER WV6 ....20 C5
Gaydon Gv *SLYOAK* B29 ....141 G5
Gaydon Pl *SCFLD/BOLD* B73 ...62 A4
Gaydon Rd *ALDR* WS9 ....44 A1
  HIA/OLT B92 ....148 B4
Gayfield Av *BRLYHL* DY5 ....119 F4
Gay Hill La *HWK/WKHTH* B38 ..177 F5
Gayhurst Dr *YDLY* B25 ....130 A4
Gayle Gv *ACGN* B27 ....163 G2
Gayton Rd *HHTH/SAND* B71 ....71 H5
Geach St *LOZ/NWT* B19 ....109 E5
Gedney Cl *SHLY* B90 ....179 E2
Geeson Cl *CVALE* B35 ....94 D2
Gee St *LOZ/NWT* B19 ....108 D3
Geneva Rd *TPTN/OCK* DY4 ......84 D2
Genge Av
  ETTPK/GDPK/PENN WV4 ......52 C4
Genners Ap *NFLD/LBR* B31 ....157 H2
Genners La *NFLD/LBR* B31 .....157 H3
Genthorn Cl
  ETTPK/GDPK/PENN WV4 ......52 C5
Gentian Cl *NFLD/LBR* B31 .....158 B4
Geoffrey Cl *WALM/CURD* B76 ..78 D4
Geoffrey Pl *SPARK* B11 * 145 E4
Geoffrey Rd *SPARK* B11 * 145 E4
George Arthur Rd
  WASH/WDE B8 ....110 B5
George Av *BLKHTH/ROWR* B65.122 D2
George Bird Cl *SMTHWK* B66 * .106 C5
George Cl *DUDS* DY2 ....103 E1
George Frederick Rd
  SCFLD/BOLD B73 ....60 C4
George Henry Rd
  TPTN/OCK DY4 ....70 C4
George Rd *CSHL/WTROR* B46 ..126 B4
  EDG B15 ....126 B4
  ERDW/GRVHL B23 ....92 A3
  HALE B63 ....138 B3
  LGLYGN/QTN B68 ....123 H5
  SCFLD/BOLD B73 ....76 B2
  SLYOAK B29 ....143 G3
  SOLH B91 ....182 A2
  TPTN/OCK DY4 ....68 D5
George Rose Gdns
  DARL/WED WS10 * 56 A3
George St *BHTH/HG* B12 ....144 B2
  BHTH/HG B12 ....7 F6
  BKHL/PFLD WV2 * 7 F6
  CBHAMW B1 ....2 C4
  DUDN DY1 ....68 B5
  HDSW B21 ....107 E1
  LOZ/NWT B19 ....108 B2
  WBROM B70 ....87 G3
  WLNHL WV13 ....39 G1
  WSL WS1 ....4 D3
George St West *WSNGN* B18 ..108 A5
Georgina Av *BILS/COS* WV14 ...53 H5
Geraldine Rd *YDLY* B25 ....129 G4
Gerald Rd *STRBR* DY8 ....118 A5
Geranium Gv *BORD* B9 ....129 E1
Geranium Rd *DUDS* DY2 ....103 E4
Gerardsfield Rd *STECH* B33 ...131 F1
Germander Dr *DSYBK/YTR* WS5.57 G5
Gerrard Cl *LOZ/NWT* B19 ....108 C3
Gerrard Rd *WLNHL* WV13 ....39 E4
Gerrard St *LOZ/NWT* B19 ......108 C3

Gervase Dr DUDN DY1 ....84 C3
Geston Rd DUDN DY1 ....101 H1
Gibbet La KINVER DY7 ....134 A3
Gibbins Rd SLYOAK B29 ....159 E1
Gibbons Dr
   DUNHL/THL/PER WV6 ....36 A1
Gibbons Hill Dr SEDG DY3 ....67 F1
Gibbons Rd
   DUNHL/THL/PER WV6 ....36 B1
   MGN/WHC B75 ....47 F2
Gibbs Hill Rd NFLD/LBR B31 ....189 H1
Gibbs Rd HAG/WOL DY9 ....137 E2
Gibbs St DUNHL/THL/PER WV6 ....36 C1
Gibb St BORD B9 ....3 K7
Gibson Dr BFLD/HDSWWD B20 ....108 B1
Gibson Rd
   BFLD/HDSWWD B20 ....108 B1
   DUNHL/THL/PER WV6 ....34 C2
Gideon Cl YDLY B25 ....146 D1
Gideons Cl SEDG DY3 ....83 F1
Giffard Rd WOLV WV1 ....53 F1
   WOLVN WV10 ....14 C5
Giggetty La WMBN WV5 ....64 C5
Gigmill Wy STRBR DY8 ....135 E3
Gilbanks Rd SLYOAK B29 ....117 H5
Gilberry Cl DOR/KN B93 ....197 E3
Gilbert Av OLDBY B69 ....103 H2
Gilbert Cl WNSFLD WV11 ....25 G3
Gilbert La WMBN WV5 ....65 F4
Gilbert Rd SMTHWK B66 ....106 C5
Gilbertstone Av
   LGN/SDN/BHAMAIR B26 ....147 E2
Gilbeys Cl STRBR DY8 ....118 A3
Gilby Rd LDYWD/EDGR B16 ....126 A3
Gilchrist Dr EDG B15 ....125 G2
Gildas Av HWK/WKHTH B38 ....177 E4
Giles Cl HIA/OLT DY2 ....165 H3
   STETCH B33 ....130 A1
Giles Rd LGLYGN/QTN B68 ....105 F4
Gildown Pl EDG D15 ....126 B5
Gillespie Cft AST/WIT B6 ....109 F2
Gillhurst Rd HRBN B17 ....124 D5
Gilling Gv BKDE/SHDE B34 ....112 C3
Gillingham Cl DARL/WED WS10 ....56 C4
Gillity Av DSYBK/YTR WS5 ....57 G3
Gillity Cl DSYBK/YTR WS5 ....42 D5
Gilliver Rd SHLY B90 ....180 B3
Gillman Cl
   LGN/SDN/BHAMAIR B26 ....148 B3
Gillott Cl SOLH B91 ....182 C2
Gillott Rd LDYWD/EDGR B16 ....125 F2
Gillows Cft SHLY B90 ....195 C1
Gillscroft Rd STETCH B33 ....111 G5
Gilt St DUDS DY2 ....121 E1
   WBROM B70 ....87 C5
Gilmorton Cl HRBN B17 ....124 D5
   SOLH B91 ....182 A4
Gilpin Cl WASH/WDE B8 ....111 C3
Gilpin Crs BLOX/PEL WS3 ....18 A3
Gilson Dr CSHL/WTROR B46 ....114 D1
Gilson Rd CSHL/WTROR B46 ....115 E1
Gilson St TPTN/OCK DY4 ....70 A3
Gilson Wy
   CHWD/FDBR/MGN B37 ....114 A4
Gilwell Rd BKDE/SHDE B34 ....113 C3
Gimble Wk HRBN B17 ....124 B4
Gipsy La ERDW/CRVHL B23 ....91 H1
   WLNHL WV13 ....39 H4
Gisborn Cl SMHTH B10 * 127 H4
Gladeside Cl RUSH/SHEL WS4 ....29 E2
The Glades ALDR WS9 ....30 E3
The Glade SHLY B90 ....22 A1
   FOAKS/STRLY B74 ....136 C2
   HAG/WOL DY9 ....136 C2
   LGN/SDN/BHAMAIR B26 ....148 C4
Gladstone Dr OLDBY B69 ....86 A3
Gladstone Gv KGSWFD DY6 ....99 H1
Gladstone Rd DOR/KN B93 ....199 E1
   ERDW/CRVHL B23 ....92 B3
   LGN/SDN/BHAMAIR B26 ....148 C4
   SPARK B11 ....144 D1
   STRBR DY8 ....134 D1
Gladstone St AST/WIT B6 ....109 G1
   DARL/WED WS10 ....55 G2
   HHTH/SAND B71 ....55 F2
   WSLW WS2 ....41 H1
Gladys Rd SMTHWKW B67 * 124 B2
   YDLY B25 ....129 F5
Gladys Ter SMTHWKW B67 * 124 C2
Glaisdale Gdns
   DUNHL/THL/PER WV6 ....22 C5
Glaisdale Rd HLGN/YWD B28 ....163 E2
Glaisedale Gv WLNHL WV13 ....40 A3
Glaisher Dr WOLVN WV10 ....12 A1
Glamis Rd SHHTH WV12 ....25 H5
Glanville Dr MGN/WHC B75 ....47 E1
Glasbury Cft HWK/WKHTH B38 ....190 C1
Glascote Cl SHLY B90 ....180 A2
Glascote Gv BKDE/SHDE B34 ....113 E3
Glaslyn Av BLKHTH/ROWR B65 ....121 H2
Glassford Dr
   DUNHL/THL/PER WV6 ....22 A4
Glasshouse Hl STRBR DY8 ....135 H4
Glastonbury Crs BLOX/PEL WS3 ....16 A5
Glastonbury Rd
   ALE/KHTH/YWD B14 ....162 A5
   HHTH/SAND B71 ....71 H3
Glaston Dr SOLH B91 ....181 G4
Gleads Cft WMSLY B62 ....140 A4
Gleave Rd SCFLD/BOLD B73 ....76 D5
Glebe Farm Rd
   BKDE/SHDE B34 ....112 C4
Glebefields Rd TPTN/OCK DY4 ....69 G2
Glebeland Cl LDYWD/EDGR B16 * 2 A7
Glebe La STRBR DY8 ....118 A3
Glebe Pl DARL/WED WS10 ....54 D2
Glebe Rd SOLH B91 ....165 F5
   WLNHL WV13 ....39 F5
Glebe St WSL WS1 ....4 D6
The Glebe HAG/WOL DY9 ....184 C2
Glenavon Rd
   ALE/KHTH/YWD B14 ....178 C2
Glen Cl RUSH/SHEL WS4 ....42 C2
Glencoe Rd LDYWD/EDGR B16 ....107 E5
Glen Ct BDMR/CCFT WV3 ....36 A3
   CDSL WV8 ....10 C3

Glencroft Rd HIA/OLT B92 ....148 B4
Glendale Cl BDMR/CCFT WV3 ....35 G5
   HALE B63 ....138 D3
Glendale Dr STETCH B33 ....130 B1
   WMBN WV5 ....65 E5
Glendene Crs
   HWK/WKHTH B38 ....190 A1
Glen Devon Cl RBRY B45 ....174 A3
Glendon Rd ERDW/CRVHL B23 ....76 B5
Glendon Wy DOR/KN B93 ....196 C5
Glendower Rd HRBN B17 ....124 A5
   PBAR/PBCH B42 ....90 C1
Gleneagles Dr GTB/HAM B43 ....58 C5
   MGN/WHC B75 ....62 C1
   OLDBY B69 ....103 G2
Gleneagles Rd BLOX/PEL WS3 ....16 B4
   DUNHL/THL/PER WV6 ....20 B5
   LGN/SDN/BHAMAIR B26 ....130 C4
Glenelg Dr STRBR DY8 ....135 H5
Glenelg Ms DSYBK/YTR WS5 ....58 B3
Glenfern Rd BILS/COS WV14 ....68 A3
Glenfield CDSL WV8 ....11 C5
Glenfield Cl SOLH B91 ....182 B3
   WALM/CURD B76 ....63 E5
Glenfield Gv SLYOAK B29 ....160 A1
Glengarry Cl RIDG/WDGT B32 ....157 F3
Glengarry Gdns
   BDMR/CCFT WV3 ....36 B4
Glenhill Dr HWK/WKHTH B38 ....177 E5
Glenhurst Cl WSLW WS2 ....40 B2
Glenmead Rd KGSTG B44 ....74 D3
Glenmore Cl BDMR/CCFT WV3 ....51 E1
Glenmore Dr HWK/WKHTH B38 ....176 B4
Glen Park Rd SEDG DY3 ....83 F4
Glenpark Rd WASH/WDE B8 ....110 C4
Glen Ri MOS/BIL B13 ....162 A4
Glen Rd SEDG DY3 ....67 G3
   STRBR DY8 ....135 F4
Glenroyd HWK/WKHTH B38 ....190 C1
Glen Side HAG/WOL DY9 ....140 D5
Glenside Av HIA/OLT B92 ....147 H4
Glenthorne Rd
   ERDE/BCHGN B24 ....93 E4
Glentworth WALM/CURD B76 ....78 C1
Glentworth Gdns
   DUNHL/THL/PER WV6 ....22 D5
Glenville Dr ERDW/CRVHL B23 ....92 C1
Glenwood Cl BRLYHL DY5 ....119 F4
Glenwood Dr SHLY B90 ....194 D4
Glenwood Rd
   HWK/WKHTH B38 ....176 B5
Globe St DARL/WED WS10 ....70 D2
Gloucester Pl WLNHL WV13 ....40 B3
Gloucester Rd DARL/WED WS10 ....56 C5
   DUDS DY2 ....120 D2
Gloucester St
   CHWD/FDBR/MGN B37 ....132 A3
Glover Cl HLGN/YWD B28 ....162 D4
Glover Rd MGN/WHC B75 ....63 F5
Glovers Cft
   CHWD/FDBR/MGN B37 ....131 H1
Glovers Field Dr
   VAUX/NECH B7 ....110 A2
Glovers Rd SMHTH B10 ....128 A4
Glover St BORD B9 ....127 G2
   WBROM B70 ....87 H5
Glyme Dr DUNHL/THL/PER WV6 ....22 A5
Glyn Av BILS/COS WV14 ....54 D5
Glyn Dr BILS/COS WV14 ....54 D5
Glyn Farm Rd RIDG/WDGT B32 ....140 C1
Glynn Crs HALE B63 ....120 B5
Glynne Av KGSWFD DY6 ....99 H5
Glyn Rd RIDG/WDGT B32 ....140 C1
Glynside Av RIDG/WDGT B32 ....140 C2
Goffs Cl RIDG/WDGT B32 ....141 F4
Goldborough Cl
   BILS/COS WV14 ....53 H5
Goldby Dr DARL/WED WS10 ....57 H2
Goldcrest Cl DUDS DY2 ....120 D2
Goldcrest Cft CBROM B36 ....114 A1
Goldencrest Dr OLDBY B69 ....104 C1
Golden Cft
   BFLD/HDSWWD B20 ....89 H5
Goldencross Wy BRLYHL DY5 ....118 D3
Golden End Dr DOR/KN B93 ....197 H2
Golden Hillock Rd DUDS DY2 ....120 C1
   SMHTH B10 ....128 B5
   SPARK B11 ....145 F2
Goldfinch Cl BVILLE B30 ....159 F2
Goldfinch Rd HAG/WOL DY9 * 136 A4
Goldicroft Rd DARL/WED WS10 ....56 A4
Goldieslie Cl SCFLD/BOLD B73 ....77 F1
Goldieslie Rd SCFLD/BOLD B73 ....77 F1
Golds Hill Gdns HDSW B21 ....107 H2
Golds Hill Rd HDSW B21 ....107 H2
Golds Hill Wy TPTN/OCK DY4 ....70 B4
Goldsmith Rd
   ALE/KHTH/YWD B14 ....161 F2
   BLOX/PEL WS3 ....28 A2
Goldstar Wy STETCH B33 ....131 E2
Goldthorn Av
   ETTPK/GDPK/PENN WV4 ....51 H3
Goldthorn Crs
   ETTPK/GDPK/PENN WV4 ....51 H3
Goldthorne Av
   LGN/SDN/BHAMAIR B26 ....148 A3
Goldthorne Wk BRLYHL DY5 ....119 F4
Goldthorn Hl BKHL/PFLD WV2 ....51 H2
Goldthorn Rd BKHL/PFLD WV2 ....51 H2
Golf La BILS/COS WV14 ....53 H1
Golson Cl MGN/WHC B75 ....63 E2
Gomeldon Av
   ALE/KHTH/YWD B14 ....178 B2
Gomer St West WLNHL WV13 ....39 G3
Gomer St WLNHL WV13 ....39 G3
Gooch St South DIG/EDG B5 ....127 F3
Gooch St North DIG/EDG B5 ....127 E4
Goodall Gv CTB/HAM B43 ....60 A3
Goodall St WSL WS1 ....5 F4
Goodby Rd MOS/BIL B13 ....143 H4
Goode Av WNSGN B18 ....108 A4
Goode Cl LGLYGN/QTN B68 ....105 G5
Goodeve Wk MGN/WHC B75 ....63 H5
Goodison Gdns
   ERDE/BCHGN B24 ....93 F1
Goodman Cl HLGN/YWD B28 ....162 D4
Goodman St CBHAMW B1 ....2 A4

Goodrest Av RMSLY B62 ....140 A2
Goodrest Cft
   ALE/KHTH/YWD B14 ....179 E1
Goodrest La ALE/KHTH/YWD B38 ....190 D2
Goodrich Av
   DUNHL/THL/PER WV6 ....35 G2
Goodrich Covert
   ALE/KHTH/YWD B14 ....177 G3
Goodrick Wy VAUX/NECH B7 * 109 H3
Goodway Ct CBHAMNE B4 ....3 G2
Goodway Rd HIA/OLT DY2 ....148 C4
   KGSTG B44 ....75 E3
Goodwood Cl CBROM B36 ....111 H1
Goodwood Dr
   FOAKS/STRLY B74 ....60 B2
Goodyear Av WOLVN WV10 ....23 C3
Goodyear Rd SMTHWKW B67 ....123 H2
Goosemoor La
   ERDW/CRVHL B23 ....76 D4
Gopsal St CBHAMNE B4 ....127 G1
Gorcott La SHLY B90 ....194 A3
Gordon Av
   ETTPK/GDPK/PENN WV4 ....52 D5
   HHTH/SAND B71 ....71 G3
   LOZ/NWT B19 ....108 D2
Gordon Cl SMTHWK B66 ....107 E5
Gordon Crs BRLYHL DY5 ....101 G4
Gordon Dr TPTN/OCK DY4 ....86 A1
Gordon Pl BILS/COS WV14 ....53 G5
Gordon Rd HRBN B17 ....142 B1
   LOZ/NWT B19 ....108 C1
Gordon St BKHL/PFLD WV2 ....7 H5
   BORD B9 ....127 H2
   DARL/WED WS10 ....55 F2
Gorey Cl SHHTH WV12 ....25 H2
Gorge Rd SEDG DY3 ....67 G3
Gorleston Gv
   ALE/KHTH/YWD B14 ....178 D3
Gorleston Rd
   ALE/KHTH/YWD B14 ....178 D3
Gorsebrook Rd
   DUNHL/THL/PER WV6 ....22 D5
   WOLVN WV10 ....23 E5
Gorse Cl
   CHWD/FDBR/MGN B37 ....131 H2
   SLYOAK B29 ....158 C2
Gorse Farm Rd GTB/HAM B43 ....73 G3
Gorsefield Rd BKDE/SHDE B34 ....113 E4
Gorse Green La HAG/WOL DY9 ....171 F5
Gorsemoor Wy WNSFLD WV11 ....15 H4
Gorse Rd DUDN DY1 ....84 A2
   WNSFLD WV11 ....25 G2
Gorsey Wy ALDR WS9 ....29 G5
Gorsly Piece RIDG/WDGT B32 ....140 C3
Gorstie Cft GTB/HAM B43 ....73 E2
Gorsty Av BRLYHL DY5 ....101 E5
Gorsty Cl HHTH/SAND B71 ....72 B3
Gorsty Hayes CDSL WV8 ....10 B4
Gorsty Rd RMSLY B62 ....121 H4
Gorsymead Gv NFLD/LBR B31 ....174 C3
Gorsy Rd RIDG/WDGT B32 ....140 D1
Gorway Cl WSL WS1 ....57 F1
Gorway Gdns WSL WS1 ....57 G1
Gorway Rd WSL WS1 ....57 G1
Goscote Cl BLOX/PEL WS3 ....28 B3
Goscote La BLOX/PEL WS3 ....28 B2
Goscote Lodge Crs
   BLOX/PEL WS3 ....28 C3
Goscote Pl BLOX/PEL WS3 ....28 C2
Goscote Rd BLOX/PEL WS3 ....28 B2
Gosford St SBTH/HG B12 ....144 B1
Gospel End Rd SEDG DY3 ....66 C3
Gospel End St SEDG DY3 ....67 F4
Gospel La ACGN B27 ....163 H2
Gospel Oak Rd TPTN/OCK DY4 ....69 H2
Gosport Cl WOLV WV1 ....53 F1
Goss Cft SLYOAK B29 ....159 F1
Gossey La STETCH B33 ....131 E2
The Goss BRLYHL DY5 ....118 C4
Gotham Rd
   LGN/SDN/BHAMAIR B26 ....147 E1
Gothersley La KINVER DY7 ....116 B2
Goths Cl BLKHTH/ROWR B65 ....104 A5
Gough Av WNSFLD WV11 ....24 C5
Gough Dr TPTN/OCK DY4 ....86 A1
Gough Rd BILS/COS WV14 ....68 C2
   EDG B15 ....126 C5
   SPARK B11 ....145 F2
Gough St CBHAMW B1 ....2 E7
   WLNHL WV13 ....40 A3
   WOLV WV1 ....7 J4
Gould Firm La ALDR WS9 ....31 E4
Gowan Rd WASH/WDE B8 ....110 C5
Gower Av KGSWFD DY6 ....100 D5
Gower Rd RMSLY B62 ....139 C1
   SEDG DY3 ....66 D2
Gower St BKHL/PFLD WV2 ....7 J7
   LOZ/NWT B19 ....108 D2
   WLNHL WV13 ....39 G3
   WSLW WS2 ....28 D1
Gozzard St BILS/COS WV14 ....54 A3

Grainger's La CDYHTH B64 ....120 C4
Grainger St DUDS DY2 ....102 D2
Graiselely Ct BDMR/CCFT WV3 ....6 D5
Graiseley Hl BDMR/CCFT WV3 ....6 D7
   BKHL/PFLD WV2 ....37 E5
Graiseley La WNSFLD WV11 ....24 C5
Graiseley Rw BKHL/PFLD WV2 ....37 E5
Graith Cl HLGN/YWD B28 ....179 G2
Grammar School La HALE B63 ....138 C3
Grampian Rd STRBR DY8 ....135 E1
Granary Cl KGSWFD DY6 ....99 E1
Granary La WALM/CURD B76 ....63 F5
Granary Rd CDSL WV8 ....22 A1
The Granary ALDR WS9 ....30 B4
Granbourne Rd SHHTH WV12 ....40 E1
Granby Av STETCH B33 ....131 E3
Granby Cl HIA/OLT B92 ....164 A3
Grandborough Dr SOLH B91 ....181 G4
Grand Cl SMTHWK B66 ....124 D1
Grand Junction Wy WSL WS1 ....56 D3
Grand Union Canal Wk
   ACGN B27 ....147 E4
   BDMR B7 ....A F2
   DOR/KN B93 ....197 H3
   SPARK B11 ....128 A3
   VAUX/NECH B7 ....3 K1
   WS1 ....146 A1
Grandys Cft
   CHWD/FDBR/MGN B37 ....131 H2
Grange Av ALDR WS9 ....30 A1
   MGN/WHC B75 ....48 B3
   WASH/WDE B8 ....111 F3
Grange Ct BDMR/CCFT WV3 ....6 D6
   HAG/WOL DY9 ....136 A4
   WSLW WS2 * 40 B3
Grange Crs HALE B63 ....138 D4
   RBRY B45 ....175 G5
   RUSH/SHEL WS4 ....28 D2
Grange Dr FOAKS/STRLY B74 ....45 F3
Grange Farm Dr
   HWK/WKHTH B38 ....176 B4
Grangefield Cl CDSL WV8 ....22 B1
Grange Hl RMSLY B62 ....139 E3
Grange Hill Rd
   HWK/WKHTH B38 ....176 C4
Grange La HAG/WOL DY9 ....136 B3
   KGSWFD DY6 ....100 D1
   MGN/WHC B75 ....47 C3
Grange Ri HWK/WKHTH B38 ....190 D1
Grange Rd
   ALE/KHTH/YWD B14 ....160 D2
   AST/WIT B6 ....109 E1
   BILS/COS WV14 ....51 H2
   CDYHTH B64 ....121 H4
   DOR/KN B93 ....198 C2
   DUDN DY1 ....84 B5
   DUNHL/THL/PER WV6 ....35 C1
   ERDE/BCHGN B24 ....93 F1
   HAG/WOL DY9 ....136 A3
   HALE B63 ....138 D4
   SLYOAK B29 ....158 D1
   SMHTH B10 ....128 B3
   SOLH B91 ....182 C2
   WBROM B70 ....87 F3
Grange St DUDN DY1 ....84 B5
   WSL WS1 ....57 F1
The Grange WMBN WV5 ....65 E4
Grangewood Ct HIA/OLT B92 * 164 A3
Granshaw Cl
   HWK/WKHTH B38 ....176 D4
Grant Cl HHTH/SAND B71 ....87 C1
   KGSWFD DY6 ....99 H1
Grantham Cl BRLYHL DY5 ....118 D5
Grantham Rd SMTHWK B66 ....124 D1
   SPARK B11 ....144 D1
Grantley Crs KGSWFD DY6 ....99 C2
Grantley Dr
   CHWD/FDBR/MGN B37 ....132 A2
Granton Cl
   ALE/KHTH/YWD B14 ....160 D5
Granton Rd
   ALE/KHTH/YWD B14 ....160 D5
Grantown Gv BLOX/PEL WS3 ....16 A5
Granville Cl BKHL/PFLD WV2 ....7 H7
Granville Rd CDYHTH B64 ....121 H4
   DOR/KN B93 ....199 E1
Granville Sq EDG B15 * 2 C7
Granville St BKHL/PFLD WV2 ....7 H7
   CBHAMW B1 ....2 D7
   WLNHL WV13 ....39 G2
   WOLV WV1 ....7 H7
Grasmere Av
   DUNHL/THL/PER WV6 ....34 D1
   FOAKS/STRLY B74 ....45 G2
Grasmere Cl
   DUNHL/THL/PER WV6 ....35 H1
   KGSWFD DY6 ....99 G4
   WNSFLD WV11 ....24 C5
Grasmere Rd HDSW B21 ....107 H2
Grasscroft Dr
   CHWD/FDBR/MGN B37 ....131 H3
Grassington Dr
   CHWD/FDBR/MGN B37 ....131 H3
Grassmere Dr STRBR DY8 ....135 F4
Grassmoor Rd
   HWK/WKHTH B38 ....176 C3
Grassy La WNSFLD WV11 ....24 B4
Gratidge Rd ACGN B27 ....146 D5
Gravel Hl WMBN WV5 ....65 G3
Gravelly Hl ERDE/BCHGN B24 ....92 C3
Gravelly Hill North
   ERDW/CRVHL B23 ....92 A3
Gravelly La ERDW/CRVHL B23 ....92 B3
Gravity Ms LGLYGN/QTN B68 ....123 G1
Grayfield Av MOS/BIL B13 ....144 B4
Grayland Cl ACGN B27 ....146 B5
Grayling Cl DARL/WED WS10 ....54 D5
Grayling Rd BRLYHL DY5 ....136 A1
Grayling Wk
   CHWD/FDBR/MGN B37 ....132 C2
   WOLVN WV10 ....38 B1
Grayshott Cl
   ERDW/CRVHL B23 ....92 C1
Grays Rd HRBN B17 ....142 B1

Gray St BORD B9 ....127 H2
Grayswood Park Rd
   RIDG/WDGT B32 ....140 C1
Grayswood Rd NFLD/LBR B31 ....189 F1
Grazebrook Cft
   RIDG/WDGT B32 ....157 H2
Grazebrook Rd DUDS DY2 ....102 C2
Greadier St SHHTH WV12 ....25 H3
Great Arthur St SMTHWK B66 ....106 B2
Great Barr St BORD B9 ....127 G2
Great Brickkiln St
   BDMR/CCFT WV3 ....6 C6
Great Br TPTN/OCK DY4 ....86 B1
Great Bridge Rd
   BILS/COS WV14 ....54 C4
Great Bridge St WBROM B70 ....86 D1
Great Brook St BRWNH WS8 ....9 F4
Great Charles Street Queensway
   CBHAMW WS1 ....2 E3
Great Colmore St EDG B15 ....126 B5
Great Cornbow HALE B63 ....138 D4
Great Farley Dr NFLD/LBR B31 ....174 D4
Great Francis St
   VAUX/NECH B7 ....109 H5
Great Hampton Rw
   LOZ/NWT B19 ....2 D1
Great Hampton St WOLV WV1 ....6 D1
   WSNGN B18 ....108 C4
Great King St LOZ/NWT B19 ....108 C4
Great King St North
   LOZ/NWT B19 ....108 C3
Great Lister St VAUX/NECH B7 ....3 K1
Great Meadow TPTN/OCK DY4 ....85 H1
Greatrex Dr HHTH/SAND B71 ....71 F3
Great Tindal St
   LDYWD/EDGR B16 ....126 A2
Great Western Ar CBHAM B2 ....3 G4
Great Western Rd WSNGN B18 ....107 G3
Great Western Dr
   CDYHTH B64 ....121 G3
Great Western St
   DARL/WED WS10 ....56 D5
   WOLV WV1 ....7 G2
Great Western Wy
   TPTN/OCK DY4 ....70 B5
Great Wood Rd BORD B9 ....128 A3
Greaves Av DSYBK/YTR WS5 ....43 E5
Greaves Cl WSL WS1 ....43 E5
Greaves Crs SHHTH WV12 ....26 A2
Greaves Rd DUDS DY2 ....102 D4
Greaves Sq HWK/WKHTH B38 ....177 F4
The Greaves WALM/CURD B76 ....79 H5
Grebe Cl ERDW/CRVHL B23 ....91 H3
Greenacre Dr CDSL WV8 ....10 C5
Greenacre Rd TPTN/OCK DY4 ....69 E2
Green Acres ACGN B27 ....146 B5
Greenacres
   DUNHL/THL/PER WV6 ....21 F5
Greenacres RIDG/WDGT B32 ....157 H1
   SEDG DY3 ....66 D2
   WALM/CURD B76 ....78 C3
Greenacres Av WOLVN WV10 ....24 D1
Greenacres Cl
   FOAKS/STRLY B74 ....45 E3
Greenacres Rd
   HWK/WKHTH B38 ....176 B5
Greenaleigh Rd
   ALE/KHTH/YWD B14 ....179 F2
Green Av HLGN/YWD B28 ....162 C1
Greenaway Ct GTB/HAM B43 ....59 C5
Green Bank Av
   HLGN/YWD B28 ....162 C1
Greenbank Gdns STRBR DY8 ....118 A2
Green Barns La LICHS WS14 ....33 C1
Greenbush Dr HALE B63 ....138 C3
Green Cl HLYWD B47 ....192 C5
Green Ct HLGN/YWD B28 ....162 D1
Greencroft BILS/COS WV14 ....53 H2
Green Cft BORD B9 ....129 E1
Greencroft KGSWFD DY6 ....99 G5
Green Dr RIDG/WDGT B32 ....157 G1
   WOLVN WV10 ....38 B2
Greenend Rd MOS/BIL B13 ....144 B5
Greenes Ri DUDS DY2 ....103 F1
Greenfield Av CDYHTH B64 ....120 D3
   STRBR DY8 ....135 F2
Greenfield Crs EDG B15 ....126 A5
Greenfield La WOLVN WV10 ....12 D2
Greenfield Rd GTB/HAM B43 ....73 E2
   HRBN B17 ....142 A2
   SMTHWKW B67 ....106 A5
Greenfields ALDR WS9 ....30 A3
   RUSH/SHEL WS4 ....28 C3
   WMBN WV5 ....81 E1
Greenfields Rd KGSWFD DY6 ....100 B4
Greenfinch Rd CBROM B36 ....114 A2
   HAG/WOL DY9 ....136 B4
Greenford Rd
   ALE/KHTH/YWD B14 ....178 D2
Green Gables
   FOAKS/STRLY B74 * 62 B1
   HLYWD B47 ....192 C1
Green Gables Dr HLYWD B47 * 192 C1
Greenhill WMBN WV5 ....65 F5
Greenhill Cl SHHTH WV12 ....25 H5
Greenhill Dr SLYOAK B29 ....159 E1
Greenhill Gdns CTB/HAM B43 ....75 F1
   RMSLY B62 ....139 F1
   WMBN WV5 ....81 F1
Greenhill Rd
   CSCFLD/WYGN B72 ....77 F3
   HDSW B21 ....89 F4
   MOS/BIL B13 ....161 F1
   RMSLY B62 ....122 B5
   SEDG DY3 ....83 C1
Greenhill WK WSL WS1 ....5 F5
Greenhill WY ALDR WS9 ....30 E1
Green Hill Wy SHLY B90 ....163 F5
Greenholm Rd KGSTG B44 ....75 E4
Greening Dr EDG B15 ....126 B5
Greenland Cl KGSWFD DY6 ....100 A1
Greenland Ri HIA/OLT B92 ....165 F3
Greenland Rd SLYOAK B29 ....160 B1
Greenlands WMBN WV5 ....64 D4

Greenlands Rd
 CHWD/FDBR/MGN B37....132 C2
Green La ALDR WS9............31 E5
 BLOX/PEL WS3.............18 A3
 BLOX/PEL WS3.............27 G4
 BORD D9.....................128 A3
 BRWNH WS8..................9 G2
 CBROM B36..................113 C1
 CSHL/WTROR B46.........115 C4
 DUDN DY1....................83 H1
 DUNHL/THL/PER WV6....22 A3
 GTB/HAM B43................73 H4
 HAG/WOL DY9...............136 B2
 HDSW B21....................107 E1
 HWK/WKHTH B38...........176 C5
 KGSWFD DY6.................99 H2
 RIDG/WDGT B32............140 C1
 RMSLY B62...................122 B3
 RUSH/SHEL WS4............18 D4
 SHLY B90......................179 G4
 WSLW WS1....................4 C2
Green Lanes BILS/COS WV14....53 C1
 SCFLD/BOLD B73..........77 F4
Greenleas Gdns HALE B63....139 E4
Green Leigh ERDW/GRVHL B23....76 D3
Greenleighs SEDG DY3....5 H2
Greenly Rd
 ETTPK/GDPK/PENN WV4....52 B3
Green Meadow DSYBK/YTR WS5....57 G4
 WNSFLD WV11................24 D5
Green Meadow CI WMBN WV5....64 C5
Green Meadow Rd
 SHHTH WV12...................25 H5
 SLYOAK B29....................132 A1
Greenoak Crs BILS/COS WV14....68 A5
 BVILLE B30......................160 C2
Green Oak Rd CDSL WV8....10 D5
Greenock Crs
 ETTPK/GDPK/PENN WV4....52 D3
Green Park Av BILS/COS WV14....38 B5
Green Park Dr BILS/COS WV14....38 C5
Green Park Rd DUDS DY2....85 F5
 NFLD B31........................175 E3
Greenridge Rd
 BFLD/HDSWWD B20........89 G1
Green Rd DUDS DY2........102 D2
 MOS/BIL S13...................88 A5
Green Rock La BLOX/PEL WS5....27 H1
Greenroyde HAG/WOL DY9....152 D1
Greensand Dr BILS/COS WV14....68 C1
Greensforge La KINVER DY7....116 B4
Greenside HRBN B17........142 A2
Greenside Rd
 ERDE/BCHGN B24...........93 G1
Greenside Av TPTN/OCK DY4....69 H5
Greenslade Crs FOAKS/STRLY B74....46 D5
Greenslade Rd DSYBK/YTR WS5....58 A1
 SEDG DY3.......................66 D1
 SHLY B90.......................179 F5
Greensleeves FOAKS/STRLY B74....46 D5
Greenstead Rd BILS/COS B13....162 B1
The Greens
 DUNHL/THL/PER WV6 *....34 C2
Green St BHTH/HG B12......127 F3
 BILS/COS WV14..............68 C3
 OLDBY B69.....................105 E2
 STRBR DY8.....................135 F2
 WBROM B70....................106 A1
Greensway WNSFLD WV11....24 B2
The Green ALDR WS9........30 C4
 BLOX/PEL WS5................27 F1
 CBROM B36....................112 D2
 CSCFLD/WYGN B72..........77 H2
 DARL/WED WS10.............55 F1
 HWK/WKHTH B38...........176 D3
 LGLYGN/QTN B68............123 F2
 NFLD/LBR B31................174 C3
 RIDG/WDGT B32.............140 A1
 SOLH B91.......................181 H4
 STRBR DY8.....................117 H2
Greenvale NFLD/LBR B31....158 C5
Greenvale Av
 LGN/SDN/BHAMAIR B26....148 B1
Green Wk HRBN B17.........19 H5
 BFLD/HDSWWD B20........73 H5
 SEDG DY5.......................5 H3
Greenway Av STRBR DY8....118 A3
Greenway Dr SCFLD/BOLD B73....61 E5
Greenway Gdns
 HWK/WKHTH B38...........190 C1
 SEDG DY5.......................5 H2
Greenways Rd BILS/COS WV14....54 A4
Greenways HALE B63........137 G2
 NFLD/LBR B31.................158 B2
 STRBR DY8......................117 G3
Greenway St B. BORD B9....128 A3
The Greenway
 CHWD/FDBR/MGN B37....149 E1
 HAG/WOL DY9.................152 B5
 SCFLD/BOLD B73............60 D5
Greenwood YDLY S25.......129 H4
Greenwood Av ACGN B27....146 A5
 BLKHTH/ROWR B65.........105 F2
 LGLYGN/QTN B68............105 F4
Greenwood Ct
 ALE/KHTH/YWD B14........161 G5
Greenwood Pk ALDR WS9....30 C1
Greenwood Pl KGSTG B44....75 H2
Greenwood Rd ALDR WS9....29 H3
 HHTH/SAND B71..............71 F3
 WOLVN WV10..................23 E3
The Greenwoods STRBR DY8....135 E2
Greethurst Dr MOS/BIL B13....145 E5
Greets Green Rd WBROM B70....86 D2
Greetville CI STETCH B33....112 C4
Gregory Av SLYOAK B29....158 C2
Gregory CI DARL/WED WS10....70 D1
Gregory Dr DUDN DY1.......84 A4
Gregory Rd STRBR DY8.....134 C2
Grendon Dr SCFLD/BOLD B73....61 H5
Grendon Gdns
 BDMR/CCFT WV3.............50 D2
Grendon Rd
 ALE/KHTH/YWD B14........178 C2
 HIA/OLT B92....................164 A2
Grenfell Dr EDG B15.........125 H4
Grenfell Rd BLOX/PEL WS3....17 F4

Grenville CI WSLW WS2......40 B2
Grenville Dr ERDW/GRVHL B23....91 H5
 SMTHWK B66..................105 H1
Grenville PI WBROM B70....86 C3
Gresham Rd DUDN DY1.....83 G5
 SHLY B90........................180 B5
Gresham Rd ALE/KHTH/YWD B28....162 D4
 LGLYGN/QTN B68............105 F3
Gresley CI FOAKS/STRLY B74....47 E1
Gressel La STETCH B33......131 E1
Crestone Av
 BFLD/HDSWWD B20........89 G3
Greswolde Dr
 ERDE/BCHGN B24............93 F2
Greswolde Park Rd ACGN B27....146 B4
Greswolde Rd SOLH B91.....164 A4
 SPARK B11......................145 G4
Greswold Gdns
 BKDE/SHDE B34..............112 C4
Greswold Rd HHTH/SAND B71....87 G1
Gretton Crs ALDR WS9......29 H5
Gretton Rd ALDR WS9.......29 H5
 ERDW/GRVHL B23...........76 B4
Greville Dr EDG B15..........143 G1
Grevis CI MOS/BIL B13.......144 B5
Grevis Rd YDLY S25...........130 A5
Greyfort Crs HIA/OLT B92....164 B1
Greyfriars CI DUDN DY1......83 H3
Greyfriars Dr SOLH B91......163 H5
Greyhound La STRBR DY8....134 C5
Greyhurst Cft SOLH B91......181 H5
Grey Mill CI SHLY B90.........195 F2
Greystoke Av CBROM B36....111 H2
Greystoke Dr KGSWFD DY6....99 H5
Greystone Pas DUDN DY1....84 C5
Greystone St DUDN DY1......84 C5
Grey Tree Crs DOR/KN B93....196 C5
Grice St WBROM B70..........105 G1
Griffen La SHLY B90...........194 A4
Griffin CI NFLD/LBR B31......158 D4
Griffin Gdns HRBN B17.......142 B3
Griffin Rd ERDW/GRVHL B23....92 A1
Griffins Brook CI BVILLE B50....159 E4
Griffins Brook La BVILLE B50....159 E4
Griffin St DUDS DY2...........102 C5
 WBROM B70....................37 H4
Griffiths Dr WMBN WV5......81 E1
 WNSFLD WV11.................25 F2
Griffiths Rd DUDN DY1.......68 A5
 HHTH/SAND B71..............71 G3
 SHHTH WV12...................26 B2
Grigg La NFLD/LBR B31......176 B3
Grimley Rd NFLD/LBR B31....176 B3
Grimpits La HWK/WKHTH B38....191 E1
Grimshaw Rd HLGN/YWD B28....163 E1
Grimstock Hi
 CSHL/WTROR B46 *.........115 E1
Grimstone St WOLVN WV10....17 H2
Grindleford Rd
 PBAR/PBCH B42...............89 G4
Gristhorpe Rd SLYOAK B29....160 A2
Grizedale CI RBRY B45.......174 B3
Grocott Rd DARL/WED WS10....54 D4
Grosmont Av BHTH/HG B12....127 H3
Grosvenor Av
 BFLD/HDSWWD B20........90 C4
 FOAKS/STRLY B74...........47 G4
 WOLVN WV10...................12 D5
Grosvenor Crs WOLVN WV10....12 D5
Grosvenor Pk
 ETTPK/GDPK/PENN WV4....51 F3
Grosvenor Rd AST/WIT B6....90 C4
 BFLD/HDSWWD B20........90 C4
 ETTPK/GDPK/PENN WV4....52 C5
 HRBN B17.......................141 G1
 LGLYGN/QTN B68............105 E5
 SOLH B91........................83 F4
 WOLVN WV10...................12 D5
Grosvenor Sq HLGN/YWD B28....162 C5
Grosvenor St EDG B5.........3 J4
 WOLVN WV10....................37 H2
Grosvenor St West EDG B15....2 A7
Grosvenor Wy BRLYHL DY5....119 F5
Grotto La
 DUNHL/THL/PER WV6.......22 A5
Groucutt St BILS/COS WV14....68 C3
Grounds Dr FOAKS/STRLY B74....46 D2
Grounds Rd FOAKS/STRLY B74....46 D2
Grout St WBROM B70.........86 C2
Grove Av HALE B63............138 B4
 MOS/BIL B13....................107 H1
 SLYOAK B29 *..................159 G1
 SOLH B91.........................165 E5
Grove Cottage Rd BORD B9....128 B2
Grove Ct PBAR/PBCH B42 *....73 H5
Grove Crs BLOX/PEL WS3....17 H4
 BRLYHL DY5.....................101 E4
Grove Farm Dr MGN/WHC B75....63 F3
Grove Gdns HDSW B21.......89 H4
Grove Hill DSYBK/YTR WS5....43 G5
Grove Hill Rd HDSW B21......89 H5
Grove House WSL WS1 *......5 F5
Grovelands Crs WOLVN WV10....12 D4
Grove La BFLD/HDSWWD B20....90 D5
 DUNHL/THL/PER WV6.......35 F3
 HRBN B17........................142 A4
 SMTHWK B66...................104 D1
 WALM/CURD B76..............79 H1
Groveley La NFLD/LBR B31....189 F2
 RBRY B45.........................188 C4
Grove Ms NFLD/LBR B31......175 H5
Grove Pk KGSWFD DY6........99 G5
Grove Rd ALE/KHTH/YWD B14....160 D3
 DOR/KN B93.....................197 F5
 HAG/WOL DY9..................136 D3
 LGLYGN/QTN B68.............105 E4
 SOLH B91.........................165 E4
 SPARK B11.......................145 E4
Groveside Wy BLOX/PEL WS3....18 A2
Grove St DUDS DY2............103 E1
 SEDG DY5.........................66 D4
 SMTHWK B66...................107 H5
 WSNGN B18......................107 F5
Grove Ter WSL WS1............5 F5
The Grove BLKHTH/ROWR B65....122 A2
 BILS/COS WV14.................119 E3

 CSHL/WTROR B46.............115 G5
 SHLY B90..........................57 H5
 ETTPK/GDPK/PENN WV4....52 C3
 FOAKS/STRLY B74.............32 B5
 GTB/HAM B43...................167 C2
 SOLH/EDGR B16 *.............125 H2
 NFLD/LBR B31..................175 H5
 RBRY B45.........................188 D4
 WASH/WDE B8..................110 A5
 WNSFLD WV11..................24 B4
Grove Vale Av GTB/HAM B43....73 E2
Grove Wy FOAKS/STRLY B74....60 B1
Grovewood Dr
 HWK/WKHTH B38............176 C4
Guardian Ct NFLD/LBR B31....174 D2
 SOLH B91..........................182 B2
Guardians Wy NFLD/LBR B31....158 A2
Guernsey Dr CBROM B36.....114 B3
Guest Av WNSFLD WV11......12 C3
Guest Gv LOZ/NWT B19.......108 C3
Guild Av BLOX/PEL WS3.......27 H3
Guild CI LDYWD/EDGR B16....126 A2
Guild Cft LOZ/NWT B19.......108 D3
Guildford Cft
 CHWD/FDBR/MGN B37....131 H4
Guildford Dr LOZ/NWT B19....108 C3
Guildford St LOZ/NWT B19....108 C3
Guild Rd ERDE/BCHGN B24....93 H2
Guillane CI NFLD/LBR B31....158 A2
Gullswood CI
 ALE/KHTH/YWD B14........177 H3
Gumbleberrys CI
 BLKHTH/ROWR B65.........122 A4
 OLDBY B69......................104 D2
Gunmakers Wk LOZ/NWT B19....108 D2
Gunner Gv MGN/WHC B75....63 G2
Gunner La RBRY B45..........187 F1
Gunns Wy HIA/OLT B92.......163 H3
Gunstone La CDSL WV8.......10 B2
Gunter Rd ERDE/BCHGN B24....94 A3
Gurnard CI SHHTH WV12......25 G4
Gurney PI WSLW WS2.........27 E5
Gurney Rd WSLW WS2........27 E5
Guthrie CI LOZ/NWT B19......108 D3
Guthrum CI
 DUNHL/THL/PER WV6.......20 D5
The Gutter HAG/WOL DY9....186 A1
Guy Av WOLVN WV10...........24 A1
Guys Cliffe Av WALM/CURD B76....78 D2
Guys La SEDG DY3.............82 D4
Gwalia Gv ERDW/GRVHL B23 *....92 D2
Gwendoline Wy ALDR WS9....19 H5
Gypsy La CSHL/WTROR B46....96 D4

H

Habberley Rd
 BLKHTH/ROWR B65.........122 B2
Habberley Cft SOLH B91.....181 H4
Hackett CI BILS/COS WV14....67 H2
Hackett Dr SMTHWK B66......105 H2
Hackett Rd
 BLKHTH/ROWR B65.........122 C1
Hackett St TPTN/OCK DY4....70 A4
Hackford Rd
 ETTPK/GDPK/PENN WV4....69 C2
Hackman's Gate La
 HAG/WOL DY9..................169 C5
Hack St B. BORD B9...........127 G3
Hackwood Rd DARL/WED WS10....71 F1
Hadcroft Gra HAG/WOL DY9....136 A3
Hadcroft Rd HAG/WOL DY9....136 A3
Haddock Rd BILS/COS WV14....53 G1
Haddon Crs SHHTH WV12....26 A1
Haddon Rd KGSTG B44.......75 G5
 PBAR/PBCH B42...............74 A2
Haden Circ BHTH/HG B12....127 F5
Haden CI CDYHTH B64........121 G5
 STRBR DY8......................117 H2
Haden Crs WNSFLD WV11....25 F4
Haden Cross Dr CDYHTH B64....121 G5
Hadendale CDYHTH B64.....121 G5
Haden Hill BDMR/CCFT WV3 *....6 A4
Haden Hill Rd CDYHTH B64....121 G5
 HALE B63.........................138 D1
Haden Park Rd CDYHTH B64....121 E2
Haden Rd CDYHTH B64.......121 G2
 TPTN/OCK DY4.................69 G2
Haden St BHTH/HG B12......144 B1
Haden Wy BHTH/HG B12......144 B1
Hadfield CI ERDE/BCHGN B24....94 A3
Hadfield Cft LOZ/NWT B19....108 C4
Hadfield Wy
 CHWD/FDBR/MGN B37....114 A5
Hadland Rd B. STETCH B33....130 D3
Hadleigh Cft
 WALM/CURD B76.............78 C5
Hadley CI DUDS DY2..........103 E5
 HLYWD B47......................192 C5
Hadley Cft SMTHWK B66.....106 C2
Hadley PI BILS/COS WV14....53 G1
Hadley Rd BILS/COS WV14....53 G1
 WSLW WS2.......................26 C4
Hadleys CI LGLYGN/QTN B68....105 F5
Hadlow Cft STETCH B33......131 F5
Hadrian Dr CSHL/WTROR B46....97 F1
Hadyn Gv
 LGN/SDN/BHAMAIR B26....147 H1
Hadzor Rd LGLYGN/QTN B68....123 H4
Hafren CI RBRY B45...........174 B3
Hafton Gv BORD B9...........128 B3
Haggar St BHL/PFLD WV2....52 A2
Hagley Cswy HAG/WOL DY9....153 E4
Hagley Gra HAG/WOL DY9....153 F3
Hagley Hall HALE B63 *......138 D4
Hagley Park Dr RBRY B45....188 A5
Hagley Rd HAG/WOL DY9....153 E2
 HALE B63.........................125 E3
 HRBN B17.........................125 E5
 STRBR DY8........................135 H4
 WSNGN B18.......................107 H5
Hagley Rd West HRBN B17....124 C2
 RIDG/WDGT B32...............140 B1
 RMSLY B62........................124 A1
Hagley View Rd DUDS DY2....102 C3

Hagley Vis BHTH/HG B12 *....144 D3
Hagley Wood La RMSLY B62....154 B4
Haig CI MGN/WHC B75........62 C1
Haig Rd DUDS DY2.............85 F5
Haig St HHTH/SAND B71......87 G1
Hailes Park CI
 ETTPK/GDPK/PENN WV4....52 B2
Hailsham Rd ERDW/GRVHL B23....92 D1
Hailstone CI
 BLKHTH/ROWR B65.........103 C3
Haines CI TPTN/OCK DY4....85 H2
Haines St WBROM B70........87 H4
Hainfield Dr SOLH B91........165 C5
Hainge Rd OLDBY B69........86 C5
Hainult CI STRBR DY8.........99 H5
Halas Ct CDYHTH B64.........121 E2
Halberton St WSNGN B18....107 F5
Haldon Gv NFLD/LBR B31....189 E1
Hale Ct WSL WS1 *............5 H6
Halecroft Av WNSFLD WV11....24 C5
Hale Gv ERDE/BCHGN B24....93 H2
Hales Crs SMTHWK B67......124 A1
Halesbury Ct HALE B63 *.....138 C4
Halescroft Sq NFLD/LBR B31....158 A4
Hales Gdns ERDW/GRVHL B23....76 A5
Hales La SMTHWK B67........106 B5
Halesmere Wy HALE B63.....139 E4
Halesowen Rd BRGRVW B61....186 D5
 CDYHTH B64.....................102 C4
 DUDS DY2........................102 C4
 RMSLY B62.......................139 G1
Halesowen St
 BLKHTH/ROWR B65.........122 A4
 OLDBY B69.......................104 D2
Hales Rd DARL/WED WS10....56 A4
 HALE B63.........................138 C3
Halesway HALE B63............104 D2
Halesworth Rd COVEN WV9....11 H5
Halewood Gv HAG/WOL DY9....163 E5
Haley St SHHTH WV12.........26 A5
Halfcot Av HAG/WOL DY9....136 A4
Halford Crs BLOX/PEL WS3....28 B5
Halford Gv ERDE/BCHGN B24....94 A2
Halford Rd SOLH B91..........164 B4
Halfords La HHTH/SAND B71....88 C5
 SMTHWK B66....................106 C2
Halfway CI KGSTG B44........75 E5
Halifax Gv NFLD/LBR B31....158 A1
Halifax Rd SHLY B90...........180 B5
Haliscombe Gv AST/WIT B6....109 E1
Hackett Gld STETCH B33....129 H1
Halladale HWK/WKHTH B38....176 D4
Hallam CI HHTH/SAND B71....88 A2
Hallam Crs WOLVN WV10....23 C4
Hallam Dr HHTH/SAND B71....87 H1
Hallam St BHTH/HG B12......144 A2
 HHTH/SAND B71...............87 H2
Hallbridge Wy STRBR DY8....117 H5
Hallbrook... OLDBY B69....85 H4
Hallchurch Rd DUDS DY2....101 H2
Hallcroft CI AST/WIT B6......90 C2
Hallcroft Gd CSCFLD/WYGN B72....77 G4
Hallcroft Wy ALDR WS9......30 C2
Hall Dale CI HLGN/YWD B28....162 D5
Hall Dr CHWD/FDBR/MGN B37....132 A5
 HAG/WOL DY9..................153 F4
Hall End DARL/WED WS10....55 F5
Hallens Dr DARL/WED WS10....55 F5
Hallet Dr BDMR/CCFT WV3....6 D6
Hallewell Rd
 LDYWD/EDGR B16............125 F2
Hall Green Rd HHTH/SAND B71....71 H2
Hallgreen St BILS/COS WV14....54 A5
Hall Gv BILS/COS WV14.......19 E5
Hall Hays Rd BKDE/SHDE B34....113 G2
Hall La ALDR WS9..............19 E5
 BILS/COS WV14................17 H4
 BLOX/PEL WS5.................54 A5
 HAG/WOL DY9..................153 F4
 TPTN/OCK DY4.................69 H5
Hall Meadow HAG/WOL DY9....153 F3
Hallmoor Rd STETCH B33....130 D1
Hallot CI ERDW/GRVHL B23....76 B3
Halloughton Rd
 FOAKS/STRLY B74.............62 A1
Hall Park St BILS/COS WV14....53 G1
Hall Rd BFLD/HDSWWD B20....108 A2
 CBROM B36.......................112 C1
 SMTHWK B67....................110 B5
 SWSNGN B18....................106 D5
Halstead Rd MOS/BIL B13....161 H5
Hall St BILS/COS WV14........54 A3
 CDYHTH B64.....................121 F2
 DUDN DY1........................84 C5
 LGLYGN/QTN B68.............105 F4
 SEDG DY3........................67 F3
 STRBR DY8.......................135 G4
 TPTN/OCK DY4.................85 E1
 WOLVN WV10....................37 G1
 WSL WS1...........................5 H4
 WSLW WS1.......................89 H4
 WNSFLD WV11..................24 D1
 WSLW WS2 *.....................41 H2
Hall St East DARL/WED WS10....55 F1
Hall St South WBROM B70....87 E5
Hallswelle Gv GTB/HAM B43....60 A4
Halton Rd SCFLD/BOLD B73....61 H5
Halton St DUDS DY2...........102 C4
Hamar Wy
 CHWD/FDBR/MGN B37....132 B4
Hamberley Ct WSNGN B18....106 D5
Hamble CI BRLYHL DY5.......100 C3
 CBROM B36.......................113 H1
Hamble Gv
 DUNHL/THL/PER WV6.......34 C1
Hamble Rd ETTPK/GDPK/PENN WV4....52 C2
 GTB/HAM B43...................73 H2
Hambleton Rd HALE B63....137 H5
Hambletts Rd WBROM B70....87 E3
Hambrook CI
 DUNHL/THL/PER WV6.......22 C5

Hambury Dr
 ALE/KHTH/YWD B14........160 D3
 RMSLY B62........................139 E4
 STRBR DY8........................134 D1
Hamilton Av HRBN B17.......124 C4
Hamilton CI SEDG DY3.......67 E3
 STRBR DY8........................117 G2
Hamilton Dr OLDBY B69......86 A4
 SLYOAK B29......................159 F2
 STRBR DY8........................117 G2
Hamilton Gdns WOLVN WV10....13 F4
Hamilton Rd HDSW B21......107 F1
 SMTHWKW B67................124 A2
 TPTN/OCK DY4.................70 A5
Hamilton St BLOX/PEL WS3....27 G1
Ham La HAG/WOL DY9........136 A5
 KGSWFD DY6....................82 A5
Hamlet Gdns HLGN/YWD B28....162 D3
Hammer Bank HALE B63.....120 A4
Hammersley CI HALE B63....120 C5
Hammond Av WOLVN WV10....23 C2
Hammond Dr
 ERDW/GRVHL B23............92 D1
Hammond Wy STRBR DY8....118 C5
Hampden CI BRLYHL DY5....120 A4
Hampden Retreat
 BHTH/HG B12...................144 A1
Hampshire Dr EDG B15.......125 C4
Hampshire Rd HHTH/SAND B71....71 E2
Hampson CI SPARK B11......144 C1
Hampstead CI WNSFLD WV11....24 D1
Hampstead Gld HALE B65....139 E4
Hampton CI SCFLD/BOLD B73....76 A1
Hampton Ct WNSFLD WV10 *....13 F5
Hampton Court Rd HRBN B17....141 G1
Hampton Dr FOAKS/STRLY B74....47 F1
Hampton Gdns HAG/WOL DY9....136 A4
Hampton Gv BLOX/PEL WS3....17 H5
Hampton La SOLH B91........182 C1
Hampton Ms AST/WIT B6....108 D1
 DOR/KN B93.....................196 ..
Hampton Rd ERDW/GRVHL B23....92 B2
 WOLVN WV10....................22 D1
Hampton St BILS/COS WV14....68 C3
 DOR/KN B93......................2 E1
 LOZ/NWT B19...................
Hams La CSHL/WTROR B46....97 F1
Hams Rd WASH/WDE B8.....110 B5
Hamstead CI WNSFLD WV11....24 D1
Hamstead Hall Av
 BFLD/HDSWWD B20........89 G2
Hamstead Hall Rd
 BFLD/HDSWWD B20........89 G2
Hamstead Hi
 BFLD/HDSWWD B20........89 H2
Hamstead Rd
 BFLD/HDSWWD B20........90 B5
 GTB/HAM B43....................73 E4
Hamstead Ter WALM/CURD B76 *...71 F1
Hanam CI MGN/WHC B75....63 F2
Hanbury CI HALE B63 *.......138 B5
Hanbury Crs
 ETTPK/GDPK/PENN WV4....51 E2
Hanbury Dr ACGN B27........147 E4
Hanbury Dr OLDBY B69.......104 B5
Hanbury Hi STRBR DY8........135 G3
Hanbury Rd BRWNH WS8....9 E2
 WBROM B70.......................87 E3
Hanch PI WSL WS1............5 G6
Hancock Rd WASH/WDE B8....110 D5
Hancox St LGLYGN/QTN B68....123 F2
Handley Gv NFLD/LBR B31....173 H1
Handley St DARL/WED WS10....56 A4
Handsworth New Rd
 HDSW B21........................107 F2
Handsworth Wood Rd
 BFLD/HDSWWD B20........89 H3
Hangar Rd
 LGN/SDN/BHAMAIR B26....149 E4
Hangleton Dr SPARK B11....145 F1
Hanley CI HALE B63............138 A3
Hanley St LOZ/NWT B19......3 F1
Hannafore Rd
 LDYWD/EDGR B16............125 F1
Hannah Rd BILS/COS WV14....54 C5
Hanney Hay Rd BNTWD WS7....9 H1
Hannon Rd
 ALE/KHTH/YWD B14........160 D5
Hanover Ct AST/WIT B6......109 E2
Hanover Ct
 DUNHL/THL/PER WV6.......35 G1
Hanover Dr ERDE/BCHGN B24....110 D1
Hanover Rd
 BLKHTH/ROWR B65.........104 B3
Hansell Dr DOR/KN B93......198 C5
Hansom Rd RIDG/WDGT B32....140 C2
Hanson Ct SMTHWK B66.....106 C2
Hanson Gv HIA/OLT B92......147 F2
Hanson's Bridge Rd
 ERDE/BCHGN B24............94 C2
Hanwell CI WALM/CURD B76....78 D4
Hanwood CI BHTH/HG B12....127 F4
Harald CI DUNHL/THL/PER WV6....20 C5
Harbeck Av KGSTG B44.......75 F3
Harberrow CI HAG/WOL DY9....152 C4
Harbet Dr BHAMNEC B40....150 A3
Harbinger Rd
 HWK/WKHTH B38.............177 F3
Harborne La SLYOAK B29....142 B5
Harborne Park Rd HRBN B17....142 A3
Harborne Rd EDG B15.........142 C1
 LGLYGN/QTN B68.............124 ..
Harborough Dr ALDR WS9....30 A5
 CBROM B36........................95 F5
Harborough Wk
 HAG/WOL DY9...................135 H5
Harbours Hi HAG/WOL DY9....186 A2
Harbury CI WALM/CURD B76....78 D5
Harbury Rd BHTH/HG B12....143 H2
Harby CI
 CHWD/FDBR/MGN B37....132 B4
Harcourt Dr FOAKS/STRLY B74....46 C1
 SEDG DY3..........................83 F4
Harcourt Rd CDYHTH B64....121 F4
 DARL/WED WS10...............55 H4
 ERDW/GRVHL B23.............76 C5

Harden Cl BLOX/PEL WS3 ....28 A3
Harden Gv BLOX/PEL WS3 ....28 A3
Harden Manor Ct HALE B63 * 139 E4
Harden Rd BLOX/PEL WS3 ....27 H3
Harding St HALE B63 * 138 A2
Harding V HALE B63 * 68 D2
Hardon Rd
ETTPK/GDPK/PENN WV4 ....52 D5
Hardware St WBROM B70 ....87 H2
Hardwick Dr CDYHTH B64 ....125 E5
Hardwicke Wy HAG/WOL DY9 .....136 B2
Hardwick Rd FOAKS/STRLY B74....45 F5
LGN/SDN/BHAMAIR B26 ....147 E3
Hardy Rd BLOX/PEL WS3 ....28 A2
DARL/WED WS10 ....85 G1
Hardy Sq BKHL/PFLD WV2 * 52 D2
Harebell Cl DSYBK/YTR WS5..........57 G5
Harebell Crs DUDN DY1 ....84 A2
Harebell Gdns
HWK/WKHTH B38 ....176 D5
Hare Gv NFLD/LBR B31 ....174 D2
Hare St BILS/COS WV14.................53 G4
Harewell Dr MGN/WHC B75 ....47 G4
Harewood AV DARL/WED WS10 ...56 C5
GTB/HAM B43 ....75 F1
Harewood Cl HLGN/YWD B28 .....162 C5
Harford St WSNGN B18 ....2 D1
Hargate La WBROM B70 * 87 G2
Hargrave Ct CSHL/WTROR B46 ......96 B3
Hargrave Rd SHLY B90 ....179 F3
Hargreave Cl WALM/CURD B76......78 B4
Hargreaves St BKHL/PFLD WV2 ....53 E1
Harland Rd FOAKS/STRLY B74 ......47 F2
Harlech Cl DUDS DY2 ....85 G5
RIDG/WDGT B32 ....157 E4
Harlech Rd SHHTH WV12..............26 A4
Harlech Wy DUDN DY1 ....85 H5
Harlequin Dr MOS/BIL B13...........144 A5
Harleston Rd KGSTG B44 ....75 F3
Harley Cl BRWNH WS8 ....19 C1
Harley Dr BILS/COS WV14 ....42 C1
Harley Gra DUDS DY2 ....102 D1
Harlow Gv HLGN/YWD B28 ....163 E4
Harlstones Cl STRBR DY8 ....118 C5
Harlyn Cl BILS/COS WV14..............69 C1
Harman Rd ERDW/GRVHL B23.......77 F4
Harmer St WSNGN B18 ....108 A4
Harmon Rd STRBR DY8 ....134 C2
Harnall Cl SHLY B90 ....195 E1
Harness Cl DSYBK/YTR WS5 ....57 E4
Harold Rd LDYWD/EDGR B16 ......125 H5
SMTHWKW B67 ....124 A1
Harold Ter LOZ/NWT B19 * 108 C1
Harper Av WNSFLD WV11 ....24 C5
Harper Gv TPTN/OCK DY4 ....84 D1
Harper Rd BILS/COS WV14 ....53 H2
Harpers Rd
ALE/KHTH/YWD B14 ....178 C4
NFLD/LBR B31 ....175 C3
Harper St WLNHL WV13 ....39 G5
Harpur Cl RUSH/SHEL WS4 ....42 C1
Harpur Rd RUSH/SHEL WS4 ....42 C1
Harrier Rd ACGN B27 ....146 D5
Harriet Cl BRLYHL DY5.................100 D4
Harringay Dr STRBR DY8 ....135 E4
Harringay Rd KGSTG B44 ....75 F1
Harrington Cft
DUNHL/THL/PER WV6 ....72 B4
Harris Dr PBAR/PBCH B42 ....74 A3
SMTHWK B66 ....124 D1
Harrison Cl BLOX/PEL WS3 ....27 G1
Harrison Rd ERDE/BCHGN B24 .....92 D2
FOAKS/STRLY B74 ....46 C5
RUSH/SHEL WS4 ....18 C5
STRBR DY8..................................118 C3
Harrison's Fold DUDS DY2 ....102 C4
Harrisons Gn EDG B15.................142 C1
Harrisons Pleck MOS/BIL B13.....144 B4
Harrison's Rd EDG B15 ....142 C1
Harrison St BLOX/PEL WS3 ....27 G1
Harrold Av
BLKHTH/ROWR B65 ....122 C1
Harrold Rd
BLKHTH/ROWR B65 ....122 C1
Harrop Wy STRBR DY8 ....118 A4
Harrowby Dr TPTN/OCK DY4 ....85 C2
Harrowby Pl WLNHL WV13 ....40 A4
Harrowby Rd BILS/COS WV14 ....54 C4
WOLVN WV10 ....12 B4
Harrow Cl HAG/WOL DY9 ....152 C4
Harrowfield Rd STETCH B33 ....112 A5
Harrow Rd KGSWFD DY6 ....81 H5
SLYOAK B29 ....142 D4
Harrow St
DUNHL/THL/PER WV6....................36 D1
Harry Perks St WLNHL WV13 ....39 G2
Hart Dr SCFLD/BOLD B73...............77 E3
Hartfield Crs ACGN B27 ....163 E1
Hartford Cl HRBN B17 ....124 C5
Hartford Rd
ETTPK/GDPK/PENN WV4 ....50 D5
Hartill St WLNHL WV13 ....39 H5
Hartington Cl DOR/KN B93 ....196 C5
Hartington Rd LOZ/NWT B19 ....108 D1
Hartland AV BILS/COS WV14 ....64 A3
Hartland Rd HHTH/SAND B71 ....72 B4
NFLD/LBR B31 ....189 E2
TPTN/OCK DY4 ....84 D1
Hartland St BRLYHL DY5 ....101 F2
Hartlebury Cl DOR/KN B93 ....196 D5
Hartlebury Rd HALE B63 ....138 B5
OLDBY B69 ....104 B4
Hartledon Rd HRBN B17 ....141 H2
Hartlepool Rd VAUX/NECH B7.......91 F1
Hartley Dr ALDR WS9 ....48 B1
Hartley Gv KGSTG B44 ....60 D5
Hartley Pl EDG B15 ....125 H4
Hartley Rd KGSTG B44 ....60 C5
Harton Wy
ALE/KHTH/YWD B14 ....160 C5
Hartopp Rd FOAKS/STRLY B74 .....46 D5
WASH/WDE B8 ....110 C5
Hart Rd ERDE/BCHGN B24 ....93 G5
WNSFLD WV11 ....38 D1
Hartsbourne Dr RMSLY B62 ....139 F3
Harts Cl HRBN B17 ....142 B1
Harts Green Rd HRBN B17 ....141 G2
Hartshill Cl BKDE/SHDE B34 ....112 C3

Hartshill Rd ACGN B27 ....146 D5
BKDE/SHDE B34 ....112 C3
Hartshorn St BILS/COS WV14 ....53 H3
Hartside Cl HALE B63 ....137 G5
Harts Rd WASH/WDE B8 ....110 C4
Hart St WSL WV1............................4 E6
Hartswell Dr MOS/BIL B13 ....161 F4
Hartwell Cl SOLH B91 ....181 H4
Hartwell Rd ERDE/BCHGN B24 .....93 F4
Hartwood Crs
ETTPK/GDPK/PENN WV4 ....51 F4
Harvard Cl DUDN DY1 ....83 H2
Harvard Rd HIA/OLT B92 ....147 H5
Harvest Cl SEDG DY3....................66 D5
Harvest Ct BVILLE B30 ....145 F4
SEDG DY3......................................83 G1
Harvesters Cl ALDR WS9 ....45 E3
Harvesters Rd SHHTH WV12 ....12 B5
Harvester Wy KGSWFD DY6 ....99 E1
Harvest Fields Wy
MGN/WHC B75 ....47 H1
Harvest Rd
BLKHTH/ROWR B65 ....121 G1
SMTHWKW B67 ....123 H1
Harvey Ct STETCH B33 * 131 F1
Harvey Dr MGN/WHC B75 ....47 G2
Harvey Rd
LGN/SDN/BHAMAIR B26 ....129 H5
WSLW WS2 ....27 F5
Harvills Hawthorn WBROM B70....70 D4
Harvine Wk STRBR DY8 ....135 E4
Harvington Dr SHLY B90 ....195 H2
Harvington Rd BILS/COS WV14 .....68 B2
HALE B63 ....138 B5
LGLYGN/QTN B68 ....123 E4
SLYOAK B29 ....158 C2
Harwin Cl
DUNHL/THL/PER WV6...................22 B3
Harwood Gv SHLY B90 ....180 C5
Harwood St WBROM B70 ....87 F5
Hasbury Cl HALE B63 ....138 A5
Hasbury Rd RIDG/WDGT B32 .....157 E2
Haseley Rd HDSW B21 ....107 C2
SOLH B91 ....164 A4
Haseler Rd SCFLD/BOLD B73 ....76 C2
Haselour Rd
CHWD/FDBR/MGN B37 ....113 H4
Haselwell Rd BVILLE B30 ....177 H2
Haskell St WSL WV1 ....5 G1
Haslucks Cl SHLY B90 ....195 G1
Haslucks Cft SHLY B90 ....180 A2
Haslucks Green Rd SHLY B90 .....193 G1
Hassop Rd PBAR/PBCH B42 ....74 D4
Hastings Ct DUDN DY1 ....83 C4
Hastings Rd ERDW/GRVHL B23 .....75 H4
Haswell Rd HALE B63 ....137 H4
Hatcham Rd KGSTG B44 ....76 A1
Hatchett St LOZ/NWT B19 ....109 E4
Hatchford Av HIA/OLT B92 ....148 A4
Hatchford Brook Rd
HIA/OLT B92 ....148 A4
Hatch Heath Cl WMBN WV5 ....64 D4
Hateley Dr
ETTPK/GDPK/PENN WV4 ....52 C4
Hatfield Cl ERDW/GRVHL B23 ....78 B4
Hatfield Rd HAG/WOL DY9 ....136 A3
LOZ/NWT B19 ....108 D1
Hathaway Cl WLNHL WV13 ....39 F5
Hathaway Ms STRBR DY8 * 117 C1
SHLY B90 ....180 B4
Hathersage Rd
PBAR/PBCH B42 ....74 D4
Hatherton Gdns WOLVN WV10 .....13 E5
Hatherton Gv SLYOAK B29 ....158 B1
Hatherton Pl ALDR WS9 ....30 A3
Hatherton Rd BILS/COS WV14 ......54 B2
WSL WV1 ....4 E3
Hatherton St WSL WV1 ....4 E2
Hattersley Gv SPARK B11 ....146 A4
Hatton Crs WOLVN WV10 ....24 A3
Hatton Gdns PBAR/PBCH B42 ......74 B4
Hatton Rd
DUNHL/THL/PER WV6 ....36 B2
Hattons Gv CDSL WV8 ....10 D5
Hatton St BILS/COS WV14 ....54 A4
Haughton Rd
BFLD/HDSWWD B20 ....90 C5
Haunch La MOS/BIL B13 ....161 G5
Haunchwood Dr
WALM/CURD B76...........................78 B4
Havacre La BILS/COS WV14 ....68 C1
Havelock Cl BDMR/CCFT WV3 ....51 E1
Havelock Rd
BFLD/HDSWWD B20 ....90 C4
SPARK B11 ....145 G3
WASH/WDE B8 ....110 C4
Haven Cft GTB/HAM B43 ....73 F5
Haven Dr ACGN B27 ....146 C1
The Haven
ALE/KHTH/YWD B14 ....179 F1
BKHL/PFLD WV2 ....37 E3
STRBR DY8 ....117 H2
Haverford Dr RBRY B45 ....188 B2
Havergal Wk HALE B63 ....137 F3
Haverhill Cl BLOX/PEL WS3 ....16 C4
Hawbridge Cl SHLY B90 ....195 H2
Hawbush Gdns STRBR DY8 ....118 C5
Hawbush Rd BLOX/PEL WS3 ....28 A4
DRVFL DY5 ....118 C2
Hawcroft Gv BKDE/SHDE B34 ....113 E3
Hawes Cl WSL WS1 ....57 F2
Hawes La BLKHTH/ROWR B65 ....105 H5
Hawes Rd WSL WS1 ....57 F2
Haweswater Dr KGSWFD DY6 ....99 H3
Hawfield Cl OLDBY B69 ....104 A2
Hawfield Gv
SCFLD/WYGN B72 ....77 G4
Hawfield Rd OLDBY B69 ....104 A2
Hawker Dr CVALE B35 ....94 B4
Hawkesbury Rd SHLY B90 ....179 H4
Hawkes Cl BVILLE B30 ....160 B2
Hawkesford Cl CBROM B36 ....112 C1
FOAKS/STRLY B74 ....47 F4
Hawkesford Rd STETCH B33 ....131 F1
Hawkes La WBROM B70 ....71 E4
Hawkesley Crs NFLD/LBR B31 ....175 F4
Hawkesley Dr NFLD/LBR B31 .....175 F5

Hawkesley End
HWK/WKHTH B38 ....176 B5
Hawkesley Mill La
NFLD/LBR B31 ....175 F3
Hawkesley Rd DUDN DY1 ....101 H1
Hawkes St SHHTH WV10 ....128 B4
Hawkestone Crs WBROM B70 ....70 D5
Hawkestone Rd SLYOAK B29 ......158 C3
Hawkeswell Cl HIA/OLT B92 ....164 A2
Hawkeswell Dr KGSWFD DY6 ....99 H1
Hawkeswell La
CSHL/WTROR B46 ....133 H1
Hawkesyard Rd
ERDE/BCHGN B24 ....92 C5
Hawkhurst Rd
ALE/KHTH/YWD B14 ....178 B3
Hawkinge Dr CVALE B35 ....94 C2
Hawkins Cl DIG/EDG B5 ....144 A1
Hawkins Cft TPTN/OCK DY4 ....85 G3
Hawkins Pl BILS/COS WV14 ....54 B5
Hawkins St WBROM B70 ....71 E3
Hawkley Cl WOLV WV1 ....38 B3
Hawkley Rd WOLV WV1 ....38 B3
Hawkmoor Gdns
HWK/WKHTH B38 ....177 E5
Hawksford Crs WOLVN WV10 ....23 F5
Hawkshead Dr DOR/KN B93 ....196 D2
Hawksmoor Dr
DUNHL/THL/PER WV6 ....34 B2
Hawkstone Ct
DUNHL/THL/PER WV6...................20 B5
Hawkswell Av WMBN WV5 ....81 E1
Hawkswell Dr WLNHL WV13 ....39 F5
Hawkswood Dr
BILS/COS WV14 ....54 D5
Hawkswood Gv
ALE/KHTH/YWD B14 ....178 D2
Hawksworth Crs
CHWD/FDBR/MGN B37 ....132 C1
Hawley Cl RUSH/SHEL WS4 ....42 B1
Hawnby Gv WALM/CURD B76........78 C1
Hawne Cl HALE B63 ....138 A1
Hawne La HALE B63 ....138 B2
Hawksford Crs WOLVN WV10 ....23 F5
Hawthorn Brook Wy
ERDW/GRVHL B23 ....76 C3
Hawthorn Cl BORD B9 ....127 H5
ERDW/GRVHL B23 ....76 D4
Hawthorn Coppice
HAG/WOL DY9 ....152 C4
Hawthorn Cft
LGLYGN/QTN B68 ....123 H5
Hawthorne Dr HLYWD B47 ....192 D2
Hawthorne Gv SEDG DY3 ....83 F4
Hawthorne La CDSL WV8 ....20 D1
Hawthorne Rd
BKHL/PFLD WV2 ....52 B2
BVILLE B30 ....177 G5
CBROM B36 ....113 C2
DUDN DY1 ....85 G5
EDG B15 ....125 G5
HALE B63 ....138 A5
SHHTH WV12 ....26 B3
WNSFLD WV11 ....15 E4
Hawthorn Pk
BFLD/HDSWWD B20 ....89 G3
Hawthorn Pl WALSALL WS9 * 40 C2
Hawthorn Rd BRLYHL DY5 ....119 G4
CSCFLD/WYGN B72 ....77 G2
DARL/WED WS10 ....55 H4
DSYBK/YTR WS5 ....57 E5
FOAKS/STRLY B74 ....45 G4
KGSTG B44 ....75 G4
RUSH/SHEL WS4 ....28 D2
TPTN/OCK DY4 ....69 G3
WOLV WV1 ....38 C5
The Hawthorns
HAG/WOL DY9 * 169 F1
MOS/BIL B13 * 144 B4
Hawthorn Ter DARL/WED WS10...55 H4
Haxby Av BKDE/SHDE B34 ....112 C3
The Haybarn WALM/CURD B76 ....78 C2
Haybridge Av STRBR DY8 ....152 B5
Haybrook Dr SPARK B11 ....145 H3
Haycock Pl DARL/WED WS10........55 E1
Haycroft Av WASH/WDE B8 ....110 C4
Haycroft Dr FOAKS/STRLY B74 ....47 E1
Haydn Sanders Sq WSL WS1 * 4 D6
Haydock Cl CBROM B36 ....111 G1
DUNHL/THL/PER WV6 ....22 D5
Haydon Cl DOR/KN B93 ....198 D1
Haydon Cft STETCH B33 ....130 C1
Haye House Gv YDLY B25 ....112 A2
Hayes Crs LGLYGN/QTN B68 ......105 H4
Hayes Cft HWK/WKHTH B38 ....190 C1
Hayes Dr ERDE/BCHGN B24 ....93 H1
Hayes La HAG/WOL DY9 ....137 E1
Hayes Meadow
SCFLD/WYGN B72 ....77 H4
Hayes St WBROM B70 ....87 E2
The Hayes HAG/WOL DY9 ....157 E2
NFLD/LBR B31 ....175 C3
SHHTH WV12 ....26 C1
Hayfield Ct MOS/BIL B13 ....144 D5
Hayfield Gdns MOS/BIL B13 ....144 D5
Hayfield Rd MOS/BIL B13 ....144 D5
Hay Gn HAG/WOL DY9 ....136 B2
Hay Green La BVILLE B30 ....159 F4
Hay Hall Rd SPARK B11 ....145 H2
Hay Hl DSYBK/YTR WS5 ....43 G5
Hayland Rd ERDW/GRVHL B23 .....76 C3
Hay La SHLY B90 ....195 G2
Hayle Cl HWK/WKHTH B38 ....177 E5
Hayley Green Rd
NFLD/LBR B31 * 157 F2
Hayley Park Rd HALE B63 ....154 C2
Hayling Cl RBRY B45 ....175 H4
Hayling Gv BDMR/CCFT WV3 ....51 H2
The Haylofts HALE B63 ....154 C1
Haymarket CDHYTH B64 * 100 C4
Hayrick Dr KGSWFD DY6 ....99 F2
Hay Rd YDLY B25 ....129 C5
Hayrick Dr KGSWFD DY6 ....99 F2
Hayseech CDYHTH B64 ....101 G3
Hayseech Rd HALE B65 ....138 B1

The Hays Kent's Moat
LGN/SDN/BHAMAIR B26 ....130 C3
Haytor Av
ALE/KHTH/YWD B14 ....160 D5
Haywain Cl COVEN WV9 ....11 H5
Hayward Pk MGN/WHC B75 ....62 C1
ERDW/GRVHL B23 ....92 C1
Hayward St BILS/COS WV14 ....68 B3
Hayward Rd BRLYHL DY5.............100 D4
Haywood Dr
DUNHL/THL/PER WV6 ....35 G1
RMSLY B62 ....122 A4
Haywood's Farm
HHTH/SAND B71 ....72 B1
Hazel Av DARL/WED WS10 ....56 A4
SCFLD/BOLD B73 ....76 A2
Hazelbank HWK/WKHTH B38 ......176 C5
Hazelbeach Rd WASH/WDE B8 ...110 D4
Hazelbeech Rd WBROM B70 ....87 F4
Hazel Cft
CHWD/FDBR/MGN B37 ....132 B3
NFLD/LBR B31 ....175 G2
Hazeldene Gv AST/WIT B6 * 109 E1
Hazeldene Rd HALE B63 ....138 A5
STETCH B33 ....131 F5
Hazel Dr HLYWD B47 ....192 D2
SLYOAK B29 ....158 B3
Hazeley Cl HRBN B17 ....124 B5
Hazel Gdns ACGN B27 ....146 C3
Hazel Gv BILS/COS WV14 ....54 A1
HOCK/TIA B94 ....198 A5
STRBR DY8 ....87 G5
WBROM B70 ....87 G5
Hazelhurst Rd
ALE/KHTH/YWD B14 ....160 D4
BVILLE B30 ....160 B3
Hazelmere Ct HLGN/YWD B28 ....162 D2
Hazelmere Dr BDMR/CCFT WV3 ...35 E4
Hazelmere Rd HLGN/YWD B28 ...162 D2
Hazeloak Rd SHLY B90 ....180 A4
Hazel Rd BDMR/CCFT WV3 ....51 E1
DUDN DY1 ....84 C4
KGSWFD DY6 ....100 A4
RBRY B45 ....187 H2
TPTN/OCK DY4 ....85 E5
WOLV WV1 ....165 F4
Hazelton Cl SOLH B91 ....181 H4
Hazeltine Cft ACGN B27 * 146 B5
Hazeltree Gv DOR/KN B93 ....196 C5
Hazelville Gv HLGN/YWD B28 .....163 E4
Hazelville Rd HLGN/YWD B28 .....163 E4
Hazelwell Crs BVILLE B30 ....160 B4
Hazelwell Dr
ALE/KHTH/YWD B14 ....160 D4
Hazelwell Fordrough
BVILLE B30 ....160 B3
Hazelwell La BVILLE B30 ....160 A4
Hazelwell Rd BVILLE B30 ....160 A4
Hazelwood Dr WNSFLD WV11 ......24 A5
Hazelwood Gv ACGN B27 ....146 B5
Hazelwood Rd BDMR/CCFT WV3 ..34 D4
DUDN DY1 ....84 A4
FOAKS/STRLY B74 ....44 D5
Hazlemere Dr
FOAKS/STRLY B74 ....47 E4
Hazlitt Gv BVILLE B30 ....159 F5
Headborough Wk ALDR WS9 ....30 B1
Headingley Dr KINVER DY7 ....116 D3
Headingley Rd BFLD/HDSWWD B20 89 G4
Headland Dr WASH/WDE B8 ....110 A4
Headland Rd BDMR/CCFT WV3 ....34 D4
The Headlands
FOAKS/STRLY B74 ....46 A2
Headley Cft HWK/WKHTH B38 ....176 B5
Headley Rd SHLY B90 ....180 D3
Headway Rd WOLVN WV10 ....12 C4
Heale Cl HALE B63.......................120 A5
Heanor Cft AST/WIT B6 ....109 H1
Heantun Ms WNSFLD WV11 ....37 E1
Heantun Ri WNSFLD WV11 * 15 F5
Heartland Ms
BLKHTH/ROWR B65 ....121 H2
Heartlands Pkwy
WASH/WDE B8 ....110 A4
Heartlands Pl WASH/WDE B8 .....110 C5
Heath Acres DARL/WED WS10......55 E4
Heath Bridge Cl
RUSH/SHEL WS4 ....28 C2
Heathbrook Av KGSWFD DY6 ....99 F2
Heathcliff Rd DUDS DY2 ....103 F2
SPARK B11 ....145 H3
Heath Cl BVILLE B30 ....159 F5
MGN/WHC B75 ....63 F1
TPTN/OCK DY4 ....85 F1
Heathcote Av SOLH B91 ....181 F2
Heathcote Rd BVILLE B30 ....160 A5
Heath Cft NFLD/LBR B31 ....175 G5
Heath Cft Rd MGN/WHC B75........47 G4
Heath End Rd HAG/WOL DY9 .....185 G1
Heather Av DSYBK/YTR WS5 ....57 H4
Heather Cl CBROM B36 ....114 A1
DARL/WED WS10 ....56 A4
SOLH B91 ....165 G4
Heather Court Gdns
FOAKS/STRLY B74 ....47 E5
Heather Cft KGSTG B44 ....75 F2
Heather Dl BILS/COS WV14 ....54 C1
Heather Dr RBRY B45 ....173 H3
SHHTH WV12 ....40 C1
SOLH B91 ....165 G4
Heatherleigh Rd CBROM B36 ......113 H1
Heather Rd BLOX/PEL WS3 ....28 C2
DUDN DY1 ....84 B2
GTB/HAM B43 ....128 D4
SMTHWKW B67 ....106 C5
Heath Farm Rd CDSL WV8 ....10 D5
STRBR DY8 ....135 E4

Heathfield Rd
ALE/KHTH/YWD B14 ....161 E2
FOAKS/STRLY B74 ....46 D2
HALE B63 ....138 A4
LOZ/NWT B19 ....108 B2
Heathfields CDSL WV8 ....20 C1
Heathfield Wy CDYHTH B64 ....121 F3
Heath Gdns SOLH B91 ....165 F4
Heath Gn DUDN DY1 ....83 H1
Heathgreen Cl
CHWD/FDBR/MGN B37 ....132 C2
Heath Green Gv WSNGN B18 *....107 C5
Heath Green Rd WSNGN B18 ......107 C5
Heath Hill Rd
DUNHL/THL/PER WV6...................34 C4
Heath House Dr WMBN WV5 ....80 B1
Heath House La CDSL WV8 ....20 C2
Heathland Av BKDE/SHDE B34 ...112 C2
Heathlands WMBN WV5 ....80 B1
Heathlands Cl KGSWFD DY6 ....100 A1
Heathlands Gv NFLD/LBR B31 ....175 G4
Heathlands Rd
SCFLD/BOLD B73 ....76 D1
The Heathlands
BLKHTH/ROWR B65 ....122 A3
WMBN WV8 ....135 H5
WSL WV1 ....80 B1
Heath La HHTH/SAND B71 ....71 H4
STRBR DY8 ....135 G3
Heathleigh Rd
HWK/WKHTH B38 ....176 A5
Heathmere Av YDLY B25 ....129 H4
Heathmere Dr
CHWD/FDBR/MGN B37 ....131 H2
Heath Mill Cl WMBN WV5 ....80 B2
Heath Mill La WMBN WV5 ....80 B2
Heath Mill Rd WMBN WV5 ....80 B2
Heath Pk WOLVN WV10 * 12 C1
Heath Ri ALE/KHTH/YWD B14 ....178 C4
Heath Rd BVILLE B30 ....176 A1
DARL/WED WS10 ....40 C5
DUDS DY2 ....120 B2
HLYWD B47 ....192 C1
SHLY B90 ....165 F4
Heath Rd South
NFLD/LBR B31 ....175 H1
Heathside Dr BLOX/PEL WS3 ....18 A3
HWK/WKHTH B38 ....177 E5
Heath St BLKHTH/ROWR B65 ......122 A3
STRBR DY8 ....135 F2
WSNGN B18 ....107 H5
Heath St South WSNGN B18 * 107 H5
Heath Ter WNLD WV5 ....112 B2
Heathway Ct BKDE/SHDE B34 ....112 C3
Heathy Farm Cl
RIDG/WDGT B32 ....157 F1
Heathy Ri RIDG/WDGT B32 ....140 A5
Heaton Cl WOLVN WV10 ....12 D2
Heaton Dr EDG B15 ....125 H4
Heaton Rd SOLH B91 ....164 B3
Heaton St WSNGN B18 ....108 B3
Hebden Gv HLGN/YWD B28 ....179 F2
SHHTH WV12 ....25 H1
Heddon Pl VAUX/NECH B7 * 127 F1
Hedera Cl DSYBK/YTR WS5 ....57 H5
Hedgefield Gv HALE B63 ....137 G3
Hedgerow Dr KGSWFD DY6 ....81 H5
The Hedgerows RMSLY B62 ....172 F2
The Hedges WMBN WV5 ....64 C5
Hedgetree Cft
CHWD/FDBR/MGN B37 ....132 C2
Hedgley Gv STETCH B33 ....112 C5
Hedingham Gv
CHWD/FDBR/MGN B37 ....132 D2
Hedley Cft CVALE B35 ....94 D2
Hednesford Rd BRWNH WS8 ....9 F2
Heeley Rd SLYOAK B29 ....142 C5
Hefford Dr SMTHWK B66 ....106 C3
Helena St CBHAMW B1 ....2 C4
Helford Cl WNSFLD WV11 ....24 A5
Helford Cl TPTN/OCK DY4 ....84 B2
Hellaby Cl SCFLD/WYGN B72 * 62 H2
Hellier Av TPTN/OCK DY4 ....85 H2
Hellier Dr WMBN WV5 ....64 C4
Hellier Rd WOLVN WV10 ....13 E5
Hellier St DUDS DY2 ....102 C1
Helming Dr WOLV WV1 ....38 B2
Helmsdale Wy SEDG DY3 ....68 A4
Helmsley Cl BRLYHL DY5 ....119 F2
Helmsley Rd WNSFLD WV11 ....24 C2
Helmswood Dr
CHWD/FDBR/MGN B37 ....132 C2
Helston Cl BLOX/PEL WS3 ....18 A3
STRBR DY8 ....135 F2
Helston Gv DSYBK/YTR WS5 ....58 A2
Helston Rd BLOX/PEL WS3 ....18 A3
Helstone Gv HLGN/YWD B28 ......146 A3
Hemery Crs GTB/HAM B43 ....75 F3
Hemingford Cft
CHWD/FDBR/MGN B37 ....132 A5
Hemlingford Rd
CHWD/FDBR/MGN B37 ....113 G3
WALM/CURD B76...........................78 D5
Hemmings Cl STRBR DY8 ....135 E2
WOLV WV1 ....37 H2
Hemmings St DARL/WED WS10 ...40 A5
Hemplands Rd STRBR DY8 ....135 F2
Hempole La TPTN/OCK DY4 ....70 B5
Hemyock Rd SLYOAK B29 ....158 B3
Henbury Dr
CHWD/FDBR/MGN B37 ....114 D5
Henbury Rd ACGN B27 ....146 D4
Henderson Wk TPTN/OCK DY4 ....69 H3
Henderson Wy
BLKHTH/ROWR B65 ....122 A3
Hendon Cl SEDG DY3 ....66 A5
WOLVN WV10 ....23 G2
Hendon Rd BSMH B11 ....144 C3
Heneage Pl VAUX/NECH B7 *......109 G5
Heneage St VAUX/NECH B7 ....109 G5
Heneage St West
VAUX/NECH B7 ....3 K2
Henfield Cl WNSFLD WV11 ....24 D4
Hengham Rd
LGN/SDN/BHAMAIR B26 ....130 C3
Henley Cl BLOX/PEL WS3 ....28 A1
SCFLD/BOLD B73 ....77 F3
Henley Crs SOLH B91 ....164 D5

Henley Dr MGN/WHC B75 .... 47 E2
Henley Rd WOLVN WV10 .... 22 D1
Henley St SPARK B11 .... 127 G5
Henley Vls BHTH/HG B12 * 144 D2
Henlow Cl TPTN/OCK DY4 * 84 D1
Henlow Rd
  ALE/KHTH/YWD B14 .... 178 B3
The Hennalls CBROM B36 .... 112 B2
Henn Dr TPTN/OCK DY4 .... 69 E3
Henne Dr BILS/COS WV14 .... 68 C2
Henn St TPTN/OCK DY4 .... 69 G3
Henrietta St LOZ/NWT B19 .... 2 E2
Henry Rd YDLY B25 .... 146 C1
Henry St WSLW WS2 .... 4 B4
Hensborough SHLY B90 .... 194 A3
Hensel Dr BDMR/CCFT WV3 .... 35 G5
Henshaw Gv YDLY DY25 .... 129 G5
Henshaw Rd SMHTH B10 .... 128 B4
Henstead St DIG/EDG B5 .... 126 D4
Henwood Cl
  DUNHL/THL/PER WV6 .... 35 H2
Henwood La SOLH B91 .... 183 F1
Henwood Rd
  DUNHL/THL/PER WV6 .... 35 H2
Hepburn Cl ALDR WS9 .... 44 A1
Hepburn Edge
  ERDE/BCHGN B24 .... 93 F2
Hepworth Cl
  DUNHL/THL/PER WV6 .... 34 D1
Herbert Rd ALDR WS9 .... 30 A1
  HDSW B21 .... 89 H5
  SMHTH B10 .... 128 A3
  SMTHWKW B67 .... 124 C3
  SOLH B91 .... 181 H2
Herbhill Cl
  ETTPK/GDPK/PENN WV4 .... 52 B4
Hereford Av BHTH/HG B12 .... 144 C1
Hereford Cl ALDR WS9 .... 30 A2
  RBRY B45 .... 174 A3
Hereford Pl HHTH/SAND B71 .... 71 F4
Hereford Rd DUDS DY2 .... 121 E1
  LGLYGN/QTN B68 .... 123 F5
Hereford Sq WASH/WDE B8 .... 110 A4
Hereford St WSLW WS2 .... 42 A1
Hereward Ri HALE B63 .... 138 D2
  RMSLY B62 .... 139 G2
Heritage Cl LGLYGN/QTN B68 .... 105 G5
Heritage Wy STETCH B33 .... 131 F1
  TPTN/OCK DY4 .... 85 H1
Hermes Rd
  LGN/SDN/BHAMAIR B26 .... 149 G3
Hermitage Dr
  WALM/CURD B76 .... 63 G4
Hermitage Rd EDG B15 .... 125 E4
  ERDW/GRVHL B23 .... 92 B3
  SOLH B91 .... 165 F4
The Hermitage SOLH B91 .... 165 G4
Hermit St SEDG DY3 .... 83 F2
Hernall Cft
  LGN/SDN/BHAMAIR B26 .... 130 C5
Herne Cl WSNGN B18 .... 108 A5
Hernefield Rd
  BKDE/SHDE B34 .... 112 C2
Hernehurst RIDG/WDGT B32 .... 140 C1
Hern Rd BRLYHL DY5 .... 136 A1
Heron Cl BRWNH WS8 .... 9 E5
  SHLY B90 .... 194 D5
Herondale Rd
  LGN/SDN/BHAMAIR B26 .... 147 F1
  STRBR DY8 .... 134 C3
Heronfield Dr NFLD/LBR B31 .... 189 F2
Heronfield Wy SOLH B91 .... 165 G5
Heron Ml BLOX/PEL WS3 .... 17 G4
Heron Rd LGLYGN/QTN B68 .... 123 E2
The Heronry
  DUNHL/THL/PER WV6 .... 34 D3
Herons Wy HRBN B17 .... 142 A4
Heronswood Dr BRLYHL DY5 .... 119 F5
Heronswood Rd RBRY B45 .... 188 B2
Heronville Dr WBROM B70 .... 71 E4
Heronville Rd WBROM B70 .... 71 E5
Heron Wy RBRY B45 .... 187 G1
Herrick Rd WASH/WDE B8 .... 110 C4
Herrick St RDMR/CCFT WV3 .... 6 D5
Herringshaw Cft
  WALM/CURD B76 .... 63 E5
Hertford St BHTH/HG B12 .... 144 C2
Hertford Wy DOR/KN B93 .... 197 F4
Hervey Gv ERDE/BCHGN B24 .... 77 H5
Hesket Av LGLYGN/QTN B68 .... 123 E3
Hesketh Crs
  ERDW/GRVHL B23 .... 92 A1
Hessian Cl BILS/COS WV14 .... 68 B1
Hestia Dr SLYOAK B29 .... 159 G2
Heston Av PBAR/PBCH B42 .... 74 A3
Hever Av KGSTG B44 .... 75 G2
Hever Cl DUDN DY1 .... 83 G4
Hewell Cl KGSWFD DY6 .... 81 H5
  NFLD/LBR B31 .... 189 F1
Hewitson Gdns
  SMTHWKW B67 * 124 B2
Hewitt St DARL/WED WS10 .... 55 E2
Hexham Wy DUDN DY1 .... 84 B4
Hexton Cl SHLY B90 .... 179 F3
Heybarnes Rd SMHTH B10 .... 129 E5
Heycott Gv HWK/WKHTH B38 .... 177 G3
Heycroft Rd BRLYHL DY5 .... 119 H5
Heyford Gv SOLH B91 .... 182 A5
Heyford Wy CVALE B35 .... 94 D1
Heygate Wy ALDR WS9 .... 30 B1
Heygesfield Rd STETCH B33 .... 131 E1
Heythrop Gv MOS/BIL B13 .... 162 B2
Hickman Av BKHL/PFLD WV2 .... 38 A5
Hickman Gdns
  LDYWD/EDGR B16 .... 125 H3
Hickman Rd BILS/COS WV14 .... 55 E3
  BRLYHL DY5 .... 101 E5
  SPARK B11 .... 144 D1
  TPTN/OCK DY4 .... 69 F3
Hickmans Av CDYHTH B64 .... 121 E2
Hickmans Ct RMSLY B62 .... 140 A1
Hickman St HAG/WOL DY9 .... 136 A1
Hickmerelands La SEDG DY3 .... 67 F3
Hickory Dr HRBN B17 .... 124 D2
Hidcote Av WALM/CURD B76 .... 78 C3

Hidcote Gv
  CHWD/FDBR/MGN B37 .... 132 A5
  STETCH B33 .... 131 E4
Hidson Rd ERDW/GRVHL B23 .... 92 A2
Higgins Av BILS/COS WV14 .... 68 D1
Higgins La RIDG/WDGT B32 .... 140 C2
Higgins Wk SMTHWK B66 .... 106 C5
Higgs Field Crs CDYHTH B64 .... 121 H5
Higgs Rd WNSFLD WV11 .... 25 C1
Higham's Cl
  BLKHTH/ROWR B65 .... 121 H1
Higham Wy WOLVN WV10 .... 23 G4
High Arcal Dr SEDG DY3 .... 67 H4
High Arcal Rd SEDG DY3 .... 82 B2
High Av CDYHTH B64 .... 121 F4
High Beeches GTB/HAM B43 .... 73 F2
Highbridge Rd DUDS DY2 .... 102 B5
  SCFLD/BOLD B73 .... 77 E2
High Brink Rd
  CSHL/WTROR B46 .... 115 F2
Highbrook Cl COVEN WV9 .... 12 A5
High Brow HRBN B17 .... 124 D5
High Bullen DARL/WED WS10 .... 70 D1
Highbury Av
  BLKHTH/ROWR B65 .... 122 B1
  HDSW B21 * 107 H1
Highbury Cl
  BLKHTH/ROWR B65 .... 122 B1
Highbury Rd
  ALE/KHTH/YWD B14 .... 160 D2
  FOAKS/STRLY B74 .... 46 A2
  LGLYGN/QTN B68 .... 105 F4
High Clere CDYHTH B64 .... 121 G5
Highcrest Cl NFLD/LBR B31 .... 189 C1
High Cft ALDR WS9 .... 19 H5
Highcroft BLOX/PEL WS5 * 18 B1
Highcroft Av STRBR DY8 .... 117 F1
Highcroft Cl HIA/OLT B92 .... 148 A5
Highcroft Dr FOAKS/STRLY B74 .... 46 C2
Highcroft Rd ERDW/GRVHL B23 .... 92 C5
Highdown Crs SHLY B90 .... 195 C2
High Ercal Av BRLYHL DY5 .... 119 E2
High Farm Rd HALE B63 .... 138 B4
  RMSLY B62 .... 122 D4
Highfield Av BILS/COS WV14 .... 54 A4
  RUSH/SHEL WS4 .... 29 E2
  WOLVN WV10 .... 13 G5
Highfield Cl HLGN/YWD B28 .... 162 B5
Highfield Crs
  BLKHTH/ROWR B65 .... 121 H4
  HALE B63 .... 137 H2
  WNSFLD WV11 .... 24 B4
Highfield Dr SCFLD/BOLD B73 .... 76 D4
Highfield La HAG/WOL DY9 .... 171 E2
  HALE B63 .... 138 C4
  RIDG/WDGT B32 .... 140 C3
Highfield Ms HALE B63 .... 137 H1
Highfield Rd
  ALE/KHTH/YWD B14 .... 162 B5
  BLKHTH/ROWR B65 .... 121 H5
  BLOX/PEL WS3 .... 18 A3
  DUDS DY2 .... 85 E5
  EDG B15 .... 126 A4
  GTB/HAM B43 .... 73 E2
  HALE B63 .... 137 H2
  MOS/BIL B13 .... 144 C4
  SEDG DY3 .... 67 F2
  SMTHWKW B67 .... 106 B4
  STRBR DY8 .... 118 C2
  TPTN/OCK DY4 .... 69 H5
  WASH/WDE B8 .... 110 C4
Highfield Rd North
  HALE B63 * 17 H2
Highfields Ct
  ETTPK/GDPK/PENN WV4 * 50 D2
Highfields Dr BILS/COS WV14 .... 53 H5
  WMBN WV5 .... 81 E1
Highfields Rd BILS/COS WV14 .... 53 H5
The Highfields
  DUNHL/THL/PER WV6 .... 35 E3
Highfield Wy ALDR WS9 .... 19 H5
Highgate FOAKS/STRLY B74 .... 45 H4
Highgate Cl
  BHTH/HG B12 .... 127 F5
  WSL WV5 * 57 F1
Highgate Dr WSL WV1 .... 57 F1
Highgate Middleway
  BHTH/HG B12 .... 127 F5
Highgate PI BHTH/HG B12 .... 127 G5
Highgate Rd BHTH/HG B12 .... 144 C1
  DUDS DY2 .... 101 H5
  WSL WV1 .... 5 F7
Highgate Sq BHTH/HG B12 .... 127 F5
Highgate St BHTH/HG B12 .... 127 F5
  CDYHTH B64 .... 121 F2
Highgrove
  DUNHL/THL/PER WV6 .... 35 G2
Highgrove Cl SHHTH WV12 .... 25 H4
Highgrove Pl DUDN DY1 .... 83 H4
High Haden Crs CDYHTH B64 .... 121 C4
High Haden Rd CDYHTH B64 .... 121 H4
High Heath Cl BVILLE B50 .... 159 F5
High Hl WNSFLD WV11 .... 15 G5
High Holborn SEDG DY3 .... 67 H4
High House Dr RBRY B45 .... 187 H5
Highland Av BILS/COS WV14 .... 68 D2
Highland Rdg RMSLY B62 .... 139 G2
High Land Rd ALDR WS9 .... 19 H5
Highland Rd CDYHTH B64 .... 121 E2
  DUDN DY1 .... 84 A3
  ERDW/GRVHL B23 .... 92 D1
  GTB/HAM B43 .... 58 C5
Highlands Rd BDMR/CCFT WV3 .... 35 H5
  SHLY B90 .... 195 E1
The Highlands SHLY B90 * 181 E5
High Leasowes HALE B63 .... 138 C3
High Meadow Rd
  HWK/WKHTH B38 .... 177 E3
High Mdw
  DUNHL/THL/PER WV6 .... 35 G3
  WMBN WV5 .... 65 G5
Highmoor Cl BILS/COS WV14 .... 53 H5
  SHHTH WV12 .... 25 C1
Highmoor Rd
  BLKHTH/ROWR B65 .... 121 H2
Highmore Dr RIDG/WDGT B32 .... 157 G2

High Oak BRLYHL DY5 .... 101 E3
Highover Dr MGN/WHC B75 .... 47 E1
Highpark Av STRBR DY8 .... 134 D2
High Park Cl SEDG DY3 .... 67 F2
  SMTHWK B66 .... 106 D4
High Park Crs SEDG DY3 .... 67 F2
High Park Rd HALE B63 .... 137 F2
High Park St VAUX/NECH B7 .... 109 H5
High Rdg ALDR WS9 .... 29 H5
High Ridge Cl ALDR WS9 .... 29 H5
  DARL/WED WS10 .... 55 E2
High Rd SHHTH WV12 .... 26 A5
High St ALDR WS9 .... 30 B4
  ALE/KHTH/YWD B14 .... 161 E2
  BILS/COS WV14 .... 53 G3
  BLKHTH/ROWR B65 .... 122 A4
  BLOX/PEL WS3 .... 18 A4
  BLOX/PEL WS3 .... 27 F1
  BRLYHL DY5 .... 119 F2
  BRWNH WS8 .... 19 E1
  CBHAMNE B4 .... 3 G5
  CDYHTH B64 .... 120 D5
  CSCFLD/WYGN B72 .... 62 C3
  CSHL/WTROR B46 .... 115 F2
  CVALE B35 .... 94 C3
  DARL/WED WS10 .... 54 C4
  DARL/WED WS10 .... 55 E2
  DOR/KN B93 .... 197 D1
  DUDN DY1 .... 102 C1
  DUNHL/THL/PER WV6 .... 35 H1
  ERDW/GRVHL B23 .... 92 D2
  HAG/WOL DY9 .... 136 C2
  HAG/WOL DY9 .... 77 F4
  HALE B63 .... 138 D5
  HIA/OLT B92 .... 167 G4
  HRBN B17 .... 142 A2
  KGSWFD DY6 .... 99 F1
  LOZ/NWT B19 .... 108 D5
  RIDG/WDGT B32 .... 140 A1
  SEDG DY3 .... 67 F2
  SEDG DY3 .... 80 C4
  SHLY B90 .... 179 E5
  SMTHWKW B67 .... 106 B5
  SOLH B91 .... 182 A1
  STRBR DY8 .... 135 E1
  TPTN/OCK DY4 .... 85 E1
  WASH/WDE B8 .... 110 B4
  WBROM B70 .... 7 J2
  WMBN WV5 .... 65 F5
  WNSFLD WV11 .... 24 C5
  WSL WV1 .... 5 F5
High Street Bordesley
  BHTH/HG B12 .... 127 G3
High Street Deritend
  BHTH/HG B12 .... 3 K7
High Street Prec
  DARL/WED WS10 * 55 F2
Highters Cl
  ALE/KHTH/YWD B14 .... 178 D3
Highters Heath La
  ALE/KHTH/YWD B14 .... 178 C4
Highters Rd
  ALE/KHTH/YWD B14 .... 178 C2
High Timbers RBRY B45 .... 173 H4
High Tower VAUX/NECH B7 * 109 H4
High Trefe Cl RIDG/WDGT B32 .... 157 F1
High Trees BFLD/HDSWWD B20 .... 89 H3
High Trees Rd DOR/KN B93 .... 197 E1
High Vw BILS/COS WV14 .... 67 G5
Highview Dr KGSWFD DY6 .... 100 B5
Highview St DUDS DY2 .... 85 G5
Highwood Av HIA/OLT B92 .... 164 D1
High Wood Cl KGSWFD DY6 .... 99 G3
Highwood Cft
  HWK/WKHTH B38 .... 176 B4
Hiker Gv
  CHWD/FDBR/MGN B37 .... 132 D2
Hilary Crs DUDN DY1 .... 68 B5
Hilary Dr ALDR WS9 .... 30 A5
  BDMR/CCFT WV3 .... 50 D1
  WALM/CURD B76 .... 62 D4
Hilary Gv NFLD/LBR B31 .... 175 F1
Hilden Rd VAUX/NECH B7 .... 109 G5
Hilderic Crs DUDN DY1 .... 101 H2
Hildicks Crs BLOX/PEL WS3 .... 28 B3
Hildicks Pl BLOX/PEL WS3 .... 28 B3
Hillaire Cl HWK/WKHTH B38 .... 177 G4
Hillary Av DARL/WED WS10 .... 55 H3
Hillary Crest SEDG DY3 * 83 C1
Hillary St WSLW WS2 .... 56 C2
Hill Av ETTPK/GDPK/PENN WV4 .... 52 D5
Hill Bank HAG/WOL DY9 .... 136 D2
Hillbank DLGBY B69 .... 104 B1
Hill Bank Dr STETCH B33 .... 111 H5
Hill Bank Rd HALE B63 .... 120 D5
  HWK/WKHTH B38 .... 177 F3
Hillborough Rd ACGN B27 .... 146 D5
Hillbrook Gv STETCH B33 .... 130 B1
Hillbury Dr SHHTH WV12 .... 25 H2
Hill Cl NFLD/LBR B31 .... 189 H1
  SEDG DY3 .... 67 G2
Hill Crest SEDG DY3 .... 82 D2
Hill Crest Av BRLYHL DY5 .... 119 E3
Hillcrest Av GTB/HAM B43 .... 73 G1
  HALE B63 .... 120 B5
  WOLVN WV10 .... 12 C3
Hillcrest Cl DUDS DY2 .... 102 C4
Hillcrest Gdns SHHTH WV12 .... 26 B5
Hill Crest Gv KGSTG B44 .... 75 G4
Hillcrest Rd CSCFLD/WYGN B72 .... 77 C3
  GTB/HAM B43 .... 73 F4
  RMSLY B62 .... 122 C4
Hill Crest Rd DUDS DY2 .... 85 E5
  MOS/BIL B13 .... 144 A5
Hill Croft Rd
  ALE/KHTH/YWD B14 .... 160 D1
Hillcroft Rd KGSWFD DY6 .... 100 A2
Hillcross Wk CBROM B36 .... 112 B2
Hilldene Rd KGSWFD DY6 .... 99 C5
Hilldrop Gv HRBN B17 .... 142 A4
Hillyers Cft
  CHWD/FDBR/MGN B37 .... 131 H2
Hillfield Ms SOLH B91 .... 181 H5
Hillfield Rd BRLYHL DY5 .... 118 D5
  SPARK B11 .... 145 F1
Hillfields SMTHWKW B67 .... 123 H1
Hillfields Rd BRLYHL DY5 .... 118 D5
Hillfield St SCDYHTH B64 .... 120 D3
Hingeston St WNSFLD WV11 .... 25 C5
Hingley Cft ALDR WS9 .... 45 F2
Hingley Rd CSCFLD/WYGN B72 .... 77 C4
Hingley St CDYHTH B64 .... 120 D3
Hinksford Gdns SEDG DY3 .... 80 C4
Hinksford La SEDG DY3 .... 80 C5

Hillhampton Cl HIA/OLT B92 .... 148 A5
Hill Hook Rd FOAKS/STRLY B74 .... 32 C4
Hill House La STETCH B33 .... 130 B1
Hillhurst Gv CBROM B36 .... 95 F5
Hillhurst Rd SCFLD/BOLD B73 .... 60 D5
Hilliards Cft PBAR/PBCH B42 .... 74 A3
Hillingford Av GTB/HAM B43 .... 59 H2
Hill La GTB/HAM B43 .... 73 G1
  HAG/WOL DY9 .... 170 C1
  MGN/WHC B75 .... 48 D3
Hillman Dr DUDS DY2 .... 103 E2
Hillman Gv CBROM B36 .... 95 G5
Hillmeads Dr DUDS DY2 .... 103 E2
Hillmeads Rd
  HWK/WKHTH B38 .... 177 H4
Hillmorton Rd DOR/KN B93 .... 197 E3
  FOAKS/STRLY B74 .... 46 D1
Hillmount Cl HLGN/YWD B28 .... 145 G5
Hill Pk ALDR WS9 .... 19 G3
Hill Pas CDYHTH B64 .... 121 E2
Hill Pl WNSFLD WV11 .... 25 F1
Hill Rd OLDBY B69 .... 85 G4
  WLNHL WV13 .... 39 G5
Hillside BRWNH WS8 .... 19 G1
Hill Side SEDG DY3 .... 83 E2
Hillside WMBN WV5 .... 64 C2
Hillside Av BLKHTH/ROWR B65 .... 121 H4
  BRLYHL DY5 .... 137 H1
  HALE B63 .... 137 H1
Hillside Cl RIDG/WDGT B32 .... 157 E2
Hillside Crs BLOX/PEL WS3 .... 18 D1
Hillside Cft HIA/OLT B92 .... 148 C3
Hillside Dr
  CHWD/FDBR/MGN B37 .... 113 H5
  FOAKS/STRLY B74 .... 60 B1
  PBAR/PBCH B42 .... 74 A5
Hillside Gdns
  CHWD/FDBR/MGN B37 * 113 H5
  WOLV WV1 .... 38 A2
Hillside Rd DUDN DY1 .... 84 A2
  ERDW/GRVHL B23 .... 92 B4
  FOAKS/STRLY B74 .... 46 D1
  GTB/HAM B43 .... 73 F1
Hillstone Gdns WOLVN WV10 .... 13 H5
Hillstone Rd BKDE/SHDE B34 .... 113 H4
Hill St BILS/COS WV14 .... 54 A5
  CBHAM B2 .... 2 E5
  DARL/WED WS10 .... 55 C5
  DIG/EDG B5 .... 3 G7
  DUDS DY2 .... 102 B4
  HAG/WOL DY9 .... 136 D2
  HALE B63 .... 138 C4
  SEDG DY3 .... 80 G1
  SMTHWK B66 .... 106 C4
  STRBR DY8 .... 135 F3
  TPTN/OCK DY4 .... 69 E5
  WNSFLD WV11 .... 14 D4
  WSL WV1 .... 5 F5
The Hill RIDG/WDGT B32 .... 140 D5
Hilltop HALE B63 .... 137 G2
Hill Top WBROM B70 .... 71 E4
Hilltop Dr CBROM B36 .... 111 H2
Hilltop Rd DUDS DY2 .... 103 E1
Hill Top Rd LGLYGN/QTN B68 .... 123 G2
  NFLD/LBR B31 .... 175 F2
Hill Top Wk ALDR WS9 .... 30 C1
Hill Vw ALDR WS9 .... 19 H5
Hillview Cl HALE B63 .... 138 A1
Hillview Rd RBRY B45 .... 173 G5
Hill Village Rd MGN/WHC B75 .... 47 E1
Hillville Gdns STRBR DY8 .... 135 H4
Hill Wd BLOX/PEL WS3 .... 17 H5
Hillwood Av SHLY B90 .... 195 G2
Hillwood Cl KGSWFD DY6 .... 99 G3
Hillwood Common Rd
  LICHS WS14 .... 33 F4
Hill Wood Rd MGN/WHC B75 .... 32 C4
Hillwood Rd NFLD/LBR B31 .... 158 A3
  RMSLY B62 .... 122 A5
Hillyfields Rd
  ERDW/GRVHL B23 .... 92 A2
Hilly Rd BILS/COS WV14 .... 69 E1
Hilsea Cl CDSL WV8 .... 22 B1
Hilston Av
  ETTPK/GDPK/PENN WV4 .... 50 C4
  HALE B63 .... 138 B3
Hilton Av HLGN/YWD B28 .... 179 G1
Hilton Cl BLOX/PEL WS3 .... 26 C5
Hilton Cross WOLVN WV10 .... 13 H2
Hilton Dr CSCFLD/WYGN B72 .... 77 G3
Hilton Pl BILS/COS WV14 .... 54 A3
Hilton Rd
  ETTPK/GDPK/PENN WV4 .... 52 D4
  OLDBY B69 .... 104 A1
  SHHTH WV12 .... 26 A2
Hilton St WBROM B70 .... 7 J1
  WSLW WS2 .... 55 G3
Himbleton Cft SHLY B90 .... 195 G2
Himley Av DUDN DY1 .... 83 H4
Himley Cl GTB/HAM B43 .... 73 E1
  SHHTH WV12 .... 25 G5
Himley Crs
  ETTPK/GDPK/PENN WV4 .... 52 A3
Himley Gdns SEDG DY3 .... 82 C2
Himley Gv RBRY B45 .... 80 D4
Himley La SEDG DY3 .... 80 B3
Himley Rd DUDN DY1 .... 83 G5
  SEDG DY3 .... 80 A5
Himley St DUDN DY1 .... 84 A5
Hinbrook Rd DUDN DY1 .... 83 G5
Hinchliffe Av BILS/COS WV14 .... 68 B1
Hinchwick Ct DOR/KN B93 .... 196 D5
Hinckes Rd
  DUNHL/THL/PER WV6 .... 21 F5
Hinckley Ct LGLYGN/QTN B68 * 123 F5
Hinckley St DIG/EDG B5 .... 2 E6
Hincks St BKHL/PFLD WV2 .... 53 E1

Hinsford Cl KGSWFD DY6 .... 100 A1
Hinstock Cl
  ETTPK/GDPK/PENN WV4 .... 51 G4
Hinstock Rd
  BFLD/HDSWWD B20 .... 89 H5
Hintlesham Av HRBN B17 .... 142 B2
Hinton Gv WNSFLD WV11 .... 25 F5
Hintons Coppice DOR/KN B93 .... 196 C2
Hipkins St TPTN/OCK DY4 .... 69 E4
Hiplands Rd RMSLY B62 .... 139 G3
Hipsley Cl CBROM B36 .... 95 E5
Hipsmoor Cl
  CHWD/FDBR/MGN B37 .... 131 H1
Hirdemonsay SHLY B90 .... 193 H3
Histons Dr CDSL WV8 .... 10 B5
Histons Hl CDSL WV8 .... 10 B5
Hitchcock Cl SMTHWKW B67 .... 105 H4
Hitches La EDG B15 .... 126 B5
Hitherside SHLY B90 .... 194 B2
Hoarstone STRBR DY8 .... 152 B5
Hobacre Cl RBRY B45 .... 174 A5
Hobart Cl VAUX/NECH B7 .... 109 G4
Hobart Dr DSYBK/YTR WS5 .... 58 A2
Hobart Rd TPTN/OCK DY4 .... 69 E2
Hobble End La GTWY WS6 .... 16 C1
Hobgate Cl WOLVN WV10 .... 37 H1
Hobgate Rd WOLVN WV10 .... 37 H1
Hob Green Rd HAG/WOL DY9 .... 136 C5
Hobhouse Cl PBAR/PBCH B42 .... 73 H4
Hobley St WLNHL WV13 .... 40 A3
Hobmoor Cft YDLY B25 .... 129 H6
Hob Moor Rd SMHTH B10 .... 129 F4
Hobnock Rd WNSFLD WV11 .... 15 E3
Hobs Hole La ALDR WS9 .... 30 D3
Hob's Meadow HIA/OLT B92 .... 147 G5
Hob's Moat Rd HIA/OLT B92 .... 147 H5
Hobson Cl WSNGN B18 .... 108 A4
Hobson Rd SLYOAK B29 .... 160 B1
Hobs Rd DARL/WED WS10 .... 56 A4
Hockley Brook Cl WSNGN B18 .... 108 A4
Hockley Brook La
  HAG/WOL DY9 .... 184 D5
Hockley Cl LOZ/NWT B19 .... 108 D3
Hockley Hl LOZ/NWT B19 .... 108 B3
Hockley La DUDS DY2 .... 120 D1
Hockley Pool Cl WSNGN B18 .... 108 B4
Hockley Rd BILS/COS WV14 .... 68 A4
  ERDW/GRVHL B23 .... 92 B2
Hockley St WSNGN B18 .... 108 C3
Hodder Gv HHTH/SAND B71 .... 72 D4
Hodge Hill Av HAG/WOL DY9 .... 136 C4
Hodge Hill Common
  BKDE/SHDE B34 .... 112 A2
Hodge Hill Rd BKDE/SHDE B34 .... 112 A4
Hodges Dr OLDBY B69 .... 85 H5
Hodgetts Cl SMTHWKW B67 .... 123 C1
Hodgetts Dr HALE B63 .... 154 C2
Hodgkins Cl BRWNH WS8 .... 19 G2
Hodnell Cl CBROM B36 .... 95 E5
Hodnet Dr BILS/COS WV14 .... 53 F3
Hodnet Dr BRLYHL DY5 .... 101 E3
Hodson Av WLNHL WV13 .... 40 A4
Hodson Cl WNSFLD WV11 .... 25 F5
Hoff Beck Ct BORD B9 .... 127 H2
Hoff Beck Court Ct BORD B9 * 127 H2
Hogarth Cl GTB/HAM B43 .... 59 H5
  WLNHL WV13 .... 39 E5
Hoggs La NFLD/LBR B31 .... 175 E1
Holbeache La KGSWFD DY6 .... 81 H5
Holbeache Rd STETCH B33 .... 130 D2
Holbeche Rd DOR/KN B93 .... 197 E1
  MGN/WHC B75 .... 47 F3
Holberg Gv WNSFLD WV11 .... 25 F5
Holborn Hl AST/WIT B6 .... 109 H1
Holbrook Cv
  CHWD/FDBR/MGN B37 .... 132 B4
Holbury Cl COVEN WV9 .... 12 B5
Holcombe Rd SPARK B11 .... 146 A4
Holcroft Rd HAG/WOL DY9 .... 136 A3
  HALE B63 .... 137 G2
  KGSWFD DY6 .... 81 G5
Holcroft St BKHL/PFLD WV2 .... 53 G1
  TPTN/OCK DY4 .... 85 G4
Holden Cl ERDW/GRVHL B23 .... 92 C4
Holden Crs BLOX/PEL WS3 .... 28 A5
Holden Cft TPTN/OCK DY4 .... 85 F5
Holden Pl BLOX/PEL WS3 .... 42 A1
Holden Rd DARL/WED WS10 .... 71 E1
  ETTPK/GDPK/PENN WV4 .... 51 G2
The Holdens HLGN/YWD B28 .... 162 C4
Holder Rd SPARK B11 .... 145 E1
  YDLY B25 .... 129 G5
Holders Gdns MOS/BIL B13 .... 143 H5
Holders La MOS/BIL B13 .... 143 G5
Holdford Rd AST/WIT B6 .... 91 F4
Holgate Rd SLYOAK B29 .... 158 D3
Hole Farm Rd NFLD/LBR B31 .... 159 E5
Hole Farm Wy
  HWK/WKHTH B38 .... 190 D1
Hole La NFLD/LBR B31 .... 176 A1
Holford Av WSLW WS2 .... 56 C2
Holford Dr PBAR/PBCH B42 .... 91 E2
Holford Wy PBAR/PBCH B42 .... 91 C5
Holifast Rd CSCFLD/WYGN B72 .... 77 C4
Holland Av DOR/KN B93 .... 183 F5
  LGLYGN/QTN B68 .... 105 G5
Holland Rd BILS/COS WV14 .... 54 A1
  CSCFLD/WYGN B72 .... 77 F5
  GTB/HAM B43 .... 73 F4
Holland Rd West AST/WIT B6 .... 109 F3
Holland St CBHAMNW B3 .... 2 C4
  CSCFLD/WYGN B72 .... 77 F5
  DUDN DY1 .... 102 B1
Hollemeadow Av
  BLOX/PEL WS3 .... 27 H3
Holliars Gv
  CHWD/FDBR/MGN B37 .... 113 H4
Holliday Rd
  ERDE/BCHGN B24 .... 93 G2
  HDSW B21 .... 107 H2
Holliday St CBHAMW B1 .... 2 D6
Hollie Lucas Rd MOS/BIL B13 .... 161 F5
Hollies Cft DIG/EDG B5 .... 143 G2
Hollies Dr DARL/WED WS10 .... 55 H5

RMSLY B62 .... 139 G1
Hollies Rd *CDYHTH* B64 .... 121 F4
Hollies St *BRWNH* WS5 .... 101 F2
The Hollies *AST/WIT* B6 .... 109 H1
  BKHL/PFLD WV2 ....
  SMTHWK B66 * 107 E5
Hollin Brow Cl *DOR/KN* B93 .. 197 F5
Hollingberry La
  WALM/CURD B76 .... 63 F5
Hollings Gv *SOLH* B91 .... 181 H5
Hollington Rd *WOLV* WV1 .... 38 B5
Hollington Wy *SHLY* B90 .... 196 A1
Hollinwell Cl *BDGC/WED* WS5 .. 16 C4
Hollister Dr *RIDG/WDGT* B32 .. 141 F4
Holloway *NFLD/LBR* B31 .... 158 A4
Holloway Bank
  DARL/WED WS10 .... 70 D3
Holloway Circ Queensway
  CBHAMW B1 .... 3 F7
Holloway Dr *WMBN* WV5 .... 80 C1
Holloway Head *EDG* B15 .... 126 D3
Holloway La *BKHL/PFLD* WV2 ... 53 E1
  SEDG DY3 .... 83 F2
Holloway St *SEDG* DY3 .... 83 F2
The Holloway
  DUNHL/THL/PER WV6 .... 35 F3
  SEDG DY3 .... 83 E5
  STRBR DY8 .... 118 B5
Hollow Cft *NFLD/LBR* B31 ..... 175 H2
Hollow Croft Rd *SHHTH* WV12 .. 25 H3
The Hollow *MOS/BIL* B13 ...... 144 A3
Holly Av *BHTH/HG* B12 .... 144 C2
  SLYOAK B29 .... 160 B1
Hollybank Av *WNSFLD* WV11 .... 15 E4
Hollybank Cl *BLOX/PEL* WS3 .... 27 E1
Hollybank Gv *HALE* B63 .... 154 D1
Hollybank Rd *MOS/BIL* B13 .... 161 G4
Hollyberry Av *SOLH* B91 .... 181 G5
Hollyberry Cl *HALE* B63 .... 138 C4
Hollyberry Cft
  BKDE/SHDE B34 .... 113 E3
Hollybrow *SLYOAK* B29 .... 158 C3
Holly Bush Gv
  RIDG/WDGT B32 .... 123 H5
Hollybush La
  ETTPK/GDPK/PENN WV4 .... 50 D4
  STRBR DY8 .... 118 B5
Holly Cl *SHHTH* WV12 .... 26 A4
  WALM/CURD B76 .... 78 B1
Hollycot Gdns *BHTH/HG* B12 .. 144 B1
Holly Ct *DSYBK/YTR* WS5 .... 57 C4
Hollycroft Rd *HDSW* B21 .... 89 F5
Hollydale Rd
  BLKHTH/ROWR B65 .... 122 B1
  ERDE/BCHGN B24 .... 93 G3
Holly Dell *HWK/WKHTH* B38 ... 177 F5
Holly Dr *ACGN* B27 .... 146 B5
  HLYWD B47 .... 192 D1
Hollyfaste Rd *STETCH* B33 ..... 130 D3
Hollyfield Av *SOLH* B91 .... 181 E2
Hollyfield Ct *MGN/WHC* B75 .... 63 E3
Hollyfield Crs *MGN/WHC* B75 ... 63 E4
Hollyfield Dr *MGN/WHC* B75 .... 63 E3
Hollyfield Rd *MGN/WHC* B75 .... 63 E3
Holly Gv *BDMR/CCFT* WV3 .... 51 F1
  BVILLE B30 .... 159 H2
  LOZ/NWT B19 .... 108 D1
  STRBR DY8 .... 118 D5
Holly Hall Rd *DUDS* DY2 .... 102 A3
Hollyhedge Cl *NFLD/LBR* B31 . 157 H4
  WSLW WS2 .... 4 A2
Hollyhedge La *WSLW* WS2 .... 4 A1
Hollyhedge Rd
  HHTH/SAND B71 .... 72 A4
Holly Hill Rd *RBRY* B45 .... 174 A3
Hollyhock Rd *ACGN* B27 .... 162 D1
  DUDS DY2 ....
Hollyhurst *CSHL/WTROR* B46 .. 96 C4
Hollyhurst Dr *STRBR* DY8 ...... 118 A1
Hollyhurst Gv
  LGN/SDN/BHAMAIR B26 ...... 147 E1
  SHLY B90 .... 180 B5
Hollyhurst Rd *SCFLD/BOLD* B73 .. 60 D5
Holly La *ALDR* WS9 .... 31 F2
  CHWD/FDBR/MGN B37 .... 131 H4
  ERDE/BCHGN B24 .... 93 C4
  FOAKS/STRLY B74 .... 45 F1
  SMTHWK B66 .... 106 A2
  SMTHWKW B67 .... 105 H5
Hollymoor Wy *NFLD/LBR* B31 .. 174 C4
Hollymount *RMSLY* B62 .... 123 E5
Hollyoak Cft *NFLD/LBR* B31 ... 175 H5
Hollyoake *LGLYGN/QTN* B68 ... 123 E1
Hollyoak Gv *SOLH* B91 .... 181 G4
Hollyoak Rd *FOAKS/STRLY* B74 .. 60 B2
Hollyoak St *HHTH/SAND* B71 .... 87 H2
Holly Park Dr *ERDE/BCHGN* B24 .. 93 F5
Holly Pl *AST/WIT* B6 * 109 E1
Holly Rd *BKHL/HDSWWD* B20 . 107 H1
  BLKHTH/ROWR B65 .... 121 H5
  BVILLE B30 .... 177 E1
  DARL/WED WS10 .... 55 H5
  HHTH/SAND B71 .... 72 A3
  LDYWD/EDGR B16 .... 125 E3
  LGLYGN/QTN B68 .... 123 E1
Holly St *DUDN* DY1 .... 101 G2
  SMTHWKW B67 ....
Hollywell Rd *DOR/KN* B93 ..... 197 E5
Hollywell St *BILS/COS* WV14 ... 68 A2
Holly Wd *GTB/HAM* B43 .... 74 A2
Hollywood By-Pass
  HLYWD B47 .... 192 A3
Hollywood Cft *PBAR/PBCH* B42 .. 73 H3
Hollywood Gdns *HLYWD* B47 . 178 C5
Hollywood La *HLYWD* B47 ...... 192 D1
Holman Cl *WLNHL* WV13 .... 38 D3
Holman Rd *WLNHL* WV13 .... 38 D3
Holmbridge Gv
  RUSH/SHEL WS4 .... 18 D5
Holme Ml *WOLV* WV10 .... 12 D3
Holmes Dr *RBRY* B45 .... 187 H2
Holmesfield Rd
  PBAR/PBCH B42 .... 74 C4
Holmes Rd *SHHTH* WV12 .... 26 B4
The Holmes *WOLV* WV10 .... 12 D4

Holme Wy *RUSH/SHEL* WS4 ..... 28 D3
Holmwood Rd *BORD* B9 .... 128 B3
Holt Cl North *VAUX/NECH* B7 * .. 3 K2
Holt Cl South *VAUX/NECH* B7 * .. 3 K2
Holte Dr *MGN/WHC* B75 .... 47 H3
Holte Rd *AST/WIT* B6 .... 109 C1
  SPARK B11 .... 145 F2
Holtes Wk *AST/WIT* B6 * 109 H1
Holt La *RMSLY* B62 .... 171 H1
Holt Rd *RMSLY* B62 .... 122 C5
Holtshill La *WSL* WS1 .... 5 G3
Holt St *VAUX/NECH* B7 * 3 J1
Holy Cross Gn *HAG/WOL* DY9 . 170 C3
Holyoak Cl *AST/WIT* B6 .... 91 F5
Holyrood Gv *AST/WIT* B6 * 109 E1
Holy Well Cl *LDYWD/EDGR* B16.. 126 A2
Holywell La *RBRY* B45 .... 187 F2
Homecroft Rd *YDLY* B25 .... 129 H4
Homedene Rd *NFLD/LBR* B31 . 158 A3
Homefield Rd *COL* WV6 .... 10 D4
Homelands *RIDG/WDGT* B32 .... 74 B4
The Homelands *WOLVN* WV10 * .. 12 C1
Homelea Rd *YDLY* B25 .... 129 H4
Homer Hill Rd *HALE* B63 .... 120 B5
Homer Rd *MGN/WHC* B75 .... 47 G5
  SOLH B91 .... 181 H2
Homers Fold *BILS/COS* WV14 .... 53 H5
Homer St *BHTH/HG* B12 .... 144 B2
Homerton Rd *KGSTG* B44 .... 75 H2
Homestead Dr *MGN/WHC* B75 ... 47 G2
Homestead Rd *STETCH* B33 .... 130 D5
Homewood Cl
  WALM/CURD B76 .... 63 E5
Honesty Cl *BRWNH* WS8 .... 8 D5
Honeswide Cl
  BFLD/HDSWWD B20 .... 108 A1
Honeyborne Rd *MGN/WHC* B75.. 62 D1
Honeybourne Cl *HALE* B63 .... 138 C4
Honeybourne Crs *WMBN* WV5 .. 80 D1
Honeybourne Rd *HALE* B63 .... 139 E4
  STETCH B33 .... 131 E4
Honeybourne Wy
  WLNHL WV13 .... 40 A3
Honeycomb Wy
  NFLD/LBR B31 .... 175 E2
Honeysuckle Cl *KGSWFD* DY6 . 100 A2
Honeysuckle Cl
  RIDG/WDGT B32 .... 140 B2
Honeysuckle Dr
  DSYBK/YTR WS5 .... 57 C5
Honeytree Cl *KGSWFD* DY6 .... 146 C2
Honiley Dr *KGSTG* B44 .... 76 A1
Honiley Rd *STETCH* B33 .... 130 C2
Honister Cl *BRLYHL* DY5 .... 119 H5
Honiton Cl *NFLD/LBR* B31 ..... 175 E1
Honiton Crs *NFLD/LBR* B31 .... 175 E1
Honiton Wy *ALDR* WS9 .... 29 H5
Honnington Ct *SLYOAK* B29 * . 158 B1
Honor Av
  ETTPK/GDPK/PENN WV4 .... 52 A3
Hood Gv *BVILLE* B30 .... 176 B1
Hook Dr *FOAKS/STRLY* B74 ..... 46 C1
Hooper St *BRWNH* WS8 .... 9 H5
Hoosen Cl *RMSLY* B62 .... 140 A1
Hopedale Rd *RIDG/WDGT* B32 . 140 C2
Hope Pl *SLYOAK* B29 * 142 D5
Hope Rd *TPTN/OCK* DY4 .... 70 A5
Hope St *DIG/EDG* B5 .... 126 D4
  DUDS DY2 .... 102 C1
  RMSLY B62 .... 137 G1
  STRBR DY8 .... 117 H1
  WBROM B70 .... 88 A4
  WSL WS1 .... 4 E6
Hopkins Ct *HHTH/SAND* B71 .... 72 A4
Hopkins St *TPTN/OCK* DY4 ...... 85 F1
Hopstone Gdns
  ETTPK/GDPK/PENN WV4 .... 51 F3
Hopstone Rd *SLYOAK* B29 ..... 158 C1
Hopton Cl
  DUNHL/THL/PER WV6 .... 34 D2
  TPTN/OCK DY4 .... 70 A1
Hopton Crs *WNSFLD* WV11 ...... 25 E4
Hopton Gdns *DUDN* DY1 .... 84 A3
Hopton Gv *MOS/BIL* B13 .... 162 A5
Hopwas Gv
  CHWD/FDBR/MGN B37 .... 113 H4
Hopwood Cl *HALE* B63 .... 138 B1
Hopwood Gv *NFLD/LBR* B31 .. 189 E2
Hopyard Cl *SEDG* DY3 .... 82 B3
Hopyard Gdns *BILS/COS* WV14.. 53 F5
Hopyard La *SEDG* DY3 .... 82 D4
Hopyard Rd *WSLW* WS2 .... 40 C3
Horace Partridge Rd
  DARL/WED WS10 .... 54 C3
Horace St *BILS/COS* WV14 ...... 68 A3
Horatio Dr *MOS/BIL* B13 .... 144 B3
Hordern Cl
  DUNHL/THL/PER WV6 .... 22 B5
Hordern Crs *BRLYHL* DY5 ...... 119 F4
Hordern Gv
  DUNHL/THL/PER WV6 .... 22 B5
Hordern Pk *WOLV* WV10 * 12 C1
Hordern Rd
  DUNHL/THL/PER WV6 ....
Hornbeam Cl *SLYOAK* B29 .... 158 D3
Hornbeam Wk *BDMR/CCFT* WV3.. 6 B5
Hornbrook Gv *HIA/OLT* B92 ... 163 G3
Hornby Gv
  ALE/KHTH/YWD B14 .... 179 E1
Hornby Rd
  ETTPK/GDPK/PENN WV4 .... 52 A4
Horne Wy *BKDE/SHDE* B34 .... 113 G4
Horning Dr *BILS/COS* WV14 .... 53 G5
Hornsey Gv *KGSTG* B44 .... 75 G1
Hornsey Rd *KGSTG* B44 .... 75 G1
Hornton Cl *FOAKS/STRLY* B74 .. 46 A3
Horrell Rd
  LGN/SDN/BHAMAIR B26 ...... 147 H3
  SHLY B90 .... 179 H3
Horsecroft Dr *HHTH/SAND* B71.. 72 C3
Horsehills Dr *BDMR/CCFT* WV3.. 36 A3
Horselea Cft *WASH/WDE* B8 .. 111 G5

Horseley Flds *WOLV* WV1 .... 7 H4
Horseley Heath *TPTN/OCK* DY4.. 85 H2
Horseley Rd *TPTN/OCK* DY4 ..... 69 H5
Horseshoe Cl *WSLW* WS2 .... 56 B1
Horse Shoes La
  LGLYGN/QTN B68 .... 123 G2
The Horseshoe
  LGLYGN/QTN B68 .... 123 G2
Horsfall Rd *MGN/WHC* B75 ...... 63 G3
Horsham Av *STRBR* DY8 .... 117 C1
Horsley Rd *FOAKS/STRLY* B74 .. 45 H3
  GTB/HAM B43 .... 59 H4
Horton Cl *DARL/WED* WS10 ..... 55 F1
  SEDG DY3 .... 67 E3
Horton Gv *SHLY* B90 .... 195 C3
Horton Pl *DARL/WED* WS10 ...... 55 F1
Horton Sq *BHTH/HG* B12 .... 127 E5
Horton St *DARL/WED* WS10 ..... 55 F1
  TPTN/OCK DY4 .... 86 B1
  WBROM B70 .... 87 G5
Hospital La *BILS/COS* WV14 .... 68 B4
Hospital St *BKHL/PFLD* WV2 ..... 7 H4
  ERDW/GRVHL B23 .... 92 C2
  LOZ/NWT B19 .... 3 F1
  WSLW WS2 .... 41 H1
Hossil La *HAG/WOL* DY9 .... 169 H5
Hothersall Dr *SCFLD/BOLD* B73.. 76 D3
Hotspur Rd *KGSTG* B44 .... 75 F2
Hough Pl *WSLW* WS2 .... 56 B1
Hough Rd
  ALE/KHTH/YWD B14 .... 160 D4
  WSLW WS2 .... 56 A1
Houghton Ct *HLGN/YWD* B28 . 179 F1
Houghton St *OLDBY* B69 .... 104 D3
  WBROM B70 .... 87 G5
Houldey Rd *NFLD/LBR* B31 .... 175 H4
Houliston Cl *DARL/WED* WS10.. 56 B5
Houndel Gv *WMBN* WV5 .... 64 D4
Houndsfield Cl *HLYWD* B47 ... 193 E2
Houndsfield Gv *HLYWD* B47 ... 192 D3
Houndsfield La *HLYWD* B47 ... 192 D3
The Houx *STRBR* DY8 .... 118 A4
Hove Rd *ACGN* B27 .... 163 F1
Howard Rd
  ALE/KHTH/YWD B14 .... 160 D3
  BFLD/HDSWWD B20 .... 90 B5
  BILS/COS WV14 .... 54 B5
  GTB/HAM B43 .... 73 E3
  HIA/OLT B92 .... 147 E4
  WNSFLD WV11 .... 25 C5
  YDLY B25 .... 146 C1
Howard Rd East
  ALE/KHTH/YWD B14 .... 161 E3
Howard St *BKHL/PFLD* WV2 .... 7 G7
  LOZ/NWT B19 .... 2 E1
  TPTN/OCK DY4 .... 85 H1
  WBROM B70 .... 70 D4
Howarth Wy *AST/WIT* B6 .... 109 G2
Howden Pl *BKDE/SHDE* B34 .. 112 C4
Howdle's La *BRWNH* WS8 .... 9 F2
Howe Crs *SHHTH* WV12 .... 26 A4
Howell Rd *BKHL/PFLD* WV2 ..... 52 C1
Howes Cft *CVALE* B35 .... 94 C4
Howe St *CBHAMNE* B4 * 3 K3
Howford Gv *VAUX/NECH* B7 ... 109 H5
Howland Cl *COVEN* WV9 .... 11 H5
Howley Av *KGSTG* B44 .... 75 F1
Howley Grange Rd
  RMSLY B62 .... 139 H3
Hoylake Cl *BLOX/PEL* WS3 ...... 16 D4
Hoylake Dr *OLDBY* B69 .... 103 G2
Hoylake Rd
  DUNHL/THL/PER WV6 .... 20 B5
Hoyland Wy *BVILLE* B30 .... 159 G2
Hubert Cft *SLYOAK* B29 .... 142 D5
Hubert Rd *SLYOAK* B29 .... 142 D5
Hubert St *AST/WIT* B6 .... 109 H4
The Hub *SOLH* B91 * 182 A2
Hucker Cl *WSLW* WS2 .... 56 A1
Hucker Rd *WSLW* WS2 .... 56 A1
Huddlestone Cl *WOLVN* WV10.. 13 G1
Huddleston Wy *SLYOAK* B29 .. 159 E1
Huddocks Vw *BLOX/PEL* WS3 .. 17 H2
Hudson Av *CSHL/WTROR* B46 . 115 F3
Hudson Gv
  DUNHL/THL/PER WV6 .... 20 C5
Hudson Rd
  BFLD/HDSWWD B20 .... 90 A2
  TPTN/OCK DY4 .... 86 A2
Hudson's Dr *BVILLE* B30 .... 177 E1
Hudswell Dr *BRLYHL* DY5 ...... 119 F4
Hughes Av *BDMR/CCFT* WV3 .... 36 B5
Hughes Pl *BILS/COS* WV14 ...... 53 H1
Hughes Rd *BILS/COS* WV14 ..... 53 H1
  DARL/WED WS10 .... 54 C3
Hugh Porter Wy
  DUNHL/THL/PER WV6 .... 22 B3
Hugh Rd *SMTHWK* B10 .... 55 D5
  SMTHWKW B67 .... 105 H4
Hugh Vls *SMHTH* B10 * 128 C3
Hulbert Dr *DUDS* DY2 .... 102 B3
Hulbert Jnl *BRLYHL* DY5 .... 119 E1
Hullbrook Rd *MOS/BIL* B13 ... 162 A5
Humber Av *WALM/CURD* B76 .. 78 C4
Humber Gdns *HALE* B63 .... 137 F2
Humber Gv *CBROM* B36 .... 95 H5
Humber Rd *BDMR/CCFT* WV3 .... 6 B5
Humberstone Rd
  ERDE/BCHGN B24 .... 94 A2
Humpage Rd *BORD* B9 .... 128 C2
Humphrey Middlemore Dr
  HRBN B17 .... 142 B3
Humphrey St *SEDG* DY3 .... 83 F3
Humphries Crs
  BILS/COS WV14 .... 69 F1
Humphries Rd *WOLVN* WV10 ... 23 F3
Hundred Acre Rd
  FOAKS/STRLY B74 .... 60 B1
Hungary Cl *HAG/WOL* DY9 ..... 136 A2
Hungary Hl *HAG/WOL* DY9 ..... 136 A2
Hungerfield Rd *CBROM* B36 .... 95 E5
Hungerford Rd *STRBR* DY8 .... 135 E5
Hunningham Gv *SOLH* B91 .... 181 H5
Hunnington Cl
  RIDG/WDGT B32 ....
Hunnington Crs *HALE* B63 .... 138 D5
Hunscote Cl *SHLY* B90 .... 195 G1
Hunslet Cl *RIDG/WDGT* B32 ... 141 F3
Hunslet Rd *RIDG/WDGT* B32 .. 141 H1
Hunstanton Av *HRBN* B17 ..... 124 B4

Hunstanton Cl *BRLYHL* DY5 ... 119 E4
Hunter Crs *BLOX/PEL* WS3 ...... 28 B4
Hunters Cl *WLNHL* WV13 .... 54 C1
Hunter's Ride *LOZ/NWT* B19 .. 117 F2
Hunters Rd *LOZ/NWT* B19 ..... 108 B3
Hunter St
  DUNHL/THL/PER WV6 .... 36 C1
Hunters V *LOZ/NWT* B19 .... 108 C3
Huntingdon Rd
  HHTH/SAND B71 .... 71 F4
Huntingdon Rd *SHHTH* WV12 ... 26 B3
Huntingtree Rd *HALE* B63 .... 138 A3
Huntlands Rd *HALE* B63 .... 138 A3
Huntley Dr *SOLH* B91 .... 181 H3
Huntly Rd *LDYWD/EDGR* B16 . 126 A4
Hunton Hl *ERDW/GRVHL* B23 .. 92 B3
Hunton Rd *ERDW/GRVHL* B23 .. 92 C3
Hunt's La *SHHTH* WV12 .... 26 B4
Huntsman Cl *BILS/COS* WV14 .. 68 D1
Hunts Mill Dr *BRLYHL* DY5 .... 83 H5
Hunts Rd *BVILLE* B30 .... 160 A3
Hurcott Rd *SHLY* B90 .... 180 A3
Hurdlow Av *WSNGN* B18 .... 108 B4
Hurley Cl
  CHWD/FDBR/MGN B37 .... 113 H4
Hurleys Fold *DUDS* DY2 .... 102 A4
Hurlingham Rd *KGSTG* B44 ..... 76 C1
Hurricane Wy *CVALE* B35 .... 94 C4
Hursey Dr *TPTN/OCK* DY4 ...... 85 G1
Hurstbourne Crs *WOLV* WV1 ... 38 B4
Hurst Cl *CBROM* B36 .... 113 G2
Hurstcroft Rd *STETCH* B33 ... 130 D1
Hurst Green Rd *DOR/KN* B93 . 196 D2
  RMSLY B62 .... 122 C4
  WALM/CURD B76 .... 78 B5
Hurst La *BKDE/SHDE* B34 ...... 113 F3
  BRLYHL DY5 .... 119 H1
  TPTN/OCK DY4 .... 84 D1
Hurst La North
  BKDE/SHDE B34 .... 113 G2
Hurst Rd *BILS/COS* WV14 .... 68 D1
  SMTHWK B67 .... 123 H2
Hurst St *DIG/EDG* B5 .... 3 F7
The Hurst *HLYWD* B47 .... 192 C2
  MOS/BIL B13 .... 162 A3
The Hurstway
  ERDW/GRVHL B23 .... 76 A3
Hurstwood Rd *KGSTG* B44 ...... 76 A3
Huskinson Cl *OLDBY* B69 .... 85 H5
Hussey Rd *BRWNH* WS8 .... 9 E4
Hutchings La *SHLY* B90 .... 194 B3
Hutton Av *WASH/WDE* B8 ...... 110 B4
Hutton Rd *BFLD/HDSWWD* B20.. 90 B5
  WASH/WDE B8 .... 110 B4
Huxbey Dr *HIA/OLT* B92 .... 165 H2
Huxley Cl *COVEN* WV9 .... 12 A4
Hyacinth Cl *DSYBK/YTR* WS5 .. 57 C5
Hyatt Sq *BRLYHL* DY5 .... 119 G5
Hyde Rd *WNSFLD* WV11 .... 24 C4
Hydes Rd *DARL/WED* WS10 ..... 71 F2
The Hyde *HAG/WOL* DY9 .... 136 B5
Hyett Wy *BILS/COS* WV14 .... 69 H1
Hylda Rd *BFLD/HDSWWD* B20 .. 90 B5
Hylstone Crs *WNSFLD* WV11 ... 24 D4
Hylton St *WSNGN* B18 .... 108 C4
  WOLV WV10 ....
Hyperion Dr
  ETTPK/GDPK/PENN WV4 .... 51 C5
Hyperion Rd *CBROM* B36 .... 95 H3
  KINVER DY7 .... 117 C5
Hyron Hall Rd *ACGN* B27 ...... 146 C5
Hyssop Cl *VAUX/NECH* B7 ..... 109 G4
Hytall Rd *SHLY* B90 .... 179 E3
Hythe Gv *YDLY* B25 .... 129 H4

I

Ibberton Rd
  ALE/KHTH/YWD B14 .... 178 D2
Ibis Gdns *KGSWFD* DY6 .... 100 C3
Ibstock Dr *STRBR* DY8 .... 135 G3
Icknield Cl *FOAKS/STRLY* B74 .. 45 G4
Icknield Port Rd
  LDYWD/EDGR B16 .... 125 G1
Icknield Sq *LDYWD/EDGR* B16.. 126 A1
Icknield St *LDYWD/EDGR* B18 ..... 2 C3
  HWK/WKHTH B38 .... 191 E3
  WSNGN B18 ....
Ida Rd *WBROM* B70 .... 87 H5
  WSLW WS2 .... 41 G4
Idbury Rd *KGSTG* B44 .... 75 G4
Idmiston Cft
  ALE/KHTH/YWD B14 .... 178 B3
Idonia Rd
  DUNHL/THL/PER WV6 .... 20 C5
Ilford Rd *ERDW/GRVHL* B23 .... 76 B5
Iliffe Wy *HRBN* B17 .... 142 B3
Ilkley Gv
  CHWD/FDBR/MGN B37 .... 131 H2
Illey Cl *NFLD/LBR* B31 .... 174 B4
Illey La *RMSLY* B62 .... 155 G2
Illshaw *COVEN* WV9 .... 12 A4
Illshaw Heath Rd
  HOCK/TIA B94 .... 206 B5
Ilmington Ct *SCFLD/BOLD* B73.. 61 E5
Ilmington Rd *SLYOAK* B29 .... 158 B1
Ilsham Gv *NFLD/LBR* B31 ...... 189 G2
Ilsley Rd *ERDW/GRVHL* B23 .... 92 C2
Imperial Ri *CSHL/WTROR* B46 . 97 F4
Imperial Rd *BORD* B9 .... 128 C3
Impsley Cl *CBROM* B36 .... 112 D1
Ince Rd *DARL/WED* WS10 .... 55 E1
Incestre Dr *GTB/HAM* B43 ...... 73 G2
Inchbrook Rd
  BFLD/HDSWWD B20 .... 90 A3
Inchford Rd *HIA/OLT* B92 ...... 165 G3
Inchlaggan Rd *WOLVN* WV10 .. 23 G2
Infantry PI *MGN/WHC* B75 ...... 63 G2
Ingatestone Dr *STRBR* DY8 ... 116 A1
Ingestre Cl *BLOX/PEL* WS3 ...... 16 B4
Ingestre Dr *GTB/HAM* B43 ...... 58 D5
Ingestre Rd *ALE/KHTH/YWD* B28.. 162 D3
  WOLVN WV10 .... 13 G2
Ingestre Rd
  ALE/KHTH/YWD B28 .... 162 D3
  WOLVN WV10 .... 13 G2
Ingham Wy *HRBN* B17 .... 124 B5
Ingleby Gdns
  DUNHL/THL/PER WV6 .... 22 C5

Ingledew Cl *WSLW* WS2 .... 40 B2
Inglefield Rd *STETCH* B33 ..... 130 B1
Inglemere Gv *SLYOAK* B29 .... 158 B3
Inglenook Dr
  BFLD/HDSWWD B20 .... 90 B4
Ingleside Vls *SPARK* B11 * 145 E2
Ingleton Rd *WASH/WDE* B8 ... 111 E2
Inglewood Av *BDMR/CCFT* WV3.. 36 B5
Inglewood Cl *KGSWFD* DY6 * ... 99 H4
Inglewood Gv
  FOAKS/STRLY B74 .... 45 E4
Inglewood Rd *SPARK* B11 ...... 145 E2
Ingoldsby Rd *NFLD/LBR* B31 .. 176 A2
Ingot Cl *WSLW* WS2 .... 27 F4
Ingram Gv *GTB/HAM* B43 .... 73 E3
Ingram Pl *BLOX/PEL* WS3 .... 27 H1
Ingram Rd *BLOX/PEL* WS3 .... 27 H1
Inhedge St *SEDG* DY3 .... 83 G1
The Inhedge *DUDN* DY1 .... 84 C5
Inkberrow Cl *OLDBY* B69 ...... 104 C5
Inkberrow Rd *HALE* B63 .... 138 B4
Inkerman St *VAUX/NECH* B7 .. 127 H1
  WOLV WV10 .... 37 H2
Inland Rd *ERDE/BCHGN* B24 ... 93 F2
Innage Rd *NFLD/LBR* B31 ...... 175 H1
The Innage *HLYWD* B47 .... 192 C3
Innsworth Dr *CVALE* B35 .... 94 C2
Inshaw Cl *STETCH* B33 .... 130 A1
Institute Rd
  ALE/KHTH/YWD B14 .... 161 F2
Instone Rd *HALE* B63 .... 138 B4
Instow Cl *SHHTH* WV12 .... 25 H3
Insull Av *ALE/KHTH/YWD* B14 . 178 D4
Intended St *HALE* B63 .... 120 C5
International Dr
  LGN/SDN/BHAMAIR B26 ...... 149 G3
International Sq
  CHWD/FDBR/MGN B37 * 149 C3
Intown *WSL* WS1 .... 5 F3
Intown Rw *WSL* WS1 .... 5 F3
Inverclyde Dr
  ETTPK/GDPK/PENN WV4 .... 52 D3
Inverclyde Rd
  BFLD/HDSWWD B20 .... 90 A3
Inverkip Wy
  ETTPK/GDPK/PENN WV4 .... 52 D3
Inverness Rd *NFLD/LBR* B31 .. 175 F2
Inworth *COVEN* WV9 .... 12 B4
Ipsley Gv *ERDW/GRVHL* B23 .... 76 A4
Ipstones Av *STETCH* B33 .... 112 B5
Ipswich Crs *PBAR/PBCH* B42 ... 74 B4
Ireland Green Rd *WBROM* B70 . 87 E3
Ireton Rd *BFLD/HDSWWD* B20.. 90 A2
  WOLV WV10 .... 12 D4
Iris Cl *DUDS* DY2 ....
  SLYOAK B29 .... 158 D2
Iris Dr *ALE/KHTH/YWD* B14 ... 177 H1
Irnham Rd *FOAKS/STRLY* B74 .. 47 E5
Iron Bridge Wk *HAG/WOL* DY9.. 152 C2
Ironmonger Rw *CBHAMW* B4 * .. 2 D4
Irvan Av *WBROM* B70 .... 86 D1
Irvine Cl *BLOX/PEL* WS3 .... 27 F3
Irvine Rd *BLOX/PEL* WS3 .... 27 F3
Irving Cl *SEDG* DY3 .... 82 C2
Irving Rd *HIA/OLT* B92 .... 148 C3
  TPTN/OCK DY4 .... 69 G2
Irving St *CBHAMW* B1 .... 126 D3
Irwin Av *RBRY* B45 .... 188 C2
Isaac Walton Pl *WBROM* B70 ... 70 C4
Isbourne Wy *BORD* B9 .... 127 H1
Isis Gv *CBROM* B36 .... 113 H1
  WLNHL WV13 .... 40 A3
Island Rd *HDSW* B21 .... 89 C5
Islington *HALE* B63 .... 138 C5
Islington Rw *EDG* B15 .... 125 H4
Ismere Rd *ERDE/BCHGN* B24 ... 93 F4
Itchen Gv
  DUNHL/THL/PER WV6 .... 34 C2
Ithon Gv *HWK/WKHTH* B38 .... 176 D5
Ivanhoe Rd *BKHL/PFLD* WV2 ... 52 B4
  GTB/HAM B43 .... 59 F5
Ivatt *TPTN/OCK* DY4 .... 102 A2
Ivatt Cl *RUSH/SHEL* WS4 .... 28 D3
Iverley Rd *HALE* B63 .... 139 E4
Iverley Wk *HAG/WOL* DY9 ..... 135 H5
Ivor Rd *SPARK* B11 .... 144 D3
Ivy Av *BHTH/HG* B12 .... 144 C2
Ivybridge Gv *PBAR/PBCH* B42 .. 90 C2
Ivy Cft *COVEN* WV9 .... 11 H4
Ivydale Av
  LGN/SDN/BHAMAIR B26 ...... 148 A2
Ivyfield Rd *ERDW/GRVHL* B23 .. 91 H1
Ivy Gv *BRWNH* WS8 .... 19 G3
Ivyhouse La *BILS/COS* WV14 ... 68 C3
Ivyhouse Rd *HWK/WKHTH* B38.. 176 A5
Ivy House Rd *OLDBY* B69 ...... 104 B3
Ivy La *CBHAMNE* B4 .... 127 G2
  RMSLY B62 .... 154 D5
Ivy Lodge Cl
  CHWD/FDBR/MGN B37 .... 132 A4
Ivy Rd *DUDN* DY1 .... 101 H1
  DUDN DY1 .... 160 A2
  HDSW B21 .... 108 B1
  SCFLD/BOLD B73 .... 76 D2
Ivy Wy *SHLY* B90 .... 194 A2
Izons La *WBROM* B70 .... 87 E5
Izons Rd *WBROM* B70 .... 87 E5

J

Jacamar Av *STETCH* B33 .... 112 B5
Jacey Rd *LDYWD/EDGR* B16 ... 125 F2
  SHLY B90 .... 180 B1
Jackdaw Cl *SEDG* DY3 .... 67 E1
Jackdaw Dr *CBROM* B36 .... 114 A1
Jackson Av *WASH/WDE* B8 ..... 110 D4
Jackson Cl *WLNHL* WV13 .... 6 E1
Jack Holden Av *BILS/COS* WV14.. 68 A1
Jackson Cl *LGLYGN/QTN* B68 . 105 F4
  SPARK B11 * 127 H5
  TPTN/OCK DY4 .... 69 G2
  WOLVN WV10 .... 13 G1
Jackson Dr *SMTHWKW* B67 ... 105 H4
Jackson Rd *WASH/WDE* B8 .... 110 D5
Jackson St
  DUNHL/THL/PER WV6 .... 36 D1

HAG/WOL DY9 ....136 C2
LGLYGCN/QTN B68 ....105 F5
Jackson Wy RIDG/WDGT B32 ....140 A2
Jacobean Cft SMTHWKW B67 ...106 A5
Jacobean La DOR/KN B93 ....183 F4
Jacoby Pl DIG/EDG B5 ....143 G2
Jaffray Crs ERDE/BCHGN B24 .....92 D3
Jaffray Rd ERDE/BCHGN B24 .....92 D3
Jakeman Rd BHTH/HG B12 ....144 A2
James Bridge Cl WSLW WS2 * 56 E1
James Cl DARL/WED WS10 ....55 H1
SMTHWKW B67 ....106 C4
James Dee Cl BRLYHL DY5 ....119 H3
James Eaton Cl
HHTH/SAND B71 ....87 G1
Jameson Rd AST/WIT B6 ....110 A1
Jameson St
DUNHL/THL/PER WV6 ....36 D1
James Ct CSHL/WTROR B46 .....115 F1
GTB/HAM B43 ....73 G4
SPARK B11 ....145 H1
James Samuel Pl
BHTH/HG B12 ....127 F5
James Scott Rd HALE B63 ....83 C2
James St BILS/COS WV14 ....54 A2
CBHAMNW B3 ....2 D3
WLNHL WV13 ....39 C4
James Turner St WSNGN B18 ...107 G3
James Watt Dr LOZ/NWT B19 ...108 B1
James Watt Queensway
CBHAMNE B4 ....3 H3
James Watt St HHTH/SAND B71 ...71 F3
Jane Lane Cl WSLW WS2 ....40 D1
Janice Gv ALE/KHTH/YWD B14 ...178 D1
Janine Av WNSFLD WV11 ....25 E3
Jaques Cl ERDW/GRVHL B23 ....73 G5
Jardine Rd AST/WIT B6 ....71 F1
Jarvis Crs ERDW/GRVHL B23 .....105 E5
Jarvis Wy ERDE/BCHGN B24 .....110 C1
Jasmin Cft
ALE/KHTH/YWD B14 ....178 A3
Jasmine Gv CDSL WV8 ....11 H4
Jasmine Gv CDSL WV8 ....10 D4
Jaques Cl DUDS DY2 ....85 F5
Jasmine Wy DARL/WED WS10 ....55 F1
Jason Rd HAG/WOL DY9 ....136 D3
Javelin Av CVALE B35 ....94 D4
Javelin Pk DARL/WED WS10 ....70 B1
Jayne Cl HHTH/SAND B71 ....72 A2
WNSFLD WV11 ....24 D3
Jay Rd KGSWFD DY6 ....99 H1
Jays Av TPTN/OCK DY4 ....85 H2
Jayshaw Av GTB/HAM B43 ....73 C3
Jean Dr TPTN/OCK DY4 ....70 B5
Jeavons Pl BILS/COS WV14 ....53 C3
Jedburgh Av
DUNHL/THL/PER WV6 ....34 C1
Jeddo St BKHL/PFLD WV2 ....6 E7
Jeffcock Rd BDMR/CCFT WV3 .....36 C5
Jefferson Cl HHTH/SAND B71 .....71 F5
Jeffrey Av
ETTPK/GDPK/PENN WV4 ....52 D2
Jeffrey Rd BLKHTH/ROWR B65 ...122 C1
Jeffs Av BKHL/PFLD WV2 ....37 F5
Jenkins Cl BILS/COS WV14 ....53 G3
Jenkinson Rd DARL/WED WS10 ...70 B2
Jenkins St SMHTH B10 ....128 A4
Jenks Av WOLVN WV10 ....23 G2
Jenks Rd WMBN WV5 ....80 D1
Jennens Rd CBHAMNE B4 ....3 J3
Jenner Cl WSLW WS2 ....27 E4
Jenner Rd WSLW WS2 ....26 D4
Jenner St BKHL/PFLD WV2 ....7 J6
Jennings St CDYHTH B64 ....121 F2
Jenny Cl BILS/COS WV14 ....69 E2
Jenny Walkers La
DUNHL/THL/PER WV6 ....34 B5
Jephcott Rd WASH/WDE B8 ....129 E1
Jephson Dr
LGN/SDN/BHAMAIR B26 ....130 D5
Jeremy Gv HIA/OLT B92 ....147 H3
Jeremy Rd
ETTPK/GDPK/PENN WV4 ....52 A3
Jerome Rd CSCFLD/WYGN B72 ....62 D4
WSLW WS2 ....41 F4
Jerrard Dr MGN/WHC B75 ....62 C3
Jerrard Rd MGN/WHC B75 * 62 C3
Jerry's La ERDW/GRVHL B23 ....76 B4
Jersey Cft CBROM B36 ....114 B3
Jersey Rd WASH/WDE B8 ....110 B2
Jervis Cl BRLYHL DY5 ....101 E2
Jervis Crs FOAKS/STRLY B74 ......46 B2
Jervis Pk FOAKS/STRLY B74 ....46 A1
Jervis Ter HDSW B21 * 107 F1
Jervoise Dr NFLD/LBR B31 ....158 D5
Jervoise La HHTH/SAND B71 ....72 A2
Jervoise Rd SLYOAK B29 ....158 B1
Jervoise St WBROM B70 ....87 E2
Jesmond Gv ERDE/BCHGN B24 ...93 H2
Jessel Rd WSLW WS2 ....40 E4
Jessie Rd ALDR WS9 ....30 A1
Jesson Cl WSL WS1 ....57 G1
Jesson Rd MGN/WHC B75 ....65 G5
SEDG DY3 ....68 A5
WSL WS1 ....5 H7
Jesson St WBROM B70 ....88 A4
Jevons Rd BILS/COS WV14 ....68 C3
Jevon St BILS/COS WV14 ....68 C3
Jew's La SEDG DY3 ....82 D3
Jiggins La RIDG/WDGT B32 ....157 G2
Jill Av GTB/HAM B43 ....73 E2
Jillcot Rd HIA/OLT B92 ....147 H4
Jinnah Cl BHTH/HG B12 ....127 F4
Joan St BKHL/PFLD WV2 ....52 C2
Jockey Fld SEDG DY3 ....67 G5
Jockey La DARL/WED WS10 ....56 A4
Jockey Rd SCFLD/BOLD B73 ....76 B1
Joeys La CDSL WV8 ....11 E4
John Bright Cl TPTN/OCK DY4 ....69 F3
John Bright St CBHAMW B1 ....3 F7
John Fletcher Cl
DARL/WED WS10 ....56 B4
John Harper St WSL WS1 ....39 H5
John Howell Dr TPTN/OCK DY4 ...85 H1
John Kempe Wy
BHTH/HG B12 ....127 G5
John Padden Cl
BLKHTH/ROWR B65 ....121 H3
John Riley Dr SHHTH WV12 ....26 A2

John Rd RMSLY B62 ....139 H3
Johns Gv GTB/HAM B43 ....73 E3
John's La OLDBY B69 ....86 A4
TPTN/OCK DY4 ....85 H2
Johnson Av WNSFLD WV11 ....25 F3
Johnson Cl DARL/WED WS10 ....55 F3
SPARK B11 ....145 G2
WASH/WDE B8 ....111 G3
Johnson Dr CVALE B35 ....94 B3
Johnson Pl BILS/COS WV14 ....54 B1
Johnson Rd DARL/WED WS10 ......71 G1
ERDW/GRVHL B23 ....92 B3
SHHTH WV12 ....26 D3
Johnsons Bridge Rd
HHTH/SAND B71 ....71 G3
Johnsons Gv LGLYGCN/QTN B68 ...123 G4
Johnson St BILS/COS WV14 ....67 H2
BKHL/PFLD WV2 ....37 F5
VAUX/NECH B7 ....110 A5
Johnstone St LOZ/NWT B19 ......108 D1
Johnston St WBROM B70 ....87 H5
John St BKHL/PFLD WV2 ....53 E2
BLKHTH/ROWR B65 ....122 A3
BRLYHL DY5 ....101 F5
LOZ/NWT B19 ....108 D3
OLDBY B69 ....105 G2
STRBR DY8 ....118 B3
WBROM B70 ....86 D1
WLNHL WV13 ....39 C4
WSLW WS2 ....4 D1
John St North HHTH/SAND B71 ...87 F1
John Wesley Wy
DARL/WED WS10 ....71 G5
Joiners Cft HIA/OLT B92 ....165 G2
Joinings Bank
LGLYGCN/QTN B68 ....105 F5
Jones Field Crs WOLV WV1 ....38 B3
Jones Rd SHHTH WV12 ....26 A4
WOLVN WV10 ....23 E4
Jones Wood Cl
WALM/CURD B76 ....78 B4
Jonquil Cl ERDW/GRVHL B23 ....76 A4
Jordan Cl MGN/WHC B75 ....47 F4
SMTHWK B66 ....106 D4
Jordan Leys TPTN/OCK DY4 ....85 H1
Jordan Pl BILS/COS WV14 ....54 A5
Jordan Rd MGN/WHC B75 ....47 F4
Jordan Wy ALDR WS9 ....30 B1
Joseph St OLDBY B69 ....104 D3
Josiah Houses BILS/COS WV14 * ...68 C3
Josiah Rd NFLD/LBR B31 ....174 D3
Jowett's La HHTH/SAND B71 ......71 F3
Joyberry Dr STRBR DY8 ....135 F4
Joynson St DARL/WED WS10 ......55 G3
Jubilee Av HHTH/SAND B71 ....71 F4
Jubilee Cl BLOX/PEL WS3 ....28 A4
Jubilee Dr ERDW/GRVHL B23 ......75 H4
Jubilee Rd BILS/COS WV14 ....54 C4
RBRY B45 ....173 G3
TPTN/OCK DY4 ....69 G4
Jubilee St HHTH/SAND B71 ....71 H4
Judge Cl OLDBY B69 ....105 G2
Judge Rd BRLYHL DY5 ....119 H5
Julia Av ERDE/BCHGN B24 ....94 B2
Julia Gdns HHTH/SAND B71 ....72 B3
Julian Cl WOLV WV1 ....38 B5
Julie Cft BILS/COS WV14 ....69 E2
Juliet Rd RMSLY B62 ....139 G3
Julius Dr CSHL/WTROR B46 ....97 F5
Junction Rd BKHL/PFLD WV2 ....53 F1
HDSW B21 ....107 E1
STRBR DY8 ....135 H5
Junction St DUDS DY2 ....102 B1
OLDBY B69 ....105 E1
WSL WS1 ....56 D1
Junction St South OLDBY B69 ...118 A4
The Junction STRBR DY8 ....118 A4
June Cft
LGN/SDN/BHAMAIR B26 ....148 B2
WALM/CURD B76 ....78 C4
Juniper Dr DSYBK/YTR WS5 ....57 H4
WALM/CURD B76 ....78 C4
Juniper Ri HALE B63 ....137 G2
Jury Rd BRLYHL DY5 ....119 H5
Jutland Rd MOS/BIL B13 ....161 H5

K

Karen Wy BRLYHL DY5 ....119 F4
Kathleen Av SMTHWKW B67 .....124 B2
Kathleen Rd
CSCFLD/WYGN B72 ....62 C4
YDLY B25 ....129 G5
Katie Rd SLYOAK B29 ....159 G1
Kayne Cl FOAKS/STRLY B74 ....60 B2
Kayne Ct KGSWFD DY6 ....99 G2
Keanscroft Dr
LGLYGCN/QTN B68 ....105 G5
Keasdon Gv WLNHL WV13 ....40 A2
Keating Gdns MGN/WHC B75 ....48 A2
Keats Av SMHTH B10 ....128 B5
Keats Cl FOAKS/STRLY B74 ....32 D4
SEDG DY3 ....83 G2
STRBR DY8 ....118 C4
Keats Dr BILS/COS WV14 ....68 D1
Keats Gv ACGN B27 ....163 F1
WOLVN WV10 ....24 A2
Keats Rd BLOX/PEL WS3 ....28 A5
SHHTH WV12 ....26 A4
WOLVN WV10 ....24 A1
Keble Gv LGN/SDN/BHAMAIR B26 ...130 C5
WSL WS1 ....57 G1
Kedleston Cl BLOX/PEL WS3 * 16 C4
Kedleston Rd
HLGN/YWD B28 ....162 D4
Keel Dr MOS/BIL B13 ....162 B1
Keeley St BORD B9 ....127 H2
Keelinge St TPTN/OCK DY4 ....85 H1
Keen St SMTHWK B66 ....107 E5
Keepers Cl ALDR WS9 ....19 F4
CSHL/WTROR B46 ....115 G5
KGSWFD DY6 ....99 F1
WSNGN B18 ....107 H4

Keepers Gate Cl
FOAKS/STRLY B74 ....62 C1
Keepers La CDSL WV8 ....21 E1
Keepers Rd FOAKS/STRLY B74 ...32 A5
Keer Ct BORD B9 * 127 H1
Kegworth Rd
ERDW/GRVHL B23 ....92 A4
Keir Pl STRBR DY8 ....118 A4
Keir Rd DARL/WED WS10 ....71 G1
Kelby Cl NFLD/LBR B31 ....175 E2
Kelby Rd NFLD/LBR B31 ....175 E1
Kelia Dr DUNHL/THL/PER WV6 ...22 B5
Kelfield Av HRBN B17 ....141 H3
Kelia Dr SMTHWKW B67 ....106 B3
Kellett Rd VAUX/NECH B7 ....109 G5
Kelling Cl BRLYHL DY5 * 119 E4
Kellington Cl WASH/WDE B8 ......110 D5
Kelmarsh Dr SOLH B91 ....181 H4
Kelmscott Rd HRBN B17 ....124 D5
Kelsall Cl WOLV WV1 ....38 D3
Kelsall Cft CBHAMW B1 ....2 A4
Kelsey Cl VAUX/NECH B7 * 109 H5
Kelso Gdns
DUNHL/THL/PER WV6 ....34 B1
Kelsull Cft
CHWD/FDBR/MGN B37 ....132 A2
Kelton Ct EDG B15 ....126 A5
Kelvedon Gv SOLH B91 ....182 A1
Kelverdale Gv
ALE/KHTH/YWD B14 ....177 G1
Kelverley Gv HHTH/SAND B71 ....72 B3
Kelvin Av WSLW WS2 ....27 F4
Kelvin Rd NFLD/LBR B31 ....175 G4
WSLW WS2 ....27 E4
Kelvin Wy WBROM B70 ....87 G3
Kelway Av GTB/HAM B43 ....59 F5
Kelwood Dr HALE B63 ....138 B2
Kelynmead Rd STETCH B33 ....131 G5
Kemberton Cl BDMR/CCFT WV3 ...35 G4
Kemberton Rd
BDMR/CCFT WV3 ....35 G4
SLYOAK B29 ....141 G5
Kemble Cl SHHTH WV12 ....40 B1
Kemble Cft DIG/EDG B5 ....127 E5
Kemble Dr CVALE B35 ....94 C3
Kemelstowe Crs HALE B63 ....154 C2
Kemerton Wy SHLY B90 ....195 F3
Kempe Rd STETCH B33 ....112 C5
Kempsey Cl HALE B63 ....138 B2
HIA/OLT B92 ....164 B2
OLDBY B69 ....104 B5
Kempsey Covert
HWK/WKHTH B38 ....190 C1
Kempson Av
HHTH/SAND B71 ....57 F1
Kempson Rd CBROM B36 ....112 B1
Kempsons Gv BILS/COS WV14 ....53 F5
Kempthorne Av WOLVN WV10 ....23 G2
Kempthorne Gdns
BILS/COS WV14 ....54 B2
Kempthorne Rd
BILS/COS WV14 ....54 B2
Kempton Park Rd CBROM B36 ...111 H1
Kempton Wy STRBR DY8 ....135 E4
Kemsey Dr BILS/COS WV14 ....54 C4
Kemshead Av NFLD/LBR B31 .....175 E5
Kemsley Rd
ALE/KHTH/YWD B14 ....178 B3
Kendal Av CSHL/WTROR B46 .....115 F2
RBRY B45 ....188 B1
Kendal Cl DUNHL/THL/PER WV6 ...22 B4
Kendal Cl ALDR WS9 * 19 F3
Kendal Gv HIA/OLT B92 ....165 H2
Kendal Ri KGSWFD DY6 ....100 B4
Kendal Rd SPARK B11 ....127 H5
Kendal Ri
DUNHL/THL/PER WV6 ....22 B4
Kendall Ri
LGLYGCN/QTN B68 ....123 F1
Kendal Rise Rd RBRY B45 ....188 B1
Kendrick Av BKDE/SHDE B34 .....113 F5
Kendrick Cl HIA/OLT B92 ....165 H1
Kendrick Pl BILS/COS WV14 ....54 C4
Kendrick Rd BILS/COS WV14 ....54 B1
WALM/CURD B76 ....94 B1
Kendricks Rd DARL/WED WS10 ...56 A5
Kenelm Ct RMSLY B62 ....172 C1
Kenelm Rd BILS/COS WV14 ....68 C2
LGLYGCN/QTN B68 ....123 E1
SCFLD/BOLD B73 ....62 B4
SMHTH B10 ....128 B1
Kenilworth Cl
FOAKS/STRLY B74 ....47 E5
STRBR DY8 ....134 D5
TPTN/OCK DY4 ....84 D2
Kenilworth Ct DUDN DY1 * 101 H2
LDYWD/EDGR B16 * 125 E1
Kenilworth Crs
ETTPK/GDPK/PENN WV4 ....52 C4
WSLW WS2 ....41 E1
Kenilworth Rd
BFLD/HDSWWD B20 ....91 E5
DOR/KN B93 ....197 H2
DUNHL/THL/PER WV6 ....34 C2
LGLYGCN/QTN B68 ....123 H1
RCOVN/BALC/EX CV7 ....151 E5
Kenley Gv BVILLE B30 ....177 E3
Kenmare Wy WOLVN WV10 ....180 C1
Kenmure Rd STETCH B33 ....131 E5
Kennedy Cft DARL/WED WS10 ...56 A5
Kennedy Crs DARL/WED WS10 ...55 F1
SEDG DY3 ....82 D3
Kennedy Gv BVILLE B30 ....160 B4
Kennedy Rd WOLVN WV10 ....7 H2
Kennerley Rd YDLY B25 ....130 A1
Kennet Cl BRWNH WS8 ....18 D3
Kennet Gv CBHAMNE B4 ....113 H1
Kenneth Gv
BFLD/HDSWWD B20 ....91 G1
Kennford Cl
BLKHTH/ROWR B65 ....104 A3
Kennington Rd WOLVN WV10 .....23 H5
Kenrick Cft CVALE B35 ....94 B4
Kenrick Wy HHTH/SAND B71 ......88 B5
SMTHWK B66 ....106 B1

Kineton Cft RIDG/WDGT B32 .....157 H2
Kineton Green Rd
HIA/OLT B92 ....163 H2
Kineton Ri SEDG DY3 ....67 E1
Kineton Rd RBRY B45 ....187 G1
SCFLD/BOLD B73 ....76 C2
Kinfare Dr
DUNHL/THL/PER WV6 ....35 F1
Kinfare Ri SEDG DY3 ....83 G2
King Av SEDG DY3 ....83 G2
King Charles Av WSLW WS2 ....40 C5
King Charles Ct KGSTG B44 ....75 H1
King Charles Rd RMSLY B62 ......139 H3
King Edmund St DUDN DY1 ....84 B4
King Edward Rd MOS/BIL B13 ...144 B4
King Edwards Cl
BFLD/HDSWWD B20 * 108 B1
King Edwards Gdns
BFLD/HDSWWD B20 * 108 B2
King Edward's Rw CBHAMW B1 ....2 B5
CBHAMW B1 ....2 A3
King Edward's Rw
BKHL/PFLD WV2 * 37 E5
King Edward's Sq
SCFLD/BOLD B73 ....62 C3
King Edward's St
DARL/WED WS10 ....55 F3
Kingfield Rd SHLY B90 ....179 E5
Kingfisher Cl BRWNH WS8 ....9 H3
LGN/SDN/BHAMAIR B26 ....147 G1
SEDG DY3 ....67 E1
Kingfisher Dr CBROM B36 ....114 A1
STRBR DY8 ....134 C3
Kingfisher Gv SHHTH WV12 ....25 H2
Kingfisher Rd
ERDW/GRVHL B23 ....76 A4
Kingfisher Vw
BKDE/SHDE B34 ....112 C4
Kingfisher Wy BVILLE B30 ....159 F2
King George Crs
RUSH/SHEL WS4 ....28 D4
King George Pl
RUSH/SHEL WS4 ....28 D4
King George Vi Av WSL WS1 ....43 E5
Kingham Cl SEDG DY3 ....83 E4
Kingham Covert
ALE/KHTH/YWD B14 ....177 H3
King's Av OLDBY B69 ....85 H4
Kingsbridge Rd
RIDG/WDGT B32 ....157 H1
Kingsbrook Dr SOLH B91 ....181 H5
Kingsbury Av
ERDE/BCHGN B24 ....93 H3
Kingsbury Cl RUSH/SHEL WS4 ...42 D1
WALM/CURD B76 ....95 F1
Kingsbury Rd
ERDE/BCHGN B24 ....92 D4
TPTN/OCK DY4 ....69 G3
WALM/CURD B76 ....78 A3
Kingscliffe Crs
BDMR/CCFT WV3 ....50 C1
Kingscliff Rd SMHTH B10 ....129 E4
Kings Cl ALE/KHTH/YWD B14 .....160 C4
Kingscote Rd DOR/KN B93 ....198 C1
EDG B15 ....142 B1
King's Cl
CHWD/FDBR/MGN B37 ....133 E3
STRBR DY8 ....135 E2
Kings Cft CBROM B36 ....114 A2
LGN/SDN/BHAMAIR B26 ....130 C5
Kingscroft Cl FOAKS/STRLY B74 ...45 G5
Kingscroft Rd
FOAKS/STRLY B74 ....60 C1
Kingsdene Av KGSWFD DY6 ....99 G5
Kingsdown Av GTB/HAM B43 ......73 H2
Kingsdown Rd
BKDE/SHDE B34...PBOR/PBCH B42 ...73 H5
Kingsdown Rd NFLD/LBR B31 ....158 A1
Kingsfield Rd
ALE/KHTH/YWD B14 ....161 E2
Kingsford Cl CBROM B36 ....95 F5
Kingsford Nouveau
KGSWFD DY6 ....100 C4
Kings Gdn BVILLE B30 ....176 C1
Kings Green Av
HWK/WKHTH B38 ....176 D3
Kingshayes Rd ALDR WS9 ....30 B1
Kingshill Dr HWK/WKHTH B38 ...176 B1
Kings Hill Fld DARL/WED WS10 ...55 E3
Kingshurst Rd NFLD/LBR B31 ....175 G2
SHLY B90 ....179 H4
Kingshurst Wy
CHWD/FDBR/MGN B37 ....113 H4
Kingsland Dr DOR/KN B93 ....196 C5
Kingsland Rd KGSTG B44 ....60 A4
WOLV WV1 ....6 C1
Kingslea Rd SOLH B91 ....181 E3
Kingsleigh Dr CBROM B36 ....114 A2
Kingsleigh Rd
BFLD/HDSWWD B20 ....90 B4
Kingsley Av
DUNHL/THL/PER WV6 ....35 F1
Kingsley Av
LGN/SDN/BHAMAIR B26 ....130 D5
Kingsley Ct YDLY B25 ....130 A4
Kingsley Gdns CDSL WV8 ....10 B4
Kingsley Gv DUDN DY1 ....84 B1
Kingsley Rd BHTH/HG B12 ....144 C2
BVILLE B30 ....176 B1
KGSWFD DY6 ....99 G4
Kingsley St DUDS DY2 ....102 C4
WSLW WS2 ....56 B1
Kingslow Av
ETTPK/GDPK/PENN WV4 ....50 D2
King's Meadow HAG/WOL DY9 ...170 C3
Kingsmere Cl ERDE/BCHGN B24 ...92 C4
Kings Mill Cl DARL/WED WS10 ...56 A3
Kingsoak Gdns DUDS DY2 ....103 E2
King's Rd ALE/KHTH/YWD B14 ...160 C4
KGSTG B44 ....92 A2
KGSTG B44 ....75 H1
RUSH/SHEL WS4 ....29 E4
SEDG DY3 ....75 H1
Kings St BILS/COS WV14 * 146 A2
Kings Street Prec
DARL/WED WS10 ....55 F2
Kingstanding Rd KGSTG B44 ....60 C4
KGSTG B44 ....75 F1
Kings Ter
ALE/KHTH/YWD B14 ....160 C4

Kingsthorpe Rd
ALE/KHTH/YWD B14........178 C2
Kingston Rd BORD B9........127 H3
MGN/WHC B75........63 F2
Kingston Rw CBHAMW B1........2 C5
Kingston Wy KGSWFD DY6........99 G2
King St ALDR WS9 *........5 E4
BILS/COS WV14........68 A3
BRLYHL DY5........119 H4
CDYHTH B64........121 F3
DARL/WED WS10........70 D2
DUDS DY2........84 C5
HAG/WOL DY9........136 D3
HALE B63........138 C3
SMTHWK B66........86 C5
SPARK B11........144 C1
STRBR DY8........135 E1
WLNHL WV13........39 H3
WOLV WV1........7 F4
WSL WS1........56 A5
King Street Pas BRLYHL DY5........120 A4
DUDS DY2........84 D5
Kingsway LGLYGN/QTN B68........123 F5
STRBR DY8........117 H4
WNSFLD WV11........25 E5
WOLV WV10........24 A4
Kingsway Av TPTN/OCK DY4........69 G3
Kingsway Dr
HWK/WKHTH B38........176 D3
Kingsway North ALDR WS9 *........29 C4
Kingsway Rd WOLV WV10........24 A4
Kingsway South ALDR WS9........29 C4
Kingsway Ter WNSFLD WV11 *........15 E3
Kingswear Av
DUNHL/THL/PER WV6........34 D2
Kingswinford Rd DUDN DY1........101 G2
Kingswood Cl BVILLE B30........178 A2
SHLY B90........180 D4
Kingswood Cft
VAUX/NECH B7........110 A2
Kingswood Dr BVILLE B30........177 G2
FOAKS/STRLY B74........60 B4
Kingswood Gdns
ETTPK/GDPK/PENN WV4........51 F2
Kingswood Rd KGSWFD DY6........99 G5
MOS/BIL B13........144 C3
NFLD/LBR B31........189 F2
Kingswood Ter YDLY B25 *........129 F5
Kington Cl SHHTH WV12........25 H2
Kington Gdns
CHWD/FDBR/MGN B37........131 H2
Kington Wy STECH B33........130 A3
King William St STRBR DY8........118 B4
Kiniths Crs HHTH/SAND B71........88 A2
Kiniths Wy HHTH/SAND B71........88 A2
RMSLY B62........122 C3
Kinlet Cl BDMR/CCFT WV3........35 E5
Kinlet Gv NFLD/LBR B31........176 A3
Kinloch Dr DUDN DY1........83 H5
Kinnerley St WSL WS1........5 H5
Kinnersley Crs OLDBY B69........104 B4
Kinsey Gv ALE/KHTH/YWD B14....178 B1
Kinsham Dr SOLH B91........181 H5
Kintore Cft RIDG/WDGT B32........157 F3
Kintyre Cl RBRY B45........173 C4
Kinver Av SHHTH WV12........25 H5
Kinver Crs ALDR WS9 *........30 C1
Kinver Cft BHTH/HG B12........144 A1
WALM/CURD B76........78 B3
Kinver Dr
ETTPK/GDPK/PENN WV4........50 C3
HAG/WOL DY9........153 E3
Kinver St NFLD/LBR B31........176 B3
Kinver St STRBR DY8........117 H3
Kinwarton Cl YDLY B25........146 D1
Kipling Av BILS/COS WV14........68 A4
Kipling Cl TPTN/OCK DY4........69 G3
Kipling Rd NFLD/LBR B31........176 A1
SEDG DY3........82 C1
SHHTH WV12........26 C3
WOLV WV10........12 D5
Kirby Cl BILS/COS WV14........54 A5
Kirby Dr DUDN DY1........83 G3
Kirby Rd WSNGN B18........107 G3
Kirkby Gn SCFLD/BOLD B73........62 A5
Kirkham Gdns BRLYHL DY5........101 E3
Kirkham Gv STECH B33........112 B5
Kirkside Gv BRWNH WS8........9 F5
Kirkstall Cl BLOX/PEL WS5........16 B5
Kirkstall Crs BLOX/PEL WS5........16 B5
Kirkstone Ct BRLYHL DY5........118 D4
Kirkstone Crs GTB/HAM B43........73 H5
WMBN WV5........64 D5
Kirkstone Wy BRLYHL DY5........118 D4
Kirkwall Rd RIDG/WDGT B32....157 H1
Kirkwood Av ERDW/GRVHL B23...76 D4
Kirstead Gdns
DUNHL/THL/PER WV6........35 F2
Kirton Gv
DUNHL/THL/PER WV6........35 E1
SOLH B91........181 G4
STECH B33........112 C5
Kitchener Rd DUDS DY2........85 E1
SLYOAK B29........160 B1
Kitchener St WSNGN B18........107 F3
Kitchen La WNSFLD WV11........25 E2
Kitebrook Cl SHLY B90........195 G1
Kitegreen Ct
CHWD/FDBR/MGN B37........114 D5
Kitsland Rd BKDE/SHDE B34....113 G3
Kitswell Gdns RIDG/WDGT B32...157 E2
Kittiwake Dr BRLYHL DY5........119 E5
Kitts Green Rd FOAKS/STRLY B74....46 D2
Kitts Green Rd STECH B33........130 D1
Kitwell La RIDG/WDGT B32........157 E3
Kitwood Dr HIA/OLT B92........165 F3
Kixley La DOR/KN B93........197 F2
Knaresdale Cl BRLYHL DY5........119 E4
Knaves Castle Av BRWNH WS8.....9 F2
Knebworth Cl KGSTG B44........75 E3
Knightcote Dr SOLH B91........181 H5
Knightley Rd SOLH B91........181 F5
Knightlow Rd HRBN B17........124 D4
Knighton Cl FOAKS/STRLY B74...46 D2
Knighton Dr FOAKS/STRLY B74...46 D3
Knighton Rd DUDS DY2........102 D5
FOAKS/STRLY B74........46 B1

NFLD/LBR B31........176 A1
Knights Av
DUNHL/THL/PER WV6........22 A4
Knightsbridge Cl
FOAKS/STRLY B74........46 D1
Knightsbridge La SHHTH WV12...25 H4
Knightsbridge Rd
HIA/OLT B92........164 B1
Knights Cl ERDW/GRVHL B23....92 C4
WNSFLD WV11........39 H1
Knights Ct
CHWD/FDBR/MGN B37........133 E4
Knights Crs
DUNHL/THL/PER WV6........22 A3
Knightsfield Cl
SCFLD/BOLD B73........61 E5
Knights Hi ALDR WS9........44 B2
Knights Rd SPARK B11........146 A3
Knightstone Av WSNGN B18....108 A5
Knights Wood Cl
MGN/WHC B75........62 D1
Knightwick Crs
ERDW/GRVHL B23........92 A1
Knipersley Rd
ERDW/GRVHL B23........77 E5
Knoll Cft ALDR WS9........30 C1
LDYWD/EDGR B16 *........126 A2
SHLY B90........194 D4
The Knoll KGSWFD DY6........100 A4
RIDG/WDGT B32........157 G1
Knottsall La LGLYGN/QTN B68..123 F1
Knotts Farm Rd KGSWFD DY6..100 C5
Knowlands Rd SHLY B90........195 G1
Knowle Cl RBRY B45........188 D1
Knowle Hill Rd DUDS DY2........103 F5
Knowle Rd
BLKHTH/ROWR B65........103 F5
SPARK B11........145 F4
Knowles Dr FOAKS/STRLY B74....62 A1
Knowles Rd WOLV WV1........37 H4
Knowles St DARL/WED WS10....56 A5
Knowle Wood Rd
DOR/KN B93........199 F1
Knox Rd BKHL/PFLD WV2........52 A2
Knutswood Cl MOS/BIL B13 *....162 B3
Kohima Dr STRBR DY8........135 C2
Kossuth Rd BILS/COS WV14........68 A2
Kyle Cl WOLV WV10........22 D1
Kyles Wy RIDG/WDGT B32........157 F3
Kynaston Crs CDSL WV8........11 G5
Kyngsford Rd STECH B33........131 F1
Kyotts Lake Rd SPARK B11........127 G5
Kyrwicks La BHTH/HG B12........127 G5
SPARK B11........144 C1
Kyter La CBROM B36........112 D1

L

Laburnham Rd KGSWFD DY6...100 A3
Laburnum Av
CHWD/FDBR/MGN B37........113 H3
SMTHWK B67........106 A5
Laburnum Cl BLOX/PEL WS5......17 H5
CHWD/FDBR/MGN B37........113 H3
HLYWD B47........192 C5
Laburnum Cft OLDBY B69........85 H4
Laburnum Dr WALM/CURD B76...63 G5
Laburnum Gv MOS/BIL B13 *....144 B4
WSLW WS2........40 D2
Laburnum Rd ALDR WS9........19 G4
DARL/WED WS10........56 B5
DSYBK/YTR WS5........58 A3
DUDN DY1........84 B2
ETTPK/GDPK/PENN WV4........52 C5
TPTN/OCK DY4........69 F4
WOLV WV1........38 B5
Laburnum St BDMR/CCFT WV3....6 B6
Laburnum Wy NFLD/LBR B31....175 G4
Ladbroke Dr WALM/CURD B76...78 B1
Ladbroke Gv ACGN B27........163 G2
Ladbrook Gv SEDC DY3........82 B2
Ladbrook Rd SOLH B91........182 A2
Ladbury Gv DSYBK/YTR WS5.....57 G4
Ladbury Rd WSLW WS2........58 A1
Ladeler Gv STECH B33........131 F2
Ladies Wk SEDC DY3........67 F3
Lady Bank RIDG/WDGT B32......157 F5
Lady Bracknell Ms
NFLD/LBR B31........176 A1
Lady Byron La DOR/KN B93....196 D1
Lady Grey's Wk STRBR DY8....134 C2
Lady La SHLY B90........194 B5
Ladymoor Rd BILS/COS WV14...68 C1
Ladypool Cl RMSLY B62........139 E3
RUSH/SHEL WS4........28 C5
Ladypool Rd BHTH/HG B12....144 C2
Ladysmith Rd HALE B63........137 G1
Ladywell Cl WMBN WV5........65 E3
Ladywell Wk DIG/EDG B5........3 G7
Ladywood Circ
LDYWD/EDGR B16........126 A2
Ladywood Cl BRLYHL DY5........119 H2
Ladywood Middleway
LDYWD/EDGR B16........126 A2
Ladywood Rd
FOAKS/STRLY B74........47 E5
LDYWD/EDGR B16........125 H3
Lake Av DSYBK/YTR WS5........57 H1
Lake Cl DSYBK/YTR WS5........58 A1
Lakedown Cl
ALE/KHTH/YWD B14........178 A4
Lakefield Cl HLGN/YWD B28...163 F3
Lakefield Rd WNSFLD WV11......25 E5
Lakeside
CHWD/FDBR/MGN B37........133 E4
FOAKS/STRLY B74........31 H5
Lakeside Cl WLNHL WV13........39 E2
Lakeside Ct BRLYHL DY5........118 D4
Lakeside Dr ERDW/GRVHL B23...91 H1

SHLY B90........195 F1
Lakeside Rd WBROM B70........71 E5
Lakes Rd ERDW/GRVHL B23......75 C5
Lake St SEDC DY3........83 F3
Lake View Cl BVILLE B30........159 C5
Lakewood Dr RBRY B45........174 B4
Lakey La HLGN/YWD B28........163 F3
Lambah Cl BILS/COS WV14........54 A1
Lamb Cl BKDE/SHDE B34........113 G4
Lamb Crs WMBN WV5........80 D1
Lambert Cl ERDW/GRVHL B23....76 B5
Lambert Ct KGSWFD DY6........99 H1
Lambert End WBROM B70........87 F3
Lambert Fold DUDS DY2........103 E1
Lambert Rd WOLV WV10........23 H4
Lambert St WBROM B70........87 F5
Lambeth Cl
CHWD/FDBR/MGN B37........114 B5
Lambeth Rd BILS/COS WV14.....54 C5
KGSTG B44........60 A5
Lambourne Gv
CHWD/FDBR/MGN B37........131 G2
Lambourne Wy BRLYHL DY5....118 D4
Lambourn Rd
ERDW/GRVHL B23........92 B2
WLNHL WV13........40 B4
Lambscote Cl SHLY B90........179 E5
Lammas Cl HIA/OLT B92........165 F1
Lammas Rd STRBR DY8........117 C1
Lammermoor Av GTB/HAM B43..73 H1
Lamont Av RIDG/WDGT B32....141 F4
Lamorna Cl BDMR/CCFT WV3....35 F5
Lanark Cl KGSWFD DY6........100 C4
Lanark Cft CVALE B35........94 D3
Lancaster Av ALDR WS9........30 B2
DARL/WED WS10........56 C5
RBRY B45........174 A5
Lancaster Circ Queensway
CBHAMNE B4........3 H2
Lancaster Cl BVILLE B30........160 A4
Lancaster Dr CVALE B35........94 D4
Lancaster Gdns
ETTPK/GDPK/PENN WV4........51 E3
Lancaster Pl BLOX/PEL WS5......17 E5
Lancaster Rd BRLYHL DY5........119 E2
Lancaster St CBHAMNE B4........3 H1
Lancelot Cl WASH/WDE B8....128 C1
Lanchester Rd
HWK/WKHTH B38........177 E4
Lanchester Wy CBROM B36........95 H5
Lander Cl RBRY B45........188 A2
Landgate Rd HDSW B21........89 F5
Land La
CHWD/FDBR/MGN B37........132 A5
Landor Rd DOR/KN B93........197 E2
Landor St BORD B9........127 H1
Landport Rd BKHL/PFLD WV2...37 H5
Landrake Rd KGSWFD DY6........100 A4
Landsdown Cl DUDS DY2........103 G1
Landsdowne St STRBR DY8........134 C2
Landsgate STRBR DY8........152 C1
Landswood Cl KGSTG B44........75 G2
Landswood Rd
LGLYGN/QTN B68........105 C5
Lane Av WSLW WS2........41 F2
Lane Cl WSLW WS2........41 F2
Lane Cft WALM/CURD B76........78 C3
Lane Green Av CDSL WV8........21 G1
Lane Green Rd CDSL WV8........21 E5
Lane Rd
ETTPK/GDPK/PENN WV4........53 E4
Lanes Cl WMBN WV5........80 B1
Lanesfield Dr
ETTPK/GDPK/PENN WV4........53 E4
Laneside Av FOAKS/STRLY B74...60 B1
Laneside Gdns WSLW WS2........41 E3
Lane St BILS/COS WV14........53 H5
Langcomb Rd SHLY B90........180 A4
Langdale Av WSNGN B18........19 E1
Langdale Cl HDSW B21........107 G2
Langdale Dr BILS/COS WV14.....54 A5
Langdale Rd GTB/HAM B43........73 H4
Langdale Wy HAG/WOL DY9....136 B5
Langdon St BORD B9........127 H1
Langfield Rd DOR/KN B93........197 E1
Langford Av GTB/HAM B43........73 G3
Langford Cl WSL WS1........5 G5
Langford Cft SOLH B91........182 A3
Langford Gv HRBN B17........142 A4
Langham Cl
LGN/SDN/BHAMAIR B26....130 C5
Langholm Dr FOAKS/STRLY B74..45 E4
Langholme Dr KGSTG B44........76 B2
Langland Dr SEDC DY3........67 E3
Langley Av BILS/COS WV14........68 C3
Langley Cl ALDR WS9........19 G4
Langley Crs LGLYGN/QTN B68....105 F5
Langley Dr CVALE B35........94 C5
Langley Gdns BDMR/CCFT WV3...50 D1
Langley Green Rd OLDBY B69...105 E5
Langley Gv SMHTH B10 *........128 B4
Langley Hall Dr MGN/WHC B75...63 H2
Langley Hall Rd HIA/OLT B92....165 E3
MGN/WHC B75........63 H2
Langley Heath Dr
WALM/CURD B76........63 F5
Langley High St OLDBY B69....105 E4
Langley Pkwy MGN/WHC B75...63 F2
Langley Ri HIA/OLT B92........148 B4
Langley Rd
ETTPK/GDPK/PENN WV4........50 C1
LGLYGN/QTN B68........105 E5
SMHTH B10........128 B4
Langleys Rd SLYOAK B29........159 G2
Langmead Cl WSLW WS2........40 B2
Langsett Rd WOLV WV10........37 G1
Langstone Rd
ALE/KHTH/YWD B14........178 D3
DUDN DY1........83 C5
Langton Cl CBROM B36........114 B3
Langton Rd BILS/COS WV14........69 E4
Langton Rd WASH/WDE B8....110 C5
Langtree Av SOLH B91........181 H4
Langwood Ct CBROM B36........112 D1
Langworth Av ACGN B27........146 C2
Lannacombe Rd
NFLD/LBR B31........189 C2
Lansbury Av DARL/WED WS10....55 E4
Lansbury Gn CDYHTH B64........121 H5
Lansbury Rd CDYHTH B64........121 H4

Lansdale Av HIA/OLT B92........165 H2
Lansdowne Av CDSL WV8........10 A5
Lansdowne Cl BILS/COS WV14...68 A4
DUDS DY2........103 F3
Lansdowne Rd BILS/COS WV14..54 D1
ERDW/GRVHL B23........92 B3
HALE B63........137 H5
HDSW B21........108 A2
RMSLY B62........122 D4
WOLV WV1........6 D2
Lansdowne St WSNGN B18....107 H5
Lansdown Pl WSNGN B18 *........108 A4
Lantern Rd DUDS DY2........120 C2
Lanton Cl BLOX/PEL WS5........16 C5
Lapal La North RMSLY B62....139 C4
Lapal La South RMSLY B62....139 C4
Lapley Cl WOLV WV1........38 B3
Lapper Av
ETTPK/GDPK/PENN WV4........67 H1
Lapwing Cl BRWNH WS8........9 E5
Lapwing Cft ERDW/GRVHL B23..76 A4
Lapwing Dr HIA/OLT B92........167 H3
Lapwood Av KGSWFD DY6........100 C4
Lapworth Gv BHTH/HG B12....144 A2
Lapworth St HAC/WOL DY9....136 C1
Lara Cl HRBN B17........124 D4
Lara Gv TPTN/OCK DY4........85 C4
Larch Av HDSW B21........89 F4
Larch Cft
CHWD/FDBR/MGN B37........132 B2
OLDBY B69........85 H4
Larch Dr NFLD/LBR B31........174 C4
Larchfield Cl HDSW B21........89 E4
Larches La BDMR/CCFT WV3........6 A4
Larches St SPARK B11........144 C1
Larchfield Cl
BFLD/HDSWWD B20........90 B3
Larch Gdns BILS/COS WV14........54 B4
Larch Gv SEDG DY3........66 D4
Larchmere Dr HLGN/YWD B28..162 D2
WNSFLD WV11........15 E4
Larch Rd KGSWFD DY6........100 A3
Larchwood Crs
FOAKS/STRLY B74........45 E5
Larchwood Gn DSYBK/YTR WS5..57 C4
Larchwood Rd DSYBK/YTR WS5..57 C4
Larcombe Dr
ETTPK/GDPK/PENN WV4........52 B3
Large Av DARL/WED WS10........55 E4
Lark Cl ALE/KHTH/YWD B14....178 C3
Larkfield Av CBROM B36........112 D1
Larkfield Rd STRBR DY8........134 C3
Larkin Cl WOLV WV10........24 A1
Lark Meadow Dr
CHWD/FDBR/MGN B37........131 G1
Larksfield Ms BRLYHL DY5........119 E5
Larks Mi BLOX/PEL WS5........17 C3
Larkspur Cft CBROM B36........111 H1
Larkspur Rd DUDS DY2........103 F1
Larkspur Wy BRWNH WS8........18 D1
Larkswood Dr
ETTPK/GDPK/PENN WV4........50 C5
SEDG DY3........67 F4
Larne Rd
LGN/SDN/BHAMAIR B26....130 C2
Latches Cl DARL/WED WS10.....55 C5
Latelow Rd STECH B33........130 C2
Latham Av GTB/HAM B43........73 C4
Latham Crs TPTN/OCK DY4........85 C5
Lath La SMTHWK B66........105 H1
Lathom Gv STECH B33........112 B4
Latimer Gdns EDG B15........126 D5
Latimer Pl WSNGN B18........107 C3
Latimer St WLNHL WV13........39 C2
Lauder Cl SEDG DY3........67 E3
WLNHL WV13........39 C5
Lauderdale Cl BRWNH WS8......19 E1
Lauderdale Gdns WOLV WV10...13 E4
Laughton Cl NFLD/LBR B31....189 H1
Launceston Cl DSYBK/YTR WS5..58 B1
Launceston Rd
DSYBK/YTR WS5........58 B1
The Launde HLGN/YWD B28....179 F2
Laundry Rd SMTHWK B66........106 D1
Laural Dr SMTHWK B66........106 D1
Laureates Wk
FOAKS/STRLY B74........47 E4
Laurel Cl DUDS DY2........103 F5
Laurel Dr FOAKS/STRLY B74.....45 E5
SMTHWK B66........106 C1
Laurel Gdns ACGN B27........145 H1
HDSW B21........89 G5
Laurel Gv BDMR/CCFT WV3.....50 C4
BILS/COS WV14........54 C4
BVILLE B30........159 G4
Laurel La HALE B63........138 D4
Laurel Rd BVILLE B30........177 E1
DSYBK/YTR WS5........58 A3
DUDN DY1........84 B2
HDSW B21........89 G5
TPTN/OCK DY4........69 F4
Leander Gdns
ALE/KHTH/YWD B14........161 F5
Leander Rd HAG/WOL DY9....136 D3
Lea Rd BDMR/CCFT WV3........51 F3
SPARK B11........145 F1
Lear Rd WMBN WV5........65 F4
Leason La WOLV WV10........24 A2
Leasow Dr EDG B15........142 B4
Leasowe Rd RBRY B45........173 H5
TPTN/OCK DY4........85 C2
Leasowes Ct HALE B63........138 B5
Leasowes Dr
DUNHL/THL/PER WV6........34 B1
Leasowes La RMSLY B62........139 C2
Leasowes Rd
ALE/KHTH/YWD B14........161 F1
The Leasowes TPTN/OCK DY4...86 A1
The Leasow ALDR WS9........20 B5
The Lea STECH B33........130 C1
Leatherhead Cl AST/WIT B6....109 F3
Lea Vale Rd STRBR DY8........135 F5
Leavesden Gv
LGN/SDN/BHAMAIR B26....147 G2
Lea Vw ALDR WS9........29 G5
SHHTH WV12........25 G5
Lea Village STECH B33........130 D2
Lea Wk RBRY B45........173 H5
Lea Yield Cl BVILLE B30........160 A3
Lechlade Rd GTB/HAM B43.....73 H3
Leckie Rd WSLW WS2........42 A1
Ledbury Cl ALDR WS9........30 C1
LDYWD/EDGR B16........126 A2
Ledbury Dr WOLV WV1........38 B4
Ledbury Wy WALM/CURD B76...78 C4

The Lawley HALE B63........154 C1
Lawn Av STRBR DY8........135 E3
Lawn La COVEN WV9........11 H2
Lawnoaks Cl BRWNH WS8.......8 D2
Lawn Rd BKHL/PFLD WV2........52 C2
Lawnsdale Ct
CSHL/WTROR B46........119 H5
Lawnsdown Rd BRLYHL DY5....119 H5
Lawnsfield Gv
ERDW/GRVHL B23........76 B4
Lawnside Gn BILS/COS WV14....55 E3
Lawn St STRBR DY8........135 E3
Lawnswood KINVER DY7........117 E2
WALM/CURD B76........78 C3
Lawnswood Av
DUNHL/THL/PER WV6........22 A2
ETTPK/GDPK/PENN WV4........52 C2
SHLY B90........180 D2
STRBR DY8........99 C5
Lawnswood Dr ALDR WS9.......19 C4
KINVER DY7........117 E2
Lawnswood Ri HDSW B21.......89 E5
Lawnswood Rd
DUNHL/THL/PER WV6........22 B2
Lawnswood Rd KINVER DY7....99 E5
SEDG DY3........83 C4
STRBR DY8........117 C1
Lawnwood Rd DUDS DY2........120 C2
Lawrence Av WNSFLD WV11....25 F4
WOLV WV10........38 A1
Lawrence Dr WALM/CURD B76...79 F5
Lawrence La CDYHTH B64......121 E3
Lawrence St HAG/WOL DY9....136 A1
WLNHL WV13........39 G2
Lawrence Wk GTB/HAM B43....59 H4
Lawson St WSNGN B18........44 B1
Lawton Cl SHHTH/SAND B71.....88 A3
Lawton Cl BLKHTH/ROWR B65..104 A3
Laxey Rd LDYWD/EDGR B16....125 E1
Laxford Cl BHTH/HG B12........144 A1
Laxton Cl KGSWFD DY6........100 C4
Laxton Gv YDLY B25........129 H3
Lazy Hi HWK/WKHTH B38........177 F3
Lazy Hill Rd ALDR WS9........30 C1
Lea Bank Av DUDN DY1........83 C5
Lea Bank Rd DUDS DY2........120 D1
Leabon Gv HRBN B17........142 A3
Leabrook
LGN/SDN/BHAMAIR B26....130 B4
Leabrook Rd DARL/WED WS10...70 B2
Leabrook Rd North
DARL/WED WS10........70 B2
Leach Green La RBRY B45.....188 A1
Leach Heath La RBRY B45.....187 H1
Leacliffe Wy ALDR WS9........45 F2
Leacote Dr
DUNHL/THL/PER WV6........35 G1
Leacroft Av WOLV WV10........25 C2
Leacroft Cl ALDR WS9........30 B1
Leacroft Gv HHTH/SAND B71....71 F3
Leacroft Rd KGSWFD DY6........100 A1
Lea End La ALSF B48........190 A4
HWK/WKHTH B38........191 F5
Leafield Crs STECH B33........112 C4
Leafield Gdns RMSLY B62........122 B4
Leafield Rd HIA/OLT B92........164 D1
Lea Ford Rd STECH B33........113 E5
Leaford Wy KGSWFD DY6........100 B4
Leafy Gld FOAKS/STRLY B74....45 G2
Lealand Ri RBRY B45........188 C1
Lea Gdns BDMR/CCFT WV3......36 D5
Lea Green Av TPTN/OCK DY4....84 C1
Lea Green Dr HLYWD B47........193 E4
Lea Green La HLYWD B47........193 E2
Lea Hall Rd STECH B33........130 C2
Leahill Cft
CHWD/FDBR/MGN B37........131 H2
Lea Hill Rd BFLD/HDSWWD B20...90 C4
Leaholme Gdns HAG/WOL DY9...135 H5
Lahurst Crs HRBN B17........142 A3
Lea Manor Dr
ETTPK/GDPK/PENN WV4........51 E5
Leam Crs HIA/OLT B92........164 D1
Leamington Rd BHTH/HG B12...144 D2
Leamore Cl WSLW WS2........27 E3
Leamore La WSLW WS2........27 E5
Leamount Dr KGSTG B44........76 A1

Ledsam Gv RIDG/WDGT B32 141 F1
Ledsam St LDYWD/EDGR B16 126 A2
Ledwell SHLY B90 194 A3
Lee Bank Middleway EDG B15 126 C4
Lee Rd HALE B63 138 A5
Leech St TPTN/OCK DY4 86 A1
Lee Crs EDG B15 126 C4
Lee Gdns SMTHWKW B67 106 A4
Lee Mt EDG B15 * 126 C4
Lee Rd CDYHTH B64 121 F4
  HLYWD B47 192 C1
Leeson Wk HRBN B17 142 B2
Lees Rd BILS/COS WV14 54 B5
Lees St WSNGN B18 107 H4
Lee Ter BILS/COS WV14 54 B5
Lee St WBROM B70 71 E3
Legge La BILS/COS WV14 68 D1
  CBHAMW B1 2 C3
Legge St BKHL/PFLD WV2 52 C2
  CBHAMNE B4 3 J1
  WBROM B70 87 H3
Legion Rd RBRY B45 187 G1
Legs La WOLVN WV10 13 F4
Leicester Cl SMTHWKW B67 124 A3
Leicester Pl HHTH/SAND B71 71 G4
Leicester St
  DUNHL/THL/PER WV6 36 D1
  WSL WS1 4 E3
Leigham Dr HRBN B17 124 B5
Leigh Cl RUSH/SHEL WS4 42 C1
Leigh Rd MGN/WHC B75 63 H2
  RUSH/SHEL WS4 42 C1
  WASH/WDE B8 110 C3
Leighs Cl RUSH/SHEL WS4 29 E1
Leighs Rd RUSH/SHEL WS4 28 D1
Leighswood Av ALDR WS9 30 B3
Leighswood Gv ALDR WS9 30 A3
Leighswood Rd ALDR WS9 30 A3
Leighton Cl DUDN DY1 83 G4
  GTB/HAM B43 59 G5
Leighton Rd BILS/COS WV14 54 C4
  ETTPK/GDPK/PENN WV4 53 F5
  MOS/BIL B13 144 B5
Leith Gv HWK/WKHTH B38 176 C5
Lelant Gv HRBN B17 141 G2
Lellow St HHTH/SAND B71 71 G3
Le More FOAKS/STRLY B74 47 E3
Lemox Rd WBROM B70 71 F2
Lench Cl RMSLY B62 122 A3
Lench's Cl MOS/BIL B13 144 B5
Lench's Cn DIG/EDG B5 127 E5
Lench St CBHAMNE B4 3 G2
Lenchs Trust Houses
  BHTH/HG B12 * 127 F1
Len Davies Rd SHHTH WV12 25 C3
Lennard Gdns SMTHWK B66 * 107 F3
Lennox Gdns BDMR/CCFT WV3 6 A7
Lennox Gv SCFLD/BOLD B73 77 E4
Lennox St LOZ/NWT B19 108 D3
Lenton Cft
  LGN/SDN/BHAMAIR B26 147 E3
Lenwade Rd LGLYGN/QTN B68 123 H4
Leominster Rd SPARK B11 145 G4
Leominster Wk RBRY B45 173 H5
Leonard Cv LOZ/NWT B19 108 C1
Leonard Rd LOZ/NWT B19 108 C1
  STRBR DY8 134 C2
Leopold Av BFLD/HDSWWD B20 89 G1
Leopold St BHTH/HG B12 127 F4
Lepid Cv SLYOAK B29 142 A5
Lerryn Cl KGSWFD DY6 100 B4
Lerwick Cl KGSWFD DY6 100 B4
Lesley Cl KGSWFD DY6 100 A3
Leslie Dr TPTN/OCK DY4 68 C4
Leslie Ri OLDBY B69 104 A1
Leslie Rd BFLD/HDSWWD B20 90 D4
  FOAKS/STRLY B74 45 H3
  LDYWD/EDGR B16 125 H2
  WOLVN WV10 37 H1
Lasscroft Cl COVEN WV9 12 A4
Lester Gv ALDR WS9 45 E3
Lester St BILS/COS WV14 54 B3
Levante Gdns STETCH B33 129 H2
Leve La WLNHL WV13 39 H4
Level St BRLYHL DY5 119 G1
Leven Av WLNHL WV13 39 G4
Leven Ct SHHTH WV12 25 H1
Levenwick Wy KGSWFD DY6 100 B3
The Leveretts HDSW B21 89 E3
Lever St BKHL/PFLD WV2 7 G7
Leverton Ri WOLVN WV10 23 E4
Leveson Cl DUDS DY2 103 E1
Leveson Dr TPTN/OCK DY4 69 E5
Leveson Rd WNSFLD WV11 25 F2
Leveson St WLNHL WV13 39 G3
Levington Ct
  DUNHL/THL/PER WV6 20 D5
Lewis Av WOLV WV1 38 B5
Lewis Cl SHHTH WV12 26 B5
Lewis Gv WNSFLD WV11 24 D4
Lewisham Rd SMTHWK B66 106 C2
  WOLVN WV10 12 B5
Lewisham St HHTH/SAND B71 87 F2
Lewis Rd BVILLE B30 160 C3
  HAG/WOL DY9 136 B2
  LGLYGN/QTN B68 123 F5
Lewis St BILS/COS WV14 54 A4
  TPTN/OCK DY4 86 B1
  WSLW WS2 41 H2
Lewthorn Ri
  ETTPK/GDPK/PENN WV4 52 B4
Lexington Gn BRLYHL DY5 119 E5
Leybourne Crs COVEN WV9 11 H4
Leybourne Gv YDLY DY25 146 B1
Leybrook Rd RBRY B45 174 B5
Leyburn Cl SHHTH WV12 40 B1
Leyburn Rd LDYWD/EDGR B16 124 D2
Leycester Cl RBRY B45 189 G1
Leycroft Av STETCH B33 131 F1
Ley Hill Farm Rd
  NFLD/LBR B31 158 A5
Ley Hill Rd MGN/WHC B75 47 G5
Leylan Cft MOS/BIL B13 162 B3
Leyland Av BDMR/CCFT WV3 36 B4
Leyland Cft BLOX/PEL WS3 17 H3
Leyman Cl
  ALE/KHTH/YWD B14 179 E1
Leys Cl RBRY B45 187 G2
Leys Crs BRLYHL DY5 118 D1

Leysdown Gv ACGN B27 163 G2
Leysdown Rd ACGN B27 163 G2
Leys Rd BRLYHL DY5 118 D1
The Leys DARL/WED WS10 55 F2
  NFLD/LBR B31 158 D5
Leys Wood Cft
  LGN/SDN/BHAMAIR B26 147 G3
Leyton Cl BRLYHL DY5 119 F4
Leyton Gv KGSTG B44 75 G2
Leyton Rd HDSW B21 107 H1
Libbards Ga SOLH B91 182 A5
Libbards Wy SOLH B91 181 H5
Library Wy RBRY B45 187 H1
Lich Av WNSFLD WV11 25 E3
Lichfield Rd ALDR WS9 19 G3
  BLOX/PEL WS3 17 E5
  BRWNH WS8 9 F4
  CSHL/WTROR B46 115 F1
  RUSH/SHEL WS4 42 C1
  WNSFLD WV11 24 D5
Lichfield St BILS/COS WV14 54 A2
  TPTN/OCK DY4 69 F5
  WOLV WV1 7 F5
  WSL WS1 5 F5
Lichwood Rd WNSFLD WV11 25 F5
Lickey Coppice RBRY B45 188 C4
Lickey Rd RBRY B45 188 D3
  STRBR DY8 135 H1
Liddon Gv ACGN B27 163 G2
Liddon Rd ACGN B27 163 G2
Lifford Cl ALE/KHTH/YWD B14 177 F1
Lifford La BVILLE B30 177 F1
Lifton Cft KGSWFD DY6 100 B4
Lighthorne Av
  LDYWD/EDGR B16 126 A1
Lighthorne Rd SOLH B91 164 D4
Lightning Wy NFLD/LBR B31 189 H1
Lightwood Cl DOR/KN B93 185 F5
Lightwood Rd DUDN DY1 83 H2
Lightwoods Hl SMTHWKW B67 124 A4
Lightwoods Rd HAG/WOL DY9 153 E1
  SMTHWKW B67 124 B3
Lilac Av BHTH/HG B12 144 C2
  DSYBK/YTR WS5 57 G4
  FOAKS/STRLY B74 60 A1
  KGSTG B44 74 D4
  TPTN/OCK DY4 69 E4
Lilac Dr WMBN WV5 64 D5
Lilac Gv DARL/WED WS10 71 E1
  WSLW WS2 40 C2
Lilac La FOAKS/STRLY B74 31 H5
Lilac Rd DUDN DY1 84 B2
  SHHTH WV12 26 C3
  WOLV WV1 38 B5
Lilian Gv BILS/COS WV14 69 E2
Lilleshall Cl RMSLY B62 121 H5
Lilleshall Rd
  LGN/SDN/BHAMAIR B26 130 D5
Lilley La NFLD/LBR B31 175 H5
Lillington Gv BKDE/SHDE B34 113 F4
Lillington Rd SHLY B90 180 B5
Lilycroft La HWK/WKHTH B38 191 E1
Lily Rd
  LGN/SDN/BHAMAIR B26 146 D1
Lily St HHTH/SAND B71 87 G1
Limberlost Cl
  BFLD/HDSWWD B20 90 A3
Limbrick Cl SHLY B90 179 F1
Limbury Gv HIA/OLT B92 165 H2
Lime Av LW SLYOAK B29 142 D5
  WSLW WS2 40 C2
Lime Cl HLYWD B47 192 C5
  TPTN/OCK DY4 69 H5
  WBROM B70 87 E2
  WSLW WS2 40 C2
Lime Ct SPARK B11 145 E3
Lime Gv BHTH/HG B12 144 B2
  BILS/COS WV14 54 A2
  CHWD/FDBR/MGN B37 132 B5
  LGN/SDN/BHAMAIR B26 146 D1
  LOZ/NWT B19 108 C1
  SCFLD/BOLD B73 77 F4
  SMTHWK B66 106 D5
Limehurst Av BDMR/CCFT WV3 35 G4
Limehurst Rd RUSH/SHEL WS4 29 E5
Limekiln La
  ALE/KHTH/YWD B14 178 C1
Lime La BLOX/PEL WS3 8 A3
Lime Rd DARL/WED WS10 55 H4
  SEDG DY3 67 H2
Limes Av BLKHTH/ROWR B65 122 A2
  BRLYHL DY5 101 E4
The Limes DUNHL/THL/PER WV6 35 G1
  ERDE/BCHGN B24 92 D3
  LDYWD/EDGR B16 * 125 H1
  SPARK B11 145 E1
  WSL WS1 5 F4
Limescroft Cl RUSH/SHEL WS4 29 E5
Limes Rd DUDN DY1 84 B3
  DUNHL/THL/PER WV6 35 G1
Lime St BDMR/CCFT WV3 6 B7
  BILS/COS WV14 68 A3
  WSL WS1 5 G4
Limes Vw SEDG DY3 67 F4
Lime Tree Av
  DUNHL/THL/PER WV6 35 G2
Lime Tree Gdns CDSL WV8 10 D4
Lime Tree Gv NFLD/LBR B31 176 A3
Lime Tree Rd ACGN B27 146 C2
  CDSL WV8 10 D4
  DSYBK/YTR WS5 57 G4
  WASH/WDE B8 110 D3
Lincoln Av WLNHL WV13 40 B3
Lincoln Cl ACGN B27 147 E4
Lincoln Gv WOLVN WV10 12 D5
Lincoln Rd
  CHWD/FDBR/MGN B37 132 A4
  DUDS DY2 120 D1
  HHTH/SAND B71 71 H2
  SMTHWKW B67 106 A4
Lincoln Rd North ACGN B27 147 E4
Lincoln St BHTH/HG B12 144 A1

Lindale Av CBROM B36 111 G3
Lindale Crs BRLYHL DY5 135 H1
Lindale Dr WMBN WV5 64 D5
Linden Av GTB/HAM B43 73 F3
  OLDBY B69 104 B1
  RMSLY B62 122 C5
Linden Cl WSLW WS2 * 40 B5
Linden Dr STRBR DY8 135 G4
Linden La SHHTH WV12 26 C3
Linden Lea BDMR/CCFT WV3 35 H4
Linden Rd BVILLE B30 159 G5
  DUDN DY1 84 B3
  SMTHWK B66 124 C2
Lindens Dr FOAKS/STRLY B74 60 B3
The Lindens
  DUNHL/THL/PER WV6 36 A2
  RIDG/WDGT B32 144 A5
Lindenwood SCFLD/BOLD B73 62 B2
Lindford Wy HWK/WKHTH B38 177 F3
Lindley Av TPTN/OCK DY4 85 F5
Lindon Cl BRWNH WS8 19 G1
Lindon Dr BRWNH WS8 19 F1
Lindon Rd BRWNH WS8 19 G1
Lindrick Cl BLOX/PEL WS3 18 A5
Lindridge Dr WALM/CURD B76 79 E5
Lindridge Rd ERDW/GRVHL B23 92 A1
  MGN/WHC B75 63 F1
  SHLY B90 179 H4
Lindrosa Rd FOAKS/STRLY B74 45 F2
Lindsay Rd PBAR/PBCH B42 74 B2
Lindsey Av NFLD/LBR B31 176 A1
Lindsey Pl BRLYHL DY5 119 F3
Lindsey Rd HHTH/SAND B71 71 G4
Lindsworth Av BVILLE B30 177 F2
Lindsworth Cl BVILLE B30 177 H2
Lindsworth Rd BVILLE B30 177 F2
Linfield Gdns SEDG DY3 67 E2
Linford Gv YDLY B25 129 H3
Linforth Dr FOAKS/STRLY B74 60 C1
Lingard Cl VAUX/NECH B7 109 H4
Lingard Rd MGN/WHC B75 63 F3
Lingfield Av KGSTG B44 75 E2
  WOLVN WV10 12 D2
Lingfield Gdns
  BKDE/SHDE B34 112 D3
Lingfield Gv
  DUNHL/THL/PER WV6 34 D1
Lingfield Wy KGSWFD DY6 100 C4
Lingham Cl HIA/OLT B92 165 F3
Lingmoor Gv ALDR WS9 30 A5
Linhope Dr KGSWFD DY6 100 C4
Link Rd ALDR WS9 19 H4
  LDYWD/EDGR B16 125 G1
  WSNGN B18 65 E4
Links Av DUNHL/THL/PER WV6 34 A5
Links Dr RBRY B45 188 A2
  SOLH B91 164 D4
  STRBR DY8 135 E5
Links Rd ALE/KHTH/YWD B14 178 C4
  ETTPK/GDPK/PENN WV4 51 G5
  LGLYGN/QTN B68 123 F4
Links Side Wy ALDR WS9 30 C2
Links Vw FOAKS/STRLY B74 45 G4
  STRBR DY8 135 E5
Linkswood Cl MOS/BIL B13 161 H1
The Link ACGN B27 162 D1
Linley Cl ALDR WS9 29 G5
Linley Dr WOLVN WV10 23 G1
Linley Gv ALE/KHTH/YWD B14 162 A5
  SEDG DY3 82 D4
Linley Rd RUSH/SHEL WS4 29 F3
Linley Wood Rd ALDR WS9 29 G5
Linnet Cl BVILLE B30 159 G2
  RMSLY B62 138 D1
Linnet Gv ERDW/GRVHL B23 75 H5
  SHHTH WV12 26 B4
Linsey Rd HIA/OLT B92 148 A5
Linslade Cl
  ETTPK/GDPK/PENN WV4 52 B4
Linthouse La WNSFLD WV11 24 D2
Lint Meadow HLYWD B47 192 D1
Linton Av SOLH B91 181 G4
Linton Cl HALE B63 137 G2
Linton Cft BILS/COS WV14 53 H4
Linton Rd CDYHTH B64 121 F1
  GTB/HAM B43 59 G4
  SPARK B11 146 B5
Linwood Rd DUDN DY1 84 B1
  HDSW B21 107 G1
  SOLH B91 163 H5
Lionel St CBHAMNW B3 2 E4
Lion Pas STRBR DY8 135 F2
Lion St STRBR DY8 135 F2
Liskeard Rd DSYBK/YTR WS5 58 B1
Lisko Cl BRLYHL DY5 118 C4
Lismore Cl RBRY B45 173 H5
Lismore Dr HRBN B17 141 G4
Lissimore Dr TPTN/OCK DY4 85 G4
Lisson Gv KGSTG B44 60 B4
Listelow Cl CBROM B36 112 D1
Lister Cl TPTN/OCK DY4 85 G3
  WSLW WS2 27 F5
Lister Rd DUDS DY2 102 C2
  WSLW WS2 27 F5
Lister St VAUX/NECH B7 3 J1
  WLNHL WV13 39 H4
Listowel Rd
  ALE/KHTH/YWD B14 160 D4
Lisures Dr WALM/CURD B76 62 D4
Little Ann St DIG/EDG B5 3 K5
Little Aston Hall Dr
  FOAKS/STRLY B74 31 G5
Little Aston La
  FOAKS/STRLY B74 32 C4
Little Aston Park Rd
  FOAKS/STRLY B74 45 G2
Little Barr St BORD B9 127 G2
Little Bell Hall Cottages
  HAG/WOL DY9 * 184 B2
Little Birches BDMR/CCFT WV3 36 B5
Little Bricklin St
  BDMR/CCFT WV3 6 E6
Little Bromwich Rd BORD B9 129 F3
Little Broom St BHTH/HG B12 127 G4
Little Caldmore WSL WS1 4 E6

Little Checkhill La KINVER DY7 98 B5
Little Clothier St WLNHL WV13 39 G2
Little Clover Cl VAUX/NECH B7 110 A3
Little Cornbow HALE B63 138 D4
Littlecote Cft
  ALE/KHTH/YWD B14 178 C2
Littlecote Dr ERDW/GRVHL B23 76 D4
Little Cottage St BRLYHL DY5 119 F2
Little Cft GTB/HAM B43 73 E2
Little Cross St DARL/WED WS10 55 F1
Little Edward St BORD B9 127 G2
Little Fields Wy OLDBY B69 104 D2
Little Francis Gv
  VAUX/NECH B7 109 H4
Little Gorway WSL WS1 5 F7
Little Green La BORD B9 128 B3
Little Gn Lanes
  SCFLD/BOLD B73 77 F4
Little Hall Rd VAUX/NECH B7 109 H5
Little Hardwick Rd ALDR WS9 44 D3
Little Heath Cft
  BKDE/SHDE B34 112 D3
Little Hl DARL/WED WS10 55 H5
Little Hill Wy RIDG/WDGT B32 140 D5
Little Johnson's La ALDR WS9 44 B4
Little John St BRLYHL DY5 101 F5
Little La HHTH/SAND B71 87 H1
  SHHTH WV12 26 A2
Little Lawns Cl BRWNH WS8 19 F2
Little London WSL WS1 57 F1
Littlemead Av NFLD/LBR B31 176 A4
Little Meadow Cft
  NFLD/LBR B31 158 B5
Littlemead Rd SHLY B90 179 G5
Little Moor Hl SMTHWK B66 106 C5
Little Newport St WSL WS1 4 D4
Little Oaks Dr KINVER DY7 117 E2
Little Oaks Rd AST/WIT B6 109 F1
Littleover Av HLGN/YWD B28 162 D4
Little Pk RIDG/WDGT B32 140 B3
Little Park St WOLV WV1 * 7 F4
Little Pitts Cl ERDE/BCHGN B24 93 H1
Little Potter St BRLYHL DY5 119 F3
Little Pountney St
  BKHL/PFLD WV2 * 7 F7
Little Shadwell St
  CBHAMNE B4 * 3 G2
Littleshaw Cft HLYWD B47 193 E4
Littleshaw La HLYWD B47 193 E4
Little's La WOLV WV1 * 7 G2
Little Station St WSLW WS2 4 D3
Little St DUDS DY2 84 D5
Little Sutton La SHHTH WV12 13 F1
Little Sutton Rd MGN/WHC B75 47 H5
Littleton Cl WALM/CURD B76 78 C1
Littleton Cft SOLH B91 182 A5
Littleton East WSL WS1 4 E2
Littleton St West WSLW WS2 4 D2
Little Wood St WLNHL WV13 39 G3
Littlewood Av DUDN DY1 68 B5
Littleworth Gv
  WALM/CURD B76 63 F4
Liveridge Cl DOR/KN B93 196 D2
Liverpool Cft
  CHWD/FDBR/MGN B37 131 H3
Liverpool St BORD B9 127 G2
Livery St CBHAMNW B3 2 E2
Livingstone Av
  DUNHL/THL/PER WV6 20 C5
Livingstone Rd
  ALE/KHTH/YWD B14 161 G4
  BFLD/HDSWWD B20 90 C5
  BILS/COS WV14 53 F3
  BLOX/PEL WS3 17 G5
  WBROM B70 87 G3
Lloyd Dr
  ETTPK/GDPK/PENN WV4 65 G1
Lloyd Hl
  ETTPK/GDPK/PENN WV4 * 50 C5
Lloyd Rd BFLD/HDSWWD B20 90 A2
  DUNHL/THL/PER WV6 35 G1
Lloyd Sq EDG B15 * 125 G4
Lloyds Rd RMSLY B62 122 A5
Lloyd St DARL/WED WS10 55 H5
  DUDS DY2 102 D1
  DUNHL/THL/PER WV6 36 D1
  HHTH/SAND B71 88 A2
  SMTHW B10 128 B4
Locarno Rd TPTN/OCK DY4 69 F5
Lochalsh Gv SHHTH WV12 13 G5
Lochranza Cft GTB/HAM B43 73 G1
Lock Dr STETCH B33 129 H1
Lock Keepers Cl
  NFLD/LBR B31 158 C2
Locke Pl VAUX/NECH B7 * 127 G1
Locket Cl WSLW WS2 40 D1
Lockfield Cl STRBR DY8 135 E1
Lockhart Dr MGN/WHC B75 47 G4
Locking Cft CVALE B35 94 D3
Lockington Cft RMSLY B62 139 H1
Lockley Cl WOLVN WV10 37 H1
Lockside ALDR WS9 30 C2
  WMBN WV5 64 C4
Locksmith Cl WLNHL WV13 39 H3
Locks Vw STRBR DY8 117 H3
Lockton Rd BVILLE B30 160 C2
Lockwood Rd NFLD/LBR B31 175 F1
Lode La SOLH B91 165 E2
Lode Mill Ct SOLH B91 164 C5
Lodge Cl DSYBK/YTR WS5 58 B2
  HALE B63 138 A4
Lodge Crs DUDS DY2 102 D5
  HAG/WOL DY9 152 D5
Lodge Cft DOR/KN B93 197 F2
  NFLD/LBR B31 158 A5
Lodge Dr
  LGN/SDN/BHAMAIR B26 130 A4
Lodge Farm Cl
  WALM/CURD B76 62 D4
Lodgefield Rd RMSLY B62 121 H5
Lodge Gv ALDR WS9 30 A5
Lodge Hill Rd SLYOAK B29 159 F3
Lodge La KGSWFD DY6 99 F5
Lodge Pool Cl KGSTG B44 60 C5
Lodge Rd AST/WIT B6 109 E1
  BILS/COS WV14 54 A4
  DARL/WED WS10 55 F3

  DOR/KN B93 197 F2
  DSYBK/YTR WS5 28 D1
  SMTHWK B66 106 B2
  WBROM B70 87 F3
  WOLVN WV10 22 D2
  WSNGN B18 107 G4
Lodge St OLDBY B69 104 A1
  SHHTH WV12 26 A5
Loeless Rd STETCH B33 130 C1
Lofthouse Crs NFLD/LBR B31 175 F2
Lofthouse Gv NFLD/LBR B31 175 F2
Lofthouse Rd
  BFLD/HDSWWD B20 89 H4
Loftus Cl SLYOAK B29 158 B2
Logan Cl WOLVN WV10 23 E4
Lomaine Dr BVILLE B30 176 C1
Lomas Dr NFLD/LBR B31 175 E2
Lomas St WOLV WV1 * 37 E1
Lombard Av DUDS DY2 120 D1
Lombard St BHTH/HG B12 127 F4
  WBROM B70 87 G3
Lombard St West
  WBROM B70 87 G3
Lombardy Cft RMSLY B62 140 A1
Lombardy Gdns SHHTH WV12 26 C3
Lomond Cl BKDE/SHDE B34 113 E3
Lomond Rd SEDG DY3 67 E2
Londonderry Gv
  SMTHWKW B67 106 B4
Londonderry La
  SMTHWKW B67 105 H5
London Hts DUDN DY1 84 A4
London Pl BDMR/CCFT WV3 6 E5
London Rd BFLD/HDSWWD B20 91 E4
  MGN/WHC B75 48 C3
London St SMTHWK B66 107 E4
Lones Rd HHTH/SAND B71 105 H4
Long Acre CDSL WV8 10 A5
  VAUX/NECH B7 109 H3
Longacre WLNHL WV13 39 G5
Longacres WLNHL WV13 39 G5
Long Acre St WSLW WS2 4 C1
Longbank Rd OLDBY B69 104 A5
Longboat La STRBR DY8 118 A4
Longboat Quay DUDS DY2 102 D5
Longbow Rd SLYOAK B29 158 B3
Longbridge La NFLD/LBR B31 175 F5
  NFLD/LBR B31 189 F1
Long Cl HAG/WOL DY9 169 G1
Long Close Wk CVALE B35 94 C4
Long Compton Dr
  HAG/WOL DY9 152 C4
Longcroft Cl CVALE B35 94 C3
The Longcroft HALE B63 138 A3
  RUSH/SHEL WS4 29 F3
Longlands Rd
  HWK/WKHTH B38 190 B1
Longdon Av
  ETTPK/GDPK/PENN WV4 52 B3
Longdon Cft DOR/KN B93 183 E5
Longdon Dr FOAKS/STRLY B74 46 C1
Longdon Rd DOR/KN B93 197 F5
Longfellow Rd NFLD/LBR B31 176 B2
  SEDG DY3 82 C1
Longfield Cl HLGN/YWD B28 162 D4
Longfield Cl FOAKS/STRLY B74 46 A2
Longfield Rd HALE B63 138 A4
  NFLD/LBR B31 158 A3
Longford Cl DOR/KN B93 197 F5
  RIDG/WDGT B32 157 E3
  WMBN WV5 80 B1
Longford Gv KGSTG B44 60 C5
Longford Rd KGSTG B44 75 G1
  WOLVN WV10 37 H1
Longham Cft RIDG/WDGT B32 141 F5
Longhurst Cft NFLD/LBR B31 189 F1
Long Hyde Rd SMTHWKW B67 124 B3
Long Innage HALE B63 137 F1
Long Knowle La WNSFLD WV11 24 B2
Longlake Av
  DUNHL/THL/PER WV6 35 E2
Longlands Rd RMSLY B62 139 G4
The Longlands WMBN WV5 65 E5
Long La BLKHTH/ROWR B65 122 A3
  RMSLY B62 122 A3
  WNSFLD WV11 15 H2
Long Leasow SLYOAK B29 158 C3
Longleat GTB/HAM B43 73 F1
Longleat Av EDG B15 126 C4
Longleat Dr DUDN DY1 83 G4
  SHLY B90 195 E3
Longleat Rd ALDR WS9 19 G5
Long Ley WOLVN WV10 37 H2
Longley Av WALM/CURD B76 79 F1
Longley Crs
  LGN/SDN/BHAMAIR B26 147 E3
Long Leys Ct
  CSHL/WTROR B46 * 96 B4
Long Leys Cft
  CSHL/WTROR B46 96 B4
Longmeadow Cl
  MGN/WHC B75 63 E3
Longmeadow Crs
  BKDE/SHDE B34 113 G3
Longmeadow Gv
  NFLD/LBR B31 189 G2
Longmeadow Rd
  DSYBK/YTR WS5 43 G5
Long Mill Av WNSFLD WV11 24 B3
Long Ml North WNSFLD WV11 24 B3
Long Ml South WNSFLD WV11 24 B3
Longmoor Cl WNSFLD WV11 25 H1
Longmoor Rd HALE B63 138 A4
  SCFLD/BOLD B73 60 D5
Longmore Av WSLW WS2 40 D4
Longmore Rd SHLY B90 180 B4
Longmore St DARL/WED WS10 55 H5
  DARL/WED WS10 127 F5
Long Mynd HALE B63 154 D1
Long Mynd Cl SHHTH WV12 25 H1
Long Mynd Rd NFLD/LBR B31 158 A5
Long Nuke Rd NFLD/LBR B31 158 A3
Long Saw Dr NFLD/LBR B31 174 D4
Longshaw Gv BKDE/SHDE B34 113 F3
Longstone Cl SHLY B90 195 G3
Longstone Rd PBAR/PBCH B42 73 H4
Long St SPARK B11 144 C1

WOLV WV1 7 G3
WSLW WS2 4 C4
Long Wd BVILLE B30 159 G5
Longwood La RUSH/SHEL WS4 43 G3
Longwood Ri SHHTH WV12 26 B5
Longwood Rd ALDR WS9 44 B3
RBRY B45 188 A1
Lonicera Cl DSYBK/YTR WS5 57 H5
Lonsdale Cl SHHTH WV12 25 H5
STETCH B33 129 H3
Lonsdale Rd BDMR/CCFT WV3 36 D5
BILS/COS WV14 54 B2
DSYBK/YTR WS5 58 A2
HRBN B17 141 H1
SMTHWK B66 105 H2
Lord's Dr WSLW WS2 4 E1
Lords La KINVER DY7 116 C3
Lordsmore Cl BILS/COS WV14 68 D2
Lord St BDMR/CCFT WV3 6 C5
BILS/COS WV14 54 A5
DSYBK/YTR WS5 57 E3
VAUX/NECH B7 3 K1
WSL WS1 56 D2
Lord St West BILS/COS WV14 54 A5
Lordswood Rd HRBN B17 141 H1
Lordswood Sq HRBN B17 * 124 D5
Lorimer Wy GTB/HAM B43 59 H3
Lorne St TPTN/OCK DY4 69 F3
Lorrainer Av BRLYHL DY5 118 C4
Lothians Rd BLOX/PEL WS3 18 A2
DUNHL/THL/PER WV6 21 H4
Lottie Rd SLYOAK B29 159 G1
Lotus Cft SMTHWKW B67 106 B5
Lotus Dr CDYHTH B64 121 F2
Lotus Wy BLKHTH/ROWR B65 103 F5
Loughton Gv HALE B63 138 B3
Louisa St CBHAMW B1 2 C4
Louise Cft
ALE/KHTH/YWD B14 178 A3
Louise Lorne Rd MOS/BIL B13 144 B3
Louise Rd HDSW B21 107 H2
Louise St SEDG DY3 82 D3
Lount Wk LOZ/NWT B19 109 E4
Lovat St BDMR/CCFT WV3 6 D4
Lovatt Cl TPTN/OCK DY4 70 A2
Loveday St CBHAMNE B4 3 G2
Lovelace Av SOLH B91 182 B5
Love La DUNHL/THL/PER WV6 21 H4
HAG/WOL DY9 136 C2
HLYWD B47 192 A1
OLDBY B69 85 G5
STRBR DY8 135 G4
VAUX/NECH B7 3 J1
WSL WS1 57 E1
Lovell Cl SLYOAK B29 158 C4
Loveridge Cl CDSL WV8 10 A4
Lovett Av OLDBY B69 104 B4
Low Av GTB/HAM B43 73 H1
Lowbridge Cl SHHTH WV12 26 A5
Lowbrook La SHLY B90 193 F4
Lowden Cft
LGN/SDN/BHAMAIR B26 147 E3
Lowe Av DARL/WED WS10 54 D1
Lowe Dr KGSWFD DY6 100 A5
SCFLD/BOLD B73 61 F5
Lower Beeches Rd RBRY B45 174 C3
Lower Chapel St OLDBY B69 86 A4
Lower Church La
TPTN/OCK DY4 85 H1
Lower City Rd OLDBY B69 86 A5
Lowercroft Wy
FOAKS/STRLY B74 32 C4
Lower Dartmouth St
BORD B9 127 H2
Lower Darwin St
BHTH/HG B12 127 F4
Lower Derry St BRLYHL DY5 119 F2
Lower Essex St DIG/EDG B5 127 E3
Lower Forster St WSL WS1 5 F2
Lower Gn
DUNHL/THL/PER WV6 22 A5
TPTN/OCK DY4 * 85 E1
Lower Ground Cl AST/WIT B6 * 91 F5
Lower Hall La WSL WS1 4 E4
Lower Hall St WSL WS1 4 E5
Lower High St CDYHTH B64 120 C4
DARL/WED WS10 70 D1
STRBR DY8 135 F1
Lower Higley Cl
RIDG/WDGT B32 141 E3
Lower Horseley Flds WOLV WV1 7 K4
Lower Lichfield St
WLNHL WV13 39 H3
Lower Loveday St LOZ/NWT B19 3 F1
Lower Moor BVILLE B30 * 159 G2
Lower North St
RUSH/SHEL WS4 42 B2
The Lower Pde
CSCFLD/WYGN B72 62 C3
Lower Prestwood Rd
WNSFLD WV11 24 C3
Lower Queen St
CSCFLD/WYGN B72 62 C4
Lower Reddicroft
SCFLD/BOLD B73 62 C3
Lower Rushall St WSL WS1 5 F3
Lower Severn St CBHAMW B1 2 E6
Lowerstack Cft
CHWD/FDBR/MGN B37 131 H1
Lower St
DUNHL/THL/PER WV6 22 A5
Lower Temple St CBHAM B2 3 F5
Lower Tower St LOZ/NWT B19 108 D4
Lower Trinity St BORD B9 127 G3
Lower Valley Rd BRLYHL DY5 118 C2
Lower Vauxhall WOLV WV1 6 A3
Lower Villiers St
BKHL/PFLD WV2 52 A1
Lower Walsall St WOLV WV1 37 H4
Lower White Rd
RIDG/WDGT B32 140 D2
Lowesmoor Rd
LGN/SDN/BHAMAIR B26 130 D5
Lowe St BHTH/HG B12 127 G4
DUNHL/THL/PER WV6 36 C1
Loweswater Dr SEDG DY3 83 F3
Lowfield Cl RMSLY B62 140 A4
Low Hill Crs WOLVN WV10 23 G2
Lowhill La RBRY B45 188 C2
Lowland Cl CDYHTH B64 121 F3
Lowlands Av
DUNHL/THL/PER WV6 22 A4
FOAKS/STRLY B74 45 E5
Lowndes Rd STRBR DY8 135 E1
Lowry Cl DUNHL/THL/PER WV6 34 D1
SMTHWKW B67 106 B3
WLNHL WV13 38 D3
Low Thatch HWK/WKHTH B38 190 C1
Low Town OLDBY B69 105 E2
Low Wood Rd
ERDW/GRVHL B23 92 C2
Loxdale Sidings BILS/COS WV14 54 B4
Loxdale St BILS/COS WV14 54 B4
DARL/WED WS10 70 D1
Loxley Av SHLY B90 179 H4
Loxley Cl NFLD/LBR B31 158 A2
Loxley Rd MGN/WHC B75 47 H2
SMTHWKW B67 124 B3
Loxton Cl FOAKS/STRLY B74 32 B5
Loynells Rd RBRY B45 188 A1
Loyns Cl
CHWD/FDBR/MGN B37 131 G1
Lozells Rd LOZ/NWT B19 108 B2
Lozells St LOZ/NWT B19 108 C2
Lozells Wood Cl LOZ/NWT B19 108 B2
Luanne Cl CDYHTH B64 121 G3
Lucas Circ LOZ/NWT B19 108 C3
Luce Cl CVALE B35 94 D2
Luce Rd WOLVN WV10 23 G4
Lucknow Rd SHHTH WV12 25 H5
Luddington Rd HIA/OLT B92 165 G3
Ludford Cl MGN/WHC B75 63 E1
Ludford Rd RIDG/WDGT B32 157 E1
Ludgate Cl CSHL/WTROR B46 96 A3
OLDBY B69 103 H1
Ludgate Hl CBHAMNW B3 2 E3
Ludgate St DUDN DY1 * 84 B5
Ludlow Cl
CHWD/FDBR/MGN B37 132 C2
SHHTH WV12 25 H4
Ludlow La WSLW WS2 41 E1
Ludlow Rd WASH/WDE B8 128 D1
Ludlow Wy DUDN DY1 83 G4
Ludmer Wy
BFLD/HDSWWD B20 90 C4
Ludstone Av
ETTPK/GDPK/PENN WV4 50 D3
Ludstone Rd SLYOAK B29 158 B1
Ludworth Av
CHWD/FDBR/MGN B37 132 B4
Lugtrout La SOLH B91 165 H4
The Lukes DUDS DY2 121 E1
Lulworth Cl HALE B63 137 G1
Lulworth Rd HLGN/YWD B28 163 E2
Lumley Gv
CHWD/FDBR/MGN B37 132 D2
Lumley Rd WSL WS1 5 J5
Lundy Vw CBROM B36 114 B3
Lunt Gv RIDG/WDGT B32 140 D2
Lunt Pl BILS/COS WV14 54 C2
Lunt Rd BILS/COS WV14 54 C1
Lupin Gv BORD B9 128 D1
DSYBK/YTR WS5 57 H4
Lupin Rd DUDS DY2 85 F5
Lusbridge Cl HALE B63 137 F3
Lutley Av HALE B63 138 A3
Lutley Cl BDMR/CCFT WV3 51 E1
Lutley Dr HAG/WOL DY9 136 A4
Lutley Gv RIDG/WDGT B32 157 F1
Lutley La HALE B63 137 G5
Lutley Mill Rd HALE B63 138 A3
Luton Rd SLYOAK B29 142 D4
Luttrell Rd FOAKS/STRLY B74 46 D5
Lyall Gdns RBRY B45 173 G4
Lyall Gv ACGN B27 146 A5
Lychgate Av HAG/WOL DY9 153 E1
Lydate Rd RMSLY B62 139 H3
Lydbrook Covert
HWK/WKHTH B38 176 C5
Lydbury Gv STETCH B33 112 C5
Lyd Cl WNSFLD WV11 24 B5
Lydd Cft CVALE B35 94 D2
Lyddington Dr RMSLY B62 121 H5
Lyde Gn HALE B63 120 C5
Lydford Gv ERDE/BCHGN B24 93 E4
Lydford Rd BLOX/PEL WS3 16 D5
Lydgate Rd KGSWFD DY6 100 B4
Lydget Gv ERDW/GRVHL B23 76 B4
Lydham Cl BILS/COS WV14 53 F4
KGSTG B44 75 G5
Lydia Cft FOAKS/STRLY B74 32 C4
Lydian Cl DUNHL/THL/PER WV6 36 D1
Lydiate Ash Rd BRGRVW B61 187 E5
Lydiate Av NFLD/LBR B31 174 D4
Lydiates Cl SEDG DY3 66 D4
Lydney Cl SHHTH WV12 40 B1
Lydney Gv NFLD/LBR B31 175 F2
Lye Av RIDG/WDGT B32 140 A5
Lye By-Pass HAG/WOL DY9 136 C1
Lye Close La RIDG/WDGT B32 139 H5
Lyecroft Av
CHWD/FDBR/MGN B37 132 D2
Lye Cross Rd OLDBY B69 103 H2
Lygon Gv RIDG/WDGT B32 141 E3
Lymedene Rd PBAR/PBCH B42 90 B1
Lyme Green Rd STETCH B33 112 B5
Lymer Rd WOLVN WV10 23 E1
Lymington Rd WLNHL WV13 40 B3
Lymsey Cft STRBR DY8 117 G1
Lynbrook Cl DUDS DY2 102 D3
HLYWD B47 192 D1
Lyncourt Gv RIDG/WDGT B32 140 B1
Lyncroft Rd SPARK B11 145 H5
Lyndale Dr WNSFLD WV11 25 F5
Lyndale Rd DUDS DY2 103 E3
SEDG DY3 66 D1
Lyndhurst Dr STRBR DY8 118 B3
Lyndhurst Rd BDMR/CCFT WV3 51 G1
ERDE/BCHGN B24 92 D4
HHTH/SAND B71 72 A4
Lyndon HHTH/SAND B71 87 H1
Lyndon Cl BFLD/HDSWWD B20 90 C4
CBROM B36 113 E1
HALE B63 138 A2
SEDG DY3 67 G2
Lyndon Cft
CHWD/FDBR/MGN B37 132 B5
Lyndon Gv HHTH/SAND B71 87 H2
KGSWFD DY6 99 F1
Lyndon Rd HIA/OLT B92 147 F5
RBRY B45 187 G1
SCFLD/BOLD B73 62 B3
STETCH B33 130 A1
Lyndworth Rd BVILLE B30 160 C3
Lyneham Gdns
WALM/CURD B76 78 D5
Lyneham Wy CVALE B35 94 B3
Lynfield Cl HWK/WKHTH B38 190 D1
Lyng La WBROM B70 87 G4
Lynmouth Cl ALDR WS9 29 H5
Lynn Gv SLYOAK B29 142 A4
Lynton Av
DUNHL/THL/PER WV6 22 A3
HHTH/SAND B71 71 G4
SMTHWK B66 106 C3
Lynton Rd AST/WIT B6 109 G2
Lynval Rd BRLYHL DY5 119 H5
Lynwood Av KGSWFD DY6 99 F1
Lynwood Cl SHHTH WV12 26 C2
Lynwood Dr KIDD DY10 168 B3
Lynwood Wk HRBN B17 142 A3
Lynwood Wy RBRY B45 188 A5
Lyons Gv SPARK B11 145 E4
Lysander Rd RBRY B45 174 A3
Lysander Wy CVALE B35 94 D4
Lysways St WSL WS1 5 F6
Lytham Cl STRBR DY8 135 G5
WALM/CURD B76 78 D5
Lytham Cft EDG B15 126 D3
Lytham Gv BLOX/PEL WS3 16 C3
Lytham Rd
DUNHL/THL/PER WV6 34 B1
Lythwood Dr BRLYHL DY5 119 E4
Lyttelton Rd
LDYWD/EDGR B16 125 F3
STETCH B33 129 H2
STRBR DY8 134 D2
Lyttleton Av RMSLY B62 122 C5
Lyttleton Cl DUDS DY2 102 C5
Lyttleton St WBROM B70 87 G4
Lytton Av
ETTPK/GDPK/PENN WV4 50 D4
Lytton Gv ACGN B27 163 F1
Lytton La RIDG/WDGT B32 141 F4

M

Maas Rd NFLD/LBR B31 175 G1
Macarthur Rd CDYHTH B64 120 C4
Macdonald Cl OLDBY B69 86 B4
Macdonald St DIG/EDG B5 127 E4
Mace St CDYHTH B64 121 E3
Machin Rd ERDW/GRVHL B23 92 D2
Mackadown La STETCH B33 131 F3
Mackay Rd BLOX/PEL WS3 17 F5
Mackenzie Rd SPARK B11 145 E5
Mackmillan Rd
BLKHTH/ROWR B65 122 A2
Macmillan Cl OLDBY B69 86 A4
Macrome Rd
DUNHL/THL/PER WV6 22 A2
Madam's Hill Rd SHLY B90 194 D1
Maddocks Hl
CSCFLD/WYGN B72 77 F1
Madehurst Rd
ERDW/GRVHL B23 76 C5
Madeira Av CDSL WV8 10 C5
Madeley Rd HAG/WOL DY9 186 A1
KGSWFD DY6 100 C5
SPARK B11 145 E2
Madin Rd TPTN/OCK DY4 85 E2
Madison Av BRLYHL DY5 119 H1
CBROM B36 111 H3
WSLW WS2 41 F3
Madley Cl RBRY B45 173 G5
Madresfield Dr HALE B63 138 D5
Maer Cl BLKHTH/ROWR B65 122 A1
Mafeking Rd SMTHWK B66 106 C2
Mafeking Vls RMSLY B62 * 121 H5
Magdala St WSNGN B18 107 G4
Magdalen Cl DUDN DY1 84 A4
Magdalene Rd WSL WS1 57 G1
Magness Crs SHHTH WV12 26 A5
Magnolia Cl SLYOAK B29 158 C3
Magnolia Dr DSYBK/YTR WS5 57 F5
Magnolia Gv CDSL WV8 10 C4
SHHTH WV12 39 H1
Magnolia Wy STRBR DY8 118 B4
Magnum Cl FOAKS/STRLY B74 * 60 B1
Magpie Cl DUDS DY2 121 E1
Maidendale Rd KGSWFD DY6 99 F2
Maidensbridge Gdns
KGSWFD DY6 81 F5
Maidensbridge Rd
KGSWFD DY6 81 F5
Maidstone Dr STRBR DY8 118 A1
Maidstone Rd
BFLD/HDSWWD B20 91 E5
Maidwell Dr SHLY B90 181 E5
Mainstream Wy
VAUX/NECH B7 110 A5
Main St SHLY B90 194 A3
SPARK B11 127 G5
Main Ter SPARK B11 * 127 G5
Mainwaring Dr MGN/WHC B75 48 A3
Maisonettes CDSL WV8 * 10 D4
The Maisonettes
ERDE/BCHGN B24 * 92 C4
Maitland Dr BKDE/SHDE B34 113 G3
Maitland Rd DUDN DY1 83 F5
WASH/WDE B8 110 D5
Majestic Wy
BLKHTH/ROWR B65 104 A5
Major St BKHL/PFLD WV2 52 C1
Majuba Rd LDYWD/EDGR B16 107 F5
Malcolm Av
ERDE/BCHGN B24 93 G1
Malcolm Gv RBRY B45 188 A1
Malcolm Rd SHLY B90 180 B3
Malcolmson Cl EDG B15 125 H5
Malfield Dr ACGN B27 147 E4
Malins Rd
ETTPK/GDPK/PENN WV4 52 B3
HRBN B17 142 B2
Malkit Cl WSLW WS2 40 C1
Mallaby Cl SHLY B90 180 A5
Mallard Cl ACGN B27 146 C4
BLOX/PEL WS3 18 A1
BRLYHL DY5 119 E5
Mallard Dr ERDW/GRVHL B23 91 H3
OLDBY B69 122 D1
Mallender Dr DOR/KN B93 196 D1
Mallen Dr OLDBY B69 85 H5
Mallin Gdns DUDN DY1 101 G1
Mallin St SMTHWK B66 105 H2
Mallory Crs BLOX/PEL WS3 17 F5
Mallory Ri MOS/BIL B13 162 A1
Mallory Rd
DUNHL/THL/PER WV6 34 C2
Mallow Cl DSYBK/YTR WS5 57 F5
Mallow Ct
DUNHL/THL/PER WV6 * 22 D5
Mallow Ri ERDW/GRVHL B23 75 H4
Mallows Cl DARL/WED WS10 * 55 F2
Malmesbury Rd SMHTH B10 145 G1
Malpas Dr RIDG/WDGT B32 157 G2
Malpass Gdns CDSL WV8 10 A3
Malpass Rd BRLYHL DY5 119 H5
Malpas Wk WOLVN WV10 38 A1
Malt Cl HRBN B17 142 B1
Malthouse Cft AST/WIT B6 109 E1
Malthouse Dr DUDN DY1 84 A4
Malthouse Gdns
LOZ/NWT B19 108 D2
Malthouse Gv YDLY B25 130 A4
Malthouse La
DUNHL/THL/PER WV6 21 H4
PBAR/PBCH B42 74 D3
WASH/WDE B8 110 C3
Malthouse Meadow SOLH B91 181 H4
Malthouse Rd TPTN/OCK DY4 85 E1
Malthouse Rw
CHWD/FDBR/MGN B37 132 A4
The Maltings ALDR WS9 * 30 C4
WMBN WV5 * 65 E5
WOLV WV1 7 G1
Malt Mill La RMSLY B62 122 A4
Malton Av OLDBY B69 104 B3
Malton Gv MOS/BIL B13 161 H3
Malvern Av HAG/WOL DY9 136 A2
Malvern Cl EDG B15 125 E4
HHTH/SAND B71 87 H1
SHHTH WV12 39 H1
Malvern Ct ACGN B27 * 146 C3
WOLVN WV10 23 F2
Malvern Crs DUDS DY2 101 H3
Malvern Dr ALDR WS9 30 C2
WALM/CURD B76 78 C3
WOLV WV1 38 B4
Malvern Hill Rd
VAUX/NECH B7 110 A2
Malvern Park Av SOLH B91 182 B2
Malvern Rd ACGN B27 146 C3
LGLYGN/QTN B68 123 F4
Malvern St BHTH/HG B12 144 C2
Malvern View Rd SEDG DY3 83 F2
Mamble Rd STRBR DY8 135 E2
Mammoth Dr WOLVN WV10 23 F4
Manby Cl DUNHL/THL/PER WV6 36 C1
Manby Rd CVALE B35 94 C2
Manby St TPTN/OCK DY4 69 F3
Mancetter Rd SHLY B90 180 C2
Manchester St AST/WIT B6 109 E4
OLDBY B69 105 F2
Mancroft Cl KGSWFD DY6 99 F2
Mancroft Gdns
DUNHL/THL/PER WV6 21 G5
Mancroft Rd
DUNHL/THL/PER WV6 21 G5
Mandale Rd WOLVN WV10 23 H4
Manderley Cl SEDG DY3 67 E1
Manders Est WOLV WV1 * 37 H2
Manderston Cl DUDN DY1 83 G3
Mander St BDMR/CCFT WV3 6 D7
Man Der Ville Gdns
KGSWFD DY6 99 G3
Mandeville Gdns WSL WS1 5 G6
Maney Cnr CSCFLD/WYGN B72 62 B4
Maney Hill Rd
CSCFLD/WYGN B72 77 H1
Manfield Rd WLNHL WV13 38 C2
Manifold Wy DARL/WED WS10 57 E5
Manilla Rd BVILLE B30 160 B1
Manitoba Cft
HWK/WKHTH B38 176 D5
Manley Cl WBROM B70 * 87 E3
Manlove St BDMR/CCFT WV3 6 B7
Manningford Rd
ALE/KHTH/YWD B14 178 B3
Manor Abbey Dr RMSLY B62 139 G4
Manor Abbey Rd RMSLY B62 139 G3
Manor Cl CDSL WV8 10 D4
ETTPK/GDPK/PENN WV4 51 F4
WLNHL WV13 39 F2
Manor Ct DOR/KN B93 * 198 D1
WSLW WS2 * 41 G4
Manor Dr NFLD/LBR B31 * 158 D3
SCFLD/BOLD B73 62 B4
SEDG DY3 80 C4
SEDG DY3 82 D3
Manor Farm Dr SHHTH WV12 26 B5
Manor Farm Rd SPARK B11 145 G3
Manorford Av HHTH/SAND B71 72 C2
Manor Gdns STETCH B33 129 H3
WMBN WV5 * 65 F4
Manor Gv NFLD/LBR B31 174 C4
Manor Hl SCFLD/BOLD B73 62 B4
Manor House Cl SLYOAK B29 158 B1
Manor House Dr
NFLD/LBR B31 158 D3
Manor House La
CSHL/WTROR B46 96 B3
LGN/SDN/BHAMAIR B26 147 E1
Manor House Pk CDSL WV8 10 D3
Manor House Rd
DARL/WED WS10 55 H4
Manor Houses RMSLY B62 * 139 H2
Manorial Rd MGN/WHC B75 48 A2
Manor La BRGRVW B61 187 E3
RMSLY B62 139 G3
STRBR DY8 134 D4
Manor Pk KGSWFD DY6 99 H3
NFLD/LBR B31 174 C3
Manor Park Cl MOS/BIL B13 144 C5
Manor Park Rd CBROM B36 113 F2
Manor Rd AST/WIT B6 91 F5
DARL/WED WS10 71 H1
DOR/KN B93 196 D5
ETTPK/GDPK/PENN WV4 51 F4
ETTPK/GDPK/PENN WV4 53 E3
FOAKS/STRLY B74 45 G5
HLYWD B47 192 C5
LDYWD/EDGR B16 125 F3
SCFLD/BOLD B73 62 B3
SMTHWKW B67 105 H4
SOLH B91 164 D5
STETCH B33 130 A1
STRBR DY8 117 H2
TPTN/OCK DY4 85 F1
WOLVN WV10 23 E3
WSLW WS2 41 G3
Manor Rd North
LDYWD/EDGR B16 125 F3
Manor Road Prec WSLW WS2 41 G3
Manor St DUNHL/THL/PER WV6 21 G5
Manor Wy HALE B63 155 F1
RMSLY B62 139 F4
Mansard Cl BDMR/CCFT WV3 36 B5
WOLVN WV10 24 B2
Mansell Cl HALE B63 120 B5
Mansell Rd TPTN/OCK DY4 69 G3
Mansel Rd SMHTH B10 128 C4
Mansfield Rd AST/WIT B6 108 D1
YDLY B25 146 C2
Mansion Cl DUDN DY1 84 A3
Mansion Crs SMTHWKW B67 106 A5
Mansion Dr TPTN/OCK DY4 86 A1
Manson Dr CDYHTH B64 121 G3
Manston Dr
DUNHL/THL/PER WV6 20 C5
Manston Rd
LGN/SDN/BHAMAIR B26 130 D5
Manton Cft DOR/KN B93 196 C5
Manway Cl BFLD/HDSWWD B20 89 H1
Manwoods Cl
BFLD/HDSWWD B20 90 B4
Maple Av DARL/WED WS10 56 C4
Maple Bank EDG B15 * 126 A5
Maplebeck Ct SOLH B91 * 165 E5
Maple Cl BILS/COS WV14 68 A4
HDSW B21 89 G5
STRBR DY8 134 D5
Maple Cft MOS/BIL B13 161 F4
Mapledene Rd
LGN/SDN/BHAMAIR B26 148 B1
Maple Dr DSYBK/YTR WS5 57 H4
KGSTG B44 75 H3
RUSH/SHEL WS4 28 D2
SEDG DY3 82 D4
Maple Gn DUDN DY1 84 A1
Maple Gv BDMR/CCFT WV3 35 G3
BILS/COS WV14 54 B4
CHWD/FDBR/MGN B37 113 H3
KGSWFD DY6 100 A3
LOZ/NWT B19 108 C1
Maple Leaf Dr
CHWD/FDBR/MGN B37 132 B4
Maple Leaf Rd
DARL/WED WS10 70 A2
Maple Ri LGLYGN/QTN B68 123 G2
Maple Rd BDMR/CCFT WV3 36 A5
BLOX/PEL WS3 17 H5
BVILLE B30 159 G2
CSCFLD/WYGN B72 62 C5
DUDN DY1 84 C3
RBRY B45 187 H2
RMSLY B62 122 B4
Maple St BLOX/PEL WS3 17 F5
Mapleton Gv HLGN/YWD B28 163 F3
Mapleton Rd HLGN/YWD B28 163 F4
Maple Tree La HALE B63 137 G1
Maple Wy NFLD/LBR B31 175 F5
Maplewood WALM/CURD B76 78 C3
Mapperley Gdns MOS/BIL B13 143 G4
Mappleborough Rd SHLY B90 179 G4
Mapps Cl HALE B63 137 G1
Marans Cft HWK/WKHTH B38 190 B1
Marbury Cl HWK/WKHTH B38 176 B3
Marbury Dr BILS/COS WV14 54 C2
Marbury Ms BRLYHL DY5 119 F3
Marchant Rd BDMR/CCFT WV3 36 B3
BILS/COS WV14 53 G1
March End Rd WNSFLD WV11 24 D5
Marchmont Rd BORD B9 129 E2
Marchmount Rd
CSCFLD/WYGN B72 77 G3
March Wy ALDR WS9 30 C1
Marcliff Crs SHLY B90 179 E3
Marcos Dr CBROM B36 95 H5
Marcot Rd HIA/OLT B92 147 F2
Marden Cl WLNHL WV13 39 F4
Marden Gv NFLD/LBR B31 189 G1
Mardon Rd
LGN/SDN/BHAMAIR B26 147 H2
Maree Gv WNSFLD WV11 25 H1
Marfield Cl WALM/CURD B76 78 C5
Margam Crs BLOX/PEL WS3 16 B5
Margam Ter BLOX/PEL WS3 16 B5
Margam Wy BLOX/PEL WS3 16 B5
Margaret Av HALE B63 138 B3
Margaret Cl BRLYHL DY5 119 G4
Margaret Dr STRBR DY8 135 H3
Margaret Gdns SMTHWKW B67 106 A4
Margaret Gv HRBN B17 125 E5
Margaret Rd DARL/WED WS10 55 E4
HRBN B17 142 A2
SCFLD/BOLD B73 76 B2
WSLW WS2 40 C2
Margaret St CBHAMNW B3 2 E4
WBROM B70 87 F4
Margaret V TPTN/OCK DY4 70 A2
Marholm Cl COVEN WV9 11 H5
Marian Cft
LGN/SDN/BHAMAIR B26 148 B3
Maria St WBROM B70 105 H1
Marie Dr ACGN B27 163 F2
Marigold Crs DUDN DY1 84 A2
Marine Crs STRBR DY8 118 A3
Marine Dr KGSTG B44 75 E5
Marine Gdns STRBR DY8 118 A3
Mariner Av LDYWD/EDGR B16 125 G3
Marion Cl BRLYHL DY5 119 H2
Marion Rd SMTHWKW B67 105 H3
Marion Wy HLGN/YWD B28 162 C3
Marita Cl DUDS DY2 121 E1
Marjoram Cl HWK/WKHTH B38 176 D5
Marjorie Av BVILLE B30 177 F2

Mark Av DARL/WED WS10 * 55 G5
Markby Rd WSNCN B18 ....107 G3
Market Pl
  BLKHTH/ROWR B65 * 122 A3
  BLOX/PEL WS3 ....27 F1
  DARL/WED WS10 ....70 D1
  TPTN/OCK DY4 ....86 B1
  WLNHL WV13 ....39 G3
Market Sq CDYHTH B64 * ...120 C4
Market St KGSWFD DY6 ......99 H5
  OLDBY B69 ....135 G2
  STRBR DY8 ....135 G2
  WOLV WV1 ....7 G4
Market Wy HAG/WOL DY9 ...153 E4
Markfield Rd
  LGN/SDN/BHAMAIR B26 ...130 D4
Markford Wk LOZ/NWT B19 ...93 G2
Markham Crs HIA/OLT B92 ...165 H1
Markham Dr WOLV WV4 .....12 A5
Markham Cft COVEN WV9 ....12 A5
Markham Rd SCFLD/BOLD B73..65 E5
Markham Rd BRLYHL DY5 ...119 H5
Marklew Cl BRWNH WS8 ....19 C2
Marklin Av WOLVN WV10 ....23 F1
Mark Rd DARL/WED WS10 ....55 C5
Marksbury Cl
  DUNHL/THL/PER WV6 ......22 C5
Marlbank Rd STRBR DY8 ...118 C3
Marlborough Cl
  FOAKS/STRLY B74 ....32 C4
Marlborough Dr STRBR DY8.135 G4
Marlborough Gdns
  DUNHL/THL/PER WV6 ......36 A1
  STRBR DY8 ....117 G2
Marlborough Gv YDLY B25 ...129 H3
Marlborough Rd CBROM B36..113 F1
  SEDG DY3 ....67 H5
  SMHTH B10 ....128 C3
Marlborough St BLOX/PEL WS3.27 F1
Marlbrook Cl HIA/OLT B92 ...148 A3
Marlbrook Dr
  ETTPK/GDPK/PENN WV4 ....51 H2
Marlburn Wy WMBN WV5 ....64 C5
Marlcliff Gv MOS/BIL B13 ...161 G4
Marldon Rd
  ALE/KHTH/YWD B14 ....160 D4
Marlene Cft
  CHWD/FDBR/MGN B37 .....132 C3
Marley Rd KGSWFD DY6 ....100 C5
Marling Cft HIA/OLT B92 ...165 G3
Marlow Cl DUDN DY1 ....120 D1
Marlowe Dr SHHTH WV12 ....25 E1
Marlow Rd ERDW/GRVHL B23..92 A1
Marlow St BLKHTH/ROWR B65.121 H3
  WSLW WS2 ....42 A1
Marlpit La MGN/WHC B75 ...47 H2
Marlpit Ri MGN/WHC B75 ....48 A2
Marlpool Dr BLOX/PEL WS3 ..28 B1
Marl Rd DUDS DY2 ....102 B5
Marl Top HWK/WKHTH B38..176 D3
Marmion Dr CTB/HAM B43 ...73 H1
Marmion Gv DUDN DY1 .....102 A1
Marmion Wy WBROM B70 ...70 D5
Marnel Dr BDMR/CCFT WV3 ..35 H5
Marquis Dr CDYHTH B64 ...121 G5
Marriott Rd DUDS DY2 .....102 C5
  SMTHWK B66 ....105 H2
Marroway St
  LDYWD/EDGR B16 ....125 H1
Marrowfat La HDSW B21 ...107 H2
Mars Cl BILS/COS WV14 .....68 A2
Marsden Cl HIA/OLT B92 ...164 A1
Marshall Cl ALDR WS9 ......44 B1
Marshall Gv KGSTG B44 .....75 F4
Marshall Lake Rd SHLY B90.180 D4
Marshall Rd LGLYGN/QTN B68.123 C5
  WLNHL WV13 ....38 D4
Marshall St CBHAMW B1 ......2 E7
  SMHTWK B67 ....105 H5
Marsham Court Rd SOLH B91.164 B3
Marsham Rd
  ALE/KHTH/YWD B14 ....178 B2
Marshbrook Cl
  DARL/WED WS10 ....94 A2
Marshbrook Rd
  ERDE/BCHGN B24 ....93 H2
Marsh Cl ERDW/GRVHL B23...92 D1
Marsh Crs STRBR DY8 ......117 H1
Marsh End HWK/WKHTH B38.177 E5
Marshfield SHLY B90 ....194 A3
Marshfield Cl
  ERDE/BCHGN B24 ....92 C4
Marsh Hl ERDW/GRVHL B23...92 A2
Marsh La CSHL/WTROR B46..96 B5
  ERDW/GRVHL B23 ....92 C1
  HHTH/SAND B71 ....71 H3
  SOLH B91 ....182 C2
  WOLVN WV10 ....12 C5
  WSLW WS2 ....42 A1
Marsh Lane Pde WOLVN WV10.12 C5
Marshmont Wy
  ERDW/GRVHL B23 ....76 B3
Marsh St WSLW WS2 ....4 D3
The Marsh DARL/WED WS10 ..55 G5
Marshwood Cft RMSLY B62 ..140 A4
Marsland Cl HRBN B17 .....125 E4
Marsland Rd HIA/OLT B92 ..164 A3
Marston Av DARL/WED WS10.55 E2
Marston Cl STRBR DY8 .....134 C3
Marston Cft
  CHWD/FDBR/MGN B37 .....131 H4
Marston Dr
  CHWD/FDBR/MGN B37 .....114 A4
Marston Gn GTB/HAM B43 ...73 E3
Marston Rd BKHL/PFLD WV2..52 A1
  DUDN DY1 ....101 F1
  SCFLD/BOLD B73 ....74 C4
  SLYOAK B29 ....158 C2
Marston St WLNHL WV13 ....40 A3
Martham Dr
  DUNHL/THL/PER WV6 ......35 F3
Martin Cl BILS/COS WV14 ...68 D4
  YDLY B25 ....146 D1
Martindale Wk BRLYHL DY5.135 H1
Martin Dr SHHTH WV12 .....26 A5
Martineau Pl CBHAM B2 * 3 H3
Martineau Sq CBHAM B2 .....3 J6
Martingale Cl DSYBK/YTR WS5.57 F4
Martin Hill St DUDS DY2 ...102 C1

Martin Ri
  CHWD/FDBR/MGN B37 .....131 H4
Martin Rd BILS/COS WV14 ...54 B5
  DSYBK/YTR WS5 ....43 E5
  TPTN/OCK DY4 ....85 G1
Martin St
  ETTPK/GDPK/PENN WV4 ....52 D2
Martlesham Sq CVALE B35 ...94 C2
Martley Cft RIDG/WDGT B32.141 E3
  SOLH B91 ....181 H5
Martley Dr HAG/WOL DY9 ...136 A3
Martley Rd OLDBY B69 ....104 B3
  RUSH/SHEL WS4 ....29 E1
Marton Cl VAUX/NECH B7 ..109 H3
Marwood Cft FOAKS/STRLY B74..45 G5
Mary Ann St CBHAMNW B3 ...2 E3
  WOLV WV1 * 7 F1
Maryland Av BKDE/SHDE B34.112 A4
Maryland Dr NFLD/LBR B31..158 D5
Maryland Rd BRLYHL DY5 ..119 H5
Marylebone Cl STRBR DY8 ..118 C5
Mary Macarthur Dr
  CDYHTH B64 ....120 C3
Mary Rd HDSW B21 ....107 G2
  OLDBY B69 ....104 A1
  STETCH B33 ....109 H1
  WBROM B70 ....87 H5
Mary St BHTH/HG B12 .....144 A2
  CBHAMNW B3 ....2 D2
  WSLW WS2 ....41 H2
Mary Vale Rd BVILLE B30 ...159 G4
Marywell Cl RIDG/WDGT B32.157 F3
Masefield Av DUDN DY1 .....68 C4
Masefield Cl BILS/COS WV14..69 F1
Masefield Ri RMSLY B62 ...139 F4
Masefield Rd BLOX/PEL WS3..28 A2
  SEDG DY3 ....82 C2
  WOLVN WV10 ....24 A1
Masefield Sq NFLD/LBR B31.176 A1
Masham Cl STETCH B33 ....130 A2
Mashie Gdns
  HWK/WKHTH B38 ....176 B4
Maslin Dr BILS/COS WV14 ...68 A2
Mason Crs
  ETTPK/GDPK/PENN WV4 ....51 E3
Masonleys Rd NFLD/LBR B31.174 D2
Mason Rd ERDE/BCHGN B24..93 E2
  WSLW WS2 ....27 F5
Masons Cl HALE B63 ....137 C1
Masons Cottages
  ERDE/BCHGN B24 * 93 F1
Mason St BILS/COS WV14 ....68 B4
  BKHL/PFLD WV2 ....52 A1
  WBROM B70 ....87 F2
Masons Wy HIA/OLT B92 ...147 E5
Massbrook Gv WOLVN WV10..23 H4
Massbrook Rd WOLVN WV10..23 H4
Masshouse La DIG/EDG B5....3 J4
  HWK/WKHTH B38 ....176 D4
Masters La RMSLY B62 ....122 C3
Matchlock Cl FOAKS/STRLY B74..60 A1
Matfen Av SCFLD/BOLD B73..76 D1
Math Meadow
  RIDG/WDGT B32 ....141 F2
Mathe Cl DUDN DY1 ....120 D1
Matlock Cl BLOX/PEL WS3 ...17 E4
  DUDN DY1 ....101 H4
Matlock Vls BHTH/HG B12 * .144 D2
Matthews Cl
  BLKHTH/ROWR B65 ....121 H5
Mattox Rd WNSFLD WV11 ...24 D4
Matty Rd LGLYGN/QTN B68 .105 G5
Maud Rd CSHL/WTROR B46...96 D3
  WBROM B70 ....87 G5
Maughan St BRLYHL DY5 ...120 A4
  DUDN DY1 ....84 A5
Maurice Gv WOLVN WV10 ...24 A4
Maurice Rd
  ALE/KHTH/YWD B14 ....161 E4
  SMTHWKW B67 ....104 A2
Mavis Gdns LGLYGN/QTN B68.123 F4
Mavis Rd NFLD/LBR B31 ...175 E4
Maw St WSL WS1 ....57 F2
Maxholm Rd FOAKS/STRLY B74..45 E5
Max Rd RIDG/WDGT B32 ...140 D2
Maxstoke Cl BLOX/PEL WS3..16 C4
Maxstoke Cft SHLY B90 ...180 C5
Maxstoke La
  CSHL/WTROR B46 ....115 C3
Maxstoke Rd BORD B9 .....127 H2
Maxted Rd ERDW/GRVHL B23..76 A3
Maxwell Av
  BFLD/HDSWWD B20 ......90 B5
Maxwell Rd BKHL/PFLD WV2..7 H7
Mayall Dr MGN/WHC B75 ...47 G1
Mayberry Rd
  ALE/KHTH/YWD B14 ....178 D3
Maybridge Dr SOLH B91 ...181 H5
Maybrook Rd BRWNH WS8 ..19 F2
  WALM/CURD B76 ....94 C1
Maybury Cl CDSL WV8 ......10 A3
Maybush Gdns WOLVN WV10..23 F1
Maydene Cft BHTH/HG B12..144 B1
Mayfair HAG/WOL DY9 .....136 B5
Mayfair Cl DUDN DY1 ....84 A4
  KGSTG B44 ....75 H5
Mayfair Dr KGSWFD DY6 ....99 G2
Mayfair Gdns BDMR/CCFT WV3..35 H3
  TPTN/OCK DY4 ....85 G2
Mayfair La HLYWD B47 ...192 B2
Mayfield Cl SOLH B91 .....182 A4
Mayfield Crs
  BLKHTH/ROWR B65 ....121 G1
Mayfield Rd BVILLE B30 ...160 A4
  DUDN DY1 ....84 B2
  FOAKS/STRLY B74 ....53 G1
  HALE B63 ....137 H5
  LOZ/NWT B19 ....108 C1
  MOS/BIL B13 ....145 C5
  RMSLY B62 ....122 D5
  SCFLD/BOLD B73 ......77 E1
  SPARK B11 ....146 A3
  WOLV WV1 ....38 B4

Mayfields Dr BRWNH WS8 .....8 B2
Mayflower Cl LOZ/NWT B19..108 D3
Mayflower Dr BRLYHL DY5 ..100 C2
Mayford Gv MOS/BIL B13 ...161 H4
Maygrove Rd KGSWFD DY6 ...99 G2
Mayhurst Cl HLYWD B47 ...193 E2
Mayhurst Av HLYWD B47 ...193 E2
Mayhurst Rd HLYWD B47 ..192 D1
Mayland Dr FOAKS/STRLY B74..60 B3
Mayland Rd
  LDYWD/EDGR B16 ....125 E2
May La ALE/KHTH/YWD B14.161 F5
  HLYWD B47 ....193 E1
Maynard Av STRBR DY8 ...134 D4
Maypole Cl CDYHTH B64 ...120 B4
Maypole Ct WMBN WV5 .....65 E5
Maypole Dr STRBR DY8 ....135 E2
Maypole Flds HALE B63 ...120 A5
Maypole Gv
  ALE/KHTH/YWD B14 ....178 D3
Maypole La
  ALE/KHTH/YWD B14 ....178 C3
Maypole St WMBN WV5 .....65 F4
May St BLOX/PEL WS3 ......27 H4
Mayswood Dr
  DUNHL/THL/PER WV6 ......34 D4
Mayswood Gv
  RIDG/WDGT B32 ....140 D3
Mayswood Rd HIA/OLT B92 .148 A5
Maythorn Av WALM/CURD B76..78 C5
Maythorn Gdns CDSL WV8 ..10 C3
  DUNHL/THL/PER WV6 ......35 G1
Maythorn Gv SOLH B91 ....181 H5
Maytree Cl
  CHWD/FDBR/MGN B37 .....132 A2
May Tree Gv
  BFLD/HDSWWD B20 ......89 H5
Maywell Dr HIA/OLT B92 ...165 H2
Maywood Cl KGSWFD DY6 ...99 F3
McBean Rd
  DUNHL/THL/PER WV6 ......36 B1
McDougall Rd DARL/WED WS10..56 C5
McGregor Cl AST/WIT B6 ....91 H4
McKean Rd OLDBY B69 ....105 E1
McKen Ct WBROM B70 * 87 C4
Meaburn Rd WOLVN WV10 ..12 C5
Meaburn Cl SLYOAK B29 ...158 C5
Mead Cl ALDR WS9 ....30 B4
Mead Crs BORD B9 ....129 F1
Meadfoot Av
  ALE/KHTH/YWD B14 ....178 B2
Meadfoot Dr KGSWFD DY6 ..99 F2
The Meadlands WMBN WV5 ..64 C5
Meadow Av HHTH/SAND B71..72 B2
Meadowbrook Gdns CDSL WV8..10 D3
Meadowbrook Rd HALE B63.137 H4
Meadow Brook Rd
  NFLD/LBR B31 ....158 B5
Meadow Cl FOAKS/STRLY B74..45 F4
  HOCK/TIA B94 ....198 A5
  HRBN B17 ....124 D1
  RUSH/SHEL WS4 ....29 E2
  WALM/CURD B76 ....78 B2
Meadow Cft
  DUNHL/THL/PER WV6 ......34 B2
  HAG/WOL DY9 ....169 F1
  HLYWD B47 ....192 C5
Meadow Dr HIA/OLT B92 ...167 G4
Meadowfield Rd RBRY B45 .188 A1
Meadowfields Cl STRBR DY8.118 A2
Meadow Ga HIA/OLT B92 ...175 E3
Meadow Grange Dr
  SHHTH WV12 ....25 H3
Meadow Gv HIA/OLT B92 ...163 H1
Meadowhill Dr STRBR DY8 .118 A2
Meadow Hill Rd
  HWK/WKHTH B38 ....176 C3
Meadowlands Dr
  RUSH/SHEL WS4 ....29 E2
Meadow La BILS/COS WV14..68 B1
  SHHTH WV12 ....25 G5
  WMBN WV5 ....65 E5
  WOLVN WV10 ....12 C1
Meadow Pk RSTR DY8 .....117 H4
Meadow Pleck La SHLY B90.193 H2
Meadow Ri BVILLE B30 ....159 F3
Meadow Rd ALDR WS9 ......44 A1
  BDMR/CCFT WV3 ....35 G5
  DUDN DY1 ....84 B2
  HLYWD B47 ....192 C5
  HRBN B17 ....124 D3
  LGLYGN/QTN B68 ......123 F4
  RIDG/WDGT B32 ......140 A1
  RMSLY B62 ....123 F5
  SMTHWKW B67 ....106 D5
Meadows Gv CDSL WV8 .....10 C3
Meadowside Cl GTB/HAM B43..73 C2
Meadowside Rd
  FOAKS/STRLY B74 ....46 D1
The Meadows ALDR WS9 ...29 G5
  HAG/WOL DY9 ....152 D3
Meadow St BDMR/CCFT WV3..6 D4
  CDYHTH B64 ....121 H4
  WSL WS1 ....4 C6
Meadowsweet Av
  HWK/WKHTH B38 ....176 D5
Meadowsweet Wy
  KGSWFD DY6 ....100 C3
Meadow V CDSL WV8 ....21 F1
Meadow Vw MOS/BIL B13 ..162 A2
  SEDG DY3 ....67 E2
Meadow Whf
  DUNHL/THL/PER WV6 * 36 A1
Meadow Wk CDYHTH B64 ...120 D4
Meadow Wy CDSL WV8 .....10 A5
  STRBR DY8 ....117 G2
Mead Ri EDG B15 ....142 B3
The Mead SEDG DY3 ....66 D3
Meadthorpe Rd KGSTG B44 .74 D5
Meadvale Rd RBRY B45 ...188 B2
Meadway STETCH B33 ....130 C2
The Meadway
  DUNHL/THL/PER WV6 ......21 G5
Mears Cl ERDW/GRVHL B23..76 B3
Mears Coppice BRLYHL DY5.135 E5
Mearse Cl LOZ/NWT B19 ...111 H5
Mearse La WSNGN B18 ....108 A4
Mearse Rd HAG/WOL DY9 ..184 D2

Mease Cft BORD B9 ....127 H2
Measham Gv
  LGN/SDN/BHAMAIR B26 ...147 E2
Measham Wy WNSFLD WV11..25 E3
Medcroft Av
  BFLD/HDSWWD B20 ......89 C2
Medina Rd SPARK B11 .....145 G3
Medina Wy KGSWFD DY6 ....99 G3
Medley Rd SPARK B11 .....145 G2
Medlicott Rd SPARK B11 ...145 E2
Medway Cl KGSWFD DY6 ...100 C5
Medway Cft CBROM B36 ...113 H2
Medway Gv HWK/WKHTH B38..176 C5
Medway Rd BRWNH WS8 .....8 C2
Medwin Gv ERDW/GRVHL B23..76 B4
Meer End HWK/WKHTH B38.190 C1
Meerhill Av SHLY B90 .....195 F2
Meeting House La
  NFLD/LBR B31 ....175 C1
Meeting La DARL/WED WS10..55 C5
  DUDS DY2 ....102 C5
  TPTN/OCK DY4 ....85 F3
Mehdi Rd OLDBY B69 ......104 C1
Melbourne Av
  BDMR/CCFT WV3 ....89 C2
  SMTHWK B66 ....106 D2
Melbourne Cl KGSWFD DY6 ..71 E5
Melbourne Gdns
  DSYBK/YTR WS5 ....57 H2
Melbourne Rd
  BKDE/SHDE B34 ....113 G3
  HALE B63 ....138 D2
  SMTHWK B66 ....106 C2
Melbourne St BKHL/PFLD WV2..6 B6
Melbury Cl BDMR/CCFT WV3 * .6 B6
Melbury Gv
  ALE/KHTH/YWD B14 ....161 E5
Melchett Rd BVILLE B30 ...176 D2
Melcote Gv KGSTG B44 .....75 E5
Meldon Dr BILS/COS WV14 ..69 C1
Melford Cl SEDG DY3 ....67 E1
Melford Hall Rd SOLH B91 .164 B3
Melfort Gv
  ALE/KHTH/YWD B14 ....178 C2
Melksham Sq CVALE B35 ....94 C3
Mellis Gv ERDW/GRVHL B23..91 G1
Mellish Dr RUSH/SHEL WS4..42 D2
Mellish Rd RUSH/SHEL WS4..42 D2
Mellor Dr FOAKS/STRLY B74..46 C2
Mellors Cl HRBN B17 ......141 H4
Mellowdew Rd STRBR DY8 .117 G1
Mell Sq SOLH B91 ....182 A1
Melplash Av SOLH B91 ....181 G1
Melrose Av BHTH/HG B12 ..144 C1
  HHTH/SAND B71 ......71 H2
  SCFLD/BOLD B73 ......76 C1
  STRBR DY8 ....152 C1
Melrose Cl HWK/WKHTH B38.176 D4
Melrose Dr
  DUNHL/THL/PER WV6 ......34 B1
Melrose Gv LOZ/NWT B19 ..108 B2
  HRBN B17 ....124 D5
  RUSH/SHEL WS4 ....29 E2
Melrose Rd
  BFLD/HDSWWD B20 ......91 E5
Melstock Cl TPTN/OCK DY4 ..84 D1
Melstock Rd
  ALE/KHTH/YWD B14 ....160 D3
Melton Av HIA/OLT B92 ...147 G5
Melton Dr EDG B15 ....126 C5
Melton Rd
  ALE/KHTH/YWD B14 ....161 F2
Melverley Gv KGSTG B44 ...75 F4
Melverton Av WOLVN WV10..23 G2
Melville Hall
  LDYWD/EDGR B16 * 125 F3
Melville Rd LDYWD/EDGR B16..125 F3
Melvina Rd VAUX/NECH B7.109 H5
Membury Rd WASH/WDE B8.110 D3
Memorial Cl WLNHL WV13 ..39 C3
Memory La DARL/WED WS10..40 B5
  WNSFLD WV11 ....24 A4
Menai Cl SHHTH WV12 ......26 A4
Mendip Av WASH/WDE B8 .110 C4
Mendip Cl BKHL/PFLD WV2..52 D2
  SEDG DY3 ....83 F5
Mendip Rd HALE B63 ....138 D1
  STRBR DY8 ....135 H1
  WASH/WDE B8 ....110 C4
Menin Crs MOS/BIL B13 ...161 H3
Menin Rd MOS/BIL B13 ....161 H3
  TPTN/OCK DY4 ....84 D1
Meon Gv
  DUNHL/THL/PER WV6 ......35 E5
  STETCH B33 ....130 D4
Meon Rd HALE B63 ....137 H5
Meon Wy WNSFLD WV11 ....25 F5
Meranti Cl SHHTH WV12 ....26 A2
Mercer Av CSHL/WTROR B46..96 A1
Mercer Gv WNSFLD WV11 ..24 D5
Mercia Dr
  ALE/KHTH/YWD B14 ....160 D4
Mere Av CVALE B35 ....94 C5
Mere Cl SHHTH WV12 ......25 C5
Merecote Rd HIA/OLT B92 .163 H3
Meredith Pool Cl
  WNSFLD WV11 ....107 H3
Meredith Rd SEDG DY3 .....82 C3
  WNSFLD WV11 ....25 F5
Meredith St CDYHTH B64 ..120 D3
Mere Dr MGN/WHC B75 .....47 C5
Mere Green Cl MGN/WHC B75..47 G5
Mere Green Rd MGN/WHC B75..47 F5
Mere Oak Rd
  DUNHL/THL/PER WV6 ......20 C5
Mere Pool Rd MGN/WHC B75..47 H4
Mere Rd ERDW/GRVHL B23..92 B1
  STRBR DY8 ....135 G3
Mereside Wy HIA/OLT B92 .164 A2
Meres Rd HALE B63 ....137 H2
Merevale Rd HIA/OLT B92 .147 H5
Mere Vw RUSH/SHEL WS4 ..29 E2
Mereways Wy SHLY B90 ...194 A3
Meriden Av STRBR DY8 ....117 C3
Meriden Cl ERDE/BCHGN B24..93 E5
  YDLY B25 ....129 F5
Meriden Dr
  CHWD/FDBR/MGN B37 .....114 A4

Meriden Ri HIA/OLT B92 ...148 B4
Meriden Rd HIA/OLT B92 ...167 H3
  WOLVN WV10 ....22 C2
Meriden St DIG/EDG B5 .....3 J6
Merino Av NFLD/LBR B31 ..175 G5
Merlin Cl CVALE B35 ....94 C3
  DUDN DY1 ....101 H1
Merlin Gv
  LGN/SDN/BHAMAIR B26 ...147 H2
Merrick Cl HALE B63 ......137 H5
Merridale Av WNSFLD WV11..25 C4
Merridale Crs BDMR/CCFT WV3..36 B3
Merridale Gdns
  BDMR/CCFT WV3 ....36 B5
Merridale Gv BDMR/CCFT WV3..36 A4
Merridale La BDMR/CCFT WV3..6 A4
Merridale Rd BDMR/CCFT WV3..6 B4
Merridale St West
  BDMR/CCFT WV3 ....6 A7
Merrill's Hall La WNSFLD WV11..39 E1
Merrington Cl SOLH B91 ...182 A5
Merrion's Cl CTB/HAM B43 ..58 C4
Merrishaw Rd NFLD/LBR B31..175 G5
Merritts Brook Cl
  NFLD/LBR B31 ....158 A5
Merritts Brook La
  NFLD/LBR B31 ....158 A4
Merritt's Hl NFLD/LBR B31.158 A4
Merrivale Rd RMSLY B62 ..122 C2
  SMTHWK B66 ....124 C2
Merryfield Cl HIA/OLT B92 .165 F3
Merryfield Gv HRBN B17 ...142 A3
Merryfield Rd DUDN DY1 ...83 F5
Merry Hl BRLYHL DY5 ......119 H3
Merryhill Dr WSNGN B18 ..107 H3
Merryhill Rd WSNCN B18 ...19 C5
Mersey Rd BLOX/PEL WS3 ..28 A1
Merstal Dr HIA/OLT B92 ...165 H3
Merstone Cl BILS/COS WV14..53 G2
Merstowe Ct ACCN B27 ....146 A4
Merton Cl LGLYGN/QTN B68.123 F2
Merton Rd MOS/BIL B13 ...145 H3
Mervyn Pl BILS/COS WV14 ..54 B5
Mervyn Rd BILS/COS WV14 ..54 B5
  HDSW B21 ....89 F5
Meryhurst Rd DARL/WED WS10..56 B4
Messenger La WBROM B70 ..87 H3
Messenger Rd SMTHWK B66.106 D3
Metchley Ct HRBN B17 ....142 B3
Metchley Dr HRBN B17 ....142 A3
Metchley La HRBN B17 ....142 B3
Metchley Park Rd EDG B15.142 B2
Metchley Ri HRBN B17 ....142 B3
Metfield Cft HRBN B17 ....142 B3
  KGSWFD DY6 ....100 B3
Metlin Gv STETCH B33 ....131 G1
Metric Wk SMTHWK B66 ..107 E2
The Mews BLKHTH/ROWR B65..121 H2
Mey Coppice CBROM B36 ..113 H2
Meyrick Rd HHTH/SAND B71..71 E5
Meyrick Wk LDYWD/EDGR B16..124 C5
Miall Park Rd SOLH B91 ...164 A5
Miall Rd HLGN/YWD B28 ..162 C5
Michael Dr EDG B15 ......126 C5
Michael Rd DARL/WED WS10..56 A7
  SMTHWKW B67 ....106 A3
Michelle Cl MOS/BIL B13 ..161 C5
Mickleholt Dr SHLY B90 ...180 B5
Mickle Meadow
  CSHL/WTROR B46 ....96 B3
Mickleover Rd WASH/WDE B8..111 G4
Mickleton Av STETCH B33 .131 E4
Mickleton Rd HIA/OLT B92 .163 H2
Mickley Av WOLVN WV10 ...23 G3
Mickley Av WOLVN WV10 ...35 H2
Middle Acre Rd
  RIDG/WDGT B32 ....141 E5
Middle Av WLNHL WV13 ....39 E5
Middle Bickenhill La
  HIA/OLT B92 ....150 C3
Middle Crs BLOX/PEL WS3 ..28 B3
Middle Cross WOLV WV1 ....7 H5
Middle Dr RBRY B45 ......188 D4
Middlefield CDSL WV8 .....11 C5
Middlefield Av DOR/KN B93.197 F3
  RMSLY B62 ....122 D5
Middlefield Cl RMSLY B62 .122 D3
Middlefield La HAG/WOL DY9..152 A3
Middle Field Rd NFLD/LBR B31..176 A3
Middlefield Rd OLDBY B69 .105 C1
Middle Gdns WLNHL WV13 ..39 H3
Middle La HLYWD B47 ....191 C1
  HWK/WKHTH B38 ....191 C1
Middle Leaford
  BKDE/SHDE B34 ....112 C4
Middle Leasowe
  RIDG/WDGT B32 ....140 C3
Middle Meadow Av
  RIDG/WDGT B32 ....140 C2
Middlemist Gv GTB/HAM B43..73 H5
Middlemore Cl ALDR WS9 ..30 C4
Middlemore La West ALDR WS9..29 C4
Middlemore Rd NFLD/LBR B31..175 H5
  SMTHWK B66 ....106 D2
Middle Park Cl SLYOAK B29.158 D2
Middle Park Rd SLYOAK B29.158 D3
Middlepark Dr DUDN DY1 ..101 C1
Middlepark Rd DUDN DY1 ..101 C1
Middleton Cl DSYBK/YTR WS5..58 B1
Middleton Gdns
  HWK/WKHTH B38 ....176 B1
Middleton Hall Rd BVILLE B30..176 C1
Middleton Rd
  ALE/KHTH/YWD B14 ....161 E3
  BRWNH WS8 ....18 D3
  FOAKS/STRLY B74 ....45 F5
  SHLY B90 ....180 A3
Middletree Rd HALE B63 ..120 C5
Middle Vauxhall WOLV WV1..37 C5
Middleway Av STRBR DY8 .117 C3
Middleway Gn BILS/COS WV14..53 C5
Middleway Rd BILS/COS WV14..38 C5
Middleway Vw WSNGN B18.108 A5
Middlewood Cl SOLH B91 ..165 F4

Midgley Dr FOAKS/STRLY B74 47 E3
Midhill Dr BLKHTH/ROWR B65 104 A3
Midhurst Gv
DUNHL/THL/PER WV6 21 G5
Midhurst Rd BVILLE B30 177 F2
Midland Cl HDSW B21 107 H2
Midland Cft STETCH B33 131 F1
Midland Dr CSCFLD/WYGN B72 62 C3
Midland Rd BVILLE B30 159 H5
DARL/WED WS10 40 A5
FOAKS/STRLY B74 62 B2
WSL WS1 4 D5
Midland St BORD B9 128 A1
Midpoint Bvd WALM/CURD B76 95 E1
Midpoint Pk WALM/CURD B76 * 95 E1
Midvale Dr
ALE/KHTH/YWD B14 177 H3
Milburn Rd KGSTG B44 60 C5
Milcote Dr SCFLD/BOLD B73 61 E5
WLNHL WV13 38 D4
Milcote Rd SLYOAK B29 158 C2
SMTHWKW B67 124 B2
SOLH B91 181 H1
Milcote Wy KGSWFD DY6 99 F2
Mildenhall Rd PBAR/PBCH B42 74 A2
Mildred Rd CDYHTH B64 121 E2
Mildred Wy
BLKHTH/ROWR B65 104 A3
Milebrook Gv RIDG/WDGT B32 157 F2
Milebush Av CBROM B36 95 F5
Mile Flat KGSWFD DY6 98 D2
Miles Gv DUDS DY2 103 F2
Miles Meadow Cl SHHTH WV12 26 A2
Milestone Dr HAG/WOL DY9 169 G1
Milestone La HDSW B21 107 F1
Milestone Wy SHHTH WV12 25 H2
Milford Av SHHTH WV12 25 G5
Milford Cl STRBR DY8 118 A1
Milford Copse HRBN B17 141 H2
Milford Ct LOZ/NWT B19 108 D4
Milford Cft
BLKHTH/ROWR B65 103 F3
Milford Gv SHLY B90 196 A1
Milford Pl
ALE/KHTH/YWD B14 * 161 E2
Milford Rd BKHL/PFLD WV2 52 A1
HRBN B17 141 H2
Milholme Gn HIA/OLT B92 165 F3
Milking Bank DUDN DY1 83 G4
Milk St DIG/EDG B5 3 K7
Millard Rd BILS/COS WV14 68 B2
Mill Bank SEDG DY3 67 F3
Millbank Gv ERDW/GRVHL B23 75 H5
Millbank St WNSFLD WV11 25 F1
Millbrook Dr NFLD/LBR B31 175 E5
Millbrook Rd
ALE/KHTH/YWD B14 160 C4
Millbrook Wy BRLYHL DY5 118 D4
Mill Burn Wy BORD B9 127 H2
Mill Cl HLYWD B47 192 C1
KIDD DY10 168 B3
SEDG DY3 67 F5
Mill Cft BILS/COS WV14 54 A2
Millcroft Cl RIDG/WDGT B32 141 E5
Millcroft Rd FOAKS/STRLY B74 45 G5
Milldale Crs WOLVN WV10 12 D4
Milldale Rd WOLVN WV10 12 D3
Mill Dr SMTHWK B66 106 D4
Millenium Pk WBROM B70 87 E1
Millennium Cl BLOX/PEL WS3 18 A3
Millennium Gdns CDYHTH B64 121 F2
Millennium Pk WBROM B70 * 87 E1
Millennium Wy CDSL WV8 10 D3
Miller Crs BILS/COS WV14 68 A2
Millers Cl WSLW WS2 40 D4
Millersdale Dr HHTH/SAND B71 72 B1
Millers Green Dr KGSWFD DY6 99 E1
Miller St AST/WIT B6 109 E4
Millers V WMBN WV5 80 B1
Millers Wk BLOX/PEL WS3 17 G4
Mill Farm Rd HRBN B17 142 A4
Millfield NFLD/LBR B31 * 175 G1
Millfield Av BLOX/PEL WS3 17 F5
RUSH/SHEL WS4 28 D1
Millfield Rd
BFLD/HDSWWD B20 89 H1
BRWNH WS8 9 G5
Millfields STETCH B33 131 G1
Millfields Rd
ETTPK/GDPK/PENN WV4 53 E3
HHTH/SAND B71 71 F2
Millfields Wy WMBN WV5 80 B1
Millfield Vw HALE B63 138 A3
Millford Cl HLGN/YWD B28 163 E5
Mill Gdns SMTHWKW B67 * 124 B2
Mill Gn WOLVN WV10 12 D3
Mill Gv CDSL WV8 11 E4
Millhaven Av BVILLE B30 160 B4
Mill Hl SMTHWKW B67 124 B1
Millhouse Rd YDLY B25 129 G4
Millichip Rd WLNHL WV13 39 E4
Millington Rd CBROM B36 112 A1
TPTN/OCK DY4 69 F2
WOLVN WV10 23 G4
Millison Gv SHLY B90 195 G1
Mill La ALDR WS9 31 G4
BRGRVW B61 186 B5
CDSL WV8 10 B2
DIG/EDG B5 3 J7
DOR/KN B93 196 D4
DUNHL/THL/PER WV6 35 E3
HALE B63 139 E3
KIDD DY10 168 B3
NFLD/LBR B31 175 F3
OLDBY B69 105 E5
RIDG/WDGT B32 141 E5
RUSH/SHEL WS4 42 B1
SEDG DY3 80 B3
SHHTH WV12 26 A5
SOLH B91 182 A2
WMBN WV5 65 F4
WNSFLD WV11 24 B3
Mill Lane Ar SOLH B91 * 182 A2
Millmead Rd
RIDG/WDGT B32 141 E5
Mill Pl BLOX/PEL WS3 42 A1
Mill Pool Cl HAG/WOL DY9 169 G1
WMBN WV5 80 B1
Millpool Gdns
ALE/KHTH/YWD B14 178 B2
Millpool Hill Alcester Rd South
ALE/KHTH/YWD B14 178 B1
Mill Pool La DOR/KN B93 199 E3
Millpool Wy SMTHWK B66 106 C5
Mill Race La STRBR DY8 135 G1
Mill Rd BRWNH WS8 9 G5
CDYHTH B64 121 E5
RUSH/SHEL WS4 28 D1
Mills Av WALM/CURD B76 63 E4
Mills Cl WNSFLD WV11 24 B2
Mills Crs BKHL/PFLD WV2 37 G5
Millside HLGN/YWD B28 179 G2
WMBN WV5 * 80 C1
Mills Rd BKHL/PFLD WV2 37 G5
Millstone Cl WALM/CURD B76 78 B2
Mill Stream Cl CDSL WV8 10 D3
Mill St AST/WIT B6 109 F4
BILS/COS WV14 53 G3
BRLYHL DY5 119 F2
CDYHTH B64 120 C5
CSCFLD/WYGN B72 62 C3
DARL/WED WS10 55 E2
STRBR DY8 118 A2
TPTN/OCK DY4 86 B1
WBROM B70 87 G2
WLNHL WV13 40 A3
WSLW WS2 42 A2
Millthorpe Cl WASH/WDE B8 110 D4
Mill Vw STETCH B33 113 E5
Millwalk Dr COVEN WV9 12 A4
The Mill Wk NFLD/LBR B31 175 F4
Millward St BORD B9 128 A3
WBROM B70 87 E3
Millwright Cl TPTN/OCK DY4 85 H1
Milner Rd SLYOAK B29 160 A1
Milner Wy MOS/BIL B13 162 B2
Milsom Gv BKDE/SHDE B34 113 F3
Milstead Rd
LGN/SDN/BHAMAIR B26 130 C3
Milston Cl ALE/KHTH/YWD B14 178 A4
Milton Cl DOR/KN B93 196 D4
SHHTH WV12 26 C3
STRBR DY8 118 C5
WSL WS1 56 D2
Milton Ct DUNHL/THL/PER WV6 34 C1
Milton Crs SEDG DY3 82 C1
YDLY B25 129 H5
Milton Dr HAG/WOL DY9 153 F3
Milton Gv HDSW B21 * 107 E1
Milton Pl WSL WS1 56 D2
Milton Rd BILS/COS WV14 68 D4
DOR/KN B93 196 D4
SMTHWKW B67 105 H4
WOLVN WV10 24 A5
Milton St BRLYHL DY5 101 F2
HHTH/SAND B71 87 F1
LOZ/NWT B19 109 E3
WSL WS1 4 C7
Milverton Cl HALE B63 138 C1
WALM/CURD B76 78 B4
Milverton Rd DOR/KN B93 197 G3
ERDW/GRVHL B23 92 C1
Mimosa Cl SLYOAK B29 158 D2
Mimosa Wk KGSWFD DY6 100 A1
Mincing La
BLKHTH/ROWR B65 122 A1
Mindelsohn Wy HRBN B17 142 B3
Minden Gv SLYOAK B29 158 D1
Minehead Rd DUDN DY1 101 F1
WOLVN WV10 12 B5
Miner St WSLW WS2 41 G2
Minerva Cl SHHTH WV12 40 C1
Minewood Cl BLOX/PEL WS3 16 B4
Minith Rd BILS/COS WV14 68 D3
Miniva Dr WALM/CURD B76 78 C1
Minivet Dr BHTH/HG B12 144 A1
Minley Av HRBN B17 124 B5
The Minories CBHAMNE B4 3 G4
DUDS DY2 84 D5
Minstead Rd ERDE/BCHGN B24 92 B5
Minster Cl BLKHTH/ROWR B65 122 C1
DOR/KN B93 183 F5
Minster Ct MOS/BIL B13 * 144 C3
Minster Dr SMHTH B10 128 A5
Minsterley Cl BDMR/CCFT WV3 36 A5
The Minster BDMR/CCFT WV3 51 F1
Mintern Rd YDLY B25 129 G3
Minton Cl WOLV WV1 38 A4
Minton Rd RIDG/WDGT B32 141 F3
Minworth Rd CSHL/WTROR B46 96 B3
Miranda Cl RBRY B45 174 A3
Mirfield Cl COVEN WV9 12 A4
Mirfield Rd SOLH B91 164 C4
STETCH B33 130 D2
Mission Cl CDYHTH B64 121 G3
Mission Dr TPTN/OCK DY4 85 G2
Mistletoe Dr DSYBK/YTR WS5 57 G5
Mitcham Gv KGSTG B44 75 H2
Mitcheldean Covert
ALE/KHTH/YWD B14 177 H3
Mitchell Av BILS/COS WV14 68 B4
Mitchel Rd KGSWFD DY6 100 B5
Mitford Dr HIA/OLT B92 165 F3
Mitre Cl SHHTH WV12 26 B3
WNSFLD WV11 15 E4
Mitre Fold WOLV WV1 6 E3
Mitre Rd HAG/WOL DY9 136 C2
Mitten Av RBRY B45 173 H4
Mitton Rd BFLD/HDSWWD B20 89 G4
Moat Brook Av CDSL WV8 10 A3
Moat Coppice
RIDG/WDGT B32 157 E1
Moat Cft
CHWD/FDBR/MGN B37 132 A2
WALM/CURD B76 78 D4
Moat Dr BKDE/SHDE B34 112 C3
RMSLY B62 122 D3
Moat Farm Dr RIDG/WDGT B32 157 E1
Moat Farm Wy BLOX/PEL WS3 18 A2
Moatfield Ter DARL/WED WS10 56 A5
Moat Green Av WNSFLD WV11 25 E3
Moat House La East
WNSFLD WV11 24 D3
Moathouse La West
WNSFLD WV11 24 D3
Moat House Rd
WASH/WDE B8 111 E5
Moat La DIG/EDG B5 3 H6
LGN/SDN/BHAMAIR B26 130 A5
SOLH B91 165 E4
Moat Mdw RIDG/WDGT B32 141 E3
Moat Rd LGLYGN/QTN B68 123 F1
TPTN/OCK DY4 69 G4
WSLW WS2 41 G3
Moatside Cl BLOX/PEL WS3 18 A2
Moat St WLNHL WV13 39 G3
The Moatway
HWK/WKHTH B38 190 C1
Mobberley Rd BILS/COS WV14 68 A2
Mob La RUSH/SHEL WS4 18 C5
Mockley Wood Rd
DOR/KN B93 197 F1
Modbury Av RIDG/WDGT B32 157 H1
Moden Cl SEDG DY3 83 F1
Moden Hl SEDG DY3 67 E5
Mogul La HALE B63 120 A5
Moillett St WSNGN B18 107 F5
Moilliett Ct SMTHWK B66 107 E3
Moira Crs ALE/KHTH/YWD B14 179 E1
Moises Hall Rd WMBN WV5 65 F5
Moland St CBHAMNE B4 3 H1
Mole St BHTH/HG B12 144 D1
Molineux St WOLV WV1 7 F2
Mollington Crs SHLY B90 180 C2
Molyneux Rd DUDS DY2 121 E2
Monarch Dr TPTN/OCK DY4 70 A5
Monarch's Wy
BLKHTH/ROWR B65 121 G2
BRGRVW B61 186 B5
CDSL WV8 20 A5
CDYHTH B64 121 F1
COVEN WV9 11 G2
DARL/WED WS10 54 D3
ETTPK/GDPK/PENN WV4 64 D1
HAG/WOL DY9 153 F2
KGSWFD DY6 98 C3
KIDD DY10 168 D4
KINVER DY7 116 C2
OLDBY B69 86 A4
RBRY B45 187 E2
RMSLY B62 173 E2
SEDG DY3 80 C4
SHHTH WV12 26 C4
STRBR DY8 135 E1
TPTN/OCK DY4 70 B5
WMBN WV5 80 C1
WNSFLD WV11 24 D2
WOLVN WV10 12 C1
WSLW WS2 41 E2
Monarch Wy DUDS DY2 102 B5
Mona Rd ERDW/GRVHL B23 92 D1
Monastery Dr SOLH B91 164 A4
Monckton Rd
LGLYGN/QTN B68 123 E5
Moncrieffe Cl DUDS DY2 103 E1
Moncrieffe St WSL WS1 5 H5
Money La BRGRVW B61 186 C2
Monica Rd SMHTH B10 128 D4
Monins Av TPTN/OCK DY4 85 G3
Monk Cl TPTN/OCK DY4 85 H3
Monkgate Dr HHTH/SAND B71 71 F5
Monk Rd WASH/WDE B8 111 F4
Monks Cl WMBN WV5 64 C5
Monkseaton Rd
CSCFLD/WYGN B72 77 F1
Monksfield Av GTB/HAM B43 73 F2
Monkshood Ms
ERDW/GRVHL B23 75 H4
Monkshood Retreat
HWK/WKHTH B38 176 D5
Monks Kirby Rd
WALM/CURD B76 63 F5
Monkspath SHLY B90 195 G2
WALM/CURD B76 78 B3
Monkspath Cl SHLY B90 194 D1
Monkspath Hall Rd SHLY B90 195 F2
Monksway HWK/WKHTH B38 177 F3
Monkswell Cl BRLYHL DY5 119 F3
SMHTH B10 128 B5
Monkswood Rd
NFLD/LBR B31 176 A3
Monkton Rd SLYOAK B29 141 G4
Monmer Cl WLNHL WV13 39 H2
Monmer La WLNHL WV13 39 H2
Monmore Rd WOLV WV1 38 A5
Monmouth Dr
HHTH/SAND B71 71 F4
SCFLD/BOLD B73 61 E4
Monmouth Rd
RIDG/WDGT B32 157 H2
SMTHWKW B67 124 A4
WSLW WS2 40 C2
Monsal Av WOLVN WV10 37 G1
Monsaldale Cl BRWNH WS8 18 D1
Monsal Rd PBAR/PBCH B42 74 C4
Mons Rd DUDS DY2 85 E5
Montague Rd
ERDE/BCHGN B24 93 E5
HDSW B21 107 H1
LDYWD/EDGR B16 125 G3
SMTHWK B66 124 D1
Montague St AST/WIT B6 109 H1
BORD B9 127 G1
Montana Av PBAR/PBCH B42 90 A1
Monteagle Dr KGSWFD DY6 81 H5
Montford Gv SEDG DY3 * 67 F4
Montfort Rd
CSHL/WTROR B46 115 F4
WSLW WS2 56 B2
Montgomery Crs BRLYHL DY5 119 H5
Montgomery Cft SPARK B11 128 A5
Montgomery Rd WSLW WS2 40 C3
Montgomery St SPARK B11 127 H5
Montgomery Wy
WASH/WDE B8 111 E5
Montpelier Rd
ERDE/BCHGN B24 93 E5
Montpellier Gdns DUDN DY1 83 G4
Montpellier St BHTH/HG B12 144 C1
Montrose Dr CVALE B35 94 C3
DUDN DY1 102 A1
Montsford Cl DOR/KN B93 196 D2
Monument Av HAG/WOL DY9 136 C3
Monument La HAG/WOL DY9 153 F3
RBRY B45 187 H4
SEDG DY3 67 G2
Monument Rd
LDYWD/EDGR B16 125 H3
Monway Ter DARL/WED WS10 55 G5
Monwood Gv SOLH B91 181 F3
Monyhull Hall Rd BVILLE B30 177 F2
Moodyscroft Rd STETCH B33 131 E1
Moorcroft Dr DARL/WED WS10 70 A1
Moorcroft Pl VAUX/NECH B7 * 109 G5
Moorcroft Rd MOS/BIL B13 143 H4
Moordown Av HIA/OLT B92 147 G5
Moore Cl DUNHL/THL/PER WV6 34 D1
FOAKS/STRLY B74 32 D4
Moore Crs LGLYGN/QTN B68 123 G1
Moorend Av
CHWD/FDBR/MGN B37 132 A3
Moor End La ERDE/BCHGN B24 93 E2
Moore Rd SHHTH WV12 26 B2
Moore's Rw DIG/EDG B5 3 K7
Moore St WOLV WV1 37 H4
Moorfield Av DOR/KN B93 196 D2
Moorfield Dr HALE B63 138 C2
SCFLD/BOLD B73 76 D3
Moorfield Rd BKDE/SHDE B34 112 C3
BKHL/PFLD WV2 51 H1
Moorfields Cl ALDR WS9 30 A3
Moorfoot Av HALE B63 154 C1
Moor Green La MOS/BIL B13 160 C1
Moor Hall Dr HAG/WOL DY9 171 E4
MGN/WHC B75 47 G4
Moorhen Cl BRWNH WS8 9 E5
Moorhills Cft SHLY B90 180 B5
The Moorings BRLYHL DY5 101 H5
COVEN WV9 * 11 H5
OLDBY B69 104 C1
WSNGN B18 107 H4
Moorland Av WOLVN WV10 23 E4
Moorland Rd BLOX/PEL WS3 27 E2
LDYWD/EDGR B16 125 F3
Moorlands Dr SHLY B90 180 C3
Moorlands Rd HHTH/SAND B71 71 G2
The Moorlands
FOAKS/STRLY B74 46 D5
Moor La AST/WIT B6 91 G3
BLKHTH/ROWR B65 121 G1
LICHS WS14 32 C1
Moor Leasow NFLD/LBR B31 176 A3
Moor Meadow Rd
MGN/WHC B75 62 D1
Moor Pk BLOX/PEL WS3 16 D4
DUNHL/THL/PER WV6 20 B5
Moorpark Rd NFLD/LBR B31 175 G4
Moor Pool Av HRBN B17 142 A1
Moors Cft RIDG/WDGT B32 157 F1
Moorside Gdns WSLW WS2 41 F2
Moorside Rd
ALE/KHTH/YWD B14 179 E1
Moors La NFLD/LBR B31 158 A2
Moors Mill La TPTN/OCK DY4 70 A4
Moorsom St AST/WIT B6 109 E4
The Moors CBROM B36 112 B1
Moor St BRLYHL DY5 118 C1
CBHAMNE B4 3 H6
DARL/WED WS10 71 F1
WBROM B70 87 G4
Moor St Queensway
CBHAMNE B4 3 H5
Moor St South BKHL/PFLD WV2 52 A1
The Moor WALM/CURD B76 78 C3
Moorville Wk SPARK B11 127 G5
Morar Cl CVALE B35 94 D2
Moray Cl RMSLY B62 122 C4
Morcom Rd SPARK B11 145 G2
Morcroft BILS/COS WV14 54 C5
Mordaunt Dr MGN/WHC B75 47 H3
Morden Rd STETCH B33 129 H1
Moreland Cft WALM/CURD B76 78 D5
The Morelands NFLD/LBR B31 175 H4
Morestead Av
LGN/SDN/BHAMAIR B26 148 A2
Moreton Av
ETTPK/GDPK/PENN WV4 52 C4
GTB/HAM B43 74 C1
Moreton Cl RIDG/WDGT B32 141 F2
TPTN/OCK DY4 69 H1
YDLY B25 129 F5
Moreton Rd SHLY B90 180 C3
WOLVN WV10 23 F1
Moreton St CBHAMW B1 2 A2
Morford Rd ALDR WS9 30 A3
Morgan Cl CDYHTH B64 121 E3
OLDBY B69 104 B1
SHHTH WV12 39 H1
Morgan Gv CBROM B36 95 H5
Morgrove Av DOR/KN B93 196 D2
Morjon Dr GTB/HAM B43 73 H1
Morland Rd GTB/HAM B43 59 G4
Morley Gv
DUNHL/THL/PER WV6 37 E1
Morley Rd WASH/WDE B8 111 F3
Morlich Ri BRLYHL DY5 118 D4
Morning Pines STRBR DY8 135 E3
Morningside SCFLD/BOLD B73 62 B2
Mornington Rd SMTHWK B66 106 D2
Morris Av WSLW WS2 40 C3
Morris Cl ACGN B27 146 D3
Morris Cft CBROM B36 95 G5
Morris Field Cft
HLGN/YWD B28 179 G1
Morrison Av WOLVN WV10 23 F2
Morrison Rd TPTN/OCK DY4 86 A2
Morris Rd WASH/WDE B8 111 F3
Morris St WBROM B70 87 G5
Mortimers Cl
ALE/KHTH/YWD B14 178 D4
Morton Rd BRLYHL DY5 119 F5
Morvale Gdns HAG/WOL DY9 136 C2
Morvale St HAG/WOL DY9 136 C2
Morven Rd SCFLD/BOLD B73 76 D1
Morville Cl DOR/KN B93 196 B5
Morville Cft BILS/COS WV14 53 F4
Morville Rd DUDS DY2 102 D5
Morville St LDYWD/EDGR B16 2 A7
Mosborough Crs
LOZ/NWT B19 108 C4
Mosedale Dr WNSFLD WV11 25 F5
Moseley Ct WNSFLD WV11 14 D4
Moseley Dr
CHWD/FDBR/MGN B37 131 H4
Moseley Old Hall La
WOLVN WV10 13 G2
Moseley Rd BHTH/HG B12 144 B2
BILS/COS WV14 39 E5
WLNHL WV13 38 D4
WOLVN WV10 13 H2
Moseley St DIG/EDG B5 127 F3
TPTN/OCK DY4 70 A4
WOLVN WV10 37 E1
Moss Cl ALDR WS9 30 A5
RUSH/SHEL WS4 42 C2
Mossdale Wy SEDG DY3 67 G4
Moss Dr CSCFLD/WYGN B72 62 C5
Mossfield Rd
ALE/KHTH/YWD B14 161 E3
Moss Gdns BILS/COS WV14 53 F5
Moss Gv ALE/KHTH/YWD B14 160 D4
KGSWFD DY6 99 H2
Moss House Cl EDG B15 126 B3
Mossley Cl BLOX/PEL WS3 26 D1
Mossley La BLOX/PEL WS3 16 B5
Mossvale Cl CDYHTH B64 121 E3
Mossvale Gv WASH/WDE B8 110 D4
Moss Wy FOAKS/STRLY B74 60 B1
Mostyn Crs HHTH/SAND B71 71 E4
Mostyn Rd HDSW B21 107 H1
LDYWD/EDGR B16 125 H3
Mostyn St WOLV WV1 36 D1
Mott Cl TPTN/OCK DY4 * 70 A3
Mottram Cl WBROM B70 87 E4
Mottrams Cl
CSCFLD/WYGN B72 77 G1
Mott St LOZ/NWT B19 2 E1
Mott's Wy CSHL/WTROR B46 115 G3
Moundsley Gv
ALE/KHTH/YWD B14 178 C2
Mountain Ash Dr
HAG/WOL DY9 136 A5
Mountain Ash Rd BRWNH WS8 19 E2
Mount Av BRLYHL DY5 101 E5
Mountbatten Cl WBROM B70 88 B4
Mountbatten Rd WSLW WS2 40 D3
Mount Cl MOS/BIL B13 144 B3
SEDG DY3 83 E4
WMBN WV5 65 E4
Mount Cottages
ETTPK/GDPK/PENN WV4 * 51 F5
Mount Ct
DUNHL/THL/PER WV6 * 35 F2
Mount Dr WMBN WV5 65 E4
Mountfield Cl
ALE/KHTH/YWD B14 178 C3
Mountford Cl
BLKHTH/ROWR B65 122 A1
Mountford Crs ALDR WS9 30 B2
Mountford Dr MGN/WHC B75 47 G5
Mountford La BILS/COS WV14 53 H1
Mountford Rd SHLY B90 179 F4
Mountford St SPARK B11 145 F2
Mount Gdns CDSL WV8 10 B3
Mountjoy Crs HIA/OLT B92 148 A4
Mount La HAG/WOL DY9 170 C1
SEDG DY3 83 E4
Mount Pleasant
ALE/KHTH/YWD B14 161 E1
BILS/COS WV14 54 A2
BKHL/PFLD WV2 * 52 D1
BRLYHL DY5 119 G3
ETTPK/GDPK/PENN WV4 * 51 F5
KGSWFD DY6 99 G5
LGLYGN/QTN B68 * 105 F5
SMHTH B10 127 H3
Mount Pleasant Av HDSW B21 89 G5
WMBN WV5 64 D4
Mount Pleasant St
BILS/COS WV14 68 B3
WBROM B70 87 G4
Mountrath St WSL WS1 4 D5
Mount Rd BLKHTH/ROWR B65 122 C1
BLOX/PEL WS3 18 A3
DUNHL/THL/PER WV6 35 E3
ETTPK/GDPK/PENN WV4 67 H1
HDSW B21 107 F2
OLDBY B69 104 A1
STRBR DY8 135 H2
WLNHL WV13 39 E5
WMBN WV5 65 E4
Mounts Rd DARL/WED WS10 70 D1
Mount St HALE B63 138 C5
STRBR DY8 135 G2
TPTN/OCK DY4 70 A5
VAUX/NECH B7 110 A3
WSL WS1 4 D6
Mounts Wy VAUX/NECH B7 110 A2
The Mount CDYHTH B64 121 G3
ERDW/GRVHL B23 92 B5
WALM/CURD B76 96 C1
Mount Vw MGN/WHC B75 63 E4
Mountwood Covert
DUNHL/THL/PER WV6 35 F2
Mousehall Farm Rd
BRLYHL DY5 119 F5
Mouse Hl BLOX/PEL WS3 17 H4
Mousesweet Cl DUDS DY2 103 E5
Mousesweet La DUDS DY2 121 E1
Mowbray Cl RBRY B45 174 A3
Mowbray St DIG/EDG B5 127 E4
Mowe Cft
CHWD/FDBR/MGN B37 132 A5
Moxhull Cl SHHTH WV12 26 A1
Moxhull Dr WALM/CURD B76 78 A3
Moxhull Gdns SHHTH WV12 26 A1
Moxhull Rd
CHWD/FDBR/MGN B37 114 A4
Moxley Rd DARL/WED WS10 54 D4
Moyle Dr HALE B63 120 B5
Moyses Cft SMTHWK B66 106 C1
Muchall Rd
ETTPK/GDPK/PENN WV4 51 G3
Mucklow Hl RMSLY B62 139 F2
Muirfield Cl BLOX/PEL WS3 16 C4
Muirfield Crs OLDBY B69 103 G2
Muirfield Gdns
HWK/WKHTH B38 176 B4
Muirville Cl STRBR DY8 117 H1
Mulberry Dr MOS/BIL B13 161 H1
Mulberry Gn DUDN DY1 83 H1
Mulberry Pl BLOX/PEL WS3 26 D1
Mulberry Rd BLOX/PEL WS3 26 D1
NFLD/LBR B31 159 E5
Mull Cl RBRY B45 173 G4
Mull Cft CBROM B36 114 A2
Mullensgrove Rd
CHWD/FDBR/MGN B37 114 A4
Mullett Rd WNSFLD WV11 24 B3
Mullett St BRLYHL DY5 100 D4

Mulliners Cl
CHWD/FDBR/MGN B37 * 132 D2
Mullion Cft HWK/WKHTH B38 .... 176 C4
Mulroy Rd FOAKS/STRLY B74 ...... 62 B2
Mulwych Rd STETCH B33 .... 131 G2
Munches La RMSLY B62 .... 171 G5
Munslow Gv NFLD/LBR B31 .... 175 F5
Muntz Crs HOCK/TIA B94 .... 198 A5
Muntz St SMHTH B10 .... 128 B4
Murcroft Rd HAG/WOL DY9 .... 153 F1
Murdoch Dr KGSWFD DY6 .... 99 G2
Murdoch Rd BILS/COS WV14 ...... 54 B2
Murdock Gv HDSW B21 .... 107 G2
Murdock Rd SMTHWK B66 .... 107 F3
Murdock Wy WSLW WS2 .... 26 D5
Murray Ct SCFLD/BOLD B73 .... 62 A5
Murrell Cl EDG/EDC B5 .... 126 D5
Musborough Cl CBROM B36 ...... 95 E5
Muscott Gv HRBN B17 .... 141 G2
Muscovy Rd ERDW/GRVHL B23 .... 92 A3
Musgrave Cl WALM/CURD B76 .... 63 E5
Musgrave Rd WSNGN B18 .... 107 H4
Mushroom Hall Rd
LGLYGN/QTN B68 .... 105 G4
Musk La SEDG DY3 .... 82 D5
Musk La West SEDG DY3 .... 82 D5
Musson Cl
CHWD/FDBR/MGN B37 .... 132 D4
Muswell Cl SOLH B91 .... 165 F5
Muxloe Cl BLOX/PEL WS3 .... 16 C4
Myatt Av ALDR WS9 .... 29 H5
BKHL/PFLD WV2 .... 52 C2
Myatt Cl BKHL/PFLD WV2 .... 52 C2
Myddleton St WSNGN B18 .... 108 A5
Myles Ct BRLYHL DY5 .... 101 F5
Mynors Crs HLYWD B47 .... 192 C3
Myring Gv MGN/WHC B75 .... 63 F3
Myrtle Av ALE/KHTH/YWD B14 .. 178 B5
BHTH/HG B12 .... 144 C2
Myrtle Cl SHHTH WV12 .... 26 C3
Myrtle Gv BDMR/CCFT WV3 ...... 51 E2
LOZ/NWT B19 .... 108 C1
Myrtle Pl SLYOAK B29 * 143 F5
Myrtle Rd DUDN DY1 .... 84 A3
Myrtle St BKHL/PFLD WV2 .... 52 D2
Myrtle Ter TPTN/OCK DY4 .... 69 F1
Myton Dr SHLY B90 .... 179 F3
Mytton Cl DUDS DY2 .... 85 E5
Mytton Gv TPTN/OCK DY4 .... 85 E1
Mytton Rd BVILLE B30 .... 159 E5
CSHL/WTROR B46 .... 95 H3
Myvod Rd DARL/WED WS10 ...... 56 A3

N

Naden Rd LOZ/NWT B19 .... 108 B3
Nadin Rd SCFLD/BOLD B73 .... 77 E3
Naesby Rd
DUNHL/THL/PER WV6 .... 34 D2
Nafford Gv
ALE/KHTH/YWD B14 .... 178 B3
Nagersfield Rd BRLYHL DY5 ...... 118 C1
Nailers Cl RIDG/WDGT B32 ...... 139 H5
Nailors Fold BILS/COS WV14 ...... 68 C1
Nailors Rw WMBN WV5 * 80 D1
Nailstone Crs ACGN B27 .... 163 G2
Nailsworth Rd DOR/KN B93 ...... 198 B1
Nairn Cl HLGN/YWD B28 .... 162 D5
Nairn Rd BLOX/PEL WS3 .... 16 C3
Nally Dr BILS/COS WV14 .... 68 A1
Nanaimo Wy KGSWFD DY6 ...... 100 C5
Nansen Rd SPARK B11 .... 145 E4
WASH/WDE B8 .... 110 C4
Nantmel Gv RIDG/WDGT B32 .. 157 G2
Naomi Wy ALDR WS9 .... 19 H3
Napier Dr TPTN/OCK DY4 .... 70 A5
Napier Rd BKHL/PFLD WV2 ...... 52 B2
WSLW WS2 .... 27 E5
Napton Gv SLYOAK B29 .... 141 F5
Narraway Gv TPTN/OCK DY4 .... 70 B3
Narrowboat Wy BRWNH WS8 .... 9 F4
Narrow La BRWNH WS8 .... 9 F4
RMSLY B62 .... 122 C5
WSLW WS2 .... 56 B1
Naseby Dr HALE B63 .... 137 H5
Naseby Rd SOLH B91 .... 164 D4
WASH/WDE B8 .... 110 D4
Nash Av DUNHL/THL/PER WV6 .. 34 C2
Nash Cl BLKHTH/ROWR B65 .... 122 A3
Nash Cft
CHWD/FDBR/MGN B37 .... 132 B4
Nash La HAG/WOL DY9 .... 184 B1
Nash Sq PBAR/PBCH B42 .... 90 D2
Nash Wk SMTHWK B66 * 107 E4
Nately Gv SLYOAK B29 .... 141 H4
Nathan Cl MGN/WHC B75 .... 47 C5
Naunton Cl SLYOAK B29 .... 158 C3
Naunton Rd WSLW WS2 .... 41 E2
Navenby Cl
ALE/KHTH/YWD B14 .... 179 E2
Navigation Dr BRLYHL DY5 ...... 102 A5
BVILLE B30 .... 177 H2
Navigation La HHTH/SAND B71 .. 72 B1
Navigation St CBHAMW B1 ...... 2 E6
WOLV WV1 * 7 H2
WSLW WS2 .... 4 C3
Navigation Wy WBROM B70 ...... 86 D4
WSNGN B18 .... 107 H4
Naylors Gv SEDG DY3 .... 83 G2
Neachells Ct WLNHL WV13 ...... 39 E4
Neachells La WLNHL WV13 ...... 38 D2
WNSFLD WV11 .... 24 D5
Neachless Av WMBN WV5 .... 81 E1
Neachley Gv STETCH B33 .... 112 B5
Neale St WSLW WS2 .... 4 A2
Near High Dr TPTN/OCK DY4 .... 85 H1
Nearhill Rd HWK/WKHTH B38 .. 160 A5
Near Lands Cl RIDG/WDGT B32 .. 140 B3
Nearmoor Rd BKDE/SHDE B34 .. 113 F4
Neasden Gv KGSTG B44 .... 75 H3
Neath Rd BLOX/PEL WS3 .... 16 B5
Neath Wy BLOX/PEL WS3 .... 16 B5
SEDG DY3 .... 68 A5
Nebsworth Cl SHLY B90 .... 163 H5
Nechells Park Rd
VAUX/NECH B7 .... 110 A2

Nechells Pkwy VAUX/NECH B7 .. 109 G5
Nechells Pl VAUX/NECH B7 ...... 109 H3
Needham St VAUX/NECH B7 .... 110 A2
Needhill Cl DOR/KN B93 .... 196 D2
Needless Aly CBHAM B2 * 3 G5
Needwood Cl BKHL/PFLD WV2 .. 51 H2
Needwood Dr
ETTPK/GDPK/PENN WV4 .... 52 D4
Needwood Gv HHTH/SAND B71 .. 72 A2
Nelson Av BILS/COS WV14 .... 53 G1
Nelson Rd AST/WIT B6 .... 96 D1
DUDN DY1 .... 84 B5
Nelson St CBHAMW B1 .... 2 B4
HHTH/SAND B71 .... 87 G1
WOLV WV1 .... 105 F3
WLNHL WV13 .... 39 H2
Nene Ct STRBR DY8 .... 135 G5
Nene Wy CBROM B36 .... 113 H1
Neptune St TPTN/OCK DY4 ...... 84 D1
Nesbit Gv BORD B9 .... 111 E1
Nesfield Gv ERDW/GRVHL B23 .. 76 C4
Nesfield Cv HIA/OLT B92 .... 167 H5
Nesscliffe Gv ERDW/GRVHL B23 .. 76 D4
Nest Common BLOX/PEL WS3 .... 17 H2
Neston Gv STETCH B33 .... 129 H2
Netheravon Cl
ALE/KHTH/YWD B14 .... 177 H4
Netherby Rd SEDG DY3 .... 67 E3
Nethercote Gdns SHLY B90 ...... 179 G2
Netherdale Cl
CSCFLD/WYGN B72 .... 77 G4
Netherdale Rd
ALE/KHTH/YWD B14 .... 178 C4
Netherend Cl HALE B63 .... 120 A5
Netherend La HALE B63 .... 120 B5
Netherend Rd HALE B63 .... 120 A5
Netherfield Gdns ACGN B27 .... 146 B4
Nethergate SEDG DY3 .... 83 H1
Netherhouse Cl KGSTG B44 ...... 60 A5
Netherstone Gv
FOAKS/STRLY B74 .... 32 D5
Netherton Gv STETCH B33 ...... 131 E1
Netherwood Cl SOLH B91 ...... 164 A4
Nethy Dr DUNHL/THL/PER WV6 .. 21 F5
Netley Gv SPARK B11 .... 145 H4
Netley Rd BLOX/PEL WS3 .... 16 A5
Netley Wy BLOX/PEL WS3 .... 16 A5
Nevada Wy
CHWD/FDBR/MGN B37 .... 132 C3
Neve Av WOLV WV10 .... 23 H1
Neville Av
ETTPK/GDPK/PENN WV4 .... 52 B2
Neville Rd CBROM B36 .... 95 G5
ERDW/GRVHL B23 .... 92 A3
SHLY B90 .... 179 H4
Nevin Gv PBAR/PBCH B42 .... 90 C1
Nevis Ct BDMR/CCFT WV3 .... 36 A3
Nevis Gv SHHTH WV12 .... 25 H1
Nevison Gv GTB/HAM B43 .... 59 F4
Newark Cft
LGN/SDN/BHAMAIR B26 .... 147 H1
Newark Rd DUDS DY2 .... 120 D2
SHHTH WV12 .... 26 A3
Newbank Gv BORD B9 .... 129 E1
New Bartholomew St
DIG/EDG B5 .... 3 J5
New Birmingham Rd
DUDS DY2 .... 85 G5
OLDBY B69 .... 104 B1
Newbold Cl DOR/KN B93 .... 196 D5
Newbold Cft VAUX/NECH B7 .... 109 H4
Newbolds Rd WOLV WV10 .... 24 A4
Newbolt Rd BILS/COS WV14 .... 54 A2
Newbolt St DSYBK/YTR WS5 .... 57 E3
New Bond St BORD B9 .... 127 H5
DUDS DY2 .... 102 D1
Newborough Gv
HLGN/YWD B28 .... 179 H1
Newborough Rd
HLGN/YWD B28 .... 179 H1
Newbridge Av
DUNHL/THL/PER WV6 .... 36 A2
Newbridge Gdns
DUNHL/THL/PER WV6 * 36 A1
Newbridge Ms
DUNHL/THL/PER WV6 * 36 B1
Newbridge Rd BORD B9 .... 129 F4
KGSWFD DY6 .... 99 G1
Newbridge St
WOLV WV10 .... 36 B1
Newburn Cft RIDG/WDGT B32 .. 140 B2
Newbury Cl RMSLY B62 .... 139 F4
Newbury La OLDBY B69 .... 104 B3
Newbury Rd STRBR DY8 .... 117 G2
WOLV WV10 .... 12 C5
Newby Gv
CHWD/FDBR/MGN B37 .... 114 B5
New Canal St DIG/EDG B5 .... 3 J6
Newcastle Cft CVALE B35 .... 95 E3
New Church Rd
SCFLD/BOLD B73 .... 77 E3
New College Cl WSL WS1 .... 57 G1
Newcombe Rd HDSW B21 .... 89 F4
Newcome Cl ERDE/BCHGN B24 .. 93 H2
Newcomen Dr TPTN/OCK DY4 .. 85 F3
Newcott Cl COVEN WV9 .... 11 H5
New Coventry Rd
LGN/SDN/BHAMAIR B26 .... 147 F2
New Cft LOZ/NWT B19 .... 109 E2
Newcroft Gv
LGN/SDN/BHAMAIR B26 .... 130 A5
New Cross Av WOLV WV10 .... 38 B1
New Cross St DARL/WED WS10 .. 55 F3
TPTN/OCK DY4 .... 85 E1
New Crown St DUDN DY1 .... 102 B3
Newdegate Rd MGN/WHC B75 .. 63 G4
New Dudley Rd KGSWFD DY6 .... 99 G1
Newells Dr TPTN/OCK DY4 ...... 70 B4
Newells Rd
LGN/SDN/BHAMAIR B26 .... 130 C4
New England RMSLY B62 .... 122 C5
New England Cl OLDBY B69 .... 86 C5
Newent Cl SHHTH WV12 .... 12 A1
Newent Rd NFLD/LBR B31 ...... 176 A1
Newey Cl RBRY B45 .... 188 B1
Newey Rd HLGN/YWD B28 ...... 162 D4
WNSFLD WV11 .... 25 G2
Newey St DUDN DY1 .... 84 A4
New Spring Gdns WSNGN B18 .. 108 A5

New Farm Rd HAG/WOL DY9 .... 136 A2
New Gas St WBROM B70 .... 71 E5
Newhall Ct CBHAMNW B3 * 2 C5
New Hall Dr MGN/WHC B75 .... 62 D4
WALM/CURD B76 .... 78 A2
New Hall Farm Ct
WALM/CURD B76 .... 62 D4
Newhall Hill CBHAMW B1 .... 2 C3
New Hall Pl DARL/WED WS10 *.. 56 A5
Newhall Rd
BLKHTH/ROWR B65 .... 122 A1
New Hall St WLNHL WV13 .... 39 G3
Newhall St CBHAMNW B3 .... 2 E4
TPTN/OCK DY4 .... 69 E3
WBROM B70 .... 87 G4
WLNHL WV13 .... 39 H4
WSL WS1 .... 4 E6
New Hampton Rd East
WOLV WV1 .... 6 C1
New Hampton Rd West
DUNHL/THL/PER WV6 .... 36 C1
Newhaven Cl VAUX/NECH B7 .. 109 G5
Newhay Cft LOZ/NWT B19 ...... 108 C2
New Heath Cl WNSFLD WV11 .. 24 B5
New Henry St
LGLYGN/QTN B68 .... 105 E5
Newhome Wy BLOX/PEL WS3 .. 27 H5
Newhope Cl EDG B15 .... 126 D4
New Hope Rd SMTHWK B66 .... 107 E5
Newhouse Farm Cl
WALM/CURD B76 .... 63 F5
Newhouse Farm Dr
NFLD/LBR B31 .... 158 D4
New Inns Cl HDSW B21 .... 107 F1
New Inns La NFLD/LBR B31 .... 175 C4
New Inns La RBRY B45 .... 173 G4
New John St AST/WIT B6 .... 109 E4
RMSLY B62 .... 122 A3
New John St West
LOZ/NWT B19 .... 108 B3
New King St DUDS DY2 * 84 C5
Newland Cl RUSH/SHEL WS4 .. 18 C5
Newland Gdns CDYHTH B64 .... 121 E4
Newland Gv DUDS DY2 .... 101 H2
Newland Rd BORD B9 .... 128 D3
Newlands Av HAG/WOL DY9 .. 153 E4
WLNHL WV13 .... 39 G4
Newlands Dr RMSLY B62 .... 122 C5
Newlands La
CHWD/FDBR/MGN B37 .... 149 F1
Newlands Rd BVILLE B30 .... 160 B3
DOR/KN B93 .... 196 C4
Newlands Wk
LGLYGN/QTN B68 * 105 F5
New Landywood La
WNSFLD WV11 .... 16 A1
Newlyn Rd CDYHTH B64 .... 120 D4
NFLD/LBR B31 .... 175 F2
Newman Av
ETTPK/GDPK/PENN WV4 .... 52 D4
Newman College Cl
RIDG/WDGT B32 * 157 G2
Newman Pl BILS/COS WV14 .... 54 B1
Newman Rd
ERDE/BCHGN B24 .... 92 D2
TPTN/OCK DY4 .... 70 A2
WOLV WV10 .... 24 A1
Newmans Cl SMTHWK B66 * .. 107 E5
Newman Wy RBRY B45 .... 188 A1
New Market St
DUNHL/THL/PER WV6 .... 22 C5
New Market St CBHAMNW B3 *.. 2 D3
New Meadow Cl
NFLD/LBR B31 .... 175 H3
New Meeting St OLDBY B69 .... 105 E1
New Mills St WSL WS1 .... 56 D1
New Mill St DUDS DY2 .... 84 C5
Newmore Gdns
DSYBK/YTR WS5 .... 58 A2
New Moseley Rd
BHTH/HG B12 .... 127 G4
Newnham Gv
ERDW/GRVHL B23 .... 76 C5
Newnham Ri SHLY B90 .... 180 D2
Newnham Rd
LDYWD/EDGR B16 .... 125 E2
New Pool Rd CDYHTH B64 ...... 120 B4
Newport Rd BHTH/HG B12 .... 144 C3
CBROM B36 .... 112 B1
Newport St WOLV WV10 .... 37 G5
WSL WS1 .... 4 D4
Newquay Cl DSYBK/YTR WS5 .. 58 C1
Newquay Rd DSYBK/YTR WS5 .. 58 B1
New Railway St WLNHL WV13 .. 39 H3
New Rd ALDR WS9 .... 30 A5
BRWNH WS8 .... 19 F5
CSHL/WTROR B46 .... 96 B2
DUDS DY2 .... 102 C2
DUNHL/THL/PER WV6 * 36 A1
HALE B63 .... 138 D3
HLYWD B47 .... 178 B5
RBRY B45 .... 187 G1
SEDG DY3 .... 80 A3
SOLH B91 .... 182 A2
STRBR DY8 .... 135 G2
TPTN/OCK DY4 .... 70 A5
WLNHL WV13 .... 40 A4
WOLV WV10 .... 24 B2
Newrow Rd DUDS DY2 * 119 G5
New Shipton Cl
WALM/CURD B76 .... 78 B2
New Spring St
WSNGN B18 .... 108 A5
New Spring St North
WSNGN B18 .... 108 A4
Newstead Rd KGSTG B44 .... 60 C5
New St BDMR/CCFT WV3 .... 50 D2
BKHL/PFLD WV2 .... 53 E2
BLOX/PEL WS3 .... 27 F1
BRLYHL DY5 .... 118 A4
CBHAM B2 .... 3 G5
CBROM B36 .... 112 D1
DARL/WED WS10 .... 70 D2
DUDN DY1 .... 84 B5
ERDW/GRVHL B23 .... 92 D1
ETTPK/GDPK/PENN WV4 .... 52 C3
KGSWFD DY6 .... 99 G1
RBRY B45 .... 174 A3
RUSH/SHEL WS4 .... 18 C5
SEDG DY3 .... 83 E3
SMTHWK B66 .... 106 D3
STRBR DY8 .... 135 G2
TPTN/OCK DY4 .... 85 F4
WBROM B70 .... 87 G3
WLNHL WV13 .... 39 E4
WNSFLD WV11 .... 15 E4
WSL WS1 .... 5 F3
New St North HHTH/SAND B71 .. 71 H5
New Summer St LOZ/NWT B19 .. 3 F1
New Swan La WBROM B70 ...... 87 E1
Newton Cl GTB/HAM B43 .... 73 E3
Newton Gdns GTB/HAM B43 .... 72 D3
Newton Gv SLYOAK B29 * 142 D5
Newton Manor Cl
GTB/HAM B43 .... 73 F3
Newton Pl WSLW WS2 .... 27 F4
WSNGN B18 .... 107 H2
Newton Rd DOR/KN B93 .... 197 F1
GTB/HAM B43 .... 144 D2
SPARK B11 .... 144 D3
WSLW WS2 .... 27 F4
Newton Sq GTB/HAM B43 ...... 73 G2
Newton St CBHAMNE B4 .... 3 H3
HHTH/SAND B71 .... 72 A4
Newton St BRLYHL DY5 .... 100 D5
DUDS DY2 .... 85 F5
Newtown Dr LOZ/NWT B19 .... 108 C3
Newtown La CDYHTH B64 ...... 120 D3
HAG/WOL DY9 .... 171 H5
RMSLY B62 .... 122 C5
Newtown Middleway
AST/WIT B6 .... 109 E4
New Town Rw AST/WIT B6 ...... 109 E4
New Summer St LOZ/NWT B19 .. 109 E4
New Village DUDS DY2 .... 120 C5
New Vis WNSFLD WV11 * 24 A4
New Wood Cl KINVER DY7 .... 117 G4
New Wood Dr NFLD/LBR B31 .. 174 D4
New Wood Gv ALDR WS9 .... 19 H2
New Wood La KIDD DY10 ...... 168 A5
Niall Cl EDG B15 .... 125 H4
Nicholas Rd FOAKS/STRLY B74 .. 45 E5
Nicholds Cl BILS/COS WV14 .... 68 B2
Nicholls Fold WNSFLD WV11 .. 24 D5
Nicholls Rd TPTN/OCK DY4 .... 69 E2
Nicholls St WBROM B70 .... 87 H4
Nigel Av NFLD/LBR B31 .... 175 H5
Nigel Rd DUDN DY1 .... 83 H4
WASH/WDE B8 .... 110 C5
Nightingale Av CBROM B36 .... 114 A1
Nightingale Cl
ERDW/GRVHL B23 .... 76 A4
Nightingale Crs BRLYHL DY5 .. 119 F5
SHHTH WV12 .... 25 H2
Nightingale Dr TPTN/OCK DY4 .. 86 A1
Nightingale Pl BILS/COS WV14 .. 53 H1
Nightingale Wk EDG B15 ...... 126 C5
Nightjar Gv ERDW/GRVHL B23 .. 76 A5
Nighwood Dr FOAKS/STRLY B74 .. 60 B1
Nijon Cl HDSW B21 .... 89 E5
Nimmings Cl NFLD/LBR B31 .. 189 F2
Nimmings Rd RMSLY B62 ...... 122 B3
Ninescares Dr
CHWD/FDBR/MGN B37 .... 132 A2
Nine Elms La WOLV WV10 ...... 37 G1
Nine Leasowes SMTHWK B66 .. 106 A2
Nine Locks Rdg BRLYHL DY5 .. 119 F2
Nineveh Av HDSW B21 .... 107 H2
Nineveh Rd HDSW B21 .... 107 G2
Ninfield Rd ACGN B27 .... 146 A3
ninth Pl DUDN DY1 .... 84 B4
Nocke Rd WNSFLD WV11 ...... 25 F1
Nock St TPTN/OCK DY4 * 70 A4
Noddy Pk ALDR WS9 .... 30 B3
Noddy Park Rd ALDR WS9 ...... 30 B3
Noele Gordon Gdns WSL WS1 * .. 4 D7
Noel Rd LDYWD/EDGR B16 .... 125 H3
Nolton Cl GTB/HAM B43 .... 73 E3
Nooklands Cft STETCH B33 .... 130 C2
The Nook BRLYHL DY5 .... 100 D4
Noose Crs WLNHL WV13 .... 39 F2
Noose La WLNHL WV13 .... 39 F2
Nora Rd SPARK B11 .... 145 E4
Norbiton Rd KGSTG B44 .... 75 G5
Norbreck Cl GTB/HAM B43 .... 73 G1
Norbury Av BLOX/PEL WS3 .... 17 H4
Norbury Crs
ETTPK/GDPK/PENN WV4 .... 52 D4
Norbury Dr BRLYHL DY5 .... 119 F3
Norbury Gv NFLD/LBR B31 .... 54 D2
Norbury Rd BILS/COS WV14 .... 54 B2
KGSTG B44 .... 60 D5
WBROM B70 .... 70 D4
WOLV WV10 .... 23 H1
Norcombe Gv
ALE/KHTH/YWD B14 .... 178 D5
Nordley Rd WNSFLD WV11 .... 24 C5
Norfolk Av HHTH/SAND B71 .. 71 H4
Norfolk Cl BVILLE B30 .... 160 B4
Norfolk Crs ALDR WS9 .... 30 B2
Norfolk Dr DARL/WED WS10 .. 56 A3
Norfolk Gdns FOAKS/STRLY B74 .. 47 F5
Norfolk New Rd WSLW WS2 .... 41 E1
Norfolk Pl BLOX/PEL WS3 ...... 27 F5
Norfolk Rd BDMR/CCFT WV3 .. 49 H4
DUDS DY2 .... 85 H1
EDG B15 .... 125 G4
ERDW/GRVHL B23 .... 92 D1
LGLYGN/QTN B68 .... 123 F2
MGN/WHC B75 .... 62 C1
RBRY B45 .... 173 H4
STRBR DY8 .... 117 H4

Norgrave Rd HIA/OLT B92 ...... 148 A5
Norian Dr ALE/KHTH/YWD B14 .. 178 B2
Norland Rd ACGN B27 .... 163 G1
Norley Gv MOS/BIL B13 .... 162 A3
Norman Av RIDG/WDGT B32 .. 124 A5
Normandy Rd
BFLD/HDSWWD B20 .... 90 D5
Norman Rd DSYBK/YTR WS5 .. 58 A1
NFLD/LBR B31 .... 175 H2
SMTHWK B67 .... 105 F3
WSNGN B18 .... 102 D1
WSNGN B18 .... 107 G4
Norman Ter
BLKHTH/ROWR B65 .... 104 A5
Normanton Av
LGN/SDN/BHAMAIR B26 ...... 148 B2
Norrington Gv RBRY B45 ...... 174 C2
Norrington Rd NFLD/LBR B31 .. 174 C2
Norris Dr STETCH B33 .... 130 A1
Norris Rd AST/WIT B6 .... 91 F5
Norris Wy MGN/WHC B75 ...... 62 D3
Northampton St WSNGN B18 .... 2 C1
Northam Wk
DUNHL/THL/PER WV6 .... 36 D1
Northanger Rd ACGN B27 ...... 146 B5
Northay Rd BHAMNEC B40 .... 150 B2
WNSFLD WV11 .... 24 C4
Northbrook Rd SHLY B90 ...... 163 G5
Northbrook St
LDYWD/EDGR B16 .... 107 H5
Northcote Rd STETCH B33 .... 111 H5
Northcote St WSLW WS2 .... 41 H1
Northcott Rd BILS/COS WV14 .. 54 D4
DUDS DY2 .... 102 D5
Northcroft Wy
ERDW/GRVHL B23 .... 92 B3
Northdown Rd SOLH B91 ...... 181 H4
North Dr BFLD/HDSWWD B20 .. 108 B1
DIG/EDG B5 .... 143 G2
SCFLD/BOLD B73 .... 62 B1
Northfield Gv BDMR/CCFT WV3 .. 50 C1
Northfield Rd BVILLE B30 ...... 176 C1
DUDS DY2 .... 102 A2
HRBN B17 .... 141 G4
Northfields Wy BRWNH WS8 .... 8 D5
Northgate ALDR WS9 .... 30 A3
CDYHTH B64 .... 120 D4
North Ga HRBN B17 .... 125 E5
Northgate Wy ALDR WS9 .... 30 A2
North Gn
ETTPK/GDPK/PENN WV4 .... 50 D2
North Holme BORD B9 .... 128 A2
Northland Rd SHLY B90 .... 180 D4
Northlands Rd MOS/BIL B13 .. 161 G1
Northleach Av
ALE/KHTH/YWD B14 .... 177 H3
Northleigh Rd WASH/WDE B8 .. 111 E3
Northmead NFLD/LBR B31 .... 175 G2
Northolt Gv PBAR/PBCH B42 .. 73 H2
Northolt Ov SEDG DY3 .... 83 G1
Northover Cl COVEN WV9 ...... 11 G4
North Park Rd
ERDW/GRVHL B23 .... 91 H3
North Pathway HRBN B17 ...... 124 D5
North Rd BFLD/HDSWWD B20 .. 90 D5
ETTPK/GDPK/PENN WV4 .... 51 H5
HRBN B17 .... 142 B1
TPTN/OCK DY4 .... 69 H3
WOLV WV1 .... 37 F1
North Roundhay STETCH B33 .. 112 C5
Northside Dr FOAKS/STRLY B74 .. 45 F5
North Springfield SEDG DY3 .. 67 F2
North St BRLYHL DY5 .... 119 F2
DARL/WED WS10 .... 55 G5
DUDS DY2 .... 84 D5
SMTHWK B67 .... 106 B4
WOLV WV1 .... 7 F3
WSLW WS2 .... 42 A1
Northumberland St
VAUX/NECH B7 .... 127 G1
North Vw Dr BRLYHL DY5 ...... 101 G4
North Warwick St BORD B9 .. 128 B3
Northway BHAMNEC B40 ...... 150 D2
SEDG DY3 .... 66 D2
North Western Ar CBHAM B2 .. 3 G4
North Western Rd
SMTHWK B66 .... 106 B3
North Western Ter
WSNGN B18 .... 107 H2
Northwick Crs SOLH B91 ...... 181 H4
Northwood Park Cl
WOLV WV10 .... 13 E4
Northwood Park Rd
WOLV WV10 .... 13 E5
North St CBHAMNW B3 .... 2 D2
North Wood St CBHAMNW B3 .. 2 C3
Northwood Wy BRLYHL DY5 .. 118 D4
North Worcestershire Pth
ALVE B48 .... 191 F5
RBRY B45 .... 187 F1
SHLY B90 .... 193 H5
Nortlycote La WOLV WV10 .... 13 F3
Norton Cl
ETTPK/GDPK/PENN WV4 .... 50 C2
Norton Crs BILS/COS WV14 .... 68 D2
BORD B9 .... 129 F1
Norton Dr RBRY B45 .... 121 E1
Norton Gn HWK/WKHTH B38 .. 160 A1
Norton Green La KIDD DY10 .. 199 F1
Norton La SHLY B90 .... 193 G4
CSHL/WTROR B46 .... 115 F1
Norton St WSNGN B18 .... 108 B2
Norton Ter BVILLE B30 * 160 A4
Norton Vw
ALE/KHTH/YWD B14 .... 160 D4
Norton Vw ALE/KHTH/YWD B14 .. 176 B5
Norwich Cft
CHWD/FDBR/MGN B37 .... 131 H3
Norwich Dr HRBN B17 .... 124 B4
Norwich Rd DUDS DY2 .... 120 D2
WSLW WS2 .... 42 A1
Norwood Av CDYHTH B64 .... 120 D4
Norwood Gv LOZ/NWT B19 .... 108 B2
Norwood Rd BORD B9 .... 128 C2
BRLYHL DY5 .... 101 F5
Nottingham Dr SHHTH WV12 .. 26 A3
Nottingham Wy BRLYHL DY5 .. 119 H2

Nova Ct GTB/HAM B43......74 B2
Nova Scotia St DIG/EDG B5......3 J4
Nowell St DARL/WED WS10......55 G5
Nugent Cl AST/WIT B6......109 E2
Nugent Gv SHLY B90......194 D5
Nursery Av ALDR WS9......30 B5
   BHTH/HG B12......144 B2
Nursery Cl BVILLE B30......159 H5
   HAG/WOL DY9......152 C5
Nursery Dr BFLD/HDSWWD B20...90 A5
   WMBN WV5......80 D2
Nursery Gdns CDSL WV8......10 B3
   SHLY B90......179 G5
   STRBR DY8......178 B1
Nursery La BRWNH WS8......47 E3
Nursery Rd BLOX/PEL WS3......27 F2
   BVILLE B30......159 G5
   EDG B15......125 F5
   LOZ/NWT B19......108 B3
Nursery View Cl ALDR WS9......30 B5
Nursery Wk
Nutbush Dr NFLD/LBR B31...157 H4
Nutfield Wk RIDG/WDGT B32...141 F2
Nutgrove Cl
   ALE/KHTH/YWD B14......161 F3
Nuthatch Dr BRLYHL DY5......119 E5
Nuthurst MGN/WHC B75......63 G4
Nuthurst Gv
   ALE/KHTH/YWD B14......178 B3
   DOR/KN B93......197 E4
Nutley Dr TPTN/OCK DY4......70 B3
Nutmeg Gv WSL SQ......5 J5
Nuttall Gv HDSW B21......107 E2

O

Oak Av BHTH/HG B12......144 C2
   WBROM B70......87 F3
   WSLW WS2......40 C2
Oak Bank WSNGN B18......108 A3
Oak Barn Rd RMSLY B62......122 B4
Oakbridge Rd NFLD/LBR B31...176 B3
Oak Ct HALE B63......138 B5
Oak Crs BLOX/PEL WS3......27 H4
   OLDBY B69......85 H5
Oak Cft
   CHWD/FDBR/MGN B37......131 G1
Oakcroft Rd MOS/BIL B13......161 H5
Oakdale Cl BRLYHL DY5......100 C2
   LGLYGN/QTN B68......123 E2
Oakdale Rd CBROM B36......112 A1
   LGLYGN/QTN B68......123 E2
Oak Dr ERDW/GRVHL B23......76 A4
Oaken Covert CDSL WV8......10 A5
Oaken Dr CDSL WV8......10 A4
   SHHTH WV12......26 C5
   SOLH B91......164 B5
Oaken Gv CDSL WV8......10 A5
Oakenhayes Crs BRWNH WS8...9 F3
   WALM/CURD B76......95 E1
Oakenhayes Dr BRWNH WS8......9 F3
Oaken Lanes CDSL WV8......10 A5
Oaken Pk CDSL WV8......10 C5
Oakenshaw Rd HAG/WOL DY9...180 D4
Oakeswell St DARL/WED WS10...56 A5
Oakeywell St DUDS DY2......85 E1
Oak Farm Cl WALM/CURD B76...78 C4
Oak Farm Rd BVILLE B30......159 G5
Oakfield Av BHTH/HG B12......144 C2
   DUDN DY1......84 A1
   KGSWFD DY6......100 A4
Oakfield Cl SMTHWK B66......107 E3
   STRBR DY8......118 B3
Oakfield Dr BLOX/PEL WS3......18 A2
   RBRY B45......122 B5
Oakfield Rd BHTH/HG B12......144 A3
   CDSL WV8......10 D5
   ERDE/BCHGN B24......92 D3
   HAG/WOL DY9......136 B5
   SLYOAK B29......143 E4
   SMTHWK B66......107 E4
   STRBR DY8......118 C3
Oakfields Wy SOLH B91......166 B5
Oak Gn DUDN DY1......84 A1
   DUNHL/THL/PER WV6......35 F2
Oak Green Wy
   LGLYGN/QTN B68......105 E5
Oak Gv NFLD/LBR B31......175 E4
   WNSFLD WV11......24 B5
Oakhall Dr DOR/KN B93......196 D4
Oakham Ct DUDS DY2......103 E3
Oakham Crs DUDS DY2......103 E2
Oakham Dr DUDS DY2......103 F2
Oakham Rd DUDS DY2......103 F2
   HRBN B17......124 D4
Oak Hill BDMR/CCFT WV3......35 G5
Oakhill Cl ACGN B27......143 G2
Oakhill Dr BRLYHL DY5......118 D5
Oak Hill Dr EDG B15......125 G5
Oakhurst Rd ACGN B27......163 F1
   CSCFLD/WYGN DY7......
Oakington Dr CVALE B35......94 C3
Oakland Cl BILS/COS WV14......33 E5
Oakland Dr SEDG DY3......82 D4
Oakland Rd BILS/COS WV14......28 A5
   HDSW B21......107 H5
   MOS/BIL B13......144 C4
Oaklands NFLD/LBR B31......175 H1
   RMSLY B62......140 A3
   STRBR DY8......118 B5
Oaklands Av HRBN B17......141 G2
Oaklands Cft WALM/CURD B76...78 D4
Oaklands Dr
   BFLD/HDSWWD B20......89 H4
Oaklands Rd BDMR/CCFT WV3...36 D5
The Oaklands
   BDMR/CCFT WV3......36 D5
   CHWD/FDBR/MGN B37......132 A5
Oaklands Wy BLOX/PEL WS3...18 B4

NFLD/LBR B31......174 C4
Oak La KGSWFD DY6......82 A5
   WBROM B70......87 F3
Oaklea Dr CDYHTH B64......121 F2
Oakleaf Cl RIDG/WDGT B32...140 C5
Oak Leaf Dr MOS/BIL B13......144 C4
Oak Leasow NFLD/LBR B31...176 A3
Oakleigh Dr CDSL WV8......10 C4
   SEDG DY3......67 E4
Oakleigh Rd STRBR DY8......135 G5
Oak Leigh Rd STRBR DY8......135 H5
Oakleighs STRBR DY8......117 G3
Oakley Av ALDR WS9......30 A5
   TPTN/OCK DY4......69 C5
Oakley Gv
   ETTPK/GDPK/PENN WV4......50 D3
Oakley Rd BVILLE B30......160 B5
   ETTPK/GDPK/PENN WV4......50 D5
   SMHTH B10......128 A5
Oak Leys BDMR/CCFT WV3......35 G4
Oakley Wood Dr SOLH B91...182 C1
Oakmeadow Av
   ERDE/BCHGN B24......93 H3
Oakmeadow Cl
   LGN/SDN/BHAMAIR B26......146 D2
   STETCH B33......131 F2
Oakmeadow Wy
   ERDE/BCHGN B24......93 H3
Oakmount Cl BLOX/PEL WS3...17 H4
Oakmount Rd
   FOAKS/STRLY B74......60 C1
Oak Park Rd STRBR DY8......118 B3
Oakridge Cl SHHTH WV12......40 A1
Oakridge Dr SHHTH WV12......40 A1
Oak Ri CSHL/WTROR B46......115 F4
Oak Rd ALDR WS9......19 H6
   BLOX/PEL WS3......17 H2
   DUDN DY1......84 C3
   LGLYGN/QTN B68......123 G5
   RUSH/SHEL WS4......29 G4
   TPTN/OCK DY4......69 C5
   WBROM B70......87 G3
   WLNHL WV13......39 E5
Oaks Crs BDMR/CCFT WV3......6 E5
Oaks Dr BDMR/CCFT WV3......6 E5
   WMBN WV5......81 E1
Oakslade Dr HIA/OLT B92......165 G2
The Oaks BDMR/CCFT WV3 *......6 B4
   BKDE/SHDE B34......112 B5
   BLOX/PEL WS3......27 E1
   HWK/WKHTH B38......190 D2
   SMTHWK B67 *......106 B4
Oak St BDMR/CCFT WV3......6 E5
   BILS/COS WV14......68 B4
   BRLYHL DY5......119 H5
   CDYHTH B64......120 D3
   DUDS DY2......103 E5
   KGSWFD DY6......99 G4
Oakthorpe Dr
   CHWD/FDBR/MGN B37......113 H4
Oak Tree Cl DOR/KN B93......196 D4
Oak Tree Crs RMSLY B62......139 H1
Oak Tree Gdns HLCN/YWD B28...179 G2
   STRBR DY8......118 C3
Oak Tree La BVILLE B30......159 G3
   HAG/WOL DY9......192 D2
Oaktree Rd DARL/WED WS10......56 B5
Oak Tree Rd WASH/WDE B8...110 B3
Oak Turn Dr HWK/WKHTH B38...176 B5
The Oak Wk NFLD/LBR B31...175 G4
Oak Wy WALM/CURD B76......78 B1
Oakwood Cl ALDR WS9......19 G4
   WNSFLD WV11......15 F4
Oakwood Crs DUDS DY2......101 H3
Oakwood Dr BLOX/PEL WS3...182 A4
Oakwood Dr
   ALE/KHTH/YWD B14......177 H1
   FOAKS/STRLY B74......45 E5
Oakwood Pl ALDR WS9......19 F4
Oakwood Rd BLOX/PEL WS3......28 A3
   HLYWD B47......192 C2
   SCFLD/BOLD B73......76 C2
   SMTHWK B67......106 B5
   SPARK B11 *......145 E4
Oakwood St WBROM B70......87 F1
The Oasis HAG/WOL DY9......152 B5
Oasthouse Cl KGSWFD DY6......99 E2
Oaston Rd CBROM B36......113 F1
Oatlands Wy
   DUNHL/THL/PER WV6......34 B2
Oatmill Cl DARL/WED WS10 *...55 G3
Oban Rd HIA/OLT B92......164 B1
Oberon Cl RBRY B45......174 A3
Oberon Dr SHLY B90......180 A4
Occupation Rd BRWNH WS8......19 G3
Occupation St DUDN DY1......84 A4
Ocean Dr DARL/WED WS10......70 B2
Ockam Cft NFLD/LBR B31......176 A2
Ocker Hill Rd TPTN/OCK DY4...69 H2
O'Connor Dr TPTN/OCK DY4......70 A2
Oddingley Rd NFLD/LBR B31...176 A3
Odell Crs BLOX/PEL WS3......27 H5
Odell Pl DIG/EDG B5......143 G2
Odell Rd BLOX/PEL WS3......27 F3
Odensil Gn HIA/OLT B92......145 H5
Odnall La HAG/WOL DY9......170 C1
Offa's Dr DUNHL/THL/PER WV6...20 C5
Offenham Covert
   HWK/WKHTH B38......176 C5
Offini Cl WBROM B70......88 B4
Offmoor Rd RIDG/WDGT B32...157 F2
Ogbury Cl HWK/WKHTH B38...177 G3
Ogley Crs BRWNH WS8......9 G5
Ogley Dr MGN/WHC B75......63 G3
Ogley Hay Rd BNTWD WS7......9 G1
Ogley Rd BRWNH WS8......9 G5
O'Keeffe Cl SPARK B11......144 D1
Okehampton Dr
   HHTH/SAND B71......71 G5
Okement Dr WNSFLD WV11......24 B5
Old Abbey Gdns HRBN B17...142 B3
Old Acre Cl WALM/CURD B76...77 H5
Old Acre Dr HDSW B21......107 G2
Oldacre Rd LGLYGN/QTN B68...123 E5
Old Bank Rd NFLD/LBR B31...175 H3
Old Barn Rd BVILLE B30......159 E3
   STRBR DY8......118 C3

Old Beeches ERDW/GRVHL B23...76 A3
Old Bell Rd ERDW/GRVHL B23...77 F5
Oldberrow Cl SHLY B90......195 G2
Old Birchills WSLW WS2......41 G2
Old Bridge St LOZ/NWT B19...108 B3
Old Bridge Wk
   BLKHTH/ROWR B65......103 F4
Old Bromford La
   WASH/WDE B8......111 F3
Old Brookside STETCH B33...130 A2
Oldbury Ring Wy OLDBY B69...104 D2
Oldbury Rd
   BLKHTH/ROWR B65......122 B2
   SMTHWK B66......105 G2
   WBROM B70......86 D3
Oldbury Road Industrial Est
   WBROM B70......86 D4
Oldbury St DARL/WED WS10...56 B5
Old Bush St BRLYHL DY5......119 G1
Old Camp HI BHTH/HG B12...127 G4
Old Castle Gv BRWNH WS8......9 F2
Old Chapel Rd SMTHWK B67...124 B1
Old Church Gn STETCH B33...130 A2
Old Church Rd
   CSHL/WTROR B46......96 B3
   HRBN B17......141 H2
Old College Dr HHTH/SAND B71...71 E2
Old Croft La CBROM B36......112 D2
Old Cross St TPTN/OCK DY4......85 E1
Old Crown Cl RIDG/WDGT B32...157 F1
Old Damson La HIA/OLT B92...148 D5
Old Dickens Heath Rd
   SHLY B90......194 A3
Old End La BILS/COS WV14......68 C4
Old Fallings Crs WOLVN WV10...23 H4
Old Fallings La WOLVN WV10...23 H2
Old Fallings La WOLVN WV10...23 H2
Old Farm Cl CDSL WV8......10 C3
Old Farm Gv
   ALE/KHTH/YWD B14......162 B5
Old Farm Mdw
   BDMR/CCFT WV3......35 G5
Old Farm Rd STETCH B33......112 A5
Oldfield Dr STRBR DY8......135 F3
Oldfield Rd BHTH/HG B12......144 C1
   BILS/COS WV14......68 A3
Oldfields CDYHTH B64......120 D4
   HAG/WOL DY9......152 D4
Old Flour Mills WBROM B70 *...87 G4
Old Fordrove WALM/CURD B76...62 D5
Old Forest Wy
   BKDE/SHDE B34......112 D3
Old Grange Rd SPARK B11......145 E3
Old Grove Gdns HAG/WOL DY9...136 B4
Old Hall Cl STRBR DY8......118 C5
Old Hall La ALDR WS9......31 G5
Old Hall St BKHL/PFLD WV2......7 G5
Old Ham La HAG/WOL DY9......136 A5
Old Hampton La WOLVN WV10...14 A5
Old Hawne La HALE B63......138 C2
Old Heath Crs WOLV WV1......38 A4
Old Heath Rd WOLV WV1......38 A3
Old High St BRLYHL DY5......119 H3
Old HI DUNHL/THL/PER WV6...21 H5
Old Hobicus La
   LGLYGN/QTN B68......105 F4
Old Horns Crs GTB/HAM B43...74 C1
Oldhouse Farm Cl
   HLCN/YWD B28......162 D4
Old House La HAG/WOL DY9......170 C1
Oldington Gv SOLH B91......181 G5
Old Kingsbury Rd
   WALM/CURD B76......95 E1
Old Landywood La
   WNSFLD WV11......15 G1
Old La BLOX/PEL WS3......27 G3
   DUNHL/THL/PER WV6......34 D3
Old Level Wy DUDS DY2......102 D5
Old Lime Gdns
   HWK/WKHTH B38......176 C5
Old Lindens Cl
   FOAKS/STRLY B74......60 A1
Old Lode La HIA/OLT B92......147 H5
The Old Mnr
   DUNHL/THL/PER WV6 *......21 H5
Old Masters Cl WSL WS1......5 H4
Old Meadow Rd
   NFLD/LBR B31......189 H1
Old Meeting Rd BILS/COS WV14...68 C3
Old Meeting St WBROM B70...87 F1
Old Mill Cl SHLY B90......179 F3
Old Mill Gdns RUSH/SHEL WS4...18 C5
Old Mill Gv
   BFLD/HDSWWD B20 *......90 C4
Old Mill House Cl
   RUSH/SHEL WS4......28 D1
Old Mill Rd CSHL/WTROR B46...115 F2
Old Moat Dr NFLD/LBR B31...175 H2
Old Moat Wy WASH/WDE B8...111 F3
Oldnall Cl HAG/WOL DY9......136 D5
Oldnall Rd HAG/WOL DY9......137 E5
Old Oak Cl ALDR WS9......30 D2
Old Oak Rd HWK/WKHTH B38...177 E3
Old Oscott HI KGSTG B44......75 E2
Old Oscott La KGSTG B44......75 E3
Old Park La OLDBY B69......105 E4
Old Park Rd DARL/WED WS10...55 E5
   DUDN DY1......83 H2
Old Park St DARL/WED WS10...56 B4
Old Penns La
   CSHL/WTROR B46......115 F2
Old Pleck Rd WSLW WS2......56 C1
Old Port Cl TPTN/OCK DY4 *...85 H4
Old Portway
   HWK/WKHTH B38......190 C1
Old Postway LOZ/NWT B19...108 D2
Old Quarry Cl RBRY B45......173 H5
Old Quarry Dr DUDS DY3......83 F1
Old Rectory Gdns ALDR WS9...30 C4
Old School Cl WLNHL WV13......39 F3
Old School Dr
   BLKHTH/ROWR B65......121 H1
Old Scott Cl STETCH B33......131 G3
Old Smithy Pl HSNGN B18......108 A4
Old Snow HI LOZ/NWT B19......3 F2
Old Sq CBHAMNE B4......3 G4
Old Stables Wk
   VAUX/NECH B7......110 A2
Old Station Rd HIA/OLT B92...167 G2

STETCH B33......111 H5
Old Stone Cl RBRY B45......173 H5
Old Stowheath La WOLV WV1 *...38 C4
Old Tokengate HRBN B17......142 B1
Old Town Cl HWK/WKHTH B38...176 C5
Old Town La BLOX/PEL WS3......17 H4
Old Vicarage Cl BLOX/PEL WS3...18 A5
   WMBN WV5......65 F4
Old Walsall Rd PBAR/PBCH B42...75 H5
Old Warwick Ct HIA/OLT B92...164 A1
Old Warwick Rd HIA/OLT B92...164 A1
Oldway Dr SOLH B91......182 C3
Old Well Cl RUSH/SHEL WS4...28 D3
Old Wharf Rd STRBR DY8......135 F1
Olga Dr TPTN/OCK DY4......69 H2
Olinthus Av WNSFLD WV11......25 E3
Olive Av
   ETTPK/GDPK/PENN WV4......52 C3
Olive Dr RMSLY B62......122 A4
Olive Hill Rd RMSLY B62......122 B4
Olive La RMSLY B62......122 A4
Olive PI ALE/KHTH/YWD B14...161 F3
Oliver Ct DUDS DY2......103 E1
Oliver Ct BLKHTH/ROWR B65...121 H2
Oliver Crs BILS/COS WV14......69 E1
Oliver Rd ERDW/GRVHL B23......76 D5
   SMTHWK B66......125 E1
Oliver St VAUX/NECH B7......109 G4
Ollerton Rd
   LGN/SDN/BHAMAIR B26......130 B5
Ollison Dr FOAKS/STRLY B74...45 F3
Olliver Cl RMSLY B62......139 H5
Olorenshaw Rd
   LGN/SDN/BHAMAIR B26......148 B2
Olton Bvd East ACGN B27......145 H4
Olton Bvd West SPARK B11...145 H4
Olton Cft ACGN B27......146 D4
Olton Mere HIA/OLT B92 *......146 B5
Olton Rd SHLY B90......163 F5
Olton Whf HIA/OLT B92......164 A1
Olympus Dr TPTN/OCK DY4 *...52 C5
Ombersley Cl OLDBY B69......104 B4
Ombersley Rd BHTH/HG B12...144 C1
   HALE B63......138 B5
Omersley Wy NFLD/LBR B31...176 B3
Onibury Rd HDSW B21......89 F5
Onslow Crs HIA/OLT B92......164 C1
Onslow Rd SPARK B11......146 A3
Ontario Cl HWK/WKHTH B38...177 E5
Oozells Sq CBHAMW B1......2 C6
Oozells St CBHAMW B1......2 C6
Opal Gdns LGLYGN/QTN B68...105 F4
Open Field Cl NFLD/LBR B31...175 H3
Openfield Cft
   CSHL/WTROR B46......96 C4
Orchard Av SOLH B91......165 F5
Orchard Cl BLKHTH/ROWR B65...121 G1
   CSHL/WTROR B46......115 F2
   HAG/WOL DY9......169 H1
   HALE B63......137 G5
   HDSW B21......89 H5
   RUSH/SHEL WS4......29 E5
   WLNHL WV13......39 H4
Orchard Ct BDMR/CCFT WV3...50 B1
   KGSWFD DY6......99 H3
Orchard Dr HLCN/YWD B28...160 C4
Orchard Gv ALDR WS9......44 B1
   ETTPK/GDPK/PENN WV4......51 H3
   FOAKS/STRLY B74......46 D2
   SEDG DY3......82 D3
Orchard La CDSL WV8......10 D4
Orchard Ri
   LGN/SDN/BHAMAIR B26......130 B5
Orchard Rd DSYBK/YTR WS5...57 H5
   DUDS DY2......120 C2
   ERDW/GRVHL B23......93 E1
   HOCK/TIA B94......39 H4
   WLNHL WV13......39 H4
   WNSFLD WV11......24 C3
The Orchards FOAKS/STRLY B74...47 E5
   HLYWD B47......192 C1
   SHLY B90......194 D4
Orchard St BRLYHL DY5......101 F5
   TPTN/OCK DY4......85 E1
Orchards Wy BHTH/HG B12...144 A1
The Orchard BILS/COS WV14...54 A3
   BLOX/PEL WS3......27 G3
   CHWD/FDBR/MGN B37......131 H4
   DUNHL/THL/PER WV6 *......22 A4
Orchard Wy ACGN B27......146 B3
   CROM B36......73 H2
   HLYWD B47......176 C5
Orchid Cl SMTHWK B66......105 H2
Orchid Dr LOZ/NWT B19......108 D3
Oregon Cl KGSWFD DY6......100 B3
Oregon Dr SHHTH WV12......26 C4
Orford Gv HDSW B21......107 E2
Oriel Cl DUDN DY1......83 G4
Oriel Dr WOLVN WV10......12 C3
Orion Cl MARH/WOL DY9......137 E3
Orkney Av BKDE/SHDE B34...112 B3
Orkney Cft CBROM B36......114 B2
Orlando Cl WSL WS1......5 J6
Ormande Cl HALE B63......120 B5
Orme Cl STRBR DY8......118 B5
Ormes La DUNHL/THL/PER WV6...35 G2
Ormond Pl BILS/COS WV14......54 A2
Ormond Rd RBRY B45......155 F5
Ormsby Gv ACGN B27......163 F5
Ormscliffe Rd RBRY B45......188 B2
Orphanage Rd
   ERDE/BCHGN B24......93 F1
Orpington Rd KGSTG B44......60 A5
Orpwood Rd STETCH B33......130 D1
Orton Av WALM/CURD B76......78 B5
Orton Cl CSHL/WTROR B46......96 A3
Orton Gv
   ETTPK/GDPK/PENN WV4......50 D4
Orton La WMBN WV5......65 E3
Orton Wy CVALE B35......94 C4
Orwell Cl STRBR DY8......134 D3
   WNSFLD WV11......25 H1
Orwell Dr HHTH/SAND B71......71 H5
Orwell Pas DIG/EDG B5......3 H6
Orwell Rd WSL WS1......5 K6
Osberton Dr DUDN DY1......83 H4
Osborne Cl AST/WIT B6......109 G2
   BRLYHL DY5......119 H4

Osborne Dr DARL/WED WS10...40 B5
Osborne Gv LOZ/NWT B19 *...108 C2
Osborne Rd ERDW/GRVHL B23...92 D1
   ETTPK/GDPK/PENN WV4......51 F3
   HDSW B21......107 H1
   WBROM B70......87 G3
Osborn Rd BHTH/HG B12......145 E1
Osbourne Cft SHLY B90......194 D5
Oscott Rd PBAR/PBCH B42......91 E5
Oscott School La KGSTG B44...75 E1
Osier Gv ERDW/GRVHL B23......75 H5
Osier PI WOLV WV1......37 H3
Osier Rd WOLV WV1......37 H3
Osler St LDYWD/EDGR B16...125 H2
Osmaston Rd HRBN B17......141 G4
   STRBR DY8......135 E5
Osmington Gv HALE B63......137 H1
Osprey Dr DUDN DY1......83 H5
Osprey Rd ACGN B27......146 D5
   ERDW/GRVHL B23......76 A5
Ostler Cl KGSWFD DY6......99 F2
Oswin PI BLOX/PEL WS3......28 B5
Oswin Rd BLOX/PEL WS3......28 B5
Othello Rd WOLVN WV10......23 G3
Otley Gv BORD B9......129 G1
Otter Cft BKDE/SHDE B34......113 F4
Otterstone Cl SEDG DY3......67 E1
Oundle Rd KGSTG B44......75 F4
Ounsdale Crs WMBN WV5......65 E4
Ounsdale Dr DUDS DY2......102 C5
Ounsdale Rd WMBN WV5......64 D4
Ounty John La STRBR DY8......152 C2
Outmore Rd STETCH B33......130 D3
Out Wood Dr NFLD/LBR B31...174 D4
Oval Rd ERDE/BCHGN B24......92 C5
   TPTN/OCK DY4......69 G4
The Oval DARL/WED WS10......55 H4
   DUDN DY1......101 G1
   SMTHWK B67......123 H2
Overbrook Cl SEDG DY3......83 E4
Over Brunton Cl
   NFLD/LBR B31......175 H3
Overbury Cl HALE B63......138 D5
   NFLD/LBR B31......176 A2
Overdale Av WALM/CURD B76...94 B1
Overdale Cl WLNHL WV13......40 A2
Overdale Dr WLNHL WV13......40 A2
Overend Rd HALE B63......137 H1
Overend St WBROM B70......87 H3
Overfield Dr BILS/COS WV14...53 G5
Overfield Rd DUDN DY1......101 G1
   RIDG/WDGT B32......158 A1
Over Green Dr
   CHWD/FDBR/MGN B37......113 H4
Overlea Av ACGN B27......146 B4
Over Mill Dr SLYOAK B29......143 G5
Overmoor Cl LOZ/NWT B19...108 C2
Over Pool Rd WASH/WDE B8...111 E3
Oversdale Rd SOLH B91......181 F5
Overseley Rd WALM/CURD B76...78 C5
Overstrand COVEN WV9......11 H5
Overton Cl HLCN/YWD B28......162 D4
Overton Dr CSHL/WTROR B46...96 C3
Overton Gv ACGN B27......163 G2
Overton PI HHTH/SAND B71......71 F1
   VAUX/NECH B7 *......109 G5
Overton Rd ACGN B27......163 F2
Overwood Cft WASH/WDE B8...128 C1
Owen Pl BILS/COS WV14......53 H2
Owen Rd BDMR/CCFT WV3......6 B7
   BILS/COS WV14......53 H1
   WLNHL WV13......39 H4
Owens Cft HWK/WKHTH B38...177 E4
Owen St DARL/WED WS10......55 H5
   DUDS DY2......105 F1
   TPTN/OCK DY4......85 E1
Owens Wy CDYHTH B64......121 G3
Ownall Rd BKDE/SHDE B34...113 E5
Oxbarn Av BDMR/CCFT WV3......51 E1
Oxenton Cft HALE B63......137 H5
Oxford Cl WASH/WDE B8......111 H4
Oxhill Rd HDSW B21......89 E5
Oxford Dr ACGN B27......146 D3
   STRBR DY8......135 F5
Oxford Rd ACGN B27......146 C4
   ERDW/GRVHL B23......92 D2
   MOS/BIL B13......144 C5
   SMTHWK B66......106 C1
   WBROM B70......87 F3
Oxford St BILS/COS WV14......54 A3
   BVILLE B30......160 A3
   DARL/WED WS10......71 F1
   DIG/EDG B5......3 J7
   DUDN DY1......84 B5
   WOLV WV1......7 H5
   WSLW WS2......56 C1
Oxford Wy TPTN/OCK DY4......84 D2
Oxley Av HDSW B21......89 E5
Oxley CI DUDS DY2......120 B2
Oxley Cl SLYOAK B29......158 C2
Oxley Gv HRBN B17......141 G3
Oxley La WOLV WV1......7 F1
Oxley Links Rd WOLVN WV10...22 C1
Oxley Moor Rd COVEN WV9...22 C2
Ox Leys Rd MGN/WHC B75......63 H4
Oxley St WOLV WV1......37 E1
Oxlip Cl DSYBK/YTR WS5......57 G5
Oxpiece Dr CBROM B36......111 H1
Oxstall Cl WALM/CURD B76......95 F1
Ox St SEDG DY3......83 F1
Oxted Cl WNSFLD WV11......25 H5
Oxted Cft ERDW/GRVHL B23...92 C3
Oxwood La RIDG/WDGT B32...173 F1

P

Pace Crs BILS/COS WV14......69 F1
Pacific Av DARL/WED WS10......70 B2
Packhorse La HLYWD B47......192 A2
   HWK/WKHTH B38......191 H1
Packington Av
   BKDE/SHDE B34......113 E4

Packington La
CSHL/WTROR B46.................115 G5
RCOVN/BALC/EX CV7...........150 D2
Packmores
DOR/KN B93..........................194 A3
Packwood Cl
BFLD/HDSWWD B20.............90 A4
DOR/KN B93..........................196 C4
WLNHL WV13........................59 F5
Packwood Cottages
DOR/KN B93..........................198 D2
Packwood Ct SLYOAK B29....158 B1
Packwood Dr GTB/HAM B43....73 F2
Packwood Rd HOCK/TIA B94..199 F4
LGN/SDN/BHAMAIR B26..........130 D4
OLDBY B69.............................85 G5
Padarn Cl SEDG DY3.................67 E2
Padbury Rd
DUNHL/THL/PER WV6............22 D5
Padgate Cl CVALE B35...............94 D3
Padstow Rd ERDE/BCHGN B24..93 H7
The Paddock
CDSL WV8..............................10 C5
DUNHL/THL/PER WV6............34 B1
HAG/WOL DY9.......................152 D2
SEDG DY3..............................83 G1
WMBN WV5............................64 C5
Paddock Vw
DUNHL/THL/PER WV6............22 D5
Padgate Cl CVALE B35...............94 D3
Padstow Rd ERDE/BCHGN B24..93 H7
Paget Cl
LDYWD/EDGR B16..................125 F1
Pagel St WOLV WV1.................9 H5
Pagham Cl COVEN WV9............11 H5
Pagnell Gv MOS/BIL B13..........162 A4
Pagoda Cl FOAKS/STRLY B74....60 B2
Paignton Rd
LDYWD/EDGR B16..................125 F1
Pailton Gv SLYOAK B29...........158 D1
Pailton Rd SHLY B90................163 F5
Painswick Cl DSYBK/YTR WS5...11 H5
Painswick Rd HLGN/YWD B28..162 C5
Paint Cup Rw DUDS DY2..........120 C2
Painters Cft BILS/COS WV14.....69 E2
Pakefield Rd BVILLE B30...........177 E2
Pakenham Cl WALM/CURD B76..78 B3
Pakenham Dr WALM/CURD B76..78 B3
Pakenham Rd EDG B15..............126 C5
Pakfield Wk AST/WIT B6 *........91 F5
Palace Cl BLKHTH/ROWR B65..104 D1
Palace Dr SMTHWK B66............105 C1
Palace Rd BORD B9..................128 C3
Palefield Rd SHLY B90..............195 F2
Pale La HRBN B17.....................124 B4
Pale St SEDG DY3.....................83 G1
Palethorpe Rd TPTN/OCK DY4..69 G3
Palfrey Rd STRBR DY8..............134 D2
Palmcourt Av HLGN/YWD B28..162 C5
Palm Cft BRLYHL DY5...............119 E4
Palmer Cl WNSFLD WV11.........25 F1
Palmers Cl CDSL WV8..............11 E5
SHLY B90................................163 F5
Palmers Gv CBROM B36...........112 A1
Palmerston Dr SLYOAK B29.......86 B4
Palmerston Rd SPARK B11........144 D1
Palmer St BORD B9..................127 G2
Palmers Wy CDSL WV8............21 G1
Palomino Pl
LGN/SDN/BHAMAIR B26..........147 G1
Pamela Rd NFLD/LBR B31.........175 G3
Pan Cft CBROM B36..................111 G2
Pangbourne Gdns SMTHWK B67 *..106 B5
Pannel Cft LOZ/NWT B19.........108 D5
Panther Cft BKDE/SHDE B34....113 F4
Paper Mill End KGSTG B44.......74 D5
Papyrus Wy CBROM B36..........94 B5
The Parade BRWNH WS8.............9 E3
CDYHTH B64...........................121 E4
DUDN DY1...............................84 B4
KGSWFD DY6..........................99 F2
WNSFLD WV11.......................24 A2
Paradise DUDS DY2...................102 D1

Paradise Circ Queensway
CBHAMNW B3........................2 D4
Paradise Cv BLOX/PEL WS3.....17 H4
Paradise La BLOX/PEL WS3.......17 H4
HLGN/YWD B28......................162 C4
Paradise Pl CBHAMNW B3 *.......2 E5
Paradise St CBHAMNW B2.........3 G4
WSLW WS2.............................42 C3
Par Gn HWK/WKHTH B38.........176 A4
Parish Gdns HAG/WOL DY9......152 D1
Park Ap ERDW/GRVHL B23........92 A4
Park Av BLKHTH/ROWR B65......122 A1
BVILLE B30.............................160 A5
CSHL/WTROR B46..................115 F3
ETTPK/GDPK/PENN WV4.......52 A3
LGLYGN/QTN B68...................123 F1
SMTHWK B67 *......................106 B5
SOLH B91...............................182 B2
TPTN/OCK DY4.......................69 G4
WLNHL WV13........................39 F5
WMBN WV5............................80 D1
WOLV WV1............................6 D3
WSNGN B18...........................108 A2
Park Cl BRWNH WS8.................9 F4
DUDN DY1..............................68 B4
ERDE/BCHGN B24...................93 H1
HIA/OLT B92...........................148 B5
OLDBY B69.............................104 A2
Park Crs HHTH/SAND B71.........87 H2
WOLV WV1............................6 D3
Park Cft HWK/WKHTH B38.......192 C3
Parkdale Av DARL/WED WS10....56 A4
Parkdale Cl ERDE/BCHGN B24....92 D4

Park Dale Ct WOLV WV1............6 A2
Parkdale Dr NFLD/LBR B31........189 G1
Park Dl East WOLV WV1.............6 A2
Parkdale Rd
LGN/SDN/BHAMAIR B26..........148 A1
Park Dl West WOLV WV1............6 A2
Park Dr
ETTPK/GDPK/PENN WV4.......52 A3
FOAKS/STRLY B74..................46 A1
Park Edge HRBN B17................125 E5
Park End DOR/KN B93..............157 H1
Parker Rd WNSFLD WV11.........25 F1
Parker St BLOX/PEL WS3..........27 E1
LDYWD/EDGR B16..................125 H3
Parkes Av CDSL WV8................10 D5
Parkes Hall Rd DUDN DY1.........84 A1
Parkes La SEDG DY3.................68 A4
TPTN/OCK DY4.......................69 F3
Parkes St BRLYHL DY5.............119 F1
SMTHWK B67........................106 B5
WLNHL WV13........................39 H4
Parkeston Crs KGSTG B44........75 H2
Park Farm Rd GTB/HAM B43.....59 E5
Parkfield RIDG/WDGT B32.........139 H5
Parkfield Chalet Land
BKHL/PFLD WV2 *..................52 B2
Parkfield Cl EDG B15................126 C5
RMSLY B62............................140 A2
Parkfield Colliery
ETTPK/GDPK/PENN WV4.......52 C3
Parkfield Crs BKHL/PFLD WV2...52 C2
Parkfield Dr CBROM B36...........95 E5
Parkfield Gv BKHL/PFLD WV2...52 C2
Parkfield Rd
CSHL/WTROR B46..................115 F2
DUDS DY2..............................102 D3
ETTPK/GDPK/PENN WV4.......52 C2
LGLYGN/QTN B68...................123 G1
STRBR DY8.............................135 H2
WASH/WDE B8.......................128 C1
Park Gv CSHL/WTROR B46.........96 C3
SMHTH B10 *.........................128 B4
Park Hall Cl DSYBK/YTR WS5.....58 A2
Park Hall Crs CBROM B36.........112 D1
Parkhall Cft BKDE/SHDE B34....113 E2
Park Hall Rd DSYBK/YTR WS5...58 B2
ETTPK/GDPK/PENN WV4.......52 B3
Park Head Crs DUDS DY2 *.......102 B1
Parkhead Locks DUDS DY2 *....102 A3
Park Head Rd DUDS DY2..........102 B1
Park Hl BLKHTH/ROWR B65......121 H5
DARL/WED WS10...................56 C4
MOS/BIL B13.........................144 A3
Park Hill Dr
BFLD/HDSWWD B20...............89 H2
Park Hill Rd HRBN B17.............142 A1
SMTHWK B67........................106 C4
Parkhill Rd WALM/CURD B76....78 B5
Park Hill St DUDS DY2..............103 E1
Parkhouse Av WNSFLD WV11...24 B4
Parkhouse Dr
ERDW/GRVHL B23...................91 G1
Parkhouse Gdns SEDG DY3......83 E2
Parklands
BDMR/CCFT WV3...................35 H3
ERDW/GRVHL B23...................76 B5
HAG/WOL DY9.......................136 B4
Park La AST/WIT B6..................109 G2
CVALE B35.............................94 D1
DARL/WED WS10...................55 H4
HALE B63................................137 E1
HDSW B21..............................88 D2
KGSWFD DY6.........................99 E5
OLDBY B69.............................105 E3
WOLVN WV10........................23 H5
Park La East TPTN/OCK DY4.....85 H2
Park La West TPTN/OCK DY4....85 G2
Park Lime Dr RUSH/SHEL WS4..42 D1
Park Meadow Av
BILS/COS WV14......................38 C5
Park Ms SLYOAK B29................158 D1
Park Pl VAUX/NECH G7............110 A2
Park Retreat SMTHWK B66........106 D5
Park Rdg FOAKS/STRLY B74.......62 A1
Park Ridge Dr HALE B63...........137 F1
Park Ri BDMR/CCFT WV3..........36 A3
Park Rd AST/WIT B6..................109 G2
BILS/COS WV14......................53 G3
BLOX/PEL WS3.......................27 F1
BRLYHL DY5..........................119 H4
CSHL/WTROR B46..................115 H4
DARL/WED WS10...................54 D2
DSYBK/YTR WS5....................58 B3
DUDN DY1..............................68 B5
DUDS DY2..............................102 C3
ERDW/GRVHL B23..................92 A4
HAG/WOL DY9.......................152 D5
HALE B63................................137 F1
MOS/BIL B13.........................144 B3
OLDBY B69.............................104 A1
RUSH/SHEL WS4....................29 E2
SCFLD/BOLD B73....................62 B3
SEDG DY3..............................82 D2
SMTHWK B67........................124 B3
SOLH B91...............................182 A2
SPARK B11............................145 E4
STRBR DY8.............................134 D2
WLNHL WV13........................39 H3
WSNGN B18...........................107 H2
Park Rd East WOLV WV1...........6 D1
Park Rd South WSNGN B18.......108 B4
Park Rd West DY8...................134 C2
Parks Crs WNSFLD WV11..........15 E3
Parkside RIDG/WDGT B32........157 H2
Parkside Av WLNHL WV13........39 E3
Parkside Cl DARL/WED WS10....56 B5
Parkside Rd
BFLD/HDSWWD B20...............89 G1
HALE B63................................137 H2
Parkside Wy
FOAKS/STRLY B74..................45 G4
NFLD/LBR B31........................174 C4

Park Sq
CHWD/FDBR/MGN B37..........132 D4
Parkstone Cl RUSH/SHEL WS4...29 E1
Park St AST/WIT B6...................109 G2
BLKHTH/ROWR B65................122 B3
CDYHTH B64...........................120 D2
DARL/WED WS10...................55 E5
DIG/EDG B5............................3 J5
HAG/WOL DY9.......................136 D2
KGSWFD DY6.........................99 H3
OLDBY B69.............................104 D3
STRBR DY8.............................135 G5
TPTN/OCK DY4.......................85 G3
WBROM B70...........................87 H3
WS1.......................................4 D3
Park St South BKHL/PFLD WV2..52 A2
Park St West
BLKHTH/ROWR B65................122 B3
Park Ter DARL/WED WS10........54 D2
HDSW B21..............................107 G1
Park Tree Wk
ERDE/BCHGN B24...................93 H2
HOCK/TIA B94.......................198 A5
SCFLD/BOLD B73....................62 A2
Parkview Ct KGSWFD DY6.........99 F1
Parkview Crs WSLW WS2..........41 E1
Parkview Dr BRWNH WS8..........9 F2
WASH/WDE B8.......................111 E3
Parkview Rd BILS/COS WV14....38 C5
Park View Rd FOAKS/STRLY B74..46 A2
HAG/WOL DY9.......................136 D3
Park Vis BORD B9 *..................127 H2
Parkville Av HRBN B17.............141 H4
Park Wk BRLYHL DY5...............119 H4
Park Wy RBRY B45...................174 B5
Parkway WASH/WDE B8..........111 E4
Park Wy WNSFLD WV11...........25 G1
Parkway Rd DUDN DY1............84 A4
The Parkway
DUNHL/THL/PER WV6............34 C2
RUSH/SHEL WS4....................29 E2
Parkwood Cl BRWNH WS8........19 G2
Parkwood Ct GTB/HAM B43.......74 B2
Parkwood Dr SCFLD/BOLD B73..61 F3
Parkyn St BKHL/PFLD WV2........37 G5
Parliament St AST/WIT B6.........109 F1
DUDS DY2..............................102 B2
SMTH B10..............................128 A4
WBROM B70...........................87 H5
Parlows End
HWK/WKHTH B38..................190 B1
Parry Rd WNSFLD WV11...........25 G2
Parsonage Dr HALE B63............120 A5
RBRY B45..............................188 D4
Parsonage St HHTH/SAND B71..71 H5
OLDBY B69.............................105 F3
Parson's Hl BVILLE B30............177 E5
LGLYGN/QTN B68...................123 F3
Parsons Rd DUDN DY1.............84 C5
Partons Rd
ALE/KHTH/YWD B14...............160 D4
Partridge Av DARL/WED WS10..54 D2
Partridge Cl
CHWD/FDBR/MGN B37..........132 C1
Partridge Rd
LGN/SDN/BHAMAIR B26.........130 C3
STRBR DY8.............................135 H4
Passey Rd MOS/BIL B13...........145 F5
Passfield Rd STETCH B33..........130 A2
The Pastures
DUNHL/THL/PER WV6............34 B1
Pasture Vw BLOX/PEL WS3.......28 B1
Patent Dr DARL/WED WS10......70 A1
Paternoster Rw DIG/EDG B5 *....3 H5
WOLV WV1............................6 A2
Paterson Pl BRWNH WS8...........19 H2
Pathlow Crs SHLY B90..............180 A4
Paton Gv BRLYHL DY5.............119 H4
Patna Cl BLOX/PEL WS3...........144 B5
Patricia Av
ALE/KHTH/YWD B14...............179 E1
ETTPK/GDPK/PENN WV4.......52 A5
Patricia Cl DUDS DY2...............68 B5
Patricia Dr TPTN/OCK DY4........85 G4
Patrick Gregory Rd
WNSFLD WV11.......................25 F3
Patrick Rd
LGN/SDN/BHAMAIR B26.........130 A5
Patriot Cl WSL WS1..................56 D3
Patshull Av WOLVN WV10.........12 C4
Patshull Cl GTB/HAM B43.........73 F2
Patshull Gv WOLVN WV10.........12 C4
Patshull Pl LOZ/NWT B19 *......108 C2
Pattenham Cl SHHTH WV12......40 B1
Patterdale Rd
ERDW/GRVHL B23...................92 B1
Patterson Cl WBRLYHL DY5......118 D4
Patterton Dr WALM/CURD B76..78 B3
Pattingham Rd
DUNHL/THL/PER WV6............34 A3
Pattison Gdns
ERDW/GRVHL B23...................92 B4
Pattison St DSYBK/YTR WS5.....57 E3
Paul Byrne Ct
BFLD/HDSWWD B20...............88 D2
Paul Pursehouse Rd
BILS/COS WV14......................53 H5
Pauls Coppice BRWNH WS8......19 F2
Paul St BILS/COS WV14.............68 A2
BKHL/PFLD WV2.....................52 A5
WOLV WV1.............................7 E1
Paul V TPTN/OCK DY4..............85 H1
Pavenham Dr DIG/EDG B5.........143 E5
Pavilion Av SMTHWK B67..........124 A1
Pavilion Dr AST/WIT B6.............91 H1
Pavilion End KINVER DY7.........116 C3
Pavilion Gdns DUDS DY2..........120 C2
Pavilion Rd AST/WIT B6............91 H1
The Pavilions CBHAMNE B4 *.....3 H5
CHWD/FDBR/MGN B37..........132 A5
Pavilion St DSYBK/YTR WS5......57 E3
Pavior's Rd BKDE/SHDE B34....112 D2
Paxford Wy NFLD/LBR B31.........174 D5
Paxton Av
DUNHL/THL/PER WV6............34 C2
Paxton Rd HAG/WOL DY9.........137 E3
WSNGN B18...........................108 A4
Payne St BLKHTH/ROWR B65...122 A3
Payton Cl OLDBY B69................86 C5

Payton Rd HDSW B21...............107 F1
Peach Av DARL/WED WS10.......55 E2
Peachley Cl HALE B63...............138 D5
Peach Ley Rd SLYOAK B29........158 B5
Peach Rd SHHTH WV12............25 G4
Peacock Av WNSFLD WV11.......25 G3
Peacock Cl TPTN/OCK DY4.......85 H2
Peacock Rd DARL/WED WS10...54 D1
MOS/BIL B13.........................161 F4
Peacocks Est CDYHTH B64 *.....120 C5
Peak Cft CBROM B36................111 H1
Peak Dr SEDG DY3....................83 F3
Peake Crs BRWNH WS8.............19 F2
Peake Dr TPTN/OCK DY4..........85 H2
Peake Rd BRWNH WS8..............19 F2
Peak House Rd GTB/HAM B43....58 C5
Peakman St RBRY B45..............188 A2
Peak Rd STRBR DY8.................135 H1
Peal St WSL WS1.......................5 F4
Pearce Cl DUDN DY1................101 G1
Pearl Gv ACGN B27..................146 B4
HDSW B21..............................107 G5
Pearman Rd RBRY B45..............175 F4
SMTHWK B66........................124 C1
Pearmans Cft HLYWD B47.........192 C2
Pearsall Dr OLDBY B69..............85 E5
Pearson St BKHL/PFLD WV2......37 E5
BRLYHL DY5..........................119 H1
CDYHTH B64...........................121 E3
HAG/WOL DY9.......................136 D3
WBROM B70...........................87 G2
Pear Tree Av TPTN/OCK DY4.....85 F1
Peartree Av WLNHL WV13.........39 H4
Pear Tree Cl
BLKHTH/ROWR B65................122 B1
HAG/WOL DY9.......................136 D3
SHLY B90................................179 E5
Pear Tree Dr
BLKHTH/ROWR B65................122 B1
GTB/HAM B43........................73 E2
Peartree Dr STRBR DY8.............135 G5
Pear Tree Gv SHLY B90.............179 F5
Pear Tree La BILS/COS WV14.....68 D3
BRWNH WS8...........................8 C2
Peartree La CDYHTH B64..........121 E3
DUDS DY2..............................101 H4
Pear Tree La WOLVN WV10......24 B1
Pear Tree Rd BKDE/SHDE B34..113 E3
GTB/HAM B43........................72 D2
SMTHWKW B67.....................106 A5
Peascroft La BILS/COS WV14.....54 A4
Peasefield Cl HDSW B21............107 E1
Pebble Cl STRBR DY8................135 H2
Pebble Mill Rd DIG/EDG B5.......143 E5
Pebworth Av SHLY B90.............195 H2
Pebworth Cl SLYOAK B29..........158 A3
Pebworth Gv DUDN DY1...........84 A5
STETCH B33...........................131 E4
Peckham Rd KGSTG B44............75 G1
Peckover Cl
BLKHTH/ROWR B65................121 H3
Pedmore La
WALM/CURD B76....................79 F5
Pedmore Court Rd STRBR DY8..152 D1
Pedmore Gv KGSTG B44............75 F1
Pedmore Hall La
HAG/WOL DY9.......................153 E1
Pedmore Rd BRLYHL DY5.........120 A3
DUDS DY2..............................120 A1
HAG/WOL DY9.......................136 D2
Peel Cl DARL/WED WS10..........40 B5
HIA/OLT B92...........................167 H4
WLNHL WV13........................39 G4
Peel St BDMR/CCFT WV3...........36 A5
DUDS DY2..............................103 E1
HHTH/SAND B71....................87 G1
TPTN/OCK DY4.......................85 G3
WLNHL WV13........................39 G4
WSNGN B18...........................107 G4
Peel Wk HRBN B17...................124 B5
Peel Wy OLDBY B69..................86 A4
Pegasus Wk SLYOAK B29..........159 F1
Pelham Dr DUDN DY1..............102 B3
Pelham Rd WASH/WDE B8........111 F5
Pelham St BDMR/CCFT WV3......6 B6
Pelsall La BLOX/PEL WS3..........17 F4
RUSH/SHEL WS4....................28 C2
Pelsall Rd BRWNH WS8............8 D5
Pemberley Rd ACGN B27...........163 E1
Pemberton Cl SMTHWK B66.....124 C1
Pemberton Crs
DARL/WED WS10...................56 C4
Pemberton Rd BILS/COS WV14..68 D2
WBROM B70...........................71 E5
Pemberton St WSNGN B18........2 B2
Pembridge Cl BRLYHL DY5.........119 E3
NFLD/LBR B31........................174 C4
Pembridge Rd DOR/KN B93.......196 C5
Pembroke Av BKHL/PFLD WV2...53 E1
Pembroke Cl HHTH/SAND B71...71 F4
HLGN/YWD B28......................162 B3
WBROM B70...........................71 F2
Pembroke Cft SHHTH WV12......40 B1
Pembroke Gdns STRBR DY8......114 C2
Pembroke Rd BHTH/HG B12......144 C3
HHTH/SAND B71....................71 F2
Pembroke Wy HHTH/SAND B71..71 F4
HLGN/YWD B28......................162 B3
Pembury Cl FOAKS/STRLY B74...60 B2
Pembury Cft KGSTG B44............75 H5
Pencombe Dr
ETTPK/GDPK/PENN WV4.......52 B3
Penda Gv
DUNHL/THL/PER WV6............20 D5
Pendeen Rd
ALE/KHTH/YWD B14...............179 E1
Pendeford Av
DUNHL/THL/PER WV6............22 A2
Pendeford Cl
DUNHL/THL/PER WV6............22 A2
Pendeford Hall La COVEN WV9..11 E4
Pendeford La COVEN WV9.........11 G3
Pendeford Mill La CDSL WV8.....11 E4
Pendennis Cl BVILLE B30..........159 F5
Pendennis Dr OLDBY B69...........86 B5
Penderel Cl WOLVN WV10.........13 G1
Penderel St BLOX/PEL WS3.......27 G1
Pendigo Wy BHAMNEC B40......150 B4

Pendinas Dr CDSL WV8..............10 D4
Pendleton Gv ACGN B27............165 F2
Pendragon Rd PBAR/PBCH B42..90 C2
Pendrell Cl
CHWD/FDBR/MGN B37..........132 A1
Pendrell Ct CDSL WV8 *..............10 C4
Pendrill Rd WOLVN WV10.........13 F4
Penfields Rd STRBR DY8............135 G3
Penge Gv KGSTG B44................60 A5
Penhallow Dr
ETTPK/GDPK/PENN WV4.......52 C3
Penhurst Av
BFLD/HDSWWD B20...............90 D5
Penkridge Cl WSLW WS2...........41 H1
Penkridge Gv STETCH B33.........112 B5
Penkridge St WSLW WS2...........41 H2
Penk Ri DUNHL/THL/PER WV6...35 F1
Penleigh Gdns WMBN WV5.......64 D4
Penley Gv WASH/WDE B8..........111 F3
Pennant Ct BDMR/CCFT WV3....36 D5
Pennant Gv SLYOAK B29..........141 G5
Pennant Rd
BLKHTH/ROWR B65................165 H1
CDYHTH B64...........................120 D3
Pennard Gv RIDG/WDGT B32....141 F3
Penn Cl BLOX/PEL WS3.............27 G1
Penn Common Rd
ETTPK/GDPK/PENN WV4.......66 A2
Penncricket La
BLKHTH/ROWR B65................122 C1
Penn Cft La
ETTPK/GDPK/PENN WV4.......66 C2
Penndale Cl ERDE/BCHGN B24...77 G5
Pennhouse Av
ETTPK/GDPK/PENN WV4.......51 F3
Pennine Dr SEDG DY3...............83 F3
Pennine Wy SHHTH WV12.........40 B1
STRBR DY8.............................114 B3
WASH/WDE B8.......................110 B3
Pennington Cl WBROM B70.......87 E4
Penn Rd BLKHTH/ROWR B65....122 C1
ETTPK/GDPK/PENN WV4.......51 F4
SEDG DY3..............................66 B2
Penn Road Island
ETTPK/GDPK/PENN WV4........6 E6
Penns Lake Rd
WALM/CURD B76....................78 A4
Penns La CSCFLD/WYGN B72....77 H4
Penn St BDMR/CCFT WV3..........6 D7
CBHAMNE B4.........................127 G1
CDYHTH B64...........................121 E3
Penns Wood Cl SEDG DY3........67 E1
Penns Wood Dr
WALM/CURD B76....................78 B4
Pennwood La
ETTPK/GDPK/PENN WV4.......51 F5
Pennyacre Rd
ALE/KHTH/YWD B14...............177 H3
Pennyfield Cft STETCH B33........130 A1
Pennyhill La HHTH/SAND B71....72 A4
Pennyroyal Cl DSYBK/YTR WS5..57 G5
Penny Royal Cl SEDG DY3.........83 F4
Penrice Dr OLDBY B69...............85 F5
Penrith Cft BRLYHL DY5............118 D4
Penrith Gv
CHWD/FDBR/MGN B37..........132 C2
Penryn Cl DSYBK/YTR WS5........58 B1
Penryn Rd DSYBK/YTR WS5......58 B1
Pensarn Vls DARL/WED WS10 *..55 F2
Pensby Cl MOS/BIL B13.............162 A2
Pens Cl SMTHWK B66................106 C5
Pensford Rd NFLD/LBR B31.......176 A2
Pensham Crt SHLY B90..............181 H2
Penshaw Cl COVEN WV9...........12 A5
Penshaw Gv MOS/BIL B13........162 B1
Pensnett Rd DUDN DY1............101 G2
Penstock Dr OLDBY B69.............104 D5
Pentland Cft BHTH/HG B12.......127 F5
Pentland Dr BDMR/CCFT WV3...36 A3
Pentos Dr SPARK B11................145 F3
Pentridge Cl WALM/CURD B76...94 B1
Penwood Gdns BILS/COS WV14..68 C3
Penzer St KGSWFD DY6.............99 H2
Peolsford Rd BLOX/PEL WS3.....18 A3
Peplins Wy BVILLE B30..............160 A5
Peplow Rd STETCH B33.............112 C5
Pepperbox Dr TPTN/OCK DY4...85 G1
Pepper Hl STRBR DY8...............135 G5
Pepperwood Cl BRGRVW B61....185 H5
Pepper Wood Dr
NFLD/LBR B31........................174 C4
Perch Av
CHWD/FDBR/MGN B37..........132 A1
Perch Rd RSLW WS2.................41 E1
Percival Rd LDYWD/EDGR B16..125 F3
Peregrine Cl DUDN DY1............85 H5
Pereira Rd HRBN B17................125 H5
Perimeter Rd BHAMNEC B40.....149 H4
Perivale Gv BILS/COS WV14.......68 D3
Perivale Wy STRBR DY8............118 C4
Periwinkle Cl BRWNH WS8.........9 E5
Perkins Cl DUDN DY1................68 C5
Perott Dr MGN/WHC D75............47 H5
Perrins Gv WASH/WDE B8.........111 E3
Perrins La HAG/WOL DY9.........136 D3
Perrins Ri HAG/WOL DY9..........136 D3
Perrott Gdns BRLYHL DY5.........118 C3
Perrott St WSNGN B18..............107 F3
Perry Av PBAR/PBCH B42.........90 C2
Perry Barr Locks
PBAR/PBCH B42 *..................74 B5
Perry Cl DUDS DY2...................102 D1
Perry Common Rd
ERDW/GRVHL B23...................75 H5
Perryford Dr SOLH B91..............181 H5
Perry Hall Dr SHHTH WV12.......25 F4
Perry Hill Crs LGLYGN/QTN B68..123 F5
Perry Hill La
LGLYGN/QTN B68...................123 F5
Perry Hill Rd LGLYGN/QTN B68..123 F5
Perry Park Crs PBAR/PBCH B42..74 D5
Perry Park Rd
BLKHTH/ROWR B65................121 H3

Perry St BILS/COS WV14 .... 54 A5
  DARL/WED WS10 .... 40 B5
  SMTHWK B66 .... 106 C2
  TPTN/OCK DY4 .... 85 G2
Perry Villa Dr PBAR/PBCH B42 .... 90 D1
Perry Wk ERDW/GRVHL B23 .... 75 H5
Perrywell Rd AST/WIT B6 .... 91 C2
Perry Wood Rd
  PBAR/PBCH B42 .... 74 A3
Persehouse St WSL WS1 .... 5 G3
Pershore Cl BLOX/PEL WS3 .... 16 B5
Pershore Rd BLOX/PEL WS3 .... 16 B5
  BVILLE B30 .... 176 D1
  HALE B63 .... 138 C5
Pershore Rd South
  BVILLE B30 .... 176 D2
Pershore St DIG/EDG B5 .... 3 G7
Pershore Wy BLOX/PEL WS3 .... 16 B5
Perth Rd SHTH WV12 .... 25 H4
Perton Brook V
  DUNHL/THL/PER WV6 .... 34 D3
Perton Gv
  DUNHL/THL/PER WV6 .... 34 D3
  SLYOAK B29 .... 158 C1
Perton Rd
  DUNHL/THL/PER WV6 .... 34 D3
Petchells Cl BRLYHL DY5 .... 119 E5
Peter Av BILS/COS WV14 .... 69 F1
Peterbrook Ri WLV B90 .... 179 F4
Peterbrook Rd SHLY B90 .... 179 F4
Peterdale Dr
  ETTPK/GDPK/PENN WV4 .... 51 F5
Peters Av NFLD/LBR B31 .... 175 F3
Petersfield Ct
  HLGN/YWD B28 * 162 D2
Petersfield Dr
  BLKHTH/ROWR B65 .... 122 C1
Petersfield Rd HLGN/YWD B28 .. 162 C3
Petersham Pl EDG B15 .... 142 C1
Petersham Rd KGSTG B44 .... 76 A2
Peter's Hill Rd BRLYHL DY5 .... 119 E5
Petershouse Dr
  FOAKS/STRLY B74 .... 32 D5
Peters St WBROM B70 .... 71 E4
Petford St CDYHTH B64 .... 121 E3
Pettyfield Cl
  LGN/SDN/BHAMAIR B26 .... 147 G1
Pettyfields Cl DOR/KN B93 .... 197 E3
Petworth Cl WLNHL WV13 .... 39 F5
Petworth Gv
  LGN/SDN/BHAMAIR B26 .... 147 G1
Pevensey Cl OLDBY B69 .... 103 F1
Peverell Dr HLGN/YWD B28 .... 162 D3
Peverill Gv WALM/CURD B76 .... 63 E4
Peverill Rd
  DUNHL/THL/PER WV6 .... 34 D1
  ETTPK/GDPK/PENN WV4 .... 52 C5
Pevril Wy GTB/HAM B43 .... 73 H1
Pheasant Cft CBROM B36 .... 114 A1
Pheasant Rd SMTHWKW B67 .. 123 H2
Pheasant St BRLYHL DY5 .... 119 E1
Philip Rd HALE B63 .... 138 B4
  TPTN/OCK DY4 .... 86 B1
Philip Sidney Rd SPARK B11 .... 144 D4
Philip St BILS/COS WV14 .... 68 D2
Philip Victor Rd
  BFLD/HDSWWD B20 .... 89 H5
Phillimore Rd WASH/WDE B8 .. 110 D2
Phillip Rd WSLW WS2 .... 56 C2
Phillips Av WOLVN WV11 .... 25 F1
Phillips St AST/WIT B6 .... 109 E3
Phipson Rd MOS/BIL B13 .... 144 D4
Phoenix Cn EDG B15 .... 125 G5
Phoenix Pk
  BLKHTH/ROWR B65 .... 122 B3
Phoenix Ri DARL/WED WS10 .... 55 F4
  ERDW/GRVHL B23 .... 75 H4
Phoenix Ri TPTN/OCK DY4 .... 69 F5
  WNSFLD WV11 .... 38 D2
Phoenix St BKHL/PFLD WV2 .... 52 B2
  WBROM B70 .... 86 D1
Piccadilly Ar CBHAMNE B2 .... 3 F5
Piccadilly Cl
  CHWD/FDBR/MGN B37 .... 132 C3
Pickenham Rd
  ALE/KHTH/YWD B14 .... 178 C4
Pickering Cft RIDG/WDGT B32 .. 157 F1
Pickering Rd WNSFLD WV11 .... 24 D5
Pickersleigh Cl HALE B63 .... 138 C4
Pickford St DIG/EDG B5 .... 3 K6
Pickrell Rd BILS/COS WV14 .... 68 B2
Pickwick Gv MOS/BIL B13 .... 145 E5
Pickwick Pl BILS/COS WV14 .... 54 A4
Picton Cft
  CHWD/FDBR/MGN B37 .... 132 D3
Picton Gv MOS/BIL B13 .... 161 H5
Picturedrome Wy
  DARL/WED WS10 .... 55 F2
Piddock Rd SMTHWK B66 .... 106 C4
Pierce Av HIA/OLT B92 .... 147 E4
Piercy St WBROM B70 .... 87 E3
Piers Rd HDSW B21 .... 108 A2
Piggots Cft
  CHWD/FDBR/MGN B37 .... 131 H1
Pike Cl BFLD/HDSWWD B20 .... 89 H5
Pike Dr CHWD/FDBR/MGN B37 . 132 C1
Pikehelve St TPTN/OCK DY4 .... 70 C4
Pikehorne Cft CBROM B36 .... 95 F4
Pike Rd WSLW WS2 .... 41 E1
The Pikes RBRY B45 .... 173 H5
Pikewater Rd BORD B9 .... 128 B2
Pilkington Av
  CSCFLD/WYGN B72 .... 62 B5
Pilson Cl CBROM B36 .... 112 B1
Pimbury Rd SHTH WV12 .... 26 B3
Pimlico Ct SEDG DY3 .... 82 A3
Pimpernel Dr DSYBK/YTR WS5 .. 57 C5
Pinbury Cft
  CHWD/FDBR/MGN B37 .... 132 B4
Pineapple Cl
  ALE/KHTH/YWD B14 .... 160 C4
Pineapple Gv BVILLE B30 .... 160 C2
Pineapple Rd BVILLE B30 .... 160 C2
Pine Av DARL/WED WS10 .... 55 H5
  SMTHWK B66 .... 106 A2
Pine Cl BDMR/CCFT WV3 .... 6 A5
  KGSWFD DY6 .... 99 H4
  SOLH B91 .... 181 F3

Pine Gn DUDN DY1 .... 84 A1
Pine Gv ALE/KHTH/YWD B14 .. 161 G5
Pinehurst Dr
  HWK/WKHTH B38 .... 176 D2
Pine Leigh FOAKS/STRLY B74 .. 47 F4
Pineneedle Cft SHHTH WV12 .. 40 C1
Pine Rd DUDN DY1 .... 84 C1
  OLDBY B69 .... 103 C1
The Pines BDMR/CCFT WV3 .... 35 H4
  RBRY B45 .... 174 A4
  SHLY B90 .... 194 D1
  WSL WS1 .... 5 F6
Pine St BLOX/PEL WS3 .... 27 G1
Pinetree Dr FOAKS/STRLY B74 . 44 D4
Pineview NFLD/LBR B31 .... 175 F5
Pine Wk CDSL WV8 .... 10 B5
  HAG/WOL DY9 .... 136 B4
  NFLD/LBR B31 .... 175 H2
Pinewall Av HWK/WKHTH B38 176 D4
Pineways FOAKS/STRLY B74 .... 46 A2
  STRBR DY8 .... 117 C2
Pineways Dr
  DUNHL/THL/PER WV6 .... 36 A2
The Pineways OLDBY B69 .... 104 A4
Pinewood Cl BDMR/CCFT WV3 .. 35 E5
  BRWNH WS8 .... 9 E2
  DSYBK/YTR WS5 .... 57 H4
  KGSTG B44 .... 75 F4
  RBRY B45 .... 173 F5
  SHTH WV12 .... 26 B3
  WMBN WV5 .... 65 G5
Pinewood Dr RIDG/WDGT B32 . 157 E2
Pinewood Gv SOLH B91 .... 181 F3
The Woods RIDG/WDGT B32 .. 140 A5
Pinewoods NFLD/LBR B31 .... 158 B2
  RMSLY B62 .... 123 E5
Pinewoods Av HAG/WOL DY9 .. 169 F1
Pinewoods Cl HAG/WOL DY9 .. 169 F1
Pinfold BLOX/PEL WS3 .... 27 C2
Pinfold Ct DARL/WED WS10 .... 55 E3
Pinfold Crs
  ETTPK/GDPK/PENN WV4 .... 50 D2
Pinfold Gdns WNSFLD WV11 .. 24 D5
Pinfold Gv
  ETTPK/GDPK/PENN WV4 .... 50 D2
Pinfold La ALDR WS9 .... 59 F3
  ETTPK/GDPK/PENN WV4 .... 51 E3
Pinfold Rd SOLH B91 .... 165 G5
Pinfold St BILS/COS WV14 .... 53 H5
  CBHAM B2 .... 3 F5
  DARL/WED WS10 .... 55 E3
  OLDBY B69 .... 105 E1
Pingle Cl HHTH/SAND B71 .... 72 B2
Pinkney Pl LGLYGN/QTN B68 .. 123 C1
Pinley Gv GTB/HAM B43 .... 59 F5
Pinley Wy SOLH B91 .... 181 G5
Pinner Gv RIDG/WDGT B32 .. 141 E5
Pinson Rd WLNHL WV13 .... 39 F4
Pintail Dr ERDW/GRVHL B23 .. 92 A4
Pinto Cl LDYWD/EDGR B16 .... 125 H2
Pinza Cft CBROM B36 .... 111 H1
Pioli Pl WSLW WS2 .... 27 H5
Pioneer Wy CVALE B35 .... 94 D4
Piper Cl DUNHL/THL/PER WV6 . 34 D1
Piper Pl STRBR DY8 .... 118 B4
Piper Rd BDMR/CCFT WV3 .... 35 F5
Pipers Gn HLGN/YWD B28 .... 162 D5
Piper's Rw WOLV WV1 .... 7 H4
Pipes Meadow
  BILS/COS WV14 .... 54 A3
Pippin Av HALE B63 .... 120 B5
Pirbright Cl BILS/COS WV14 .. 54 A5
Pirrey Cl BILS/COS WV14 .... 68 D2
Pitcairn Cl DVILLE B30 .... 160 D4
Pitcairn Dr RMSLY B62 .... 138 D1
Pitcairn Rd SMTHWKW B67 .. 123 H3
Pitclose Rd NFLD/LBR B31 .... 175 H4
Pitfield Rd STETCH B33 .... 112 B5
Pitfield Rw DUDN DY1 .... 84 B5
Pitfields Cl LGLYGN/QTN B68 . 123 E4
Pitfields Rd LGLYGN/QTN B68 . 123 E4
Pitfield St DUDN DY1 * 84 B5
Pithall Rd BKDE/SHDE B34 .... 113 F4
Pit Leasow Cl BVILLE B30 .... 160 B2
Pitman Rd RIDG/WDGT B32 .. 140 C2
Pitmaston Rd HLGN/YWD B28 . 163 E4
Pitsford St WSNGN B18 .... 2 B1
Pitt La HIA/OLT B92 .... 149 H5
Pitts Farm Rd
  ERDE/BCHGN B24 .... 93 C1
Pitt St CBHAMNE B4 .... 127 G1
Pixall Dr EDG B15 .... 143 F1
Pixhall Wk CVALE B35 .... 94 D3
Plainview Cl ALDR WS9 .... 45 E3
Plaistow Av CBROM B36 .... 111 G2
Plane Gv
  CHWD/FDBR/MGN B37 .... 132 B3
Planetary Rd WLNHL WV13 .... 38 C2
Plane Tree Rd DSYBK/YTR WS5 . 57 F5
Planetree Rd FOAKS/STRLY B74 . 44 D5
Planet Rd BRLYHL DY5 .... 101 F5
Planks La WMBN WV5 .... 64 D5
Plantation Dr HAG/WOL DY9 .. 63 F2
Plantation La DSYBK/YTR WS5 . 81 F2
Plantation Rd DSYBK/YTR WS5 . 58 A1
The Plantation BRLYHL DY5 .. 100 D2
Plants Brook Rd
  WALM/CURD B76 .... 78 B5
Plants Cl SCFLD/BOLD B73 .... 76 B2
Plants Gv ERDE/BCHGN B24 .. 77 H5
Plants Hollow BRLYHL DY5 .... 119 F3
Plant St CDYHTH B64 .... 120 C3
  STRBR DY8 .... 118 A2
Plant Wy BLOX/PEL WS3 .... 17 H5
Plascom Rd WOLV WV1 .... 38 A4
Platts Crs STRBR DY8 .... 118 A4
Platts Dr STRBR DY8 .... 118 A4
Platts Rd STRBR DY8 .... 118 A4
Platt St DARL/WED WS10 .... 55 F3
Playdon Gv
  ALE/KHTH/YWD B14 .... 178 C2
Pleasant Cl KGSWFD DY6 .... 99 C5
Pleasant St WBROM B70 .... 87 G5
Pleasant Vw SEDG DY3 .... 81 F5
Pleck Rd WSLW WS2 .... 41 G5
Pleck Wk HWK/WKHTH B38 .. 177 E4
Plestowes Cl SHLY B90 .... 163 F5
Plimsoll Gv RIDG/WDGT B32 .. 140 C3
Plough Av RIDG/WDGT B32 .. 140 C5

Plough & Harrow Rd
  LDYWD/EDGR B16 .... 125 H3
Ploughmans Pl MGN/WHC B75 . 47 H1
Ploughmans Wk KGSWFD DY6 . 99 E2
Ploverdale Crs KGSWFD DY6 .. 100 C5
Plowden Rd STETCH B33 .... 112 B5
Plume St AST/WIT B6 .... 109 H2
Plumstead Rd KGSTG B44 .... 75 C3
Plym Cl WNSFLD WV11 .... 24 C5
Plymouth Cl NFLD/LBR B31 .. 189 G1
Plymouth Rd BVILLE B30 .... 160 B5
Pocklington Pl
  NFLD/LBR B31 * 159 H2
Pointon Cl BILS/COS WV14 .... 67 H1
Polden Cl HALE B63 .... 154 C1
Polesworth Gv
  BKDE/SHDE B34 .... 112 D3
Pollard Rd ACGN B27 .... 145 G3
The Pollards ERDW/GRVHL B23 . 76 C5
Polo Flds HAG/WOL DY9 .... 152 D1
Pomeroy Rd GTB/HAM B43 .... 59 H4
  RIDG/WDGT B32 .... 157 G1
Pommel Cft DSYBK/YTR WS5 .. 57 F4
Pond Crs BKHL/PFLD WV2 .... 52 C1
Pond Gv BKHL/PFLD WV2 .... 52 C1
Pond La BKHL/PFLD WV2 .... 52 C1
Poole Crs BILS/COS WV14 .... 68 C2
  BRWNH WS8 .... 8 D5
  HRBN B17 .... 142 A4
Poolehouse Rd GTB/HAM B45 . 58 C5
Pool End Cl DOR/KN B93 .... 196 D2
Pooles La SHHTH WV12 .... 26 C3
Poole St STRBR DY8 .... 135 E3
Pool Farm Rd ACGN B27 .... 163 G1
Poolfield Dr SOLH B91 .... 181 F2
Pool Furlong HAG/WOL DY9 .. 170 C4
Pool Gn ALDR WS9 .... 30 A5
Pool Hall Crs BDMR/CCFT WV3 . 34 D5
Pool Hall Rd BDMR/CCFT WV3 . 34 D5
Pool Hayes La SHHTH WV12 .. 25 G5
Pool House Rd WMBN WV5 .. 64 B5
Pool La OLDBY B69 .... 104 D5
Pool Meadow WALM/CURD B76 . 78 C5
Pool Meadow Cl MOS/BIL B13 . 162 A1
  SOLH B91 .... 182 D4
Pool Rd BRWNH WS8 .... 9 E2
  HALE B63 .... 138 D4
  SMTHWK B66 .... 106 D4
  WNSFLD WV11 .... 25 G4
Pool St BKHL/PFLD WV2 * 109 F3
  BKHL/PFLD WV2 .... 6 F4
  DUDN DY1 .... 68 A5
  WSL WS1 .... 5 G5
Pool Vw RUSH/SHEL WS4 .... 29 F3
Pope Rd WOLVN WV10 .... 24 A2
Popes La DUNHL/THL/PER WV6 . 21 E4
  HWK/WKHTH B38 .... 176 B2
  OLDBY B69 .... 105 F3
Pope St SMTHWK B66 .... 106 B1
  WSNGN B18 .... 2 A4
Poplar Av ALE/KHTH/YWD B14 . 161 E2
  BHTH/HG B12 .... 144 C3
  BRWNH WS8 .... 9 G4
  CHWD/FDBR/MGN B37 .. 133 E2
  DSYBK/YTR WS5 .... 57 C4
  ERDW/GRVHL B23 * 92 D2
  HRBN B17 .... 124 D2
  LOZ/NWT B19 * 108 C1
  MGN/WHC B75 .... 63 F1
  OLDBY B69 .... 103 H1
  TPTN/OCK DY4 .... 85 H4
  WBROM B70 .... 87 G1
  WNSFLD WV11 .... 24 B5
  WSLW WS2 .... 40 B1
Poplar Cl OLDBY B69 .... 86 B5
  WMBN WV5 .... 65 F5
  WSLW WS2 .... 40 C1
Poplar Crs DUDN DY1 .... 84 B3
  WASH/WDE B8 .... 110 B3
Poplar Dr OLDBY B69 .... 68 A5
  WALM/CURD B76 .... 79 C1
  SMTHWK B66 * 124 D1
Poplar La RMSLY B62 .... 172 C2
Poplar Ri FOAKS/STRLY B74 .. 32 B5
  OLDBY B69 .... 104 A1
  PBAR/PBCH B42 .... 74 C4
Poplar Rd ALE/KHTH/YWD B14 . 161 E2
  BDMR/CCFT WV3 .... 51 C2
  BILS/COS WV14 .... 54 B4
  BRWNH WS8 .... 9 G4
  DARL/WED WS10 .... 56 A2
  DOR/KN B93 .... 196 A5
  KGSWFD DY6 .... 100 A4
  OLDBY B69 .... 105 E1
  SMTHWK B66 .... 124 C5
  SOLH B91 .... 182 A1
  SPARK B11 .... 144 D2
  STRBR DY8 .... 135 E4
Poplars Dr CBROM B36 .... 112 D1
  CDSL WV8 .... 10 C5
The Poplars
  LDYWD/EDGR B16 * 125 H1
  STRBR DY8 .... 118 B2
Poplar St BKHL/PFLD WV2 .... 52 B2
  SMTHWK B66 .... 107 E4
Poplarwoods RIDG/WDGT B32 140 B5
Poppy Dr DSYBK/YTR WS5 .... 57 F5
Poppyfields CDYHTH B64 .... 135 H4
Poppy La ERDE/BCHGN B24 .. 93 G1
Poppymead ERDW/GRVHL B23 . 75 H3
Porchester Cl ALDR WS9 .... 19 G5
Porchester Dr LOZ/NWT B19 . 108 D3
Porchester St LOZ/NWT B19 . 108 D3
Porlock Crs NFLD/LBR B31 .. 174 D2
Porlock Rd STRBR DY8 .... 135 C1
Portal Rd WSLW WS2 .... 40 D3
Porchester Dr WNSFLD WV11 . 24 D5
Porters Cft HRBN B17 .... 124 C1
Porters Dr
  ALE/KHTH/YWD B14 .... 177 G1
Porters Fld DUDS DY2 .... 84 D5
Portersfield Rd CDYHTH B64 . 120 C4
Portershill Dr SHLY B90 .... 180 C5
Porter St DUDS DY2 .... 84 D5
Porter St South DUDS DY2 .... 84 D5
Porters Wy BORD B9 .... 128 C2

Portfield Dr TPTN/OCK DY4 .... 85 G3
Portfield Gv ERDW/GRVHL B23 . 77 E5
Porthkerry Gv SEDG DY3 .... 66 D4
Port Hope Rd SPARK B11 .... 127 C5
Porthouse Gv BILS/COS WV14 * . 53 F5
Portia Av SHLY B90 .... 180 B3
Portland Av ALDR WS9 .... 30 B5
Portland Crs HAG/WOL DY9 .. 152 D1
Portland Dr HAG/WOL DY9 .. 152 D1
  OLDBY B69 .... 86 B5
Portland Pl BILS/COS WV14 .. 68 B4
Portland Rd ALDR WS9 .... 30 B5
  LDYWD/EDGR B16 .... 125 E2
Portland St AST/WIT B6 .... 109 G2
  WSL WS1 .... 4 D1
Portland Ter WSNGN B18 .... 108 A4
Port la COVEN WV9 .... 10 D1
Portman Rd MOS/BIL B13 .... 161 F3
Portobello Cl WLNHL WV13 .. 38 C4
Portobello Rd WBROM B70 .... 70 D3
Portrush Av HWK/WKHTH B38 . 176 B4
Portrush Rd
  DUNHL/THL/PER WV6 .... 34 B1
Portsdown Cl WOLVN WV10 .. 23 H5
Portsdown Rd HALE B63 .... 154 D1
Portsea St BLOX/PEL WS3 .... 27 G4
Portswood Cl COVEN WV9 .... 22 B1
Portway Cl KGSWFD DY6 .... 100 A4
  SOLH B91 .... 181 H1
Portway HI OLDBY B69 .... 103 H5
Portway Rd BILS/COS WV14 .. 54 A1
  BLKHTH/ROWR B65 .... 103 H5
  DARL/WED WS10 .... 70 C1
  OLDBY B69 .... 104 D2
The Portway KGSWFD DY6 .. 100 A4
Posey Cl HDSW B21 .... 89 E3
Poston Cft
  ALE/KHTH/YWD B14 .... 177 H1
Potter Cl ERDW/GRVHL B23 .. 76 B3
Potters La AST/WIT B6 .... 109 E2
  DARL/WED WS10 .... 70 C1
Potterton Wy SMTHWK B66 .. 106 B1
Pottery Rd LGLYGN/QTN B68 . 123 H5
Pouk Hill Cl WSLW WS2 .... 41 E2
Poultney St WBROM B70 .... 70 D4
Poulton Cl MOS/BIL B13 .... 144 C5
Pound Cl LGLYGN/QTN B68 .. 122 D1
Pound La CSHL/WTROR B46 .. 115 C1
  RIDG/WDGT B32 .... 173 H2
Poundley Cl CBROM B36 .... 113 E1
Pound Rd ALE/KHTH/YWD B14 . 178 A4
  DARL/WED WS10 .... 56 A5
  LGLYGN/QTN B68 .... 122 D1
Pountney St BKHL/PFLD WV2 . 7 F7
Powell Av RIDG/WDGT B32 .. 140 A1
Powell Pl BILS/COS WV14 .... 54 A5
  TPTN/OCK DY4 .... 86 A1
Powells Cl CSCFLD/WYGN B72 . 77 F1
Powell St CBHAMW B1 .... 2 B3
  HALE B63 .... 138 A4
  WOLVN WV10 .... 37 H1
Power Crs
  LDYWD/EDGR B16 .... 126 A3
Power Wy TPTN/OCK DY4 .... 70 B3
Powick Pl LOZ/NWT B19 * 108 C2
Powick Rd ERDW/GRVHL B23 . 92 B5
Powis Av TPTN/OCK DY4 .... 69 H4
Powke La CDYHTH B64 .... 121 F1
Powlers Cl HAG/WOL DY9 .... 153 E5
Powlett St BKHL/PFLD WV2 .. 7 G6
Poxon Rd ALDR WS9 .... 19 G4
The Poynings
  DUNHL/THL/PER WV6 .... 21 C5
The Precinct SHHTH WV12 * .. 25 H5
Premier Ct BVILLE B30 .... 177 G2
Premier St VAUX/NECH B7 .. 110 B1
Prescot Rd HAG/WOL DY9 .. 136 A4
Prestbury Rd AST/WIT B6 .... 109 E1
Presthope Rd SLYOAK B29 .. 158 D3
Preston Av WALM/CURD B76 . 63 H5
Preston Rd
  WNSFLD WV11 .... 24 A4
Prestons Rw BILS/COS WV14 .. 53 E5
Prestwick Cl MGN/WHC B75 .. 47 G2
Prestwick Rd CVALE B35 .... 94 D2
Prestwood Av WNSFLD WV11 . 24 D2
Prestwood Dr KINVER DY7 .. 116 D4
Prestwood Rd SLYOAK B29 .. 158 D2
  WNSFLD WV11 .... 24 D3
Prestwood Rd West
  WNSFLD WV11 .... 24 B4
Pretoria Rd BORD B9 .... 128 C1
Priam Gv BLOX/PEL WS3 .... 18 B2
Price Crs BILS/COS WV14 .... 54 D5
Price Rd DARL/WED WS10 .... 56 C5
  HAG/WOL DY9 .... 137 E1
Prices Rd SEDG DY3 .... 83 E3
Price St BILS/COS WV14 .... 54 A5
  CBHAMNE B4 .... 3 G2
  DUDS DY2 .... 105 E1
  SMTHWK B66 .... 106 D4
  WBROM B70 .... 88 A3
Priestfield Cl KGSTG B44 .... 74 D1
Priestfield St BILS/COS WV14 . 53 F2
Priestland Rd BKDE/SHDE B34 . 112 D2
Priestley Cl
  BFLD/HDSWWD B20 .... 90 A5
  HALE B63 .... 137 H1
Priestley Rd SPARK B11 .... 127 C5
  WSLW WS2 .... 27 E5
Priest St CDYHTH B64 .... 121 F3
Primley Av CBROM B36 .... 111 H2
  WSLW WS2 .... 41 F5
Primrose Av SPARK B11 .... 127 F5
  TPTN/OCK DY4 .... 70 A3
  WOLVN WV10 .... 24 A4
Primrose Bank
  LGLYGN/QTN B68 .... 105 F5
Primrose Cl BLOX/PEL WS3 .... 16 A3
  CDYHTH B64 .... 120 B4
Primrose Crs DUDN DY1 .... 84 C2
Primrose Cft ERDW/GRVHL B25 . 76 A4
  HLGN/YWD B28 .... 162 C4
Primrose Gdns CDSL WV8 .... 10 C4
  HWK/WKHTH B38 .... 176 D5
Primrose HI HWK/WKHTH B38 . 176 H4
  SMTHWKW B67 .... 105 H5

STRBR DY8 .... 118 A2
  WOLVN WV10 .... 23 H2
Primrose La HLGN/YWD B28 . 162 D5
Primrose Pk BRLYHL DY5 .... 101 E2
Primrose Rd DUDS DY2 .... 102 C5
The Primroses DSYBK/YTR WS5 .. 57 H4
Primrose Woods
  RIDG/WDGT B32 .... 140 B5
Primsland Cl SHLY B90 .... 196 A1
Prince Albert St BORD B9 .... 128 B3
Prince Andrew Crs RBRY B45 . 173 C3
Prince Charles Cl RBRY B45 .. 173 G3
Prince Charles Rd
  BILS/COS WV14 .... 54 B5
Prince Edward Dr RBRY B45 . 173 G3
Prince George Rd
  DARL/WED WS10 .... 56 A3
Prince of Wales La
  ALE/KHTH/YWD B14 .... 179 E3
Princep Cl GTB/HAM B43 .... 59 H4
Prince Philip Cl RBRY B45 .... 173 G3
Prince Rd RBRY B45 .... 176 D2
Prince's Av WSL WS1 .... 5 J6
Princess Dr CDSL WV8 .... 10 C4
Princes Gdns CDSL WV8 .... 10 C4
Princes Sq BILS/COS WV14 .. 181 H1
  WBROM B70 .... 88 A4
Prince's Rd OLDBY B69 .... 85 C4
  STRBR DY8 .... 118 C4
Princess Alice Dr
  SCFLD/BOLD B73 .... 76 B1
Princess Aly WOLV WV1 .... 7 C4
Princess Anne Rd
  BILS/COS WV14 .... 54 B5
  WSLW WS2 .... 27 H5
Princess Crs HALE B63 .... 138 A1
Princess Gv HHTH/SAND B71 . 71 H4
Princess Pde WBROM B70 * .. 87 H3
Princess Rd DIG/EDG B5 .... 144 A1
  LGLYGN/QTN B68 .... 123 H2
Princess Sq BILS/COS WV14 .. 54 B5
Princess Wy DARL/WED WS10 . 40 A5
Prince St ALDR WS9 .... 19 F5
  CDYHTH B64 .... 121 E4
  DUDS DY2 .... 102 C3
  WSL WS1 .... 41 G5
Prince's Wk SOLH B91 .... 181 H2
Princethorpe Cl
  BKDE/SHDE B34 .... 113 F2
  SHLY B90 .... 180 A3
Princethorpe Rd SLYOAK B29 . 158 D1
Prince Thorpe Rd WLNHL WV13 . 39 H5
Princeton Gdns COVEN WV9 . 11 H5
Prince William Cl
  ERDW/GRVHL B23 .... 92 B4
Printing House St CBHAMNE B4 . 3 G3
Priors MI SEDG DY3 .... 67 G5
Priory Av SLYOAK B29 .... 143 F5
Priory Chambers DUDN DY1 * . 84 C5
Priory Cl CSHL/WTROR B46 * . 115 G4
  DUDN DY1 .... 84 B4
  SMTHWK B66 .... 107 E5
  WBROM B70 .... 88 B4
Priory Dr LGLYGN/QTN B68 .. 105 C4
Priory Field Cl BILS/COS WV14 . 67 H2
Priory Gdns HLGN/YWD B28 . 179 F1
Priorygate Wy BORD B9 .... 128 C1
Priory La SEDG DY3 .... 67 F4
The Priory Queensway
  CBHAMNE B4 .... 3 H4
Priory Rd ALE/KHTH/YWD B14 . 160 C3
  AST/WIT B6 .... 109 F1
  DUDN DY1 .... 84 C4
  EDG B15 .... 143 F1
  HLGN/YWD B28 .... 179 F1
  RMSLY B62 .... 137 G5
  STRBR DY8 .... 135 H4
Priory Sq CBHAMNE B4 .... 3 H5
Priory St DUDN DY1 .... 84 C5
The Priory SEDG DY3 .... 67 F5
Priory Wk CBHAMNE B4 .... 3 H4
  CSCFLD/WYGN B72 .... 77 C4
Pritchard Av WNSFLD WV11 .. 25 E4
Pritchard Cl SMTHWK B66 .. 106 D4
Pritchard St BRLYHL DY5 .... 118 D1
  DARL/WED WS10 .... 55 H5
Pritchatts Rd EDG B15 .... 142 D2
Pritchett Av
  ETTPK/GDPK/PENN WV4 .... 52 D5
Pritchett Rd NFLD/LBR B31 . 189 H1
Pritchett St AST/WIT B6 .... 3 G1
Private Wy RBRY B45 .... 188 C4
Privet Cl KGSTG B44 .... 60 A5
Proffitt Cl WSLW WS2 .... 42 A1
Proffitt St WSLW WS2 .... 42 A1
Prole St WOLVN WV10 .... 37 G1
The Promenade BRLYHL DY5 . 119 F2
Prospect Gdns STRBR DY8 .. 135 G3
Prospect HI STRBR DY8 .... 135 G3
Prospect La SOLH B91 .... 163 H5
Prospect PI BHTH/HG B12 * .. 144 B2
Prospect Rd MOS/BIL B13 .... 161 F1
  RMSLY B62 .... 122 A1
  SEDG DY3 .... 82 D4
Prospect Rw DUDS DY2 .... 102 C3
  STRBR DY8 .... 135 G4
Prospect St BILS/COS WV14 .. 54 A2
  TPTN/OCK DY4 .... 70 A3
Prosper Meadow
  KGSWFD DY6 .... 100 B2
Prospero Cl RBRY B45 .... 174 A3
Prosser St BILS/COS WV14 .... 53 H5
  WOLVN WV10 .... 37 H1
Prossers Wk
  CSHL/WTROR B46 .... 115 F2
Prouds La BILS/COS WV14 .... 53 H1
Provence Cl WOLVN WV10 .... 37 H1
Providence Cl BLOX/PEL WS3 . 27 G3
Providence Dr HAG/WOL DY9 . 136 C1
Providence La BLOX/PEL WS3 . 27 G3
Providence Rw
  BILS/COS WV14 .... 68 B3
Providence St CDYHTH B64 .. 120 D3
  HAG/WOL DY9 .... 136 C1
  TPTN/OCK DY4 .... 86 A1

Providence Ter
DARL/WED WS10 * 55 G2
Pruden Av
ETTPK/GDPK/PENN WV4....52 D5
Pryor Rd LGLYGN/QTN B68...123 C1
Pudsey Dr MGN/WHC B75.....47 G2
Pugh Crs WSLW WS2 ....40 C3
BILS/COS WV14 ....67 H1
Puglin Cl DUNHL/THL/PER WV6..54 B2
Pugh Rd AST/WIT B6 ....109 G2
Pugin Cl DUNHL/THL/PER WV6..34 B2
Pugin Gdns ERDW/GRVHL B23..76 B3
Pumphouse Wy OLDBY B69...104 D5
Pump St BKHL/PFLD WV2....53 E1
Pump Gn TPTN/OCK DY4.....85 E4
Purbeck Cl HALE B63 ....69 E2
Purbeck Cft RIDG/WDGT B32..141 F2
Purbrook Rd WOLV WV1......38 A5
Purcell Rd WOLVN WV10.....23 C2
Purdy Rd BILS/COS WV14....69 E2
Purefoy Rd BILS/COS WV14..162 A5
Purley Gv ERDW/GRVHL B23..91 G1
Purnells Whf DUDS DY2 ......121 E1
Purnells Wy DOR/KN B93....197 E3
Purslet Rd WOLV WV1 ....58 A4
Purslow Gv FILLBR B31......175 G4
Putney Av BFLD/HDSWWD B20..90 C5
Putney La RMSLY B62 ....172 D3
Putney Rd BFLD/HDSWWD B20..90 C5
Pype Hayes Cl
ERDE/BCHGN B24 ....93 H2
Pype Hayes Rd
ERDE/BCHGN B24 ....93 H2
Pytman Dr WALM/CURD B76..78 C4

Q

The Quadrangle BVILLE B30 *...159 H4
The Quadrant SEDG DY3.......67 F2
Quadrille Lawns COVEN WV9...11 H5
Quail Gn DUNHL/THL/PER WV6..34 D3
Qualcast Rd WOLV WV1.......37 H5
Quantock Cl BRWNH WS8.....19 G2
HALE B63...137 H5
RBRY B45...174 B3
Quantock Rd STRBR DY8.....135 H1
Quantry La HAG/WOL DY9.....186 A1
Quarrington Gv
ALE/KHTH/YWD B14........178 C2
Quarry Brow SEDG DY3.......83 G1
Quarry Hl HALE B63..........137 F5
Quarry House Cl RBRY B45...173 H4
Quarry La HALE B63.........138 B5
NFLD/LBR B31........175 F2
Quarry Park Rd STRBR DY8...152 C2
Quarry Ri OLDBY B69.........103 H1
Quarry Rd DUDS DY2.........120 B2
SLYOAK B29........158 B1
Quarry Wk RBRY B45.........188 A1
Quasar Centre WSL WS1......4 D3
Quayle Cv STRBR DY8........117 H1
Quayside WSNGN B18........100 A4
Quayside Cl OLDBY B69......104 C1
Quayside Dr WSLW WS2.......4 A6
Queen Eleanors Dr
DOR/KN B93........183 F5
Queen Elizabeth Av WSLW WS2..40 D3
Queen Elizabeth Rd RBRY B45..173 G3
Queen Mary St WSL WS1......56 D2
Queens Ar WOLV WV1 ....7 F4
Queens Av
ALE/KHTH/YWD B14 *.....161 E2
OLDBY B69........85 H5
SHLY B90........180 B3
WSNGN B18........100 C4
Queensbridge Rd MOS/BIL B13..143 H5
Queens Cl ERDE/BCHGN B24...92 D4
SMTHWKW B67........106 C4
Queens Ct RIDG/WDGT B32...140 A5
STRBR DY8........118 C5
Queens Crs BILS/COS WV14...68 A2
Queens Dr BLKHTH/ROWR B65..104 B5
BVILLE B30........177 E1
DIG/EDG B5........3 G6
Queens Gdns BILS/COS WV14..53 H1
CDSL WV8........10 B4
DUDS DY2........102 B5
ERDW/GRVHL B23........92 A3
Queens Head Rd HDSW B21...107 G2
Queens Hospital Cl EDG B15...126 C3
Queens Lea SHHTH WV12.....26 A4
Queens Md SMTHWKW B67 *...106 C4
Queen's Park Rd
RIDG/WDGT B32........141 F1
Queen Sq WOLV WV1 ....7 F4
Queens Ride DIG/EDG B5.....143 G3
Queens Rd AST/WIT B6 ......109 G1
DSYBK/YTR WS5........57 H2
ERDW/GRVHL B23........92 A3
LGN/SDN/BHAMAIR B26...130 B3
RUSH/SHEL WS4........29 E3
SEDG DY3........67 E5
SMTHWKW B67........105 H5
STRBR DY8........135 F1
Queens Tower
VAUX/NECH B7 *........109 H4
Queen St ALDR WS9..........19 F5
BHTH/HG B12........144 D2
BILS/COS WV14........54 A3
BRLYHL DY5........120 A4
CSCFLD/WYGN B72........62 B4
HALE B63........137 H5
KGSWFD DY6........99 H2
OLDBY B69........105 E1
STRBR DY8........135 F1
TPTN/OCK DY4........69 F3
WBROM B70........87 H3
WOLV WV1........7 G4
WSLW WS2........56 A2
Queensway FOAKS/STRLY B74..45 G5
HAG/WOL DY9........136 C5
OLDBY B69........85 H5
LGLYGN/QTN B68........123 F4
Queensway Cl
LGLYGN/QTN B68........123 F4

Queensway Ml HALE B63 *...138 D4
Queenswood Rd
MGN/WHC B75........47 F4
MOS/BIL B13........144 C3
Quenby Dr DUDN DY1........84 A3
Quendale WMBN WV5........64 C5
Quentin Dr DUDN DY1........101 H2
Queslade Cl GTB/HAM B43...73 H2
Queslett Rd ERDE/BCHGN B24..92 A2
Queslett Rd East
FOAKS/STRLY B74........60 A3
Quicksand La ALDR WS9......43 H1
Quigley Av BORD B9.........127 H2
Quillets Rd STRBR DY8.......117 C1
Quilter Cl BILS/COS WV14...68 A3
WSLW WS2........40 D2
Quilter Rd ERDE/BCHGN B24..93 C1
Quincey Dr ERDE/BCHGN B24..93 C3
Quinton Ri BRLYHL DY5.......119 E5
Quinton Cl HIA/OLT B92......148 B3
Quinton Expy
RIDG/WDGT B32........140 B3
Quinton La RIDG/WDGT B32...140 D1
Quinton Rd HRBN B17........141 H4
Quinton Rd West RIDG/WDGT B32..140 B2
Quorn Crs STRBR DY8........117 C1
Quorn Gv ERDE/BCHGN B24...93 F4

R

Rabone La SMTHWK B66......106 D3
Raby Cl OLDBY B69..........103 F1
Raby St BKHL/PFLD WV2......7 H4
Racecourse La STRBR DY8...152 A1
Racecourse Rd
DUNHL/THL/PER WV6........22 C5
Racemeadow Crs DUDS DY2...120 C3
Rachael Gdns DARL/WED WS10..56 C4
Rachel Cl TPTN/OCK DY4.....70 A2
Rachel Gdns SLYOAK B29....142 B5
Radbourn Dr FOAKS/STRLY B74..62 C2
Radbourne Dr HALE B63......136 A5
Radbourne Rd SHLY B90......180 D2
Radcliffe Dr RMSLY B62......139 G1
Raddens Rd RMSLY B62......139 H4
Raddington Dr HIA/OLT B92...163 H2
Raddlebarn Farm Dr
SLYOAK B29........159 H1
Raddlebarn La SLYOAK B29...159 H1
Raddlebarn Rd SLYOAK B29...159 H1
Radford Dr RUSH/SHEL WS4...18 C5
Radford Ri SOLH B91........165 G5
Radford La SLYOAK B29......158 C3
Radley Gv SLYOAK B29......141 G5
Radley Rd HAG/WOL DY9.....136 D3
RUSH/SHEL WS4........29 E4
The Radleys STETCH B33...131 G4
Radlow Crs
CHWD/FDBR/MGN B37........132 B4
Radnor Cl RBRY B45.........174 B3
Radnor Cft DSYBK/YTR WS5...58 A5
Radnor Rd HHTH/SAND B71...71 C4
BFLD/HDSWWD B20........108 B1
LGLYGN/QTN B68........123 F5
SEDG DY3........67 E3
Radstock Av CBROM B36......111 C2
Radstock Rd SHHTH WV12...26 A1
Radway Rd SHLY B90.........195 E1
Raeburn Rd GTB/HAM B43...58 D5
Raford Rd ERDW/GRVHL B23...76 B5
Ragees Rd KGSWFD DY6......118 B1
Raglan Av
DUNHL/THL/PER WV6........34 C3
SMTHWK B66........107 E5
Raglan Cl ALDR WS9.........45 F2
SEDG DY3........66 D4
Raglan Rd BDMR/CCFT WV3...6 D4
BRLYHL DY5........143 H1
SMTHWK B66........107 E5
Raglan Wy
CHWD/FDBR/MGN B37........132 D2
Ragley Cl BLOX/PEL WS3.....27 E1
DOR/KN B93........197 F1
Ragley Dr GTB/HAM B43.....73 H1
LGN/SDN/BHAMAIR B26........148 A1
Ragnall Av STETCH B33......131 F5
Railswood Dr BLOX/PEL WS3..18 A4
Railway Cl SHMTH WV12......26 D1
Railway Dr BILS/COS WV14...54 A3
Railway St DARL/WED WS10...70 D1
PBAR/PBCH B42........87 H1
TPTN/OCK DY4........70 B2
WOLV WV1........7 H3
Railway Ter DARL/WED WS10..70 D1
Railwharf Sidings DUDS DY2..102 D5
Rainbow St BILS/COS WV14...54 A3
BKHL/PFLD WV2........52 B1
Rainham Cl TPTN/OCK DY4...84 D1
Rainsbrook Dr SHLY B90......195 F2
Rake Wy EDG B15...........2 A7
Raleigh Cft GTB/HAM B43...88 D5
Raleigh Rd BILS/COS WV14...54 B5
BORD B9........128 B2
Raleigh St HHTH/SAND B71...87 C2
Ralph Rd SHLY B90..........180 D1
WASH/WDE B8........114 B5
Ralphs Meadow
RIDG/WDGT B32........140 D5
Ralston Cl BLOX/PEL WS3...16 C3
Ramp Rd
CHWD/FDBR/MGN B37........149 C2
Ramsay Cl HHTH/SAND B71...71 C4
Ramsay Rd LGLYGN/QTN B68..123 C4
TPTN/OCK DY4........69 E4

WSLW WS2........27 E5
Ramsden Cl SLYOAK B29.....158 D3
Ramsey Cl RBRY B45.........173 C4
Ramsey Rd VAUX/NECH B7....110 A2
Randall Cl KGSWFD DY6......100 D5
Randle Dr MGN/WHC B75.....47 G2
Randle Rd HAG/WOL DY9.....136 A3
Randwick Gv KGSTG B44.....74 D2
Rangeview Cl
FOAKS/STRLY B74........60 B2
Rangeways Rd KGSWFD DY6...118 B1
Ranleigh Av KGSWFD DY6....100 D5
Rann Cl LDYWD/EDGR B16...126 A3
Rannoch Cl BRLYHL DY5......118 D4
Ranscombe Dr SEDG DY3.....83 E4
Ransom Rd ERDW/GRVHL B23..92 A2
Ranworth Ri
ETTPK/GDPK/PENN WV4........52 B4
Ratcliffe Av BVILLE B30.....177 H2
Ratcliffe Cl SEDG DY3.......67 H4
Ratcliffe Dr WLNHL WV13....39 H3
Ratcliffe Rd SOLH B91......165 E5
WNSFLD WV11........25 H1
Ratcliff Wk DARL/WED WS10 *..104 D2
Ratcliff Wy TPTN/OCK DY4...70 D3
Rathbone Cl BILS/COS WV14..53 H5
DIG/EDG B5........127 E5
Rathbone Rd SMTHWKW B67...124 B2
Rathlin Cl COVEN WV9.......12 A4
Rathlin Cft CBROM B36......114 B4
Rathmore Cl STRBR DY8......135 E5
Rathwell Cl COVEN WV9......12 A5
Rattle Cft STETCH B33......130 C1
Ravenal Cl ERDE/SHDE B34...112 D2
Raven Crs WNSFLD WV11......25 G1
Ravenfield Cl WASH/WDE B8..113 H4
Ravenhayes La
RIDG/WDGT B32........157 E4
Raven Hays Rd NFLD/LBR B31..174 C3
Ravenhill Dr CDSL WV8......10 C4
Ravenhurst Dr GTB/HAM B43..73 E1
Ravenhurst Ms
ERDW/GRVHL B23........92 C3
Ravenhurst Rd HRBN B17...125 C1
Ravenhurst St BHTH/HG B12..127 C4
Raven Rd DSYBK/YTR WS5....57 H1
Ravenscourte Gv
WLNHL WV13........40 A3
Ravenscroft STRBR DY8 *...135 E5
Ravenscroft Cl DSYBK/YTR WS5..57 H1
Ravensdale Gdns
DSYBK/YTR WS5........57 H1
Ravensdale Rd SMHTH B10...128 D5
Ravenshaw La SOLH B91......183 E1
Ravenshaw Rd
LDYWD/EDGR B16........125 E2
Ravenshaw Wy DOR/KN B93...183 E5
Ravenshill Rd
ALE/KHTH/YWD B14........179 E1
Ravensitch Wk BRLYHL DY5...119 G3
Ravenswood EDG B15.........125 G5
Ravenswood Cl
FOAKS/STRLY B74........47 F5
Ravenswood Dr SOLH B91....181 E4
Ravenswood Hl
CSHL/WTROR B46........115 F2
Rawlings Rd SMTHWKW B67...124 C2
Rawlins Cft CVALE B35......94 D3
Rawlins St LDYWD/EDGR B16..126 A3
Rayboids Bridge Rd WSLW WS2..41 G1
Rayboids Bridge St WSLW WS2..41 G1
Raybon Cft RBRY B45 *......188 C1
Raybould's Fold DUDS DY2...102 C4
Rayford Dr HHTH/SAND B71...72 B1
Ray Hall La GTB/HAM B43...72 D3
Rayleigh Rd BDMR/CCFT WV3..36 D5
Raymond Av PBAR/PBCH B42..74 B5
Raymond Cl WSLW WS2.......27 H5
Raymond Gdns WNSFLD WV11..25 E5
Raymond Rd WASH/WDE B8...114 C5
Raymont Gv GTB/HAM B43...58 D5
Rayners Cft
LGN/SDN/BHAMAIR B26........130 B2
Raynor Rd WOLVN WV10......23 H4
Rea Av RBRY B45...........173 C2
Reabrook Rd NFLD/LBR B31...175 F5
Rea Cl NFLD/LBR B31........189 C1
Readers Wk GTB/HAM B43...58 C5
Rea Fordway RBRY B45.......174 B2
Reansway Sq
DUNHL/THL/PER WV6........36 C1
Reapers Cl SHHTH WV12......26 C1
Reaside Crs
ALE/KHTH/YWD B14........160 B5
Reaside Cft BHTH/HG B12 *..144 B3
Reaside Dr RBRY B45........174 B3
Rea St DIG/EDG B5.........127 F3
Rea St South DIG/EDG B5...127 E4
Rea Ter DIG/EDG B5........3 K6
Rea Valley Dr NFLD/LBR B31..175 H5
Reaview Dr SLYOAK B29......143 F5
Reaymer Cl WSLW WS2.......27 H4
Reay Nadin Dr
SCFLD/BOLD B73........60 D4
Rebecca Dr SLYOAK B29......142 C5
Rebecca Gdns
ETTPK/GDPK/PENN WV4........50 D2
Recreation St DUDS DY2.....102 D4
Rectory Av DARL/WED WS10...55 H3
Rectory Cl STRBR DY8.......135 H4
Rectory Gdns SOLH B91......182 B2
STRBR DY8........135 H4
Rectory La CBROM B36......112 C1
Rectory Park Av
MGN/WHC B75........63 E4
Rectory Park Cl MGN/WHC B75..63 E4
Rectory Park Rd
LGN/SDN/BHAMAIR B26........148 A2
Rectory Rd MGN/WHC B75...63 E4
NFLD/LBR B31........175 H1
SOLH B91........182 A2
STRBR DY8........135 H4

Rectory St STRBR DY8........117 H1
Redacre Rd SCFLD/BOLD B73..76 D1
Redacres DUNHL/THL/PER WV6..22 A4
Redbank Av ERDW/GRVHL B23..92 A5
Redbourn Rd BLOX/PEL WS3..16 C3
Red Brick Cl CDYHTH B64...120 D5
Redbrook Covert
HWK/WKHTH B38........190 C1
Red Brook Rd WSLW WS2.....27 E5
Redbrooks Cl SOLH B91......181 G4
Redburn Dr
ALE/KHTH/YWD B14........177 H3
Redcar Cft CBROM B36......111 C1
Redcar Rd WOLVN WV10......12 D5
Redcliffe Dr WMBN WV5......65 F5
Redcotts Cl WOLVN WV10...24 A3
Redcroft Dr ERDE/BCHGN B24..93 G1
Reddal Hill Rd CDYHTH B64..121 E3
Reddicap Heath Rd
MGN/WHC B75........63 F4
Reddicap Hl WALM/CURD B76..62 D4
Reddicap Trading Est
MGN/WHC B75........63 F3
Reddings La HLGN/YWD B28...145 G5
Reddings Rd MOS/BIL B13...143 H5
The Reddings HLYWD B47....192 C5
Redditch Rd ALVE B48.......189 H5
HWK/WKHTH B38........176 C4
NFLD/LBR B31........175 H5
Redfern Cl HIA/OLT B92......164 D1
Redfern Park Wy SPARK B11...146 A2
Redfern Rd SPARK B11.......146 A2
Redfly La BRLYHL DY5.......119 E1
Redford Cl MOS/BIL B13.....144 D5
Redgate Cl HWK/WKHTH B38...176 C5
Redhall Rd RIDG/WDGT B32...140 A4
SEDG DY3........83 E4
Redhill Av WMBN WV5.......65 H5
Redhill Cl STRBR DY8........135 H3
Redhill Gdns NFLD/LBR B31...190 A1
Red Hill Gv HWK/WKHTH B38...190 D1
Redhill La BRGRVW B61......187 E5
Redhill Rd HWK/WKHTH B38...190 B1
NFLD/LBR B31........175 H5
YDLY B25........129 H3
Red Hill St WOLV WV1........7 F1
Red House Av DARL/WED WS10..56 B5
Red House Cl HALE B63.......137 C5
Red House La WALM/CURD B76..79 G5
Red House Park Rd
GTB/HAM B43........73 G1
Redhouse Rd
DUNHL/THL/PER WV6........21 F5
Red House Rd STETCH B33...130 A1
Redhurst Dr WOLVN WV10...12 B4
Redlake Rd HAG/WOL DY9...152 D1
Redlands Cl SOLH B91.......165 F5
Redlands Rd SOLH B91......165 F5
Redliff Av CBROM B36.......95 F5
Red Lion Cl OLDBY B69......85 G5
Red Lion St WOLV WV1......6 E2
Redmead Cl NFLD/LBR B31...176 A1
Redmoor Gdns
ETTPK/GDPK/PENN WV4........51 G3
Rednal Hill La RBRY B45....188 A2
Rednall Dr MGN/WHC B75....47 G2
Rednal Mill Dr RBRY B45....188 C1
Rednal Rd HWK/WKHTH B38...176 A5
Redpine Crest SHHTH WV12...40 D1
Red River Rd WSLW WS2......41 E1
Red Rock Dr CDSL WV8......10 B5
Redruth Cl DSYBK/YTR WS5...58 B1
KGSWFD DY6........99 H1
Redruth Rd DSYBK/YTR WS5...58 B1
Redstone Dr WNSFLD WV11...25 F5
Redstone Farm Rd
HLGN/YWD B28........163 F4
Redthorn Gv STETCH B33...129 H1
Redvers Rd BORD B9.........128 C5
Redwing Gv ERDW/GRVHL B23..91 H1
Redwood Cl BVILLE B30......176 C1
FOAKS/STRLY B74........45 F3
Redwood Cft
ALE/KHTH/YWD B14........161 G3
Redwood Dr OLDBY B69......85 H4
Redwood Gdns ACGN B27....146 A3
Redwood Rd BILS/COS WV14...68 B3
BVILLE B30........176 C1
DSYBK/YTR WS5........58 B1
Redwood Wy SHHTH WV12...25 H2
Reedham Gdns
ETTPK/GDPK/PENN WV4........50 D2
Reedly Rd SHHTH WV12......26 B1
Reedmace Cl
HWK/WKHTH B38........176 D5
Reedswood Cl WSLW WS2.....41 G2
Reedswood Gdns WSLW WS2...41 G2
Reedswood La WSLW WS2.....41 G2
Reedswood Wy WSLW WS2.....41 G1
Rees Dr WMBN WV5..........65 F4
Reeves Cl TPTN/OCK DY4....85 H5
Reeves Gdns CDSL WV8......10 C3
Reeves Rd
ALE/KHTH/YWD B14........160 C4
Reeves St BLOX/PEL WS3....27 F2
Reflex Cl SHHTH WV12......26 D1
Reform St WBROM B70.......87 G3
Regal Cft CBROM B36.......111 F1
Regal Dr WSLW WS2.........41 H2
Regan Av SHLY B90.........180 A4
Regan Crs ERDW/GRVHL B23...92 B2
Regan Dr OLDBY B69........104 B1
Regency Cl BORD B9........128 B3
Regency Ct WSL WS1........57 G1
Regency Dr HWK/WKHTH B38...176 C4
Regency Gdns
ALE/KHTH/YWD B14........179 E2
Regent Av LGLYGN/QTN B68...85 G5
Regent Cl BILS/COS WV14...69 G1
DIG/EDG B5........143 H1
HALE B63........138 C5

KGSWFD DY6........99 G3
Regent Dr OLDBY B69........103 G1
Regent Gv WSLW WS2........85 G5
Regent Park Rd SMHTH B10...128 A4
Regent Pl CBHAMW B1........2 C2
OLDBY B69........85 H4
Regent Rd
ETTPK/GDPK/PENN WV4........51 E3
HDSW B21........107 F1
HRBN B17........142 A1
OLDBY B69........85 G5
Regents Cl BKHL/PFLD WV2 *..7 F6
Regent St BILS/COS WV14...53 H2
BVILLE B30........160 A3
CBHAMW B1........2 C2
CDYHTH B64........121 F2
DUDN DY1........84 C3
SMTHWK B66........106 C3
TPTN/OCK DY4........69 E5
WLNHL WV13........39 G2
Regents Wy MGN/WHC B75...63 E3
Regina Av KGSTG B44.......74 D3
Regina Cl RBRY B45........173 G4
Regina Crs
DUNHL/THL/PER WV6........35 F1
Regina Dr PBAR/PBCH B42...90 C3
RUSH/SHEL WS4........42 C1
Reginald Rd SMTHWKW B67...124 B2
WASH/WDE B8........110 B5
Regis Beeches
DUNHL/THL/PER WV6 *........21 G5
Regis Gdns
BLKHTH/ROWR B65........122 A3
Regis Heath Rd
BLKHTH/ROWR B65........122 B2
Regis Rd BLKHTH/ROWR B65...122 A2
DUNHL/THL/PER WV6........21 F5
Reid Av SHHTH WV12.......26 B4
Reid Rd LGLYGN/QTN D68...123 G5
Reigate Av WASH/WDE B8...111 G5
Relko Dr CBROM B36.......111 G2
Remembrance Rd
DARL/WED WS10........56 C5
Remington Pl WSLW WS2....27 F4
Remington Rd WSLW WS2....27 F4
Renfrew Cl STRBR DY8......117 G1
Renfrew Sq CVALE B35......94 D2
Rennie Gv RIDG/WDGT B32...140 D2
Rennison Dr WMBN WV5......65 E5
Renown Cl BRLYHL DY5......100 D2
Renton Gv WOLVN WV10.....22 C1
Renton Rd WOLVN WV10.....22 C1
Repington Wy MGN/WHC B75...63 H5
Repton Av
DUNHL/THL/PER WV6........34 B2
Repton Dr COVEN WV9......13 G1
Repton Gv BORD B9........129 F1
Reservoir Cl WSLW WS2.....41 F5
Reservoir Pas DARL/WED WS10..55 H5
Reservoir Retreat
LDYWD/EDGR B16........125 H3
Reservoir Rd
BLKHTH/ROWR B65........122 B1
ERDW/GRVHL B23........92 B2
HALE B63........137 G2
LDYWD/EDGR B16........125 H2
LGLYGN/QTN B68........105 G5
RBRY B45........188 C5
SLYOAK B29........142 A4
Retallack Cl SMTHWK B66...106 D1
Retford Dr WALM/CURD B76...63 E4
Retford Gv YDLY B25.......146 C1
Retreat Gdns SEDG DY3.....67 G4
The Retreat CDYHTH B64...121 E5
Revesby Wk VAUX/NECH B7...109 G5
Revival St BLOX/PEL WS3...27 F1
Reynards Cl SEDG DY3......68 A4
Reynolds Cl SEDG DY3......80 C5
Reynolds Cv
DUNHL/THL/PER WV6........20 D5
Reynolds Rd HDSW B21......107 G2
Reynoldstown Rd
CBROM B36........111 G1
Reynolds Wk WNSFLD WV11...25 G2
Rhayader Rd NFLD/LBR B31...158 A5
Rhodes Cl SEDG DY3........82 C2
Rhone Cl SPARK B11........145 G5
Rhys Thomas Cl SHHTH WV12..40 D1
Rian Ct CDYHTH B64.......120 D4
Ribbesford Av WOLVN WV10...22 D2
Ribbesford Cl HALE B63.....137 H2
Ribbesford Crs BILS/COS WV14..68 B1
Ribblesdale Rd BVILLE B30...160 A3
Richard Pl DSYBK/YTR WS5...43 E5
Richards Cl
BLKHTH/ROWR B65........104 C5
NFLD/LBR B31........189 F2
Richardson Dr STRBR DY8...118 A4
Richards Rd TPTN/OCK DY4...69 F2
Richard St DARL/WED WS10...55 H5
Richard St VAUX/NECH B7...109 F4
WBROM B70........87 F3
Richard St West WBROM B70..87 F3
Richard Watts Dr
DARL/WED WS10........55 H3
Richard Williams Rd
DARL/WED WS10........71 F1
Richborough Dr DUDN DY1...83 G3
Riches St DUNHL/THL/PER WV6..36 B2
Richford Gv STETCH B33...131 F2
Richmond Aston Dr
TPTN/OCK DY4........85 G3
Richmond Av BDMR/CCFT WV3..36 B4
BHTH/HG B12 *........144 B2
Richmond Cl
BFLD/HDSWWD B20........90 A4
HDSW B21........107 F1
Richmond Cft PBAR/PBCH B42..73 H5
Richmond Dr
DUNHL/THL/PER WV6........34 D2
MGN/WHC B75........63 G2
Richmond Gdns WMBN WV5...81 E1
Richmond Gv STRBR DY8....118 A4
Richmond Hl LGLYGN/QTN B68..105 G5
Richmond Hill Gdns EDG B15..142 C1

Richmond Hill Rd *EDG* B15.... 142 D1
Richmond Pk *KGSWFD* DY6.... 99 G1
Richmond Pl
ALE/KHTH/YWD B14.... 161 F2
Richmond Rd
BDMR/CCFT WV3.... 36 A4
DUDN DY1.... 102 B1
HIA/OLT B92.... 147 E5
HLYWD B47.... 193 E1
RBRY B45.... 187 G1
SCFLD/BOLD B73.... 62 A2
SEDG DY5.... 67 G4
SMTHWK B66.... 124 C2
STETCH B33.... 129 H2
WSNGN B18.... 108 B3
Richmond St *HALE* B63.... 138 C5
WBROM B70.... 86 C1
WSL WS1.... 5 G5
Richmond St South
WBROM B70.... 86 C1
Richmond Wy
CHWD/FDBR/MGN B37.... 132 C1
Rickard Cl *DOR/KN* B93.... 196 C3
Rickman Dr *EDG* B15.... 126 D4
Rickyard Cl *SLYOAK* B29.... 158 C4
YDLY B25.... 129 H3
Rickyard Piece
RIDG/WDGT B32.... 141 E3
Riddfield Rd *CBROM* B36.... 112 A1
Ridding La *WALM/CURD* WS10.. 70 D1
Riddings Crs *BLOX/PEL* WS3.... 17 H3
The Riddings *HAG/WOL* DY9.136 B5
STETCH B33.... 112 A5
WALM/CURD B76.... 70 D3
WOLVN WV10.... 24 A3
Ridgacre La *RIDG/WDGT* B32.. 140 C2
Ridgacre Rd *HHTH/SAND* B71.. 71 F5
RIDG/WDGT B32.... 140 B1
Ridgacre Rd West
RIDG/WDGT B32.... 140 A1
WSLW WS2.... 47 H5
Ridgefield Rd *RMSLY* B62.... 122 A4
Ridge Gv *HAG/WOL* DY9.... 136 A2
Ridge La *WNSFLD* WV11.... 24 D3
Ridgemount Dr
HWK/WKHTH B38.... 190 B1
Ridge Rd *KGSWFD* DY6.... 99 G4
Ridge St *STRBR* DY8.... 134 C1
Ridgewater Cl *RBRY* B45.... 188 B2
Ridge Wy *ALDR* WS9.... 31 E1
Riding Wy *SHHTH* WV12.... 26 A1
Ridley St *CBHAMW* B1.... 126 C3
Ridpool Rd *STETCH* B33.... 130 D1
Rifle St *BILS/COS* WV14.... 68 A3
Rigby St *DARL/WED* WS10.... 70 D2
Riland Rd *MGN/WHC* B75.... 48 A2
Riley Crs *BDMR/CCFT* WV3.... 51 G2
Riley Dr *CBROM* B36.... 96 A5
Riley Rd *ALE/KHTH/YWD* B14... 179 F2
Riley St *WLNHL* WV13.... 39 H5
Rilstone Rd *RIDG/WDGT* B32.. 141 F2
Rindleford Av
ETTPK/GDPK/PENN WV4.... 50 C4
Ringhills Rd *CDSL* WV8.... 10 C5
Ringinglow Rd *KGSTG* B44.... 74 C1
Ringmere Av *CBROM* B36.... 112 D1
Ring Rd North *EDG* B15.... 142 D3
Ring Road St Andrews
WOLV WV1.... 6 D4
Ring Road St Davids
WOLV WV1.... 7 H3
Ring Road St Georges
BKHL/PFLD WV2.... 7 G6
Ring Road St Johns
BKHL/PFLD WV2.... 6 E6
Ring Road St Marks
WOLV WV1.... 7 G2
Ring Rd South *EDG* B15.... 142 D4
Ringswood Rd *HIA/OLT* B92... 147 E5
The Ring *YDLY* B25.... 129 G4
Ringwood Av *ALDR* WS9.... 30 B5
Ringwood Dr *RBRY* B45.... 174 A4
Ringwood Rd *WOLVN* WV10... 23 F1
Ripley Cl *OLDBY* B69.... 103 F1
Ripley Gv *ERDW/GRVHL* B23.. 91 H1
Ripon Dr *HHTH/SAND* B71.... 71 H4
Ripon Rd *ALE/KHTH/YWD* B14... 179 E1
WOLVN WV10.... 23 E3
WSL WS2.... 41 F3
Rippingille Rd *GTB/HAM* B43... 59 G4
Ripple Rd *BVILLE* B30.... 160 B5
Rischale Wy *RUSH/SHEL* WS4... 29 E2
Rise Av *RBRY* B45.... 188 A1
Riseley Crs *DIG/EDG* B5.... 143 H1
The Rise *ALVE* B48.... 189 H4
CHWD/FDBR/MGN B37.... 132 A5
KGSWFD DY6.... 100 A4
PBAR/PBCH B42.... 74 A3
Rising Brook
DUNHL/THL/PER WV6.... 35 F1
Rissington Av *SLYOAK* B29... 160 A2
Ritchie Cl *MOS/BIL* B13.... 161 C1
Rivendell Gdns
DUNHL/THL/PER WV6.... 21 F5
Riverbank Rd *WLNHL* WV13... 40 B3
River Brook Dr *BVILLE* B30.... 160 B3
River Lee Rd *SPARK* B11 *.... 145 G2
Rivermead Pk
BKDE/SHDE B34.... 112 C4

Riversdale Rd
ALE/KHTH/YWD B14.... 179 F2
Riverside Cr *HWK/WKHTH* B38 .176 B2
Riverside Crs *HLGN/YWD* B28 ..179 F1
Riverside Dr *SOLH* B91.... 182 C3
SPARK B11.... 111 H5
Riverside Gdns *CDSL* WV8..... 10 D2
Riversleigh Dr *STRBR* DY8.... 118 A4
River St *DIG/EDG* B5.... 127 G2
River Wk *DARL/WED* WS10.... 71 E2
Riverway *DARL/WED* WS10.... 71 H1
Rivington Ct *STRBR* DY8.... 135 E3
Rivington Crs *KGSTG* B44.... 76 A2
Roach Cl *BRLYHL* DY5.... 101 F4
CHWD/FDBR/MGN B37.... 132 C1
Roach Crs *WNSFLD* WV11 *... 25 F2
Roach Pool Cft
LDYWD/EDGR B16.... 125 E2
Robert Av *ERDW/GRVHL* B23.. 76 C5
Robert Rd *BFLD/HDSWWD* B20.. 90 B5
TPTN/OCK DY4.... 69 F5
Roberts Cl *ALDR* WS9.... 19 F5
Roberts Green Rd *SEDG* DY5.. 83 G2
Roberts La *HAG/WOL* DY9.... 152 D2
Roberts Knoll *CBROM* B36.... 112 B2
Robertsons Gdns
VAUX/NECH B7.... 110 A2
Roberts Rd *ACGN* B27.... 146 C1
BLOX/PEL WS3.... 28 B5
DARL/WED WS10.... 57 E5
Robert St *SEDG* DY3.... 83 G2
Robert Wynd *BILS/COS* WV14... 67 H2
Robeson Cl *TPTN/OCK* DY4.... 84 D1
Robin Cl *CBROM* B36.... 114 A1
KGSWFD DY6.... 100 C3
Robin Gv *WNSFLD* WV11.... 24 C3
Robin Hood Crs
HLGN/YWD B28.... 162 C3
Robin Hood Cft
HLGN/YWD B28.... 162 D5
Robin Hood La
HLGN/YWD B28.... 162 C3
Robin Hood Rd *BRLYHL* DY5 ..119 H2
Robin Rd *ERDW/GRVHL* B23.... 92 C2
Robin's Cl *STRBR* DY8.... 135 C4
Robinsfield Dr *NFLD/LBR* B31.. 189 C1
Robinson's Wy
WALM/CURD B76.... 95 F1
Robottom Cl *WSLW* WS2.... 27 F4
Rocester Av *WNSFLD* WV11.... 25 E3
Rochdale Wk *SMHTH* B10.... 128 A5
Roche Rd *BLOX/PEL* WS3.... 26 D1
Rochester Cft *WSL* WS2.... 41 E1
Rochester Rd *NFLD/LBR* B31.. 175 C1
Roche Wy *BLOX/PEL* WS3.... 26 D1
Rochford Cl *HALE* B63.... 138 B5
RBRY B45.... 187 G1
WALM/CURD B76.... 78 C3
WSLW WS2.... 56 C1
Rochford Gv
ETTPK/GDPK/PENN WV4.... 50 D3
Rock Av *RBRY* B45.... 188 C1
Rocket Pool Dr *BILS/COS* WV14.. 69 C1
Rockford Rd *PBAR/PBCH* B42.. 74 A4
Rock Gv *HIA/OLT* B92.... 147 E4
Rockingham Cl
BLOX/PEL WS3 *.... 27 F1
DOR/KN B93.... 198 B1
SEDG DY3.... 82 D3
Rockingham Dr
DUNHL/THL/PER WV6.... 34 C2
Rockingham Gdns
FOAKS/STRLY B74.... 62 B2
Rockingham Hall Gdns
HAG/WOL DY9.... 153 F3
Rockingham Rd *YDLY* B25.... 129 H4
Rockland Dr *STETCH* B33.... 112 A5
Rockland Gdns *WLNHL* WV13.. 39 F5
Rocklands Dr *MGN/WHC* B75.. 47 F5
Rockley Gv *RBRY* B45.... 188 B1
Rockley Rd
BLKHTH/ROWR B65.... 103 C3
Rockmead Av *KGSTG* B44.... 75 F1
Rockmoor Cl
CHWD/FDBR/MGN B37.... 131 C1
Rock Rd *BILS/COS* WV14.... 67 H3
Rock St *SEDG* DY3.... 83 G1
The Rock *DUNHL/THL/PER* WV6.. 21 H5
Rockville Rd *WASH/WDE* B8... 111 E5
Rockwood Rd *ACGN* B27.... 146 B3
Rocky La *AST/WIT* B6.... 109 G5
PBAR/PBCH B42.... 74 C3
Rodborough Rd *DOR/KN* B93.. 198 C1
Rodbourne Rd *HRBN* B17.... 142 A4
Roddis Ct *ERDW/GRVHL* B23.. 76 B3
Roderick Dr *WNSFLD* WV11.... 24 D3
Roderick Rd *SPARK* B11.... 145 E2
Rodlington Av *KGSTG* B44.... 75 E1
Rodman Cl *EDG* B15.... 125 F4
Rodney Cl *HIA/OLT* B92 *.... 164 D1
LDYWD/EDGR B16.... 126 A2
Rodney Rd *HIA/OLT* B92.... 164 D1
Rodway Cl *BRLYHL* DY5.... 119 G4
ETTPK/GDPK/PENN WV4.... 52 B5
LOZ/NWT B19.... 108 D2
Rodwell Gv *KGSTG* B44.... 75 F3
Roebuck Cl *BKDE/SHDE* B34.. 113 C5
Roebuck Gld *SHHTH* WV12.... 40 C1
Roebuck La *SMTHWK* B66.... 106 B2
WBROM B70.... 88 A5
Roebuck Pl *BLOX/PEL* WS3.... 28 A4
Roebuck St *WBROM* B70.... 88 B5
Roedean Cl *KGSTG* B44.... 75 H4
Roford Ct *SEDG* DY3.... 83 C1
Rogerfield Rd
ERDW/GRVHL B23.... 77 E5
Rogers Cl *WNSFLD* WV11.... 25 G1
Rogers Rd *WASH/WDE* B8.... 111 F4
Rokeby Cl *WALM/CURD* B76... 63 E4
Rokeby Rd *GTB/HAM* B43.... 73 H1
Rokewood Cl *KGSWFD* DY6... 81 H5
Rolan Dr *SHLY* B90.... 179 C5
Roland Rd *LOZ/NWT* B19.... 108 C1
Roland Vernon Wy
TPTN/OCK DY4.... 70 A4
Rolfe St *SMTHWK* B66.... 106 C3

Rollason Rd *DUDS* DY2.... 102 D1
ERDE/BCHGN B24.... 93 E3
Rollesby Dr *WLNHL* WV13.... 39 F5
Rolling Mill Cl *DIG/EDG* B5 *.. 127 E5
Rolling Mill Rd *CNCK/NC* WS11.. 8 A1
Rollingmill St *WSLW* WS2.... 4 A5
Rollswood Dr *SOLH* B91.... 181 F1
Roman Cl *BRWNH* WS8.... 9 E2
Roman Gra *FOAKS/STRLY* B74.. 32 A5
Roman La *FOAKS/STRLY* B74.... 46 A2
Roman Pk *FOAKS/STRLY* B74... 45 H1
Roman Rd *FOAKS/STRLY* B74... 46 A2
STRBR DY8.... 134 D3
Roman Wy
BLKHTH/ROWR B65.... 122 A1
CSHL/WTROR B46.... 97 E4
EDG B15.... 142 B4
Romany Rd *RBRY* B45.... 173 F4
Romany Wy *STRBR* DY8.... 134 C4
Roma Rd *SPARK* B11.... 145 G2
Romford Cl
LGN/SDN/BHAMAIR B26.... 147 H1
Romilly Av *BFLD/HDSWWD* B20.. 90 B4
Romilly Cl *STRBR* DY8.... 117 F4
WALM/CURD B76.... 63 C4
Romney Cl *HLGN/YWD* B28... 162 D3
Romney Wy *GTB/HAM* B43.... 59 H4
Romsey Rd *WOLVN* WV10.... 12 C4
Romsey Wy *WOLVN* WV10.... 12 C4
Romsey Wy *BLOX/PEL* WS3.... 16 B4
Romsley Cl *HALE* B63.... 138 D5
RBRY B45.... 173 G5
RUSH/SHEL WS4.... 30 A2
Romsley Rd *HAG/WOL* DY9.. 136 A2
LGLYGN/QTN B68.... 123 F2
RIDG/WDGT B32.... 157 F2
Romulus Cl
BFLD/HDSWWD B20.... 90 B3
Ronald Gv *CBROM* B36.... 95 F5
Ronald Pl *BORD* B9.... 128 C2
Ronald Rd *BORD* B9.... 128 B2
Ron Davis Cl *SMTHWK* B66 *.. 106 D4
Rood End Rd
LGLYGN/QTN B68.... 105 C3
Rooker Av *BKHL/PFLD* WV2.... 52 C2
Rooker Crs *BKHL/PFLD* WV2.. 52 D2
Rookery Av *BRLYHL* DY5.... 118 C2
ETTPK/GDPK/PENN WV4.... 53 E5
Rookery La *BKHL/PFLD* WV2.... 51 G2
Rookery Pk *BRLYHL* DY5.... 100 D4
Rookery Rd *WMBN* WV5.... 65 F5
Rookery Rd
ETTPK/GDPK/PENN WV4.... 53 E5
HDSW B21.... 89 G5
SLYOAK B29.... 142 D5
WMBN WV5.... 65 F5
Rookery St *WNSFLD* WV11.... 24 C5
The Rookery *RMSLY* B62.... 140 A5
Rooks Meadow *HAG/WOL* DY9..152 D4
Rookwood Dr
DUNHL/THL/PER WV6.... 34 C4
Rooth St *DARL/WED* WS10.... 56 B4
Roper Wy *SEDG* DY3.... 67 H5
Rosafield Av *RMSLY* B62.... 139 H4
Rosalind Av *DUDN* DY1.... 68 B5
Rosalind Gv *WNSFLD* WV11... 25 G5
Rosamond St *WSL* WS1.... 56 D1
Rosary Rd *ERDW/GRVHL* B23.. 92 B4
Rosary Vls *SPARK* B11 *.... 145 G2
Rose Av *KGSWFD* DY6.... 100 D4
LGLYGN/QTN B68.... 123 C5
Rose Bank Dr *BLOX/PEL* WS3 *.. 42 A1
Rosebay Av *HWK/WKHTH* B38..176 D5
Roseberry Rd *SMTHWK* B66... 124 A1
Rosebery St *BDMR/CCFT* WV3.. 6 C6
WSNGN B18.... 108 A5
Rosebury Gv *WMBN* WV5.... 64 C5
Rose Cl *SMTHWK* B66.... 107 E4
Rose Cottage Dr *STRBR* DY8...117 H1
Rose Cottages *SLYOAK* B29 *..142 D5
Rosecroft Rd
LGN/SDN/BHAMAIR B26.... 148 A1
Rosedale Av *ERDW/GRVHL* B23.. 92 C5
SMTHWK B66.... 107 E4
Rosedale Gv *YDLY* B25.... 129 G4
Rosedale Pl *WLNHL* WV13.... 39 G5
Rosedene Dr
BFLD/HDSWWD B20.... 89 H4
Rose Dr *BRWNH* WS8.... 19 E2
Rosefield Ct *SMTHWK* B66.... 107 F2
Rosefield Rd *SMTHWKW* B67.. 106 D5
Rosefield St *SOLH* B91.... 181 F4
Rose Hi *BRLYHL* DY5.... 119 G5
RBRY B45.... 188 A4
WLNHL WV13.... 39 G4
Rose Hill Cl *CBROM* B36.... 112 D1
Rose Hill Gdns *WLNHL* WV13... 39 G4
Rose Hill Rd *HDSW* B21.... 108 A2
Roseship Cl *DSYBK/YTR* WS5... 57 C5
Roseland Av *EDG* B15.... 85 F5
Roseland Wy *EDG* B15.... 126 B3
Roseleigh Rd *RBRY* B45.... 188 B2
Rosemary Av *BILS/COS* WV14... 54 B2
ETTPK/GDPK/PENN WV4.... 52 A3
Rosemary Crs *BRWNH* WS8... 18 D1
Rosemary Crs *WNSFLD* WV11... 25 F5
Rosemary Crs *DUDN* DY1.... 67 H5
ETTPK/GDPK/PENN WV4.... 52 A3
Rosemary Crs West
ETTPK/GDPK/PENN WV4.... 51 H3
Rosemary Dr *FOAKS/STRLY* B74.. 46 A3
Rosemary Hill Rd
FOAKS/STRLY B74.... 46 A3
Rosemary La *STRBR* DY8.... 134 D4
Rosemary Nook
FOAKS/STRLY B74.... 32 B5
Rosemary Rd *HALE* B63.... 137 H5
STETCH B33.... 130 B2
TPTN/OCK DY4.... 85 G5
Rosemoor Dr *BRLYHL* DY5.... 118 C5
Rose Rd *CSHL/WTROR* B46.... 115 F1
HRBN B17.... 142 B1
Rose St *BILS/COS* WV14.... 69 F1
Rose Vls *RBRY* B45 *.... 129 E5
Roseville Gdns *CDSL* WV8.... 10 B5
Roseville Prec *BILS/COS* WV14 *.. 68 C5
Rosewood Dr
ERDW/GRVHL B23.... 92 B4
SHHTH WV12.... 25 H2
Rosewood Gdns *WNSFLD* WV11.. 15 F4

Rosewood Rd *DUDN* DY1.... 84 B1
Roshven Rd *BHTH/HG* B12.... 144 C3
Roslin Gv *LOZ/NWT* B19.... 108 C2
Roslyn Cl *SMTHWK* B66.... 106 C5
Ross *BLKHTH/ROWR* B65.... 103 H4
Ross Cl *BDMR/CCFT* WV3.... 36 A5
Ross Dr *KGSWFD* DY6.... 99 G2
Rosse Ct *HIA/OLT* B92.... 165 H2
Rossendale Cl *HALE* B63.... 137 H1
Ross Hts *BLKHTH/ROWR* B65.. 121 H1
Rosslyn Rd *WALM/CURD* B76.. 78 B5
Ross Rd *BLOX/PEL* WS3.... 28 A5
Rostrevor Rd *SMHTH* B10.... 128 D3
Rotherby Gv
CHWD/FDBR/MGN B37.... 132 B5
Rotherfield Rd
LGN/SDN/BHAMAIR B26.... 130 D4
Rothesay Cft *RIDG/WDGT* B32..157 F3
Rothesay Dr *STRBR* DY8.... 117 G1
Rothesay Gdns
ETTPK/GDPK/PENN WV4.... 52 C3
Rothesay Wy *SHHTH* WV12.... 25 H4
Rothwell Dr *SOLH* B91.... 180 D1
Rotten Park Rd
LDYWD/EDGR B16.... 125 H1
Rotton Park St *WSNGN* B18 *... 55 E1
Rough Hay Pl *DARL/WED* WS10.. 55 E1
Rough Hay Rd
DARL/WED WS10.... 55 E1
Rough Hills Rd *BKHL/PFLD* WV2.. 52 D2
Roughlea Av *CBROM* B36.... 112 B2
Roughley Dr *MGN/WHC* B75... 47 C3
Roughley Farm Rd
MGN/WHC B75.... 48 A2
Rough Rd *KGSTG* B44.... 60 C5
Rouncil La *HIA/OLT* B92.... 165 F3
The Roundabout
NFLD/LBR B31.... 174 D4
Round Cft *WLNHL* WV13.... 39 F5
Round Hl *SEDG* DY3.... 67 F1
Round Hill Av *HAG/WOL* DY9...153 E1
Roundhill Cl *WALM/CURD* B76.. 63 E4
Roundhill Ter *RMSLY* B62.... 122 D4
Roundhill Wy *BRWNH* WS8.... 9 G2
Round House Rd *SEDG* DY3.... 83 G2
Roundlea Cl *SHHTH* WV12.... 25 H3
Roundlea Rd *NFLD/LBR* B31... 158 A4
Round Rd *ERDE/BCHGN* B24.... 93 F4
Round Saw Cft *RBRY* B45.... 173 H5
Rounds Green Rd *OLDBY* B69..104 D4
Rounds Hill Rd *BILS/COS* WV14.. 68 D5
Rounds Rd *BILS/COS* WV14.... 53 H5
Round St *DUDS* DY2.... 102 C3
Roundway Down
DUNHL/THL/PER WV6.... 34 C2
Rousay Cl *RBRY* B45.... 173 H4
Rousdon Gv *GTB/HAM* B43.... 73 F3
Rover Dr *ACGN* B27.... 146 D3
CBROM B36.... 95 H5
Rowallan Rd *MGN/WHC* B75... 48 B1
Rowan Cl *HLYWD* B47.... 192 D5
WALM/CURD B76.... 78 B1
Rowan Ct *BVILLE* B30.... 177 E3
SMTHWKW B67 *.... 105 C5
Rowan Crs *BDMR/CCFT* WV3.. 51 E1
BILS/COS WV14.... 68 B2
WNSFLD WV11.... 15 F4
Rowan Ri *KGSWFD* DY6.... 100 A3
Rowan Rd *SCFLD/BOLD* B73... 61 C1
DSYBK/YTR WS5.... 57 F4
SEDG DY3.... 67 H2
Rowantrees *RBRY* B45.... 188 B3
Rowan Wy
CHWD/FDBR/MGN B37.... 132 C3
NFLD/LBR B31.... 189 E3
Roway La *OLDBY* B69.... 86 D5
Rowbrook Cl *SHLY* B90.... 179 C5
Rowchester Ct *CBHAMNE* B4 *... 3 G3
Rowcroft Covert
ALE/KHTH/YWD B14.... 177 G2
Rowdale Rd *PBAR/PBCH* B42.. 74 C4
Rowden Dr *ERDW/GRVHL* B23.. 77 E5
SOLH B91.... 181 E5
Rowena Gdns *SEDG* DY3.... 67 E1
Rowheath Rd *BVILLE* B30.... 176 D1
Rowington Av
BLKHTH/ROWR B65.... 122 B1
Rowington Rd
BKDE/SHDE B34.... 96 B4
Rowington Ter *YDLY* B25 *.... 129 F5
Rowland Gdns *WSLW* WS2.... 42 A3
Rowley Gv *STETCH* B33.... 131 E1
Rowley Hall Av
BLKHTH/ROWR B65.... 122 A1
Rowley Pl *RUSH/SHEL* WS4.... 28 D3
Rowley Rd *BILS/COS* WV14.... 54 C5
DARL/WED WS10.... 55 E4
WBROM B70.... 87 F3
Rowley Village
BLKHTH/ROWR B65.... 122 A1
Rowney Cft *HLGN/YWD* B28... 179 G1
Rowood Dr *HIA/OLT* B92.... 165 E3
Rowthorn Cl *FOAKS/STRLY* B74.. 46 C1
Rowthorn Dr *SHLY* B90.... 195 C3
Rowton Av
DUNHL/THL/PER WV6.... 34 C2
Rowton Dr *FOAKS/STRLY* B74.. 60 B3
Roxall Cl *KIDD* DY10.... 168 C3
Roxburgh Gv *GTB/HAM* B43.. 59 G4
Roxburgh Rd *SCFLD/BOLD* B73.. 62 A4
Roxby Gdns
DUNHL/THL/PER WV6.... 22 C5
Royal Cl *BLKHTH/ROWR* B65... 104 A4
BRLYHL DY5.... 119 E4

Royal Gv *ERDW/GRVHL* B23.... 75 H4
Royal Mail St *CBHAMW* B1.... 2 E6
Royal Oak Rd
BLKHTH/ROWR B65.... 103 F4
RMSLY B62.... 139 H5
Royal Scot Gv *WSL* WS1.... 56 D3
Royal Scot Gv *WSL* WS1.... 56 D3
Royal Star Cl *STETCH* B33.... 131 E2
Royal Wy *TPTN/OCK* DY4.... 85 G4
Roydon Rd *ACGN* B27.... 163 G2
Royden Crs
SCFLD/BOLD B73.... 76 A1
Royston Cha *FOAKS/STRLY* B74.. 45 G2
Royston Cft *BHTH/HG* B12.... 144 B2
Royston Wy *SEDG* DY3.... 67 E3
Rubens Cl *SEDG* DY3.... 83 F1
Rubery Farm Gv *RBRY* B45.... 173 H5
Rubery Field Cl *RBRY* B45.... 174 A4
Rubery La *RBRY* B45.... 173 H4
Rubery La South *RBRY* B45.... 173 H5
Rubery St *DARL/WED* WS10.... 40 B5
Ruckley Av *LOZ/NWT* B19 *.... 108 C2
Ruckley Rd *SLYOAK* B29.... 158 D2
Rudd Gdns *WOLVN* WV10.... 12 C3
Ruddington Wy *LOZ/NWT* B19.. 109 E4
Rudge Av *WOLV* WV1.... 38 B2
Rudge Cl *SHHTH* WV12.... 40 C3
Rudge Wk *WSNGN* B18 *.... 126 A1
Rudgewick Cft *AST/WIT* B6.... 109 F3
Rudyard Cl *WOLVN* WV10.... 13 E3
Rudyard Gv *STETCH* B33.... 130 D1
Rudyngfield Dr *STETCH* B33... 130 B1
Rufford Cl *ERDW/GRVHL* B23... 76 B3
Rufford Rd *HAG/WOL* DY9.... 136 B3
Rufford St *HAG/WOL* DY9.... 136 B3
Rufford Wy *ALDR* WS9.... 29 C2
Rugby St *WOLV* WV1.... 6 C1
Rugeley Av *SHHTH* WV12.... 26 B2
Rugeley Gv *SPARK* B11.... 85 E1
Ruislip Cl *CVALE* B35.... 94 C2
Ruiton St *SEDG* DY3.... 83 E2
Rumbow *HALE* B63.... 138 D3
Rumbow La *RMSLY* B62.... 171 H1
Rumbush La *HOCK/TIA* B94.... 193 H5
Runcorn Cl
CHWD/FDBR/MGN B37.... 114 C5
Runcorn Rd *BHTH/HG* B12.... 144 C2
Runnymede Rd *SPARK* B11.... 145 G4
Rupert St *BDMR/CCFT* WV3.... 6 A4
VAUX/NECH B7.... 109 G4
Rushall Cl *RUSH/SHEL* WS4.... 42 D1
STRBR DY8.... 118 A4
Rushall Manor Cl
RUSH/SHEL WS4.... 42 D1
Rushall Manor Rd
RUSH/SHEL WS4.... 42 D1
Rushall Rd *WOLVN* WV10.... 13 E5
Rushbrook Cl *BRWNH* WS8.... 18 B1
HIA/OLT B92.... 147 E5
Rushbrooke Cl *MOS/BIL* B13... 144 B1
Rushbrooke Dr
SCFLD/BOLD B73.... 61 E4
Rushbury Cl *BILS/COS* WV14.... 53 F3
SHLY B90.... 180 D1
Rushden Cft *KGSTG* B44.... 75 F2
Rushes Ml *BLOX/PEL* WS3.... 17 G4
Rushey La *SPARK* B11.... 146 A2
Rushford Av *WMBN* WV5.... 65 E5
Rushford Cl *SHLY* B90.... 195 E2
Rush Gn *RIDG/WDGT* B32.... 141 E5
Rushleigh Rd *SHLY* B90.... 179 C5
Rushmead Gv *RBRY* B45.... 188 A1
Rushmere Rd *TPTN/OCK* DY4.. 69 G3
Rushmoor Cl *FOAKS/STRLY* B74.. 62 B2
Rushwater Cl *WMBN* WV5.... 64 C5
Rushwick Gv *SHLY* B90.... 195 G2
Rushwood Cl *RUSH/SHEL* WS4.. 42 C2
Rushy Piece *RIDG/WDGT* B32..140 D4
Ruskin Av *BLKHTH/ROWR* B65... 122 B2
ETTPK/GDPK/PENN WV4.... 67 H1
SEDG DY3.... 82 C1
Ruskin Cl *ASTN* B6.... 109 F2
Ruskin Gv *ACGN* B27.... 146 B5
Ruskin Hall Gv *AST/WIT* B6.... 109 F2
Ruskin Rd *WOLVN* WV10.... 23 H2
Ruskin St *HHTH/SAND* B71.... 87 F1
Russell Bank Rd
FOAKS/STRLY B74.... 46 C1
Russell Cl *OLDBY* B69.... 86 B4
TPTN/OCK DY4.... 25 F1
WNSFLD WV11.... 143 H4
Russell Rd *BILS/COS* WV14.... 54 B1
MOS/BIL B13.... 143 H4
Russell's Hall Rd *DUDN* DY1... 83 C5
The Russells *MOS/BIL* B13.... 143 H4
Russell St *BDMR/CCFT* WV3.... 6 D6
DARL/WED WS10.... 70 D1
DUDN DY1.... 84 B5
WLNHL WV13.... 39 G5
Russett Cl *DSYBK/YTR* WS5.... 43 F5
Russett Wy *BRLYHL* DY5.... 100 C2
Russett Gv *NFLD/LBR* B31.... 158 A4
Ruston St *LDYWD/EDGR* B16... 126 A3
Ruthall Cl *SLYOAK* B29.... 159 F3
Ruth Cl *TPTN/OCK* DY4.... 70 A1
Rutherford Rd
ERDW/GRVHL B23.... 76 C4
WSLW WS2.... 27 C4
Rutland Av
ETTPK/GDPK/PENN WV4.... 50 D4
Rutland Crs *ALDR* WS9.... 30 B3
BILS/COS WV14.... 53 H1
Rutland Dr
LGN/SDN/BHAMAIR B26.... 130 A5
Rutland Pl *STRBR* DY8.... 117 H4
Rutland Rd *DARL/WED* WS10.. 56 A4
HHTH/SAND B71.... 71 G4
SMTHWK B66.... 124 C3
Rutland St *BLOX/PEL* WS3.... 28 A4
Rutland Ter *WSNGN* B18 *.... 108 A4
Rutters Meadow
RIDG/WDGT B32.... 140 B3
Rutter St *WSL* WS1.... 57 E1
Ryan Av *WNSFLD* WV11.... 25 G3

Ryan Pl *DUDS* DY2 ....102 C5
Rycroft Gv *STECH* B33 ....131 E2
Rydal Cl *FOAKS/STRLY* B74 ......45 F3
  WNSFLD WV11 ....24 C3
Rydal Dr *DUNHL/THL/PER* WV6....34 D1
Rydding La *HHTH/SAND* B71 ......71 F3
Ryde Gv *ACGN* B27 ....163 E1
Ryde Park Rd *RBRY* B45 ....188 C2
Ryders Green Rd *WBROM* B70 ....86 C2
Ryders Hayes La
  BLOX/PEL WS3 ....18 A3
Ryder St *CBHAMNE* B4 * 3 H3
  STRBR DY8 ....117 H2
  WBROM B70 ....86 D1
Ryebank Cl *BVILLE* B30 ....159 E5
Ryeclose Cft
  CHWD/FDBR/MGN B37 ....132 D1
Rye Cft *ACGN* B27 ....146 C2
  HAG/WOL DY9 ....136 C5
  HLYWD B47 ....192 C3
Ryecroft Av
  ETTPK/GDPK/PENN WV4 ....51 H3
Ryecroft Cl *SEDG* DY3 ....67 E3
Ryecroft Pk *WOLV* WV1 ....9 G2
Ryecroft Pl *BLOX/PEL* WS3 ......28 B4
Ryecroft St *WSLW* WS2 ....42 A2
Ryefield *CDSL* WV8 ....22 A1
Ryefield Cl *HAG/WOL* DY9 ......169 G1
  SOLH B91 ....164 A5
Ryefield Wy *KGSWFD* DY6 ....99 G5
Rye Grass Wk *CVALE* B35 ....94 D3
Rye Gv *SPARK* B11 ....145 H3
Ryknild Cl *FOAKS/STRLY* B74 ...32 A4
Ryknild Dr *FOAKS/STRLY* B74 ....60 C1
Ryland Cl *HALE* B63 ....138 A5
  TPTN/OCK DY4 ....85 H1
Ryland Rd *EDG* B15 ....126 C5
  ERDE/BCHGN B24 ....92 D5
  SPARK B11 ....145 F3
Rylands Dr
  ETTPK/GDPK/PENN WV4 ....51 G4
Ryland St *LDYWD/EDGR* B16......2 A7
Ryle St *BLOX/PEL* WS3 ....17 F5
Rymond Rd *BKDE/SHDE* B34 .....112 A3
Ryton Cl *SCFLD/BOLD* B73 ....62 B5
  WNSFLD WV11 ....24 A5
Ryton Gv *BKDE/SHDE* B34 ....113 F2

S

Sabell Rd *SMTHWKW* B67 ....106 B3
Sabrina Rd
  DUNHL/THL/PER WV6 ....34 C4
Saddlers Cl *HALE* B63 ....137 F2
Saddlers Ms *SOLH* B91 ....182 A4
The Saddlestones
  DUNHL/THL/PER WV6 ....34 B1
Saddleworth Rd
  BLOX/PEL WS3 ....16 C3
Sadler Rd *BRWNH* WS8 ....9 G4
  MGN/WHC B75 ....63 F1
Sadlers Ct *WSLW* WS2 ....56 B1
Sadlers MI *BRWNH* WS8 ....9 G5
Sadlers Wk *LDYWD/EDGR* B16...126 A3
Saffron Gdns
  ETTPK/GDPK/PENN WV4 ....51 C4
Sage Cft *NFLD/LBR* B31 ....158 B5
St Agatha's Rd *WASH/WDE* B8 ..111 F4
St Agnes Cl *MOS/BIL* B13 ......144 D5
St Agnes Rd *MOS/BIL* B13 ......144 D5
St Aidans Wk *SMHTH* B10 ....144 B2
St Albans Cl *SMTHWKW* B67 * ..106 A3
  WNSFLD WV11 ....25 G2
St Albans Rd *MOS/BIL* B13 ......144 C3
  SMTHWKW B67 ....106 A3
St Alphege Cl *SOLH* B91 * 182 A2
St Ambrose Cl *RMSLY* B62 ......121 H4
St Andrews Av *BLOX/PEL* WS3...18 A2
St Andrews Cl
  DUNHL/THL/PER WV6 ....36 C1
  RIDG/WDGT B32 ....141 G4
  SEDG DY3 ....82 C3
  STRBR DY8 ....135 F5
St Andrews Dr
  DUNHL/THL/PER WV6 ....34 B1
  OLDBY B69 ....103 H2
St Andrew's Rd *BORD* B9 ....127 H2
  MGN/WHC B75 ....62 C1
St Andrew's St *BORD* B9 ....127 H2
  DUDS DY2 ....102 C4
St Annes Cl
  BFLD/HDSWWD B20 ....89 H2
St Anne's Ct *MOS/BIL* B13 ......144 A3
St Annes Gv *DOR/KN* B93 ....197 G2
St Anne's Rd *DUDS* DY2 ....120 C3
  WLNHL WV13 ....39 H2
  WOLVN WV10 ....22 D1
St Annes Wy *KGSTG* B44 ....75 C4
St Anthonys Dr *BLOX/PEL* WS3...18 B2
St Athan Cft *CVALE* B35 ....94 D3
St Augustine's Rd
  LDYWD/EDGR B16 ....125 F3
St Augustus Cl *WBROM* B70 ......88 B4
St Austell Rd *DSYBK/YTR* WS5...58 B1
St Bartholomew Ter
  DARL/WED WS10 ....55 H5
St Benedict's Cl *WBROM* B70 ....88 B4
St Benedicts Rd *SMHTH* B10 ....128 D4
Saint Benedicts Rd *WMBN* WV5..65 C4
St Bernards Rd
  CSCFLD/WYGN B72 ....77 G1
  HIA/OLT B92 ....163 H5
St Blaise Av *CSHL/WTROR* B46...96 C4
St Blaise Rd *MGN/WHC* B75 ......47 H2
St Brades Cl *OLDBY* B69 ....104 A2
St Brides Cl *SEDG* DY3 ....67 E3
  WMBN WV5 ....64 D5
Saintbury Dr *SOLH* B91 ....196 A1
St Caroline Cl *WBROM* B70 ....88 B3
St Catharines Cl *WSL* WS1 ....57 G1
St Catherines Cl *DUDS* DY2 * 85 G5
  MGN/WHC B75 ....63 F1
St Catherine's Crs
  ETTPK/GDPK/PENN WV4 ....51 F4
St Chad's Circ *CBHAMNW* B3......3 F3
St Chad's Cl *SEDG* DY3 ....82 D3

St Chads Queensway
  CBHAMNE B4 ....3 C2
St Chads Rd *BILS/COS* WV14 ....54 B1
  MGN/WHC B75 ....63 E3
  RBRY B45 ....187 H1
  WOLVN WV10 ....23 H2
St Christopher Dr *WBROM* B70...88 A4
St Christophers
  BFLD/HDSWWD B20 ....89 H2
St Clement's Av *BLOX/PEL* WS3..27 G3
St Clement's La
  HHTH/SAND B71 ....87 G2
St Clements Rd
  VAUX/NECH B7 ....110 A3
St Columbas Dr *RBRY* B45 ....188 D1
St Cuthbert's Cl *WBROM* B70 ....88 B4
St Davids Cl *BLOX/PEL* WS3 .....18 B2
  WBROM B70 ....88 B4
St Davids Dr *RIDG/WDGT* B32 ..140 B2
St Davids Gv
  BFLD/HDSWWD B20 ....89 H2
St David's Pl *BLOX/PEL* WS3 ....17 F5
St Denis Rd *SLYOAK* B29 ....158 C4
St Dominic's Rd
  DUNHL/THL/PER WV6 * 36 B2
  WBROM B70 ....88 B4
St Edburghs Rd *YDLY* B25 ......130 A3
St Edmund's Cl
  DUNHL/THL/PER WV6 * 36 B2
  WBROM B70 ....88 B4
St Edward's Rd *SLYOAK* B29....142 D5
St Eleanor Cl *WBROM* B70 ....88 B3
St Francis Av *SOLH* B91 ....164 A4
St Francis Cl *BLOX/PEL* WS3 ....18 B2
St Francis Dr *BVILLE* B30 ....177 H2
St George Dr *SMTHWK* B66 * ...106 C2
St Georges Av
  ERDW/GRVHL B23 ....93 E1
St Georges Cl *DARL/WED* WS10..55 F1
  EDG B15 ....126 A5
  MGN/WHC B75 ....63 F2
St Georges Ct
  FOAKS/STRLY B74 ....32 C5
St George's Pde *BKHL/PFLD* WV2..7 C5
St Georges Pl *WBROM* B70 ....87 G2
St Georges Rd *DUDS* DY2 ....102 D3
  SHLY B90 ....180 D5
  STRBR DY8 ....134 D5
St Georges St *DARL/WED* WS10..55 F1
  LOZ/NWT B19 ....114 A4
St Gerards Rd *SOLH* B91 ....180 A4
St Giles Av *BLKHTH/ROWR* B65..103 H5
St Giles Cl *BLKHTH/ROWR* B65..103 H5
St Giles Crs *WOLV* WV1 ....38 A3
St Giles Rd *STECH* B33 ....131 F2
  WLNHL WV13 ....39 H4
  WOLV WV1 ....38 A3
St Giles Rw *STRBR* DY8 * 135 G1
St Giles St *DUDS* DY2 ....102 C4
St Helens Av *TPTN/OCK* DY4 .....86 A1
St Helen's Rd *SOLH* B91 ....164 C4
St Heliers Rd *NFLD/LBR* B31 ....175 E1
St Ives Rd *DSYBK/YTR* WS5 .....58 B1
St James Av
  BLKHTH/ROWR B65 ....103 C5
St James Cl *BLOX/PEL* WS3 * 18 B2
  WBROM B70 ....88 B4
St James Pl *SHLY* B90 ....180 B3
  VAUX/NECH B7 ....127 G1
St James Rd *EDG* B15 ....126 B4
  HDSW B21 ....107 F1
  MGN/WHC B75 ....47 G5
  OLDBY B69 ....104 B1
St James's Rd *DUDN* DY1 ....84 B4
St James's Ter *DUDN* DY1 ....84 A4
St James St *DARL/WED* WS10 ....70 C1
  SEDG DY3 ....85 F3
  WOLV WV1 ....7 J5
Saint James Wk *BRWNH* WS8 ....9 F5
St John Bosco Cl
  HHTH/SAND B71 ....71 F4
St John Cl *MGN/WHC* B75 ....47 H2
St Johns Av
  BLKHTH/ROWR B65 ....103 H5
St John's Cl *ALDR* WS9 ....19 F2
  DOR/KN B93 ....197 F2
  SEDG DY3 ....80 B4
  WBROM B70 ....87 F3
St Johns Ct *NFLD/LBR* B31 .....175 H4
St Johns
  CHWD/FDBR/MGN B37 ....131 H1
St Johns Rd *BLOX/PEL* WS3 .....18 B2
  BRWNH WS8 ....19 G2
  DARL/WED WS10 ....55 E3
  DUDS DY2 ....102 D1
  HALE B63 ....138 A3
  HRBN B17 ....142 B1
  LGLYGN/QTN B68 ....105 G4
  SPARK B11 ....145 E2
  STRBR DY8 ....135 G1
  TPTN/OCK DY4 ....69 F4
  WNSFLD WV11 ....15 E4
  WSLW WS2 ....41 F5
St John's Sq *BKHL/PFLD* WV2.....7 F6
St John's St *DUDS* DY2 ....102 C4
St Johns Wd *MGN/WHC* B75 ......47 H2
St Johns Wk *PBAR/PBCH* B42....90 D2
St Johns Wd *RBRY* B45 ....188 B3
St Josephs Av *NFLD/LBR* B31 ..158 D5
St Josephs Ct *BLOX/PEL* WS3...18 A3
St Josephs Rd *WASH/WDE* B8 ..111 F4
St Joseph St *DUDS* DY2 ....84 D5
St Judes Cl
  ALE/KHTH/YWD B14 ....178 B3
  MGN/WHC B75 ....63 F2
St Jude's Pas *DIG/EDG* B5 * 3 F7
St Jude's Rd
  DUNHL/THL/PER WV6 ....36 B2
St Jude's Rd West
  DUNHL/THL/PER WV6 ....36 B2
St Katherine's Rd
  LGLYGN/QTN B68 ....123 C2
St Kenelms Av *HALE* B63 ....154 D1
St Kenelm's Cl *WBROM* B70 ......88 B3
St Kenelm's Rd *RMSLY* B62 ....172 C1
St Kilda's Rd *WASH/WDE* B8 * ..111 G4
St Laurence Rd
  NFLD/LBR B31 ....158 C5
St Lawrence Cl *DIG/EDG* B5 ....126 D5
  DOR/KN B93 ....197 F3
St Lawrence Wy
  DARL/WED WS10 ....55 F2

St Leonards Cl
  CHWD/FDBR/MGN B37 ....132 A5
St Loye's Cl *RMSLY* B62 ....122 B5
St Lukes Cl
  BLKHTH/ROWR B65 ....103 H5
St Lukes Rd *DARL/WED* WS10 ....56 B5
Saint Lukes Rd
  DARL/WED WS10 ....71 E1
St Luke's Rd *DIG/EDG* B5 ....127 E5
St Lukes St *CDYHTH* B64 ....120 D3
St Margaret's Av *FOAKS/STRLY* B74..46 A2
St Margarets Av
  WASH/WDE B8 ....111 F3
St Margarets Dr *HALE* B63 ......138 B5
St Margarets Rd *BLOX/PEL* WS3..17 H3
  GTB/HAM B43 ....73 H1
  HIA/OLT B92 ....164 A1
  WASH/WDE B8 ....111 E3
St Marks Crs *CBHAMW* B1 ......126 A1
St Mark's Rd *BDMR/CCFT* WV3....6 C5
  BLOX/PEL WS3 ....18 A3
  BRWNH WS8 ....19 G2
  DUDS DY2 ....85 F5
  HAG/WOL DY9 ....136 B2
  SMTHWKW B67 ....106 C2
  TPTN/OCK DY4 ....69 G5
St Mark's St *BDMR/CCFT* WV3.....6 D5
  CBHAMW B1 ....2 A3
St Martin's Cl *BKHL/PFLD* WV2..52 C2
  WBROM B70 ....88 B4
St Martin's Dr *TPTN/OCK* DY4 ...85 G1
St Martin's Queensway (below)
  DIG/EDG B5 ....3 G6
St Martins Dr *MGN/WHC* B75 .....63 F3
St Martin's St *EDG* B15 ....126 B5
St Martin's Ter *BILS/COS* WV14..54 A5
St Marys Cl *ACGN* B27 ....146 B4
  ERDE/BCHGN B24 ....93 H2
  SEDG DY3 ....67 H3
St Marys Ct *WLNHL* WV13 * 39 G3
St Mary's La *STRBR* DY8 ....135 H4
St Marys Rd *DARL/WED* WS10 ...55 H5
  HRBN B17 ....142 B2
St Mary's Rw *CBHAMNE* B4 ....3 G3
  MOS/BIL B13 ....144 B4
St Marys Vw *ERDW/GRVHL* B23..76 B3
St Mary's Wy *ALDR* WS9 ....30 A5
St Matthews Cl
  BLOX/PEL WS3 * 18 B2
  WSL WS1 ....5 F5
Saint Matthews Rd
  LGLYGN/QTN B68 ....125 E2
St Matthews Rd *SMHTH* B10 ....126 B5
St Matthew St *WOLV* WV1 ....37 H4
St Mawes Rd
  DUNHL/THL/PER WV6 ....34 D2
St Mawgen Cl *CVALE* B35 ....95 E2
St Michael's Cl *BLOX/PEL* WS3..17 H5
St Michael's Ct
  DUNHL/THL/PER WV6 ....22 A5
St Michael's Crs *OLDBY* B69 ...104 D5
St Michael's Gv *DUDS* DY2 ....85 F5
St Michael's Rd
  SCFLD/BOLD B73 ....76 D3
  SEDG DY3 ....82 B1
  WSNGN B18 ....108 A2
St Michael St *WSL* WS1 ....4 E7
St Michael St West
  WBROM B70 ....87 G3
St Michaels Wy *TPTN/OCK* DY4..85 G3
St Nicholas Cl *BLOX/PEL* WS3...18 A3
St Nicolas Gdns
  HWK/WKHTH B38 ....176 D3
St Oswalds Rd *SMHTH* B10 .....128 C4
St Patricks Cl
  ALE/KHTH/YWD B14 ....161 E4
St Paul's Av *BHTH/HG* B12 ......144 C2
St Pauls Crs *BLOX/PEL* WS3 .....18 B2
  CSHL/WTROR B46 ....115 G2
  WBROM B70 ....70 C4
St Pauls Dr *RMSLY* B62 ....122 B3
  TPTN/OCK DY4 ....86 A4
St Paul's Rd *BHTH/HG* B12 ......144 B1
  DARL/WED WS10 ....56 B3
  DUDS DY2 ....102 D4
  SMTHWK B66 ....105 H2
St Paul's Sq *CBHAMNW* B3 ....2 E2
St Paul's St *WSL* WS1 ....4 E3
St Peter Cft *DARL/WED* WS10 ...57 E5
St Peters Cl *CSCFLD/WYGN* B72..62 B5
  CSHL/WTROR B46 ....96 B4
Saint Peters Ct
  HLGN/YWD B28 ....162 B4
St Peter's Cl *TPTN/OCK* DY4 .....69 F3
St Peters Ct *BLOX/PEL* WS3 .....27 F1
St Peters Cft
  SCFLD/BOLD B73 * 62 B5
St Peters Dr *BLOX/PEL* WS3 .....18 A3
St Peters La *HIA/OLT* B92 ....166 D2
St Peter's Rd
  BFLD/HDSWWD B20 ....90 C5
  DUDS DY2 ....102 D1
  HAG/WOL DY9 ....153 E1
  HRBN B17 ....141 H2
St Peters Sq *WOLV* WV1 ....7 H1
St Peters Ter *WSLW* WS2 ....42 A1
St Philips Av *BDMR/CCFT* WV3..51 G1
St Phillips Av *BDMR/CCFT* WV3..51 F1
St Phillips Gv *BDMR/CCFT* WV3..51 F1
St Quentin St *WSLW* WS2 ....41 G5
St Saviour's Cl *BKHL/PFLD* WV2..52 D2
St Saviour's Rd *WASH/WDE* B8..128 C1
St Silas' Sq *LOZ/NWT* B19 ......108 B2
St Simons Cl *MGN/WHC* B75 ....63 G3
St Stephen's Av *WLNHL* WV13 ..39 F3
St Stephens Gdns
  WLNHL WV13 * 39 G4
St Stephens Rd
  HHTH/SAND B71 ....106 D1
  SLYOAK B29 ....160 B2
St Stephens St *AST/WIT* B6 .....109 E3
St Thomas' Cl *ALDR* WS9 ....30 B1
  WSL WS1 ....28 A4
St Thomas' Rd
  ERDW/GRVHL B23 ....92 B4
St Thomas St *DUDS* DY2 ....102 C4
St Valentines Cl *WBROM* B70 ....88 B4
St Vincent Crs *WBROM* B70 ......70 C5

St Vincent St West
  LDYWD/EDGR B16 ....126 A2
Saladin Av *OLDBY* B69 ....104 C4
Salcombe Av
  LCN/SDN/BHAMAIR B26 ....148 A2
Salcombe Dr *BRLYHL* DY5 ......119 E4
Salcombe Gv *BILS/COS* WV14 ...68 D2
Salcombe Rd *SMTHWK* B66 .....106 D4
Salem St *TPTN/OCK* DY4 ....86 B1
Salford St *AST/WIT* B6 ....110 A1
Salisbury Chambers
  MOS/BIL B13 * 144 B3
Salisbury Cl *DUDN* DY1 ....83 H3
  MOS/BIL B13 ....144 B3
Salisbury Dr *CSHL/WTROR* B46..96 C3
Salisbury Gv
  CSCFLD/WYGN B72 ....77 G4
Salisbury Rd *LOZ/NWT* B19 ....108 D1
  MOS/BIL B13 ....144 B3
  SMTHWK B66 ....106 D4
  WASH/WDE B8 ....110 C4
  WBROM B70 ....88 A5
Salisbury St *BDMR/CCFT* WV3.....6 C6
  DARL/WED WS10 ....55 G1
Sallow Gv *BRWNH* WS8 ....9 F3
Sally Ward Dr *ALDR* WS9 ....19 C5
Salop Cl *HHTH/SAND* B71 ....71 F3
Salop Dr *LGLYGN/QTN* B68 .....123 C2
  OLDBY B69 ....104 D1
Salop Rd *BHTH/HG* B12 ....127 E4
  BILS/COS WV14 ....54 A4
  DUDN DY1 ....83 C4
  OLDBY B69 ....104 D1
  WOLV WV1 ....6 E5
Salstar Cl *AST/WIT* B6 ....109 E3
Saltash Gv *YDLY* B25 ....129 G3
Saltbrook Rd *HALE* B63 ....120 A5
Salter Rd *TPTN/OCK* DY4 ....69 F4
Salter's La *HHTH/SAND* B71 .....88 B2
  HALE B63 ....138 B2
  WBROM B70 ....88 C1
Salters V *WBROM* B70 ....88 C4
Saltley Cottages
  ERDE/BCHGN B24 * 110 D1
Saltley Rd *VAUX/NECH* B7 ......110 A4
Saltley Viad *VAUX/NECH* B7 ....110 A4
Saltney Ct *ERDE/BCHGN* B24 ....93 H1
Saltwells La *BRLYHL* DY5 ....120 A2
Saltwells Rd *DUDS* DY2 ....120 A2
Salwarpe Gv *SLYOAK* B29 ....141 F5
Sambourn Cl *SOLH* B91 ....165 G4
Sambourne Dr
  BKDE/SHDE B34 ....113 F2
Sambrook Rd *WOLVN* WV10 .....24 A4
Sampson Cl *HDSW* B21 ....89 E5
  OLDBY B69 ....104 A2
Sampson Rd *SPARK* B11 ....127 G4
Sampson Rd North
  SPARK B11 ....127 G4
Sampson St *DARL/WED* WS10 ...56 B5
Sams La *WBROM* B70 ....88 A3
Samuels Rd *RIDG/WDGT* B32 ..140 A2
Samuel St *BLOX/PEL* WS3 ....27 F1
Sanda Cft *CBROM* B36 ....114 B3
Sandalls Cl *NFLD/LBR* B31 .....174 D4
Sandal Ri *SOLH* B91 ....182 C2
Sandals Ri *RMSLY* B62 ....139 F4
Sandalwood Cl *SMHTH* WV12 ....25 H2
Sand Bank *BLOX/PEL* WS3 ....18 A4
Sandbarn Cl *SHLY* B90 ....195 F2
Sandbeds Rd *SHHTH* WV12 ......40 A1
Sandbourne Rd
  WASH/WDE B8 ....111 E5
Sanderling Ri *KGSWFD* DY6 ...100 C3
Sanders Cl *DUDS* DY2 ....103 E2
Sanders Crs *TPTN/OCK* DY4 .....85 H1
Sandfield Br *BRLYHL* DY5 ....82 D5
Sandfield Cl *SHLY* B90 ....180 A5
Sandfield Gv *SEDG* DY3 ....82 D4
Sandfields Av *SMHTH* B10 ......127 H4
Sandfields Rd
  LGLYGN/QTN B68 ....123 G2
Sandford Av
  BLKHTH/ROWR B65 ....122 A1
Sandford Ri
  DUNHL/THL/PER WV6 ....22 A4
Sandford Rd *DUDN* DY1 ....83 G5
  MOS/BIL B13 ....144 C4
Sandgate Rd *HLGN/YWD* B28 ..179 H1
  TPTN/OCK DY4 ....69 G3
Sandhills Crs *SOLH* B91 ....181 H5
Sandhurst St *BLOX/PEL* WS3 ....27 E1
Sandhurst Av *CBROM* B36 ......111 H3
  HAG/WOL DY9 ....136 B5
Sandhurst Rd
  FOAKS/STRLY B74 ....32 D5
  KGSWFD DY6 ....100 C5
  MOS/BIL B13 ....144 A5
Sandland Cl *BILS/COS* WV14 .....54 B2
Sandland Rd *SHHTH* WV12 ....26 A2
Sandmartin Cl *DUDS* DY2 ....120 C2
Sandmeadow Pl *KGSWFD* DY6 ..99 G4
Sandmere Gv
  ALE/KHTH/YWD B14 ....179 F2
Sandmere Ri *WOLVN* WV10 ......23 C1
Sandmere Rd
  ALE/KHTH/YWD B14 ....179 F2
Sandon Gv *ERDE/BCHGN* B24 ...93 E2
Sandon Rd *HAG/WOL* DY9 ......136 D3
  HRBN B17 ....124 D3
  WOLVN WV10 ....12 B5
Sandown Dr
  DUNHL/THL/PER WV6 ....34 D1
Sandown Rd *CBROM* B36 ....111 H1
Sandpiper Cl *HAG/WOL* DY9 ...136 D2
Sandpiper Gdns
  HWK/WKHTH B38 ....190 D1
Sandpiper Wy
  ERDW/GRVHL B23 ....76 A5
Sandpit Bldgs *SEDG* DY3 * 159 G2
Sand Pits Pde *CBHAMW* B1 ....2 B4
The Sandpits *BVILLE* B30 ....159 G2
Sandra Cl *ALDR* WS9 ....30 B5
Sandringham Av *SHHTH* WV12 ..25 H4
Sandringham Dr *ALDR* WS9 ......30 B1

  BLKHTH/ROWR B65 ....104 A5
Sandringham Pl *STRBR* DY8 ....117 H3
Sandringham Rd
  ETTPK/GDPK/PENN WV4 ....51 G4
  PBAR/PBCH B42 ....74 B5
  RMSLY B62 ....138 D5
  STRBR DY8 ....117 G3
  WMBN WV5 ....64 D5
Sandringham Wy *BRLYHL* DY5..119 E4
Sandstone Av *RBRY* B45 ....174 A5
Sandstone Cl *SEDG* DY3 ....83 F2
Sand St *WBROM* B70 ....86 C2
Sandway Gdns *WASH/WDE* B8..110 B3
Sandway Gv *MOS/BIL* B13 ....162 A3
Sandwell Av *DARL/WED* WS10 ...54 A5
Sandwell Pl *SMHTH* WV12 ....26 B3
Sandwell Rd *HDSW* B21 ....89 F5
  WBROM B70 ....87 G2
  WOLVN WV10 ....22 D1
Sandwell Rd North
  HHTH/SAND B71 ....87 H2
Sandwell St *WSL* WS1 ....5 F6
Sandwell Wk *WSL* WS1 ....5 F7
Sandwood Dr *KGSTG* B44 ....75 F3
Sandyacre Wy *STRBR* DY8 ....135 H2
Sandy Crs *WNSFLD* WV11 ....25 G2
Sandy Cft *SCFLD/WYGN* B72 ....62 C5
  MOS/BIL B15 ....162 A3
Sandyfields Rd *SEDG* DY3 ....82 E1
Sandy Gv *BRWNH* WS8 ....9 F3
Sandy Hill Ri *SHLY* B90 ....180 A1
Sandy Hill Rd *SHLY* B90 ....180 A1
Sandy Hollow
  DUNHL/THL/PER WV6 ....35 G3
Sandy La *AST/WIT* B6 ....109 G2
  BRGRVW B61 ....186 B3
  DSYBK/YTR WS5 ....10 B3
  DUNHL/THL/PER WV6 ....22 A4
  PBAR/PBCH B42 ....74 D3
  WOLVN WV10 ....23 C1
Sandy Mt *WMBN* WV5 ....65 G4
Sandy Mount Rd *WSL* WS5 ....5 C7
Sandys Gv *TPTN/OCK* DY4 ....85 E1
Sandy Wy *EDG* B15 ....2 C7
Sangwin Rd *BILS/COS* WV14 .....68 C4
Sansome Rd *SHLY* B90 ....179 H3
Sansome Rd *SHLY* B90 ....179 H3
Sanstone Rd *BLOX/PEL* WS3 ....17 E4
Sanstone Rd *BLOX/PEL* WS3 ....16 D4
Santolina Dr *DSYBK/YTR* WS5...57 C5
Sant Rd *NFLD/LBR* B31 ....189 H1
The Saplings *WALM/CURD* B76 ..78 C3
Saracen Dr *MGN/WHC* B75 ....63 F2
Sara Cl *FOAKS/STRLY* B74 ....49 E2
Sarah Cl *BILS/COS* WV14 ....69 F2
Sarah Gdns *DSYBK/YTR* WS5 ....57 F4
Saredon Cl *BLOX/PEL* WS3 ....28 C1
Saredon Rd *BLOX/PEL* WS3 * ...162 C2
Sarehole Rd *HLGN/YWD* B28 ...162 C2
Sargent Cl *GTB/HAM* B43 ....59 H4
Sark Dr *CBROM* B36 ....114 B3
Saunton Wy *SLYOAK* B29 ....159 E1
Saville Ms *WALM/CURD* B76 .....63 E4
Savernake Cl *RBRY* B45 ....174 A5
Saville Cl *RBRY* B45 ....188 B1
Savoy Cl *RIDG/WDGT* B32 ....141 F2
Saw Mill Cl *RUSH/SHEL* WS4 .....4 F1
Saxelby Cl
  ALE/KHTH/YWD B14 ....178 A3
Saxoncourt
  DUNHL/THL/PER WV6 ....21 C5
Saxondale Av
  LCN/SDN/BHAMAIR B26 ....147 F5
Saxon Dr *BLKHTH/ROWR* B65 ..104 A5
Saxonfields
  DUNHL/THL/PER WV6 ....21 G5
Saxons Wy
  ALE/KHTH/YWD B14 ....178 C3
Saxon Wy
  CHWD/FDBR/MGN B37 ....131 H1
Saxon Wood Cl *NFLD/LBR* B31..175 G1
Saxon Wood Rd *SHLY* B90 ....194 D3
Saxton Dr *FOAKS/STRLY* B74 ...32 D4
Scafell Dr *BILS/COS* WV14 ....54 B1
  ERDW/GRVHL B23 ....92 A1
Scafell Rd *STRBR* DY8 ....135 H1
Scampton Cl
  DUNHL/THL/PER WV6 ....20 C5
Scarborough Cl *WSLW* WS2 ......41 F5
Scarborough Rd *WSLW* WS2 .....41 G5
Scarecrow La *MGN/WHC* B75 ....48 A1
Scarsdale Rd *PBAR/PBCH* B42..74 D3
Schofield Av *HHTH/SAND* B71 ...71 F3
Schofield Rd
  CHWD/FDBR/MGN B37 ....113 H4
Scholars Ga *STECH* B33 ....130 D2
Scholars Rd *HRBN* B21 ....107 H2
Schoolacre Ri
  FOAKS/STRLY B74 ....45 E4
Schoolacre Rd
  BKDE/SHDE B34 ....112 D3
School Av *BRWNH* WS8 ....9 F4
School Cl *BDMR/CCFT* WV3 ....50 B1
  CDSL WV8 ....10 C3
  CHWD/FDBR/MGN B37 ....114 A3
  CVALE B35 ....94 D3
  NFLD/LBR B31 ....175 E3
  OLDBY B69 ....104 A2
  WMBN WV5 ....64 A2
School Cottages
  WOLVN WV10 * 12 D5
School Dr *BILS/COS* WV14 * 68 C2
  BKDE/SHDE B34 ....115 G4
  HLYWD B47 ....192 C5
  STRBR DY8 ....118 B1
The School Dr *DUDS* DY2 ....102 D2
Schoolgate Cl *RUSH/SHEL* WS4..29 F1
  WASH/WDE B8 ....111 E3
School Gn *BILS/COS* WV14 ....38 C5
Schoolhouse Cl
  BVILLE B30 ....177 F3
School La *BKDE/SHDE* B34 ......112 D2
  BLOX/PEL WS3 ....17 H3
  BRLYHL DY5 ....100 D5
  HAG/WOL DY9 ....166 A4
  HALE B63 ....138 B5
  SOLH B91 ....182 B1
  STECH B33 ....130 B3
  WOLVN WV10 ....12 D5

School Rd
 ALE/KHTH/YWD B14............**178** D1
 BRLYHL WV5............**120** A2
 DARL/WED WS10............**71** H1
 DUNHL/THL/PER WV6............**35** E1
 HLGN/YWD B28............**162** D2
 MOS/BIL B13............**161** F1
 RBRY B45............**187** G2
 SEDG DY3............**81** F3
 SHLY B90............**180** B3
 WMBN WV5............**64** A2
 WNSFLD WV11............**24** C4
School St BDMR/CCFT WV3............**6** E6
 BRLYHL DY5............**101** F2
 CDYHTH B64............**120** D3
 DARL/WED WS10............**71** H1
 DUDN DY1............**84** B5
 RUSH/SHEL WS4............**29** F1
 SEDG DY3............**67** G3
 STRBR DY8 *............**135** F1
 WLNHL WV13............**39** F3
School West BILS/COS WV14............**68** C3
School Ter SLYOAK B29 *............**142** D5
School Wk BILS/COS WV14............**38** C5
Scorers Cl SHLY B90............**194** D3
The Scotchings CBROM B36............**112** A1
Scotland La RIDG/WDGT B32............**157** G3
Scotland St CBHAMNW B1............**2** C4
Scott Av DARL/WED WS10............**72** A4
Scott Cl WALM/CURD B76............**51** E4
Scott Gv HIA/OLT B92............**147** E4
Scott Rd DSYBK/YTR WS5............**58** B2
 GTB/HAM B43............**73** H1
 HIA/OLT B92............**147** E5
Scott's Green Cl DUDN DY1............**101** H1
Scott's Rd STRBR DY8............**135** F1
Scott St TPTN/OCK DY4............**86** A1
Scotwell Cl
 BLKHTH/ROWR B65............**121** H1
Scout Cl STETCH B33............**131** E2
Scribbans Cl SMTHWK B66............**106** D5
Scribers La HLGN/YWD B28............**179** G1
Scribers Meadow
 HLGN/YWD B28............**179** G1
Sculthorpe Rd KIDD DY10............**168** B3
Seacroft Av YDLY B25............**130** A3
Seafield Cl KGSWFD DY6............**100** A5
Seaforth Gv SHHTH WV12............**25** H1
Seagar St BRLYHL DY5............**87** H2
Seager's La BRLYHL DY5............**119** F2
Seagull Bay Dr BILS/COS WV14............**68** D2
Seal Cl WALM/CURD B76............**65** H3
Seals Gn HWK/WKHTH B38............**190** B1
Seamless Dr WNSFLD WV11............**38** D1
Searton Cl WNSFLD WV11............**25** F5
Seaton Gv MOS/BIL B13............**160** D1
Seaton Pl STRBR DY8............**117** G2
Seaton Rd SMTHWK B66............**106** D4
Second Av BORD B9............**128** C3
 BRWNH WS8............**9** G4
 KGSWFD DY6............**100** C2
 SLYOAK B29............**143** F4
 WOLVN WV10............**23** H4
Second Exhibition Av
 BHAMNEC B40............**149** H3
Sedge Av HWK/WKHTH B38............**176** D2
Sedgeberrow Covert
 HWK/WKHTH B38............**176** C5
Sedgeberrow Rd HALE B63............**138** C5
Sedgeborne Wy
 NFLD/LBR B31............**174** C4
Sedgefield Cl DUDN DY1............**83** G3
Sedgefield Gv
 DUNHL/THL/PER WV6............**34** D1
Sedgeford Cl BRLYHL DY5............**119** F4
Sedgehill Av HRBN B17............**141** H5
Sedgemere Gv RUSH/SHEL WS4............**29** E2
Sedgemere Rd
 LGN/SDN/BHAMAIR B26............**130** A3
Sedgley Gv BFLD/HDSWWD B20............**89** G2
Sedgley Hall Av SEDG DY3............**67** E3
Sedgley Rd
 ETTPK/GDPK/PENN WV4............**66** B1
Sedgley Rd East TPTN/OCK DY4............**85** G2
Sedgley Rd West
 TPTN/OCK DY4............**68** C5
Sedgley St BKHL/PFLD WV2............**52** A1
Seedhouse Ct CDYHTH B64............**121** G4
Seeds La BRWNH WS8............**9** F4
Seeleys Rd SPARK B11............**145** G2
Sefton Dr BLKHTH/ROWR B65............**103** F5
Sefton Gv TPTN/OCK DY4............**70** A1
Sefton Rd LDYWD/EDGR B16............**115** H5
Segbourne Rd RBRY B45............**187** E3
Segundo Cl DSYBK/YTR WS5............**57** E4
Segundo Rd DSYBK/YTR WS5............**57** E4
Selborne Cl WSL WS1 *............**5** H4
Selborne Gv MOS/BIL B13............**162** A5
Selborne Rd
 BFLD/HDSWWD B20............**90** A4
 DUDS DY2............**102** D2
Selborne St WSL WS1............**5** H4
Selbourne Crs WOLV WV1............**38** B4
Selby Cl
 LGN/SDN/BHAMAIR B26............**130** B3
Selby Gv MOS/BIL B13............**162** A5
Selby Wy BLOX/PEL WS3............**16** A5
Selcombe Wy
 HWK/WKHTH B38............**190** D1
Selco Wy WALM/CURD B76............**94** C1
Selcroft Av RIDG/WDGT B32............**141** F2
Selecta Av KGSTG B44............**73** G5
Selkirk Cl HHTH/SAND B71............**71** G5
Selly Av SLYOAK B29............**143** E5
Selly Cl SLYOAK B29............**143** F5
Selly Hall Cft BVILLE B30............**159** H1
Selly Hill Rd SLYOAK B29............**142** D5
Selly Oak Rd SLYOAK B29............**159** G5
Selly Park Rd SLYOAK B29............**160** B1
Selly Wharf SLYOAK B29............**159** G1
Selly Wick Dr SLYOAK B29............**143** E5
Selly Wick Rd SLYOAK B29............**143** E5
Sellywood Rd BVILLE B30............**159** G3
Selma Gv ALE/KHTH/YWD B14............**162** B5
Selman's Hill BLOX/PEL WS3............**17** E4
Selmans Pde BLOX/PEL WS3 *............**17** E5
Selsdon Cl HLYWD B47............**193** E3
Selsdon Rd BLOX/PEL WS3............**16** B4
Selsey Av HRBN B17............**124** D1
Selsey Rd HRBN B17............**124** D1

Selston Rd AST/WIT B6............**109** E2
Selvey Av GTB/HAM B43............**59** F5
Selworthy Rd CBROM B36............**113** H2
Selwyn Cl BKHL/PFLD WV2............**52** A1
Selwyn Rd BILS/COS WV14............**54** B2
 LDYWD/EDGR B16............**115** E1
Selwyn Wk FOAKS/STRLY B74............**46** A1
Senneleys Park Rd
 NFLD/LBR B31............**158** B1
Sennen Cl WLNHL WV13............**39** F4
Sensall Rd HAG/WOL DY9............**136** D4
Sentry Wy MGN/WHC B75............**63** G2
Serpentine Rd AST/WIT B6............**91** G5
 HALE B63............**142** A2
 SLYOAK B29............**143** E4
Settle Av BKDE/SHDE B34............**112** B3
Settle Cft
 CHWD/FDBR/MGN B37............**131** H5
Setton Dr SEDG DY3............**67** G4
Seven Acres ALDR WS9............**30** B5
Seven Acres Rd NFLD/LBR B31............**176** A4
 RMSLY B62............**140** A2
Sevendwellings Vw
 BRLYHL DY5............**119** E3
Seven Star Rd SOLH B91............**164** D5
Seven Stars Rd OLDBY B69............**105** E2
Severn Cl CBROM B36............**113** H2
 DY5............**85** F1
 TPTN/OCK DY4............**85** H5
Severn Dr BRLYHL DY5............**100** D2
 DUNHL/THL/PER WV6............**34** C1
Severne Gv ACGN B27............**163** G1
Severne Rd ACGN B27............**163** G2
Severn Gv LOZ/NWT B19 *............**108** C2
 SPARK B11 *............**145** E1
Severn St BLOX/PEL WS3............**27** H2
 BRWNH WS8............**9** H4
 HALE B63............**137** F2
 STRBR DY8............**135** F4
Severn St CBHAMW B1............**2** E7
Sevington Cl SOLH B91............**182** A5
Seymour Cl SLYOAK B29............**143** F5
Seymour Gdns
 FOAKS/STRLY B74............**46** C3
Seymour Rd HAG/WOL DY9............**136** D2
 OLDBY B69............**105** G2
 TPTN/OCK DY4............**86** A3
Seymour St DIG/EDG B5............**3** J5
Shackleton Dr
 DUNHL/THL/PER WV6............**20** B5
Shackleton Rd BLOX/PEL WS3............**17** F5
Shadowbrook La HIA/OLT B92............**166** D3
Shadwell Dr SEDG DY3............**83** F4
Shadwell St CBHAMNE B4............**3** G2
Shady La KGSTG B44............**74** C3
Shadymoor Dr BRLYHL DY5............**119** E4
Shaftesbury Av HAG/WOL DY9............**136** A4
Shaftesbury Rd
 DARL/WED WS10............**71** H1
Shaftesbury Sq
 HHTH/SAND B71............**87** G1
Shaftesbury St
 HHTH/SAND B71............**87** G2
Shaftmoor La HLGN/YWD B28............**145** G5
Shaftsbury Av HALE B63............**120** B5
Shaftsbury Cl BILS/COS WV14............**54** B1
Shaftsbury Rd
 LGN/SDN/BHAMAIR B26............**148** A2
Shahjalal Rd WASH/WDE B8............**110** B4
Shakespeare Crs
 BLOX/PEL WS3............**28** A2
Shakespeare Dr SHLY B90............**180** B4
Shakespeare Pl BLOX/PEL WS3............**28** A3
Shakespeare Rd
 ERDW/GRVHL B23............**91** H3
 SEDG DY3............**82** C2
 SMHY B67............**180** B4
 SMTHWK B67............**105** H5
 TPTN/OCK DY4............**69** G4
Shakespeare St SPARK B11............**145** E2
 WOLV WV1............**7** J5
Shaldon Wk SMTHWK B66............**106** D4
The Shales WMBN WV5 *............**80** C1
Shale St BILS/COS WV14............**53** G5
Shalford Rd HIA/OLT B92............**147** E3
Shalicross La SEDG DY3............**83** F3
Shalnecote Gv
 ALE/KHTH/YWD B14............**160** C5
Shambles DARL/WED WS10............**70** D1
Shandon Cl RIDG/WDGT B32............**141** H2
Shannon Dr BRWNH WS8............**8** C2
Shannon Rd HWK/WKHTH B38............**190** C1
Shapinsay Dr RBRY B45............**173** H4
Shard End Crs
 BKDE/SHDE B34............**113** E4
Shardlow Rd WNSFLD WV11............**25** E2
The Shardway
 BKDE/SHDE B34............**113** E4
Sharesacre St WLNHL WV13............**39** H2
Sharington Cl DUDS DY2............**103** E1
Sharman Rd WOLVN WV10............**23** C4
Sharmans Cross Rd SOLH B91............**181** F1
Sharon Cl
 ETTPK/GDPK/PENN WV4............**52** C3
Sharps Cl RBRY B45............**187** E3
Sharrat Fld MGN/WHC B75............**47** H3
Sharrocks St WOLV WV1............**7** J6
Shawberry Av CVALE B35............**94** D3
Shawberry Rd
 CHWD/FDBR/MGN B37 *............**113** H4
Shawbrook Gv
 ALE/KHTH/YWD B14............**178** C2
Shawbury Gv BHTH/HG B12............**127** F4
 DUNHL/THL/PER WV6............**20** C5
Shawbury Rd WOLVN WV10............**23** C5
Shaw Dr STETCH B33............**130** A2
Shawfield HLYWD B47............**192** C3
Shawhellier Av BRLYHL DY5............**119** G2
Shaw Hill Rd WASH/WDE B8............**111** E5
Shawhurst Cft HLYWD B47............**192** C1
Shawhurst Gdns HLYWD B47............**192** D1
Shawhurst La HLYWD B47............**192** C2
Shaw La DUNHL/THL/PER WV6............**35** F2
Shawley Cft ACGN B27............**146** C1
Shaw Rd BILS/COS WV14............**68** B2
 BKHL/PFLD WV2............**52** A2
 DUDS DY2............**102** B2
 TPTN/OCK DY4............**86** A2
 WOLVN WV10............**23** H4

Shawsdale Rd CBROM B36............**112** B2
Shaw's Pas DIG/EDG B5............**3** J5
Shaw St WBROM B70............**70** C3
 WSLW WS2............**4** D3
Shaw Wy BKHL/PFLD WV2............**52** B1
Sheaf La
 LGN/SDN/BHAMAIR B26............**147** H3
Shearers Pl MGN/WHC B75............**48** A2
Shearwater Cl RBRY B45............**187** H2
Shearwater Wk
 ERDW/GRVHL B23............**75** H5
Sheaves Cl BILS/COS WV14............**53** E5
Shedden Cl DUDS DY2............**102** D1
Sheddington Rd
 ERDW/GRVHL B23............**76** B4
Sheen Rd KGSTG B44............**60** A4
Sheepclose Dr
 CHWD/FDBR/MGN B37............**132** A1
Sheepcote St LDYWD/EDGR B16............**2** A5
Sheepfold Cl
 BLKHTH/ROWR B65............**105** G5
Sheepmoor Cl HRBN B17............**124** B4
Sheepwash La TPTN/OCK DY4............**86** B1
Sheerwater Dr BRLYHL DY5............**119** E5
Sheffield Rd SCFLD/BOLD B73............**77** E4
Sheffield St BRLYHL DY5............**120** A3
Shefford Rd AST/WIT B6............**109** F4
Sheila Av WNSFLD WV11............**25** F5
Shelah Rd HALE B63............**138** C1
Shelbourne Cl OLDBY B69............**86** B4
Sheldon Av DARL/WED WS10............**56** A4
Sheldon Cl BILS/COS WV14............**53** H5
Sheldon Dr NFLD/LBR B31............**174** D4
Sheldonfield Rd
 LGN/SDN/BHAMAIR B26............**148** B3
Sheldon Gv
 LGN/SDN/BHAMAIR B26............**147** H2
Sheldon Hall Av STETCH B33............**131** F1
Sheldon Heath Rd
 LGN/SDN/BHAMAIR B26............**130** C2
Sheldon Rd HHTH/SAND B71............**72** A5
 WOLVN WV10............**22** C1
Sheldrake Cl HOCK/TIA B94............**205** H5
Shelfield Rd
 ALE/KHTH/YWD B14............**177** C2
Shelley Av TPTN/OCK DY4............**69** G5
Shelley Cl SEDG DY3............**82** C1
 STRBR DY8............**118** C4
Shelley Dr ERDW/GRVHL B23............**91** H3
 FOAKS/STRLY B74............**37** H4
Shelley Rd SHHTH WV12............**26** C1
 WOLVN WV10............**12** D5
Shelly Cl
 CHWD/FDBR/MGN B37............**131** H2
Shelly Crs SHLY B90............**195** H2
Shelly Cft STETCH B33............**130** C1
Shelly La SHLY B90............**195** H2
Shelsley Av OLDBY B69............**104** B4
Shelsley Dr MOS/BIL B13............**161** H1
Shelsley Wy SOLH B91............**181** H4
Shelton Cl DARL/WED WS10............**56** C3
Shelton La HALE B63............**138** A2
Shelwick Gv DOR/KN B93............**196** D4
Shenley Av DUDN DY1............**68** B5
Shenley Fields Dr
 NFLD/LBR B31............**158** B3
Shenley Fields Rd SLYOAK B29............**158** B3
Shenley Gdns SLYOAK B29............**158** C4
Shenley Hl NFLD/LBR B31............**158** A4
Shenley La NFLD/LBR B31............**158** A2
Shenstone Av RMSLY B62............**138** D3
 STRBR DY8............**134** D5
Shenstone Cl FOAKS/STRLY B74............**32** C4
Shenstone Ct BDMR/CCFT WV3............**51** G2
Shenstone Dr ALDR WS9............**30** A2
Shenstone Rd
 ALE/KHTH/YWD B14............**178** C4
 GTB/HAM B43............**73** G3
 LDYWD/EDGR B16............**115** E1
Shenstone Valley Rd
 RMSLY B62............**139** H1
Shenton Wk
 CHWD/FDBR/MGN B37............**113** H4
Shephard Rd
 LGN/SDN/BHAMAIR B26............**148** B2
Shepherd Dr SHHTH WV12............**25** H5
Shepherds Brook Rd
 HAG/WOL DY9............**136** B2
Shepherds Fold
 BLKHTH/ROWR B65............**121** H2
Shepherds Gdns EDG B15............**126** B3
Shepherds Green Rd
 ERDE/BCHGN B24............**92** D4
Shepherds Pool Rd
 MGN/WHC B75............**48** A3
Shepherds Standing
 BKDE/SHDE B34............**112** D3
Shepherds Wy
 ERDW/GRVHL B23............**76** A3
Shepley Rd RBRY B45............**188** B2
Sheppey Dr CBROM B36............**114** B4
Shepwell Gn WLNHL WV13............**40** A4
Sherard Cft CBROM B36............**114** B3
Sheraton Cl ALDR WS9............**30** B4
Sheraton Gra STRBR DY8............**135** F5
Sherborne Cl BLOX/PEL WS3............**28** B2
 CSHL/WTROR B46............**115** G5
Sherborne Gdns CDSL WV8............**10** C4
Sherborne Gv BRWNH WS8............**9** F4
Sherborne Rd LDYWD/EDGR B16............**2** A6
Sherborne St ACGN B27............**146** C5
Sherbourne Dr
 BHTH/HG B12............**127** G4
 CDYHTH B64............**121** G4
 STRBR DY8............**135** H3
Sherdmore Cft SHLY B90............**195** F2
Sheridan Cl WSLW WS2............**56** B1
Sheridan Gdns SEDG DY3............**82** B1
Sheridan St HHTH/SAND B71............**87** H2
 WSLW WS2............**56** B1
Sheridan Wk CVALE B35 *............**94** C3
Sheriff Dr BRLYHL DY5............**119** H2
Sherifoot La MGN/WHC B75............**47** F2
Sheringham B15............**125** C4
Sheringham Rd BVILLE B30............**177** E2
Sherington Dr
 ETTPK/GDPK/PENN WV4............**52** B3
Sherlock Cl SHHTH WV12............**26** B1
Sherlock St DIG/EDG B5............**127** E4

Sherrans Dell
 ETTPK/GDPK/PENN WV4............**52** B5
Sherratt Cl WALM/CURD B76............**78** B3
Sherringham Dr WNSFLD WV11............**26** A1
Sherron Gdns BHTH/HG B12............**144** A1
Sherston Covert BVILLE B30............**177** G3
Shervale Cl
 ETTPK/GDPK/PENN WV4............**51** G2
Sherwin Av BILS/COS WV14............**68** A1
Sherwood Av TPTN/OCK DY4............**85** F2
Sherwood Cl HIA/OLT B92............**164** B2
 HLGN/YWD B28............**162** D5
Sherwood Dr BRLYHL DY5............**119** H5
Sherwood Ms HLGN/YWD B28............**162** C4
Sherwood Rd HLGN/YWD B28............**162** C3
 SMTHWKW B67............**124** C3
 STRBR DY8............**118** A5
Sherwood St WOLV WV1............**6** E1
Sherwood Wk ALDR WS9............**29** F3
Shetland Cl
 DUNHL/THL/PER WV6............**22** D4
 LDYWD/EDGR B16............**125** H2
Shetland Dr SMTHWK B66............**105** H2
Shidas La OLDBY B69............**104** C2
Shifnal Wy MOS/BIL B13............**63** F1
Shillcock Gv LOZ/NWT B19............**109** E4
Shilton Cl SHLY B90............**195** F2
Shilton Gv SLYOAK B29............**158** B3
Shinwell Crs OLDBY B69............**86** D4
Shipbourne Cl
 RIDG/WDGT B32............**141** F2
Shipley Flds ERDE/BCHGN B24............**93** E5
Shipley Gv SLYOAK B29............**158** C2
Shipston Rd NFLD/LBR B31............**175** H4
Shipton Cl DUDN DY1............**83** G3
Shipton Rd CSCFLD/WYGN B72............**77** G1
Shipway Rd YDLY B25............**129** E5
Shirebrook Cl AST/WIT B6............**109** E1
Shire Cl LDYWD/EDGR B16............**125** H2
 LCLYGN/QTN B68............**123** G5
Shireland Brook Gdns
 WSNGN B18 *............**107** F5
Shireland Cl
 BFLD/HDSWWD B20............**89** G3
Shireland Rd SMTHWK B66............**106** D5
Shire Rdg ALDR WS9............**19** G5
Shirestone Rd STETCH B33............**131** G2
Shireview Gdns
 BLOX/PEL WS3............**18** B5
Shireview Rd BLOX/PEL WS3............**18** B5
Shirland Rd
 CHWD/FDBR/MGN B37............**132** A3
Shirley Dr CSCFLD/WYGN B72............**62** C4
Shirley Park Rd SHLY B90............**180** B4
Shirley Rd ACGN B27............**160** A5
 BVILLE B30............**160** C3
 DUDS DY2............**103** E1
 HLGN/YWD B28............**163** E2
 LGLYGN/QTN B68............**105** G3
Shirral Dr POL/KGSB/FAZ B78............**49** H1
Shirral Gv
 CHWD/FDBR/MGN B37............**113** H4
Shirrall Dr MGN/WHC B75............**49** F1
Sholing Cl CDSL WV8............**22** B1
Shooters Cl DIG/EDG B5............**143** H1
Shooters Hl CSCFLD/WYGN B72............**77** H1
Shop La CDSL WV8............**20** B1
Shopton Rd BKDE/SHDE B34............**112** C3
Shoreham Cl WLNHL WV13............**38** D4
Short Acre St WSLW WS2............**4** D1
Shorters Av
 ALE/KHTH/YWD B14............**178** D1
Short Heath Rd
 ERDW/GRVHL B23............**76** C2
Shortland Cl DOR/KN B93............**197** E2
Shortlands Cl BVILLE B30............**177** E3
Shortlands La BLOX/PEL WS3............**17** H5
Short Rd SMTHWKW B67............**123** H1
 WOLVN WV10............**23** C1
Short St BILS/COS WV14............**53** H2
 BLKHTH/ROWR B65............**122** A3
 CDSL WV8............**10** C5
 DARL/WED WS10............**55** C5
 DUDN DY1............**84** A4
 HALE B63............**138** B3
 SHHTH WV12............**26** C1
 SHLY B90............**194** A5
 STRBR DY8............**135** F2
 TPTN/OCK DY4............**69** E3
 WOLV WV1............**7** G3
 WSLW WS2............**4** D3
Shorwell Pl BRLYHL DY5............**119** E3
Shottery Gv WALM/CURD B76............**78** B2
Shottery Rd SHLY B90............**180** B4
Shotteswell Rd SHLY B90............**194** B1
Showell Circ WOLVN WV10............**23** G3
Showell Green La SPARK B11............**144** D4
Showell La
 ETTPK/GDPK/PENN WV4............**50** A5
Showell Rd WOLVN WV10............**23** F5
Showells Gdns VAUX/NECH B7............**110** A2
Shrawley Cl HALE B63............**138** C5
 RBRY B45............**187** H1
Shrawley Rd NFLD/LBR B31............**176** A3
Shrewley Crs STETCH B33............**131** G3
Shrewsbury Cl BLOX/PEL WS3............**26** D1
Shrewton Av
 ALE/KHTH/YWD B14............**177** H3
Shrubbery Av TPTN/OCK DY4............**84** D1
Shrubbery Cl WALM/CURD B76............**77** H5
The Shrubbery DUDN DY1............**84** B4
 LDYWD/EDGR B16 *............**125** H1
Shrublands Av
 LCLYGN/QTN B68............**123** F5
Shrub La ERDE/BCHGN B24............**93** E2
Shugborough Dr DUDN DY1............**83** G4
Shustoke La DSYBK/YTR WS5............**57** H4
Shustoke Rd BKDE/SHDE B34............**113** E3
 SOLH B91............**165** F5
Shutlock La MOS/BIL B13............**160** D2
Shut Mill La RMSLY B62............**171** H4
Sibdon Gv NFLD/LBR B31............**175** H5
Sidaway Cl
 BLKHTH/ROWR B65............**104** A3
Sidaway St CDYHTH B64............**121** E3
Sidbury Gv DOR/KN B93............**196** C5
Sidcup Cl BILS/COS WV14............**53** G4
Sidcup Rd KGSTG B44............**75** G2
Siddons Rd BILS/COS WV14............**68** D1
Siddons Wy WBROM B70............**71** E4

Sidenhill Cl SHLY B90............**180** B5
Sidestrand COVEN WV9............**11** H4
The Sidings STRBR DY8............**152** C4
 WBROM B70............**87** G4
Sidlaw Cl HALE B63............**137** H5
 WOLVN WV10............**22** C4
Sidney St BKHL/PFLD WV2............**6** E7
Sidwick Crs BKHL/PFLD WV2............**53** F2
Sigmund Cl WOLV WV1............**38** B2
Signal Gv BLOX/PEL WS3............**27** E1
Signal Hayes Rd
 WALM/CURD B76............**78** C2
Silesbourne Cl CBROM B36 *............**95** E5
Silhill Hall Rd SOLH B91............**164** D2
Silva Av KGSWFD DY6............**100** D5
Silver Birch Cl WASH/WDE B8............**110** C5
Silver Birch Coppice
 FOAKS/STRLY B74............**32** B5
Silver Birch Dr HLYWD B47............**192** D2
Silver Birch Rd BKHL/PFLD WV2............**52** C1
 CHWD/FDBR/MGN B37............**113** H3
 ERDW/GRVHL B23............**77** F5
 FOAKS/STRLY B74............**46** F4
Silverbirch Rd SOLH B91............**182** C2
Silvercroft Av HDSW B21............**89** E2
Silverdale Dr WOLVN WV10............**37** G1
Silverdale Gdns STRBR DY8............**117** G1
Silverdale Rd ERDE/BCHGN B24............**93** H2
Silverfield Cl
 ALE/KHTH/YWD B14............**161** G2
Silver Innage HALE B63............**120** C5
Silverlands Av
 LCLYGN/QTN B68............**123** F1
Silverlands Cl HLGN/YWD B28............**162** D1
Silvermead Ct HLYWD B47............**192** D3
Silvermead Rd
 SCFLD/BOLD B73............**77** E2
Silvermere Rd
 LGN/SDN/BHAMAIR B26............**148** B1
Silver's Cl BLOX/PEL WS3............**17** H2
Silverstone Dr WSLW WS2............**40** B2
Silverstone Dr
 FOAKS/STRLY B74............**60** B2
Silver St ALE/KHTH/YWD B14............**161** G2
 BRLYHL DY5............**118** D5
 B **9** E5
 HLYWD B47............**192** A3
Silverthorne Av TPTN/OCK DY4............**84** D1
Silverthorne La CDYHTH B64............**120** B3
Silverton Cr MOS/BIL B13............**162** B1
Silverton Hts SMTHWKW B67............**106** B3
Silverton Rd SMTHWKW B67............**106** B3
Silverton Wy WNSFLD WV11............**25** F5
Silvester Rd BILS/COS WV14............**54** A2
Silvester Wy BRLYHL DY5............**118** D4
Silvington Cl SLYOAK B29............**159** E3
Simcox Gdns RIDG/WDGT B32............**140** D5
Simcox Rd DARL/WED WS10............**55** H3
Simeon Bissell Cl
 TPTN/OCK DY4............**85** G1
Simeon's Wk BRLYHL DY5............**119** H5
Simmonds Cl BLOX/PEL WS3 *............**17** F4
Simmonds Pl DARL/WED WS10............**55** H1
Simmonds Rd BLOX/PEL WS3............**17** F4
Simmonds Wy BRWNH WS8............**19** G2
Simmons Dr RIDG/WDGT B32............**140** D3
Simmons Leasow
 RIDG/WDGT B32............**140** D5
Simmons Rd WNSFLD WV11............**25** H1
Simms La DUDS DY2............**102** C4
 HLYWD B47............**192** C3
Simon Rd HLYWD B47............**192** C1
Simpkins Cl ALDR WS9............**19** G4
Simpson Gv WOLVN WV10............**23** G4
Simpson Rd CSCFLD/WYGN B72............**62** D3
 WOLVN WV10............**23** G4
 WSLW WS2............**56** A2
Simpson St OLDBY B69............**105** E2
Singer Cft CBROM B36............**95** H5
Sir Alfreds Wy
 WALM/CURD B76............**63** E5
Sir Harrys Rd DIG/EDG B5............**143** C1
Sir Hilton's Rd NFLD/LBR B31............**189** H1
Sir John's Rd SLYOAK B29............**143** C4
Sir Richards Dr HRBN B17............**124** B5
Sisefield Rd HWK/WKHTH B38............**177** E4
Siskin Cl LCLYGN/QTN B68............**122** C2
Siskin Dr DIG/EDG B5............**144** A1
Siskin Rd HAG/WOL DY9............**136** B4
Sister Dora Buildings WSL WS1 *............**4** E5
Sister Dora Gdns WSL WS1............**4** D5
Siviter's Cl BLKHTH/ROWR B65............**121** H1
Siviter's La
 BLKHTH/ROWR B65............**121** H1
Siviter St HALE B63............**138** C3
Six Acres RIDG/WDGT B32............**140** C3
Skelcher Rd SHLY B90............**180** A1
Skemp Cl BILS/COS WV14............**53** H4
Sketchley Cl SMTHWK B66............**106** C4
Skidmore Av BDMR/CCFT WV3............**36** B5
Skidmore Rd BILS/COS WV14............**67** H3
Skinner La DIG/EDG B5............**127** E3
Skinner St WOLV WV1............**6** E3
Skip La DSYBK/YTR WS5............**58** C3
Skipton Gv
 DUNHL/THL/PER WV6............**22** C5
Skipton Rd LDYWD/EDGR B16............**125** A3
Skomer Cl RBRY B45............**173** G4
Skye Cl CBROM B36............**114** B3
Skylark Cl BRLYHL DY5............**85** E5
 ERDW/GRVHL B23............**76** A4
Slack La BFLD/HDSWWD B20............**89** E4
Slacky La BLOX/PEL WS3............**28** B1
Sladefield Rd WASH/WDE B8............**111** E4
Slade Gdns CDSL WV8............**10** C3
Slade Gv DOR/KN B93............**196** C3
Slade Hl
 DUNHL/THL/PER WV6 *............**36** B2
Slade La HLGN/YWD B28............**179** G2
 MGN/WHC B75............**48** C2
Slade Lanker BKDE/SHDE B34............**112** C4
Sladepool Farm Rd
 ALE/KHTH/YWD B14............**178** B2
Slade Rd ERDW/GRVHL B23............**92** B1
 HALE B63............**137** G1
 MGN/WHC B75............**48** A2
 WOLVN WV10............**12** C4

Slaithwaite Rd
  HHTH/SAND B71 ....87 H2
Slaney Ct WSLW WS2 ....56 C1
Slaney Rd WSLW WS2 ....56 B2
Slatch House Rd
  SMTHWKW B67 ....124 A2
Slateley Crs SHLY B90 ....195 F2
Slater Cl CDYHTH B64 ....121 F3
Slater Rd DOR/KN B93 ....196 C4
Slaters La WSLW WS2 ....56 B1
Slaters Pl WLNH WS1 ....56 B1
Slater St BILS/COS WV14 ....54 A5
  DARL/WED WS10 ....55 F2
  TPTN/OCK DY4 ....85 G2
  WLNHL WV13 ....40 A2
Sleaford Gv HLGN/YWD B28 ....163 E3
Sleaford Rd HLGN/YWD B28 ....163 E3
Sledmore Rd DUDS DY2 ....102 D2
The Slieve BFLD/HDSWWD B20 ....90 A3
Slim Av BILS/COS WV14 ....54 A5
Slimbridge Cl SHLY B90 ....195 G2
Slim Rd WSLW WS2 ....40 C3
Slims Ga HALE B63 ....138 C5
Slingfield Rd NFLD/LBR B31 ....176 A4
The Sling DUDS DY2 ....102 C5
Sloane St CBHAMW B1 ....2 A3
Smallbrook La WMBN WV5 ....65 F4
Smallbrook Queensway
  DIG/EDG B5 ....3 G7
Small Cl SMTHWKW B67 ....105 H4
Smalldale Rd PBAR/PBCH B42 ....74 D4
Small Heath Br SPARK B11 ....127 H5
Small Heath Hwy SMHTH B10 ....145 H1
Smallshire Cl WNSFLD WV11 ....25 F5
Smallshire Wy STRBR DY8 ....117 H4
Small St HHTH/SAND B71 ....87 F1
  ....4 D6
Smallwood Cl
  ERDE/BCHGN B24 ....93 H3
  WALM/CURD B76 ....63 E5
Smallwood Rd CDSL WV8 ....11 G5
Smarts Av LICHS WS14 ....13 H1
Smeaton Gdns WSNGN B18 ....107 G5
Smeed Gv ERDE/BCHGN B24 ....93 F3
Smestow La SEDG DY3 ....80 A2
Smestow St WOLVN WV1 ....7 G1
Smirrells Rd HLGN/YWD B28 ....162 C5
Smith Cl BILS/COS WV14 ....55 F4
Smith Cl BILS/COS WV14 ....68 A2
  SMTHWKW B67 ....123 H1
Smithfield Rd BLOX/PEL WS3 ....27 H1
Smithmoor Crs
  HHTH/SAND B71 ....72 B3
Smith Pl TPTN/OCK DY4 ....85 H2
Smith Rd DARL/WED WS10 ....70 D2
  WSLW WS2 ....56 C2
Smiths Cl RIDG/WDGT B32 ....157 F1
Smiths La DOR/KN B93 ....196 C2
Smith St BILS/COS WV14 ....53 H3
  LOZ/NWT B19 ....108 C4
Smiths Wy CSHL/WTROR B46 ....96 A3
Smithy Dr BLOX/PEL WS3 ....18 A3
Smithy La BRLYHL DY5 ....100 D1
The Smithy
  LGN/SDN/BHAMAIR B26 ....147 H1
Smout Crs BILS/COS WV14 ....67 H1
Snapdragon Dr
  DSYBK/YTR WS5 ....57 F5
Snape Rd WNSFLD WV11 ....25 H3
Sneyd Hall Cl BLOX/PEL WS3 * 27 E2
Sneyd Hall Rd BLOX/PEL WS3 ....26 D1
Sneyd La WNSFLD WV11 ....26 A1
Snowberry Dr BRLYHL DY5 ....83 E5
Snowberry Gdns ACGN B27 * 146 C2
Snowdon Gv HALE B63 ....154 D1
Snowdon Rd SEDG DY3 ....67 F5
Snowdon Rd STRBR DY8 ....135 H1
Snow Hv SHHTH WV12 ....25 H1
  WOLVN WV10 ....24 A2
Snowdrop Cl BRWNH WS8 ....18 D1
Snowford Cl SHLY B90 ....179 H4
Snow Hl BKHL/PFLD WV2 ....7 G5
Snow Hill Jct BKHL/PFLD WV2 ....7 G6
Snow Hill Queensway
  CBHAMNE B4 ....3 F3
Snows Hill Dr SHLY B90 ....194 D3
Snowshill Gdns DUDN DY1 ....83 H2
Soberton Cl WNSFLD WV11 ....25 F3
Soho Av WSNGN B18 ....108 A2
Soho Cl SMTHWK B66 ....107 E5
Soho Hl HDSW B21 ....108 A2
Sohopoolway WSNGN B18 ....108 A3
Soho Rd HDSW B21 ....107 H2
Soho Wy SMTHWK B66 ....106 D5
Solari Cl TPTN/OCK DY4 ....70 A3
Solcum St COVEN WV9 ....11 H5
Solihull By-Pass SOLH B91 ....182 D2
Solihull La HLGN/YWD B28 ....163 E4
Solihull Pkwy
  CHWD/FDBR/MGN B37 ....133 E5
Solihull Rd HIA/OLT B92 ....166 D4
  SHLY B90 ....180 D2
  SPARK B11 ....145 F4
Solihull Wy CBROM B36 ....112 C1
  HIA/OLT B92 ....165 E1
  SHLY B90 ....180 C2
Solly Gv TPTN/OCK DY4 ....70 B4
Solva Cl WOLV WV1 ....38 B4
Solway Cl DARL/WED WS10 ....56 C4
Somerby Dr SOLH B91 ....181 G5
Somercotes Rd
  PBAR/PBCH B42 ....74 D3
Somerdale Rd NFLD/LBR B31 ....176 A1
Somerfield Cl RUSH/SHEL WS4 ....29 E1
Somerfield Rd BLOX/PEL WS3 ....27 E2
Somerford Gdns WOLVN WV10 ....13 E5
Somerford Pl WLNHL WV13 ....39 F4
Somerford Rd RIDG/WDGT B32 ....158 B2
Somerford Wy BILS/COS WV14 ....68 B3
Somerland Rd
  LGN/SDN/BHAMAIR B26 ....130 C3
Somerset Crs DARL/WED WS10 ....56 D4
Somerset Dr NFLD/LBR B31 ....189 F1
  STRBR DY8 ....117 H5
Somerset Rd
  BFLD/HDSWWD B20 ....89 H4
  EDG B15 ....142 C1
  ERDW/GRVHL B23 ....76 C5
  HHTH/SAND B71 ....71 H5

RUSH/SHEL WS4 ....42 C1
  WLNHL WV13 ....40 B3
Somers Rd RMSLY B62 ....139 E2
  WSLW WS2 ....56 A1
Somerton Dr
  CHWD/FDBR/MGN B37 ....132 B5
  ERDW/GRVHL B23 ....77 E5
Somerville Rd SCFLD/BOLD B73 ....62 A4
  SMHTH B10 ....128 D4
Somery Rd DUDN DY1 ....84 C3
  RIDG/WDGT B32 ....141 G5
Sommerfield Rd
  RIDG/WDGT B32 ....140 D4
Sommerville Dr
  SCFLD/BOLD B73 ....62 A4
Sonning Dr COVEN WV9 ....11 H5
Sopwith Cft CVALE B35 ....94 C4
Sorrel Cl OLDBY B69 ....85 H4
Sorrel Dr ACGN B27 ....146 B5
  DSYBK/YTR WS5 ....57 G5
Sorrel Gv ERDE/BCHGN B24 ....93 H5
Sorrell Dr ACGN B27 * 146 B5
Southacre Av DIG/EDG B5 ....127 E4
Southall Crs BILS/COS WV14 ....68 C2
Southall Rd WNSFLD WV11 ....25 G5
Southall's La DUDN DY1 ....84 B5
Southampton St WOLV WV1 ....7 G2
Southam Rd HLGN/YWD B28 ....162 C2
South Av DIG/EDG B5 ....135 F3
  WNSFLD WV11 ....24 C5
South Bank Rd CDYHTH B64 ....121 F4
Southbank Vw KGSWFD DY6 ....100 A5
Southbourne Av
  BKDE/SHDE B34 ....111 H3
  WSLW WS2 ....41 F4
Southbourne Cl SLYOAK B29 ....143 E5
Southbourne Rd WOLVN WV10 ....12 C4
South Car Park Rd
  BHAMNEC B40 ....150 B4
Southcote Gv
  HWK/WKHTH B38 ....176 B4
Southcott Av BRLYHL DY5 ....119 F4
South Crs WOLVN WV10 ....14 A1
Southcroft Rd
  ERDW/GRVHL B23 ....92 C3
South Dene SMTHWKW B67 * 106 B4
Southdown Av WSNGN B18 ....108 A3
South Dr CSHL/WTROR B46 ....115 E3
  DIG/EDG B5 ....143 C5
  MGN/WHC B75 ....62 C2
Southern Cl KGSWFD DY6 ....118 B1
Southernwood Rd SEDG DY3 ....66 D3
Southern Dr
  ALE/KHTH/YWD B14 ....177 H5
Southern Rd WASH/WDE B8 ....111 G4
Southern Wy DARL/WED WS10 ....55 E5
Southey Cl SHHTH WV12 ....26 C2
  SOLH B91 ....181 H5
Southfield Av CBROM B36 ....112 D1
  LDYWD/EDGR B16 ....125 F1
Southfield Cl ALDR WS9 ....30 A5
Southfield Dr HLGN/YWD B28 ....163 E5
Southfield Gv BDMR/CCFT WV3 ....50 C1
Southfield Rd
  LDYWD/EDGR B16 ....125 F1
  WNSFLD WV11 ....25 F5
Southfields Cl
  CSHL/WTROR B46 ....115 G4
Southfields Rd SOLH B91 ....181 F4
South Gdns HAG/WOL DY9 ....169 G1
Southgate CDYHTH B64 ....120 D4
  WOLV WV1 ....6 E5
Southgate Rd KGSTG B44 ....75 E1
South Gn
  ETTPK/GDPK/PENN WV4 ....50 D3
South Gv ERDW/GRVHL B23 ....92 D1
  LOZ/NWT B19 ....108 B3
South Holme BORD B9 ....128 A5
Southlands Rd MOS/BIL B13 ....161 G1
Southminster Dr
  ALE/KHTH/YWD B14 ....161 E4
South Ov SEDG DY3 ....83 G1
South Pde CSCFLD/WYGN B72 ....62 D1
South Park Ms BRLYHL DY5 ....119 E2
South Range SPARK B11 ....144 D1
South Rd ALE/KHTH/YWD B14 ....161 E2
  ERDW/GRVHL B23 ....92 D2
  ETTPK/GDPK/PENN WV4 ....52 D4
  HAG/WOL DY9 ....169 G1
  NFLD/LBR B31 ....175 F3
  SMTHWKW B67 ....106 B4
  SPARK B11 ....127 H5
  STRBR DY8 ....135 F3
  TPTN/OCK DY4 ....69 H3
  WSNGN B18 ....108 A3
South Road Av WSNGN B18 ....108 A3
South Roundhay STETCH B33 ....130 C1
South St BRLYHL DY5 ....119 G2
  HRBN B17 ....142 B1
  WLNHL WV13 ....39 E4
  WOLVN WV10 ....23 E4
  WSL WS1 ....4 C7
South Street Gdns WSL WS1 * 4 C7
South Tower VAUX/NECH B7 * 109 H5
South View Cl CDSL WV8 ....10 D5
  WOLVN WV10 ....13 H1
Southview Rdg BRLYHL DY5 ....119 F5
South View Rd SEDG DY5 ....66 D3
Southville Bungalows
  ALE/KHTH/YWD B14 * 178 D1
South Wy BHAMNEC B40 ....150 B4
Southway Ct KGSWFD DY6 ....100 B5
Southwick Pl BILS/COS WV14 ....53 H1
Southwick Rd RMSLY B62 ....138 B3
Southwold Av BVILLE B30 ....177 G2
Southwood Av
  BKDE/SHDE B34 ....112 C2
Southwood Cl KGSWFD DY6 ....100 A4
Southwood Covert
  ALE/KHTH/YWD B14 ....177 G3
Sovereign Dr DUDN DY1 ....83 F4
Sovereign Hts NFLD/LBR B31 ....174 C4
Sovereign Rd BVILLE B30 ....176 D1
Sovereign Wk WSL WS1 ....5 G3
Sovereign Wy MOS/BIL B13 ....144 B3
Sowerby March
  ERDE/BCHGN B24 ....93 H2

Sowers Cl SHHTH WV12 ....26 B5
Sowers Ct MGN/WHC B75 ....47 H1
Sowers Gdns SHHTH WV12 ....26 B5
Spa Gv BVILLE B30 ....160 C2
Spark St SPARK B11 ....144 C1
Sparrey Dr BVILLE B30 ....160 A2
Sparrow Cl DARL/WED WS10 ....56 B3
Speakers Cl OLDBY B69 ....85 E3
Speed Rd TPTN/OCK DY4 ....69 E5
Speedwell Cl ALDR WS9 ....29 H5
  WNSFLD WV11 ....25 E5
Speedwell Gdns BRLYHL DY5 ....118 C5
Speedwell Rd DIG/EDG B5 ....143 H1
  YDLY B25 ....146 A1
Spencer Av BILS/COS WV14 ....68 C3
Spencer Cl ERDE/BCHGN B24 ....93 H2
  HHTH/SAND B71 ....72 B5
  OLDBY B69 ....103 H1
  SEDG DY3 ....82 C2
Spencer St WSNGN B18 ....2 C1
Spenser Av
  DUNHL/THL/PER WV6 ....34 C1
Spernall Gv SLYOAK B29 ....158 C1
Spey Cl DIG/EDG B5 ....143 H1
Spiceland Rd NFLD/LBR B31 ....158 B4
Spiers Cl DOR/KN B93 ....197 G2
Spies Cl RMSLY B62 ....139 H1
Spies La RMSLY B62 ....139 H2
Spills Meadow SEDG DY3 ....83 G1
Spilsbury Cft SOLH B91 ....181 G5
Spindle La SHLY B90 ....194 A2
Spinners End Dr CDYHTH B64 ....120 D3
Spinney Cl BLOX/PEL WS3 ....18 A5
  NFLD/LBR B31 ....175 G2
  STRBR DY8 ....117 F1
Spinney Dr SHLY B90 ....194 D4
The Spinney BDMR/CCFT WV3 ....35 H4
  BFLD/HDSWWD B20 ....89 G2
  FOAKS/STRLY B74 ....31 H4
  HLYWD B47 ....192 D4
  SEDG DY3 ....83 E4
  SOLH B91 ....182 A5
Spiral Cl RMSLY B62 ....122 C4
Spiral Gn ERDE/BCHGN B24 ....93 G2
Spitfire Rd ERDE/BCHGN B24 ....93 C4
Spitfire Wy CVALE B35 ....94 C4
Spondon Rd BKDE/SHDE B34 ....113 E4
Spon Croft WBROM B70 ....87 H5
Spon La South SMTHWK B66 ....105 H1
Spoon Dr HWK/WKHTH B38 ....176 B3
Spooner Cft DIG/EDG B5 ....142 D5
Spooners Cl HIA/OLT B92 ....165 H5
Spouthouse La GTB/HAM B43 ....73 G4
Spout La WSL WS1 ....4 E7
Spreadbury Cl HRBN B17 ....124 B4
Sprig Cft CBROM B36 ....111 G1
Spring Av BLKHTH/ROWR B65 ....122 B2
Springavon Cft HRBN B17 ....141 H1
Springbank BORD B9 ....128 D1
Springbank Rd BILS/COS WV14 ....126 C5
Springbrook Cl CBROM B36 ....95 F5
Spring Cl HAG/WOL DY9 ....169 F1
  RUSH/SHEL WS4 ....18 C5
  SOLH B91 ....181 F2
Spring Coppice Dr
  DOR/KN B93 ....197 E5
Spring Ct WSL WS1 ....5 J7
Spring Crs CDYHTH B64 ....121 F5
Springcroft Rd SPARK B11 ....145 H5
Springfield ERDW/GRVHL B23 ....76 C5
Springfield Av BHTH/HG B12 ....144 C1
  HAG/WOL DY9 ....136 C3
  SEDG DY3 ....67 G2
Springfield Cl
  BLKHTH/ROWR B65 ....103 G4
Springfield Crs DUDS DY2 ....103 F1
  HIA/OLT B92 ....148 A4
  WALM/CURD B76 ....63 H4
  WBROM B70 ....88 A5
Springfield Dr
  ALE/KHTH/YWD B14 * 161 E1
Springfield Gv SEDG DY3 ....67 F2
Springfield La
  BLKHTH/ROWR B65 ....103 G4
  WOLVN WV10 ....12 D3
Springfield Rd
  ALE/KHTH/YWD B14 ....161 F2
  BILS/COS WV14 ....54 A1
  CBROM B36 ....118 B5
  LGLYGN/QTN B68 ....105 G5
  MOS/BIL B13 ....162 B1
  RMSLY B62 ....122 B5
  WALM/CURD B76 ....78 B1
  WOLVN WV10 ....37 G1
Springfields
  CSHL/WTROR B46 ....115 F4
  RUSH/SHEL WS4 ....28 D4
Springfields Rd BRLYHL DY5 ....118 D2
Springfield St WSNGN B18 ....126 A1
Springfield Ter
  BLKHTH/ROWR B65 ....103 F4
Spring Gdns DUDS DY2 ....102 D1
  HDSW B21 ....107 H2
Spring Gv LOZ/NWT B19 * 108 B3
Spring Grove Gdns
  WSNGN B18 ....107 H3
Spring Head DARL/WED WS10 ....70 D1
Spring Hl ERDE/BCHGN B24 ....92 D3
  WSNGN B18 ....108 A5
Springhill Av
  ETTPK/GDPK/PENN WV4 ....50 C5
Spring Hill Circ WSNGN B18 ....2 A3
Springhill Cl RUSH/SHEL WS4 ....29 F1
  SHHTH WV12 ....26 D5
Springhill Gv
  ETTPK/GDPK/PENN WV4 ....50 C4
Springhill La
  ETTPK/GDPK/PENN WV4 ....50 A4
Springhill Pk
  ETTPK/GDPK/PENN WV4 ....50 B5
Spring Hill Pas WSNGN B18 ....126 A1
Springhill Rd BRWNH WS8 ....9 H1
  WNSFLD WV11 ....24 D3
  WSL WS1 ....5 K5
Spring La ERDE/BCHGN B24 ....93 E3
  RMSLY B62 ....171 H1
  RUSH/SHEL WS4 ....18 C5

SHHTH WV12 ....39 H1
  HALE B63 ....138 B5
  TPTN/OCK DY4 ....70 A5
Spring Meadow CDYHTH B64 ....121 F3
Spring Meadow Rd DUDS DY2 ....120 C2
Spring Parklands DUDN DY1 ....102 A1
Spring Parklands DUDN DY1 ....102 A1
Spring Rd DUDS DY2 ....102 D3
  EDG B15 ....126 D5
  ETTPK/GDPK/PENN WV4 ....53 E4
  RUSH/SHEL WS4 ....29 F1
  SMTHWK B66 ....105 H1
  SPARK B11 ....145 H4
Springside RIDG/WDGT B32 ....141 F2
Springslade Dr
  ERDE/BCHGN B24 ....93 H3
The Springs CDYHTH B64 ....121 G3
Spring St EDG B15 ....126 D4
  HAG/WOL DY9 ....136 C5
  HALE B63 ....137 G1
  TPTN/OCK DY4 ....85 G1
Springthorpe Gn
  ERDE/BCHGN B24 ....93 G2
Springthorpe Rd
  ERDE/BCHGN B24 ....93 H3
Springvale Av BILS/COS WV14 ....53 F4
  DSYBK/YTR WS5 ....58 A1
Springvale St WLNHL WV13 ....68 A2
Spring Vale Rd
  BLKHTH/ROWR B65 * 103 G4
Springvale St WLNHL WV13 ....39 H2
Spring Wk HALE B63 ....154 D1
  OLDBY B69 ....105 E4
  WSLW WS2 ....41 F2
Sproat Av DARL/WED WS10 ....55 E3
Spruce Gv ERDE/BCHGN B24 ....93 F4
Spruce Rd DSYBK/YTR WS5 ....57 H5
Spruce Wy BDMR/CCFT WV3 ....35 H4
Spur Tree Av BDMR/CCFT WV3 ....35 E4
Squadron Cl CVALE B35 ....95 E2
Square Cl RIDG/WDGT B32 ....140 C4
The Square BKHL/PFLD WV2 ....7 F5
  CDSL WV8 ....10 B3
  HRBN B17 ....141 H1
  SHHTH WV12 ....26 B2
  SOLH B91 ....182 A2
  TPTN/OCK DY4 ....70 B4
Squires Ct BRLYHL DY5 ....119 E3
Squires Cft WALM/CURD B76 ....78 C1
Squires Gate Rd WLNHL WV13 ....39 H3
Squirrel Hollow
  WALM/CURD B76 ....78 C1
Squirrels Hollow
  LGLYGN/QTN B68 ....123 G3
Squirrel Wk
  ETTPK/GDPK/PENN WV4 ....51 G4
  FOAKS/STRLY B74 ....32 A5
Stable Cft SEDG DY3 ....67 G5
Stable Ct HHTH/SAND B71 ....72 B4
Stableford Cl RIDG/WDGT B32 ....141 H4
The Stables SLYOAK B29 ....143 E5
Stacey Cl CDYHTH B64 ....121 E4
Stacey Grange Gdns
  RBRY B45 * 188 A2
Stackhouse Cl ALDR WS9 ....19 G4
Stackhouse Dr RUSH/SHEL WS4 ....18 A3
Stadium Cl WLNHL WV13 ....39 H2
Stadium Dr DUDS DY2 ....120 C3
Stafford Cl BLOX/PEL WS3 ....17 E5
Stafford Dr HHTH/SAND B71 ....71 F4
Stafford La CDSL WV8 ....10 B4
Stafford Rd DARL/WED WS10 ....54 D2
  GTWY WS6 ....16 C5
  HDSW B21 ....107 H1
  WOLVN WV10 ....23 E3
Staffordshire Pool Cl
  AST/WIT B6 ....91 F5
Staffordshire Wy CDSL WV8 ....10 B2
Stafford St BILS/COS WV14 ....53 H3
  DARL/WED WS10 ....70 C1
  DUDN DY1 ....84 B5
  WLNHL WV13 ....39 G3
  WOLV WV1 ....7 G3
  WSLW WS2 ....4 D2
Stafford Street Jct WOLV WV1 ....7 F2
Staff Wy ERDW/GRVHL B23 ....77 G2
Stag Crs BLOX/PEL WS3 ....28 A4
Stag Hill Rd BLOX/PEL WS3 ....28 A3
Stag Wk WALM/CURD B76 ....78 C4
Stainsby Av LOZ/NWT B19 ....108 C4
Stainsby Cft SHLY B90 ....195 F1
Stakenbridge La KIDD DY10 ....168 C1
Stalling's La KGSWFD DY6 ....82 C5
Stambermill Cl HAG/WOL DY9 ....136 B2
Stamford Cft SOLH B91 ....181 H3
Stamford Gv
  BFLD/HDSWWD B20 ....90 C4
Stamford Rd
  BFLD/HDSWWD B20 ....90 C5
  BRLYHL DY5 ....135 H2
  STRBR DY8 ....135 H2
Stamford St STRBR DY8 ....118 B5
Stambrook Rd SHLY B90 ....195 G3
Stanbury Av DARL/WED WS10 ....54 D2
Stanbury Rd
  ALE/KHTH/YWD B14 ....178 D1
Stancroft Gv
  LGN/SDN/BHAMAIR B26 ....130 C4
Standard Wy
  ERDE/BCHGN B24 ....110 D1
Standbridge Wy
  TPTN/OCK DY4 ....85 G1
Standhills Rd KGSWFD DY6 ....100 B4
Standlake Av CBROM B36 ....111 H2
Stanfield Rd GTB/HAM B43 ....59 H5
  RIDG/WDGT B32 ....124 A5
Stanford Av PBAR/PBCH B42 ....74 A4
Stanford Gv HALE B63 ....154 C1
Stanford Rd BKHL/PFLD WV2 ....52 A3
  BLKHTH/ROWR B65 ....121 H1
Stanhoe Cl BRLYHL DY5 ....119 H4
Stanhope Rd SMTHWKW B67 ....124 B1
Stanhope St BDMR/CCFT WV3 ....6 B5
  BHTH/HG B12 ....127 G5
  DUDS DY2 ....103 E3

Stanhope Wy GTB/HAM B43 ....59 H4
Stanhurst Wy HHTH/SAND B71 ....72 C1
Stanier Cl RUSH/SHEL WS4 ....28 D3
Stanier Gv BFLD/HDSWWD B20 ....90 B4
Stanier St CBHAMNE B4 ....3 H1
Stanley Av MGN/WHC B75 ....63 F4
  RIDG/WDGT B32 ....124 A5
  SHLY B90 ....180 B1
Stanley Cl HLGN/YWD B28 ....163 F5
  WNSFLD WV11 ....25 F2
Stanley Ct
  DUNHL/THL/PER WV6 ....34 C1
Stanley Dr SEDG DY3 ....80 C4
Stanley Pl BILS/COS WV14 ....53 F3
  MOS/BIL B13 * 144 B4
  RUSH/SHEL WS4 ....28 D4
Stanley Rd
  ALE/KHTH/YWD B14 ....160 D3
  DARL/WED WS10 ....55 F3
  HHTH/SAND B71 ....72 A4
  LGLYGN/QTN B68 ....123 G5
  NFLD/LBR B31 ....175 F5
  STRBR DY8 ....135 F4
  VAUX/NECH B7 ....110 A2
  WOLVN WV10 ....23 G3
Stanley St BLOX/PEL WS3 ....27 G2
Stanmore Gv HALE B63 ....154 B1
Stanmore Rd
  LDYWD/EDGR B16 ....125 E3
Stanton Av DUDN DY1 ....67 H5
Stanton Gv
  LGN/SDN/BHAMAIR B26 ....130 B4
  SHLY B90 ....180 A1
  TPTN/OCK DY4 ....85 G1
Stanton Rd GTB/HAM B43 ....73 F3
  SHLY B90 ....180 A1
  WOLV WV1 ....37 H3
Stanville Rd
  LGN/SDN/BHAMAIR B26 ....148 A1
Stanway Gdns HHTH/SAND B71 ....71 H5
Stanway Gv KGSTG B44 ....60 B5
Stanway Rd HHTH/SAND B71 ....71 H5
  SHLY B90 ....180 D1
Stanwell Gv ERDW/GRVHL B23 ....76 C5
Stanwick Av STETCH B33 ....131 G1
Stapenhall Rd SHLY B90 ....195 G3
Stapleford Cft
  ALE/KHTH/YWD B14 ....177 G3
Stapleford Gv STRBR DY8 ....118 A2
Staple Hall Rd NFLD/LBR B31 ....175 F2
Staplehurst Rd
  HLGN/YWD B28 ....162 D2
Staple Lodge Rd
  NFLD/LBR B31 ....175 H4
Stapleton Cl WALM/CURD B76 ....78 D5
Stapleton Dr
  CHWD/FDBR/MGN B37 ....132 A1
Stapleton Rd ALDR WS9 ....29 H5
Stapylton Av HRBN B17 ....141 H2
Starbank Rd SMHTH B10 ....129 E4
Starbold Crs DOR/KN B93 ....197 F3
Star Cl TPTN/OCK DY4 ....86 A1
  WSLW WS2 ....40 D1
Starcross Rd ACGN B27 ....146 C5
Star Hl EDG B15 ....126 B4
Starkey Cft
  CHWD/FDBR/MGN B37 ....132 C2
Starkie Dr LGLYGN/QTN B68 ....105 G5
Starley Wy
  CHWD/FDBR/MGN B37 ....149 G1
Star St BDMR/CCFT WV3 ....36 A5
  HAG/WOL DY9 ....136 D2
Statham Dr LDYWD/EDGR B16 ....125 E2
Station Ap DOR/KN B93 ....196 D5
  FOAKS/STRLY B74 ....32 D4
  SCFLD/BOLD B73 ....62 B2
  SOLH B91 ....181 G1
Station Buildings
  DUNHL/THL/PER WV6 * 36 A1
Station Cl BLOX/PEL WS3 ....27 F2
  CDSL WV8 ....10 A4
Station Dr BRLYHL DY5 ....118 D3
  FOAKS/STRLY B74 ....47 F5
  HAG/WOL DY9 ....152 C5
  HIA/OLT B92 ....164 A1
  KIDD DY10 ....168 B5
  TPTN/OCK DY4 ....85 H2
Station Link Rd
  CHWD/FDBR/MGN B37 ....149 H5
Station Dr BLOX/PEL WS3 ....27 F2
Station Rd ACGN B27 ....146 C4
  ALDR WS9 ....30 A5
  ALE/KHTH/YWD B14 ....160 D2
  AST/WIT B6 ....91 F5
  BLKHTH/ROWR B65 ....54 A3
  BLKHTH/ROWR B65 ....103 E5
  BLOX/PEL WS3 ....18 A4
  BRLYHL DY5 ....101 E5
  BVILLE B30 ....176 C1
  CDSL WV8 ....10 A4
  CDYHTH B64 ....121 G4
  CHWD/FDBR/MGN B37 ....131 G5
  CSHL/WTROR B46 ....115 F1
  DOR/KN B93 ....197 F4
  ERDW/GRVHL B23 ....92 D2
  HAG/WOL DY9 ....152 C4
  HDSW B21 ....107 E1
  HIA/OLT B92 ....167 G3
  HRBN B17 ....142 B5
  HWK/WKHTH B38 ....176 D1
  NFLD/LBR B31 ....175 G3
  OLDBY B69 ....105 E4
  SCFLD/BOLD B73 ....28 C4
  SCFLD/BOLD B73 ....62 C3
  SOLH B91 ....181 H1
  STETCH B33 ....129 H1
  WMBN WV5 ....65 E3
  WSLW WS2 ....42 D4
Station Sr BLOX/PEL WS3 ....16 C4
  CBHAMW B1 ....3 F7
  CDYHTH B64 ....120 C4
  DARL/WED WS10 ....55 G2
  SCFLD/BOLD B73 ....62 C3
  TPTN/OCK DY4 ....85 G1
  WSLW WS2 ....4 D5
Staunton Rd ALE/KHTH/YWD B14 ....160 D4
  WOLV WV1 ....37 E1
Staveley Rd
  ALE/KHTH/YWD B14 ....160 D4
  WOLV WV1 ....37 E1

Stead Cl TPTN/OCK DY4 ....69 H2
  WSLW WS2 ....23 C1
Steadman Cft TPTN/OCK DY4 * ...70 B3
Stechford La WASH/WDE B8 ....111 G4
Stechford Rd BKDE/SHDE B34 ..111 H4
Steel Bright Rd SMTHWK B66 ...107 E3
Steel Dr WOLVN WV10 ....19 F2
Steel Gv YDLY B25 ....129 G5
Steelhouse La BKHL/PFLD WV2 ...2 J7
  CBHAMNE B4 ....3 H5
Steelpark Rd RMSLY B62 ....121 H5
Steelpark Wy WNSFLD WV11 ....38 D1
Steel Rd NFLD/LBR B31 ....175 F3
Steene Gv NFLD/LBR B31 ....174 C2
The Steeples STRBR DY8 ....135 H4
Steepwood Cft BVILLE B30 .....176 B1
Stella Cft
  CHWD/FDBR/MGN B37 ....132 C2
Stella Gv GTB/HAM B43 ....73 E3
Stella Rd TPTN/OCK DY4 ....69 H5
Stenbury Cl WOLVN WV10 ....13 F3
Stencils Dr RUSH/SHEL WS4 ....42 D2
Stennels Av RMSLY B62 ....139 G3
Stennels Crs RMSLY B62 ....139 G3
Stephens Cl WNSFLD WV11 .....25 F2
Stephenson Av WSLW WS2 ......27 E4
Stephenson Dr
  CHWD/FDBR/MGN B37 ....132 B2
  DUNHL/THL/PER WV6 ....20 C5
Stephenson Pl CBHAM B2 ....3 G6
Stephenson Sq WSLW WS2 ......27 F5
Stephenson St BDMR/CCFT WV3 ..6 D5
  CBHAM B2 ....2 E6
Stephens Rd WALM/CURD B76 ..63 G4
Stepping Stone Cl WSLW WS2 ..40 D1
Stepping Stones STRBR DY8 ...135 H2
Steppingstone St DUDN DY1 ....83 G5
Sterling Pk BRLYHL DY5 * 101 H5
Sterndale Rd PBAR/PBCH B42 ..74 C5
Steven Dr BILS/COS WV14 .....52 A2
Stevens Av BKHL/PFLD WV2 ....37 E5
Stevens Ga BKHL/PFLD WV2 ....37 E5
Stevens Rd HAG/WOL DY9 .....136 B5
Steward St WSNGN B18 ....126 A1
Stewart Rd ALDR WS9 ....16 C4
  KGSWFD DY6 ....99 H5
Stewarts Rd RMSLY B62 ....122 B5
Stewart St BKHL/PFLD WV2 ......7 F7
Stewkins STRBR DY8 ....118 A4
Steyning Rd
  LGN/SDN/BHAMAIR B26 ....147 E2
Stickley La SEDG DY3 ....83 E2
Stilehouse Crs
  BLKHTH/ROWR B65 ....122 A2
Stilthouse Gv RBRY B45 ....188 A1
Stirling Crs SHHTH WV12 ....25 H5
Stirling Rd BILS/COS WV14 .....54 B5
  DUDS DY2 ....85 F2
  LDYWD/EDGR B16 ....115 H3
  SCFLD/BOLD B73 ....76 B1
  SHLY B90 ....181 E5
Stirrup Cl DSYBK/YTR WS5 .....57 F4
Stockbridge Cl
  DUNHL/THL/PER WV6 ....34 D3
Stockdale Pl EDG B15 ....125 F4
Stock Exchange Buildings
  CBHAMNW B3 * 2 E5
Stockfield Rd ACGN B27 ....146 B3
Stockhill Dr RBRY B45 ....187 H2
Stocking St HAG/WOL DY9 ....136 D2
Stockland Rd
  ERDW/GRVHL B23 ....92 B2
Stockley Crs SHLY B90 ....180 D2
Stockmans Cl
  HWK/WKHTH B38 ....176 C5
Stockton Cl DOR/KN B93 ......197 H4
  WALM/CURD B76 ....95 E1
  WSLW WS2 ....27 H5
Stockton Gv STECH B33 ....131 F3
Stockwell Av BRLYHL DY5 .....119 F4
Stockwell End
  DUNHL/THL/PER WV6 ....21 H4
Stockwell Ri HIA/OLT B92 ....165 F3
Stockwell Rd
  DUNHL/THL/PER WV6 ....21 H5
  HDSW B21 ....89 G4
Stokes Av TPTN/OCK DY4 ....69 H5
  WLNHL WV13 ....59 F5
Stokesay Av
  DUNHL/THL/PER WV6 ....34 D2
Stokesay Cl OLDBY B69 ....103 G1
Stokesay Gv NFLD/LBR B31 ....175 F5
Stokes St WOLVN WV10 ....37 G1
Stoke Wy EDG B15 ....85 H2
Stom Rd BILS/COS WV14 ....53 F3
Stonacre Cl BDMR/CCFT WV3 ..35 E4
Stone Av MGN/WHC B75 ....63 G3
Stonebow Av SHLY B90 ....181 H5
Stonebridge Crs
  CHWD/FDBR/MGN B37 ....113 H5
Stonebridge Rd
  CSHL/WTROR B46 ....133 G4
Stonebrook Wy SLYOAK B29 ...141 F5
Stonechat Dr
  ERDW/GRVHL B23 ....92 A4
Stone Cl HWK/WKHTH B38 .....176 D3
Stonecroft Av RBRY B45 ....188 A1
Stonecrop Cl BRWNH WS8 ....9 G1
  HWK/WKHTH B38 ....176 D5
Stone Cross CSHL/WTROR B46 ..86 B5
Stonedown Cl BILS/COS WV14 ..53 E5
Stonefield Dr BRLYHL DY5 .....100 C2
Stonefield Rd BILS/COS WV14 * ..53 H1
Stoneford Rd SHLY B90 ....180 A1
Stonehaven Gv
  HLGN/YWD B28 ....163 F2
Stonehenge Cft
  ALE/KHTH/YWD B14 ....177 H4
Stonehill Cft SHLY B90 ....195 F2
Stonehouse Av WLNHL WV13 ...39 F2
Stonehouse Crs
  DARL/WED WS10 ....71 F1
Stonehouse Dr
  FOAKS/STRLY B74 ....45 H1
Stonehouse Hl SLYOAK B29 ...141 G5
Stonehouse La
  RIDG/WDGT B32 ....140 D5

Stonehouse Rd
  SCFLD/BOLD B73 ....61 H5
Stonehurst Rd GTB/HAM B43 ...59 G5
Stonelea ALDR WS9 ....30 B5
Stonelea Cl HHTH/SAND B71 ....72 A3
Stoneleigh Cl FOAKS/STRLY B74 ..46 D5
Stoneleigh Gdns CDSL WV8 ....10 B3
Stoneleigh Rd
  BFLD/HDSWWD B20 ....91 E5
  SOLH B91 ....163 H5
Stoneleigh Wy SEDG DY3 ....66 D1
Stonepine Pl SEDG DY3 ....67 G5
Stone Rd EDG B15 ....126 D5
Stonerwood Av
  HLGN/YWD B28 ....162 C3
Stones Gn ERDW/GRVHL B23 ...76 D5
Stone St DUDN DY1 ....84 C5
  OLDBY B69 ....105 E2
Stoneton Gv SLYOAK B29 ......158 C2
Stoney La BHTH/HG B12 ....17 F4
  DUDS DY2 ....85 F1
  HHTH/SAND B71 ....87 H2
  KIDD DY10 ....169 E2
  RIDG/WDGT B32 ....140 B1
  STRBR DY8 ....130 A3
Stony La SMTHWKW B67 ....106 B3
Stony St SMTHWK B66 ....106 C3
Stornoway Rd CVALE B35 ....94 D2
Storrs Cl BORD B9 ....128 A3
Storrs Pl SMHTH B10 ....128 B3
The Storrs Wy
  RIDG/WDGT B32 ....157 F3
Stot Fold Rd
  ALE/KHTH/YWD B14 ....178 B3
Stourbridge Rd BRGRVW B61 ..185 H3
  BRLYHL DY5 ....101 G4
  DUDN DY1 ....84 A5
  ETTPK/GDPK/PENN WV4 ....50 C5
  HAG/WOL DY9 ....185 G2
  HALE B63 ....138 B3
  HALE B63 ....138 C4
  WMBN WV5 ....64 D3
Stour Cl HALE B63 ....138 A1
Stourdale Rd CDYHTH B64 ....120 C5
Stourdell Rd HALE B63 ....138 A1
Stour Hl BRLYHL DY5 ....120 A5
Stourmore Cl SHHTH WV12 ....26 B4
Stour Vale Rd WBROM B70 .....86 C3
  WSNGN B18 ....126 A1
Stourton Cl DOR/KN B93 ......197 F1
  WALM/CURD B76 ....63 F4
Stourton Dr
  ETTPK/GDPK/PENN WV4 ....50 C3
Stourton Rd RIDG/WDGT B32 ..140 B2
Stour Valley Cl BRLYHL DY5 ...119 F5
Stow Dr BRLYHL DY5 ....135 H1
Stowell Rd KGSTG B44 ....75 F4
Stowe St BLOX/PEL WS3 ....27 G3
Stow Gv CBROM B36 ....112 A2
Stow Heath La WOLV WV1 ......53 F1
Stow Heath Pl WOLV WV1 ......53 F1
Stowmans Cl BILS/COS WV14 ..53 F5
Straight Rd SHHTH WV12 ....26 A4
Straits Gn SEDG DY3 ....82 D2
Straits Rd SEDG DY3 ....82 D3
The Straits SEDG DY3 ....82 C2
Stratford Cl DUDN DY1 ....83 G4
Stratford Pl BHTH/HG B12 .....127 G3
  SPARK B11 ....127 G4
Stratford Rd HLGN/YWD B28 ...162 D3
  HOCK/TIA B94 ....198 A5
  SHLY B90 ....194 D1
  SPARK B11 ....127 G4
Stratford St SPARK B11 ....127 G4
Stratford St North SPARK B11 .127 G4
Strathdene Rd SLYOAK B29 ....142 A5
Strathern Dr BILS/COS WV14 ...68 A2
Strathmore Crs WMBN WV5 ....65 E2
Strathmore Rd TPTN/OCK DY4 ..69 G3
Stratton St WOLVN WV10 ......37 G1
Strawberry Cl DUDN DY1 ......104 A2
Strawberry La WLNHL WV13 ...38 C2
Stream Meadow
  RUSH/SHEL WS4 ....29 E1
Stream Pk KGSWFD DY6 ....99 H5
Stream Rd KGSWFD DY6 ....99 H5
Streamside Wy HIA/OLT B92 ..148 B5
  RUSH/SHEL WS4 ....29 E1
Streatham Gv KGSTG B44 ......75 G1
Streather Rd MGN/WHC B75 ...47 G4
Streetly Crs FOAKS/STRLY B74 ..46 B2
Streetly Dr FOAKS/STRLY B74 ..46 B2
Streetly La FOAKS/STRLY B74 ..46 C3
Streetly Rd ERDW/GRVHL B23 ..92 B1
Streetly Wd FOAKS/STRLY B74 ..46 B2
Streetsbrooke Rd SOLH B91 ...147 G1
Streets Corner Gdns ALDR WS9 ..19 F1
Strensham Hl BHTH/HG B12 ...144 A3
Strensham Rd BHTH/HG B12 ...144 A3
Stretton Gdns CDSL WV8 ....10 B3
Stretton Gv LOZ/NWT B19 * ...108 C2
  SPARK B11 ....145 E1
  WASH/WDE B8 ....111 F3
Stretton Pl BILS/COS WV14 ....68 C1
  DUDS DY2 ....102 D5
Stretton Rd OLDBY B69 ....103 G2
  SHLY B90 ....180 B5
Stringer Cl MGN/WHC B75 .....47 E1
Stringes Cl WLNHL WV13 ......39 H2
Stringes La WLNHL WV13 ......39 H3
Strode Rd BKHL/PFLD WV2 ....52 A2
Stronsay Cl RBRY B45 ....173 H4
Stroud Av WLNHL WV13 ....40 A1
Stroud Cl WLNHL WV13 ....40 A1
Stroud Rd SHLY B90 ....179 H3

Strutt Cl EDG B15 ....125 F4
Stuart Crs DUDS DY2 ....85 E5
Stuart Rd
  BLKHTH/ROWR B65 ....104 A5
  RMSLY B62 ....139 H2
Stuarts Dr STETCH B33 ....129 H3
Stuarts Gn HAG/WOL DY9 .....152 D2
Stuarts Rd STETCH B33 ....129 H2
Stuart St BLOX/PEL WS3 ......27 F2
  VAUX/NECH B7 ....110 A2
Stuarts Wy RIDG/WDGT B32 ...157 F3
Stubbers Green Rd
  RUSH/SHEL WS4 ....29 F2
Stubbington Cl WLNHL WV13 ...38 D4
Stubbs Rd BDMR/CCFT WV3 ....51 G1
Stubby La WNSFLD WV11 ....25 G4
Stubley Dr WOLVN WV10 ....19 G5
Studland Rd HLGN/YWD B28 ...163 E2
Stud La STETCH B33 ....130 B1
Studley Cft HIA/OLT B92 ......148 A4
Studley Dr BRLYHL DY5 ....119 E4
Studley Ga STRBR DY8 ....134 D2
Studley Rd BDMR/CCFT WV3 ...35 G5
Sturman Dr
  BLKHTH/ROWR B65 ....121 H3
Suckling Green La CDSL WV8 ..10 B5
Sudbury Cl WNSFLD WV11 .....25 F2
Sudbury Gv KGSTG B44 ....75 H1
Sudeley Cl CBROM B36 ....94 D5
Sudeley Gdns DUDN DY1 ....83 F4
Suffield Gv ERDW/GRVHL B23 ..91 H1
Suffolk Cl LGLYGN/QTN B68 ...105 F5
  WNSFLD WV11 ....24 C4
Suffolk Dr BRLYHL DY5 ....119 E5
Suffolk Gv ALDR WS9 ....30 B2
Suffolk Pl CBHAM B1 * 5 F7
  WSLW WS2 ....27 H5
Suffolk Rd DARL/WED WS10 ...56 C5
  DUDS DY2 ....102 A2
Suffolk St Queensway
  ....2 E6
Suffrage St SMTHWK B66 .....106 D4
Sugden Gv DIG/EDG B5 ....127 E4
Sulgrave Cl DUDN DY1 ....84 A3
Sumburgh Cft CVALE B35 ......94 C3
Summercourt Dr KGSWFD DY6 ..99 G4
Summercourt Sq KGSWFD DY6 ..99 G4
Summer Cft LOZ/NWT B19 ....108 C2
Summer Dr SEDG DY3 ....83 E3
Summerfield Av KGSWFD DY6 ...99 G2
Summerfield Crs
  LDYWD/EDGR B16 ....125 G1
Summerfield Dr SLYOAK B29 ..158 C2
Summerfield Rd DUDS DY2 ....102 D2
  HAG/WOL DY9 ....170 C3
  HIA/OLT B92 ....164 C1
  LDYWD/EDGR B16 ....125 G1
  WOLV WV1 ....6 C4
Summerfields Av RMSLY B62 ..122 D4
Summergate SEDG DY3 ....83 F3
Summer Hl HALE B63 ....138 C2
  KGSWFD DY6 ....99 G3
Summer Hill Rd CBHAMW B1 ....2 A3
Summerhill Rd BILS/COS WV14 ..68 D2
  TPTN/OCK DY4 ....69 F3
Summer Hill St CBHAMW B1 ....2 B4
Summerhouse Rd
  BILS/COS WV14 ....68 A2
Summer La LOZ/NWT B19 ....3 F1
  RUSH/SHEL WS4 ....30 B5
  SEDG DY3 ....83 E3
  WALM/CURD B76 ....79 F5
Summerlee Rd
  ERDE/BCHGN B24 ....93 F4
Summer Rd ACGN B27 ....146 A5
  BLKHTH/ROWR B65 ....122 B1
  DUDN DY1 ....84 A2
  EDG B15 ....126 C5
  ERDW/GRVHL B23 ....92 B2
Summer Row BKHL/PFLD WV2 ...7 F5
  CBHAMNW B3 ....2 D4
Summer St HAG/WOL DY9 .....136 C2
  HHTH/SAND B71 ....87 H2
  KGSWFD DY6 ....99 G2
  STRBR DY8 ....135 F2
  WLNHL WV13 ....39 F5
Summerton Rd OLDBY B69 ....104 B1
Summervale Rd HAG/WOL DY9 .152 C5
Summerville Ter HRBN B17 * ..142 A2
Summit Crs SMTHWK B66 .....106 A1
Summit Gdns HALE B63 ....138 B3
Summit Pl SEDG DY3 ....82 D4
The Summit HAG/WOL DY9 ....136 B3
Sumner Rd CSHL/WTROR B46 .115 G3
Sunbeam Cl CBROM B36 ......95 H2
Sunbeam St BKHL/PFLD WV2 ..52 A4
Sunbeam Wy STETCH B33 .....131 E2
Sunbury Cl BILS/COS WV14 ....68 D2
Sunbury Rd HALE B63 ....138 B3
  NFLD/LBR B31 ....189 E1
Sunbury Rd NFLD/LBR B31 ....158 D5
Sunderland Dr STRBR DY8 ....118 C4
Sunderton Rd
  ALE/KHTH/YWD B14 ....178 A1
Sundew Cft CBROM B36 ....111 H1
Sundial La GTB/HAM B43 ....73 H2
Sundour Crs WNSFLD WV11 ...24 B1
Sundridge Rd KGSTG B44 ......60 A4
Sunleigh Gv ACGN B27 ....147 E5
Sunningdale RMSLY B62 ......139 G3
Sunningdale Av
  DUNHL/THL/PER WV6 ....20 B5
Sunningdale Cl
  BFLD/HDSWWD B20 ....89 G2
  SCFLD/BOLD B73 ....77 E1
  STRBR DY8 ....135 F5
Sunningdale Dr OLDBY B69 ...103 G2
Sunningdale Rd SEDG DY3 ....66 D2
  SPARK B11 ....145 H2
Sunny Av BHTH/HG B12 ....144 C2
Sunnybank Av KGSTG B44 .....75 H4

Sunnybank Cl ALDR WS9 ......45 E3
Sunny Bank Rd
  LGLYGN/QTN B68 ....123 G5
Sunnybank Rd
  SCFLD/BOLD B73 ....77 E3
  SEDG DY3 ....83 G1
Sunnydene WASH/WDE B8 ....111 E4
Sunny Hill Cl WMBN WV5 ......65 F5
Sunnymead Rd
  LGN/SDN/BHAMAIR B26 ....147 F1
Sunnymead Wy
  FOAKS/STRLY B74 ....60 B1
Sunnymede Rd KGSWFD DY6 ..100 C5
Sunnyside ALDR WS9 ....19 F5
  OLDBY B69 ....103 H2
Sunnyside Av
  ERDW/GRVHL B23 ....92 C3
Sunridge Av LOZ/NWT B19 ....108 D3
  WMBN WV5 ....65 G4
Sunset Pl
  ETTPK/GDPK/PENN WV4 ....52 D5
Sun St BRLYHL DY5 ....119 H3
  WOLVN WV10 ....7 J2
Surfeit Hl CDYHTH B64 ....121 E4
Surfeit Hill Rd CDYHTH B64 ...120 D4
Surrey Crs HHTH/SAND B71 ....71 E3
Surrey Dr BDMR/CCFT WV3 ....50 C3
  KGSWFD DY6 ....100 A5
Surrey Rd DUDS DY2 ....102 A2
  KGSTG B44 ....60 A4
Surrey Wk ALDR WS9 ....30 A2
Sussex Av DARL/WED WS10 ...56 D4
  HHTH/SAND B71 ....71 G5
Sussex Dr BDMR/CCFT WV3 ...36 A4
Sutherland Av BKHL/PFLD WV2 ..37 H5
  SHLY B90 ....180 C2
Sutherland Cl GTB/HAM B43 ...59 H4
Sutherland Dr MOS/BIL B13 ...144 B3
  WMBN WV5 ....65 E3
Sutherland Gv
  DUNHL/THL/PER WV6 ....34 D1
Sutherland Pl BKHL/PFLD WV2 ..7 H6
Sutherland Rd CDYHTH B64 ...121 E4
  ETTPK/GDPK/PENN WV4 ....51 H3
  SEDG DY3 ....83 G1
Sutherland St BORD B9 ....127 H1
Sutton Ap WASH/WDE B8 .....111 E5
Sutton Ct
  ETTPK/GDPK/PENN WV4 ....67 G1
  MGN/WHC B75 ....62 B1
Sutton Crs WBROM B70 ....87 E5
Sutton New Rd
  ERDW/GRVHL B23 ....92 D2
Sutton Oak Rd
  SCFLD/BOLD B73 ....60 C4
Sutton Rd ALDR WS9 ....64 B4
  DARL/WED WS10 ....56 C5
  ERDE/BCHGN B23 ....93 E1
Sutton's Dr GTB/HAM B43 .....58 D4
Sutton Sq WALM/CURD B76 ...79 G5
Sutton St AST/WIT B6 ....109 F5
  CBHAMW B1 ....2 B5
  STRBR DY8 ....118 A3
Swains Gv KGSTG B44 ....60 B4
Swale Gv HWK/WKHTH B38 ...176 D5
  WLNHL WV13 ....40 B3
Swale Rd WALM/CURD B76 ....78 C2
Swallow Av CBROM B36 ....114 A1
Swallow Cl BHTH/HG B12 .....144 B4
  DARL/WED WS10 ....56 B4
  DUDS DY2 ....120 D2
Swallow Ct WOLVN WV10 ......19 G3
Swallowdale ALDR WS9 ....19 G3
  DUNHL/THL/PER WV6 ....20 A3
Swallowfall Av STRBR DY8 ....134 C3
Swallowfields Rd SEDG DY3 ...65 H4
Swallows Cl BILS/COS WV14 ...54 A2
Swallows Meadow SHLY B90 ..180 D5
Swallow St CBHAMW B1 ....2 B7
  WBROM B70 ....87 E1
Swanage Rd SMHTH B10 ......128 B4
Swan Av SMTHWK B66 ....106 A2
Swan Bank
  ETTPK/GDPK/PENN WV4 ....51 F4
Swan Cl KIDD DY10 ....168 B4
  WMBN WV8 ....110 D5
Swan Copse YDLY B25 ....146 C2
Swancote Dr
  ETTPK/GDPK/PENN WV4 ....50 C3
Swancote Rd DUDN DY1 ......102 A1
  STETCH B33 ....129 H3
Swan Crs OLDBY B69 ....104 D3
Swancroft Rd TPTN/OCK DY4 ..69 E5
Swanfield Rd STRBR DY8 ......118 C3
Swan Gdns ERDW/GRVHL B23 ..92 D2
Swan La BRGRVW B61 ....185 H5
  STRBR DY8 ....118 C3
  WBROM B70 ....87 E1
Swanley Cl RMSLY B62 ....140 A4
Swanmore Cl BDMR/CCFT WV3 ..51 E1
Swann Rd BILS/COS WV14 .....68 A1
Swan Pool Gv RUSH/SHEL WS4 .29 F1
Swansbrook Gdns
  HWK/WKHTH B38 ....177 G3
Swanshurst La MOS/BIL B13 ..162 A2
Swan St BRLYHL DY5 ....101 G5
  DUDS DY2 ....102 C2
  STRBR DY8 ....135 E2
  WOLV WV1 ....7 H3
Swanswell Rd HIA/OLT B92 ...163 H5
Swan Village
  CHWD/FDBR/MGN B37 * 132 C1
Swarthmore Rd SLYOAK B29 ..158 D3
Sweetbriar La SHHTH WV12 ...26 B5
Sweetbriar Rd BKHL/PFLD WV2 .52 B1
Sweetbrier Dr STRBR DY8 .....118 A3
Sweetman Pl
  DUNHL/THL/PER WV6 ....6 B1
Sweetman St
  DUNHL/THL/PER WV6 ....35 F2
Sweetmoor Cl CBROM B36 ....113 E1
Sweetpool La STRBR DY8 .....152 B5
Swift Cl CBROM B36 ....114 A1
Swinbrook Gv KGSTG B44 ......75 F2
Swinbrook Wy SHLY B90 ......180 D1

Swincross Rd STRBR DY8 ......135 H4
Swindell Rd HAG/WOL DY9 ....153 E1
Swindon Rd HRBN B17 ....124 D1
  KGSWFD DY6 ....98 D1
Swinford Gv DOR/KN B93 .....196 C5
Swinford Leys WMBN WV5 .....80 B1
Swinford Rd SLYOAK B29 .....141 G4
  STRBR DY8 ....135 G5
  WOLVN WV10 ....23 G5
Swin Forge Wy SEDG DY3 .....80 C4
Swiss Dr STRBR DY8 ....118 B2
Swynnerton Dr WNSFLD WV11 ..14 D3
Sycamore Av ERDE/BCHGN B24 ..92 D3
  RUSH/SHEL WS4 ....28 D2
  STRBR DY8 ....134 D5
  WALM/CURD B76 ....78 B1
Sycamore Crs
  CHWD/FDBR/MGN B37 ....132 A4
  ERDE/BCHGN B24 ....92 D3
Sycamore Dr BDMR/CCFT WV3 .35 H4
  HLYWD B47 ....192 D5
Sycamore Gn DUDN DY1 ....83 H1
Sycamore Paddock
  STRBR DY8 ....118 C3
Sycamore Pl BILS/COS WV14 ..54 C5
Sycamore Rd AST/WIT B6 .....109 G1
  BVILLE B30 ....159 H3
  DARL/WED WS10 ....71 E1
  DSYBK/YTR WS5 ....57 F3
  ERDW/GRVHL B23 ....76 C4
  GTB/HAM B43 ....58 C5
  HDSW B21 ....107 F1
  KGSWFD DY6 ....100 A3
  OLDBY B69 ....105 E5
  RUSH/SHEL WS4 ....28 D2
  SMTHWK B66 ....124 D1
  TPTN/OCK DY4 ....69 F4
The Sycamores STRBR DY8 ...152 B5
  WOLVN WV10 ....23 H2
Sycamore Ter
  ALE/KHTH/YWD B14 * 160 C3
Sycamore Wy ACGN B27 ......146 C5
Sydenham Rd SMTHWK B66 ...106 C2
  SPARK B11 ....145 E1
  WOLV WV1 ....38 B3
Sydney Cl WBROM B70 ....71 E4
Sydney Rd BORD B9 ....128 A2
  CDYHTH B64 ....120 B3
  SMTHWKW B67 ....124 A2
Sydney Wy BKDE/SHDE B34 ..113 G3
Sylvan Av NFLD/LBR B31 .....175 F2
Sylvan Gn RMSLY B62 ....139 G4
Sylvia Av NFLD/LBR B31 .....175 H5
Symphony Ct
  LDYWD/EDGR B16 ....2 B6
Sytch La WMBN WV5 ....81 E1

T

Tack Farm Rd STRBR DY8 .....117 H3
Tackford Cl CBROM B36 ....95 E5
Tackley Cl SHLY B90 ....180 B5
Tadmore Cl BILS/COS WV14 ....53 G3
Tadworth Cl WOLV WV1 ....38 A3
Tait Cft HIA/OLT B92 ....165 H2
Talaton Cl COVEN WV9 ....12 A3
Talbot Cl FOAKS/STRLY B74 ...45 H2
Talbot Cl ERDW/GRVHL B23 ....76 B3
  WSLW WS2 ....27 G4
Talbot Pl BILS/COS WV14 ......53 G3
Talbot Rd BKHL/PFLD WV2 ....52 A2
  DUDS DY2 ....102 B5
  SMTHWK B66 ....124 C1
Talbots La BRLYHL DY5 ....119 G3
Talbot St BRLYHL DY5 ....119 F1
  HAG/WOL DY9 ....137 G1
  HALE B63 ....137 G3
  STRBR DY8 ....135 G2
  WSNGN B18 ....107 H3
Talfourd St BORD B9 ....128 B3
Talgarth Covert
  HWK/WKHTH B38 ....190 C1
Talke Rd DSYBK/YTR WS5 .....57 F3
Talladale RIDG/WDGT B32 ....157 F3
Tallington Rd STETCH B33 ....131 E5
Tall Trees Cl FOAKS/STRLY B74 .46 B1
  SHHTH WV12 ....26 B4
Tall Trees Dr HAG/WOL DY9 ..136 B5
Talton Cl SHLY B90 ....194 D5
Tamar Cl BRWNH WS8 ....8 C2
Tamar Dr CBROM B36 ....113 H1
  DUDS DY2 ....102 B5
  WALM/CURD B76 ....78 C2
Tamar Gv DUNHL/THL/PER WV6 ..34 C1
  WLNHL WV13 ....40 A3
Tamarisk Cl SLYOAK B29 ......158 D2
Tamar Ri STRBR DY8 ....118 C4
Tame Av DARL/WED WS10 .....56 C4
  WSL WS1 ....57 E2
Tame Crs HHTH/SAND B71 ....71 G5
Tame Dr BLOX/PEL WS3 ....28 C5
Tame Rd AST/WIT B6 ....93 E4
  LGLYGN/QTN B68 ....123 E4
  TPTN/OCK DY4 ....86 A1
Tamerton Rd RIDG/WDGT B32 .157 H1
Tameside Cl WLNHL WV13 .....39 F3
Tameside Dr AST/WIT B6 ......91 H2
  CVALE B35 ....94 A5
Tame St BILS/COS WV14 ....54 A5
  WBROM B70 ....70 D2
  WSL WS1 ....57 E2
Tame St East WSL WS1 ....57 F2
Tamworth Cl BRWNH WS8 .....9 F1
Tamworth Rd MGN/WHC B75 ...62 D1
Tanacetum Dr DSYBK/YTR WS5 .57 G5
Tanfield Cl
  DUNHL/THL/PER WV6 ....35 F2
Tanfield Rd DUDS DY2 ....102 B5
  STETCH B33 ....130 B1
Tanford Rd HIA/OLT B92 .....148 A4
Tanglewood Cl
  BKDE/SHDE B34 ....113 G4
  RIDG/WDGT B32 ....140 B3
Tanglewood Gv SEDG DY3 ....67 E1

Tangmere Cl DUNHL/THL/PER WV6 ...... 20 C5
Tangmere Dr CVALE B35 ...... 94 C3
Tanhouse Av GTB/HAM B43 ...... 73 E4
Tanhouse Farm Rd HIA/OLT B92 ...... 148 A5
Tanhouse La HALE B63 ...... 137 G2
Tanners Cl MGN/WHC B75 ...... 63 E1
Tansey Green Rd BRLYHL DY5 ...... 100 D1
Tansley Cl DOR/KN B93 ...... 196 D4
Tansley Gv KGSTG B44 ...... 75 F2
Tansley Hill Av DUDS DY2 ...... 103 F1
Tansley Hill Rd DUDS DY2 ...... 103 F1
Tansley Rd KGSTG B44 ...... 75 F3
Tansley Vw BKHL/PFLD WV2 ...... 52 B1
Tantany La HHTH/SAND B71 ...... 87 G2
Tantarra St WSL WS1 ...... 5 G4
Tanwood Cl SOLH B91 ...... 181 H5
Tanworth Gv BHTH/HG B12 ...... 144 B1
Tanworth La SHLY B90 ...... 194 B2
Tanyards ACGN B27 ...... 146 D4
Tapestries Av WBROM B70 ...... 87 E2
Tapton Cl BLOX/PEL WS3 ...... 17 E4
Tarmac Rd ETTPK/GDPK/PENN WV4 ...... 53 F5
Tarragon Gdns RBRY B45 ...... 174 C3
Tarrant Gv RIDG/WDGT B32 ...... 141 F2
Tarrington Covert HWK/WKHTH B38 ...... 176 C5
Tarry Hollow Rd BRLYHL DY5 ...... 100 D1
Tarry Rd SALTLY B8 ...... 110 C5
Tarvin Ms BRLYHL DY5 ...... 119 F3
Taryn Dr DARL/WED WS10 ...... 55 F1
Tasker St WBROM B70 ...... 86 C2
WSL WS1 ...... 4 C6
Tasman Gv DUNHL/THL/PER WV6 ...... 20 C5
Tat Bank Rd OLDBY B69 ...... 105 F3
Taunton Av WOLVN WV10 ...... 12 D5
Taunton Cl NFLD/LBR B31 ...... 174 C2
Taunton Rd BHTH/HG B12 ...... 144 C3
Taverners Cl SHHTH WV12 ...... 26 A1
Taverner's Gn BFLD/HDSWWD B20 ...... 89 H3
Tavistock Rd ACGN B27 ...... 163 G3
Taw Cl CBROM B36 ...... 113 H2
Tay Cft CHWD/FDBR/MGN B37 ...... 114 C5
Tay Gv HWK/WKHTH B38 ...... 176 D5
RMSLY B62 ...... 122 C2
Taylor Av BLOX/PEL WS3 ...... 27 H2
Taylor Rd DUDS DY2 ...... 121 E2
ETTPK/GDPK/PENN WV4 ...... 52 D3
MOS/BIL B13 ...... 161 F5
OLDBY B69 ...... 104 C2
SMTHWKW B67 ...... 106 B4
Taylor's La HHTH/SAND B71 ...... 87 F2
OLDBY B69 ...... 104 C2
SMTHWKW B67 ...... 106 B4
Taylors Orch ERDW/GRVHL B23 ...... 91 H2
Taylor St WNSFLD WV11 ...... 24 C5
Taylor Wy OLDBY B69 ...... 103 H1
Tay Rd RBRY B45 ...... 174 B4
Taysfield Rd NFLD/LBR B31 ...... 158 A4
Taywood Dr SMHTH B10 ...... 128 A5
Tealby Gv SLYOAK B29 ...... 160 A1
Teal Dr ERDW/GRVHL B23 ...... 91 H5
Teal Gv DARL/WED WS10 ...... 54 D5
Teall Rd WASH/WDE B8 ...... 110 C4
Tean Cl SPARK B11 ...... 146 A4
Teasdale Wy HAG/WOL DY9 ...... 136 B5
Teasel Rd WNSFLD WV11 ...... 25 E5
Teazel Av BVILLE B30 ...... 159 F4
Tebworth Cl COVEN WV9 ...... 11 H5
Tedbury Crs ERDW/GRVHL B23 ...... 76 C5
Tedder Rd WSLW WS2 ...... 40 B3
Teddesley Gv STECH B33 ...... 113 E5
Teddesley St RUSH/SHEL WS4 ...... 5 J1
Teddington Gv PBAR/PBCH B42 ...... 90 C3
Tedstone Rd RIDG/WDGT B32 ...... 141 E2
Teesdale Av BDR/SHDE B34 ...... 112 B3
Teesdale Cl WOLV WV1 ...... 38 A3
Tees Gv HWK/WKHTH B38 ...... 176 D5
Teignmouth Rd SLYOAK B29 ...... 142 D5
Telford Cl HHTH/SAND B71 ...... 71 F3
SMTHWKW B67 ...... 123 H3
WSLW WS2 ...... 27 E5
Telford Gdns BDMR/CCFT WV3 ...... 50 D1
Telford Rd WSLW WS2 ...... 27 E5
Telford Wy SMTHWK B66 ...... 106 B2
Teme Gv WLNHL WV13 ...... 40 B3
Teme Rd HALE B63 ...... 137 F2
STRBR DY8 ...... 135 F4
Tempest St BKHL/PFLD WV2 ...... 7 F5
The Templars OLDBY B69 ...... 104 C4
Templars Wk WLNHL WV13 ...... 39 G3
Templefield Gdns BORD B9 ...... 128 A3
Templefield Sq EDG B15 ...... 126 B5
Templefield St BORD B9 ...... 128 A3
Temple Meadows Rd HHTH/SAND B71 ...... 88 A1
Templemore Dr GTB/HAM B43 ...... 73 G4
Temple Pas CBHAM B2 ...... 3 F5
Temple Rd DOR/KN B93 ...... 197 F5
WLNHL WV13 ...... 39 G2
Temple Rw CBHAM B2 ...... 3 G5
Temple Rw West CBHAM B2 ...... 3 F4
Temple Sq WLNHL WV13 ...... 39 G2
Temple St BILS/COS WV14 ...... 54 A3
BKHL/PFLD WV2 ...... 7 F5
CBHAM B2 ...... 3 G5
SEDG DY3 ...... 83 F5
WBROM B70 ...... 87 G2
Templeton Cl DOR/KN B93 ...... 197 E5
Templeton Rd KGSTG B44 ...... 75 E1
Temple Wy CSCL/WTROR B46 ...... 97 F5
OLDBY B69 ...... 86 A4
Tenacre La SEDG DY3 ...... 83 G1
Ten Acres End BVILLE B30 ...... 160 B2
Ten Acres Ms SLYOAK B29 ...... 160 B2
Ten Ashes La RBRY B45 ...... 188 C4
Tenbury Cl ALDR WS9 ...... 30 C2
WSLW WS2 ...... 40 B2
Tenbury Ct ETTPK/GDPK/PENN WV4 ...... 50 D3
Tenbury Gdns ETTPK/GDPK/PENN WV4 ...... 50 D4
Tenbury Rd ALE/KHTH/YWD B14 ...... 160 D4
Tenby Cl MOS/BIL B13 ...... 145 E5

Tenby St CBHAMW B1 ...... 2 B2
Tenby St North CBHAMW B1 ...... 2 B2
Tenlands Rd HALE B63 ...... 138 B4
Tennal Dr RIDG/WDGT B32 ...... 141 E1
Tennal Gv RIDG/WDGT B32 ...... 141 E1
Tennal La RIDG/WDGT B32 ...... 141 E2
Tennal Rd RIDG/WDGT B32 ...... 141 E1
Tennant St EDG B15 ...... 126 B3
Tennis Ct BVILLE B30 ...... 176 B1
Tennis Cts EDG B15 * 143 E2
Tennyson Av FOAKS/STRLY B74 ...... 32 D4
Tennyson Rd BLOX/PEL WS3 ...... 28 A2
SEDG DY3 ...... 82 C1
SHHTH WV12 ...... 26 D1
SMHTH B10 ...... 128 C5
WOLVN WV10 ...... 24 A1
Tennyson St BRLYHL DY5 ...... 101 F3
Tenter Ct HALE B63 ...... 138 D3
Tenter Dr HALE B63 ...... 139 E4
Tenterfields HALE B63 ...... 138 D3
Terminal Rd LGN/SDN/BHAMAIR B26 ...... 148 D4
Tern Cl ETTPK/GDPK/PENN WV4 ...... 52 B5
Tern Gv HWK/WKHTH B38 ...... 176 C5
Terrace Rd LOZ/NWT B19 ...... 108 A2
Terrace St BRLYHL DY5 ...... 101 G4
CDYHTH B64 ...... 121 H5
DARL/WED WS10 ...... 55 H5
The Terrace BDMR/CCFT WV3 ...... 35 G4
CDYHTH B64 ...... 121 E4
Terrence Vls DARL/WED WS10 * 55 F1
Terret Cl WSL WS1 ...... 5 F2
Terry Dr WALM/CURD B76 ...... 78 B2
Terrys La ERDE/BCHGN B24 ...... 93 C3
Terry St DUDS DY2 ...... 84 D5
Tessall La NFLD/LBR B31 ...... 174 D3
Tetbury Gv NFLD/LBR B31 ...... 174 D2
Tetley Av RUSH/SHEL WS4 ...... 42 C1
Tetley Rd SPARK B11 ...... 145 G4
Tetnall St DUDS DY2 ...... 102 D1
Tettenhall Rd BDMR/CCFT WV3 ...... 6 A2
DUNHL/THL/PER WV6 ...... 34 C1
Teviot Gdns BRLYHL DY5 ...... 100 C3
CDSL WV8 ...... 10 C2
Teviot Gv HWK/WKHTH B38 ...... 176 C5
Tewkesbury Dr DUDS DY2 ...... 120 D1
Tewkesbury Rd BFLD/HDSWWD B20 ...... 91 E5
BLOX/PEL WS3 ...... 16 A5
Tew Park Rd HDSW B21 ...... 107 H4
Thackeray Rd BVILLE B30 ...... 159 F5
Thames Cl BRLYHL DY5 ...... 100 D2
Thames Rd BLOX/PEL WS3 ...... 27 H2
Thames St BORD B9 * 127 H5
Thanet Cl PBAR/PBCH B42 ...... 74 D4
Thanet Gv PBAR/PBCH B42 ...... 74 C4
The Thatchers RMSLY B62 ...... 122 C4
Thatchway Gdns HWK/WKHTH B38 ...... 190 C1
Theatre Rd STETCH B33 ...... 131 G1
Theatre Ap DIG/EDG B5 ...... 3 G7
Thelbridge Rd NFLD/LBR B31 ...... 189 E2
Thelma Rd TPTN/OCK DY4 ...... 69 E5
Thelma St WSL WS1 ...... 56 D1
Thetford Wy HIA/OLT B92 ...... 165 F2
Theodore Cl HRBN B17 ...... 142 B3
OLDBY B69 ...... 86 C5
Theresa Rd SPARK B11 ...... 127 H5
Thetford Cl TPTN/OCK DY4 ...... 68 C5
Thetford Gdns WNSFLD WV11 ...... 24 D4
Thetford Rd PBAR/PBCH B42 ...... 74 A3
Thetford Wy DSYBK/YTR WS5 ...... 58 A5
Thickett Cl WSLW WS2 ...... 41 F5
Thicknall Dr HAG/WOL DY9 ...... 135 H5
Thicknall La HAG/WOL DY9 ...... 169 H2
Thicknall Ri HAG/WOL DY9 ...... 169 G1
Thimble Dr WALM/CURD B76 ...... 78 B2
Thimble End Rd WALM/CURD B76 ...... 78 C1
Thimble Mill La AST/WIT B6 ...... 109 H2
Thimblemill Rd SMTHWKW B67 ...... 124 B1
SMTHWKW B67 ...... 124 B1
BRWNH WS8 ...... 9 C3
KGSWFD DY6 ...... 100 B1
SLYOAK B29 ...... 143 G4
WOLVN WV10 ...... 23 H3
Third Exhibition Av BHAMNEC G40 ...... 149 H2
Third Rd BRGRVW B61 ...... 186 B4
Thirlemere Cl DUNHL/THL/PER WV6 ...... 21 H2
Thirlmere Dr MOS/BIL B13 ...... 144 C2
WNSFLD WV11 ...... 15 E5
Thirlmere Gv DUNHL/THL/PER WV6 ...... 34 D1
Thirsk Wk BRLYHL DY5 ...... 118 B5
Thirsk Cft CBROM B36 ...... 111 G1
Thirston Cl WNSFLD WV11 ...... 25 C5
Thistle Cft SEDG DY3 ...... 67 H5
Thistle Cft WNSFLD WV11 ...... 39 G2
Thistle Down Cl FOAKS/STRLY B74 ...... 45 G3
Thistledown Rd BKDE/SHDE B34 ...... 113 E2
Thistle Gn HWK/WKHTH B38 ...... 190 C1
Thistlegreen Cl BLKHTH/ROWR B65 ...... 103 E4
Thistlegreen Rd DUDS DY2 ...... 103 E5
Thistle La NFLD/LBR B31 ...... 157 F2
Thomas Benson Pl BHTH/HG B12 ...... 127 F5
Thomas Crs SMTHWK B66 ...... 107 E4
Thomas Guy Rd WBROM B70 ...... 70 C4
Thomas Mason Cl WNSFLD WV11 ...... 24 D3
Thomas St AST/WIT B6 ...... 109 F5
BKHL/PFLD WV2 ...... 7 F7
SMTHWK B66 ...... 106 H4
WBROM B70 ...... 87 H4
WSLW WS2 ...... 4 E4
Thompson Av BKHL/PFLD WV2 ...... 52 B1
Thompson Cl DUDS DY2 ...... 120 B2
WLNHL WV13 ...... 39 G2
Thompson Dr ERDE/BCHGN B24 ...... 110 D1
Thompson Gdns SMTHWKW B67 ...... 106 B5
Thompson Rd LGLYGN/QTN B68 ...... 105 F5

SMTHWKW B67 ...... 106 B5
Thompson St BILS/COS WV14 ...... 53 H1
WLNHL WV13 ...... 39 G2
Thomson Av HWK/WKHTH B38 ...... 176 A4
Thoresby Cft DUDN DY1 ...... 83 H3
Thornberry Dr DUDN DY1 ...... 101 F1
Thornberry Wk VAUX/NECH B7 ...... 110 A3
Thornbridge Av PBAR/PBCH B42 ...... 74 D4
Thornbridge Gv ALDR WS9 ...... 19 F4
Thornbury Ct DUNHL/THL/PER WV6 ...... 35 E2
Thornbury Rd BFLD/HDSWWD B20 ...... 90 D4
Thornby Av SOLH B91 ...... 164 D5
Thornby Rd ERDW/GRVHL B23 ...... 76 A3
Thorncliffe Rd KGSTG B44 ...... 75 E1
Thorn Cl DARL/WED WS10 ...... 55 H4
Thorncroft Wy DSYBK/YTR WS5 ...... 57 H4
Thorne Av WOLVN WV10 ...... 23 C3
Thorne Rd WLNHL WV13 ...... 39 G1
Thorneycroft La WOLVN WV10 ...... 24 A5
Thorneycroft Rd BILS/COS WV14 ...... 54 C5
Thorney Rd FOAKS/STRLY B74 ...... 45 F4
Thornfield Cft SEDG DY3 ...... 67 G4
Thornfield Rd ACGN B27 ...... 146 C5
Thorngrove Av SOLH B91 ...... 182 A5
Thornham Wy ALE/KHTH/YWD B14 ...... 177 H4
Thornhill Gv HDSW B21 ...... 107 H1
Thornhill Pk FOAKS/STRLY B74 ...... 45 C5
Thornhill Rd BRLYHL DY5 ...... 119 H3
DUDN DY1 ...... 84 C2
FOAKS/STRLY B74 ...... 45 G5
HALE B63 ...... 138 A4
HDSW B21 ...... 107 H1
SOLH B91 ...... 165 E3
SPARK B11 ...... 145 H4
Thornhurst Av RIDG/WDGT B32 ...... 124 A5
Thornleigh SEDG DY3 ...... 83 F1
Thornley Cl MOS/BIL B13 ...... 161 G1
WNSFLD WV11 ...... 25 F1
Thornley Gv WALM/CURD B76 ...... 79 C5
Thornley Rd WNSFLD WV11 ...... 25 F1
Thornley St WOLV WV1 ...... 7 G2
Thorn Rd BVILLE B30 ...... 159 G3
Thorns Av BRLYHL DY5 ...... 119 C5
Thornsett Gv SHLY B90 ...... 163 F4
Thorns Rd BRLYHL DY5 ...... 119 G5
Thornthwaite Cl RBRY B45 ...... 174 B3
Thornton Cl WNSFLD WV11 ...... 24 D2
Thornton Dr BRLYHL DY5 ...... 119 G5
Thornton Rd SHLY B90 ...... 195 F2
WASH/WDE B8 ...... 111 H4
WOLV WV1 ...... 38 B4
Thornwood Cl LGLYGN/QTN B68 ...... 105 G4
Thornyfield Cl SHLY B90 ...... 180 C2
Thornyfield Rd SHLY B90 ...... 180 C2
Thorpe Cl MGN/WHC B75 ...... 62 C1
Thorpe Rd WSL WS1 ...... 56 D4
Thorpe Rd WSL WS1 ...... 57 E1
Thorp St CBHAMW B1 ...... 3 F7
Three Acres La SHLY B90 ...... 193 F5
Three Broadway EDG B15 * 126 B3
Three Corner Cl SHLY B90 ...... 179 G5
Three Oaks Rd HLYWD B47 ...... 192 D4
Three Shires Oak Rd SMTHWKW B67 ...... 124 B2
Three Tuns La WOLVN WV10 ...... 12 C5
Threshers Dr SHHTH WV12 ...... 26 D4
Throne Cl BLKHTH/ROWR B65 ...... 104 A4
Throne Crs BLKHTH/ROWR B65 ...... 104 B5
Throne Rd BLKHTH/ROWR B65 ...... 104 B5
Throstles Ct GTB/HAM B43 ...... 73 C4
Thrush Rd LGLYGN/QTN B68 ...... 122 D2
Thruxton Cl ALE/KHTH/YWD B14 ...... 178 B2
Thunderbolt Wy TPTN/OCK DY4 ...... 68 D5
Thurcroft Cl SMTHWK B38? WASH/WDE B8 ...... 110 D5
Thuree Rd SMTHWKW B67 ...... 123 H2
Thurleigh Cl HAG/WOL DY9 ...... 135 H5
Thurlestone Rd NFLD/LBR B31 ...... 189 E1
Thurloe Crs RBRY B45 ...... 173 H1
Thurlston Av HIA/OLT B92 ...... 147 F3
Thurstone Dr ETTPK/GDPK/PENN WV4 ...... 51 F1
Thurstone Rd BLOX/PEL WS3 ...... 16 D4
Thursfield Rd HHTH/SAND B71 ...... 72 A4
TPTN/OCK DY4 ...... 69 G5
Thurston Av OLDBY B69 ...... 104 D3
Thynne St WBROM B70 ...... 88 A3
Tibbats Cl RIDG/WDGT B32 ...... 140 C4
Tibberton Cl BDMR/CCFT WV3 ...... 50 D1
HALE B63 ...... 139 E4
SOLH B91 ...... 181 G5
Tibbets La HRBN B17 ...... 141 C5
Tibbington Rd TPTN/OCK DY4 ...... 69 E4
Tibbington Ter TPTN/OCK DY4 ...... 69 F4
Tiberius Cl CSCL/WTROR B46 ...... 97 H5
Tibland Rd ACGN B27 ...... 163 H1
Tiddington Cl CBROM B36 ...... 94 C5
Tideswell Rd PBAR/PBCH B42 ...... 74 C5
Tidworth Cft ALE/KHTH/YWD B14 ...... 178 C2
Tierney Dr TPTN/OCK DY4 ...... 70 A5
Tiffany La COVEN WV9 ...... 11 H5
Tiffield Rd YDLY B25 ...... 146 D2
Tigley Av RIDG/WDGT B32 ...... 157 H1
Tilbury Cl BDMR/CCFT WV3 ...... 35 F5
Tilbury Gv MOS/BIL B13 ...... 160 D1
Tildasley St WBROM B70 ...... 87 H1
Tildesley Dr SHHTH WV12 ...... 26 A1
Tile Cross Rd STETCH B33 ...... 131 G3
Tiled House La BRLYHL DY5 ...... 100 D3
Tile Gv CHWD/FDBR/MGN B37 ...... 114 A4
Tilehouse Green La DOR/KN B93 ...... 195 G5
Tilehouse La SHLY B90 ...... 193 G1
Tiller Gv MGN/WHC B75 ...... 47 H1
Tilley St DARL/WED WS10 ...... 55 H2
Tillyard Cft SLYOAK B29 ...... 159 F2

Tilshead Cl ALE/KHTH/YWD B14 ...... 178 A2
Tilsley Gv ERDW/GRVHL B23 ...... 91 H1
Tilston Dr BRLYHL DY5 ...... 119 F3
Tilton Rd BORD B9 ...... 128 A3
Timberdine Cl HALE B63 ...... 137 H1
Timberlake Cl SHLY B90 ...... 195 H2
Timberley Cft BKDE/SHDE B34 ...... 113 F2
Timberley La BKDE/SHDE B34 ...... 94 B2
Timbers Wy ERDE/BCHGN B24 ...... 93 H2
SPARK B11 ...... 144 C1
Timbertree Cl CDYHTH B64 ...... 121 E5
Timbertree Rd CDYHTH B64 ...... 121 E5
Times Square Av BRLYHL DY5 ...... 119 H2
Timmins Cl SOLH B91 ...... 165 G5
Timmins Rd HAG/WOL DY9 ...... 136 A1
Timothy Rd OLDBY B69 ...... 104 A2
Tinacre Hl DUNHL/THL/PER WV6 ...... 34 C3
Tinchbourne St DUDN DY1 * 84 B1
Tindal St BHTH/HG B12 ...... 144 B2
Tinkers Farm Gv NFLD/LBR B31 ...... 175 E2
Tinkers Farm Rd NFLD/LBR B31 ...... 158 D1
Tinmeadow Crs RBRY B45 ...... 188 C1
Tinsley St TPTN/OCK DY4 ...... 71 E1
Tintagel Cl DUNHL/THL/PER WV6 ...... 34 D2
Tintagel Dr DUDN DY1 ...... 83 C4
Tintagel Wy ALDR WS9 ...... 29 C4
Tintern Cl FOAKS/STRLY B74 ...... 46 C1
Tintern Ct DUNHL/THL/PER WV6 ...... 34 C1
Tintern Crs BLOX/PEL WS3 ...... 16 B5
Tintern Rd BFLD/HDSWWD B20 ...... 91 E5
Tintern Vls BHTH/HG B12 * 144 D2
Tintern Wy BLOX/PEL WS3 ...... 16 B5
Tipperary Cl CBROM B36 ...... 112 A1
Tipps Stone Cl TPTN/OCK DY4 ...... 85 E2
Tipton Rd DUDN DY1 ...... 85 E3
OLDBY B69 ...... 86 A4
SEDG DY3 ...... 67 C5
Tirley Rd STETCH B33 ...... 112 C4
Titania Cl RBRY B45 ...... 174 A2
Titchfield Cl WOLVN WV10 * 13 E3
Titford La BLKHTH/ROWR B65 ...... 104 C5
Titford Rd OLDBY B69 ...... 104 C5
Tithe Ct WOLVN WV10 ...... 37 H2
Tithe Rd WNSFLD WV11 ...... 25 H1
Titterstone Rd NFLD/LBR B31 ...... 175 C5
Tiverton Cl KGSWFD DY6 ...... 118 C1
Tiverton Dr HHTH/SAND B71 ...... 71 E5
Tiverton Gv BLKHTH/ROWR B65 ...... 104 B4
SMTHWK B66 ...... 106 D4
Tividale Rd OLDBY B69 ...... 85 E5
Tividale St TPTN/OCK DY4 ...... 85 G4
Tixall Rd HLGN/YWD B28 ...... 162 C5
Toberland WSLW WS2 * 27 F3
Toll End Rd TPTN/OCK DY4 ...... 70 A3
Tollgate Cl NFLD/LBR B31 ...... 175 E4
Tollgate Dr BFLD/HDSWWD B20 ...... 108 A2
Toll House Rd RBRY B45 ...... 188 D1
Tollhouse Wy SMTHWK B66 ...... 106 B2
Tolworth Gdns BKHL/PFLD WV2 ...... 52 C1
Tolworth Hall Rd ERDE/BCHGN B24 ...... 93 F5
Tomey Rd SPARK B11 ...... 145 F3
Tomlan Rd NFLD/LBR B31 ...... 190 A1
Tomlinson Rd CBROM B36 ...... 95 F3
Tompstone Rd HHTH/SAND B71 ...... 72 B3
Tonadine Cl WNSFLD WV11 ...... 25 G1
Tonbridge Rd ERDE/BCHGN B24 ...... 93 E5
Tong St WSL WS1 ...... 5 J4
Top Croft Rd ERDW/GRVHL B23 ...... 76 D4
Topland Gv NFLD/LBR B31 ...... 174 A5
Top Rd BRGRVW B61 ...... 186 C4
Topsham Cft ALE/KHTH/YWD B14 ...... 160 D5
Topsham Rd SMTHWKW B67 ...... 106 A5
Torfield CDSL WV8 ...... 11 C5
Toronto Gdns RIDG/WDGT B32 ...... 141 E1
Torre Av NFLD/LBR B31 ...... 174 D3
Torrey Gv WASH/WDE B8 ...... 111 C5
Torridge Dr WNSFLD WV11 ...... 24 C5
Torridon Cft MOS/BIL B13 ...... 143 H4
Torvale Rd DUNHL/THL/PER WV6 ...... 35 E3
Tor Wy BLOX/PEL WS3 ...... 17 H4
Totnes Gv SLYOAK B29 ...... 142 B5
Totnes Rd SMTHWKW B67 ...... 106 B3
Tottenham Crs KGSTG B44 ...... 75 H1
Touchwood Hall Cl SOLH B91 ...... 182 A1
Towcester Cft CBROM B36 ...... 111 H1
Tower Cft CHWD/FDBR/MGN B37 ...... 114 C5
Tower Hl PBAR/PBCH B42 ...... 74 B5
Tower Ri OLDBY B69 ...... 104 A4
Tower Rd AST/WIT B6 ...... 109 F2
ERDW/GRVHL B23 ...... 92 C3
MGN/WHC B75 ...... 47 C5
OLDBY B69 ...... 104 A2
Tower St DUDN DY1 ...... 84 C5
LOZ/NWT B19 ...... 108 B2
SEDG DY3 ...... 67 G4
WOLV WV1 ...... 7 G4
WSL WS1 ...... 4 E4
Townend Sq WSL WS1 ...... 4 E3
Townfold BLOX/PEL WS3 ...... 18 A5
Townley Gdns AST/WIT B6 ...... 91 H4
Townsend Av SEDG DY3 ...... 67 F3
Townsend Dr WALM/CURD B76 ...... 78 B4
Townsend Wy CSHL/WTROR B46? 2 C5
Townshend Gv CHWD/FDBR/MGN B37 ...... 113 H5
Townwell Fold WOLV WV1 * 6 E4
Towpath Wy ALE/KHTH/YWD B14 ...... 177 G1
Towyn Rd MOS/BIL B13 ...... 144 D5
Toys La HALE B63 ...... 137 G2

Tozer St TPTN/OCK DY4 ...... 69 F4
Traceys Meadow RBRY B45 ...... 188 A1
Trafalgar Gv YDLY B25 * 146 A1
Trafalgar Rd ERDE/BCHGN B24 ...... 92 D3
HDSW B21 ...... 107 G1
MOS/BIL B13 ...... 144 B4
OLDBY B69 ...... 85 H5
SMTHWK B66 ...... 106 D5
Trajan HI CSHL/WTROR B46 ...... 97 F1
Tram Wy SMTHWK B66 ...... 105 G2
Tramway Cl BILS/COS WV14 ...... 54 B1
DARL/WED WS10 ...... 55 G1
Tranter Rd WASH/WDE B8 ...... 111 E4
Tranwell Cl COVEN WV9 ...... 11 H5
Traquain Dr DUDN DY1 ...... 84 A3
Treaford La WASH/WDE B8 ...... 111 F5
Tredington Cl SLYOAK B29 ...... 158 C3
Tree Acre Gv HALE B63 ...... 137 G3
Treeford Cl SOLH B91 ...... 181 F4
Trees Rd WSL WS1 ...... 57 F2
Treeton Cft STETCH B33 ...... 130 C2
Tree Tops WMBN WV5 ...... 64 C3
Treetops Dr SHHTH WV12 ...... 26 C5
Trefoil Cl SLYOAK DY9 ...... 135 E5
Trefoil Gdns STRBR DY8 ...... 135 G1
Tregaron Rd HALE B63 ...... 137 G2
Tregea Ri GTB/HAM B43 ...... 73 E4
Trehern Cl DOR/KN B93 ...... 197 E3
Treherne Dr RIDG/WDGT B32 ...... 152 D1
Trehurst Av PBAR/PBCH B42 ...... 74 C4
Trejon Rd CDYHTH B64 ...... 121 E4
Tremont St WOLVN WV10 ...... 7 K2
Trenchard Cl MGN/WHC B75 ...... 63 C1
Trent Cl DUNHL/THL/PER WV6 ...... 34 C1
STRBR DY8 ...... 135 H1
Trentham Av SHHTH WV12 ...... 25 C5
Trentham Gv LGN/SDN/BHAMAIR B26 ...... 147 G2
Trentham Ri BKHL/PFLD WV2 ...... 52 D1
Trent Pl BLOX/PEL WS3 ...... 27 H1
Trent Rd BLOX/PEL WS3 ...... 28 B5
Trent St DIG/EDG B5 ...... 3 K6
Trenville Av BHTH/HG B12 ...... 144 D2
Tresco Cl RBRY B45 ...... 173 G4
Trescott Rd NFLD/LBR B31 ...... 174 D2
Tresham Rd KGSTG B44 ...... 75 G1
Trevanie Av RIDG/WDGT B32 ...... 140 C1
Trevorne Cl BHTH/HG B12 ...... 144 B1
Trevor Rd BLOX/PEL WS3 ...... 17 H3
Trevor St VAUX/NECH B7 ...... 110 A5
Trevor St West VAUX/NECH B7 ...... 110 A5
Trevose Cl BLOX/PEL WS3 ...... 16 B4
Trevose Retreat BHTH/HG B12 ...... 144 B2
Trewman Cl WALM/CURD B76 ...... 78 B3
Treyamon Rd DSYBK/YTR WS5 ...... 58 C1
Treynham Cl WOLV WV1 ...... 38 C4
The Triangle WSNGN B18 ...... 107 H3
Trickley Dr MGN/WHC B75 ...... 63 F2
Trident Bvd CVALE B35 ...... 94 C3
Trident Cl ERDW/GRVHL B23 ...... 77 E4
WALM/CURD B76 78
Trident Ct LGN/SDN/BHAMAIR B26 ...... 149 G3
Trigo Cft CBROM B36 ...... 112 A1
Trimpley Cl DOR/KN B93 ...... 196 C5
Trimpley Gdns ETTPK/GDPK/PENN WV4 ...... 51 E5
Trimpley Rd RIDG/WDGT B32 ...... 157 F2
Trinder Rd SMTHWKW B67 ...... 123 H3
Trindle Rd DUDN DY1 ...... 84 D4
Tring Ct DUNHL/THL/PER WV6 ...... 36 B1
Trinity Cl HIA/OLT B92 ...... 164 D1
STRBR DY8 ...... 117 H2
Trinity Ct BRLYHL DY5 ...... 101 H5
Trinity Hl BHTH/HG B12 ...... 127 G4
Trinity Rd NORTH WBROM B70 ...... 87 H4
Trinity Rd South WBROM B70 ...... 87 H5
Trinity St BRLYHL DY5 ...... 101 H5
CDYHTH B64 ...... 121 E3
OLDBY B69 ...... 105 E4
SMTHWKW B67 ...... 106 C3
WBROM B70 ...... 87 H5
Trinity Wy BFLD/HDSWWD B20 ...... 90 B5
WBROM B70 ...... 87 H5
Trippleton Av RIDG/WDGT B32 ...... 157 H4
Tristram Av NFLD/LBR B31 ...... 175 H4
Trittiford Rd MOS/BIL B13 ...... 161 G3
Troon Cl CDYHTH B64 ...... 121 E5
FOAKS/STRLY B74 ...... 47 H5
Troon Ct DUNHL/THL/PER WV6 ...... 20 D5
Trostrey Rd BVILLE B30 ...... 159 F5
Trotter's La HHTH/SAND B71 ...... 71 E4
Trouse La DARL/WED WS10 ...... 55 G5
Troutbeck Dr BRLYHL DY5 ...... 118 D4
Troy Gv ALE/KHTH/YWD B14 ...... 160 D4
Truda St WSL WS1 ...... 5 J3
Truemans Heath La HLYWD B47 ...... 192 D1
Truro Cl BLKHTH/ROWR B65 ...... 104 C5
Truro Rd DSYBK/YTR WS5 ...... 58 B1
Trustin Crs HIA/OLT B92 ...... 165 G2
Tryon Pl BILS/COS WV14 ...... 54 A2
Trysull Av LGN/SDN/BHAMAIR B26 ...... 148 A3
Trysull Gdns BDMR/CCFT WV3 ...... 50 D1
Trysull Rd BDMR/CCFT WV3 ...... 50 D1
WMBN WV5 ...... 64 C2
Trysull Wy DUDS DY2 ...... 102 C5
Tudbury Rd NFLD/LBR B31 ...... 157 H3
Tudman Cl WALM/CURD B76 ...... 78 C4
Tudor Av COVEN WV9 ...... 11 H5
Tudor Cl ALE/KHTH/YWD B14 ...... 161 H4
MOS/BIL B13 ...... 161 H1

SCFLD/BOLD B73 .... 76 B1
Tudor Ct TPTN/OCK DY4 .... 85 G2
  WNSFLD WV11 .... 14 D3
Tudor Crs BKHL/PFLD WV2 .... 51 H2
Tudor Cft
  CHWD/FDBR/MGN B37 .... 131 H3
Tudor Gdns ERDW/GRVHL B23 .... 92 C5
  STRBR DY8 .... 135 G2
Tudor Gv SEDG DY3 .... 67 G5
Tudor Hl SCFLD/BOLD B73 .... 62 A2
Tudor Pl SEDG DY3 .... 67 G5
Tudor Rd BILS/COS WV14 .... 54 D4
  BLKHTH/ROWR B65 .... 104 A4
  LGLYGN/QTN B68 .... 105 G5
  MOS/BIL B13 .... 125 H5
  SCFLD/BOLD B73 .... 62 B5
  SEDG DY3 .... 67 G5
  WOLVN WV10 .... 38 A1
Tudors Cl SMHTH B10 * 128 A4
Tudor St TPTN/OCK DY4 .... 85 G2
  WSNGN B18 .... 107 F5
Tudor Ter DUNHL/THL/PER WV6 .... 35 E5
  HRBN B17 * 142 A1
Tudor V SEDG DY3 .... 67 G5
Tudor Wy CSCFLD/WYGN B72 .... 77 F1
Tufnell Gv WASH/WDE B8 .... 111 E2
Tugford Rd SLYOAK B29 .... 159 E3
Tulip Gv FOAKS/STRLY B74 .... 60 B2
Tulyar Cl CBROM B36 .... 111 G1
Tunnel La ALE/KHTH/YWD B14 .... 177 G1
Tunnel Rd WBROM B70 .... 71 E3
Tunnel St BILS/COS WV14 .... 68 C3
Tunstall Rd KGSWFD DY6 .... 100 C4
Turchill Dr WALM/CURD B76 .... 78 C3
Turfpits La ERDW/GRVHL B23 .... 76 B5
Turf Pitts La MGN/WHC B75 .... 48 B2
Turks Headway WBROM B70 .... 87 G4
Turls St DUDN DY1 .... 68 A5
Turls Hill Rd BILS/COS WV14 .... 67 H5
Turls St SEDG DY3 .... 67 G4
Turnberry Gv
  DUNHL/THL/PER WV6 .... 20 B5
Turnberry Rd BLOX/PEL WS3 .... 16 D3
  PBAR/PBCH B42 .... 74 B3
Turner Av
  ETTPK/GDPK/PENN WV4 .... 67 H1
Turner Dr BRLYHL DY5 .... 119 F5
Turner Gv
  DUNHL/THL/PER WV6 .... 35 E1
Turners Cft HHTH/SAND B71 .... 72 C3
Turner St SEDG DY3 .... 83 E2
Turner's Hl
  BLKHTH/ROWR B65 .... 103 H3
Turner's La BRLYHL DY5 .... 119 E4
Turner St DUDN DY1 .... 68 C5
  SEDG DY3 .... 83 F3
  SPARK B11 .... 144 C1
  TPTN/OCK DY4 .... 69 F4
  WBROM B70 .... 87 F5
Turney Rd STRBR DY8 .... 135 F1
Turnham Gn
  DUNHL/THL/PER WV6 .... 34 C2
Turnhouse Rd CVALE B35 .... 94 D2
Turnley Rd BKDE/SHDE B34 .... 113 E5
Turnpike Cl SPARK B11 .... 144 C1
Turnpike Dr CSHL/WTROR B46 .... 96 C5
Turton Cl BLOX/PEL WS3 .... 16 C5
Turton Rd TPTN/OCK DY4 .... 69 F4
  WBROM B70 .... 87 F4
Turtons Cft BILS/COS WV14 .... 53 F5
Turves Gn NFLD/LBR B31 .... 175 G4
Turville Rd
  BFLD/HDSWWD B20 .... 90 C5
Tustin Gv ACGN B27 .... 163 G2
Tutbury Av
  DUNHL/THL/PER WV6 .... 34 D2
Tuxford Cl SMHTH WV10 * 37 G1
Tweeds Well RIDG/WDGT B32 .... 157 F3
Twickenham Ct STRBR DY8 .... 117 G5
Twickenham Dr MOS/BIL B13 .... 144 A5
Twickenham Rd KGSTG B44 .... 75 H2
Two Gates HALE B63 .... 137 G2
Two Gates La HALE B63 .... 137 G2
Two Locks BRLYHL DY5 .... 101 H5
Two Woods La BRLYHL DY5 .... 119 G3
Twycross Gv CBROM B36 .... 111 H2
Twydale Av OLDBY B69 .... 85 H5
Twyford Cl ALDR WS9 .... 30 B5
Twyford Gv WNSFLD WV11 .... 25 F3
Twyford Rd WASH/WDE B8 .... 111 G4
Twyning Rd BVILLE B30 .... 160 B5
  LDYWD/EDGR B16 .... 107 F5
Tyber Dr BFLD/HDSWWD B20 .... 90 B3
Tyberry Cl SHLY B90 .... 180 A4
Tyburn Gv ERDE/BCHGN B24 .... 93 H3
Tyburn Rd ERDE/BCHGN B24 .... 93 H5
  WOLV WV1 .... 38 C4
Tyburn Sq ERDE/BCHGN B24 .... 93 H5
Tyebeams BKDE/SHDE B34 .... 113 G4
Tye Gdns HAG/WOL DY9 .... 152 D1
Tyler Ct ERDE/BCHGN B24 .... 92 D5
Tyler Gdns WLNHL WV13 .... 39 G5
Tyler Gv GTB/HAM B43 .... 74 A2
Tyler Rd WLNHL WV13 .... 39 G5
Tylers Gn HWK/WKHTH B38 .... 177 F4
Tylers Gv SHLY B90 .... 195 F2
Tylney Cl DIG/EDG B5 .... 126 D5
Tyndale Crs GTB/HAM B43 .... 59 G5
Tyne Cl BRWNH WS8 .... 8 C2
Tynedale Crs
  ETTPK/GDPK/PENN WV4 .... 52 C5
Tyne Gv YDLY B25 .... 129 H4
Tyne Pl BRLYHL DY5 .... 119 H2
Tyning Cl COVEN WV9 .... 12 A5
Tyninghame Av
  DUNHL/THL/PER WV6 .... 21 H4
Tynings La ALDR WS9 .... 30 A5
Tyrley Cl DUNHL/THL/PER WV6 .... 34 C1
Tyrol Cl STRBR DY8 .... 134 D1
Tyseley Hill Rd SPARK B11 .... 146 A3
Tyseley La SPARK B11 .... 146 A3
Tysoe Cl HOCK/TIA DY4 .... 100 A1
Tysoe Dr WALM/CURD B76 .... 63 F4
Tysoe Rd KGSTG B44 .... 75 F4
Tythebarn Dr KGSWFD DY6 .... 99 E2
Tythe Barn La SHLY B90 .... 193 G2
  SHLY B90 .... 194 A2

Tythebarn La SHLY B90 .... 194 A2
Tyzack Cl BRLYHL DY5 .... 119 E2

U

Udall Rd BILS/COS WV14 .... 53 H5
Uffculme Rd BVILLE B30 .... 160 D2
Uffmoor Est HALE B63 .... 155 E1
Uffmoor La HALE B63 .... 155 E1
  RMSLY B62 .... 154 D4
Ufton Cl SHLY B90 .... 181 G2
Ufton Crs SHLY B90 .... 180 D2
Ullenhall Rd DOR/KN B93 .... 197 E2
  WALM/CURD B76 .... 78 B3
Ullenwood HDSW B21 .... 107 F2
Ulleries Rd HIA/OLT B92 .... 147 G5
Ullrik Gn ERDE/BCHGN B24 .... 92 D4
Ullswater Cl RIDG/WDGT B32 .... 141 F5
Ullswater Gdns KGSWFD DY6 .... 99 H5
Ullswater Ri BRLYHL DY5 .... 102 A1
Ullswater Rd SMHTH WV12 .... 25 H1
Ulster Dr KGSWFD DY6 .... 100 A5
Ulverley Crs HIA/OLT B92 .... 164 B2
Ulverley Green Rd
  HIA/OLT B92 .... 164 C2
Ulwine Dr NFLD/LBR B31 .... 175 G1
Umberslade Rd SLYOAK B29 .... 160 A2
Uncle Ben's Cl OLDBY B69 .... 104 D5
Underhill La WOLVN WV10 .... 13 C5
Underhill Rd TPTN/OCK DY4 .... 70 A5
  WASH/WDE B8 .... 128 D1
Underhill St OLDBY B69 .... 105 E4
Underley Cl KGSWFD DY6 .... 99 F2
The Underpass BHAMNEC B40 .... 150 A3
Underwood Cl EDG B15 .... 142 B4
  ERDW/GRVHL B23 .... 92 A2
Underwood Rd
  BFLD/HDSWWD B20 .... 89 C1
Unett St LOZ/NWT B19 .... 108 C4
  SMTHWK B66 .... 107 E5
Unett St North LOZ/NWT B19 .... 108 C4
Unett Wk LOZ/NWT B19 .... 108 C4
Union La WMBN WV5 .... 64 B2
Union Mill St WOLV WV1 * 7 J4
Union Pas CBHAM B2 .... 3 G5
Union Pl SLYOAK B29 .... 143 F5
Union Rd AST/WIT B6 .... 109 H1
  OLDBY B69 .... 86 C4
  SHLY B90 .... 180 C3
  SOLH B91 .... 182 A1
Union Rw HDSW B21 .... 107 H1
Union St BILS/COS WV14 .... 53 G5
  BLKHTH/ROWR B65 .... 122 A3
  CBHAM B2 .... 3 G5
  DARL/WED WS10 .... 70 D1
  DUDN DY1 .... 68 C4
  HAG/WOL DY9 .... 136 C2
  STRBR DY8 .... 135 G3
  TPTN/OCK DY4 .... 85 F1
  WBROM B70 .... 87 G4
  WLNHL WV13 .... 39 C5
  WOLV WV1 .... 7 H4
  WSL WS1 .... 5 G3
Unitt Dr CDYHTH B64 .... 121 E4
Unity Cl DARL/WED WS10 .... 55 F4
Unity Pl OLDBY B69 * 105 E1
  SLYOAK B29 * 142 D5
Unketts Rd SMTHWKW B67 .... 124 A1
Unwin Crs STRBR DY8 .... 135 E2
Upavon Cl CVALE B35 .... 94 D2
Upland Rd SLYOAK B29 .... 143 E5
Uplands HALE B63 .... 137 H5
Uplands Av BDMR/CCFT WV3 .... 35 H5
  BLKHTH/ROWR B65 .... 121 H4
  WLNHL WV13 .... 38 D4
Uplands Cl DUDS DY2 .... 103 E2
Uplands Dr BDMR/CCFT WV3 .... 36 A5
  SEDG DY3 .... 67 F3
Uplands Gv WLNHL WV13 .... 38 C4
Uplands Rd DUDS DY2 .... 103 E2
  HDSW B21 .... 89 F4
  WLNHL WV13 .... 38 C4
The Uplands SMTHWKW B67 .... 106 B5
Upper Ashley St RMSLY B62 .... 122 A3
Upper Balsall Heath Rd
  BHTH/HG B12 .... 144 B1
Upper Brook St WSLW WS2 * 4 B4
Upper Chapel St OLDBY B69 .... 85 H4
Upper Church La TPTN/OCK DY4 .... 69 F4
Upper Clifton Rd
  SCFLD/BOLD B73 .... 62 B3
Upper Cl RIDG/WDGT B32 .... 140 D4
Upper Coneybere St
  BHTH/HG B12 .... 127 F5
Upper Dean St DIG/EDG B5 .... 3 G7
Upper Ettingshall Rd
  BILS/COS WV14 .... 68 A3
Upper Forster St
  RUSH/SHEL WS4 .... 5 F1
Upper Gough St CBHAMWW B1 .... 126 D3
Upper Gn
  DUNHL/THL/PER WV6 .... 21 H5
Upper Green La WSLW WS2 * 41 G1
Upper Grosvenor Rd
  BFLD/HDSWWD B20 .... 90 B4
Upper Hall La WSL WS1 * 4 E5
Upper Highgate St
  BHTH/HG B12 .... 127 F5
Upper High St CDYHTH B64 .... 120 D3
  DARL/WED WS10 .... 55 H5
Upper Holland Rd
  CSCFLD/WYGN B72 .... 62 C4
Upper Lichfield St
  WLNHL WV13 .... 39 G3
Upper Marshall St
  CBHAMW B1 .... 2 E7
Upper Meadow Rd
  RIDG/WDGT B32 .... 140 C2
Upper Navigation St
  WSLW WS2 .... 4 C3
Upper Rushall St WSL WS1 .... 5 F4
Upper Russell St
  DARL/WED WS10 .... 70 D1
Upper St Mary's Rd
  SMTHWKW B67 .... 124 B3
Upper Short St WSLW WS2 * 4 B4
Upper Sneyd Rd WNSFLD WV11 .. 15 F3

Upper Stone Cl
  WALM/CURD B76 .... 63 E4
Upper St
  DUNHL/THL/PER WV6 .... 21 H5
Upper Sutton St AST/WIT B6 .... 109 F2
Upper Thomas St AST/WIT B6 .... 109 F3
Upper Trinity St BORD B9 .... 127 G3
Upper Vauxhall WOLV WV1 .... 6 B3
Upper Villiers St
  BKHL/PFLD WV2 .... 51 H2
Upper William St CBHAMW B1 .... 2 C7
Upper Zoar St
  BDMR/CCFT WV3 .... 6 C7
Upton Gdns BILS/COS WV14 .... 53 G5
Upton Gn WOLVN WV10 .... 12 B4
Upton Gv STETCH B33 .... 129 G3
Upton Rd STETCH B33 .... 129 G3
Upton St DUDS DY2 .... 102 C4
Upwey Av SOLH B91 .... 181 G1
Usk Cl BLOX/PEL WS3 .... 27 H2
Usk Wy TPTN/OCK DY4 .... 113 H1
Uttoxeter Cl
  DUNHL/THL/PER WV6 .... 22 D5
Uxbridge Cl SEDG DY3 .... 82 D5
Uxbridge St LOZ/NWT B19 .... 108 D4

V

Valbourne Rd
  ALE/KHTH/YWD B14 .... 177 G1
Vale Av ALDR WS9 .... 44 D3
  SEDG DY3 .... 83 E3
Vale Cl RIDG/WDGT B32 .... 141 F4
Vale Ct CDYHTH B64 * 120 D5
Vale Head Dr
  DUNHL/THL/PER WV6 .... 35 E3
Valencia Cft CVALE B35 .... 94 D2
Valentine Cl FOAKS/STRLY B74 .... 60 D2
Valentine Rd
  ALE/KHTH/YWD B14 .... 161 E1
  LGLYGN/QTN B68 .... 123 G2
Valepits Rd STETCH B33 .... 131 E5
Vale Rd Gv GTB/HAM B43 .... 75 E3
Vale Rd DUDS DY2 .... 103 E5
Vale Rw SEDG DY3 .... 83 F1
Vales Cl WALM/CURD B76 .... 78 A4
Vale St BKHL/PFLD WV2 .... 51 H3
  HHTH/SAND B71 .... 72 A5
  SEDG DY3 .... 83 F1
  STRBR DY8 .... 118 B4
The Vale SPARK B11 .... 144 D5
Vale Vw ALDR WS9 .... 44 B2
Valley Farm Rd RBRY B45 .... 187 H2
Valley La HOCK/TIA B94 .... 199 H4
Valley Rd BLOX/PEL WS3 .... 27 H2
  CDYHTH B64 .... 121 E3
  FOAKS/STRLY B74 .... 60 D1
  GTB/HAM B43 .... 74 D1
  HAG/WOL DY9 .... 136 D1
  HIA/OLT B92 .... 148 A3
  SEDG DY3 .... 67 G5
  SMTHWKW B67 .... 124 B1
  SOLH B91 .... 181 H5
  WNSFLD WV11 .... 24 D4
  WOLVN WV10 .... 23 H5
Valley Side BLOX/PEL WS3 * 18 A5
Valley Vw BRWNH WS8 .... 9 G5
Vallian Cft CBROM B36 .... 112 B2
Vanborough Wk DUDN DY1 .... 84 A4
Vanbrugh Ct
  DUNHL/THL/PER WV6 .... 34 C2
Van Diemans Rd WMBN WV5 .... 80 C1
Vanguard Cl CBROM B36 .... 112 A1
Vanguard Rd
  LGN/SDN/BHAMAIR B26 .... 149 C3
Vann Cl SMHTH B10 .... 128 A4
Vantage Point WBROM B70 * 87 G4
Varden Cft DIG/EDG B5 .... 126 D5
Vardon Wy HWK/WKHTH B38 .... 176 B4
Varley Rd ERDE/BCHGN B24 .... 93 H2
Varlins Wy HWK/WKHTH B38 .... 190 B2
Varney Av WBROM B70 .... 87 H4
Vaughan Cl FOAKS/STRLY B74 .... 32 D4
Vaughan Gdns CDSL WV8 .... 10 B5
Vaughan Rd WLNHL WV13 .... 38 D4
Vaughton Dr MGN/WHC B75 .... 63 E2
Vaughton St STRBR DY8 * 127 F4
Vaughton St South
  BHTH/HG B12 .... 127 E5
Vauxhall Av WOLV WV1 .... 6 B3
Vauxhall Crs CBROM B36 .... 95 H5
Vauxhall Gdns DUDS DY2 .... 103 E2
Vauxhall Gv VAUX/NECH B7 .... 127 G1
Vauxhall Pl VAUX/NECH B7 * 127 G1
Vauxhall Rd STRBR DY8 .... 135 G2
  VAUX/NECH B7 .... 127 G1
Vauxhall St DUDN DY1 .... 102 B1
Velsheda Rd SHLY B90 .... 180 A5
Venetia Rd BORD B9 .... 128 A2
Venning Gv GTB/HAM B43 .... 73 F4
Ventnor Av CBROM B36 .... 111 H2
  LOZ/NWT B19 .... 108 C2
Ventnor Cl LGLYGN/QTN B68 .... 123 G5
Ventnor Rd HIA/OLT B92 .... 148 A4
Venture Wy VAUX/NECH B7 .... 3 K1
Vera Rd
  LGN/SDN/BHAMAIR B26 .... 130 A5
Verbena Gdns VAUX/NECH B7 .... 109 G4
Verbena Rd NFLD/LBR B31 .... 158 B5
Vercourt FOAKS/STRLY B74 .... 45 H2
Verdun Crs DUDS DY2 .... 85 H5
Vere St DIG/EDG B5 .... 126 D5
Verity Wk STRBR DY8 .... 118 A3
Verney Av STETCH B33 .... 131 F5
Vernier Av KGSWFD DY6 .... 100 C4
Vernolds Cft DIG/EDG B5 * 127 E4
Vernon Av BFLD/HDSWWD B20 .... 89 G5
  BRWNH WS8 .... 9 G5
  TPTN/OCK DY4 .... 69 G2
Vernon Cl FOAKS/STRLY B74 .... 32 C5
  RMSLY B62 .... 122 A4
  SHLY B90 .... 39 E4
  WNSFLD WV11 .... 14 D3
Vernon Ct LDYWD/EDGR B16 .... 125 G5
  LGLYGN/QTN B68 .... 123 F5
Vernon Rd BILS/COS WV14 .... 54 B2
  LDYWD/EDGR B16 .... 125 F5

  LGLYGN/QTN B68 .... 105 G3
  RMSLY B62 .... 122 A4
Vernon St WBROM B70 .... 86 C5
Vernon Wy BLOX/PEL WS3 .... 26 C1
Veronica Av
  ETTPK/GDPK/PENN WV4 .... 52 C5
Veronica Cl SLYOAK B29 .... 158 B4
Veronica Rd KGSWFD DY6 .... 100 C5
Verstone Cft NFLD/LBR B31 .... 175 G3
Verstone Rd SHLY B90 .... 180 C1
Verwood Cl WLNHL WV13 .... 38 C4
Vesey Rd SCFLD/BOLD B73 .... 77 F2
  FOAKS/STRLY B74 .... 46 D5
Vesey St CBHAMNE B4 .... 3 G2
Vestry Cl CDYHTH B64 .... 121 F3
Vestry Ct STRBR DY8 .... 135 E1
Viaduct Dr
  DUNHL/THL/PER WV6 .... 22 D4
Viaduct St VAUX/NECH B7 .... 127 G1
Vibart Rd
  LGN/SDN/BHAMAIR B26 .... 130 B4
  BRWNH WS8 .... 9 C4
  BVILLE B30 .... 160 B2
  PBAR/PBCH B42 .... 74 D4
Vicarage Cl AST/WIT B6 .... 109 F2
  BILS/COS WV14 .... 53 F3
  BRWNH WS8 .... 9 G5
  TPTN/OCK DY4 .... 85 G2
Vicarage Gdns RMSLY B62 .... 122 B3
  WALM/CURD B76 .... 78 B4
Vicarage La BRLYHL DY5 .... 101 F1
Vicarage Pl WSL WS1 .... 5 F5
Vicarage Prospect DUDN DY1 .... 84 B5
Vicarage Rd
  ALE/KHTH/YWD B14 .... 160 D3
  BILS/COS WV14 .... 68 C4
  BKHL/PFLD WV2 .... 7 H7
  BLOX/PEL WS3 .... 18 A5
  BRWNH WS8 .... 9 G5
  DARL/WED WS10 .... 55 H5
  EDG B15 .... 125 H4
  HAG/WOL DY9 .... 136 C5
  HHTH/SAND B71 .... 71 H5
  HOCK/TIA B94 .... 198 D4
  HRBN B17 .... 141 H2
  LGLYGN/QTN B68 .... 105 G4
  RMSLY B62 .... 122 A4
  SEDG DY3 .... 83 G1
  SMTHWK B66 .... 106 C4
  SMTHWKW B67 .... 117 H5
  WNSFLD WV11 .... 24 B4
  YDLY B25 .... 130 A3
Vicarage Rd West DUDN DY1 .... 68 C5
Vicarage St LGLYGN/QTN B68 .... 105 F4
Vicarage Ter WSL WS1 .... 41 G5
Vicarage Wk WSL WS1 .... 5 F4
Vicar St DARL/WED WS10 .... 56 A1
  DUDS DY2 .... 102 C1
  SEDG DY3 .... 83 G1
Vicars Wk HAG/WOL DY9 .... 136 C5
Vicenza Ct DIG/EDG B5 .... 143 G1
  KGSWFD DY6 .... 100 C4
Victor Cl BKHL/PFLD WV2 .... 53 F2
Victoria Ar WOLV WV1 .... 6 E5
Victoria Av BLOX/PEL WS3 .... 27 G1
  RMSLY B62 .... 139 H1
  SMHTH B10 * 128 B5
  SMTHWK B66 .... 106 C4
Victoria Gdns CDYHTH B64 * 121 E2
Victoria Gv WMBN WV5 .... 65 E3
  WSNGN B18 .... 107 G5
Victoria Ms OLDBY B69 .... 87 H2
  RUSH/SHEL WS4 .... 42 C2
Victoria Wy
  BFLD/HDSWWD B20 .... 90 A5
Victoria Park Rd
  SMTHWK B66 .... 106 D4
Victoria Pas WOLV WV1 .... 7 F4
Victoria Pk DARL/WED WS10 * 40 D5
Victoria Rd ACGN B27 .... 146 C5
  AST/WIT B6 .... 109 G2
  BDMR/CCFT WV3 .... 35 H4
  BLOX/PEL WS3 .... 18 A4
  BVILLE B30 .... 159 H3
  CDYHTH B64 .... 121 F2
  CSCFLD/WYGN B72 .... 62 C3
  DARL/WED WS10 .... 55 F2
  DUNHL/THL/PER WV6 .... 22 A5
  ERDW/GRVHL B23 .... 92 B3
  HDSW B21 .... 107 H2
  HRBN B17 .... 141 H2
  LGLYGN/QTN B68 .... 105 G5
  RMSLY B62 .... 122 B4
  SEDG DY3 .... 67 F3
  STETCH B33 .... 129 H1
  TPTN/OCK DY4 .... 70 A5
  WNSFLD WV11 .... 24 D4
  WOLVN WV10 .... 23 H5
Victoria Sq CBHAMW B1 * 2 E5
Victoria St BORD B9 .... 128 B2
  BRLYHL DY5 .... 119 F1
  DARL/WED WS10 .... 71 F1
  HALE B63 .... 138 C3
  KGSWFD DY6 .... 99 E1
  STRBR DY8 .... 135 F3
  WBROM B70 .... 86 D1
  WLNHL WV13 .... 39 G2
  WOLV WV1 .... 7 F5
Victoria Ter HDSW B21 * 107 H2
Victor Rd HIA/OLT B92 .... 147 H5
  AST/WIT B6 .... 109 C4
Victor St BLOX/PEL WS3 .... 19 F1
  WSL WS1 .... 57 E1
Victory Av DARL/WED WS10 .... 55 E5
Victory La WSLW WS2 .... 41 E1
Victory Ri HHTH/SAND B71 .... 87 H1
View Dr DUDS DY2 .... 103 E1
Viewfield Crs SEDG DY3 .... 81 H1
View Pt OLDBY B69 .... 105 H1
Vigo Cl ALDR WS9 .... 19 H3
Vigo Pl ALDR WS9 .... 30 A5
Vigo Rd ALDR WS9 .... 19 H3
Vigo Ter ALDR WS9 .... 19 F5

Viking Ri BLKHTH/ROWR B65 .... 104 A5
Village Ms RIDG/WDGT B32 .... 140 A1
The Village KGSWFD DY6 .... 100 A2
Village Wy BILS/COS WV14 .... 53 H2
Villa Rd LOZ/NWT B19 .... 108 B2
Villa St LOZ/NWT B19 .... 108 C3
  STRBR DY8 .... 118 C4
Villa Wk LOZ/NWT B19 .... 108 C3
Villette Gv ALE/KHTH/YWD B14 .... 179 E1
Villiers Av BILS/COS WV14 .... 53 H1
Villiers Sq BILS/COS WV14 .... 53 H1
Villiers St WLNHL WV13 .... 57 E1
  WSL WS1 .... 57 E1
  WSNGN B18 .... 107 G4
Vimy Rd DARL/WED WS10 .... 56 A4
  MOS/BIL B13 .... 144 D4
Vincent Cl BHTH/HG B12 .... 144 B1
Vincent Dr EDG B15 .... 142 B1
Vincent Pde BHTH/HG B12 .... 144 B1
Vincent Rd MGN/WHC B75 .... 63 E1
Vincent St BHTH/HG B12 .... 144 A1
  WSL WS1 .... 57 F1
Vince St SMTHWK B66 .... 124 C1
Vinculum Wy WLNHL WV13 .... 39 H5
Vine Av DIG/EDG B5 .... 143 H1
Vine Cl WOLVN WV10 .... 12 C4
Vine Crs HHTH/SAND B71 .... 71 H5
Vine Gdns CDYHTH B64 .... 121 F2
Vine La HAG/WOL DY9 .... 170 D2
  HALE B63 .... 138 C4
  STRBR DY8 .... 118 A3
The Vineries ACGN B27 .... 147 E3
Vine St AST/WIT B6 .... 109 H2
  BRLYHL DY5 .... 101 G4
  DUDN DY1 .... 118 A5
Vineyard Rd NFLD/LBR B31 .... 175 F2
Vinnall Gv RIDG/WDGT B32 .... 157 F2
Vintage Cl BKDE/SHDE B34 .... 112 C4
Vinyard Ct HDSW B21 .... 107 H2
Violet Cft TPTN/OCK DY4 .... 69 H2
Violet La HAG/WOL DY9 .... 170 C1
Virginia Dr
  ETTPK/GDPK/PENN WV4 .... 51 F4
Viscount Cl CVALE B35 .... 94 C4
Viscount Dr CVALE B35 .... 94 D4
Vista Gn HWK/WKHTH B38 .... 177 F4
The Vista SEDG DY3 .... 66 D3
Vittoria St CBHAMW B1 .... 2 C2
  SMTHWK B66 .... 107 F3
Vivian Cl HRBN B17 .... 142 A2
Vivian Rd HRBN B17 .... 142 A2
Vixen Cl WALM/CURD B76 .... 77 H4
Vowles Rd HHTH/SAND B71 .... 71 H5
Vulcan Rd BILS/COS WV14 .... 54 B3
  SOLH B91 .... 165 E4
Vyrnwy Gv HWK/WKHTH B38 .... 176 B4
Vyse St AST/WIT B6 .... 109 H1
  WSNGN B18 .... 2 C1

W

Wadbarn SHLY B90 .... 194 A3
Waddams Pool DUDS DY2 .... 86 B5
Waddell Cl BILS/COS WV14 .... 67 H2
Waddens Brook La
  WNSFLD WV11 .... 25 E5
Waddington Av GTB/HAM B43 .... 73 G2
Wadesmill Lawns WOLVN WV10 .. 13 E5
Wadham Cl
  BLKHTH/ROWR B65 .... 104 A3
Wadhurst Rd HRBN B17 .... 124 D2
Wadleys Rd SOLH B91 .... 164 D4
Waen Cl TPTN/OCK DY4 .... 69 G1
Waggon La KIDD DY10 .... 168 A2
Waggon St CDYHTH B64 .... 121 E2
Waggoners Wk HWK/WKHTH B38 .. 176 A5
Wagoners Cl WASH/WDE B8 .... 110 D3
Wagon La HIA/OLT B92 .... 147 G5
Wagstaff Cl BILS/COS WV14 .... 68 D3
Wagstaff Wy
  CHWD/FDBR/MGN B37 .... 132 A4
Wainwright Cl KGSWFD DY6 .... 99 E2
Wainwright St AST/WIT B6 .... 109 G2
Waite Rd WLNHL WV13 .... 38 C5
Wakefield Cl SCFLD/BOLD B73 .... 77 F1
Wakefield Ct MOS/BIL B13 .... 144 D5
Wakefield Gv CSHL/WTROR B46 .. 96 B3
Wakeford Rd NFLD/LBR B31 .... 176 A4
Wake Green Pk MOS/BIL B13 .... 144 D5
Wake Green Rd MOS/BIL B13 .... 144 C5
  MOS/BIL B13 .... 162 A1
  TPTN/OCK DY4 .... 69 G2
Wakelam Gdns GTB/HAM B43 .. 73 F2
Wakeley Hl
  ETTPK/GDPK/PENN WV4 .... 51 G3
Wakelin Rd SHLY B90 .... 194 B1
Wakeman Dr OLDBY B69 .... 103 H1
Wakeman Gv STETCH B33 .... 131 G1
Wakes Cl WLNHL WV13 .... 39 H4
Wakes Rd DARL/WED WS10 .... 71 F1
Walcot Cl MGN/WHC B75 .... 47 F2
Walcot Dr GTB/HAM B43 .... 73 G5
Walcot Gdns BILS/COS WV14 .... 53 F5
Walcot Gn DOR/KN B93 .... 199 E1
Waldale Cl SHHTH WV12 .... 26 A1
Walden Gdns
  ETTPK/GDPK/PENN WV4 .... 51 E2
Walden Rd SPARK B11 .... 146 A2
Waldeve Gv HIA/OLT B92 .... 165 H2
Waldley Gv ERDE/BCHGN B24 .... 93 G3
Waldron Av BRLYHL DY5 .... 118 D2
Waldron Cl DARL/WED WS10 .... 55 H2
Waldrons Moor
  ALE/KHTH/YWD B14 .... 160 C5
Walford Av DUNHL/THL/PER WV6 .. 35 E2
Walford Dr HIA/OLT B92 .... 148 B4
Walford Gv MGN/WHC B75 .... 63 F2
Walford Rd BORD B9 .... 128 B2
  SPARK B11 .... 145 F1
Walford St OLDBY B69 .... 85 E5
Walhouse Cl WSL WS1 .... 5 G3
Walhouse Rd WSL WS1 .... 5 G3
Walker Av BRLYHL DY5 .... 119 F5
  HAG/WOL DY9 .... 136 D4
  OLDBY B69 .... 104 B2

WOLVN WV10 .... 23 G2
Walker Dr ERDE/BCHGN B24 .... 110 C1
Walker Pl BLOX/PEL WS3 .... 28 A2
Walker Rd BLOX/PEL WS3 .... 27 H2
Walkers Fold SHHTH WV12 .... 26 B4
Walkers Heath Rd
    HWK/WKHTH B38 .... 177 F4
Walker St DUDS DY2 .... 102 C5
    TPTN/OCK DY4 .... 70 A4
Walk La WMBN WV5 .... 65 E5
The Walk SEDC DY3 .... 67 F2
Wallace Cl OLDBY B69 .... 104 B3
Wallace Ri CDYHTH B64 .... 121 E5
Wallace Rd BILS/COS WV14 .... 54 C5
    WOLVN WV10 .... 69 F1
    OLDBY B69 .... 104 B3
The Wallows ALDR WS9 .... 30 B5
Walmer Wy
    CHWD/FDBR/MGN B37 .... 132 C1
Walmesley Wy NFLD/LBR B31 .. 175 C2
Walnut Av
    WALM/CURD B76 .... 78 B4
Walmley Cl HALE B63 .... 120 D5
    WALM/CURD B76 .... 78 B5
Walnut Av CDSL WV8 .... 10 D4
Walnut Cl
    BDMR/CCFT WV3 .... 132 B3
    HAG/WOL DY9 .... 152 D1
Walnut Dr BDMR/CCFT WV3 ..... 35 H4
    SMTHWK B66 .... 106 D4
Walnut La DARL/WED WS10 ...... 71 E1
Walnut Wy NFLD/LBR B31 .... 175 F5
Walpole St
    DUNHL/THL/PER WV6 .... 6 B1
Walpole Wk WBROM B70 .... 87 H5
Walsall Rd ALDR WS9 .... 30 A5
    ALDR WS9 .... 43 H1
    BLOX/PEL WS3 .... 18 A5
    DARL/WED WS10 .... 55 G2
    DSYBK/YTR WS5 .... 57 F4
    FOAKS/STRLY B74 .... 46 C2
    HHTH/SAND B71 .... 72 A4
    PBAR/PBCH B42 .... 74 A3
    RUSH/SHEL WS4 .... 19 E5
    WLNHL WV13 .... 40 A3
Walsall Wood Rd ALDR WS9 ..... 30 D5
Walsgrave Dr HIA/OLT B92 .... 165 F5
Walsham Cft BKDE/SHDE B34 .. 113 E4
Walsh Dr WALM/CURD B76 .... 63 F4
Walsh Gv ERDW/GRVHL B23 ..... 76 B5
Walsingham St WSL WS1 .... 5 H5
Walstead Rd West
    DSYBK/YTR WS5 .... 57 E3
Walt Dr
    DSYBK/YTR WS5 .... 57 E3
Waltdene Cl GTB/HAM B43 .... 73 G1
Walter Cobb Dr
    SCFLD/BOLD B73 .... 77 E2
Walter Rd BILS/COS WV14 .... 54 A5
    SMTHWK B67 .... 106 A3
Walters Cl NFLD/LBR B31 .... 189 F2
Walters Rd LGLYGN/QTN B68 .. 123 E5
Walters Rw DUDN DY1 .... 84 A5
Walter St BLOX/PEL WS3 .... 28 C1
    VAUX/NECH B7 .... 109 H5
    WBROM B70 .... 88 C5
Waltham Gv KGSTG B44 .... 75 H1
Walthamstow Ct BRLYHL DY5 .. 119 F3
Walton Av BLKHTH/ROWR B65 . 121 H4
Walton Cl BLKHTH/ROWR B65 . 103 C5
    HALE B63 .... 138 B5
Walton Crs
    ETTPK/GDPK/PENN WV4 .... 52 C3
Walton Ct SOLH B91 .... 181 H4
Walton Dr HAG/WOL DY9 .... 153 H2
Walton Gdns CDSL WV8 .... 10 B3
Walton Gv BVILLE B30 .... 177 F3
Walton Heath BLOX/PEL WS3 .... 16 B4
Walton Pool La HAG/WOL DY9 . 170 D3
Walton Ri HAG/WOL DY9 .... 171 E2
Walton Rd ALDR WS9 .... 30 A1
    DARL/WED WS10 .... 71 G1
    ETTPK/GDPK/PENN WV4 .... 52 D3
    LGLYGN/QTN B68 .... 123 G5
    STRBR DY8 .... 95 E2
Walton St TPTN/OCK DY4 .... 85 F1
Wanderers Av BKHL/PFLD WV2 .. 52 A2
Wanderer Wk CBROM B36 .... 94 A5
Wandle Gv SPARK B11 .... 146 A4
Wandsworth Rd KGSTG B44 .... 60 A5
Wannerton Rd KIDD DY10 .... 180 C5
Wansbeck Gv
    HWK/WKHTH B38 .... 176 C5
Wansbeck Wk DUDS DY3 .... 67 H5
Wanstead Gv KGSTG B44 .... 75 G2
Wantage Rd
    CSHL/WTROR B46 .... 97 E5
Ward Cl WASH/WDE B8 .... 111 E4
Warden Av SCFLD/BOLD B73 ..... 76 D3

Ward End Cl WASH/WDE B8 ..... 110 D3
Ward End Hall Gv
    WASH/WDE B8 .... 111 E3
Ward End Park Rd
    WASH/WDE B8 .... 110 D4
Wardend Rd WASH/WDE B8 ...... 111 E3
Wardle Rd SCFLD/BOLD B73 ..... 76 D3
Wardlow Cl
    ETTPK/GDPK/PENN WV4 .... 52 D5
Wardle Cl MGN/WHC B75 .... 47 E1
Wardlow Ct
    ETTPK/GDPK/PENN WV4 .... 51 H2
Wardlow Rd VAUX/NECH B7 .... 109 G4
Wardour Dr
    CHWD/FDBR/MGN B37 .... 132 C2
Wardour Gv KGSTG B44 .... 76 A3
Ward Rd CDSL WV8 .... 10 B4
    ETTPK/GDPK/PENN WV4 .... 52 B3
Ward St BILS/COS WV14 .... 68 B3
    BKHL/PFLD WV2 .... 53 F2
    ERDW/GRVHL B23 .... 92 C2
    LOZ/NWT B19 .... 3 G1
    WLNHL WV13 .... 39 H2
    WSL WS1 .... 7 J4
    WSL WS1 .... 5 F4
Wareham Cl BLOX/PEL WS3 ...... 28 B5
Wareham Rd RBRY B45 .... 174 B3
Wareing Dr ERDW/GRVHL B23 .. 76 B3
Warewell Cl WSL WS1 .... 5 F3
Warewell St WSL WS1 .... 5 F4
Waring Cl TPTN/OCK DY4 .... 69 E3
Waring Rd TPTN/OCK DY4 .... 69 G3
The Warings WMBN WV5 .... 80 D2
War La HRBN B17 .... 141 H2
Warley Cft LGLYGN/QTN B68 .. 123 H4
Warley Hall Rd
    LGLYGN/QTN B68 .... 123 H3
Warley Rd LGLYGN/QTN B68 .. 105 G4
Warmington Dr
    SCFLD/BOLD B73 .... 62 B4
Warmington Rd HLYWD B47 .... 192 C2
    LGN/SDN/BHAMAIR B26 .... 148 A2
Warmley Cl
    DUNHL/THL/PER WV6 .... 22 D5
    SOLH B91 .... 165 F5
Warner Dr BRLYHL DY5 .... 119 F3
Warner Pl BLOX/PEL WS3 .... 28 C4
Warner Rd BLOX/PEL WS3 .... 28 C4
    CDSL WV8 .... 10 B4
    DARL/WED WS10 .... 71 G1
Warner St BHTH/HG B12 .... 127 G4
Warners Wk SMHTH B10 .... 128 A4
Warple Rd RIDG/WDGT B32 .... 140 C2
Warren Cl TPTN/OCK DY4 .... 69 F4
Warren Dr BLKHTH/ROWR B65 . 103 F4
    DOR/KN B93 .... 197 E5
    SEDC DY3 .... 67 E1
Warren Farm Rd KGSTG B44 ..... 75 F3
Warren Gdns KGSWFD DY6 .... 99 G3
Warren Gv WASH/WDE B8 .... 110 C3
Warren Hill Rd KGSTG B44 .... 75 G4
Warren House Wk
    WALM/CURD B76 .... 78 B2
Warren La RBRY B45 .... 188 B5
Warren Pl BRWNH WS8 .... 9 G2
Warren Rd BVILLE B30 .... 160 A3
    KGSTG B44 .... 75 G5
    WASH/WDE B8 .... 110 C3
Warrens Cft DSYBK/YTR WS5 .... 58 B3
Warrens End
    HWK/WKHTH B38 .... 176 D5
Warrens Hall Rd DUDS DY2 .... 103 E2
Warrington Cl
    WALM/CURD B76 .... 78 C2
Warrington Dr
    ERDW/GRVHL B23 .... 76 B4
Warsash Cl WOLV WV1 .... 38 B5
Warstock La
    ALE/KHTH/YWD B14 .... 178 C1
Warstock Rd
    ALE/KHTH/YWD B14 .... 178 C1
Warstone Dr RIDG/WDGT B32 . 140 D4
Warstone Dr HHTH/SAND B71 .. 88 A2
Warstone La WSNGN B18 .... 2 C2
Warstone Ms WSNGN B18 * 2 C2
Warstone Pde East WSNGN B18 .. 2 B2
Warstones Crs
    ETTPK/GDPK/PENN WV4 .... 50 D3
Warstones Dr
    ETTPK/GDPK/PENN WV4 .... 50 C3
Warstones Gdns
    ETTPK/GDPK/PENN WV4 .... 50 C2
Warstones Rd
    ETTPK/GDPK/PENN WV4 .... 50 D4
Warstone Ter HDSW B21 .... 107 G1
Wartell Bank KGSWFD DY6 .... 99 H2
Warwards La SLYOAK B29 .... 160 A1
Warwell La
    LGN/SDN/BHAMAIR B26 .... 146 D1
Warwick Av DARL/WED WS10 .... 56 C5
    DUDN DY1 .... 84 D2
    WLNHL WV13 .... 39 E3
Warwick Cl LGLYGN/QTN B68 . 123 F2
    WBROM B70 .... 70 C4
Warwick Crest EDG B15 * 126 B5
Warwick Dr CDSL WV8 .... 10 A4
Warwick Gdns OLDBY B69 .... 86 A4
Warwick Gra SOLH B91 .... 164 B3
Warwick Gv HIA/OLT B92 .... 163 H1
Warwick Pas CBHAM B2 .... 3 G5
Warwick Rd DOR/KN B93 .... 183 F5
    DOR/KN B93 .... 197 F1
    DUDS DY2 .... 121 E1
    LGLYGN/QTN B68 .... 123 H5
    SCFLD/BOLD B73 .... 76 A1
    SOLH B91 .... 164 B3
    SPARK B11 .... 145 G3
    STRBR DY8 .... 117 H3
Warwick St BHTH/HG B12 .... 127 G3
    BILS/COS WV14 .... 54 A3
    RUSH/SHEL WS4 .... 54 A3
    WOLV WV1 .... 7 J5
Waseley Rd RBRY B45 .... 173 G5
Washbrook Rd
    WASH/WDE B8 .... 111 E3

Washford Gv YDLY B25 .... 129 F4
Washington Dr
    BFLD/HDSWWD B20 .... 90 B3
Washington St CBHAMW B1 .... 2 D7
    DUDS DY2 .... 120 D1
Washington Whf CBHAMW B1 .. 129 G5
Washwood Heath Rd
    WASH/WDE B8 .... 110 C3
Wasperton Cl CBROM B36 .... 112 D1
Wassell Ct HALE B63 .... 138 A5
Wassell Grove La
    HAG/WOL DY9 .... 137 F5
Wassell Grove Rd
    HAG/WOL DY9 .... 153 H1
Wassell Rd BILS/COS WV14 ...... 53 H1
    HAG/WOL DY9 .... 137 G5
    HALE B63 .... 138 A5
Wast Hill Gv HWK/WKHTH B38 . 190 D1
Wasthill La HWK/WKHTH B38 . 190 B3
Wastwater Ct
    DUNHL/THL/PER WV6 .... 34 D1
Watchbury Cl CBROM B36 .... 95 E5
Watchman Av BRLYHL DY5 ..... 119 H5
Waterbridge La WMBN WV5 ...... 64 C4
Water Dt BDMR/CCFT WV3 .... 36 A3
Waterdale SHLY B90 .... 194 D5
    WMBN WV5 .... 80 C1
Waterfall Cl SMTHWK B66 .... 106 A2
Waterfall La CDYHTH B64 .... 121 G3
Waterfall Rd BRLYHL DY5 .... 119 E5
Waterfield Cl TPTN/OCK DY4 .... 84 C1
Waterfield Wy
    LGN/SDN/BHAMAIR B26 .... 131 E5
Waterford Pl STETCH B33 .... 131 E1
Waterford Rd KGSWFD DY6 ...... 99 H2
Waterfront East BRLYHL DY5 .. 101 G5
    The Waterfront BRLYHL DY5 *.. 101 G5
Waterfront Wy BRLYHL DY5 ... 101 H5
    WSLW WS2 .... 4 B5
Waterfront West BRLYHL DY5 . 119 G1
Waterglade La WLNHL WV13 .... 39 G4
Waterhaynes Cl RBRY B45 ...... 188 C2
Waterhead Cl WOLVN WV10 ..... 13 G5
Waterhead Dr WOLVN WV10 ..... 13 H5
Water La HHTH/SAND B71 .... 72 B4
Water Lily Gv BRWNH WS8 .... 8 D5
Waterlinks Bvd AST/WIT B6 .... 109 G2
Waterloo Av
    CHWD/FDBR/MGN B37 .... 114 B5
Waterloo Rd
    ALE/KHTH/YWD B14 .... 161 E2
    SMTHWK B66 .... 124 D1
    WOLV WV1 .... 6 E3
    YDLY B25 .... 146 B1
Waterloo St CBHAM B2 .... 3 F5
    DUDN DY1 .... 102 A1
    TPTN/OCK DY4 .... 85 F1
Waterloo St East
    TPTN/OCK DY4 .... 85 F1
Watermead Gra BRWNH WS8 ..... 9 E5
Watermeadow Dr
    RUSH/SHEL WS4 .... 29 F1
Watermere RUSH/SHEL WS4 .... 29 F2
Water Mill Cl SLYOAK B29 .... 142 B4
Watermint Cl WOLVN WV10 ...... 12 D4
Water Mill Crs WALM/CURD B76 . 78 B2
Water Orton La
    WALM/CURD B76 .... 95 F1
Water Orton Rd CBROM B36 ... 113 F1
Water Rd SEDC DY3 .... 83 G4
Waters Dr FOAKS/STRLY B74 .... 46 B2
The Waters Edge CBHAMW B1 ... 2 B6
Waterside CTB/HAM B43 .... 73 G4
Waterside Av DARL/WED WS10 . 71 E2
Waterside Cl BKHL/PFLD WV2 .. 52 B1
    BORD B9 .... 127 H2
    ERDE/BCHGN B24 .... 94 C2
Waterside Ct OLDBY B69 .... 104 D5
Waterside Dr WSNGN B18 .... 107 H4
Waterside Orch ALVE B48 *.... 189 H5
Waterside Pk TPTN/OCK DY4 * . 70 B4
Waterside Vw BRLYHL DY5 ..... 118 D3
    WSNGN B18 .... 108 A4
Water Side Wy COVEN WV9 .... 12 A5
Waterson Cft
    CHWD/FDBR/MGN B37 .... 132 D1
Water St CBHAMNW B3 .... 2 E3
    KGSWFD DY6 .... 99 H2
    WBROM B70 .... 87 H4
    WOLVN WV10 .... 7 H1
Waters Vw BLOX/PEL WS3 .... 18 B2
Waterward Cl HRBN B17 .... 142 A2
Waterway Ct
    ALE/KHTH/YWD B14 .... 179 E2
Waterways Dr OLDBY B69 .... 86 C5
Waterways Gdns STRBR DY8 ... 118 A3
Waterworks Dr NFLD/LBR B31 . 157 H3
Waterworks Rd
    LDYWD/EDGR B16 .... 125 H3
Watery La DOR/KN B93 .... 197 H1
    SHLY B90 .... 194 C4
    SMTHWK B67 .... 106 C4
    STRBR DY8 .... 118 A2
    TPTN/OCK DY4 .... 85 F1
    WLNHL WV13 .... 39 E2
    WSL WS1 .... 4 D7
Watery La Middleway
    BORD B9 .... 127 H3
Watford Rd BVILLE B30 .... 159 H5
Wathan Av BILS/COS WV14 ...... 67 H1
The Wathcroft HRBN B17 .... 141 H1
Watkins Gdns NFLD/LBR B31 .. 175 H2
Watkins Rd SHHTH WV12 .... 26 A5
Watland Gn BKDE/SHDE B34 .. 113 C4
Watling St CNCK/NC WS11 .... 8 A2
Watney Gv KGSTG B44 .... 76 A3
Watson Cl SCFLD/BOLD B73 ..... 77 F1
Watson Rd BILS/COS WV14 ...... 67 G1
    DARL/WED WS10 .... 57 E3
    WASH/WDE B8 .... 110 B2
    WOLVN WV10 .... 12 B5
Watson Rd East
    VAUX/NECH B7 .... 110 B2
Watsons Cl DUDS DY2 .... 103 E1
Watson's Green Flds
    DUDS DY2 .... 103 F1

Watson's Green Rd DUDS DY2 . 103 E1
Wattisham Sq CVALE B35 .... 94 C2
Wattis Rd SMTHWK B67 .... 124 C2
Wattle Rd WBROM B70 .... 87 E3
Watton Cl BILS/COS WV14 .... 68 A2
Watton Gn CVALE B35 .... 94 C4
Watton La CSHL/WTROR B46 .... 96 C4
Watton St WBROM B70 .... 87 G4
Watt Rd ERDW/GRVHL B23 ...... 92 C2
    TPTN/OCK DY4 .... 69 H3
Watts Cl TPTN/OCK DY4 .... 84 C1
Watt's Rd SMHTH B10 .... 128 B4
Watt St HDSW B21 .... 107 E1
    SMTHWK B66 .... 106 D3
Wattville Av HDSW B21 .... 107 E1
Wattville Rd HDSW B21 .... 107 E1
Watwood Rd HLGN/YWD B28 . 179 H2
Waugh Cl
    CHWD/FDBR/MGN B37 .... 132 B2
Waugh Dr HALE B63 .... 154 D2
Waveil Rd BRLYHL DY5 .... 119 H5
    SMTHWK B66 .... 106 C4
    WSLW WS2 .... 40 C3
Waveney Av
    DUNHL/THL/PER WV6 .... 34 C1
Waveney Crt CBROM B36 .... 113 H1
Waverhill Rd HDSW B21 .... 107 H2
Waverley Av GTB/HAM B43 .... 59 F4
Waverley Crs BKHL/PFLD WV2 .. 51 H2
    ETTPK/GDPK/PENN WV4 .... 52 D5
    RMSLY B62 .... 122 C1
Waverley Gv SOLH B91 .... 181 E2
Waverley Rd BLOX/PEL WS3 ..... 16 B5
    DARL/WED WS10 .... 55 F2
    SMHTH B10 .... 128 A3
    WOLV WV1 .... 38 B1
Waverley St DUDS DY2 .... 102 A1
Wavers Marston CHWD/FDBR/MGN
    B37 .... 132 A4
Waxland Rd HALE B63 .... 138 D5
Wayfield Cl SHLY B90 .... 180 C2
Wayfield Rd SHLY B90 .... 180 C2
Wayford Dr CSCFLD/WYGN B72 . 77 H4
Wayford Gld WLNHL WV13 .... 39 F5
Waynecroft Rd GTB/HAM B43 ... 73 G1
Wayside
    CHWD/FDBR/MGN B37 .... 132 A4
Wayside Acres CDSL WV8 .... 10 B5
Wayside Dr FOAKS/STRLY B74 .. 46 A2
Wayside Gdns SHHTH WV12 ..... 26 C5
Wayside Wk WSLW WS2 .... 41 E2
Waystone La HAG/WOL DY9 ... 184 B5
Wealden Hatch WOLVN WV10 .. 13 E3
Wealdstone Dr SEDC DY3 .... 83 F4
Weaman St CBHAMNE B4 .... 3 G3
Weatheroak Rd SPARK B11 ...... 145 E2
Weatheroaks ALDR WS9 .... 19 H5
Weather Oaks HRBN B17 .... 141 H2
Weatheroaks RMSLY B62 .... 123 E5
Weaver Av
    LGN/SDN/BHAMAIR B26 .... 147 H1
    WALM/CURD B76 .... 78 C2
Weaver Cl BRLYHL DY5 .... 100 D5
Weaver Gv WLNHL WV13 .... 40 D3
Weavers Ri DUDS DY2 .... 120 D1
Webb Av DUNHL/THL/PER WV6 . 20 C5
Webbcroft Rd STETCH B33 ..... 112 A5
Webb La HLGN/YWD B28 .... 179 F3
Webb Rd TPTN/OCK DY4 .... 70 A4
Webb St BILS/COS WV14 .... 68 C1
    WLNHL WV13 .... 39 F3
Webley Ri WOLVN WV10 .... 13 F3
Webster Cl CSCFLD/WYGN B72 . 77 F4
    SPARK B11 .... 144 D1
Webster Rd WLNHL WV13 .... 39 G2
    WSLW WS2 .... 27 H5
Webster Wy WALM/CURD B76 .. 78 D4
Weddell Wynd BILS/COS WV14 . 69 E2
Wedgbury Cl DARL/WED WS10 . 71 E2
Wedgbury Wy BRLYHL DY5 ... 118 D3
Wedge St WSL WS1 .... 5 G3
Wedgewood Av WBROM B70 .... 70 D4
Wedgewood Dr
    BFLD/HDSWWD B20 .... 90 B4
    WOLV WV1 .... 38 A4
Wedgewood Pl WBROM B70 ..... 70 D4
Wedgewood Rd
    RIDG/WDGT B32 .... 140 C2
Wedgwood Cl WMBN WV5 .... 64 D4
    WOLV WV1 .... 38 A4
Wedmore Rd SCFLD/BOLD B73 . 76 D3
Wednesbury Oak Rd
    TPTN/OCK DY4 .... 69 G2
Wednesbury One
    DARL/WED WS10 * 55 F5
    WSLW WS2 .... 54 C1
Wednesfield Rd WLNHL WV13 .. 25 E5
    WOLVN WV10 .... 7 K2
Wednesfield Wy WNSFLD WV11 . 25 E5
    WOLVN WV10 .... 38 A1
Weeford Dell MGN/WHC B75 ... 48 A2
Weeford Dr
    BFLD/HDSWWD B20 .... 89 H2
Weeford Rd MGN/WHC B75 ...... 48 C3
Welbeck Av DUDN DY1 .... 84 D2
Welbeck Cl RMSLY B62 .... 139 E2
Welbeck Dr RUSH/SHEL WS4 .... 29 F3
Welbeck Gv ERDW/GRVHL B23 . 91 H1
Welbury Gdns
    DUNHL/THL/PER WV6 .... 22 B5
Welby Rd HLGN/YWD B28 .... 162 D1
Welch Cl TPTN/OCK DY4 .... 85 F3
Welches Cl NFLD/LBR B31 ...... 158 D5
Welcombe Gv SOLH B91 .... 181 F2
Welford Av
    LGN/SDN/BHAMAIR B26 .... 130 B4
Welford Rd
    BFLD/HDSWWD B20 .... 108 A1
    SCFLD/BOLD B73 .... 76 C2
    SHLY B90 .... 180 C1
Welham Cft SHLY B90 .... 195 G2
Welland Cl CSHL/WTROR B46 .. 98 B1
Welland Dr STRBR DY8 .... 118 C4
Welland Rd HALE B63 .... 138 C5
Welland Wy WALM/CURD B76 .. 78 C2
Well Cl CBROM B36 .... 112 A1

Wellcroft Rd BKDE/SHDE B34 . 112 C2
Wellcroft St DARL/WED WS10 .. 55 H5
Wellesbourne
    BDMR/CCFT WV3 .... 35 F5
Wellesbourne Dr
    BILS/COS WV14 .... 68 B4
Wellesbourne Rd
    BFLD/HDSWWD B20 .... 90 B5
Wellesley Dr TPTN/OCK DY4 .... 85 F1
Wellesley Gdns MOS/BIL B13 .. 162 B1
Wellesley Rd LGLYGN/QTN B68 . 105 F3
Wellfield Gdns DUDS DY2 ...... 103 E5
Wellfield Rd ALDR WS9 .... 30 B2
    HLGN/YWD B28 .... 163 F4
Wellhead La PBAR/PBCH B42 .. 91 E4
Wellington Av
    BDMR/CCFT WV3 .... 51 F1
Wellington Cl KGSWFD DY6 ... 100 A5
Wellington Gv SOLH B91 .... 164 B4
Wellington Pl WLNHL WV13 ..... 39 F2
Wellington Rd
    BFLD/HDSWWD B20 .... 90 B4
    BILS/COS WV14 .... 54 B3
    DSYBK/YTR WS5 .... 58 A2
    DUDN DY1 .... 84 B5
    EDG B15 .... 143 G1
    SMTHWK B67 .... 124 C4
    TPTN/OCK DY4 .... 85 F5
Wellington St CDYHTH B64 .... 121 F2
    HHTH/SAND B71 .... 87 G2
    OLDBY B69 .... 105 F3
    SMTHWK B66 .... 106 F4
    WSLW WS2 .... 56 B1
Wellington St South
    WBROM B70 .... 87 G2
Wellington Ter
    LOZ/NWT B19 * 108 B2
    WLNHL WV13 * 39 G2
Wellington Wy CVALE B35 .... 94 D4
Well La BLOX/PEL WS3 .... 28 A3
    DIG/EDG B5 .... 3 H6
    WNSFLD WV11 .... 38 C1
Wellman Cft SLYOAK B29 .... 159 F1
Wellman's Rd WLNHL WV13 ..... 40 A4
Well Meadow RBRY B45 .... 188 A2
Well Pl BLOX/PEL WS3 .... 28 A3
Wells Av DARL/WED WS10 .... 54 D2
Wells Cl DUNHL/THL/PER WV6 . 34 B1
    HHTH/SAND B71 .... 71 H3
    TPTN/OCK DY4 .... 69 F5
Wellsford Av HIA/OLT B92 ...... 147 G3
Wells Green Rd HIA/OLT B92 . 147 G3
Wells Rd BILS/COS WV14 .... 54 A5
    BLKHTH/ROWR B65 .... 122 C1
    BRLYHL DY5 .... 118 D1
    ETTPK/GDPK/PENN WV4 .... 51 F3
    HIA/OLT B92 .... 148 A3
Well St COVEN WV9 .... 119 C4
Welney Gdns COVEN WV9 .... 12 A4
Welsby Av GTB/HAM B43 .... 73 G4
Welsh House Farm Rd
    RIDG/WDGT B32 .... 141 F3
Welshmans Hl KGSTG B44 .... 75 H1
    SCFLD/BOLD B73 .... 61 G5
Welton Cl WALM/CURD B76 ...... 78 C1
Welwyndale Rd
    CSCFLD/WYGN B72 .... 77 G5
Wembley Gv YDLY B25 .... 129 G4
Wem Gdns WNSFLD WV11 .... 24 D4
Wendell Crest WOLVN WV10 .... 13 F4
Wendover Rd
    BLKHTH/ROWR B65 .... 103 G3
    ERDW/GRVHL B23 .... 76 A4
    ETTPK/GDPK/PENN WV4 .... 67 G1
Wendron Gv
    ALE/KHTH/YWD B14 .... 177 H1
Wenlock Av BDMR/CCFT WV3 ... 36 A5
Wenlock Cl HALE B63 .... 137 H5
    SEDC DY3 .... 67 E4
Wenlock Gdns BLOX/PEL WS3 .. 28 A5
Wenlock Rd
    BFLD/HDSWWD B20 .... 91 E5
    STRBR DY8 .... 135 H1
Wenman St BHTH/HG B12 ...... 144 B1
Wensley Cft HLGN/YWD B28 .. 163 F4
Wensleydale Rd
    PBAR/PBCH B42 .... 74 B5
Wensley Rd
    LGN/SDN/BHAMAIR B26 .... 147 F1
Wentbridge Rd WOLV WV1 .... 38 A5
Wentworth Av CBROM B36 ..... 112 D1
Wentworth Dr OLDBY B69 ...... 105 G2
Wentworth Ga HRBN B17 .... 141 H1
Wentworth Gv
    DUNHL/THL/PER WV6 .... 20 B5
Wentworth Park Av
    HRBN B17 .... 141 H1
Wentworth Ri RMSLY B62 .... 139 F4
Wentworth Rd BLOX/PEL WS3 .. 16 B3
    FOAKS/STRLY B74 .... 47 E5
    HIA/OLT B92 .... 147 F4
    HRBN B17 .... 141 H1
    STRBR DY8 .... 117 H5
    WOLV WV10 .... 13 F5
Wentworth Wy
    RIDG/WDGT B32 .... 157 E3
Weoley Av SLYOAK B29 .... 142 A5
Weoley Castle Rd SLYOAK B29 . 158 C1
Weoley Hill SLYOAK B29 .... 158 D3
Weoley Park Rd SLYOAK B29 . 158 D2
Wergs Dr DUNHL/THL/PER WV6 . 21 E3
Wergs Gdns CDSL WV8 * 20 D1
Wergs Hall Rd CDSL WV8 .... 20 D1
Wergs Rd
    DUNHL/THL/PER WV6 .... 21 E4
Werneth Gv BLOX/PEL WS3 ...... 16 C3
Wesley Av CDSL WV8 .... 10 D5
    HALE B63 .... 120 B5
Wesley Cl CDYHTH B64 .... 121 F3
Wesley Gv DARL/WED WS10 ..... 70 A4
Wesley Pl TPTN/OCK DY4 .... 70 A4
Wesley Rd BRLYHL DY5 .... 100 D4
    CDSL WV8 .... 10 D5
    ERDW/GRVHL B23 .... 92 D1
Wesleys Fold DARL/WED WS10 . 55 F2
Wesley St BILS/COS WV14 .... 69 E1
    BKHL/PFLD WV2 .... 53 E2
    OLDBY B69 .... 105 E3

WBROM B70....................................87 F3
Wessex Cl BRWNH WS8...................9 F5
Wessex Rd BKHL/PFLD WV2.........52 D2
Wesson Gdns HALE B63..............138 C4
Wesson Rd DARL/WED WS10........55 E1
West Acre WLNHL WV13................39 F4
Westacre Crs BDMR/CCFT WV3....35 F5
Westacre Dr BRLYHL DY5..........119 H4
Westacre Gdns STETCH B33.......130 B2
West Av BFLD/HDSWWD B20..........89 H2
  CBROM B36........................113 F1
  OLDBY B69........................105 H1
  WNSFLD WV11.......................24 C4
Westbook Wy WMBN WV5.............80 D1
West Bvd RIDG/WDGT B32..........141 E1
Westbourne Av
  BKDE/SHDE B34....................112 A3
Westbourne Crs EDG B15...........126 A4
Westbourne Gdns EDG B15.........126 A5
Westbourne Gv HDSW B21 *........107 H2
Westbourne Rd
  DARL/WED WS10......................55 H1
  EDG B15..........................125 H4
  ETTPK/GDPK/PENN WV4.............51 G3
  HDSW B21...........................93 E1
  HIA/OLT B92......................164 B3
  RMSLY B62........................139 G1
  RUSH/SHEL WS4.....................42 B1
  WOLVN WV10.........................87 F5
Westbourne St
  RUSH/SHEL WS4.....................42 B2
West Bromwich Ringway
  WBROM B70.........................87 H3
West Bromwich Rd
  DSYBK/YTR WS5......................57 E2
West Bromwich St OLDBY B69......86 D5
  WSL WS1.............................4 E7
Westbrook Av ALDR WS9.............29 H5
Westdean Cl RMSLY B62...........139 E3
Wester Dr BFLD/HDSWWD B20 *.....89 H2
  DIG/EDG B5.......................143 G3
West End Av SMTHWK B66..........105 H2
Westerdale Cl SEDG DY3.............68 A4
Westerham Cl DOR/KN B93.........196 D2
Westeria Cl CBROM B36...........113 E1
Westering Pkwy WOLVN WV10.......13 E5
Westerings
  BFLD/HDSWWD B20...................90 C4
Western Av BRLYHL DY5...........118 D2
  RMSLY B62........................139 C3
  SEDG DY3...........................66 D3
  WSLW WS2...........................40 B2
Western Cl WSLW WS2................40 B2
Western Rd CDYHTH B64...........120 C4
  ERDE/BCHGN B24....................93 E3
  HAG/WOL DY9......................169 H1
  OLDBY B69........................105 F4
  SCFLD/BOLD B73.....................77 E2
  STRBR DY8........................135 F2
  WSNGN B18........................107 H5
Western Wy DARL/WED WS10........55 G5
Westfield Av
  ALE/KHTH/YWD B14................178 D3
Westfield Cl DOR/KN B93.........198 C1
Westfield Dr ALDR WS9.............30 A4
  WMBN WV5...........................64 D4
Westfield Gra
  ALE/KHTH/YWD B14................161 E1
Westfield Gv BDMR/CCFT WV3......35 C5
Westfield Mnr MGN/WHC B75.......47 E1
Westfield Rd ACGN B27...........146 B4
  ALE/KHTH/YWD B14................160 D2
  BILS/COS WV14.....................61 H3
  BRLYHL DY5.......................119 H4
  DUDS DY2.........................102 D2
  EDG B15..........................125 F5
  RMSLY B62........................122 C3
  SEDG DY3...........................67 E4
  SMTHWKW B67......................106 B5
  WLNHL WV13.........................39 E5
Westford Gv HLGN/YWD B28......179 G2
Westgate ALDR WS9.................29 C3
  EDG B15..........................142 D3
West Ga LDYWD/EDGR B16.........125 G1
Westgate Cl SEDG DY3..............67 G4
West Gn
  ETTPK/GDPK/PENN WV4.............50 C3
West Green Cl EDG B15...........126 B4
Westgrove Av SHLY B90...........195 F2
Westhaven Dr NFLD/LBR B31.....158 A3
Westhaven Rd
  CSCFLD/WYGN B72...................62 C2
Westhay Rd HLGN/YWD B28.......163 F3
West Heath Rd NFLD/LBR B31....175 H4
  WSNGN B18........................107 F5
Westhill BDMR/CCFT WV3...........35 G3
Westhill Cl HIA/OLT B92.........164 B2
  SLYOAK B29.......................159 F1
Westhill Rd HWK/WKHTH B38.....176 D2
West Holme BORD B9..............128 A2
Westholme Cft BVILLE B30........159 C3
Westhouse Ga
  ALE/KHTH/YWD B14................177 F1
Westland Av BDMR/CCFT WV3.......36 B3
Westland Cl ERDW/GRVHL B23....92 D1
Westland Gdns
  BDMR/CCFT WV3.....................36 B3
  STRBR DY8........................118 B5
Westland Rd BDMR/CCFT WV3.....36 B3

Westlands Rd MOS/BIL B13.......161 G1
  WALM/CURD B76.....................78 B5
Westleigh Rd WMBN WV5...........80 D1
Westley Brook Cl
  LGN/SDN/BHAMAIR B26...........147 H2
Westley Cl HLGN/YWD B28.......163 H4
Westley Rd ACGN B27.............146 B4
Westley St BORD B9..............127 G2
  DUDN DY1.........................102 B1
Westmead Crs
  ERDE/BCHGN B24....................93 G2
West Mead Dr
  ALE/KHTH/YWD B14................161 E4
Westmead Dr
  LGLYGN/QTN B68...................105 F5
West Ms KGSTG B44.................74 D1
West Mill Cft
  HWK/WKHTH B38....................190 C1
Westminster Av
  ETTPK/GDPK/PENN WV4.............51 H3
Westminster Cl DUDN DY1.........84 A3
Westminster Dr
  ALE/KHTH/YWD B14................160 D4
Westminster Rd
  BFLD/HDSWWD B20...................90 C4
  HHTH/SAND B71.....................71 H2
  RUSH/SHEL WS4.....................28 D5
  SLYOAK B29.......................160 A1
  STRBR DY8........................117 G2
Westmore Wy
  DARL/WED WS10......................56 D3
Westmorland Rd
  HHTH/SAND B71.....................71 G5
Weston Av LOZ/NWT B19 *........108 C2
  OLDBY B69.........................85 H5
Weston Cl DOR/KN B93...........199 E1
  WSL WS1............................57 E2
Weston Crs ALDR WS9...............44 B1
Weston Dr BILS/COS WV14.........53 G4
  TPTN/OCK DY4.......................70 A1
Weston La SPARK B11.............145 G3
Weston Rd LOZ/NWT B19.........108 B2
  SMTHWKW B67......................106 B5
Weston St WSL WS1.................57 E2
Weston Ter LOZ/NWT B19 *.......108 D1
Westover Rd
  BFLD/HDSWWD B20...................89 C2
West Park Av NFLD/LBR B31......175 E3
West Park Cl ALDR WS9............29 C5
West Park Rd SMTHWKW B67.....105 H3
West Pathway HRBN B17..........142 A1
Westport Crs WNSFLD WV11.......25 F5
Westray Cl RBRY B45.............173 G4
Westridge SEDG DY3...............67 E3
Westridge Rd MOS/BIL B13......162 A4
West Ri MGN/WHC B75.............62 C2
West Rd
  ETTPK/GDPK/PENN WV4.............52 D3
  GTB/HAM B43.......................73 G4
  HALE B63.........................137 F1
  TPTN/OCK DY4.......................69 H5
West Rd South HALE B63.........137 F1
Westside Dr RIDG/WDGT B32......157 H1
West St BLKHTH/ROWR B65.......122 A3
  BLOX/PEL WS3.......................27 G5
  BRLYHL DY5.......................119 H4
  DUDN DY1..........................84 B4
  DUNHL/THL/PER WV6................23 F5
  STRBR DY8........................135 F2
  VAUX/NECH B7 *.....................3 K2
Westthorpe Gv LOZ/NWT B19....108 C4
West Vw WASH/WDE B8.............111 G5
West View Dr MGN/WHC B75.......63 E2
West View Rd MGN/WHC B75.......63 E2
Westville Rd WSLW WS2............41 E2
Westward Cl KGSTG B44............75 F3
West Wy RUSH/SHEL WS4...........18 B5
Westwood Av SPARK B11.........145 G5
  STRBR DY8........................134 D4
Westwood Dr RBRY B45...........174 B4
Westwood Gv SOLH B91...........181 F2
Westwood Rd AST/WIT B6..........91 G4
  SCFLD/BOLD B73....................60 C4
Westwood St BRLYHL DY5........118 C3
Westwood Vw
  ERDE/BCHGN B24....................93 G3
Wetherby Cl CBROM B36.........111 H1
  WOLVN WV10........................12 D5
Wetherby Rd ACGN B27..........146 C5
  BLOX/PEL WS3......................16 C3
Wetherfield Rd SPARK B11......146 A4
Wexford Cl DUDN DY1.............83 H4
Weybourne Rd KGSTG B44..........75 E1
Weycroft Rd ERDW/GRVHL B23...75 H4
Weyhill Cl COVEN WV9...........11 G5
Weymoor Rd HRBN B17...........141 G4
Weymouth Dr
  FOAKS/STRLY B74...................46 D1
Wharf Ap ALDR WS9................29 H3
Wharfdale Rd SPARK B11........146 B2
Wharfdale Cl KGSWFD DY6.........99 F2
Wharfdale St
  DARL/WED WS10......................70 D1
Wharf La SOLH B91...............165 F4
  WSNGN B18........................108 A4
Wharf St AST/WIT B6.............109 G2
  WOLV WV1............................7 J5
  WSLW WS2...........................4 A5
  WSNGN B18........................108 A3
Whar Hall Rd HIA/OLT B92.......165 G2
Wharton Av HIA/OLT B92.........165 G2
Wharton St VAUX/NECH B7.......110 B1
Whatcote Gn HIA/OLT B92........165 F2
Whateley Av BLOX/PEL WS3......28 B4
Whateley Crs CBROM B36........113 F1
Whateley Gn FOAKS/STRLY B74....47 E5
Whateley Hall Cl
  DOR/KN B93 *.....................197 G1
Whateley Hall Rd
  DOR/KN B93.......................197 F1
Whateley Rd BLOX/PEL WS3 *.....28 B4
Whateley Rd BLOX/PEL WS3.......28 B4
  HDSW B21.........................107 G1
Wheatcroft Cl MGN/WHC B75......48 A2
  RMSLY B62........................122 D4

Wheatcroft Dr
  CHWD/FDBR/MGN B37.............132 D3
Wheatcroft Gv DUDS DY2..........85 F5
Wheatcroft Rd STETCH B33......130 B2
Wheaten Cl
  CHWD/FDBR/MGN B37.............132 D1
Wheatfield Cl CBROM B36........114 A2
Wheatfield Vw NFLD/LBR B31....157 H5
Wheat Hl DSYBK/YTR WS5..........43 G5
Wheathill Cl
  ETTPK/GDPK/PENN WV4.............51 E5
Wheatland Av ALDR WS9............44 C1
Wheatlands Cft STETCH B33.....131 G1
The Wheatlands
  DUNHL/THL/PER WV6................34 B2
Wheatley Cl HIA/OLT B92.........165 G2
  LGLYGN/QTN B68...................123 C4
  MGN/WHC B75.......................47 G2
Wheatley Gra
  CSHL/WTROR B46...................115 F3
Wheatley Rd LGLYGN/QTN B68...123 C4
Wheatley St BKHL/PFLD WV2......52 C2
  WBROM B70.........................87 E2
Wheatmill Cl KIDD DY10.........168 B5
Wheatmoor Ri MGN/WHC B75......48 E2
Wheatmoor Rd MGN/WHC B75......63 F1
Wheaton Cl WOLVN WV10...........23 E3
Wheaton V
  BFLD/HDSWWD B20...................89 C3
Wheatridge Cl KGSWFD DY6.......99 E2
Wheats Av HRBN B17.............141 H4
Wheatsheaf Cl MGN/WHC B75.....48 A1
Wheatsheaf Rd CDSL WV8.........22 A1
  LDYWD/EDGR B16...................125 F2
  OLDBY B69........................103 G1
Wheatstone Cl SEDG DY3..........67 G5
Wheatstone Gv STETCH B33......112 B4
Wheatstone Rd SEDG DY3..........67 H4
The Wheel Cft CDSL WV8..........10 B4
Wheeler Cl CDSL WV8.............10 A3
Wheeler Rd WNSFLD WV11..........24 C3
Wheeler's Fold WOLV WV1..........7 F3
Wheeler's La MOS/BIL B13......161 E4
Wheeler St LOZ/NWT B19........108 D3
  STRBR DY8........................135 E2
Wheeley Moor Rd
  CHWD/FDBR/MGN B37.............114 A4
Wheeley Rd HIA/OLT B92.........165 F3
Wheeleys La EDG B15............126 C4
Wheeleys Rd EDG B15............126 B5
Wheelock Cl FOAKS/STRLY B74....60 B1
Wheelwright Cl
  DARL/WED WS10......................55 E2
Wheelwright Rd
  ERDE/BCHGN B24....................92 D5
Wheldrake Av
  BKDE/SHDE B34....................113 E4
Whernside Dr
  DUNHL/THL/PER WV6................22 C5
Wherretts Well La SOLH B91....165 G5
Whetstone Cl EDG B15 *.........142 D2
Whetstone Gn WOLVN WV10 *......23 F1
Whetstone La ALDR WS9...........44 B1
Whetstone Rd WOLVN WV10........23 F2
Whettybridge Rd RBRY B45.....187 G2
Whetty La RBRY B45.............187 G1
Whichford Cl WALM/CURD B76.....77 H5
Whichford Gv BORD B9...........129 F2
Whilmot Cl FSTR/WYGN B72.......62 B4
Whilmot Cl WOLVN WV10...........13 H1
Whinberry Ri BRLYHL DY5..........83 E5
Whisley Brook La
  HLGN/YWD B28....................145 H5
Whiston Av WNSFLD WV11..........25 G5
Whiston Gv SLYOAK B29.........158 D2
Whitacre Rd BORD B9............128 C1
  DOR/KN B93.......................197 F1
Whitbourne Cl BHTH/HG B12.....144 B5
Whitburn Av PBAR/PBCH B42......90 A1
Whitburn Cl COVEN WV9..........12 A5
Whitby Cl BLOX/PEL WS3..........16 B4
Whitby Rd BHTH/HG B12.........144 C3
Whitchurch La SHLY B90..........165 H5
Whitcot Gv NFLD/LBR B31 B5 *.175 F5
Whitebeam Cl BRWNH WS8.........19 E1
  SEDG DY3...........................83 E1
Whitebeam Cft
  HWK/WKHTH B38...................176 C5
White Beam Rd
  CHWD/FDBR/MGN B37.............132 D3
White City Rd BRLYHL DY5......120 A3
White House Gv SHLY B90........179 F2
Whitecrest GTB/HAM B43...........73 H1
Whitecroft Rd
  LGN/SDN/BHAMAIR B26...........148 B2
White Falcon Ct SOLH B91......181 F3
White Farm Rd
  FOAKS/STRLY B74...................46 C1
Whitefield Cl CDSL WV8...........10 D5
Whitefields Crs SOLH B91......181 G1
Whitefields Gv SOLH B91........181 G4
Whitefields Rd SOLH B91.........181 G4
Whitefriars Dr HALE B63........138 C3
Whitegates Rd BILS/COS WV14....68 D1
Whitehall Dr DUDN DY1...........84 A4
  HALE B63.........................138 B3
Whitehall Rd BORD B9...........128 B3
  CDYHTH B64.......................120 C4
  ETTPK/GDPK/PENN WV4.............51 H4
  HALE B63.........................138 B3
  HDSW B21.........................108 A2
  KGSWFD DY6.........................99 G3
  STRBR DY8........................135 H5
  TPTN/OCK DY4.......................84 B2
  WSL WS1............................57 E1
Whitehead Dr
  WALM/CURD B76.....................79 F5
Whitehead Rd AST/WIT B6.......109 G2
White Hl NFLD/LBR B31..........158 D5
Whitehill La SLYOAK B29........158 C5
White Hollies BLOX/PEL WS3.....17 C3
White Horse Rd BRWNH WS8........9 E2
Whitehouse Av
  DARL/WED WS10......................55 G5
  DARL/WED WS10......................54 D1
White House Av
  WNSFLD WV11........................25 F3
White House Cl SOLH B91.......181 F2

Whitehouse Common Rd
  MGN/WHC B75.......................63 E1
Whitehouse Crs MGN/WHC B75....48 A5
  WNSFLD WV11........................25 F1
Whitehouse Dr SMTHWK B66.....106 C2
White House Gn SOLH B91.......181 F2
Whitehouse La CDSL WV8.........10 C2
Whitehouse Pl RBRY B45........187 G2
White Houses La WNSFLD WV10...13 G1
Whitehouse St AST/WIT B6......109 F5
  BILS/COS WV14......................68 C3
  TPTN/OCK DY4.......................85 G4
Whitehouse Wy ALDR WS9.........43 H1
White House Wy SOLH B91.......181 G2
Whitemoor Dr SHLY B90..........195 G1
White Oak Dr BDMR/CCFT WV3....35 G4
  KGSWFD DY6.........................99 G5
Whitepoplars Cl BRLYHL DY5....101 E5
White Rd RIDG/WDGT B32........140 D1
  SMTHWKW B67......................106 B3
  SPARK B11........................128 A5
White Rw WMBN WV5................64 A2
White St Dr SEDG DY3.............67 G3
Whiteslade Cl DOR/KN B93......197 E1
Whitesmith Cl SEDG DY3..........67 F3
White's Rd HHTH/SAND B71.......71 G5
Whitestone Rd HALE B63........138 C1
White St BHTH/HG B12..........144 C2
  CDSL WV8...........................8 B4
Whites Wd WMBN WV5..............81 E1
Whitethorn Crs
  FOAKS/STRLY B74...................44 D4
Whitethorn Rd STRBR DY8......118 C5
Whitewood Gld SMHTH WV12.......48 A1
Whitford Dr SHLY B90...........195 H1
Whitgreave Av WOLVN WV10.......23 G2
Whitgreave Ct WBROM B70.........86 C5
  WOLVN WV10.........................13 F4
Whitgreave St WBROM B70........86 C3
Whitland Cl RBRY B45...........188 B2
Whitland Dr
  ALE/KHTH/YWD B14................178 D2
Whitley Cl
  DUNHL/THL/PER WV6................35 F3
Whitley Court Rd
  RIDG/WDGT B32...................140 C1
Whitley Dr FOAKS/STRLY B74......45 G5
Whitley St DARL/WED WS10........55 G5
Whitlock Gv
  ALE/KHTH/YWD B14................178 C2
Whitminster Av
  ERDE/BCHGN B24....................93 F3
Whitminster Cl SHHTH WV12.......40 A1
Whitmore Hl WOLV WV1..............6 E3
Whitmore Rd SMHTH B10.........128 A4
  STRBR DY8........................134 D2
Whitmore St WOLV WV1..............7 G3
  WSL WS1............................5 D1
  WSNGN B18........................108 B4
Whitney Av STRBR DY8...........134 D1
Whittaker St BKHL/PFLD WV2.....52 C1
Whittall St CBHAMNE B4............3 G3
Whittimere St WSL WS1.............5 F3
Whittingham Gv
  WNSFLD WV11........................25 F4
Whittingham Rd HALE B63.......138 C2
Whittington Cl
  ALE/KHTH/YWD B14................161 E5
  HHTH/SAND B71.....................72 B3
Whittington Gv STETCH B33.....130 B2
Whittington Hall La
  KINVER DY7.......................134 B4
Whittington Ov STETCH B33.....131 G1
Whittington Rd STRBR DY8......134 D4
Whittle Cft CVALE B35............94 B3
Whittleford Gv CBROM B36........95 E5
Whitton St DARL/WED WS10........55 G5
Whitwell Cl SHLY B90...........195 G2
Whitworth Cl DARL/WED WS10....55 G1
Whitworth Dr HHTH/SAND B71....72 A2
Whyley St WBROM B70.............86 A4
Whyley Wk OLDBY B69...........105 E4
Whynot St HALE B63.............137 F2
Wibert Cl SLYOAK B29...........160 A1
Wichnor Rd HIA/OLT B92........147 F2
Wicket La KINVER DY7...........116 C3
Wickham Gdns WNSFLD WV11.....24 A4
Wicklow Cl HALE B65...........154 D1
Widdecote Dr KGSTG B44..........75 E4
Wide Acres RBRY B45...........173 H4
Widney Av ALDR WS9..............30 B1
  SLYOAK B29.......................142 A5
Widney Cl BILS/COS WV14.......196 D3
Widney La SOLH B91.............181 F4
Widney Manor Rd
  DOR/KN B93.......................196 B1
  SOLH B91.........................182 A3
Widney Rd DOR/KN B93..........196 B2
Wiggin Cotts HRBN B17...........142 C1
Wiggins Cft WALM/CURD B76......63 F5
Wiggins Hill Rd
  WALM/CURD B76.....................79 H3
Wigginsmill Rd
  DARL/WED WS10......................70 B2
Wiggin St LDYWD/EDGR B16.....125 H1
Wight Cft CBROM B36...........114 B3
Wightman Cl
  DUNHL/THL/PER WV6................34 D3
Wightwick Bank
  DUNHL/THL/PER WV6................34 B3
Wightwick Gv
  DUNHL/THL/PER WV6................35 E3
Wightwick Hall Rd
  DUNHL/THL/PER WV6................34 C4
Wigmore Gv KGSTG B44............75 H3
Wigmore La HHTH/SAND B71.......72 C3
Wigorn La HAG/WOL DY9.........152 D2
Wigorn Rd SMTHWKW B67.......106 B3
Wilberforce Wy HIA/OLT B92...165 G3
Wilbraham Rd WSLW WS2..........41 G4
Wilcote Gv ACGN B27...........164 C2
Wildacres STRBR DY8...........134 C1
Wilday Cl TPTN/OCK DY4..........85 G1
Wilde Cl ALE/KHTH/YWD B14....177 G1
Wilden Cl NFLD/LBR B31........174 C2
Wilderness La
  GTB/HAM B43.......................58 B5
Wildmoor Cl BGRVW B61.......186 C4
Wildmoor La BRGRVW B61.......186 B4
Wildmoor Rd SHLY B90..........163 F5
Wildtree Av WOLVN WV10.........13 G5
Wiley Av DARL/WED WS10.........55 E3

Wiley Av South
  DARL/WED WS10......................55 E3
Wilford Rd SOLH B91...........181 H3
  WALM/CURD B76.....................78 D5
Wilford Rd HHTH/SAND B71.......71 H5
Wilkes Av WSLW WS2..............40 D3
Wilkes Cl BLOX/PEL WS3..........17 G4
Wilkes Cft SEDG DY3.............67 F4
Wilkes Rd CDSL WV8..............10 B4
Wilkes St HHTH/SAND B71........71 H5
  LOZ/NWT B19.......................39 G4
Wilkin Rd BRWNH WS8.............8 C2
Wilkinson Av BILS/COS WV14......69 E1
Wilkinson Cl SCFLD/BOLD B73....77 F1
Wilkinson Cft WASH/WDE B8.....111 G3
Wilkinson Rd DARL/WED WS10....54 C5
Wilkinson Rd BILS/COS WV14....53 G1
Willard Rd YDLY B25............146 C1
Willaston Rd STETCH B33.......131 F5
Willclare Rd
  LGN/SDN/BHAMAIR B26...........147 G1
Willcock Rd BKHL/PFLD WV2......52 C1
Willenhall La SHHTH WV12........26 D3
Willenhall Rd BILS/COS WV14....54 B2
  DARL/WED WS10......................55 H3
  WOLV WV1..........................38 B4
Willenhall St DARL/WED WS10....55 E2
Willerby Fold WOLVN WV10.......13 F5
Willersey Rd MOS/BIL B13......162 B2
Willes Rd WSNGN B18...........107 G5
Willett Rd HHTH/SAND B71.......72 A5
Willetts Dr HALE B63..........137 F5
Willetts Rd NFLD/LBR B31......175 G4
Willett's Wy CDYHTH B64.......121 F2
Willey Gv ERDE/BCHGN B24......93 F4
William Booth La CBHAMNE B4....3 F2
William Cook Rd
  WASH/WDE B8.....................111 F4
William Edward St
  BHTH/HG B12.....................127 F5
William Green Rd
  DARL/WED WS10......................56 C5
William Harper Rd
  WLNHL WV13........................39 H4
William Henry St
  VAUX/NECH B7.....................109 G5
William Ker Rd TPTN/OCK DY4....86 A1
William Rd SMTHWKW B67........123 E1
Williams Cl SBDMR/CCFT WV3....6 D7
William St BRLYHL DY5..........119 F1
  EDG B15..........................126 C5
  RUSH/SHEL WS4.....................42 B2
  WBROM B70.........................86 C1
William St North LOZ/NWT B19....3 F1
William St West SMTHWK B66...106 D2
William Wiggin Av
  BLOX/PEL WS3......................16 D5
Willingsworth Rd
  DARL/WED WS10......................70 A2
Willingworth Cl BILS/COS WV14..53 E3
Willis Pearson Av
  BILS/COS WV14.....................69 F1
Willmore Gv HWK/WKHTH B38...176 D5
Willmore Rd
  BFLD/HDSWWD B20...................90 D4
Willmott Cl MGN/WHC B75........47 H2
Willmott Rd MGN/WHC B75........47 H1
Willoughby Dr SOLH B91.........181 H4
Willoughby Gv SLYOAK B29.....158 C1
Willow Av DARL/WED WS10........55 H4
  HRBN B17.........................124 C2
  WNSFLD WV11........................24 B2
Willow Bank BDMR/CCFT WV3.....35 G4
Willow Bank Rd DOR/KN B93....196 D2
Willow Cl CDYHTH B64..........121 E3
  HAG/WOL DY9......................152 B5
Willow Coppice
  RIDG/WDGT B32...................157 G1
Willow Ct SMTHWK B66..........105 H1
Willowdale Gra
  DUNHL/THL/PER WV6................22 A5
Willow Dr CDSL WV8..............10 D4
  HDSW B21...........................89 E5
  OLDBY B69........................104 A2
  SHLY B90.........................194 D4
Willow End HAG/WOL DY9........136 B4
Willow Gdns
  LDYWD/EDGR B16...................107 H5
Willow Gv WLNHL WV13............39 H4
  WNSFLD WV11........................11 F1
Willow Hts CDYHTH B64.........121 G4
Willowherb Wy DSYBK/YTR WS5....57 G5
Willowherb Wy SHLY B90.........194 B5
Willow Ms SLYOAK B29..........158 D1
Willow Park Dr STRBR DY8......135 G5
Willow Ri BRLYHL DY5..........119 E3
Willow Rd BDMR/CCFT WV3.......35 H5
  DUDN DY1..........................84 A2
  GTB/HAM B43.......................73 G2
  SOLH B91.........................181 H4
Willowsbrook Rd RMSLY B62....122 D4
Willows Crs BHTH/HG B12.......143 H2
Willowside RUSH/SHEL WS4.......29 E2
Willows Rd BHTH/HG B12.......144 A2
  RUSH/SHEL WS4.....................29 E2
  WSL WS1............................5 J4
The Willows ACGN B27...........146 B5
  DUDS DY2.........................103 E4
  HLYWD B47........................192 C2
  WALM/CURD B76.....................78 B1
  WMBN WV5...........................80 D1
Willow Wy
  CHWD/FDBR/MGN B37.............132 B2
Wills Av HHTH/SAND B71..........71 H4
Willsbridge Covert
  ALE/KHTH/YWD B14................177 G2
Wilson Cft HLGN/YWD B28.......179 F2
Wilson St LOZ/NWT B19.........108 C2
  WOLV WV1..........................7 F3
Wils Wy SMTHWK B66............105 H2
Wilmcote Cl BHTH/HG B12......144 A3
Wilmcote Dr MGN/WHC B75.......47 F2
Wilmcote Rd SOLH B91.........164 B4
Wilmington Rd
  RIDG/WDGT B32...................140 B1
Wilmore La HLYWD B47..........192 A4
Wilmot Av CSHL/WTROR B46.....115 F3
Wilmot Dr ERDW/GRVHL B23......77 F5
  TPTN/OCK DY4.......................69 E5

Wilmot Gdns *DUDN* DY1 ....84 A4
Wilnecote Gv
  PBAR/PBCH B42 ....90 C2
Wilner's Vw *BLOX/PEL* WS3 .....17 H2
Wilsford Cl
  ALE/KHTH/YWD B14....177 H4
  RUSH/SHEL WS4 ....29 E2
Wilson Dr *MGN/WHC* B75 ....63 C3
  OLDBY B69 ....86 A3
Wilson Rd *BILS/COS* WV14 ....68 C4
  BRLYHL DY5 ....101 E5
  HRBN B17 ....124 D1
  LGLYGN/QTN B68 ....123 H4
  LOZ/NWT B19 ....108 C1
Wilsons Rd *SHLY* B90 ....197 G2
Wilson St *TPTN/OCK* DY4 ....85 C2
Wilton Cl *SEDG* DY3 ....67 G4
Wilton Rd *BFLD/HDSWWD* B20 ...90 B5
  ERDW/GRVHL B23 ....92 D1
  SPARK B11 ....144 D2
Wiltshire Cl *WSLW* WS2 ....41 H1
Wiltshire Dr *HALE* B63 ....120 B5
Wiltshire Wy *HHTH/SAND* B71 ...71 G4
Wimbledon Dr *STRBR* DY8 ....135 H5
Wimborne Rd *WOLVN* WV10 .....24 A4
Wimbourne Rd
  LDYWD/EDGR B16 ....125 F1
  WALM/CURD B76 ....63 C4
Wimperis Wy *GTB/HAM* B43 ......59 C4
Wimpole Gv *KGSTG* B44 ....75 H4
Wimshurst Meadow
  WOLVN WV10 ....13 F5
Wincanton Cft *CBROM* B36 ......111 C1
Wincey Rd
  DUNHL/THL/PER WV6............34 D2
  HIA/OLT B92 ....147 H5
Winchcombe Rd *HIA/OLT* B92 ..147 H5
Winchester Cl
  BLKHTH/ROWR B65 ....104 C5
  HAG/WOL DY9 ....152 C3
Winchester Dr
  CHWD/FDBR/MGN B37 .....132 A2
  STRBR DY8 ....135 G4
Winchester Gdns
  NFLD/LBR B31 ....175 G2
Winchester Ms *ALDR* WS9 ....30 D5
Winchester Ri *DUDN* DY1 ....84 A4
Winchester Rd
  BFLD/HDSWWD B20 ....90 D5
  HHTH/SAND B71 ....71 F3
  WOLVN WV10 ....12 C5
Winchfield Dr *HRBN* B17 ....124 B5
Wincote Dr
  DUNHL/THL/PER WV6............35 C1
Wincrest Wv *BKDE/SHDE* B34 ...113 E4
Windermere Dr
  FOAKS/STRLY B74 ....45 F2
  KGSWFD DY6 ....99 H3
Windermere Rd
  DUNHL/THL/PER WV6............21 H2
  HDSW B21 ....89 C4
  MOS/BIL B13 ....161 H1
Windfall Ct *ERDE/BCHGN* B24 ...93 H2
Windhill Cl
  BRLYHL DY5 * 119 C5
Winding MI North
  BRLYHL DY5 * 119 C5
Winding MI South
  BRLYHL DY5 * 119 C5
Windlass Cft *NFLD/LBR* B31 .....175 F1
Windleaves Rd *CBROM* B36 ......113 C2
Windmill Av
  CSHL/WTROR B46 ....115 F2
  RBRY B45............................173 C5
Windmill Bank *WMBN* WV5.........65 E4
Windmill Cl *NFLD/LBR* B31 ......159 E5
Windmill Cottages
  PBAR/PBCH B42 * 90 A1
Windmill Crs *BDMR/CCFT* WV3 ..35 E4
  SMTHWK B66 ....87 G4
Windmill End *DUDS* DY2 ....103 E4
Windmill Gv *KGSWFD* DY6 ....99 E1
Windmill HI *HALE* B63 ....137 H2
  NFLD/LBR B31 ....157 H5
Windmill La *BDMR/CCFT* WV3....35 E4
  DOR/KN B93 ....198 D2
  HOCK/TIA B94 ....199 E3
  SMTHWK B66 ....106 D5
Windmill Prec *SMTHWK* B66 ...106 D4
Windmill Rd *SHLY* B90 ....179 C3
Windmill St *CBHAMW* B1 ....126 D3
  DARL/WED WS10 ....55 H5
  DUDN DY1 ....84 A4
  SEDG DY3 ....82 C5
  WSL WS1 ....4 E6
Windmill Vw *WALM/CURD* 68 B4
Windridge Crs *HIA/OLT* B92 ....165 H2
The Windrow
  DUNHL/THL/PER WV6............34 B1
Windrush Cl *BLOX/PEL* WS3 ....28 C1
Windrush Gv *SLYOAK* B29 ....160 A2
Windrush Rd *HLYWD* B47 ....192 D1
Windsor Av
  ETTPK/GDPK/PENN WV4 .....51 E2
  LGLYGN/QTN B68 ....123 E1
Windsor Cl
  BLKHTH/ROWR B65 ....104 A5
  HALE B63 ....138 B4
  NFLD/LBR B31 ....189 C2
  RBRY B45............................174 A3
  SEDG DY3 ....82 D5
Windsor Crs *DUDS* DY2 ....102 D5
Windsor Dr *ERDE/BCHGN* B24 ...93 C2
  HIA/OLT B92 ....147 H5
Windsor Gdns *BDMR/CCFT* WV3 ..50 A1
  CDSL WV8 ....10 B4
Windsor Ga *SHHTH* WV12 ....40 A1
Windsor Gv *RUSH/SHEL* WS4 ......18 C5
  STRBR DY8 ....118 A3
Windsor Pl *ERDW/GRVHL* B23 ....92 C5
  VAUX/NECH B7 * 127 C1
Windsor Rd
  BLKHTH/ROWR B65 ....104 A4
  BVILLE B30 ....160 B5
  CBROM B36 ....113 H2
  ETTPK/GDPK/PENN WV4 .....51 E2
  HALE B63 ....138 B3
  HHTH/SAND B71 ....71 F3
  LGLYGN/QTN B68 ....123 E1

SCFLD/BOLD B73 ....76 B2
STRBR DY8 ....134 D4
TPTN/OCK DY4 ....69 C3
WMBN WV5 ....64 D5
Windsor St *BILS/COS* WV14 ......53 C2
  VAUX/NECH B7 ....109 G5
  WSL WS1 ....57 E1
Windsor St South
  VAUX/NECH B7 ....109 G5
Windsor Ter
  LDYWD/EDGR B16 * 125 H3
Windsor Vw *RIDG/WDGT* B32 ...157 F5
Windsor Wk *DARL/WED* WS10 ....40 B5
Windsor Wy *RUSH/SHEL* WS4 ....29 F3
Winds Point *HAG/WOL* DY9 .....152 C4
Windward Wy *CBROM* B36 ....113 H2
Windy Arbor Rd
  WALM/CURD B76 ....78 B5
Winford Av *KGSWFD* DY6 ....100 A5
Wingate Cl *HWK/WKHTH* B38 ..176 D1
Wingate Rd *WSLW* WS2 ....40 C3
Wing Cl *WSLW* WS2 ....27 H5
Wingfield Cl
  CHWD/FDBR/MGN B37 .....131 H1
Wingfield Rd
  CSHL/WTROR B46 ....115 F4
  PBAR/PBCH B42 ....74 C4
Wingfoot Av *WOLVN* WV10 ....23 F2
Winleigh Rd
  BFLD/HDSWWD B20 ....89 H4
Winnall Cl *BILS/COS* WV14 ....68 D1
Winnie Rd *SLYOAK* B29 ....159 G1
Winnington Rd
  WASH/WDE B8 ....111 E2
Winnipeg Rd
  HWK/WKHTH B38 ....177 E5
Winrush Cl *SEDG* DY3 ....83 E3
Winscar Cft *SEDG* DY3 ....83 C3
Winsford Cl *HALE* B63 ....138 C1
  WALM/CURD B76 ....63 F2
Winsham Gv *HDSW* B21 ....107 F1
Winslow Dr
  DUNHL/THL/PER WV6 ....36 A1
Winson Green Rd *WSNGN* B18...107 C4
Winson St *WSNGN* B18 ....107 F5
Winstanley Rd *STETCH* B33 .....129 H2
Winster Av *DOR/KN* B93 ....196 C4
Winster Gv *KGSTG* B44 ....74 D1
Winster Rd *GTB/HAM* B43 ....75 F3
  WOLVN WV10 ....24 D5
Winston Dr
  BFLD/HDSWWD B20 ....90 B5
  RMSLY B62 ....122 C1
Winston Rd *SEDG* DY3 ....80 C4
Winterbourne Cft
  ALE/KHTH/YWD B14..........177 G1
Winterbourne Rd *SOLH* B91 .....181 F1
Winterley Gdns *SEDG* DY3 ....67 G5
Winterley La *RUSH/SHEL* WS4 ...29 E3
Winterton Rd *KGSTG* B44 ....60 C5
Winthorpe Dr *SOLH* B91 ....182 A5
Wintney Cl *HRBN* B17 ....124 C5
Winton Gv *WALM/CURD* B76 ....78 C5
Winwood Heath Rd
  RMSLY B62 ....172 A3
Winwood Rd
  BLKHTH/ROWR B65 ....122 C1
Winwoods Gv
  RIDG/WDGT B32 ....157 E2
Wiremill Cl *KGSTG* B44 ....75 E5
Wirral Rd *NFLD/LBR* B31 ....158 B4
Wiseacre Cft *SHLY* B90 ....179 C3
Wiseman Gv *KGSTG* B44 ....76 B2
Wisemeadow *SHLY* B90 ....179 G3
Wisemore *WSLW* WS2 ....4 D2
Wishaw Cl *SHLY* B90 ....179 C4
Wishaw Gv
  CHWD/FDBR/MGN B37 .....113 H4
Wishaw La *WALM/CURD* B76 ......79 G4
Wisley Wy *RIDG/WDGT* B32 .....141 F2
Wistaria Cl *NFLD/LBR* B31 ....158 C4
Wisteria Dr *DSYBK/YTR* WS5 .....57 F4
Wisteria Gv *KGSTG* B44 ....75 E1
Wistmans Cl *DUDN* DY1 ....83 F5
Wistwood Hayes
  WOLVN WV10 ....13 F5
Witham Cl *WALM/CURD* B76 ....78 C2
Witham Cft *SOLH* B91 ....182 A4
Withdean Cl *SPARK* B11 ....145 E2
Witherford Cl *SLYOAK* B29 ......159 E2
Witherford Cft *SOLH* B91 ....180 D3
Witherford Wy *SLYOAK* B29 ....159 E2
Withern Wy *SEDG* DY3 ....83 F3
Withers Rd *CDSL* WV8 ....10 D4
Withers Wy *HHTH/SAND* B71 ...87 H2
Withington Covert
  ALE/KHTH/YWD B14..........177 H3
Withington Gv *DOR/KN* B93 .....196 C4
Withybrook Rd *SHLY* B90 ....180 A5
Withy Gv
  CHWD/FDBR/MGN B37 .....113 G4
Withy Hill Rd *MGN/WHC* B75 .....63 C1
Withymoor Rd *DUDS* DY2 ....103 G5
  STRBR DY8 ....118 C5
Witley Av *BILS/COS* WV14 ....53 G2
Witley Crs *OLDBY* B69 ....104 C4
Witley Farm Cl *SOLH* B91 ....182 A3
Witley Rd *NFLD/LBR* B31 ....176 B3
Witney Dr
  CHWD/FDBR/MGN B37 .....131 H2
Witney Gv *WOLVN* WV10 ....12 B4
Witton Bank *RMSLY* B62 * 138 C1
Witton La *AST/WIT* B6 ....91 F5
  HHTH/SAND B71 ....71 E3
Witton Lodge Rd
  ERDW/GRVHL B23 ....76 H4
Witton Rd *AST/WIT* B6 ....109 E1
  ETTPK/GDPK/PENN WV4 .....51 G2
Witton St *BORD* B9 ....127 H2
  STRBR DY8 ....135 G5
Wixford Gv *SHLY* B90 ....180 D3
Wobaston Rd *CDSL* WV8 ....11 F4
Woburn Av *SHHTH* WV12 ....25 H4

Woburn Crs *GTB/HAM* B43 ....73 F2
Woburn Dr *BRLYHL* DY5 ....118 D4
  RMSLY B62 ....121 G5
Woburn Gv *ACGN* B27 ....165 G1
Wodehouse Cl *WMBN* WV5 ....80 C1
Wodehouse La *SEDG* DY3 ....66 A3
Woden Av *WNSFLD* WV11 ....24 C4
Woden Cl *WMBN* WV5 ....64 D4
Woden Crs *WNSFLD* WV11 ....24 C4
Woden Rd *WOLVN* WV10 ....37 H1
Woden Rd East
  DARL/WED WS10 ....56 B3
Woden Rd North
  DARL/WED WS10 ....55 C3
Woden Rd South
  DARL/WED WS10 ....70 D2
Woden Rd West
  DARL/WED WS10 ....55 F4
Wold Wk *MOS/BIL* B13 ....161 H4
Wolfsbane Dr *DSYBK/YTR* WS5...57 G5
Wolfson Dr *HRBN* B17 ....142 B3
Wollaston Ct *STRBR* DY8 ....134 C1
Wollaston Crs *WNSFLD* WV11 ....24 C2
Wollaston Rd *KINVER* DY7 ....117 G5
  STRBR DY8 ....118 A5
Wollerton Gv *MGN/WHC* B75 ....63 F7
Wollescote Rd *HAG/WOL* DY9 ..136 B4
Wollscote Dr *SOLH* B91 ....181 H4
Wolmer Rd *WNSFLD* WV11 ....14 D5
Wolseley Av *ACGN* B27 ....146 D3
Wolseley Bank *WOLVN* WV10 ....23 H5
Wolseley Cl *CBROM* B36 ....96 A5
  WOLVN WV10 ....23 H4
Wolseley Dr *WASH/WDE* B8 .....111 E2
Wolseley Ga *WOLVN* WV10 ....23 H5
Wolseley Rd *BILS/COS* WV14 .....53 F1
  WBROM B70 ....70 D5
Wolseley St *BORD* B9 ....127 H2
Wolston Cl *SHLY* B90 ....163 F5
Wolverhampton Rd
  BLOX/PEL WS3 ....17 G4
  BLOX/PEL WS3 ....17 C4
  CDSL WV8 ....10 A4
  KGSWFD DY6 ....99 C1
  KINVER DY7 ....116 D5
  LGLYGN/QTN B68 ....123 E1
  SEDG DY3 ....52 B5
  WNSFLD WV11 ....14 D4
  WOLVN WV10 ....37 H2
  WSLW WS2 ....41 G3
Wolverhampton Rd East
  ETTPK/GDPK/PENN WV4 .....52 C4
Wolverhampton Rd South
  RIDG/WDGT B32 ....124 A5
Wolverhampton Rd West
  WLNHL WV13 ....40 B3
Wolverhampton St
  BILS/COS WV14 ....53 C2
  DARL/WED WS10 ....54 D2
  DUDN DY1 ....84 B5
  WLNHL WV13 ....39 F4
  WSLW WS2 ....4 C3
Womberley Av
  ETTPK/GDPK/PENN WV4 .....50 D3
Wombourne Cl *SEDG* DY3 ....67 E3
Wombourne Pk *WMBN* WV5 ......80 D2
Wombourne Rd *SEDG* DY3 ....80 D3
Wombrook Dr *WMBN* WV5 ....64 B5
Woodacre Rd
  ERDE/BCHGN B24 ....93 G2
Woodall Rd *AST/WIT* B6 ....91 F5
Woodall St *BLOX/PEL* WS3 ....27 G2
  CDYHTH B64 ....120 C3
Woodard Rd *TPTN/OCK* DY4 ......70 A4
Wood Bank Rd
  WNSFLD WV11 ....24 C4
Woodbank Rd *SEDG* DY3 ....67 E4
Woodbine Av
  WALM/CURD B76 ....78 C1
Woodbourne Wk *ACGN* B27 .....146 D4
Woodbine Av *SHHTH* WV12 ......128 B4
Woodbine Cft
  LGN/SDN/BHAMAIR B26 ....147 G1
Woodbourne *EDG* B15 ....125 F4
Woodbourne Rd
  SMTHWK B66 ....124 A2
Woodbridge Cl *BLOX/PEL* WS3 ..16 C4
  RUSH/SHEL WS4 ....29 F1
Woodbridge Rd *MOS/BIL* B13 ..144 B4
Woodbrooke Gv
  NFLD/LBR B31 ....158 D4
Woodbrooke Rd *BVILLE* B30 ....159 F3
Woodburn Rd *SMTHWK* B66 ...107 F2
Woodbury Cl *BKDE/SHDE* B34 ..112 C3
  BRLYHL DY5 ....119 G3
  RMSLY B62 ....122 A3
Woodbury Gv *SOLH* B91 ....181 H5
Woodbury Rd *RMSLY* B62 ....123 E4
Woodchester *HAG/WOL* DY9 ...169 H1
Woodchester Rd *DOR/KN* B93 ..198 C1
Woodchurch Gra
  SCFLD/BOLD B73 ....76 D3
Wood Cl *CSHL/WTROR* B46 ......115 F2
Woodclose Rd
  CHWD/FDBR/MGN B37 .....131 H1
Woodcock Cl *NFLD/LBR* B31 ....174 C4
Woodcock La *ACGN* B27 ....146 D4
  NFLD/LBR B31 ....158 A2
Woodcock La North
  ACGN B27 ....146 D3
Woodcock St *CBHAMNE* B4 ....5 J2
Woodcombe Cl *BRLYHL* DY5 ...118 D5
Wood Common Gra
  BLOX/PEL WS3 ....17 G3
Woodcote Dr *DOR/KN* B93 ......196 C5
  WASH/WDE B8 ....110 D4
Woodcote Pl *LOZ/NWT* B19 * ..108 C2

Woodcote Rd
  DUNHL/THL/PER WV6 ....35 G1
  ERDE/BCHGN B24 ....93 H1
Woodcote Wy
  FOAKS/STRLY B74 ....60 B2
  WSNGN B18 ....108 A5
Wood Ct *BFLD/HDSWWD* B20 ...90 A4
Wood Cft *HLYWD* B47 ....192 D2
Woodcroft Av
  BFLD/HDSWWD B20 ....89 G3
  TPTN/OCK DY4 ....84 C1
Woodcroft Cl *BLOX/PEL* WS3 ...18 A3
  CDYHTH B64 ....121 F4
Woodcross La *BILS/COS* WV14 ...53 E1
Woodcross St *BILS/COS* WV14 ...67 H1
Woodend *BFLD/HDSWWD* B20 ..75 F4
Woodend Pl
  DUNHL/THL/PER WV6 ....35 F1
Wood End Rd *DSYBK/YTR* WS5...55 H5
  ERDE/BCHGN B24 ....92 D3
Wood End La *ERDE/BCHGN* B24..92 D3
Woodend Pl
  DUNHL/THL/PER WV6 ....35 F1
Woodfall Av *BVILLE* B30 ....159 H5
Woodfield *HAG/WOL* DY9 ....184 B1
Woodfield Av *BRLYHL* DY5 ....100 D2
  OLDBY B69 ....105 E5
Woodfield Cl *DSYBK/YTR* WS5 ...58 C3
  FOAKS/STRLY B74 ....47 F5
Woodfield Crs *BHTH/HG* B12 ...144 C1
Woodfield Hts
  DUNHL/THL/PER WV6 ....35 H1
Woodfield Rd
  ALE/KHTH/YWD B14...........161 F2
  BHTH/HG B12 ....144 C1
  SEDG DY3 ....83 E2
  SOLH B91 ....164 D4
Woodfold Cft *ALDR* WS9 ....30 B3
Woodford Av *CBROM* B36 ....112 C1
Woodford Cl *COVEN* WV11 ....11 H5
Woodford Green Rd
  HLGN/YWD B28 ....163 G2
Woodford La *WMBN* WV5 ....64 D3
Woodfort Rd *GTB/HAM* B43 ....73 C4
Woodgate Dr *RIDG/WDGT* B32 ..157 E4
Woodgate Gdns
  RIDG/WDGT B32 ....140 A5
Woodgate La
  RIDG/WDGT B32 ....140 A5
Woodgate Wy *HAG/WOL* DY9 ..184 C1
Woodglade Cft
  HWK/WKHTH B38 ....176 C3
Woodgreen Cft
  LGLYGN/QTN B68 ....123 G5
Woodgreen Rd
  LGLYGN/QTN B68 ....123 G5
Wood Green Rd
  DARL/WED WS10 ....55 H5
  WSNGN B18 ....107 F5
Woodhall Cl *TPTN/OCK* DY4 ......69 G3
Woodhall Cft *HIA/OLT* B92 ......147 F4
Woodhall Rd
  ETTPK/GDPK/PENN WV4 .....51 E4
Woodham Cl *RBRY* B45 ....173 G4
Woodhaven *RUSH/SHEL* WS4 ....29 F1
Wood Hayes Cft *WOLVN* WV10 ..14 A5
Wood Hayes Rd *WNSFLD* WV11 ..24 C1
  WOLVN WV10 ....13 H5
Woodhill Cl *WMBN* WV5 ....64 D5
Wood Hill Dr *WMBN* WV5 ....64 D5
Woodhouse Fold
  WNSFLD WV11 ....24 D5
Woodhouse Orch
  HAG/WOL DY9 ....184 C1
Woodhouse Rd North
  DUNHL/THL/PER WV6 ....34 C5
Woodhouse Wy *CDYHTH* B64 ..120 C5
Woodhurst Rd *MOS/BIL* B13 ....144 C3
Wooding Crs *TPTN/OCK* DY4 ....69 H2
Woodington Rd
  MGN/WHC B75 ....63 C5
Woodland Av *BRLYHL* DY5 ....120 A3
  DUDN DY1 ....84 A4
  DUNHL/THL/PER WV6 ....35 F2
  STRBR DY8 ....152 B5
Woodland Centre
  SHHTH WV12 * 26 C3
Woodland Cl *HAG/WOL* DY9 ....153 F1
  SHHTH WV12 ....26 B4
Woodland Cottages
  ETTPK/GDPK/PENN WV4 * ...51 E4
Woodland Ct *LICHS* WS14 ....33 E3
Woodland Crs
  BDMR/CCFT WV3 ....51 F3
Woodland Dr *SMTHWK* B66 .....106 A2
Woodland Gv *GTB/HAM* B43 .....58 C5
  SEDG DY3 ....82 D3
Woodland Rd *CDYHTH* B64 ....121 F4
  SCFLD/BOLD B73 ....62 B4
Woodland Rd *NFLD/LBR* B31 ....50 D1
  HDSW B21 ....107 F1
  NFLD/LBR B31 ....175 H2
  RMSLY B62 ....122 B4
Woodlands Av
  CSHL/WTROR B46 ....96 B4
  DSYBK/YTR WS5 ....58 C5
Woodlands Cottages
  ETTPK/GDPK/PENN WV4 * ...51 E4
Woodlands Crs *BLOX/PEL* WS3 ..17 H2
Woodlands Farm Rd
  ERDE/BCHGN B24 ....78 B4
Woodlands La *SHLY* B90 ....180 B5
Woodlands Paddock
  ETTPK/GDPK/PENN WV4 .....51 E4
Woodlands Park Rd
  BVILLE B30 ....159 E5
Woodlands Rd *RBRY* B45 ....145 E4
  SPARK B11 ....145 F4
  WASH/WDE B8 ....128 D1
  WMBN WV5 ....81 E1
Woodlands St *SMTHWK* B66 ....107 G5
The Woodlands *CDYHTH* B64 ...121 G5
  MGN/WHC B75 ....63 C3
  STRBR DY8 ....135 G5

Woodlands Wy
  CHWD/FDBR/MGN B37 .....132 D1
Wood La ALDR WS9 ....31 G2
  BFLD/HDSWWD B20 ....90 B4
  BLOX/PEL WS3 ....17 H2
  BRGRVW B61 ....185 G5
  CHWD/FDBR/MGN B37 .....132 A4
  ERDE/BCHGN B24 ....93 F5
  FOAKS/STRLY B74 ....45 E4
  HRBN B17 ....141 G1
  RIDG/WDGT B32 ....157 F1
  SHHTH WV12 ....26 C3
  WOLVN WV10 ....12 D5
Wood Lane Cl *SHHTH* WV12 * ...26 C3
Woodman Gv *KGSWFD* DY6 ....99 H4
Woodlea Dr *ERDE/BCHGN* B24 ..92 D4
  SOLH B91 ....164 A5
Wood Leasow
  RIDG/WDGT B32 ....140 D5
Woodleaves *HLYWD* B47 ....178 B5
Woodleigh Av *HRBN* B17 ....142 B5
Woodleigh Cl *HALE* B63 ....138 C1
Woodleigh Rd
  CSCFLD/WYGN B72 ....77 F2
The Woodleys
  RIDG/WDGT B32 ....178 D1
Woodloes Rd *SHLY* B90 ....178 B5
Woodman Cl *DARL/WED* WS10 ...56 B4
  HALE B63 ....138 D1
Woodman Gv *MGN/WHC* B75 ....48 A2
Woodman La *HAG/WOL* DY9 ....170 B1
Woodman Rd
  ALE/KHTH/YWD B14..........178 C4
  HALE B63 ....138 D1
Woodmeadow Rd *BVILLE* B30 ..177 D2
Woodnorton Dr *MOS/BIL* B13 ..144 A5
Woodnorton Rd
  BLKHTH/ROWR B65 ....122 D2
Woodpecker Gv *CBROM* B36 ....114 A2
Woodpecker Rd *STETCH* B33....113 G5
Woodperry Av *SOLH* B91 ....182 A4
Woodridge Av *RIDG/WDGT* B32 ..91 E5
Woodridge Rd
  RIDG/WDGT B32 ....140 B3
Woodridge Rd *HALE* B63 ....138 C3
Wood Rd *DUNHL/THL/PER* WV6 ..35 F2
  SEDG DY3 ....83 F5
  WMBN WV5 ....79 G5
Woodrough Dr *MOS/BIL* B13....144 B5
Woodrow Crs *DOR/KN* B93 ......197 G5
Woodruff Wy *DSYBK/YTR* WS5 ..57 G5
Woodrush Dr *HLYWD* B47 ....192 C3
Woods Bank Ter
  DARL/WED WS10 ....55 F3
Woods Crs *BRLYHL* DY5 ....120 A3
Woodsetton Cl *DUDN* DY1 ....68 B5
Woodshires Rd *HIA/OLT* B92 ...164 A5
Woodside
  CHWD/FDBR/MGN B37 .....113 G5
  FOAKS/STRLY B74 ....46 C3
Wood Side *WNSFLD* WV11 ....25 G2
Woodside Cl *DSYBK/YTR* WS5 ....58 B5
Woodside Crs *DOR/KN* B93 ......197 E4
Woodside Dr *FOAKS/STRLY* B74...45 E4
Woodside Gv *CDSL* WV8 ....10 D3
Woodside Rd *DSYBK/YTR* WS5 ...58 C2
  NFLD/LBR B31 ....160 A1
Woodside Wy *ALDR* WS9 ....30 B5
  RIDG/WDGT B32 ....157 E2
  SHHTH WV12 ....26 B4
  SOLH B91 ....164 A5
Woods La *BRLYHL* DY5 ....119 F5
  CDYHTH B64 ....120 C3
Woodsome Gv
  ERDW/GRVHL B23 ....76 A4
Woodsorrel Rd *DUDN* DY1 ....83 H2
The Woods
  ALE/KHTH/YWD B14...........161 F1
Woodstile *BKDE/SHDE* B34 ......112 D3
Woodstile Cl *MGN/WHC* B75 .....47 H2
Woodstock Cl *DSYBK/YTR* WS5 ...57 G5
  DUDN DY1 * 102 A1
  STRBR DY8 ....117 G3
Woodstock Crs *DOR/KN* B93 ....196 D5
Woodstock Dr
  FOAKS/STRLY B74 ....46 B1
  STRBR DY8 ....117 G2
Woodstock Rd *HDSW* B21 ....107 H1
  MOS/BIL B13 ....144 C3
  WOLVN WV10 ....12 B5
Wood St *DARL/WED* WS10 ....55 H2
  DUDS DY2 ....101 H3
  ETTPK/GDPK/PENN WV4 .....55 E5
  HAG/WOL DY9 ....136 D3
  STRBR DY8 ....117 H5
  TPTN/OCK DY4 ....69 E5
  WLNHL WV13 ....39 G3
  WOLVN WV10 ....12 D5
Woodthorne Cl *SEDG* DY3 ....83 E2
Woodthorne Rd South
  DUNHL/THL/PER WV6 ....21 E6
Woodthorpe Dr
  HAG/WOL DY9 ....136 B4
Woodthorpe Gdns
  ALE/KHTH/YWD B14...........161 E5
Woodthorpe Rd
  ALE/KHTH/YWD B14...........160 D5
Woodvale Rd *HLGN/YWD* B28 ..179 G1
  RIDG/WDGT B32 ....157 E1
Woodview Dr *EDG* B15 ....126 C5
Woodville Gdns *SEDG* DY3 ....67 F2
Woodville Rd
  ALE/KHTH/YWD B14...........161 G2
  HRBN B17 ....124 D1
Woodward Pl *HAG/WOL* DY9 ...136 A3
Woodwards Cl *WSLW* WS2 ....41 F5
Woodwards Pl *WSLW* WS2 ....41 F5
Woodwards Rd *WSLW* WS2 ....41 F5
Woodward St
  HHTH/SAND B71 ....87 H2
Woodway *ERDE/BCHGN* B24 .....93 G5
Woodwells Rd *WASH/WDE* B8 ..111 E4
Woolacombe Lodge Rd
  SLYOAK B29 ....142 A5

Woolmore Rd
ERDW/GRVHL B23 ....92 A2
Woolpack Cl
BLKHTH/ROWR B65 ....103 C5
Wooton Gv *KGSTG* B44.............76 A3
Wootton Av *WNSFLD* WV11 ....24 D5
Wootton Rd *BDMR/CCFT* WV3....50 C1
NFLD/LBR B31........................189 C1
Worcester Bar *CBHAMW* B1 *......2 C6
Worcester Cl *HAG/WOL* DY9 ...152 C5
WALM/CURD B76..................47 H2
Worcester Cn *BDMR/CCFT* WV3..36 A5
Worcester Gn *HHTH/SAND* B71 ..71 C4
Worcester Gv
DUNHL/THL/PER WV6.............34 B1
Worcester La *HAG/WOL* DY9 ....152 D2
MGN/WHC B75.......................47 H2
Worcester Ri *SLYOAK* B29 ....160 B1
Worcester Rd *DUDS* DY2 ....121 E1
HAG/WOL DY9.....................168 D1
LGLYGN/OTN B68 ....123 E4
WLNHL WV13........................40 B3
Worcester St *BKHL/PFLD* WV2 ....6 E6
CBHAM B2 ....5 G3
DUDS DY8 ....135 G3
Worcester Wk *CBHAM* B2 *.........5 C6
Word Hl *HRBN* B17 ....124 B5
Wordsworth Av
ETTPK/GDPK/PENN WV4.........52 C4
Wordsworth Cl *TPTN/OCK* DY4..69 F3
Wordsworth Ct
DUNHL/THL/PER WV6.............34 B1
Wordsworth Rd *BLOX/PEL* WS3 ..28 A2
SEDG DY3...............................82 D1
SHHTH WV12..........................26 C3
SMHTH B10...........................128 B5
WOLVN WV10.........................24 A2
Wordsworth St
HHTH/SAND B71 ....87 C1
Worfield Cl *RUSH/SHEL* WS4 ....42 C1
Worfield Gdns
BDMR/CCFT WV3....................51 F2
Works Rd
LGN/SDN/BHAMAIR B26 ......149 E4
World's End Av
RIDG/WDGT B32 ....140 D1
World's End La
RIDG/WDGT B32 ....140 D2
Worlds End Rd
BFLD/HDSWWD B20..............90 A3
Worleys Wharf Av
DARL/WED WS10 ....72 A1
Worsey Gv *TPTN/OCK* DY4 ....70 B5
Worthen Gv *NFLD/LBR* B31 .....175 C5
The Worthings *BVILLE* B30.......160 B4
Worthy Down *WNSFLD* WV11 ....23 C4
Wortley Av *WOLVN* WV10 *........23 C4
Worton Rd *HAG/WOL* DY9 ....136 C5
Wragby Cl *COVEN* WV9 ....12 B4
Wrekin Cl *HALE* B63.................154 C1
Wrekin Dr *BDMR/CCFT* WV3......36 A5
DUNHL/THL/PER WV6.............21 E5
HAG/WOL DY9.......................136 B3
Wrekin Gv *SHHTH* WV12 ....25 H1
Wrekin La
DUNHL/THL/PER WV6.............21 E5
Wrekin Rd *KGSTG* B44.............75 F5
SCFLD/BOLD B73...................77 E2

Wrekin Vw *BRWNH* WS8.............19 C2
Wrekin View Rd *SEDG* DY3..........67 E3
Wren Av *DUNHL/THL/PER* WV6 ..34 B2
Wrenbury Dr *BILS/COS* WV14 ....54 C1
Wrens Av *KGSWFD* DY6 ....100 C5
TPTN/OCK DY4 ....84 C1
Wrens Hill Rd *DUDN* DY1 ....84 B1
Wren's Nest Cl *SHLY* B90 ....194 A3
Wrens Nest Rd *DUDN* DY1..........84 B1
Wrens Park Av
WALM/CURD B76...................78 A4
Wren St *DUDN* DY1....................68 B5
DUDS DY8 ....102 B4
Wrentham St *DIG/EDG* B5 ....127 E4
Wretham Rd *LOZ/NWT* B19 .....108 B5
Wrexham Av *WSLW* WS2............40 D4
Wright Av *WNSFLD* WV11 ....24 D3
Wrighton Cl *SHHTH* WV12 ....26 A2
Wrighton Dr *BRLYHL* DY5...........85 E5
Wright Rd *WASH/WDE B8*.........110 C4
Wright's La *CDYHTH* B64............121 F2
Wright St *BILS/COS* WV14...........54 A4
HALE B63...............................138 D5
SMHTH B10...........................128 B4
WOLVN WV10 *........................37 F1
Wrottesley Park Rd
DUNHL/THL/PER WV6.............34 B1
Wrottesley Rd
DUNHL/THL/PER WV6.............21 F5
GTB/HAM B43........................73 F2
Wrottesley Rd West
DUNHL/THL/PER WV6.............20 D4
Wrottesley St *DIG/EDG* B5 ....3 G7
Wroxall Cl *BRLYHL* DY5...........118 D4
Wroxall Gv *MOS/BIL B13..........161 G4
Wroxall Rd *SOLH* B91..............164 A5
Wroxham Gdn *WNSFLD* WV13....39 F5
Wroxton Rd *YDLY* B25 ....130 A4
Wulfruna Gdns
BDMR/CCFT WV3....................36 B4
Wulfruna St *WOLV* WV1...............7 F3
Wulfrun Sq *WOLV* WV1...............7 G5
Wulfrun Wy *WOLV* WV1...............7 F4
Wyatt Cl *DIG/EDG* B5...............143 G2
Wyatt Rd *MGN/WHC* B75...........63 H2
Wychall Dr *WOLVN* WV10...........13 E3
Wychall La *WLNHL* WHB38 ......176 B3
Wychall Park Gv
HWK/WKHTH B38 ....176 B3
Wychall Rd *NFLD/LBR* B31 ....175 H2
Wychbold Cl *SHHTH* WV12 ....26 B1
Wychbold Ct *HAG/WOL* DY9 ....155 E2
Wychbold Crs *STETCH* B33 ....131 E1
Wychbury *WALM/CURD* B76........78 C2
Wychbury Ct *HALE* B63............138 C4
Wychbury Dr *HAG/WOL* DY9 ....155 E3
Wychbury Rd *BDMR/CCFT* WV3 ..50 C1
BRLYHL DY5 ....119 C4
HAG/WOL DY9......................155 C5
RIDG/WDGT B32 ....140 B1
Wyche Av *ALE/KHTH/YWD* B14..177 H1
Wychelm Farm Rd
ALE/KHTH/YWD B14............178 C4
Wych Elm Rd *BRWNH* WS8.........18 D2
Wycherley Gv *CDYHTH* B64.......121 E4
Wychnor Gv *HHTH/SAND* B71...72 A1
Wychwood Av
*DOR/KN B93...........................183 F5

Wychwood Crs
LGN/SDN/BHAMAIR B26 ......147 G1
Wyckham Cl *HRBN* B17............141 G3
Wyckham Rd *CBROM* B36 ....113 H2
Wycome Rd *HLGN/YWD* B28 ....162 D4
Wye Cliff Rd
BFLD/HDSWWD B20..............108 B1
Wye Cl *DUNHL/THL/PER* WV6 ....34 D1
WALM/CURD B76...................78 C4
Wyegate Cl *CBROM* B36 ....114 A1
Wyemanton Rd *CTB/HAM* B43..75 F2
Wye Rd *BLOX/PEL* WS3 ....28 A1
Wykeham Gv
DUNHL/THL/PER WV6.............34 B2
Wykin Gv *WOLVN* WV10 ....29 G5
Wyld Cl *HHTH/SAND B71..........71 E3
Wylde Crs *BLKHTH/ROWR* B65..104 A5
Wylde Green Rd
CSCFLD/WYGN B72.................77 C2
Wymering Av *WNSFLD* WV11......25 F5
Wynall La *HAG/WOL* DY9.........136 D4
Wynall La South *HAG/WOL* DY9.137 E4
Wynbrook Gv *SHLY* B90...........195 G2
Wynchcombe Av
ETTPK/GDPK/PENN WV4.........50 D4
Wyndcliff Rd *BORD* B9.............128 B3
Wyndham Gdns *BVILLE* B30......176 C1
Wyndham Rd *LDYWD/EDGR* B16..125 H5
Wyndhurst Rd *STECH* B33........112 A5
Wyndley Cl *FOAKS/STRLY* B74....32 D4
Wyndley Dr *SCFLD/BOLD* B73....62 B4
Wyndley Gv *CSCFLD/WYGN* B72..77 C1
Wyndley La *SCFLD/BOLD* B73....62 A4
Wyndmill Crs *HHTH/SAND* B71...72 B2
Wynds Covert
ALE/KHTH/YWD B14............177 H3
Wyndshiels *CSHL/WTROR* B46...115 C3
Wynds Point *NFLD/LBR* B31 ....158 D5
The Wynd *SEDG* DY3..................67 F2
Wynfield Gdns
ALE/KHTH/YWD B14............161 F5
Wynford Rd *ACGN* B27.............146 C2
Wyn-Griffith Dr *TPTN/OCK* DY4..85 G3
Wynne Crs
ETTPK/GDPK/PENN WV4.........50 C5
Wynn Rd
ETTPK/GDPK/PENN WV4.........51 F2
Wynn St *EDG* B15....................126 D4
Wynstead Covert
ALE/KHTH/YWD B14............177 G3
Wyntor La *HHTH/SAND* B71 ......71 F3
Wyre Cl *ALDR* WS9......................19 F3
Wyre Rd *STRBR* DY8 ....118 A5
Wyrley Cl *BRWNH* WS8................9 F1
SHHTH WV12..........................26 A3
Wyrley Rd *AST/WIT* B6 ....91 C5
MGN/WHC B75........................47 H4
WNSFLD WV11........................25 G5
Wyrley St *WOLV* WV10...............37 H5
Wyrley Wy *ERDW/GRVHL* B23....75 C5
Wythall Green Wy *HLYWD* B47...193 H5
Wythall Rd *HALE* B63...............138 C5
Wythwood Cl *HAG/WOL* DY9 ....153 F1
Wythwood Gv *HLYWD* B47 ....193 E2
TPTN/OCK DY4 ....69 G5
Wythwood Rd *HLYWD* B47 ....192 D2
Wyton Av *LGLYGN/OTN* B68 ....123 G2
Wyvern Cl *FOAKS/STRLY* B74.....62 B1

LGLYGN/OTN B68...................105 F5
WLNHL WV13..........................25 C3
Wyvern Gv *SLYOAK* B29...........142 A5
Wyvern Rd *FOAKS/STRLY* B74....62 B1
Wyvis Cl *BDMR/CCFT* WV3.........36 A3

Y

Yale Dr *WNSFLD* WV11...............25 E5
Yale Rd *WLNHL* WV13.................54 C1
Yardley Cl *LGLYGN/OTN* B68....123 F5
Yardley Fields Rd *STETCH* B33..129 H2
Yardley Green Rd *BORD* B9 ......128 D5
Yardley Rd *ACGN* B27...............146 C1
Yardley St *DARL/WED* WS10.......55 E1
HAG/WOL DY9.......................136 A1
Yardley Wood Rd
ALE/KHTH/YWD B14.............178 D1
*MOS/BIL B13.........................161 H5
Yare Gv *WLNHL* WV13................40 B4
Yarnborough Hl *STRBR* DY8 ....155 G5
Yarnbury Cl
ALE/KHTH/YWD B14.............178 A4
Yarn Cl *HLYWD* B47.................192 C3
Yarner Cl *DUDN* DY1...................83 C5
Yarnfield Rd *SPARK* B11...........146 A4
Yarningale La *BVILLE* B30.........177 H2
Yarningale Rd
ALE/KHTH/YWD B14.............160 C5
Yarn La *SHLY* B90....................194 A2
Yarrow Cl *BLOX/PEL* WS3...........18 A2
WNSFLD WV11........................25 E5
Yarrow Dr *HWK/WKHTH* B38 ...176 D5
Yarwell Cl *WOLV* WV10...............37 F1
Yateley Av *PBAR/PBCH* B42.......74 A4
Yateley Crs *PBAR/PBCH* B42......74 A4
Yateley Rd *EDG* B15.................125 G5
Yatesbury Av *CVALE* B35............94 B3
Yates Cft *FOAKS/STRLY* B14......32 D4
Yates La *BLKHTH/ROWR* B65....122 C2
Yeadon Gdns *BDMR/CCFT* WV3..35 H5
Yeames Cl *CTB/HAM* B43............50 D1
Yelverton Cl *BLOX/PEL* WS3 ....16 D5
Yelverton Dr *EDG* B15.............125 C5
Yeman Rd *LGLYGN/OTN* B68....123 H1
Yemscroft Flats
RUSH/SHEL WS4 *.....................28 C4
Yenton Gv *ERDE/BCHGN* B24...77 G5
Yeomanry Cl *MGN/WHC* B75......63 C2
Yeomans Wy *MGN/WHC* B75......63 F2
Yerbury Gv *ERDW/GRVHL* B23...91 G1
Yewcroft Av *HRBN* B17.............141 C1
Yewdale *HRBN* B17..................142 A3
Yewhurst Rd *SOLH* B91............180 D1
Yew St *BDMR/CCFT* WV3.............6 B5
Yew Tree Av *HAG/WOL* DY9 .....170 B5
Yew Tree Gdns *CDSL* WV8 ....10 C3
Yew Tree Hills *DUDS* DY2.........120 C1
Yewtree La
BLKHTH/ROWR B65...............121 H2
Yew Tree La *BILS/COS* WV14......68 D2
DARL/WED WS10 *..................71 E1
DUNHL/THL/PER WV6.............35 F1
LGN/SDN/BHAMAIR B26 ......130 A5
RIDG/WDGT B32 ....173 H2

Yew Tree Pl *RMSLY* B62...........155 F5
Yew Tree Ri *WALM/CURD* B76....63 F5
Yewtree Rd *FOAKS/STRLY* B74...44 D5
SCFLD/BOLD B73....................77 E4
Yew Tree Rd *AST/WIT* B6...........91 C5
CBROM B36..........................113 C1
DSYBK/YTR WS5.....................57 G3
DUDS DY2 ....102 C5
EDG B15 ....126 C4
HALE B63...............................158 A4
MOS/BIL B13........................143 H5
RUSH/SHEL WS4 ....28 D1
WSNGN B18.........................107 A5
Yew Tree Vls
SCFLD/BOLD B73 *..................77 E4
Yockleton Rd *STETCH* B33........131 E1
York Av *BDMR/CCFT* WV3..........36 A4
WLNHL WV13..........................40 B3
WSLW WS2.............................41 F5
Yorkbrooke Dr
LGN/SDN/BHAMAIR B26 ......147 H2
York Cl *BVILLE* B30..................177 E5
TPTN/OCK DY4 ....84 D2
York Crs *BDMR/CCFT* WV3........35 H4
*BKDE/SHDE B34....................113 G4
DARL/WED WS10....................55 F2
STRBR DY8 ....117 H5
WBROM B70...........................71 E5
Yorkdale Cl *SEDG* DY3...............83 F5
York Dr *CBROM* B36................111 F1
Yorke Av *BRLYHL* DY5.............118 C3
York Gdns *BDMR/CCFT* WV3......36 A4
Yorkleq Cl
CHWD/FDBR/MGN B37.........131 H2
Yorklea Cft
CHWD/FDBR/MGN B37.........131 H2
Yorkminster Dr
CHWD/FDBR/MGN B37.........132 D1
York Rd *ALE/KHTH/YWD* B14...161 G2
BDMR/CCFT WV3....................35 F5
BLKHTH/ROWR B65...............122 C1
DUDS DY2 ....121 E1
ERDW/GRVHL B23..................92 D2
HDSW B21 ....107 H1
HRBN B17 ....142 D1
LDYWD/EDGR B16................125 F5
RUSH/SHEL WS4.....................29 F3
York St *HRBN* B17...................142 B1
WOLV WV1...............................7 J5
Yorks Wood Dr
CHWD/FDBR/MGN B37.........113 G4
York Ter *WSNGN* B18...............108 C4
Young St *WBROM* B70................87 E3
Yoxall Gv *STETCH* B33.............130 C1
Yoxall Rd *SHLY* B90.................180 D5

Z

Zions Cl *CDYHTH* B64...............121 F3
Zoar St *TPTN/OCK* DY4...............69 F3
Zoar St *BDMR/CCFT* WV3...........6 B5
SEDG DY3 ....83 C5
Zouche Cl *STRBR* DY8 ....118 A4

Index - featured places

The 3b Business Village
HDSW B21 ....107 F2
A1 Trading Estate
SMTHWK B66.......................106 C2
SMTHWK B67.......................124 C3
Abberley Industrial Centre
SMTHWK B66.......................107 F4
Abbey CP School
BLOX/PEL WS3 ....16 A4
Abbey Infant School
SMTHWK B67.......................124 A2
Abbey Junior School
SMTHWK B67.......................124 A3
Abbey Tutorial College
CBHAMNW B3..........................2 E5
Abu Bakr Girls School *WSL* WS1 ..4 B7
Ace Business Park
STECH B33 ....131 E2
Acupoint Magneto Clinic
SMHTH B10..........................128 C5
Adderley Primary School
WASH/WDE B8 ....128 B1
Adderley Industrial Estate
BORD B9 ....110 A5
Albert Bradbeer Infant School
NFLD/LBR B31 ....189 F1
Albert Bradbeer Junior School
NFLD/LBR B31 ....189 F1
Albert Pritchard Infant School
DARL/WED WS10 ....56 A3
Albion Business Park
SMTHWK B66.......................106 A1
Albion Industrial Estate
WBROM B70...........................87 E4
Albion Junior School
HHTH/SAND B71...................106 C1
Albion Road Junior School
WLNHL WV13..........................39 H3
Alcott Hall Primary School
CHWD/FDBR/MGN B57.........132 B3
Alderbrook School *SOLH* B91....181 F5
Alder Coppice Primary School
SEDG DY3...............................67 E2
Aldersley High School
CDSL WV8................................22 A1
Aldersley Leisure Village
DUNHL/THL/PER WV6.............22 B4
Aldridge School *ALDR* WS9.........30 A5
Alexander Industrial Park
BILS/COS WV14.......................53 G4
Alexandra High School &
Sixth Form Centre
TPTN/OCK DY4.......................69 H5
Alexandra Industrial Estate
TPTN/OCK DY4.......................69 F5

Alexandra Medical Centre
HALE B63.............................138 B2
Alexandra Theatre *DIG/EDG* B5 ...3 F6
Al-Furqan Community College
SPARK B11 ....145 H3
Al Furqan Primary School
SPARK B11 ....145 H3
Al Hijjrah School *BORD* B9 ....128 B2
Al-Hira School *BHTH/HC* B12 ...144 B3
Al Huda Girls School
WASH/WDE B8 ....110 B4
Alison Nicholas Golf Academy
PBAR/PBCH B42.....................74 C3
Allens Croft Primary School
ALE/KHTH/YWD B14.............160 B5
All Saints CE J & I School
HHTH/SAND B71 ....71 C5
All Saints Industrial Estate
WSNGN B18.........................108 A4
Alma Industrial Estate
DARL/WED WS10 ....55 E2
Alston Primary School
BORD B9 ....129 E1
Alumrock Medical Centre
WASH/WDE B8 ....110 C5
Alumwell Community School
WSLW WS2.............................41 E4
Alumwell Infant School
WSLW WS2.............................41 E3
Alumwell Junior School
WSLW WS2.............................41 E3
Amblecote Primary School
STRBR DY8 ....118 B4
AMC Cinema
LDYWD/EDGR B16................126 A3
Amptronik Trading Estate
WMBN WV5.............................80 B2
Anchor Brook Industrial Park
ALDR WS9...............................30 B4
Anderton Park Primary
School
BHTH/HC B12 ....144 C3
Anglesey Primary School
LOZ/NWT B19 ....108 C2
Anglo African Industrial Park
OLDBY B69.............................86 C4
Anita Myatt Health Centre
ETTPK/GDPK/PENN WV4.........50 D1
Annie Lennard Infant School
SMTHWK B67.......................124 A1
Arcadian Shopping Centre
DIG/EDG B5.............................3 G7
Archbishop Grimshaw
RC School
CHWD/FDBR/MGN B57.........131 H1

Archbishop Ilsey Catholic
Technology College &
Sixth Form Centre
ACGN B27 ....146 C4
Arden Hotel & Leisure Club
HIA/OLT B92 ....149 F5
Arden Industrial Estate
WASH/WDE B8 ....111 F2
Arden Primary School
SPARK B11 ....145 E2
Arden School
*DOR/KN B93.........................197 F3
Armoury Trading Estate
SPARK B11 ....145 F1
Arran Medical Centre
CBROM B36 ....114 A2
Arrow Industrial Estate
WNSFLD WV11........................25 H3
Arthur Terry School
FOAKS/STRLY B74..................47 E3
Ashbourne Centre
ERDW/GRVHL B23..................92 C3
Ashford Industrial Estate
BKHL/PFLD WV2 ....52 D1
Ashfurlong Health Centre
MGN/WHC B75.......................48 A5
Ashmore Park Clinic
WNSFLD WV11........................25 G2
Ashmores Industrial Estate
DUDN DY1.............................84 D3
Ashtree Medical Centre
BILS/COS WV14.....................160 A4
Ashwood Park Primary School
STRBR DY8 ....117 H3
Aston Cross Business Park
AST/WIT B6 ....109 G3
Aston Expressway
Industrial Estate
AST/WIT B6 ....109 E4
Aston Health Centre
AST/WIT B6 ....91 E5
Aston Manor Cricket &
Lucas Sports Club
PBAR/PBCH B42.....................90 D1
Aston Manor School
AST/WIT B6 ....109 F3
Aston Science Park
VAUX/NECH B7 ....3 K2
Aston Tower Primary School
AST/WIT B6 ....109 F2
Aston University
CBHAMNE B4 ....3 J5
Aston Villa FC (Villa Park)
AST/WIT B6 ....91 F5

Aston Wood Golf Club
FOAKS/STRLY B74..................32 C4
Astoria Hotel
LDYWD/EDGR B16................125 F3
Atlas Trading Estate
BILS/COS WV14.......................69 F1
SPARK B11 ....145 F2
Attock Community Sports & CC
MOS/BIL B13........................162 A1
Attwood Business Centre
HAG/WOL DY9......................136 D2
Autobase Industrial Estate
TPTN/OCK DY4 ....85 H3
Avery Dell Industrial Estate
BVILLE B30...........................159 H4
Axcess 10 Business Park
DARL/WED WS10....................40 C5
Baggeridge Country Park
SEDG DY3 ....66 A5
Bagley Industrial Park
SEDG DY3 ....102 D5
Balliol Business Park
COVEN WV9..............................11 C4
Banners Gate Infant School
SCFLD/BOLD B73....................60 D4
Banners Gate Junior School
SCFLD/BOLD B73....................60 C4
Bantock House & Park
BDMR/CCFT WV3....................36 B4
Barber Institute of Fine Arts
EDG B15 ....142 D3
Barford Primary School
LDYWD/EDGR B16................125 G1
Barnfield Trading Estate
TPTN/OCK DY4 ....69 E4
Baron Business Centre
HAG/WOL DY9......................136 C2
Barons Court Industrial Estate
HAG/WOL DY9......................136 D2
Barons Court Trading Estate
EDG B15 ....19 E5
The Barr Beacon School
ALDR WS9...............................59 F3
Bartley Green FC
RIDG/WDGT B32 ....157 G1
Bartley Green Health Centre
RIDG/WDGT B32 ....157 F1
Bartley Green Technology
College *RIDG/WDGT* B32 .....157 G1
Barton Industrial Estate
BILS/COS WV14.......................54 A1
Baskerville Special School
HRBN B17 ....141 G1
Bath Walk Industrial Estate
BHTH/HC B12 ....144 A3

Baverstock GM School
ALE/KHTH/YWD B14.............178 A3
Bayer Hall Clinic
BILS/COS WV14......................68 C3
Beacon CP School
SHHTH WV12..........................26 B2
Beacon Hill Cemetery
ETTPK/GDPK/PENN WV4........67 G1
Beaconside Primary School
RBRY B45 ....187 G2
Beacon Trading Estate
ALDR WS9..............................29 H4
Bean Road Industrial Estate
TPTN/OCK DY4 ....68 C5
Bearwood Medical Centre
SMTHWK B67.......................124 C2
Bearwood Primary School
SMTHWK B66.......................124 C2
Bearwood Shopping Centre
SMTHWK B66.......................124 C2
Beaufort Special School
CBROM B36..........................111 H4
Beautiform College
ALE/KHTH/YWD B14.............160 D2
Beauty Bank Primary School
STRBR DY8 ....135 F1
Beechdale CP School
WSLW WS2.............................27 G5
Beeches Hospital
WSNGN B18.............................6 A2
Beeches Pool & Fitness Centre
PBAR/PBCH B42.....................74 B4
Belbroughton CE First School
HAG/WOL DY9......................184 C2
Belfont Trading Estate
RMSLY B62 ....139 E3
Bell Barn Shopping Centre
EDG B15 ....126 C3
Belle Vue Medical Centre
EDG B15 ....126 D5
Belle Vue Primary School
STRBR DY8 ....117 G1
Bellfield J & I School
NFLD/LBR B31 ....175 F1
Bartley Green Health Centre
ALE/KHTH/YWD B14.............157 F1
The Bell Shopping Centre
NFLD/LBR B31 ....175 G1
Bennetts Well Primary School
CHWD/FDBR/MGN B37.........131 H1
Benson Community School
WSNGN B18.........................107 H3
Benson Industrial Estate
WSNGN B18.........................107 H3

Bentley Bridge Business Park
WNSFLD WV11 .... 24 C5
Bentley Bridge Leisure Park
WNSFLD WV11 .... 38 B1
Bentley Cemetery
WLNHL WV13 .... 40 B3
Bentley Drive Primary School
WSLW WS2 .... 41 F2
Bentley Heath CE
Primary School
DOR/KN B93 .... 196 D3
Bentley Lane Industrial Park
WSLW WS2 .... 41 F2
Bentley Mill Industrial Estate
WSLW WS2 .... 40 D3
Bentley West Primary School
WSLW WS2 .... 40 C2
Berrybrook Primary School
WOLVN WV10 .... 24 B1
Bescot Industrial Estate
DARL/WED WS10 .... 55 F5
Best Western Premier Moor Hall
Hotel & Spa
MCN/WHC B75 .... 47 H4
Best Western The Fairlawns
at Aldridge *ALDR* WS9 .... 31 E4
Best Western Westley Hotel
ACCN B27 .... 146 B4
Bevan Industrial Estate
BRLYHL DY5 .... 118 C2
Beverley Hotel
RUSH/SHEL WS4 .... 42 C1
Bhylls Acre Primary School
WOLVSE WV3 .... 50 B1
Bickenhill Trading Estate
CHWD/FDBR/MGN B37 .... 149 H2
Bickford Road Industrial Estate
AST/WIT B6 .... 91 G5
Bilberry CE Middle School
CDSL WV8 .... 10 D4
Bilbrook Medical Centre
CDSL WV8 .... 10 D4
Billesley Primary School
MOS/BIL B13 .... 162 A4
Bilston Cemetery
BILS/COS WV14 .... 53 G1
Bilston Central Industrial Estate
BILS/COS WV14 .... 54 A3
Bilston CE Primary School
BKHL/PFLD WV2 .... 53 F2
Bilston Health Centre
BILS/COS WV14 .... 53 H2
Bilston High School
BILS/COS WV14 .... 53 H5
Bilston Industrial Estate
BILS/COS WV14 .... 54 C4
Bingle Primary School
BDMR/CCFT WV3 .... 36 C5
Bilston Key Industrial Estate
BILS/COS WV14 .... 54 C3
Bilston Leisure Centre
BILS/COS WV14 .... 53 H2
Bilston Public Library &
Art Gallery *BILS/COS* WV14 .... 54 A2
Bilston Town FC
BILS/COS WV14 .... 54 B2
Bilton Industrial Estate
HWK/WKHTH B38 .... 176 C5
Birches First School *CDSL* WV8 .... 21 F1
Birches Green J & I School
ERDE/BCHGN B24 .... 93 F3
Birchfield Independent
Girls School *AST/WIT* B6 .... 109 E1
Birchfield Primary School
AST/WIT B6 .... 90 D5
Birchills CE Primary School
WSLW WS2 .... 4 B2
Birchills Health Centre
WSLW WS2 .... 4 A1
Birchley Industrial Estate
OLDBY B69 .... 104 C4
Birch Road East
Industrial Estate
AST/WIT B6 .... 91 H4
Birmingham Alexander
Stadium *PBAR/PBCH* B42 .... 74 C5
Birmingham Area Civil Service
Sports Club *HIA/OLT* B92 .... 149 E5
Birmingham Botanical
Gardens & Glasshouses
EDC B15 .... 125 H5
Birmingham Business Centre
WBROM B70 .... 88 B4
Birmingham Business Park
CHWD/FDBR/MGN B37 .... 133 E4
Birmingham Christian Centre
CBHAMNW B5 .... 3 F4
Birmingham City College
BORD B9 .... 129 E1
Birmingham City FC
(St Andrews Stadium)
BORD B9 .... 127 H3
Birmingham College of Food,
Tourism & Creative Studies
CSCFLD/WYGN B72 .... 62 C3
Birmingham Community College
CSCFLD/WYGN B72 .... 62 C3
Birmingham Conservatoire
(University of Central England)
CBHAMNW B5 .... 2 D4
The Birmingham Crematorium
PBAR/PBCH B42 .... 90 C1
Birmingham Heartlands
Hospital *BORD* B9 .... 129 F2
Birmingham Hebrew
Congregation *CBHAMW* B1 .... 2 E7
Birmingham international
Airport
LGN/SDN/BHAMAIR B26 .... 149 G3
Birmingham Marriott Hotel
EDC B15 .... 126 B4
The Birmingham & Midland
Hospital for Woman
SPARK B11 .... 145 E4
The Birmingham Mint
WSNCN B18 .... 2 B1
Birmingham Museum &
Art Gallery *CBHAMNW* B3 .... 2 E5
The Birmingham Nuffield
Hospital *EDG* B15 .... 142 D2

Birmingham One Industrial
Estate *CBHAMW* B1 .... 2 B4
Birmingham Repertory Theatre
CBHAMW B1 .... 2 D5
Birmingham Wheels
Adventure Park *BORD* B9 .... 128 A2
Birmingham Womens Hospital
HRBN B17 .... 142 B2
Birmingham (Yardley)
Crematorium *YDLY* B25 .... 146 D2
Bishop Ashbury's Cottage
GTB/HAM B43 .... 72 D2
The Bishop Challoner RC School
ALE/KHTH/YWD B14 .... 161 E2
Bishop Milner RC Secondary
School *DUDN* DY1 .... 84 A3
Bishop Veseys Grammar School
FOAKS/STRLY B74 .... 62 C2
Bishop Walsh Catholic School
WALM/CURD B76 .... 77 H1
Bishop Wilson CE
Primary School
CHWD/FDBR/MGN B37 .... 132 C1
Bi-Tec Industrial Park
WOLV WV1 .... 37 H4
Blackbrook Valley
Industrial Estate
DUDS DY2 .... 102 A3
Blackbrook Valley
Industrial Park
BRLYHL DY5 .... 102 A4
Black Country Living Museum
DUDN DY1 .... 84 D3
Blackheath Primary School
BLKHTH/ROWR B65 .... 121 H3
Blackheath Trading Estate
BLKHTH/ROWR B65 .... 122 C2
Black Lake Industrial Estate
WBROM B70 .... 71 E5
Blackwood School
FOAKS/STRLY B74 .... 45 E4
Blakedown CE First School
KIDD DY10 .... 168 C4
Blakeley Heath Primary School
WMBN WV5 .... 81 E1
Blakenall CE *BLOX/PEL* WS3 .... 27 G3
Blakenall Heath Junior School
BLOX/PEL WS3 .... 27 G2
Blakenhale Infant School
STECH B33 .... 130 D3
Blakenhale Junior School
STECH B33 .... 130 D3
Blakenhall Industrial Estate
BDMR/CCFT WV3 .... 51 H1
Blakesley Hall *YDLY* B25 .... 130 A3
Blakesley Hall Primary School
STECH B33 .... 129 H3
Blanford Mere Primary School
KGSWFD DY6 .... 100 A2
Bleakhouse Clinic
LGLYGN/QTN B68 .... 123 C3
Bleakhouse Junior School
LGLYGN/QTN B68 .... 123 C3
Blossomfield Infant School
SHLY B90 .... 180 D2
Blowers Green Primary School
DUDS DY2 .... 102 B1
Bloxwich Business Park
WSLW WS2 .... 27 F3
Bloxwich CE Primary School
BLOX/PEL WS3 .... 27 F1
Bloxwich Golf Club
BLOX/PEL WS3 .... 16 D3
Bloxwich Hospital
BLOX/PEL WS3 .... 27 F2
Bloxwich Lane Industrial Estate
WSLW WS2 .... 41 E2
Bloxwich Leisure Centre
BLOX/PEL WS3 .... 27 G2
Blue Coat CE Comprehensive
School *WSL* WS1 .... 5 F5
Blue Coat CE Infant School
WSL WS1 .... 5 F6
Blue Coat CE Junior School
WSL WS1 .... 5 G5
The Blue Coat School
HRBN B17 .... 142 C1
Blythe Business Park
SHLY B90 .... 195 F5
Blythe Special School
CSHL/WTROR B46 .... 115 G5
BMI Priory Hospital
DIG/EDG B5 .... 143 F2
Boddis Industrial Park
CDYHTH B64 .... 121 G2
Boldmere Clinic
SCFLD/BOLD B73 .... 76 D2
Boldmere Golf Club
SCFLD/BOLD B73 .... 61 C5
Boldmere J & I School
SCFLD/BOLD B73 .... 76 D2
Boldmere St Michaels FC
SCFLD/BOLD B73 .... 76 D3
Bordesley Green Girls School
WASH/WDE B8 .... 128 C1
Bordesley Green Primary
School *BORD* B9 .... 129 E2
Bordesley Green Trading
Estate *WASH/WDE* B8 .... 128 B1
Borough Cemetery
DUDS DY2 .... 102 B1
Bosworth Wood Primary
School *CBROM* B36 .... 95 H5
Boulton Industrial Centre
WSNGN B18 .... 108 B4
The Boundary Hotel
WSL WS1 .... 57 H1
Boundary Industrial Estate
WOLVN WV10 .... 12 C2
Bournelle Infant School
BVILLE B30 .... 159 G3
Bournville Junior School
BVILLE B30 .... 159 G3
Bournville College of Further
Education *SLYOAK* B29 .... 159 E3
Bournville School of
Art & Craft *BVILLE* B30 .... 159 F3
Bournville School &
Sixth Form Centre
NFLD/LBR B31 .... 159 E4

Bowlplex *LDYWD/EDGR* B16 .... 126 A3
Brackendale Shopping Centre
SHHTH WV12 .... 40 B1
Bradford Street Clinic *WSL* WS1 .... 4 D5
Braidwood School for
Deaf Children
ERDW/GRVHL B23 .... 75 H5
Bramford Primary School
BILS/COS WV14 .... 68 A5
Brandhall Clinic
LGLYGN/QTN B68 .... 123 F4
Brandhall Golf Club
LGLYGN/QTN B68 .... 123 E2
Brandhall Primary School
LGLYGN/QTN B68 .... 123 F3
Brandon Way Industrial Estate
WBROM B70 .... 86 D3
Brandwood End Cemetery
ALE/KHTH/YWD B14 .... 178 A1
Brasshouse Infant School
SMTHWK B66 .... 106 C2
Brasshouse Language Centre
LDYWD/EDGR B16 .... 2 B7
Brays Special School
LGN/SDN/BHAMAIR B26 .... 147 G1
Breener Industrial Estate
BRLYHL DY5 .... 118 D3
Brickhouse J & I School
BLKHTH/ROWR B65 .... 121 G1
Bridge Industrial Estate
SOLH B91 .... 165 E2
Bridge Special School
ERDW/GRVHL B23 .... 92 C2
Bridge Street Industrial Estate
DARL/WED WS10 .... 70 D2
The Bridge Trading Estate
SMTHWK B66 .... 106 D2
Brierley Hill Cemetery
BRLYHL DY5 .... 118 D2
The Brierley Hill Health Centre
BRLYHL DY5 .... 119 F1
Brierley Hill Primary School
BRLYHL DY5 .... 119 F2
The Brierley Trading Estate
BRLYHL DY5 .... 119 E1
Brierly Hill Leisure Centre
BRLYHL DY5 .... 119 G1
The Brier Special School
BRLYHL DY5 .... 119 G1
Brindley Place *CBHAMW* B1 .... 2 C6
Brineton Industrial Estate
LDYWD/EDGR B16 .... 4 A6
Bristnall Hall High School
LGLYGN/QTN B68 .... 123 H1
Broadcott Industrial Estate
CDYHTH B64 .... 121 G3
Broadfield House Glass Museum
KGSWFD DY6 .... 99 H4
Broadmeadow J & I School
BVILLE B30 .... 177 F5
Broadwalk Retail Park
WSL WS1 .... 56 D2
Broadway Medical Centre
WSL WS1 .... 57 F2
Broadway Plaza
LDYWD/EDGR B16 .... 126 A3
Broadway School
BFLD/HDSWWD B20 .... 91 E4
Broadwell Industrial Park
OLDBY B69 .... 87 E5
Brockmoor Industrial Estate
KGSWFD DY6 .... 100 D1
Brockmoor Primary School
BLOX/PEL WS3 .... 118 C1
Brockmoor Primary School
BRLYHL DY5 .... 119 E1
Bromford Road Industrial
Estate *OLDBY* B69 .... 87 E5
Bromley Hills Primary School
KGSWFD DY6 .... 100 B5
Bromley Primary School
BRLYHL DY5 .... 100 D4
Brookfields Primary School
WSNGN B18 .... 2 A1
Brooklands Hospital
CHWD/FDBR/MGN B37 .... 132 B4
The Brook Primary School
STRBR DY8 .... 118 B3
Brookside Industrial Estate
DARL/WED WS10 .... 56 B5
Brook Street Business Centre
TPTN/OCK DY4 .... 69 E5
Brookvale Primary School
ERDW/GRVHL B23 .... 91 H2
Brookvale Trading Estate
AST/WIT B6 .... 91 G3
Brownhills Business Park
BRWNH WS8 .... 19 F2
Brownhills Clinic *BRWNH* WS8 .... 9 F5
Brownhills Comprehensive
School *BRWNH* WS8 .... 9 F3
Brownhills West JMI School
BRWNH WS8 .... 8 C1
Brownhills West Station
BRWNH WS8 .... 8 C1
Browning Street Industrial
Estate *LDYWD/EDGR* B16 .... 2 A6
Brownmead Primary School
BKDE/SHDE B34 .... 112 D3
Brunswick Park Trading Estate
WBROM B70 .... 56 B4
Brymill Industrial Estate
TPTN/OCK DY4 .... 69 E4
BSA Business Park *SPARK* B11 .... 145 F1
BT Tower *CBHAMNW* B3 .... 2 E3
Bullring Shopping Centre
DIG/EDG B5 .... 3 H6
Bull Ring Trading Estate
BHTH/HG B12 .... 3 K7
Bull Street Trading Estate
BRLYHL DY5 .... 118 D3
Burman Infant School
SHLY B90 .... 180 A3
Burnt Tree Industrial Estate
TPTN/OCK DY4 .... 85 H4
Burnt Tree J & I School
OLDBY B69 .... 85 G4
Burton Industrial Estate
CDYHTH B64 .... 121 E4

Bushbury Baths
WOLVN WV10 .... 23 G1
Bushbury Cemetery
WOLVN WV10 .... 13 F5
Bushbury Health Centre
WOLVN WV10 .... 13 F5
Bushbury Hill J & I School
WOLVN WV10 .... 23 H1
Busill Jones JMI School
BLOX/PEL WS3 .... 26 D2
The Business Centre
SPARK B11 .... 145 H1
Butts JMI School
RUSH/SHEL WS4 .... 5 F1
Cadbury College
HWK/WKHTH B38 .... 176 D4
Cadbury World *BVILLE* B30 .... 159 H5
Calderfields Golf Club &
Academy *RUSH/SHEL* WS4 .... 43 E3
Caldmore JMI School *WSL* WS1 .... 4 E7
Caldmore Medical Centre
WSL WS1 .... 4 E7
Calthorpe Special School
BHTH/HG B12 .... 127 G4
Cambrian Wharf *CBHAMW* B1 .... 2 C5
Cambridge Tutorial College
SMHTH B10 .... 128 B4
Campanile Hotel
VAUX/NECH B7 .... 109 F4
Camp Hill Old Edwardians
RFC *SHLY* B90 .... 180 B2
Canal Side Industrial Estate
BRLYHL DY5 .... 118 D3
Canal View Industrial Estate
STRBR DY8 .... 118 C3
Canning Wharf *CBHAMW* B5 .... 2 D4
Cannon Business Park
BILS/COS WV14 .... 68 C2
Canterbury Cross
Primary NC School
BFLD/HDSWWD B20 .... 90 D4
Cape Hill Medical Centre
SMTHWK B66 .... 107 E5
Cape Primary School
SMTHWK B66 .... 107 E5
Cardinal Wiseman
Catholic School *KGSTG* B44 .... 75 F1
Carlton Business Centre
VAUX/NECH B7 .... 110 A4
Carlyle Business Park
WBROM B70 .... 86 D1
Carters Green Medical Centre
WBROM B70 .... 87 G2
Caslon Primary School
HALE B63 .... 137 F3
Castle Bromwich Business
Park *CVALE* B35 .... 94 B5
Castle Bromwich CC
CBROM B36 .... 113 E1
Castle Bromwich Hall
Gardens *CBROM* B36 .... 112 C1
Castle Bromwich Infant
School *CBROM* B36 .... 113 G1
Castle Bromwich Junior
School *CBROM* B36 .... 113 F2
Castlecroft J & I School
BDMR/CCFT WV3 .... 35 F4
Castlefort JMI School
ALDR WS9 .... 19 H4
Castle High School
DUDN DY1 .... 84 B4
The Castle Pool &
Adventure Play Centre
CVALE B35 .... 95 E4
Castle Special School
BLOX/PEL WS3 .... 27 F3
Castle Vale Health Centre
WALM/CURD B76 .... 94 C1
Castle Vale Industrial Estate
CVALE B35 .... 94 B3
Castle Vale Shopping Centre
CVALE B35 .... 94 B3
Castle View Industrial Estate
TPTN/OCK DY4 .... 85 F3
Causeway Green
Primary School
LGLYGN/QTN B68 .... 122 D1
C&CC Site *RMSLY* B62 .... 121 E2
Cemetery of St Joseph
VAUX/NECH B7 .... 109 H2
Central Business Park
STECH B33 .... 131 F3
Central Clinic *DUDS* DY2 .... 84 D5
Central Hall *CBHAMNE* B4 .... 3 H3
Central Industrial Estate
BKHL/PFLD WV2 .... 52 D1
Central Park Industrial Estate
DUDS DY2 .... 121 E1
Central Trading Estate
BRLYHL DY5 .... 118 C1
Centre Link Industrial Estate
VAUX/NECH B7 .... 109 H3
Century Industrial Estate
KGSTG B44 .... 60 A5
Chad Vale Primary School
EDG B15 .... 125 F5
Chamber of Commerce
WSL WS1 .... 5 G2
Chamber of Commerce &
Industry *BDMR/CCFT* WV3 .... 6 A3
Chancel Industrial Estate
DARL/WED WS10 .... 55 G5
KGSWFD DY6 .... 81 H5
KGSWFD DY6 .... 100 A1
WLNHL WV13 .... 39 H3
WOLV WV1 .... 37 H4
Chancel Way Industrial Estate
AST/WIT B6 .... 91 F1
Chandos Primary School
DIG/EDG B5 .... 127 G5
Chapel Fields Junior School
HIA/OLT B92 .... 147 F4
Chapel Street Industrial Estate
DUDS DY2 .... 102 D5
Charlemont Primary School
HHTH/SAND B71 .... 72 A3
Charles Street Industrial Estate
TPTN/OCK DY4 .... 86 C1
Charnwood Business Park
BILS/COS WV14 .... 53 G2

Charterfield Shopping Centre
KGSWFD DY6 .... 99 H1
Chase Watersports Centre
BRWNH WS8 .... 8 C1
Cheapside Industrial Estate
BHTH/HG B12 .... 127 F3
Chelmsley Wood Industrial
Estate
CHWD/FDBR/MGN B37 .... 114 A4
Chelmsley Wood Shopping
Centre
CHWD/FDBR/MGN B37 .... 132 B2
Chelsea Trading Estate
AST/WIT B6 .... 109 G3
Cherry Oak Special School
SLYOAK B29 .... 142 B5
Cherry Orchard Primary
School *BFLD/HDSWWD* B20 .... 90 A3
Cherry Trees Special School
WMBN WV5 .... 64 D5
Cherrywood Industrial Estate
WASH/WDE B8 .... 111 G1
Cheston Industrial Estate
AST/WIT B6 .... 109 H2
Cheswick Green Primary
School *SHLY* B90 .... 195 E3
Chilcote Primary School
HLGN/YWD B28 .... 179 H1
Chillington Works Industrial
Estate *WOLV* WV1 .... 37 H4
The Chiropody Surgery
YDLY B25 .... 129 H3
Chivenor Primary School
CVALE B35 .... 94 C4
Christ Church CE Infant School
HAG/WOL DY9 .... 36 D1
Christ Church CE Junior School
DUNHL/THL/PER WV6 .... 35 G1
Christ Church CE
Primary School
BLOX/PEL WS3 .... 27 H3
OLDBY B69 .... 105 E1
SPARK B11 .... 127 H5
Christ Church Infant School
DUNHL/THL/PER WV6 .... 35 E2
Christ Church Primary School
BILS/COS WV14 .... 68 D2
Christ the King RC
Primary School *KGSTG* B44 .... 75 G2
Chuckery Primary School
WSL WS1 .... 5 H4
Churchbridge Industrial Estate
OLDBY B69 .... 104 D3
Churchfield Industrial Estate
DUDS DY2 .... 102 C1
Churchill & Blakedown
Golf Club *KIDD* DY10 .... 168 A3
Church Hill Primary School *DUDN* DY1 .... 84 D5
Church Lane Health Centre
STECH B33 .... 130 B1
Church Lane Industrial Estate
HHTH/SAND B71 .... 71 G5
Church of Ascension CE
Primary School
KGSWFD DY6 .... 99 F1
Cineworld *SOLH* B91 .... 182 A2
City College *ACGN* B27 .... 146 C4
City College Birmingham
BKDE/SHDE B34 .... 113 F3
HDSW B21 .... 108 A2
HRBN B17 .... 142 B1
STECH B33 .... 130 D4
City Hospital *WSNGN* B18 .... 107 H5
City of Wolverhampton College
BKHL/PFLD WV2 .... 7 G5
City Plaza Shopping Centre
CBHAM B2 .... 3 F5
City Road Primary School
LDYWD/EDGR B16 .... 125 F1
The City Technology College
CHWD/FDBR/MGN B37 .... 114 A5
City Trading Estate
LDYWD/EDGR B16 .... 125 H1
Claregate Primary School
DUNHL/THL/PER WV6 .... 22 B3
Clarkes Industrial Estate
SCFLD/BOLD B73 .... 77 E2
Clearwater Industrial Estate
BKHL/PFLD WV2 .... 52 D1
Clent Hills HAG/WOL DY9 .... 154 A5
Clent Hills Country Park (NT)
HAG/WOL DY9 .... 171 E1
Clent Parochial First School
HAG/WOL DY9 .... 170 D3
Cleton Street Business Park
TPTN/OCK DY4 .... 85 H3
Clifton Infant School
BHTH/HG B12 .... 144 C2
Clifton Junior School
BHTH/HG B12 .... 144 C2
Clifton Primary School
BHTH/HG B12 .... 144 B2
Clothier Street Primary School
WLNHL WV13 .... 39 G2
CMT Industrial Estate
OLDBY B69 .... 105 E1
Coalpool Clinic *BLOX/PEL* WS3 .... 28 B4
Coal Pool Lane Cemetery
BLOX/PEL WS3 .... 42 B1
Cobham Business Centre
WASH/WDE B8 .... 128 B1
Cockshut Hill Technology
College
LGN/SDN/BHAMAIR B26 .... 130 C4
Cocks Moors Woods
Leisure Centre
ALE/KHTH/YWD B14 .... 178 B1
Codsall Cemetery
CDSL WV8 .... 10 B2
Codsall Clinic *CDSL* WV8 .... 10 C4
Codsall Middle School
CDSL WV8 .... 10 C4
Cofton Medical Centre
NFLD/LBR B31 .... 189 G1
Cofton Primary School
NFLD/LBR B31 .... 189 G2
Coldland Colts FC
SOLH B91 .... 165 H4
Colebourne Primary School
BKDE/SHDE B34 .... 112 A4

Coleshill Cemetery
  CSHL/WTROR B46 .... 115 G3
Coleshill CE Primary School
  CSHL/WTROR B46 .... 115 F3
Coleshill Clinic
  CSHL/WTROR B46 .... 115 G3
Coleshill
  Primary School
  CHWD/FDBR/MGN B37 ...... 132 C3
Coleshill Hotel
  CSHL/WTROR B46 .... 115 G5
Coleshill Industrial Estate
  CSHL/WTROR B46 .... 97 F4
Coleshill Leisure Centre
  CSHL/WTROR B46 .... 115 F3
Coleshill School
  CSHL/WTROR B46 .... 133 G1
Coleshill Town FC
  CSHL/WTROR B46 .... 133 G1
The College High School
  KGSTG B44 .... 75 G3
College of Continuing
  Education
  WSL WS1 .... 57 E1
Colley Lane Health Clinic
  HALE B63 .... 137 G3
Colley Lane Primary School
  HALE B63 .... 137 F1
Collingwood Primary School
  WOLVN WV10 .... 13 E5
Colmers Farm J & I School
  RBRY B45 .... 174 B5
Colmers Farm Secondary
  School *RBRY* B45 .... 174 B5
Colmore J & I School
  ALE/KHTH/YWD B14 .... 160 D3
Colonial Industrial Park
  CDYHTH B64 .... 120 C5
Colton Hills School
  ETTPK/GDPK/PENN WV4 .. 51 H4
Comfort Inn
  LDYWD/EDGR B16 .... 125 F3
Community High School
  CDSL WV8 .... 10 C5
Community Leisure Centre
  TPTN/OCK DY4 .... 68 D5
Coneygre Industrial Estate
  TPTN/OCK DY4 .... 85 F4
Connect Business Park
  WASH/WDE B8 .... 128 A2
Conway Primary School
  SPARK B11 .... 144 D1
Cookley Wharf Industrial
  Estate *BRLYHL* DY5 .... 118 C1
Cooper & Jordan CE J & I
  School *ALDR* WS9 .... 30 C4
Copperfield House Hotel
  SLYOAK B29 .... 143 E4
Coppice High Community
  School *WNSFLD* WV11 .... 25 H2
Coppice Junior School
  HIA/OLT B92 .... 165 G3
Coppice Primary School
  HLYWD B47 .... 192 C2
  MGN/WHC B75 .... 47 G4
Coppice Side Industrial Estate
  BRWNH WS8 .... 8 D5
Copt Heath Golf Club
  DOR/KN B93 .... 183 E5
Copthorne Hotel *BRLYHL* DY5 . 101 G5
  CBHAMNW B3 .... 2 D5
Corbett Hospital *STRBR* DY8 .. 118 C5
Corbett Industrial Estate
  DUDS DY2 .... 102 C3
Corngreaves Hall Golf Club
  CDYHTH B64 .... 121 F4
Corngreaves J & I School
  CDYHTH B64 .... 120 D3
Corngreaves Trading Estate
  CDYHTH B64 .... 120 D5
Cornwall Industrial Estate
  SMTHWK B66 .... 107 E2
  WASH/WDE B8 .... 110 A5
Cornwall Road Industrial
  Estate *SMTHWK* B66 ...... 107 E2
Corpus Christi RC Primary
  School *STETCH* B33 .... 129 H2
  WNSFLD WV11 .... 25 G2
Corus Hotel Solihull *SHLY* B90 . 195 E1.5
Coseley Medical Centre
  BILS/COS WV14 .... 68 C3
The Coseley School
  BILS/COS WV14 .... 68 B2
Coseley Swimming Pool
  BILS/COS WV14 .... 68 C3
Cotteridge Primary School
  BVILLE B30 .... 160 A5
Cottesbrooke Infant School
  ACGN B27 .... 146 D3
Cottesbrooke Junior School
  ACGN B27 .... 146 C3
Cotwall End Primary School
  SEDG DY3 .... 67 G4
County Bridge Primary School
  WLNHL WV13 .... 40 C4
Courtfarm Primary School
  ERDW/CRVHL B23 .... 76 C5
Crabtree Clinic
  CHWD/FDBR/MGN B37 .... 131 H2
Cradley Cemetery *HALE* B63 .. 120 C5
Cradley CE Primary School
  HALE B63 .... 120 C5
Cradley Heath Community
  Recreation Centre
  DUDS DY2 .... 121 E2
Cradley High School
  HALE B63 .... 137 F1
Cradley Town FC *HALE* B63 .. 137 G3
Craig Croft Child Health Clinic
  CHWD/FDBR/MGN B37 .... 132 C2
Craig Croft Medical Centre
  CHWD/FDBR/MGN B37 .... 132 C2
Cranmore Industrial Estate
  SHLY B90 .... 181 E5
Cransmore Infant School
  SOLH B91 .... 181 E4
Crescent Industrial Park
  DUDS DY2 .... 102 B2
Crescent Theatre
  LDYWD/EDGR B16 .... 2 B6

Crescent Works Industrial Park
  DARL/WED WS10 .... 40 B4
Crestwood Park Primary
  School *KGSWFD* DY6 ...... 100 C4
The Crestwood Secondary
  School *KGSWFD* DY6 ...... 100 B4
Crocketts Lane Primary
  School *SMTHWK* B66 ...... 106 C4
Croft Foundry Industrial
  Estate *WLNHL* WV13 ...... 39 G3
Croft Industrial Estate
  CHWD/FDBR/MGN B37 .... 132 B2
Croft Street JMI School
  WSLW WS2 .... 41 H1
Cromwell Primary School
  VAUX/NECH B7 .... 109 G3
Cronehill Primary School
  WBROM B70 .... 87 G2
Cronehills Health Centre
  WBROM B70 .... 87 H3
Crossings Industrial Estate
  BLOX/PEL WS3 .... 27 E2
Cross Quays Business Park
  OLDBY B69 .... 86 A4
Cross Street Health Centre
  DUDN DY1 .... 84 C5
Crossways Shopping Centre
  WOLVN WV10 .... 38 A2
Crown Wharf Shopping Centre
  WSLW WS2 .... 4 C2
Crown Wharf Shopping Park
  WSLW WS2 .... 41 G1
Crystal Leisure Centre
  STRBR DY8 .... 135 F2
Culwell Industrial Park
  WOLVN WV10 .... 7 J2
Culwell Trading Estate
  WOLVN WV10 .... 37 H1
Dadsford Bridge Industrial
  Estate *STRBR* DY8 .... 118 A2
Dame Elizabeth Cadbury
  School *BVILLE* B30 .... 159 G3
Dame Ellen Pinsent School
  HRBN B17 .... 124 D2
Damson Wood Infant School
  HIA/OLT B92 .... 165 F3
Danescourt Cremetorium &
  Cemetery
  DUNHL/THL/PER WV6 ...... 21 F4
Danesmore Park Primary
  School *WNSFLD* WV11 .... 25 F1
Darlaston Central Trading
  Estate *DARL/WED* WS10 .. 55 C1
Darlaston Clinic
  DARL/WED WS10 .... 55 F2
Darlaston Community School
  DARL/WED WS10 .... 54 D2
Darlaston FC *DARL/WED* WS10 . 55 F2
Darlaston Road Industrial
  Estate *DARL/WED* WS10 .. 55 F3
Dartmouth Golf Club
  HHTH/SAND B71 .... 72 A5
Dartmouth High School
  GTB/HAM B43 .... 58 B5
David Lloyd Birmingham
  KGSTG B44 .... 60 A5
Daw End School
  RUSH/SHEL WS4 .... 28 D4
Dawley Brook Primary
  School *KGSWFD* DY6 ...... 99 G2
Dawley Trading Estate
  KGSWFD DY6 .... 99 H1
Daylesford Infant School
  HIA/OLT B92 .... 147 G4
Days Inn *SPARK* B11 .... 128 A5
Deanery CE Primary School
  WALM/CURD B76 .... 78 B3
Deansfield High School
  WOLV WV1 .... 38 C3
Deeleys Industrial Estate
  WSLW WS2 .... 27 F4
Deepdale Industrial Estate
  DUDN DY1 .... 83 G3
The Dell Stadium *BRLYHL* DY5 . 100 D4
Delph Road Industrial Estate
  BRLYHL DY5 .... 119 E3
Delph Road Industrial Park
  BRLYHL DY5 .... 119 F3
Delta Trading Estate
  BKHL/PFLD WV2 .... 37 H5
Delves J & I School
  DSYBK/YTR WS5 .... 57 G3
Dental Health Centre
  KGSTG B44 .... 75 F1
Dental Hospital
  KGSTG B44 .... 3 G2
Department of Art (University
  of Central England)
  CBHAMNW B3 .... 2 E4
Devonshire J & I School
  SMTHWK B67 .... 106 A4
Devkin Avenue J & I School
  AST/WIT B6 .... 91 G4
D'Eyncourt Primary School
  WOLVN WV10 .... 24 B3
Diana (Princess of Wales
  Hospital for Children)
  CBHAMNE B4 .... 3 G3
Dickens Heath Primary School
  SHLY B90 .... 193 H2
Digbeth Coach Station
  DIG/EDG B5 .... 3 J7
Dingle Primary School
  KGSWFD DY6 .... 100 C5
Dock Lane Industrial Estate
  DUDN DY1 .... 84 B5
Dock Meadow Drive
  Industrial Estate
  ETTPK/GDPK/PENN WV4 .. 53 E4
Doranda Way Industrial Park
  HHTH/SAND B71 .... 88 B5
Dormston Secondary School
  SEDG DY3 .... 67 G3
Dormston Trading Estate
  DUDN DY1 .... 83 H2
Dorothy Pattison Hospital
  WSLW WS2 .... 41 F4
Dorothy Purcell Junior School
  BILS/COS WV14 .... 54 D5
Dorridge CC *DOR/KN* B93 .. 198 C2

Dorridge J & I School
  DOR/KN B93 .... 197 E5
Dorrington Primary School
  PBAR/PBCH B42 .... 74 A5
Doulton Trading Estate
  BLKHTH/ROWR B65 .... 103 F5
Dovecote J & I School
  CDSL WV8 .... 22 A1
The Dovecote Surgery
  LGLYGN/QTN B68 .... 123 H5
Downing Close Health Clinic
  DOR/KN B93 .... 197 E4
Dreamwell Industrial Estate
  SPARK B11 .... 145 H1
Droicon Industrial Estate
  BLKHTH/ROWR B65 .... 103 H5
Droicon Trading Estate
  BLKHTH/ROWR B65 .... 103 H4
Druids Heath Golf Club
  ALDR WS9 .... 30 C2
Duddeston Mill Trading Estate
  WASH/WDE B8 .... 110 A5
Dudley Castle & Zoological
  Gardens *DUDN* DY1 .... 84 D4
Dudley Central Trading Estate
  DUDS DY2 .... 102 B1
Dudley College *BRLYHL* DY5 .. 119 E1
Dudley Central Trading Estate
  DUDN DY1 .... 84 C5
Dudley College
  (Mons Hill Campus)
  DUDN DY1 .... 84 B2
Dudley Golf Club
  BLKHTH/ROWR B65 .... 103 G3
Dudley Kingswinford RFC
  KGSWFD DY6 .... 99 E2
Dudley Leisure Centre
  DUDN DY1 .... 84 B5
Dudley Museum & Art Gallery
  DUDN DY1 .... 84 C5
Dudley Town Hall
  DUDN DY1 .... 84 C4
Dudley Water Sports Centre
  DUDS DY2 .... 120 B1
Dudley Wood Primary School
  DUDS DY2 .... 120 C2
Dunstall Hill Industrial Estate
  DUNHL/THL/PER WV6 ...... 23 E5
Dunstall Hill Primary School
  DUNHL/THL/PER WV6 ...... 37 E1
Durberville Road Industrial
  Estate *BKHL/PFLD* WV2 .. 52 D1
Eagle Industrial Estate
  TPTN/OCK DY4 .... 70 B4
Eagle Trading Estate
  HALE B63 .... 138 C3
Earls High School *HALE* B63 .. 138 D3
Eastbourne House School
  ACGN B27 .... 146 C3
Eastfield Primary School
  WOLV WV1 .... 37 H3
East Park J & I School
  WOLV WV1 .... 38 B5
East Park Trading Estate
  BKHL/PFLD WV2 .... 37 H5
Eaton Wood Medical Centre
  ERDW/CRVHL B23 .... 93 H3
Ebrook Adult Training Centre
  CSCFLD/WYGN B72 .... 62 D5
Eclipse Industrial Estate
  TPTN/OCK DY4 .... 85 E1
Eclipse Trading Estate
  TPTN/OCK DY4 .... 85 E1
Edgar Stammers Primary
  School *BLOX/PEL* WS3 ...... 28 B3
Edgbaston Golf Club *EDG* B15 . 145 F1
Edgbaston Health Clinic
  EDG B15 .... 142 C2
  SOLH B91 .... 164 B4
Edgbaston High School for Girls
  & Preparatory Department
  EDG B15 .... 125 H5
Edgbaston Shopping Centre
  LDYWD/EDGR B16 .... 126 A4
Edgewood Road Clinic
  RBRY B45 .... 188 B2
Edward Street Hospital
  WBROM B70 .... 87 G3
Electra Park Industrial Estate
  AST/WIT B6 .... 91 H5
Electric Cinema *DIG/EDG* B5 .... 3 F6
The Ellowes Hall School
  SEDG DY3 .... 81 H3
Elmdon Trading Estate
  CHWD/FDBR/MGN B37 .... 149 G1
Elmore Green JMI School
  BLOX/PEL WS3 .... 27 E1
Elms Farm Primary School
  STETCH B33 .... 131 E5
Elms Health Centre *HALE* B63 . 137 F1
Elm Terrace Clinic *OLDBY* B69 . 85 H5
Elston Hall Primary School
  WOLVN WV10 .... 12 D5
Embassy Industrial Estate
  HAG/WOL DY9 .... 136 D2
Emmanuel School *WSL* WS1 .... 4 E5
Empire Industrial Park
  ALDR WS9 .... 29 H2
English Martyrs RC Primary
  School *SPARK* B11 .... 145 E3
Enterprise Trading Estate
  BRLYHL DY5 .... 119 H1
Erdington Hall Primary School
  ERDE/BCHGN B24 .... 92 D4
Erdington Industrial Estate
  ERDE/BCHGN B24 .... 94 B3
Erdington Medical Centre
  ERDW/CRVHL B23 .... 92 C4
Erdington Pool & Turkish Suite
  ERDW/CRVHL B23 .... 93 E2
Essington Light Industrial
  Estate *WNSFLD* WV11 .... 14 D3
Ettingshall Primary School
  BKHL/PFLD WV2 .... 53 F1
Euro Business Park *OLDBY* B69 . 86 C5
European Business Park
  OLDBY B69 .... 104 C3
Eversfield Preparatory School
  SOLH B91 .... 182 A1

Express by Holiday Inn
  HLGN/YWD B28 .... 163 E4
Expressway Industrial Estate
  AST/WIT B6 .... 109 E3
Eye Infirmary
  BDMR/CCFT WV3 .... 6 B4
Fairfax Road *MGN/WHC* B75 .. 63 F3
Fairfield First School
  BRCRVW B61 .... 185 H5
Fairfield Villa FC *BRCRVW* B61 . 185 H5
Fairhaven Primary School
  STRBR DY8 .... 117 H1
Fairway Primary School
  NFLD/LBR B31 .... 176 B3
Falcon Lodge Clinic
  MGN/WHC B75 .... 63 G3
Fallings Heath Cemetery
  DARL/WED WS10 .... 55 H1
Fallings Park Industrial Estate
  WOLVN WV10 .... 23 H5
Fallings Park Primary School
  WOLVN WV10 .... 24 A3
Fazeley Industrial Estate
  DIG/EDG B5 .... 3 K5
Featherstone Primary School
  ERDW/CRVHL B23 .... 92 C2
Feldon Lane Clinic *RMSLY* B62 . 122 C5
Fernbank Medical Centre
  WASH/WDE B8 .... 111 E5
Ferndale Primary School
  GTB/HAM B43 .... 73 G3
Field Road Cemetery
  BLOX/PEL WS3 .... 27 G1
Field Road Industrial Estate
  BLOX/PEL WS3 .... 27 G1
Firs Primary School
  CBROM B36 .... 112 A1
Fir Tree Primary School
  DSYBK/YTR WS5 .... 57 G4
Five Ways Shopping Centre
  EDG B15 .... 126 B3
The Foot Clinic *CBHAMNW* B3 .. 2 E4
Fordhouse Road Industrial
  Estate *WOLVN* WV10 ...... 23 E2
Fordhouses CC *WOLVN* WV10 . 12 D3
Forest Oak School *CBROM* B36 . 95 G5
Forge Trading Estate
  RMSLY B62 .... 139 E2
Formans Trading Estate
  SPARK B11 .... 145 F4
Fort Industrial Park *CVALE* B35 . 94 B5
The Fort Shopping Centre
  ERDE/BCHGN B24 .... 94 C3
Foundry Primary School
  WSNGN B18 .... 107 F3
Fountain Court Hotel
  LDYWD/EDGR B16 .... 125 E3
Four Dwellings High School
  RIDG/WDGT B32 .... 140 B2
Four Dwellings Infant School
  RIDG/WDGT B32 .... 140 B2
Four Oaks J & I School
  FOAKS/STRLY B74 .... 46 C1
Four Oaks Medical Centre
  MGN/WHC B75 .... 47 F3
Four Oaks Saints CC
  FOAKS/STRLY B74 .... 32 C5
Four Seasons Art Gallery
  ERDE/BCHGN B24 .... 93 E1
Fox & Goose Shopping Centre
  WASH/WDE B8 .... 111 G1
The Fox Hollies Leisure Centre
  HLGN/YWD B28 .... 163 E1
Fox Hollies Special School
  ACGN B27 .... 163 E1
Foxhill Estate *SPARK* B11 .... 145 F5
Foxyards Primary School
  TPTN/OCK DY4 .... 84 C1
Frank F Harrison
  Comprehensive School
  SHHTH WV12 .... 26 D5
Frankley Community High
  School *RBRY* B45 .... 173 H5
Frankley Health Centre
  RBRY B45 .... 174 A4
Frankley Industrial Park
  RBRY B45 .... 174 B4
Friar Park Clinic
  DARL/WED WS10 .... 56 A1
Frogmill Junior School
  RBRY B45 .... 174 B3
Gainsborough Trading Estate
  STRBR DY8 .... 135 H3
Garretts Green Trading Estate
  STETCH B33 .... 131 E3
Gas Street Basin *CBHAMW* B1 .. 2 C6
Gatehouse Trading Estate
  BRWNH WS8 .... 9 G3
Gate Medical Centre
  WASH/WDE B8 .... 110 D5
Gay Hill Golf Club *HLYWD* B47 . 178 C5
George Auden School
  NFLD/LBR B31 .... 158 B5
George Betts Primary School
  SMTHWK B66 .... 105 G2
George Dixon School &
  Sixth Form *HRBN* B17 .... 125 E2
George Fentham Endowed
  Primary School
  HIA/OLT B92 .... 167 G4
George Salter High School
  WBROM B70 .... 87 F3
Gibbons Industrial Park
  KGSWFD DY6 .... 100 C2
The Giffard RC Primary School
  DUNHL/THL/PER WV6 ...... 22 B5
Gig Mill Primary School
  STRBR DY8 .... 135 E4
Gilbertstone Primary School
  LGN/SDN/BHAMAIR B26 .. 146 D2
GK Davies Industrial Estate
  HALE B63 .... 137 E1
Glebefields Health Centre
  TPTN/OCK DY4 .... 69 G3
Glebe Fields Primary School
  TPTN/OCK DY4 .... 69 G2
Glenmead J & I School
  KGSTG B44 .... 74 D3
Glynne Primary School
  KGSWFD DY6 .... 99 G5

Golden Hillock School
  SPARK B11 .... 145 F1
Goldtel Industrial Estate
  ETTPK/GDPK/PENN WV4 .. 53 E3
Goldthorne Medical Centre
  BKHL/PFLD WV2 .... 52 A2
Goldthorn Park Primary School
  ETTPK/GDPK/PENN WV4 .. 52 B3
Good Hope Hospital
  MGN/WHC B75 .... 62 D2
Gornal Wood Cemetery
  SEDG DY3 .... 82 D5
Gornal Wood Crematorium
  SEDG DY3 .... 82 D5
Goscote Hospital
  BLOX/PEL WS3 .... 28 B2
Goscote Industrial Estate
  BLOX/PEL WS3 .... 28 A1
Gossey Lane J & I School
  STETCH B33 .... 131 E2
Gracechurch Shopping Centre
  CSCFLD/WYGN B72 .... 62 D5
Grace Mary Primary School
  OLDBY B69 .... 104 A2
Graiseley Primary School
  BKHL/PFLD WV2 .... 37 G5
Granada Industrial Estate
  OLDBY B69 .... 104 D3
Granby Business Park
  STETCH B33 .... 131 F5
Grand Theatre *WOLV* WV1 ...... 7 G4
The Grange Arts & Media
  Centre *WSL* WS1 .... 4 E2
The Grange Playhouse
  WSL WS1 .... 42 D4
The Grange School
  HAG/WOL DY9 .... 136 B3
Gravel Hill Surgery
  WMBN WV5 .... 65 F5
Gravelly Industrial Park
  ERDE/BCHGN B24 .... 110 C1
Grazebrook Industrial Estate
  DUDS DY2 .... 102 B3
Grazebrook Industrial Park
  DUDS DY2 .... 102 B3
Great Barr Business Park
  PBAR/PBCH B42 .... 90 A1
Great Barr Golf Club
  GTB/HAM B43 .... 58 D4
Great Barr Hotel & Conference
  Centre *GTB/HAM* B43 ...... 72 D2
Great Bridge Industrial Estate
  TPTN/OCK DY4 .... 70 A4
Great Bridge Primary School
  TPTN/OCK DY4 .... 70 A4
Great Western Industrial
  Estate *WSNGN* B18 .... 107 G3
Green Acres Primary School
  BILS/COS WV14 .... 54 B2
Greenfield Primary School
  RUSH/SHEL WS4 .... 29 E2
  STRBR DY8 .... 135 F2
Greenfield Surgery
  STRBR DY8 .... 135 F2
Greenholm J & I School
  KGSTG B44 .... 74 B4
Green Lane Industrial Estate
  BORD B9 .... 128 C2
Green Meadow Primary
  School *SLYOAK* B29 .... 158 B3
Green Rock J & I School
  BLOX/PEL WS3 .... 28 A1
Greet Primary School
  SPARK B11 .... 145 F4
Greets Green Road Industrial
  Estate *WBROM* B70 .... 86 D2
Gregston Industrial Estate
  OLDBY B69 .... 105 F1
Grendon Primary School
  ALE/KHTH/YWD B14 ...... 178 C2
Grestone Primary School
  BFLD/HDSWWD B20 .... 89 G2
Greswold Primary School
  SOLH B91 .... 164 D4
Griffin Business Park
  ERDE/BCHGN B24 .... 94 A2
Griffin Industrial Estate
  BLKHTH/ROWR B65 .... 122 D1
Griffins Brook Medical Centre
  SLYOAK B29 .... 159 E3
Grimstock Country House
  Hotel *CSHL/WTROR* B46 .. 97 E5
Grosvenor Shopping Centre
  NFLD/LBR B31 .... 175 C1
Grove Medical Centre
  BKHL/PFLD WV2 .... 37 G5
Grove Primary School
  BKHL/PFLD WV2 .... 52 C1
Grove School *HDSW* B21 ...... 107 H1
Grove Vale Primary School
  GTB/HAM B43 .... 73 F2
Guardian Angels RC Primary
  School *BKDE/SHDE* B34 .. 113 F3
Guest Hospital *DUDN* DY1 .... 85 E5
Gun Barrel Industrial Centre
  CDYHTH B64 .... 138 C1
Guns Village Primary School
  WBROM B70 .... 87 E3
Gunter Primary School
  ERDE/BCHGN B24 .... 94 A2
Gupta Trading Estate
  OLDBY B69 .... 86 D5
Guru Nanak Sikh Temple
  SMTHWK B67 .... 36 D5
Guy Motors Industrial Park
  WOLVN WV10 .... 23 G5
GWS Industrial Estate
  DARL/WED WS10 .... 70 B2
GWS Trading Estate
  TPTN/OCK DY4 .... 70 B2
Haden Hill Leisure Centre
  CDYHTH B64 .... 121 F4
Hadley Stadium *SMTHWK* B66 . 124 C1
Hagley Cemetery
  HAG/WOL DY9 .... 152 D5
Hagley Golf & Country Club
  HAG/WOL DY9 .... 154 A2
Hagley Hall *HAG/WOL* DY9 .. 153 F4
Hagley RC High School
  STRBR DY8 .... 152 B4

Halas Industrial Estate
HALE B63 .....138 D2
Halcyon Gallery *CBHAM* B2 .....3 F6
Halesbury Special School
RMSLY B62 .....122 C4
Halesowen CC *HALE* B63 .....138 D5
Halesowen Cemetery
HALE B63 .....138 C3
Halesowen CE Primary
School *HALE* B63 .....138 C3
Halesowen College *HALE* B63 .....138 C2
Halesowen FC (The Grove
Recreation Ground)
HALE B63 .....138 C2
Halesowen Golf Club
RMSLY B62 .....139 F2
Halesowen Harriers FC
HALE B63 .....137 F2
Halesowen Health Centre
HALE B63 .....138 D1
Halesowen Industrial Park
RMSLY B62 .....138 D1
Halesowen Leisure Centre
HALE B63 .....138 D4
Hall Trading Estate
TPTN/OCK DY4 .....85 H1
Hallfield School *EDG* B15 .....126 A5
Hall Green Cemetery
BILS/COS WV14 .....69 E1
Hall Green J & I School
HHTH/SAND B71 .....71 G2
Hall Green Little Theatre
ACGN B27 .....146 A5
Hall Green Secondary School
HLGN/YWD B28 .....162 C3
Hall Green Stadium
HLGN/YWD B28 .....162 D1
Halimpor Special School
STETCH B33 .....130 D1
Hall of Memory *CBHAMW* B1 .....2 D5
Hamd House School
SMHTH B10 .....128 C4
Ham Dingle Primary School
HAG/WOL DY9 .....136 C5
Hamilton Special School
HDSW B21 .....107 F1
Hams Hall International Freight
Terminal
CSHL/WTROR B46 .....97 G3
Hams Hall National
Distribution Park
CSHL/WTROR B46 .....97 H2
Hamstead Hall School
BFLD/HDSWWD B20 .....75 G5
Hamstead J & I School
GTB/HAM B43 .....73 F4
Handsworth Boys Grammar
School *HDSW* B21 .....107 G1
Handsworth Cemetery
HDSW B21 .....88 D4
Handsworth Golf Club
BFLD/HDSWWD B20 .....89 F2
Handsworth Leisure Centre
BFLD/HDSWWD B20 .....107 H1
Handsworth RFC
GTB/HAM B43 .....58 B4
Handsworth Wood Girls
School & Sixth Form Centre
BFLD/HDSWWD B20 .....89 H4
Harborne Church Farm Golf
Club *HRBN* B17 .....141 H3
Harborne Golf Club
RIDG/WDGT B32 .....141 G2
Harborne Hill School *EDG* B15 .....142 C1
Harborne Pool & Fitness
Centre *HRBN* B17 .....141 H2
Harborne Primary School
HRBN B17 .....142 A1
Harden Primary School
BLOX/PEL WS3 .....28 A3
Hargate Primary School
HHTH/SAND B71 .....87 G2
The Harper Bell School
BHTH/HG B12 .....127 C4
Harry Mitchell Leisure Centre
SMTHWKW B67 .....106 B4
Harvey Road Health Centre
LGN/SDN/BHAMAIR B26 .....130 A5
Harvey Works Industrial
Estate *HALE* B63 .....138 B1
Harvills Hawthorn Primary
School *WBROM* B70 .....70 D4
Hasbury CE Primary School
HALE B63 .....138 B5
Haslucks Green Junior School
SHLY B90 .....180 A2
Hastingwood Industrial Park
ERDE/BCHGN B24 .....93 F5
Hatchford Brook Golf Club
LGN/SDN/BHAMAIR B26 .....148 C3
Hatchford Brook Primary
School *HIA/OLT* B92 .....148 A4
Hatchford Gm Primary School
CHWD/FDBR/MGN B37 .....131 H2
Hateley Heath Primary School
HHTH/SAND B71 .....71 F4
Hatherton Lane Primary
School *WSLW* WS2 .....26 D4
Hawbush Primary School
BRLYHL DY5 .....118 D2
Hawkesley Church Primary
School *HWK/WKHTH* B38 .....190 C1
Hawkesley Health Centre
HWK/WKHTH B38 .....190 C1
Hawksmill Industrial Estate
SMHTH B10 .....128 A3
Hawthorne Primary School
KGSTG B44 .....75 C4
Hawthorns Business Centre
SMTHWK B66 .....106 C1
Hawthorns Industrial Estate
SMTHWK B66 .....106 D1
Haybridge High School &
Sixth Form
STRBR DY8 .....152 B4
Hayes Trading Estate
HAG/WOL DY9 .....137 E1
The Hayes Trading Estate
HAG/WOL DY9 .....137 E1

Hayley Green Hospital
HALE B63 .....154 D2
Hayward Industrial Park
ALDR WS9 .....30 A3
Hazel Oak School *SHLY* B90 .....180 A3
Healthcare Clinic
CSCFLD/WYGN B72 .....77 F3
The Heartlands High School
VAUX/NECH B7 .....109 G5
Heath Clinic *SOLH* B91 .....165 F5
Heathfield Foundation Technology
College *CDYHTH* B64 .....121 F2
Heathfield Primary School
LOZ/NWT B19 .....108 C1
Heathlands Primary (NC)
School *BKDE/SHDE* B34 .....112 B2
Heath Lane Cemetery
HHTH/SAND B71 .....71 H4
Heath Lane Hospital
HHTH/SAND B71 .....71 H4
Heath Lodge Hotel
CHWD/FDBR/MGN B37 .....132 D4
Heath Mount Primary School
BHTH/HG B12 .....144 A1
Heath Park High School
WOLVN WV10 .....24 A5
Heath Street Industrial Estate
SMTHWK B66 .....107 F4
Heath Town Leisure Centre
WOLVN WV10 .....38 A1
The High Arcal Secondary
School *SEDG* DY3 .....67 H5
Highclare St Paul's School
FOAKS/STRLY B74 .....62 B1
Highclare School
CSCFLD/WYGN B72 .....77 G2
Highclare the Abbey School
ERDW/GRVHL B23 .....92 B3
Highcroft Hospital
ERDW/GRVHL B23 .....92 B3
Highfield Primary School
WASH/WDE B8 .....110 C4
Highfields Primary School
BILS/COS WV14 .....68 C1
BLKHTH/ROWR B65 .....122 A4
Highfields School
ETTPK/GDPK/PENN WV4 .....50 B3
Highgate Business Centre
BHTH/HG B12 .....144 D1
Highgate Medical Centre
BHTH/HG B12 .....127 F5
Highgate Primary School
DUDS DY2 .....101 H5
Highgate Retail Park
BHTH/HG B12 .....127 F5
Highgate Trading Estate
BHTH/HG B12 .....127 G5
Highgate United FC *SHLY* B90 .....193 G2
High Meadow Infant School
CSHL/WTROR B46 .....115 F1
Highters Heath J & I School
ALE/KHTH/YWD B14 .....178 D2
Hillary Primary School
WSLW WS2 .....56 C1
Hill Avenue Primary School
ETTPK/GDPK/PENN WV4 .....52 D5
Hillcrest Business Park
DUDS DY2 .....102 C2
Hillcrest Industrial Estate
CDYHTH B64 .....120 D4
Hillcrest School & Community
College *DUDS* DY2 .....102 B4
Hillcrest School & Sixth Form
Centre *RIDG/WDGT* B32 .....141 E4
Hillmeads Health Centre
HWK/WKHTH B38 .....177 E4
Hillstone Primary School
BKDE/SHDE B34 .....113 F4
Hill Top Industrial Estate
WBROM B70 .....70 D3
Hilltop Medical Centre
LGLYGN/QTN B68 .....123 G2
Hilltop Public Golf Course
HDSW B21 .....89 E2
Hilton Cross Business Park
WOLVN WV10 .....13 H1
Hilton Main Industrial Estate
WNSFLD WV11 .....14 A2
Hilton Trading Estate
ETTPK/GDPK/PENN WV4 .....52 D4
Himley Country Hotel
SEDG DY3 .....81 F3
Himley Hall Golf Centre
SEDG DY3 .....82 A2
Himley Hall & Park *SEDG* DY3 .....81 H2
Himley House Hotel *SEDG* DY3 .....81 C3
Himley Plantation
Nature Reserve *WMBN* WV5 .....81 E3
Hingley Industrial Park
DUDS DY2 .....120 C3
Hive Industrial Centre
WSNGN B18 .....108 A3
HM Prison *WSNGN* B18 .....107 G4
Hobden Primary School
HAG/WOL DY9 .....136 C5
Hobmoor Primary School
YDLY B25 .....129 H4
Hobs Moat Medical Centre
HIA/OLT B92 .....147 G5
Hockley Brook Trading Estate
WSNGN B18 .....108 A3
Hockley Heath Pavilion
(Sports Centre)
HOCK/TIA B94 .....198 A5
Hockley Hill Industrial Estate
WSNGN B18 .....108 A4
Hodge Hill Girls School
CBROM B36 .....111 G2
Hodge Hill School
CBROM B36 .....111 G2
Holiday Inn *SOLH* B91 .....181 H2
Hollemeade Infant School
CSCFLD/WYGN B72 .....62 C4
Holland Industrial Park
DARL/WED WS10 .....40 B5
Holliday Wharf *CBHAMW* B1 .....2 D7
The Hollies Clinic
LGLYGN/QTN B68 .....105 F5
Hollies Industrial Estate
BDMR/CCFT WV3 .....6 D7

Holloway Bank Trading Estate
DARL/WED WS10 .....70 D2
Holly Bush Medical Centre
RIDG/WDGT B32 .....123 H5
Hollyfield Primary School
MGN/WHC B75 .....63 F4
Holly Hall Clinic *DUDN* DY1 .....101 H2
Hollyhedge Primary School
HHTH/SAND B71 .....72 A3
Holly Hill Infant School
RBRY B45 .....173 H5
Holly Lane Cemetery
SMTHWKW B67 .....105 H4
Holly Lodge High School
SMTHWKW B67 .....105 H4
Holly Park Industrial Estate
ERDE/BCHGN B24 .....93 C4
Hollywood Primary School
ALE/KHTH/YWD B14 .....178 C4
Holte School *LOZ/NWT* B19 .....108 D2
Holt Farm Primary School
RMSLY B62 .....122 C3
Holy Child School *EDG* B15 .....126 B4
Holy Cross Catholic Primary
School *WALM/CURD* B76 .....63 C5
Holy Family RC Primary School
SMHTH B10 .....128 C5
Holyhead Primary School
DARL/WED WS10 .....55 F5
Holyhead School *HDSW* B21 .....107 F1
Holy Name RC Primary School
GTB/HAM B43 .....73 G2
Holy Rosary RC Primary School
WOLV WV1 .....38 A4
Holy Souls RC Primary School
ACGN B27 .....146 C4
Holy Trinity Catholic Primary
School *WOLV* WV1 .....38 A4
Holy Trinity CE Primary School
BFLD/HDSWWD B20 .....90 C4
BRWNH WS8 .....18 D1
WBROM B70 .....87 H5
Holy Trinity RC School
SMHTH B10 .....128 A4
Holywell Primary School
RBRY B45 .....187 F1
Horrell Road Health Centre
LGN/SDN/BHAMAIR B26 .....130 C5
Horse Shoe Associated FC
SHLY B90 .....193 H2
Hotel Clarine
LDYWD/EDGR B16 .....125 G3
Hotel du Vin & Bistro
CBHAMNW B3 .....3 F4
Hotel Ibis *CBHAMW* B1 .....126 D3
DIG/EDG B5 .....3 G7
SMHTH B10 .....127 H3
Howard Street Industrial
Estate *WBROM* B70 .....70 D4
Howley Grange Primary
School *RMSLY* B62 .....140 A2
HRS Business Park
STETCH B33 .....130 D3
HRS Industrial Estate
STETCH B33 .....131 E3
Hudson Industrial Estate
BKHL/PFLD WV2 .....52 D1
Hulbert Industrial Estate
DUDS DY2 .....102 B3
Huntingtree Primary School
HALE B63 .....138 A3
Hurst Business Park
BRLYHL DY5 .....101 H5
Hurstgreen Primary School
RMSLY B62 .....122 C4
Hurst Hill Primary School
BILS/COS WV14 .....68 A3
Hydesville Tower School
WSL WS1 .....5 H2
IKEA store Wednesbury
DARL/WED WS10 .....56 A2
Ikon Gallery *CBHAMW* B1 .....2 C5
IMAX Cinema *DIG/EDG* B5 .....3 K4
Imex Business Park
BKHL/PFLD WV2 .....52 A1
BORD B9 .....128 B2
SPARK B11 .....145 H1
STETCH B33 .....111 H4
TPTN/OCK DY4 .....85 G3
Imex Industrial Estate
WSNGN B18 .....108 A5
Indian High Commission
WSNGN B18 .....2 C1
Industrial Kingston Estate
BORD B9 .....127 G3
Industrial Weston Estate
SPARK B11 .....145 G3
Infant Welfare Clinic
DARL/WED WS10 .....73 C1
Inkeeper's Hotel *DOR/KN* B93 .....197 H5
Innkeeper's Lodge
HIA/OLT B92 .....147 H3
KGSWFD DY6 .....99 G3
RIDG/WDGT B32 .....123 H5
The Innkeeper's Lodge Hotel
SCFLD/BOLD B73 .....60 C3
International Convention
Centre *CBHAMW* B1 .....2 C5
International School &
Community College
STETCH B33 .....131 F1
Izons Lane Industrial Estate
WBROM B70 .....86 D5
Jack o'Watton Business Park
CSHL/WTROR B46 .....96 D3
Jack o'Watton Industrial
Estate *CSHL/WTROR* B46 .....96 D3
James Bridge Cemetery
DARL/WED WS10 .....40 D5
James Watt Industrial Park
SMTHWK B66 .....107 E3
Jamia Mosque
DUNHL/THL/PER WV6 .....6 A1
Jane Lane Special School
DARL/WED WS10 .....40 B5
Janet Shaw Clinic
CHWD/FDBR/MGN B37 .....132 A4
JAS Industrial Park
OLDBY B69 .....104 C5
Jerome Retail Park *WSL* WS1 .....4 C5

Jervoise J & I School
SLYOAK B29 .....158 C1
Jessons CE First & Middle
School *DUDN* DY1 .....84 A5
Jewellery Quarter *WSNGN* B18 .....2 C1
The Jewellery Quarter
Discovery Centre
WSNGN B18 .....108 B4
Jewish Cemetery *AST/WIT* B6 .....91 G1
JFK Memorial *CBHAMNE* B4 .....3 F3
John Black Day Hospital
CHWD/FDBR/MGN B37 .....132 B4
John Willmott School
WALM/CURD B76 .....63 F4
Joseph Chamberlain Sixth
Form College
BHTH/HG B12 .....127 F5
Joseph Leckie Comprehensive
School *WSL* WS1 .....57 E3
Joseph Turner Primary School
TPTN/OCK DY4 .....69 H4
Josiah Mason College
CVALE B35 .....94 D3
DUDN DY1 .....101 H1
KGSTG B44 .....74 D2
MOS/BIL B13 .....144 A5
Jubilee Business Park
HAG/WOL DY9 .....136 D2
Jubilee Park Primary School
TPTN/OCK DY4 .....69 H5
Junction 2 Industrial Estate
OLDBY B69 .....104 D3
Junction 6 Industrial Park
AST/WIT B6 .....91 H4
Junction Industrial Estate
SMTHWK B66 .....106 B2
Jurys Inn
CBHAMW B1 .....2 C6
Karis Medical Centre
LDYWD/EDGR B16 .....125 H3
Kates Hill Primary School
DUDS DY2 .....103 E1
Kelvin Way Trading Estate
WBROM B70 .....105 F1
Key Business Park
ERDE/BCHGN B24 .....93 H3
Key Hill Cemetery
WSNGN B18 .....2 B1
Key Industrial Park
WLNHL WV13 .....38 D2
Keyway Retail Park
WLNHL WV13 .....39 H5
Khalsa Industrial Estate
SMTHWK B66 .....107 F5
Kineton Green Infant School
ACGN B27 .....163 H1
King Charles Primary School
WSLW WS2 .....40 D3
King David Primary School
MOS/BIL B13 .....144 B5
King Edwards School (Boys)
EDG B15 .....143 E3
King Edwards VI Aston School
AST/WIT B6 .....109 E1
King Edwards VI Handsworth
School *BFLD/HDSWWD* B20 .....108 A2
King Edward VI Camp Hill
School for Boys
ALE/KHTH/YWD B14 .....160 D3
King Edward VI Camp Hill
School For Girls
BVILLE B30 .....160 D2
King Edward VI College
STRBR DY8 .....135 G1
King Edward VI Five Ways
School *RIDG/WDGT* B32 .....157 G2
King Edward VI Girls High
School *EDG* B15 .....143 E3
Kingfisher Industrial Estate
WBROM B70 .....86 C2
Kingfisher Primary School
CBROM B36 .....114 A1
King George V Primary School
HHTH/SAND B71 .....88 A3
Kingsbury Business Park
WALM/CURD B76 .....79 G5
Kingsbury School
ERDE/BCHGN B24 .....92 D4
Kings Business Park
GTB/HAM B43 .....59 H5
The Kings CE School
DUNHL/THL/PER WV6 .....21 F5
Kings Cinema *WBROM* B70 .....87 H3
Kings Heath Boys School
MOS/BIL B13 .....161 G4
Kings Heath CC
ALE/KHTH/YWD B14 .....161 H1
Kings Hill Business Park
DARL/WED WS10 .....55 G4
Kings Hill Clinic
DARL/WED WS10 .....55 G3
Kings Hill JMI School
DARL/WED WS10 .....55 G3
Kingshurst City Technology
College
CHWD/FDBR/MGN B37 .....132 B1
Kingshurst Clinic
CHWD/FDBR/MGN B37 .....114 A4
Kingshurst J & I School
CHWD/FDBR/MGN B37 .....114 A3
Kingsland Primary School
KGSTG B44 .....60 B4
Kings Norton Boys School
BVILLE B30 .....176 C1
Kings Norton Business Centre
BVILLE B30 .....176 D1
Kings Norton Girls School
BVILLE B30 .....159 C5
Kings Norton High School
HWK/WKHTH B38 .....176 C4
Kings Norton Primary School
BVILLE B30 .....177 E2
Kingsrise Community Primary
School *KGSTG* B44 .....75 H1
Kings Road Industrial Estate
YDLY B25 .....145 H1
Kingstanding Leisure Centre
KGSTG B44 .....75 H3
Kingstanding Special School
KGSTG B44 .....75 E2

Kingsthorne Primary School
KGSTG B44 .....75 G2
The Kingswinford Secondary
School *KGSWFD* DY6 .....99 F3
Kingswood School
SHLY B90 .....180 B3
Kitwell J & I School
RIDG/WDGT B32 .....157 E3
Klaxon Industrial Estate
SPARK B11 .....145 H3
Knowle CE Primary School
DOR/KN B93 .....197 G1
Knowle & Dorridge CC
DOR/KN B93 .....197 E4
Knowle FC *DOR/KN* B93 .....197 G1
Knowle Village CC
DOR/KN B93 .....197 G1
La Caverna Hotel
LGN/SDN/BHAMAIR B26 .....148 A3
Ladypool Primary School
SPARK B11 .....144 D1
Ladywood Arts & Leisure
Centre *LDYWD/EDGR* B16 .....125 G2
Ladywood Middleway Health
Centre *CBHAMW* B1 .....126 A1
Lakeside JM School
WLNHL WV13 .....39 E2
Lakeside Medical Centre
DUNHL/THL/PER WV6 .....34 C1
Lane Lane Primary School
HLGN/YWD B28 .....163 E2
Lanchester School *CBROM* B36 .....95 C5
Lane Green First School
CDSL WV8 .....10 D3
The Lane Medical Centre
BHTH/HG B12 .....144 D2
Lanesfield Primary School
ETTPK/GDPK/PENN WV4 .....53 E5
The Lanes Shopping Centre
SCFLD/BOLD B73 .....77 F4
Langley High School
LGLYGN/QTN B68 .....105 F5
Langley Primary School
HIA/OLT B92 .....163 H3
OLDBY B69 .....104 D4
Langley School *HIA/OLT* B92 .....163 H3
Langley Special School
LGLYGN/QTN B68 .....63 G2
Langley Swimming Centre
LGLYGN/QTN B68 .....105 F5
Lansdowne Health Centre
WSNGN B18 .....107 H5
Lapal Primary School
RMSLY B62 .....139 H5
Lasercare Clinics *EDG* B15 .....126 B4
Laurie Pike Health Centre
AST/WIT B6 .....108 D1
Leamore Industrial Estate
WSLW WS2 .....27 E3
Leamore Primary School
BLOX/PEL WS3 .....27 G3
Lea Road Medical Practice
BDMR/CCFT WV3 .....36 C5
Leasowes Community College
RMSLY B62 .....139 G1
Leaverstock Industrial Estate
STETCH B33 .....131 E3
Lee Bank Business Centre
CBHAMW B1 .....2 E7
Lego Brothers Industrial
Estate
ETTPK/GDPK/PENN WV4 .....52 D5
Leigh J & I (NC) School
WASH/WDE B8 .....110 C3
Leighswood Junior School
ALDR WS9 .....30 B3
Leighswood School *ALDR* WS9 .....30 B3
Lemar Industrial Estate
BVILLE B30 .....160 C1
Lennon Indoor Market
KGSTG B44 .....60 C5
Leona Industrial Estate
RMSLY B62 .....122 B3
Leviss Industrial Estate
STETCH B33 .....111 H5
Lewisham Industrial Estate
SMTHWK B66 .....106 C2
Leyhill Health Centre
NFLD/LBR B31 .....158 A4
Ley Hill Primary School
NFLD/LBR B31 .....157 H5
Leys Industrial Estate
BRLYHL DY5 .....118 C4
Lickey Hills Country Park
RBRY B45 .....188 A4
Lickey Hills Golf Club
RBRY B45 .....188 A4
Lifford Trading Estate
BVILLE B30 .....177 E1
Light Hall School *SHLY* B90 .....180 B4
Light House Cinema
WOLV WV1 .....7 G3
Lightwoods Primary School
LGLYGN/QTN B68 .....123 H4
Linden Road Instruction
Swimming Pool
BVILLE B30 .....159 H3
Lindens Primary School
FOAKS/STRLY B74 .....60 B2
Lindley Lodge Industrial Estate
ALDR WS9 .....29 G4
Lindsworth North School
ERDW/GRVHL B23 .....77 E5
Lindsworth School
BVILLE B30 .....177 G2
Link One Industrial Park
TPTN/OCK DY4 .....70 C5
Linkwood Industrial Estate
STRBR DY8 .....135 F2
Lion Industrial Park *ALDR* WS9 .....30 A1
Little Aston CP School
FOAKS/STRLY B74 .....32 A4
Little Aston Golf Club
FOAKS/STRLY B74 .....45 H1
Little Bloxwich CE (V) School
BLOX/PEL WS3 .....17 F4
Little London JMI School
WLNHL WV13 .....39 G3
Locarno Primary School
TPTN/OCK DY4 .....69 F5

The Lock Museum
WLNHL WV13 .... **39** F4
Lode Heath School *SOLH* B91 ...**165** E4
Lodge Farm Primary School
SHHTH WV12 .... **40** C1
Lodge Forge Trading Estate
CDYHTH B64 .... **120** C5
Lodge Hill Cemetery
SLYOAK B29 .... **158** D1
Lodge Hill Crematorium
SLYOAK B29 .... **141** H5
Lodge Primary School
WBROM B70 .... **87** F3
Long Acre Trading Estate
VAUX/NECH B7 .... **109** H2
Long Knowle Primary School
WNSFLD WV11 .... **24** C2
Long Lane Medical Centre
RMSLY B62 .... **122** B3
Long Lane Trading Estate
RMSLY B62 .... **122** B3
Longmoor Special School
SCFLD/BOLD B73 .... **60** D4
Longwill Special School
HRBN B17 .... **158** C5
Lordswood Boys School
HRBN B17 .... **124** C4
Lordswood Girls School
HRBN B17 .... **124** D4
Lordswood Medical Practice
HRBN B17 .... **141** H1
Lower Farm JMI School
BLOX/PEL WS3 .... **17** E3
Lower Gornal Health Centre
SEDG DY3 .... **82** D4
Low Hill Medical Centre
WOLVN WV10 .... **23** G3
Loxdale Industrial Estate
BILS/COS WV14 .... **54** A4
Loxdale Primary School
BILS/COS WV14 .... **54** B4
Lozells Primary School
LOZ/NWT B19 .... **108** D2
Lugman Medical Centre
WSL WS1 .... **56** D1
Lutley Primary School
HALE B63 .... **154** D1
Lye Business Centre
BRLYHL DY5 .... **119** H5
Lye CC *HAG/WOL* DY9 .... **136** B2
Lye Town FC *HAG/WOL* DY9 .... **136** B2
Lye Valley Industrial Estate
HAG/WOL DY9 .... **136** D1
Lye & Wollescote Cemetery
HAG/WOL DY9 .... **136** C3
Lyndon Green J & I School
LGN/SDN/BHAMAIR B26 ....**147** F1
Lyndon School *HIA/OLT* B92 .....**147** G4
Lyng Primary School
WBROM B70 .... **87** G5
Macdonald Burlington Hotel
CBHAM B2 .... **3** F5
Magmeal Industrial Estate
LDYWD/EDGR B16 ....**125** H1
Maidensbridge Primary School
KGSWFD DY6 .... **81** F5
The Mailbox *CBHAMW* B1 ....**2** E6
Mainstream Forty Seven
Industrial Park
VAUX/NECH B7 .... **110** A4
Mainstream Industrial Park
VAUX/NECH B7 .... **110** A5
Malmaison Hotel *CBHAMW* B1 .....**2** E7
Malt Mill Lane Trading Estate
RMSLY B62 .... **122** B4
Mander Shopping Centre
WOLV WV1 .... **7** F4
Manders Industrial Estate
WOLVN WV10 .... **37** H2
Maney Hill Primary School
CSCFLD/WYGN B72 .... **71** H1
The Manor General Hospital
WSLW WS2 .... **41** G4
Manor High School (Foundation)
DARL/WED WS10 .... **56** D5
Manor Industrial Estate
WSLW WS2 .... **4** A4
Manor Park Primary School
AST/WIT B6 .... **109** C1
Manor Primary School
BILS/COS WV14 .... **68** B1
FOAKS/STRLY B74 .... **45** C4
Manor Way Primary School
HALE B63 .... **139** E4
Mansfield Green Primary School
WSLW WS2 .... **41** F2
Maple Business Park
VAUX/NECH B7 .... **109** H3
Maple Leaf Industrial Estate
WSL2 .... **41** F2
Marlborough J & I School
SMHTH B10 .... **128** C3
Marlow Estate
BLKHTH/ROWR B65 ....**121** H3
Marshalls Industrial Estate
BKHL/PFLD WV2 .... **52** A1
Marsh Hill Primary School
ERDW/GRVHL B23 .... **91** H2
Marston Green Clinic
CHWD/FDBR/MGN B37 .....**132** A5
Marston Green Infant School
CHWD/FDBR/MGN B37 .....**132** A5
Marston Green Junior School
CHWD/FDBR/MGN B37 .....**132** A5
Marston Road Industrial Estate
BKHL/PFLD WV2 .... **52** A1
Mary Elliot School
WSLW WS2 .... **42** A1
Maryvale Catholic Primary
School *KGSTG* B44 .... **75** F1
Maryvale Institute *KGSTG* B44 .....**75** F1
Maternity Welfare Clinic
ETTPK/GDPK/PENN WV4 .....**50** D2
Matthew Boulton College of
Further & Higher Education
CBHAMNE B4 .... **3** J3
DIG/EDG B5 .... **126** D4
Matthew Boulton Community
Primary School
HDSW WV1 .... **107** G2

Maybrook Industrial Estate
BRWNH WS8 .... **19** F2
The Mayfair Centre *CBHAM* B2 ...**3** G6
Mayfield Preparatory School
WSL WS1 .... **5** H6
Mayfield Special School
LOZ/NWT B19 .... **108** C1
Maypole Health Centre
ALE/KHTH/YWD B14 ....**178** B2
Meadow Green Primary School
HLYWD B47 .... **192** C5
Meadows Primary School
NFLD/LBR B31 .... **175** E3
Meadow View JMI School
GTB/HAM B43 .... **59** H3
Meadwood Industrial Estate
BILS/COS WV14 .... **54** A3
Media Centre *WOLV* WV1 ....**7** G3
Meeting Lane Industrial
Estate *BRLYHL* DY5 .... **118** D3
Megabowl *BRLYHL* DY5 .... **119** F2
Menzies High School
HHTH/SAND B71 .... **71** C3
Mere Green Combined School
MGN/WHC B75 .... **47** F3
Merridale Cemetery
BDMR/CCFT WV3 .... **6** A7
Merridale Primary School
BDMR/CCFT WV3 .... **6** A6
Merry Hill Shopping Centre
BRLYHL DY5 .... **119** H2
Merstone School
CHWD/FDBR/MGN B37 .....**132** A3
Mesty Croft Primary School
DARL/WED WS10 .... **56** A5
Metalloys Industrial Estate
WALM/CURD B76 .... **94** D1
Middlemore Business Park
ALDR WS9 .... **29** C4
Middlemore Industrial Estate
HDSW B21 .... **88** D5
SMTHWK B66 .... **106** D1
Middleton Trading Estate
WLNHL WV13 .... **39** E3
Middleway Industrial Estate
BHTH/HG B12 .... **127** F5
Midland House Dawley
Trading Estate *KGSWFD* DY6 .**99** H1
Midland Institute *CBHAMW* B5 ...**2** E4
Midlands Arts Centre Cinema
BHTH/HG B12 .... **143** H3
Milking Bank Primary School
DUDN DY1 .... **83** G4
Millard Industrial Estate
WBROM B70 .... **87** E5
Millbrook Industrial Estate
WOLVN WV10 .... **23** F3
Millfield CP School *BRWNH* WS8 ...**9** C5
Millfield Special School
HHTH/SAND B71 .... **71** H5
Mill Lodge Primary School
SHLY B90 .... **179** C3
Minworth Industrial Park
WALM/CURD B76 .... **78** D5
WALM/CURD B76 .... **95** F1
Minworth J & I School
WALM/CURD B76 .... **95** F1
Moat Farm J & I School
LGLYGN/QTN B68 .... **123** C1
Mobarak Health Centre
BHTH/HG B12 .... **144** A2
Monarch Industrial Estate
SPARK B11 .... **146** A2
Monkspath Business Park
SHLY B90 .... **181** E5
Monkspath Primary School
SHLY B90 .... **195** H2
Mommer Close Industrial Estate
WLNHL WV13 .... **39** H2
Monmore Business Park
BKHL/PFLD WV2 .... **52** D1
Monmore Green Greyhound Stadium
BKHL/PFLD WV2 .... **38** A5
Monmore Park Industrial Estate
BKHL/PFLD WV2 .... **52** D1
Montgomery Primary School
SPARK B11 .... **128** A5
Montgomery Street Business Centre
SPARK B11 .... **145** F1
Monway Industrial Estate
DARL/WED WS10 .... **55** F5
Monyhull Hospital *BVILLE* B30 ...**177** H2
The Moore Group Business
Centre *WSL* WS1 .... **4** E7
Moor Green FC
HLGN/YWD B28 .... **162** C3
Moor Green J & I School
MOS/BIL B13 .... **160** C1
Moor Green Sports Centre
SLYOAK B29 .... **143** C5
Moor Green Sports Centre
WSL WS1 .... **4** E7
Moor Hall Golf Club
MGN/WHC B75 .... **47** H4
Moor Hall Primary School
MGN/WHC B75 .... **47** H3
Moorlands Primary School
HHTH/SAND B71 .... **71** F3
Moor Lane Trading Estate
AST/WIT B6 .... **91** F2
Moor Street Industrial Estate
BRLYHL DY5 .... **119** C2
Moreton Community School
WOLVN WV10 .... **23** H1
Moseley CC *SHLY* B90 .... **163** C5
Moseley CE Primary School
MOS/BIL B13 .... **144** B5
Moseley Golf Club
ALE/KHTH/YWD B14 ....**161** C2
Moseley Hall Hospital
MOS/BIL B13 .... **144** A1
Moseley Old Hall (NT)
WOLVN WV10 .... **13** C2
Moseley Park School &
Technology College
BILS/COS WV14 .... **39** E1
Moseley School *MOS/BIL* B13 ...**145** E5
Mossley Clinic *BLOX/PEL* WS3 ...**26** D1
Mossley Primary School
BLOX/PEL WS3 .... **16** B5

The Mount Hotel
DUNHL/THL/PER WV6 ....**35** E3
Mount Pleasant Primary
School *BRLYHL* DY5 .... **119** C3
Mount Street Business Centre
VAUX/NECH B7 .... **110** A3
Mount Street Business Park
VAUX/NECH B7 .... **110** B2
Moxley Industrial Centre
DARL/WED WS10 .... **55** E5
Moxley Medical Centre
DARL/WED WS10 .... **55** E2
Mucklow Hill Industrial Estate
RMSLY B62 .... **139** E2
Mucklow Hill Trading Estate
RMSLY B62 .... **139** E2
Municipal Art Gallery
WOLV WV1 .... **7** F3
Munrow Sports Centre
EDG B15 .... **142** D3
Nansen J & I School
WASH/WDE B8 .... **110** D4
National Exhibition Centre
BHAMNEC B40 .... **150** A2
National Indoor Arena
CBHAMW B1 .... **2** B5
National Institute of
Conductive Education
MOS/BIL B13 .... **143** H3
National Motorcycle Museum
HIA/OLT B92 .... **150** C4
National Sea Life Centre
LDYWD/EDGR B16 .... **2** B5
The Natural Health Centre
HW/WKHTH B38 .... **176** D3
Nature Park *WALM/CURD* B76 ...**94** C1
Neachells Lane Industrial
Estate *WNSFLD* WV11 ....**38** D1
Nechells Primary School
VAUX/NECH B7 .... **110** A1
Nelson Mandela Primary
School *BHTH/HG* B12 ....**144** C2
Nelson Primary School
CBHAMW B1 .... **2** A4
Neptune Industrial Estate
WLNHL WV13 .... **39** H5
Netherbrook Primary School
DUDS DY2 .... **84** A2
Netherton Business Park
DUDS DY2 .... **120** D1
Netherton CC *DUDS* DY2 ....**102** B5
Netherton CE Primary School
DUDS DY2 .... **102** B4
Network Park Industrial
Estate *VAUX/NECH* B7 ....**110** A5
The New Art Gallery Walsall
WSLW WS2 .... **4** C3
Newbridge Preparatory School
DUNHL/THL/PER WV6 ....**36** A1
New Cross Hospital
WNSFLD WV11 .... **24** B5
New Cross Industrial Estate
WOLV WV1 .... **38** A2
Newfield Park Primary School
HALE B63 .... **138** C2
New Hall Hotel
WALM/CURD B76 .... **78** A1
New Hall J & I School
MGN/WHC B75 .... **63** H3
Newhampton Arts Centre
WOLV WV1 .... **6** D2
New Invention Junior School
SHHTH WV12 .... **26** A3
Newman College of Higher
Education *RIDG/WDGT* B32 ..**157** G2
Newshire Industrial Estate
SPARK B11 .... **145** F1
Newton Industrial Estate
BORD B9 .... **128** B2
Newtown Health Centre
LOZ/NWT B19 .... **108** D3
Newtown Primary School
WBROM B70 .... **86** B3
Newtown Shopping Centre
LOZ/NWT B19 .... **109** E3
Ninestiles School
ACGN B27 .... **163** F1
Nonsuch Primary School
RIDG/WDGT B32 .... **140** D5
Norfolk House School
EDG B15 .... **125** F4
Norman Green Sports Centre &
Athletics Track *SOLH* B91 ...**181** G2
Northbrook Health Centre
SHLY B90 .... **163** G5
Northfield Manor Primary
School *SLYOAK* B29 .... **158** D3
Northfield Pool & Fitness
Centre *NFLD/LBR* B31 ....**175** F2
Northfield Road Primary
School *DUDS* DY2 .... **102** D4
Northicote Secondary School
WOLVN WV10 .... **13** E4
Northmoor Industrial Estate
BRLYHL DY5 .... **119** F1
Northside Business Centre
WSNGN B18 .... **107** C4
North Solihull Sports Centre
& Track
DARL/WED WS10 .... **56** A5
North Street Industrial
Estate *BRLYHL* DY5 .... **119** E2
North Worcestershire Golf
Club *NFLD/LBR* B31 ....**174** D3
Novotel
CBHAMW B1 .... **2** B6
LGN/SDN/BHAMAIR B26 .....**149** G3
WOLV WV1 .... **7** H4
Oak Cottage Primary School
SOLH B91 .... **164** A4
Oakdale Trading Estate
KGSWFD DY6 .... **81** H5
KGSWFD DY6 .... **100** A1
Oakeswell Health Centre
DARL/WED WS10 .... **56** A5
Oakham Primary School
OLDBY B69 .... **103** H2
Oak House *WBROM* B70 ....**87** F4
The Oak Industrial Park
KGSWFD DY6 .... **82** A5

Oaklands Primary School
ACGN B27 .... **146** C5
Oakleigh Trading Estate
BILS/COS WV14 .... **68** B1
Oak Meadow Primary School
WNSFLD WV11 .... **25** G3
The Oaks Primary School
ALE/KHTH/YWD B14 ....**177** H3
Oak Street Industrial Estate
CDYHTH B64 .... **120** D3
Oak Street Trading Centre
BRLYHL DY5 .... **119** H5
Oakwood Special School
ALDR WS9 .... **19** G4
Ocker Hill J & I School
TPTN/OCK DY4 .... **70** A3
Odeon Cinema *CBHAM* B2 ....**3** G6
CSCFLD/WYGN B72 .... **62** B5
Ogley Hay Infant School
BRWNH WS8 .... **9** F4
Oldbury Business Centre
OLDBY B69 .... **123** E2
Oldbury Green Retail Park
OLDBY B69 .... **104** D1
Oldbury Health Centre
OLDBY B69 .... **105** E1
Oldbury Leisure Centre
OLDBY B69 .... **104** C3
Oldbury Road Industrial
Estate *SMTHWK* B66 ....**105** H2
WBROM B70 .... **86** D4
Oldbury United FC
BLKHTH/ROWR B65 ....**122** C1
Old Bush Trading Estate
BRLYHL DY5 .... **119** C1
Old Church CE Primary School
DARL/WED WS10 .... **55** E2
Old Edwardians Sports Club
SHLY B90 .... **163** G5
Oldfield Trading Estate
CDYHTH B64 .... **120** D4
Old Forge Trading Estate
HAG/WOL DY9 .... **135** H2
Old Halesonians RFC
BLOX/PEL WS3 .... **153** H2
Old Hall Industrial Estate
BLOX/PEL WS3 .... **27** G2
Oldhall Special School
WSLW WS2 .... **26** C5
Old Hill CC *CDYHTH* B64 ....**121** F4
Old Hill Primary School
CDYHTH B64 .... **121** F3
Oldknow Junior School
SMHTH B10 .... **128** C5
Old Limberlost Sports Club
BFLD/HDSWWD B20 ....**90** A3
Old Park Industrial Estate
DARL/WED WS10 .... **55** C3
Old Park Primary School
DARL/WED WS10 .... **55** C3
Old Park Special School
DUDN DY1 .... **101** H1
Old Rep Theatre *DIG/EDG* B5 .....**3** J7
The Old Square Shopping
Centre *WSL* WS1 .... **4** E4
Oldswinford CE Primary
School *STRBR* DY8 .... **135** G4
Old Swinford Hospital School
STRBR DY8 .... **135** G5
Olive Hill Primary School
RMSLY B62 .... **122** B5
Olton Golf Club *SOLH* B91 ....**164** C3
One Stop Retail Park
PBAR/PBCH B42 .... **90** D3
Open University *HRBN* B17 ....**142** B1
Oratory RC Primary School
LDYWD/EDGR B16 .... **125** H2
Orchard Lane Clinic
HAG/WOL DY9 .... **136** C1
The Orchard School
SMTHWK B66 .... **106** A2
Orthodontists Surgery
SPARK B11 .... **146** A4
Osborne Primary School
ERDW/GRVHL B23 .... **93** E1
Ounsdale High School
WMBN WV5 .... **64** D4
Ounsdale Sports Centre
WMBN WV5 .... **64** D4
Our Lady of Compassion RC
Primary School
HIA/OLT B92 .... **163** H3
Our Lady of Fatima RC Primary
School *HRBN* B17 .... **124** B5
Our Lady of Lourdes RC
Primary School
MOS/BIL B13 .... **162** B5
Our Lady of the Wayside RC
Primary School *SHLY* B90 ...**180** C5
Our Lady & St Chad RC
Secondary School
WOLVN WV10 .... **23** H2
Our Lady & St Kenelm RC
Primary School *HALE* B63 ...**138** C4
Our Lady & St Rose of Lima RC
Primary School
SLYOAK B29 .... **158** D1
Our Ladys RC Primary School
STETCH B33 .... **131** F2
The Oval Primary School
STETCH B33 .... **130** B2
Owen Road Industrial Estate
WLNHL WV13 .... **40** A4
Owen Road Trading Estate
WLNHL WV13 .... **40** A4
Oxbarn Social & Sports Club
BDMR/CCFT WV3 .... **51** F1
Oxford Street Industrial Park
DIG/EDG B5 .... **54** B3
Oxley Park Golf Club
WOLVN WV10 .... **23** E3
Paddys Wide Water Industrial
Estate *BRLYHL* DY5 ....**101** C4
Paget Primary School
ERDE/BCHGN B24 .... **93** G2
Palfrey Girls School *WSL* WS1 .....**4** D4
Palfrey Infant School
WSL WS1 .... **56** D1
Palfrey Junior School
WSL WS1 .... **56** D1

Pallasades Shopping Centre
CBHAM B2 .... **3** F6
Palmers Cross Primary School
DUNHL/THL/PER WV6 ....**21** H2
Paper Mill End Industrial Estate
KGSTG B44 .... **74** D5
Parkbrook Industrial Estate
HAG/WOL DY9 .... **136** D2
Parkfield Clinic
BKHL/PFLD WV2 .... **52** B2
Parkfield High School
ETTPK/GDPK/PENN WV4 ...**52** C3
Parkfield Primary School
ETTPK/GDPK/PENN WV4 ...**52** C3
WASH/WDE B8 .... **128** C1
Park Hall Hotel & Conference
Centre
ETTPK/GDPK/PENN WV4 ...**52** A4
Park Hall Infant School
DSYBK/YTR WS5 .... **58** A1
Park Hall Junior School
DSYBK/YTR WS5 .... **58** A1
Park Hall School *CBROM* B36 ...**95** C5
Park Hill Primary School
DARL/WED WS10 .... **56** C4
SMTHWK B66 .... **144** B3
Park Lane Industrial Estate
HHTH/SAND B71 .... **88** C5
Park Lane Trading Estate
OLDBY B69 .... **105** E2
WOLVN WV10 .... **23** C5
Park Medical Centre
SMHTH B10 .... **128** C5
Parkrose Industrial Estate
SMTHWK B66 .... **106** D1
Parkside Industrial Estate
WOLV WV1 .... **37** H4
Park Trading Estate
WSNGN B18 .... **108** A3
Park View School
WASH/WDE B8 .... **110** C4
Parkway Industrial Centre
VAUX/NECH B7 .... **109** G5
Pavilions Shopping Centre
CBHAMNE B4 .... **3** H5
Pdh Industrial Estate
DARL/WED WS10 .... **55** E4
WLNHL WV13 .... **38** D2
Peartree Industrial Park
DUDS DY2 .... **102** A3
Pedmore CE Primary School
HAG/WOL DY9 .... **152** D1
Pedmore Road Industrial
Estate *BRLYHL* DY5 ....**101** H5
Pegasus Primary School
CVALE B35 .... **94** D3
Pelsall Clinic *BLOX/PEL* WS3 .....**18** A3
Pelsall Village School
BLOX/PEL WS3 .... **17** H3
Pendeford Business Park
COVEN WV9 .... **11** H4
Pendeford Health Centre
COVEN WV9 .... **12** A5
Pendeford High School
WOLVN WV10 .... **12** A5
Pendeford Mill Nature
Reserve *COVEN* WV9 ....**11** G3
Pendene Complimentary
Medical Centre *WOLV* WV1 ...**6** C3
Penn Cemetery
ETTPK/GDPK/PENN WV4 ...**50** D5
Pennfields Health Centre
BDMR/CCFT WV3 .... **6** C7
Penn Fields School
BDMR/CCFT WV3 .... **51** F1
Penn Golf Club
ETTPK/GDPK/PENN WV4 ...**66** C1
Penn Hall Special School
ETTPK/GDPK/PENN WV4 ...**51** E4
Penn Hospital
ETTPK/GDPK/PENN WV4 ...**51** E4
Penn Industrial Estate
DUDS DY2 .... **120** C3
Penn Manor Medical Centre
ETTPK/GDPK/PENN WV4 ...**51** E4
Penn Road Retail Park
BKHL/PFLD WV2 .... **36** D5
Penns Primary School
CSCFLD/WYGN B72 .... **77** C5
Pens Meadow Special School
STRBR DY8 .... **118** A3
The Pennsett School of
Technology *BRLYHL* DY5 ......**100** D3
Pensnett Trading Estate
KGSWFD DY6 .... **100** B1
The Pennsett Trading Estate
KGSWFD DY6 .... **100** C1
Percy Business Park
OLDBY B69 .... **104** D2
Percy Shurmer Primary
School *DIG/EDG* B5 .... **127** E5
Perry Barr Greyhound
Stadium *PBAR/PBCH* B42 ....**90** D3
Perry Beeches J & I School
PBAR/PBCH B42 .... **74** C3
Perry Common Primary
School *ERDW/GRVHL* B23 ....**75** H4
Perryfields High School
RMSLY B62 .... **123** E4
Perryfields Primary School
RMSLY B62 .... **123** E5
Perry Hall Primary School
WNSFLD WV11 .... **25** F4
Perry Street Industrial Estate
BILS/COS WV14 .... **54** A5
Personal & Child Health
Centre *BVILLE* B30 ....**160** A4
Perton Clinic
DUNHL/THL/PER WV6 ....**34** C1
Perton First School
DUNHL/THL/PER WV6 ....**20** C5
Perton Middle School
DUNHL/THL/PER WV6 ....**35** E1
Perton Park Golf Club
DUNHL/THL/PER WV6 ....**34** A2
Peterbrook Primary School
SHLY B90 .... **179** F3
Peters Hill Primary School
BRLYHL DY5 .... **119** E5

Pheasey Clinic
GTB/HAM B43 .... 59 G5
Pheasey Park Farm Primary
School *GTB/HAM* B43 .... 59 G4
Phillips Street
Industrial Estate
AST/WIT B6 .... 109 E3
Phoenix Business Park
VAUX/NECH B7 .... 109 G3
Phoenix Industrial Estate
BILS/COS WV14 .... 54 B4
Phoenix International
WBROM B70 .... 86 D1
Phoenix Road Industrial
Estate *WLNHL* WV13 .... 38 D2
Phoenix Works Industrial
Estate *DARL/WED* WS10 ...... 40 C5
Piccadilly Cinema
SPARK B11 .... 144 D2
The Picture House
STRBR DY8 .... 135 G3
WASH/WDE B8 .... 111 E4
Pines Special School
CBROM B36 .... 112 B1
Pinfold Industrial Estate
BLOX/PEL WS3 .... 27 G2
Pinfold Street Primary School
DARL/WED WS10 .... 55 E3
Planetary Industrial Estate
WLNHL WV13 .... 38 C1
Planet Ice Arena *DIG/EDG* B5 ... 3 H7
Plantsbrook School
CSCFLD/WYGN B72 .... 62 C4
Pleck Business Park *WSLW* WS2 ... 4 A4
Pleck Industrial Estate
WSLW WS2 .... 41 G5
Pool Hayes Comprehensive
School *SHHTH* WV12 .... 25 H5
Pool Hayes Primary School
WNSFLD WV11 .... 25 H4
Poplar Road Clinic
ALE/KHTH/YWD B14 .... 161 F1
Poplar Trading Estate
AST/WIT B6 .... 91 F1
Portersfield Industrial Estate
CDYHTH B64 .... 120 C4
Portland Hotel
LDYWD/EDGR B16 .... 125 E3
Portway Road Industrial
Estate *OLDBY* B69 .... 104 C3
Powke Lane Industrial Estate
BLKHTH/ROWR B65 .... 121 G2
Premier Business Centre
HAG/WOL DY9 .... 136 D2
Premier Business Park
WSLW WS2 .... 4 B5
Premier Lodge *MGN/WHC* B75 ... 63 F1
Premier Partnership Industrial
Estate *KGSWFD* DY6 .... 100 C5
Premier Trading Estate
VAUX/NECH B7 .... 109 F4
Premier Travel Inn
AST/WIT B6 .... 109 F4
BHAMNEC B40 .... 133 F5
CBHAMW B1 .... 2 D6
CNCK/NC WS11 .... 8 A1
EDG B15 .... 3 J4
HAG/WOL DY9 .... 153 H5
KGSWFD DY6 .... 100 B2
OLDBY B69 .... 104 B2
RBRY B45 .... 174 B5
SHLY B90 .... 182 D2
SHLY B90 .... 195 F3
WBROM B70 .... 86 D1
WOLN WV10 .... 12 D2
WSLW WS2 .... 40 C4
Preston College *WLNHL* WV13 ... 39 G4
Priestley Smith Special School
ERDW/GRVHL B23 .... 75 H5
Primrose Hill Primary School
HWK/WKHTH B38 .... 158 A1
Primrose Hill Trading Estate
DUDS DY2 .... 102 D5
Primrose Lane Health Centre
WOLN WV10 .... 24 A2
Primrose Trading Estate
DUDS DY2 .... 102 D5
Prince Albert Primary School
BILS/COS WV14 .... 69 E2
Princes End Industrial Park
BILS/COS WV14 .... 69 G2
Princethorpe J & I School
SLYOAK B29 .... 158 C2
Priory Clinic *DUDN* DY1 .... 84 B3
Priory Courts *CBHAMNE* B4 .... 3 G4
Priory Green Primary School
COVEN WV9 .... 12 A5
Priory House Industrial Estate
WSNGN B18 .... 108 B4
Priory Junior Mixed & Infants
School *BLOX/PEL* WS3 .... 27 F3
Priory New Way Industrial
Estate *AST/WIT* B6 .... 109 E4
Priory Primary School
DUDN DY1 .... 84 B3
The Priory Primary School
DARL/WED WS10 .... 71 H1
Prospect Trading Estate
CBHAMW B1 .... 2 C4
Providence Industrial Estate
HAG/WOL DY9 .... 136 C1
Pype Hayes Golf Club
WALM/CURD B76 .... 78 A5
Qualcast Road Industrial Estate
WOLV WV1 .... 37 H3
Quality Hotel *BDMR/CCFT* WV3 ... 36 D5
WSLW WS2 .... 40 D3
Quarry Bank Primary School
BRLYHL DY5 .... 120 A3
Queen Alexandra College
HRBN B17 .... 141 G1
Queen Elizabeth Hospital
EDG B15 .... 142 C2
Queen Elizabeth Psychiatric
Hospital *EDG* B15 .... 142 C3
Queen Marys Grammar School
CBHAMNE B1 .... 3 F2
Queen Marys High School
RUSH/SHEL WS4 .... 5 G1

Queensbury Special School
ERDE/BCHGN B24 .... 92 D3
Queens College *EDG* B15 ...... 142 D2
Queens Court Trading Estate
WBROM B70 .... 86 D3
Queen Street Cemetery
WSLW WS2 .... 4 A6
Queensway Trading Estate
DIG/EDG B5 .... 3 J4
Queen Victoria Primary School
SEDG DY3 .... 67 F3
Quinton Business Park
RIDG/WDGT B32 .... 140 A2
Quinton Cemetery
RMSLY B62 .... 122 D5
Quinton CE Primary School
RIDG/WDGT B32 .... 140 A1
Racecourse Road Industrial
Estate
DUNHL/THL/PER WV6 .... 22 C5
Raddlebarn J & I School
SLYOAK B29 .... 159 H1
Radleys Primary School
RUSH/SHEL WS4 .... 29 E3
Radway Industrial Estate
SHLY B90 .... 195 E1
Rainbow Business Park
WLNHL WV13 .... 39 H2
Rake Gate Infant School
WOLN WV10 .... 22 D1
Rake Gate Junior School
WOLN WV10 .... 22 D1
Raleigh Industrial Estate
HDSW B21 .... 88 D5
Ramada Hotel *SOLH* B91 .... 182 A2
WALM/CURD B76 .... 78 A4
Rathville School
NFLD/LBR B31 .... 175 H2
Rea Business Park
VAUX/NECH B7 .... 109 H5
Reaside Clinic *RBRY* B45 .... 174 A4
Reaside Junior School
RBRY B45 .... 173 G4
Reddal Hill Primary School
CDYHTH B64 .... 121 E3
Reddicap Trading Estate
MGN/WHC B75 .... 62 D4
Red Hall Primary School
STRBR DY8 .... 83 E3
Redhill J & I School *OLDLY* B25 ... 129 E5
Redhill Secondary School
STRBR DY8 .... 135 H2
Red Hill Street Clinic
WOLV WV1 .... 37 E1
The Red House Glass Cone
STRBR DY8 .... 118 A2
Redhouse Industrial Estate
ALDR WS9 .... 29 F4
Redhouse JMI School
ALDR WS9 .... 29 G5
Rednal Hill J & I School
RBRY B45 .... 188 B1
Red Rooster Industrial Estate
ALDR WS9 .... 29 G4
Redwood Business Park
SMTHWK B66 .... 105 G2
Reedswood Retail Park
WSLW WS2 .... 41 F1
Reflex Industrial Park
WLNHL WV13 .... 39 F2
Regents Park Primary School
SMHTH B10 .... 128 A4
Regent Special School
OLDBY B69 .... 85 G5
Regis Medical Centre
BLKHTH/ROWR B65 .... 122 A3
Reliance Trading Estate
ETTPK/GDPK/PENN WV4 ...... 53 F3
Renaissance Solihull Hotel
SOLH B91 .... 181 H1
Reynalds Cross School
SOLH B91 .... 181 H3
The Ridge Primary School
STRBR DY8 .... 134 C2
Ridgewood High School
STRBR DY8 .... 134 C1
Ridpool Primary School
STETCH B33 .... 130 D1
Riland Industrial Estate
MGN/WHC B75 .... 62 C3
River Brook Medical Centre
BVILLE B30 .... 160 B2
RMW Business Centre
HAG/WOL DY9 .... 136 D2
Robert Clinic *BVILLE* B30 ...... 159 G5
Roberts Primary School
SEDG DY3 .... 83 G2
Robin Hood Cemetery
SHLY B90 .... 163 F5
Robin Hood Golf Club
HIA/OLT B92 .... 163 G4
Robin Hood Primary School
HLGN/YWD B28 .... 163 H4
Robins Business Park
TPTN/OCK DY4 .... 70 C4
Rocky Lane Trading Estate
VAUX/NECH B7 .... 109 G3
Rollingmill Business Park
WSLW WS2 .... 4 A5
Romney House Industrial
Estate *DARL/WED* WS10 ...... 54 D1
Rood End Cemetery
LGLYGN/QTN B68 .... 105 G2
Rood End Primary School
LGLYGN/QTN B68 .... 105 H2
Rookery Primary School
HDSW B21 .... 89 G5
Rosary RC Primary School
WASH/WDE B8 .... 128 C1
Rosedale CE Infant School
SHHTH WV12 .... 26 B5
Rosewood Special School
DUDN DY1 .... 83 G5
Rosslyn School
HLGN/YWD B28 .... 163 E5
Rotton Park Medical Centre
LDYWD/EDGR B16 .... 125 F1
Rotunda *CBHAM* B2 .... 3 G6
Rough Hay Primary School
DARL/WED WS10 .... 55 E1

Rough Wood Nature Reserve
SHHTH WV12 .... 26 C4
Rounds Green Primary School
OLDBY B69 .... 104 C1
Rovex Business Park
SPARK B11 .... 145 H2
Rowley Hall Primary School
BLKHTH/ROWR B65 .... 104 A5
Rowley Regis Cemetery &
Crematorium
BLKHTH/ROWR B65 .... 121 G2
Rowley Regis College
BLKHTH/ROWR B65 .... 121 H1
Rowley Regis Hospital
BLKHTH/ROWR B65 .... 121 H1
Royal Birmingham Society of
Arts *CBHAMNW* B3 .... 2 D2
Royal Brierley Trading Estate
BRLYHL DY5 .... 119 E1
Royal Orthopaedic Hospital
NFLD/LBR B31 .... 158 D5
Royal Theatre *CDYHTH* B64 ... 120 D3
The Royal Wolverhampton
Junior School
BDMR/CCFT WV3 .... 51 G1
The Royal Wolverhampton
School *BDMR/CCFT* WV3 ..... 51 H1
RSPB Sandwell Valley Nature
Reserve *GTB/HAM* B43 .... 73 E5
Rubery Clinic *RBRY* B45 .... 187 G1
Ruckleigh School *SOLH* B91 ... 182 A1
Rufford Primary School
HAG/WOL DY9 .... 136 A2
Rushall Community College
RUSH/SHEL WS4 .... 28 D4
Rushall JM School & Education
Development Centre
BLOX/PEL WS3 .... 28 C1
Russell Medical Centre
DARL/WED WS10 .... 70 D1
Russells Hall Hospital
BRLYHL DY5 .... 101 F2
Russells Hall Primary School
DUDN DY1 .... 83 G5
Ryders Green Primary School
WBROM B70 .... 87 E2
Ryders Hayes JMI School
BLOX/PEL WS3 .... 18 A2
Sacred Heart RC Primary
School *BFLD/HDSWWD* B20 ... 90 D5
TPTN/OCK DY4 .... 85 F2
Saddlers Shopping Centre
WSL WS1 .... 4 D4
Sai Medical Centre *WSLW* WS2 ... 4 A3
St Albans CE Primary School
WNSFLD WV11 .... 25 H2
St Albans CE School
BHTH/HG B12 .... 127 F5
St Albans RC Primary School
ALE/KHTH/YWD B14 .... 178 B1
St Alphege CE Infant School
SOLH B91 .... 182 A2
St Alphege CE Junior School
SOLH B91 .... 182 A3
St Ambrose Barlow RC
Primary School
HLGN/YWD B28 .... 163 E4
St Andrews CE Infant School
DUNHL/THL/PER WV6 .... 36 B1
St Andrews Industrial Estate
BORD B9 .... 126 D5
St Andrews Primary School
BORD B9 .... 127 H2
St Annes Industrial Estate
HIA/OLT B92 .... 147 G5
St Annes RC JMI School
WLNHL WV13 .... 39 H2
St Anne's RC School
FOAKS/STRLY B74 .... 45 E5
St Annes RC Primary School
BHTH/HG B12 .... 127 G4
CHWD/FDBR/MGN B37 .... 132 A2
St Anthonys RC Primary
School
CHWD/FDBR/MGN B37 .... 114 A4
WOLN WV10 .... 12 D4
St Augustines Catholic Primary
School *HDSW* B21 .... 89 F4
St Augustines Primary School
SOLH B91 .... 181 G3
St Barnabas CE Primary
School *ERDE/BCHGN* B24 ..... 93 F3
St Bartholomews CE Primary
School
ETTPK/GDPK/PENN WV4 ...... 51 E5
St Benedict Biscop CE Primary
School *WMBN* WV5 .... 65 G4
St Benedicts Infant School
SMHTH B10 .... 128 D5
St Bernadettes RC JMI School
BRWNH WS8 .... 9 F4
St Bernadettes RC Primary
School *SMHTH* B10 .... 129 F4
WMBN WV5 .... 64 D5
St Bernards RC Primary School
MOS/BIL B13 .... 162 A1
St Brigids RC Primary School
NFLD/LBR B31 .... 175 F2
St Catherine of Siena RC
School *EDG* B15 .... 126 D4
St Chads Industrial Estate
LOZ/NWT B19 .... 109 E4
St Chad's RC Cathedral
CBHAMNE B4 .... 3 F2
St Chads RC Primary School
LOZ/NWT B19 .... 108 D4
St Christophers RC Primary
School *CDSL* WV8 .... 10 C5
St Clares Primary School
BFLD/HDSWWD B20 .... 90 B5
St Clements CE Primary
School *VAUX/NECH* B7 .... 109 H2
St Columbas RC School
CBROM B36 .... 188 D1
St Cuthberts RC Primary
School *WASH/WDE* B8 .... 111 G5
St Dunstans RC
Primary School
ALE/KHTH/YWD B14 .... 161 E2

St Edmund Campion RC
School *ERDW/GRVHL* B23 ..... 77 F5
St Edmunds Catholic School
BDMR/CCFT WV3 .... 35 H2
St Edmunds RC Primary
School *WSNGN* B18 .... 108 A5
St Edward's RC Primary
School *CSHL/WTROR* B46 ... 115 G4
St Edwards CE Primary
School *CSHL/WTROR* B46 ... 133 G1
STRBR DY8 .... 160 B1
St Francis CE Primary School
BVILLE B30 .... 159 F4
St Francis of Assisi RC School
ALDR WS9 .... 30 C5
St Francis RC Primary School
LOZ/NWT B19 .... 108 B3
RUSH/SHEL WS4 .... 29 E1
St Francis Xavier RC Primary
School *WSNGN* B18 .... 108 A5
St George & St Teresa RC
Primary School
DOR/KN B93 .... 197 E4
St Georges CE Primary School
EDG B15 .... 125 H3
St Georges School Edgbaston
EDG B15 .... 126 B4
St Georges Sixth Form & CE
Primary School
LOZ/NWT B19 .... 108 D4
St Gerards Orthopaedic
Hospital
CSHL/WTROR B46 .... 115 G4
St Gerards RC Primary School
CVALE B35 .... 94 D2
St Giles CE Primary School
WLNHL WV13 .... 39 H3
St Gregorys RC Primary School
SMTHWK B67 .... 124 B2
St Huberts RC Primary School
LGLYGN/QTN B68 .... 123 G3
St James CE Junior School
SHLY B90 .... 180 B3
St James CE Primary School
HDSW B21 .... 89 F5
OLDBY B69 .... 104 B4
STRBR DY8 .... 117 H5
St James Medical Centre
HDSW B21 .... 107 F1
St James Primary School
BRWNH WS8 .... 9 F4
St James RC Primary School
RBRY B45 .... 188 A1
St John Bosco RC Primary
School *HHTH/SAND* B71 ...... 71 H4
St John Fishers RC Primary
School *NFLD/LBR* B31 .... 189 H1
St John & St Monica RC
Primary School
MOS/BIL B13 .... 144 A3
St John CE JMI School
ALDR WS9 .... 19 F4
St Johns CE Primary School
DARL/WED WS10 .... 70 D1
LDYWD/EDGR B16 .... 126 A2
SEDG DY3 .... 80 C4
SPARK B11 .... 145 E4
WNSFLD WV11 .... 15 E3
St Johns Retail Park
BKHL/PFLD WV2 .... 7 F6
St John the Baptist RC Primary
School *CBROM* B36 .... 114 A2
St John Wall RC School
HDSW B21 .... 89 F3
St Josephs Catholic Primary
School *DARL/WED* WS10 ...... 55 E1
FOAKS/STRLY B74 .... 62 C1
STRBR DY8 .... 135 F5
St Josephs RC Primary School
BVILLE B30 .... 159 G5
DUDS DY2 .... 85 E5
VAUX/NECH B7 .... 109 H3
St Judes CE Primary School
DUNHL/THL/PER WV6 .... 36 B2
St Judes RC Primary School
ALE/KHTH/YWD B14 .... 178 B3
St Kenelms CE First School
RMSLY B62 .... 172 C1
St Laurence CE J & I School
NFLD/LBR B31 .... 175 H1
St Lukes CE Aided Primary
School *BKHL/PFLD* WV2 .... 51 H1
St Margaret Mary RC Primary
School *ERDW/GRVHL* B23 .... 76 A5
St Margarets CE Primary
School *GTB/HAM* B43 .... 58 C4
HIA/OLT B92 .... 147 F5
St Margarets Hospital
DSYBK/YTR WS5 .... 43 G5
St Marks CE Primary School
BRLYHL DY5 .... 101 E2
St Marks RC Primary School
PBAR/PBCH B42 .... 73 H4
St Martin de Porres RC
Primary School
MOS/BIL B13 .... 144 C4
St Martins CE Primary School
BILS/COS WV14 .... 69 C1
TPTN/OCK DY4 .... 85 H1
St Martins Industrial Estate
OLDBY B69 .... 105 E3
St Martins Market *DIG/EDG* B5 ... 3 H7
St Martins School *SOLH* B91 ... 182 B2
St Mary & Johns RC Primary
School *BKHL/PFLD* WV2 .... 37 F5
St Mary Magdalene CE Primary
School *HHTH/SAND* B71 ...... 72 C5
St Mary of the Angels RC JMI
School *ALDR* WS9 .... 30 B5
St Mary's Abbey (Remains)
RMSLY B62 .... 139 F5
St Mary & St John RC Primary
School *ERDW/GRVHL* B23 .... 92 C3
St Mary & St Margarets CE
Primary School
CBROM B36 .... 112 D1
St Marys CE Primary School
BFLD/HDSWWD B20 .... 90 B4
KGSWFD DY6 .... 99 H2
SLYOAK B29 .... 159 H1

St Marys RC Primary School
BRLYHL DY5 .... 119 G2
DARL/WED WS10 .... 55 H4
HRBN B17 .... 142 A1
WOLV WV1 .... 24 A3
St Marys the Mount RC School
WSL WS1 .... 5 H7
St Matthews CE Primary School
SMTHWK B66 .... 106 D4
VAUX/NECH B7 .... 109 G5
St Michaels CE High School
BLKHTH/ROWR B65 .... 104 B4
St Michaels CE Primary School
BLOX/PEL WS3 .... 17 F5
DUNHL/THL/PER WV6 .... 22 A5
HDSW B21 .... 108 A2
RIDG/WDGT B32 .... 157 G2
St Michaels RC Primary School
BDMR/CCFT WV3 .... 50 D1
St Nicholas CE VC First School
WSL WS1 .... 10 B3
St Nicholas RC JMI School
SCFLD/BOLD B73 .... 76 D1
St Patricks Catholic Primary
School
CHWD/FDBR/MGN B37 .... 132 C2
WSLW WS2 .... 4 C1
St Patricks RC Primary School
WNSFLD WV11 .... 24 C5
WSNGN B18 .... 107 H5
St Pauls CE (A) Primary School
COVEN WV9 .... 12 A5
St Pauls CE Primary School
TPTN/OCK DY4 .... 69 F5
St Pauls Nursery School
HWK/WKHTH B38 .... 177 E4
St Pauls School BHTH/HG B12 ... 144 C2
St Pauls School for Girls
LDYWD/EDGR B16 .... 125 G3
St Peter & Paul RC Primary
School *ERDE/BCHGN* B24 ..... 93 G3
St Peters CE Junior School
HRBN B17 .... 142 A3
St Peters CE JMI School
BLOX/PEL WS3 .... 16 D5
St Peters Collegiate Secondary
School *BDMR/CCFT* WV3 ..... 36 A2
St Peters RC Primary School
RIDG/WDGT B32 .... 157 G1
St Peters RC School *SOLH* B91 ... 181 H5
St Philips Cathedral
CBHAMNW B3 .... 3 F4
St Philips RC Primary School
SMTHWK B66 .... 106 D3
St Philips RC Sixth Form
College *LDYWD/EDGR* B16 ... 125 H4
St Saviours CE Primary School
WASH/WDE B8 .... 110 B4
St Stephens CE Primary
School *WOLN* WV10 .... 37 G1
St Teresas RC Primary School
BFLD/HDSWWD B20 .... 90 A4
ETTPK/GDPK/PENN WV4 ...... 52 C3
St Thomas Aquinas RC School
HWK/WKHTH B38 .... 176 B2
St Thomas CE Primary School
EDG B15 .... 126 D4
WNSFLD WV11 .... 24 D5
St Thomas Community
Network *DUDS* DY2 .... 85 G5
St Thomas More Catholic
School *WLNHL* WV13 .... 39 H5
St Thomas More RC Primary
School
LGN/SDN/BHAMAIR B26 ... 147 H2
St Thomas of Canterbury RC
JMI School *BLOX/PEL* WS3 ... 28 B4
St Vincents RC Primary
School *VAUX/NECH* B7 .... 127 H1
St Wilfrids RC Primary School
CBROM B36 .... 112 B1
Salafi Independent School
SMHTH B10 .... 128 B4
Salford Trading Estate
AST/WIT B6 .... 110 A1
Salisbury Place Industrial
Estate *BDMR/CCFT* WV3 .... 6 C6
Salisbury Primary School
DARL/WED WS10 .... 55 G1
Saltbrook Trading Estate
HALE B63 .... 120 A5
Saltley Business Park
WASH/WDE B8 .... 110 D3
Saltley Health Centre
WASH/WDE B8 .... 110 C4
Saltley Industrial Centre
WASH/WDE B8 .... 110 D3
Saltley Leisure Centre
BORD B9 .... 129 E1
Saltley School *WASH/WDE* B8 ... 129 E1
Saltley Trading Estate
WASH/WDE B8 .... 110 A4
Salvation Army *CBHAMNE* B4 ... 3 F2
Sandown First School
DUNHL/THL/PER WV6 .... 34 D1
Sandwell Borough FC
OLDBY B69 .... 104 C2
Sandwell Business
Development Centre
OLDBY B69 .... 105 G2
Sandwell Business Park
SMTHWK B66 .... 105 G2
Sandwell Business &
Technology Centre
LGLYGN/QTN B68 .... 122 D2
Sandwell College
LGLYGN/QTN B68 .... 123 E1
SMTHWK B66 .... 106 C4
WBROM B70 .... 87 G3
Sandwell District General
Hospital
HHTH/SAND B71 .... 87 H1
Sandwell Health Authority
Clinic *CDYHTH* B64 .... 121 E3
Sandwell Park Golf Club
HHTH/SAND B71 .... 88 B4
Sandwell Park Industrial
Estate *HHTH/SAND* B71 .... 88 B5
Sandwell Valley
HHTH/SAND B71 .... 72 C5

Sandyhill Industrial Estate
HLGN/YWD B28 ....180 A1
Sapcote Business Centre
SMHTH B10 ....145 G1
Sapcote Industrial Estate
CDYHTH B64 ....121 F1
Sapcote Trading Centre
AST/WIT B6 ....91 G3
CDYHTH B64 ....121 F1
SMHTH B10 ....145 G1
Sarehole Mill *MOS/BIL* B13 ....162 B2
Sarephed Medical Centre
SMTHWKW B67 ....106 C4
Sargent Turner Trading
Estate *HAG/WOL* DY9 ....136 D1
Satellite Industrial Park
WNSFLD WV11 ....38 C1
School of Jewellery (University
of Central England)
CBHAMW B1 ....2 C2
Scott Arms Shopping Centre
GTB/HAM B43 ....75 G2
Sears Retail Park *SHLY* B90 ....124 C4
Sedgley Golf Centre *SEDG* DY3 ....66 D5
Selly Manor Museum
BVILLE B30 ....159 H3
Selly Oak Health Centre
SLYOAK B29 ....159 G1
Selly Oak Hospital
SLYOAK B29 ....159 H1
Selly Oak Industrial Estate
SLYOAK B29 ....159 G1
Selly Oak School *SLYOAK* B29 ....159 G2
Selly Park Technology College
for Girls *SLYOAK* B29 ....160 B1
Seth Somes Track *RMSLY* B62 ....139 E5
Severne Primary School
ACGN B27 ....163 G2
Shaftmoor Industrial Estate
HLGN/YWD B28 ....145 H5
Sharmans Cross Junior School
SOLH B91 ....181 E1
Shaw Hill Primary School
WASH/WDE B8 ....110 C5
Shaw Park Business Village
WOLVN WV10 ....23 F4
Sheldon CC *YDLY* B25 ....129 H4
Sheldon Country Park
LGN/SDN/BHAMAIR B26 ....148 C1
Sheldon Heath Community
School
LGN/SDN/BHAMAIR B26 ....131 E4
Shelfield Clinic
RUSH/SHEL WS4 ....29 E2
Shelfield Sports & Community
College *RUSH/SHEL* WS4 ....18 C5
Shell Corner Trading Estate
RMSLY B62 ....122 B4
Shelter Waterside
Industrial Estate
ETTPK/GDPK/PENN WV4 ....53 E3
Shenley Court School
SLYOAK B29 ....158 B3
Shenley Lane Community
Association Sports Centre
SLYOAK B29 ....158 C4
Shenstone Trading Estate
HALE B63 ....139 E3
Sherborne Wharf
LDYWD/EDGR B16 ....2 A6
Shireland Hall Primary School
SMTHWK B66 ....125 E1
Shireland Language College
SMTHWK B66 ....124 C1
Shire Oak School *BRWNH* WS8 ....19 G2
Shirestone Primary School
STETCH B33 ....131 F2
Shirley Clinic *SHLY* B90 ....180 B2
Shirley Heath Junior School
SHLY B90 ....180 C4
Shirley Park Sports Club &
Golf Club *SHLY* B90 ....195 G4
Shirley Road Health Clinic
ACGN B27 ....163 F1
Short Heath Clinic
SHHTH WV12 ....26 B4
Short Heath Primary School
ERDW/GRVHL B23 ....76 B5
Shorth Heath Junior School
SHHTH WV12 ....26 B5
Showcase Cinema *DUDN* DY1 ....85 E3
WSLW WS2 ....40 D4
Showcase Cinemas
ERDE/BCHGN B24 ....93 H4
Showell Road Industrial
Estate *WOLVN* WV10 ....23 F4
The Shrubbery School
WALM/CURD B76 ....78 B4
Silhill FC *SOLH* B91 ....181 E1
Silver End Business Park
BRLYHL DY5 ....118 D4
Silver End Industrial Estate
BRLYHL DY5 ....118 D3
Sladefield Infant School
WASH/WDE B8 ....111 E4
Slade Primary School
ERDW/GRVHL B23 ....92 B4
Sledmere Primary School
DUDS DY2 ....102 D3
Small Heath Business Park
SMHTH B10 ....128 D5
Small Heath Lower School
SMHTH B10 ....128 B5
Smestow Bridge Industrial
Estate *WMBN* WV5 ....64 A5
Smestow Secondary School
BDMR/CCFT WV3 ....35 F4
Smethwick Medical Centre
SMTHWKW B67 ....106 C3
Smethwick Swimming Centre
SMTHWKW B67 ....124 B2
Smith's Wood School
CBROM B36 ....114 A3
Sneyd Community School
BLOX/PEL WS3 ....16 A5
Snow Hill Clinic *BKHL/PFLD* WV2 ....7 C5
Soho Health Centre
HDSW B21 ....107 H2

Soho House *WSNGN* B18 ....108 A2
Solihull College *SOLH* B91 ....181 G2
Solihull Hospital *SOLH* B91 ....182 B1
Solihull Ice Rink *HIA/OLT* B92 ....147 H4
Solihull Retail Park *SHLY* B90 ....180 D4
Solihull School *SOLH* B91 ....182 B1
Solihull Sixth Form College
SOLH B91 ....182 B3
Somerville Primary School
SMHTH B10 ....128 B4
South Birmingham College
BHTH/HG B12 ....3 K7
HLGN/YWD B28 ....162 C2
Southside Business Centre
BHTH/HG B12 ....144 C2
South Staffordshire Golf Club
DUNHL/THL/PER WV6 ....21 G4
Sovereign Trading Estate
STRBR DY8 ....135 E2
Sparkbrook Health Centre
SPARK B11 ....127 H5
Sparkhill Pool & Fitness
Centre *SPARK* B11 ....145 E3
Spartan Industrial Centre
WBROM B70 ....70 C5
Speedwell Trading Estate
SPARK B11 ....146 A1
Spines Clinic *WMBN* WV5 ....64 D5
Spinners End Industrial
Estate *CDYHTH* B64 ....120 D3
Spon Lane Industrial Estate
SMTHWK B66 ....105 H1
Spon Lane Trading Estate
WBROM B70 ....87 G4
Springdale J & I School
ETTPK/GDPK/PENN WV4 ....50 C3
Springfield Industrial Estate
OLDBY B69 ....105 F2
Springfield Infant School
MOS/BIL B13 ....145 F5
Springfield Junior School
BLKTH/ROWR B65 ....103 G5
Springfield Primary School
BLKTH/ROWR B65 ....103 G5
Spring Hill Industrial Estate
SMHTH B10 ....108 A5
Spring Lane Industrial Estate
SHHTH WV12 ....40 A1
Spring Road Industrial Estate
ETTPK/GDPK/PENN WV4 ....53 E4
Springvale Business Park
BILS/COS WV14 ....53 F4
Springvale Industrial Park
BILS/COS WV14 ....53 F4
Spring Vale Primary School
ETTPK/GDPK/PENN WV4 ....52 C4
Stafford Road Sports Club
BLOX/PEL WS3 ....16 D5
Stag Industrial Estate
BILS/COS WV14 ....54 C4
Stambermill Industrial Estate
HAG/WOL DY9 ....136 A1
Stanhope Road Clinic
SMTHWKW B67 ....124 B1
Stanville Primary School
LGN/SDN/BHAMAIR B26 ....147 H1
Starbank Primary School
SMHTH B10 ....129 F4
Start Point Trading Estate
SPARK B11 ....145 F3
Station Road Industrial
Estate *BLKTH/ROWR* B65 ....122 B2
CSHL/WTROR B46 ....115 F1
Stechford Cascades
STETCH B33 ....130 A1
Stechford Health Centre
STETCH B33 ....130 A2
Stechford Primary School
STETCH B33 ....129 H2
Stechford Retail Park
STETCH B33 ....112 A5
Stechford Trading Estate
STETCH B33 ....112 A5
Steetley Industrial Estate
BILS/COS WV14 ....68 C4
Stephens Industrial Estate
SPARK B11 ....145 H3
Stevens Dental Health Centre
SPARK B11 ....135 F3
Stirchley Primary School
BVILLE B30 ....160 A4
Stirchley Trading Estate
BVILLE B30 ....160 B5
Stock Exchange *CBHAMNW* B3 ....2 E4
Stockland Clinic
ERDW/GRVHL B23 ....92 B2
Stockland Green Health Centre
ERDW/GRVHL B23 ....92 B2
Stockland Green School
ERDW/GRVHL B23 ....92 A2
Stone Cross Clinic
HHTH/SAND B71 ....72 A2
Stourbridge CC *STRBR* DY8 ....118 B5
Stourbridge Cemetery
STRBR DY8 ....134 D3
Stourbridge Clinic *STRBR* DY8 ....135 H3
Stourbridge College
HAG/WOL DY9 ....136 B2
STRBR DY8 ....135 E2
Stourbridge Crematorium
STRBR DY8 ....134 D3
Stourbridge FC *STRBR* DY8 ....135 F1
Stourbridge Golf Club
STRBR DY8 ....152 C1
Stourbridge Industrial Estate
STRBR DY8 ....135 G1
Stourbridge RFC *KINVER* DY7 ....134 B1
Stourbridge Trading Estate
HAG/WOL DY9 ....136 D1
Stourvale Trading Estate
HALE B63 ....137 H1
Stowheath Industrial Estate &
New Enterprise Centre
BKHL/PFLD WV2 ....38 A5
Stow Heath J & I School
WLNHL WV13 ....38 D4
Stowlawn Primary School
WOLV WV1 ....38 C5
Straits Primary School
SEDG DY3 ....82 D1

Stratford Road School Clinic
SPARK B11 ....145 F5
Strawberry Lane Industrial
Estate *WLNHL* WV13 ....38 C2
The Streetley School
FOAKS/STRLY B74 ....60 B2
Streetly Cemetery
ALDR WS9 ....44 D3
Streetly Clinic
FOAKS/STRLY B74 ....45 E5
Streetly Crematorium
ALDR WS9 ....44 D3
Streetly Hockey & CC
FOAKS/STRLY B74 ....45 G4
Streetly Methodist Recreation
Centre *FOAKS/STRLY* B74 ....45 F5
Streetsbrook Infant School
SHLY B90 ....180 C1
Stuart Bathurst RC High School
DARL/WED WS10 ....56 B3
Stuart Crystal *STRBR* DY8 ....118 A3
Summerfield Hospital
WSNGN B18 ....107 H5
Summerfield Primary School
WSNGN B18 ....107 G5
Summer Hill Industrial Park
CBHAMW B1 ....2 A3
The Summerhill Secondary
School *KGSWFD* DY6 ....99 F4
Sundridge Primary School
KGSTG B44 ....60 A4
Sunfield School
HAG/WOL DY9 ....170 C1
Sunrise Business Park
STRBR DY8 ....118 A5
Sunshine Infant School
BLOX/PEL WS3 ....27 G2
Sutton Arts Theatre
CSCFLD/WYGN B72 ....62 C4
Sutton Coldfield College
ERDE/BCHGN B24 ....93 E2
ERDW/GRVHL B23 ....92 A2
FOAKS/STRLY B74 ....72 C4
KGSTG B44 ....75 E4
MGN/WHC B75 ....47 H2
WASH/WDE B8 ....110 D2
Sutton Coldfield Crematorium
MGN/WHC B75 ....48 C3
Sutton Coldfield Girls School
SCFLD/BOLD B73 ....62 B5
Sutton Coldfield Golf Club
FOAKS/STRLY B74 ....45 H4
Sutton Coldfield Hospital
SCFLD/BOLD B73 ....62 B4
Sutton Coldfield Town FC
CSCFLD/WYGN B72 ....62 C5
Sutton Coldfield Town Hall
CSCFLD/WYGN B72 ....62 C5
Sutton Coldfield Cemetery
MGN/WHC B75 ....62 D2
The Sutton Special School
DUDN DY1 ....101 H1
Sutton Town Sports Club
CSCFLD/WYGN B72 ....62 C4
Sutton United FC
MGN/WHC B75 ....63 E3
The Swallows Industrial Estate
SHLY B90 ....194 D1
Swallows Rise Business Park
BRLYHL DY5 ....119 G1
Swan Lane Industrial Estate
WBROM B70 ....87 E1
Swan Medical Centre
YDLY B25 ....129 H5
Swanpool Medical Centre
TPTN/OCK DY4 ....69 G3
Swanshurst Girls School
MOS/BIL B13 ....161 G3
Sycamore Green Primary
School *DUDN* DY1 ....83 H1
Sycamore House Medical
Centre *WSL* WS1 ....5 J7
Sycamore Industrial &
Trading Estate
HDSW B21 ....107 F2
Symphony Hall *CBHAMW* B1 ....2 C5
Talbots Lane Trading Estate
BRLYHL DY5 ....119 G3
Tamar Medical Centre
DUNHL/THL/PER WV6 ....34 C1
Tamebridge Industrial Estate
PBAR/PBCH B42 ....91 E2
Tame Road Industrial Estate
AST/WIT B6 ....91 H5
Tame Valley Primary School
CBROM B36 ....111 H1
Tandon Medical Centre
SEDG DY3 ....83 G1
Tansey Green Trading Estate
BRLYHL DY5 ....100 D1
Teisen Industrial Centre
AST/WIT B6 ....109 F3
Temple Meadow Primary
School *CDYHTH* B64 ....121 F3
Tenterfields Primary School
HALE B63 ....139 E3
Tettenhall College
DUNHL/THL/PER WV6 ....35 H1
Tettenhall Wood Special School
DUNHL/THL/PER WV6 ....35 F2
Thameside Primary School
DARL/WED WS10 ....71 G1
Thinktank at Millennium Point
CBHAMNE B4 ....3 K4
Thistle Hotel *CBHAMNE* B4 ....3 F3
LDYWD/EDGR B16 ....125 G3
Thornleigh Trading Estate
DUDS DY2 ....102 A2
Thorns Community College
BRLYHL DY5 ....119 F4
Thorns Primary School
BRLYHL DY5 ....119 G5
Thornton Junior School
WASH/WDE B8 ....111 F4
Three Crowns Special School
DSYBK/YTR WS5 ....43 H4
Tidbury Green Primary School
SHLY B90 ....193 G4
Tile Cross Trading Estate
STETCH B33 ....131 F3

Timberley Primary School
BKDE/SHDE B34 ....113 F3
Timbertree Primary School
CDYHTH B64 ....121 E5
Tindal Primary School
BHTH/HG B12 ....144 B2
Tipper Trading Estate
HALE B63 ....137 E2
Tipton Green Junior School
TPTN/OCK DY4 ....85 F2
Tipton Sports Academy
TPTN/OCK DY4 ....69 H2
Tiverton J & I School
SLYOAK B29 ....142 D5
Tiverton Road Pool & Fitness
Centre *SLYOAK* B29 ....159 H1
Tividale Business Park
TPTN/OCK DY4 ....85 H3
Tividale Comprehensive School
OLDBY B69 ....86 A5
Tividale FC *OLDBY* B69 ....85 H5
Tividale Hall Primary School
OLDBY B69 ....85 G5
Tividale Medical Centre
OLDBY B69 ....104 B1
Tividale Primary School
OLDBY B69 ....85 H4
Tollgate Shopping Precinct
SMTHWKW B67 ....106 B3
Topcliffe Primary School
CVALE B35 ....94 C3
Touchwood Shopping Centre
SOLH B91 ....182 A1
Tower Hill Health Centre
PBAR/PBCH B42 ....74 A5
Tower Works Industrial Estate
BDMR/CCFT WV3 ....6 A6
Town Gate Retail Park
DUDN DY1 ....85 F4
Town Junior School
CSCFLD/WYGN B72 ....62 C4
Town Wharf Business Park
WSLW WS2 ....4 B3
T P Riley Community School
BLOX/PEL WS3 ....17 E5
Tractor Spares Industrial
Estate *WLNHL* WV13 ....38 D3
Trading Estate Parkview
HWK/WKHTH B38 ....176 C5
Travelodge *BRLYHL* DY5 ....101 G5
EDG B15 ....2 C7
LGN/SDN/BHAMAIR B26 ....147 E1
OLDBY B69 ....86 B2
RIDG/WDGT B32 ....156 D3
SCFLD/BOLD B73 ....76 D1
Trescott Primary School
NFLD/LBR B31 ....174 D2
Trevor Street Industrial Estate
VAUX/NECH B7 ....110 A3
Trident Retail Park
BORD B9 ....127 G2
Trident Shopping Centre
DUDN DY1 ....84 C5
Trinity Business Park
HIA/OLT B92 ....149 H4
Trinity CE Primary School
WOLVN WV10 ....37 H1
Tromans Industrial Estate
DUDS DY2 ....120 D1
Truck Stop Business Park
SPARK B11 ....146 B1
Tudor Grange School
SOLH B91 ....181 G3
Tudor Grange Sports Centre &
Pool *SOLH* B91 ....181 H2
Tudor Industrial Estate
SPARK B11 ....146 B2
Turves Green Boys School
NFLD/LBR B31 ....175 G5
Turves Green Girls School
NFLD/LBR B31 ....175 G4
Turves Green Primary School
NFLD/LBR B31 ....175 G4
Twickenham Primary School
KGSTG B44 ....76 A2
Two Woods Industrial Estate
BRLYHL DY5 ....119 G3
Two Woods Trading Estate
BRLYHL DY5 ....119 H3
Tybum Industrial Estate
ERDE/BCHGN B24 ....93 H4
Tyseley Industrial Estate
SPARK B11 ....145 G2
Tyseley Locomotive Works
Visitor Centre *SPARK* B11 ....145 H2
UCI Cinema *BRLYHL* DY5 ....119 G2
SHLY B90 ....195 E1
Uffculme Clinic *MOS/BIL* B13 ....143 H5
Uffculme Special School
MOS/BIL B13 ....161 E1
Ulverley Primary School
HIA/OLT B92 ....164 D2
Union Business Park
WSLW WS2 ....4 C4
Unisant Trading Estate
CDYHTH B64 ....121 F2
University of Birmingham
CBHAMNE B4 ....3 G2
EDG B15 ....142 D4
University of Central England
CBHAMNE B4 ....3 J2
CBHAMNW B3 ....2 E5
EDG B15 ....126 A4
PBAR/PBCH B42 ....90 D3
University of Central England
(Institute of Art & Design)
CBHAMNE B4 ....3 J1
University of Central England
(Technology Innovation Centre)
CBHAMNE B4 ....3 K3
University of Wolverhampton
BDMR/CCFT WV3 ....35 H3
WOLVN WV10 ....23 E4
WOLV WV1 ....38 D1
WSL WS1 ....57 G4
WSLW WS2 ....41 G4
University of Wolverhampton
(North Site) *WOLV* WV1 ....7 F2
University of Wolverhampton
(South Site) *WOLV* WV1 ....7 F3

Uplands Cemetery
SMTHWK B67 ....124 A1
Uplands Junior School
BDMR/CCFT WV3 ....35 H5
Uplands Manor Primary School
SMTHWK B67 ....124 A1
Upper School & Sixth Form
WOLVN WV10 ....128 B4
Usam Trading Estate
WOLVN WV10 ....12 D5
Valley Infant School
HIA/OLT B92 ....148 B4
Valley Park Campus
DUNHL/THL/PER WV6 ....22 B5
Vaughan Trading Estate
TPTN/OCK DY4 ....85 H3
Vauxhall Trading Estate
VAUX/NECH B7 ....109 H5
Vector Industrial Park
HHTH/SAND B71 ....71 F5
Venkat Medical Centre
RMSLY B62 ....122 A4
Vernon Trading Estate
HALE B63 ....137 G1
Victoria Health Centre
SMTHWK B66 ....106 D5
Victoria Infant School
TPTN/OCK DY4 ....85 E1
Victoria Park Primary School
SMTHWK B66 ....106 D4
Victoria School
NFLD/LBR B31 ....158 C5
Villiers Primary School
BILS/COS WV14 ....53 H1
Villiers Trading Estate
BKHL/PFLD WV2 ....52 A1
Visit Centre *WSNGN* B18 ....107 G4
Viva! Health & Leisure Club
SOLH B91 ....196 A1
Vulcan House Industrial
Estate *SOLH* B91 ....165 E4
Vulcan Industrial Estate
WSL WS2 ....27 G4
Wake Green FC *SHLY* B90 ....179 G5
Walbrook Primary School
BILS/COS WV14 ....69 E3
The Wallows Industrial Estate
BRLYHL DY5 ....101 F4
Walmley CC *WALM/CURD* B76 ....78 A4
Walmley Golf Club
CSCFLD/WYGN B72 ....77 G3
Walmley Infant School
WALM/CURD B76 ....78 C4
Walsall Business Park
ALDR WS9 ....30 B5
ALDR WS9 ....43 G1
Walsall CC *WSL* WS1 ....57 G1
Walsall College of Arts &
Technology *WSLW* WS2 ....41 G4
Walsall College of Arts &
Technology *WSLW* WS2 ....4 D2
Walsall FC (Bescot Stadium)
WSL WS1 ....56 D3
Walsall Gala Baths *WSL* WS1 ....4 E3
Walsall Golf Club *WSL* WS1 ....57 H2
Walsall Leather Museum
WSLW WS2 ....4 D1
Walsall Museum & Library
WSLW WS2 ....5 F3
Walsall RFC *WSL* WS1 ....57 F2
Walsall Wood Cemetery
ALDR WS9 ....19 F5
Walsall Wood Primary School
ALDR WS9 ....19 F3
Ward End Medical Centre
WASH/WDE B8 ....111 F4
Ward End Primary School
WASH/WDE B8 ....111 F3
Warley High School
LGLYGN/QTN B68 ....123 E2
Warley Infant School
LGLYGN/QTN B68 ....123 G2
Warley Woods Golf Club
SMTHWKW B67 ....124 A5
Warner Village Star City
VAUX/NECH B7 ....110 B1
Warren Farm Primary School
KGSTG B44 ....75 H3
Warstones Primary School
ETTPK/GDPK/PENN WV4 ....51 E2
Warteil Bank Industrial Estate
KGSWFD DY6 ....99 H1
Warwick Road Trading Estate
SPARK B11 ....145 F3
Warwickshire CCC (Edgbaston)
EDG B15 ....143 H2
Waseley Hills Country Park
BRGRVW B61 ....173 E5
Waseley Hills High School
RBRY B45 ....187 F1
Washington Street Industrial
Estate *DUDS* DY2 ....120 D1
Washwood Heath Technology
College *WASH/WDE* B8 ....111 G4
Waterfall Lane Trading Estate
CDYHTH B64 ....121 G3
Waterfront Business Park
BRLYHL DY5 ....119 G1
Waterloo Industrial Estate
CHWD/FDBR/MGN B37 ....114 B4
Watermill Primary School
SLYOAK B29 ....142 B4
Water Orton CC
CSHL/WTROR B46 ....96 B3
Water Orton Primary School
CSHL/WTROR B46 ....96 B4
Waterside Industrial Estate
BKHL/PFLD WV2 ....53 E2
Watery Lane Industrial Estate
WLNHL WV13 ....38 D2
Watling Street Business Park
CNCK/NC WS11 ....8 A2
Watling Street JMI School
BRWNH WS8 ....9 E3
Wattville Primary School
SMTHWK B66 ....106 D1
Wattville Road Industrial
Estate *SMTHWK* B66 ....106 D2
Waverley School
SMHTH B10 ....129 E4

Webnor Industrial Estate
BKHL/PFLD WV2 ....53 E2
Wednesbury CC
DARL/WED WS10 ....56 A4
Wednesbury Chiropody Surgery
DARL/WED WS10 ....55 H5
Wednesbury Leisure Centre
DARL/WED WS10 ....55 G5
Wednesbury Medical Centre
DARL/WED WS10 ....70 C1
Wednesbury Oak Primary
School *TPTN/OCK* DY4 ....69 F2
Wednesbury Rugby Club
DARL/WED WS10 ....70 D2
Wednesbury Trading Estate
DARL/WED WS10 ....55 G4
Wednesfield FC
WNSFLD WV11 ....24 C4
Wednesfield High School
WNSFLD WV11 ....25 E5
Wednesfield Village Primary
School *WNSFLD* WV11 ....24 D5
Wednesfield Way Industrial
Estate *WNSFLD* WV11 ....38 D1
Welford Primary School
BFLD/HDSWWD B20 ....108 B1
Wellington Industrial Estate
BILS/COS WV14 ....68 C4
Welsh House Farm Primary
School *RIDG/WDGT* B32 ...141 F3
Welsh RFC *HIA/OLT* B92 ...149 C5
Weoley Castle Health Centre
SLYOAK B29 ....158 C1
Weoley Castle Ruins &
Museum *SLYOAK* B29 .....141 G5
Wergs Golf Club
DUNHL/THL/PER WV6 ....21 E3
Westacre Infant School
BDMR/CCFT WV3 ....35 H4
West Bromwich Albion FC
(The Hawthorns)
HHTH/SAND B71 ....88 C5
West Bromwich Dartmouth CC
HHTH/SAND B71 ....88 B5
Westcroft Special School &
Sports College
WOLVN WV10 ....13 H5
West Cross Shopping Centre
SMTHWK B66 ....105 H2
Western Business Park
RMSLY B62 ....121 H5
WSNGN B18 ....107 G3
Westfield Primary School
WMBN WV5 ....65 E4
Westgate Trading Estate
ALDR WS9 ....29 G4
West Heath Hospital
HWK/WKHTH B38 ....176 A5
West House School
EDG B15 ....126 C4
The Westmead Hotel
ALVE B48 ....189 H4
West Midlands Hospital
HALE B63 ....137 H2
Westminster Industrial Estate
DUDS DY2 ....120 D2
Westminster Primary School
BFLD/HDSWWD B20 ....90 C5

Westminster School
TPTN/OCK DY4 ....69 G5
West Park Hospital *WOLV* WV1 ....6 C3
West Park Primary School
WOLV WV1 ....6 C1
Westwood Business Park
AST/WIT B6 ....91 H4
Wharton Street Industrial
Estate *VAUX/NECH* B7 .....110 B1
Wheelers Lane Technology
College *MOS/BIL* B13 .....161 F3
Wheeler Street Shopping
Centre *LOZ/NWT* B19 .....108 C3
Whetstone Field Primary
School *ALDR* WS9 ....44 B1
Whitecrest Primary School
GTB/HAM B43 ....74 A1
Whitehall Industrial Park
TPTN/OCK DY4 ....86 C1
Whitehall Infant School
WSL WS1 ....57 F1
Whitehall Junior School
WSL WS1 ....57 F1
Whiteheath Clinic
OLDBY B69 ....104 B4
Whitehouse Common
Primary School
MGN/WHC B75 ....62 D1
Whitesmore School
CHWD/FDBR/MGN B37 .....131 H3
Whitgreave J & I School
WOLVN WV10 ....23 G2
Whitmore Medical Centre
WOLV WV1 ....6 E1
Whitmore Reans Health Centre
DUNHL/THL/PER WV6 ....36 C1
Whitworth Industrial Park
BORD B9 ....128 A2
Wholesale Markets
DIG/EDG B5 ....3 H7
Widney Junior School
SOLH B91 ....181 F4
Widney Manor Cemetery
DOR/KN B93 ....196 C2
Widney Manor Golf Club
SHLY B90 ....196 A1
Wightwick Hall Special School
DUNHL/THL/PER WV6 ....34 C3
Wightwick Manor (NT)
DUNHL/THL/PER WV6 ....34 D4
Wilkes Green J & I School
HDSW B21 ....89 G5
Wilkinson Primary School
BILS/COS WV14 ....54 B5
Willenhall Industrial Estate
WLNHL WV13 ....40 A2
Willenhall Lane Industrial
Estate *BLOX/PEL* WS3 .....27 E2
Willenhall Lawn Cemetery
SHHTH WV12 ....26 C5
Willenhall Leisure Centre
WLNHL WV13 ....39 H4
Willenhall School Sports
College *SHHTH* WV12 ....26 C5
Willenhall Town FC
WLNHL WV13 ....39 F2
Willenhall Trading Estate
WLNHL WV13 ....39 F4

William Cowper Primary
School
LOZ/NWT B19 ....109 E3
William Hanke Industrial
Estate
BRLYHL DY5 ....119 G3
Willingsworth High School
TPTN/OCK DY4 ....69 H1
Wilson Stuart Special School
ERDW/GRVHL B23 ....76 A5
Windmill Hill (Look out)
RBRY B45 ....173 E5
Windmill Works Industrial Park
DUDS DY2 ....102 B2
Windsor High School
HALE B63 ....138 B3
Windsor Industrial Estate
VAUX/NECH B7 ....109 G4
Windward Way Industrial
Estate
CBROM B36 ....113 H1
Windy Arbor Primary School
CHWD/FDBR/MGN B37 .....132 D1
Winster Grove Industrial
Centre *KGSTG* B44 ....74 D1
Winster Grove Industrial
Estate *KGSTG* B44 ....75 E1
Wishaw Golf Course
WALM/CURD B76 ....79 F1
Withymoor Primary School
BRLYHL DY5 ....119 F3
Withy Road Industrial Estate
BILS/COS WV14 ....53 G5
Witton Industrial Estate
AST/WIT B6 ....91 G4
Witton Park Industrial Estate
AST/WIT B6 ....91 G5
Woden Primary School
WOLVN WV10 ....37 G1
Wodensborough Community
Technology College
DARL/WED WS10 ....71 F1
Wodensfield Primary School
WNSFLD WV11 ....24 B4
Wollescote Business Park
HAG/WOL DY9 ....136 D2
Wollescote Primary School
HAG/WOL DY9 ....136 D3
Wolverhampton Business Park
WOLVN WV10 ....12 D2
Wolverhampton CC
DUNHL/THL/PER WV6 ....21 G4
Wolverhampton Central Baths
WOLV WV1 ....6 D3
Wolverhampton College
WOLV WV1 ....53 F1
Wolverhampton Girls High
School
DUNHL/THL/PER WV6 ....36 B2
Wolverhampton Grammar
School *BDMR/CCFT* WV3 .....36 B3
Wolverhampton Healthcare
WOLVN WV10 ....38 B1
The Wolverhampton Nuffield
Hospital
DUNHL/THL/PER WV6 ....35 G2
Wolverhampton Racecourse
DUNHL/THL/PER WV6 ....22 C4

Wolverhampton Wanderers FC
(Molineux Stadium)
WOLV WV1 ....6 E1
Wombourne Cricket Tennis &
Bowling Club *WMBN* WV5 ...65 E4
Wombrook Business Centre
WMBN WV5 ....64 C4
Wombrook Industrial Estate
WMBN WV5 ....64 C5
Woodbourne Priory Hospital
HRBN B17 ....125 E3
Woodcock Hill Primary
School
NFLD/LBR B31 ....158 A3
Woodcock Sports Centre
CBHAMNE B4 ....3 J2
Woodcross Clinic
BILS/COS WV14 ....68 A1
Wood End Primary School
WNSFLD WV11 ....24 C3
Woodfield J & I School
ETTPK/GDPK/PENN WV4 ...51 F2
Woodgate Business Park
RIDG/WDGT B32 ....140 B5
Woodgate Primary School
RIDG/WDGT B32 ....157 F1
Woodgate Valley
RIDG/WDGT B32 ....140 C3
Woodgate Valley Health
Centre *RIDG/WDGT* B32 ...140 C5
Wood Green High School
College of Sport
DARL/WED WS10 ....56 B3
Wood Green Junior School
DARL/WED WS10 ....55 H4
Woodhouse J & I School
RIDG/WDGT B32 ....141 E1
Woodlands Cemetery
CBROM B36 ....114 C4
Woodlands Hotel *HRBN* B17 ...124 D3
Woodlands Infant School
SHLY B90 ....180 B5
Woodlands Primary School
SHHTH WV12 ....26 B4
The Woodrush High School
HLYWD B47 ....192 C2
Woodrush Rugby Club
HWK/WKHTH B38 ....191 F4
The Woodsbank Industrial
Estate *DARL/WED* WS10 .....55 F4
The Woodsbank Trading
Estate *DARL/WED* WS10 .....55 F4
The Woodsetton Special
School *SEDG* DY3 ....67 H4
Woodside Industrial Estate
DUDS DY2 ....101 H4
Woodstock Girls School
MOS/BIL B13 ....144 C3
Woodthorne Primary School
DUNHL/THL/PER WV6 ....35 E1
Woodthorpe Primary School
ALE/KHTH/YWD B14 ....161 E5
Woodview Primary School
EDG B15 ....126 C4
Wordsley Green Health
Centre *STRBR* DY8 ....117 H2
Wordsley Green Shopping
Centre *STRBR* DY8 ....117 H2

Wordsley Hospital
STRBR DY8 ....118 A1
Works Trading Estate
SMTHWK B66 ....106 C2
Worlds End J & I School
RIDG/WDGT B32 ....140 D2
The Worsley School
KGSWFD DY6 ....118 B1
Wren's Nest National Nature
Reserve *DUDN* DY1 ....84 B2
Wrens Nest Primary School
DUDN DY1 ....84 A2
Wrottesley Hall
CDSL WV8 ....20 A2
Wulfrun Shopping Centre
WOLV WV1 ....7 F5
Wulfrun Trading Estate
WOLV WV1 ....23 E5
Wychall Farm Primary School
NFLD/LBR B31 ....176 A3
Wylde Green Primary School
SCFLD/BOLD B73 ....77 F4
Wyndcliffe Primary School
BORD B9 ....128 B3
Wyndley Leisure Centre
FOAKS/STRLY B74 ....62 A3
Wyndley Swimming Baths
SCFLD/BOLD B73 ....62 A4
Wynford Industrial Trading
Estate *ACGN* B27 ....146 C2
Wynford Road Industrial
Estate *ACGN* B27 ....146 C2
Wythall Cemetery
HLYWD B47 ....192 A5
Wythall Health Centre
HLYWD B47 ....192 C1
Yardley Cemetery
YDLY B25 ....146 D2
Yardley Green Health Centre
SMHTH B10 ....128 D3
Yardley Green Medical Centre
SMHTH B10 ....128 A4
Yardley Medical Centre
YDLY B25 ....129 F5
Yardleys School
SPARK B11 ....145 G4
Yardleys Secondary School
SPARK B11 ....145 H3
Yardley Wood Health Centre
MOS/BIL B13 ....162 A5
Yardley Wood Primary School
ALE/KHTH/YWD B14 ....179 F1
Yarnfield Primary School
SPARK B11 ....146 A4
Yenton Junior School
ERDE/BCHGN B24 ....77 F5
Yew Tree Community
Junior School
AST/WIT B6 ....91 G5
Yew Tree Primary School
DSYBK/YTR WS5 ....57 H4
SOLH B91 ....165 G5
York Mead Primary School
HLGN/YWD B28 ....145 G5
Yorks Wood Primary School
CHWD/FDBR/MGN B37 .....113 H4
Zip Theatre
WOLV WV1 ....6 D1

Acknowledgements

Schools address data provided by Education Direct

Petrol station information supplied by Johnsons

Garden centre information provided by:

Garden Centre Association  Britains best garden centres

Wyevale Garden Centres

The statement on the front cover of this atlas is sourced, selected and quoted
from a reader comment and feedback form received in 2004

Notes

AA Street by Street · QUESTIONNAIRE

Dear Atlas User
Your comments, opinions and recommendations are very important to us.
So please help us to improve our street atlases by taking a few minutes
to complete this simple questionnaire.

You do not need a stamp (unless posted outside the UK). If you do not want to remove this page from your street atlas, then photocopy it or write your answers on a plain sheet of paper.

Send to: Marketing Assistant, AA Publishing, 14th Floor Fanum House, Freepost SCE 4598, Basingstoke RG21 4GY

ABOUT THE ATLAS...

Please state which city / town / county you bought:

Where did you buy the atlas? (City, Town, County)

For what purpose? (please tick all applicable)

To use in your local area ☐   **To use on business or at work** ☐

Visiting a strange place ☐   **In the car** ☐   **On foot** ☐

Other (please state)

Have you ever used any street atlases other than AA Street by Street?

Yes ☐   **No** ☐

If so, which ones?

Is there any aspect of our street atlases that could be improved?
(Please continue on a separate sheet if necessary)

Please list the features you found most useful:

_____

_____

Please list the features you found least useful:

_____

_____

_____

LOCAL KNOWLEDGE...

Local knowledge is invaluable. Whilst every attempt has been made to make the information contained in this atlas as accurate as possible, should you notice any inaccuracies, please detail them below (if necessary, use a blank piece of paper) or e-mail us at _streetbystreet@theAA.com_

_____

_____

_____

ABOUT YOU...

Name (Mr/Mrs/Ms) _____

Address _____

                                        Postcode _____

Daytime tel no _____

E-mail address _____

Which age group are you in?

Under 25 ☐   **25-34** ☐   **35-44** ☐   **45-54** ☐   **55-64** ☐   **65+** ☐

Are you an AA member?   YES ☐   **NO** ☐

Do you have Internet access?   YES ☐   **NO** ☐

_____

Thank you for taking the time to complete this questionnaire. Please send it to us as soon as possible, and remember, you do not need a stamp (unless posted outside the UK).

We may use information we hold about you to, telephone or email you about other products and services offered by the AA, we do NOT disclose this information to third parties.

Please tick here if you do not wish to hear about products and services from the AA. ☐